Theories of Personality

Understanding Persons

Susan C. Cloninger
Russell Sage College

PEARSON

Prentice
Hall

Upper Saddle River, New Jersey 07458

Library of Congress Cataloging-in-Publication Data

Cloninger, Susan C., 1945-
  Theories of personality : understanding persons / Susan C. Cloninger. -- 5th ed.
    p. cm.
  Includes bibliographical references and indexes.
  ISBN-13: 978-0-13-243409-6 (alk. paper)
  ISBN-10: 0-13-243409-1 (alk. paper)
  1. Personality--Textbooks. I. Title.
  BF698.C543 2008
  155.2--dc22

                                                2007011348

Executive Editor: Jeff Marshall
Editor-in-Chief: Leah Jewell
Project Manager (Editorial): LeeAnn Doherty
Editorial Assistant: Jennifer Puma
Marketing Manager: Jeanette Moyer
Marketing Assistant: Laura Kennedy
Associate Managing Editor: Maureen Richardson
Project Manager (Production): Kathy Sleys
Senior Operations Supervisor: Sherry Lewis
Interior Design: GGS Book Services
Cover Design: Kiwi Design
Cover Illustration/Photo: 3poD Animation/Shutterstock
Production Editor: Karpagam Jagadeesan
Full-Service Project Management: GGS Book Services
Printer/Binder: Quebecor World Book Services
Cover Printer: Coral Graphics

Credits and acknowledgments borrowed from other sources and reproduced, with permission, in this textbook appear on page 561.

Pearson Prentice Hall™ is a trademark of Pearson Education, Inc.
Pearson® is a registered trademark of Pearson plc
Prentice Hall® is a registered trademark of Pearson Education, Inc.

Pearson Education Ltd.   Pearson Educación de Mexico, S.A. de C.V.
Pearson Education Australia PTY, Ltd.   Pearson Education–Japan
Pearson Education Singapore, Pte. Ltd.   Pearson Education Malaysia, Pte. Ltd.
Pearson Education North Asia Ltd.   Pearson Education, Upper Saddle River, NJ
Pearson Education, Canada, Ltd.

10 9 8 7 6 5 4 3 2 1
ISBN-13: 978-0-13-243409-6
ISBN-10: 0-13-243409-1

To the Memory
of my mother and father.

Brief Contents

Preface   xv

Chapter 1   Introduction to Personality Theory   1

PART I   The Psychoanalytic Perspective   23

Chapter 2   Freud: Classical Psychoanalysis   25
Chapter 3   Jung: Analytical Psychology   63

PART II   The Psychoanalytic-Social Perspective   93

Chapter 4   Adler: Individual Psychology   95
Chapter 5   Erikson: Psychosocial Development   122
Chapter 6   Horney and Relational Theory: Interpersonal   149
               Psychoanalytic Theory

PART III   The Trait Perspective   183

Chapter 7   Allport: Personological Trait Theory   185
Chapter 8   Cattell and the Big Five: Factor Analytic Trait Theories   215
Chapter 9   Evolution and Temperament: Biological Theories   245

PART IV   The Learning Perspective   279

Chapter 10   Skinner and Staats: The Challenge of Behaviorism   281
Chapter 11   Dollard and Miller: Psychoanalytic Learning Theory   313

PART V   The Cognitive Social Learning Perspective   337

Chapter 12   Mischel and Bandura: Cognitive Social Learning Theory   339
Chapter 13   Kelly: Personal Construct Theory   368

PART VI   The Humanistic Perspective   395

Chapter 14   Rogers: Person-Centered Theory   398
Chapter 15   Maslow: Need Hierarchy Theory   422
Chapter 16   Buddhist Psychology: Lessons from Eastern Culture   451
Chapter 17   Conclusion   488

Contents

Preface   xv

1 Introduction to Personality Theory   1
Personality: The Study of Individuals   2
Description of Personality   2
Personality Dynamics   5
Personality Development   6
The Scientific Approach   8
Methods in Personality Research   13
One Theory or Many? Eclecticism and the Future of Personality Theory   18
Summary   19
Thinking about Personality Theory   20
Study Questions   21

PART I   THE PSYCHOANALYTIC PERSPECTIVE   23

2 Freud: Classical Psychoanalysis   25
Preview: Overview of Freud's Theory   28
The Unconscious   30
Structures of the Personality   37
Intrapsychic Conflict   41
Personality Development   47
Psychoanalytic Treatment   52
Psychoanalysis as a Scientific Theory   56
Summary   61
Thinking about Freud's Theory   62
Study Questions   62

3 Jung: Analytical Psychology   63
Preview: Overview of Jung's Theory   66
The Structure of Personality   68
Symbolism and the Collective Unconscious   78
Therapy   81
Synchronicity   83
Psychological Types   84

Summary   90
Thinking about Jung's Theory   91
Study Questions   91

PART II   THE PSYCHOANALYTIC-SOCIAL PERSPECTIVE   **93**

4 Adler: Individual Psychology   **95**
Preview: Overview of Adler's Theory   98
Striving from Inferiority toward Superiority   101
The Unity of Personality   104
The Development of Personality   107
Psychological Health   113
Interventions Based on Adler's Theory   116
Summary   120
Thinking about Adler's Theory   120
Study Questions   121

5 Erikson: Psychosocial Development   **122**
Preview: Overview of Erikson's Theory   125
The Epigenetic Principle   128
The Psychosocial Stages   128
The Role of Culture in Relation to the Psychosocial Stages   134
Racial and Ethnic Identity   137
Gender   140
Research on Development through the Psychosocial Stages   142
Toward a Psychoanalytic Social Psychology   146
Summary   147
Thinking about Erikson's Theory   147
Study Questions   148

6 Horney and Relational Theory: Interpersonal Psychoanalytic Theory   **149**
Preview: Overview of Interpersonal Psychoanalytic Theory   152
Interpersonal Psychoanalysis: Horney   **153**
Basic Anxiety and Basic Hostility   155
Three Interpersonal Orientations   156
Major Adjustments to Basic Anxiety   160
Secondary Adjustment Techniques   162
Cultural Determinants of Development   163
Therapy   167
Parental Behavior and Personality Development   168

The Relational Approach within Psychoanalytic Theory   **169**
The Sense of Self in Relationships   172
Narcissism   173
Attachment in Infancy and Adulthood   174
Parenting   179
Therapy   179
Summary   179
Thinking about Horney's Theory and the Relational Approach   180
Study Questions   181

PART III   THE TRAIT PERSPECTIVE   183

7 Allport: Personological Trait Theory   **185**
Preview: Overview of Allport's Theory   187
Major Themes in Allport's Work   190
Allport's Definition of Personality   191
Personality Traits   194
Personality Development   202
Influence of Personality on Social Phenomena   208
Eclecticism   212
Summary   213
Thinking about Allport's Theory   214
Study Questions   214

8 Cattell's 16 Factors and the Big Five: Factor Analytic Trait Theories   **215**
Preview: Overview of Factor Analytic Trait Theories   219
Factor Analysis   219
The 16 Factor Theory: Cattell   **221**
Personality Measurement and the Prediction of Behavior   222
Because Personality Is Complex: A Multivariate Approach   224
Psychological Adjustment   226
Three Types of Traits   227
Predicting Behavior   230
Determinants of Personality: Heredity and Environment   234
The Role of Theory in Cattell's Empirical Approach   235
The Five-Factor Theory: McCrae and Costa   **235**
Extraversion   237
Agreeableness   238
Neuroticism   238
Conscientiousness   239
Openness   239

More about These Five Factors   240
Summary   242
Thinking about Factor Analytic Trait Theories   243
Study Questions   244

9 **Evolution and Temperament: Biological Theories**   **245**
Preview: Overview of Biological Theories   248
Evolutionary Approaches   **248**
Emotions   250
Altruism   251
Sexual Behavior   252
Parental Behavior   255
Aggression and Dominance   256
Culture   256
Language and Thought   257
Genetics and Personality   **259**
Temperament   **259**
Biological Contributors to Personality   **263**
The Brain   263
Emotional Arousal   264
Cortical Arousal   265
Biological Factor Theories: Eysenck, Gray, and Others   **267**
Eysenck's "PEN" Biological Model   267
Gray's Reinforcement Sensitivity Theory   271
Cloninger's Tridimensional Model   273
Biological Mechanisms in Context   **275**
Summary   276
Thinking about Biological Personality Theories   277
Study Questions   277

PART IV   THE LEARNING PERSPECTIVE   279

10 **Skinner and Staats: The Challenge of Behaviorism**   **281**
Preview: Overview of Skinner's and Staats's Theories   284
Radical Behaviorism: Skinner   **285**
Behavior as the Data for Scientific Study   288
Learning Principles   290
Schedules of Reinforcement   293
Applications of Behavioral Techniques   294
Radical Behaviorism and Personality Theory: Some Concerns   296

Psychological Behaviorism: Staats   **297**
Reinforcement   299
Basic Behavioral Repertoires   300
Situations   305
Psychological Adjustment   306
The Nature-Nurture Question from the Perspective   307
of Psychological Behaviorism
Personality Assessment from a Behavioral Perspective   **308**
The Act Frequency Approach to Personality Measurement   309
Contributions of Behaviorism to Personality Theory and Measurement   310
Summary   310
Thinking about Skinner's Theory   311
Thinking about Staats's Theory   312
Study Questions   312

11 Dollard and Miller: Psychoanalytic Learning Theory   **313**
Preview: Overview of Dollard and Miller's Theory   316
Four Fundamental Concepts about Learning   319
The Learning Process   321
Learning by Imitation   322
The Four Critical Training Periods of Childhood   323
Conflict   324
Frustration and Aggression   327
Language   330
Neurosis   331
Psychotherapy   331
Suppression   332
Psychoanalytic Learning Theory Reconsidered   334
Summary   334
Thinking about Dollard and Miller's Theory   335
Study Questions   335

PART V   THE COGNITIVE SOCIAL LEARNING PERSPECTIVE   337

12 Mischel and Bandura: Cognitive Social Learning Theory   **339**
Preview: Overview of Mischel's and Bandura's Theories   342
Traits in Cognitive Social Learning Theory: Mischel   **342**
The Trait Controversy: Mischel's Challenge   343
Cognitive Person Variables   347

Delay of Gratification   350
Performance in Cognitive Social Learning Theory: Bandura   **352**
Reciprocal Determinism   353
Self-Regulation of Behavior: The Self-System   354
Self-Efficacy   355
Processes Influencing Learning   358
Observational Learning and Modeling   360
Therapy   363
The Person in the Social Environment   365
Summary   366
Thinking about Mischel's and Bandura's Theories   366
Study Questions   367

13 Kelly: Personal Construct Theory   **368**
Preview: Overview of Kelly's Theory   372
Constructive Alternativism   374
The Process of Construing   376
The Structure of Construct Systems   379
The Social Embeddedness of Construing Efforts   381
The Role Construct Repertory (REP) Test   382
Cognitive Complexity   384
Personality Change   385
Therapy   387
Research Findings   390
Constructivism, Social Constructionism, and Postmodernism   391
Summary   391
Thinking about Kelly's Theory   392
Study Questions   392

PART VI   THE HUMANISTIC PERSPECTIVE   **395**

14 Rogers: Person-Centered Theory   **398**
Preview: Overview of Rogers's Theory   401
The Actualizing Tendency   404
The Self   406
Development   407
Therapy   409
Other Applications   416
Criticisms of Rogers's Theory   419

Summary 420
Thinking about Rogers's Theory 420
Study Questions 421

15 **Maslow: Need Hierarchy Theory** 422
Preview: Overview of Maslow's Theory 425
Need Hierarchy Theory: Maslow **425**
Maslow's Vision of Psychology 428
Hierarchy of Needs 430
Self-Actualization 435
Applications and Implications of Maslow's Theory 443
Maslow's Challenge to Traditional Science 446
Other Growth Themes in Psychological Theory **447**
Self-Determination Theory and Intrinsic Motivation 448
Positive Psychology 448
Summary 449
Thinking about Maslow's Theory 450
Study Questions 450

16 **Buddhist Psychology: Lessons from Eastern Culture** 451
Preview: Overview of Buddhist Psychology 455
The Relevance of Buddhism for Personality Psychology 455
A Brief History of Buddhism 457
The Buddhist Worldview: The Four Noble Truths 459
Buddhism and Personality Concepts 462
Spiritual Practices 471
Buddhism and Psychotherapy 481
The Importance of the Dialogue, and Some Cautions 484
Summary 486
Thinking about Buddhist Psychology 487
Study Questions 487

17 **Conclusion** 488
Contributions of the Theories to Various Topics 489
Choosing or Combining Theories 493
Theories as Metaphors 496
What Lies Ahead? 499
Summary 499
Thinking about Personality Theory 500
Study Questions 500

Glossary 501

References 513

Photo Credits 561

Author Index 563

Subject Index 573

Preface

Understanding persons is both my academic passion and my personal fascination. People are at the same time so diverse and so similar. Theories of personality never explain all the particulars of individual lives; but theories do open our eyes to nuances and themes that we might otherwise overlook. Whatever else may change in my life, I personally expect to be revising my understanding of persons without ceasing, and both academic reading and real people feed this obsession. I invite you to do the same. The more we understand, the better we can live.

This fifth edition adds a new chapter on Buddhist personality theory, in response to suggestions from reviewers and increased attention to Buddhism among modern psychologists. I first encountered Buddhism when I was still a teenager, taking a summer school course on religions of the world. (I doubt that Professor Jerry Ball is still out there or reading this, but if so, thanks! Your enthusiasm and the field trip to the Buddhist center in San Francisco gave me lifelong memories and respect for that spiritual tradition.) As I have written this new chapter, friends have spontaneously loaned me books from their personal collections and have engaged me in conversations. So I know that Buddhist approaches are vital and evolving in the American experience, and I hope that the spirituality and tolerance of this approach will add to whatever religious-spiritual traditions each of us brings, to help make a better world. From a scientific point of view, the current dialogue between modern neuroscience and ancient Buddhism is truly thrilling. For therapists, Buddhism offers a model of a healthy personality and practices for achieving that state.

Within the remaining chapters, material has been updated. For example, Erikson's classic eight-stage model of psychosocial development, which is all that had been published when he died, is now expanded to include a ninth stage, described by his wife and collaborator based on their previously unpublished conversations. Current research has been added in several places, most extensively in the scientific study of meditation.

As I once again have immersed myself in the Illustrative Biography section of these chapters, revising biographies previously analyzed and adding new ones, I am struck that a life story looks quite different, depending on the theoretical viewpoint that is adopted. It's a bit like putting on different colored lenses when looking at a richly colored picture: Different parts jump out or fade into obscurity. Each of the life stories that is analyzed here would change, viewed from a different theory, but to present that with enough detail to be comprehensible is beyond the scope of this book. (I tried, to some extent, to do this in the previous edition by applying two or three theories to each biography, but it seemed a step backward. This edition returns to the earlier format of interpreting each biography from only one theoretical perspective, but this time only one biography per chapter, instead of two.) Some new biographies have been added: Hillary Rodham Clinton, Oprah Winfrey, and the 14th Dalai Lama of Tibet. Some illustrative biographies that were in some previous editions but not the most recent one have returned. Adolf Hitler would not remain buried. Mahatma Gandhi has resumed his previous place to illustrate Erikson's theory—a choice that is natural, given Erikson's well-known book on Gandhi. Many biographies are continued from the fourth edition but revised into a new and more systematic format: Maya Angelou, Albert Einstein, Frida Kahlo, Martin Luther King, Jr., Marilyn Monroe, Richard Nixon, David Pelzer, Eleanor Roosevelt, Mother Teresa, and Tiger Woods. These brief illustrative biographies are intended to introduce the theories of each chapter, and they don't do justice to the complexity of each person, so I encourage interested readers and students to delve into the sources I have cited and others, to expand and challenge my interpretations and to add the lens of another theory. For example, I've presented Albert Einstein from a factor theory perspective (Chapter 8), but what about his Eriksonian identity issues, as a person born into a Jewish family in Germany who also lived in Italy and the United States, and who worked as a patent officer, private tutor, and professor as well as a physicist? There's another lens, to be sure.

Notice that although many of the chapters cover only one theory (e.g., Chapters 2 on Freud and 3 on Jung), others combine two closely related theories. For example, Chapter 6 presents both Karen Horney's interpersonal theory and the newer relational or object relations approach. These combinations can be confusing; occasionally my own students, for example, refer erroneously to "Cattell's five-factor theory" when in fact, Cattell's 16-factor theory and the newer five-factor theory are distinct, although presented in the same chapter (Chapter 8). To add to the difficulty, many current approaches, such as biological approaches (Chapter 9), combine contributions from several theorists, so it isn't sensible to refer to them by a single theorist's name in the chapter title. These trends, although confusing, represent the evolution of personality theory from major statements by individual theorists to a more advanced state in which several theoretical contributors share fundamental assumptions to a greater extent than in the past.

Admittedly, I most enjoy the reading and research that goes into book writing, and I find the final writing stressful. The research is a delightful treasure hunt, aided by the electronic search capacities that our libraries provide and also the joys of bookstores. For my taste, it's far better when libraries and bookstores dedicate an entire section to biographies, instead of interspersing them with other content. I'd rather find Martin Luther King, Jr. shelved between Frida Kahlo and Marilyn Monroe than between the Pilgrims and the history of colonial America (as in the Library of Congress system). Public libraries have been a great resource for biographies that are no longer current enough to warrant shelf space on major bookstores (although for me, there are allergy repercussions when reading old books, which may explain my new delight with electronic books).

The increased availability of scholarly literature searching through the Internet is bound to make for more integrated theories in personality and other areas. We, and our students, are no longer limited to reading familiar journals but can readily search topics and combinations of topics and thus discover what scholars in different fields, on different continents, with different approaches, have written about topics of interest.

One of the challenges of a personality theory course or text is to do justice to historical theories while also conveying the vitality of new theories and research. Time and page limits mandate compromise between depth and breadth of coverage, and between empirical research studies and application of theory to understanding individual persons. Professors and students with different judgments than mine may skip here and supplement there, and forge connections between the study of personality and other disciplines. We cannot, I am convinced, understand individual personalities without also studying history and society. Our understandings are bound to influence our interpretations of people we meet and of those we know only from news reports.

Many reviewers and other advisers have offered helpful suggestions for this and previous editions. I have not been able to incorporate all of their advice, unfortunately, but even the suggestions not explicitly incorporated in this edition are incubating in my thoughts about personality and may surface later. Particular thanks to these reviewers, who helped make the transition from the previous edition:

Clay Peters, Liberty University
Carol Miller, Anne Arundel Community College

Paul Murray, Southern Oregon University

Spencer McWilliams, California State University, San Marcos

Nicholas Carnagey, Iowa State University

Melinda C. R. Burgess, Southern Oklahoma State University

Elissa Koplik, Bloomfield College

Beverly Goodwin, Indiana University of Pennsylvania

Their advice adds to suggestions made by others, as reviewers of previous editions and, less formally, others who have generously offered advice: Kurt D. Baker (Emporia State University); Mary Louise Cashel (Southern Illinois University at Carbondale); George Domino (University of Arizona); Bernadette Tucker Duck (Chicago State University); Jeanine Feldman (San Diego State University); Ehsha G. Klirs (George Mason University); Maria J. Lavooy (University of Central Florida); Thomas J. Martinez, III (private practice); Tom M. Randall (Rhode Island College); Eric Shiraev (George Mason University); Arthur W. Staats (University of Hawaii); Eunkook Suh (University of California, Irvine); and Julie Ann Suhr (Ohio University). Others have also helped by sending papers and books.

I am fortunate to work with great editors and their assistants at Prentice Hall. Thank you, LeeAnn Doherty, Jeff Marshall, Jennifer Puma, and many others, for attention to myriad details, for watching the calendar and prodding me into overdue delivery of this manuscript, and for helping to make this process fun. Thanks to the production editor, Karpagam Jagadeesan, whose conscientious and prompt oversight of the final manuscript preparation have made the world seem smaller, indeed. The time difference between her work in Chennai, India, and mine in upstate New York have made for round-the-clock activity on the final book preparations, as her responses to my late afternoon and evening electronic communications routinely appeared in my electronic mailbox the following morning before breakfast.

PowerPoints and other teaching resources are available to faculty through the publisher. Contact your local representative for details. In addition, I maintain a personal Web site at http://www.suecloninger.com where I post materials for the various courses I teach. Students and faculty may find there some links to Web resources and additional material related to personality. (Despite the dot-com ending, nothing is for sale on my site!) It's hard to predict what additional electronic developments will change the way we learn and teach in the near future. Nor would I predict too specifically the directions the field of personality is heading, except to anticipate thoughtful integrations of the various levels, from biology to culture, that make us who we are.

Susan C. Cloninger

Introduction to Personality Theory

Chapter
Overview

Personality: The Study of Individuals
Description of Personality
Personality Dynamics
Personality Development
The Scientific Approach
Methods in Personality Research
One Theory or Many? Eclecticism and the Future of Personality Theory
Summary

Writers and philosophers have reflected about personality for centuries. They describe various types of people.

> The true artist will let his wife starve, his children go barefoot, his mother drudge for his living at seventy, sooner than work at anything but his art. (George Bernard Shaw, *Major Barbara*, act 1)

> A fool uttereth all his mind. (Prov. 29:11)

They tell us about the dynamic motivations and emotions of human nature.

> We would all be idle if we could. (Samuel Johnson, quoted in Boswell's *Life of Johnson*)

> Unlimited power is apt to corrupt the minds of those who possess it. (William Pitt, speech, House of Lords, January 9, 1770)

Sayings tell us how personality develops down various paths.

> Train up a child in the way he should go: and when he is old, he will not depart from it. (Matt. 22:6)

> Spare the rod and spoil the child. (Samuel Butler, *Hudibras*, pt. ii, c. I, 1. 844).

With centuries of such commentary about personality, we might think we already know about people and that we may leave scientific investigation for other problems, perhaps to explore the mysteries of the physical universe and biological processes. Personality seems so close to common sense that theorists and scientists seem unnecessary. Yet formal study is needed, perhaps here more than anywhere, for there are contradictions in culture's lessons about personality.

Virtue is bold, and goodness never fearful. (Shakespeare, *Measure for Measure*, act 3, line 215)

Boldness is a child of ignorance and baseness. (Francis Bacon, *Essays*, line 12)

How can we know, given such contradictory observations, whether boldness should be admired or pitied? Perhaps when we and our friends are bold, we will agree with Shakespeare and leave Bacon's skepticism aside until we confront a bold enemy. After all, our understandings may be self-serving.

An Englishman thinks he is moral when he is only uncomfortable. (George Bernard Shaw, *Major Barbara*, act 3)

Such sayings, although charming, are disconcerting because there seems to be a saying to support any belief. Cultural sayings do not offer a systematic understanding of human nature that reliably tells us when we are wise and when we are only entertained. For that, we turn to psychology.

Personality: The Study of Individuals

Psychology for more than a century has used the methods of science to come to some clearer and less ambiguous (if, alas, less literary) understandings of human nature. Personality is the field within this scientific psychology that studies individuals. How is one person different from another, or are people fundamentally similar rather than different? How can we understand the dynamics that motivate us to act in one way or another? How do we develop from childhood on?

DEFINITION OF PERSONALITY

personality the underlying causes within the person of individual behavior and experience

Personality may be defined as *the underlying causes within the person of individual behavior and experience.* Personality psychologists do not all agree about what these underlying causes are, as the many theories in this text suggest. They offer a variety of answers to three fundamental questions. First, how can personality be described? Personality **description** considers the ways in which we should characterize an individual. Should we describe personality traits by comparing people with one another or use some other strategy, such as studying an individual? What terms, beyond those offered in everyday language, should be used to describe people? Second, how can we understand personality **dynamics?** How do people adjust to their life situations? How are they influenced by culture and by their own cognitive (thought) processes? Third, what can be said about personality **development?** How does it reflect the influence of biological factors and experience in childhood and beyond? How does personality change over the life of an individual, from childhood to adulthood? Although some theories emphasize one question rather than another, these three questions are so fundamental that each theory considers them in some way. Furthermore, the issues are interrelated: The way a theory describes personality has implications for personality dynamics and development, and vice versa.

description theoretical task of identifying the units of personality, with particular emphasis on the differences between people

dynamics the motivational aspect of personality

development formation or change (of personality) over time

Description of Personality

The most fundamental theoretical question is this: What concepts are useful for describing personality? Should we concentrate on identifying and labeling the stable differences between people? Or should we avoid comparisons, instead focusing on intensive understanding of one person? Should we assume that personality is more or less fixed, or instead focus on the transient states that come and then pass?

DIFFERENCES BETWEEN PEOPLE: GROUPS OR GRADATIONS?

Personality researchers have devoted considerable effort to identifying the ways that individuals differ from one another—that is, of describing **individual differences**. Essentially, we have the choice of classifying people into a limited number of separate groups, a type approach. Or we can decide that people vary in gradations and describe people by saying how much of the basic dimensions they possess, a trait approach. For comparison, trees can be described in types: oak, maple, eucalyptus, gingko, and so on. Each tree belongs entirely to one type. There are no gradations of types. Alternatively, trees can be described in quantitative dimensions: height, hardiness, and so on, where gradations are possible. One tree can be very tall, another moderately tall, and so on.

individual differences qualities that make one person different from another

Types

The *type approach* proposes that personality comes in a limited number of distinct categories (qualitative groupings). Such personality **types** are categories of people with similar characteristics. A small number of types suffice to describe all people. In ancient Greece, for example, Hippocrates described four basic types of temperament: sanguine (optimistic), melancholic (depressed), choleric (irritable), and phlegmatic (apathetic) (Merenda, 1987). Each person is a member of only one of these type categories. In modern psychology, when clinicians classify people into a diagnostic category—such as schizophrenia or panic disorder—they are using diagnostic categories as types (Blashfield & Livesley, 1991).

type a category of people with similar characteristics

Traits and Factors

Nature often presents us with more gradual transitions (quantitative dimensions). Consider "cruelty": Between Mother Teresa and Stalin lie many intermediate levels of cruelty. Therefore, personality researchers generally prefer **quantitative measures**, which give each person a score, ranging from very low to very high or somewhere in between. A personality **trait** is a characteristic that varies from one person to another and causes a person's more or less consistent behavior. In contrast to types, traits describe a narrower scope of behavior. Traits permit a more precise description of personality than types because each trait refers to a more focused set of characteristics.

quantitative measures measures that permit expression of various amounts of something, such as a trait

More traits than types are necessary to describe a personality. In fact, the number of traits can be astonishing. One classic study counted nearly 18,000 traits among words listed in the dictionary (Allport & Odbert, 1936). Do we really need that many? To eliminate unnecessary redundancy (e.g., by combining synonyms such as "shy" and "withdrawn"), researchers rely on statistical procedures that compute correlations among trait scores, and on that basis they have proposed broad **factors** of personality. Factors differ from most traits by being broader, but, like traits, they are quantitative. People receive a score, rather than simply being placed into one category or another. Factors are often thought to derive from underlying biological variables.

trait personality characteristic that makes one person different from another and/or that describes an individual's personality

Types, traits, and factors all have a role in personality theory and research. The terms are sometimes used imprecisely, but knowing their differences (summarized in Table 1.1) helps us understand the variety of ways that personality can be described and measured.

factor a statistically derived, quantitative dimension of personality that is broader than most traits

TABLE 1.1	Types, Traits, and Factors: Three Ways of Describing Personality
Types	Type membership is an all-or-nothing thing (a qualitative variable). A person belongs to one and only one category.
	Theoretically, a small number of types describe everyone.
	A person fits into only one type.
Traits	Trait scores are continuous (quantitative) variables. A person is given a numeric score to indicate how much of a trait the person possesses.
	Theoretically, there are a great many traits to describe everyone.
	A person can be described on every trait.
Factors	Factor scores are also continuous (quantitative) variables. A person is given a numeric score to indicate how much of a factor the person possesses.
	Theoretically, a small number of factors describe everyone.
	A person can be described on every factor.

COMPARING PEOPLE OR STUDYING INDIVIDUALS: NOMOTHETIC AND IDIOGRAPHIC APPROACHES

nomothetic involving comparisons with other individuals; research based on groups of people

Personality traits and types allow us to compare one person with another: the **nomothetic** approach. Groups of individuals are studied, often by comparing their trait or factor scores on personality tests and relating these scores to different behaviors or background experiences. For example, we can give several hundred people a test to measure their self-confidence and then study the correlation of this trait with one or more other variables (such as sex, how they were disciplined in childhood, score on an extraversion test, or other variables). Most personality research is nomothetic.

Despite its scientific advantages, the nomothetic method has drawbacks. It studies many people and compares them on only a few numerical scores, which makes it difficult to understand one whole person because many aspects combine to form personality (Carlson, 1971). Much personality research is also limited because it often investigates college students (Carlson, 1971; Sears, 1986), who differ from the general adult population of employed adults on many personality characteristics (Ward, 1993).

idiographic focusing on one individual

In contrast to nomothetic research, the **idiographic** approach studies individuals one at a time, without making systematic comparisons with other people. Strictly idiographic approaches may be difficult because any description of a person (e.g., "Mary is outgoing") implies comparison with other people, if only in the memory of the one doing the analysis. Although implicit comparisons with other people are unavoidable, we call research idiographic if it focuses on the particularities of an individual case, for example, in a case study or a psychobiographical analysis. William McKinley Runyan reminds personality psychologists of Kluckhohn and Murray's (1953) classic assertion: "Every man is in certain respects (a) like all other men, (b) like some other men, (c) like no other man" (1988, p. 53). Today we would broaden this assertion to include women as well as men, but the fundamental point remains valid. Personality psychology can discover truths about unique individuals, as well as typical group characteristics and universal principles.

Both nomothetic and idiographic approaches contribute something to personality psychology (Hermans, 1988). Only by doing both kinds of research can we understand the individual and know whether this understanding can be generalized—that is, applied to understand other people, too. Sometimes relationships between variables are different in nomothetic research than in idiographic research (S. Epstein, 1983). For example, nomothetic research shows a positive relationship between self-focused attention and negative mood. People who are more self-focused in their attention are likely to report a negative mood. However, idiographic research does not replicate this relationship. Becoming focused on oneself does not, generally, put a person in a bad mood. That is, within individuals, there is no tendency for changes in self-focus to be associated with changes in mood (Wood et al., 1990). So we find both idiographic and nomothetic information useful but not interchangeable. In part, what seem to be discrepancies can occur because nomothetic research focuses on description, whereas idiographic research is often concerned with personality dynamics.

Personality Dynamics

The term *personality dynamics* refers to the mechanisms by which personality is expressed, often focusing on the motivations that direct behavior. Motivation provides energy and direction to behavior. If you see a person running energetically toward a door, you may ask, "*Why* is that person running?" What is the motivation? Theorists discuss many motives. Some theorists assume that the fundamental motivations or goals of all people are similar. Sigmund Freud suggested that sexual motivation underlies personality; Carl Rogers proposed a tendency to move toward higher levels of development. Other theorists suggest that motives or goals vary from one person to another. For example, Henry Murray (1938) listed dozens of motives that are of varying importance to different people, including achievement motivation, power motivation, nurturance, and so on.

Personality dynamics include individuals' adaptation or adjustment to the demands of life and so have implications for psychological health. Modern personality theory considers cognitive processes as a major aspect of personality dynamics. How we think is an important determinant of our choices and adaptation. In addition, culture influences us through its opportunities and expectations.

ADAPTATION AND ADJUSTMENT

Personality encompasses an individual's way of coping with the world, of adjusting to demands and opportunities in the environment—that is, **adaptation**. Many theories of personality have historical roots in the clinical treatment of patients. Observations of their symptoms, and of increasing adjustment with treatment, suggested more general ideas about personality that have been applied broadly to nonclinical populations; conversely, studies of nonclinical populations have implications for therapy.

adaptation coping with the external world

COGNITIVE PROCESSES

What role does thinking play? Theories vary considerably on this question. Based on clinical experience, Sigmund Freud proposed that conscious thought plays only a limited role in personality dynamics; unconscious dynamics are more important in his psychoanalytic theory. Other approaches disagree, emphasizing conscious experience and investigating various thought patterns that predict behavior and coping. The ways that we label experience and the ideas we have about ourselves have substantial effects on our personality dynamics.

CULTURE

Historically, personality theories focused on the individual, leaving culture and society in the background. This left an incomplete picture of personality and prevented theories from adequately explaining gender, ethnic, and cultural differences. Influenced by greater awareness of cultural change, researchers have increasingly considered the role of culture in personality. For example, the individualism of U.S. culture encourages extraverted and assertive behavior that would be frowned on in more interdependent collectivist societies (Triandis, 2001). Personality traits also change from one generation to the next; for example, based on test scores, U.S. students have been increasing in self-esteem and extraversion but also in anxiety and neuroticism (Twenge, 2000, 2001a; Twenge & Campbell, 2001). Much remains to be done to understand adequately the role of social influences on personality, but we can be sure that some of the motivations that direct people are shaped by their culture.

Personality Development

Another major issue in personality theory concerns the formation and change of personality. To what extent is personality influenced by biological factors, such as heredity? To what extent can personality change as a result of learning? How critical are the childhood years for personality development, and how much change can occur in adulthood? Besides "how much" is the question of how: How do we change personality in the direction we would like, to turn high-risk children toward healthier paths of development or to teach ordinary folk to be creative or to be leaders?

BIOLOGICAL INFLUENCES

temperament
consistent styles of behavior and emotional reactions present from early life onward, presumably caused by biological factors

Some children seem to be quiet or energetic or whatever from the moment of birth. Could it be that personality is genetically determined? The term **temperament** refers to consistent styles of behavior and emotional reactions that are present from infancy onward, presumably because of biological influences. As long ago as ancient Greece, philosophers and physicians believed that inborn predispositions lead one person to be melancholic and another sanguine (Kagan, 1994). Developmental psychologists have been observing temperament differences in children for quite some time, but within personality theory, biological predispositions were ignored or acknowledged without detailed considerations, until recently.

Evidence is accumulating to an impressive degree to support the claim that personality is significantly influenced by heredity. With the explosion of research in genetics and neuroscience, modern personality researchers are moving beyond the speculation of classic theorists about the role of biology, identifying biological mechanisms that contribute to such aspects of personality as the tendency for some people to be outgoing and others to be shy. However, we should keep in mind that biology plays out its influence in the environment, and different environments can make quite different personalities out of the same biological potential.

TABLE 1.2   Major Issues Addressed by Personality Theories

Issue	*Examples of Approaches to These Issues*
Descriptive Issues	
Individual Differences	What are the traits that distinguish people?
	How can these traits be measured?
	Should we look at what people say, or what they do, to describe how they are unique?
	Are people consistent?
Dynamic Issues	
Adaptation and Adjustment	How do people adapt to life's demands?
	How does a mentally healthy person act?
	What behaviors or thoughts are unhealthy?
Cognitive Processes	Do our thoughts affect our personality?
	What kinds of thoughts are important for personality?
	Do unconscious processes influence us?
Culture	How does culture influence our functioning?
	Does culture affect us by its expectations for men and women?
	For different classes?
Society	How does society influence our functioning?
	Does society affect us by its expectations for men and women?
	For different races and classes?
Developmental Issues	
Biological Influences	How do biological processes affect personality?
	Is personality inherited?
Child Development	How should children be treated?
	What do children learn that matters for personality?
	Does childhood experience determine adult personality?
Adult Development	Do adults change? Or has personality been determined earlier?
	What experiences in adulthood influence personality?

These categories are presented for purposes of an overview. In many personality theories, the topics listed under each issue also are related to other issues.

EXPERIENCE IN CHILDHOOD AND ADULTHOOD

Personality develops over time. Experience, especially in childhood, influences the way each person develops toward his or her unique personality. Many of the major personality theories described in this text make statements about the development of personality. Theorists in the psychoanalytic tradition, for example, emphasize the experience of the preschool years in forming personality. Theories in the learning tradition focus primarily on change, but even some of them (e.g., Staats, 1996) propose that early learning can significantly influence the course of personality throughout life by developing essential skills on which later experience builds. In the emotional domain, early development of bonds of attachment with the parents is receiving considerable attention and is widely thought to influence relationships with people into adulthood. Although people do change, considerable evidence indicates the stability of personality over a person's lifetime (e.g., McCrae & Costa, 1984).

To the Student

At the beginning of each chapter is a preview of its theory based on several of the issues just discussed. The issues often overlap. For example, cognitive processes not only are dynamic but also can be considered descriptive, because individuals differ in them, and developmental, because they change over time. You might begin your study of personality by considering what you believe about these issues based on your own life experience, trying to answer the questions in Table 1.2. Then, to get a preview of the field of personality, browse through the summaries at the beginning of each chapter. Do some theories match your ideas more than others do? Do you find new or puzzling ideas in these preview tables? This formal study of personality ideally will offer you new ideas and help you think critically about those you already believe.

The Scientific Approach

scientific method the method of knowing based on systematic observation

Personality theorists, like psychology theorists more generally, test their assertions about people through the scientific method. The **scientific method** requires systematic observations and a willingness to modify understanding based on these observations. The assumption of **determinism** is central to the scientific method. Determinism refers to the assumption that the phenomena being studied have causes and that empirical research can discover these causes.

determinism the assumption that phenomena have causes that can be discovered by empirical research

In the scientific method, two different levels of abstraction are important. In Figure 1.1, two abstract concepts are proposed at the theoretical level, "high self-esteem" and "social responsibility." The theoretical proposition "High self-esteem causes social responsibility" asserts that a cause-and-effect relationship exists between these two concepts. Abstract concepts cannot be directly observed. They do, however, correspond to observable phenomena, indicated at the observable level in Figure 1.1.

Notice in Figure 1.2 that the constructs and observations can be phrased in reverse without changing the meaning. However phrased, these figures suggest that at the observable level, people who score high on a self-esteem test should like themselves, talk about their successes, smile, and dress nicely; the opposite behaviors will be observable among people who score low on a self-esteem test. Furthermore, the high self-esteem people should also be observed engaging in behaviors that are observable evidences of the abstract concept of social responsibility. They should obey laws, join political groups,

Figure 1.1 Levels of Thinking in Theory

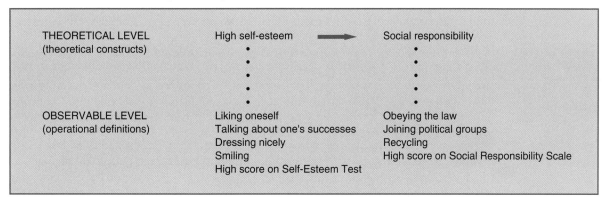

recycle, and score high on a test of social responsibility. People who are low in self-esteem should engage in the opposite behaviors. Clear scientific language makes explicit what we observe and what abstract theoretical ideas predict and explain those observations.

THEORY

A **theory** is a conceptual tool for understanding certain specified phenomena. It includes concepts (theoretical constructs) and statements about how they are related (theoretical propositions). The concepts of a theory are called theoretical **constructs**. One kind of theoretical construct already mentioned is a personality trait. Traits are often considered to be the underlying units of personality. Examples of traits include shy, intelligent, athletic, and so on. Because traits are assumed to remain constant and determine behavior, people are expected to behave consistently at different times and in different situations.

Traits, like all theoretical constructs, are not themselves directly observable. They are related to observable behaviors through **operational definitions**, statements identifying what observable phenomena are evidence of a particular trait. In Figures 1.1 and 1.2, the trait self-esteem is operationally defined to correspond to various observable behaviors: talking about successes (rather than failures), dressing nicely (rather than poorly), and

theory a conceptual tool, consisting of systematically organized constructs and propositions, for understanding certain specified phenomena

construct a concept used in a theory

operational definition procedure for measuring a theoretical construct

Figure 1.2 Levels of Thinking in Theory: Another View

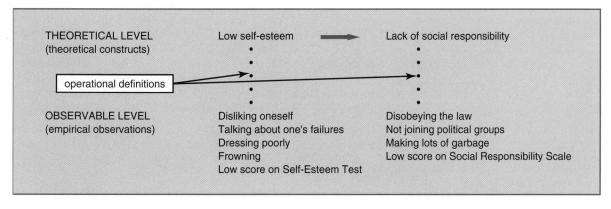

scoring high on a self-esteem test (rather than scoring low). Each trait or other theoretical construct can have many different operational definitions. Because they all correspond to the same trait, we would expect these observations to be positively correlated with one another.

theoretical proposition theoretical statement about relationships among theoretical constructs

A theory contains various **theoretical propositions**, which tell how the constructs are related. For example, in Figure 1.1 the theoretical proposition diagrammed hypothesizes that "self-esteem causes social responsibility." Both self-esteem and social responsibility are theoretical constructs, and as such they are abstract conceptual tools that cannot be directly observed. Theoretical propositions are also abstract statements and are not themselves directly observable (cf. Clark & Paivio, 1989).

To test a theory, predictions about observable phenomena are logically derived from the theoretical propositions. Consider the example of a classic theoretical proposition in psychology that states, "Frustration leads to aggression." When this proposition is stated in terms of observable phenomena (i.e., in terms of the constructs as operationally defined), we have a **hypothesis**, which can be tested by **empirical** observation (see Figure 1.3).

hypothesis a prediction to be tested by research

empirical based on scientific observations

Research tests whether hypotheses derived from theory make predictions that are confirmed by actual empirical observations. Does the abstract theoretical world accurately predict what actually takes place in the real world? The more reliably hypotheses derived from a theory are tested and confirmed by empirical research, the more confidence we have in the theory. When observations differ from prediction, the theory is disconfirmed. If this occurs often, the theory will be revised to make it more accurate, or it may even be abandoned.

Figure 1.3 Hypotheses Derived from a Theoretical Position

THEORETICAL CONSTRUCTS:	Frustration Aggression
THEORETICAL PROPOSITION:	Frustration leads to aggression.
OPERATIONAL DEFINITIONS:	
Frustration	Losing 75 cents in a soda machine. Failing an exam. Losing one's job.
Aggression	Kicking the soda machine. Rating the instructor as "poor." Beating one's spouse.

HYPOTHESES:

1. Subjects who lose 75 cents in a soda machine (which is rigged by the experimenter) will kick the soda machine more often than a control group, which does not lose money.

2. Students who are told that they have failed an exam will rate their instructor lower than students who are told they have passed the exam.

3. When unemployment rises, the number of reported spouse beatings will increase.

CRITERIA OF A GOOD THEORY

Theories are always somewhat tentative. Elementary students of science know this when they differentiate between theories and facts, the latter being more definite and less arguable than theories. (Such elementary students commonly have the misconception that when we become certain of our theories, they will be considered facts. This misunderstanding stems from ignorance of the difference between the theoretical level and the level of observables presented earlier in this chapter. Facts are always at the level of observables; theories never are.) Because theories are abstract, a certain amount of ambiguity can be expected, compared to the concrete details that come as factual observations. Not all theories are equally valuable, however. How can we decide whether a theory is worthwhile?

Several criteria are generally accepted for evaluating scientific theories. Philosophers of science suggest these criteria, and they are commonly used to argue for or against various theories in psychology. Some psychologists disagree about how to apply the criteria (e.g., McMullin, 1990; Meehl, 1990), and others argue that the prevailing philosophies of science are too restricted to the assumptions of the natural sciences and do not address specifically psychological issues such as free will (Rychlak, 1988), but at least philosophers of science have given us some ground rules for debate. That is not to say that individuals always base their personal theoretical preferences on these criteria. Psychology majors, for example, report that they prefer theories that help them understand themselves (Vyse, 1990). It may take effort to apply the more impersonal criteria that we discuss next, but the effort is worthwhile. These criteria guide psychology from intuitive knowledge toward a firmer scientific base.

Verifiability

The most important criterion is that a theory should be **verifiable**, that is, testable through empirical methods. If we specify what evidence would support a theory and what evidence would refute it, we can test the theory scientifically. This requires, first, that the theoretical constructs be defined with precision so it is clear what is meant by the construct. Consider the frustration-aggression example in Figure 1.3. Is "kicking a soda machine" really aggression? Is "rating a teacher as poor" an example of aggression? Vaguely defined constructs are of little use in a scientific theory.

verifiable the ability of a theory to be tested by empirical procedures, resulting in confirmation or disconfirmation

Next, the operational definitions must be clear and reliably measurable. Operational definitions may include written tests, clinical judgments, interpersonal ratings, observations of behavior, and other well-specified ways of making observations.

Finally, the theory must predict relationships among these measurements so clearly, in the form of hypotheses, that observations can be made to support or refute the prediction. **Disconfirmation** is particularly important for advancing science. It is always possible to find supportive evidence for a vaguely formulated theory. The criterion of verifiability requires that we also identify evidence that would refute the theory.

disconfirmation evidence against a theory; observations that contradict the predictions of a hypothesis

Comprehensiveness

Other things being equal, a good theory is characterized by **comprehensiveness**. That is, it explains a broad range of behavior. Most traditional personality theories are broad, comprehensive theories dealing with many phenomena: developmental processes in childhood, adaptation or mental health, self-image, social interactions with other people, biological influences, and so forth. All else being equal, theories that explain a wider

comprehensiveness the ability of a theory to explain a broad variety of observations

range of phenomena are better theories. In practice, however, if a theory attempts to explain too much, its concepts tend to become fuzzy and ill defined so the theory cannot be tested adequately. Although comprehensiveness is a desirable characteristic in a theory, it is less important than empirical verifiability.

Applied Value

applied value the ability of a theory to guide practical uses

A theory that has **applied value**, offering practical strategies for improving human life, has an edge over theories that are simply intellectually satisfying. For example, personality theories may suggest therapeutic interventions; guide child care; help select the best employees for a particular job; or even predict what will happen in politics, based on the leader's personality (Immelman, 1993). As in many fields, personality psychology has both basic and applied interests that are not always integrated. **Applied research** is conducted to solve practical problems. **Basic research** is conducted for the purpose of advancing theory and scientific knowledge.

applied research research intended for practical use

basic research research intended to develop theory

Other Considerations: Parsimony and Heuristic Value

Besides the three important criteria of verifiability, comprehensiveness, and applied value, theories that are parsimonious and have heuristic value are preferred. A *parsimonious* theory is one that does not propose an excessive number of narrow constructs or propositions if a smaller number of broad constructs could explain the phenomena under consideration. To do so makes the theory unnecessarily complicated. However, humans are complex creatures, so a theory with too few constructs or propositions may be too simplistic to permit detailed prediction.

The ability of a theory to suggest new ideas for further theory and research is called its *heuristic value*. Another term for heuristic value is *fertility* (e.g., Howard, 1985). Scientific understanding is not static. Scientists build on the work of earlier scientists, moving toward an improved understanding. Just as artists replace rough sketches with more elaborate drawings, theories are replaced by their more polished successors.

RELATIONSHIP BETWEEN THEORY AND RESEARCH

Research and theory building in personality ideally go hand in hand. At the level of theory, constructs and theoretical propositions are proposed. By a process of deductive reasoning, hypotheses are derived and, through research, tested.

Theory leads to research. The converse is also true: Research leads to theory (Gigerenzer, 1991). Unexplained observations lead scientists to think inductively. They then suggest new or revised theoretical constructs and propositions. Theory without adequate research becomes stagnant. Research without adequate theory can wander aimlessly.

Scientific development of theories must advance against the complication that people are, in their everyday lives, informal personality theorists. Making distinctions among individuals is second nature to people in their everyday lives (cf. Lupfer, Clark, & Hutcherson, 1990). Everyday unscientific beliefs about personality are sometimes called **implicit theories of personality**. We assume that certain phenomena that we have seen are accompanied by other personality characteristics, even though we may not have had an opportunity to observe them. Attractive people, for example, are often assumed to be warm and trustworthy. Implicit theories are especially important when we judge people we don't know (Vonk & Heiser, 1991). For example, many undergraduates base sexual

implicit theories of personality ideas about personality that are held by ordinary people (not based on formal theory)

decisions on implicit personality theories, believing they can assess HIV status by appearance and other irrelevant factors (Williams et al., 1992).

Implicit personality theories are not necessarily incorrect. Some researchers believe they often correspond to the formal theories that have been derived from extensive research (Sneed, McCrae, & Funder, 1998). There is no guarantee of their accuracy, though. Well-planned research studies are necessary to test, and sometimes to correct, many errors emanating from implicit theories.

Methods in Personality Research

Throughout its history, personality research has used a variety of research methods: personality scales and questionnaires, projective techniques, observer judgments, and laboratory methods. In addition, biographical analyses and case studies permit investigations of individuals, and various physiological measures, such as genetic analysis and studies of immune system functioning, attest to the increasing attention to biological aspects of personality.

PERSONALITY MEASUREMENT

Measurement of personality involves operationally defining theoretical constructs by specifying how they will be assessed. The most common type of measurement is the self-report personality test, which asks many questions, often in multiple-choice format, under a standard set of instructions. It is not difficult to write personality test items; you have probably seen so-called pop psychology personality tests in magazines or on the Internet. However, establishing their value is more difficult. What constitutes sound measurement? Some qualities are described next.

Reliability

Measurement should yield consistent scores from one time to another. Such **reliability** is determined in several ways. *Test-retest reliability* is determined by testing the same subjects on two occasions and calculating the extent to which the two scores agree. Do the same people who score high on the first occasion also score high the second time? They will if the test is reliable. Could it be, though, that they simply remember how they answered the first time (even if they were guessing), which is why the scores do not change? The method of *alternate forms reliability* gets around this problem by giving different versions of the questionnaire on each occasion. If subjects are tested only once, researchers can estimate reliability by calculating subscores based on the two halves of the questionnaire. Generally, all the odd-numbered items are added together for one score and all the even-numbered items for the other score. The correlation between these two subscores is computed; this correlation is called *split-half reliability*.

Problems of unreliability can result from several factors. Short tests are generally less reliable than longer tests. Tests combining unrelated items are less reliable than those composed of closely correlated items, or *homogeneous items*. Other factors that reduce reliability are ambiguously worded test items and uncontrolled factors in the test-taking situation that influence responses. In addition, real change can occur between the two times that the psychological characteristic is measured, although perhaps in this last case it would be better to speak of personality change rather than unreliability of measurement.

reliability consistency, as when a measurement is repeated at another time or by another observer, with similar results

Validity

Someone could claim to assess your intelligence by measuring the circumference of your head, or your morality by examining your skull for bumps in particular locations, as phrenologists once did. Undoubtedly, except in very unusual cases, these would be quite reliable measures. Yet we would not accept them. Such measures might be reliable, but they are not valid.

validity desirable characteristic of a test, indicating it actually does measure what it is intended to measure

Validity is present if a test really measures what it claims to measure. Whereas reliability can be assessed straightforwardly, determining validity requires careful specification of the theoretical construct to clearly indicate what is supposed to be measured. *Predictive validity* is established if a test predicts a behavior that the researcher accepts as a *criterion* for the construct being measured (e.g., if a test of assertiveness predicts the number of times a person initiates conversations). In the known groups method, a test is given to different groups of people who are known to differ in what the test measures. For example, a test of mental well-being should produce higher scores among college students than among psychiatric patients (Hattie & Cooksey, 1984). Employers use a variety of tests when they are deciding which job applicant to hire, and researchers have studied these tests to determine which have the best validity as predictors of effective employee selection. They have found that tests do improve selection over simply using employment interviews (Schmidt & Hunter, 1998). However, test validity can be reduced by several factors, including respondents' intentional distortion of responses (Furnham, 1990b), their misunderstanding of test items, and their lack of knowledge or insight about the material being asked.

Predictive validity focuses primarily on the validity of a particular test. What about the validity of the theoretical construct? This question goes beyond measurement. If a theoretical construct is valid, it will be possible to define it operationally in a variety of ways, and we would expect these various measures to be correlated. Furthermore, the relationships of the construct with other variables, which are predicted by theory, should be similar regardless which particular measure is used. Consider this imaginary example: If a researcher finds that a new form of therapy reduces patients' anxiety when measured by a self-report but increases their anxiety when a behavioral observation is used instead, we would doubt the construct validity of anxiety. Perhaps one or both of the measures is defective. Perhaps anxiety is not the one unified combination of behavior and experience that we thought. Until compelling evidence indicates that two measures are comparable, it is best to limit our claims of validity to each measure separately, or, to use Jerome Kagan's apt phrase, "validity is local" (1990, p. 294). However, if several research studies using a variety of measures present converging lines of evidence for the usefulness of a theoretical construct—for example, if many studies using various measurement methods find that the new therapy reduces anxiety—we can make the important and bold claim that **construct validity** (of anxiety) has been established (Cronbach & Meehl, 1955).

construct validity the usefulness of a theoretical term, evidenced by an accumulation of research findings

Measurement Techniques

Various measurement techniques have been used in personality research. Usually, subjects are asked to provide some sorts of verbal statements that are analyzed.

Direct self-report measures ask subjects to respond to specific questions, generally in multiple-choice format. They may be either questionnaires (that measure one trait or construct) or inventories (that measure several traits or constructs, e.g., the California Personality Inventory and the Minnesota Multiphasic Personality Inventory). Self-report measures are easy to administer and often reliable, but they have disadvantages. Subjects may not have enough self-knowledge to provide accurate information. They may intentionally give false responses, or they may be influenced by response sets, such as the tendency to agree with items regardless of content.

Alternatively, personality can be measured through *indirect* methods. When people talk or write without having to pick a multiple-choice answer, many of the sources of distortion are reduced. *Open-ended questions* (e.g., "Tell me about your experiences at college") or other materials (journals, diaries, letters, etc.) can provide data for researchers to interpret (C. P. Smith, 1992). *Projective tests* present subjects with ambiguous stimuli (such as pictures or inkblots) to which they respond. The indirect approach can avoid some of the shortcomings of verbal reports. (What sort of imaginative story would you make up about an inkblot to look well adjusted, for example? It's hard to say!) The indirect approach may reveal material of which the person is unaware, and thus it avoids intentional deception and the limitations of conscious experience. Projective tests include the famous Rorschach inkblot test and the Thematic Apperception Test (TAT), which asks subjects to make up stories based on pictures.

Behavioral measures are sometimes included in personality research. This type of measurement helps develop an understanding of personality in its real-world context. Observers may watch people in real life or in a laboratory, or subjects can be asked to provide information about their real-life experiences. We have to keep in mind, though, that such self-reports may not always be accurate reports of experience because of forgetting, inattention, distortion, or a variety of other reasons.

Test scores are important data in personality research, but they can be misleading. Any test score may be inaccurate for a variety of reasons. Tests that are valid for adults may not be valid for children; tests that are valid for majority cultures may be biased when applied to minorities. Failure to recognize such limitations as this can lead to racial and ethnic bias in psychological tests when they are used to predict individual outcomes, and can limit the development of theories.

CORRELATIONAL STUDIES

Much personality research is correlational. **Correlational research**, which measures two or more variables to study how they are related, is vital to refining descriptions of personality. Sometimes two measures are studied for a single theoretical construct; in such a case, these measures should be correlated. At other times, two different theoretical constructs are predicted to be correlated because theoretical propositions describe one as causing the other (e.g., "Frustration causes aggression").

correlational research research method that examines the relationships among measurements

Causes and effects should be correlated; but there is no guarantee that when two variables are correlated, one is the cause and the other is the effect. Correlational research cannot provide strong proof of causation. Two observations can be correlated because one causes another, or because both are caused by a third variable. For example, suppose a correlational research study finds that two variables are associated in a study of elementary school children: number of hours of television watched (variable A) and children's aggressiveness, determined by observing behavior on the playground (variable B). What can we conclude based on this correlational research? First, it is possible that A causes B; that is, watching television increases the children's aggressive behavior. Second, it is possible that B causes A: Friends may reject aggressive children after school, and, having no one to play with, they watch television instead. Third, it is possible that another variable, C, causes both A and B, leading to their correlation without either causing the other. What might such a third variable be? Perhaps having neglectful parents causes children to watch more television (because they are not encouraged in other activities that would place more demands on their parents) and also causes them to be aggressive on the playground (because they have not been taught more mature social skills). The point is that correlational research is always ambiguous about the causes underlying the associations observed. From such a study it is not clear that aggressiveness could be reduced by limiting television, by increasing parental attention, or by changing any of the other potential causes that could account for the relationship. Causal ambiguities can be resolved through another research strategy: experimentation.

EXPERIMENTATION

true experimental research research strategy that manipulates a cause to determine its effect

In **true experimental research**, hypothesized cause-and-effect relationships are put to a direct test. An **independent variable**, which the researcher suspects is the cause, is manipulated by the researcher. An **experimental group** is exposed to the independent variable. A **control group** is not exposed to the independent variable. These groups, formed by random assignment to make everything else equal, are then compared to see whether they have different scores on the **dependent variable**, which is the hypothesized effect.

independent variable in an experiment, the cause that is manipulated by the researcher

An experiment could be conducted for the preceding example to test whether watching a lot of television causes an increase in aggressive behavior. An experimental group would be assigned to watch a great deal of television. A control group would watch little television. Then their aggressive behavior on the playground would be observed. If watching television (the independent variable) is the cause, there will be differences between the two groups in their level of aggression (the dependent variable). If some other **variable** is the cause, the two groups will not differ in aggression.

experimental group in an experiment, the group exposed to the experimental treatment

control group in an experiment, the group not exposed to the experimental treatment

Logically, it is easier to imagine situations as independent variables in an experiment than personality. It is fairly easy to manipulate television viewing. In contrast, how could we manipulate aggressiveness, a personality trait, if we believe the trait of aggressiveness is the cause of aggressive behavior? Most often, this is not possible because research participants bring their personalities to the research, and all the researcher can do is measure them. One strategy, however, is to change personality for an experimental group through some kind of situational manipulation or therapy program. Mischel (1992) and Bandura (1986b) have conducted much experimental research in which situations or training interventions are manipulated to change aspects of personality and then effects on behavior are observed. Similarly, a program of research by McClelland and Winter (1969) changed businessmen's trait of "need for achievement" through a training program and found that this change brought about changes in their business activities. Experimental techniques have occasionally been used by psychoanalytically oriented researchers who have experimentally aroused unconscious material to investigate psychodynamics (e.g., Shulman & Ferguson, 1988; Silverman, 1976, 1983). Nonetheless, experimental research in personality is conducted less often than correlational research, in which personality is measured rather than manipulated.

dependent variable the effect in an experimental study

variable in research, a measurement of something across various people (or times or situations), which takes on different values

Constructs derived from experimental research are not necessarily interchangeable with those derived from correlational research (Brogden, 1972; West, 1986). For example, a generally anxious person (with a trait of anxiety) may not be comparable to a generally calm person who is temporarily anxious because of a crisis (with a temporary *state* of anxiety).

The importance of experimentation for testing cause-and-effect relationships cannot be emphasized enough, but it isn't always practical or even ethical to subject people to experiments. Fortunately, we can also gain evidence from quasi experiments in which people are exposed to interventions that are expected to reveal personality processes, but where experimenters don't exert all the usual controls (especially random assignment). One intervention that has been important throughout the history of personality research is *psychotherapy*. In therapy, the intent is to change (improve) the functioning of an individual's personality. If therapy can be shown to have this positive effect, it offers evidence supporting the theory on which it is based. The evidence has to be evaluated critically. There may be factors beyond those suggested by the theory that cause therapy to be effective: the expectation of improving, for example, and the relationship with a therapist. Because these factors influence many therapies, they should cause all of them to have beneficial effects that are not limited to a particular mode of therapy, and much evidence exists for this interpretation. Also, because there are limitations to the scientific controls that can be put in place during therapy for establishing cause-and-effect relationships, a mature science of personality must also conduct experiments outside of this setting, where necessary controls can be put in place.

STUDYING INDIVIDUALS: CASE STUDIES AND PSYCHOBIOGRAPHY

When researchers study individuals instead of groups, they often describe their observations in ways that remind us of people telling their life stories. These narratives are often rich in detail and imagery, and they can convey emotional insights in ways that more statistical data cannot. A **case study** is an intensive investigation of a single individual. For example, a clinician may describe an individual client (Gedo, 1999), or an educational psychologist may describe an individual child. When the focus is on theoretical considerations, case studies are called **psychobiography**. In psychobiography, the researcher often works from archival data, such as letters, books, and interviews, rather than directly interacting with the person being described.

case study an intensive investigation of a single individual

psychobiography the application of a personality theory to the study of an individual's life; different from a case study because of its theoretical emphasis

The analysis of individuals is occasionally prompted by practical, even political, considerations. For example, in 1943 U.S. government officials requested a psychological analysis of Adolf Hitler (Runyan, 1982), an analysis that was later published (Langer, 1972). In the early 1960s, a similar request was made for an analysis of the Soviet leader Nikita Khrushchev (Mack, 1971). When a person has died and suicide is suspected, a "psychological autopsy" may be carried out to help determine whether the case was a suicide, and if so, why it occurred (Brent, 1989; Kewman & Tate, 1998; Otto et al., 1993).

Psychobiographical studies need not be limited to one person. They can investigate several individuals representing a particular group, such as women (H. M. Buss, 1990) or homosexuals (G. Sullivan, 1990). The emphasis is still on individual personality, though, except that the various members of the group are considered similar. In contrast, psychohistory looks beyond the individuals to the larger world stage of history. Many of the theories we study in this book, especially the psychoanalytic theories (Freud, Jung, and Adler), offer insights into history as well as biography (Goldwert, 1991).

Studies of individuals using nonexperimental methods lack both the statistical advantages of large correlational studies and the advantages stemming from control of independent variables in the experimental method. Without these controls, alternate interpretations of the same material are possible (Runyan, 1981), making definitive analyses elusive. Principles for case study research differ from those for studying groups (Edwards, 1998). Despite the difficulties, case studies are invaluable if we are to be sure that our theoretical concepts do indeed help us understand individual personality dynamics.

William McKinley Runyan defines psychobiography as "the explicit use of formal or systematic psychology in biography" (1982, p. 233). Much psychobiography in the past has been based on psychoanalytic theory. The founder of psychoanalysis, Sigmund Freud (1910/1957), wrote the first psychobiography: a study of Leonardo da Vinci. Ironically, Freud did not follow the standards of sound psychobiography that he set out in the same work (Elms, 1988). Psychoanalysis warns that subjective factors (transference) can be a source of error in psychobiography (Schepeler, 1990). Psychoanalytic theory has been the predominant theory guiding psychobiographical analyses ever since Freud's initial effort (e.g., Baron & Pletsch, 1985; Ciardiello, 1985; Erikson, 1958b; Freud & Bullitt, 1966). It has shortcomings, however. For one thing, evidence about childhood experience, which is so important in psychoanalytic formulations, is often poor (Runyan, 1982). The theory often leads to overemphasizing a particular period, the "critical period fallacy," or specific life events, "eventism" (Mack, 1971). Also, psychoanalytic theory does not call attention to historical and cultural factors that influence personality (L. Stone, 1981).

Other theories have also guided psychobiography. For example, Raymond Cattell's theory has been used to analyze Martin Luther and other Reformation leaders (Wright, 1985), and Henry Murray's theory has been applied to a psychobiographical study of Richard Nixon (Winter & Carlson, 1988). Researchers have developed systematic ways to analyze existing materials, such as personal documents, diaries, letters, and dream records (Alexander, 1988, 1990; Carlson, 1981, 1988; Gruber, 1989; McAdams, 1990; Ochberg, 1988; Stewart, Franz, & Layton, 1988). Computer methods for analyzing verbal materials exist, but human judges are still essential in these narrative approaches, making such research extremely labor intensive.

One Theory or Many? Eclecticism and the Future of Personality Theory

eclectic combining ideas from a variety of theories

paradigm a basic theoretical model, shared by various theorists and researchers

Most personality psychologists prefer an **eclectic** approach, one that combines insights from many different theories. Empirical research does not validate one theoretical perspective so convincingly that others are made obsolete. In the language of Thomas Kuhn (1970), no single **paradigm** serves as a theoretical model accepted by the entire field of personality. There are, instead, competing perspectives, including psychoanalysis, learning theory, trait approaches, and humanistic psychology. Some attempts have been made to integrate theories. For the most part, though, theories simply coexist, each developing its own theoretical and research literature. Why?

First, some of this fragmentation is related to larger divisions in psychology between what have traditionally been called the "two disciplines" (Cronbach, 1957, 1975) or "two cultures" (Kimble, 1984) of psychology. One side emphasizes experimentation and studies groups of people. The other side is more interested in individuals and content to compromise experimental rigor to focus on aspects of the person that cannot be studied experimentally. Gregory Kimble (1984) undoubtedly spoke for many psychologists when he expressed pessimism about the chances for achieving an integration of the two orientations (see Table 1.3).

Second, theories may have different areas of usefulness. For example, one theory may be useful for understanding people's subjective experiences of life, another for predicting how people will behave in given situations. Some theories may help us understand the mentally ill or individuals distraught from overwhelming stress; other theories may be

TABLE 1.3	Kimble's Analysis of "Scientific" versus "Humanistic" Psychology	
	Scientific Culture	*Humanistic Culture*
Research Setting	Laboratory	Field study and case study
Generality of Laws	Nomothetic	Idiographic
Level of Analysis	Elementism	Holism
Scholarly Values	Scientific	Humanistic
Source of Knowledge	Observation	Intuition

Kimble, G. A. (1984). Psychology's two cultures. *American Psychologist, 39*, 833–839. Copyright 1984 by the American Psychological Association. Adapted by permission.

more useful in understanding the creative heights of those who have become highly developed. Some theories may seem to apply only to males or to those with enough food to be concerned with less mundane issues than mere survival.

Besides the different areas of application, theories specialize in different influences on personality. Some focus on early experience; others on the impact of thought; others on biological influences; and so on. Because diverse psychological processes influence individual personality, and because influences range from the biological to the social, the field of personality may always be more comprehensive than any single theory can encompass, unless it is very broad in scope indeed. Consider what must be included: cognitive processes, people's goals and sense of human agency; cultural, ethnic, and gender influences; heredity and other biological influences. In all this, one wonders whether personality theories will always remain as diverse as they are at present, or whether some day a unified theory, with multiple levels and applications, may emerge.

To be sure, it would be easy to get lost in such theoretical debates, but the subject matter of our discipline always brings us back to people. Past and current personality theories both help and hinder progress toward new theories that explain people. They help to the extent that they provide useful and heuristic concepts. They hinder to the extent that theoretical preconceptions, like implicit personality theories, blind us to new directions. How can we remove such blinders? One suggestion, to borrow advice from the British statesman Benjamin Disraeli, is to

> Read . . . biography, for that is life without theory. (*Contarini Fleming*, pt. i, chap. 23)

Summary

- *Personality* is defined as the underlying causes within the person of individual behavior and experience.
- Three areas are addressed by personality theory: *description, dynamics*, and *development*.
- Personality can be described in terms of broad types or more numerous, and narrower, traits.

- Using statistical techniques, traits can be combined into personality *factors*.
- The *nomothetic approach* describes personality by making comparisons among people.
- Studies of single individuals use the *idiographic approach*.
- Personality *dynamics* refers to the motivational aspect of personality. Some theorists emphasize common motivations, which influence all people, whereas others focus on individual differences.
- Personality dynamics permit *adaptation* to the world and may be studied in terms of adjustment or mental health.
- Personality *development* in childhood and adulthood is also described by the various theories, recognizing biological and social influences on development.
- The scientific approach assumes *determinism* and makes systematic observations to test and revise theories.
- Theoretical *constructs* and *propositions* are made testable through operational definitions and hypotheses.
- Theories are evaluated according to the criteria of *verifiability, comprehensiveness*, and *applied value*.
- Theory and research mutually influence one another.
- Personality measurement, which should be *reliable* and *valid*, uses various techniques, including self-report measures, projective measures, measures of life experiences, and behavioral measures.
- Research techniques include *correlational* research, in which associations are examined among various measures, and *experimental* research, in which cause-and-effect relationships are tested by manipulating an *independent* variable to examine its effect on a *dependent variable*.
- Two methods, *case studies* and *psychobiography*, study one individual intensively. Psychobiography, in which theory is systematically used to understand one individual, can offer suggestions for theory development.
- People have informal *implicit theories of personality* with which they try to understand others.
- Personality psychologists use many *paradigms* for understanding personality. Many adopt an *eclectic* approach, whereas others seek to integrate competing theories.

Thinking about Personality Theory

1. Look again at the literary sayings at the beginning of the chapter. Discuss them in terms of the concerns of personality theory. For example, do they relate to description, dynamics, or development? Can they be verified? Can you think of any sayings about personality in addition to those quoted at the beginning of the chapter?

2. How important do you think it is for personality theory to be evaluated according to scientific criteria? Is the scientific method too limiting?

3. What implicit ideas about personality, besides those mentioned in the text, might produce bias when we think about personality?

4. Look at the preview tables for the coming chapters. Which of these theories most appeal to you? Why?

Study Questions

1. Define personality.
2. List and explain the three issues that personality theory studies.
3. Contrast types, traits, and factors as units of description in personality.
4. Explain the difference between idiographic and nomothetic approaches.
5. Explain what is meant by personality dynamics.
6. Explain the term *adaptation*.
7. Describe how cognitive processes and culture are related to personality dynamics.
8. What are some important influences on personality development?
9. Explain what is meant by temperament.
10. Describe the scientific approach to personality. Include in your answer theoretical constructs, propositions, operational definitions, and hypotheses.
11. List and explain the criteria of a good theory.
12. Discuss the relationship between theory and research.
13. Describe some ways in which personality can be measured.
14. Explain reliability and validity of measurement.
15. Explain the difference between correlational studies and experimental studies.
16. What is psychobiography? Discuss the strengths and weaknesses of this approach to understanding personality.
17. What is an implicit theory of personality? How is it different from a formal personality theory?
18. What is eclecticism? Why might someone prefer to have more than one theory?

The Psychoanalytic Perspective

The psychoanalytic perspective on personality has become one of the most widely known approaches outside of psychology. Within psychology, it has steadfast adherents and forceful critics. The central idea of the psychoanalytic perspective is the unconscious. Simply put, this concept says that people are not aware of the most important determinants of their behavior. Self-understanding is quite limited and often incorrect. This concept of an unconscious, proposed by Freud, gives patients in therapy a way of thinking about their behavior, moods, or other symptoms that seem out of touch with their conscious intentions; thus it has been a valuable concept in the therapeutic setting (Piers, 1998).

All psychoanalytic approaches maintain the concept of a dynamic unconscious—that is, one that has motivations or energies and so can influence behavior and experience. Various psychoanalytic theories describe the unconscious differently. Sigmund Freud (see Chapter 2) proposed that the unconscious consists of sexual and aggressive wishes that are unacceptable to the conscious personality. For Carl Jung (see Chapter 3), the unconscious is not primarily sexual; it consists of more general motivations, which have spiritual content. Other theorists, including Melanie Klein (1946) and Harry Stack Sullivan (1953), have described the unconscious as consisting of primitive concepts about the self and relationships with other people, especially the mother as the first "other" the infant encounters.

Despite these variations, psychoanalysts share characteristic assumptions:

1. Personality is strongly influenced by unconscious determinants.
2. The unconscious is dynamic, or motivational, and is in conflict with other aspects of the unconscious and with consciousness.
3. The unconscious originates in early experience.

Psychoanalysis originated and has continued to be developed in the context of psychotherapy. Its professional communications were historically largely restricted to journals and organizations that are outside of the academic scientific tradition of empirical testing of theoretical propositions, but in recent years more effort has been made to test psychoanalytic ideas, such as repression and defense mechanisms, in controlled studies. The primary data for psychoanalysts consist of reports by patients in therapy, in which they are encouraged to express thoughts that would otherwise be dismissed. The fact that these inferences are not generally checked for historical accuracy with outside evidence has been the focus of considerable controversy when inferences about sexual abuse have led patients to confront their alleged abusers. Psychoanalysts generally doubt that the complexities of personality, especially unconscious processes, can be measured by objective instruments (cf. Sugarman, 1991). When formal measurement is used, psychoanalysts often employ projective techniques. Projective techniques present ambiguous stimuli, such as inkblots in the well-known Rorschach test, and ask the patients (or research subjects) to say what they see in them. Such techniques are generally reputed to be less reliable than questionnaires, but their advocates claim that they provide access to deeper levels of motivation not available to conscious awareness.

Psychoanalytic personality theory assumes that these projective test reports provide information that is broadly applicable, not only to those who seek therapeutic assistance but also to the general population. However, this assumption is challenged by those outside the psychoanalytic framework. Another objection is that psychoanalytic theorists have not clearly specified the types of evidence that would refute psychoanalytic theory. Psychoanalysts often are aware of conflicts between one kind of conscious motivation (e.g., self-control) and an opposite unconscious motivation (e.g., sexual freedom). In such a case, any observed behavior is consistent with the theory, simply by interpreting the observation flexibly. If a person behaves with self-control, the conscious is presumed to be the cause; if promiscuity is observed, the unconscious is said to determine this behavior. Scientifically, a theory cannot be tested if no observation is inconsistent with it. It is not verifiable, as explained in Chapter 1. In potentially explaining every observation, psychoanalysis has weakened its scientific status. In terms of the model of theory presented in Chapter 1, psychoanalytic theory has not clearly specified the operational definitions of its theoretical constructs. Because these operational definitions are vague, empirical observations are not linked to theoretical constructs in a way that can be clearly specified in advance. Instead, intuition ("clinical insight") makes these links. Metaphorical thinking occurs where the hard-nosed scientist would prefer concrete, rigorous thinking. This criticism has been levied against psychoanalytic theory for many decades, but in recent years, research on defense mechanisms and other psychoanalytic constructs has increased, bridging the gap between clinical theory and science.

Outside of psychology, psychoanalytic theory has influenced art and literature, film, and popular culture. With the decline of traditional religion and of mystical thinking, psychoanalysis has, for many, become a way of contacting the irrational forces within the human personality, which is sufficiently "scientific" to be permissible today. Whether this is a legitimate function and whether psychoanalysis fulfills it adequately are matters of debate.

Study Questions

1. What are the fundamental assumptions of the psychoanalytic perspective?
2. What objections have been raised against the psychoanalytic perspective?

Freud
Classical Psychoanalysis

Chapter
Overview

Preview: Overview of Freud's Theory
The Unconscious
Structures of the Personality
Intrapsychic Conflict
Personality Development
Psychoanalytic Treatment
Psychoanalysis as a Scientific Theory
Summary

ILLUSTRATIVE BIOGRAPHY

Adolf Hitler

Adolf Hitler was probably the most infamous tyrant of the 20th century, perhaps of all time. This charismatic dictator was responsible for the deaths of millions of Jews and others in the extermination camps of Nazi Germany during World War II. Many biographers, often using psychoanalytic theory, have attempted to understand Hitler. One of these analyses, commissioned by the U.S. government during the war in an attempt to learn how to overthrow Hitler, remained secret for decades (Murray, 1943).

Adolf Hitler was born in 1889 in Austria, near the German border. He aspired to be an artist but failed the entrance exam for art school, although he deceived family and friends into thinking he was a student. He earned a meager existence as a so-called artist, selling postcards and small paintings. Later he moved to Germany, which he adopted as his homeland, and where he served in the Bavarian army in World War I, although without much success. In the period of discontent following Germany's defeat in the war, he became active in politics and dreamed of a restoration of German glory. Elected as chancellor of Germany in 1933, he soon invaded neighboring countries; the hostilities escalated to become World War II. Far from restoring German glory, the result of Hitler's ambitions was the destruction of cities throughout Europe and the extermination of millions of Jews and other prisoners in concentration camps. In the face of defeat in May 1945, Hitler; his lover, Eva Braun; and some close associates committed suicide.

Development

For Freud, childhood experience shapes personality. The conditions of physical drive satisfaction in early life determine character structure. A strong ego, capable of umpiring the forces of the unconscious, must develop gradually, protected from psychic trauma and supported by nurturant and guiding parents in areas it cannot yet master. From a Freudian perspective, the parents are credited or (more often) blamed for the child's personality. Three important stages before the age of 5 shape personality. If a child's needs are met in these early years, and if there is not traumatic experience, then healthy development occurs. The third of these stages occurs from about age 3 to 5, a critical time for the development of masculinity (in boys) and a sense of morality (superego).

Hitler's abusive father and overprotective mother failed to nurture healthy development. His mother's overprotectiveness, in part a result of the death of her other children, contributed to what Freud termed "oral fixation," an exaggerated need for oral pleasure, evidenced by Hitler's cravings for sweets, his vegetarianism, and his habit of sucking his fingers, and even his energy for public speaking, which is also an oral expression—in his case, primitive and tantrum-like, providing more evidence of its childhood basis. His father was a severe disciplinarian who frequently beat his son. When Hitler was 3 years old, he thought he saw his drunk father rape his mother, a traumatic incident because of the physical aggression and a premature exposure to adult sexuality. Hitler feared and hated his father and lacked the positive role model essential for normal development of a secure masculine identity and a moral sense (superego). Besides the abuse, Hitler's father lived apart from the family for a year when Adolf was 5, further depriving him of a male role model. His father, a custom's officer, wanted his son to also pursue a career as a government official, but instead Hitler became a failed artist and then a tyrannical head of state, even more abusive than his father. Murray (1943) concludes that Hitler's love for his mother and hatred for his father constitutes a Freudian "Oedipus complex."

Description

Freud's theory describes people in terms of their failed or successful development through the stages of psychosexual development. Thus we speak of "oral characters" and "anal characters" and "phallic characters" (as explained in this chapter). Additional psychiatric labels can be applied to the seriously disturbed.

Hitler's personality is so disturbed that, although he does evidence problems at all of the first three psychosexual developmental stages, he warrants a more serious label. Psychiatrist Henry Murray (1943) describes him as having all the symptoms of paranoid schizophrenia.

Adjustment

Health comes from a strong ego that can control impulses (id) and follow the rules of morality without being overburdened by guilt (superego). Evidence of health comes from two main areas of life: the ability to love (including sexual expression) and to work.

Hitler did not have a healthy balance between impulses (id) and conscience (superego). His ego (which for Freud is the source of mental health and the hope of civilization) never was strong enough to contain his destructive id impulses. According to the analysis that Henry Murray (1943) delivered to the American government, Hitler was periodically energized by impulsive outbursts from his id, whereas the superego, which in a healthy person would oppose such outbursts, was repressed. He did not have the steady, sustained motivation of a healthy personality. In terms of love, reports of his sexual encounters with women are replete with tales of perversity (Waite, 1977). According to Murray's (1943) report, before he came to power, several sexual incidents got Hitler into trouble and warranted a police record as a sexual pervert. His perversions are described as masochistic (self-punishing) and anal, but their exact nature remained a government secret. Murray describes Hitler as impotent. He buoyed up his sense of self-worth by injecting himself with bull testicles and by projecting onto women his fear of sexuality. Even the Nazi salute, a stiff raised hand, has been described as a symbolic erect penis. Once Hitler boasted to a female visitor, "I can hold my arm like that for two solid hours. I never feel tired . . . . I never move. My arm is like granite—rigid and unbending. . . . That is four times as long as Goering . . . . I marvel at my own power" (Waite, 1977, p. 49). He was, symbolically, claiming sexual potency.

Cognition

If a person is healthy, then the world is perceived accurately. Mild disturbances may cause forgetfulness or wishful thinking, whereas serious pathology can leave a person in a fantasy world that has little resemblance to reality.

Hitler's unrealistic perception of the Jewish people is but one aspect of his distorted thought. He exhibited other delusions (false beliefs). Once, firmly believing the lottery ticket he had purchased would win, he responded to its failure to do so with a childish tantrum. Late in the war, he suffered delusions about the movements of fantasy troops. These false beliefs are typical of psychotics. It is possible, however, that some of his later symptoms were caused by drugs prescribed by his doctor, reportedly made more powerful through tampering by spies. Interestingly, Henry Murray credits Hitler with skillful use of metaphor in his speeches. Metaphor, like art, can convey the primitive, non-logical thoughts of the unconscious.

Society

In Freud's theory, society restricts the individual's impulses for satisfaction of primitive drives. Learning to cope with these restrictions, by building a healthy ego, is essential to healthy development.

Hitler, however, did not learn to cope with society but rather projected his own pathology onto the external world. For Hitler, Germany, his "Motherland," symbolized his own mother (Murray, 1943), and his efforts to purify and defend her were motivated by his childhood perceptions of his family. Murray interprets Austria as symbolic of the father, so his military actions against that country are motivated by his hatred of his father. That he continued his delusional projections for so long without being institutionalized for mental illness, is evidence that his projections resonated with the German people (Murray, 1943). Hitler echoed and amplified the anti-Semitic feelings of his era, and the Jewish people became projective targets for repressed characteristics. Some biographers have argued that Hitler's own grandfather was Jewish and denial of this ancestry intensified his persecution of the Jewish people. Loewenberg (1988) suggests that Hitler was aware "the real enemy lay within" (p. 143); perhaps Hitler's projection of evil onto Jews was not entirely unconscious but rather a political strategy. Anti-Semitism was not unique to Hitler; it contributed to his popularity as a charismatic leader.

Indeed, whenever the citizenry of a country feel frustrated (as the German people did because of the oppressive political conditions imposed on Germany after World War I), they are likely to elevate a leader who gives expression to their unresolved conflicts.

Biology

Freud turned to biology as the source of human motivation, providing the energy that motivates behavior. Through development, this energy is transformed from its primitive urges (oral, anal, and phallic) to simply fulfill bodily functions, and it takes forms that are expressed in mature relationships and activities. In maladjusted people, impulses remain stuck in their primitive forms. The instinctual energy can be categorized as that which affirms life and love (*eros*) and that which propels toward aggression and death (*thanatos*).

The mass murders of the Holocaust give evidence of a greater measure of death instinct than life instinct. Hitler's difficulty with sexual love confirms this interpretation. His body was also inferior (a point that would be of even greater interest to one of Freud's followers, Alfred Adler). Hitler is famous for his single testicle, which, combined with a frail and effeminate body (Murray, 1943), accentuated his conflict over masculinity. According to Murray (1943), he was rejected for military service in Austria (although others speculate that he left that country to avoid the draft). In Freud's theory, the biological urges of an infant and toddler should be transformed into adult sexual expressions, but Hitler's masochistic anal sexual perversions are evidence that he was stuck with childish drives throughout adulthood, impotent and incapable of normal adult sexual behavior (according to Murray, 1943). His rhetoric about race and the importance of a pure Aryan gene pool stands in stark contrast to his own biological shortcomings.

Final Thoughts

The topic of many psychobiographical books, Hitler's personality is so disturbed that it shocks us even in the next millennium. We may analyze him from the perspective of personality theory, but the magnification of his pathology on the pages of history requires an historical understanding.

Preview: Overview of Freud's Theory

Freud's theory has implications for major theoretical questions, as presented in Table 2.1. From a scientific point of view, this theory has been long criticized as deficient because of excessive vagueness in operational definitions that makes it difficult to verify. However, increasing research, in nonclinical as well as therapeutic settings, has been designed to test some psychoanalytic propositions, as studies described in this chapter illustrate. Although the theory is in some ways comprehensive, including artistic productions and other symbolism, it is not comprehensive enough because of its focus on early life to encompass many environmental and social influences. Its applied value focuses particularly on psychotherapy and implications for childrearing.

Probably no theory of personality is as widely known or as controversial as that proposed by Sigmund Freud. Freud compared his theory to those of Copernicus, who claimed that humans do not live at the center of the universe, and of Darwin, who discredited the idea that humans are a separately created species. Humanity was further humbled by Freud's (1925/1958, p. 5) assertion that reason does not rule behavior. He proposed that unconscious psychological forces powerfully affect human thought and behavior. These forces originate in the emotions of childhood and continue their influence throughout life. Freud portrayed humans as driven by instincts that "in themselves

TABLE 2.1	Preview of Freud's Theory
Individual Differences	People differ in their ego defense mechanisms, which control expression of primitive forces in personality.
Adaptation and Adjustment	Mental health involves the ability to love and to work. Psychoanalysis provides a method for overcoming unconscious psychological conflict.
Cognitive Processes	Conscious experience often cannot be trusted because of distortions produced by unconscious defense mechanisms.
Society	All societies deal with universal human conflicts and lead to repression of individual desires. Traditional religion is challenged as a shared defense mechanism.
Biological Influences	Psychiatric symptoms are explained in psychodynamic terms, instead of in biological terms. Biological drives, in particular sexual motivation, provide the basis of personality. Hereditary differences may influence level of sexual drive (libido) and phenomena such as homosexuality.
Development	Experience in the first 5 years is critical for personality formation. The oral, anal, and phallic (Oedipal) psychosexual conflicts are central. Adult personality changes very little.

are neither good nor evil" (p. 213) but have both kinds of effects. These forces fuel the positive achievements of culture but also lead to war, crime, mental illness, and other human woes. Psychoanalytic theory has transformed our understanding of sex and aggression and has led people in the post-Freudian era never to quite trust their conscious experience.

BIOGRAPHY OF SIGMUND FREUD

Sigmund Freud was born in 1856 into a Jewish family in predominantly Catholic Freiberg, Moravia (then part of the Austro-Hungarian Empire but now part of the Czech republic). By the time he was 4 years old, his family moved to Vienna, which remained his home until near his death.

SIGMUND FREUD

Freud was one of eight children, including two older half brothers by his father's first marriage. Freud's father remarried at age 40, and his young wife bore six children. Sigmund was the oldest and by all accounts the favorite of his mother. She expected him to be great, gave him the only oil lamp in the house, and did not permit his sister to disturb him by practicing the piano when he was studying. His father, a not particularly successful wool merchant, was a strict authority figure within the family.

Freud studied medicine at the University of Vienna, specializing in neurology. He intended to become an academician and had published five research studies by the age of 26. In the light of his later theory, known for its emphasis on sex, an interesting historical footnote is that one of his neurological research papers reported the discovery of the testes in an eel. He studied the anesthetic properties of cocaine, narrowly missing fame when a colleague published in this area before he did. Realistically, though, academic medicine did not pay well, and discrimination against Jews made it unlikely that he would achieve as high a position as he wished. Thus Freud took the advice of a professor, turned to private practice as a clinical neurologist, and soon was able to marry his fiancée of 4 years, Martha Bernays. The union produced five children, including a daughter, Anna, who followed her father's footsteps as a psychoanalyst.

In his practice, Freud saw a variety of psychiatric patients, including many diagnosed as suffering from hysteria, a psychological disorder that produces physical symptoms without physical damage to the body. Over a long career, he developed new ways of thinking about these disorders, formulating the theory of psychoanalysis. His explorations were also turned to an understanding of his own symptoms; for example, he suffered a fear of travel and especially of flying, interpreted by one commentator (Scherr, 2001) as evidence that Freud feared women and sexuality, despite his psychoanalytic sophistication. His reputation grew beyond Vienna. He was well received in the United States, especially after his lecture series in 1909 at Clark University in Massachusetts. His theory was controversial because of its emphasis on childhood sexuality. It was also criticized as a Jewish science, dealing with psychiatric disturbances, then thought to affect Jews particularly. Undoubtedly, the anti-Semitism of his society greatly influenced both Freud and his patients (Blum, 1994). The Nazis burned the works of Freud and others in 1933, part of their attacks against Jewish intellectuals (including Einstein), and they raided his house in Vienna frequently in the years prior to World War II. Freud's personal health was failing at this time; he had cancer of the mouth, aggravated by his addiction to cigars. He finally fled Vienna in 1938, at the age of 82, and went to London, where he died in 1939.

The Unconscious

When people are asked why they did something, they usually can answer without much difficulty. Why did you decide to read this chapter? Why did you decide to study psychology? Although, like many people, you may think you know the answers to these questions and to many others that could be asked, Freud suggested that the most important determinants of behavior are not available to our conscious thought. If this is true of routine decisions in life, it is even more true of psychological disturbances, such as those that motivate people to seek professional help.

PSYCHIC DETERMINISM

At first Freud, like psychiatrists of his day, looked for physical causes of psychiatric disorders. As a neurologist, he knew that damage to the brain and neurons could cause individuals to behave in strange ways, including physical symptoms, such as loss of sensation (anesthesia) or loss of motion (paralysis), and emotional symptoms, such as anxiety and depression. For some patients, though, physical causes could not be found. Freud's colleagues thought such patients were shamming, or faking, their symptoms. Forces outside of mainstream medicine were already preparing the way for another, psychodynamic approach (Ellenberger, 1970). Popular healers treated physical and psychological disorders by the laying on of hands and by "animal magnetism." A few French psychiatrists treated patients with hypnosis, although the medical mainstream regarded it as quackery. At Salpêtrière, a hospital in Paris where Freud studied for 4 months during 1885 and 1886, Freud saw Jean-Martin Charcot demonstrate that psychiatric symptoms could be induced through hypnosis. Later, he was impressed by Josef Breuer's discovery that a patient who recalled earlier memories while in a hypnotic trance was relieved of her symptoms when the trance was ended. They published the case history of this woman, known as "Anna O.," to document the importance of catharsis in therapy (Breuer & Freud, 1895/1955). It is historically ironic that this woman, now known by her actual name Bertha Pappenheim, was a social activist who worked against the sexual victimization of women in the external world, as opposed to Freud's emphasis on internal conflict (Kimball, 2000).

These evidences of hypnosis converted Freud from the purely physical model of psychiatric disorder to "dynamic" (psychological) psychiatry (Ellenberger, 1970). Freud became convinced that unconscious forces have the power to influence behavior, an assumption called psychic determinism. The term *determinism* refers to the fundamental scientific assumption of lawful cause and effect. The concept of psychic determinism allows psychological factors to be causes.

At first, Freud (1895/1966b) tried to understand how psychic factors, such as traumatic events, produce physical changes in the nervous system. For example, he postulated that the anxiety of a traumatic sexual encounter could, by modifying connections in the nervous system, produce anxiety symptoms in later life. Freud realized that the microscope would not be an appropriate investigative tool for his theory. Neurologists would not know where to look; after all, these changes were far more subtle than the gross lesions with which they generally dealt. So Freud turned to less direct investigative methods through the analysis of clinical material. The clinical method is well accepted within neurology, where nerve damage is often diagnosed on the basis of behavioral symptoms such as paralysis and pain rather than by physical examination of the neurons.

As his theory developed, Freud turned away from neurology, which rests on a physical model of human behavior, and founded a new science, based on mental causes (Sulloway, 1979). He named this new science **psychoanalysis**. Psychoanalysis pays close attention to the content of thought rather than the neurons that make thought possible. If a physiologically oriented neurologist can be thought of as tracking neural pathways, then the psychoanalytic practitioner can be thought of as tracking pathways of ideas. As Freud discovered, much thought is hidden, even from the thinker.

psychoanalysis Freud's theory and its application in therapy

LEVELS OF CONSCIOUSNESS

Some of our thoughts are easily known, and it may seem that that is all there is to our minds. Freud saw the limits of this view. "What is in your mind is not identical with what you are conscious of; whether something is going on in your mind and whether you hear of it are two different things" (S. Freud, 1925/1958, p. 8).

Freud postulated three levels of consciousness and compared the mind to an iceberg floating in the water. Like an iceberg, only a small part of the mind is readily seen: the **conscious** mind. Just at the water's surface, sometimes visible and sometimes submerged, is the **preconscious** mind. Like an iceberg, great dangers lurk in what is not seen. Finally, there is a great mass, which is most of the mind, that is hidden, like the bulk of an iceberg that is under water: the **unconscious** mind.

conscious aware; cognizant; mental processes of which a person is aware

The Conscious

The *conscious* level refers to experiences of which a person is aware, including memories and intentional actions. Consciousness functions in realistic ways, according to the rules of space and time. We are aware of consciousness and accept it as us; we identify with it.

preconscious mental content of which a person is currently unaware but that can readily be made conscious

The Preconscious

Some material that is not in awareness at a particular time can be brought to awareness readily; this material is called *preconscious*. It includes information that is not at the moment being thought about but can be easily remembered if needed—for example, your mother's middle name. The content of the preconscious is not fundamentally different from that of consciousness. Thoughts move readily from one to the other.

unconscious mental processes of which a person is unaware

The Unconscious

The third level of consciousness is different. Its contents do not readily move into consciousness. The *unconscious* refers to mental processes of which a person is not aware. Such material remains in the unconscious because making it conscious would produce too much anxiety. This material is said to be repressed; that is, it resists becoming conscious.

Among the contents of the unconscious are forgotten traumatic memories and denied wishes. A child who has been sexually abused, for example, often represses this memory, having amnesia for the terrifying event. This forgetting protects the victim from the anxiety that would accompany the recall of traumatic experiences. Desires also may cause anxiety if we are ashamed of what we wish. For example, a child may wish that a younger sibling were dead, so there would be no competition for the love of the parents. This wish is rejected by consciousness as horrid and evil, so it is repressed. These wishes are called *denied wishes* by Freudians because we deny that we have them. The unconscious becomes, in effect, the garbage pile of what consciousness throws away. It is emotionally upsetting and less civilized than consciousness.

A comment is in order about wording: What is the difference between "unconscious" and "nonconscious"? In this book, we use the term *unconscious* to refer to the unconscious or, literally, "unknown" (*Unbewusst*) as Freud used it: a dynamic unconscious, that is, one with forces that produce symptoms and motivation. (Sometimes people refer to this Freudian unconscious as "the dynamic unconscious.") A broader term, referring to everything of which we are unaware, is *nonconscious*. For example, we might say that people breathe and walk "nonconsciously" because these processes do not require conscious attention—without implying any Freudian repression.

EFFECTS OF UNCONSCIOUS MOTIVATION

Behavior is determined by a combination of conscious and unconscious forces. These may act together smoothly so a person's actions appear comprehensible and rational, as though consciousness alone determined behavior. Alternatively, unconscious forces may interfere with conscious intentions. This conflict produces irrational thoughts and behavior. Freud's particular interest, as a clinician, was in cases in which the forces of the conscious and the unconscious mind were conflicted.

Physical Symptoms

conversion hysteria
form of neurosis in which psychological conflicts are expressed in physical symptoms (without actual physical damage)

Many of Freud's patients had physical symptoms for which no organic cause could be found. Influenced by his study of hypnosis under Charcot, Freud argued that cases of **conversion hysteria** represent the impact of unconscious forces on the body to produce physical symptoms of paralysis, mutism, deafness, blindness, tics, or other maladies that resemble physical diseases but occur in physically normal, undamaged bodies (Breuer & Freud, 1925/1955). The diagnosis is less often made today (M. M. Jones, 1980), and its appearance is influenced by beliefs about disease, which vary across time and culture (Fabrega, 1990).

One particularly striking example of such a conversion hysteria is *glove anesthesia*. In this disorder, a patient has no physical sensation of touch or pain on the hand in the area a glove would cover. Sensation on the arm above the wrist is normal. There is no pattern of neurons that, if damaged, could produce this disorder because those nerve cells responsible for sensation in the thumb also affect feeling in part of the forearm above the wrist, and those neurons that affect the fingers also serve other parts of the forearm. Glove anesthesia is impossible, physically. So why does it occur in some patients? Freud argued that glove anesthesia is produced by psychological forces. A patient thinks of the hand as a unit and the arm as another unit; they are psychological units (although not neurological ones). A person who is very anxious about what the hand might feel or do could be driven by this psychological reason to have glove anesthesia as a symptom.

Hypnosis

In hypnosis, an individual (the subject) experiences a highly suggestible state, often called a *trance*, in which the suggestions of a hypnotist strongly influence what is experienced or recalled. The hypnotist may suggest that the subject's arm will rise in the air automatically, without the subject intending it, or that the subject will be unable to do something that is usually easy to do, like bending an arm. Suggestions can also alter perceptions, causing subjects to see things that are not there, to not see things that are there, or to not feel pain. In the popular mind, hypnosis can be used to compel people to do what they otherwise would not do, including criminal or sexual acts. In fact, the research evidence does not support these claims (Gibson, 1991), but through *posthypnotic suggestion*, in which the hypnotist suggests that a particular action or experience (sensation) will occur when the hypnotic trance is ended, therapeutic benefits can occur. For example, a hypnotist may suggest that a subject will feel a choking sensation when puffing a cigarette; after the trance is ended, the subject will experience the choking sensation, making hypnosis a way to quit smoking (Spanos et al., 1992–1993). Hypnosis is also used to treat anxiety, asthma, skin diseases (psoriasis and warts), nausea, bulimia and anorexia nervosa, and other diseases (Frankel, 1987). It is used to provide relief from headaches and other types of pain (Bowers, 1994; Kraft, 1992; Patterson et al., 1992; Primavera & Kaiser, 1992). Hypnosis is even used to reduce the length of hospitalization after surgery (Blankfield, 1991). Overall, research confirms that adding hypnosis to other forms of therapy, psychodynamic and cognitive-behavioral therapy, improves treatment outcomes (Kirsch & Lynn, 1995; Kirsch, Montgomery, & Sapirstein, 1995).

These therapies seem to attest to the ability of hypnosis to harness the power of the unconscious for helpful purposes, but hypnosis remains a controversial phenomenon. According to Ernest Hilgard (1976, 1994), hypnosis is a state of consciousness that is dissociated from normal experience. That is, consciousness is divided into two (or more) simultaneous parts, and a barrier between them produces amnesia. As a result of this barrier, one part, the part that acts out a hypnotic suggestion, for example, will not recall what happened when the person was in the other state of consciousness, the part that received the suggestion from the hypnotist (Kirsch & Lynn, 1998).

Others have questioned Hilgard's neodissociation theory (cf. Kirsch & Lynn, 1998; Orne, 1959, 1971; Stava & Jaffa, 1988), arguing that social factors such as expectation must be considered to understand hypnosis and other alleged dissociative states such as multiple personality disorder (Spanos, 1994). Hypnotized subjects often behave similarly to people who are not hypnotized but are instructed to act as though they had been. This finding at least raises the possibility that hypnosis could simply be a well-played role, not a separate state of consciousness.

Brain waves and other physiological measurements are not different under hypnosis than in normal consciousness (Silverstein, 1993). Many of the phenomena reported under hypnosis could result from a desire to comply with the requests of the hypnotist (Orne, 1959, 1971; Spanos et al., 1993). Hypnotized subjects' reports of their experience may result from suggestion, in which they bias their reports as the situation seems to demand. For example, when researchers hypnotized experimental subjects and gave them a hypnotic suggestion for deafness, the subjects judged auditory tones to be less loud than when they were not hypnotized. In a subsequent trial when they were not hypnotized, the experimenter's statement that they might have drifted back into hypnosis led subjects to also judge the sounds as less loud, even though they were not hypnotized either when they heard the suggestion or when they heard the tone they were now judging. Control subjects without the suggestion of drifting back into hypnosis judged the sounds as louder. If they were hooked up to a bogus pipeline apparatus that purportedly served as a sort of lie detector to indicate to the experimenter what they had really experienced, subjects changed their story and reported the tones more accurately (Perlini, Haley, & Buczel, 1998). Research such as this clearly shows that hypnotic reports are influenced by suggestion and that hypnotized subjects bias their reports to fit what they believe is expected of them. Contrary to what most people, including many psychotherapists, believe, hypnotically recalled memories are often inaccurate, and it is not possible to be sure when they are accurate and when not (Kihlstrom, 1994, 1995; Lindsay & Read, 1995; Lynn et al., 1997; Nash, 1987; Steblay & Bothwell, 1994; Yapko, 1994).

Psychosis

An extreme form of mental disorder is termed a *psychosis*. Psychotics lose touch with reality and experience the unconscious in raw form through hallucinations, seeing and hearing things that are not actually present. The irrationality of psychotic behavior, said Freud, reflects the underlying irrationality of the unconscious.

Dreams

Freud praised dreams as "the royal road to the unconscious." In waking life, conscious forces powerfully restrain the unacceptable forces of the unconscious. During sleep, the restraining forces of consciousness are relaxed, and the unconscious threatens to break into awareness. This triggers anxiety, which threatens to waken the dreamer. Sleep is protected by disguising the unconscious into less threatening symbolic form in a dream.

Usually, a dream disguises the fulfillment of a repressed wish (S. Freud, 1900/1953). Consider this dream of a young man:

> I was on a beach with my girl and other friends. We had been swimming and were sitting on the beach. My girl was afraid that she would lose her pocketbook and kept saying that she felt certain she would lose it on the beach. (Hall, 1966, pp. 57–58)

manifest content the surface meaning of a dream

latent content the hidden, unconscious meaning of a dream

The recalled dream (here, the story of the beach and the pocketbook) is termed the **manifest content** of the dream. *Dream interpretation* is the process of inferring the unconscious wishes disguised in the dream. Its hidden meaning, revealed by interpreting the dream symbols, is termed the **latent content** of the dream. A pocketbook is a Freudian symbol for female genitals, so the dream symbolizes the dreamer's wish that his girlfriend would lose her virginity on the beach. Dream interpretation is like decoding. The coding process, which has produced the dream, is called *dream work*. Ideas are expressed by symbols, and so they can be visualized. A larger amount of material is often condensed to a much briefer form. Troublesome ideas are displaced from their original objects to disguise ideas that would produce conflict (S. Freud, 1935/1963a, pp. 86–87).

Although Freud's theory suggests that dreams respond to life's events, they do not do so in a clear and obvious way. Dreams reported by people who have experienced traumatic events do not even reveal the realistic kind of trauma (Brenneis, 1997). To understand the emotional meaning of dreams, it is necessary to follow the dreamer's associations to see where they lead. Freud, for example, asked an American woman who had written him a letter about a troubling dream to tell what the name "Mildred Dowl" meant. In the dream, the woman's romantic partner had sent her a cruel note saying he had married Miss Mildred Dowl, and she had (in the dream) stabbed herself in despair. As

Freud said, without knowing the source of the name, only a limited interpretation of the dream was possible (Benjamin & Dixon, 1996).

Psychoanalysts emphasize the importance of dreams as ways of dealing with emotions, such as the anxiety and guilt that may follow traumatic events (Hartmann, 1998; Hartmann et al., 2001). Researchers confirm that dreams contain much emotion (Hobson, Pace-Schott, & Stickgold, 2000; Merritt et al., 1994). During dream sleep, there is a shift from an emphasis on thinking to an emphasis on hallucination-like experiences, which brain researchers suggest comes from a shift to a different neurotransmitter pathway in the brain (Fosse, Stickgold, & Hobson, 2001). People whose personality tests indicate they are repressors report dreams with relatively high levels of aggression, which supports the interpretation that dreams express what is repressed in waking life (Bell & Cook, 1998). Alternatives to Freud's model of dream interpretation have been developed by Carl Jung (see Chapter 3) and others (e.g., Blagrove, 1993; Hermans, 1987). One suggestion is that dreams function to promote attachment relationships (about which we say more in Chapter 6), for example by promoting mother–infant relationships and sexual pair bonding (Zborowski & McNamara, 1998).

Dreams have also been investigated from a biological viewpoint, and the relationship between psychological meaning and biological brain mechanisms presents a modern version of the philosophical mind–body problem. Dreams seem to occur when lower brain centers, especially the pons, and possibly a "curiosity-interest-expectancy" area in the ventromedial forebrain, stimulate activity in higher cortical areas (Hobson, 1988; Hobson & McCarley, 1977; Reiser, 2001). Although some influential neuroscientists deny that dreams have any significance (Crick & Mitchison, 1986), other psychologists have proposed models for understanding dreams that draw on modern cognitive theory, an enhanced understanding of neurology, and the suggestion that emotion may bridge the "mind–body" process in dreaming (Antrobus, 1991; Cicogna, Cavallero, & Bosinelli, 1991; Hobson, 1988; Hobson & Stickgold, 1994; Reiser, 2001). Dreams could be expressions of a more primitive, emotional-narrative mode of functioning that has only been partially displaced by the development of higher human consciousness.

The characteristics of dream work that Freud described (condensation, displacement, and symbolism) represent the functioning of the unconscious more generally. Freud understood not only dreams and psychosis but even aspects of everyday normal behavior as results of unconscious motivation.

The Psychopathology of Everyday Life

Freud described the impact of the unconscious in a wide variety of behaviors of normal people. He termed such phenomena, in German, *Fehlleistungen*, which could be translated, according to Strachey (S. Freud, 1933/1966a, p. 25), as "faulty acts" or "faulty functions." The unfortunate English translation for this concept is an invented word, **parapraxes**. More commonly, people refer to them as **Freudian slips**, or "the psychopathology of everyday life."

One of the most common of these Freudian slips is a misstatement, or slip of the tongue. For example, in parting from a boring party, one might say, "I'm so glad I have to leave now," intending to say, "I'm so sorry I have to leave now." The unconscious tells the truth, lacking the tact of consciousness. Errors of memory are another kind of Freudian slip (e.g., forgetting the birthday of a disliked relative). Other Freudian slips include errors of hearing, losing or misplacing objects, and errors of action. In 1935 Alfred Stieglitz wrote letters to his wife, Georgia O'Keeffe, and to his lover, Dorothy Norman, but he placed each letter into the wrong envelope so his wife received the letter intended for

parapraxis (plural: -es) a psychologically motivated error, more commonly called a *Freudian slip*

Freudian slip a psychologically motivated error in speech, hearing, behavior, and so forth (e.g., forgetting the birthday of a disliked relative)

his lover (Lisle, 1980, p. 227). Was this merely an error, or did Stieglitz unconsciously wish to confront his wife with his other relationship? Such so-called accidents, to a Freudian, are not random but are motivated by unconscious wishes. Psychic determinism holds us strictly accountable for all our actions. An alternative cognitive explanation, however, holds that wishes are not the cause of such slips; rather, they are a result of actions becoming sufficiently automated that conscious control is not required, opening the possibility of feedback errors in the control of behavior (Heckhausen & Beckmann, 1990).

Humor

Freud (1916/1963b) described humor as a safe expression of repressed conflict, deriving its pleasure from the release of tension through a joke. We laugh at jokes if they express issues or conflicts that are unconsciously important but consciously unacceptable. A bigot, for example, finds racial jokes particularly amusing. Freud gave many examples of jokes in his writing. One that survives translation from the German is the following:

> Two Jews met in the neighborhood of the bath-house. "Have you taken a bath?" asked one of them. "What?" asked the other in return, "is there one missing?" (S. Freud, 1916/1963b, p. 49).

condensation
combining of two or more images; characteristic of primary processes (e.g., in dreams)

Like a dream, the joke is terse. Both dreams and humor often use the technique of **condensation**, in which two or more images are combined to form an image that merges the meanings and impulses of both. The humor of this joke is achieved by the double meaning of the word *taken*, providing a way of expressing the anti-Semitic attitude (or impulse) that Jews are thieves rather than clean. Because the anti-Semitism is indirect and disguised, the joke may be acceptable to those who would not consciously confess to anti-Semitism. A research study, supporting this idea that humor makes prejudice acceptable, finds that sexist social interactions are more acceptable when they are presented as jokes (Ford, 2000). Robert Wyer and James Collins (1992) criticize Freud's analysis as untenable because we find too many things funny to be accounted for without an unreasonably long list of repressed emotions. (They present an extensive theory of humor that includes concepts from cognitive research.)

A master of humor, Charlie Chaplin expressed an opinion consistent with the psychoanalytic view that the irrational is the key to humor:

> Through humor, we see in what seems rational, the irrational; in what seems important, the unimportant. It . . . preserves our sanity. Because of humor we are less overwhelmed by the vicissitudes of life. It activates our sense of proportion and reveals to us that in an overstatement of seriousness lurks the absurd. (1964, pp. 211–212)

On that note, let us be glad that the unconscious, the irrational, is part of the experience of all of us and not only of psychiatric patients.

projective test a test that presents ambiguous stimuli such as inkblots or pictures, so responses will be determined by the test taker's unconscious

Projective Tests

Finally, both clinicians and researchers seek a method for revealing unconscious material on their request so they may diagnose individuals and test psychoanalytic hypotheses. For this purpose, they have developed **projective tests**. Among the most widely used projective tests in clinical practice are the Rorschach inkblot method and the Thematic Apperception Test (TAT), each of which can be scored in a variety of ways (Bornstein

& Masling, 2005; Butcher & Rouse, 1996). Most (nonprojective) tests ask explicit questions. For example, a test may ask, "Do you feel happy most of the time?" In contrast, a projective test presents the client or research subject with an ambiguous stimulus, such as an inkblot or a picture, and gives only minimal directions for responding. "What do you see in this inkblot?" "Tell me a story about this picture." The assumption is that responses in such minimally constrained conditions will reveal unconscious material, unknown even to the respondent. On the nonprojective test a person may say that he or she is happy most of the time yet make up a story about a picture that describes weeping and grief. If other people make up happier stories to the same picture, isn't it reasonable to presume that the grief is in the storyteller? Sometimes the story told to a projective stimulus almost speaks for itself, without professional interpretation. Consider a man shown a picture of a boy with a violin, whose story included this: "Up on my wall there is a picture of a boy staring at a violin. I stare at my violin too and think and dream of one day playing the violin. On the table stretched out *like a dead corpse* is a music book" (Pam & Rivera, 1995; italics added). The evaluators, who had much more extensive information than this, concluded that the young man was seriously disturbed and potentially dangerous, perhaps suicidal, and recommended long-term hospitalization. Perhaps you agree; after all, not many people compare music books with corpses.

Researchers have also used projective tests to investigate motives for achievement, affiliation and intimacy, power, and other social motives—not described by Freud, but theorized to be unconscious. Evidence indicates that these unconscious or implicit motives are not correlated with people's consciously known motives and that the unconscious measures are better predictors of various behaviors, including entrepreneurial business activity (McClelland, Koestner, & Weinberger, 1989; Winter et al., 1998).

ORIGIN AND NATURE OF THE UNCONSCIOUS

Where does this powerful, pervasive unconscious come from? Freud asserted that it was created primarily by experience, especially in childhood. This happens through the all-important mechanism of **repression**. No one likes to focus on unpleasant thoughts if they can be avoided. According to Freud's hedonic hypothesis, people seek pleasure and avoid pain. This simple idea has been included in many psychological theories, in a variety of forms (Higgins, 1997). In Freud's theory, hedonic impulses for pleasure often are accompanied by painful thoughts because pleasure would violate the moral restrictions we have learned. Repression is a mechanism for removing unpleasant thoughts, including unacceptable impulses, from consciousness. Thoughts and memories are repressed (i.e., made unconscious) if they are painful or if they are associated with something painful.

repression defense mechanism in which unacceptable impulses are made unconscious

id the most primitive structure of personality; the source of psychic energy

Structures of the Personality

To state more clearly the tension between the unconscious, which seeks expression, and consciousness, which tries to hold back unconscious forces, Freud described three structures of personality. The **id** is primitive and the source of biological drives. It is unconscious. The **ego** is the rational and coping part of personality. It is the most conscious structure of personality (although not entirely conscious). The **superego** consists of the rules and ideals of society that have become internalized by the individual. Some of the superego is conscious, but much of it remains unconscious.

ego the most mature structure of personality; mediates intrapsychic conflict and copes with the external world

superego structure of personality that is the internal voice of parental and societal restrictions

Although they have become among the best known of his concepts, Freud introduced the terms *id*, *ego*, and *superego* (his structural hypothesis) rather late in the development of his theory. His book *The Ego and the Id*, which describes these structures, was not published until 1923 when he was already in his late 60s.

Each structure serves a different function. For example, consider the various aspects of eating. A person feels hungry and wants to eat. That motivational function belongs to the id. Before hunger can be satisfied, it is necessary to cook or go to a restaurant, perhaps even to plant a crop and harvest it. These planning and coping functions belong to the ego. In addition, there are "oughts" to be considered: advice about what is nutritious or fattening and standards of gourmet cuisine. These ideal and moral standards belong to the superego.

In the metaphor of driving, the id corresponds to the motor of a car, the ego corresponds to the steering wheel, and the superego represents the rules of the road. In the metaphor of Freud's day, the ego

> is like a man on horseback, who has to hold in check the superior strength of the horse. . . . Often a rider, if he is not to be parted from his horse, is obliged to guide it where it wants to go; so in the same way the ego is in the habit of transforming the id's will into action as if it were its own. (S. Freud, 1923/1962b, p. 15)

Like Freud's horseback rider, the ego may seem to be steering more than it truly is.

THE ID

The *id*, which contains biological drives, is the only structure of personality present at birth. It functions according to the **pleasure principle**. That is, it is hedonistic and aims to satisfy its urges, which reduces tension and thus brings pleasure.

pleasure principle the id's motivation to seek pleasure and to avoid pain

Psychic Energy: Libido

Freud proposed that the id is the source of psychic energy, called **libido**, which is sexual. Motivation for all aspects of personality is derived from this energy, which can be transformed from its original instinctive form through socialization. All energy for cultural achievements—for works of art, for politics, for education—is sexual energy transformed. Conversely, repression ties up energy, making it unavailable for higher achievements.

libido psychic energy, derived from sexuality

Life and Death Instincts: Eros and Thanatos

Psychic energy is of two kinds. **Eros**, the "life instinct," motivates life-maintaining behaviors and love. At first, Freud felt that all libido was of this kind, and it is the usual energy described in his theory. Later he postulated a second form of psychic energy, also innate. **Thanatos**, the "death instinct," is a destructive force directing us inevitably toward death, the ultimate release from the tension of living. It motivates all kinds of aggression, including war and suicide. Most often, Freud emphasized erotic, sexual energy and conflict over its expression. Death and conflict about it, according to some theorists, should receive more attention (e.g., Arndt et al., 1997; Becker, 1973).

Eros the life instinct

Thanatos the death instinct

Characteristics of Instincts

Because Freud understood all personality functioning as derived from instinctive energy, knowing the fundamental principles regulating instincts provides a basic framework for understanding personality. These can be summarized as four basic aspects of instincts: source, pressure, aim, and object.

1. *Source.* All psychic energy is derived from biological processes in some part or organ of the body. There is no separate, exclusively mental energy. The amount of energy a person has does not change throughout a lifetime, although it is transformed so it is "invested" differently. At first, psychic energy is directed toward biological needs. As development occurs, this same energy can be redirected into other investments, such as interpersonal relationships and work.

2. *Pressure.* The pressure of an instinct refers to its force or motivational quality. It corresponds to the strength of the instinctual drive; it is high when the drive is not satisfied and falls when the need is met. For example, a hungry infant has a high pressure of the hunger drive; one just fed has hunger at a low pressure. When the pressure is low, the instinct may not have noticeable effects; but when the pressure is high, it may break through, interrupting other activities. A hungry baby wakes up, for example.

3. *Aim.* Instincts function according to a principle of homeostasis, or steady state, a principle borrowed from biology. Instincts aim to preserve the ideal steady state for the organism. Changes moving away from this steady state are experienced as tension. The aim of all instincts is to reduce tension, which is pleasurable. (Think of the good feeling of eating when you are hungry.) Instincts operate according to what Freud called the *pleasure principle*; they aim simply to produce pleasure by reducing tension, immediately and without regard to reality constraints.

   Tension reduction occurs when the original biological instinct is directly satisfied—for example, when a hungry infant is fed or when a sexually aroused adult achieves orgasm. It would be a mistake, however, to conclude that only direct biological drive satisfaction can reduce tension. Some transformations of libido also allow tension reduction. An artist may experience tension reduction when a creative problem is solved. In his filmmaking, Charlie Chaplin (1964) stated,

   > The solution [to a creative problem] would suddenly reveal itself, as if a layer of dust had been swept off a marble floor—there it was, the beautiful mosaic I had been looking for. *Tension was gone.* (p. 188; emphasis added)

   Such healthy, socially acceptable ways of reducing tension are termed *sublimation*. However, indirect expressions of libido do not always reduce the pressure of the instinct. Thus a chronic deviation from a restful homeostatic state occurs in individuals who have not found ways to reduce tension, such as neurotics.

4. *Object.* The object of an instinct is the person or thing in the world that is desired so the instinct can be satisfied. For example, the object of the hunger drive of an infant is the mother's breast: It brings satisfaction. The object of a sexually aroused adult is a sexual partner. Investment of psychic energy in a particular object is called **cathexis**.

cathexis investment of psychic energy in an object

What kind of partner? It is with respect to the object of an instinct that there is the most variation, the most influence of experience on a person's fundamental motivations. Some sexually aroused men look for a woman just like Mother; others look for a very different kind of woman or for a man, or even for underwear or a child or any of a vast assortment of sexual objects. Women, of course, also vary widely in their choice of sexual objects.

The fact that libido is capable of being directed toward so many diverse objects, not fixed biologically, is termed the *plasticity* of the instinct. This plasticity is much greater in humans than in lower animals, who seem to come with instincts prewired to very specific objects. Learning from experience—selecting objects from the possibilities in the environment and learning to adapt to reality—occurs in the ego. The id, in contrast, functions according to a very primitive mechanism, called *primary process*.

Primitive Functioning: Primary Process

primary process unconscious mental functioning in which the id predominates; characterized by illogical, symbolic thought

The id functions according to the purely instinctive and unsocialized **primary process**. Primary process is as blind and inflexible as the instinctive impulses that draw a moth to a candle flame, and its consequences can be as deadly. Primary process ignores time, recognizing no past and no future, only the present moment. It demands immediate gratification; it cannot wait or plan. If reality does not satisfy its urges, it may resort to hallucinatory wish fulfillment, that is, simply imagine that its needs are met. As a sexually aroused dreamer conjures up a lover, a psychotic individual might hallucinate a boat in a stormy sea. This, of course, is not adaptive in the real world.

Simple organisms in natural environments may be able to function quite well with only their biological drives (or id) operating according to the primary process. Humans, however, must adapt to a complex social environment, and the id, functioning according to primary process and blind instinct, cannot adapt or learn. It is the ego that can profit from experience.

THE EGO

reality principle the ego's mode of functioning in which there is appropriate contact with the external world

The ego is the structure of personality that brings about the unity of personality and is in touch with the real world. It operates according to the **reality principle**. That is, it can accurately understand reality and can adapt itself to the constraints of the real world. The ego can delay gratification and plan. These abilities are termed **secondary process**.

Mental health requires a strong ego, one that can defend against anxiety while still allowing the individual to thrive in the real external world with enjoyment. A weak ego may not adequately defend against anxiety, or it may require a person to behave in rigid ways to avoid anxiety. If the ego breaks down altogether, a psychotic episode occurs.

secondary process conscious mental functioning in which the ego predominates; characterized by logical thought

THE SUPEREGO

The third structure of personality, the *superego*, is the internal representative of the rules and restrictions of family and society, originating based on the authority of the father. Freud regarded it as the civilizing force that tames our savage nature (Frank, 1999). It generates guilt when we act contrary to its rules. In addition, the superego presents us with an ego ideal, which is an image of what we would like to be, our internal standards. Because the superego develops at a young age, it represents an immature and rigid form of morality. In psychoanalytic jargon, the superego is "archaic" and largely unconscious. Freud argued that our sense of guilt is often out of touch with current reality, representing the immature understandings of a young child.

Anna Freud (1935) gives examples that illustrate the archaic nature of the superego. One case is a man who, as a child, stole sweets. He was taught not to do so and internalized the prohibition in his superego. As an adolescent, he blushed with guilt every time he ate sweets, even though they were no longer forbidden (p. 97). In another case, a woman could not select "an occupation which would necessitate sharing a room with companions" (p. 99) because of an early punishment for nakedness. In both these cases, the superego was based on parental restrictions in childhood and failed to adapt to the adult situation.

Sigmund Freud dismissed much religion as similarly immature. For Freud, mature ethics are not achieved through the superego but rather through the ego, the only structure of personality that adapts to current reality.

Intrapsychic Conflict

The id, ego, and superego do not always coexist peacefully. The id demands immediate satisfaction of drives, whereas the superego threatens guilt if any pleasurable satisfaction of immoral impulses is attempted. Thus there is **intrapsychic conflict**. The ego tries to repress unacceptable desires, but it does not always succeed. The repressed materials have energy, and this energy tries to return the repressed material to consciousness. It is like an ice cube that is pushed completely under the surface of the water: It keeps bobbing up again. Like a forgotten bill or dentist appointment, repressed material threatens to return. Because pain is associated with repressed material, we keep trying to repress it, like a hand pushing the ice back under the water. The ego tries to reconcile the conflicting demands of the id and superego while at the same time taking into account external reality with its limited opportunities for drive satisfaction.

intrapsychic conflict conflict within the personality, as between id desires and superego restrictions

ENERGY HYPOTHESIS

Freud understood these phenomena in terms of his energy hypothesis. Repression of unacceptable thoughts or impulses requires psychic energy. The force of the impulse that seeks expression must not exceed the repressive force or repression will fail and the repressed material will become conscious. The more energy tied up in such intrapsychic conflict, the less available for dealing with current reality.

Although the energy hypothesis is generally dismissed as an outdated metaphor from 19th-century physics, it does aptly describe the experience of exhaustion that can come from unresolved psychological stress or from the ego's need to direct activities (the "executive function of the ego," in Freud's language). Muraven, Tice, and Baumeister (1998) report that requiring experimental subjects to suppress their thoughts (about a white bear) or emotions led to impaired performance on a variety of experimental tasks (such as squeezing a handgrip and solving anagrams), as though their energy had been depleted by the effort of self-regulation. In another study, they found that experimental subjects gave up sooner when trying to solve problems if they had earlier forced themselves to eat radishes instead of chocolates—a choice that seems to have depleted their ego of energy (Baumeister et al., 1998). Emotional suppression also has adverse effects on performance in laboratory tasks (Baumeister et al., 1998), and in life.

ANXIETY

Anxiety signals that the ego may fail in its task of adapting to reality and maintaining an integrated personality. *Neurotic anxiety* signals that id impulses may break through (overcome repression) and be expressed. A person who does not accept sexual desires would be expected to suffer from neurotic anxiety. *Moral anxiety* indicates fear that one's own superego will respond with guilt. A person who rationally believes it is acceptable to take the afternoon off, putting off work until the next day, may nonetheless suffer from moral anxiety if the superego demands more work. *Reality anxiety* indicates that the external world threatens real danger. Knowing that automobile accidents are more likely when the driver is tired may produce reality anxiety when someone drives too many hours.

DEFENSE MECHANISMS

defense mechanisms ego strategies for coping with unconscious conflict

The ego uses various strategies to resolve intrapsychic conflict. These **defense mechanisms** are adopted if direct expression of the id impulse is unacceptable to the superego or dangerous in the real world. All defense mechanisms begin with repression of unacceptable impulses, that is, forcing them to be unconscious. However, repression ties up energy. To conserve energy, the ego uses a variety of defense mechanisms that disguise the unacceptable impulse. By distorting the source, aim, and/or object of the impulse, they avoid the retaliation of the superego, allowing the impulse, in effect, to sneak past the censor. In this way, total repression of the impulse is not necessary. This reduces the energy requirements for repression, analogous to the way that letting steam out of a pressure cooker reduces the force required to hold on the lid. Furthermore, it avoids the experience of anxiety, which is an underlying issue in all defense mechanisms (Paulhus, Fridhandler, & Hayes, 1997; Turvey & Salovey, 1993–1994).

Defense mechanisms range from primitive ones, first developed in infancy, to more mature ones, developed later (Kernberg, 1994; Vaillant, 1971, 1992, 1993). Empirical research finds that the most seriously disturbed individuals, psychotics, use the most primitive defenses: denial and distortion of reality. Other immature defenses include projection, dissociation, and acting out. Less primitive (neurotic) defenses include intellectualization and isolation, repression, reaction formation, displacement, and rationalization. Finally, suppression and sublimation, as well as altruism and humor, are the most mature defenses (Vaillant, 1994). Although everyone needs defense mechanisms to cope with life, people who are better adapted use more mature defenses, and extensive use of primitive defenses is unhealthy (Cramer, 2002). When patients with various diagnoses switch from less mature to more mature defense mechanisms, their functioning improves (Cramer, 2000). Couples who use more mature defense mechanisms adjust better to parenthood when their first children are born (Ungerer, Waters, & Barnett, 1997). The maturity of defense mechanisms is unrelated to intelligence, education, and social class (Vaillant, 2000), and mature defenses help people overcome disadvantages in these areas. In a longitudinal study, 14-year-old inner-city boys who scored low (mean of 80) on an IQ measure were, nonetheless, likely to mature into well-adapted 65-year-olds with good incomes and educated children if they had mature defenses; those with less mature defenses fared less well (Vaillant & Davis, 2000).

denial primitive defense mechanism in which material that produces conflict is simply repressed

Denial is a primitive defense mechanism in which an individual does not acknowledge some painful or anxiety-provoking aspect of reality or of the self. For example, a person may deny that smoking is contributing to his or her health problems despite clear statements to that effect by a competent physician. Denial is a normal defense mechanism in preschool children, but as they grow to 7, 8, and 9 years old, children use denial much less often, turning to more mature defense mechanisms such as projection instead (Cramer, 1997; Cramer & Block, 1998). When denial continues to adulthood, it is maladaptive because it involves a major distortion of reality.

In **reaction formation**, an unacceptable impulse is repressed and its opposite is developed in exaggerated form. For example, a child who hates a younger sister may repress it and instead feel love for the sister. The defense may be diagrammed thus:

I hate sister *(unconscious)* → I love sister *(conscious)*

reaction formation defense mechanism in which a person thinks or behaves in a manner opposite to the unacceptable unconscious impulse

When only love is acknowledged, but not its opposite, a psychoanalyst suspects that hatred is also present but denied. Similarly, highly modest persons may be suspected of defending against exhibitionism. People who are raised to very strict moral codes, not allowed to enjoy the normal pleasures of childhood, sometimes turn against themselves and use reaction formation as a defense against adult impulses for gratification; thus they become excessively "good" and prone to moral outrage against other people's flaws (Kaplan, 1997). The defense mechanism of reaction formation contributes to prejudice against homosexuals; that is, men who are unconsciously sexually aroused by other men defend themselves against this threatening impulse by exaggerated anti-gay attitudes. Researchers offer evidence of this; in a laboratory, homophobic men had erections when they watched sexually explicit erotic male homosexual films, but nonhomophobic men did not (Adams, Wright, & Lohr, 1996).

In **projection**, the person's own unacceptable impulse is instead thought to belong to someone else. A man who is tempted to steal but whose strong ethical sense (superego) will not allow him to even think of stealing may project his unacceptable impulse onto another person:

I want to steal *(unconscious)* → That person is stealing *(conscious)*

projection defense mechanism in which a person's own unacceptable impulse is incorrectly thought to belong to someone else

In experiments, people who have been misled to believe they possess an undesirable personality trait but asked not to think about it (which can be thought of as experimental repression) are likely to project their fault onto another person whom they are asked to rate on that trait (Newman, Duff, & Baumeister, 1997). In society, cultural scapegoats often become projective targets, accused of crimes and immoral acts that are really the accuser's own repressed impulses. In this way, individual intrapsychic conflict contributes to prejudice.

The defense mechanism of **displacement** distorts the object of the drive. Displacement is less primitive than projection because the impulse is correctly seen as belonging to the individual; only the object is distorted. For example, a child who is angry with the father may not consciously be able to acknowledge the anger because of fear of retaliation and guilt. The aggressive impulse may be disguised by directing it toward a brother:

displacement defense mechanism in which energy is transferred from one object or activity to another

I want to hurt Dad *(unconscious)* → I want to hurt my brother *(conscious)*

We suspect that the feelings are related to displacement, rather than caused by the brother's actual behavior, if they are disproportionately strong compared to that which the current situation would warrant or if a person frequently has aggressive impulses in a wide variety of situations. Displacement of other emotions, such as dependency and sexuality, can also occur.

identification defense mechanism in which a person fuses or models after another person

Identification is a process of borrowing or merging one's identity with that of someone else. It is part of normal development; boys identify with their fathers, girls with their mothers, and all of us with cultural heroes. It can also be a defense mechanism—avoiding the recognition of one's own inadequacies and wishfully adopting someone else's identity instead. An example of identification as a pervasive defense mechanism is Grey Owl, an Englishman who identified so strongly with stories of Indians in the West that he moved to Canada, lived with the native people, and eventually became so like them in manner and appearance that he passed as an Indian (Dickson, 1973). Identification is important during the third psychosexual stage, when sex roles are an issue, and experimental research confirms that threats to gender identity (based on false information about scores on the Bem Sex-Role Inventory) increase the use of identification as coded from TAT tests (Cramer, 1998c). Identification sometimes functions to overcome feelings of powerlessness. Adopting the identity of someone who has power over us, even if that power is not used for our benefit, is termed *identification with the aggressor*. For example, children may identify with abusive parents or hostages with their captors.

isolation defense mechanism in which conflictful material is kept disconnected from other thoughts

In the defense mechanism of **isolation**, thoughts related to some unpleasant occurrence are disassociated from other thinking and thus do not come to mind. In addition, emotions that would ordinarily be connected with the thoughts are gone. For example, a person who has lost a loved one through death may isolate this experience, not thinking of the loved one because of the grief it might bring.

rationalization defense mechanism in which reasonable, conscious explanations are offered rather than true unconscious motivations

The defense mechanism of **rationalization** involves giving plausible, but false, reasons for an action to disguise the true motives. For example, a parent might rationalize spanking a child, saying it will teach the child to be more obedient, although the true motivation may be that the parent resents the child. Rationalization involves relatively little distortion, so it is considered a relatively mature defense mechanism.

intellectualization defense mechanism in which a person focuses on thinking and avoids feeling

The defense mechanism of **intellectualization** prevents clear, undistorted recognition of an impulse through excessive or distorted explanation. A person who overeats may give many reasons: "I need extra vitamins to deal with stress," "I always gain weight in the winter," and so on. Sometimes intellectualization works like a sour grapes attitude; we intellectually convince ourselves that we did not want what we cannot have. Margaret Sanger described the loss of her newly built home to fire:

> I was neither disappointed nor regretful. . . . In that instant I learned the lesson of the futility of material substances. Of what great importance were they spiritually if they could go so quickly? . . . I could. . . be happy without them. (1938/ 1971, p. 64)

This defense mechanism is adaptive, although defensive in that it distorts the grief of the tragedy.

SUBLIMATION

sublimation defense mechanism in which impulses are expressed in socially acceptable ways

Sublimation is the most desirable and healthy way of dealing with unacceptable impulses. It occurs when the individual finds a socially acceptable aim and object for the expression of an unacceptable impulse. This allows indirect discharge of the impulse, so its pressure is reduced. Sublimation occurs when artists transform primitive urges into works of art. Aggressive impulses may be sublimated into athletic competitiveness. A Freudian would even interpret Mother Teresa's acts of love, bathing and feeding the "poorest of the poor" (Gonzalez-Balado & Playfoot, 1985), as sublimation of sexual motivation. Within Freudian theory, this is the most laudatory interpretation that can be made about anyone.

Creativity

Creative individuals are particularly interesting models of sublimation, and they have been of interest to psychoanalysis, beginning with Sigmund Freud (1910/1957). They retain the ability, lost by most of us, to access the fantasy world of the id. Unlike psychotics, they do not get caught irretrievably in the id, and unlike children, they can function with a mature ego. Creative people are capable of what psychoanalysis describes as "regression in the service of the ego" (Kris, 1952/1964). Research confirms the psychoanalytic hypothesis that creative artists can shift readily between controlled thinking (an ego function) and unregulated thought (the unconscious). Psychotic individuals can access unconscious material, too, but they have difficulty returning to controlled thinking (Wild, 1965). The schizophrenic, in contrast to the poet, cannot use metaphor as a bridge between reality and imagination (Reinsdorf, 1993–1994). Religious mystics, like creative individuals, may have an affinity for the unconscious (Stifler et al., 1993).

Surrealistic artists, such as Salvador Dali, explicitly portray images of unconscious material in their work. Freud, however, valued the ego more than the id, and so he only came to respect Dali after he became convinced of the artist's capacity for control as well as for expression (Romm & Slap, 1983; Rose, 1983). Creative pursuits such as painting and writing can release unconscious conflict in a safe way, which is the purpose of defense mechanisms.

EMPIRICAL STUDIES OF DEFENSES

Descriptions of defense mechanisms were originally derived from clinical case histories. Based on extensive interviews with a client, the therapist describes the ego's efforts to transform unacceptable unconscious material through ego defense mechanisms. Such case histories, however, have shortcomings for research purposes. For one thing, they are extremely time consuming, requiring dozens or even hundreds of hours of investigation for each person studied. In addition, there is a problem of reliability. Because the therapist is both the interviewer and the interpreter of the material, it is difficult to know the extent to which another independent observer would have come to the same interpretations.

Consider sexual identity disorders that are so severe that people resort to sexual reassignment surgery to correct what they perceive to be the wrong-sex body. With sexuality so central to psychoanalytic theory, and identification so clearly described in the Oedipal stage, it is no surprise that psychoanalysts interpreted such disorders, and the voluntary castration that beckons as a cure, to result from a boy's excessive identification with his mother, especially in the absence of a strong father to serve as a model of the male role. Empirical support for such interpretations of transgender disorders, however, is not compelling. Research designs have been inadequate for decades, in the analysis of Midence and Hargreaves (1997), marred by inadequate controls and measurements that permit researchers' preconceptions to bias their results.

For research, a more systematic assessment of defense mechanisms can be made, using psychological tests. Projective tests, including the TAT and the Rorschach test, can be scored for defense mechanisms. Research using the TAT has found that patients had healthier defense patterns after therapy than before (Cramer & Blatt, 1990). Clinical interview methods are also useful for monitoring changes in defenses over the course of therapy (Perry & Ianni, 1998).

Despite their many limitations for measuring unconscious processes such as defenses (Davidson & MacGregor, 1998), self-report inventories have also been developed to assess defense mechanisms, including the Defense Mechanism Inventory (Gleser & Ihilevich, 1969) and the Defense Style Questionnaire (Bond, 1995). A related concept is coping (considered by many to be less unconscious than are defense mechanisms; e.g., Cramer, 1998a), and self-report methods also exist for measuring coping strategies (Amirkhan, 1990, 1994; Turvey & Salovey, 1993–1994). Some studies indicate that experimental manipulations affect defensiveness (Cramer, 1991; Cramer & Gaul, 1988), which increases confidence that the test is valid. Studies also indicate that people who are repressors are likely to claim they are not anxious even when their bodies show signs of physiological arousal. When observers rate them as anxious, they put a positive spin on interpreting their own behavior (Derakshan & Eysenck, 1997). It has not been demonstrated, however, that these various measures of defenses, both self-report and projective tests, are valid indicators of the use of defense mechanisms in people's everyday lives. For example, when researchers have asked subjects to report coping in everyday life at the time when they were stressed, using a portable palm-top computer, these reports didn't correspond very well with later retrospective reports (Stone et al., 1998). Without better assessment, this aspect of psychoanalytic theory cannot be tested adequately. Unfortunately, there is a chasm between the retrospective reports of coping that researchers measure by questionnaire and the clinical observations of coping that therapists observe.

What could be more threatening than awareness that we will die? *Terror management theory* describes the impact of the anxiety of death, proposing that people make defensive efforts to maintain positive self-images and cling to their cultural worldviews to ward off such anxiety. By maintaining the belief that "I am a valuable participant in a meaningful universe," a person defends against unconscious death anxiety. For example, death threats triggered by terrorist attacks lead to an increase in patriotism and religious sentiment. If death threatens more immanently, active suppression or cognitive distortions also are activated, such as disbelieving reports that behaviors we engage in have been found to lead to premature death (Pyszczynski, Greenberg, & Solomon, 1999).

In addition to correlational measures of defense, researchers have further explored defensive processes in experimental laboratory studies. Consider a repressive coping style: people whose bodies show physiological signs of anxiety but who score low on written measures of anxiety. Correlational studies show that repressors have fewer memories of adverse childhood events than do nonrepressors, even though more negative things have happened in their childhood. Laboratory experiments suggest that they may be using emotional cues to signal repression. In one study, research subjects were directed to recall certain types of stimuli that they are shown and to forget others. Overall, subjects were able to remember more of the information that they had been told to remember, but most exciting for the study of defenses were differences between people. *Repressors* were especially able to forget stimuli that they had been told to forget when such stimuli were associated with negative emotions (Myers, Brewin, & Power, 1998). They seem able to use negative emotion as an unconscious cue.

In an extensive review of personality and social psychological research, including many studies that were not designed by their originators as studies of defense mechanisms but that could be interpreted as providing evidence about such processes, Roy Baumeister and colleagues concluded that there was substantial evidence for several defense mechanisms: projection, undoing, isolation, and denial. However, very limited evidence could be found for displacement and none whatsoever for sublimation (Baumeister, Dale, & Sommer, 1998). Cross-cultural studies of defense mechanisms are relevant for testing Freud's claim that his theory describes universal aspects of personality. Although there is much to be done, a large-scale empirical study of defense mechanisms in Thailand, using self-report measures, found similar kinds of defenses to those in U.S. samples. Some, though, were used less frequently in Thailand (regressive or immature emotional behavior), and some were used more frequently (projection, reaction formation, projection, and other indicators of a high level of control), reflecting the different cultural values of the two countries (Tori & Bilmes, 2002).

Personality Development

One of Freud's legacies is that childhood experience potently influences adult personality. Personality development involves a series of conflicts between the individual, who wants to satisfy instinctual impulses, and the social world (especially the family), which constrains this desire. Through development, the individual finds ways to obtain as much hedonic gratification as possible, given the constraints of society. These adaptational strategies constitute the personality. The common saying "As the twig is bent, so grows the tree" aptly describes this psychoanalytic theory of development. Like a tree that has grown crooked under adverse conditions of wind and terrain, the adult human shows the permanent distorting effects of childhood struggles.

Freud proposed that the mucous membranes of the body could be the physical source of id impulses, the *erogenous zones* where libido is focused. These zones are highly responsive to sensation and can be associated with increased tension and reduction of tension, as the libido model requires. Different zones are central at different ages because of maturational changes (i.e., physical changes associated with age). For the adult, the erogenous zone is the genital area. In early life, though, other zones give more pleasure: in infancy, the mouth; in toddlerhood, the anus. Driven by maturational factors, all people develop through the same *psychosexual stages* (see Table 2.2.).

The infant, under the tyranny of the pleasure principle, wants to be fed immediately whenever hungry. In reality, feeding is sometimes delayed, and ultimately the child is weaned. This is the conflict of the first psychosexual stage, the **oral stage**. In the second, or **anal stage**, the toddler enjoys controlling the bowels, retaining and expelling feces according to his or her own will; but conflict with the restrictive forces of society arises because the family demands toilet training. Conflict over drive satisfaction in the third psychosexual stage, the **phallic stage**, focuses on punishment for masturbation and the child's complex fantasy of a sexual union with the opposite-sex parent—a wish that is frustrated because it conflicts with the universal taboo of incest.

Personality development occurs as the ego finds new strategies to cope with the frustrations imposed by socialization. If socialization is too severe or too sudden, the young ego cannot cope, and personality development is impaired. Sudden, severe shocks that are beyond the child's capacity to cope, called psychic trauma, include sexual abuse and early witnessing of adults' sexual intercourse (the "primal scene"). The primal scene has been compared with the attempts of young children of Holocaust survivors to understand their parents' Holocaust experience: "a knowledge that engulfs the child who does not know what to do with a knowledge that he or she cannot yet grasp"

oral stage the first psychosexual stage of development, from birth to age 1

anal stage the second psychosexual stage of development, from age 1 to 3

phallic stage the third psychosexual stage of development, from age 3 to 5

TABLE 2.2   Stages of Psychosexual Development

Stage	*Age*	*Conflict*	*Outcomes*
Oral Stage	Birth to 12 months	Weaning	Optimism or pessimism
			Addictions to tobacco, alcohol
Anal Stage	1 to 3 years	Toilet training	Stubbornness
			Miserliness
Phallic Stage	3 to 5 years	Masturbation and Oedipus/	Sex-role identification
		Electra conflict	Morality (superego) vanity
Latency	5 years to puberty		
Genital Stage	Puberty to adulthood		

fixation failure to develop normally through a particular developmental stage

(Auerhahn & Laub, 1998, p. 371). Such events produce **fixation**, in which impulses are repressed rather than outgrown.

Traumatic stress exceeds the ego's ability to integrate the traumatic experience with the rest of personality, so it remains separate, dissociated from ordinary consciousness. Such dissociations occur in the clinical condition called *posttraumatic stress disorder*. One extreme form of dissociation occurs in *multiple personality disorder*. Recent researchers have challenged the psychoanalytic dissociation explanation of these disorders, and have not found a strong enough link between trauma and dissociative symptoms to be sure that one causes the other (Piers, 1998; Tillman, Nash, & Lerner, 1994; Yehuda & McFarlane, 1995). In support of the possibility that trauma may cause dissociation, however, are findings that changes in neurotransmitters brought about by drugs do produce temporary amnesia (Nissen, Knopman, & Schacter, 1987). Trauma could produce amnesia if it is severe enough to disrupt normal neurotransmitter functioning that is necessary to form permanent memories.

The effects produced by fixation are usually much milder than these severe disorders and are evidenced by less dramatic symptoms. The specific effects of fixation depend on when, in the progression of development through several stages, the fixation occurs. Let's look at these stages.

THE FIVE PSYCHOSEXUAL STAGES

There are five universal stages of development. Freud believed that personality is essentially formed by the end of the third stage, at about age 5. By then, the individual has developed basic strategies for expressing impulses, strategies that constitute the core of personality.

The Oral Stage

The oral stage of development occurs from birth to about age 1. During this stage, the erogenous zone is the mouth, and pleasurable activities center around feeding (sucking). At first, in the oral erotic phase, the infant passively receives reality, swallowing what is good or (less passively) spitting out what is distasteful. Later in the oral stage, a second phase, termed *oral sadism*, involves the development of a more active role, epitomized by biting.

Because the infant's needs are met without effort, he or she is said to feel omnipotent. This feeling passes in normal development but is retained in some psychoses. The feeling of infantile omnipotence normally gives way to realization that needs are satisfied through loved objects in the world, not magically. As the infant learns to associate the mother's presence with satisfaction of the hunger drive, the mother becomes a separate object, and the first differentiation of self from others occurs. Fixation in the first psychosexual stage results in development of an **oral character** personality type, whose traits have traditionally been said to include *optimism*, *passivity*, and *dependency*. Conflicts over these traits can sometimes produce the opposite characteristics; for example, because of reaction formation, the person fixated at the oral stage may become pessimistic instead of optimistic, leading to depression (Lewis, 1993).

oral character personality type resulting from fixation in the first psychosexual stage; characterized by optimism, passivity, and dependency

The hypothesized relationship between oral fixation and behavior that is conforming and dependent is sometimes supported. People with oral imagery on the Rorschach test conform more to others' judgments on an Asch-type judgment task, particularly in the presence of a high-status authority figure (Masling, Weiss, & Rothschild, 1968; Tribich & Messer, 1974), and they are more likely to indicate on personality tests the need for help (O'Neill & Bornstein, 1990). They are capable of disagreeing too, though, if that will create a favorable impression to an authority figure, according to Bornstein (1997), who advocates understanding dependency in terms of relationships with other people (object relations), instead of orality (Bornstein, 1996). Studies suggest that oral concerns in the most literal sense, that is, "preoccupation with food and eating," might be unrelated to dependency (Bornstein, 1992, p. 17), contrary to Freud's theory (Young-Bruehl, 1990). Developments in psychoanalysis since Freud's time have emphasized interpersonal relationships more than libido (see Chapter 6). Consistent with this modern revision, unhealthy patterns of interpersonal attachments have been found in those whose weight concerns put them at risk for eating disorders (Sharpe et al., 1998). Other personality factors that predispose people to eating disorders include perfectionism, negative emotionality, and obsessive-compulsive tendencies (Lilenfeld et al., 2005).

The Anal Stage

During the second and third years, the toddler's pleasure is experienced in a different part of the body: the anus. The toddler's desire to control his or her own bowel movements conflicts with the social demand for toilet training. Pleasure is experienced at first through the newly formed ability to retain feces, the anal retentive phase, and then in the experience of willful defecation, the anal expulsive phase. Lifelong conflicts over issues of control, of holding on and letting go, may result if there is fixation at this stage. The **anal character** is characterized by three traits, *orderliness*, *parsimony*, and *obstinacy*, which are correlated in many empirical studies (Greenberg & Fisher, 1978; but see a contrary opinion by Hill, 1976). Anal fixation may be expressed by issues related to money—hoarding it or spending it—as symbolic feces (Wolfenstein, 1993). As predicted by Freud's proposal that humor expresses unconscious conflict (described earlier), experimental

anal character personality type resulting from fixation at age 1 to 3, characterized by orderliness, parsimony, and obstinacy

subjects who score high on the anal traits (obstinacy, orderliness, and parsimony) find jokes on anal themes to be particularly funny (O'Neill, Greenberg, & Fisher, 1992).

The Phallic Stage

From age 3 to 5 (or a bit later), the primary erogenous area of the body is the genital zone. Freud called this stage of development the phallic stage, reflecting his conviction that the phallus (penis) is the most important organ for the development of both males and females. (Critics chastise Freud for being phallocentric.) The child's desire for sexual pleasure is expressed through masturbation, which is accompanied by important (and, to critics, incredible) fantasies. At this stage, males and females follow different developmental paths.

Oedipus conflict
conflict that males experience from age 3 to 5 involving sexual love for the mother and aggressive rivalry with the father

castration anxiety
fear that motivates male development at age 3 to 5

Male Development: The Oedipus Conflict.   According to Freud, the young boy wants to kill his father and to replace him as his mother's sexual partner. This **Oedipus conflict** is derived from Sophocles' play *Oedipus Rex*, in which Oedipus unwittingly murders his father and takes his own mother as his wife. The young boy fears, however, that this desire will be found out and punished, and so he represses the incestuous desire. In addition, Freud speculated that the male's rivalry with his father is aided by brothers who join with him to overthrow the patriarch, and who would be his rivals for an incestuous relationship with the mother, if their joint assault against the father were successful. If all of them obeyed an *incest taboo* so they did not compete with one another, then the social order would be preserved (Winter, 1999). **Castration anxiety**, the fear that his penis will be cut off, is the motivating anxiety of the young boy at this stage. Although such castration anxiety may seem an incredible idea, threats of castration do occur in some bizarre circumstances. We are told, for example, that Adolf Hitler ordered artists to be castrated if they used the wrong colors for skies and meadows (Waite, 1977, p. 30). It has also been suggested that many of the sexual problems that patients bring to medical clinics that treat sexual dysfunction are derived from castration anxiety. In other cultures, castration anxiety is expressed differently; for example, in Southeast Asia, the phenomenon of *koro* is the sudden anxiety that the penis (or, in females, the vulva and nipples) will recede into the body (American Psychiatric Association, 1994; Kirmayer, 1992). Freud asserted that the Oedipus complex was universal throughout all human societies, but others have argued that it is a reflection of the father–son competition characteristic of Freud's cultural and historical time, reflecting the competition of an educated and upwardly mobile capitalist culture (Winter, 1999), that an Oedipus complex does not occur everywhere (Wax, 2000) and that incest itself, especially mother–son incest, is unusual among humans across the world, and also in animals, because it is maladaptive from an evolutionary viewpoint (Sugiyama, 2001).

In normal development, castration anxiety is repressed. Unconscious castration anxiety may be displaced, experienced as the fear of tonsillectomy (Blum, 1953, p. 87) or as the fear of disease. Freud believed that syphilidophobia, fear of being infected with syphilis, is derived from castration anxiety (Freud, 1933/1966a, p. 552). Presumably, he would regard exaggerated fear of AIDS as evidence of a similar displacement today.

In a healthy resolution of the Oedipal conflict, the boy gives up his fantasy of replacing his father and instead decides to become *like* his father. By this identification, the boy achieves two important developments: (1) appropriate male sex typing, and (2) the internalization of conscience, called superego. Conscience is fueled by castration anxiety: The stronger the castration fear, the stronger the superego. Or as Freud (1923/1962b, p. 38) so memorably phrased it, "The superego . . . is the heir of the Oedipus complex."

Female Development: The Electra Conflict. Girls develop differently. Seeing that they lack a penis, girls believe they have been castrated. According to Freud, girls interpret their clitoris as inferior to a penis and wish for the latter (penis envy). Like boys, girls in the phallic stage fantasize sexual union with the opposite-sex parent. Unlike boys, girls must shift their erotic attachment from the mother (the first, pre-Oedipal love object for both sexes) to the father. This change of object is facilitated by the girl's anger toward her mother for not being powerful enough to protect her from castration.

Freud (1933/1966a, p. 590) lists three possible outcomes of the girl's castration complex: sexual inhibition or neurosis, a masculinity complex, or normal femininity. By *masculinity complex*, Freud meant that the woman strives for achievements considered in his day to be inappropriate for females, such as career advances to the exclusion of traditional feminine family commitments. Normal feminine development, according to Freud, results in accepting the role of wife and mother and developing the "normal" feminine traits of passivity and masochism. Many psychoanalysts today reject Freud's claim that healthy women need to become wives and mothers to satisfy their innate cravings (M. G. Morris, 1997). Without castration anxiety to motivate their development, girls are theoretically less psychologically developed than males, with a weaker superego. Naturally, this assertion has been rejected by those who argue that cultural factors can adequately explain the acceptance of suffering that Freud described as biologically determined masochism (e.g., Caplan, 1984). It also contradicts the empirical record of sex differences: that women report more shame and guilt (interpreted as evidence of moral development), have more empathy for other people's feelings (Tangney, 1990, 1994), and score higher than males on the level of ego development (e.g., Mabry, 1993).

Incest: Freud's Abandonment of the Seduction Hypothesis. Freud developed and revised his theory over many decades. In his final view, the girl's fantasy of a sexual relationship with her father is just that: fantasy. Earlier, Freud had believed that actual, rather than imagined, incest was important in the histories of his female patients (the *seduction hypothesis*). His seduction hypothesis, which he later abandoned, held that the father's sexual behavior with his daughter was responsible for her development of psychiatric problems, specifically, hysteria (Freud, 1896/1962a; McGrath, 1986). Why did Freud change his mind, first believing that his patients had been sexually assaulted and later concluding this had been their imagination? Could he have been defending himself against a suspicion that his own father had seduced Freud himself and his siblings (Kupfersmid, 1992)? One critic, Jeffrey Masson (1984, p. 134), thought so, and he accused Freud of a "loss of courage," putting career interests ahead of his patients.

Others disagree. Orthodox Freudians accept Freud's abandonment of the seduction hypothesis as the correction of an earlier error (e.g., Gleaves & Hernandez, 1999; Lawrence, 1988; Paul, 1985; Rosenman, 1989). Throughout Freud's theory, thoughts and wishes are centrally important and actual events are less important. Thoughts and fantasies can be changed through therapy, as facts cannot (Birch, 1998), and so the analysis concentrates on what the abusive memory means for the patient, now, rather than the abuse simply as an historical fact. Recollections of abuse become, in effect, narratives that serve as organizing metaphors for experience; but a theory that focuses on fantasized incest while ignoring actual incest invites criticism (Mack, 1980).

Effects of Fixation. Psychoanalytic theory says that fixation at the phallic stage results in difficulties of superego formation; sex-role identity; and sexuality, including sexual inhibition, sexual promiscuity, and homosexuality. Historically, Freud argued that homosexuality is understandable because people all have some attraction to both men and women (bisexuality), but that a heterosexual outcome was more mature and healthy (Freud, 1905/1962b, 1920/1978; Jacobo, 2001). Problems with sex role identification (accepting cultural standards for male or female behavior) may stem from difficulties at this stage. This classic formula assumes that cultural sex norms will be accepted by healthy individuals; it does not allow for the possibility that sex-role norms are themselves in need of change. More recently, psychoanalysts have attempted to describe the dynamics of the Oedipus conflict in modified form to relate to gay men (Lewes, 1998; Schwartz, 1999). In addition, other research implicates biological causes of sexual orientation, including prenatal hormone exposure (Meyer-Bahlburg et al., 1995) and brain structure (LeVay, 1991).

Freud asserted that personality is largely formed during these first three psychosexual stages when the basic ego mechanisms for dealing with libidinal impulses are established. If fixation has occurred, the specific neurosis will depend on the stage at which development was impaired. The earlier the fixation, the more serious the resulting disorder. Freud suggested that schizophrenia, paranoia or obsessional neurosis, and hysteria result from serious fixation at the first three stages, respectively (Sulloway, 1979).

The Latency Stage

Middle childhood is a period of relative calm for the sexual instincts, so Freud's model of libidinal tension says little about this stage. (It is, however, an important period of development according to other theories.)

The Genital Stage

genital stage the adult psychosexual stage

genital character healthy personality type

The **genital stage** begins at puberty. In contrast to the autoerotic and fantasy sexual objects of the phallic child, the genital adult develops the capacity to experience sexual satisfaction with an opposite-sex object. The **genital character** is Freud's ideal of full development. It develops if fixations have been avoided or if they have been resolved through psychoanalysis. Such a person has no significant pre-Oedipal conflicts; enjoys a satisfying sexuality; and cares about the satisfaction of the love partner, avoiding selfish narcissism. Sublimated psychic energy is available for work, which brings enjoyment.

Freud regarded neurosis as essentially a sexual dysfunction. Because of the inherent conflict between biological demands and the requirements of civilization, some degree of neurotic conflict is inevitable, but it could be minimized through enlightened acceptance of sexual needs. In the post-Freudian era, sexual performance and enjoyment are widely accepted as standards to be attained.

Psychoanalytic Treatment

In the healthy adult, both direct sexual satisfaction and indirect sublimation of sexual instincts occur, leading to Freud's famous criterion of mental health, *Lieben und Arbeiten*, that is, "love and work." Such an outcome is possible if there are no major fixations in development or if fixations are resolved through psychoanalytic treatment. Freud described psychoanalysis with the metaphor of archaeology. The analytic process tries to "dig up" primitive material long "buried" by repression and to bring it to the surface, to consciousness, so it can be considered with the skills of the more developed ego. Freud's formula for achieving health is "Where id was, there shall ego be" (1933/1966a, p. 544).

PSYCHOANALYTIC THERAPY TECHNIQUES

The psychoanalyst uses the principle of psychic determinism to discover the unconscious ideas and conflicts of the patient that originated in the past, thus helping the patient to become free of the neurotic compulsion to repeat the past, and instead to be able to live in the present (Covington, 2001). The basic technique of psychoanalysis is **free association**, which requires the patient "to say whatever came into his head, while ceasing to give any conscious direction to his thoughts" (Freud, 1935/1963a, p. 75). Suspension of conscious control allows the forces of the unconscious, which are usually obscured by the consciousness, to be observed directing thoughts and memories. In addition to the interview, some clinicians also use psychological tests to guide their diagnosis (Jaffe, 1992).

The emergence of buried feelings from the unconscious is called **catharsis**. These feelings, including fear and grief, often accompany the recall of forgotten memories. Like the removal of infectious material when a wound is lanced, catharsis frees the unconscious of troublesome repressions.

Psychoanalytic treatment produces **insight**, that is, understanding of true motives, which are unconscious conflicts. To be therapeutic, insight must be accompanied by emotional awareness. Although the insight into unconscious motivations, even if accompanied by emotional catharsis, is a major step toward overcoming the symptoms produced by the unconscious, it does not provide a magical once-and-for-all cure. In addition to this dramatic recall, modern psychoanalysis recognizes that unconscious conflicts must be confronted again and again in a psychoanalytic treatment. The patient must "work through" the conflict, discovering the many circumstances that have been influenced by it and essentially reconstructing personality to replace these unconscious irrational determinants with more reasonable and mature motivations.

A major phenomenon in psychoanalytic treatment is **transference**. During the course of psychoanalytic treatment, the patient develops a relationship to the therapist based on unconscious projections from earlier life. The patient perceives the therapist erroneously and experiences emotions that were repressed when felt toward earlier significant others. It is common, for example, for a female patient to "fall in love with" her male analyst because of transference of the love she felt for her father during childhood. Negative as well as positive emotions occur. Transference is, strangely enough, desirable, according to psychoanalysts. It permits the earlier unresolved issues to be present in the analytic session, where they can be resolved. More problematic are the analyst's emotional reactions to the patient, termed **countertransference**, which may interfere with treatment because they represent the analyst's unresolved complexes.

In his day, Freud's theory was a force for the humane treatment of the mentally ill because it interpreted their disorders as the consequence of disease (the medical model) rather than of moral failure. Today, critics argue that the medical model has adverse implications. It treats people as passive victims of pathological forces, undermining their active effort and responsibility for their own psychological well-being. An outspoke critic of the medical model, Thomas Szasz argues that the mental illness model ignores the truth that even people who have abnormal biological or unconscious states can, like others, make moral choices; to theorize otherwise is to ignore the evidence of science and to deprive them of their humanity (Szasz, 2001). The medical model tends to place

free association psychoanalytic technique in which the patient says whatever comes to mind, permitting unconscious connections to be discovered

catharsis therapeutic effect of a release of emotion when previously repressed material is made conscious

insight conscious recognition of one's motivation and unconscious conflicts

transference in therapy, the patient's displacement onto the therapist of feelings based on earlier experiences (e.g., with the patient's own parents)

countertransference the analyst's reaction to the patient, as distorted by unresolved conflicts

the wisdom of the physician over the experience of the patient and is insensitive to the role of social factors in causing psychopathology. How ironic that Freud, whose theory began with the premise that the experience of patients must be taken seriously, should be criticized for such a shortcoming.

Considerable effort has been made in recent years to investigate the effectiveness of various modes of psychotherapy (Westen & Morrison, 2001). Therapy comes in many forms today, and psychoanalytic treatment is considerably more time consuming and expensive than alternative modes of treatment. A typical analysis may take 3 to 7 years, three sessions each week. Some alternative treatments may take only a few weeks. Is psychoanalysis more effective, justifying the extra cost and commitment? There has been much skepticism even about Freud's own therapeutic effectiveness (e.g., Ellenberger, 1972; Mahony, 1986). Evidence for analytic therapy's effectiveness is mixed, favoring psychoanalysis for psychosomatic disorders (Fisher & Greenberg, 1977) but not for anxiety and phobias (Goldfried, Greenberg, & Marmar, 1990) or depression (Westen & Morrison, 2001). We should be cautious, though, because it is not easy to evaluate therapy effectiveness, especially to compare different approaches. The requirements of data collection may constrain therapists from their usual procedures (Busch et al., 2001). Some research indicates that, if patients are assessed after a longer time period, the advantage of psychodynamic therapy increases (Blomberg, Lazar, & Sandell, 2001), which makes sense if we grant that this approach aims at more fundamental personality change. However, investigation of the effectiveness of therapy is just beginning, and until methodological difficulties have been addressed and more studies conducted, using diverse methodologies, we really do not know scientifically what works and what does not (Westen & Morrison, 2001).

In addition to outcome studies, researchers study the process of psychoanalytic therapy, using clinicians' notes and even recordings of sessions to understand what particular techniques work (e.g., Jones & Windholz, 1990; Wallerstein & Sampson, 1971; Weiss, 1988; Wolpe & Rachman, 1960). These systematic studies of psychotherapy suggest that insight is less important to successful treatment than psychoanalytic theory predicts (Wallerstein, 1989). Such studies promise to improve therapy, whether or not more global empirical validation of treatment outcomes is feasible (Strupp, 2001).

THE RECOVERED MEMORY CONTROVERSY

One controversial technique that was used by a small minority of therapists has now been discredited: recovered memory therapy. The idea behind this therapy, consistent with psychoanalytic ideas, was that traumatic sexual experiences in childhood had led patients to develop a variety of symptoms (depression, promiscuity, eating disorders, and others) and also to repress the memory of the abuse. If memory for the traumatic event could be restored, it was thought, a therapeutic benefit would be obtained aim (Blume, 1995; Freyd, 1994, 1996; Whitfield, 1995). Unfortunately, belief in this model was so zealous among a few therapists that they jumped to a conclusion of sexual abuse with minimal evidence, even over the objections of patients (who were thought to be actively repressing the memory), and through suggestion, therapists gradually convinced many patients of their traumatic past. Sometimes these inferences are true. Sometimes they are false. Occasional reports are so bizarre, including reports of Satanic ritual abuse, cult mass murders of newborns, and childbirth in women whose physicians find no evidence of pregnancy, that they are patently absurd. Often there is no reliable way of knowing whether a particular client's memories are true or false or a mixture of truth and falsehood (Genoni, 1994; Lindsay & Read, 1995; Scheflin & Brown, 1996), and that is a particularly troublesome consequence of this debate: the likelihood that it has made some truly abused victims less credible. In those rare cases in which recovered memories can be validated, they seem to be so different from the typical therapeutically recovered memory that one clinician suggests most recovered memory tales told in therapy are not really about the past at all but rather some metaphor for events that are actually happening within therapy itself (Brenneis, 2000).

The controversy has moved to the courts, too, where trials pit children who claim to have been abused against their parents. The legal system, of course, requires decisions about what behavior actually occurred, and psychoanalysis, because it is concerned instead with "subjective truth," is not well suited to provide the needed information (Birch, 1998). Judges and juries are deciding whether the abuse was real or imagined, whether questioning by therapists and others helped uncover repressed memories or created them by the power of suggestion (Ceci & Bruck, 1993; Ofshe & Watters, 1994; Pressley & Grossman, 1994). Occasionally, substantial financial awards are given to fathers who sue therapists for implanting false memories of abuse into their daughters' minds (Ceci & Bruck, 1995; Genoni, 1995; Loftus, 1993; Pope & Hudson, 1996; *Ramona v. Isabella* et al., 1994; *State v. Michaels*, 1993).

Although in many cases the past cannot be known, many scientists are convinced that some of these constructed memories were false, given the extreme claims that were sometimes made and also given scientific evidence about memory. They argue that some allegedly recalled memories of abuse are, in fact, the result of suggestion by therapists to gullible clients (e.g., Bowers & Farvolden, 1996). Such suggested memories are called the *false memory syndrome*. One study finds that defendants accused of child abuse, after the victim recovered memory of the abuse in therapy, passed a polygraph exam 96% of the time; in contrast, only 22% of the accused passed the exam if their victims had not repressed memory of the abuse (Abrams, 1995).

Many experts doubt that sexual abuse would be forgotten as frequently as the recovered memory advocates claim. Victims of other traumas, such as natural disasters, are often troubled by intrusive memories instead of forgetting the pain, although some soldiers who have experienced the stress of combat are unable to recall their experiences (Karon & Widener, 1997). However, sexual trauma is often kept secret, which may interfere with memory. A prospective study, in which abuse was documented in childhood, indicates that 38% did not recall the abuse 17 years later (Williams, 1994).

This controversy has unfortunately pitted psychologists against one another as they debate the relevance of scientific studies for clinical treatment. On the one hand, scientific skepticism is supported by many laboratory studies that show that people can be led to believe things that never happened, even in their own personal histories. Through the power of suggestion, some research subjects came to believe they had been lost in a shopping mall in childhood, and over time they reported these incidents with increasing (but incorrect) detail. Their families asserted that such events had never happened (Loftus & Pickrell, 1995). On the other hand, as therapists point out, a memory for childhood sexual abuse is quite different from a memory for being lost in a mall. Shrouded in secrecy and with the perpetrator's demand for silence, a childhood abuse incident is not validated or acknowledged by the family or others, and society often turns a deaf ear as well. Furthermore, the extreme distress caused by sexual abuse can produce emotional and accompanying biochemical changes that can profoundly impact memory, which is outside the scope of the cognitive social experiments used to discredit such amnesia. There is still much to learn about trauma and memory.

Could real incest ever seem to be only fantasized or imagined incest? At first glance, it would seem impossible to confuse the two. An experimental study, though, shows that sometimes stressful experiences are misremembered as imagined rather than real (Kunzendorf & Moran, 1993–1994). A controlled laboratory study, of course, cannot expose subjects to sexual victimization. Instead, a milder event was substituted: solving anagram puzzles under stress. Some subjects received problems that could be solved (e.g., the letters CYJOKE can be rearranged to make the word JOCKEY); others received unsolvable anagrams (such as CYSOKE). During part of the testing, subjects could see clues to help solve the anagrams (such as RACE) projected on a screen. Later in the testing, clues were read to them and they were instructed to imagine seeing them on the screen. There were other experimental manipulations in some groups designed to produce high levels of anxiety about succeeding; they were told the test measured intelligence, and in contrast to their own difficulties (because their own anagrams were impossible), they could see others solving the anagrams more quickly. Some subjects, those whose personality tests indicated they were afraid of failure, were likely to report that clues to the anagrams they had failed to solve had been "imagined" clues, rather than actually seen. If this distortion in memory occurs in college students with the relatively innocuous task of solving verbal puzzles, could some similar process occur among victims of childhood sexual abuse? Could they sometimes recall the incest as an imagined event? The evidence is sparse, so we can only speculate. But if processes similar to this controlled experiment occur in the more important setting of life itself, it would help explain why Freud came to believe incest was fantasized.

Two points are established beyond controversy: Sexual abuse of children occurs all too frequently, and it has long-term negative effects on psychological functioning (Cahill, Llewelyn, & Pearson, 1991). David Finkelhor and his colleagues report a national survey of Americans in which 27% of the women and 16% of the men reported some type of sexual abuse when they were children. Overall, 13% of the women and 9% of the men reported a history of actual or attempted intercourse (Finkelhor et al., 1990). Those who have been sexually abused as children are at increased risk for a variety of disorders, including posttraumatic stress disorder, anxiety, depression, suicide, borderline personality disorder, multiple personality disorder, dissociation, drug and alcohol abuse, sexual victimization, difficulty in relationships, and poor self-esteem (Alter-Reid et al., 1986; Barnard & Hirsch, 1985; Browne & Finkelhor, 1986; Connors & Morse, 1993; deChesnay, 1985; Kendall-Tackett, Williams, & Finkelhor, 1993; Kiser et al., 1991; Leifer et al., 1991; Saltman & Solomon, 1982; Shapiro et al., 1990; Silon, 1992; Trickett & Putnam, 1993). There is more damage when the abuse is more invasive, when the abuser uses physical force or is coercive, and when parents do not believe the child's reports of abuse (Spaccarelli, 1994).

Psychoanalysis as a Scientific Theory

Psychoanalysis is more than a therapy. It is a theory of personality. Does the personality theory fare any better than the therapy when subjected to the objective evaluation of the scientific method? Most psychologists today would say no. The main difficulty is that Freud's concepts were not described precisely enough to guide scientists toward a definitive test; that is, they fall short on the criterion of *verifiability*. For Freud, the psychoanalytic method of talking with an individual patient provided sufficient data to verify his theory. He was not interested in independent scientific evaluation, which would have required advance prediction about what would be observed, in precise enough terms to say what did and what did not confirm his theory. Many analysts defend clinical observation as evidence, despite its difficulties (Arlow, 1977; Jaffe, 1990; Meissner, 1990; Rubinstein,

1980; Wallace, 1989). Others, however, have conducted empirical studies (e.g., Bellak, 1993), and after a long history of separation between clinical and research efforts, some significant convergences are now developing, for example, in the literature on coping (Lazarus, 2000). The call for more systematic research to supplement clinical observation has been voiced not only by critics of psychoanalysis but also by many psychoanalysts themselves (e.g., Grünbaum, 1984, 1990).

Many therapists are indifferent to, or even antagonistic to, scientific research (Williams & Irving, 1999), unless that research is specifically targeted to clinical practice (Williams & Hill, 2001). As therapists, psychoanalysts listen intuitively, prepared to synthesize diverse, vague clues into a picture of the client's personality. However, science does not tolerate such loosely defined methods. Science demands verifiability. That is, science predicts what observations would confirm its hypotheses and also what observations would constitute disconfirmation. In contrast, an intuitive therapist may be able to explain any observation. For example, either optimism or pessimism can be interpreted as evidence of an oral personality. Even a middle level between these two opposites is consistent with the diagnosis of oral fixation because both extremes may be present but in equal proportions. Such a flexible theory cannot be disconfirmed and so is not science. Instead, critics describe psychoanalysis as myth or pseudoscience. Robert Langs (1993) describes psychoanalysis as a mythology that legitimizes treatment, building on the traditions of "hominid healers, shamans and priests" (p. 559). Others agree that psychoanalysis builds on these nonscientific mythic origins, but they admire the mythic connection (e.g., Walsh, 1994).

When researchers test psychoanalytic ideas outside of the therapeutic setting, other difficulties emerge. Most psychological tests rely on self-report measures, in which people say what they experience. These are problematic, however, because psychoanalytic theory itself is based on the premise that people have little insight into their own psychodynamics. Projective tests such as the Rorschach inkblot test (Pichot, 1984), which are commonly used to measure unconscious motivations, have often been accused of suffering low reliability, which impedes research. Nonetheless, some striking results have been reported with the Rorschach method, and a variety of scoring methods based on empirical research, instead of simply clinical intuition, have increased reliability and validity (Bornstein & Masling, 2005). In one study, the medical school Rorschach protocols of those physicians who later committed suicide or came down with cancer were strikingly distinctive (Thomas, 1988). In another, Rorschach tests of women who killed their abusive husbands were found to be similar to tests of combat veterans suffering from posttraumatic stress disorder (Kaser-Boyd, 1993). Rorschach tests have also been reported to change as psychotherapy progresses, so the patients' scores indicate increasing adjustment over time and greater improvement with long-term than short-term therapy (Exner & Andronikof-Sanglade, 1992; Weiner & Exner, 1991).

SILVERMAN'S EXPERIMENTS

Lloyd Silverman (1976, 1983) has conducted a series of evaluations that offer experimental tests of the unconscious. Calling his method *subliminal psychodynamic activation*, Silverman presented stimuli with a tachistoscope, which is essentially a slide projector beamed through a camera shutter. This device allows very brief presentations (4 milliseconds) of stimuli. Subjects reported that they could see only brief flickers of light. Although they could not consciously identify the subliminal messages, they were influenced by them. Schizophrenics exposed to a conflict-arousing stimulus, "I am losing Mommy," increased their psychotic symptoms. This response is predicted by Freud's theory because a schizophrenic uses hallucination, a primitive ego defense mechanism of infancy, to deal with conflicts about losing the mother, the object just developing in the oral stage. When Silverman's tachistoscope conveyed the unconscious message "Mommy and I are one," psychotic symptoms were reduced, presumably because the conflict was unconsciously reduced as a symbiotic merger with the mother was activated in the unconscious. Silverman later tested the cue "Mommy and I are one" in a variety of populations and reported that it had many beneficial effects in reducing phobias (Silverman, Frank, & Dachinger, 1974), reducing homosexual threat (Silverman et al., 1973) and facilitating weight loss in obese women (Silverman, Martin, et al., 1978).

Using other cues with other patient populations, Silverman claimed that unconscious arousal of the specific conflict identified by psychoanalytic theory to be associated with each diagnosis (e.g., oral conflict for schizophrenics and anal conflict for stutterers) could produce an increase or decrease of the symptoms (Silverman, Bronstein, & Mendelsohn, 1976). Among women with eating disorders, subliminal arousal of abandonment conflict led to increased eating in a bogus cracker-rating task (Patton, 1992). An appropriate stimulus ("Beating Dad is OK") was even reported to improve dart-throwing performance in college males (Silverman, Ross, et al., 1978). If the stimuli were presented at longer exposures, so they could be consciously recognized, there was no effect on the symptoms; only unconscious dynamics produced changes.

Some researchers have not replicated Silverman's findings and have called for more stringent controls (Balay & Shevrin, 1988; Brody, 1987; Fudin, 1986, 2001; Malik et al., 1996). Other critics are more positive. One systematic statistical review of research using the subliminal activation technique concluded that it is effective in reducing pathology and that replications by other researchers not associated with Silverman's laboratory also confirm the effect (Hardaway, 1990). If it is effective, it is still unclear whether the mechanism is the hypothesized unconscious return to an infantile symbiosis with the mother, before the burdens of becoming a separate self. It might instead occur because this stimulus produces a positive mood, which in turn has a variety of beneficial effects (Sohlberg, Billinghurst, & Nylén, 1998). Further complicating the issue, other researchers report that the Silverman procedure sometimes results in suffering instead of comfort, presumably because for some individuals, increasing merger with the mother may arouse conflict (Sohlberg, Samuelberg, Sidén, & Thöm, 1998).

Silverman's work represents the most elaborate, but not the only, attempt to verify hypotheses derived from psychoanalytic theory through experimental research. Many experimental studies of repression have been conducted, although they often do not correspond precisely to Freud's conceptualization (Geisler, 1985). Other approaches, reviewed by Shulman (1990), include hypnotic induction of unconscious ideas to test their behavioral effects (e.g., Reyher, 1962) and examination of situational effects on Freudian slips (e.g., Motley, Baars, & Camden, 1983). Although others have criticized psychoanalytic concepts for being too vague to verify empirically, Shulman expressed optimism that psychoanalytic theory can be tested with well-controlled experimental studies.

UNCONSCIOUS COGNITION

Freud explored the unconscious from an assumption that consciousness was the usual mode of experience, and unconscious phenomena were the oddities to be explained. He proposed that repression provides the energy to move material from consciousness to the unconscious. Both of these assumptions, the primacy of consciousness and the energy model, have been replaced by more modern explanations.

Freud proposed the unconscious and repression to explain why emotional reactions in his patients, obvious from their behavior and physiological reactions, were not accompanied by appropriate awareness (Lang, 1994). However, material may be unconscious for other reasons besides repression. Sometimes it is simply not the focus of attention or is not available to conscious thought because of competing associations, for example. Several researchers have investigated unconscious cognition without the assumptions of conflict that Freud's dynamic model describes (Kihlstrom, 1985, 1987, 1990; Kihlstrom, Barnhardt, & Tataryn, 1992; Natsoulas, 1994). We can do many things without consciously knowing the details, such as knowing how to type or dance (Bowers, 1985). Also, while we are consciously paying attention to one thing, other information may be presented that does not become conscious but is still perceived at some level. When research subjects are asked to determine whether briefly presented stimuli are members of a specific category, such as "mammal," or not, their electroencephalograph (EEG) brain scans show different activity for category members ("horse") than for stimuli that are not members of the category ("apple"), even when they fail consciously to make the correct identification; this provides evidence of semantic processing of which we are not conscious (Stenberg et al., 2000). Subliminal presentations of smiling faces can cause experimental subjects to form more positive attitudes about people (Krosnick et al., 1992). The emotions associated with subliminal messages in advertising are thought to change consumer's attitudes toward products, and experimental evidence supports this claim, although subliminal advertising does not seem to have much impact on actual purchases (Aylesworth, Goodstein, & Kalra, 1999; Trappey, 1996). Even under anesthesia, people can be influenced by auditory stimuli. One study reports that tapes of therapeutic suggestions played to patients during abdominal surgery reduced the amount of pain medication required after surgery, even though patients could not consciously recall the tapes (Caseley-Rondi, Merikle, & Bowers, 1994).

The cognitive interpretation of such unconscious cognition does not require a sophisticated process of repression or censorship based on anxiety, such as Freud proposed. Instead of mental processes being conscious intrinsically, unless repressed to keep them unconscious, many modern theorists have proposed much the opposite: that mental processes are nonconscious unless they are made conscious by some additional action (Natsoulas, 1993), such as focusing attention (Velmans, 1991). In one model, consciousness may occur when information in the nonconscious part of the brain (which is most of the brain) is represented again in a system of the brain devoted to consciousness (Olds, 1992). In this model, unconscious suggestion is readily explained. Events that do not reach awareness can activate or strengthen neural networks that are related to certain ideas, so they are more easily activated by subsequent events and then become conscious (Greenwald, 1992).

Unconscious cognition and memory can be understood as cognitions that are not expressed verbally. Often they are emotional. Memory researchers in cognitive psychology distinguish between explicit (controlled, conscious) memories and implicit (automatic, unconscious) memories, and this distinction offers an understanding of the unconscious if we consider explicit memories to be conscious—such as our ability to tell about episodes from childhood experience—and implicit memories to be unconscious—such as the emotions that we experience but cannot verbalize (Brainerd, Stein, & Reyna, 1998).

The modern theory of a cognitive unconscious offers a substitute for Freud's dynamic unconscious. The cognitive alternative does not invoke questionable assumptions of psychic energy, and it can be reconciled with recent cognitive research and theory. Individual differences in defenses can also be understood without a psychic energy model. Repression is an example. Experiments show that people who are classified as repressors because written tests indicate that they avoid threatening thoughts are particularly attentive to emotional information, both pleasant and unpleasant. When circumstances allow, they distance themselves from emotional events (Mendolia, Moore, & Tesser, 1996). Individual differences in responses to emotion do not require a psychic energy model; they can be understood as differences in emotional reactivity, perhaps caused by a genetically predisposed physiological pattern combined with learned ways of behaving.

UNCONSCIOUS INFLUENCES AND THE BODY

Freud's work began in neurology, and it became psychological because the clinical phenomena he confronted were incomprehensible with the medical knowledge of that time. Today, neurologists suggest that some of the clinical symptoms Freud observed do have a neurological basis. For example, consider traumatic memory loss. Traumatic experience, in Freud's theory, can cause repression of the traumatic events, so they are unavailable to memory. Neural imaging of the brain shows decreased functioning in the hippocampus and some other areas in people who have been exposed to combat stress and other traumas (Conway & Pleydell-Pearce, 2000).

We know from controlled studies that when experimental animals are exposed to very high levels of stress, the brain responds physiologically in ways that can alter memory, producing amnesia. In studies of rats, stress created by a painful shock to the animals' feet caused them to forget how to escape from a tank of water. Unshocked rats swam to a submerged platform whose location they had previously learned, but rats shocked before the test could not find it. Stress caused an increase in the hormone glucocorticoid, which interfered with neural messages in the hippocampus of the brain, an area known to be important for memory (de Quervain, Roozendaal, & McGaugh, 1998). These or other biochemical consequences of severe stress, especially in an immature brain, could cause amnesia for biological reasons (Bremner et al., 1995, 1996; van der Kolk & Fisler, 1995). What about the claim of some therapists that bodily symptoms result from forgotten traumatic events (Ratican, 1996)? It is even possible, neurologically, that emotions and bodily responses could register the effects of the trauma while the memory for events is lost because the brain processes such memories in different ways: through the hippocampus for the event and through the amygdala for the emotions and bodily memory (Byrd, 1994). The psychoanalytic claim that stress can cause amnesia is partly correct in that stress in the rat study just described did interfere with memory. The mechanism, though, was not as psychoanalysts thought. Stress disrupted memory for a biological reason and not because the rat's memory would have been too painful. In this study, in fact, the memory would have been a relief. Perhaps, in focusing on the pain of the memory instead of the biological mechanisms, psychoanalysis has been incorrect.

Modern neurology has progressed considerably since Freud's time, and some anticipate that it may be possible to understand some of the mind as Freud described it in terms of modern cognitive neuroscience (Kandel, 1999). The separation of classical psychoanalysis from neurology may now be less necessary, according to Hobson and Leonard's call for a new psychiatry that they call "neurodynamic" (Hobson & Leonard, 2001)—an approach that is already well under way (Shapiro, 2002). Neuroscientists have mapped many brain areas, including those involved in the primitive sexual and aggressive drives that Freud emphasized. The right hemisphere is often described as the creative hemisphere, in contrast to the more logical left side of the brain; perhaps the right hemi-sphere is the anatomical site of Freud's dynamic unconscious (Schore, 2001). Some evidence from brain-imaging studies suggests that psychotic delusions of persecution are accompanied by disturbed neural functioning in several brain areas (Blackwood et al., 2001).

Research thus supports the idea that unconscious processes influence behavior, although this is a more encompassing unconscious than Freud proposed. Rather than criticizing him for being wrong about many of the details of personality and its unconscious foundation, it is more sensible to credit him with suggesting areas worthy of investigation and for opening doors for those who followed—those who were intrigued by the unconscious but dissatisfied with Freud's description of it. After all, theories are not meant to last forever. If they pave the way to better theories, is that not enough?

Summary

- Freud's psychoanalytic theory proposes that behavior is caused by psychological forces, according to the assumption of *psychic determinism*.
- Unconscious forces often overpower consciousness, producing symptoms of neurosis, dreams, and mistakes in everyday life.
- *Dreams* can be interpreted by seeking their symbolic meanings (latent content).
- The unconscious develops from *repression* of unacceptable thoughts.
- Personality can be described in terms of three structures: id, ego, and superego.
- The *id* functions according to primary process and the pleasure principle, unconsciously seeking immediate satisfaction of biologically based drives, and it is the source of psychic energy (libido).
- The *ego* functions according to secondary process and the reality principle; it adapts to reality by using defense mechanisms to cope with intrapsychic conflict.
- The *superego* represents society's restrictions and produces guilt and an ego ideal.
- Personality develops through five psychosexual stages. The first three stages are most influential. These are the *oral, anal,* and *phallic* stages, which occur from birth to age 5.
- The *latency* stage provides a lull before the final, *genital*, stage of adulthood.
- Fixation, especially at the first three stages, impedes development and may produce symptoms treatable by *psychoanalysis*.
- The basic technique of psychoanalysis is *free association*, which permits the discovery of unconscious material.
- Other key elements of treatment are dream interpretation, catharsis, and insight.
- Memory recovery in therapy is a controversial technique that may result in false memories.
- Although many psychoanalysts share Freud's belief that the observations of psychoanalytic treatment provide sufficient evidence for the theory, others have attempted empirical verification through research, with mixed results.
- Alternative explanations of unconscious phenomena have been offered, such as the cognitive (instead of dynamic) unconscious.

Thinking about Freud's Theory

1. Have you observed behavior that fits Freud's description of unconscious motivation? Describe it. Could the behavior be explained in any other way, without referring to unconscious motivation?
2. Does Freud's idea that conflict over sexual motivation is central to personality make sense in our time, or have more permissive social attitudes toward sexuality made this idea obsolete?
3. Is Freud's theory biased against women? Why or why not?
4. Would you make any changes in Freud's description of mental health as the ability to love and work?
5. Consider recalled memories of sexual abuse that emerge during therapy and the decision by some to accuse their abusers through the judicial system. Do you think this is a wise action? What responsibilities should the therapist have to the patient and to the accused?
6. Can you suggest research to test some aspect of Freud's psychoanalytic theory, beyond the tests described in the text?
7. If neuroscience comes to demonstrate a physical basis for Freud's observations, such as the impact of traumatic childhood experiences on memory and defense mechanisms, do you think psychoanalytic theory should be replaced by neuroscience or integrated with it?

Study Questions

1. Describe what Freud claimed was revolutionary about his theory of personality.
2. Explain the concept of psychic determinism.
3. Briefly describe what is found in the conscious, preconscious, and unconscious levels of the mind. How are these levels like an iceberg?
4. How does conversion hysteria illustrate psychic determinism?
5. Describe a Freudian approach to dream interpretation. Explain, in your answer, the terms *manifest content* and *latent content*.
6. Describe how repression produces the unconscious.
7. List the three structures of personality. Describe each one.
8. List and explain the four characteristics of instincts.
9. Distinguish between primary process and secondary process.
10. What is intrapsychic conflict? Describe the roles of the id, ego, and superego in this conflict.
11. Explain the energy hypothesis. How does it interpret the benefits of psychoanalytic therapy?
12. List and explain the three types of anxiety.
13. What is the purpose of defense mechanisms? List several defense mechanisms and give examples.
14. Explain sublimation. Give an example.
15. Describe development through the five psychosexual stages.
16. Discuss the controversy over Freud's seduction hypothesis.
17. Describe psychoanalytic treatment. What is its basic technique?
18. What does research indicate about the effectiveness of psychoanalytic treatment?
19. Describe empirical evidence that tests psychoanalytic theory, including Silverman's studies of subliminal psychodynamic activation.
20. Explain the difference between Freud's dynamic unconscious and the modern cognitive unconscious.

3

Jung
Analytical Psychology

Chapter
Overview

Preview: Overview of Jung's Theory
The Structure of Personality
Symbolism and the Collective Unconscious
Therapy
Synchronicity
Psychological Types
Summary

ILLUSTRATIVE BIOGRAPHY

Martin Luther King, Jr.

Carl Jung's theory portrays an unconscious that is shared by all humanity rather than contained solely within an individual psyche. The impact of that collective unconscious is felt through powerful archetypal symbols that can be projected onto individuals and influence history. This is one interpretation of the larger than life events that surrounded the life and death of an American hero, Dr. Martin Luther King, Jr.

Born January 15, 1929, in Atlanta, Georgia, deep in the racially segregated South of the United States, M. L. (as he was called as a child) grew up the second child (first son) of a Baptist minister, Martin Luther King, Sr., a strict disciplinarian whose hard work had elevated him from poverty. His maternal grandfather, too, had been a minister, and eventually Martin, Jr., became minister in the same segregated Ebenezer Baptist church where his father and grandfather had served. His concern for civil rights was also a family legacy.

With the encouragement and support of his family, King attended Morehouse College, where he graduated with a degree in sociology, and then studied for the ministry at Crozer Seminary in Pennsylvania, where he was valedictorian, and at Boston University, where he earned his PhD in theology. He developed from these studies an intellectual foundation for integrating social justice concerns with religious beliefs. Early in the civil rights movement, Dr. King's potential for leadership was recognized, and in those divisive times, many thought of him as a safer alternative to those who advocated violence as a means to combat racism. His leadership role in the nonviolent civil rights movement was honored with a Nobel Peace Prize in 1964 (Garrow, 1986), although others distrusted him, tracked his movements and ultimately murdered him. Within less than 4 years (1969), at the age of 39, King was assassinated, leaving his widow, Coretta Scott King, to raise their four young children and his fellow civil rights activists to continue the struggle for racial justice in the United States.

Development

Carl Jung's theory, unlike that of Freud, is little concerned with childhood. Instead, he focuses on the developments that occur in adulthood. During midlife, according to Jung, a person has the task of becoming a unique person whose unconsciously accepted psychological qualities are now examined and revised. This is the *individuation* process, and it is one that draws on the deep unconscious reservoir of personality that Jung called the *collective unconscious*, as well as on a strong ego.

Although Dr. King was still young when he died, he may have been further along in the individuation process because of his spiritual background. (For Jung, psychological and spiritual development had much in common.) During the individuation process, an adult explores aspects of his personality that were neglected earlier in life, and then integrates them into a more whole personality.

most famous speech, delivered in August 1963, described his dream from the mountaintop, his vision of racial equality. King worked to make his dreams real in the world, but he described that as a future potential rather than a current reality. To be concerned with future potentialities is characteristic of intuitive types, using Jung's psychetype theory. On the third dimension of Jung's descriptive model, King may have emphasized thinking somewhat more than feeling, given his intense motivation for education, which prompted him to complete a doctorate degree, despite the early disadvantage of an inferior education in segregated schools. But the emotional richness of his speeches suggests that both of these poles, thinking and feeling, had been already well developed.

Description

Jung's theory describes differences between people along three dimensions. First, a person is classified as an introvert or an extravert. Next, the theory describes two ways of making decisions: thinking and feeling. Finally, Jung suggested that there are two ways of getting information: through the details of the five senses (sensation) or more intuitively (intuition). All combinations of these three dimensions are possible.

King, analyzing himself, claimed to be partly introvert and partly extravert: an "ambivert" in King's words (Oates, 1982, p. 40), but his greater strength is introversion, his connection with his own inner life. Within the types listed by Jung, King could best be classified as an intuitive introvert. Jung (1971, p. 400) said that introverted intuitive types are often *prophets* (see also Maidenbaum & Thomson, 1989), and many, including King himself, applied this term to his ministry. King drew richly from this symbolic realm in his sermons. He turned prayerfully inward at critical moments—for example, when deciding whether to take a leading role in the Southern Christian Leadership Conference, despite the conflicting demands of his congregation and his young family. King's

Adjustment

The healthy person, according to Jung, has developed all four of the psychological functions (thinking and feeling, sensation and intuition). (Introversion or extraversion do not change.) The unconscious provides sources of healthy energy and not only the maladjustment that Freud described. In fact, a healthy person needs to draw from both the unconscious and from consciousness. Consciousness alone is not sufficient. The challenge is to find ways to tap into this unconscious without being driven to pathology in the process.

King's success in his ministry and family are evidence of health, but along the way, there were times of great trouble. He attempted suicide twice, a biographer relates (Oates, 1982, p. 36). Until a person can forge a new relationship with the unconscious, the limitations of conscious life may seem unbearable, and the unconscious too dangerous and destructive. Once past this stage, though, King drew from his unconscious and spiritual side and found ways to make its energies available not only to himself but to others. The unconscious into which he tapped, Jung would say, was not only his personal unconscious but the collective unconscious of humankind; and so his journey was not only to heal himself but to help humanity. All the psychological functions came into play. With the help of others in the civil rights movement, he paid attention to the details of the campaign as well as the vision of the future, thus using the sensation as well as the intuition function. Feeling as well as thinking was clearly evident in his inspiring sermons and speeches. This ability to use all of the psychological functions is a characteristic of healthy personality in Jung's theory.

Cognition

Jung's theory values not only the logical, scientific way of thinking (drawing on the sensation function), but even more the more wholistic way of thinking that derives from the intuitive function. He describes *archetypes* as basic cognitive units in the unconscious, on which symbols and mythology and religious imagery are built. These archetypes are not only cognitive but also have a tremendous amount of energy, tapping much deeper into the unconscious than the sexual energies that Freud proposed. One archetype is that of the *hero*, a person whose individuation process confronts the powerful forces of the unconscious and taps into their riches without being destroyed in the process.

Dr. Martin Luther King, Jr.'s success in mobilizing and challenging the moral conscience of the nation can be understood from Jung's theory as this: He functioned for many as a concrete representation of the *hero archetype*. Throughout his ministry, King spoke to his congregation and to the world in symbols that mobilized the energies of the unconscious, symbols that often were found in the Christian images of his faith. In addition, the public's own unconscious hero archetype was projected onto him, recognizing that his work resonated with something not yet named (for many but not all of them) within their own psyche. Archetypes are powerful because of this shared nature, and they energize much human activity and history.

Jungian theory helps us understand the public's response to King. Jung described the archetype of The Hero. This concept suggests that people would be ready to project onto certain leaders, such as King, the combination of several characteristics: a promise of a better life; the expectation that the hero will fight difficult battles on behalf of others; and in many myths, the tragic finale in which the hero, once crowned as king, must die. Jung recommended that people stay within the symbols and mythology of their own heritage, and King did so. He borrowed the ideas of nonviolence from Gandhi's teachings in India and South Africa, but he presented them within the Christian framework of his own Baptist heritage.

Society

Jung, himself an introvert, was more interested in the inner world of archetypes than in external social reality, and so he tended to regard social behavior as a consequence of inner psychological experience, rather than to think of social causes. He suggested that racial bigotry can occur when people project their own unacceptable unconscious qualities (their "shadow," in his terminology) onto cultural scapegoats, which is an argument with considerable merit. But is the solution to racism, then, to psychoanalyze the bigots? What about economic and legal reforms?

King, in contrast, actively worked in society on the front lines of the civil rights movement, and he paid dearly for that effort. Among other speeches is a noteworthy one in 1967, when he addressed a national meeting of psychologists about their potentional contributions to the civil rights movement (King, 1968). To the extent that he can be considered not just an individual but a part of the collective whole, the benefit of his prophetic leadership lives on.

Biology

In contrast to Freud's emphasis on sexuality, Jung described a more psychological and even spiritual unconscious, but one that also is inherited as part of our biological nature. The unfortunate consequence of this proposed genetic basis for the collective unconscious was a certain blindness to racial issues, and he allowed his writing to be used to support racist Nazi propaganda.

Final Thoughts

From prophecy to assassination, King's life story reads as hauntingly archetypal. The myth of the hero, an archetypal story shared across cultures, seems to define the life and work of Martin Luther King, Jr. better than any strictly individual interpretation as he was cast into the role of a hero in the struggle against racial injustice in the United States. The fact that he has become world famous attests to the resonance in many people to the universal archetypal energies that he represents for us. It was Jung's life work to explore the archetypes so they could coexist with rational consciousness rather than blindly driving human experience. As long as masses of people are unconscious of the archetypal realm, we will continue to act out these various tragic scripts.

Preview: Overview of Jung's Theory

Jung's theory has implications for major theoretical questions, as presented in Table 3.1. From a scientific viewpoint, Jung's theory contains some of the most elusive concepts to measure objectively, yet his theory of personality psychetypes has stimulated considerable empirical testing. The breadth or comprehensiveness of the theory encompasses not only individual functioning but also many cultural symbols and myths. The theory has not only influenced analytical psychotherapy. In addition, its statements about personality type have been widely applied to interpersonal training in business.

Like Freud, Carl Jung proposed a theory of personality that gives a prominent role to the unconscious. For Jung, however, the libido was not primarily sexual but was a broad psychic energy with spiritual dimensions. Jung believed that the most interesting personality developments occur in adulthood, not in childhood. This emphasis reflects his concern with the future directions toward which personality is developing, in contrast with Freud's emphasis on the past. Like Freud, Jung allowed himself to experience the unconscious firsthand through dreams and fantasies, comparing his role to that of an explorer. He considered himself strong enough to make this dangerous voyage and to come back to tell others what he found there. Unlike Freud, who aspired to understand the unconscious from the objective perspective of a scientist, Jung felt that science is an inadequate tool for knowing the psyche.

TABLE 3.1	Preview of Jung's Theory
Individual Differences	Individuals differ in their tendency to be introverts or extraverts, which is stable throughout life. They also differ in the extent to which they make use of four psychological functions (thinking, feeling, sensation, and intuition).
Adaptation and Adjustment	The unconscious has an important role in healthy maturity and should be explored through symbolism. Health requires a balance between conscious and unconscious functioning.
Cognitive Processes	Rational thinking, intuition, and emphasis on concrete details all provide useful information and should be developed. Unconscious images influence perceptions and may distort our perception of reality.
Society	Cultural myths and rituals provide ways of dealing with the unconscious. Important differences exist among cultures and should be preserved.
Biological Influences	Mental contents (a "collective unconscious") as well as physical characteristics are inherited.
Development	Early experience was of little interest to Jung. Midlife change (individuation) involves exploration of the creative potentials of the unconscious.

Jung preferred to describe the psyche in the language of mythology rather than of science. He rejected "rational, scientific language" in favor of "a dramatic, mythological way of thinking and speaking, because this is not only more expressive but also more exact than an abstract scientific terminology, which is wont to toy with the notion that its theoretical formulations may one fine day be resolved into algebraic equations" (1959, p. 13). This is ironic because Jung's international fame first came from his empirical studies of word associations (Naifeh, 2001).

Needless to say, this antiscientific attitude places Jung outside mainstream psychology. Don McGowan's (1994) criticism represents the view of mainstream science. He dismisses Jung's work as a "pseudoscience" (p. 12). That is, it masquerades as science, although not using the scientific methods of empirical verification to determine what is true and what is not. (Other nonscientific areas, such as literature and art, are not pseudoscience because they make no pretense about being scientific.) Jung's unique perspective strengthens the bridge Freud had begun between psychology and symbolic expressions in literature, art, and religion. Jung goes further than Freud, though, in abandoning scientific constraints. Even Freud, who referred to the Oedipus story and other myths in his theorizing, vehemently opposed Jung's mysticism. Nonetheless, Jung's theory has attracted many followers. Jungian psychotherapy and applications of his ideas in career guidance, organizational development, and literary criticism attest to his influence.

BIOGRAPHY OF CARL JUNG

Carl Gustav Jung was born in Switzerland in 1875, the son of a Protestant minister and grandson of a physician who was alleged to be the illegitimate son of the renowned German poet Goethe. Jung had one sister, who was 9 years his junior. His father and several uncles were Protestant clergymen. Jung suspected, even as a child, that his father did not genuinely believe the church's teachings but was afraid to face his doubts honestly. Like many in her family, Jung's mother was emotionally unstable (Noll, 1994) and, according to Jung, psychic.

As a young psychiatrist, Jung lectured at the University of Zurich, developed a word association technique for uncovering the emotional complexes of his patients, and had a private practice. He greeted

CARL JUNG

Freud's controversial work on psychoanalysis enthusiastically and supported it in his own professional writing. After a period of mutually admiring correspondence, the two met at Freud's office in Vienna. This first meeting lasted 13 hours, attesting to the breadth of their mutual interest and respect. They continued an active correspondence, which has been published (McGuire, 1974). Together they traveled to the United States in 1909 to present psychoanalysis at the G. Stanley Hall Conference at Clark University, and both were well received (Jung, 1910/1987). This trip had particular psychological significance for Jung because the United States was an important symbol for Jung's own personal growth (Martinez & Taylor, 1998; Taylor, 1998). In addition, the trip, which in that era was a long journey by sea, gave Jung and Freud plenty of time to discuss psychoanalysis and dreams. These discussions revealed a small crack in their relationship that later became a huge split. Freud, to protect his authority, would not reveal personal associations to a dream he was telling Jung. These mental connections would have disclosed a sexual indiscretion, and to protect his authority, Freud chose to violate a cardinal rule of psychoanalysis by censoring his associations (Rosen, 1993).

Jung presided over a psychoanalytic association in Zurich, and Freud intended to have Jung succeed him as president of the International Psychoanalytic Association, thinking it would be advantageous to broaden psychoanalysis beyond its Jewish circle. He conveyed this intent to Jung in a letter in which he referred to Jung as a "crown prince," and Jung responded with gratitude, referring to Freud as a father figure.

Before this could be achieved, however, the personal relationship between Freud and Jung was disrupted. There were intellectual disagreements, to be sure; Jung felt that Freud overemphasized the role of sexuality in his theory and underestimated the potential of the unconscious to contribute positively to psychological growth. However, it was a personal conflict as well as an intellectual one (Goldwert, 1986; Marcovitz, 1982; Stern, 1976), part of a midlife crisis in which Jung withdrew from his academic pursuits and devoted himself to introspection. His own personal conflicts, explored in this period, have been interpreted in terms of fragmentation of the self. Jung himself described his two personalities (Rosen, 1996). In Jung's case, this dissociation did not lead to the pathology that such splits sometimes produce (Ticho, 1982). Jung believed that Freud's emphasis on maintaining his authority prevented him (Freud) from dealing fully with his own unconscious conflicts; Freud feared that Jung had abandoned science for mysticism. One critic, Richard Noll (1994), portrays Jung as a charismatic cult leader. This accusation is challenged by another historian (Shamdasani, 1998), who points out that Jung instituted the requirement of a training analysis, so psychoanalysts must themselves experience the process of psychoanalysis before becoming full-fledged members of the psychoanalytic community, but this is not equivalent to a cult initiation.

Jung had long been interested in mystical phenomena. His doctoral dissertation had reported experiments on his cousin, a spiritualistic "medium" (Ellenberger, 1991), one of many of Jung's relatives who experienced spiritualistic or psychic tendencies (Las Heras, 1992). In later life, he continued subjective explorations of the unconscious, read esoteric texts on mysticism and alchemy, and built a primitive retreat at Bollingen, on Lake Zurich. He reported several personal experiences of psychic phenomena, which he understood as manifestations of a broad, transpersonal "collective unconscious." For example, Jung is said to have dreamt of Winston Churchill whenever the English politician came near Switzerland, even though Jung had no conscious awareness of his arrival (G. Wehr, 1987, p. 357). Understanding this collective unconscious was Jung's major life task. Indeed, legend has it that many of Jung's students had nightmares before learning of his death in 1961. Jung's development of his own archetypal psychology was something he portrayed in the language of a hero, confronting great threats to accomplish good. This portrayal can be understood as a personal myth that Jung developed, describing escape from historical time to a timeless and more glamorous alternative (Pietikainen, 1999).

The Structure of Personality

Like all psychoanalysts, Jung recognized that personality contains both conscious and unconscious elements. Like Freud, Jung referred to the ego when describing the more conscious aspects of personality. His description of the unconscious, though, differed from Freud's id and superego structures. Furthermore, he did not seek to increase the role of consciousness in personality and to minimize unconscious influence, as Freud did.

Rather, Jung sought a balance in which unconscious elements were given an equal role, complementary to that of consciousness.

THE PSYCHE AND THE SELF: THE PERSONALITY AS A WHOLE

Jung generally did not refer to personality but rather to the *psyche*, a Latin word that originally meant "spirit" or "soul" (Hall & Nordby, 1973, p. 32). This term avoids the connotation of a scientific dissection of personality into unrelated functions, suggesting instead the integration of all aspects of personality. Jung referred to the total integrated personality as the **Self**. (In Jungian writing, Self is usually capitalized, which helps distinguish it from the more conscious and social self of other theorists.) The Self includes all of a person's qualities and potentials, even those that are not yet apparent at a particular stage of life.

Self the total integrated personality

Throughout life, we sometimes emphasize conscious growth (e.g., in developing a career identity); at other times we focus more on inner development. Jung compared this flow of libido outward (adapting consciously to the world) and then inward (to serve inner needs) to the ebb and flow of the tides. In contrast to the aim of Freud, Jung did not believe it was possible or desirable to live entirely consciously; that would be like trying to build a dike to hold back the ocean. It is not healthy to give all energy to the unconscious either; that would be like a flood. Learning from the tides, people should expect sometimes to deal consciously with the external world and at other times to turn to the inner world for psychic rejuvenation.

Consciousness and the unconscious coexist in individuals. Jung described this relationship as one of **compensation**. Consciousness is necessary for dealing with the real world, as Freud had pointed out, but it is not enough. The unconscious compensates for the one-sidedness of consciousness by emphasizing those aspects of psychic totality that have been neglected by consciousness. For example, a person who has developed a conscious attitude of rational and logical thought but who has neglected emotional issues will have these feelings in the unconscious. A research investigation of dreams, for example, finds that repressors, who deny aggressive feelings, are more likely to dream about aggression (Bell & Cook, 1998). The unconscious has much to offer. It has the "missing pieces" to allow the development of the Self toward psychic wholeness. A healthy condition requires both consciousness and unconscious, and compensation serves as a homeostasis-like mechanism to restore this balance, often through dreams (Beebe, Cambray, & Kirsch, 2001).

compensation principle of the relationship between the unconscious and consciousness, by which the unconscious provides what is missing from consciousness to make a complete whole

Individuation

People develop the various aspects of their psyche unevenly. Along the way, we may identify disproportionately with our ego or with some aspect or another of our unconscious; this excessive identification is often referred to as "inflation" (Edinger, 1972). Modern humans, according to Jung, are particularly vulnerable to ego inflation, and unlike our ancestors who lived more unconsciously, we suppress the unconscious to an unhealthy extent (Drob, 1999). **Individuation** is the process of restoring wholeness to the psyche in adult development. In early life, the psyche begins as a unified whole, although unconscious. During the course of development, various aspects of the psyche come into consciousness and are developed while other areas remain unconscious. For example, in childhood and adolescence, the person develops and becomes aware of a social identity (the persona, discussed later) but tends to ignore personal shortcomings

individuation the process of becoming a fully developed person, with all psychic functions developed

and failures (the shadow, described later). As parts of the personality are developed in consciousness, an imbalance in the original wholeness is inevitable.

This imbalance is restored during adult development in midlife. Unconscious potentials are explored and reintegrated with the total Self in a process Jung called individuation. The goal of individuation, in Jung's metaphor, is to move the center of personality from the ego to some midpoint between the ego and the unconscious. In the later phases of the individuation process, the **transcendent function** is the aspect of personality that integrates the diverse aspects into a unified whole.

The unconscious plays an active role in directing this process by selectively offering material to consciousness and by reintegrating developments into the whole Self. If new experiences are not allowed into consciousness, because of such factors as anxiety or personality type, individuation is impeded. If the unconscious is consistently ignored, it may act in extreme ways to block consciousness, creating symptoms (including psychogenic illness and neurosis) that force attention to neglected issues. Only through the adult development of individuation can the person become truly an individual and not simply a carrier of unconscious images and other people's projections. When this developmental process does not proceed, tragic consequences can result. For example, Marilyn Monroe's inability to individuate herself left her trapped in her cultural image as a sex goddess, without a genuinely individual identity.

EGO

Jung (1959), like Freud, described the ego as the aspect of personality that is most conscious. Nothing can become conscious without going through the ego, which serves as "the gatekeeper to consciousness." The ego is essential for a feeling of personal identity, without which we would be overwhelmed by the perceptions, thoughts, feelings, and memories of day-to-day life. In the midst of his own intense explorations into the unconscious, Jung stabilized his identity by reminding himself of the bases of his ego identity—that is, his role as a therapist and family member.

The ego is also the center of our will. It enables us to strive for conscious goals. However, there are limits to willpower because of limitations to consciousness itself. To use Jung's metaphor, the ego is part of personality, but it is not the center of personality. Many people identify too closely with their consciousness, in effect putting it at the center of their personality. Probably the most common way of being out of balance, especially in the first half of life, is to identify too closely with conscious experience and intentions. Jung called this **ego inflation**. In Jung's theory, being overly focused on the ego is not desirable. In fact, growth forces within the psyche work to undo such identifications, by bringing about such dramatic evidence of ego limitations as job burnout (Garden, 1991) or marital setbacks. Many midlife crises occur when people finally realize the limitations of their consciousness, often because of adverse circumstances such as a career setback or a failed marriage.

Alternatively, but less often, psychic inflation can result from overvaluing the unconscious. Mystics and spiritualistic mediums, as well as psychotics, suffer from this kind of psychic imbalance. The remedy for either type of psychic inflation is individuation, which involves finding a proper balance between consciousness and the unconscious.

PERSONA

The **persona** is the aspect of personality that adapts to the world. The term originally meant the mask that actors wore in the theater, and it still reflects the roles that we play, not in the theater but in society. The persona is shaped by the reactions we elicit in other

transcendent function the process of integrating all opposing aspects of personality into a unified whole

ego inflation overvaluation of ego consciousness, without recognizing its limited role in the psyche

persona a person's social identity

people. To the extent that people respond to us as good looking or bright or athletically skilled, that becomes our self-image, or persona. We strive to behave in ways that will earn for us a positive social image, emphasizing aspects of ourselves that are valued by others and trying to ignore or deny the rest. Such efforts succeed only temporarily. Franz Fanon (1967), an African political activist, described the attempts of black Africans to adopt the speech and social mannerisms of white colonialists to earn a positive persona, but that effort was doomed to failure because of racism. When social roles change, we may experience great discontinuity in personality. For example, when a person retires, the persona based on the work role, which has been the basis of identity and social interaction for decades, is no longer relevant.

Changes in persona are celebrated throughout life with publicly visible symbols of the new status. Rites of initiation among primitive societies are occasions in which members are given a symbol of their entry into adulthood. Marriage ceremonies celebrate a change of persona, marked often by a change of name for the bride or, in modern times, sometimes for both parties. New clothes or costumes, as at a wedding or graduation, underscore the change in persona. Because clothing often symbolizes the persona, an inadequate persona may be symbolized by the common dream of being naked, and embarrassed, in a public place.

The persona is generally well established by young adulthood. Two other psychic elements, the shadow and the anima (in men) or animus (in women), are more problematic. Bringing these elements to awareness and integrating them with consciousness are major tasks of adult development.

SHADOW

While consciousness has been occupied with creating a socially acceptable persona, other potentials in personality have been neglected or actively repressed. The term **shadow** refers to those aspects of the psyche that are rejected from consciousness by the ego because they are inconsistent with one's self-concept. Unacceptable sexual and aggressive impulses are especially characteristic of the shadow, and these are reminiscent of Freud's theory of repressed id impulses. Other characteristics may be found in some people's shadows: stupidity in a person who takes pride in intelligence, ugliness in one who is handsome, and so on.

shadow the unconscious complement to a person's conscious identity, often experienced as dangerous and evil

A classic literary portrayal of the shadow is Robert Louis Stevenson's tale of Dr. Jekyll and Mr. Hyde. The respectable gentleman, Dr. Jekyll, represents the socially desirable persona, whereas the evil Mr. Hyde represents the shadow. Another literary portrayal of the shadow appears in Oscar Wilde's story "The Picture of Dorian Gray." Dorian Gray maintained the outward appearance of a fine and upstanding citizen. His hidden portrait of himself, meanwhile, took on the hideous look of his secret crimes. His picture represented his shadow—hidden and evil. Like Dorian Gray, we show our persona to the world and hide the shadow. As we do so, the shadow gets uglier and uglier, and the split between persona and shadow, which for a time disrupts our wholeness, widens. If we were instead to deal more consciously with shadow issues, as Jungians advocate (Zweig & Wolf, 1997), the shadow would not become so ugly.

The shadow mediates between consciousness and unconsciousness and can be regarded as "the gatekeeper to the unconscious." Emergence of the shadow from the unconscious produces the experience of moral conflict. Our shadow is experienced as frightening or evil when we fear our unconscious. This perception does not represent truth, however, but only the attitude of consciousness, which is reluctant to share center stage with the unconscious. According to David Rosen (1993), a Jungian psychiatrist and scholar, the shadow assists psychological growth by helping to bring about an *egocide* (a symbolic suicide or an ego sacrifice); this helps the person find a center of personality that is not so overly identified with consciousness but instead is more open to the unconscious. When a person comes to terms with the unconscious and recognizes that it has positive contributions to make to personality as a whole, experience changes. The shadow then is less repulsive and more playful, and it brings zest and liveliness to experience. The shadow, when integrated with consciousness, is a source of creativity and pleasure.

According to Jung (1959, p. 8), there are some rare exceptions to the general rule that the shadow is negative. A few people have an identity that is consciously evil and have repressed their own positive qualities into a positive shadow. For example, powerful tyrants may pride themselves on brutality and reject humane qualities as "weak."

Projection of the Shadow

The shadow is symbolized in literature and in dreams by various images of evil, disturbed, and repulsive people: criminals, psychotics, and others whom we despise or pity, including disliked racial groups. Jung asserted that in dreams, the shadow is symbolized by a figure who is the same sex as the dreamer. The specific repulsive qualities of a shadow figure give clues to the material that the person has repressed in forming a conscious self-concept. Thus a man who is proud of his intelligence may represent his shadow in a dream as a mentally retarded man; a sexually controlled woman may symbolize her shadow in a dream of a prostitute.

The tendency to project shadow elements onto persons of other races in waking life, as well as in dreams, obviously contributes to racial prejudice. Fanon (1967, p. 165) suggested that people project their instinctive animal characteristics onto blacks and their threatening intellectual qualities onto Jews, an interpretation that Jung would probably have accepted.

ANIMA AND ANIMUS

People consciously reject not only qualities that are evil or inconsistent with their persona (the shadow) but also qualities they consider incompatible with their identity as males or females. These sex-inappropriate qualities, traditionally exemplified by traits such as emotionality for males and power for females, constitute the **anima** (a man's repressed or undeveloped feminine-typed qualities) and the **animus** (a woman's repressed or undeveloped masculine-typed qualities). Jung referred to the anima as "a man's inner woman." The animus is "a woman's inner man."

Sometimes a person becomes "possessed" by his anima or her animus, which is Jung's way of describing a condition in which unconscious qualities control behavior without being integrated into consciousness. Jung interpreted the anima to represent Eros, the principle of relatedness. Men possessed by their anima act moody and emotional. Jung referred to the animus as "the paternal Logos," claiming that logic and reason (Logos) are masculine qualities. He believed women were possessed by the animus if they were opinionated and preoccupied with power.

Jung's focus on masculinity and femininity seems, to some researchers, consistent with key dimensions of individual differences measured by self-report inventories (Coan, 1989). Others, though, are offended by Jung's emphasis on sex differences and accuse him of sexism. Although Jung stressed the importance for each sex to develop psychological androgyny, he described women's animus development more harshly than men's

anima the femininity that is part of the unconscious of every man

animus the masculinity that is part of the unconscious of every woman

explorations of the anima (Torrey, 1987). He seemed to accept cultural realities rather than urging progress toward an improved, less sexist society. This position typifies psychoanalytic emphasis on the individual rather than on society and cultural determination.

Projection of the Anima or Animus

The unconscious anima or animus is projected onto people of the opposite sex, including parents and lovers. These individuals trigger various emotions (such as fear, rejection, or longing), depending on one's attitude toward one's own unconscious anima or animus. A man may project either negative or positive qualities onto women, depending on whether he is at the early stage of rejecting his "inner femininity" or at a more developed stage of acceptance. A man who belittles a woman for her sentimentality is, by projection, rejecting his own unacknowledged sentimentality. When he is ready to integrate it, he will stop criticizing women in whom he sees that quality. Similarly, women may project their own rejected animus by fearing or attacking qualities such as dominance and independence in men. These projections, too, will become more positive as the animus is integrated into consciousness.

One of the most common, and potentially healthy, instances of projection of the anima or animus is the experience of falling in love (Jung, 1931/1954). Falling in love promises to restore the missing piece of the psyche that was left behind in the unconscious when the conscious personality was developed. This experience is, of course, outside the realistic, willful planning of the ego and in that sense is irrational. Such a projection is the essence of romance, whether it progresses positively, as in the fairy tale of Cinderella, or tragically, as in Shakespeare's *Romeo and Juliet*. Each lover feels psychologically whole when with the beloved. The anima or animus, not yet consciously developed, is felt to be present with the loved one. Gradually, through this love relationship, the woman develops her own masculine potentials and the man becomes more conscious of his own repressed feminine qualities. Then love can move from a basis in projection to a basis in more accurate knowledge of the other. In a psychologically healthy love relationship, the shadow is also accepted into consciousness. The lover accepts the other in his or her entirety, even rejected aspects of the shadow. Thus love facilitates psychological development.

PERSONAL UNCONSCIOUS

The anima or animus and the shadow together constitute what Jung called the **personal unconscious**. This is the unconscious of each individual that is developed because of the person's unique experiences. The shadow is somewhat closer to consciousness than the anima (or animus), and it can and should be assimilated to consciousness. During this process, the person becomes more aware of personal shortcomings and more accepting of them in himself or herself and in others on whom they may have been projected. The anima or animus is somewhat deeper in the personal unconscious, but much of it, too, can be differentiated and made conscious. As this occurs, the individual develops more androgynous qualities.

In describing the personal unconscious, Jung and Freud used different language, but both agreed that the content of this unconscious is determined by the experience of a person in the world. There are differences, however: Freud assumed consciousness as the starting point and explained how some material is repressed into the unconscious because of emotional conflict; Jung presumed at the outset an unconscious totality from which consciousness emerges.

personal unconscious that part of the unconscious derived from an individual's experience

COLLECTIVE UNCONSCIOUS

Jung also described a deeper layer to the unconscious. It was symbolized, in a dream he reported, as a concealed basement deep below a house, approached down dusty stairs and finally to an ancient room below the ordinary cellar, filled with prehistoric bones and pottery (Jung, 1989; reported in Noll, 1994, pp. 177–178). Jung interpreted this dream as portraying a deep level of the unconscious, shared by everyone despite differences in personal experience. This contrasts with Freud's interpretation of dreams as reflecting simply personal dreams and wishes: In this case, Jung's wish that some of the people he knew would be dead and deeply buried (Noll, 1994, p. 178).

collective unconscious the inherited unconscious

Jung called this deeper unconscious (symbolized by the deeper cellar) the **collective unconscious**. This collective unconscious is the core of Jung's mysticism and is the concept least accepted by mainstream psychology. Jung described the collective unconscious as inherited, contained in human brain structure and not dependent on personal experience to develop. It can be described as prewired circuits in our brain, to use an electrical metaphor, or ROM (read-only memory) chips, to use a computer metaphor—content that is built into the machine at the factory and not changed by the user. The collective unconscious can also be illustrated with imagery from science fiction. Human beings, no matter how far they might travel to distant galaxies, bear the imprint of ancestors who originated on a planet with seasons and with 24-hour days, even if they have been born in a spaceship somewhere in space and have never personally experienced life on Earth. The collective unconscious is shaped by the remote evolutionary experiences of the human species and transmitted to each individual through genetic inheritance.

Beyond the rhythms of the seasons and the days, physiological psychology tells us that there are basic neural units of sensation and perception. Certain neurons respond only to particular colors, shapes, or angles. We know from animal psychology that some rather complex behaviors occur instinctively, without individual experience; for example, a bird, raised entirely in isolation, nonetheless at maturity will build a species-appropriate nest, although it has never seen one. If an instinct can tell an animal how to behave, why can't it tell a human how to think?

archetype a primordial image in the collective unconscious; an innate pattern that influences experience of the real world

Jung suggested that it can. He claimed that the collective unconscious contains "primordial images," called **archetypes**, which are similar in all people. These archetypes are the basic units of the collective unconscious, and they function as "psychic instincts" that predispose us to experience the world in certain universally human ways. Archetypes have both an emotional, psychosomatic component and a cognitive component of associated images and ideas, and they influence behavior. According to Jung, we have images that tell us what a mother is, what a spiritual leader is, even what God is. All personal experience is interpreted through these archetypal patterns. This is a particularly strange concept for modern psychology, which has been profoundly influenced by behaviorism and its emphasis on environmental determinism. A more palatable interpretation may be that archetypes are not themselves full blown and inherited, but rather that they are likely to emerge through the self-organization of the mind and brain, based on more fundamental emotional and cognitive processes that are inherited (Saunders & Skar, 2001).

Biological determination of mental imagery sounds farfetched to many, although some suggest that archetypes can be reconciled with neuroscience (Stevens, 1995). Neuroscientists who do not discuss Jungian ideas at all sometimes use language that could be interpreted as referring to archetypes; in describing the role of the amygdala in the emotional reactions of monkeys, for example, one brain researcher (Amaral, 2002) referred to this brain center's theorized reaction to "innate templates of species-specific emotional elicitors (such as snakes)"—which certainly sounds like an archetypal image of a snake (in the monkey psyche). Furthermore, lesions of this brain area in the monkey sometimes produced fearfulness and sometimes unusual lack of fear, which varied with the age of the animal at the time of the lesion and the object or social stimulus to which the animal was exposed. Jungians describe an ambivalent aspect of archetypes, which seems to fit this still unexplained inconsistency in the role of the amygdala. It is obviously too early in the neurological research to draw definitive correspondences between archetypes and specific brain areas, but the possibility is intriguing.

Mainstream psychologists generally ignore Jung's theory of archetypes because of its lack of rigor, leaving the theory to flourish and grow, "unchecked by reasoned and thoughtful scrutiny" (Neher, 1996, p. 63). However, if the assumption of inheritance is set aside and archetypes are considered to represent important symbolic forms, perhaps determined by culture instead of genetics, then the concept of archetypes may be more acceptable (Pietikainen, 1998). Archetypal images have been investigated in studies of people's perceptions and some significant results have been obtained, but the data could also be interpreted more parsimoniously as learned concepts; so the challenge of demonstrating, to the satisfaction of rigorous scientific methods, that people inherit archetypal images is still not accomplished (Jones, 2000; Maloney, 1999).

Genetics and the Collective Unconscious

One of Jung's controversial ideas is that the collective unconscious follows the laws of genetic inheritance. It is different in humans than in other animal species, of course. Jung suggested that various races and families inherit somewhat different variations of the collective unconscious, just as they inherit different physical characteristics. This notion of a "racial unconscious" was exploited in the Nazi era as a scientific rationalization for the racially motivated extermination of so-called non-Aryan people, especially Jews. Psychologists in the post–World War II era, horrified by the concentration camps, naturally avoided Jung's unfortunate genetic hypotheses. The concept has not entirely disappeared, however; some psychoanalysts still refer to an "ethnic unconscious," not necessarily inherited but nonetheless different for each ethnic group in a multicultural society (Herron, 1995). On balance, though, Jung was more preoccupied with demonstrating similarity of unconscious material across diverse cultures than differences.

The Shadow and the Anima or Animus as Archetypes

As described earlier, the *content* of the shadow and the anima or animus, with associated emotional conflicts or complexes, is part of the personal unconscious. The content of the shadow would be different if a person were raised with different messages about what is right and wrong. (For a vegetarian Hindu, such as Mahatma Gandhi, eating meat is a shadow characteristic; for most Americans, it is not.) In a similar way, the content of the anima or animus varies according to the sex roles taught in a culture.

The predisposition to develop a shadow and an anima or animus, however, is collective and universal. Personal experience shapes its particular content for an individual, making one person's shadow a horrid satanic figure and another's a minor criminal. Besides the shadow and the anima or animus, in the collective unconscious there are many more archetypes.

Other Archetypes

Because the shadow and the anima or animus are closest to consciousness, they are the archetypes with the most noticeable effects on experience. The other archetypes discussed here are said to be deeper in the collective unconscious and influence conscious experience less often. When they do, they feel more foreign. Archetypes may be experienced individually in dreams or projections onto other people. In addition, they are reflected in stories and myths.

The Great Mother.   The archetype of the Great Mother reflects the ancestral experience of being raised by mothers. Humans are not, for example, hatched from an egg on a lonely shore, like a turtle or a Dali vision. The Great Mother is widely represented in mythology and art, from the carved fertility symbols of ancient cultures to paintings of the Virgin Mary and modern sculptures by Henry Moore. Even the rock star Madonna borrows from this archetype of the Great Mother and, in so doing, illustrates the diversity of particular forms that an archetype can inspire.

All archetypes have an ambivalent quality, with both positive and negative aspects. Sentimentality about motherhood and apple pie is positive, but the Great Mother also encompasses negative elements. The archetypal feminine principle encompasses not only the fertile womb but also death and the grave. The Hindu goddess Kali symbolizes the archetype with both positive and negative aspects. Not only does she nurse infants but she also drinks blood (Neumann, 1963, p. 152). Many primitive myths relate the fertility of the harvest and human reproduction with death, thus expressing both aspects of the archetype. For example, the myth of Demeter and Persephone celebrates the coming of spring only after a woman's journey to the underworld.

The Spiritual Father.   In his descriptions of the father archetype, Jung contrasted instinctive qualities, which he claimed were more feminine, with the spiritual qualities of the archetypal father. The association of spirituality with masculinity did not originate with Jung; it has a long history in the Judeo-Christian tradition (Daly, 1978; Lacks, 1980; Patai, 1967), which has traditionally portrayed God and spiritual leaders as masculine. Sometimes even classroom teachers may be perceived to have more wisdom than they actually have because students project the archetype (sometimes called a "wise old man") onto them (Mayes, 1999).

The Hero.   The hero of mythology and folklore conquers great enemies and wins mighty battles. He or she is often, like Daniel in the lion's den or Parsifal of the Grail myth, a relatively weak individual, but heroes and heroines are in touch with special forces that allow them to conquer great opponents. For Jung, the hero myth was central as a description of psychological development, a myth of continuing to confront the unconscious and emerge from it stronger and more developed, much as the sun (mythically, at least) descends into darkness and reemerges with each sunrise (Haule, 2000). Many varieties of the hero myth are described by a Jungian scholar, Joseph Campbell (1949). Jung believes this archetype is associated with the internal psychic struggle to become an individual, separate from regressive ties to the mother. It also relates to external battles with threatening forces in the world.

The Trickster.   The Trickster appears in various cultures as a simple-minded prankster who seems to be outwitted but who ultimately brings good results. The Grimms' fairy tale of Stupid Hans is an example. In literature, trickster figures disrupt (sometimes violently) an order that has become sterile and in so doing, they bring characters back to reality (Schaum, 2000). Trickster figures are less common in our culture than in some others (e.g., in Native American mythology), but they can be seen in the revelries of Mardi Gras and in circus clowns. Because of the frequent representation of mythic Trickster figures as criminals, such as murderers, rapists, and thieves (Carp, 1998), it seems possible that more cultural attention to Trickster figures could help transform psychic energies that are acted out as crime into more integrated and healthy forms. Carp (1998) suggests that clown therapy may be a way to help integrate the shadow. Jung (1969) referred to the trickster as "a collective shadow figure, a summation of all the inferior traits of character in individuals" (p. 150). Because they provide a symbolic expression of this shadow, trickster myths may assist individuals to incorporate the shadow to find creative energies for growth in previously repressed material.

Mandala.   A **mandala** is an archetype of order, usually symbolized by a circle or a square or often a square within a circle. Many religions include mandalas as symbols facilitating spiritual development (Coward, 1989). Examples are found in Tibetan Buddhism, the World Wheel of Hinduism, the Rose Window of Notre Dame cathedral in Paris, and many other places (see Figure 3.1).

mandala symbolic representation of the whole psyche, emphasizing circles and/or squares

Dreams of mandalas often occur when people are experiencing great conflict. Such dreams can be interpreted to mean that the unconscious has developed more of a solution to the conflict than the person yet consciously recognizes. Thus the symbol anticipates the development of a more well-rounded, balanced Self (Coward, 1989). Because the mandala represents emerging psychic wholeness, the goal of the development of the Self, we can also speak of the archetype of the Self (Edinger, 1968) or the archetype of wholeness.

Figure 3.1 A Mandala, a Symbol of Psychic Wholeness

In Eastern religious tradition, these monks are preparing a mandala as an aid to meditation. For Carl Jung, this image affirmed the value of unconscious processes. He was influenced by Buddhist ideas.

transformation
modification of psychic energy to higher purposes (e.g., through ritual)

Transformation.   **Transformation** is symbolized by many mythic and individual symbols. Alchemists, predating modern chemists, struggled to find the secret that would transform base metal into gold: the quest for the philosophers' stone. Myths of great journeys, such as Odysseus's wanderings in ancient Greece, are classic parallels to more mundane images of crossing bridges or crossing streets. Such crossings symbolize psychological transformation, the changes that occur with continued development (Jung, 1944/1968b).

Psychosis: Dangers of the Collective Unconscious

Jung's (1960a) theory interprets psychotic hallucinations and delusions as direct expressions of the collective unconscious. Without the conscious ego to act as a mediator, this powerful collective unconscious overwhelms the individuality of the person and makes manifest what is latent in the rest of us. Drugs can trigger psychosis by chemically inducing an encounter with images of the archetypal unconscious. Direct experience is dangerous, but the collective unconscious can be approached cautiously, with the aid of symbols and myths.

Symbolism and the Collective Unconscious

Like Freud, Jung believed that the unconscious manifests itself in symbols. Whereas symbolic expression may be modified by an individual's unique experience (the personal unconscious), symbols also reach deep into the psyche, into the collective unconscious. A symbol is formed at the meeting point between the unconscious and consciousness, shaped by both conscious experience and unconscious material, including archetypes. Because the collective unconscious is determined by heredity rather than personal experience, its contents are similar from person to person, although they may live in different environments, even different centuries. Symbols tap this shared archetypal substratum and thus have some more or less universal meanings (cf. Chetwynd, 1982; Cirlot, 1971). Archetypes are not themselves symbols but are rather the underlying raw material, which is often expressed symbolically.

Jung took great delight in finding similarities between the experiences of psychotic patients and the symbols of ancient art and mythology. For him, this similarity confirmed the existence of the collective unconscious. For example, he reported parallels between hallucinations and drawings of a psychiatric patient and symbols on a newly discovered Greek papyrus. Jung said the modern drawing could not have come from any knowledge based on experience, so it must have come from the collective unconscious. There is, however, some doubt about Jung's report; a historian suggests that the ancient Greek images were publicized before this patient's images and so could have been their source and that other patients alleged by Jung to have spontaneously produced images like those of ancient peoples could also have learned of these images beforehand (Noll, 1994). Another critic finds several alternative explanations for this report, including simple coincidence, that do not constitute evidence for Jung's theory of archetypes (Neher, 1996).

Many of Jung's concepts, such as archetypes and the collective unconscious, are difficult or impossible to test empirically. Jung made no effort to do so by using well-controlled scientific procedures as we know them, and his followers likewise emphasize nonempirical methods. One exception, an experimental study of archetypal symbolism, is reported by D. H. Rosen and others (Rosen et al., 1991). They developed an Archetypal

Symbol Inventory consisting of 40 visual images portraying symbols associated with Jungian archetypes. Undergraduate psychology students were administered a paired learning task in which they tried to learn to associate these symbols with words. Unknown to the subjects, half of the words matched the accepted archetypal meaning of the symbols, and half were mismatched (associated with the incorrect symbol). The results supported the validity of the archetypal symbols. An image of a snake, for example, matched "health," as might seem sensible when we consider that the caduceus, the symbol of the medical profession, features a snake. Furthermore, the symbol of a crescent moon matches the word "feminine," as those aware of lunar imagery may readily see. When symbols were presented with their matching words, recall accuracy was significantly higher than recall of mismatched symbol-word pairs. Other analyses showed that subjects were not consciously aware of the meaning of the symbols (Huston, Rosen, & Smith, 1999). This research does not definitively demonstrate the Jungian assertion that archetypal symbols are innate because there may be other reasons why some pairs are more memorable than others, but it is, nonetheless, a praiseworthy step in applying scientific methods to the elusive concept of the collective unconscious.

The collective unconscious has a feeling that Jung called **numinous**, meaning "spiritual" or "awesome." It can never be totally assimilated into individual consciousness, but it is important for individual consciousness to have some relationship to this collective unconscious. This can be accomplished through symbols, which give access to the energy of the unconscious. When unconscious contents are symbolized, they can become known to the conscious mind. Analysis of symbols is not intended, though, to make them entirely conscious because doing so would diminish their power, which comes from the unconscious and fuels creative living. Bettelheim (1976) found that when he exposed young boys only to "safe" versions of traditional fairy stories, with all monsters, witches, and frightening episodes removed, the boys were much more disruptive than were children exposed to the traditional frightening stories by the Brothers Grimm. Symbolic representation of fearsome emotions through fairy tales brings these issues to consciousness, where they can be dealt with by ego strengths. If these negative forces are not symbolized, they remain unchanged in the primitive unconscious, from which they emerge untransformed and uncivilized. This produces psychological difficulties such as the antisocial acting out behaviors of these disturbed boys. Some Jungian analysts use fairy tales as a way of encouraging creativity in developing new ways of thinking about life's issues (Kast, 1996).

numinous experience of spiritual or transpersonal energies

MYTHS AND RELIGION

How can we tap the energies of the unconscious without being destroyed by them? That is the function of mythology, religion, and the arts, which provide cultural symbols. Myths provide a means of tapping the deeper, creative levels of human potential, without being destroyed by it (as in psychosis). Jung encouraged people to participate in the religious traditions in which they had been raised. (He discouraged Westerners from switching to Eastern religions, based on his premise that a somewhat different unconscious was represented in each.) Perhaps another caution in cross-cultural religious studies is the danger of distorting other traditions because we see the world through the lens of our own background, as one Jesuit priest is indicted for doing when he interpreted Native Americans' religious tradition of the Sacred Pipe from a Christian viewpoint (Bucko, 2000).

In our scientific era, we sometimes misinterpret myth as merely primitive science. A myth of the sun rising, for example, is dismissed as an outdated statement before people knew that the earth revolved around the sun. Fertility rites are, from this view, outdated by our increased understanding of natural science. For Jung, however, myths are far more than primitive science because they deal with human experience of the events of nature. A myth of the sun "setting" not only describes the sun going deep into the earth but also expresses people's grief of seeing the departure of the sun and their fear of the dangers that come with the night. Science, which is intentionally neutral in the emotional sphere, cannot replace this emotional function of myth. Perhaps a sense of this loss has contributed to antiscience tendencies in our modern era.

Religious myths are probably the most important myths, providing valuable guidance for living and for development. Jung's theory is influenced by mystical thought in both Christian and Jewish traditions (Drob, 1999). This is not to say that religious prophecy has a specific magical quality; rather, the archetypal language of religious writing—for example, the apocalypse in the biblical book of Revelation (Edinger, 1999)—expresses symbolic insights. Interest in ancient gods and goddesses reflects a modern hunger for myths (May, 1991). Some people take offense at the labeling of religion as myth and try to defend religious assertions by scientific standards. The debate over creationism versus evolution is an example. To judge religion by scientific criteria is to misunderstand, and underestimate, the nature of myth and is really no more sensible than sending a dishwasher to the repair shop because it cannot bake a cake.

MODERN MYTHS

Old myths, therefore, are not made obsolete by scientific advances. They, and the collective unconscious that they tap, contain "the wisdom of the ages lying dormant in the brain" and so offer valuable guidance for human life. Influenced by Jungian theory, many scholars are investigating old myths for wisdom. There is particular interest in myths of the feminine, to balance what is perceived as an overemphasis on masculine values in Western culture (e.g., Bolen, 1984; Lauter & Rupprecht, 1985; D. S. Wehr, 1987; Whitmont, 1982). However, old myths may not suffice; we also need new myths to guide us through the new challenges of our age (Atkinson, 1991; DeCarvalho, 1992; May, 1991). At its best, myth making is an active and vital process in human culture. According to Jung, when humans lose the capacity for myth making, they lose touch with the creative forces of their being.

Modern myths are described by various Jungian scholars, including the mythologist Joseph Campbell (1972). Examples include the *Star Wars* films (Ryback, 1983) and other science fiction works. One of Campbell's students, George Lucas, produced several well-known movies that are modern myths, including *Raiders of the Lost Ark, Indiana Jones and the Temple of Doom,* and *Indiana Jones and the Last Crusade.* (The last of these extends a medieval legend, the Holy Grail.)

Technological and social change have made some old myths obsolete and the consciousness they foster dangerous in the face of new perils, such as nuclear holocaust, that demand new ways of thinking (Kull, 1983; Mack, 1986; Perlman, 1983). Creative new myths, in the Jungian tradition, may be our guide to the development of new ways of relating to the collective human unconscious and to the historical experiences of our own time. A Jungian analyst, for example, praises Spielberg's (1993) film *Schindler's List* for its approach to the Holocaust. The story allows the viewer to experience mourning and shame without a confrontation with these emotions that is so direct as to be overpowering, providing "a healing rite of vision" (Beebe, 1996).

Myths are central to the psychoanalytic process as Jung understood it. Outside of the mainstream, in alternative training centers, flows a respect for mythology as a necessary tool for understanding the psyche and for training psychotherapists (Lukoff, 1997). This contrasts with mainstream psychology, which emphasizes scientific attitudes. There may be some basis for increasing dialogue between these two camps, however. Even as psychotherapy is described as a process of helping clients construct a new life story or narrative (Frank & Frank, 1991), some research-oriented psychologists are analyzing subjects' life stories to gain insights into their lives (Lukoff, 1997; McAdams, 1988).

Therapy

Jungian therapy aims to assist the unconscious in claiming its rightful role, challenging the inflation of the ego (Singer, 1994). Like Freudian psychoanalysis, Jungian therapy focuses largely on dreams and symbolic material. Unlike Freud, Jung did not emphasize the past or childhood origins of psychological difficulty. Jung dispensed with Freud's couch. He preferred a face-to-face encounter between the therapist and the patient. This reflected his conviction that the therapist should not hide behind authority and a guise of scientific objectivity.

Jung regarded the unconscious as an ally rather than the enemy. Its energies can be creative, not destructive. The direction of growth, in therapy and outside, is toward greater wholeness. Parts of the psyche that have been broken off from the whole must be retrieved and integrated with the rest of the personality. Often these isolated pieces take the form of **complexes**, that is, networks of emotions and thoughts that are conflictful and unconscious. They center around a common theme (such as a mother complex or a hero complex), which is often archetypal (Edinger, 1968). Unresolved complexes cause maladaptive behavior, as when a complex based around an uninvolved father causes a person to become involved with distant spouses or bosses (Van Eenwyk, 1997). Therapy aims to integrate this material with the rest of the personality.

> **complexes** emotionally charged networks of ideas (such as those resulting from unresolved conflicts)

How are complexes uncovered? They may appear in symptoms or dreams. They also can be elicited through the **Word Association Test**, which Jung (1973) devised—an approach that brought him, at that time, international fame for his experimental work and has been described as a precursor of modern cognitive science (Noll, 1994). In this test, the patient listens to a word and is instructed to say whatever comes to mind. Unusual associations and delays in responding indicate that a psychological complex may have been activated. Jung's Word Association Test was, incidentally, an influence on Hermann Rorschach, Jung's colleague at the Burgholzli hospital, in his development of the famous Rorschach inkblot test (Pichot, 1984).

> **Word Association Test** method devised by Jung to reveal complexes by asking people to say whatever comes to mind when they hear a word

The word association technique has been elaborated on in subsequent research (Zivkovic, 1982). In one study, undergraduate subjects served as judges. They were instructed to decide which of several word association protocols was produced by a "suspect" who had role-played a thief. The results suggested that people who approached the task in a playful, heuristic manner, rather than more logically, were most successful (Dollinger, Levin, & Robinson, 1991). Clinical interpretation, too, requires intuition.

DREAMS

Jung, like Freud, regarded dreams as products of the unconscious. Often patients have dreams early in analysis that, in effect, are statements by the unconscious of the therapeutic task. Because the Jungian unconscious contains multiple levels, personal and collective, various kinds of dreams can be distinguished. Many dreams reveal the individual's unresolved emotional complexes. These dreams, which tap the personal unconscious, are comparable to Freudian dreams, although Jung (1974) did not interpret them sexually. Other dreams reach into the collective unconscious and incorporate archetypal imagery, especially when the dreamer's personality is intuitive and low in neuroticism (Cann & Donderi, 1986). Occasionally, according to Jung, dreams are not personal at all but are like the "big dreams" of Native Americans: messages to humanity at large, with the individual only a receiving medium.

Interpretation of dreams involves three stages. First, the dreamer recalls the dream, retelling it in detail. Second, in the **amplification** of the dream, the dreamer elaborates on the dream images, describing associations of the people and symbols contained in the dream (Mattoon, 1978). In the third stage, **active imagination**, the dreamer continues with the dream imagery in waking imagination, adding new episodes or otherwise continuing the symbolic work toward the personal growth that was begun in the dream. For example, if a dream includes a woman, who may symbolize unconscious potentials in the dreamer's psyche, then having an imagined conversation with that woman can further the psychological development begun by the dream (Beebe et al., 2001).

Jung interpreted all persons and symbols of a dream as aspects of the dreamer's psyche. The way they interact in the dream describes efforts and obstacles in the developmental task of individuation. For example, a dream of exploring a long-forgotten basement and being frightened at the monsters that live there may reflect a person's fear of exploring the unconscious. Many dreams can be interpreted according to the principle of compensation (Jung, 1974; M. F. Mahoney, 1966). That is, the dream presents ideas or emotions that supplement the limitations of consciousness. Such dreams, if understood, prompt the dreamer to have a more balanced approach to current life issues. Jung (1961) described one of his own dreams in which he looked across a valley and, straining to look up, saw one of his patients. He interpreted this dream, according to the principle of compensation, to mean that in real life he had been "looking down on" the patient with a condescending attitude. That interpretation, which he shared with the patient, prompted a change in Jung's attitude toward her, which facilitated therapeutic progress.

OTHER SYMBOLIC THERAPY TECHNIQUES

Besides dreams, other techniques are available to encourage a dialogue with the unconscious. Play therapy is used with children by Jungians and therapists from some other theoretical traditions (Allan & Brown, 1993). Among both children and adults, artistic creations provide a way of expressing images from the unconscious, especially as they may have appeared in dreams. Sometimes these visual images can be interpreted in a way that links the dreamer's experience to larger myths (Johnson, 1991; Nez, 1991).

Myths can provide meanings for patients' problematic behaviors, too. For example, the self-starvation eating disorder anorexia nervosa can be given larger meaning by interpreting this behavior as an unconscious acting out of the ascetic ritual of fasting, which is intended as a spiritual exercise (Barrett & Fine, 1990). Thus the symptom, the illness, provides an unconscious connection with larger, and more healthy, spiritual meaning.

Attention to symbols should not end with the conclusion of therapy. Further symbolic exploration through structured workshops (e.g., Progoff, 1975) may be useful. At its most desirable conclusion, Jungian therapy prepares individuals to create new symbolic forms. They actively participate in the ongoing human task of tapping the creative energies of the unconscious, thus contributing to an evolving human destiny. One who has successfully completed a Jungian analysis must lead a "symbolic life." Through the numinous

amplification
elaboration of dream images as a step toward dream interpretation

active imagination
technique for exploring the unconscious by encouraging waking fantasies

power of symbols and myths, the psyche grows beyond the limitations of the ego to a larger consciousness (Hollis, 2000).

Synchronicity

Jung and others claim that the collective unconscious is not simply a shared human inheritance but a psychic reality that transcends individual consciousness in the moment, forming the basis for paranormal phenomena that have no causal explanation in a deterministic science. Mainstream scientists dismiss phenomena such as extrasensory perception (ESP), spiritualism, and mental telepathy as superstitious or fraudulent. In contrast, Jung found them fascinating. He studied spiritualistic séances; he wrote in laudatory terms about J. B. Rhine's controversial experiments into ESP; he wrote about flying saucers (Jung, 1964).

Had Jung abandoned science and common sense altogether, as Freud feared? Writers sympathetic to Jung argue that he was not really a believer in these phenomena (e.g., Hall & Nordby, 1973). Rather, he felt that prescientific explanations offered a target onto which people projected their preexisting concepts and ideas, especially their archetypal images. Medieval alchemists described their search for the process of transforming base metal into gold, and their descriptions used symbols that provided clues to their archetypal patterns of thought (Jung, 1959, 1968a, 1944/1968b, 1970). This view of Jung, although it is accurate, is incomplete. It tends to present Jung as a more objective observer than, by his own account, he was. He experienced a world in which events sometimes had no deterministic explanation. Jung's (1961) autobiography reports many incidents of paranormal experience. For example, he reported waking from sleep with a pain in his head at the time when, unknown to him, a patient shot himself in the head. He dreamed bloody forebodings of war. He discovered that a story he made up about fictitious criminal activity was actually the real-life story of a man he had just met. These are only a few of Jung's self-reported paranormal experiences. He did not dismiss such experiences as meaningless coincidences. In fact, he used such experiences in his work as a therapist, and they helped free his patients from being stuck in their apparently rational but limiting views (Haule, 2000).

Jung (1960b) proposed the term **synchronicity** to describe experiences that logically can be only coincidental but in a feeling sense have meaning. In short, these are meaningful coincidences. In addition to the examples just cited, Jung reported the following incident. One of his patients related a dream of a scarab, a sacred beetle in Egyptian lore. At that instant, an insect banged on his window and he let it in. It was the closest insect relative in Switzerland to the Egyptian scarab (p. 22). Another meaningful coincidence occurred when he was talking to Freud. They both heard a loud, startling sound emanating from the bookcase and wondered what it was. Jung said it was the forces of their contact, and to prove it, he predicted it would happen again. It did (Jung, 1961). Jung interpreted such synchronistic events as manifestations of the collective unconscious that occur when this level of experience is activated by circumstances, such as the meeting of the two analysts. To most people, though, it is simply a coincidence that the bookcase settled or perhaps cracked at that moment.

Jung was interested in the **I Ching**, a traditional Chinese method of "consulting an oracle" or, more bluntly, of fortunetelling (Wilhelm, 1960). The I Ching is based on a number system, with 64 hexagrams corresponding to various phases in the ever-changing conditions of human experience (Phillips, 1980). Traditionally, the Chinese draw straws to select the relevant answer to their question. Alternatively, Jung used a method of flipping coins. He carried a bag of special coins for this purpose. It was his way of transcending the

synchronicity the acausal principle, in which events are determined by transpersonal forces instead of by causes generally understood by science

I Ching ancient Chinese method of fortune-telling

limitations of ego consciousness when life posed difficulties irresolvable through reason. Even if an oracle provides random advice (although Jung was not so rationally cynical), there probably is something to be said for having a way out of the ever-deepening ruts of imperfect conscious decision-making strategies.

Jung's mystical side, like all paranormal thinking, is at odds with the deterministic assumptions of science (Blackmore, 1994; Gallo, 1994; Grey, 1994; Tart, 1992). When empirical studies of the I Ching have been reported, results are not convincing by traditional scientific standards; occasional significant results are reported (Storm & Thalbourne, 2001), but they do not replicate reliably from one study to another. Some have argued that most personality theory is based on a model of reality derived from outmoded physics. Developments in relativity theory and in quantum physics, they argue, provide a better model for psychology, one that allows indeterminism and free will and is more compatible with subjective and even mystical approaches (Keutzer, 1984; Mansfield, 1991; Mansfield & Spiegelman, 1991; von Franz, 1964). Is a new philosophy of science emerging that will validate Jungian mystical ideas? Possibly. However this reference to new models of physics may also be a modern parallel to the medieval alchemists, whose objectivity was clouded by their own presuppositions.

Another way to interpret Jung's mysticism derives from his theory of psychological types (presented in the next section). Traditional science is based on logical and concrete thinking. Jung's theory of psychological types proposes that such thought represents only a partial use of the potential of the psyche. It uses only two of four psychological functions that he identifies (the sensation and thinking functions), neglecting the other two (intuition and feeling). Jung's theory holds that any approach that does not use all four functions is incomplete. His mystical side can be viewed as exploring the implications of the underrepresented functions. Should personality theory encompass this mystical material, or does its commitment to science require excluding Jung's mysticism and the work of others who write of human potential in nonempirical ways (e.g., Washburn, 1990; Wilber, 1990)? Perhaps considering Jung's theory of psychological types, discussed next, will help explain his sympathy toward mysticism.

Psychological Types

Jung's description of personality types is one of the more straightforward, least mystical aspects of his theory. Among other things, it helps explain why some people seize on his descriptions of mystical and mythological experience with enthusiasm and others dismiss them as nonscientific nonsense. The difference depends on a person's **psychological type**, that is, the person's grouping based on Jung's three major dimensions of personality. The three dimensions are introversion versus extraversion, thinking versus feeling, and sensation versus intuition.

psychological type
a person's characteristic pattern of major personality dimensions (introversion-extraversion, thinking-feeling, and sensation-intuition)

To identify psychological type, it is first necessary to determine whether a person is oriented primarily toward the inner world (introversion) or toward external reality (extraversion). Jung called introversion or extraversion the *fundamental attitude* of the individual to emphasize its importance. Next, one assesses which of four *psychological functions* (thinking, feeling, sensation, or intuition) the person prefers. This is labeled the **dominant function**. The dominant function is directed toward external reality if the person is an extravert or toward the inner world if the person is an introvert (O'Roark, 1990). The fundamental attitudes (introversion and extraversion) can be combined with the four functions (thinking, feeling, sensation, and intuition) in eight different ways, constituting eight psychetypes (see Table 3.2).

dominant function
a person's predominant psychological function

TABLE 3.2   Personality Psychetypes

Introverted Thinking	Interested in ideas (rather than facts); interested in inner reality; pays little attention to other people
Introverted Feeling	Superficially reserved, but sympathetic and understanding of close friends or of others in need; loving, but not demonstrative
Introverted Sensation	Emphasizes the experience that events trigger, rather than the events themselves (e.g., musicians and artists)
Introverted Intuition	Concerned with possibilities, rather than what is currently present; in touch with the unconscious
Extraverted Thinking	Interested in facts about objects external to the self; logical; represses emotion and feelings; neglects friends and relationships
Extraverted Feeling	Concerned with human relationships; adjusted to the environment (especially frequent among women, according to Jung)
Extraverted Sensation	Emphasizes the objects that trigger experience; concerned with facts and details; sometimes with pleasure seeking
Extraverted Intuition	Concerned with possibilities for change in the external world, rather than with the familiar; an adventurer

Adapted from Fordham, 1966.

To give a more complete description, we can also identify the function that the individual uses for dealing with the less preferred direction (internal reality for an extravert, external reality for an introvert). This is labeled the **auxiliary function** (see Figure 3.2).

Jung described the four psychic functions as constituting two pairs of functions. The two rational functions, thinking and feeling, enable us to make judgments or decisions. The two irrational functions, sensation and intuition, provide us with information on which to base these judgments. If the dominant function is a rational (decision) function, the auxiliary function will be an irrational (information-gathering) function, and vice versa (McCaulley, 1990). Altogether, considering both the psychetype and the auxiliary function, 16 different patterns are possible.

auxiliary function
the second most developed function of an individual's personality

INTROVERSION AND EXTRAVERSION

Even people with no psychological training use the terms *introvert* and *extravert* to indicate whether people are shy or sociable. Introverts withdraw from company, whereas extraverts mix easily with other people. Jung described the subjective experience of these types. Introverts turn their attention and their libido inward, to their own thoughts and inner states, whereas extraverts direct their energy and attention outward, to people and experiences in the world. The orientations of these two types are so fundamentally different that they often do not understand each other. The extravert, unaware of his or her own inner dynamics, thinks the introvert is "egotistical and dull." The introvert, minimally concerned with other people, regards the extravert as "superficial and insincere" (Fordham, 1966, p. 33). Jung believed that introverts and extraverts are so fundamentally

Figure 3.2 The Dominant and Auxiliary Functions in Extraverts and Intraverts

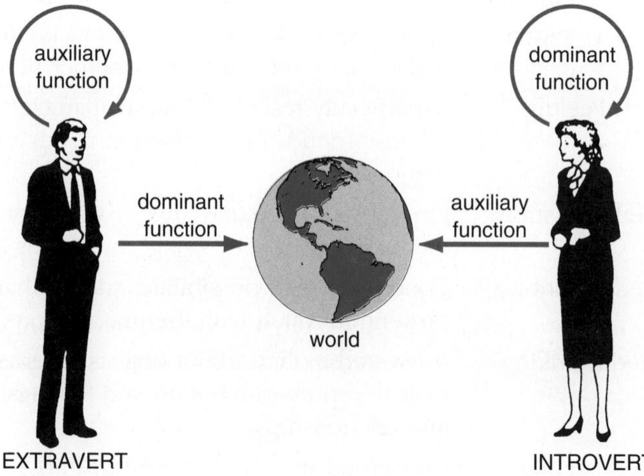

EXTRAVERT   INTROVERT

An extraverted type uses the dominant function to deal with the external world and the auxiliary function to deal with inner reality. An introverted type uses the dominant function to deal with inner reality and the auxiliary function to deal with the external world.

different in orientation that they cannot be close friends in the long run. He understood his own personal conflict with Freud as an example of such a clash of types. Jung's introversion was always suspect to the extravert Freud. Knowing the basis for such interpersonal conflicts cannot eliminate them, but it can at least provide a counterforce against the tendency to devalue the other type of person.

Jung believed that a person remains an introvert or an extravert, without change, for a lifetime. Heredity determines whether the libido is directed to "flow inward" to the inner world or to "flow outward" to external reality. This hypothesized stability of the introversion-extraversion trait is consistent with empirical research using non-Jungian measures of introversion and extraversion. However, the particular description of extraversion that Jung offered has been criticized by researchers because it is multidimensional—that is, it combines more than one trait (Watson & Clark, 1997). An introvert thinks about inner thoughts and feelings but is also unsociable. An extravert turns attention toward other people but is also active instead of reflective. What about someone who is unreflective and also unsociable? That combination does not fit either extraversion or introversion, and research-oriented theorists would prefer that they not be combined into the same theoretical construct.

THE FOUR FUNCTIONS

thinking
psychological function in which decisions are based on logic

The four psychological functions describe fundamental cognitive processes that everyone uses (but to varying degrees). How do we make decisions? Do we emphasize logical thinking or emotional feeling? How do we get information on which to base those decisions? Do we emphasize the details of sensation or the big picture of intuition?

Thinking and Feeling

feeling psychological function in which decisions are based on the emotions they arouse

Like Freud, Jung observed that emotion and thought are not always consistent. **Thinking** and **feeling** are alternative ways of making value decisions or judgments. Some people decide what is worthwhile by how they feel emotionally. They make choices that increase positive emotions, such as excitement, pleasure, or joy. They avoid doing what brings negative emotions, such as anxiety, pain, or sorrow. Other people think things through logically, considering reasons and principles. The difference between thinking and feeling types is portrayed in the *Star Trek* television series by Mr. Spock, a logical and unemotional thinking-type Vulcan, contrasted with Dr. McCoy, a feeling-type human (Barry, 1991). Typical of opposite types, they struggle to relate to the other's experience, and their interactions tend to be abrasive because of their psychological differences. Michael Malone (1977) lists additional examples of feeling types (Emily Dickinson, Albert Schweitzer, and Vincent van Gogh) and of thinking types (Sigmund Freud, Aristotle, and Albert Einstein). Benjamin Franklin, who led a carefully organized life and kept systematic records of his efforts toward his goals, was also a thinking type.

Although emotion and thinking have often been described as in conflict, even theorists outside of Jung's followers are now proposing that they work together—for example, in the realm of interpersonal relationships (Planalp & Fitness, 1999). Emotion is not limited to the overpowering, undifferentiated force that results from early repression (portrayed by Freud) or that impels blind passion. Emotion can be developed and even intelligent, much like the concept of emotional intelligence proposed by Peter Salovey and John Mayer (1990). If development continues toward a healthy maturity, an adult should develop a balance between thinking and feeling. A person who, in youth, makes decisions emotionally must learn to think things through logically as well, and a coldly logical person must learn to pay attention to feelings.

Sensation and Intuition

Sensation and **intuition** are complementary ways of getting information about the world. Do we focus on specific details or the big picture? The sensation type pays attention to details and knows what comes through the five senses: what is seen, heard, touched, tasted, or smelled. The sensation type is unlikely to take hints, for to do so requires making an inference beyond the concrete details. President Harry Truman, famous for his "I'm from Missouri, show me!" attitude, exemplifies the sensation type's concern with concrete details. This type risks becoming so focused on the particularities of a situation that he or she may miss the big picture. Among sensation types Michael Malone (1977) includes Richard Nixon. Perhaps if President Nixon had been less focused on particular details, he would have grasped the potential harm of the infamous political Watergate break-in when there was time to handle this scandal differently.

In contrast to the sensation type, the intuitive-type person grasps the big picture, although often unable to say exactly why he or she understands it. Intuition may sound intangible, but even laboratory research on cognition has studied intuition as a process that enables people to make correct guesses on tasks without being able to identify the correct answers in words (e.g., Wippich, 1994). Jung suggested that intuitive types are skilled at knowing what other people experience, almost seeming like mind readers in their ability to get on the same wavelength as others. That's because the other person gives off cues unconsciously and unintentionally, and the intuitive-type person picks those up, often with uncanny accuracy. Given this ability, they often recognize potential developments in situations that the detail-oriented sensation type misses. Intuition is higher among creative and artistic people (Sundberg, 1965). Among intuitive types Malone (1977) includes Walt Disney, Marilyn Monroe, and Carl Jung himself. Like the thinking-feeling dimension, the sensation-intuition dimension develops through adulthood. Eventually, an adult should develop both skills, however one-sided he or she may have been when younger.

sensation
psychological function in which material is perceived concretely, in detail

intuition
psychological function in which material is perceived with a broad perspective, emphasizing future possibilities rather than current details

MEASUREMENT AND APPLICATION

Theorizing about psychological type is not difficult. It is more challenging to measure the different personality dimensions and then to demonstrate that these measures predict behavior as the theory describes.

Measurement: The Myers-Briggs Type Indicator

Myers-Briggs Type Indicator (MBTI)
psychological test for measuring the psychic functions in an individual

The most commonly used psychological test for measuring the Jungian functions is the **Myers-Briggs Type Indicator (MBTI)** (McCaulley, 1990; Myers & McCaulley, 1985). This test gives scores for introversion-extraversion and the four paired functions (thinking-feeling and sensation-intuition). It determines which of the four functions is dominant by means of a fourth scale that measures whether the external world is approached by a judging function (thinking or feeling, whichever is higher) or a perceiving function (sensation or intuition, whichever is higher). For extraverts, the function identified by this judging-perceiving scale is the dominant function. For introverts, it identifies the auxiliary function because their dominant function is turned inward rather than toward the outer world (McCaulley, 1990). Because the MBTI specifies the auxiliary function in addition to the basic psychetype, it produces 16 types rather than only 8.

Researchers have debated the best way to measure Jung's psychological functions. He proposed types, not traits (as described in Chapter 1); however, research evidence based on the MBTI and other measures of Jungian types supports continuous trait dimensions instead (Arnau et al., 2003; McCrae & Costa, 1989). In addition, the test's forced-choice format forces thinking and feeling and sensing and intuiting to be bipolar opposites, which may be less accurate than considering them as four separate traits (Cowan, 1989; Girelli & Stake, 1993; Lorr, 1991; J. B. Murray, 1990; O'Roark, 1990). Some people may have developed both of the supposed opposites in a pair; others may have developed neither.

Research using the MBTI confirms that it is a reliable and valid measure (J. G. Carlson, 1985; J. B. Murray, 1990; Thompson & Borrello, 1986) that correlates with other psychological tests as one would expect (e.g., Campbell & Heller, 1987). Extraversion is correlated with other psychological measures of that trait (Apostal & Marks, 1990; Sipps & Alexander, 1987). Extraverts are higher in self-monitoring than introverts (Hicks, 1985; Mill, 1984), are more likely to work in sales (Sundberg, 1965), and are happier with their lives than introverts (Harrington & Loffredo, 2001). Feeling types can perceive photographs of emotional faces more quickly than thinking types when the faces are presented very briefly using a tachistoscope (Martin et al., 1996). Higher scores on Intuition are correlated with more frequent recall of archetypal dreams (Cann & Donderi, 1986), greater creativity (Myers & McCaulley, 1985; cf. Tegano, 1990), and innovation as business managers (Berr, Church, & Waclawski, 2000). Sensation types are overrepresented among people with coronary heart disease (Thorne, Fyfe, & Carskadon, 1987). Other analyses consider combinations of these dimensions: For example, Thinking types score high on a psychological test of assertiveness—if they are also extraverted (Tucker, 1991).

Some questions have been raised about specific scales. Perhaps the extraversion dimension is simply sociability rather than the more general "turning energy outward," which Jung proposed. The judgment-perception scale seems to tap impulsivity (Sipps & Alexander, 1987; Sipps & DiCaudo, 1988). Despite these concerns and ongoing revision of the instrument based on empirical analysis of its scales (e.g., Harvey & Hammer, 1999), the Myers-Briggs instrument has stood up well to empirical testing. It is said by one reviewer to be "the most widely used personality instrument for nonpsychiatric populations" (J. B. Murray, 1990, p. 1187).

Business and Education Applications

The MBTI has been used extensively in research, guidance, and especially in business (Bubenzer, Zimpfer, & Mahrle, 1990). It is reported that over 3 million people a year take the MBTI test, and nearly 40% of these are taken in corporations for personnel training (Gardner & Martinko, 1996). By teaching people about their psychological type and its implications, trainers hope to make people aware that others may see the world quite differently than they do and to make allowances for this when they work and live together, enabling them to be more successful in their businesses (Bringhurst, 2001; Olson, 1990; Rideout & Richardson, 1989). For example, financial planners are advised to present life insurance decisions to thinking types with numbers and data but to downplay this strategy in favor of an emphasis on personal values when selling to feeling types (Hanlon, 2000).

In business and other organizations, training advocates propose that decision making can be improved through awareness that a person's decision-making style varies with psychological type. Testing permits the identification of intuitive-type executives, who are particularly well suited for creative brainstorming about new ideas (Agor, 1991). Sensation types perform better than Intuitive types on computer-simulated business decisions (Davis, Grove, & Knowles, 1990), although they prefer lecture-style classes over computer-assisted teaching (Wheeler, 2001). Despite such evidence, carefully controlled research measuring managerial performance in an international airline found no significant correlations with MBTI scores (Furnham & Stringfield, 1993).

The Myers-Briggs instrument has been used successfully in stress-reduction interventions, based on the assumption that people of different psychological types do not experience stress in the same way (Goodspeed & DeLucia, 1990). Depending on psychological type, students approach their work differently. Whether students approach academic advisement with an emphasis on detail (sensation types) or breadth of information (intuitive types) varies with psychological type (Crockett & Crawford, 1989). Sensation-type students are more likely to choose applied fields than are intuitive-type students (Myers & McCaulley, 1985), and they also learn a computer program more quickly from videodisc instruction (Matta & Kern, 1991). Some evidence indicates that judgment types settle down to study with a more focused work ethic (Schurr et al., 1997) and use career services offered by the college more often than perceiving types (Nelson & Roberge, 1993). Some researchers have recommended tailoring educational activities to students of different psychological types, although this is probably a premature application of the research. At any rate, the theory of Jungian types helps us understand the diversity of ways in which students experience the educational environment.

Experimental Studies of Judgments

The psychological functions also have implications for phenomena studied by social psychologists, such as eyewitness testimony. Ward and Loftus (1985) reported that when eyewitnesses were questioned about what they had seen, introverted and intuitive types (measured by the MBTI) were particularly influenced by the wording of questions. If questions were misleading (e.g., referring to a stop sign that was not really there), introverted and intuitive subjects made more errors of recollection. However, if questions were consistent with what was seen, these types gave more accurate testimony than did their opposite (extraverted and sensation) types. The researchers suggest that intuitive introverts are particularly unlikely to trust their own senses and hence are influenced by immediate information from questions.

Another experiment also demonstrates that environmental manipulations have different impact on people depending on psychological type. A robust finding in social psychology is the fundamental attribution error (Ross, 1977), a finding of particular interest to personality psychologists. What is the fundamental attribution error? Most people attribute too much importance to personality and too little importance to situations when they give reasons for other people's behavior. For example, when they read student essays that take a position on a social issue (such as abortion or nuclear arms), research subjects typically judge that the essay accurately reflects the writer's attitude, even if they are told that the position expressed in the essay was assigned by the instructor (Jones & Nisbett, 1972). Hicks (1985) found that one personality type is relatively resistant to this error: the intuitive-thinking type. In a setting in which most students hold antinuclear positions, intuitive-thinking types judge that an essay writer probably does too, even if the essay was pronuclear, because they have been told that the essay position was assigned. Other types overlook the constraint of the situation (the essay assignment) and judge that the person who wrote a pronuclear essay must have a pronuclear attitude. Another study suggests a consistent finding: Intuitive types, compared to sensation types, are less likely to exaggerate their control over the outcomes of their actions (Thomson & Martinko, 1995). Hicks (1985) notes that intuitive-thinking types are especially likely to enter scientific careers, which is consistent with their more objective judgments.

Possible Causes of Psychological Type.   Like many personality measures, the Myers-Briggs is largely influenced by genetics, based on twin studies (Bouchard & Hur, 1998). Shiflett (1989) reports that the Sensation-Intuition and Judging-Perceiving scales are related to hemispheric dominance, but it would be premature to conclude a physiological basis for psychological types without further research. Little research has been done on other determinants of psychological type, such as experience. Sex differences are minimal, except that females tend to score higher on the Feeling scale and males on the Thinking scale (Myers & McCaulley, 1985). For example, males are more likely than females to say that they usually "keep your feelings to yourself" rather than "show your feelings freely" (Harvey & Hammer, 1999).

Despite the enthusiasm with which researchers have adopted the MBTI and the Jungian concept of psychological types, Hillman (1980) cautions that Jung never intended his types to be used to differentiate among people. Rather, the types present descriptions of psychic functions existing in everyone that need to be recognized and developed in each person if the task of becoming a fully developed human being is to be achieved.

Summary

- Jung proposed a theory of personality in which the unconscious contains broad psychic energy, rather than simply sexual energy as Freud postulated.
- Consciousness and the unconscious exist in a relationship of *compensation*.
- During the *individuation* process of adulthood, unconscious aspects of personality are developed and integrated with those of consciousness in the development of a mature *Self*. In this process, the center of personality is shifted away from the ego.
- The *persona* is challenged by the emergence of the *shadow* and the *anima* or *animus* from the unconscious.
- Projection of the shadow contributes to racism. Projection of the anima or animus occurs in romantic love.
- The *personal unconscious* contains material repressed during individual experience.

- The *collective unconscious* contains transpersonal inherited material, including several *archetypes* that serve as patterns for experience.
- Jung encouraged people to encounter the unconscious through symbols in dreams, myths, religion, and cultural rituals. Modern myths, as well as ancient ones, are valuable and should continue to be developed by individuals leading a creative symbolic life.
- Jung discussed mystical, paranormal phenomena in his concept of *synchronicity*, or meaningful coincidence.
- Jung developed a *Word Association Test* to reveal complexes.
- He interpreted dreams as compensatory to conscious awareness.
- Jung's theory of psychological types comprises eight *psychetypes*, based on the dimension of introversion-extraversion and the functions of thinking-feeling and sensing-intuition. These dimensions can be measured by the widely used Myers-Briggs Type Indicator. Research in business, education, and laboratory settings has confirmed that the types vary in their experience and behavior.

Thinking about Jung's Theory

1. Do you think that the unconscious can be creative? If so, why does it sometimes lead to creativity and sometimes to maladjustment?
2. What observations about society (such as events in the news) can be understood through Jung's concept of the shadow?
3. Do you think that Jung's interpretation of religious mythology has any implications about the value of religion? (Is it an insult to religion? Does it make religion more important?)
4. Can you suggest a way to test Jung's archetypal theory through research?
5. Do you think that paranormal phenomena (such as ESP and astrology) should be included in a scientific theory of personality? If so, would you suggest any changes from Jung's description of the paranormal?
6. Does the concept of psychological types help you understand yourself or anyone you know? Does it have implications for your career plans?

Study Questions

1. Contrast Jung's description of the unconscious with that of Freud.
2. Explain Jung's concept of the Self. What is the relationship between consciousness and the unconscious in the Self?
3. Describe the process of individuation.
4. What is ego inflation?
5. Explain the term *persona*.
6. Describe the shadow. How can it contribute to racial prejudice? What can it contribute, in a positive way, to personality?
7. Describe the anima and the animus. Discuss Jung's understanding of sex differences, androgyny, and falling in love.
8. Explain the term *collective unconscious*. List several of its archetypes.
9. Why are symbolism and mythology important for personality?
10. Describe Jung's understanding of religion.
11. Contrast Jungian therapy with Freudian psychoanalysis.
12. Describe the Word Association Test.
13. Explain Jung's approach to dream interpretation.
14. What is meant by the symbolic life?
15. Discuss Jung's mystical concepts, including synchronicity.
16. List the three dimensions Jung used to determine a person's psychological type (psychetype). Describe them.
17. Describe the MBTI. Describe a few research results from this instrument.

The Psychoanalytic-Social Perspective

Freud's psychoanalytic theory inspired many clinicians and theorists to consider personality in dynamic terms. Their extensions of Freud's theory led to new developments in psychoanalytic theory. In particular, many theorists emphasized ego functions to a greater extent than Freud did (Hartmann, 1939/1958). They stressed the capacity of the individual to delay gratification, not simply to be driven by unconscious id impulses. Freud had developed the description of the ego in the later years of his theorizing, from the 1923 publication of *The Ego and the Id* onward (Rapaport, 1959), so these developments follow reasonably from his theory.

Many theorists who regarded themselves as orthodox Freudians are now labeled psychoanalytic-social theorists. Freud's daughter, Anna Freud, elaborated on his concept of ego defenses in her classic book *The Ego and the Mechanisms of Defense* (A. Freud, 1936/1966). Heinz Hartmann (1939/1958) stressed the role of the ego in organizing or integrating personality. Alfred Adler, a member of Freud's inner circle, emphasized the striving aspects of personality and the social context of development, which are characteristic of the psychoanalytic-social perspective.

The ego's role includes adapting to relationships with other people. Infancy is reinterpreted to emphasize the development of a relationship with the mother (E. H. Erikson, 1950; H. S. Sullivan, 1953). An infant nursing at the mother's breast, for example, is viewed by Sigmund Freud as satisfying libidinal drives. In contrast, Alfred Adler and the ego psychologists emphasized the infant's relationship of cooperation with the mother, each needing the other (T. Davis, 1986). This emphasis on relationships with people is reflected in object relations approaches, so named because people are the "objects" of instinctive desire, or the related *relational approaches* in psychoanalysis (discussed in Chapter 6).

Theorists in the psychoanalytic-social tradition also call our attention to cultural factors that influence individuals. Social categories such as race and gender influence personality development and well-being, and these influences were not examined in Freud's and Jung's theories.

Theorists presented in the next three chapters—Alfred Adler, Erik Erikson, and Karen Horney, with later relational theorists—discussed interpersonal aspects of the ego's functioning, beginning in the family and extending to society generally. Culture, not simply biology, determines sex differences, according to Adler and Horney. Erik Erikson remained traditionally psychoanalytic in his biological explanation of sex differences, although he stressed cultural influences in other respects. Besides reinterpreting sex roles as cultural products, the social emphasis has encouraged the development of typologies of interpersonal behavioral styles. Adler ("getting," "ruling," and "avoiding" types) and Horney ("moving toward," "moving against," and "moving away" types) each offered such typologies. Thus, in addition to emphasis on the ego within personality, these theorists gave more attention to society, the context in which personality develops.

The psychoanalytic-social theorists agree with theorists in the psychoanalytic perspective on two important points. The unconscious is a useful concept for understanding personality, and childhood experience is important in determining personality. In addition, theorists in the psychoanalytic-social perspective have distinctive assumptions:

1. The *ego*, the adaptational force in personality, is more important than in Freud's theory.
2. The development of a sense of *self* is described.
3. *Interpersonal relationships*, beyond the relationships with one's parents, are important aspects of personality.
4. *Social and cultural factors* influence personality in important ways.

Most psychoanalytic-social theorists, like Freudian and Jungian psychoanalysts, have based their theories on clinical data. However, a research tradition in ego development has also emerged. Many studies of Erikson's theory have been conducted by using self-report data, as we see in Chapter 5. In addition, Jane Loevinger (1966, 1976, 1979, 1985) has developed an extensive theoretical and research program that measures ego development through questionnaires, thus enabling researchers to investigate ego development in nonclinical populations.

Theorists in the psychoanalytic-social tradition have presented an approach that is not as narrowly biological as classical psychoanalysis. They stress the adaptational and interpersonal aspects of personality and have provided concepts for understanding the ways society shapes human development.

Study Questions

1. What assumptions does the psychoanalytic-social perspective share with the psychoanalytic perspective?
2. What are the distinctive assumptions of the psychoanalytic-social perspective?

4

Adler

Individual Psychology

Chapter Overview

Preview: Overview of Adler's Theory

Striving from Inferiority toward Superiority

The Unity of Personality

The Development of Personality

Psychological Health

Interventions Based on Adler's Theory

Summary

ILLUSTRATIVE BIOGRAPHY

Oprah Winfrey

Adler's theory focuses on choice and goals as more important than unconscious conflict. Oprah Winfrey's spectacular success as a television celebrity, earning her fame and wealth, and her inspiration to help others to achieve their dreams, makes her a great example of the positive healthy functioning that Adler described. Internal conflicts and external societal restrictions need not prevent healthy functioning.

Oprah Winfrey's own life and her role as a model for others focus on the theme of self-improvement by personal effort, a central idea in Adler's theory. Born in 1954 to an 18-year-old unmarried mother, Oprah Winfrey's childhood environment was a mixture of economic hardship, neglect, and abuse. As an adult, she is wealthy and loved by millions in her audience and by a longtime male companion. Her personal qualities were already apparent before school age—her intelligence and her strong will to succeed. The child guidance clinics that Adler offered in schools were more structured and formal than the guidance that Oprah received from her father and from some of her teachers, but the importance of intervention to help a child find a socially useful life course is a central lesson in Adler's theory. Above all, his theory would credit her choices and personal striving for her success.

Development

Adler called attention to parental behavior, which could influence a child to develop in a healthy way that recognized other people's interests as well as her own or to be more selfish. He cautioned against pampering or giving in to the child's wishes but also against neglecting a child. The desirable path was to set standards and teach the child responsibility. Adler also recognized that a child interacts with sisters and brothers, and those interactions influence the developing personality, in part because of the different experiences of those who are the oldest, middle, or youngest in a family, and also in part because of the unique sibling relationships of a particular family.

The parenting that Oprah experienced was varied. In her earliest years, she was raised by her grandparents on a poor farm without indoor plumbing. They were not demonstrative of affection and beat her frequently to punish her (as was the practice in that place and time), but they encouraged her reading and church participation and so provided a solid base for her personality growth. At age 6 she went to live with her mother and a younger half sister in a one-room ghetto rooming house in Milwaukee (Mair, 1994), and she was sent back and forth a few times between that environment and her father's more disciplined home in Nashville. Her mother's neglect left her vulnerable. She was raped by an older cousin (who was visiting and, in the crowded home, shared her bed) when she was 9 years old (King, 1987). She was falling into undisciplined and promiscuous habits, having sex with several men, stealing money from her mother, and running away. She became pregnant, but the baby died. Faced with an increasingly out of control young teenager, her mother (who by now had another child) sent her again to live with her father, where she had lived previously during her third-grade year. Her family configuration, because of moving from one parental home to another and because of the absence of a consistent father figure in her mother's home, did not give her the stable sibling and parent relationships on which to base her development. That inconsistency changed with the return to Nashville. Vernon Winfrey and his wife gave Oprah the discipline that she needed: a curfew, advice about dealing with boys, restrictions about clothing, and homework. She thrived, becoming popular at school and responsible enough to earn the respect of her father and to set her on course for success in life. Her achievements have included spectacular fame and wealth as a radio and then television talk show celebrity, movies, and a magazine.

Description

In Adler's theory, each person develops a unique style of life that is formed early and remains consistent through life, directed by goals for self-improvement. He was particularly interested in the interpersonal style of the individual; for example, was the person too dependent, too domineering, or appropriately cooperative?

Oprah's life story attests to her intelligence and speaking ability and to her warmth toward other people. Already at age 3 she was able to read and write and gave a much admired speech about Easter at church. She skipped first grade because of her ability and later was sent to a better high school than the neighborhood school, again because her achievement surpassed that of her classmates. She loved to give speeches—first to the barnyard chickens and pigs at her grandmother's farm and later to other children and to adults. She entered public-speaking contests. Her style of life seems to be one of getting attention, love, and admiration by speaking to a group of people—radio at first, and later the *Oprah Winfrey Show* on television. She talks easily with others, assertively interviewing them and expressing her opinion but with empathy.

Adjustment

Adler's theory describes compensation for previous inadequacies and disappointments as the motivating force behind healthy adjustments. In addition to love and work, the criteria that Freud proposed, he pointed out that social interaction is also an important component of good adjustment. A well-adjusted person does not pursue only selfish goals, but also contributes to society ("social interest").

Adler's criterion of social interest is fulfilled in Oprah's life. Her television shows frequently offer helpful support and information to help others deal with adversity. Among the topics she has explored are divorce, homosexuality, transgender parents, terminal illness, sexual abuse and incest, as well as lighter themes like beauty and exercise. She is popular in part because of the generous gifts that she bestows on her television audience. Off air, she has been present for teenage girls to help them avoid unplanned pregnancy, with the life of poverty and despair that too often follows. She is helpful to others, especially in areas that draw from her own background. For example, she advocated for legislation to register child molesters as sex offenders. Over the years she has also conquered a problem with obesity, slimming down and exercising regularly. Overall, these self-improvement efforts and contributions to others constitute what Adler would call a healthy style of life.

Cognition

Although we do not always clearly think about it, each of us has an image of what would be desirable, what would make up for what is lacking (our "felt minus"). Adler called this our "fictional finalism" and suggested that it guides our efforts in life and gives a consistency to our motivation. Hints of what is felt to be lacking are often contained in a person's early memories. Over time, we may get a clearer idea of this goal. It's so important that, once we understand a person's unique fictional finalism, we understand that person's personality. It influences the choices that we make.

The first descriptions of a "felt minus" that Adler proposed were based on physical features, and Oprah describes her dissatisfaction with her hair, which did not bounce like that of her white classmates; her nose, which she tried to reshape by pinching it with clothespins while she slept (Waldron, 1987); and her dark skin, especially upsetting because her lighter-skinned half sister was considered the pretty one. She also had few toys—only a doll made out of corncobs. One of her early memories is of "drawing water from the well every morning and playing with corncob dolls" (Waldron, 1987, p. 171), a clear indication that a simple and poor life was the situation from which she wished to rise. Throughout descriptions of her early life is evidence of a fictional finalism that became ever clearer and propelled Oprah Winfrey to her adult life. In part, this view of her goal was based on social class and privilege. Early, she describes the television images of privileged children, unlike her: white and not beaten, when she caught glimpses on friends' television sets (because their family had no television). Later, she saw upper-middle-class families in person when she visited friends from high school. These experiences helped focus her fictional finalism, her goal. She says, "Somewhere in my spirit, I always knew I was going to be exactly where I am" (Waldron, 1987, p. 18). Another important part of her goal was public performance. When she visited Hollywood and admired the sidewalk stars that commemorate celebrities, she told her father that she would be famous one day.

Society

Adler's theory recognizes the society to a greater extent than classical psychoanalysis. Influences from society, such as schools, offer opportunities for healthy growth. In turn, a healthy individual contributes to society. He criticized the way that society sometimes limits personal growth, for example through restrictive gender roles.

Although racial prejudice and unequal economic opportunity clearly existed, there were also positive influences concerning racial issues in Oprah's background. The small town where she lived in her early years (Kosciusko, Mississippi) had a history of supporting black opportunity. The town was, in fact, named for a Revolutionary War soldier who had left money on his death for the purpose of buying slaves to set them free (Waldron, 1987). She also lived at a time when antidiscrimination and equal opportunity laws made it easier for blacks and women to succeed in America, enhancing her early job opportunities in radio and television. Another positive influence in her life was the church. As a preschooler, she spoke at church. Later, she gave impromptu sermons to kids on the playground, earning the nickname of "The Preacher." She considered, at one point, becoming a missionary. The church as a social institution presents a vision of a better world and provides guidelines to supplement the sometimes inadequate parental guidance of its members. Education also contributed importantly to her success, and she has encouraged reading by suggesting books on her television show.

Biology

Adler's theory does not focus on biology as a determinant of personality but rather as one of the factors that creates the basis for positive striving. Feelings of inferiority about our physical bodies provide one source of motivation for self-improvement.

As just described, Oprah felt dissatisfied with her nonwhite physical features in childhood. In adulthood, she successfully, but not easily, battled obesity. These "felt minus" aspects of her body were the basis for positive striving, epitomizing a central theme in Adler's theory. Her movie roles, particularly the Oscar-nominated role of Sophie in *The Color Purple*, contributed to public awareness of the experience of black Americans.

Final Thoughts

Adler's theory and his therapeutic work challenge people to take responsibility for their lives and not to blame others for what is lacking. He stressed the value of intervention to redirect troubled youth and urged people to contribute usefully to society. All these are major themes in Oprah Winfrey's life, which stands as a positive example of personality and an inspiration for many of her fans.

Preview: Overview of Adler's Theory

Adler's theory has implications for major theoretical questions, as presented in Table 4.1. His theoretical ideas are easier to test scientifically than those of Freud and Adler, and researchers have developed tests to measure style of life, early memories, and others of his theoretical constructs. In addition, his hypothesized relationship between birth order and personality has generated many empirical studies. The theory extends the comprehensiveness of psychoanalytic theory by including more conscious thought and future goals into the scope of the theory. It has been applied to school interventions for troubled youth and has generated an Adlerian version of psychotherapy.

Alfred Adler was one of the earliest and most influential dissenters from Freud's inner circle of early psychoanalysts. Unlike Freud, who emphasized the universal conflicts that all people experience, Adler focused attention on the uniqueness of each person. He named his theory "individual psychology." His ideas have so influenced other psychoanalysts, including Karen Horney, Erich Fromm, and Harry Stack Sullivan, that they should perhaps be called neo-Adlerians rather than neo-Freudians (Wittels, 1939). Even Freud was influenced. He borrowed many Adlerian ideas, although often calling them by a new name: defense mechanisms (from Adler's safeguarding tendencies), ego-ideal (from Adler's self-ideal), and superego (from Adler's counter-fiction) (Ansbacher & Ansbacher, 1956, pp. 21–22). Adler's discussions of masculine protest contributed to Freud's postulate of the Oedipus complex.

TABLE 4.1	Preview of Adler's Theory
Individual Differences	Individuals differ in their goals and in how they try to achieve them, their "style of life."
Adaptation and Adjustment	Health involves love, work, and social interaction and is the responsibility of each individual. Social interest, rather than selfishness, is required for health.
Cognitive Processes	Conscious experience and thought are important and generally trustworthy.
Society	Society influences people through social roles, including sex roles. Schools are especially influential.
Biological Influences	Organ inferiority provides the direction of personality development as the individual attempts to compensate for the inferiority.
Development	Parents have an important influence on children, and better parenting techniques can be taught. Extensive guidelines for child rearing are provided, especially the caution to avoid pampering. Relationships with siblings are important; birth order affects personality. Throughout life, people create their own personalities through goal setting.

Adler argued that people must be understood from a social perspective, not a biological one. He opposed Freud's exclusive emphasis on sex as a source of energy, and he asserted that any deterministic approach that does not consider the individual's goals is incomplete and cannot provide an effective therapy. Adler's emphasis on the innate tendency toward social interest and on a holistic approach to personality is a historical precursor to the humanistic psychologists' concept of self-actualization (Runyon, 1984). We may say that Adler defended the role of the soul or the self in psychological theory (cf. Ansbacher & Ansbacher, 1956, p. 62; Weiss-Rosmarin, 1958/1990). His emphasis on growth and free will is an important counterforce to the deterministic attitude of Freud.

Throughout the subsequent history of personality theory, Adler's influence is clear. His emphasis on the whole person is reflected in the work of Allport, Maslow, and Rogers. His attention to the social context is echoed in the work of Horney and modern social psychologists. Some Adlerian concepts have become so popular that they seem more like common sense than psychological theory (e.g., the inferiority complex).

BIOGRAPHY OF ALFRED ADLER

Alfred Adler was born in a suburb of Vienna (Penzing), Austria, in 1870, the second son in a family of four boys and two girls. His father was a grain merchant. His family was financially comfortable and one of the few Jewish families in his village. In protest against the isolation of orthodox Judaism, Alfred later converted to Christianity.

ALFRED ADLER

As a young child, Alfred was unhealthy and suffered from rickets. His earliest reported memory is as a 2-year-old, bandaged so he could barely move while his older brother moved freely about. His childhood, he said, was often made unhappy by the greater achievements of his older brother, with whom Alfred unsuccessfully competed. At the age of 5, Alfred heard a doctor tell his father that Alfred's pneumonia was so serious that he would die; treatment was useless. This seemed credible because Alfred's younger brother, with whom he shared a room, had died in bed 2 years earlier. On the advice of a second physician, however, treatment was given, and Alfred recovered. He decided to become a doctor himself "in order to overcome death and the fear of death" (Ansbacher & Ansbacher, 1956, p. 199). In addition to all this, he was run over twice when he was 4 or 5.

Eventually, with the courage that he later was to urge on his patients, Adler overcame his physical difficulties. He was active in sports and became popular with his classmates (but not with his older brother). He also compensated for early shortcomings in the academic area, especially in mathematics, becoming, as Bottome (1947) said, a "mathematical prodigy, solving problems as fast as they could be put to him" (p. 28). Throughout life, Adler loved music, attending various performances and singing in a wonderful tenor voice that, some thought, should have made him an opera singer.

Adler married a Russian émigré, a member of the intelligentsia whose ideas were far more liberal than those typical in Austria at the time. She undoubtedly influenced Adler to deplore the restrictions of traditional attitudes toward women. For example, he reported one study he conducted that found that successful girls often had mothers with careers. Adler and his wife, Raissa, had four children.

Adler received his medical degree from Vienna University in 1895. He began practice as an ophthalmologist, later becoming a general practitioner. He was interested in the contribution of psychological factors to illness and its cure, but he did not limit his practice to psychiatry until 1910, after his break with Freud. As a general practitioner, his life-long concern with the social context of illness is exemplified by his pamphlet "The Health of Tailors," in which he exposed the working conditions leading to high rates of disease in this occupational group. During World War I, Adler served as a physician in the Austrian army, treating war neuroses (later to be called shell shock).

Adler (like Jung) was impressed by Freud's book on dreams and defended it in print against critics, although at the time he did not know Freud personally. Freud responded with gratitude. In 1902 Freud invited Adler to join his weekly discussion group, later known as the Vienna Psychoanalytic Society. Although Adler was not psychoanalyzed by Freud or anyone else, he did participate in these discussions. He became Freud's successor as president of the group in 1910 and coedited its journal. He took over many of Freud's cases and was Freud's personal physician.

In 1911, however, Freud broke with Adler, unable to reconcile Adler's theoretical contributions with his own. Freud questioned Adler's intellectual ability and accused Adler of failing to recognize the importance of the unconscious, thereby fundamentally missing the point of psychoanalysis. Adler, from his side, regarded Freud as a pampered child who had never overcome the self-indulgence of childhood and who clung to authority out of defensiveness.

Adler had many supporters. When he left Freud's circle, resigning the presidency of the Psychoanalytic Society in 1911, 9 of the 35 other members left with him. In 1912 he established an independent psychoanalytic association, the Society for Individual Psychology, and in 1914, he founded his own journal.

Adler was particularly interested in intervening to resolve problems with children, including the prevention of delinquency and of psychological difficulties related to physical handicaps, poor parenting, and problems in getting along with other children (Ansbacher, 1992). He set up nearly 50 child-guidance clinics in Vienna and elsewhere in Europe. In these interventions, he did not emphasize punishment but instead tried to find ways to encourage children's inherent creativity (Hoffman, 1997). He is reported to have established rapport with astonishing success, even in difficult cases. Surgeons summoned him to calm their juvenile patients, and he was especially effective with depressive patients. However, he directed his message more to the public than to medical experts and did not like empirical research studies. This popular orientation impeded his recognition among academicians, although it is echoed by those who urge psychologists to "give psychology away" (G. Miller, 1969) to the public.

Adler wrote extensively, publishing over 300 articles and books (Dinkmeyer & Dinkmeyer, 1989). His reputation spread internationally, and he lectured both in the United States and throughout Europe. Like many Europeans during the politically troubled times prior to World War II, Adler moved to the United States in 1935. He taught at the Long Island College of Medicine. In 1937, at the age of 67, he died of cardiac problems, with little forewarning and after a healthy adulthood, while on a lecture tour in Scotland.

Adler acknowledged that his theory drew on his own life experiences. It is easy to see how a boy who was ill, and diagnosed as a terminal case, would aspire to become a physician and would describe the overcoming of physical defects as a major motivating force.

Adler's theory, in contrast to those of Freud and Jung, emphasizes individuals' conscious striving to improve their lives. It offers concepts for understanding people who, through hard work, become successful. What about those who do not try? Rather than accepting their lack of effort as a consequence of forces beyond their conscious control, Adler's theory holds these individuals responsible for their faulty choices.

Striving from Inferiority toward Superiority

The fundamental motive in Adler's theory is the never-ending effort to move on to a better way of life. The struggle takes different forms for different people, and it seems impossible to some, who resign themselves to defeat.

INFERIORITY

Almost everyone has heard the term *inferiority complex*, which describes being overcome by a feeling of lack of worth. This concept was developed and popularized by Alfred Adler, although he may not have originated the particular term (Ansbacher & Ansbacher, 1956, p. 256). For Adler, the basic human motivation is to strive "from a felt minus situation towards a plus situation, from a feeling of inferiority towards superiority, perfection, totality" (p. 1). This is a process triggered by the dissatisfaction of the "felt minus."

Adler's Evolving Ideas about Striving to Improve

What is this "felt minus"? All people begin life as infants. They feel inferior and helpless because their survival depends on others. Each person's sense of what is negative and what would be more positive emerges in a unique and personal way. Adler's terminology changed as he developed his theory over the years, grappling to understand this process. These five stages of Adler's thought are all more or less synonymous as he struggled to describe personality development more precisely, culminating in his final description: perfection striving.

Organ Inferiority. At first, influenced by his medical practice, Adler (1923/1929) referred to organ inferiority as the source of the felt minus. Inherited inferiorities intensify "the normal feeling of weakness and helplessness" all young children experience (p. 18). A person with weak limbs (like Adler himself, having suffered from rickets) considers his legs inferior. A child with hearing problems would feel inferior in auditory capacity. Delayed puberty can also be a source of this sense of organ inferiority, leading to the notion that one will always remain a child (Adler, 1921/1927, p. 72).

It is subjective experience that is important in determining the sense of inferiority. The child makes comparisons with other children and the demands of the social world. Severe socialization and environmental demands can produce a sense of inferiority that would be avoided, given the same physical condition, in a more benign environment. The weak organ may become the basis of a neurotic maladjustment, in which the person exploits the physical deficiency as an excuse for avoiding life's tasks. Children with physical disabilities face this psychological danger. It takes a particularly skilled parent or teacher, like Anne Sullivan (Helen Keller's inspired teacher), to help such a child live more courageously.

However, in a healthy adjustment, the child strives to compensate for the organ inferiority. Adler (1926/1988c) suggested that children with defective ears may compensate by developing a musical capacity, citing Beethoven, who became totally deaf in adulthood, as an example. Early research suggested that people with deficient color vision or hearing compensate for these organ inferiorities, confirming Adler's theory (Overton, 1958).

Not everyone with an organ inferiority, of course, is able to compensate for it successfully. Nonetheless, the attempt to do so directs motivation. If compensation fails, the individual may instead develop an incapacitating sense that the inferiority cannot be overcome—hence an *inferiority complex*.

Aggressive Drive.   The second term Adler used for this process, as his theory evolved, was **aggressive drive**. The struggle toward the felt plus may take the form of fighting and cruelty, or it may be expressed in a more socialized form as athletic competition or other striving for dominance, including politics. It is in this sense that we speak of "aggressive sports" or an "aggressive campaign" or even an "aggressive business deal." Consciously, the aggressive drive may be experienced as anger.

> **aggressive drive**
> one of Adler's terms for positive striving, emphasizing anger and competitiveness

Masculine Protest.   In a third stage of his thinking, Adler referred instead to **masculine protest**, an assertion of manliness that implies greater competence, superiority, and control. Such traits as aggressiveness and activity are seen as masculine, whereas submissiveness and obedience are feminine. Adler noted that traditional sex roles in culture, which give females a subordinate position, contribute to the experience of masculine protest. He did not accept the sex roles of his culture as ideal because they have adverse effects on both sexes (Adler, 1917/1988a). He wrote critically of "the arch evil of our culture, the excessive pre-eminence of manliness" (Ansbacher & Ansbacher, 1956, p. 55). Adler's criticism of traditional sex roles has earned him the label of "an early feminist" (Stein & Edwards, 1998).

> **masculine protest**
> one of Adler's terms for positive striving, emphasizing manliness

Females, as well as males, are motivated by masculine protest as they struggle against the constraints of the less socially valued female role. Physical problems may result, including menstrual difficulties, difficulties with pregnancy and childbirth, and sexual disorders. Or masculine protest may lead women to become career oriented, marry late or not at all, have fewer children, become lesbians, or become nuns as a rejection of their feminine role. Despite the value judgments implicit in these so-called symptoms, Adler (1978, p. 35) warned the therapist to "not bring his own value judgments about masculine and feminine traits to the analysis."

Superiority Striving.   In yet another stage of thought, Adler spoke of **superiority striving**. He did not mean eminence so much as self-improvement. He meant striving to achieve one's own personal best, rather than striving to be better than others.

> **superiority striving**
> effort to achieve improvement in oneself

Perfection Striving.   The final term Adler used for the process is *perfection striving*. Perhaps more than any of his previous terms, this connotes an inherent growth process within the individual. It refers to an effort to improve that is realistic, in contrast to a neurotic perfectionism (Lazarsfeld, 1991). Later theorists, Rogers and Maslow, described a process that sounds quite similar to Adler's basic motivation. They called it self-actualization.

Inferiority Complex

> **inferiority complex**
> stagnation of growth in which difficulties seem too immense to be overcome

When the growth process stagnates, a person may fall victim to an **inferiority complex**. In this case, the felt-minus situation is too powerful to be overcome and the person accepts an exaggerated sense of inferiority as an accurate self-description. All neurotics have an inferiority complex, according to Adler. Even non-neurotic people have inferiority feelings; but only in their exaggerated form, when they overwhelm attempts to move to the felt plus and stagnate growth, are they called a complex. This exaggerated sense of inferiority may result from physical disabilities, family dynamics, or societal influences that are overwhelming (Stein & Edwards, 1998).

Superiority Complex

Some neurotics repress their feelings of inferiority and believe themselves better than others. This outcome is termed a **superiority complex**. Because it masks an unconscious sense of inferiority, it is not a healthy outcome. People with a superiority complex often behave arrogantly; they exaggerate their achievements, which may be intellectual, athletic, or emotional, depending on the unique strengths of the individual. They may adopt idiosyncratic behavior that sets them apart from others. Adler suggests that claims of telepathic powers may spring from a superiority complex. An exaggerated sense of one's superiority over other races and nationalities is another form of superiority complex. One historical example is Adolf Hitler, who claimed an exaggerated sense of his own superiority and that of the German people (Murray, 1943).

superiority complex a neurotic belief that one is better than others

FICTIONAL FINALISM

As described in Chapter 2, Freud was committed to the scientific assumption of determinism in even the psychological realm. This assumption led to a theory that treated humans as passive products of various forces, primarily biological. In contrast, Adler viewed individuals as causes rather than effects. He argued that personality is creative. People make choices and determine their own outcomes in life. External factors present challenges and choices but do not wholly determine the outcomes. Or, to use an Adlerian phrase that captures this point of view, the person is a **creative self** who is trying to discover or create experiences that lead to fulfillment. This creativity is compensatory, that is, a creative way of compensating for feelings of inferiority (Lemire, 1998). For Adler, each person is "the artist of his own personality" (Ansbacher & Ansbacher, 1956, p. 177).

creative self the person who acts to determine his or her own life

In his or her life situation, each person imagines a better situation than the present. This ideal situation is different for each person. It is an image of the fulfillment of what is lacking at the present time: a strong healthy body, if the person is ill; a fortune, if the person feels held back by lack of money; admiration, if the person feels unappreciated; and so forth. Doctors, according to Adler, are often compensating for some early experience with death, trying to overcome it through their careers. Others are directed by a "redeemer complex," trying (not necessarily consciously) to save someone, perhaps by entering medicine or the ministry.

This imagined goal, the desirable future state, Adler called the **fictional finalism** of the individual. (Adler credited this term to the philosopher Hans Vaihinger.) The fictional finalism is a subjective experience rather than an objective reality. It gives direction to the individual's striving. Because an individual's fundamental motivation is to move toward this fictional finalism, a person cannot be understood without knowing the unique goal. Once it is understood, it explains the consistency of a person's striving.

fictional finalism a person's image of the goal of his or her striving

People do not ordinarily have a clear and complete idea of the fictional finalism that directs them. This goal is "dimly envisaged," partly known and partly not known. The unknown part of the goal constitutes the unconscious. (Obviously, this is a far different unconscious from Freud's, which emphasized the past rather than the future.)

Throughout life, the general direction of striving remains, but the specific understanding of the goal may change. Whereas a healthy person modifies the goal, a neurotic may have such an inflexible fictional finalism that behavior is not adaptive.

The Unity of Personality

Adler (1937/1982b, 1932/1988b) emphasized the unity of personality. Before separating from Freud, he explained this unity as resulting from a "confluence of drives." As his theory evolved, he abandoned the drive model and described personality as held together by the fictional finalism and unique style of life.

This emphasis on unity contrasts sharply with Freud's description of conflict within personality. According to Freud, unity is a facade created by the defense mechanism of overcompensation; it masks deeper conflicts within the personality. Freud suggested that Adler did not understand the importance of repression and the unconscious. To be blunt, he missed the point of the psychoanalytic revolution. Adler rejected the idea of conflict between the conscious and the unconscious as "an artificial division . . . that has its origin merely in psycho-analytic fanaticism" (Adler, 1936/1964, p. 93). He believed that the conscious and the unconscious work together more often than they conflict (Ansbacher, 1982).

STYLE OF LIFE

style of life a person's consistent way of striving

A person's goal directs a unique **style of life**. The style of life begins as a compensatory process, making up for a particular inferiority. It leads to consistency of personality as the person compensates, even overcompensates, for this inferiority. Besides the goal, the style of life includes the individual's concepts about the self and the world and his or her unique way of striving toward the personal goal in that world. Some people adopt antisocial styles of life, cheating and aggressively seeking their own satisfaction; others are cooperative and hardworking.

First Memories

A person's style of life, according to Adler, is established by the age of 4 or 5. In this, he agreed with Freud about the importance of early experience in determining personality. A key to identifying the style of life is a person's first memory, which on average dates back to age $3\frac{1}{2}$ (Mullen, 1994). Few people can remember events before age 3, and for many people, nothing is remembered until 6 or 7 years of age. Early memories are often erroneous, and adults seem to confuse what they truly remember with what they have later been told about the past (Eacott & Crawley, 1998). Events that occur very early in life are not recalled years later, even if they could be reported a few weeks later (as in one study of a fire alarm at a preschool), presumably because of changes in cognitive processing (Pillemer, Picariello, & Pruett, 1994), or the self-concept (Howe & Courage, 1993), or perhaps because the hippocampus in the brain has not matured sufficiently to allow permanent memories to be developed (Nadel & Zola-Morgan, 1984). Researchers can assess memory by watching whether children interact with objects differently, having interacted with them in the past, than when the object is first experienced. If the behavior has changed—for example, by making movements toward a part of a play object that in the past produced interesting events when manipulated—there is memory. Using this method, researchers report that even at age 1 and 2 years, children remember events of their lives for weeks and even months. This memory, though, is not in the form that older children and adults can manage, narrative stories expressed in words, so it is not generally accessible to adult recall (Bauer, 1996). As researchers develop a better understanding of memory systems, expanding what they already know about the distinction between memory about events (episodic memory) and memory that is more closely tied to language (semantic memory), we appreciate that childhood memories are selective (Wheeler, Stuss, & Tulving, 1997).

The first memory sticks out because a person has thought about it repeatedly over the years, and it captures what has been subjectively important for that person. The key to the importance of this early memory is not the objective facts recalled but rather the psychological importance of the early memory for the individual. Researchers suggest that early memories are influenced by talking with adults about the events. This occurs more often for firstborns and for girls, which makes their first memories earlier (Mullen, 1994).

Mary Mullen also reports that whites report earlier average memories than Asians, interpreting this difference as a result of the greater emphasis on individuality in Western than in Asian culture. Research supports this cultural difference more directly by asking 4- and 6-year-old boys and girls in China, Korea, and the United States to tell about their lives. Compared to the two Asian countries, U.S. children more often mentioned themselves and their feelings in these recollections (Han, Leichtman, & Wang, 1998).

Adler regarded patients' reports of incredibly early events, such as memories of their own birth or maternal care in early infancy, as factually suspect but psychologically revealing. Adler himself reported an erroneous early memory. He recalled, as a child, running back and forth across a cemetery to overcome his fear of death. The memory must have been inaccurate because there was no cemetery in the place he described. Nonetheless, the false memory is an important clue to Adler's own consistent efforts to overcome death (Bruhn, 1992a; Monte, 1980).

Adler said that a person's "memories represent his 'Story of My Life': a story he repeats to himself to warn him or comfort him, to keep him concentrated on his goal, and to prepare him by means of past experiences, so that he will meet the future with an already tested style of action" (Ansbacher & Ansbacher, 1956, p. 351). Memories are thus a key to one's style of life. Memories of accidents may suggest a lifestyle based on avoiding danger. Memories of one's mother may suggest issues concerned with her care or lack of it. Memories of the first day at school may suggest "the great impression produced by new situations" (p. 354).

Adler said he would always include questions about first memories in a personality analysis. People are willing to report them because they do not realize how much they disclose to a psychologist. Any early memories, even if they are not the very first memories, provide valuable clues to a person's unique style of life. Early memories are routinely assessed in Adlerian counseling and are useful with clients of all ages, including the elderly (Sweeny & Myers, 1986). The Early Memories Procedure (Bruhn, 1990) asks systematic questions about early memories and interprets these as clues to a person's current life attitudes. By briefly stating the essential structure of the memory, its meaning for one's current life becomes apparent (Bruhn, 1992a). For example, early school memories are interpreted as attitudes toward achievement and independence. A memory of running away from playmates after falling off the jungle gym is restated more generally: "When I encounter difficulties with an achievement task . . . I withdraw" (Bruhn, 1992b, p. 327). Psychiatric patients (all men) who had committed felonies reported more early memories of abuse and aggression than did nondangerous psychiatric patients. Those who recalled early psychological abuse were almost 14 times more likely to be in the dangerous group than in the nondangerous group (Tobey & Bruhn, 1992).

Early memories reflect our basic and ongoing emotional schemas. Early memories are significantly related to vocational interest and vocational choice (Elliott, Amerikaner, & Swank, 1987), to delinquency (Davidow & Bruhn, 1990) and criminality (Hankoff, 1987), and to depression (Acklin, Sauer, et al., 1989; Allers, White, & Hornbuckle, 1990). Correlations with various clinical scales—including the Minnesota Multiphasic Personality Inventory (MMPI) and the Symptom Checklist 90-Revised—confirm the hypothesis that early memories express "relationship paradigms" and thus can reflect adjustment or maladjustment (Acklin et al., 1991).

MISTAKEN AND HEALTHY STYLES OF LIFE

A person's style of life is unique. Adler did not like the practice of presenting typologies because they ignore this uniqueness of each individual. For teaching purposes, however, he described four different types (Adler, 1935/1982a), including three "mistaken" (or unhealthy) styles of life and one that was to be recommended. His intent was not to classify people but to make it easier to grasp this concept; therefore, we should realize that these categories are only rough indications of the many styles of life that people adopt.

Mistaken Styles of Life

Not all styles of life are equally desirable. Sometimes, early in life, people develop strategies for improving their situations that are, in the long run, maladaptive. For example, a child may become overly dependent on doting parents or overly rebellious. Adler referred to these as "mistaken styles of life." He listed several types, which we examine here.

Ruling Type.   Ruling types seek to dominate others. They may actively confront life's problems in a selfish way, becoming "delinquents, tyrants, sadists" (Ansbacher & Ansbacher, 1956, p. 168). Adler (1998) described, for example, a schoolgirl who acted sarcastically and arrogantly toward her peers, seeking satisfaction there because she was unable to do her schoolwork. Or, if less active, ruling types may attack others indirectly through suicide, drug addiction, or alcoholism, according to Adler. Not all people of this type are despicable. Some, with talent and hard work, are high achievers, but they are vain and overly competitive. They may express their sense of superiority over others by belittling them, a tendency that Adler (1921/1927, p. 161) called the **deprecation complex**.

deprecation complex unhealthy way of seeking superiority by belittling others

Getting Type.   Getting types lean on others. They are dependent. They adopt a passive, rather than active, attitude toward life, and they may become depressed. Adler said that pampered children and females are subject to environmental pressures that encourage this neurotic style, but it is always the choice of the individual, rather than external circumstances, that determines the style of life.

Avoiding Type.   Avoiding types try not to deal with problems, thereby avoiding the possibility of defeat. Agoraphobia, an irrational fear that confines people to their homes, is one form of this maladaptive style of life. The avoiding type tends to be isolated and may strike others as cold. This outward appearance hides an underlying, but fragile, superiority belief. Whole classes, religious groups, and nations may adopt this style, which hinders the progress of civilization (Adler, 1921/1927, p. 186).

The Healthy Style of Life: The Socially Useful Type

If the lifestyle is adaptive, Adler referred to it as a **socially useful type**. To be so characterized, a person must act in ways beneficial to others. This does not necessarily imply economic productivity or acts generally considered altruistic. Adler included artists and poets as people who "serve a social function more than anyone else. They have taught us how to see, how to think, and how to feel" (Ansbacher & Ansbacher, 1956, p. 153). These people have a well-developed sense of "social interest," which is described in a later section of this chapter. In addition, they feel a sense of internal control (Minton, 1968), an attitude that is especially important in the cognitive social learning theories of Rotter, Mischel, and Bandura.

Longitudinal research confirms Adler's prediction that style of life is consistent from childhood to adulthood (Pulkkinen, 1992). Identification of lifestyle in childhood is particularly important because intervention may prevent undesirable patterns from becoming resistant to change (Ansbacher, 1988).

socially useful type a personality that is well adjusted

The Development of Personality

Although Adler said that each person was fully responsible for his or her own choices in life, he did recognize that circumstances could incline people toward either undesirable or desirable styles of life. He was critical of restrictive sex roles (especially for women), of warlike orientations in government, and of poverty and adverse living conditions. These societal factors impede the development of a psychologically healthy lifestyle. Because style of life is developed early, the family is a particularly important influence. Adler, like Freud, described relationships with parents. In addition, he considered the impact of siblings on personality development.

PARENTAL BEHAVIOR

A child begins life in a helpless state. Parents can help or hinder the development of a healthy lifestyle to compensate for this fundamental felt minus. They can help prevent neurosis by protecting the child from tasks too difficult to be successfully completed and by ensuring that appropriate tasks are available. Parents err if they try to make their children always superior to everyone else, more symbols of parental worth than individuals in their own right. Dreikurs and Soltz (1964) have summarized Adler's advice for raising healthy children (see Table 4.2).

The mother, in particular, influences the development of social feeling, the cooperative attitude that distinguishes healthy from unhealthy styles of life. The father, traditionally the authority in the family, teaches the child about power and its selfish or socially responsible expression. (Adler, like Freud, developed his theory in the context of the traditional two-parent nuclear family.) However, the mother usually spends more time with children, and research suggests that maternal behavior is more closely linked with aggressive and other problematic behavior by children (Rothbaum & Weisz, 1994).

The Pampered Child

Some of Adler's most critical remarks were directed toward parental **pampering**. Children who are treated with overindulgence come to expect that others will cater to their needs. They are, in a word, spoiled. Ultimately, because the real world is far less

pampering parental behavior in which a child is overindulged, spoiled

TABLE 4.2	Advice for Raising Healthy Children, Derived from Adler's Approach

Encourage the child, rather than simply punishing.

Be firm, but not dominating.

Show respect for the child.

Maintain routine.

Emphasize cooperation.

Don't give the child too much attention.

Don't become engaged in power struggles with the child.

Show by your actions, not by your words.

Don't offer excessive sympathy.

Be consistent.

(Adapted from Dreikurs & Soltz, 1964).

indulgent than they have come to demand, they will not be loved. Adler criticized Freudian theory as the construction of a pampered child. Who but a spoiled child, he asked, would propose a universal Oedipus complex in which the child wanted complete possession of the mother?

The Neglected Child

neglect parental behavior in which a child's needs are not adequately met

Parental **neglect** also contributes to maladaptive development. Children who have been neglected, including orphans and unwanted or illegitimate children, are likely to believe others will not support them. The tasks of life seem overwhelmingly difficult.

Strangely, parental neglect can lead a child to adopt a pampered style of life. It is the desire to be pampered, the fictional goal of being cared for, rather than the fact of having been pampered, that characterizes the pampered style of life. Thus neglected children, as well as overindulged children, can become overly dependent on others for recognition and for nurturance.

Parenting Training Programs

Training parents to be more effective can prevent and help solve problems that might appear at school and elsewhere. One study reports, for example, that adding a parenting training component to a Head Start program brought about better outcomes. As parents learned to be more positive and less critical and punitive, children became happier and behaved more cooperatively (Webster-Stratton, 1998). Many parenting training programs based on Adlerian principles have been developed (Dinkmeyer & McKay, 1976; Dreikurs & Soltz, 1964). A major goal of these programs is to teach parents to understand the reasons for their children's misbehavior so they can more effectively influence it. Dreikurs (1950) identified four goals of children's behavior: "attention-getting, struggle for power or superiority, desire to retaliate or get even, and a display of inadequacy or assumed disability" (Dinkmeyer & Dinkmeyer, 1989, p. 28). Overall, although they have not been evaluated as thoroughly as we might hope (Wiese & Kramer, 1988), the evidence suggests that parents can be taught more effective ways of parenting, based on Adlerian concepts (Utay & Utay, 1996).

FAMILY CONSTELLATION

Interactions among sisters and brothers in childhood have important influences on the development of personality. Because other psychoanalysts have emphasized parent–child interactions, only infrequently considering sibling relationships (e.g., Agger, 1988), this emphasis on **family constellation** (the number, age, and sex of siblings) was an important and distinct contribution of Adler. In proposing the effects of birth order, Adler recognized that many other factors in any particular family would need to be considered. He offered general observations about birth order, described later, but he also expected there would be many exceptions.

family constellation
the configuration of family members, including the number and birth order of siblings

Firstborn Child

The firstborn child begins life with the full attention of the parents, and this child is often pampered or spoiled. Then, when other children arrive, the eldest must share the parents' attention with the new baby. Only the oldest child has had the full attention of the parents, and so only the firstborn feels so acutely the loss of parental, especially maternal, love. Adler (1936/1964, p. 231) described the eldest child as "dethroned" by the arrival of later children and noted, with some derision toward his former colleague, that even Freud had adopted his phrasing. Often, according to Adler, oldest children do not cope well with dethronement. They are likely to become "problem children, neurotics, criminals, drunkards, and perverts" (Ansbacher & Ansbacher, 1956, p. 377). Most problem children, he claimed, are firstborns (although research, described later, does not generally confirm this prediction).

To compensate for having to share the mother with a new baby, the oldest child may turn to the father. Or he or she may take on a somewhat "parental," protective (and, not incidentally, powerful) role in relationship to the younger siblings. Eldest children may long for the past (i.e., the time before competition), and they tend to overvalue authority and hold conservative values.

Second-Born Child

The second-born child, seeing the head start that the older sibling has on life, may feel envious, experiencing "a dominant note of being slighted, neglected" (Adler, 1921/1927, p. 127). This often makes him or her rebellious, even revolutionary. This experience presents a challenge that can usually be successfully overcome.

The older sibling serves as a "pacemaker," Adler's analogy with a racer. Thus the second-born child is stimulated to higher achievement. Observing the pace set by the older sibling, the second-born child does not waste energy by trying an impossible pace. (In contrast, the firstborn may become exhausted by trying too hard, like a long-distance runner without a pacer.) Unlike the oldest child, the second child always has had to share parental love and therefore is unlikely to have been spoiled. Adler regarded the second child as having the most favorable position.

Youngest Child

Youngest children, said Adler (1921/1927, p. 123), often become problem children. The youngest child, as the baby of the family, is likely to grow up in a warmer atmosphere than the older children. This poses the risk of being pampered and, as a spoiled child, lacking the incentive to develop independence. With too many pacemakers, the youngest child may compete in many directions, leading to a diffuseness and sense of inferiority.

Results can be more positive, though; success may be attainable if an area of effort not already claimed by other family members can be found. This is less true of female children, owing (at the time of Adler's writing) to the fewer opportunities available to women (1936/1964, p. 239).

Only Child

The only child never competes with siblings for parental attention. This child is likely to be pampered and overly attached to the mother, who is often overprotective, so the only child develops a "mother complex" (Ansbacher & Ansbacher, 1956, p. 381). Constant parental attention gives the only child an unrealistic sense of personal worth.

Other Aspects of the Family Environment

In addition to sibling position, many particular aspects of the family environment may modify these outcomes. Children whose talents are quite different from those of their siblings are in a far different situation from those who compete more directly. The spacing between children is significant. If many years pass between the births of various children, they will all have some characteristics of an only child. The number of boys and girls also influences the encouragement of masculinity or femininity in each child.

Research on Birth Order

Adler's observations about birth order have stimulated many studies, probably because it is so easy to measure family constellation. Research on birth order and personality has shown some relationships but not always in the direction hypothesized by Adler; the effects are weak and inconsistent (Jefferson, Herbst, & McCrae, 1998), and sometimes no effects are found at all (Guastello & Guastello, 2002).

Several studies show that parents treat children in the various sibling positions differently. Parents are typically more anxious and critical of their first child than of later children, giving the firstborn more responsibility and pressure to live up to parental expectations (Falbo, 1987; L. W. Hoffman, 1991; Newman, Higgins, & Vookles, 1992). Lasko (1954), in a longitudinal study observing families at their homes, found that firstborns received a great deal of attention until a sibling was born, at which point the firstborn received very little attention, which is just what Adler's concept of dethronement describes. A study exploring the relationship between sibling position and the perception that one is the mother's or father's favorite child (Kiracofe & Kiracofe, 1990) found that sibling position was not very important; instead, children perceived favoritism by the parent of the opposite sex.

Adler's expectation that firstborns would be oriented toward the parents is consistent with the research finding that oldest children are more likely than those born later to search the Internet for their genealogical roots (Salmon & Daly, 1998). Among Chinese American children, it is the eldest child who most often has a strong ethnic identity because this reflects the greater influence of parents on this sibling position (Cheng & Kuo, 2000).

Confirming Adler's prediction that firstborns have more difficulty than second-born children in pacing their work realistically, one study found firstborn teachers more susceptible to teacher burnout (Forey, Christensen, & England, 1994). Firstborns are also more often type A (time-pressured, coronary-prone) persons (Ivancevich, Matteson, & Gamble, 1987; Phillips, Long, & Bedeian, 1990; Strube & Ota, 1982). Firstborns are reported to be higher in narcissism (self-absorption), which is consistent with Adler's negative portrayal of them (Curtis & Cowell, 1993; Joubert, 1989a). Research using a Knowing Styles Inventory suggests that firstborns more often adopt a Separate Knowing style in which they distance themselves from others' ideas, which they challenge and doubt, whereas later-born children scored higher on a Connected Knowing scale, suggesting that they take the perspective of others (Knight et al., 2000).

Research does not support Adler's claim that second-born children are the highest achievers; firstborns generally achieve the most (Goertzel, Goertzel, & Goertzel, 1978; Schachter, 1963), are most intelligent (Sulloway, 1996), and are overrepresented among world political leaders (Hudson, 1990).

Only children tend to be similar to firstborn children: high achievers with high "locus of control, autonomy, leadership, and maturity" (Falbo, 1987, p. 165). In China, however, only children have undesirable social characteristics, including dependency and egocentrism, perhaps because of parental overindulgence (Falbo, 1987). This cultural difference stems, presumably, from the one-child policy of the Chinese government. Families are strongly encouraged to limit family size to one child because of the fear that overpopulation will lead to famine and other social problems. However, couples often wish to have additional children; when they have only one child, parents tend to indulge rather than discipline this one precious child. In contrast, the culture in which Adler developed his theory was one where families were typically larger, and birth control was not available. If anything, later children might be resented rather than prized because of the increased financial burden they placed on the family, and they would feel less loved than the first or second child (Chen & Goldsmith, 1991). No automatic and universal effect stems from being an only child (or any other birth order); the particular cultural and familial circumstances must always be considered. The example of China makes us realize that such phenomena as birth-order effects may vary significantly from one culture to another.

Middle children say they are more likely to turn to siblings when stressed, in contrast to the oldest and youngest children in the family, who turn to their parents (Salmon & Daly, 1998). Having an older sibling teaches the middle child to comprehend the idea of a "false belief" at an earlier age than do firstborn children (Ruffman et al., 1998). (Whether you wish to interpret this as the educational benefit of playing "let's pretend" games with someone a little bit older or a self-protective lesson learned early to protect against the older child's teasing is a matter you may wish to discuss with your siblings, if you have any.)

Some evidence suggests that later-born males have better psychological well-being than males in other positions (Fullerton et al., 1989), which is inconsistent with Adler's portrayal of a pampered child. Although the difference is small, later-born children tend to be rated by their peers as more extraverted than their older siblings; they also are more trusting and innovative (Jefferson, Herbst, & McCrae, 1998). In a study of early memories, later-born children were more likely than firstborns to include family members in their recollections, whereas firstborns were more likely to recall people outside the family and traumatic events such as injury; otherwise, the memories were similar (Fakouri & Hafner, 1984).

Research on sibling relationships is especially promising when it goes beyond the simple hypothesis that birth order determines personality and instead looks at the quality of relationships among siblings. Sisters and brothers may be buddies, caretakers of one another, or have more casual relationships (Stewart, Verbrugge, & Beilfuss, 1998). When there is much conflict, adverse effects on psychosocial functioning result; when there is more support, sibling relationships have more benign consequences, as may happen when children support one another to make up for the lack of support from parents and stepparents (Brody, 1998). Although Adler described birth-order effects quite clearly, his theory was not as simplistic as it has often been presented, and he emphasized that external conditions do not determine outcomes. Ultimately, individuals create their own styles of life.

Sulloway's Analysis of Scientific Revolutions

Extending Adlerian ideas about birth order, a modern historian of science, Frank Sulloway (1996), theorizes that the history of science has been shaped by birth-order effects. He suggests that for their survival, as an evolutionary mechanism, different children in the same family develop divergent personalities because each child strives to compete for parents' attention and must find a unique way to do so. The oldest child may adopt parental standards and achieve within the established values of the parents' generation, but the next child needs to find a different strategy. Sulloway (1996) hypothesizes that scientists who are later-born children are predisposed to rebellion, leading revolutions against the establishment. Two famous later-born scientists exemplify this strategy: Copernicus rebelliously argued that the earth revolves around the sun, a revolutionary idea when the earth was considered flat, and Darwin's theory of evolution challenged the idea that humans are entirely separate from animals. One psychobiographer chose to interpret the life of Francis Galton from an Adlerian perspective in part because that youngest child's scientific theories of hereditary genius seemed to illustrate his position as a youngest child and also to compensate for his own inferiority feelings about intelligence and reproduction (Fancher, 1998). Also confirming the idea that later-born children challenge the status quo, later-born college students were found more likely to have been arrested in support of a labor dispute at a Kmart Distribution Center than were firstborns (Zweigenhaft & von Ammon, 2000).

Although Sulloway presents impressive historical data to support his thesis—he is, after all, an historian and not a psychologist—history is subject to multiple interpretations, and his work has been criticized as scientifically biased to support his theory, selecting from among the myriad of data those that fit his predictions (e.g., Dalton, 2004; Townsend, 2000). In addition, research using self-report questionnaires casts doubt on his theory. An analysis of sociological data does not support these predictions. Social attitudes on such issues as conservatism, support for authority, and tough-mindedness are not predicted by birth order (Freese, Powell, & Steelman, 1999). Similarly, a study of undergraduates found no association between birth order and various personality measures (Guastello & Guastello, 2002). Another study analyzed birth-order effects among adopted children, enabling the researchers to look at biological birth order separately from the sibling position in which a child was raised into an adoptive family. In this study, Sulloway's predictions were not supported. So, although some biographical data and selected empirical research support the hypothesized rebelliousness of later-born siblings, it would be premature to accept the idea as proven. One issue to consider, as this controversy continues, is that the confirming evidence comes largely from reports of behavior, whereas questionnaire measures of personality do not support the hypotheses. (Recall that projective tests often do not correlate with questionnaire measures of personality, either, although they may be superior in predicting behavior.) In addition, we must realize that birth order is only one factor that influences people's behavior. It has to be considered in the context of the particular family, as Adler cautioned, and in the social context with all of its complexities; overly simplified hypotheses may be easy to understand and exciting to ponder, but they do not do justice to human complexities (Rosenberg, 2000).

Psychological Health

Adler's description of psychological health was phrased in more social, less purely individual terms than Freud's intrapsychic model.

SOCIAL INTEREST

Humans are inherently social. A sense of community is essential for human survival. The more **social interest** the person has, the more that person's efforts are channeled into shared social tasks, rather than selfish goals, and the more psychologically healthy that person is. The concept of social interest helps correct for the overemphasis on individualism in Western culture (Richardson & Guignon, 1988; Triandis, 1989).

social interest innate potential to live cooperatively with other people

In German, Adler used the term *Gemeinschafsgefühl*, which has been translated as "social interest," "social feeling," "community feeling," and so forth. Perhaps "feeling of community" is the best description for social interest (Stein & Edwards, 1998). It should not be confused with extraversion. Nor is it simply the need for affection, although Adler did use that concept earlier in the development of his theory (Ansbacher & Ansbacher, 1956, p. 40). Social interest is the innate potential to live cooperatively with other people. It enables the person to value the common good above personal welfare. It is not a matter of sacrificing self for other, though. Social connections with others and individual development each enhance the other (Guisinger & Blatt, 1994; Stein & Edwards, 1998). Although social interest is an inborn potential, it must be fostered. In early life, the mother serves as the "first bridge to social life" (p. 372) by being trustworthy and loving, but not possessive, and by fostering cooperative interactions with others. As a felt experience, social interest has been described as a distinct subjective condition as real as anger or grief (Hanna, 1996).

We can compare Adlerian social interest with *empathy*, defined as concern for the experience of another person. Empathic individuals respond emotionally, sharing the joys and sorrows of others. They are also cognitively concerned, trying to imagine situations from the perspective of others. According to Carolyn Zahn-Waxler and Marian Radke-Yarrow (1990), empathy is found in children as young as 2 years old. They respond to others' emotions even earlier, from the first few days after birth (Zahn-Waxler et al., 1992). These observations are consistent with Adler's view of social interest as an inborn potential. Research also confirms Adler's warning that social interest must be nurtured. Empathy declines under adverse conditions, including parents who are depressed or in conflict with one another or who mistreat the child (Zahn-Waxler & Radke-Yarrow, 1990). It provides the basis for moral development, according to a theory proposed by Martin Hoffman (1975). Without social interest, life seems purposeless and the self feels empty (Richardson & Manaster, 1997). Social interest may even contribute to spirituality by encouraging a loving attitude toward all of life (Eriksson, 1992).

Social interest is a core concept for Adler, who says that all neurosis stems from inadequate social feeling. An extreme lack of social feeling occurs in schizophrenia, according to Adler; schizophrenics are very low in empathy, as one might expect (Zahn-Waxler & Radke-Yarrow, 1990). Criminals, too, lack sufficient social interest, as do those who commit suicide (Adler, 1937/1958). Roy Baumeister (1990, p. 107) lists "feelings of responsibility and fear that others will disapprove" as one of several deterrents to suicide. Such feelings correspond closely to Adler's concept of social interest, although Baumeister's theory is considerably broader. Some studies report that females have higher social interest than males (Joubert, 1989b; Kaplan, 1991). This is consistent with reports of higher empathy in females, evidenced as early as age 1 to 2 years (Zahn-Waxler et al., 1992).

Groups, as well as individuals, can be described by social interest or the lack thereof. Lack of social interest leads "groups and nations toward the abyss of self-extermination" (Ansbacher & Ansbacher, 1956, p. 449). Societies impede the development of social interest through the glorification of war, the death penalty, physical punishment and abuse, and failure to provide humane conditions for all classes and categories of people (Adler, 1936/1964, pp. 280–281). Healthy social institutions, including religious institutions, teach "Love thy neighbor" (Ansbacher & Ansbacher, 1956, p. 449), thus fostering social interest. Researchers have compared Adler's concept of social interest to the teachings of various religious traditions, including Christianity, Judaism, and Buddhism (Kaplan & Schoeneberg, 1987; Leak, Gardner, & Pounds, 1992; Watts, 1992).

Adler assessed social interest through interview and history (see Table 4.3). Since then, researchers have developed several self-report scales to measure social interest. The most commonly used are the Social Interest Scale (Crandall, 1975/1991) and the Social Interest Index (Greever, Tseng, & Friedland, 1973). Unfortunately, however, five self-report measures of social interest have low correlations (averaging 0.08 to 0.22) (Bass et al., 2002).

Although not all measures of social interest yield the same results, several studies confirm theoretical predictions. People who score high on social interest score low on narcissism (Miller et al., 1987), low on alienation (Leak & Williams, 1989), and low on MMPI scales that indicate maladjustment (Mozdzierz, Greenblatt, & Murphy, 1988). They score high on the Affiliation, Nurturance, and Aggression scales of the Personality Research Form and on scales of the Life Styles Inventory thought to be associated with self-actualization (Leak et al., 1985). Students high in social interest have attitudes toward love that emphasize companionship ("storge") and reject egocentric game playing ("ludus") (Leak & Gardner, 1990). Some studies report that measures of social interest correlate with prosocial behaviors: volunteering in legal advocacy agencies (but not other kinds) (Hettman & Jenkins, 1990) and having more friends (Watkins & Hector, 1990).

High scorers are also more satisfied with their jobs (Amerikaner, Elliot, & Swank, 1988), suggesting that they have dealt better with this life task than have those low in

---

TABLE 4.3   Examples of Questions Suggested by Adler to Measure Psychological Health in Children

1. Did the child make friends easily, or was the child unsociable, perhaps tormenting people and animals?

2. Is the child inclined to take the lead or to stand aside?

3. Does the child have rivalries with siblings?

4. Does the child interrupt other children's games?

5. In what respect is the child discouraged? Does the child feel slighted? Does the child react favorably to appreciation and praise?

6. Does the child speak openly of a lack of ability, of "not being gifted enough" for school, for work, for life? Has the child expressed thoughts of suicide?

(Adapted from Adler, 1936/1964, pp. 299–307.)

social interest. They are also healthier. Perhaps they can resist the effects of negative life experiences and hassles on health. In a correlational study, though, it is also possible that causality is reversed, that is, that health leads to social interest (Zarski, Bubenzer, & West, 1986).

Overall, researchers in the area of social interest are convinced that this construct is useful and Adler's conceptualization was sound, although they have some unresolved questions about its measurement.

THE THREE TASKS OF LIFE

Life in society requires cooperation and, therefore, social interest. This is readily seen by considering the three fundamental tasks of life: work, love, and social interaction. Success in all three areas is evidence of mental health.

Work

Work refers to having an occupation, earning a living by some socially useful job. Division of labor is a means for organizing cooperation among people in providing for the necessities and wants of everyone. Any occupation that contributes to the community is desirable. When children describe their occupational aspirations, they provide insight into their whole style of life. Occupational aspirations may change as the child learns more about reality. This, said Adler, is a healthy sign (Ansbacher & Ansbacher, 1956, pp. 430–431). Criminals fail in the work task (as also in the other two tasks), and this failure can usually be observed from early in their life histories (p. 412).

Love

The love task refers to sexual relationships and marriage between men and women, including the decision to have children (Ansbacher & Ansbacher, 1956, p. 432). Adler recommended monogamy as the best solution to the love task (p. 132) and remonstrated against premarital sex, saying it detracts from "the intimate devotion of love and marriage" (p. 434). Someone who falls in love with two people simultaneously is, by doing so, avoiding the full love task (p. 437). Today, Adlerians voice less traditional views about the love task, including the view that love tasks can be met in homosexual as well as heterosexual relationships (Schramski & Giovando, 1993).

Adler thought that many sexual dysfunctions and perversions, and even disinterest in one's partner, stem from lack of social interest rather than from purely physical causes. Equality between men and women is essential for success in the task of love, according to Adler. Successful love affirms the worth of both partners. In other ways, his attitudes sound less modern. Although he did suggest that birth control and abortion should be a woman's choice (Ansbacher & Ansbacher, 1956, p. 434), Adler criticized the decision of some women not to have children. It is interesting to speculate how he would resolve this issue now, on an overpopulated planet. Is there a conflict between his recommendation of parenthood as the norm of healthy individual choice and the need for humankind to maintain a habitable planet?

Social Interaction

The task of social interaction refers to "the problems of communal life" (Adler, 1936/1964, p. 42)—that is, social relationships with others, including friendship. Unlike the two preceding tasks, social interaction is not one that Freud listed when he described a healthy person as someone who can "love and work." People perform this life task better if they are high in social interest. All social relationships should be based on a strong sense of social interest, which prevents a self-centered, narcissistic attitude.

All three tasks are interrelated. None can be solved in isolation. None can be solved adequately unless there is sufficient social interest. If there is a fourth life task, Adler suggested, it is art (Bottome, 1947, p. 81). He even hinted at a fifth task, spirituality (Mosak & Dreikurs, 1967/2000).

Interventions Based on Adler's Theory

Like all psychoanalysts, Adler discussed the role of formal psychotherapy in overcoming psychological distress. Some specific intervention is often needed to overcome developmental errors from childhood. We do not learn readily from life itself because we interpret life experience according to the often erroneous directions of our style of life (Adler, 1921/1927, p. 222).

Besides formal psychotherapy, the principles of individual psychology can be applied in other interventions as well, such as schools, making Adler a pioneer in modern community psychology interventions. In fact, Adler thought psychologists should advocate social change to prevent mental disorders (Ansbacher, 1990a).

SCHOOL

Adler's ideas have been applied in schools, where they are called *individual education* (Clark, 1985). Adler thought that schools had great potential for personality growth, but only if traditional authoritarian methods were replaced by practices designed to foster social interest. Corporal punishment, according to Adler, is ineffective and "shows that the educator is not very eager to be interested in the particular child's problems" (1998, p. 125). It may stop misbehavior for a time but does not change the child's style of life. Teachers should encourage cooperation among students. When problems arise—even problems traditionally handled by teachers, such as laziness—the students should discuss them. The problem child should not be personally identified but will learn from the group (Ansbacher & Ansbacher, 1956, p. 402). Adler recommended having classmates help teach slower learners. He favored clubs. He thought it was a good idea for a teacher to have the same students for several years to permit more effective intervention in personality development.

Adler taught his concepts of individual psychology in over 30 Child Guidance Clinics that he established in Vienna during the 1920s. In these clinics, he interviewed a problem child in front of an audience of teachers, using this demonstration to instruct them in the principles of his psychology. These clinics were well attended and successful, but in the early 1930s political changes in Europe forced their closure. During the years the clinics operated, court cases of juvenile delinquency and neuroses in Vienna substantially decreased (Bottome, 1947, p. 51).

The city of Vienna also established a public Individual Psychology Experimental School as a place for Adlerian ideas to be applied. The original school operated only from 1931 to 1934 when, along with the Child Guidance Clinics, it was closed. Demonstration schools were reopened after World War II (Ansbacher & Ansbacher, 1956, p. 404). Subsequent generations of Adlerians have continued to develop new intervention programs in schools (Corsini, 1989; Dinkmeyer, McKay, & Dinkmeyer, 1982; Morse,

Bockoven, & Bettesworth, 1988; Turk, 1990). School interventions are not, of course, always based on Adlerian principles; sometimes they deal with issues that are not intrinsically related to school problems, such as helping children whose parents are divorced (Grych & Fincham, 1992). Many of the democratic practices in education that focus on individual student needs, though, stem historically from Adler's influence, even if that connection has been forgotten (Pryor & Tollerud, 1999).

THERAPY

Adlerian therapy aims to change thinking, emotion, and behavior through progressive stages (see Table 4.4). Because individual psychology believes all personality failures result from a lack of social interest, Adlerian therapy aims to foster the individual's social interest, that is, to take over a maternal function (Ansbacher & Ansbacher, 1956, p. 119). His approach appeals to some feminists because it emphasizes freedom and purposefulness, and in addition because Adler often emphasized the importance of gender equality (Morris, 1997). In stressing the social nature of the human, Adlerians have also been highly involved in family therapy (Dinkmeyer & Dinkmeyer, 1989; Sherman & Dinkmeyer, 1987).

TABLE 4.4   Stages of Adlerian Psychotherapy

1. **Empathy and Relationship Stage:** Offer empathy to the client and establish a working relationship.

2. **Information Stage:** Gather information about the problem and the client's past history, early memories, and current functioning.

3. **Clarification Stage:** Clarify the client's core beliefs about self, others, and life.

4. **Encouragement Stage:** Encourage the client for progress.

5. **Interpretation and Recognition Stage:** Interpret the client's behavior and help the client recognize and reconsider his or her fictional goal.

6. **Knowing Stage:** The client knows more about his or her behavior and goals, without so much therapist interpretation.

7. **Emotional Breakthrough Stage:** Old, unhealthy patterns are expressed in emotional breakthroughs and are replaced by new ones, sometimes aided by imagery and role play.

8. **Doing Differently Stage:** The client gradually starts to behave differently in life.

9. **Reinforcement Stage:** The client begins paying more attention to other people's needs, not only his or her own.

10. **Social Interest Stage:** A feeling of community is strengthened.

11. **Goal Redirection Stage:** The client finds a new goal to strive toward.

12. **Support and Launching Stage:** The client is striving toward the new goal in a spirit of social interest.

(Prepared from Stein, 1988, and Stein & Edwards, 1998.)

The client's style of life is assessed at the beginning of therapy, often in the first consultation. It provides a context for understanding the patient's specific problem. By asking a patient, "What would you do if you had not got this trouble?" Adler was able to determine what the patient was trying to avoid (Bottome, 1947, p. 148). The style of life provides a general strategy for avoiding life's tasks, and the specific problem that the patient presents in therapy is often intertwined with the style of life. The symptom, therefore, cannot be removed without modifying the latter.

Changing to a healthier lifestyle necessarily involves increased social interest. Benefits are expected not only for the client but also for others. Tinling (1990) suggested that the mother of a female incest victim unwittingly contributed to the family problem by an unhealthy, victimized style of life; an increase in her social feeling would make incest less likely in the family. (Obviously, this is only one perspective on a complex issue; the mother is not the only one to blame or to change.)

Adler (1921/1927, pp. 30–31) gave the example of a man unrealistically distrustful that his fiancée would break their engagement. The man's first memory (always an important clue to the style of life) was of being picked up by his mother in a crowd but then put down again so his younger brother could be picked up. This memory suggests a lifestyle based on a sense of not being the favorite one, which of course would contribute to later doubts about the earnestness of his intended spouse.

Dreams are interpreted as indicators of the individual's unique style of life. For Adler, the key to understanding dreams is the emotion they create. These emotions are the ones needed by the dreamer to solve life's current problems. Adler cited the example of a man who dreamed that his wife had failed to take care of their third child, so the child became lost. He awoke feeling critical of his wife. This emotion, although triggered by a dream that was not accurate in terms of facts, was the emotion the man needed to deal with his own dissatisfaction with his marriage (Ansbacher & Ansbacher, 1956, p. 361). Dreams in this approach are not concerned so much with the unconscious, but instead with present problems in life, in relationship to the person's style of life (Lombardi & Elcock, 1997).

Like Freud, Adler considered it important to understand childhood experiences. Unlike Freud, he tried to avoid developing a transference relationship, which he thought unnecessarily complicates and prolongs psychotherapy. Adlerian therapy is typically brief (Ansbacher, 1989). Adler thought that treatment should show some success within the first 3 months. As in schools, Adler recommended avoiding an authoritarian approach in analysis. The therapist can coach and advise, but it is the effort and courage of the client that determine whether there will be a favorable outcome (cf. Sizemore & Huber, 1988). Adler explicitly encouraged his patients to accept this responsibility. He did not intimidate patients with his scholarly expertise, preferring to talk to them "like an old grandmother," according to a close friend (Bottome, 1947, p. 41).

Adlerian therapy aims to enhance the self-esteem of the client. A sense of inferiority is the basis of all unhealthy styles of life. Adler said, "I believe that by changing our opinion of ourselves we can also change ourselves" (Bottome, 1947, p. 83). He, of course, challenged the false self-presentations of his patients, but he did his "unmasking . . . with love" (p. 42). The atmosphere in Adler's sessions was supportive, with minimal tension.

Adler used humor frequently. He told his biographer that a chapter should be titled "Therapeutic Jokes" (p. 119). Other therapists have agreed that humor can be effective in therapy (Baker, 1993; Richman, 2001). Perhaps surprisingly, a formal therapeutic intervention using humor has been devised (Prerost, 1989) although not within a specifically Adlerian context. One therapist recounts the case of a 71-year-old man suffering from depression that stemmed from the death of a friend. A joke helped him overcome his own death anxiety. The joke tells of a physician who is trying, at the request of a patient's family, to inform his elderly patient that he had won $10 million in the lottery. The family was afraid that the shock of the good news would kill the old man. As the joke goes, "The doctor visited and said to the old man, 'What would you say if I told you that you won ten million dollars?' 'I would give half of it to you,' said the old man. And the doctor dropped dead" (Richman, 2001, p. 421).

Adler respected the religious commitments of his patients. He regarded the idea of God as a reflection of the basic human striving for a better condition. The patients' religious commitments could facilitate this growth process. (Freud, in contrast, emphasized the defensive function of religion.) Many therapists avoid following up on mention of religion by their patients, thus conveying the idea that religious experience should not be a part of the therapeutic experience; in doing so, they miss therapeutic opportunities (LaMothe, Arnold, & Crane, 1998).

Physical as well as psychological improvement can result from therapy. Adler (1936/1964, p. 78) reported relief from "nervous headaches, migraine, trigeminal neuralgia, and epileptiform attacks" in cases not caused by organic problems. He claimed that even thyroid problems can respond to psychological treatment (p. 181), but he also recognized genuine physical components to disease and insisted that psychotherapists be supervised by a physician if they were not medically trained themselves. Yet psychological factors are involved in many physical conditions.

Adler's claims of the importance of psychological factors in physical disease are more persuasive because of his many years as a general practitioner preceding his specialization in psychiatry. He had a reputation for competence as a medical doctor (Bottome, 1947). We may regard Adler as a pioneer in the field of psychosomatic medicine, which recognizes psychogenic components in many physical illnesses. Recent research demonstrates that psychological factors often contribute to physical health and disease (e.g., Kiecolt-Glaser et al., 2002; L. Sperry, 1992). Longitudinal research shows that pessimistic explanatory style predicts poor health some decades later (Peterson, Seligman, & Vaillant, 1988); it seems reasonable to interpret the health-producing optimistic explanatory style as indicating Adlerian creative striving.

Adler was innovative in his therapeutic techniques. He once got a patient whose speech was extremely slow, the result of depression, to speak more quickly simply by continuing to ask questions at a normal pace, whether the patient had finished responding yet or not (Dreikurs, 1940/1982). A behaviorist might say that he succeeded by withholding reinforcement (attention) for slow speech. Indeed, Adlerian therapy is essentially a primitive version of operant conditioning (Pratt, 1985). It seems reasonable, then, that behavioral psychology journals have been the major publication outlet for studies of one of Adler's emphases, parenting training programs (Wiese & Kramer, 1988). Behavioral psychologists have also applied their methods to interventions in schools, another of Adler's primary efforts (Kratochwill & Martens, 1994; Repp, 1994). Behaviorists emphasize that it is important to analyze the function of a student's undesirable behavior, for example, by seeing how it influences the teacher (Taylor & Romanczyk, 1994). This functional analysis is essentially the same as Adler's advice to see what the problem child is trying to achieve. Adlerian therapists continue to explore new techniques, including hypnosis as a means of producing lifestyle change (Fairfield, 1990). W. O'Connell (1990) claims that his "natural high" approach encompasses Adlerian principles of holism and transcendence.

Adler's therapeutic approach has been compared to various modern therapeutic techniques, including family systems approaches (Carich & Willingham, 1987), cognitive therapy (Elliott, 1992), and rational-emotive therapy (Ellis, 1989). These developments in therapy and in school psychology show that psychologists have judged Adler's ideas positively.

Summary

- Adler emphasized conscious striving and the *creative self*, in contrast to Freud's unconscious determinism.
- He described the fundamental motivation to strive from a *felt minus* to a *felt plus*.
- A person with an *inferiority complex* feels overcome by a lack of worth and ceases striving.
- In this striving, a person is guided by *fictional finalism*, the image of the goal.
- Adler viewed personality as a unity.
- A person's unique *style of life* is evidenced by *early memories*.
- Although he thought of each person as unique, Adler listed types of *mistaken styles of life*: ruling type, getting type, and avoiding type of person.
- In contrast, a healthy style of life is *socially useful*.
- Parents contribute to unhealthy styles of life by *pampering* or *neglecting* their children.
- Adler's theory has inspired training programs for parents.
- *Family constellation*, particularly birth order, influences personality development.
- Adler regarded the second-born position as the most desirable, although research does not generally confirm his prediction of higher achievement for this sibling position.
- *Social interest* is the key factor in psychological health.
- A healthy person succeeds in *three tasks of life*: work, love, and social interaction.
- Adler intervened in schools to deal with problem children.
- Adlerian therapy supports self-esteem and aims to change the style of life to a socially useful one.
- Adler described physical as well as psychological benefits of therapy.

Thinking about Adler's Theory

1. Does Adler's emphasis on social aspects of personality problems have any particular relevance for today's problems?
2. How would Adler's concept of inferiority apply to people with physical disabilities?
3. Do you think Adler's use of the term *masculine protest* would be relevant to today's society?
4. Imagine that you are writing open-ended questions for a research project. What would you ask to assess people's fictional finalisms?
5. Do you have a first memory or an early memory that can be interpreted from the perspective of Adler's theory?
6. Families have changed considerably in many cultures, including the United States and other Western cultures and China (with its one-child policy), since Adler wrote his theory. What additions to his theory would you suggest to describe the effects of these changes?
7. Western cultures emphasize individualism. How might Adler's theory help correct the problems created by too much self-interest?

Study Questions

1. How does Adler's approach to personality differ from that of Freud?
2. Describe a person's fundamental motivation, according to Adler. List five terms he used in the development of this idea.
3. Distinguish between a feeling of inferiority and an inferiority complex.
4. Explain the term *fictional finalism*. Give an example.
5. Explain how early memories are a key to personality.
6. What is a style of life? List three mistaken styles of life. What did Adler call a healthy style of life?
7. How do parents contribute to their children's development of unhealthy styles of life?
8. Explain how children can be helped by sending their parents to parenting training programs.
9. Discuss Adler's theory of the relationship between birth order and personality. What did he expect would be the typical personality of the oldest child? The middle child? The youngest child?
10. Describe how Adler's predictions hold up or are refuted by research on birth order.
11. Describe Sulloway's proposal about birth order and scientific revolution.
12. Explain what is meant by social interest.
13. List and explain the three tasks of life.
14. Describe Adler's interventions in schools.
15. Describe Adlerian therapy. Why is it compared to family therapy rather than to individual approaches?

5

Erikson
Psychosocial Development

Chapter Overview

Preview: Overview of Erikson's Theory
The Epigenetic Principle
The Psychosocial Stages
The Role of Culture in Relation to the Psychosocial Stages
Racial and Ethnic Identity
Gender
Research on Development through the Psychosocial Stages
Toward a Psychoanalytic Social Psychology
Summary

ILLUSTRATIVE BIOGRAPHY

Mahatma Gandhi

Mahatma Gandhi was a political figure in 19th- and 20th-century India when it was ruled by Great Britain. He used nonviolent civil disobedience methods that became a model for other civil rights activists, including Dr. Martin Luther King, Jr. in the United States. Erik Erikson, an influential theorist in the fields of psychohistory (Pois, 1990) and psychobiography, himself wrote a book analyzing our chosen personality. His analysis, *Gandhi's Truth: On the Origins of Militant Nonviolence*

(1969), won the Pulitzer Prize and the National Book Award.

Mohandas Gandhi (later called Mahatma, or "Great Soul," to honor his spiritual leadership) was born in 1869 in Porbandar, India, to the young fourth wife of a government administrator. His father's family had for several generations served in government offices under British rule. According to the custom of his large Hindu family, Gandhi was married at age 13. This was a real marriage not simply an engagement. Mohandas and his bride, Kasturba, lived together and conceived a child, who died shortly after birth. This occurred not long after the death of Gandhi's father, when Gandhi was 16. Later, he and Kasturba had four sons.

Gandhi went to England for his law degree. Members of his caste refused approval of this voyage. In leaving he became an outcast, and he was socially ostracized on his return. His mother's consent was given only after he had vowed to abstain from meat, wine, and women, to honor their religious values. Gandhi promised, not confessing that he had already eaten meat with a friend. He honored this vow to his mother in England and thereafter. He refused meat, meat broth, eggs, and milk, even when doctors prescribed them. There was one exception, when he took goat's milk, legalistically reasoning that he had only promised his mother to refrain from the milk of cows and buffalo; but he regretted this action. In fact, his dietary restrictions expanded, so for the most part his diet consisted of fruit and nuts.

After earning his law degree, and because it was difficult to become established as a lawyer in India, Gandhi worked as a lawyer for an Indian company in South Africa. There he was the victim of racial prejudice. Indians were resented for their economic threat and different living habits. Despite his British education, he was refused hotel accommodation and first-class train travel. Once he was beaten simply for being in the wrong neighborhood. Gandhi embarked on a larger career of public service and political activism on behalf of Indians in South Africa and, later, in India. He was influential in ending the practice of indentured labor. In India he founded an ashram (a traditional communal living arrangement) and boldly admitted an Untouchable family to membership, violating traditional Indian caste practices. He organized Indian fabric workers against exploitation by their employers, and he organized a civil disobedience movement to protest the British salt tax. He went to prison for his political activities. He fasted as a political strategy. Throughout, he was guided by the principle of *ahimsa*, or nonviolence, which seeks to do no harm to others (Gandhi, 1957, p. 349; Teixeira, 1987). He died by assassination in 1948, having lived to see India become independent from Britain.

Much in the life of this world-renowned leader invites psychoanalytic analysis. His focus on concerns of eating and of sexual restraint match two of the areas of libidinal focus named by Freud. The other, anality, is also well represented in Gandhi's autobiography, with frequent concern about unsanitary conditions, which were prevalent in India because of lack of indoor plumbing. To explain how his personal psychology relates to the public and political arenas, however, it is necessary to theorize beyond the psychosexual level, as Erikson's psychosocial theory does.

Description

Erikson's theory is a developmental theory, so it describes people by identifying the developmental stages that a person has experienced and suggesting whether growth was healthy or left personality flaws.

Mahatma Gandhi lived a long life, and so his personality could be shaped at all the stages of development that Erikson theorized. The major legacies of this development left him with a fervent commitment to a cause (as a result of identity development) but enduring difficulties about trust or nurturance and love for women. Erikson describes a personality he admires, but he describes it as also flawed.

Development

Erikson's theory describes eight stages of development that occur in sequence throughout life (with a ninth stage added later, based on his ongoing revision of his model). Each has a typical age of occurrence, and Erikson believed these stages to occur in all cultures.

The concept of identity is the central concept by which Erikson attempted to understand Gandhi. Identity is the developmental issue that prevails in adolescence, according to Erikson's theory, and it typically involves career choice and racial identity issues. Erikson interpreted Gandhi's period of study in England as a psychosocial moratorium, a period in which he explored his identity, which is (in Erikson's theory) a healthy process. Gandhi's connection with his mother and with his Indian motherland was strengthened by his dietary vows, which continued to remind him of that connection in a strange land. (How ironic that Gandhi's return to India brought him the news of his mother's death.) Deciding to study law provoked identity issues beyond those of career choice because it required travel to another country. His caste was opposed, fearing the corrupt practices of the British (eating meat, drinking wine, etc.), and it banned him as an outcast when he left. His minority position in London made him more conscious of his identity as an Indian, which he explored by reading about vegetarianism and Hinduism. The greatest identity crisis, however, Erikson (1969, p. 47) suggested, occurred when Gandhi was first in South Africa. He was thrown off a train and denied the right to travel first class, despite having purchased a ticket, because of his race. His reaction was to devote himself to the political and religious cause of improving the life of poor Indians, solidifying his identity. There were strongly proud and egoistic aspects to this identity. Gandhi repeatedly showed that he felt himself to be the only one who could achieve what needed to be done (p. 166), a belief that had its origins in his position as a favored youngest child in his family, one who, unlike his older brothers, largely escaped his father's punitiveness.

Adjustment

In Erikson's theory, each stage of life involves a conflict between a positive pole and a negative pole, and if it is resolved in a healthy way, the ego is strengthened. His theory proposes that the identity crisis, if resolved well (as Gandhi did), enhances the ego with a stronger ability of what Erikson called "fidelity," by which he meant being faithful to a cause. Thus Gandhi's fidelity to the cause of nonviolent protest is a consequence of his identity development.

Although Erikson admired Gandhi, he also criticized him. Erikson suggested that Gandhi did not come to a good resolution of the next two crises, which typically occur in young adulthood (the crisis of intimacy) and middle adulthood (the crisis of generativity). Gandhi gave no evidence of psychological intimacy with his wife, Kasturba. According to Erikson (1969, p. 121), "one thing is devastatingly certain: nowhere is there any suggestion of joyful intimacy." On the contrary, Gandhi deplored his sexuality and treated Kasturba and other women as temptresses who aroused regrettable desires. He decided to give up a sexual relationship with her to devote himself to "higher" purposes (and, incidentally, to prevent conceiving another child) without consulting her. Erikson says that Gandhi retained "some vindictiveness, especially toward woman as the temptress" (p. 122) and even sadism (p. 234).

Cognition

Like Freud, Erikson believed the major determinants of personality are not conscious. They are the result of conflict through the various stages of development.

In Gandhi's personality, the development of his identity as a lawyer and an Indian obviously had some conscious components. He could answer the question "Who am I?" appropriately and in ways that others would accept. The unconscious legacy of this stage, though, was the energy for his political efforts on behalf of Indians, and later of other oppressed people. His failure to resolve the young adult stage of intimacy adequately left more harmful unconscious tendencies to blame women for problems. Erikson relates one incident on Gandhi's commune as an example. Gandhi directed young boys and girls to bathe together, which to his naive surprise led to difficulties, with some boys making fun of the girls. (The details are not given in Gandhi's autobiography.) Gandhi's solution was to cut the girls' beautiful long hair, thus making them less tempting to the boys, a solution Erikson criticizes (1969, pp. 237–242). Had Gandhi been able to confront his own sexuality more honestly, rather than denying it, he would not have, in essence, punished the girls for their sexual attractiveness.

Society

Erikson (1958b, 1975) proposed that the conflicts of the person studied in psychobiography are not simply individual conflicts but represent the conflicts of the society in which the person lived. Thus the study of individuals can enlighten historical understanding. Erikson (1969) honored Gandhi immensely for his work toward a more inclusive identity for humankind. Gandhi worked to rise above the divisions that mark what Erikson called *pseudospeciation* by envisioning a more inclusive identity. Pseudospeciation is inherent in colonialism, causing individuals to experience "guilt and rage which prevent true development" (p. 433). At this particular historical moment, then, Gandhi's solution to the problem of identity moved history forward toward greater peace and mutual acceptance.

Erikson (1969, p. 251) expressed disappointment that Gandhi's sexual renunciation would be unacceptable to the West, limiting the extent to which we could learn from his nonviolent political activism. Yet we must ask whether Erikson's stages can be used, without modification, as universal developmental standards against which to evaluate someone from such a different culture. To criticize Gandhi for failing to develop all the strengths that Erikson outlined presumes that the strengths described in this Western theory apply even in the quite different cultures of the East. Is intimacy, as described in the context of a tradition of Western love and marriage, to be expected in a culture where child marriage, arranged by parents, is accepted? Or would such a psychological interpretation be parallel to the economic colonialism against which Gandhi and other leaders of his country struggled so courageously?

Biology

Erikson's theory builds on that of Freud, presuming that biology provides the motivation for personality through the psychosexual stages that Freud outlined. However, biological sexual energy is not the only consideration. He also describes psycho*social* issues.

The linking of biological and social issues is evident in Gandhi's life in issues around eating and his mother. Gandhi sought throughout his life for a relationship to take the place of the disrupted relationships with his mother and father (cf. Muslin & Desai, 1984, who interpret this in terms of Kohut's psychoanalytic theory). Erikson (e.g., 1969, p. 110), noted that Gandhi did not acknowledge the extent of his dependency on his mother, even refusing to cry openly when he learned of her death. His dietary restrictions served as a ritual to preserve hope, the ego strength that develops in the first developmental stage, in which there is a conflict between trust and mistrust (p. 154). This stage corresponds to Freud's psychosexual oral stage. The extremity of his dietary control suggests unacknowledged mistrust. His dietary restrictions can be considered obsessive (p. 152), though Erikson observes that "it is always difficult to say where, exactly, obsessive symptomatology ends and creative ritualization begins" (p. 157). Surely the physicians who urged Gandhi unsuccessfully to drink milk or eat meat for his health would have agreed with the more negative clinical label.

Final Thoughts

Erikson's approach to psychobiography emphasizes the immediacy of the person's experience, rather than reducing the person to an object to be studied with distancing and judgmental categories (Schnell, 1980). His theory calls attention to the cultural context in which an individual develops, and it acknowledges the potential of an individual, through a highly developed ego, to have an impact on culture (Nichtern, 1985), as Mahatma Gandhi did.

Erikson's (1969) respect for Gandhi and openness to learn from him is clear in his book. He even addressed a long section to Gandhi in conversational terms, as "I" to "you" (pp. 229–254). Erikson described his task in his analysis of Gandhi: "to confront the spiritual truth as you have formulated and lived it with the psychological truth which I [Erikson] have learned and practiced" (p. 231). Erikson suggested that psychoanalysis is the counterpart of Gandhi's philosophy of *Satyagroha* (roughly meaning "passive resistance" or "militant nonviolence") "because it confronts the inner enemy nonviolently" (p. 244). Lorimer (1976) suggested that Erikson's objectivity was compromised in this analysis. Erikson (1975), though, did not claim objectivity, instead characterizing his method as "disciplined subjectivity" (p. 25). It requires undistorted self-knowledge, which can be achieved by undergoing psychoanalysis.

Besides Gandhi, Erikson wrote brief analyses of George Bernard Shaw (1968), and of Hitler and Gorky (1963). His 1958 book, *Young Man Luther*, analyzed the Protestant theologian Martin Luther and triggered renewed interest in applying psychological theory to historical figures, becoming a model for psychohistorians (Coles, 1970; Hutton, 1983; Schnell, 1980). It helped move psychohistory beyond a stage in which it documented the impact of great people on history and toward a stage that recognizes the mutual influences of psychological and historical forces (Fitzpatrick, 1976).

Preview: Overview of Erikson's Theory

Erikson's theory has implications for major theoretical questions, as presented in Table 5.1. Like other psychoanalytic theories, it proposes a number of broad concepts for understanding individual development that are not easily captured within the precise hypothesis-testing language of verifiable scientific research. Some of his concepts, however, have been operationally defined in ways that have generated many research studies. Most notably, identity statuses are measured by interview and questionnaire. Additionally, many empirical studies of racial and ethnic identity have been conducted, testing theoretical ideas proposed by others but owing an historical debt to Erikson's ground-breaking work on identity. Some of his clinical observations, such as differences between the play constructions of boys and girls, have not been confirmed by carefully controlled scientific studies. His theory is more comprehensive than classical psychoanalysis because it encompasses cultural phenomena. Erikson's theory has been applied to therapy with children and adolescents. It also has suggested attention to identity issues in a multicultural society.

TABLE 5.1	Preview of Erikson's Theory
Individual Differences	Individuals differ in their ego strengths. Males and females differ in personality because of biological differences.
Adaptation and Adjustment	A strong ego is the key to mental health. It comes from good resolution of eight stages of ego development, in which positive ego strengths predominate over the negative pole (trust over mistrust, etc.).
Cognitive Processes	The unconscious is an important force in personality. Experience is influenced by biological modes, which are expressed in symbols and in play.
Society	Society shapes the way in which people develop. (Thus the term *psychosocial* development.) Cultural institutions continue to support ego strengths (religion supports trust or hope, and so forth).
Biological Influences	Biological factors are important determinants of personality. Sex differences in personality are strongly influenced by differences in the "genital apparatus."
Development	Children develop through four psychosocial stages, each of which presents a crisis in which a particular ego strength is developed. Adolescents and adults develop through four additional psychosocial stages. Again, each involves a crisis and develops a particular ego strength.

Each person develops within a particular society, which, through its culturally specific patterns of child rearing and social institutions, profoundly influences how that person resolves conflicts. The ego is concerned not only with biological (psychosexual) issues but also with interpersonal concerns, which Erikson termed **psychosocial**. His emphasis on culture was Erikson's fundamental contribution to psychoanalysis.

In contrast to Freud's emphasis on sexuality, Erikson (1968) proposed that the prime motivation for development is social:

> Personality . . . can be said to develop according to steps determined in the human organism's readiness to be driven toward, to be aware of, and to interact with a widening radius of significant individuals and institutions. (p. 93)

Many psychologists consider social determinants to be important. Perhaps that explains the widespread popularity of Erikson's theory of psychosocial development.

psychosocial
Erikson's approach to development, offered as an alternative to Freud's psychosexual approach

BIOGRAPHY OF ERIK ERIKSON

Erik Homberger Erikson (as we now call him) was born near Frankfurt, Germany, in 1902. He was raised by his mother, who was Jewish and of Danish ancestry, and his stepfather, a Jewish pediatrician whom his mother met when she sought care for 3-year-old Erik.

Erikson did not know that he was conceived ille-
gitimately. He believed his stepfather was his biological
father and was given his last name, Homberger
(Hopkins, 1995). His biological father, a Danish
Protestant, had left his mother before he was born, but
Erikson's mother had not told him about his biological
father. Erikson was not accepted as fully Jewish because
of the physical appearance that was the legacy of his
Danish parents: tall, blond, and blue eyed. Yet he had
not been raised to think of himself as Danish. This
somewhat confused background contributed to his own
keen interest in identity, as he later said.

Erikson studied art and wandered through Europe in
his youth, trying to become an artist (Wurgaft, 1976). In
a job found at the suggestion of a friend, Erikson taught
art to children of Freud's entourage. His future wife,
Joan Serson, was studying to be a psychoanalyst, and
she introduced him to psychoanalysis. Interestingly, in
later years he became the psychoanalyst and she the artist. They had three children,
including a son who unfortunately suffered from Down syndrome. Erikson was analyzed
by Freud's daughter, Anna, for 3 years and was recruited as an analyst, a "lay analyst"
because of his nonmedical training. In 1933 he and his wife left Germany, where anti-
Semitism was becoming increasingly overt. They went briefly to Denmark, his ancestral
home, and then to the United States. To mark the identity change in his own life, he took
Erikson as a last name at this time.

Although he had no college degree (not even an undergraduate degree), Erikson
became a child analyst and taught at Harvard. There he was affiliated with the Harvard
Psychological Clinic, under Henry Murray (E. H. Erikson, 1963), and was the author of the
Dramatic Productions Test in Murray's (1938, pp. 552–582) well-known research report,
Explorations in Personality. He was part of a team that prepared an analysis of enemy
leader Adolf Hitler for the American government during World War II. He also was affili-
ated, at various stages in his career, with the Yale Institute of Human Relations, the
Guidance Study in the Institute of Human Development at the University of California at
Berkeley, and the Austen Riggs Center in western Massachusetts. Besides his clinical and
developmental studies, his association with anthropologists permitted him to observe
development among two Native American cultures, the Sioux at Pine Ridge, South
Dakota, and the Yurok, a California fishing tribe.

At the time that Erikson was a professor of psychology and a lecturer in psychiatry at the
University of California at Berkeley, the United States was undergoing a wave of concern
about communist infiltration in the schools. Faculty members were required to sign an additional loyalty oath, besides the oath in which they had already routinely pledged to uphold
the national and state constitutions. Erikson and several others refused, resulting in their
dismissal, although this was overturned in court. Because Erikson had become a U.S. citizen as an adult and conducted psychological research for the government during World
War II, analyzing Hitler's speeches and conducting other war-related studies (Hopkins,
1995), he cannot be accused of anti-Americanism for his stance. In explaining his action,
Erikson (1951b) argued that the anticommunist hysteria that had prompted the requirement
of a loyalty oath was dangerous to the university's historical role as a place where truth and
reason can be freely sought and where students learn critical thinking. Undoubtedly, his
experience with German nationalism under the Nazis figured in his position.

Although he considered himself a Freudian, Erikson proposed many theoretical innovations that emphasized the ego and social factors. Most notably, he theorized that ego development continues throughout life. In his 80s, he and his wife were still active, interviewing a group of elderly Californians to learn more about this last stage of life (Erikson, Erikson, & Kivnick, 1986). He died at a nursing home in Massachusetts on May 12, 1994, at the age of 91. After his death, his daughter published a critical memoir of her parents, faulting them for hiding from her the secret of a brother institutionalized with Down syndrome, whom they told her had died (Bloland, 2005).

Although Erikson had "neither medical training nor an advanced degree of any kind except a certificate in Montessori education" (Fitzpatrick, 1976, p. 298), his contributions to psychology have transformed our understanding of human development and of the relationship between the individual and society. Erikson's most important contribution was a model of personality development that extends throughout the life span. The concept of ego development, although by no means exclusively Erikson's contribution (cf. Hartmann, 1958; Loevinger, 1966), has become much more popular as a consequence of his work.

The Epigenetic Principle

epigenetic principle the principle for psychosocial development, based on a biological model, in which parts emerge in order of increasing differentiation

Erikson (1959) based his understanding of development on the **epigenetic principle**: "that anything that grows has a *ground plan,* and that out of this ground plan the *parts* arise, each part having its *time* of special ascendancy, until all parts have arisen to form a *functioning whole*" (p. 52). This principle applies to the physical development of fetuses before birth (where it is easy to visualize the gradual emergence of increasingly differentiated parts) and to the psychological development of people throughout their lives. For a whole, healthy ego to develop, several parts must develop sequentially. These parts are the ego strengths Erikson identified, and they develop in stages. At each stage, there is a particular focus on one aspect of ego development: trust in infancy, autonomy in toddlerhood, and so on.

The Psychosocial Stages

Erikson (1959) reinterpreted Freud's psychosexual stages, emphasizing the social aspects of each. Further, he extended the stage concept throughout life, giving a life-span approach to development in a classic set of eight stages. Erikson's first four stages correspond to Freud's oral, anal, phallic, and latency stages. Freud's genital stage encompasses Erikson's last four stages (see Table 5.2). Later (Erikson, 1997), his wife and collaborator Joan Erikson described a ninth stage that they had been discussing when her husband died.

Each stage involves a crisis, and conflict centers on a distinctive issue. A crisis can be thought of as a developmental turning point (Erikson, 1964). Just as, biologically, heart, arms, and teeth develop most rapidly at different times, so it is with the ego strengths of hope, will, purpose, and so on. Out of each crisis emerges an ego strength, or "virtue," that corresponds specifically to that stage (Erikson, 1961). The strength then becomes part of the repertoire of ego skills for the individual throughout life. Each strength develops in relation to an opposite, or negative, pole. The strength of trust develops in relation to

TABLE 5.2   Stages of Psychosocial Development Compared with Psychosexual Development

Psychosocial Stage	Comparable Psychosexual Stage and Mode	Freudian Stage	Age
1. Trust vs. Mistrust	Oral-Respiratory, Sensory-Kinesthetic (Incorporative Mode)	Oral	Infancy
2. Autonomy vs. Shame, Doubt	Anal-Urethral, Muscular (Retentive-Eliminative Mode)	Anal	Early childhood
3. Initiative vs. Guilt	Infantile-Genital Locomotor (Intrusive, Inclusive Mode)	Phallic	Play age
4. Industry vs. Inferiority	Latency	Latency	School age
5. Identity vs. Identity Diffusion	Puberty	Genital	Adolescence
6. Intimacy vs. Isolation	Genitality	Genital	Young adulthood
7. Generativity vs. Self-Absorption	Procreativity	Genital	Adulthood
8. Integrity vs. Despair	Generalization of Sensual Modes	Genital	Old age

(Adapted from *The Life Cycle Completed: A Review,* by Erik H. Erikson, by permission of W. W. Norton & Company, Inc. Copyright © 1982 by Rikan Enterprises Ltd.)

mistrust, the strength of autonomy in relation to shame, and so forth. In healthy development, there is a larger ratio of the strength (the syntonic element) than of the weakness (the dystonic element). Furthermore, these strengths develop in relationships with significant people, beginning with the mother and expanding more broadly throughout life (see Table 5.3).

Although each ego skill has its period of greatest growth at a distinct period in life, earlier developments pave the way for that strength, and later developments can to some extent modify an earlier resolution (see Figure 5.1). For example, being a grandparent offers many older people a second chance at developing the ego strength (generativity) that had its primary focus of development in the previous stage (Erikson, Erikson, & Kivnick, 1986).

Each of these stages must be considered not simply from the individual's point of view but also from a social point of view. An adolescent's identity develops in relationship to the older generation's ideals and values. Significant others, as members of society, are inextricably involved at each stage. Infant development implies not only the infant's needs but also the complementary need of the mother to nurture (Erikson, 1968; Erikson, Erikson, & Kivnick, 1986). Erikson's theory offers a rationale for enhancing programs that increase intergenerational contact (ReVille, 1989).

TABLE 5.3   Strengths Developed at Each Stage of Psychosocial Development and Their Social Context

Psychosocial Stage	Strength	Significant People	Related Elements in Society
1. Trust vs. Mistrust	Hope	Maternal person	Cosmic order (e.g., religion)
2. Autonomy vs. Shame, Doubt	Will	Parental persons	Law and order
3. Initiative vs. Guilt	Purpose	Basic family	Ideal prototypes (e.g., male, female, socioeconomic status)
4. Industry vs. Inferiority	Competence	Neighborhood, school	Technological order
5. Identity vs. Identity Diffusion	Fidelity	Peer groups and outgroups, Models of leadership	Ideological worldview
6. Intimacy vs. Isolation	Love	Partners in friendship, sex, competition, cooperation	Patterns of cooperation and competition
7. Generativity vs. Self-absorption	Care	Divided labor and shared household	Currents of education and tradition
8. Integrity vs. Despair	Wisdom	Mankind and My kind	Wisdom

(Adapted from *The Life Cycle Completed: A Review,* by Erik H. Erikson, by permission of W. W. Norton & Company, Inc. Copyright © 1982 by Rikan Enterprises Ltd.)

STAGE 1: TRUST VERSUS MISTRUST

trust the positive pole of the first psychosocial stage

During the first year of life, the infant develops basic **trust** and basic **mistrust**. Basic trust is the sense that others are dependable and will provide what is needed, as well as the sense that one is trustworthy oneself (Erikson, 1968, p. 96). It is based on good parenting (traditionally, Erikson emphasized good mothering), with adequate provision of food, caretaking, and stimulation. The infant approaches the world with an *incorporative* mode, taking in not only milk and food but also sensory stimulation, looking, touching, and so on. This begins relatively passively at first but becomes increasingly active in later infancy. This stage is one of mutuality, not simply of receiving; the infant seeks the mother's care and seeks to explore the environment tactilely, visually, and so on.

mistrust the negative pole of the first psychosocial stage

To the extent that the infant does not find the world responsive to his or her needs at this stage, basic mistrust develops. Some mistrust is inevitable because no parental nurturing can be as reliable as the umbilical connection. Some amount of basic mistrust is even necessary for later adaptation. The world the individual confronts after infancy will not always be trustworthy, and the capacity to mistrust will be required for realistic adaptation. In a healthy resolution of the crisis between basic trust and basic mistrust, trust predominates, providing strength for continued ego development in later stages. In adult life, the ability to trust others, even though they could betray that trust, is an important quality that contributes to adjustment and happiness (Jones, Couch, & Scott, 1997).

STAGE 2: AUTONOMY VERSUS SHAME AND DOUBT

autonomy the positive pole of the second psychosocial stage

During the second year of life, the toddler develops a sense of **autonomy**. This period includes toilet training, which Freud emphasized, but also broader issues of control of the musculature in general (becoming able to walk well) and control in interpersonal

Figure 5.1 The Epigenetic Chart

		1	2	3	4	5	6	7	8
Old Age	VIII								INTEGRITY vs. DESPAIR
Adulthood	VII							GENERATIVITY vs. STAGNATION	
Young Adulthood	VI						INTIMACY vs. ISOLATION		
Adolescence	V	Temporal Perspective vs. Time Confusion	Self-Certainty vs. Self-Consciousness	Role Experimentation vs. Role Fixation	Apprenticeship vs. Work Paralysis	IDENTITY vs. IDENTITY CONFUSION	Sexual Polarization vs. Bisexual Confusion	Leader- and Followership vs. Authority Confusion	Ideological Commitment vs. Confusion of Values
School Age	IV				INDUSTRY vs. INFERIORITY	Task Identification vs. Sense of Futility			
Play Age	III			INITIATIVE vs. GUILT		Anticipation of Roles vs. Role Inhibition			
Early Childhood	II		AUTONOMY vs. SHAME, DOUBT			Will to be Oneself vs. Self-Doubt			
Infancy	I	TRUST vs. MISTRUST				Mutual Recognition vs. Autistic Isolation			

Adapted from *Identity, Youth and Crisis* by Erik H. Erikson, by permission of W. W. Norton & Company, Inc. Copyright © 1968 by W. W. Norton and Company, Inc.

relationships. The toddler experiments with the world through the modes of *holding on* and *letting go.* He or she requires the support of adults to develop, gradually, a sense of autonomy. If the toddler's vulnerability is not supported, a sense of **shame** (of premature exposure) and a sense of doubt develop. As in the first stage, a higher ratio of the positive pole (autonomy) should prevail, but some degree of shame and doubt are necessary for health and for the good of society.

shame the negative pole of the second psychosocial stage

STAGE 3: INITIATIVE VERSUS GUILT

Four- and 5-year-old children face the third psychosocial crisis: **initiative** versus **guilt**. The child can make choices about what kind of person to be, based in part on identifications with the parents. Erikson agreed with Freud that the child at this age is interested in sexuality and in sex differences and is developing a conscience (superego). The young child acts in an intrusive mode, physically and verbally intruding into others' space. The child approaches the unknown with curiosity. For the boy, this intrusion is congruent with early awareness of sexuality, described by Freud's phallic stage. For the girl, awareness of her different physical sexual apparatus is significant at this stage, according to Erikson, who claimed that children reflect these different sexualities in their play (described in a later section). If the stage is resolved well, the child develops more initiative than guilt.

initiative the positive pole of the third psychosocial stage

guilt the negative pole of the third psychosocial stage

STAGE 4: INDUSTRY VERSUS INFERIORITY

industry the positive pole of the fourth psychosocial stage

inferiority the negative pole of the fourth psychosocial stage

The remainder of childhood, until puberty, is devoted to the school-age task of stage 4: the development of a sense of **industry**. The negative pole is **inferiority**. The child at this stage "learns to win recognition by *producing things*" (Erikson, 1959, p. 86). A child who works at tasks until completion achieves satisfaction and develops perseverance. The quality of the product matters. If the child cannot produce an acceptable product or fails to obtain recognition for it, a sense of inferiority prevails. Teachers are especially important at this stage because much of this development occurs at school.

STAGE 5: IDENTITY VERSUS IDENTITY CONFUSION

identity sense of sameness between one's meaning for oneself and one's meaning for others in the social world; the positive pole of the fifth psychosocial stage

Erikson's best known concept is the identity crisis, the developmental stage of adolescence. In this time of transition toward adult roles, the adolescent struggles to attain a sense of **identity**. Erikson (1968) defined the sense of ego identity as "the awareness of the fact that there is a self-sameness and continuity to the ego's synthesizing methods, the *style of one's individuality,* and that this style coincides with the sameness and continuity of one's *meaning for significant others* in the immediate community" (p. 50). The task is to find an answer to the question "Who am I?" that is mutually agreeable to the individual and to others. Earlier identifications with parents and other role models provide a basis, and these identifications become increasingly evident in the defensive behaviors of adolescents (Cramer, 2001), but the adolescent must develop a personal identity that goes beyond these identifications. Attaining identity can be described as the development of a personal narrative or life story; adolescents, unlike children, are capable of the abstract thinking about their values that can give meaning to their life stories (Barresi, 1999; Habermas & Bluck, 2000). An occupation is often an important core of identity, and exploring different career possibilities is part of the process of achieving an identity, especially in the college populations that are typically studied.

identity confusion the negative pole of the fifth psychosocial stage

negative identity identity based on socially devalued roles

identity foreclosure inadequate resolution of the fifth psychosocial stage, in which an identity is accepted without adequate exploration

Identity confusion occurs if a coherent identity cannot be achieved in a reasonable time. No one identity prevails as the core. Another undesirable resolution of the identity crisis is the development of a **negative identity**, that is, an identity based on undesirable roles in society, such as the identity as a juvenile delinquent. When young offenders are imprisoned with criminals, this mixing of the generations may encourage the development of such a negative identity (Erikson, 1962/1988). Culture, unfortunately, provides clear images of such negative identities, making them appealing for those who find that a positively valued identity seems unattainable (Erikson, 1968). Finally, **identity foreclosure** (discussed later in the chapter) occurs if commitment is made too quickly, without adequate exploration.

moratorium period provided by society when an adolescent is sufficiently free of commitments to be able to explore identity; also, a stage of identity development when such exploration is occurring, before identity achievement

Society can assist the healthy resolution of this stage by providing a **moratorium**, a period when the adolescent is free to explore various possible adult roles without having the obligations that will come with real adulthood. Having the opportunity to study various fields, even to change majors, in college before settling down to a career commitment provides a moratorium. Erikson stressed the importance of exploration, fearing that too early a commitment to a particular identity would risk a poor choice. Further, it would not provide an opportunity to develop the ego strength of this stage: *fidelity,* which he defined as "the ability to sustain loyalties freely pledged in spite of the inevitable contradictions of value systems" (Erikson, 1964, p. 125). Before identity resolution, the adolescent questions and experiments; afterward, the adult "has made commitments and is striving to honor them" (Newman & Newman, 1988, p. 551).

STAGE 6: INTIMACY VERSUS ISOLATION

The first of three stages of adulthood is the crisis of **intimacy** versus **isolation**. Psychological intimacy with another person cannot occur, according to Erikson, until individual identity is established. Intimacy involves a capacity for psychological fusion with another person, whether a friend or lover, secure that individual identity will not be destroyed by the merger. This intimacy is selective. Erikson (1959) referred to *distantiation* as the counterpart of intimacy, defining it as "the readiness to repudiate, to isolate, and, if necessary, to destroy those forces and people whose essence seems dangerous to one's own" (pp. 95–96). The adult who does not satisfactorily resolve this crisis remains self-absorbed and isolated.

intimacy the positive pole of the sixth psychosocial stage

isolation the negative pole of the sixth psychosocial stage

Intimacy increases during the early adult years (Reis et al., 1993). For many young adults, this crisis is experienced through the social role of marriage, although marriage is no guarantee that the crisis will resolve successfully. Furthermore, psychological intimacy is not the same as sexual intimacy, and a spouse is not the only significant other who may play a role in resolving this stage.

STAGE 7: GENERATIVITY VERSUS STAGNATION

The seventh task is to develop the ego strength of **generativity**, "the interest in establishing and guiding the next generation" (Erikson, 1959, p. 97). Current researchers have offered this description of a high level of generativity: *"Generative* individuals are highly involved in their work and the growth of young people, and are concerned about broader societal issues. They are tolerant of different ideas and traditions, and able to strike a balance between care and consideration for the self and for others" (Bradley & Marcia, 1998, p. 42). Generativity is often but not necessarily expressed through the role of parenting. To be a teacher or a mentor may substitute. Failure to develop optimally in this stage leaves a person with a sense of **stagnation**, not being able to be fully involved in caring for others in a nurturing way.

generativity the positive pole of the seventh psychosocial stage

stagnation the negative pole of the seventh psychosocial stage

STAGE 8: INTEGRITY VERSUS DESPAIR

The task of old age is to resolve the crisis of integrity versus despair. The sense of **integrity** means being able to look back on one's own life and decide that it is meaningful as it has been lived, without wishing that things had been different. Periods of life when important transitions and choices were made are salient in this reminiscence. Among famous psychologists, according to researchers who analyzed their autobiographies, retrospection focuses on the college and graduate school years, which launched their professional lives (Mackavey, Malley, & Stewart, 1991). Not all focus is on the past, however; people at this stage who are successfully accomplishing the task of integrity also believe they have learned lessons that they can now apply (Brown & Lowis, 2003). The elderly, whose bodies of course are less robust than in the past, report to researchers that they feel less in control (Geppert & Halisch, 2001), so integrity is about the present, not only the past. In the absence of a sense of integrity, **despair** occurs instead, as well as unwillingness to accept death.

integrity the positive pole of the eighth psychosocial stage

despair the negative pole of the eighth psychosocial stage

A NINTH STAGE: DYSTONIC RESURGENCE OR GEROTRANSCENDENCE

After his death, Erik Erikson's wife Joan described the ideas that they had been developing in their studies of the very old. Their observations and personal experience with aging suggested that people in their 80s and 90s face ego developmental issues beyond the integrity versus despair crisis (Brown & Lowis, 2003; Erikson, 1997). This period of life does not pose a new crisis comparable to those of the traditional eight stages. Rather, the very old return to the issues of earlier stages, confronting more directly the negative poles of those stages (mistrust, shame, guilt, etc.) as their frail selves and losses of loved ones no longer sustain the level of strength attained in their younger years. Shame, for example, may grow as a result of forgetfulness, incontinence, and other age-related declines. This stage is not simply disengagement from life, although people do typically withdraw from the busy activities of earlier stages. Now, the elderly struggle to accept death and kinship with those who have passed on. It is a time of spiritual, often but not always religious, reflection and growth. When the outcome is positive, grappling with the dystonic elements (mistrust, shame, etc.) as demanded by the physical declines of life but courageously maintaining the positive syntonic elements, it brings peace of mind and a concern with cosmic rather than material values, and it may be called **gerotranscendence**, or, as creative Joan Erikson playfully suggests with her image of dancing, *gerotranscendance* (Erikson, 1997).

gerotranscendence the ninth stage of psychosocial development, referring to the very elderly

The Role of Culture in Relation to the Psychosocial Stages

The stages themselves, Erikson said, are universal, but each culture organizes the experience of its members. The way people resolve each stage internalizes the culture's particular characteristics. Culture not only provides the setting in which psychosocial crises are encountered and mastered: It also provides continuing support for the ego strengths when they are threatened in later life. Each stage has its own cultural institution to support continuation of the strength that emerges at that stage. Erikson (1963) listed these relationships and observed,

> [J]ust as there is a basic affinity of the problem of basic trust to the institution of religion, the problem of autonomy is reflected in basic political and legal organization and that of initiative in the economic order. Similarly, industry is related to technology; identity to social stratification; intimacy to relationship patterns; generativity to education, art, and science; and integrity, finally, to philosophy. (pp. 278–279)

Influence goes both ways. The individual is supported by the social institutions. In addition, "each generation can and must revitalize each institution even as it grows into it" (p. 279).

THE FIRST STAGE: RELIGION

hope fundamental conviction in the trustworthiness of the world; the basic virtue developed during the first psychosocial stage

Positive developments in the first psychosocial stage leave one with the capacity for **hope**. Erikson (1959) was respectful of religion and spirituality; he observed that "religion through the centuries has served to restore a sense of trust at regular intervals in the form of faith while giving tangible form to a sense of evil which it promises to ban" (p. 65). In this way, religion supports the ego developments of the first stage of psychosocial development: basic trust and basic mistrust. Other cultural supports for these ego strengths may substitute for religion. Erikson listed "fellowship, productive work, social action, scientific pursuit, and artistic creation" as sources of faith for some people (p. 64).

THE SECOND STAGE: LAW

Positive developments in the second psychosocial stage leave one with the capacity for **will**, or will power, which develops out of the toddler's struggle between autonomy and shame. Institutional support for will is found in the law, which legitimizes and provides boundaries for an individual's autonomy. The law also provides punishments. In the past, punishment sometimes consisted of public shaming. Those caught misbehaving could be locked in a pillory, hands and head immobilized in a wooden frame, exposed to public scorn. Nowadays, jail and/or a fine are the expected punishments. Some have suggested that judges be permitted to order public shaming as modern punishment, but the idea is controversial (Massaro, 1997).

> **will** conviction that what one wants to happen can happen; the basic virtue developed during the second psychosocial stage

THE THIRD STAGE: IDEAL PROTOTYPES

The third stage of psychosocial development leaves the child with the basic virtue of **purpose**. The corresponding element of the social order for this stage consists of the *ideal prototypes* of society. Erikson said that primitive cultures provide a small number of unchanging prototypes that are close to the economy of the tribe—for example, the buffalo hunter of the Sioux. These provide straightforward models for children to channel their initiative in play (e.g., playing at buffalo hunting with a toy bow and arrow) and for adults to channel and support their initiative in the serious versions of these roles. In contrast, in civilized cultures, prototypes are numerous, fragmented, and changing. What roles shall children play that will continue to be significant in their adulthood?

> **purpose** orientation to attain goals through striving; the basic virtue developed during the third psychosocial stage

Americans value socioeconomic status, and they respond with guilt when it is threatened, as third-stage development would predict (cf. Erikson, 1959, p. 28). Such socioeconomic status is abstract and fragmented, however, compared with the whole person of the buffalo hunter prototype. Another ideal prototype that Erikson discussed is the military prototype (p. 27), which channels the aggressive ideals important at this stage (1968, p. 122). Sex roles, central to psychoanalytic theory at this age, provide ideal prototypes to support the ego strength of initiative.

THE FOURTH STAGE: TECHNOLOGICAL ELEMENTS

The sense of **competence** that develops in the fourth stage is supported by technological elements in culture, particularly the way that labor is divided among people. Opportunities unfairly limited by discrimination are particularly harmful to the developments of this stage, as is an overemphasis on work as a basis of identity (cf. Erikson, 1968, pp. 122–128).

> **competence** sense of workmanship, of perfecting skills; the basic virtue developed during the fourth psychosocial stage

THE FIFTH STAGE: IDEOLOGICAL PERSPECTIVES

The virtue of **fidelity**, which emerges from the fifth psychosocial stage, enables the individual to be faithful to an ideology. Thus the ideological perspectives of a society support, sometimes even exploit, this ego strength. The cause may be political, social, or occupational, or it may take another form. Erikson (1968) outlined a complex relationship between developmental stages and cultural change:

> **fidelity** ability to sustain loyalties freely pledged; the basic virtue developed during the fifth psychosocial stage

> It is through their ideology that social systems enter into the fiber of the next generation and attempt to absorb into their lifeblood the rejuvenative power of

youth. Adolescence is thus a vital regenerator in the process of social evolution, for youth can offer its loyalties and energies both to the conservation of that which continues to feel true and to the revolutionary correction of that which has lost its regenerative significance. (p. 134)

This stage permits reassessing the role of technology and finding its appropriate limits (cf. Côté & Levine, 1988c; Erikson, 1968, p. 259). Another potential is the creation of a more inclusive identity that can encompass both the racial identity and the American identity of black Americans (Erikson, 1968, p. 314). Because the individual and society are interrelated, identity cannot be solved wholly at an individual level. However, the personal identity developments of especially developed people, such as Mahatma Gandhi, may help point the way in which society should be directed.

THE SIXTH STAGE: PATTERNS OF COOPERATION AND COMPETITION

love ability to form an intimate mutual relationship with another person; the basic virtue developed during the sixth psychosocial stage

Successful resolution of the sixth stage brings the ego strength that Erikson called a capacity to **love**. This strength is supported and channeled through what Erikson (1982) termed "patterns of cooperation and competition" (p. 33). For many, marriage serves this role, although cultures may provide other forms besides the nuclear family for shaping the sense of community. It can also be developed in homosexual relationships (Sohier, 1985–1986) and in nonsexual relationships.

THE SEVENTH STAGE: CURRENTS OF EDUCATION AND TRADITION

care ability to nurture the development of the next generation; the basic virtue developed during the seventh psychosocial stage

The strength of **care** develops in the seventh stage of development. In this stage one plays the nurturing role of the older generation toward the younger generation, for example, as parents, teachers, and mentors. Societal involvement is clearly evident in such institutionalized forms as school systems. Erikson suggested that the psychosexual procreative urge (which he felt that Freud did not emphasize sufficiently) can be channeled into career paths like teaching if, by choice or for other reasons, an individual does not become a parent. Even people who are biological parents can channel generativity impulses into their careers. According to one analysis, the famous architect Frank Lloyd Wright expressed his generativity more fully as an architect than toward his biological children, whom he neglected (de St. Aubin, 1998).

THE EIGHTH STAGE: WISDOM

wisdom mature sense of the meaningfulness and wholeness of experience; the basic virtue developed during the eighth psychosocial stage

Given demographic changes, culture is becoming more aware of its oldest members. What does society offer them for their continuing psychological development, and what do they have to offer society? The ego strength developed during old age is **wisdom**, described by Erikson as "informed and detached concern with life itself in the face of death itself" (1982, p. 61). The individual, ideally, becomes connected with the "wisdom of the ages," which seeks to understand the meaning of individual and collective human life. This interest is expressed in religious and/or philosophical areas. Elderly Californians interviewed by Erikson and his wife and a younger collaborator generally expressed this development by saying, in essence, "There are no regrets that I know of for things that have happened or that I've done" (Erikson, Erikson, & Kivnick, 1986, p. 70). Unfortunately, for many of the elderly, reminiscing about their lives brings regret, instead, which is not healthy (McKee et al., 2005).

These relationships, which Erikson proposed between individual ego development and cultural supports (religion, law, etc.), have been neglected in empirical research. His suggestion that personality and culture are intertwined is widely applauded, but it should be explored in more detail in research as well. Cross-cultural research is a logical approach. Any theory that attempts to discuss cultural factors risks bias because of the experience and values of the theorist, and Erikson's list of ego strengths has been criticized as reflecting middle-class Western ideology (Henry, 1967).

Different societies practice different **rituals**, each supporting the ego strengths of its members in a unique way. Prayer and atonement—for example, in the ritual Sun Dance of the Dakota Sioux—support "the paradise of orality," the trust of the first stage (Erikson, 1963, p. 147). Cultural rituals tend to enhance the ego strengths necessary for the specific needs of the culture. For example, the Yurok, who depend on catching abundant salmon during the brief period in the year when the fish can be netted in the river, practice rituals that develop oral character traits, including strict eating rituals. These prepare them for the unpredictability of each salmon catch. Such cultural rituals are adaptive.

> **ritual** cultural practice or tradition that supports ego strengths

Individuals may also develop their own, often unhealthy, rituals for maintaining certain ego strengths (e.g., obsessive hand-washing). When such rituals stagnate, defending the ego rather than strengthening it, Erikson (1977) called them **ritualisms**.

> **ritualism** an individual's maladaptive repetitive actions intended to make up for weak aspects of ego development

Racial and Ethnic Identity

Erikson remarked that identity first became noticeable to him in his psychiatric practice when he immigrated to the United States. People here, coming from diverse backgrounds (especially in large urban centers), must define themselves anew, as Erikson did himself when he changed his name. This issue is particularly salient during adolescence. A study of Chinese immigrants to the United States, for example, found that those who came alone (without family) during adolescence emphasized their Chinese cultural orientation more than did those who came with family earlier in life or those who came when they were older when identity issues were not so acute (Ying, 2001). Even among those who have not themselves immigrated, racial and ethnic minorities have a distinctiveness to integrate in their identity formation. Erikson (1968, pp. 295–320), writing in the 1960s, observed that black Americans had particular difficulties with identity because of society's unresponsiveness to them.

Other theorists propose that individuals have various ways of resolving this mixed message that comes from society. They may submerge their ethnicity and instead choose *assimilation* into the mainstream culture. They may emphasize their ethnicity. Or they may become bicultural or multicultural, celebrating unique and beneficial aspects of their ethnic background(s) and the mainstream culture, perhaps in different social groupings or contexts, without choosing one over the other, although this is more difficult to achieve (LaFromboise, Coleman, & Gerton, 1993).

Ethnic identity may be defined as "an enduring, fundamental aspect of self that includes a sense of connection in a social group . . . or ethnic group, and the attitudes and feelings associated with that membership" (Yeh & Hwang, 2000). It is not simply an individual accomplishment but inherently involves connection with the group. Most researchers have emphasized the individual accomplishment aspect of identity, which may be especially misleading for understanding identities in cultures that emphasize interdependence, such as Hispanic, Filipino, African, Chinese, and Indian cultures (Yeh & Hwang, 2000).

Racism in society poses obstacles to the identity development of minorities but also opportunities. When others see the person's race through stereotyped eyes, they fail to validate the individuality of the person, which can contribute to an "invisibility syndrome" that interferes with a developing sense of self (Franklin, 1999). In the past, cross-cultural studies have reported lower identity statuses among some national and ethnic groups. For example, black adults in South Africa scored lower on identity, compared to whites (Ochse & Plug, 1986), and Mexican Americans were reported more often as identity-foreclosed than Anglo-Americans on ideological, but not interpersonal, identity (Abraham, 1986). With cultural change, however, minorities have more support for their identity formation. Black South Africans, for example, have more recently scored higher than whites on identity, probably as a consequence of more visible and respected black role models and a greater pride in their culture (Thom & Coetzee, 2004).

Since Erikson's introduction of identity as a seminal idea, others have expanded the concept to better understand racial and ethnic identities. A person may develop a strong identification with his or her ethnic, racial, or cultural group: an *ethnic identity* or *gender identity*. This identification can provide the basis of strength and enhanced self-esteem, helping the individual reject racism, instead of internalizing racism into his or her own identity when it is confronted in society (Alvarez & Helms, 2001; Helms, 1990; Miller, 1999). Thus ethnic identity fosters psychological well-being and protects against depression and loneliness (Roberts et al., 1999). For those who can develop identities in both the majority culture and the minority culture—for example, mainstream American and a Native American tribe—self-esteem and psychological well-being tend to be even higher than those who develop identities in either culture alone or neither one (Moran et al., 1999). It may also, however, have adverse consequences on self-esteem because the group may be evaluated either positively or negatively (cf. Deaux, 1993). The impact of minority status is positive when ethnic identity involves a strong sense of membership with the ethnic group and when the group is positively valued by the larger culture (Phinney, 1990, 1991), or when the group has developed a sense of its own positive worth. This can happen when the language, traditions, and values that are characteristic of that group are respected. Today, difficulties of minority adolescents in resolving identity issues are sometimes addressed through special programs to enhance minority identity (Spencer & Markstrom-Adams, 1990).

Recent history has recorded changes in the public image of racial minorities in the United States, including the adoption of *African American* in place of *black* as a preferred designation to emphasize culture rather than race (Philogene, 1994; T. W. Smith, 1992). Especially in pluralistic societies, many individuals can claim legitimate connections with more than one cultural group. Many Native Americans ("Indians") have Indian ancestors from different tribes, and they also have African American and other ancestral lines (Mihesuah, 1998). Mixed ancestry can produce conflict, particularly if one of these identifications is devalued. In seeking a personal identity that is positively valued, adolescents of mixed heritage may devalue one ancestral root and in the process devalue part of themselves. Because identity resolution occurs in dialogue between the individual and the society, such conflicts and suppressions are more likely when society devalues minority groups. Another source of difficulty comes when society lumps together groups that, to their members, are seen as distinct: Chicano, Mexican, and Cuban as Hispanic, for example. For those who can resolve the value conflicts that occur when they belong to two different cultures, there may even be psychological advantages compared to those with only mainstream, monocultural experience; for example, they may pursue achievement opportunities in the mainstream culture while finding support from the extended family and sense of community that characterize various ethnic minorities (LaFromboise et al., 1993).

The process of resolving identity for minority groups involves additional considerations than for mainstream youth because the collective group identity must be established and also integrated with one's personal identity. Perception of their parents' beliefs about ethnicity influences adolescents as they forge their own ethnic identity (Okagaki & Moore, 2000). Along the way, the minority group identity may cause stress—for example, when a Jewish young person confronts anti-Semitism—as well as ultimately providing coping resources (Dubow et al., 2000). Stage descriptions of this process have been theorized. According to Cross (1991), the first stage is *pre-encounter:* A black youth gives little thought to race issues or may even judge minority status to be an obstacle, taking over the white culture's devaluation of blacks. In the second stage, *encounter,* the person confronts his or her blackness and begins to develop a black identity. This stage may be precipitated by personal experience of discrimination or by historical events such as the death of a black leader. The third stage, *immersion-emersion,* is a time of considerable involvement in black culture: clothing, speech, holidays, and so on. In the final stage, *internalization,* the person becomes inwardly confident and secure about his or her black identity. African American college students who are at a more advanced level of these stages are also more mature in the psychological defense mechanisms that they report using, supporting the theory that racial identity contributes to ego identity (Nghe & Mahalik, 2001). Research on South African blacks suggests that this model would need to be modified to accurately describe those who have experienced a recent history of apartheid—for example, the low awareness of race in Cross's early pre-encounter stage may not occur in the more racially charged atmosphere of South Africa (Hocoy, 1999).

Various ethnic groups may go through similar stages although facing greater difficulty if a sufficient cultural group is unavailable to provide supportive traditions for identification, as is the case for many Native American groups (Mihesuah, 1998). And it is not only nonwhites whose race plays a role in identity formation; white racial identity, too, occurs (Clark & O'Donnell, 1999). However, we should not simply take for granted that theoretical ideas about identity can be transposed cross-culturally. Many psychologists in personality and other fields have explored differences between *individualism* and *collectivism* cross-culturally. Identity is inherently an individualistic issue. This implies that the task of forming an identity that is considered healthy, evaluated according to the individualistic Western theory of Erikson, would be particularly problematic for adolescents with mixed cultural affiliations, one individualistic (such as white American) and another collectivistic (such as Latina or Asian). For individuals, the developmental task is to integrate the relevant social identities or categories, as well as more individual traits and interests, into a unified individual identity (Deaux, 1993).

Ethnic identity is a mixture of various components, too. For example, the ethnic identities of Chinese Americans include various factors that can be teased apart by statistical analysis: Ethnic Friendship and Affiliation, EthnoCommunal Expression, Ethnic Food Orientation, and Family-Collectivism; individuals may accept one or more of these factors more than others (Kwan, 2000). We can best understand what it means to have a particular ethnic identification if we listen to how people describe their own group. For example, in one study Mexican Americans emphasized their own greater protective closeness to their children, contrasting what they perceived to be greater distancing in Anglo-American and African American families (Niemann et al., 1999).

Erikson envisioned each generation's grappling with identity to be a force that changes the world, as well as changing the individual. We anticipate, then, that among these adolescents with mixed allegiances are some who will help psychology, and society, to become more inclusive of everyone's perspectives (Sampson, 1993). This inclusive goal is in the spirit of Erikson's expressed values. A clear statement of his ethical judgments is given in his discussion of **pseudospeciation** (Erikson, 1968, 1985). This term refers to the exaggerated sense of many groups, especially national and ethnic groups, that they are different from others, as though they were a separate species. It is, of course, prejudicial and has been described as "the arrogant placing of one's nation, race or culture, and/or society ahead of those of others" (Hanson, 2001). In times of primitive cultures, when intergroup contact was less than it is today, that was not such a dangerous belief. In the nuclear age, though, Erikson warned that such beliefs increase tensions and the threat of nuclear war. As a solution, he suggested the development of a broader, more inclusive sense of identity that would include all of the human species with its diverse members, overcoming tendencies toward pseudospeciation.

Since Erikson's analysis, historical changes have brought increasing globalization to our planet because of population patterns and communication through television and more recently the Internet. As a consequence, traditional cultures are no longer isolated. Increasing numbers of people are connected with more than one ethnic or racial culture and with a *global culture* (Arnett, 2002).

Gender

Erikson, like the other theorists we have considered so far, has been criticized for not adequately understanding women (e.g., Gergen, 1990). Despite his awareness of the social context of development, Erikson nonetheless agreed with the psychoanalytic proposition that the personality differences between males and females are fundamentally determined by biology. Sensitive as he was to the importance of culture, he underestimated its role in creating (and potentially modifying) differences between males and females. Let us consider children at play and adolescents resolving identity issues.

CHILDREN'S PLAY

Erikson's description of children's play illustrates his biological orientation. Erikson (1951a, 1968, 1975) observed 300 boys and girls, ages 10 to 12, over a period of 2 years. He provided a variety of toys, including human figures and blocks, and asked each child to construct an exciting scene, like one from a movie. Girls, he reported, built interior peaceful scenes with elaborate doorways. Boys built high towers and portrayed more movement and activity, sometimes leading to the collapse of the structures. Erikson (1965) interpreted these differences as projections of the children's own genital apparatus: Enclosures symbolized the womb; towers, the penis. Womanhood, from childhood on, emphasizes the "inner space," leaving the "out world space" to males, for good or ill (see Figure 5.2).

Paula Caplan (1979) reanalyzed Erikson's own data and concluded that they do not support his broad claims of sex differences. Those of his claims that were statistically significant accounted for less than 2% of the variance, and in any event, boys built three to four times as many enclosures as towers. Furthermore, Erikson's subjects were ages 11 to 13, yet he made general interpretations for all ages. He assumed, for example, that these differences existed in the preschool years as well.

Next, Paula Caplan suggested that sex-role socialization could explain the remaining differences. Based on the sex-typed toys they had been given for years, she reasoned that boys felt more comfortable playing with blocks and girls with furniture and figures of people. Blocks are more easily made into towers, and furniture and people encourage

Figure 5.2 Play Configurations Erikson Described for Boys and Girls

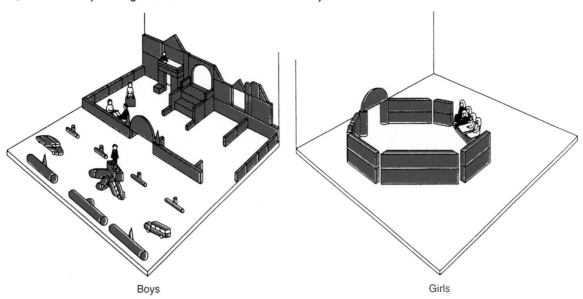

Boys   Girls

(Reproduced from *Childhood and Society, Second Edition*, by Erik H. Erikson, by permission of W. W. Norton & Company, Inc., and Faber and Faber Ltd. Copyright 1950, © 1963 by W. W. Norton & Company, Inc. Copyright renewed 1978, 1991 by Erik H. Erikson.)

the building of a room to contain them. When boys and girls used the same toys, girls built towers and other structures that were just as high as those built by boys, and both sexes were equally likely to build towers or enclosures. Other researchers also report that the specific play materials are significant (Budd, Clance, & Simerly, 1985). It does seem that Erikson's findings are less robust than he claimed, which casts doubt on his anatomical interpretation.

MALE AND FEMALE IDENTITY RESOLUTION

Erikson (1985) consistently asserted that males and females are, and should remain, distinct. Even in his futuristic vision of a world community not divided by conflicting group identities, he described men's contribution as changing technology from destructive to nurturing applications and women's role as developing "the powerful potential of protective mothering." Although he parenthetically included both sexes in both the technological and parenting roles, his message clearly differentiated the sexes into traditional roles.

Erikson, like Freud, accepted an anatomical basis for sex differences in personality. This biological interpretation contrasts with the more social emphasis of feminist and social role theorists (e.g., Eagly, 1987; Eagly & Wood, 1991; Gilligan, 1982), who say the sexes are different because of their different experiences in a world that has gender-based expectations. Critics say that Erikson did not go far enough in replacing Freudian biological determinism with a recognition of the impact of culture on sex roles (Lerman, 1986a, 1986b). Perhaps the biological metaphor of the epigenetic principle itself prevents Erikson's theory from being fully cultural.

What is the evidence? Although many have argued that important sex differences exist in identity development, the evidence favors similarity instead. On the "difference" side, many researchers suggest that women resolve identity issues differently from men, emphasizing interpersonal issues more, in contrast to men's emphasis on occupational and ideological issues (Josselson, 1973, 1987; Levitz-Jones & Orlofsky, 1985). They propose that the sequence of development from identity to intimacy may describe the development of men but not women (Lobel & Winch, 1988; Ochse & Plug, 1986). According to this argument, women defer resolution of identity until intimacy issues have been more fully developed (Douvan & Adelson, 1966; Hodgson & Fischer, 1979), and they may experience identity crises when relationships, rather than occupations, are in crisis (Josselson, 1987).

This argument, however, is refuted by research that shows identity development is similar in the two sexes. The sexes do not differ in level of identity and other measures of individualism (self-actualization, internal locus of control, and principled moral reasoning). Furthermore, these measures predict positive psychological functioning equally well for women and men, which suggests the sexes are really quite similar in the processes of identity resolution and psychological individualism (Archer, 1982, 1989; Archer & Waterman, 1988; Pulkkinen & Rönkä, 1994; Streitmatter, 1993; Waterman, 1982).

One way of resolving this apparent conflict is to distinguish between the process of identity resolution (which may be similar for everyone) and the content of identity, which may emphasize different aspects of life for males and females. Some people may resolve identity through other roles, such as religion, family, or politics (Kroger, 1986). Despite cultural changes, the relative importance of career and family remains a more important issue for girls anticipating their adulthood than for boys (Curry et al., 1994). Consistent with this, some studies report females to be more advanced in resolving identity issues in the areas of family roles (Archer, 1989) and sexuality (Orlofsky, 1978a; Waterman & Nevid, 1977).

As in the case of ethnic identity, cultural supports can facilitate identity development. Female models of achievement (Cella, DeWolfe, & Fitzgibbon, 1987) and the women's movement support personality growth. Women in one longitudinal study who found the women's movement more personally meaningful developed more confidence, initiative, and self-esteem in the years after college (Agronick & Duncan, 1998).

We might expect that masculine males and feminine females would be more advanced in identity resolution (cf. Lobel & Gilat, 1987), but research on sex typing and identity does not confirm this. In contrast, masculinity on personality tests is usually associated with identity resolution and well-being for both sexes (Della Selva & Dusek, 1984; Lamke & Peyton, 1988; Markstrom-Adams, 1989; Schiedel & Marcia, 1985). The term *masculinity* is misleading. "Masculinity" scales measure personality characteristics that reflect individualism and autonomy, which enhance personality development for both sexes. Identity does proceed to a more advanced level in women who break out of more restrictive female roles. Longitudinal studies show that women who occupy many roles have achieved more advanced identities than those with fewer roles (Vandewater, Ostrove, & Stewart, 1997).

Research on Development through the Psychosocial Stages

Erikson (1958a) based his theory on clinical evidence. Perhaps because of this, like other psychoanalytic approaches, his theory has been criticized as elusive and therefore difficult to verify (Chess, 1986; Fitzpatrick, 1976; Wurgaft, 1976). This criticism is probably more justified when applied to his psychohistorical work than to his developmental stages, which have stimulated substantial empirical research, particularly in adolescent identity development.

IDENTITY STATUS

Identity research has been dominated by studies focusing on identity statuses—that is, levels of development. This *identity status paradigm* has developed along its own path, becoming somewhat separate from Erikson's theory (Côté & Levine, 1988b; Waterman, 1988). Most frequently, identity is assessed from an interview. Questions probe crisis and commitment in the areas of occupation and ideology (Marcia, 1966). James Marcia reasoned that complete identity development occurs if an individual has experienced a crisis and has come through it with a reasonably firm commitment to an occupation and/or ideology. This mature outcome Marcia calls **identity achievement**. Three less mature outcomes are also possible: **identity diffusion**, in which neither a crisis nor a commitment has been experienced (the least mature outcome); *moratorium,* in which a crisis is being currently experienced but no commitment has yet been made; and *identity foreclosure,* in which a commitment has been made without a crisis and without much exploration of alternatives, often by simply accepting parental choices. (Marcia used the term *identity diffusion,* rather than *identity confusion,* because that was Erikson's earlier term, which he was still using when the scale was developed.)

When researchers who have published in this field responded to a survey asking them to describe the prototypical person in each identity status (Mallory, 1989), these were among the most descriptive characteristics they chose:

> *Identity achiever:* clear, consistent personality; productive
>
> *Moratorium:* philosophically concerned; rebellious, nonconforming
>
> *Identity diffusion:* unpredictable; reluctant to act
>
> *Foreclosure:* conventional; moralistic

Marcia reasoned that people begin in a state of identity diffusion and must pass through moratorium to identity achievement to develop optimally. Cramer's research indicates that strong identification with the father is typical of adolescents in the foreclosure identity status (Cramer, 2001). Foreclosure is an undesirable outcome; it can be a permanent dead end, or it can be temporary if exploration (moratorium) is later chosen on the way to identity achievement. This theoretical developmental sequence is not always found. Sometimes people become less certain of their identities as they mature (Côté & Levine, 1988a, 1988c).

It has been suggested recently, however, that the "foreclosed" status may not be so adverse for mental health in other cultural contexts, such as Greece, which emphasize norms and traditions to a greater extent. There, the lack of individual exploration is acceptable, and the commitment to an identity, which foreclosed individuals share with identity achieved status individuals, brings positive well-being (Vleioras & Bosma, 2005). Sexual orientation, too, has an impact on identity exploration. It is not such an issue for heterosexuals as for homosexuals because of the cultural assumption of heterosexuality, and some evidence indicates that the increased sexual identity explorations of homosexuals could stimulate greater identity exploration overall, resulting in a more mature identity-achieved status (Konik & Stewart, 2004). More research is needed to see whether this result applies more generally, or only to the atypical, politically aware group that was studied.

identity achievement status representing optimal development during the fifth (adolescent) psychosocial stage

identity diffusion the negative pole of the fifth psychosocial stage (earlier terminology)

OTHER PSYCHOSOCIAL STAGES

Erikson's proposal of stage sequences predicts that people will become more preoccupied with certain themes at appropriate periods in their lives: identity in adolescence, generativity in adulthood, and so on. One way to test this hypothesis is to analyze the writings of someone who has continued writing for many years. One such person is the British novelist and diarist Vera Brittain (1893–1970), whose diaries and fictional works have been analyzed for Eriksonian themes of identity, intimacy, and generativity. As predicted by Erikson's theory, as she became older, her writing turned from identity and intimacy issues to generative themes (Peterson & Stewart, 1990).

Age changes are also found using objective tests. George Domino and Dyanne Affonso (1990) developed a self-report questionnaire assessing positive and negative aspects of the original eight stages of development. This Inventory of Psychosocial Balance requires subjects to rate the extent to which they agree with each of 120 items. Sample items are as follows:

> *I can usually depend on others.* (Trust scale)
> *I genuinely enjoy work.* (Industry scale)
> *Sometimes I wonder who I really am.* (Identity scale)
> *Life has been good to me.* (Ego Integrity scale)

As expected, scores on the Inventory of Psychosocial Balance generally increased in older groups of subjects. In fact, longitudinal research using the Inventory of Psychosocial Development indicates that adults in their 20s continue to develop not only on identity and intimacy, as we would expect, but also on earlier stages, which would have been expected to be stable since childhood (Whitbourne et al., 1992). Other measures also revealed more advanced stages with age (Adams & Fitch, 1982; Archer, 1982; Marcia, 1966; Ochse & Plug, 1986; Waterman, Geary, & Waterman, 1974).

CORRELATES OF STAGE MEASURES

Higher scores on measures of the psychosocial stages are associated with better functioning in several studies. Howard Protinsky (1988) reported that problem adolescents scored lower on three of the first five psychosocial stages (trust, initiative, and identity) compared with other adolescents.

Identity is the most frequently studied of Erikson's stages. Many studies report that subjects who score high on various measures of ego identity function better. Among college students, those with more advanced identity statuses are more likely to have chosen a career (Cohen, Chartrand, & Jowdy, 1995). They use more mature defense mechanisms (Cramer, 1998b), perform better under stress (Marcia, 1966), get better grades (Cross & Allen, 1970), have higher self-concepts (Lobel & Winch, 1988), and score higher on a measure of moral judgment (Podd, 1972). They have greater recall of personal memories (Neimeyer & Rareshide, 1991), and their early memories reflect themes that are more mature when scored for psychodynamic imagery (Orlofsky & Frank, 1986).

Moratorium stage students are less committed to an occupational choice (Blustein, Devenis, & Kidney, 1989). They also experience higher anxiety, which can slow their performance (Marcia, 1967; Podd, Marcia, & Rubin, 1970), and they are less satisfied with college (Waterman & Waterman, 1970). Foreclosed subjects are more authoritarian (Marcia, 1967) and impulsive (Cella, DeWolfe, & Fitzgibbon, 1987).

Intimacy resolution is correlated with self-reported interpersonal behaviors. College men who score low on resolution of the intimacy stage (isolates) report having had fewer friends when growing up (Orlofsky, 1978b). Resolution of intimacy issues correlates with femininity on the Bem Sex-Role Inventory among male undergraduates but not among women (Schiedel & Marcia, 1985).

Generativity has been measured by a self-report scale, the Loyola Generativity Scale, which includes items like "I try to pass along the knowledge I have gained through my experiences" (Peterson, 2006). Men who are fathers score higher than those who have not had children (McAdams & de St. Aubin, 1992), and high scores are associated with better parenting (Pratt et al., 2001). Generativity influences the style of parenting; compared to authoritarian parents, who are punitive, generative parents are more authoritative: That is, they guide rather than coerce and so have a better outcome (Peterson, Smirles, & Wentworth, 1997). They have children who are more conscientious and agreeable than others, and who themselves are high in generativity (Peterson, 2006). Generativity concerns are especially high during midlife, as would be expected from Erikson's model (McAdams, de St. Aubin, & Logan, 1993). Adults who are highly generative, a sample of schoolteachers and community volunteers, describe their lives with narratives of commitment to alleviate others' suffering and improve their lives and benefit society (McAdams et al., 1997). In their families and in their work, generative women express prosocial attitudes, helping others (Peterson & Klohnen, 1995). Generativity combines individual action (agency) with social concern (communion), as a person actively does something (agency) for others (communion). It is higher in people whose TAT projective tests reveal a need for power (agency) and intimacy (communion) (McAdams, Ruetzel, & Foley, 1986; Peterson & Stewart, 1993). Some people express generativity through their work, others in their role as parents, and some channel their generativity into political activity and social activism (Peterson, Smirles, & Wentworth, 1997; Peterson & Stewart, 1996). Among younger adults, not yet parents, generativity is associated with attachment to pets (Marks & Koepke, 1994), perhaps as a way of practicing their nascent generativity potential.

Ego integrity (stage 8), as assessed by a written measure, was investigated among elderly men and women living in a nursing home and in a residential apartment complex. Those with higher scores reported less fear of death (Goebel & Boeck, 1987). Domino and Hannah (1989) studied Elderhostel participants. High scores on the Generativity scale of the Inventory of Psychosocial Balance (Domino & Affonso, 1990) predicted Self-Realization, measured by the California Personality Inventory. However, virtually all of the other seven developmental stages were also predictive, even when their positive intercorrelations were taken into account. One interpretation of this finding is that the strengths and weaknesses of each stage continue to influence functioning throughout life as Erikson's epigenetic principle predicts.

The conflicts described by Erikson's stage theory do not begin and end at the times he described, but they have their precursors in earlier stages, and subsequent implications and developments later. (Incidentally, one suggested revision of Erikson's model—by Capps, 2004—would assign each of his stages to a separate decade of life, so the trust issue would be the focus of development until age 10, the autonomy issue until age 20, the identity crisis at the time of life sometimes referred at as the midlife crisis, and so on.) In Erikson's stage theory, a person who does not successfully resolve the conflict at any one stage will be handicapped in following stages (somewhat like a student who does not master a basic math or language course and consequently finds later courses more difficult). Researchers have studied the prediction that people whose personality test scores indicate that they did not master one stage also score low on later stages

(Domino & Affonso, 1990; Domino & Hannah, 1989; Hannah et al., 1996). Aside from theoretical prediction, such positive correlations could also occur if the scores measuring the various stages inadvertently and inappropriately included some general factor such as social desirability.

Toward a Psychoanalytic Social Psychology

Like many theorists, Erikson believed that his theoretical concepts had implications for improving the human condition as well as understanding it (Wurgaft, 1976). Erikson clearly envisioned a psychoanalytic approach that would consider social and cultural realities rather than focusing exclusively on the individual, as Freud had done. James Côté and Charles Levine have developed such a *psychoanalytic social psychology* in their research and theorizing (Côté, 1993; Côté & Levine, 1988a, 1988b, 1988c). How does society influence personality and its development? How does personality influence society? These are core questions for a personality theory that includes the social context.

From such a perspective, psychological processes are affected by culture. Gender differences depend on the cultural context and are not likely to be universal. Ethnic and cross-cultural differences are understood in terms of social processes, not by misapplied biological concepts such as (pseudo)speciation. How are psychic structures (the id, ego, and superego) reflected in culture? James Côté (1993, pp. 43–44) speculates that social institutions reflect and direct these psychic structures. For example, the id is expressed in music and dance, sports, and brothels; the superego in religion, the judiciary, and the military; and the ego in work, government, and education.

Personality development is influenced by culture, which (for example) provides a moratorium period for exploration of identity, especially for college students in the humanities rather than in technological fields (Côté & Levine, 1988a, 1988c). The moratorium is not simply a time to select an occupation. It is also a time for wrestling with questions of values, which in psychoanalytic parlance is a struggle between the superego (representing values presented to the individual by family and society) and the ego (representing the individual's own accepted values) (cf. Côté & Levine, 1989). The humanities encourage more pondering of the human condition and human dilemmas (Côté & Levine, 1992, p. 392).

This relationship between individual identity development and cultural career paths is an example of an explicitly social perspective, which enables investigation of the ways in which "culture, social structure, social class, interaction networks, and so forth, may function to aid or hinder certain forms of development" (Côté & Levine, 1988b, p. 216). Such studies of the individual in the social context fulfill Erikson's (1968) vision: "We are in need . . . of concepts which throw light on the *mutual complementation* of ego synthesis and social organization, the cultivation of which on ever higher levels is the aim of all therapeutic endeavor, social and individual" (p. 53).

Psychoanalytic social psychology should understand culture without being constrained by any specific set of cultural values, but that may not be easy. Erikson has been criticized for not sufficiently separating his own values from his theory. Heinz Kohut, an intellectual rival, complained that "his description of the various developmental phases are really value judgments disguised in scientific terms" (Elson, 1987, p. 22; quoted in Cornett, 2000). These values are not simply Erikson's personal values but the values of Western culture: autonomy, industry, and individuality (Cornett, 2000; Eagle, 1997), despite his claim that the psychosocial stages are universal. As for Erikson's claim that the psychosocial ego strengths are not simply Western, but universal—we need more evidence before accepting that claim.

Summary

- Erikson proposed a theory of *psychosocial development* that described eight stages in the life span. A ninth stage was later added to reflect his final thoughts.
- According to the *epigenetic principle,* these stages build on one another and occur in invariant sequence across cultures.
- In each stage, the individual experiences a *crisis*, which is resolved in the context of society.
- The original eight stages are trust versus mistrust, autonomy versus shame and doubt, initiative versus guilt, industry versus inferiority, identity versus identity confusion, intimacy versus isolation, generativity versus stagnation, and integrity versus despair. The ninth stage is gerotranscendence.
- In each stage, culture influences development. Conversely, individuals also influence culture through the way they develop at each stage, particularly through their identity development.
- Considerable research has been conducted on the psychosocial stages. Predicted age changes have been found, and measures of identity formation show predicted positive personality correlates of higher identity status.
- Considerable research on racial and ethnic identity illustrates the relationship between individual development and culture.
- Erikson's cross-cultural studies of the Sioux and Yurok explored the relationship between individual ego development and the culture, a theme that identity status researchers have continued.
- Erikson claimed that biological factors strongly influence sex differences, and he supported his point with observations of children's play structures. However, his conclusions have been criticized for methodological flaws.
- Erikson warned that conflict among groups is increased because of *pseudospeciation,* and he urged the development of more inclusive identities to help reduce political and social conflict in the world.

Thinking about Erikson's Theory

1. How do Erikson's stages help you understand the people you know who are older or younger than you are? Explain, giving a few examples.
2. Do you think your culture fails to provide adequate supports at any particular stage? What should it do better?
3. Have you observed any prejudices that fit Erikson's concept of pseudospeciation?
4. Do you think Erikson's theory is equally applicable to females and males? What do you think are the differences in the way the two genders develop in your culture?
5. Do you think that an early choice of a career and technological majors are obstacles to identity achievement and that a delayed choice of major and humanities majors facilitate the process (as Erikson and Côté and Levine suggest)?
6. If you have lived in another country, compare that culture with your own. Does it have a different impact on the resolution of any of the psychosocial stages?

Study Questions

1. Contrast Erikson's view of motivation with Freud's psychosexual model.
2. Explain Erikson's epigenetic principle.
3. List Erikson's psychosocial stages. Describe the crisis of each stage. Describe the consequences of each stage for ego development.
4. List and explain various outcomes of the identity crisis. What is the healthiest outcome?
5. What is a psychosocial moratorium? Give an example.
6. Discuss the importance of the negative pole of the crisis at various Eriksonian stages. How does the negative pole contribute to healthy ego development?
7. Discuss the way culture contributes to ego development at various stages, from childhood to adulthood.
8. What is the difference between a ritual and a ritualism? Give an example.
9. Explain Erikson's ideas about the relationship between identity and race.
10. Explain Erikson's concept of pseudospeciation.
11. How did Erikson understand sex differences? Describe his report of sex differences in play constructions. Summarize research that challenged his conclusions.
12. Describe research on sex differences in identity development.
13. Describe Marcia's measure of identity status.
14. Summarize research on Erikson's stages of development.

Horney and Relational Theory
Interpersonal Psychoanalytic Theory

Chapter
Overview

Preview: Overview of Interpersonal
   Psychoanalytic Theory
Interpersonal Psychoanalysis: Horney
Basic Anxiety and Basic Hostility
Three Interpersonal Orientations
Major Adjustments to Basic Anxiety
Secondary Adjustment Techniques
Cultural Determinants of Development
Therapy

Parental Behavior and Personality Development
**The Relational Approach Within Psychoanalytic
   Theory**
The Sense of Self in Relationships
Narcissism
Attachment in Infancy and Adulthood
Parenting
Therapy
Summary

ILLUSTRATIVE BIOGRAPHY

Marilyn Monroe

Karen Horney's theory is popular for its insights into gender. It confronted the male bias of the earlier generation of psychoanalysts. As an icon of femininity in American popular culture, Marilyn Monroe portrays a person trapped in the gender role of her time, and so she can be understood from the perspective of Horney's interpersonal theory and of the subsequent relational theory that further develops these ideas.

Although she has been dead since 1962, the movie actress Marilyn Monroe is a timeless embodiment of the image of femininity. She epitomizes sexual beauty; her picture on a nude calendar was admired by many men and envied by many women. She also had a tragic side, arousing sympathy for the helpless victim.

Born in Los Angeles, California, in 1926, Norma Jeane Mortenson (her birth name) was not told the truth about her paternity, the product of an extramarital affair. She grew up without a father or mother. Mental illness ran in her family, and her mother and grandmother were institutionalized (Steinem, 1986). After living in several foster homes and an orphanage and having no other stable home, Norma Jeane married at age 16 (a marriage that lasted 4 years). With her husband off to war, she worked in a factory until a photographer taking pictures to boost the troops' morale discovered her there. She quickly became a model, on her way to becoming a movie actress, under the name of Marilyn Monroe. Along the way, she posed as the first *Playboy* magazine centerfold, married baseball star Joe DiMaggio (a union that lasted only 8 months), and then married playwright Arthur Miller (for 4 years). She also was the lover of President John F. Kennedy (among others). Marilyn Monroe had many lovers and three, possibly four, husbands. As much as she sought love, her longest marriage lasted

149

only 4.5 years. She loved children but never raised her own. Many were conceived; reportedly she had over a dozen abortions. (She reported that she bore an illegitimate child as a teenager, but it is unclear whether this is fact or imagination.) When motherhood was acceptable, as Arthur Miller's wife, she miscarried.

Throughout adulthood, Monroe took very high doses of barbiturates and attempted suicide on several occasions. It is likely that her death was either an intentional suicide or an accidental overdose. Theories of murder are favored by some, who argue that the FBI, the Kennedys, and the Mafia all had reasons to be involved in her death. Whatever the circumstances, her death occurred on the fifth anniversary of her much-mourned miscarriage.

Development

Karen Horney's theory emphasizes childhood parental love as essential for healthy development, whereas neglect produces a fundamental conflict that endures. Conflict is between basic anxiety (fear of not being loved or lovable) and basic hostility (anger about the lack of love).

Marilyn Monroe was neglected by her parents. She did not know her father. Her mother suffered serious depression and was institutionalized when Monroe was 7 and for most of her life thereafter. Monroe then grew up in foster homes and an orphanage, never experiencing a stable, loving family that would help her establish healthy interpersonal relationships. This insecure beginning, according to Horney's theory, would leave her with lifelong unconscious feelings of being unloved and angry.

Description

Horney's interpersonal psychoanalysis and subsequent developments in object relations theory emphasize that the most important aspect of personality is the relationships we have with other people. If they are not secure, then no

amount of fame or success can replace them. Personality is described in terms of relationship styles. Some people have a style of an exaggerated need for love and acceptance ("moving toward" style). Others have exaggerated needs for competition or aggression ("moving against" style). A third style is an exaggerated need for isolation ("moving against" style).

Of these three styles, Marilyn Monroe clearly has an exaggerated need for love. In her case, this need took the form of seeking sexual love and admiration for her physical beauty. She had a childlike innocence in her physical appearance and also a childlike hunger for love without the stabilizing anchor of mature self-esteem. Her childlike persona elicited love and protective impulses in others. Like many "moving toward" women, she chose for her male partners powerful men (including baseball player Joe DiMaggio, playwright Arthur Miller, and President John Fitzgerald Kennedy). Gloria Steinem describes her as "the child-woman who offered pleasure without adult challenge; a lover who neither judged nor asked anything in return" (1986, p. 22).

Adjustment

In Horney's theory, well-adjusted people have an ability to use all three interpersonal styles appropriately, as circumstances require. A poorly adjusted person, though, creates a defensive idealized self that resists awareness and does not permit flexibility. A person whose idealized self demands always being loved will not be able to move against others by appropriate assertive behavior or to move away from them to be alone when that is needed. A variety of defense mechanisms maintain this style, defending against any unconscious impulses for the repressed material to emerge—in this case, for repressed anger that could lead to competitiveness or assertiveness. Defense mechanisms also prevent the individual from realizing the unconscious feelings of anger and lack of love.

Physical beauty can be a way of ensuring love; it therefore takes on great value for those with a neurotic need for affection (Horney, 1950, p. 138). Monroe's exhibitionist tendencies trace back to childhood (Steinem, 1986). Horney (1937/1967d, pp. 256–257) suggested that a neurotic need for love can also be expressed as a series of sexual relationships, surely characteristic of Monroe, whose promiscuity was legendary.

In people who have adopted this pattern of a neurotic, compulsive need for love, hostility is repressed. If expressed, it would interfere with being loved. Thus feeling hostility leads to anxiety. One anecdote strongly suggests how much suppressed hostility must have pervaded her lovemaking. At a party, where a game required disclosing personal fantasies, "she said she imagined disguising herself in a black wig, meeting her father, seducing him, and then asking vindictively, 'How do you feel now to have a daughter that you've made love to?'" (Steinem, 1986, p. 144). How clearly this says that she thought her father's love could only be obtained by trickery, and she was mad about it. From an object relations theory point of view, this fantasy discloses an unhealthy pattern of relationships, and we would expect the fantasy to also contaminate her lovemaking.

Cognition

As in other psychoanalytic theories, Horney's theory describes defense mechanisms that distort thinking and interfere with accurate self-perception. Some of these defense mechanisms (e.g., repression) are the same as those described in previous chapters, whereas others (e.g., blind spots and externalization) are first described by Horney.

Marilyn Monroe showed an exaggerated concern for the suffering of animals and even plants that can be interpreted as a defense mechanism (externalization) that distorted accurate self perception. She externalized her own sense of being unloved and helplessness in a hostile world, not realizing it was she herself who felt the need to be rescued. For example, when she found boys trapping pigeons to sell in New York City, she bought the birds from the boys every week to set the birds free. Another rather bizarre externalization occurred when she saw nasturtiums cut by a lawn mower. As her husband, Arthur Miller, tells it, "crying as if she were wounded," Marilyn demanded that they stop the car as they drove past. "Then she rushed about picking up the fallen flowers, sticking the stalks back into the ground, to

see if they might recover" (Summers, 1985, p. 200; cf. Horney, 1945, p. 116).

Society

Horney's most important contribution to psychoanalysis was her recognition that culture contributes significantly to mental health problems by encouraging certain neurotic tendencies. By relegating women into society's accepted gender roles, culture produces unconscious conflict and neurosis. Early psychoanalysts did not recognize this, and so their supposed expertise had the unfortunate effect of endorsing the unhealthy gender messages of society. Freud's theory describes masochism as part of normal feminine development, whereas Horney said this trait is a product of culture. It is not inevitably part of being a normal female, and it is not healthy.

The particular style of femininity that Marilyn Monroe epitomized, the sex goddess of her age, was a product of her culture. Marilyn Monroe paints, in bold strokes, themes that typify the feminine personality of her time, in her culture, suggests Gloria Steinem (1986). Her self-doubt and need to be loved, her inability to express anger appropriately, were widespread issues for women of that era (and, to a lesser extent, today). Although Marilyn Monroe was treated by a Freudian analyst, a psychiatrist internationally known for his scholarly publications and a former close friend of the Freud family, her therapist missed this opportunity to put her on a less dependent, healthier track (Steinem, 1986). Rather than challenging her need for love as neurotic, apparently he played along, at times even taking the patient into his home. Of course, it is impossible to judge analysis from a distance; but if the therapy did not get beneath the neurotic need for affection, it was not addressing the core neurosis and could not hope to achieve a personality reconstruction. One suspects that Horney would even criticize the therapist for allowing "morbid dependency" in the doctor–patient relationship (cf. Horney, 1950, p. 243). Cultural assumptions can blind even the experts.

Biology

Although Horney added a cultural component to psychoanalytic theory, she did not deny the underlying assumption that biology provides the energy for personality. Thus she suggested that physical as well as psychological symptoms can be produced by unresolved unconscious conflict. She also realized that some people turn to physical substances to alleviate psychological suffering.

Marilyn Monroe tried to drown her hostility and anxiety with drugs. Horney (1950, p. 152) proposed that drug use stems from the underlying problem of self-contempt. Even Monroe's physical difficulties are consistent with Horney's theory. Monroe suffered extreme menstrual pain. She was reportedly frigid, compulsively seeking intercourse but not experiencing orgasm. If Horney's paper had not originally been published in 1926, we might have thought Horney had Marilyn Monroe in mind when she observed "that frigid women can be even erotically responsive and sexually demanding, an observation that warns us against equating frigidity with the rejection of sex" (Horney, 1926/1967c, p. 74). Horney reported that frigid women may convert their sexual functioning into a variety of menstrual disorders, including pain and miscarriage.

Final Thoughts

It took a woman, Karen Horney, to see cultural bias in misunderstanding women in the psychoanalytic theory that she otherwise admired and practiced. Her insights help us understand the psychological flaws of Marilyn Monroe, not simply to admire or desire her. We must remember that culture has continued to change, and that the typical neuroses of our era have undoubtedly given way to new culturally produced conflicts. Still, the core conflict, in Horney's theory, stems from inadequate parental love. We may defend against that conflict in culturally driven ways, varying from one century to the next and from one subgroup within society to another, but our basic needs are the same.

Preview: Overview of Interpersonal Psychoanalytic Theory

Interpersonal approaches in psychoanalysis, raised by Karen Horney and continued in the modern relational approach within psychoanalytic theory, have implications for major theoretical questions, as presented in Table 6.1. Both Horney's theory and

TABLE 6.1	Preview of Horney's Theory and Object Relations Theory
Individual Differences	Individuals differ in the way they define themselves in relationships. Horney described a balance among three interpersonal orientations: moving toward, moving against, and moving away (from people). People have different idealized selves and use different ways of adjusting to anxiety.
Adaptation and Adjustment	Healthy interpersonal relationships are a key to adjustment, and they are based on acceptance of the true self instead of some defensive idealized self. Horney provides full descriptions of neurotic trends. Psychoanalysis is the preferred therapy; self-analysis can be an important supplement.
Cognitive Processes	Blind spots and other defense mechanisms limit insight, but courageous self-examination can lead to growth. Developmental and object relations theorists are studying specific cognitions, such as those related to emotion.
Society	Culture is very important in shaping personality, especially through sex roles.
Biological Influences	Biology is far less important than orthodox psychoanalysis claims.
Development	Love and nurturance are key to a child's development. In Horney's theory, basic anxiety and hostility are the fundamental emotions of childhood. Without adequate parental love, the child develops unhealthy interpersonal modes and a defensive sense of self. Few major changes in personality occur after childhood (except through therapy).

relational psychoanalytic approaches have inspired empirical research, not only within clinical settings but beyond, in developmental and social investigations of personality, studying infants and children as well as adults. In addition to implications for adjustment and therapy, interpersonal approaches help us understand the variety of interpersonal styles that occur in everyday life. Formal applications of the approach focus on therapeutic settings at this time.

Interpersonal Psychoanalysis: Horney

The emphasis on society that Adler and Erikson contributed to psychoanalytic theory continued into the next generation of analysts, of whom one of the most widely known is Karen Horney. Like traditional Freudian psychoanalysts, Karen Horney firmly believed that the unconscious is a powerful determinant of personality and that childhood conflicts are important. However, she questioned Freud's emphasis on sexual conflict. According to Horney, the most important conflicts are based on unresolved interpersonal issues, not libidinal fixations. She argued that cultural forces must be considered and the personality differences between men and women are influenced more by society than by anatomy.

The interpersonal emphasis that Horney advocated has been the foundation of other psychoanalytic theories, as well—too many to cover thoroughly in this book. The *relational approach* draws from many of these theoretical developments and has forged connections with advances in developmental and social psychology. This approach, which has too many contributors to single out one "great name" with which to label it, is presented later in this chapter.

BIOGRAPHY OF KAREN HORNEY

Karen Danielson was born near Hamburg, Germany, on September 15, 1885. She was the second child in an unhappy marriage of an often absent Norwegian sea captain and his beautiful, somewhat higher-class wife. Danielson and her older brother Berndt (who later became a lawyer) were disciplined strictly by their tyrannical Lutheran father when he was home from his long sea voyages around Cape Horn to the Pacific coast of South and Central America. She retained a strongly independent character, regarded her father's outspoken religious attitudes as hypocritical, and questioned the fundamentalist teachings of her church.

KAREN HORNEY

The secondary education traditionally available to German girls would have precluded attending a university, but this was a time of social change in Germany. Young Danielson prevailed on her father to allow her to attend a newly opened nontraditional school that offered girls the course work necessary to prepare for the university entrance exams. Her father agreed, and she entered the University of Freiburg in 1906, in a class of 58 women and 2,292 men. There she studied medicine. She was popular and included in the partying and study sessions of her male classmates. She married one frequent companion, Oskar Horney, in 1909.

They moved to Berlin, where she continued her medical studies and he began a business career.

Karen Horney was a psychoanalytic patient of the famous Freudian analyst Karl Abraham. This was an avant-garde interest at that time. It was characteristic of her to explore new ideas, but she sought relief from personal problems as well. Horney was experiencing depression, fatigue, and dissatisfaction with her marriage, which she expressed by having an affair with her husband's friend. Her father died about this time, and she had ambivalent feelings toward him to sort out: anger because of the unhappiness of her parents' marriage, which had culminated in separation a few years before, but also more fondness for him than she admitted. The demands of combining a medical education with family life, without much encouragement from her husband, also required coping. Besides the analytic sessions, she kept a personal diary at this time, as she had in past years.

Although the medical and psychiatric establishment held psychoanalysis in low esteem, Horney made it her professional specialty. After receiving her traditional psychiatric degree in 1915, she dared to lecture on the controversial Freudian theory and to defend it against critics including, interestingly, Adler and Jung (Quinn, 1988, p. 151). Her own challenges to the theory were still brewing. Unlike many psychoanalysts of this time, however, she did not visit Freud in Vienna and so did not know him personally (Quinn, 1988). Freud did, however, chair a session in 1922 in which Horney presented a paper, "The Genesis of the Castration Complex in Women" (O'Connell, 1980).

Karen and Oskar Horney had three daughters. (One, Marianne Horney Eckardt, became a Horneyan analyst.) But the couple continued to have a troubled marriage and finally separated. Horney poured increasing energy into her career. She became one of the founding members of the Berlin Psychoanalytic Institute in 1920 and published several papers on male and female development, relationships, and marriage. Her 14 papers between 1922 and 1935 outlined a theory of female psychology that was clearly critical of Freud's theory. Horney's first suggestions were presented in a spirit of intellectual debate within classic Freudian theory, the sort of challenge that fosters the development of any science. The psychoanalytic community, however, dismissed her points and attacked her motivations. Freud is reported to have said of her, "She is able but malicious—mean" (Quinn, 1988, p. 237). He accused her of an inadequate analysis, saying that she did not accept her own penis envy (Symonds, 1991).

Given this hostile professional environment in Germany, it is no wonder that Horney accepted an invitation to become associate director of a new Institute for Psychoanalysis in Chicago, under Franz Alexander, in 1932. Horney became dissatisfied with her position at the institute, and in 1934 she moved to New York. Ironically, the same sort of professional debates over theoretical orthodoxy that had impelled her to leave Germany divided the New York Psychoanalytic Institute. Finally, the orthodox Freudians could no longer tolerate Horney's dissenting views, and in 1941 the New York Psychoanalytic Society voted to remove her from her role as a teacher and clinical supervisor, demoting her to instructor.

Horney and her followers quickly formed a new organization, the Association for the Advancement of Psychoanalysis, and founded the *American Journal of Psychoanalysis*. The announcement of the new training institute contained a statement of commitment to nonauthoritarian teaching: "Students are acknowledged to be intelligent and responsible adults. . . . It is the hope of the Institute that it will continue to avoid conceptual rigidities, and to respond to ideas, whatever the source, in a spirit of scientific and academic democracy" (cited in Quinn, 1988, p. 353).

It was not only the orthodox Freudians who were suspicious of her. The Federal Bureau of Investigation (FBI) kept a file on her because of her alleged communist sympathies, and because of this she was for a while denied a passport to travel to Japan (Quinn, 1988). The basis for this accusation seems to have been her affiliation with the liberal New School for Social Research in New York City. She was ultimately granted the passport, and in Japan she stayed at several Zen monasteries (O'Connell, 1980). In Zen Buddhism, Horney found support for the idea of a striving, healthy *real self* within the individual that Freudian theory, with its biological and genetic views, did not offer (Morvay, 1999). On December 4, 1952, within months of her return from Japan, she died of abdominal cancer, which had not been previously diagnosed.

As a person, Karen Horney seems to have had a capacity for enjoying life, despite the seriousness of her career and the disappointments of her marriage. She liked to eat in the best restaurants and to attend concerts and parties. During Prohibition, she at least once spiked the punch by writing her own prescription for "medicinal" alcohol (Quinn, 1988). She enjoyed relationships with men and had several affairs. Her lovers included the famous psychoanalyst Erich Fromm and, it was rumored, a trainee at the Chicago Institute for Psychoanalysis, who was also her patient (Quinn, 1988).

Horney challenged Freud's claim that he had discovered universal developmental conflicts. Instead, she argued that personality and its development are greatly influenced by culture and therefore vary from one society to another. This energetic and nontraditional woman proposed new understandings of women, and of men, which today are more widely accepted than the classical Freudian theory she challenged. For women in psychology, she is praised as an important role model (O'Connell & Russo, 1980), and her writings had a major influence on feminist theory (Gilman, 2001). Yet from her early interest in feminine psychology, Karen Horney turned later to the development of a general systematic theory of neurosis in which sex differences were not inevitable but rather developments that occur only in particular cultural contexts (Eckardt, 1991; Symonds, 1991).

Basic Anxiety and Basic Hostility

Infants and young children are highly dependent on their parents, not only for physical survival but also for psychological security. In the ideal case, the infant senses that he or she is loved and protected by the parents and therefore is safe. Under less than ideal circumstances, the child feels intensely vulnerable. This helplessness in childhood, in the absence of adequate parenting, produces a feeling of **basic anxiety**, which Horney (1945, p. 41) described as "the feeling a child has of being isolated and helpless in a potentially hostile world."

Parental neglect and rejection make the child angry, a condition Horney called **basic hostility**. However, the young child is not able to express the hostility because it would result in punishment or loss of love. This repressed hostility increases the anxiety. The neurotic, then, develops a basic conflict between "fundamentally contradictory attitudes he has acquired toward other persons" (Horney, 1945, pp. 40–41). On the one hand, the child needs the parents and wants to approach them but, on the other hand, hates them and wants to punish them. This conflict is the driving force behind neurosis: an interpersonal conflict, in contrast to Freud's libidinal conflict between sexual desire and the restricting forces of society (see Figure 6.1).

basic anxiety feeling of isolation and helplessness resulting from inadequate parenting in infancy

basic hostility feeling of anger by the young child toward the parents, which must be repressed

Figure 6.1 Horney's Model of Neurotic Conflict

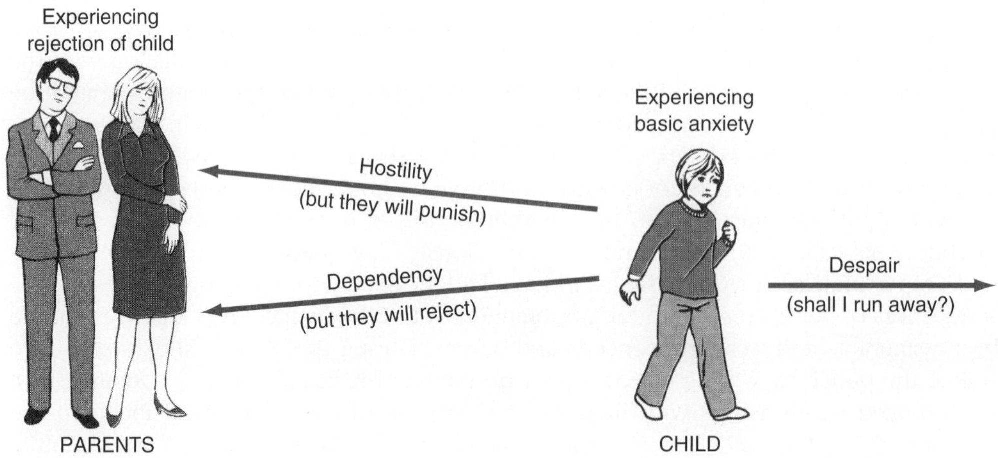

The child, needing to be loved, wants to move toward the parents but fears rejection. The child also feels hostility and wants to retaliate by moving against the parents but fears punishment. The child may give up and move away from the parents.

Three Interpersonal Orientations

moving toward interpersonal orientation emphasizing dependency

moving against interpersonal orientation emphasizing hostility

moving away interpersonal orientation emphasizing separateness from others

self-effacing solution attempting to solve neurotic conflict by seeking love; moving toward people

expansive solution attempting to solve neurotic conflict by seeking mastery; moving against people

What is the child to do? Three choices are available: Accentuate dependency and move toward the parents, accentuate hostility and move against them, or give up on the relationship and move away from them. The young child resolves the conflict with the parents by using whichever of these strategies seems best to fit his or her particular family environment. This choice becomes the person's characteristic interpersonal orientation.

Ideally, a healthy person should be able to **move toward** people, **move against** them, or **move away** from them, flexibly choosing the strategy that fits the particular circumstances. Paris (1989) observed that these three orientations, moving toward or against or away from people, correspond to "the basic mechanisms of defense in the animal kingdom—fight, flight, and submission" (p. 186). In contrast to healthy flexibility, neurotics are imbalanced in their interpersonal behavior. Some choices cause so much anxiety that they simply are not options. The young child who was never permitted to express any criticism of the parents, for example, is unlikely to be able to compete wholeheartedly against others in adulthood. The rejected child will continue to have difficulty depending on people. Neurotics are not necessarily restricted to only one interpersonal orientation. Horney's theory is not, strictly speaking, a typology of different kinds of neurotics; it describes neurotic trends that exist in complexly interacting ways within the same individual (Ingram, 2001).

Horney said that neurotics who emphasize moving toward people adopt the **self-effacing solution** to neurotic conflict, seeking love and minimizing any apparently selfish needs that could interfere with being loved. Neurotics who emphasize moving against people adopt the **expansive solution** to neurotic conflict, seeking mastery even if it impedes close relationships with others. Finally, neurotics who emphasize moving away

---

TABLE 6.2   Horney's Three Neurotic Solutions

---

1. Self Effacing Solution: The Appeal of Love ("The Compliant Personality")

"Moving toward" people

Morbid dependency: the need for a partner (friend, lover, or spouse)

"Poor little me": feeling of being weak and helpless

Self-subordination: assumption that others are superior

Martyrdom: sacrifice and suffering for others

Need for love: desire to find self-worth in a relationship

2. Expansive Solution: The Appeal of Mastery ("The Aggressive Personality")

"Moving against" people

Narcissistic: in love with idealized self-image

Perfectionistic: high standards

Arrogant-vindictive: pride and strength

Need to be right: to win a fight or competition

Need for recognition: to be admired

3. Resignation: The Appeal of Freedom ("The Detached Personality")

"Moving away from" people

Persistent resignation and lack of striving: the aversion to effort and change

Rebellious against constraints or influences: the desire for freedom

Shallow living: an onlooker at self and life, detached from emotional experiences and wishes

Self-sufficient and independent: uninvolved with people

Need for privacy: keeping others outside the magic circle of the self

---

(Adapted from Horney, 1945, 1950.)

---

from people adopt the **resignation solution**, seeking freedom even at the expense of relationships and achievement (see Table 6.2).

A measure of Horney's three interpersonal orientations, the Horney-Coolidge Type Indicator (HCTI; Coolidge et al., 2001), assesses three facets of each orientation, based on factor analysis (see Table 6.3). In a study of normal adults (Coolidge et al., 2004), scores on a scale measuring personality disorders were correlated with HCTI scores. Those with higher Cluster A (eccentric) scores, comprising the paranoid, schizoid, and schizotypal personality disorder scales, scored higher on the Detachment scale and, to a lesser extent, the Aggression scale. Those with higher Cluster B (emotional) scores, comprising the antisocial, borderline, histrionic, and narcissistic personality disorder scales, scored higher on the Aggression scale. People with higher Cluster C (fearful) scores, reflecting avoidant, dependent, and obsessive-compulsive personality disorders, scored higher on the Detachment and Compliance scales. These results are consistent with Horney's view that imbalanced interpersonal orientations are maladaptive, although the research needs to be replicated among clinically diagnosed individuals. Interestingly, the Malevolence facet of the Aggression scale was positively correlated with all three clusters of personality disor-

resignation solution attempting to solve neurotic conflict by seeking freedom; moving away from people

TABLE 6.3	Horney-Coolidge Measure of Interpersonal Orientations: Facets and Sample Items
1. Compliance Scale	
Altruism	*"I like to help others."*
Need for Relationships	*"I feel better when I'm in a relationship."*
Self-Abasement	*"I am self-sacrificing."*
2. Aggression Scale	
Malevolence	*"Beggars make me angry."*
Power	*"I like to be in command."*
Strength	*"I test myself in fearful situations to make myself stronger."*
3. Detachment Scale	
Need for Aloneness	*"I prefer to be alone."*
Avoidance	*"I avoid questions about my personal life."*
Self-Sufficiency	*"I don't really need people."*

(Prepared from information in Coolidge, Moor, Yamazaki, Stewart, & Segal, 2001, and Coolidge, Segal, Benight, & Danielian, 2004.)

ders, which, according to the researchers, "captures the maladaptive relational aspect of the personality disorders and suggests that underlying the differing relational postures of Horney's theory is a basic belief that people hurt other people and cannot be trusted" (Coolidge et al., 2004, p. 372). Other research using this questionnaire examines its relationships to biological factor models of personality (see Chapter 9), suggesting that the Compliant scale is related to Eysenck's Neuroticism measure, and the Aggressive and Detached scales to his Psychoticism (or antisocial) scale (Shatz, 2004).

MOVING TOWARD PEOPLE: THE SELF-EFFACING SOLUTION

Some people turn to others for the love and protection lacking in their early life. Because of this dependency, they must be careful to do nothing to alienate others. Horney (1945) referred to these as *compliant types*. Some are dominated by a need for affection, living as though their motto were "If you love me, you will not hurt me" (Horney, 1937, p. 96). Others are characterized by their submissive attitude, as though they felt, "If I give in, I shall not be hurt" (p. 97).

To be lovable, a person will do things to endear others: becoming sensitive to their needs; seeking their approval; and acting in unselfish ways, generous to a fault. The need for love may be expressed in an exaggerated need to be "in love" or involved in sexual relationships in which the partner takes control. Women, especially, are subjected to cultural pressures toward this need for love.

The compliant type of person makes few demands on others, instead playing a "poor me" role that emphasizes helplessness and subordination. This produces low self-esteem. Such a person "takes it for granted that everyone is superior to him, that they are more attractive, more intelligent, better educated, more worthwhile than he" (Horney, 1945, pp. 53–54).

MOVING AGAINST PEOPLE: THE EXPANSIVE SOLUTION

A second strategy for resolving the conflict over unmet early needs is to emphasize the mastery of tasks and power over others, which seem to offer protection from the vulnerability of being helpless. Horney (1945) refers to those who adopt this strategy as *aggressive types*, who seem to live by the motto "If I have power, no one can hurt me" (Horney, 1937, p. 98). Less subtle domination over others, or more subtle power through competitive mastery, both achieve the desired protection against humiliation.

Career competitiveness and perfectionism tap this trend. In politics, the expansive solution can lead to vigorous campaigning or it can make military action seem more appealing (Swansborough, 1994). From her clinical experience, Horney noted that patients of this type seem to have particular difficulty when they begin to come close to other people in love or friendship.

MOVING AWAY FROM PEOPLE: THE RESIGNATION SOLUTION

A third strategy for resolving childhood conflicts is epitomized by the fox in Aesop's fable who could not reach the grapes hanging over his head. After all attempts to reach them failed, the fox finally gave up, avoiding disappointment by telling himself that the grapes were probably sour anyway. In Horney's theory, some people try to do without other people, having given up on solving the problem of basic anxiety through love or power. Horney (1945) refers to these as *detached personality types* and says they seem to live by the motto "If I withdraw, nothing can hurt me" (Horney, 1937, p. 99). In the effort to be self-sufficient, detached types may develop considerable resourcefulness and independence; Horney cites the example of Robinson Crusoe. Or they may restrict their needs and protect their privacy. Creative people are often detached types.

HEALTHY VERSUS NEUROTIC USE OF INTERPERSONAL ORIENTATIONS

Harmonious interpersonal relationships are an important source of life satisfaction cross-culturally, although to a greater extent in some cultures than others (Kwan, Bond, & Singelis, 1997). How do we achieve this? The healthy person adopts, when appropriate, any of the three orientations toward people because each is adaptive in certain situations. The neurotic individual is limited in using these orientations. Consider aggression. Although it is pathological to be aggressive toward everyone, the healthy person must be capable of "adequate aggressiveness," by "taking initiative; making efforts; carrying things through to completion; attaining success; insisting on one's rights; defending oneself when attacked; forming and expressing autonomous views; recognizing one's goals and being able to plan one's life according to them" (Horney, 1935/1967e, p. 228). The current term would be *assertiveness* rather than *aggressiveness*. Similarly, although excessive dependency (moving toward) is neurotic, the inability to ask for appropriate help (a deficit in the moving-toward orientation) is also maladaptive (cf. Bornstein, 1992).

Interpersonal orientations also influence physical health. Horney reported that repressed hostility may cause physical symptoms, such as headaches and stomach problems (1945, p. 58). Research confirms that high levels of hostility ("moving against" orientation) contribute to coronary heart disease (T. Q. Miller et al., 1996; Roemer, 1987). Excessive dependency, too, puts people at increased risk for many physical diseases, including ulcers, asthma, epilepsy, and heart disease—perhaps in part because unmet dependency needs arouse anxiety, which impairs the immune system (Bornstein, 1998, 2000). If these relationships were found only after people became ill, we might dismiss them as only indicating that sick people become dependent. The fact that the relationships are also found in *prospective* studies (that is, that earlier dependency predicts later illness) indicates that the dependency–illness relationship is not simply an artifact of the sick role. On the positive side, Robert Bornstein (2000) points out that dependency can have a protective effect, too, when it stimulates people to seek early treatment and to comply with medical instructions. It is not simply the trait of dependency but the way it plays out in an interpersonal context that produces health outcomes.

Major Adjustments to Basic Anxiety

To solve conflicts over basic anxiety, an individual adopts defense mechanisms, including many of the defense mechanisms that previous analysts had described, such as repression, and Horney's expanded list of defensive maneuvers. All neurotics use some mixture of four major strategies for resolving the basic conflict between helplessness and hostility. These strategies do not solve the conflict or lead to growth, but they may allow a person to adapt sufficiently to cope with daily life.

ECLIPSING THE CONFLICT: MOVING TOWARD OR AGAINST OTHERS

First, the neurotic may "eclipse part of the conflict [between helplessness and hostility] and raise its opposite to predominance" (Horney, 1945, p. 16). Some eclipse hostility and emphasize helplessness, turning dependently toward others. Others eclipse helplessness and emphasize hostility against other people. These constitute two of the basic interpersonal orientations: moving toward and moving against people.

DETACHMENT: MOVING AWAY FROM OTHERS

A second major adjustment strategy is to become detached from others. Because the conflicts are inherently interpersonal, simply moving away from people reduces the experience of conflict. If this tendency is much stronger than eclipsing, it leads to Horney's third interpersonal orientation, moving away from people.

THE IDEALIZED SELF: MOVING AWAY FROM THE REAL SELF

idealized self an image of what a person wishes to be

real self the vital, unique center of the self, which has growth potential

actual self what a person really is at a given time, seen objectively

The third major neurotic adjustment strategy is to turn away from the real self toward some seemingly better (less helpless, less angry) **idealized self**. The **real self** is "the alive, unique, personal center of ourselves" (Horney, 1950, p. 155) and is involved in healthy psychological growth. It is the self that would have developed if we had been nurtured properly as we were developing or that we may become once we overcome our neurosis (Paris, 1999). For clarity, Horney offered a different term to describe everything that we really are at a given time (neurotic as well as healthy): the **actual self** (p. 158). The neurotic turns away from growth potential (the real self), not from reality (the actual self).

A healthy adult who is neglected or rejected can turn to other relationships, confident in his or her own self-worth, but the young child does not have the resources to do so. Consequently, the sense of self, which is just in the process of developing, emerges already wounded. The child develops a low self-esteem. The person may feel like a counterfeit, having "lost touch with essential aspects of self," that is, alienated from the true self (Ingram, 2001). Instead, the neurotic turns to an imagined idealized self, which would not be despised. The idealized self varies depending on the interpersonal orientation of the individual. "Perhaps if I am very, very good and kind, I will be lovable," thinks one child. "Or," imagines another, "if I impress people with my achievements and power, they will not be able to hurt me, and they may even admire me." "Or," muses a third, "maybe I don't need people after all; I can manage alone."

The idealized self may become the basis for intense striving; for example, Lyndon Johnson's idealized self channeled his political career, ultimately leading to the presidency (Huffman, 1989). Some incest victims form an idealized self that denies their helplessness by emphasizing their special power over the abusing parent (Price, 1994). However, it is a struggle to maintain the pretense that one is like one's idealized self, rather than like one's rejected real self. When the effort fails, a person must confront the underlying conflict, and anxiety or even panic may result.

The profoundly disturbing consequences of turning from the real to the idealized self are suggested by the comparison Horney (1950) makes. The process corresponds to "the devil's pact . . . the selling of one's soul" (p. 155). The neurotic is like Faust, who sold his soul to the devil for a bit of fleeting pleasure and power. The healthier choice is to turn away from false pride and instead to accept the "ordinariness" of one's real self (Horner, 1994).

However, neurotics try instead to strengthen the idealized self and avoid painful confrontation with the repressed real self. "I should be kind to everyone" or "I should be able to do the work better than anyone else" or "I should not have to depend on other people." These are the sorts of demands, often not fully conscious, that people make of themselves. Horney called these demands the **tyranny of the shoulds**. They urge us ever closer to the idealized self but at the expense of increased alienation from the real self. Perfectionism causes people to strive vigorously toward high standards, and it can produce the sort of high performance that many jobs reward, but the cost is great. Bieling et al. (2004), based on empirical data, describe perfectionism as "an underlying factor across several disorders and categories of psychopathology" (p. 194). When people ruminate over unobtainable goals, they become anxious, depressed, dissatisfied with life (Flett et al., 1998; Hewitt, Flett, & Ediger, 1996; Minarik & Ahrens, 1996; Shafran & Mansell, 2001), and sometimes suicidal (Blatt, 1995; Chang, 1998; Hewitt et al., 1997; Orbach, 1997). The poet Sylvia Plath, who tragically committed suicide, has been described as a perfectionist (Schulman, 1998; Van Pelt, 1997).

Not all perfectionists are suicidal, of course. Some have high self-esteem and are able to strive successfully for achievement, and they are not at risk (Adkins & Parker, 1996; Rice, Ashby, & Slaney, 1998). Perfectionism may be healthy and contribute to socially valued achievements, as it does in some Asian populations that have been studied (Chang, 2003). It is when perfectionism is accompanied by other indicators of dysfunction, such as mood disorders, anxiety, and substance abuse or dependence, that it may turn self-destructive (Dean & Range, 1996; Gould et al., 1998). For example, exercise is healthy, but the extreme exercise patterns of some eating-disordered patients and male body builders are not (Blouin & Goldfield, 1995; Davis et al., 1998; Shafran & Mansell, 2001). Even if they succeed, perfectionists may feel like "impostors" (Henning, Ey, & Shaw, 1998). Bernard Paris (1999, p. 165) conveys wise advice: "Horney recognized that the absolute best is the enemy of the good, that we must not disregard our accomplishments because we have failed to attain perfection."

tyranny of the shoulds inner demands to live up to the idealized self

EXTERNALIZATION: PROJECTION OF INNER CONFLICT

externalization
defense mechanism in
which conflicts are projected outside

In the fourth major adjustment strategy, the neurotic projects inner conflicts onto the outside world, a process Horney called **externalization**. Externalization refers to "the tendency to experience internal processes as if they occurred outside oneself and, as a rule, to hold these external factors responsible for one's difficulties" (Horney, 1945, p. 115). It includes the defense mechanism of projection, as traditional psychoanalysis understands it, in which our own unacceptable tendencies (such as anger or sometimes ambition) are perceived as characteristic of other people but not ourselves. In one case study, for example, a woman was interpreted to have selected her ambitious but narcissistic husband because she could externalize onto him "power, competence, and a capacity for success" that she could not see in herself (Horwitz, 2001). This defensive choice by the self-effacing wife, combined with the husband's own expansive and narcissistic solution to conflict, led to considerable marital discord.

Externalization can also include our unrecognized feelings. Horney cited the example of a man unaware of his own feeling of oppression, who, through externalization, was "profoundly disturbed by the oppression of small countries" (1945, p. 116). Neurotics often externalize feelings of self-contempt, either by thinking that others despise them (projection of the impulse) or by despising others (displacement of the object of contempt). Compliant types (those who move toward others) are likely to externalize in the first way, and aggressive types (those who move against others) in the second way. In either case, the neurotic is protected from becoming aware of deep self-contempt. Rage is also externalized in various ways: by irritation against other people, by fear that others will be irritated with us, and by converting the rage into bodily disorders.

These four attempts at solution occur in all neuroses, although not with equal strength. The neurotic attempts only to "create an artificial harmony" (Horney, 1945, p. 16) rather than actually resolving the problem.

Secondary Adjustment Techniques

In addition to the major defensive strategies (eclipsing, detachment, the idealized self, and externalization), there are many auxiliary strategies for reducing anxiety. Horney believed these secondary adjustment techniques, like the major adjustment techniques, do not really solve the neurotic problem in any lasting way, as she made clear in the title by which she introduced the concepts: "Auxiliary Approaches to Artificial Harmony" (1945, p. 131).

blind spots secondary
adjustment technique in
which a person is
unaware of behavior
inconsistent with the idealized self-image

People are often unaware of aspects of their behavior that are blatantly incompatible with their idealized self-image. Horney (1945) cited the example of a patient who "had all the characteristics of the compliant type and thought of himself as Christlike" but who blindly failed to recognize the aggression expressed by his symbolic murders of co-workers. "At staff meetings he would often shoot one colleague after another with a little flick of his thumb" (p. 132). Such **blind spots** prevent conscious awareness of the conflict between the behavior and our self-image.

**compartmentaliza-
tion** secondary adjust-
ment technique in which
incompatible behaviors
are not simultaneously
recognized

Another way to prevent the recognition of conflict is by **compartmentalization**, allowing the incompatible behaviors to be consciously recognized but not at the same time. Each is allowed to be experienced in a separate "compartment" of life: family or outsiders, friends or enemies, work or personal life, and so forth. For example, a person may be loving within the family but a ruthless business competitor outside the family.

Horney (1945, p. 135) called **rationalization** "self-deception by reasoning." We explain our behaviors so they seem consistent with what is socially acceptable and with our idealized self-image. Horney provided these examples: A compliant type who is helpful will rationalize this action as due to feelings of sympathy (ignoring a tendency to dominate, which may also be present); an aggressive type will explain his or her helpfulness as expedient behavior.

Excessive self-control prevents people from being overwhelmed by a variety of emotions, including "enthusiasm, sexual excitement, self-pity, or rage" (Horney, 1945, p. 136). When emotions threaten to break through, people may fear they are going crazy. Rage is particularly dangerous and is most actively controlled. People using this defense mechanism typically avoid alcohol because it would be disinhibiting, and they have difficulty with free association in psychotherapy.

Arbitrary rightness "constitutes an attempt to settle conflicts once and for all by declaring arbitrarily and dogmatically that one is invariably right" (Horney, 1945, p. 138). Inner doubts are denied, and external challenges are discredited. The rigidity of these people makes them avoid psychoanalysis, which challenges a person's core defensive beliefs.

Elusiveness is quite the opposite of arbitrary rightness. These people do not commit themselves to any opinion or action because they "have established no definite idealized image" (Horney, 1945, p. 139) to avoid the experience of conflict. The person who is elusive does not stick with a conflict long enough to really work at resolution. "You can never pin them down to any statement; they deny having said it or assure you they did not mean it that way. They have a bewildering capacity to becloud issues" (p. 138). They are reminiscent of the joke about the neighbor who, asked to return a borrowed bucket, says he did not borrow it, and besides it was leaking when he borrowed it, and besides he already returned it.

Cynicism avoids conflict by "denying and deriding . . . moral values" (Horney, 1945, p. 139). A Machiavellian-type person is consciously cynical, seeking to achieve his or her goals without moral qualms. Others use cynicism unconsciously; they consciously accept society's values but do not live by them.

rationalization secondary adjustment technique in which a person explains behaviors in socially acceptable ways

excessive self-control secondary adjustment technique in which emotions are avoided

arbitrary rightness secondary adjustment technique in which a person rigidly declares that his or her own view is correct

elusiveness secondary adjustment technique in which a person avoids commitment to any opinion or action

cynicism secondary adjustment technique in which the moral values of society are rejected

Cultural Determinants of Development

Horney stressed social and cultural determinants of personality and neurosis, in addition to orthodox Freudian biological forces. She stated that "there is no such thing as a normal psychology that holds for all mankind" (1937, p. 19). Specific family experiences, such as having domineering or self-sacrificing mothers, only occur under particular cultural conditions (p. viii). In contrast with Freud's description of universal family psychodynamics, for Horney, even the Oedipal complex occurs because of rivalry within the family that is characteristic only of certain cultural conditions, not universal. In other ways, though, her thinking was consistent with the psychoanalytic tradition. She accepted more biological determinism than some feminist critics would wish, and she remained focused on changing individuals rather than becoming an activist for social change (Garrison, 1981; Lerman, 1986b).

With current awareness of cross-cultural issues in psychology, psychoanalysts have noted that family ties are much closer and more central to the patients' sense of self in Asian countries influenced by Confucian values, including China, Japan, Korea, and Vietnam (Slote, 1992). Cultural factors even influence labeling certain behavior patterns as abnormal. Unlike medical disorders, such as broken bones, Horney argued that behaviors such as seeing visions or shame about sexuality are neurotic in some cultures but quite normal in others. Horney (1937, p. 62) argued that sexual conflict was becoming less important as a source of anxiety at the time she wrote than in Freud's somewhat earlier era, and the conflict between competitiveness and love was becoming more important. "In our culture," she wrote, "the most important neurotic conflict is between a compulsive and indiscriminate desire to be the first under all circumstances and the simultaneous need to be loved by everybody" (1937/1967d, p. 258). This conflict is exacerbated by the feminine role. Because cultures can change, Horney's emphasis on culture appeals to feminists and others who advocate change.

GENDER ROLES

Whereas biology determines sex (male or female), it is culture that defines the accepted traits and behaviors for men and women. Who should care for children? Who should take on dangerous jobs? The answers are provided by society, not by our chromosomes. To recognize that we are discussing cultural rather than biological phenomena, it is customary to use the terms *masculine* and *feminine* instead of *male* and *female* and the term *gender* instead of *sex*. According to *social role theory*, cultures define what is masculine and what is feminine (Eagly, 1987; Eagly & Wood, 1991), and these gender definitions are central components of the sense of self (H. M. Buss, 1990; Menaker, 1990). For example, the importance of machismo to the masculine identity of Chicano men results from cultural influences (Segura & Pierce, 1993). The contrasting high levels of dependency among males in China shows that culture can produce different gender roles (Dien, 1992). Much research has documented differences between women and men in their attitudes about social issues; women, according to these studies, are more socially compassionate and sympathetic to minorities than men (Eagly et al., 2004).

Achievement

Horney described sex roles concerning achievement in ways that anticipated later psychological research. Women, she claimed, are especially likely to become compliant types who do not risk achievement because "our cultural situation . . . stamps success a man's sphere" (1937, p. 204). The roles of women and of men also vary. In her time, Horney (1939, p. 181) noted that a woman who sacrificed her own career for her husband's career was considered "normal," even if the wife was more gifted, but cultures can change. Women may even develop a "fear of success" (pp. 210–214). Research confirms that males are more likely to perceive situations as competitive than females and that for females, but not for males, competition reduces affection for others (Deberry, 1989).

Karen Horney originally used the term *fear of success*. She suggested that it may come from a conflict between competition and the need for affection. For example, a woman motivated by fear of success may feel that if she succeeds, she will lose her friends. Fear of success can be measured for research purposes by a projective test (Horner, 1972), conceptualizing the fear of success as a motive to avoid achievement.

Social Dominance

Traditionally, gender roles prescribe dominance or power for males and submissiveness or nurturance for females. This is true to such an extent that the short form of the Bem Sex-Role Inventory "masculine" scale is virtually identical to a scale derived by factor analysis called Interpersonal Potency, and the Bem "feminine" scale is virtually identical to an Interpersonal Sensitivity scale (Brems & Johnson, 1990).

Gender roles profoundly influence the development of social power or dominance, and this affects other aspects of personality, including masochism (the enjoyment of pain and suffering). Freud had attributed female masochism to biology. Horney disagreed. As she put it, "in our culture it is hard to see how any woman can escape becoming masochistic to some degree" (Horney, 1935/1967e, p. 231). She suggested that "masochistic phenomena represent the attempt to gain safety and satisfaction in life through inconspicuousness and dependency" (1939, p. 113).

An empirical study of couples provides evidence that social power determines interpersonal behavior. The strategies people use to influence their intimate partners were found to vary with the person's structural strength or weakness in the relationship, as indicated by income, education, and age. The more powerful member of a couple was more likely to use bullying and autocratic tactics to influence the partner, whereas the weaker partner was more likely to use supplication and manipulation. This association held for both heterosexual and homosexual couples. In the former, the more powerful partner was usually the man, but it was power, rather than sex or gender role, that best predicted behavior (Howard, Blumstein, & Schwartz, 1986).

Valuing the Feminine Role

Horney rejected Freud's assertion that women reject their bodies as inferior. Horney argued that culture, rather than anatomy, is the important force behind the "penis envy" Freud had postulated. Women envy the power and privilege that humans with penises have, rather than the organ itself. Penis envy represents an avoidance of the feminine role (Horney, 1926/1967a, 1923/1967b; Siegel, 1982). She countered, "Is not the tremendous strength in men of the impulse to creative work in every field precisely due to their feeling of playing a relatively small part in the creation of living beings, which constantly impels them to an overcompensation in achievement?" (quoted in Gilman, 2001). This argument, well known by the catchy term **womb envy**, questions the assumption that men have the enviable position, and instead it suggests that they feel inferior to women's reproductive capacity.

> **womb envy** men's envy of women's reproductive capacity (the complement of Freud's penis envy)

Beyond this biological image, what might women have that could compete with the dominance and achievement of men's social roles? A prime candidate is women's greater interpersonal connectedness (Lang-Takac & Osterweil, 1992), the proposal that feminine values, especially relationship-oriented values like nurturance and empathy, should be more highly valued (Gilligan, 1982; J. B. Miller, 1976; Symonds, 1991). This argument has not gone unchallenged. Marcia Westkott contends that women's valuing of relationships often takes the form of an idealized self, one who unselfishly nurtures. In Horney's theory, the idealized self is neurotic. Feminist theory and therapy, by affirming relationship values, unwittingly confirm a neurotic idealized self and perpetuate a cultural expectation that women should take care of men. This makes it more difficult for women to become the well-balanced ideal that Horney envisaged for healthy people (Westkott, 1986a, 1986b, 1989). For example, when feminine nurturant values are emphasized, family members of alcoholics may inadvertently enable the alcoholic to continue drinking by taking care of the problems that the addiction creates. This enabling, or codependent, role is unhealthy for both the alcoholic and the codependent family member (Haaken, 1993).

Mental Health and Gender Roles

The prevailing view among psychologists used to be that women who work and have professions suffer personality disturbances (labeled penis envy or otherwise) and that traditionally feminine women are psychologically healthier than less traditional women. Research does not support this view (Helson & Picano, 1990; Yogev, 1983). A review of the research relating sex roles to mental health indicated that psychological masculinity (as measured on sex-typing instruments such as the Bem Sex-Role Inventory) is associated with better mental health, in both men and women; femininity is not consistently related to mental health (Bassoff & Glass, 1982; Taylor & Hall, 1982; Whitley, 1984). It is not the presence of "feminine" characteristics, such as empathy and nurturance, but rather the absence of "masculine" qualities, such as assertiveness, that interferes with healthy adaptation for women and, equally, for men, at least in the United States and similar cultures.

Gender roles bring a price. In men, they contribute to defense mechanisms such as restrictions in emotionality (Mahalik et al., 1998) and to gender-related problems, including violence, fear of homosexuals, detached fathering, and neglect of health needs (Levant, 1996). Feminine people, even if they are men, tend to use defense mechanisms that turn against themselves rather than against others (Lobel & Winch, 1986). Women use such a defensive style more, and this along with other aspects of gender roles contributes to their higher incidence of depression, compared to men (Nolen-Hoeksema, 1987; Nolen-Hoeksema & Girgus, 1994).

CROSS-CULTURAL DIFFERENCES

The emphasis on individual achievement is, as Horney hinted, particularly characteristic of Western culture. Harry Triandis and his colleagues have studied cultural differences in **individualism**, a value that emphasizes individual accomplishments and privileges. The United States and Britain are particularly high in individualism. Countries are more likely to be individualistic if they are affluent and if people within the country are socially and geographically mobile (Triandis, McCusker, & Hui, 1990). In contrast, countries that are less affluent, in which people depend on cooperation to share resources, are characterized by **collectivism**, which values the relationships between people and their shared goals and mutual responsibilities (Triandis, 1996). Collectivist cultures emphasize conformity, social harmony, group tasks, and family obligations. Many countries in Africa, Asia, and Latin America are collectivist. Studying demographic groups within the same country is also enlightening (Triandis, 1996), and the insight gleaned from such comparisons can be invaluable for understanding personality in pluralistic societies. Within the United States, some groups, including Hispanics and Hawaiians, are less individualistic and more collectivist than the dominant culture (Hui & Triandis, 1986; Triandis, 1988, 1989).

Individualism and collectivism obviously influence social behavior, but they are also important influences on a person's self-concept (Bochner, 1994). The assumption that the self is separate rather than connected to others pervades Western thought and psychological theory and treatment. Having harmonious relationships with other people is less important as a source of life satisfaction in the United States, an individualistic culture, than in Hong Kong (Kwan, Bond, & Singelis, 1997). Their individualist bias contributes to therapists' misperception of clients who come from other cultures or minority groups that emphasize collectivism (Landrine, 1992). For example, the passive dependency described by the Japanese concept of *amae* has been misinterpreted as pathological when therapists presumed the Western value of individualism (Bradshaw, 1990). Training programs for clinicians have added increased attention to cultural diversity to avoid such misunderstandings (Allison et al., 1994; Bernal & Castro, 1994; Clarkson & Nippoda, 1997). Individualistic cultures have norms that encourage Horney's moving-against orientation,

individualism values, predominant in many Western cultures, of individual goals and achievement (in contrast to shared group goals and cooperation)

collectivism values, predominant in some cultures, of social cooperation and group goals

emphasizing achievement and accepting aggressive behavior. In contrast, collectivist cultures are more supportive of a moving-toward orientation. Thus cultures vary in the conflicts they present to individuals. Of course cultures influence personality, but we should also bear in mind that the variations within a given culture are great (Triandis, 1997).

Therapy

In her emphasis on the role of culture in the development of neurosis, Horney opened the door for realizing that the therapist, too, is influenced by culture, bringing assumptions and perhaps biases to the understanding of the client (Miletic, 2002). In criticizing Freud's patriarchal biases, she set a model for later clinicians to question whether therapists could also fail to understand patients because of their own limited experience of race, sexual orientation, or other factors. She wrote for a broader, more popular audience than previous psychoanalysts, yet she did accept the value of analysis.

Therapy must analyze the entire personality. No quick interventions, focused only on specific presenting symptoms, are possible in any psychoanalytic therapy. Horney (1945, p. 240) acknowledged that briefer psychotherapies may have some promise, but not for neurosis.

The therapist must uncover the unconscious strategies the patient has been using to deal with neurotic conflict. These have implications for interpersonal relationships, self-image, and perception of the world. Then the detailed implications of these strategies for living are explored with the patient. These insights provide guidance for building new, less neurotic ways of resolving the conflict. The idealized self must be given up, replaced by the real self with its sense of "felt aliveness" (Lerner, 1986).

Although orthodox in her acceptance of the importance of childhood experience in developing personality, Horney did not believe all psychoanalytic treatment required delving into childhood recollections. Horney criticized the Freudian overemphasis on the exploration of childhood origins of neurosis, although she would doubtless agree that interpersonal relationships based on faulty parent–child interacting can be mended in therapy (Morgan, 1997). She believed that the important insight for therapy is to understand unconscious tendencies and their functions, and exploring childhood is only useful to the extent that it enlightens this understanding. Sometimes focus on the present is more effective in producing change. Patients may try to avoid confronting their neurotic conflicts through an exaggerated interest in past origins in childhood. Horney advised the therapist to keep bringing the patient back to the present, seeing how neurotic trends influence current life. This is painful for the patient but pertinent to the task of therapy, which is personality change.

Inevitably, the patient's idealized image must he challenged, but this must be done carefully and slowly because it is the basis for the personality, wounded but not destroyed, that the patient brings to analysis. Eventually, the idealized image must be replaced by a more realistic self-concept. The term *shrink*, applied to the analyst, seems particularly fitting for this function.

Psychotherapy's ultimate goal is to make fundamental changes in personality. This involves many aims: to increase self-responsibility; to become more genuinely independent of others; to experience feelings more spontaneously; and to become "wholehearted," unpretentious, and fully and sincerely involved in life (Horney, 1945, pp. 241–242).

SELF-ANALYSIS

Although Horney recommended professional analysis for neurosis, she did think that some progress could be achieved by a person working alone. For example, in intervals between the end of one analysis and the beginning of another, the momentum of growth begun in psychotherapy could be continued by the individual alone.

Self-analysis can be undertaken occasionally to deal with a particular problem that presents itself. Horney (1950, pp. 101–102) cited the example of a woman who analyzed her own foolish behavior in one incident when she persisted climbing a mountain path under dangerous circumstances. Through self-analysis she traced it to an adolescent experience. Or self-analysis can be done systematically, with a commitment to regular individual work. For example, some people analyze all their dreams; others regularly note their emotional reactions and observe how they deal with life. Horney herself systematically kept a diary of self-exploration.

Sometimes the function of a symptom can be analyzed rather simply. Horney (1942, pp. 157–158) offered the example of a patient whose self-analysis revealed that his headaches were always related to anger. He cured his headaches by this self-analysis, but he did not achieve the deeper insights and more fundamental personality reconstructions that a professional analysis might have engendered. There are limits to what can be achieved through self-analysis. The blind spots accompanying neurotic defenses are particularly resistant, even in professional psychotherapy, and they are unlikely to yield to an individual working alone. All therapy, professional as well as self-analysis, leaves some problems unsolved. According to Horney (1942, p. 303), "There is no such thing as a complete analysis."

Parental Behavior and Personality Development

Neurotic problems begin early in life, within the family, where the "basic evil is invariably a lack of genuine warmth and affection" (Horney, 1937, p. 80). Parental behavior that undermines a feeling of safety will lead to neurotic development. This includes parental neglect, indifference, and even active rejection of the child. If the environment is loving, the sorts of traumas identified by Freud, such as premature weaning or toilet training or witnessing the primal scene, could be tolerated.

The ideal family atmosphere provides warmth, goodwill, and "healthy friction with the wishes and wills of others" (Horney, 1950, p. 18). Such an environment allows the child to develop a secure feeling of belonging, instead of basic anxiety. Healthy parenting requires that the parents themselves be capable of genuinely loving the child, which is not possible if they have emotional problems. Many parents fall short of this ideal. One of the goals Horney described for psychoanalysis was to advise parents how to raise healthy youths, thus breaking the repeating cycle of neurosis through each generation. Psychoanalysts exploring these issues suggest it is important for parents to pay attention to their infants' emotional experiences. This requires that the mother (or other caregiver) be able to understand the infant's emotion and to respond appropriately, for example, by mirroring an infant's distress or joy. If this experience is deficient, the child will develop with deficits in affective regulation (Glucksman, 2000).

Research supports her ideas. The trait of neuroticism in parents contributes to their abuse of children, apparently by making the parents less able to tolerate the negative emotions that come from stressful interactions with their children (Belsky, 1993; McCrae & Costa, 1988). Longitudinal research shows that parental acceptance and nonauthoritarian punishment in childhood predict higher ego development at age 30, particularly for women (Dubow, Huesmann, & Eron, 1987). One particularly impressive study, using Block and Block's longitudinal sample, correlated parental behavior during preschool and the children's development as young adults. Fathers and mothers were evaluated according to the "poisonous pedagogy" formulation of psychoanalyst Alice Miller, whose ideas are similar to those of Karen Horney. As predicted, parents who treated their children with criticism and excessive control produced anxious, poorly adjusted children; parents who expressed affection and encouraged their children produced warm and socially well-adjusted young adults (Harrington, 1993). Studies of parenting styles have been based on Baumrind's (1967, 1971) descriptions of various types of parenting. As Horney expected, neglectful parents have children who have greater difficulties. Authoritative parents, who provide both direction and acceptance, rear children who are better adjusted (Lamborn et al., 1991).

The Relational Approach within Psychoanalytic Theory

Theories build on earlier theories. In contrast to Freud's emphasis on the unconscious and intrapsychic conflict, many of his successors today stress disturbances in the relationships that people have developed, beginning with early family experience, a theme that Horney and others emphasized (see Table 6.4). The relational model was presented as an alternative to Freud's drive model (Greenberg & Mitchell, 1983; Mitchell & Aron, 1999). Even many therapists who were trained in a more Freudian tradition have come to emphasize more sociocultural issues and relationship issues in their current practice (Sudak, 2000).

One of the most significant of these current psychoanalytic theories is the **relational approach**, which emphasizes interpersonal relationships, especially the impact of early relationships with parents (Greenberg & Mitchell, 1983). The mother is more important in this approach, in contrast to Freud's emphasis on the father (Grotstein, 1993). Relationship needs are seen as fundamental (in contrast to Freud's emphasis on libidinal satisfaction). Early relationships are particularly influential because the very young do not yet have a sense of themselves as separate persons. Early relationships are the basis for developing internal representations of self and others that will guide relationships throughout life. They prepare us to expect love or rejection, nurturance or disappointment, from people throughout life. These expectations may become self-fulfilling prophecies, or they are inappropriate and so cause us to behave inappropriately in later relationships. Whether people seek support from others in adulthood or avoid doing so and dwell on depression and self-criticism is related to the way they describe their parents, even though they are old enough to have moved on to new relationships (Mongrain, 1998). A relationship with an empathic, nurturant parent begins this process in a healthy way. But rejecting or abusive parenting sets the stage for internalizing much more negative images of others and of the self.

Although the relational approach is a relatively recent development within psychoanalysis, Freud did recognize the importance of interpersonal relationships—for example, in his description of the transference (see Chapter 2)—and some psychoanalysts argue relational theorists do not give Freud the credit he deserves for his insights. He did, of course, propose that, in seeking a marriage partner, men seek someone similar to their own mother, and women seek someone like their father. This prediction can be tested scientifically, and it finds some support. A widely used test of personality (the Five Factor

relational approach
approach in modern psychoanalysis that emphasizes interpersonal relationships

TABLE 6.4	Important Persons in the History of the Relational Approach
Theorist	**Theoretical Ideas**
Melanie Klein	Young children are very needy; they relate to "part objects" (such as the breast) instead of the whole parent; their ambivalent feelings cause guilt about their negative feelings about their parents.
W. R. D. Fairbairn	People have a fundamental need for relatedness. Maternal indifference and lack of love for the child contribute to the development of child pathology. The child defensively splits the rejecting mother (which is internalized) from the hoped-for loving mother, which impedes development from immature to mature dependency.
Harry Stack Sullivan	Children attempt to avoid anxiety in interpersonal relationships by constructing an understanding of self that includes a *good me*, a *bad me*, and a *not me*.
Otto Kernberg	Borderline and psychotic patients suffer disturbed identity and interpersonal relationships. Early severe frustration leads to unmanageable aggression and narcissistic personality disorders. Especially in borderline personality disorder, narcissistic frustrations lead to a splitting of the "good" and "bad" self and object relations, which are kept isolated from one another, and a grandiose self is defensively formed.
Heinz Kohut	A *grandiose self* is part of normal, healthy development, based on a desire for merger with omnipotent caretakers, whose admiration is sought. A healthy, integrated self structure will be formed if the adults respond empathically to the child. If less than optimal parenting is available, the child will construct an *idealized parental imago* to support the grandiose self.
Mary Ainsworth and John Bowlby	Infants develop secure attachment, in which they derive comfort from the presence of the mother (or substitute); or insecure attachment, in which they are not comforted.
Nancy Chodorow	Children's gender development is influenced by the different roles that the mother and father play in caring for children (in contrast to Freud's proposed anatomical determinants of gender).

Inventory) was administered to participants (mostly college students) and to their parents, and on several traits, the participants' opposite-sex parent had a personality similar to their chosen romantic partner (Geher, 2000).

object relations term used in psychoanalysis for relationships with people, based originally on the idea that people serve as objects to satisfy libidinal drives

Relationships are often referred to as **object relations** in psychoanalysis, based on Freud's idea that other people serve as the objects that can satisfy libidinal desire. The relational approach considers the cognitive and affective (emotional) processes that allow people to form healthy interpersonal relationships or that impede such relationships. For example, sociopaths have defective object relationships in that they exploit others for their own selfish purposes. People suffering from borderline personality disorder have another kind of disturbed object relationship pattern: They manipulate others and may quickly become intensely attached to someone who is not suitable to meet this irrational need (Westen, 1991).

The sense of self, instead of libido, is central to the understanding of defense mechanisms in relational theory. Instead of serving to defend against unacceptable impulses and to prevent material from becoming conscious, as Freud had described, defenses serve to protect a person's self-esteem (Cooper, 1998).

Emotions triggered in interpersonal situations are especially important in object relationships, as we might expect given the role of infantile anxiety and hostility that Horney
described. The emotions we expect from relationships can be measured by projective
tests as well as by interview measures (Barends et al., 1990). By providing ways of measuring individuals' capacity for healthy relationships—methods that are more systematic
than clinical impressions and can also be used to study people who are not in therapy—
researchers are contributing to the dialogue between clinical and research-oriented psychologists (see Table 6.5).

In a cross-sectional study of children, Westen and his colleagues (Westen et al.,
1991) report evidence for increasing maturity from grade 2 to grade 5 (about age 8 to 11
years) on three dimensions of relationships: complexity of representations, capacity for
emotional investment, and understanding social causality. As predicted, there were no
changes in the affect-tone of relationship paradigms. Another cross-sectional sample in
the same report showed additional progress on the same three dimensions from ninth to
twelfth grade, and once again, no change in the affect-tone dimension. It is clear from
these results that object relationships are not so fixed in the preschool years as Freud theorized, but instead they continue to develop for many years thereafter.

Dreams can be analyzed to describe the dreamers' object relationships. Evidence from
a cross-cultural study shows that among both Chicano and Anglo university students,
women's dreams portrayed more interactions among people, especially more benevolent
interactions, than men's dreams. This gender difference was particularly strong among
Chicanos (Kern & Roll, 2001).

TABLE 6.5 Measurement of Object Relations from TAT Stories

Scale	Description	Description of Low Score	Description of High Score
Complexity	Complexity, differentia-tion, and integration of representations of people	Poor differentiation between people	Complex, multifaceted, integrated representa-tions of people's subjec-tive experience and enduring dispositions
Affect-tone of rela-tionship paradigms	Expectation that relation-ships will be safe and enriching or destructive and threatening	Expectation that relationships will be destructive and threatening	Expectation that rela-tionships will be safe and enriching
Capacity for emotional investment in relationships and moral standards	Emotional orientation that is selfish, or that unselfishly invests in people, values and ideals	Investment in one's own need gratification and desires	Commitment to values and relationships that acknowledge needs of self and others
Understanding of social causality	Logic, complexity, accuracy, and psycho-logical mindedness of attributions	Absence of causal understanding	Complex understanding of the role mental events play in social causation

(Adapted from information in Westen, Klepser, Ruffins, Silverman, Lifton, & Boekamp, 1991.)

Being with other people influences us emotionally. Others may calm us when we are distressed or arouse anxiety when we are not. Just what this effect is depends on our individual experience with relationships, especially early relationships. Drew Westen and his colleagues have developed an instrument to measure affect regulation styles, using a Q-sort technique in which clinical judges sort statements describing each patient's emotions into nine piles, according to how well they describe the person: the Affect Regulation and Experience Q-Sort (the AREQ). They suggest that psychological problems are more severe among people who have difficulty regulating strong negative emotions (Westen et al., 1997).

It is worth noting, too, that object relationships affect the body as well as behavior. Research subjects watched a film and then responded to projective tests; those who described relationships that were benevolent showed healthy changes in immune function, although those who described malevolent relationships showed unhealthy immune system changes (McKay, 1991).

The Sense of Self in Relationships

Our sense of self is rooted in relationships. Early disturbances, coming from relationships with inadequate parents, leave a person with a weakened or enfeebled sense of self (Kohut, 1984). Children who have not been adequately nurtured or loved develop a belief (which may be unconscious) that they are not worthy, and this impaired self is at the heart of much pathology. Patients diagnosed with borderline personality disorder report what Westen and his colleagues call "malevolent" early memories, in which people were injured (e.g., being pushed to the ground in an early school experience) and little help was given (Nigg et al., 1992). In contrast, adolescents who describe their parents as warm and fostering independence, as "ideal parents," are less likely to suffer from a variety of personality disorders than those who recall less benign parenting (Brennan & Shaver, 1998).

Relational theorist Stephen Mitchell (1970/1999) suggests that the early parent–child relationship is one in which parents' more or less distorted views of themselves and their child set up a distorted, grandiose self-image in the child. For example, the parents might create an unrealistically good and obedient image of their child, which is too limiting for a real child to have room to develop his or her full personality. Object relations theorist Fairbairn (Celani, 1999) describes the defense mechanism of "splitting" as a result of inadequate parenting. The parental object is seen as two separate objects: the bad object that has been rejecting or abusive and the good object that the child longs to please. The child introjects both good and bad aspects into an ego structure that is not integrated, and so he or she has a despised self that in a warped sense justifies the parental rejection or abuse and a grandiose good self that could ideally be the basis for earning parental respect and love. These ideas are quite similar to Horney's description of the despised real self and the grandiose self, and in both theories, the split stems from bad parenting.

Our role relationships with other people throughout life are based on early relationships, and they recapitulate the weaknesses and the defective sense of self that are the legacy of the past. People whose early object relationships are unhealthy because of early physical, sexual, and emotional abuse or other mistreatment are vulnerable to self-destructive behaviors, including suicide (Twomey, Kaslow, & Croft, 2000). They remain in relationships that seem obviously unhealthy. Why would this be? The need to maintain a relationship with an important object, such as the parent, is so strong that extreme measures are taken to maintain the relationship. Perhaps the faults of the object must be overlooked. Sometimes the person must view herself or himself as deficient in some way, so the fiction can be maintained that love would be available, of only one were worthy (Grand & Alpert, 1993). A sexual abuse victim, for example, may develop the idea, perhaps unconsciously, that she is to blame for the abuse, by acting as a seductress and may then enact this self-image through later promiscuous relationships (cf. Westen, 1991). The other person is also perceived in distorted ways to maintain the illusion.

The sense of self can be radically threatened by the loss of a significant other. When a loved one dies, the relationship with that "object" (person) and one's own sense of self as defined by that relationship are disrupted. To work through the grief, the mourner must give up or transform the relationship with the loved one (Baker, 2001). This may take a variety of forms, including reminiscences, talking with the one who has died, thinking of the person as a ghost, and other forms.

Although psychoanalytic theorists emphasize close interpersonal relationships, such as those in families and intimate bonds, the idea that a disturbed sense of self impairs relationships has also been investigated for our less intimate encounters. Group dynamics researchers report that people with low self-esteem are more drawn to groups that seem to offer little of value, but where acceptance is assured, whereas those with higher self-esteem have the confidence to choose groups that offer more, but that are more selective (Haupt & Leary, 1997).

Narcissism

Whether we develop a sense of self through relationships (as many current theorists, including relational theorists, believe) or whether the sense of self comes first and relationships follow (as Freud proposed), in either case too much focus on the self gets in the way of healthy relationships. An unhealthy self-focus and self-admiration constitutes **narcissism**. In less than 1 in 100 people, narcissism is severe and impairs the person so much that it can be diagnosed as a mental disorder, *narcissistic personality disorder* (American Psychiatric Association, 1994). People who suffer from this disorder are extremely self-focused; they do not have much empathy for other people's experience. Their sense of being special, that they deserve attention and admiration, leads them to use other people as admiring audiences and supporters instead of as separate individuals. Narcissistic students tend to overestimate the grades they will receive (Farwell & Wohlwend-Lloyd, 1998). When undergraduates who score high on a measure of narcissism are asked to describe a shameful early memory (a manipulation theorized to confront the early basis of their narcissism), they subsequently express considerable hostility on an ambiguous projective picture of a child; but those in the experimental group asked to recall a positive memory projected much less hostility onto the picture. Non-narcissists did not show these effects, which supports the interpretation that narcissists' hostility is tied to early shameful experiences (Heiserman & Cook, 1998). It is easy to see why narcissism, which is based on disturbed relationships, may lead to domestic violence (Zosky, 1999).

narcissism unhealthy self-focus that impairs the ability to have healthy, empathic relationships with other people

The insight that a disturbed sense of self is closely related to disturbed relationships with others helps us understand puzzling findings reported by researchers. High *self-esteem*, that is, thinking you are a worthwhile person, is generally a healthy characteristic. High self-esteem has its downside, though. For one thing, people with high self-esteem sometimes take on tasks that are too difficult, apparently trying to prove how much they can do (Baumeister, Heatherton, & Tice, 1993). They also may persist too long at tasks that cannot be finished and are prone to other self-defeating behaviors (Baumeister,

1997a). Surprisingly, it has also been found that people with high self-esteem may also be more aggressive than other people (Baumeister, Smart, & Boden, 1996). Why? One factor to consider is that "self-esteem" is operationally defined as a person's score on a self-report measure. Some people who score high on such measures truly accept who they are, but others have a fragile, grandiose image of themselves hiding a deeper self-doubt. For them, high self-esteem scores are not so much accurate as they are defensive statements. When challenged, they feel vulnerable and so may behave aggressively in an effort to bully their way to being seen as worthwhile. That interpretation suggests that narcissism, not true self-esteem, leads to aggression when a person is insulted or provoked. This interpretation is supported by experimental evidence. Subjects who score high on a test of narcissism behave aggressively toward someone who has insulted them by criticizing essays they had written. When given the opportunity to do so in a laboratory setting, narcissists blast the other person with a loud noise in a computer game (Bushman & Baumeister, 1998). People with a secure, stable self-esteem are not so volatile when insulted, but narcissistic people are readily angered (Rhodewalt & Morf, 1998). Their self-esteem is insecure, subject to the supports and attacks of life's transient events (Rhodewalt, Madrian, & Cheney, 1998), and so they must defend their self-worth, even with aggression.

Attachment in Infancy and Adulthood

Whether we turn to relational theorists, Horney, or even Freud, the experts continue to point to the importance of early relationships between parents and children. Developmental psychologists have long studied this important phenomenon. At first, researchers considered the bonds of love and nurturance that are established between parents and children in infancy. More recently, they have extended this attachment research to include adulthood, investigating the impact of attachment on love relationships at that phase of life.

INFANT ATTACHMENT

attachment bonds of affection in which an infant turns to the mother or other caretaker for comfort and security; by extension, close interpersonal styles in adulthood

Infants develop bonds of affection with their mother, called **attachment** (Ainsworth et al., 1978; Bowlby, 1988a). Attachment functions, in an evolutionary sense, to ensure children's survival by keeping them near to their parents, on whom they depend for survival. John Bowlby, a pioneer of the attachment literature, compares the parents' role to that of a commanding officer in the military who sends out an expeditionary force. If all goes well, the expedition does its task, but if there is trouble, the base provides a secure place to which to retreat. In Bowlby's view, parents should provide "a secure base from which a child or an adolescent can make sorties into the outside world and to which he can return knowing for sure that he will be welcomed when he gets there, comforted if distressed, reassured if frightened. In essence this role is one of being available, ready to respond when called upon to encourage and perhaps assist, but to intervene actively only when clearly necessary" (1988b, p. 11).

Attachment is a basic survival need. In historic observations, René Spitz (1945) observed that orphanage babies deprived of human touch and love became ill and even died, despite adequate food and medical care. Mary Ainsworth (1972; Ainsworth et al., 1978) studied infant attachment to the mother (as the primary caretaker) by observing infants' responses to strangers. The development of a secure attachment between infant and parent provides a basis for emotional health and coping in later life. It facilitates cognitive development in childhood, presumably because the securely attached child has self-confidence to investigate the world (Jacobsen, Edelstein, & Hofmann, 1994). Later love relationships are also healthier when they build on secure attachment.

In the infant attachment studies, researchers observed how infants behaved when in the presence of a stranger. Some infants were frightened; others seemed comforted by their mothers' presence. The various attachment patterns can be interpreted as confirming Horney's patterns of moving toward or away from people (Feiring, 1984). Some infants resist being comforted (Ainsworth's type A), analogous to Horney's moving-away types. Others show anger toward a stranger (Ainsworth's type C), early evidence perhaps of Horney's moving-against mode of relationship. Type B infants are considered securely attached and are likely to show positive indexes of interpersonal relationships and development later in life. This group can be subdivided, however; those who are most likely to cling to the mother (Ainsworth's type B$_4$) may be interpreted (according to Feiring, 1984) as showing Horney's pattern of moving toward, whereas those who explore a new environment rather than clinging to the mother (Type B$_1$) have the balanced interpersonal mode that Horney regarded as most healthy (see Table 6.6).

Parental behaviors found in developmental research to be associated with these types seem to confirm Horney's statements (Feiring, 1984). However, the Ainsworth experimental situation is quite unusual for the infant and so may result in misleading observations (Chess, 1986). Also, we should be cautious about blaming the parents entirely for attachment disturbances. Childhood temperament, produced by genetics, is partly responsible for the greater security of one child compared to another. In the ideal world, parents might be so wise in their parenting skills that they could nurture sufficiently to make all securely attached. However, in the real world, the same parental behavior that is adequate for the average child may leave a temperamentally vulnerable child anxious about attachment. Infant attachments are not only important in themselves, for an infant's survival and well-being, but in addition, they provide a formative model of what relationships are.

TABLE 6.6   Ainsworth's Description of Infant Temperament Types Compared with Horney's Model of Interpersonal Orientations

Infant Type	Infant Behavior	Horney's Interpersonal Orientation
Type A	• Resists being comforted	Moving Away
Type B$_1$	• Securely attached • Comforted by mother • Explores new environment	Balance of the three Interpersonal Orientations
Type B$_4$	• Securely attached • Stays near mother for comfort	Moving Toward
Type C	• Ambivalent toward mother • Shows anger toward stranger	Moving Against

(Adapted from Feiring, 1984.)

ADULT ATTACHMENTS AND RELATIONSHIPS

Attachment styles continue after infancy (Hazan & Shaver, 1994). Attachment in adulthood helps regulate emotion and reduce stress (Feeney & Kirkpatrick, 1996; Silverman, 1998). In the language of another theorist, Erik Erikson, infant relationships provide a person with an enduring sense of trust or mistrust of people that remains significant throughout life. Researchers have found that, indeed, securely attached adults feel more trust toward their partners than do those without secure attachment (Mikulincer, 1998b) and are able to resolve conflicts within relationships more maturely (Corcoran & Mallinckrodt, 2000). They also describe their parents more positively (Levy, Blatt, & Shaver, 1998). Adolescents hospitalized for psychiatric disorders are reported to be insecurely attached, as are their mothers (Rosenstein & Horowitz, 1996). Furthermore, the specific kind of insecure attachment predisposes individuals to particular kinds of psychiatric disorders. *Dismissing attachment*, in which a person minimizes the emotions and thoughts connected with attachment difficulties, predisposes adolescents to conduct disorder or substance abuse and is more typical of males. *Preoccupied attachment* strategies emphasize emotions and lead to affective disorders such as depression; this attachment style is more often found in females (Rosenstein & Horowitz, 1996).

Various kinds of adult attachment resemble infant attachment styles. A person who falls in love, marries, and stays in a stable relationship throughout adulthood exemplifies secure attachment. Another, who is hesitant about love, marries, but divorces not long after and thereafter avoids long-term relationships, illustrates an avoidant attachment style (Klohnen & Bera, 1998). Insecure attachment, too, occurs in adulthood as well as infancy. Michael Sperling describes "desperate love" in some college students as a style of love with high anxiety and the desire to be extremely close to the loved one; this corresponds to insecure attachment in infancy (Sperling & Berman, 1991).

Sperling and his colleagues have suggested a model of four types of adult attachment that emphasizes both dependence and anger. Their model corresponds well to Horney's three interpersonal styles, with an additional category reflecting ambivalence between moving toward and moving against (Sperling, Berman, & Fagen, 1992) (see Table 6.7).

More frequently, however, researchers have adopted a three-category model of adult attachment, corresponding to the infant research (see Table 6.8). It is not only simpler but more optimistic, in that it includes a "secure" category. In this model, *securely attached*

TABLE 6.7   A Model of Adult Attachment Styles

	High Anger	*Low Anger*
High Dependency	Resistant-ambivalent attachment style (compare to Horney's description of conflict between achievement and love, that is, moving against and moving toward)	Dependent attachment style (compare to Horney's moving toward orientation)
Low Dependency	Hostile attachment style (compare to Horney's moving against orientation)	Avoidant attachment style (compare to Horney's moving away orientation)

(Adapted in part from Sperling, Berman, & Fagen, 1992. The comparisons with Horney's theory are added.)

TABLE 6.8   Questions to Measure Three Attachment Styles

One way of classifying adults' attachment style is to simply have them choose which description is most like them. Which of these paragraphs is most like you?

1. I find it relatively easy to get close to others and am comfortable depending on them and having them depend on me. I don't often worry about being abandoned or about someone getting too close to me.

2. I am somewhat uncomfortable being close to others; I find it difficult to trust them completely, difficult to allow myself to depend on them. I am nervous when anyone gets too close and often love partners who want me to be more intimate than I feel comfortable being.

3. I find that others are reluctant to get as close as I would like. I often worry that my partner doesn't love me or won't want to stay with me. I want to merge completely with another person, and this desire sometimes scares people away.

The first paragraph describes a secure attachment style, the second on avoidant attachment style, and the third an anxious-ambivalent attachment style. It would not be surprising if none of these paragraphs described you completely, or if your answer might change from one relationship to another.

(Based on Hazan & Shaver, 1987.)

adults report that they are comfortable with others, can get close to others relatively easily, and do not worry about being abandoned or smothered in a relationship. *Avoidantly attached* adults report difficulty trusting others and avoid becoming dependent on or too close to others. *Anxious-ambivalent* adults worry about not being loved enough by others and want to get close to others, but others seem reluctant to get close to them (Hazan & Shaver, 1987). Personality tests show securely attached adults to be higher on extraversion and lower on neuroticism than anxious and avoidant adults (Shaver & Brennan, 1992). Securely attached adults are also less prone to anger and deal with it more constructively (Mikulincer, 1998a). Adults who are not securely attached have difficulty expressing anger toward their romantic partners; those who are securely attached, in contrast, can express anger appropriately and maintain the relationship (Sharpsteen & Kirkpatrick, 1997). Securely attached college students, as yet unmarried, look forward to having more children and are more confident about their ability to be effective parents, compared to insecurely attached college students (Rholes et al., 1997). In one study, anxiously attached male undergraduates wrote TAT stories containing violent imagery almost twice as frequently as securely attached men did. Stories describing violence of men toward female victims occurred more than seven times as often as in the secure group (and were also rare in the avoidant group), perhaps reflecting the frustrations of anxiously attached men about intimacy (Woike, Osier, & Candela, 1996).

Some studies of attachment examine people's views of themselves and of the other person, as well as the connection between them (Bartholomew, 1990). Does the person think of himself or herself as worthwhile? Does he or she expect others to be supportive? Ideally, the answer to both questions is "yes," giving a positive-self/positive-others view and resulting in a secure attachment style. Unfortunately, either the self or the others, or both, may also be viewed negatively, leading to impaired attachment. A person may have a positive view of self and a negative view of others, leading to a dismissing or counter-dependent attachment style; these people have problems in relationships because they lack warmth. Or a person may think positively of others but negatively of the self, becoming preoccupied with relationships. These people value relationships but have problems in relationships by depending too much on others for their self-esteem, trying too hard to be noticed and involved with others. Perhaps surprisingly, these preoccupied individuals describe conflict in personal relationships less negatively than other types; the conflict, even though painful, helps forge intimacy and get the partner to respond (Pietromonaco & Barrett, 1997). If the views of both self and others are negative, the person is fearful of intimacy and socially avoidant. These people have problems interpersonally by being overly passive in relationships, and they strike others as introverted and unexpressive (Bartholomew & Horowitz, 1991). On psychological measures of self-confidence, well-being, and psychological defenses, people with the securely attached style come across as most mature (Diehl et al., 1998).

LONGITUDINAL STUDIES OF ATTACHMENT

Longitudinal studies of attachment verify that disturbed attachment relationships from early life carry over to adulthood. One study tracked down college students up to 31 years later when they were in their early 50s. In middle age, the women selected one of several paragraphs that best described them (using the method of Hazan & Shaver, 1987), and this allowed researchers to classify their attachment style. Those classified as "avoidantly attached" (that is, insecure in their attachments) had already expressed more ambivalence about marriage and family when they were in college. As the years passed, they were less likely to marry than the securely attached group and more likely to be divorced if they had married. Their files suggested to researchers that, compared to the securely attached, the avoidantly attached were less interpersonally close, more defensive and repressive, and less tolerant to stress from college onward (Klohnen & Bera, 1998). In this study, coming from a larger family and a smaller town were conducive to more secure attachment; childhood loss of a parent through death brought attachment difficulties.

In another study, which gathered data on subjects for 70 years of their lives, subjects whose parents had divorced (a major disruption of attachment relationships for a child) were adversely affected. They were more likely to become divorced themselves, as we might expect from attachment theory. In addition, they were more likely to die earlier, at least in part because stable marriage tends to increase longevity (Tucker et al., 1997).

A representative sample of U.S. adults provides considerable support for the claim that parents have an impact on their children's attachment. Having warm parents and protective fathers bodes well for adult attachment. Adults were less likely to be securely attached if, in childhood, their parents had suffered various forms of psychopathology (including depression, anxiety, and substance abuse), committed suicide, died, or were absent for long periods of time. Other traumas and hardships also were related to insecure attachment: physical and sexual abuse, neglect, accidents, natural disaster, financial adversity, and other distressing events. This same study also finds that adults who are securely attached are more mentally healthy. They are less likely than avoidant or anxiously attached individuals to suffer from depression, phobias, alcohol or drug abuse, and other psychological problems (Mickelson, Kessler, & Shaver, 1997). Securely attached adults marry other securely attached adults; those insecurely attached also tend to marry people with similar attachment problems, which bodes ill for their ability to provide a secure relationship for their children (van Ijzendoom & Bakermans-Kranenburg, 1996).

Parenting

Both relational approaches and Horney's interpersonal psychoanalytic approach agree that parent–child relationships have an immense impact on the emotional development of the child. Developmental researchers are investigating messages about emotion that are conveyed in the family. Parents' understanding of their children's emotional states influences their interactions with the child in ways that can benefit or harm the child's physiological emotional reactions (Gottman, Katz, & Hooven, 1996). And children must learn to understand these emotional messages; for example, it is important to distinguish whether parents are rejecting the child or whether they are simply angry (Eisenberg, 1996).

Drew Westen (1991; Westen et al., 1991) notes that developmental psychologists researching social cognition deal with some of the same issues as psychoanalytic relational theorists. In some cases, the research findings from the developmental psychologists, who are studying children, suggest that the psychoanalytic ideas about development, which were based on retrospective reports by adults and the framework suggested by Freud, need to be modified. For example, object relations in Freud's theory focused on the first five years of life, but developmental research shows that important developments occur later. In addition, developmental research has suggested that several categories of object relationships develop somewhat separately. It is this dialogue between nonclinical researchers and clinical practitioners that is probably the most exciting and propitious aspect of these theories.

Therapy

The knowledge gained from therapists and researchers can be put to practical use to prevent or to treat problems. Stella Chess (1986) noted that "there is no simple and direct correlation between early life experiences and later development" (p. 142); humans are remarkably adaptable, and sometimes they overcome severe environmental deficits. Knowing how early attachment difficulties predispose people to later problems in life gives us insight to develop intervention strategies.

Relational therapists suggest that the patient–therapist relationship provides an opportunity for transformation of old maladaptive relationship patterns to new healthy ones. The transference relationship should be similar enough to old patterns to put these disturbances in the arena of therapy, even if the old relationships were unhealthy, but different enough to stimulate change (Greenberg, 1986/1999). Paradoxically, a patient may need to cast the therapist in the role of the bad parent to experience that warped attachment—for example, acting out anger against a therapist perceived as hostile and rejecting like the patient's parent, before being able to move on to healthier relationships (Knight, 2005).

Summary

- Karen Horney revised psychoanalytic theory to emphasize interpersonal factors.
- The child experiences *basic anxiety* as a result of parental rejection or neglect.

- This anxiety is accompanied by *basic hostility*, which cannot be expressed because of the child's dependence on the parents.
- The child attempts to resolve the conflict by adopting one of three interpersonal orientations: *moving toward* people (the self-effacing solution), *moving against* them (the expansive solution), or *moving away* from them (the resignation solution).
- The healthy person can flexibly use all three orientations, but the neurotic person cannot.
- Horney described four basic strategies for resolving neurotic conflict: *eclipsing* the conflict, *detachment*, the *idealized self*, and *externalization*.
- The neurotic individual turns away from the real self, which has the potential for healthy growth, to an *idealized self*. The *tyranny of the shoulds* supports the idealized self.
- In addition, Horney described several *secondary adjustment mechanisms:* blind spots, compartmentalization, rationalization, excessive self-control, arbitrary rightness, elusiveness, and cynicism.
- Horney emphasized the *cultural determinants* of development. Parenting patterns vary from society to society; even the Oedipus complex is not a universal human experience in her theory.
- Horney discussed sex roles as developments shaped by particular cultures, which can change if cultures change.
- Horneyan therapy seeks to uncover unconscious conflicts originating in childhood but emphasizes their implications for present life. *Self-analysis* can be a useful supplement to psychoanalysis.
- *Relational theorists* (a newer approach than Horney's theory) also emphasize early parent–child relationships and their implications for a sense of self and for interpersonal relationships throughout life.
- Disturbances in *object relationships* contribute to many disorders, including narcissism, and to disturbed relationships in adulthood.
- In addition to contributors from psychoanalysis, developmental researchers investigating *attachment* have contributed to our understanding of object relations.

Thinking about Horney's Theory and the Relational Approach

1. Do you know people who represent each of the three interpersonal orientations that Horney describes? Which orientation best describes you?
2. Horney describes perfectionism critically, saying it can be a defense mechanism. Do you agree, or is it desirable to set very high standards?
3. How would you modify Horney's theory, given the changes in gender roles that have occurred since her work?

4. What can be done in society to give infants and children the kind of parenting that Horney and relational theorists recommend?
5. What are the characteristics of a narcissistic personality?
6. How do attachment styles provide a way of thinking about adjustment?

Study Questions

1. Contrast Horney's understanding of the unconscious with that of Freud.

2. Describe the emotional conflicts of early life. Include an explanation of basic anxiety and basic hostility.

3. List and describe the three interpersonal orientations. Give an example of each.

4. Explain the terms *self-effacing solution, expansive solution*, and *resignation solution* in relation to the three interpersonal orientations.

5. Explain the difference between healthy and neurotic use of the interpersonal orientations.

6. Discuss the research on Horney's interpersonal orientations.

7. List and explain the four major adjustments to basic anxiety.

8. Describe the neurotic's attitude toward the real self.

9. Explain the tyranny of the shoulds. Give a hypothetical example.

10. List and explain the seven secondary adjustment techniques. Give an example of each.

11. Discuss the role of culture in determining development. What did Horney say was the most important conflict of her time?

12. How did Horney explain female masochism?

13. Explain what is meant by womb envy.

14. Describe Horneyan therapy. How does it differ from other therapies we have considered so far?

15. Explain the role and limitations of self-analysis.

16. Explain how parental behavior contributes to neurosis.

17. What is the relational approach?

18. What is narcissism?

19. Describe healthy and unhealthy patterns of attachment in infancy.

20. Describe healthy and unhealthy patterns of attachment in adulthood.

21. Discuss research on attachment from the perspective of relational theory.

22. How do attachment difficulties contribute to anger and aggressive behavior in relationships?

The Trait Perspective

The trait perspective focuses on one of the most fundamental questions in personality: How will we describe people? What are the basic units of personality? One place to begin is with everyday language. People have been talking about one another, labeling one another, since before history was recorded. Raymond Cattell (1943a) remarked, "all aspects of human personality which are or have been of importance, interest, or utility have already become recorded in the substance of language" (p. 483; quoted by Borkenau, 1990). The "lexical approach" attempts to derive a description of personality by systematically examining language, usually beginning with words in the dictionary (Allport & Odbert, 1936; Cattell, 1943b; John, Angleitner, & Ostendorf, 1988). Everyday language, however, is full of subtleties, such as connotations of evaluation (Borkenau, 1990) and causality (Hoffman & Tchir, 1990), that make it less straightforward than scientific constructs should be.

A *trait* is a theoretical construct describing a basic dimension of personality. Although they differ more widely than is generally acknowledged, trait theories agree on some basic assumptions:

1. Trait approaches emphasize *individual differences* in characteristics that are more or less stable across time and across situations.
2. Trait approaches emphasize the *measurement* of these traits through tests, often self-report questionnaires.

Trait measurement has taken a variety of forms. Proposed single traits are often based on observations of behaviors. The traits and their measuring instruments then undergo a process of theoretical refinement and research before they are accepted into the field of personality (Furnham, 1990a). Researchers refine the personality measures by using the statistical technique of factor analysis. Sometimes this is done simply to be sure that a measuring instrument does not contain unrelated questions. Other times factor analysis aims to broaden the measurement to seek general traits that affect a wide variety of behaviors.

The attempt to find the basic, broad dimensions of personality has motivated many researchers. One popular model proposes five basic factors (the "big five"): extraversion, agreeableness, neuroticism, conscientiousness, and openness (Digman, 1990; McCrae & Costa, 1987). Another approach identifies sixteen dimensions, rather than five (Cattell, 1979). Yet another approach proposes only three factors (Eysenck, 1990). The apparent discrepancy can be resolved by considering a hierarchical model, in which a larger number of more specific factors—not entirely uncorrelated with one another—correspond to a smaller number of more general factors (Boyle, 1989). By way of analogy, a person who claims there are only two things to study in college, liberal arts or professional training, does not really disagree with a person who says there are several dozen things to study and then lists all the departments in the college. They are simply speaking at different levels of generality. In the study of personality, the number of "basic dimensions" uncovered depends on how general or specific are the dimensions sought (Marshall, 1991).

Personality trait and factor theories have advanced considerably in recent years, seeking theoretical connections with our expanding understanding of the biological foundations of behavior. Some theories propose specific neurotransmitter variations that cause people to be introverted or extraverted, excitable or calm, and so on (see Chapter 9). It has been argued that a trait approach provides the basis for a coherent paradigm of personality theory in the natural science tradition because "in any science, taxonomy precedes causal analysis" (Eysenck, 1991, p. 774).

Whether trait research ultimately makes such theoretical contributions, it has great value for practical applications. For example, measurement of vocational interest traits helps predict who is suited for particular occupations; those who enter careers that suit their personality are happier and more successful (Dawis, 1996; Hogan, Hogan, & Roberts, 1996; Holland, 1996). Using tests to screen applicants for employment, however, is a practice that has sometimes resulted in lawsuits when candidates claim that tests are biased, resulting in racial or other discrimination (Tenopyr, 1995). Such lawsuits remind us of the importance of validity in testing (as described in Chapter 1), not only for abstract theoretical reasons, but as a fundamental principle of fairness (Lubinski, 1995). Perhaps the prevalence of testing for traits indicates that, whatever theoretical debates remain unresolved, traits exist in the public's eye.

Study Questions

1. What are the assumptions of the trait perspective?
2. Why do some models propose as few as three traits, whereas other approaches propose many more?

ALLPORT
Personological Trait Theory

Chapter
Overview

Preview: Overview of Allport's Theory
Major Themes in Allport's Work
Allport's Definition of Personality
Personality Traits
Personality Development
Influence of Personality on Social Phenomena
Eclecticism
Summary

ILLUSTRATIVE BIOGRAPHY

Mother Teresa

Gordon Allport was especially interested in the healthy functioning of a whole person and particularly interested in the implications of religious attitudes for our behavior toward other people in the world. Clearly he would have found Mother Teresa an example of the positive contributions that he thought could stem from religious motivations.

Mother Teresa, born in Skopje, Serbia, on August 26, 1910 (Spink, 1997), was a world-renowned Roman Catholic nun, mourned worldwide when she died in 1997 (only a few days after the death of Diana, Princess of Wales). She was widely admired by people of many faiths for her charitable work among those she called

the "poorest of the poor" in India and elsewhere. Mother Teresa gained permission from Pope Paul II to establish a new order, the Sisters of Charity, to serve the very poor, including lepers and others, adults and children, whose basic physical needs were not being met. Over time, missions were established in many countries, and her concern for the sick and dying of the world, the "poorest of the poor," mobilized charitable acts by others. Despite her personal humility, the drive to declare her an official "saint" has proceeded at an unusual pace.

Development

Gordon Allport described personality development in terms of stages in the self-concept. Throughout life, he proposed, we move from lack of awareness of a self, to a primitive understanding that our body or physical self is who we are, and then include ever more details to this view. Our possessions (such as childhood toys) are concrete aspects of self, but as we grow to middle childhood we also "own" our intentions and goals, and by adolescence we can become reflective about a more inclusive view of self. Of course, our particular life experiences, especially our experiences in the social world, influence the content of this self-concept. We are influenced by social models, including our parents, but we come to take responsibility for our own behavior, no matter how it originated ("functional autonomy").

As a girl, Agnes Bojaxhiu (Mother Teresa's birth name) was the youngest of three children. She witnessed political upheavals in Albania that led to the First World War, and her father died—possibly murdered for his political views—when Agnes was only 8. Her mother was devoutly religious in the minority Roman Catholic religion of Albania, and she modeled charity to her daughter by helping those who were even poorer than they were. The future Mother Teresa reports feeling called to the life of a nun when she was 12. At 18, with her mother's blessing, she left home and began the process of becoming a postulant and eventually a nun, learning English and traveling to India to help combat illness and poverty. She did not construe the missionary work as social work, however, but instead as a religious contemplation, in which she and the other nuns with whom she served encountered the divine and suffering Jesus through the needy persons they served. She witnessed suffering not only from poverty and illness, but from violent conflict in Calcutta between Muslim and Hindu Indians.

Description

Allport emphasized the uniqueness of each person's traits as they develop ways of adjusting to the world, and he suggested that some people have such clear and cohesive styles of personality (cardinal traits) that their name conjures up a clear image of their personality. Surely that is so for Mother Teresa, world renowned for her life of charitable service toward the poor.

Allport's personological trait theory offered a less formal, more holistic version of trait theory than the more empirically focused trait models that followed. He would use the language of everyday life to describe Mother Teresa's traits: saintly, self-sacrificing, dedicated, well organized, and so on. Allport theorized religion can be used for self-serving reasons or it can inspire genuine love for others (and we would include Mother Teresa in this group). Allport envisioned traits within a model of humanistic development and integration of personality, and so he would emphasize the unifying vision of her religious commitment.

Allport's theory describes consistency of personality, because of a person's enduring traits, even as a person develops a sense of self. Throughout Mother Teresa's life we can find evidence of salient traits. Her trait of humility is evidenced in responses to public acclaim. For example, when she was awarded the much-esteemed Nobel Peace Prize in 1979, she traveled to Norway to accept the prize but stated that the recognition was for the poor, not for herself personally. Certainly Mother Teresa was pious in subjugating selfish pleasure for service to others.

Adjustment

Allport considered a healthy person to have a consistency or unity of personality (in contrast to conflicts among various parts of personality, as described by psychoanalytic theories). He suggests that unification is based on a person's philosophy of life, which for many is a religious philosophy. He suggested additional characteristics of healthy personalities: having interests beyond themselves, interacting with others warmly, emotional security, realistic perceptions, insight and a sense of humor.

Mother Teresa's selfless concern for others is grounded on a unifying focus defined by her religious commitment and her conviction of the importance of love. In the sick and dying, she saw the presence of the suffering Jesus of her faith, and loving them was her calling. She viewed lack of love and prayer in the family as root causes of larger social problems, including loss of world peace (Spink, 1997, p. 132). Personality, in Allport's theory, provides a person's unique adaptation to the world, so we cannot expect that Mother Teresa's way of life is for everyone, but she has raised the world's awareness of the plight of the "poorest of the poor."

Cognition

Besides self concept and a realistic sense of self, already mentioned, Allport's theory includes other cognitive concepts. Social attitudes and values are often analyzed from a cognitive viewpoint. Allport developed a questionnaire to measure values on six scales: Aesthetic, Economic, Political, Religious, Social, and Theoretical.

It is clear that Mother Teresa would have scored high on the Religious scale. Despite her contributions to world social issues, she would likely have scored low on the Political scale; in fact, she avoided politics and is described by her biographer as having been uninformed about apartheid in South Africa (Spink, 1997, p. 214).

Society

A social psychologist as well as personality psychologist, Allport studied some topics of interest to the war effort (World War II), especially rumor transmission, but the best known social applications of his theory concern racial prejudice. Allport realized that people who proclaim themselves to be religious are sometimes cruel, and so he explored various kinds of religious orientation to see whether he could untangle the "brotherhood and bigotry" that he found intertwined. The result has been a classic analysis of religious orientation and prejudice. He predicted, and found, that people are less racially prejudiced if their religion is one in which they have accepted the religious teachings to give selflessly to others ("intrinsic religious orientation"). In contrast, people who see religion as a utilitarian means to improve their condition ("extrinsic religious orientation") are often racially prejudiced. Thus intrinsic religious orientation predicts love for one's neighbor (although, as the chapter points out, there are exceptions).

Mother Teresa's orientation is clearly the more favorable intrinsic religious orientation. Sometimes missionaries can be disrespectful of others' traditions, and because of that, there were some angry protests against the first arrival of her nuns in India. However, despite her own firm commitment to Roman Catholicism, Mother Teresa tolerated the religious views of others, providing for their own religious practices to also be included in celebrations at her charitable institutions (Spink, 1997, p. 123).

Biology

Allport taught that personality traits are physical as well as psychological, but at the time of his theorizing, he could not be more precise than that. He did suggest that an infant's first sense of self begins with the sense of the physical body, but soon cognitive and social issues rise into focus.

Mother Teresa obviously tended to the physical needs of the very poor, feeding them and caring for their wounded bodies. Most important from her point of view, though, was the love.

Final Thoughts

Allport envisioned a theory of personality that was comprehensive in scope, from the physiological to the social and even religious. In his time, he could not fill in all the details, including the physical aspect of traits. His ideas about religious orientation and prejudice, though, have inspired researchers to the present day, and we see that they help us understand the loving acts of Mother Teresa, who met the world as a place to act lovingly on her religious convictions, and not as a place to find converts or to punish evil others.

Preview: Overview of Allport's Theory

Allport's theory has implications for major theoretical questions, as presented in Table 7.1. Allport's work contributed to empirical research on traits and on the relationship of religious orientation to behavior and so can be evaluated positively based on the criterion that a theory should be verifiable. As expected in science, research in subsequent years has built on his early suggestions and has suggested revisions. His contributions also get high marks for comprehensiveness, in that he extended personality consideration to many areas of social behavior, including prejudice, rumor transmission, and intergroup relations. In these areas, his theory also has applied value, suggesting ways to help alleviate social problems.

As an early personality theorist in an academic (as opposed to clinical) setting, Gordon Allport taught the first personality course in the United States and wrote a text for it. In the preface to his 1937 text, *Personality*, he wrote that the study of personality was then a new and increasingly popular area in colleges. "The result of this rising

TABLE 7.1	Preview of Allport's Theory
Individual Differences	Individuals differ in the traits that predominate in their personalities. Some traits are common (shared by various people); others are unique (belonging only to one person).
Adaptation and Adjustment	Psychology errs if it looks too much for illness. Allport listed several characteristics of a healthy personality.
Cognitive Processes	People's self-statements can generally be taken at face value.
Society	Adaptation to society is of central importance. Allport made important contributions to our understanding of prejudice, rumor, and religion.
Biological Influences	All behavior is influenced, in some part, by heredity, but the mechanisms are not specified.
Development	The proprium (ego or self) develops through stages that are outlined but not researched in detail. Adult development consists of integrating earlier developments.

tide of interest is an insistent demand for a guide book that will *define* the new field of study—one that will articulate its objectives, formulate its standards, and test the progress made thus far" (Allport, 1937b, p. vii). Thus he formulated some of the issues that the field of personality has continued to debate, including the nature and role of personality traits, the relationship between personality and social behavior, and the self.

Allport's theory is called *personological,* a term that emphasizes the development of a *person,* a unified and conscious whole (cf. Barresi, 1999). This theme is important for the humanistic movement in psychology (considered later in this book). In fact, Allport was one of the early founders of a formal humanistic organization in psychology, and Roy DeCarvalho (1991a) reports that Allport was the first to use the term *humanistic psychology.* Allport urged personality theorists to use concepts that take into account the unique capacities of humans (as opposed to animals) and emphasize healthy functioning. His emphasis on the whole person, the self, has continued in the humanistic movement (Maddi & Costa, 1972), although his own theoretical focus could more accurately be portrayed as eclectic (Nicholson, 1997).

Allport's eclectic approach included contributions from various schools of psychology. "Better to expand and refashion one's theories until they do some measure of justice to the richness and dignity of human personality, than to clip and compress personality until it fits one closed system of thought" (Allport, 1937b, p. vii). Although he taught both psychoanalysis and learning theory, he viewed these approaches as limited. Psychoanalysis overemphasized the unconscious and did not pay enough attention to conscious motivation, whereas learning theory missed uniquely human qualities that cannot be understood through an animal model. Allport challenged the excessive emphasis on scientific methodology of the behaviorist school, represented by John Watson and by B. F. Skinner, his colleague at Harvard.

Allport conducted research as well as proposing theoretical ideas, and he hoped science would enhance psychology's applied contributions to human welfare. Nonetheless, Allport argued that it was a mistake for methodology to overshadow the content of a field. In its early years, he said, personality was better served by paying attention to common sense and to philosophy and the liberal arts. Despite his own attitude, he correctly predicted that methodological issues would dominate the future of personality. To many, Allport's emphasis on a commonsense approach and on global personality traits makes his ideas obsolete and primarily of historical interest, but others defend his intuitively meaningful insights as theoretically helpful even in modern times (e.g., Funder, 1991).

BIOGRAPHY OF GORDON ALLPORT

GORDON ALLPORT

Gordon Allport was born in 1897 in Montezuma, Indiana, the fourth son of a salesman who was changing careers to become a country doctor. The family moved several times when Allport was very young. They finally settled in Cleveland, Ohio, where Allport grew up in a hardworking, midwestern, Protestant environment. His mother, who had been a schoolteacher, encouraged the educational and religious interests of her four sons and hoped that Gordon would become a missionary (Nicholson, 1998), and his father expected them to help out in the office. Allport remained, in adulthood, a devout Episcopalian (Pettigrew, 1999).

Allport graduated second in his high school class of 100. He then followed his second brother, Floyd, who was 7 years older, to Harvard University, where Floyd was a graduate student in psychology. Gordon Allport was a subject in his brother's research on social influence. After a shockingly poor set of first exam grades, he began working to the higher standards expected at Harvard and earned A's. He studied psychology and social ethics. He did volunteer work at a Boston boys club throughout college. After graduation, he taught English and sociology briefly overseas, in Constantinople; later he returned to Harvard with a fellowship for graduate study in psychology.

On his return trip to the United States, Allport stopped in Vienna to visit his brother Fayette. While there, he requested a meeting with Sigmund Freud. Allport was only 22 at the time. Looking back on the visit later, Allport (1967, p. 8) said he was motivated to meet with Freud by "rude curiosity and youthful ambition." In his naiveté, he had not thought to prepare an introductory statement to Freud explaining the reason for the meeting. Freud sat in silence, probably expecting that this was a therapeutic consultation because his reputation drew many patients from distant places. As Allport tells it,

> I was not prepared for silence and had to think fast to find a suitable conversational gambit. I told him of an episode on the tram car on my way to his office. A small boy about four years of age had displayed a conspicuous dirt phobia. He kept saying to his mother, "I don't want to sit there . . . don't let that dirty man sit beside me." To him everything was schmutz. His mother was a well-starched Hausfrau, so dominant and purposive looking that I thought the cause and effect apparent.

> When I finished my story Freud fixed his kindly therapeutic eyes upon me and said, "And was that little boy you?" Flabbergasted and feeling a bit guilty, I contrived to change the subject. . . . Freud's misunderstanding of my motivation was amusing. . . . This experience taught me that depth psychology. . . may plunge too deep, and that psychologists would do well to give full recognition to manifest motives before probing the unconscious. (p. 8)

Freud's clinical intuition suggested to him that Allport feared being "dirtied" by this contact with psychoanalysis. Allport argued that it was not a therapeutic meeting, and the manifest (conscious) level of his experience, which was simply a desire to impress Freud with his powers of observation, was the appropriate level at which to interpret his anecdote about the little boy. This theme, that psychology should pay more attention to conscious self-reports, became a major element of Allport's theory as it developed over the next several decades.

For his doctoral dissertation, Allport investigated personality traits. This was then a new topic, one criticized by more traditional, experimentally minded psychologists. His first publication on personality traits was jointly authored with his brother Floyd (Allport & Allport, 1921). Gordon received his doctorate in 1922, at the age of 24. He then did postdoctoral study in Europe. There he learned more about Gestalt psychology and the German doctrine of types, themes reflected in his later consideration of holism and his development of a type inventory. He accepted a teaching position at Harvard in social ethics in 1924. In 1925 Allport married Ada Lufin Gould, a clinical psychologist. They had one son, Robert, who became a pediatrician.

Allport taught at Harvard, his alma mater, for most of his professional life, with the exception of 4 years at Dartmouth College beginning in 1926. He developed a new course called "Personality: Its Psychological and Social Aspects," which he reported was probably the first personality course taught in the United States. He did much writing and research on social psychology as well as personality. For a time, he chaired Harvard's Department of Psychology. He joined the University's Department of Social Relations when, in 1946, it separated from the Psychology Department. There he pursued interdisciplinary work with sociology and anthropology.

Allport rose to prominence in national circles. He edited the major journal in the field, the *Journal of Abnormal and Social Psychology* (1937–1948), and was president of the American Psychological Association (1939). He was one of the founders, in 1936, of the Society for the Psychological Study of Social Issues (SPSSI), an organization that applies psychological insights to practical social issues, and he became its president in 1944. The organization continues to commemorate Allport's memory by awarding an annual prize for a paper on intergroup relations. Allport was one of several U.S. psychologists who assisted intellectuals in Europe to find work in the United States so they could flee Nazi Germany. Another contribution at the time of the war was his effort to help control wartime rumors, reflected in his daily newspaper column and his later book on rumors (Allport & Postman, 1947). He was awarded many professional honors. Gordon Allport died of lung cancer on October 9, 1967, at age 69.

Major Themes in Allport's Work

Allport had a major influence on the selection of issues that would concern the field of personality as it developed during the following decades. Here are some of the issues identified by Allport, which personality theorists have grappled with ever since.

PERSONALITY CONSISTENCY

The concept of personality consistency across time and across situations is central to the field of personality. Allport (1937b) argued strongly that from infancy on, humans are consistent, or "remarkably recognizable," even though they vary from situation to situation and across time.

SOCIAL INFLUENCE

Allport, who was quite aware that people live in a social environment that exerts a significant influence, considered specific social issues. For example, he wrote a major work on prejudice that has become a classic text (Allport, 1954), and he studied rumor transmission (Allport & Postman, 1947). At a time when mass communication was quaint by modern standards, he and his former student Hadley Cantril wrote a book called *The Psychology of Radio* (Cantril & Allport, 1935; Pandora, 1998).

THE CONCEPT OF SELF

In an age when many other psychological approaches were reductionistic, Allport argued for the notion of self as a major focus of personality growth. The self is now a major theoretical concept in personality and social psychology, widely used in areas as diverse as humanistic clinical psychology and cognitive social psychology.

INTERACTION OF PERSONALITY WITH SOCIAL INFLUENCE

It is no surprise that a psychologist who was both a personality psychologist and a social psychologist would not think of personality and situations as either-or causes but would rather consider how they work together as joint influences. Situations influence people, but they influence individuals in different ways, as the interactionist approach to personality recognizes (Endler & Magnusson, 1976). In Allport's (1937b) words, "The same heat that melts the butter hardens the egg" (pp. 102, 325). He did not, however, develop the notion of the interaction between personality and environment beyond this brief sketch. He acknowledged that in his emphasis on personality traits, he had "neglect[ed] the variability induced by ecological, social, and situational factors" (Allport, 1966b, p. 9). He recognized that further theoretical advances were needed to develop this concept of interactionism (Zuroff, 1986).

In summary, Allport anticipated many of the themes that would concern personality psychology in the decades since his classic personality text was first published. Current approaches are more sophisticated in their analysis of empirical data, certainly. Nonetheless, the basic themes of consistency, social influence, the self, and the interaction of personality with the environment have remained important foci.

Allport's Definition of Personality

After a review of 49 other definitions of personality in psychology, theology, philosophy, law, sociology, and common usage, Allport (1937b) proposed what has become a classic definition of **personality**: *Personality is the dynamic organization within the individual of those psychophysical systems that determine his unique adjustments to the environments"*

personality for Gordon Allport, "the dynamic organization within the individual of those psychophysical systems that determine his unique adjustments to the environment"

(p. 48; emphasis in original). Although the definition is much quoted, it is not universally accepted because it contains assumptions that not all personality theorists concede. Let us look in detail at Allport's explanation of the five major concepts in his definition of personality because it provides a broad outline of his theory.

DYNAMIC ORGANIZATION

Allport (1937b) referred to "the dynamic organization" of personality in order "to stress active organization" (p. 48). Healthy people become integrated, "getting it all together." Dynamic organization evolves as a developmental process, and a failure of integration is a mark of psychopathology.

This theme of organization, or unity, is not shared by all theories. Traditional learning theories deal, instead, with discrete behavioral units, or stimulus–response associations. Psychoanalysis tends to fragment people into conflicting parts. Allport believed that psychoanalysis has a restricted view of personality because it is based on clinical populations and studies people who have not become wholly integrated, whose symptoms do not seem to fit with the rest of their personality. In contrast, healthy personality becomes an organized and self-regulating whole.

PSYCHOPHYSICAL SYSTEMS

temperament innate emotional aspects of personality

Personality is subject to biological as well as psychological influences. Mind and body are inextricably united. **Temperament** refers to biologically based differences in personality, often evidenced as emotional reactivity to new or potentially frightening stimuli. It is the basis, for example, of one person's shyness and another's bold adventurousness. Allport accepted the empirical research available in his day, indicating that temperament constitutes an inherited biological foundation for personality. Since that time, additional evidence further supports the importance of biologically based temperament, already observable in infancy (e.g., Kagan, 1989; Kagan & Snidman, 1991a, 1991b). Allport (1937b) listed inherited physique and intelligence, together with temperament, as "the three principal raw materials of personality" (p. 107).

How important is heredity as a determinant of personality? Allport asserted that it is always important. "*No feature of personality is devoid of hereditary influences*" (Allport, 1937b, p. 105; emphasis in original). All are influenced by experience, too. Allport offered a mathematical expression of this pervasive influence of heredity through a multiplicative equation:

$$\text{Personality} = f(\text{Heredity}) \times (\text{Environment})$$

"The two causal factors are not added together, but are interrelated as multiplier and multiplicand. If either were zero there could be no personality," he stated (p. 106). The mathematical properties of an alternative, *additive* model (which adds heredity and environment instead of multiplying them) would be different because then heredity and environment could have independent effects, and either could be zero without negating the effect of the other.

This was a theoretical statement, based on reasoning rather than research, at this early time in the history of personality as an academic area. Allport anticipated later biological and medical research to understand biological contributions to personality. Allport commented, "I believe . . . we'll never have a complete psychology of personality until we have a much better knowledge of genetic factors" (Evans, 1981b, p. 49).

DETERMINATIVE

For some theorists, personality concepts are useful predictors but are not themselves real. Allport disagreed, using the word *determine* to emphasize that personality is a cause of behavior. Allport (1937b) said that this term "is a natural consequence of the biophysical view. Personality is something and does something" (p. 48). Traits are real in a physical sense. "Traits are not creations in the mind of the observer, nor are they verbal fictions; they are here accepted as biophysical facts, actual psychophysical dispositions related—though no one yet knows how—to persistent neural systems of stress and determination" (p. 339).

This assertion of traits as determinative distinguishes Allport's view of personality from two alternatives. The first alternative is the view that personality traits are simply conceptual abstractions—that is, useful conceptual tools for predicting behavior. This argument recognizes that the concepts of personality are useful because they summarize many observations. Nonetheless, it denies that personality is real and determinative; it simply is convenient to speak as if it were real. By way of analogy, astronomers know that stars we refer to as constellations (Orion, the Big Dipper, etc.) are not near one another in the universe and so do not constitute any real group. Nonetheless, it is convenient to refer to them as a group because that is how they appear from Earth, and the group can help orient travelers who may be without a compass.

The second alternative to Allport's assertion that traits are determinative is more pessimistic. This objection states that using personality traits to explain behavior is a meaningless circular argument. For example, you see a man talking to a lot of people, so you say he is outgoing. Then, asked why he talks to a lot of people, you say it is because he is outgoing. This is circular reasoning (see Figure 7.1). If the same behavior that prompts inference of the trait is predicted to result from it, the trait cannot fail. Without the possibility of disconfirmation, a theoretical construct is not useful. Allport was not ignorant of the potential problem of circular reasoning, that labeling is not really an answer. He discussed this issue in relationship to the question of whether the

Figure 7.1 Circular Reasoning

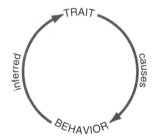

Critics of trait concepts argue that it is circular reasoning to say a trait causes the same behavior that is the basis for inferring the trait exists.

concept of a self is necessary in psychology (Allport, 1955, pp. 54–55), but he did not think that the circular reasoning argument invalidated the usefulness of his personality concepts.

The idea that traits determine behavior has been involved in heated theoretical debates in personality and social psychology. Within modern social psychology, many studies have investigated the idea that behavior is less related to the actor's personality traits than it is to the influence of the situation. To a large extent, this research suggests that situations are more important and personality traits are less important than Allport thought (e.g., Bem & Allen, 1974; Mischel & Peake, 1982). In addition, considerable research effort has been devoted to understanding the everyday tendency to infer traits from behavior—for example, inferring that a person who gives to charity has a trait of generosity. Researchers have established that most people do erroneously infer traits from behavior too readily, underestimating the extent to which situations determine behavior: an error called the "correspondence bias" (Gilbert & Malone, 1995). (Psychologists avoid this error by making repeated observations that would reveal disconfirming evidence if the trait was not there.)

UNIQUE

For Allport, traits are highly individualized, or unique. He explicitly disagreed with theorists who asserted that one or a few motives, or instincts, are determinative for all people (as, for example, Freud attributed personality to sexual motivation). Rather, people are motivated by diverse traits reflecting the differences in their learning.

> But are not the purposes of different people far too diverse and too numerous to be traced to a few primal motives shared by all the species? Are the directions of striving after all innately determined? Is it not necessary to allow for the learning of new motives and for the acquisition of novel interests as personality matures? (Allport, 1937b, p. 113)

ADJUSTMENTS TO THE ENVIRONMENT

Allport (1937b) emphasized the adaptive, coping functions of personality. "Personality results from the attempts of the central nervous system to establish security and comfort for the individual torn between his own affective cravings and the harsh demands of his environment" (p. 118). Allport was far more interested in these, which would be called ego functions by psychoanalysts, than in the internal conflicts preventing adaptation that occur in the mentally unhealthy. These adaptations are unique to each individual because of differences in heredity and environment.

Personality Traits

According to Allport (1931, 1937b), the primary unit of personality is the trait. Listing a person's traits provides a description of that person's personality. What are these crucial units?

ALLPORT'S DEFINITION OF TRAIT

Allport (1937b) defined a **trait** as "a generalized and focalized neuropsychic system (peculiar to the individual), with the capacity to render many stimuli functionally equivalent, and to initiate and guide consistent (equivalent) forms of adaptive and expressive behavior" (p. 295).

In this definition, he reiterated themes from his definition of personality: the psychophysical emphasis, the uniqueness of the individual, the focus on adaptation, and the concept of the trait as a determinative entity. Traits develop over time, with experience. They may change as the individual learns new ways of adapting to the world (p. 146). They are, however, relatively stable, in contrast to *states*, which change quickly—for example, a moment of anger (state) on being cut off in traffic, in contrast with a chronic trait of hostility (cf. Chaplin, John, & Goldberg, 1988).

Allport identified various kinds of traits, thus outlining for later theorists and researchers the different perspectives from which personality can be studied.

> **trait** a characteristic of a person that makes a person unique, with a unique style of adapting to stimuli in the world

CAN WE ALL BE DESCRIBED BY THE SAME TRAITS?

Does everyone have different traits? Or do we have the same traits, only in different amounts? Most researchers base their work on the second alternative, but Allport did not rule out either possibility. Based on the work of the German philosophers Windelband and Stem (Hermans, 1988), Allport distinguished **individual traits**, which are possessed by only one person, from **common traits**, which are possessed by many people, each to a varying extent. He intended to distinguish "the study of *persons* on the one hand and the study of *person variables*, that is, variables with respect to which persons have been differentiated, on the other" (Lamiell, 1997, p. 123). The distinction may appear simple at first, but its implications are enormous.

In everyday speech, we often describe people by using common traits, comparing how much of a trait each person has. For example, we may describe Walt Disney as more creative than others or Albert Einstein as more intelligent than the rest of us. Creativity and intelligence, and many other traits, too, can be applied to all of us in common, although some have more of each trait and others have less. Psychologists recognize that various people seem to have traits similar enough to be called by the same name and considered together. Allport (1937b, p. 298) regarded such inquiry as legitimate.

However, such common traits are not the ultimate real units of personality in Allport's theory. The real units of personality are **unique traits**, which exist within an individual and have status as psychophysical realities. Thus the psychologist comparing people on ascendance-submission or on any other common trait,

> **individual trait** a trait that characterizes only the one person who has it (i.e., a trait considered from the idiographic point of view)

> **common trait** a trait characterizing many people (i.e., a trait considered from the nomothetic point of view)

> **unique trait** a trait that only one person has (also called individual trait)

> does not measure directly the full-bodied individual trait that alone exists as a neuro-psychic disposition and as the one irreducible unit of personality. What he does is to measure a common aspect of this trait, such a portion thereof as takes common cultural forms of expression and signifies essentially the same manner of adjusting within the social group. (Allport, 1937b, p. 298)

Allport asserted, "In the strict sense of the definition of traits . . . the common (continuum) trait is not a true trait at all, but is merely a measurable aspect of complex individual traits" (p. 299).

Traits are individualized adaptive entities, unique to each person. Allport (1937b) argued, "Strictly speaking, no two persons ever have precisely the same trait" (p. 297). In principle, all traits are unique to the individual. According to his argument, it is not possible to describe fully differences between people by simply scoring them on a set of universally applied traits. To understand an individual fully, it would be necessary to have a list of traits specifically chosen for that person. That is, only an idiographic approach can adequately describe an individual. Although Allport accepted nomothetic research as a rough approximation for research purposes, he believed it would never result in identifying the fundamental drives of all people (Allport, 1940). However appealing this argument may be, the distinction between unique traits (idiographic research) and common traits (nomothetic research) is difficult to translate into precise research methods. A reviewer of his 1937 book complained that Allport's explanation of individual traits was not clear and that the examples he used were simply extreme scores on common traits (Paterson, 1999).

Allport did not differentiate between idiographic methods (single-subject research) and idiography as a theoretical position (that each person is unique), which has further confused the debate over the value of an idiographic approach (Marceil, 1977). Many objections have been raised against a theory of idiographic traits. One argument is that such studies of individuals can provide ideas and generate hypotheses but that actually testing hypotheses requires the traditional nomothetic methods of science (Eysenck, 1954). Another objection is that it is logically impossible to be genuinely idiographic because implicit comparisons with others are always made. Finally, when individuals are studied, what is learned may not apply to other people, which is disappointing for a science that seeks general laws (Emmerich, 1968; Holt, 1962). Conversely, for reasons that are rather subtle, the relationships found by studying groups of people do not necessarily apply to the study of individuals (Lamiell, 1987).

Understanding individuals' behavior and functioning is a primary task of personality theory (Lamiell, 1997; Runyan, 1983), and this requires studying individuals, not only groups. Allport emphasized the need to individualize trait conceptions. In one study (Conrad, 1932), which Allport described, teachers rated students on various traits. Reliability of these ratings was not particularly high overall. However, if teachers indicated with a star which traits particularly described the child, those starred ratings had a much higher agreement (Allport, 1937b, p. 301). Thus the same set of traits is not useful for describing every person, but the central traits of an individual can be rated reliably. Other researchers since Allport have essentially replicated this finding (Cheek, 1982; Markus, 1977). Baumeister and Tice (1988; Baumeister, 1991) offer a statistical approach for dealing with Allport's belief that not everyone possesses the same traits. Each trait can be thought of as having an associated "metatrait," which is simply whether the individual has the trait (at any level—low, medium, or high). If the metatrait indicates that the trait is relevant to the individual, a trait measure is meaningful. If the metatrait indicates the trait is not relevant, no trait measure is meaningful, just as it is sensible to skip a question asking "How well do you get along with your sister?" if you do not have one.

INFERRING TRAITS

How do we know what traits a person possesses? Allport suggested several methods for inferring a person's traits. He began, sensibly enough, with the wisdom of everyday language.

Inferring Traits from Language: The Dictionary Study

Gordon Allport and Henry Odbert (1936) conducted a study in which they listed all of the trait words in the 1925 edition of *Webster's New International Dictionary* used to describe individuals. Excluding obsolete terms, they identified 17,953 trait names, which was 4.5% of the total words in the dictionary. They classified these trait names into four categories:

1. Neutral Terms Designating Personal Traits (e.g., "artistic," "assertive")
2. Terms Primarily Descriptive of Temporary Moods or Activities (e.g., "alarmed," "ashamed")
3. Weighted Terms Conveying Social or Characterial Judgments of Personal Conduct, or Designating Influence on Others (e.g., "adorable," "asinine")
4. Miscellaneous: Designations of Physique, Capacities, and Developmental Conditions; Metaphorical and Doubtful Terms (e.g., "alone," "Anglican")

They suggested that the first, purely descriptive, category would be most useful to personality psychologists as a compilation of nonevaluative terms for enduring traits.

Researchers have developed this method further, searching the language that people use every day for words that describe personality and having research subjects make judgments about how well these terms describe various people. By statistically analyzing these judgments, researchers have determined that certain major dimensions of personality are represented in everyday language. These dimensions are often referred to as the "big five" dimensions of personality: extraversion, agreeableness, neuroticism, openness, and conscientiousness (Angleitner, Ostendorf, & John, 1990; John, 1990; John, Angleitner, & Ostendorf, 1988), and they are further described in Chapter 8.

Inferring Traits from Behavior

Traits may also be inferred from behavior. People who talk a lot are judged to be outgoing; people who exercise regularly are called athletic. Allport suggested that *interests* are a good clue to personality. Behavioral inferences can be made in natural circumstances. For example, children can be observed in their everyday lives, using a time-sampling procedure (Allport, 1937b, pp. 315–316). Or observations can be made in an experimental setting if subjects are given a diverse set of tasks.

Allport and Vernon (1933) conducted such an experimental study to determine whether **expressive traits** could be inferred. Expressive traits are concerned with one's style of behavior—for example, how fast or slow, energetic, or graceful is an action. Allport and Vernon intensively studied 25 male subjects. They obtained exhaustive measures of handwriting, walking, tapping, reading, and so on, and had raters code these behaviors (e.g., measuring the length of check marks). They concluded that their subjects had consistent expressive traits, such as expansiveness or emphasis, that affected these various measures. Few researchers have continued such research. One source of embarrassment is that Allport and Vernon provided personality sketches of people based on handwriting (graphology), which many in academic psychology banish to the realm of pseudoscience.

A review of research finds that, although handwriting analysis is popular in lay circles and even widely used as a part of personnel selection in European companies, it has not stood up to scientific tests of validity (Greasley, 2000). As in many popularly researched hypotheses, some studies do provide support for the idea that handwriting correlates

expressive traits
traits concerned with the style or tempo of a person's behavior

with personality traits, such as extraversion (Riggio, Lippa, & Salinas, 1990; cf. Wellingham-Jones, 1989), but overall, science does not support handwriting as an indicator of personality. Other expressive traits may have more value, for example, as predictors of coronary heart disease. Specifically, the expressive style with which interviewees respond to the structured interview, used to assess type A behavior (a coronary risk factor), is more important than the content of responses in predicting heart disease (Friedman & Booth-Kewley, 1987). In the practical world where terrorists and criminals threaten the public, law enforcement personnel turn to handwriting analysts not only to match handwriting samples but also to develop personality profiles of yet unidentified criminals (Grossman, 2001).

Inferring Traits from Documents: Letters from Jenny

We can infer traits from many documents or records of people's lives, including diaries, letters, public statements, and so forth. Sometimes existing documents, those not produced specifically for research purposes, are unusually rich. Allport had kept a collection of 301 letters written to him and his wife by Jenny Grove Masterson, who was the mother of Allport's roommate in college and had turned to Gordon as a "good son," in contrast to her own disappointing child (Winter, 1997). The letters covered a period of 11 years, beginning in 1926, until her death at the age of 70. They disclose an interesting but sad tale of a woman who found life difficult, worried about money, and complained frequently about her son's neglect. Allport and his students interpreted these letters from assorted theoretical perspectives, including various psychoanalytic approaches (Freudian, Jungian, Adlerian, and ego approaches) and learning theory.

Allport's own approach, which he called *structural-dynamic*, was in essence a content analysis of the letters. Content analysis is a research strategy in which material is coded to summarize what it contains, with minimal interpretation. For example, a content analysis of dream transcripts might count the number of aggressive acts, animals, people talking, and so on, but would not interpret these as symbols. Allport and his research assistants and students read Jenny's letters and listed adjectives describing the personality traits they inferred from them. Combining analyses by 36 raters, Allport (1965, pp. 193–194) concluded that Jenny's personality could be summarized by eight traits: quarrelsome-suspicious; self-centered; independent-autonomous; dramatic-intense; aesthetic-artistic; aggressive; cynical-morbid; and sentimental.

Content coding requires considerable time. It can be simplified by using a computer. One of Allport's students, Jeffrey Paige (1966), used a computer procedure called the General Inquirer to analyze Jenny's letters. He described eight recurring themes: acceptance, possessiveness, need for affiliation, need for autonomy, need for familial acceptance, sexuality, sentience, and martyrdom (Allport, 1965, pp. 200–201). Allport noted that this list of factors was remarkably similar, although not identical, to the categories he had earlier derived "from common-sense interpretation" (p. 201).

Aided by computers, researchers can code material more quickly and reliably than by hand (Rosenberg, Schnurr, & Oxman, 1990). Even with computers, though, content analysis requires coders to spend much more time than would be needed to score objective self-report questionnaires. It is a valuable method that permits analysis of existing letters, diaries, speeches, and so on, without requiring subjects to respond to a researcher's questions, and it allows researchers to study materials from people such as political leaders, who would be unlikely to agree to fill out research questionnaires (e.g., D. G. Winter, 1993; Winter & Carlson, 1988; Winter et al., 1991a, 1991b), or historical figures long dead, who could not do so (e.g., Broehl & McGee, 1981; Craik, 1988).

Inferring from Personality Measurement: The Study of Values

We can also infer traits from personality tests. Allport did some of this nomothetic type of research. Crediting the influence of German philosophers, especially Spranger, Allport (1937b, pp. 227–228) said among the most important characteristics that distinguish people from one another are their values—that is, those things toward which they strive. With colleagues, he developed a scale to measure values, named (in its revised form) the Allport-Vernon-Lindzey Study of Values (Allport & Vernon, 1931; Allport, Vernon, & Lindzey, 1951) (see Table 7.2).

This self-report instrument consists of 60 questions. Scores are compared with normative data to determine which values are relatively high for an individual. Allport (1966b) reported that college students who entered different occupations had different value scores. For example, those who entered business scored higher on economic values. Later research confirms that scores on the Study of Values taken during college were associated with occupations of male students 25 years later (Huntley & Davis, 1983).

Despite considerable stability, values can change over time. Baird (1990) reported a 20-year longitudinal study indicating that Religious scale scores declined during the 4 years of college, with little change thereafter, except that graduates who moved away from their conservative college regions became more liberal. In another study, a group of talented 13-year-old students participating in a program for gifted youth at Johns Hopkins University took the Study of Values at that early age and again at age 33. Although there were of course some continuities, there also were changes; overall, as these youth matured, they rated Aesthetic and Economic values more highly and decreased the relative emphasis on Political and Social values (Lubinski, Schmidt, & Benbow, 1996). Studies such as these demonstrate both stability and change in values.

Allowing for Inconsistency in Making Trait Inferences

Traits and behavior do not have a one-to-one correspondence. Even optimists sometimes cry, and a person who offers to help may not always turn out to be altruistic. *Phenotypical* appearances or behaviors do not always correspond to underlying motives or traits, which are called *genotypical* (Allport, 1937b, p. 325). As Allport observed, "Perfect consistency will never be found and must not be expected" (p. 330). There are several reasons for this. For one thing, more than one trait influences any particular behavior, and people often possess traits that are themselves contradictory. Consider a person who possesses the traits of domineering and respectful. These traits could cause

TABLE 7.2   The Allport-Vernon-Lindzey Study of Values

Scale	Description of Value	Typical Occupation
Social	Helping people	Social work
Theoretical	Search for truth	College professor
Economic	Pragmatic, applied	Business
Aesthetic	Artistic values	Artist
Political	Power and influence	Politics
Religious	Religion, harmony	Clergy

the person to be submissive toward authority figures but domineering over others. Also, behavior is influenced by several traits at a time, even if they are not contradictory. Any given trait may not always be active. For example, a usually generous person might not give to someone in need when he or she is in a hurry. In this example, traits of goal achievement are in "a state of active tension" (p. 330), while the trait of generosity is momentarily dormant.

Allport's Attitude toward Methodology

Allport raised serious concerns about methodology in trait measurement, clearly addressing the philosophical basis of psychological research. Should psychology be based on methodologically rigorous experimental-positivistic philosophy or on humanistic experiential-phenomenological philosophy (DeCarvalho, 1990a)? Allport favored the latter. Animal research cannot, he argued (Allport, 1940), give complete understanding of human psychology. He was not enthusiastic about computers and methodology, although he acknowledged the importance of "corrective empiricism" as a contribution of psychology (Allport, 1937b, p. 231). However, he distrusted complicated statistical procedures, such as factor analysis, as a way of discovering traits. Factor analysis, he argued, loses the individual in the average. He remarked that "factors often seem remote from psychological fact, and as such they risk the accusation that they are primarily mathematical artifacts" (p. 245). He praised content analysis, such as he used to analyze Jenny's letters (described "above"), because it kept researchers close to the data. Allport said we need to be guided by theory and common sense, not by data alone. To expect truth to emerge from study after study not guided by theory and common sense is folly and can yield quite bizarre results. He cited as one "example of empiricism gone wild" an empirically derived scale in which "children who give the response word 'green' to a stimulus word 'grass' receive a score of +6 for 'loyalty to the gang'" (p. 329). He preferred to ask people rather directly about their traits and to take responses at face value instead of reading too much into the replies. That preference also caused him to argue for traits as the basic units of personality, in contrast to another tradition, represented by Henry Murray and a host of researchers on TAT-based research, that emphasized motives (Winter et al., 1998).

Allport's objection to methodological excess reflects his concern for the uniqueness of the individual, who gets lost in the nomothetic, measurement-oriented approach. Allport (1940) expressed dismay at the decline in reporting individual case histories. Although acknowledging there is a place for methodological concerns within psychology, he argued, along with other humanistic psychologists such as Abraham Maslow, that psychology should be not method centered but problem centered. To overvalue methods, losing sight of the questions being asked about personality, is "methodolatry" (Evans, 1981b, p. 88).

THE PERVASIVENESS OF TRAITS: CARDINAL, CENTRAL, AND SECONDARY TRAITS

How pervasive is the influence of a particular trait? It varies. For example, you may have the trait of being a drinker of decaffeinated coffee, but that would be noticeable only occasionally, such as when you are drinking coffee or buying it. However, if you have a trait of being self-confident, it affects many more aspects of your life: how you behave with others, what risks you choose to take, and so forth.

Allport categorized traits as cardinal, central, or secondary, depending on how extensively they influence personality. The most pervasive are cardinal traits; the least pervasive are secondary traits. The usual terms we use to describe someone are at the intermediate level: central traits.

Central Traits

In the preceding example, self-confident would be a **central trait** because it pervasively affects many behaviors. Allport's analysis of Jenny's letters led to the inference that she had eight central traits, as we have seen. Someone who knows you well could summarize your personality in a small number of central traits, perhaps six to ten adjectives.

central trait one of the half dozen or so traits that best describe a particular person

The specific traits, of course, vary from person to person. A characteristic that is a central trait for one person might not even be relevant for another. Therefore, it is not the trait of self-confidence that makes it central but rather the fact that many behaviors are affected by it. If a person is self-confident in playing chess but not in many other things, for that person self-confidence would not be a central trait because its influence is not pervasive. It would be a secondary trait.

Secondary Traits

Secondary traits describe ways in which a person is consistent but do not affect so much of what that person does as a central trait. Secondary traits are "less conspicuous, less generalized, less consistent, and less often called into play than central traits" (Allport, 1937b, p. 338). Liking decaffeinated coffee in the example discussed above is an instance of a secondary trait. So, too, would be most tastes and personal preferences: "John likes spinach"; "Sarah's favorite color is mauve"; "David always orders almond fudge ice cream." Such personal preferences do not affect many behaviors, although they are consistent. Of course, for some people a personal preference may be a central trait; consider Popeye's preference for spinach. In his case, the trait is not secondary; it is at least central or perhaps even a cardinal trait.

secondary trait a trait that influences a limited range of behaviors

Cardinal Traits

A **cardinal trait** is so pervasive that it dominates just about everything a person does. It is "the eminent trait, the ruling passion, the master-sentiment, or the radix of a life" (Allport, 1937b, p. 338). Most people do not have such a highly pervasive single trait. When they do, the trait often makes its possessor famous, a prototype for a disposition that others may resemble to a lesser extent. Allport provided examples of traits so pervasive that they dominated all of their original possessors' behavior. Each of the following adjectives used to describe people originated as a cardinal trait in one person: *Calvinistic, chauvinistic, Christlike, Dionysian, Faustian, lesbian, Machiavellian, puckish, quixotic,* and *sadistic* (pp. 302–303). Only very rarely do people have a cardinal trait. Other psychologists have challenged the usefulness of this concept. They suggest it is not the pervasiveness of the trait (as Allport claimed) that is distinctive; rather, what appear to be cardinal traits are simply extreme scores on a nomothetic trait.

cardinal trait a pervasive personality trait that dominates nearly everything a person does

LEVELS OF INTEGRATION OF PERSONALITY

Cardinal, central, and secondary traits are not three discrete types; actually, traits appear on a continuum of pervasiveness (Allport, 1937b, p. 338). For Allport, these various traits exist on a broader spectrum of aspects of personality, which includes much less pervasive

Figure 7.2 Levels of Integration in Personality

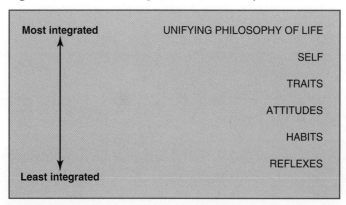

influences (reflexes and habits) and higher-order levels of integration (selves). Personality is arranged in a hierarchical structure (see Figure 7.2). At the lowest level of integration are simple conditioned reflexes. These become associated over time to form habits. A higher level of integration is the notion of self or, as sociologists sometimes refer to it, a sub-identity—for example, one's sense of oneself as a sister, as a professional, and so on. The fact that we can have multiple selves suggests that integration can occur on some higher level. At least some people have an even higher level of integration, "a thoroughly unified system of personality at the top of the pyramid" (p. 142).

Personality Development

In his description of personality development, Allport emphasized the later, more developed, stages.

FUNCTIONAL AUTONOMY

Although traits begin as adaptive strategies to satisfy needs, ultimately the traits lose their close connection with their origins, whether these origins are in physical drives per se or in some later developments, such as identification with parents. Thus motivation becomes fully *contemporaneous* (Allport, 1937a). To understand the significance of this approach, recall the psychoanalytic view that motivation is determined by fixation in early childhood. For psychoanalysts, even adult motivation is understood in terms of its developmental origins. A highly gullible adult, for example, is still described as orally fixated rather than being given some contemporaneous description (such as gullible or naive). To Allport, and many others, this approach unnecessarily emphasizes the past.

In reaction to this preoccupation with the past, Allport (1937a, 1950b) proposed an alternative theoretical concept: **functional autonomy** of motivation. Whatever the original cause for developing a motive or trait, at some point it begins to function independently of its origins. For example, consider a woman who as a child really wanted to be like her mother and admired her. As she grew up, she continued to dress like her mother and to imitate her; as an adult, she styled her hair as her mother did, entered her mother's profession, and aimed to marry someone just like her own father. One interpretation of

functional autonomy a trait's independence of its developmental origins

this behavior is that the woman's motivation is stuck in a childhood identification with her mother. However, Allport argued that for the adult, the motivation is no longer to "be like mother." The particular interests and values have been internalized; they are now her own. They are, Allport would say, "functionally autonomous" from their origins. Allport (1937b, p. 196) cited workmanship as another example of a trait that has become functionally autonomous of its origins. Although one learns to do a job well because it brings praise or security, later the work itself is satisfying. Similarly, hobbies and artistic or intellectual interests show functional autonomy (p. 207).

Allport (1955) criticized psychology for its preoccupation with the past. "People, it seems, are busy leading their lives into the future, whereas psychology, for the most part, is busy tracing them into the past" (p. 51). Real people are *becoming* themselves, rather than finding themselves by looking backward. The psychoanalytic preoccupation with fixation from the past does not allow understanding of the integrated, forward-directed functioning of healthy persons, whose personality is still developing, as Allport (1955) argues in his aptly titled book, *Becoming*. Allport (1937b) thought the principle of functional autonomy was so important that he referred to it as "a declaration of independence for the psychology of personality" (p. 207), allowing us to study individual differences from a contemporaneous perspective. Not incidentally, this approach is particularly suitable for studying psychologically healthy individuals.

QUALITIES OF A NORMAL, MATURE ADULT

Allport (1937b, 1961) listed several characteristics of a mature (i.e., healthy) personality.

Extension of the Sense of Self

The developed person "has a variety of autonomous interests: that is, he can lose himself in work, in contemplation, in recreation, and in loyalty to others" (Allport, 1937b, p. 213). In explaining this capacity of a healthy adult for self-extension, Allport remarked that "the sign of cultivation in a man is his ability to talk for half a day without betraying [revealing] his occupation" (p. 218). Such an individual is not egocentric but rather is involved in goals that are "extensions of the self."

Warm Human Interaction

The healthy person has a capacity for warm human interaction. Social interactions are sincere and friendly rather than prescribed by rigid roles and expectations.

Emotional Security (Self-Acceptance)

Healthy individuals are emotionally secure and accept themselves, having high self-esteem.

Realistic Perception, Skills, and Assignments

The healthy person realistically perceives the world. Both unrealistic optimism, such as the conviction that this lottery ticket is going to be a winner, and unrealistic pessimism, such as the expectation of failing at everything, are avoided.

Self-Objectification: Insight and Humor

Mature individuals are capable of self-objectification, seeing themselves accurately from an objective perspective, with insight, and often with a sense of humor.

Unifying Philosophy of Life

unifying philosophy of life an attitude or set of values, often religious, that gives coherence and meaning to life

Finally, the mature person has a **unifying philosophy of life** (Allport, 1937b, p. 214). For many people this is a religious philosophy of life, but it need not be.

Ravenna Helson and Paul Wink (1987) used Allport's criteria as a theoretical framework to examine maturity in a longitudinal study of women ages 21 to 43. Most of Allport's criteria were correlated significantly with two alternate measures of maturity, one stressing adaptation to society (competence) and the other stressing intrapsychic development (ego level). Emotional security (measured by the Minnesota Multiphasic Personality Inventory, the MMPI), however, correlated only with competence (Allport's realistic perception and self-objectification) and not with ego level. Ego level was related to individuality of personality integration (Allport's unifying philosophy of life). These findings suggest that Allport's criteria of healthy maturity do not take into account the distress that may result from conflict between individual development and the demands of society.

UNITY OF PERSONALITY

With maturity comes integration or unification of personality. To some extent, of course, all of us are different in different social roles—as friend, student, worker, and so on—but we also develop consistency across these various roles (Roberts & Donahue, 1994), except in disturbances such as multiple personality disorder (Barresi, 1999). Where does this unity come from? For Allport, the answer lies within the personality, which to be healthy must forge unity from within, because it is not guaranteed from society or from one's personal history. Integration occurs through the formation of "master-sentiments" (Allport, 1937b, p. 191). These may be religious or nonreligious philosophies of life that constitute a person's core consistency. Allport offered the example of Leo Tolstoy, who approached everything from his master-sentiment, the simplification of life (pp. 190–191). To bring about this unification, earlier motives are transformed. With maturity, the individual becomes more purposive, less pushed from the past (Allport, 1950b).

For many people, such unification of personality is fostered by religious practices. A research review reports that those who are active in practicing their religion report higher subjective well-being in life (Diener et al., 1999). People experience a crisis of values when unification is threatened. Such disunity is unpleasant, but it can provide the opportunity for personal growth (Hermans & Oles, 1996). On the one hand, research supports Allport's claim that integrated personalities are better adjusted and more effective (Behrends, 1986; Donahue et al., 1993). On the other hand, Allport has also been criticized for not recognizing that cultural messages make it much more difficult for minorities to achieve unity (Gaines & Reed, 1995), for ambiguity about how this unification is achieved, and for not realizing that it is not always a sign of maturity (Marsh & Colangelo, 1983). The person's goals matter; unity of personality toward some goals is not mature. Even religious orientations are only sometimes associated with higher mental health (Ryan, Rigby, & King, 1993). The problem of unity of personality, or the organization of any complex systems, for that matter, is still a theoretical puzzle. We can observe such apparent cases of disunity as patients suffering from multiple personality disorder, but theorizing the nature of the "glue" that binds healthy people is an elusive question (Eidelson, 1997).

Unitas Multiplex

In referring to the unity of personality, Allport used the Latin phrase ***unitas multiplex***, the "unity of multiples." In the healthy person, there is integration of diverse elements: interests, traits, biological predispositions, and so forth. Allport urged psychologists to consider people as a whole, rather than analyzing them into isolated parts: habits, conflicts, and so forth. He stressed that the various parts are somehow directed by the individual to work together toward some adaptive purpose. Kenneth Craik (1988) credits Allport with envisioning personality "as that branch of psychology that takes the person as the unit of analysis, rather than selected processes (such as cognition, perception, learning, or interpersonal relations, etc.), and attempts to pull together the scientific achievements of these other branches of psychology, plus those from the biological and social sciences, to understand individuals and their fates" (pp. 196–197).

unitas multiplex the Latin phrase indicating that a person makes a unified whole out of many diverse aspects of personality

The Proprium

Allport (1955) suggested a theoretical concept, the **proprium**, which "includes all aspects of the personality that make for unity" (p. 40). The proprium serves the functions that other theorists describe as belonging to the ego or the self. It is the striving part of our being that gives us our intentionality and direction.

proprium all aspects of a person that make for unity; a person's sense of self or ego

STAGES OF DEVELOPMENT

The proprium develops gradually through a lifetime. According to Allport (1937b), "The newborn infant *lacks* personality, for he has not yet encountered the world in which he must live, and has not developed the distinctive modes of adjustment and mastery that will later comprise his personality. He is almost altogether a creature of heredity" (p. 107). The most important hereditary bases of personality, observable in infancy, are *activity level* (motility) and *emotionality* (temperament) (p. 129). On this inherited basis, personality develops through interaction with the environment.

Allport (1937b) suggested a list of stages of development, but he warned that any stages identified by a theory are somewhat arbitrary. "For the single person there is only *one* consecutive, uninterrupted course of life" (p. 131). Allport did not conduct developmental research to test whether his hypothesized stages really exist and whether they represent the order in which personality develops. The theoretical significance of this model is its emphasis on the self.

1. *Bodily Sense.* The proprium begins developing in infancy with the sense of the bodily self. An infant discovers, for example, that putting his or her own hand in the mouth feels quite different from mouthing a toy. This experience contributes to the development of a sense of "the bodily me."
2. *Self-Identity.* The second achievement of propriate development begins in the second year of life, from age 1 to 2. The child develops a sense of *self-identity*, a sense of his or her existence as a separate person. Children begin to recognize themselves by name, signifying recognition of continuing individuality.

3. *Ego-Enhancement.* From age 2 to 3, the child begins working on self-esteem. The capacity for pride through achievement starts to develop, as well as the capacity for humiliation and selfishness.

4. *Ego-Extension.* Next, perhaps beginning as early as age 3 to 4, the child begins to identify with his or her **ego-extensions**, such as personal possessions: "That is my toy." Of course, this process continues into adulthood, especially in a consumer-oriented culture such as ours. Besides possessions, the maturing individual identifies with "loved objects, and later . . . [with] ideal causes and loyalties" (Allport, 1955, p. 45).

5. *Self-Image.* The self-image includes both evaluation of our present "abilities, status, and roles" and our aspirations for the future (Allport, 1955, p. 47). Children between the ages 4 and 6, Allport suggested, begin to become capable of formulating future goals and are aware of being good and bad.

6. *Rational Agent.* During the middle childhood years (age 6 to 12) the child may be thought of as a **rational coper**. The child is busy solving problems and planning ways of doing things, skills that are practiced at school. In his description of these ego skills, Allport contrasted his attention to the adaptive functions of the ego with Freud's emphasis on ego defenses.

7. *Propriate Striving.* The seventh stage of development is labeled **propriate striving**, derived from Allport's term *proprium*. Propriate striving, which begins in adolescence, is "ego-involved" motivation that has "directedness or intentionality," to use Allport's phrasing. At this time, some defining object becomes the "cement" holding a life together, as the person becomes capable of genuine ideology and career planning.

8. *The Knower.* Allport described the development in adulthood of the **self as knower**. The adult cognitively integrates the previous seven aspects of the self into a unified whole, a view that emphasizes Allport's conviction that unity is characteristic of mature personalities. Many other theorists have also referred to a self that integrates personality. Raymond Cattell, whose theory is presented in Chapter 8, refers to the self as a "master-sentiment." The self as a unifying and highly developed part of personality has also been described by many humanistic psychologists, including Carl Rogers and Abraham Maslow and others not presented in this book (e.g., Frick, 1993; Tloczynski, 1993).

ego-extensions objects or people that help define a person's identity or sense of self

rational coper a stage in middle childhood in which problem-solving ability is important to one's sense of self

propriate striving effort based on a sense of selfhood or identity

self as knower a stage in adulthood in which a person integrates the self into a unified whole

Although Allport sketched out a description of personality development, he believed that psychology is very far from being able to predict outcomes. Children growing up in the same family, for example, may turn out quite differently from one another and from their parents. We know too little about the way heredity, learning, and social factors work to predict an individual's adult personality accurately. Ultimately, though, Allport (1940) asserted that a science of psychology ought to be able to predict individual outcomes more precisely and not settle for probabilities based on studies of groups.

CONTINUITY AND CHANGE IN PERSONALITY DEVELOPMENT

Allport (1937b, p. 143) stated that most people have little personality change after age 30. In this he agreed with the well-known psychologists of his day, including John Watson and William James. Unlike some approaches (e.g., Freud), Allport did not claim that the earlier stages of development were necessarily the most important. Optimally, earlier stages are transformed into a new integration of personality, but sometimes they remain relatively unchanged, in isolated "archaic" (Freud would say "fixated") components (Allport, 1955, p. 28).

Since Allport's day, many researchers have reconsidered the question of consistency and change in personality. Data from longitudinal studies that retest participants at various times in their lives to see how much they have changed add further insights. Evidence indicates both consistency and change. Many studies show significant consistency of personality measures, such as tests of extraversion, from one measurement period to another. That is, compared with others in the group being studied, the same persons tend to be among the highest, or among the lowest, on the trait being considered. For some traits, people as a whole tend to change over time; for example, the whole group may become more conscientious (e.g., Warr, Miles, & Platts, 2001), but there still is consistency in an individual's score relative to others in the group.

The degree of consistency, understandably, is reduced when a long time passes between measures. Furthermore, the degree of consistency is less in the younger years and increases over time, so people in their 50s are more consistent than those in their 40s or 20s (Roberts & DelVecchio, 2000). Still, consistency is imperfect even at that age, leaving room for change. Many reasons have been suggested for consistency (see Table 7.3).

In addition to information about continuity of individuals across time, modern developmental studies are accumulating evidence that there are marked differences in personality from one cohort to another—that is, from a generation that experiences childhood

TABLE 7.3 Factors Contributing to Consistency in Personality

Environment	Stable environments, such as consistent job demands and stable family influences
Genes	Unchanging genetic influence throughout life; evidence of similarity of personalities of identical twins (even if raised apart)
Psychological factors	Various components of adjustment and ego resiliency that produce consistency; planful competence; emotional stability
Person-environment transactions	"Good fit" between personality and environment
Reactive transactions:	The person interprets experience in a way that is consistent with personality
Evocative transactions:	Reactions elicited from others are caused by a person's characteristics and, in turn, influence the person
Proactive transactions:	The person selects environments and roles that fit his or her personality
Manipulative transactions:	The person tries to change the environment to suit his or her preferences
Identity structure	Strong identity; consistent messages from others based on one's identity

(Based on categories described by Roberts & DelVecchio, 2000.)

and adolescence in different historical times. Even the popular press talks about "Generation X" and "the baby boomers," for example. Jean Twenge (2001b, 2002) reports increasing levels of depression and anxiety in recent decades, along with increases in self-esteem (based on self-reports), extraversion, and (among women) assertiveness. Cultural pressures toward individualism, along with declines in social support and changes in gender roles, may account for these changes. Although such studies do not address the question of consistency of an individual's personality, they do point out that individuals develop their personality in a social context, which personality theories have generally neglected, focusing instead on causes in the family and (more recently) in biology.

Influence of Personality on Social Phenomena

Allport viewed humans as social beings. He, unlike psychoanalysts, cannot be accused of ignoring the social world. Nonetheless, in contrast to behaviorists, he looked for the causes of behavior within the individual rather than in the social environment and historically was influential in establishing the field of personality as separate from either clinical or social psychology (Barenbaum, 2000). Thus his contributions to the understanding of prejudice, religion, and rumor transmission emphasize personality rather than social causation. Individual differences in personality, including those based on biology, influence how a person functions within a culture, and simply to focus on the "main effects" of culture without considering these variations is insufficient (Oishi, 2004).

PREJUDICE

Allport's classic book, *The Nature of Prejudice* (1954), examined such factors as in-group and out-group influences, ego defenses, cognitive processes, the role of language, stereotypes in culture, scapegoating, and learning prejudice in childhood. Allport understood prejudice from the point of view of the individual, instead of from a social historical viewpoint that emphasizes oppression of groups, such as the analysis by W. E. B. Du Bois (Gaines & Reed, 1995). His ideas about loyalty to in-groups continue to be discussed by social psychologists (Brewer, 1999). Allport offered practical strategies for reducing prejudice. He thought, for example, that when different races worked together for the common good in the war effort (World War II), this cooperation would reduce prejudice. He listed four conditions for groups to interact without prejudice (equal status contact, common goals, no intergroup competition, and authority sanction), and subsequent research supports this analysis (Pettigrew, 1999). Allport's description of prejudice is a classic that is still frequently cited; for example, it provides principles for understanding the persistence of the Israeli-Palestinian conflict (Kelman, 1999), the conditions for reducing prejudice against the elderly (Schwartz & Simmons, 2001), and the positive influence of models on academic achievement of minorities (Marx, Brown, & Steele, 1999). Allport did not realize, though, that prejudiced attitudes and discriminatory behavior often do not go together (Katz, 1991).

RELIGION AND PREJUDICE

Allport (1950a) criticized psychologists for ignoring the role of religion in personality. He was particularly interested in how religion relates to racial prejudice. On the one hand, because religion teaches love, it should reduce prejudice. On the other hand, Allport reported research showing that people who attend church, on the average, are more prejudiced than those who do not attend. How could these contradictory trends be reconciled?

Recognizing that brotherhood and bigotry are intertwined in religion (Allport, 1966a), Allport tried to understand when each would prevail. He distinguished two types of religious orientation, which he called intrinsic and extrinsic. People with an **extrinsic religious orientation** used religion for a selfish purpose—for example, raising their status in the community (Allport & Ross, 1967). They were likely to agree, on a Religious Orientation Survey, with such self-report statements as this: "One reason for my being a church member is that such membership helps to establish a person in the community." These were the churchgoers who were more racially prejudiced, he found.

Others held an **intrinsic religious orientation**, having presumably incorporated the religious values of loving others into their own belief system. Such people agree with self-report statements such as this: "My religious beliefs are what really lie behind my whole approach to life" (Allport & Ross, 1967) (see Table 7.4). An intrinsic religious orientation can have beneficial effects for an individual. It seems to protect against depression, at least in some studies (Genia, 1993; Park, Cohen, & Herb, 1990; Park & Murgatroyd, 1998).

Other researchers have confirmed Allport's finding that extrinsic religious orientation predicts higher racial prejudice (Donahue, 1985; Herek, 1987). In addition, they have distinguished two aspects of extrinsic orientation. One of these is socially oriented—for

extrinsic religious orientation attitude in which religion is seen as a means to a person's other goals (such as status or security)

intrinsic religious orientation attitude in which religion is accepted for its own sake rather than as a means to an end

TABLE 7.4   Concepts Associated with Intrinsic and Extrinsic Religiousness in Allport's Writings

Intrinsic	*Extrinsic*
Relates to all of life (a, b, c, d, f, g, h, j)	Compartmentalized (a, c, d, h)
Unprejudiced; tolerance (a, b, c, h, i)	Prejudiced; exclusionary (a, b, c, d, e, h)
Mature (a, d)	Immature; dependent; comfort; security (a, b, d, f, g, h, i, j)
Integrative; unifying; meaning endowed (a, c, d, f, g, h, i)	Instrumental; utilitarian; self-serving (a, c, d, e, f, g, h, i, j)
Regular church attendance (e, g, h)	Irregular church attendance (c, g, h, i)
Makes for mental health (f, g)	Defense or escape mechanism (d, f, g)

Note: Letters in parentheses refer to the following references: (a) Allport (1950a), (b) Allport (1954), (c) Allport (1959), (d) Allport (1961), (e) Allport (1962), (f) Allport (1963), (g) Allport (1964), (h) Allport (1966a), (*i*) Allport (1966b), (j) Allport & Ross (1967).
(From M. J. Donahue (1985). Intrinsic and extrinsic religiousness: Review and meta-analysis. *Journal of Personality and Social Psychology, 48*, 400–419. Copyright 1985 by the American Psychological Association. Adapted by permission.)

example, "I go to church because it helps me to make friends," whereas the other is personally oriented—for example, "What religion offers me most is comfort in times of trouble and sorrow" (Gorsuch & McPherson, 1989). In contrast, intrinsic religious orientation does not consistently predict low prejudice (Donahue, 1985). With correlational studies, as noted in Chapter 1, cause and effect cannot be clearly identified. It is not certain that intrinsic religious orientation per se is the cause of racial tolerance; perhaps the cause is empathy, which is correlated with intrinsic orientation (Watson et al., 1984), or some other correlated personality trait (Francis, 1991, 1992; Francis & Pearson, 1993).

When we consider other forms of prejudice besides racial prejudice, Allport's positive portrait of intrinsic religious orientation becomes even more sullied. Intrinsically religious people have been found to have higher than average prejudice against homosexuals (Herek, 1987) (see Figure 7.3). Because this group of intrinsically religious people was more tolerant of racial minorities in his study, Herek interpreted the increased prejudice against homosexuals as a direct result of intolerant religious teachings about homosexuality. Batson and colleagues also found that intrinsically religious undergraduates discriminated against gays, in one experiment, by being less willing to help them win money in a contest, even when the prize would be used for personal needs unrelated to sexual orientation, namely, to visit grandparents (Batson et al., 1999). In another experiment, however, intrinsically religious female subjects discriminated in apparently the opposite way; that is, they discriminated against those who are overtly anti-gay (Batson, Eidelman, & Higley, 2001). Studies of prejudice against homosexual persons have produced complex relationships with

Figure 7.3 Religious Orientation as a Predictor of Religious Fundamentalism and Prejudice against Racial Minorities, Gays, and Lesbians

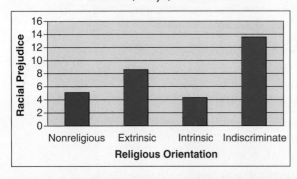

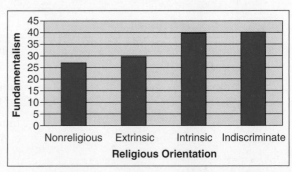

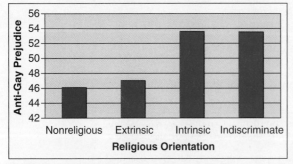

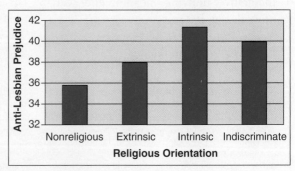

Note: Higher scores indicate more prejudice against racial minorities, higher religious fundamentalist ideology, and more prejudice against gay men and lesbian women. Prepared from data reported by Herek (1987).

religious orientation, suggesting the need to measure various components of both religious orientation and prejudice (e.g., stereotyping and discriminatory behaviors) to understand the processes more accurately (Wilkinson, 2004).

Gender issues are also pertinent to understanding the relationship of religious orientation to a person's biases. Intrinsically religious people, if their religion teaches sexist attitudes, would be expected to accept such attitudes, and the traditional religions from which research samples are drawn have long been criticized for a patriarchal bias. One study reports that it is the subtler, protective paternalistic attitudes toward women that are typical of those high in intrinsic religious orientation; although these attitudes seem more benign than hostile sexism, they are also more difficult to challenge (Burn & Busso, 2005). In one study, undergraduates with high intrinsic religious orientation scores were more accepting of a man's abusive behavior toward a girlfriend who rejected his marriage proposal and said she might be a lesbian than those with other religious orientations, although they did not excuse such abusive behavior when he was rejected because of religious differences (Burris & Jackson, 1999). In another study, intrinsically religious people were less likely to devalue a rape victim (Joe, McGee, & Dazey, 1977). The association of religious orientation with prejudice seems to depend, in part, on the target of the potential prejudice.

Other research also casts doubt on Allport's suggestion that intrinsically religious people are wholeheartedly, unselfishly helpful to others. Correlations between the Religious Orientation Survey and other personality measures suggest that intrinsically religious people are motivated by conscious impression management and unconscious self-deception (Leak & Fish, 1989). From his experimental study of helping, Batson (1990) argued that intrinsically religious subjects were motivated primarily by the desire to enhance their own esteem rather than by pure altruism. Another suggestion is that religious prejudice, like other forms of favoring in-groups over out-groups, is best understood from a group dynamics perspective, rather than as a consequence of personality (Jackson & Hunsberger, 1999).

Batson suggests that a *religion as quest* orientation comes closer to the nonjudgmental concern for helping others that Allport was trying to convey in his concept of intrinsic religious orientation. In both of the helping studies cited earlier (Batson et al., 1999; Batson, Eidelman, & Higley, 2001), those scoring high on the religion as quest orientation helped without discriminating. Another study also finds prejudice against homosexuals is more common among students at a conservative Christian school who were low in religious quest orientation and high in fundamentalist beliefs, but prejudice was not predicted from Allport's intrinsic or extrinsic religious orientations (Fulton, Gorsuch, & Maynard, 1999). The quest orientation describes people who are open ended in their search for answers to existential-religious questions, who question the contradictions and tragedies of life, facing existential issues personally (Batson, 1976; Batson & Schoenrade, 1991a, 1991b; Batson, Schoenrade, & Ventis, 1993). For example, how do we deal with life's tragedies? A person with a high quest orientation is disinclined to simply depend on God to deal with the tragedy of a drive-by shooting of an infant who was held in the arms of her praying grandmother (Burris et al., 1996). For such a person, active questioning is part of religion's meaning.

Other dimensions of religious orientation have been studied since Allport. Understandably there is overlap among these measures, and several of them are correlated with other variables, such as happiness and low levels of depression (Tsang & McCullough, 2003). Allport did suggest that religion can be the basis for a unifying philosophy of life, and it does seem to protect people against fear of death, which may be one reason it is associated with greater happiness (Cohen et al., 2005).

The dimension of *immanence* is a religious orientation that involves "motivation to transcend boundaries [such as the boundaries among various religious groups], awareness and acceptance of experience, and emphasis on the present moment" (Burris & Tarpley, 1998, p. 55). A measure of religious immanence gives points for agreeing with statements such as these: "Learning to appreciate one's dark or 'sinful' side is essential to spiritual growth," and "What my religious tradition labels falsehood is often misunderstood truth" (Burris & Tarpley, 1998, p. 63). Religious immanence is proposed to be another route to low levels of prejudice. It is positively associated with other religious orientations that eschew traditional orthodoxy: extrinsic religious orientation and religion as a quest (Burris et al., 1996; Burris & Tarpley, 1998). Researchers continue to analyze religious attitudes and prejudice to understand the inconsistent relationship between these two aspects of personality.

RUMOR TRANSMISSION

Motivated by concerns about controlling the spread of rumors during World War II, Allport and Postman (1947) studied rumors in the laboratory and offered advice to the government. Their book, *The Psychology of Rumor*, illustrates the interplay between history and psychological work, beginning with classifying the rumors that circulated following the Japanese attack on Pearl Harbor in 1941. It is an early example of applied social psychological research, and it interweaves experimental laboratory studies of basic processes with socially relevant descriptions of real rumors and strategies in an effort to prevent them from undermining the national interest. With his brother Floyd Allport and others, Allport considered broader public relations issues, too; for example, their work showed that newspaper headlines with a positive image about progress in the war were an impediment to recruiting soldiers; pessimistic headlines encouraged more soldiers to enlist (Johnson & Nichols, 1998).

One set of concepts Allport and Postman (1947) investigated concerned the cognitive processes of leveling and sharpening, which cause information to change, becoming more general or more specific as rumors are repeated. In a classic study, they found that information that begins with an eyewitness and then is passed on by word of mouth can change considerably. One subject viewed a slide in which a white man holding a knife was apparently arguing with a black man in a subway car. The subject, while looking at the slide, described it to another subject, who could not see it. Based on this description, the second subject described it to a third subject, and so on, until, like the child's game of telephone, the rumor had been passed on to several subjects. In over half the replications, the black man was erroneously reported as holding the knife at some point in the rumor transmission. This study has become a classic one supporting the idea that stereotypes lead to erroneous eyewitness reporting. Ironically, the original study is often exaggerated (Boon & Davis, 1987) and distorted (Treadway & McCloskey, 1987) in making this point.

Eclecticism

Allport believed that psychology, especially the psychology of personality, should gain truth from many areas. He called his approach eclectic. According to Allport, who drew his distinction from the German poet Goethe, we can distinguish "jackdaw" eclecticism from systematic eclecticism. A jackdaw is a bird that, like a pack rat, collects everything. **Jackdaw eclecticism** is not selective. *Systematic eclecticism*, in contrast, is selective and tries to make one unified whole out of all that is taken. Because most psychologists consider themselves eclectic with respect to personality theory, we should take Allport's advice to heart and consider how we select what to keep and what to discard from each theory.

Allport accepted insights from various theories. He accepted Freud's assertion that sexual conflict is particularly important in the formation of personality (Allport, 1937b, p. 116), although this was a passing remark that he did not often restate. He included many psychoanalytic mechanisms in his eclectic approach, including *"rationalization, projection, fantasy, infantilism, regression, dissociation, trauma, the complex, and the ego-ideal"* (p. 183). He also included Adler's concept of inferiority, even investigating the frequency of various types of inferiority complexes in college students. He reported that 48% of men and 55% of women suffer from persistent feelings of inferiority about physical matters; 58% of men and 65% of women feel inferior about social matters; 29% of men and 64% of women feel inferior about intellectual matters; and only 17% of men and 18% of women feel inferior about moral matters (p. 174). Thus Allport, with his eclectic approach, borrowed from diverse sources.

> **jackdaw eclecticism** considering concepts from diverse theories, without making careful selection from and evaluation of these concepts

Summary

- Gordon Allport emphasized several major themes: personality consistency, social influence, the concept of self, and the interaction of personality with social influence in determining behavior.

- Allport defined *personality* as "the dynamic organization within the individual of those psychophysical systems that determine his unique adjustments to the environment."

- The primary unit of personality is the *trait*.

- Traits can be studied *idiographically* (individual traits) or *nomothetically* (common traits).

- Evidence of traits comes from many sources: language, behavior, documents (such as letters), and such questionnaires as the Study of Values.

- Allport emphasized that the subject matter should take precedence over methodological issues.

- Traits vary in pervasiveness. *Cardinal traits* have extremely pervasive influences but occur in only a few people. *Central traits* have broad influences and occur in everyone. In addition, people have *secondary traits* that influence only a few behaviors.

- Traits are in the middle of a spectrum of aspects of personality, ranging from very narrow reflexes through highly integrated selves.

- As personality develops, traits become *functionally autonomous* from their developmental origins. Thus the study of personality should focus on contemporaneous issues.

- Allport listed several characteristics of a mature, healthy adult: extension of the sense of self, warm human interactions, emotional security (self-acceptance), realistic perceptions, self-objectification, and a unifying philosophy of life. The healthy personality is unified, combining various elements into a *unitas multiplex*.

- Personality development, the development of the unifying *proprium* (or self), proceeds through stages: bodily sense, self-identity, ego-enhancement, ego-extensions, self-image, rational agent, propriate striving, and the self as knower.
- Allport studied prejudice, which he said was more frequent among *extrinsically religious individuals* and less frequent among *intrinsically religious individuals*. Subsequent research has found that Allport's predictions generally hold for racial prejudice but not for anti-homosexual prejudice.
- Allport conducted applied social research on rumor transmission.
- Overall, Allport's approach was *eclectic*.

Thinking about Allport's Theory

1. Allport's point of view is quite different from that of psychoanalytic theorists. What implications does this have for the issues that we should concentrate on when trying to understand an individual's personality?
2. Do you believe it is possible to focus on one individual without comparing that person with others? That is, can we really do idiographic as well as nomothetic personality research?
3. Allport considered the relationship between personality and social psychology (e.g., in his description of prejudice). Are there other social issues or social phenomena that should also be studied in this way?
4. Do you think that expressive traits, such as the analysis of handwriting, have a place in a science of personality? What research would you suggest to explore expressive traits?
5. Allport inferred personality by analyzing Jenny's letters. If you have access to personal letters or diaries or journals, look at them as a personality psychologist might. What inferences would you make from particular documents?
6. Propose a research hypothesis using the Allport-Vernon-Lindzey Study of Values as one measure.
7. Reflect on Allport's description of a normal mature adult. Do you think these criteria are adequate, or would you suggest any change?
8. How do you think religion contributes to prejudice or to the reduction of prejudice in today's world?

Study Questions

1. List and briefly describe some of the ways in which Allport influenced the study of personality.
2. How did Allport define personality? Explain the significance of this definition.
3. Discuss Allport's concept of a trait. Explain the difference between an individual trait and a common trait.
4. What sources provide evidence about traits? Discuss, in particular, Allport's *Letters from Jenny* and his Study of Values.
5. Explain how cardinal traits, central traits, and secondary traits differ in the pervasiveness of their influence.
6. Explain Allport's concept of functional autonomy.
7. List and explain the characteristics of a mature healthy adult.
8. Explain the importance of the unity of personality for good adjustment, according to Allport's theory.
9. List and explain the stages in the development of the proprium.
10. Explain what Allport meant by intrinsic and extrinsic religious orientation.
11. Discuss the relationship between religious orientation and prejudice.
12. Summarize Allport's advice about theoretical eclecticism.

Cattell's 16 Factors and the Big Five
Factor Analytic Trait Theories

Chapter Overview

Preview: Overview of Factor Analytic Trait Theories

Factor Analysis

The 16 Factor Theory: Cattell

Personality Measurement and the Prediction of Behavior

Because Personality Is Complex: A Multivariate Approach

Psychological Adjustment

Three Types of Traits

Predicting Behavior

Determinants of Personality: Heredity and Environment

The Role of Theory in Cattell's Empirical Approach

The Five Factor Theory: McCrae and Costa

Extraversion

Agreeableness

Neuroticism

Conscientiousness

Openness

More about These Five Factors

Summary

ILLUSTRATIVE BIOGRAPHY

Albert Einstein

Without question, Albert Einstein was the best known theoretical physicist of the 20th century. His theory of relativity is generally lauded as one of the highest achievements of human intelligence. Although we may interpret Einstein's personality as an academic exercise, Einstein's second wife cautioned, "You cannot analyze him, otherwise you will misjudge him" (Clark, 1971/1984, p. 645).

Einstein was born in Ulm, Germany, in 1879. He had a younger sister. He worried his parents by being very slow to start talking, and he did poorly in school subjects that required rote memorization. Despite these apparent weaknesses, he showed a talent for mathematics and a high level of general intelligence from an early age. He reportedly taught himself calculus by the age of 16 and was reading the abstruse philosopher Kant at 13. His family moved from Germany to Italy, and after some delay because of his schooling and difficulties for a young man to obtain an exit visa, Einstein followed at the age of 15, finishing his studies in Italy. He graduated from the University of Zurich (Switzerland) in 1900 but was unable to find a teaching job in physics. During this delay, he fathered a child of a woman who later became his first wife, but because of the impracticality of becoming married without a stable position and over parental objection, they gave up the daughter and hid the scandal (Brian, 1996). Later they married and had two sons (and much later, they divorced and Einstein remarried). After much looking and a few brief teaching jobs, he accepted a position in the Swiss Patent Office evaluating new inventions. After hours (and during work hours when no one was looking), he worked on theoretical physics. He began publishing a series of papers in physics journals while in this nonacademic position.

As the world knows (but few really understand), these theoretical developments culminated in the theory of relativity, which states that matter and energy are interrelated (the famous $e = mc^2$) and questions the fundamental concepts of space and time that had been taken for granted by Newtonian physics. Einstein was awarded the Nobel Prize in Physics in 1921 (but not for his work on relativity), after being nominated several times. International events brought this internationally acclaimed (but still controversial) physicist to the United States, where he assisted other scientists in developing the world's first atomic bomb ahead of the feared German enemy of World War II. The consequences of dropping two bombs on Japan to finally end the war triggered much debate until his death in 1955, and beyond.

Development

Unlike the various psychoanalytic perspectives, which focus considerably on development, factor theories are primarily descriptive. Many of the personality factors are presumed to be influenced by heredity, and there is evidence to support this, as there is for the general stability of personality over time. Life experience also has an impact, but the primary focus of the theories is description and measurement of individual differences.

Einstein's (second) wife remarked that his personality as an adult was the same as when they were childhood playmates (Brian, 1996, p. 151). Although this contrasts with the detailed analysis of development offered by many theories, it is consistent with the point of view of factor and trait approaches, which emphasize stability of personality. Undoubtedly the excellent education valued by his family and available in

Germany allowed his innate potential to develop.

Description

In applying factor theories to Albert Einstein, our task is to suggest a profile of scores on major personality factors. Ideally, we would have inventory scores for a proper assessment. Lacking that, let us venture a rough profile based on inferences from biographical information. Considering Cattell's list of 16 personal factors, Einstein's most noteworthy trait was, of course, intelligence (a high score on factor B, Reasoning). He would also score as artless, rather than shrewd (a low score on factor N, renamed Privateness in the current terminology). One biographer said that "Einstein despised the careful cultivation of men or women for particular ends, the balancing of interest against interest . . . and the ability to judge the right moment for dropping the right hint into the right ear" (Clark, 1971/1984, p. 379). His independent-mindedness and preference, from childhood, for solitary pleasures would warrant a high score on factor Q_2, Self-reliance. His famous absent-mindedness, his sloppiness of dress and failure to wear socks—sometimes even underwear, forgetting keys, and his carelessness with money constitute evidence for a high score on Cattell's factor M, Abstractness. His daughter recounted a time when she became worried that her father had been in the bathroom for a very long time without a sound. On checking, she found he was sitting in the bathtub, immersed in a solving a physics problem, saying that he thought he was at his desk (Brian, 1996, p. 98)!

On one of the major dimensions in several factor theories, introversion-extraversion, Einstein appears inconsistent. On the one hand, he behaved in quite introverted ways when he was focused on a difficult problem in physics, withdrawing from social contact for sometimes days at a stretch. His career required him to attend academic dinners, but he reported that "On occasions like this I retire to the back of my mind and there I am happy" (Clark, 1971/1984, p. 388). According to

Einstein's son, "his father was withdrawn from the world even as a boy—a pupil for whom teachers held out only poor prospects" (Clark, 1971/1984, p. 27). On the other hand, Einstein seemed to blossom socially after his move as a teenager from Germany to Italy (Brian, 1996). As an adult he routinely spent great amounts of time with friends, discussing physics especially, but also politics and personal matters. Did he change from an introvert to an extrovert? Was he fundamentally an extrovert but one whose Jewishness and lack of respect for German authority suppressed that behavior until he left Germany? Was he an extrovert but one who also had an intense intellectual curiosity that sometimes required solitude? A theoretical challenge for factor theories is to specify how the underlying personality factors may change over time, or change their expression from one setting to another, and how traits combine in predicting behavior.

The five-factor theory includes a factor of Conscientiousness. Einstein had a well-deserved reputation for being sloppy and forgetful, and so he would likely score low on this factor. He wore the same clothes for many days, even though clean and pressed clothes were ready for him, and his wife reported that he would return from trips without having opened his suitcase. On the Agreeableness factor, Einstein would likely receive a middle score: He did not stir up conflict (like someone very low in Agreeableness), but neither did he refrain, out of tactfulness, from expressing opinions directly. In fact, he could be quite sarcastic and tactless, even arrogant (Brian, 1996). His inquiring and creative mind suggests a high score on the Openness factor.

Adjustment

Although the theories in this chapter are designed to measure primarily normal personality variations, they do include a few factors that reflect adjustment. The Neuroticism factor in the five-factor model assesses readiness to become anxious or depressed; other models have similar factors.

On Neuroticism, Einstein seems low. Situations that would make someone else anxious tended to provoke a humorous remark from Einstein. He is described as someone who could be quite relaxed and uninhibited (Clark, 1971/1984, p. 397), enjoying the pleasures of a pipe, wine, music, and sailing. His biographer gives no indication that he was embarrassed by his unkempt appearance and relates that a colleague described him as possessing "perfect goodwill, . . . gaiety and instinctive kindliness" (p. 440). He did describe the "agony of mathematical torment" (Clark, 1971/1984, p. 743) and the dismay he felt

at imagining that subatomic physics could be described in probabilities instead of certainties, but these are not the sort of negative emotions that psychologists generally intend when they describe negative emotionality. Psychotic tendencies can also be measured, and some critics who mocked his theory of relativity quite publicly did accuse him of being insane. His nonconforming dress and manners, such as appearing at important functions in rumpled pants, surely enforced such accusations. Yet ultimately, the truth of his analyses and his contributions, although unconventional, to society suggest that he was not insane but one of those geniuses that folklore tells us is very close. There was a family history of schizophrenia, and one of his sons had that disease. Some research finds a link between a family history of schizophrenia and creativity. Perhaps this creative physicist profited from a particular biochemical inheritance that, had it been combined with other genes in the formation of his particular genetic code or had it occurred in an environment that did not give him an outlet for the theoretical obsessions he himself compared to insanity, would have brought devastating results. For there is, ironically, indeterminacy in hereditary neurobiology, as in the subatomic physical universe.

Cognition

Factor theories sometimes include intelligence as one component (e.g., in Cattell's theory), and clearly Einstein was a genius. Beyond that, because intelligence can take many forms, we may ask what was Einstein's cognitive style. Certainly he favored a wholistic, intuitive approach to the problems in physics that so intrigued him. He said of himself "I g[r]asp things in a broad way easily. I cannot do mathematical calculations easily. I do them not willingly and not readily. Others perform these details better" (Clark, 1971/1984, p. 658). The tedious detail orientation of mathematics was not so attractive in the beginning, but as he appreciated that his grand models required mathematics, he came to appreciate that cognitive approach. In his early schooling, he detested classes that required rote memory and performed poorly in them. Later, when a brash reporter asked him how fast sound travels, a question like the ones that the esteemed American inventor Thomas Edison expected his employees to know, under threat of being fired, Einstein confessed that he did not know but could easily look it up. Instead of memory, he valued thinking, which he argued is best obtained from a liberal arts rather than a technical education like that favored by Edison: "A person doesn't need to go to college to learn facts. He can get them from books" (Clark, 1996, p. 129)—or now, from the Internet.

Society

Factor theories are primarily concerned with identifying and measuring people's personality traits (or broad factors), but to predict how these will be expressed in behavior, some also consider the environment. Cattell's theory is most explicit about this. He proposes that a specific behavior can be predicted from personality only if the predictive equation also includes the situation. Sometimes the situation is narrowly defined, as in the difference between a party and a classroom, when predicting the behavior of talking. Broader environments, such as cultures, can also be studied. Although it is not a major theme, Cattell suggested there are often differences from one country or social group to another in their typical personality.

Einstein lived during a time of political unrest and war. He was born in Germany, but during his lifetime he lived in other countries as well. As a young man, he followed his parents to Italy. Motivated by poverty, he also followed sparse job opportunities to Switzerland, where he became a naturalized citizen, and Austria, which he disliked. He found the intellectual climate and scientific opportunities of Germany suitable for his scientific work, and returned there, but he was troubled by anti-Semitism and was often at odds with the expectation of respect for authority that was typical there. Teaching in the university, for example, he offended his colleagues by conducting informal classes in which he treated students respectfully and by socializing with students outside of class, although it did make him popular among students (Brian, 1996). This informal behavior was characteristic of his general indifference to social status.

Einstein's last years were in the United States, where he supported the development of the first nuclear bomb and worked with other scientists on the project. As a Jewish celebrity, he was sought out to help raise money for the (at that time) new nation of Israel. His Jewish ancestry had been an issue in receiving academic appointments and as a magnet for anti-Semitic prejudice, even though personally he was not actively religious (Brian, 1996).

Attitudes toward the social issues of the day are influenced by personality. Cattell's theory suggests that individuals learn to channel their basic motives into specific sentiments and attitudes. Einstein clearly had a sentiment against power and status issues in interpersonal relationships. He disliked dealing with people of power, according to Robert Oppenheimer (Clark, 1971/1984, p. 719), and he was unimpressed by social status, speaking as easily with common folk as with powerful individuals (Brian, 1996). He was a pacifist concerning war, although he did encourage the American president to develop a nuclear bomb before the German enemy could do so. After the war, Einstein opposed the arms race (Cuny, 1965). He did not care for fame or praise, or for money, and he had a reputation of helping people with financial difficulties and finding jobs.

The fact that people belong to groups with different national characters, which Cattell investigated in his concept of syntality, was a pervasive theme in Einstein's life. Abba Eban, former Israeli ambassador to the United States, claimed that Einstein was one example of "the Hebrew mind [which] has been obsessed for centuries by a concept of order and harmony in the universal design. The search for laws hitherto unknown which govern cosmic forces" (Clark, 1971/1984, p. 36) was the guiding vision of Einstein's quest for a unifying theory of physics. Eban's description of "the Hebrew mind" corresponds to Cattell's general concept of syntality. To avoid discrimination in hiring, however, one supporter argued that he was not at all like the typical Jew (Brian, 1996, p. 74). The whole attempt to specify the typical characteristics of a group of people is obviously controversial, although it is easy enough to compute average scores on a standard test and compare across groups. The question is, should we do this, and do the tests even measure valid personality characteristics in each group?

Biology

Factor theories that have developed more elaborate biological models are considered in Chapter 9. Even the theories in this chapter, though, are influenced by heredity, according to research. Intelligence is one obvious example. Intelligence is the most highly heritable personality factor, according to Cattell (1973, p. 147).

Reportedly, Einstein's brain (and also his eyes) were saved at autopsy from cremation, and over the years some scientists have examined them for clues to his genius. According to biographer Denis Brian (1996), results of these analyses have been mixed. They were, after all, based on slices of brain tissue, and not on the dynamic monitoring of living brains that neuroscientists can now investigate.

Final Thoughts

Although factor models can be intuitively applied to Albert Einstein, we do not have the kind of systematic assessment, using tests, that factor theorists would require for a proper analysis. Nor do factor theories focus on the uniqueness of each person, so they can never fully capture an individual life.

Preview: Overview of Factor Analytic Trait Theories

Cattell's theory and the more recent Big Five model both have implications for major theoretical questions, as presented in Table 8.1. The major strength of these approaches is their sophisticated description of personality through clearly defined factors assessed through questionnaires. This measurement provides clear operational definitions, contributing to the verifiability of the theory or model. Both Cattell's factor theory and the Big Five model emphasize description over theoretical statements about development, so in that sense the theories are less comprehensive than we might hope. Applied uses of the factor theories are a strength of this approach because empirically validated tests can be used to select people for various positions and to predict performance.

Factor Analysis

Factor analysis, the essential tool of factor analytic trait theories, is a statistical procedure based on the concept of correlation. A **correlation coefficient** measures the relationship between two sets of numbers. There is a positive correlation if high numbers in one set are associated with high numbers in the other set and low numbers in each set are

correlation coefficient a measure of the association between two variables, in which 0 indicates no association, and +1 or −1 a strong association (positive or negative)

TABLE 8.1	Preview of Factor Analytic Trait Theories
Individual Differences	Individuals differ in their traits, which are measured by personality tests. The two models considered in this chapter include sixteen (Cattell) or five (Big Five) major personality traits.
Adaptation and Adjustment	Neurosis and psychosis can be described as combinations of traits, can be measured by valid new tests (better than clinical interviews), and are influenced by heredity. Biologically based traits, such as predisposition to anxiety, contribute to maladjustment.
Cognitive Processes	Mental abilities can be measured objectively; culture-free intelligence can be measured. Self-report measures are generally valid.
Society	Differences among groups and nations (syntality) exist and can be measured. Factor structures of tests are generally universal, across different cultures.
Biological Influences	Heredity affects many personality traits.
Development	Some traits are influenced by early experience, interacting with biological predispositions. Some traits change in adulthood, but for the most part, adult personality is stable.

Figure 8.1 Scatterplots Illustrating Positive and Negative Correlations

Positive Correlation

Negative Correlation

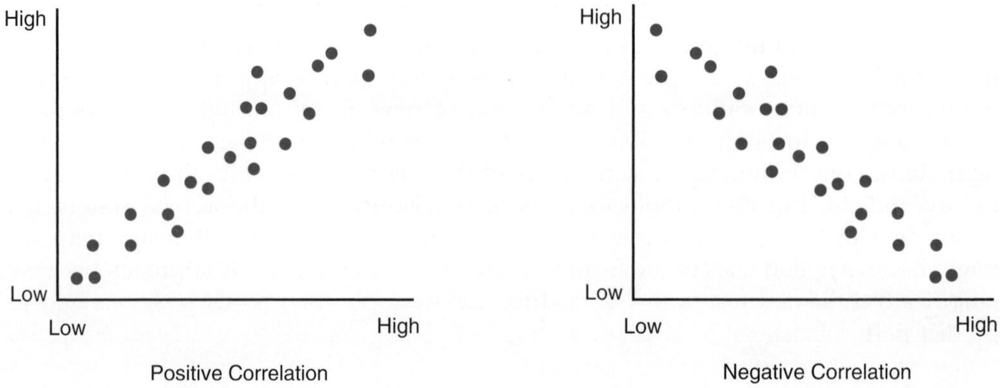

associated with each other. If low numbers in one set go with high numbers in the other, there is a negative correlation (see Figure 8.1).

A correlation coefficient may range from −1 to +1, indicating the direction and strength of the association between two variables. Several correlation coefficients are computed during the course of a factor analysis. The correlations among all pairs of variables are computed to form a **correlation matrix**. Patterns of correlations often disclose redundant information, which may be systematically described. **Factor analysis** then provides a way of more simply describing large numbers of variables by identifying a smaller number of dimensions (factors).

The procedure involves complicated mathematics, but the idea is simple. We do a similar sort of thinking, although less systematically, whenever we intuitively combine lots of detailed information about people into more general trait statements. For example, rather than saying, "Dave is great at football, wonderful at tennis, and a great runner but average in math, average in English, and mediocre in history," we would say, "Dave is a great athlete and an average academic student." We have combined six pieces of information (variables) into two more general dimensions (factors).

Before this method was applied to personality traits, factor analysis was used to study intelligence. If people are tested for various abilities, some scores are highly related. Tests of mathematical abilities are positively correlated, including geometry, algebra, spatial relations, and so forth. Tests of verbal abilities correlate highly together (e.g., vocabulary, grammar, and spelling), but they have lower correlations with tests of mathematical abilities. Factor analysis of these variables reveals two factors, mathematical ability and verbal ability.

Factor analysis combines variables in a linear equation, only adding or subtracting the effect of each variable. In principle, it would be possible to use other mathematical relationships, such as multiplying variables. (Recall that Allport suggested that heredity and environment should be multiplied.) These mathematical options would profoundly affect the results. Factor analysis is not a magical procedure, and even experts debate its proper uses. Still, factor analysis is a sophisticated mathematical tool for identifying patterns of related observations, and Cattell and the researchers who have followed his lead have used this tool brilliantly to search for the fundamental traits of personality. Cattell (1957) considered factor analysis "a research tool as important to psychology as the microscope was to biology" (p. 4).

correlation matrix
a chart of the correlations between all pairs of a set of variables

factor analysis
statistical procedure for determining a smaller number of dimensions in a data set from a large number of variables

The 16 Factor Theory: Cattell

Factor analytic trait theories have become increasingly popular in personality as computer technology and data analysis methods have become readily available. In essence, these approaches use the power of computers to examine and organize data systematically into simpler form. A leader in the development of factor theories, Raymond Cattell (1979) claimed that the study of personality passed through two earlier phases before reaching its current scientific status. "From biblical times until the early nineteenth century," he wrote, "it was a matter for intuitive insights expressed in the realm of literature" (p. 6), marked by such giants as Plutarch, Bacon, and Goethe. Then came a century of clinically oriented theorists (Freud, Adler, and Jung), with some experimental work (Jung and McDougall). Ever since World War I, the study of personality has been in the third, "experimental and quantitative" phase. Cattell saw his work as building on the valuable insights of earlier theories "but subjecting them to independent judgment on the basis of modern methods" (p. 8). We will see that Cattell's emphasis on research methods did, indeed, add considerably to the theoretical foundations built by the earlier theorists. Other factor analytic models that followed, most notably the Big Five factor theory, built on his attempt to measure the basic dimensions of personality, and some further specified the underlying biological dimensions of some aspects of personality (see Chapter 9).

BIOGRAPHY OF RAYMOND CATTELL

Raymond B. Cattell was born in 1905 in Staffordshire, England, the son and grandson of engineers. He had two brothers and was a bright student. As a boy, he witnessed the carnage and casualties of World War I.

RAYMOND CATTELL

In college, Cattell studied science. Shortly before graduating from the University of London, he decided, to the dismay of friends, that psychology was the field he really wished to pursue. He attended the University of London (King's College), completing his doctoral degree in 1929 at the age of 23. There he learned Spearman's factor analysis, a mathematical procedure developed to study intelligence but that Cattell would later apply to personality research.

Prospects for a professorship in psychology in England were slight. Cattell reported in his autobiography that only six faculty positions existed in the country, and they were all held by men who were healthy and showed no signs of vacating them. So Cattell accepted an applied position, moving to Leicester to set up a school psychological service. Of these 5 years of clinical work, he later said, "Though . . . I felt a charlatan it gave me many leads for personality research" (Cattell, 1984, p. 123).

Besides long hours of administrative work, Cattell did research in those years. He studied the relationship of intelligence to family size and social status (a research question that offended liberal critics). He developed a projective test at the same time as Henry Murray, who is generally credited for developing this testing strategy. Cattell commented that, to his best knowledge, he himself may be the one who first used the term *projective test*.

In 1937 Cattell accepted an invitation from E. L. Thorndike to work in social psychology in New York for a year. The proposed year became, in fact, a permanent immigration. Cattell became a professor at Clark University, where he worked on culture-fair intelligence tests, and then, in 1941, at the invitation of Gordon Allport (American Psychological Association, 1997), he accepted a lectureship at Harvard University. His office was next door to Allport's (Cattell, 1984, p. 141), and he remarked that "in personality theory, Allport and I spoke a different language, which . . . was tough on students" (Cattell, 1974, p. 71). During World War II, he developed objective personality tests for officer selection.

Cattell's next move, in 1945, was to the University of Illinois, where he was appointed to a research position. Freed from teaching responsibilities and with access to a new and (for the times) powerful computer (which they fondly dubbed the Sacred Illiac), these were very productive years for Cattell. He continued to work hard, remarking, "For many years I rarely left the laboratory before 11 P.M., and then was generally so deep in thought or discussion that I could find my car only because it was the last still in the parking lot!" (Cattell, 1974, p. 75).

To facilitate distribution of his many new psychological tests, Cattell set up a private organization, the Institute for Personality and Ability Testing (IPAT), in 1949. The institute still provides Cattell's tests and manuals to interested researchers and practitioners. He also founded the Society for Multivariate Experimental Psychology in 1960 to foster the kind of research he felt was necessary to advance personality theory scientifically.

Cattell eventually left academia and retired to Hawaii, where he continued to advocate statistical approaches to theory development (Cattell, 1990a) and to develop computer methods for personality research (McArdle & Cattell, 1994) until his death in 1998 (Horn, 2001). In 1997 he was recognized with an award for lifetime achievement by the American Psychological Foundation. The citation praised his work for its inclusion of many areas, saying, "Cattell stands without peer in his creation of a unified theory of individual differences integrating intellectual, temperamental, and dynamic domains of personality in the context of environmental and hereditary influences" (American Psychological Association, 1997, p. 797).

Personality Measurement and the Prediction of Behavior

Earlier theories were rich in words and understanding but sparse in the specific predictions we would hope to make from a science. Science that cannot make predictions is scarcely worthy to be called science. Cattell emphasized the methodological issues that Allport regarded as relatively less important. Cattell's background in science, contrasting with Allport's background in social ethics, explains the contrasting emphasis.

Cattell's (1950, p. 2) definition of personality neatly summarizes his theoretical and empirical approach:

> Personality is that which permits a prediction of what a person will do in a given situation.

trait that which defines what a person will do in a particular situation

Traits are the units of personality that have predictive value. Cattell (1979, p. 14) defined a trait as "that which defines what a person will do when faced with a defined situation." Unlike Allport, he did not feel it was necessary to define traits in psychophysical terms. For Cattell, traits are abstract concepts, conceptual tools useful for predictive purposes, but not necessarily corresponding to any specific physical reality. He believed, though, that personality traits are not purely statistical phenomena. Although his method was correlational rather than experimental, the sophistication of the studies and the patterns emerging from so many led him to believe "traits exist as determiners of behavior" (p. 98).

Science is advanced by new tools, new measurement devices. For example, physiology has been advanced by sophisticated procedures (such as magnetic resonance imaging) that show images of body structures, and astronomy has progressed rapidly as a result of the giant Hubble telescope. In the same way, personality research is greatly enhanced by improved measurement. Cattell gave us a new set of instruments, demanding that personality tests themselves be tested to provide extensive evidence of reliability and validity before they were used to make decisions about people. The value of tests sometimes becomes a matter of dispute in court trials (Pope, 1993–1994).

One technique Cattell (1957) discarded was the interview, which he described as "an anachronism in psychology, for the preservation of which, as an assessment device, there are many excuses but few justifications" (p. 761). Research reviewed by Robyn Dawes (1994) confirms Cattell's pessimism about the worth of interviews for making clinical diagnostic decisions, predicting whether a person will be violent or even anticipating which students will succeed in college. According to Dawes, interviews may be useful to gather data, but for making predictions it is better to trust a computer model. Cattell was a pioneer in that method.

PERSONALITY TESTS

Cattell's most important contribution to personality is his systematic description and measurement of personality. He argued that such description, a taxonomy of individual differences, is essential before investigating the causes of personality can sensibly begin.

To assess personality differences in the population at large, Cattell developed his best known and most widely used test, the 16 Personality Factor Questionnaire (16PF); "PF" stands for "personality factors," a term used prominently in his theory to refer to important traits. This test is described more fully later in this chapter. In addition, several tests have been specifically devised for clinical use—including the Neuroticism Scale Questionnaire, the Clinical Analysis Questionnaire, and the Marriage Counseling Report—and measures of anxiety and depression. Cattell also developed various kinds of intelligence tests, most notably the Culture Fair Intelligence Test, intended to measure a person's innate capacity to learn. These are only a sampling of the many tests that Cattell devised and validated. The catalog of his Institute for Personality and Ability Testing (IPAT) contains many others and is an impressive testament to the practical applications of Cattell's work in clinical, vocational, educational, and research settings.

BEYOND PERSONALITY TESTS

The most widely used type of personality test asks people to describe themselves in response to a set of standard questions, choosing among multiple-choice or true-and-false answers. Such pencil-and-paper self-report tests provide "questionnaire data," which Cattell called **Q-data**. (To avoid confusing Cattell's terminology, you may find it helpful to call these ordinary measures questionnaires rather than tests.) Although much useful information can be gained from such questionnaires, the procedure also has shortcomings. For example, a subject may distort test responses to present a certain image to the questionnaire administrator, or the subject's conscious self-understanding may be different from his

Q-data data from self-report tests or questionnaires

or her true underlying personality. Dare we trust self-reports? Cattell looked for other evidence to support their validity.

T-data data collected from objective tests, such as reaction times

A second type of data is **T-data**, or "objective test data." Unlike questionnaire data, these involve measuring instruments that are indirect; the purpose of the test is hidden. This type of test cannot be faked because the subject does not know how answers will be interpreted. Projective measures, such as inkblot tests, fall into this category. So do objective behavioral measures observed in the laboratory, such as finger tapping and reaction time, and physiological tests, such as blood pressure and urinalysis.

Personality would be of limited value, however, if it referred only to personality test scores, whether self-report Q-data or objective T-data. Personality should also relate to behavior in the real world. So Cattell also studied a third type of data: objective information about the life history of the individual. Cattell called this **L-data**, or "life record data."

L-data objective information about the life history of the individual

School records, grade-point average, driving history, ratings by supervisors about job performance, letters of recommendation, records of books checked out of the library—all of these data can be obtained without necessarily requiring subjects to answer a questionnaire or respond to a test in a standard setting. However, as other researchers have noted, the inclusion of life events as research data can pose challenging measurement problems (Stone, Kessler, & Haythornthwaite, 1991).

Cattell looked for patterns of personality that could be independently confirmed in the three types of data. For example, a person with low emotional stability has distinctive responses in all three kinds of data. In Q-data, low emotional stability is reflected in scores on Factor C of the 16PF personality questionnaire, a trait called ego strength. In T-data, low emotional stability is associated with an objective test factor called self-sentiment control, which involves components such as verbal explicitness and performance skill. In L-data, low emotional stability is reflected in "low occupational stability, high automobile accident rate, and many clinical visits" (Cattell, 1957, p. 54). Confirmation across these three very different types of data increases certainty that meaningful personality traits are being measured.

Because Personality Is Complex: A Multivariate Approach

Personality is complex. To attempt to explain it by considering only a small number of concepts would distort by oversimplifying, yet much personality research considers only one or two predictors at a time. Cattell recommended against the oversimplification of predicting from one variable at a time—for example, predicting how well a person will do in school from knowledge about the person's intelligence but nothing about motivation, educational background, health, and so forth. Life, of course, is multivariate. Any theorist will agree that people are affected by many things at one time, yet very few theories describe this in a formal sense.

Multivariate prediction would never have been possible before modern computers. With computers to do the tedious computations, it is possible to specify formally, in a mathematical model, how that many variables are related to one another and how they predict behavior (Cattell, 1979). Cattell pioneered **multivariate** research methods, using several variables at one time to predict behavior. People can keep only a limited number of concepts in mind at the same time, but computers can keep track of many variables simultaneously. What is more, computers can combine many pieces of information,

multivariate a research strategy that includes many variables

keeping each in proper perspective, better than humans can (Dawes, 1994; Grove & Meehl, 1996).

SURFACE TRAITS AND SOURCE TRAITS

The term *trait* roughly means "patterns of observations that go together." If we make these observations systematically and find sets of variables that are positively correlated, we have identified **surface traits**. The term indicates that, although they appear on the surface to be a trait, no evidence indicates they are really a trait in any enduring sense. The pattern of correlations might not reappear under different situations—for example, in a different population, under different testing conditions, or at a different time.

surface traits traits as defined simply at the level of observable behavior

Through many studies, Cattell identified some correlation clusters that are quite *robust*, that is, they reappear over and over again. They emerge despite differences in population, in testing situations, and so forth. Cattell argued that such a robust pattern must have a single source of variance. It corresponds to one "cause" within personality, a fundamental trait of personality. He searched for such robust traits by using factor analysis, and he called them **source traits**.

source traits basic, underlying personality traits

MEASUREMENT OF SOURCE TRAITS: THE 16PF

Cattell developed questionnaires to measure the source traits as directly as possible. His best known personality test, the **16PF**, represents the culmination of many factor analytic studies (Cattell, Eber, & Tatsuoka, 1970). It has sixteen multiple-choice scales, each measuring one underlying source trait of normal personality (see Table 8.2).

16PF Cattell's questionnaire designed to measure the major source traits of normal personality

The set of scores on all factors is the **profile** of an individual. Sometimes a distinct group of people are averaged together, and their averaged profile can be compared to general population norms for descriptive purposes. Occupational groups have been thus described. Similarly, another personality measure can be correlated with each of the 16 factors; for example, based on correlations with an attitude toward Christianity measure, religious youths have a profile that includes conformity (high factor G), tender-mindedness (high factor I), self-discipline (high factor Q_3), submissiveness (low factor E), and sobriety (low factor F) (Francis & Bourke, 2003).

profile the pattern of a person's scores on several parts of a personality test

FIVE SECOND-ORDER FACTORS

It is possible to reduce further the number of factors by factor-analyzing scores on the 16 personality factors themselves. This is a **second-order factor analysis**. Cattell (1957) described five second-order global factors: extraversion, stability (low anxiety), receptivity (low tough-mindedness), accommodating (low independence) and self-control. These five factors are "strikingly similar to the Big-Five factors proposed today, and they are the basis for today's five-factor model" (American Psychological Association, 1997, p. 799).

second-order factor analysis factor analysis in which the data are factor scores (rather than raw data); produces more general personality factors

Each second-order factor is calculated by combining an individual's scores from certain of the 16 source traits of personality. For example, the second-order factor Extraversion includes points from the 16PF factor A (liking people), factor F (talkativeness and optimism), and factor H (adventurous boldness). Extraversion scores are increased if subjects are told to answer the questionnaire with a "good personality," whatever that is. Cattell

TABLE 8.2	Cattell's 16 Personality Factors (16PF)
A	Warmth
B	Reasoning
C	Emotional stability
E	Dominance
F	Liveliness
G	Rule-consciousness
H	Social boldness
I	Sensitivity
L	Vigilance
M	Abstractness
N	Privateness
O	Apprehension
Q_1	Openness to change
Q_2	Self-reliance
Q_3	Perfectionism
Q_4	Tension

(*Note*: The names of these factors were different in Cattell's original descriptions. These names correspond to the current revision of the 16PF, as described in H. E. P. Cattell & Schuerger, 2003.)

(1957) suggested that extraversion has a genetic basis. Specifically, people who inherit a tendency to react more strongly to ideas than to external stimuli tend to develop into introverts. It is as though introverts march to a different (i.e., internal) drummer, compared to extraverts, who respond more to stimuli in the external world.

It is tempting to focus on second-order factors because there are fewer of them; therefore, it seems easier to comprehend Cattell's research at this level. But Cattell (1978, p. 225) cautioned against the error of "thinking that higher-strata factors are higher in importance" and maintained that they predict behavior less well than the 16 primary factors.

Psychological Adjustment

Some of the traits that Cattell measured contribute to a person's psychological adjustment. The terms *neurosis* and *psychosis* are already familiar from psychoanalytic theory. Both refer to adjustment difficulties, which are more serious in psychosis.

Neurotics differ from the general population on several traits. Of particular interest are the "controlling triumvirate" of personality, three factors involved in impulse control and emotional adjustment: Factors C (Ego Strength), G (Superego Strength), and Q_3 (Self-Sentiment Integration). Anxiety is high among neurotics, partly because of family conflict, inconsistent discipline, and insufficient affection. Heredity also plays a significant role in the development of personality characteristics related to neurosis.

Psychosis is a more serious form of disturbance. There are several different types of psychoses, and Cattell found different patterns of traits for various diagnoses. Schizophrenics have low ego strength, low drive tension, and high introversion. People with manic depression have low intelligence, conservative temperament, and high super-ego (i.e., an inclination to feel guilty).

Cattell developed clinical scales similar to the 16PF but focusing specifically on differences among diagnostic groups. He was highly critical of clinicians for not supplementing their unreliable clinical diagnoses with empirically validated scales, which could improve the reliability of diagnosis (Cattell, 1979, p. 110).

Three Types of Traits

It is customary in personality theory to distinguish various types of traits, including dynamic traits (motives), temperament, and ability. Cattell adopted these concepts as well.

ABILITY TRAITS

Ability traits define various types of intelligence and determine how effectively a person works toward a desired goal. Both heredity and learning affect intelligence, and Cattell and others have struggled to disentangle these two influences. Cattell was concerned that existing intelligence tests did not measure simply a person's innate ability to learn but also included effects of experience. Most intelligence tests are biased in favor of those with a good education and underestimate those who are innately brilliant but not well educated in vocabulary and mathematical content that are learned in school. Is it possible to test for innate intelligence without underestimating the abilities of those with a poor education? Cattell tried.

Cattell (1971) distinguished two types of intelligence. One, which he called **fluid intelligence**, is the innate ability to learn. It is "fluid" because it can be expressed in different kinds of learning, depending on the educational opportunities of the individual. Researchers have suggested that fluid intelligence is related to the capacity of working memory (Engle et al., 1999) and perhaps even to brain size (Wickett, Vernon, & Lee, 2000). In contrast, **crystallized intelligence** includes the effects of education: what has been learned. As we might expect, by middle age, adults know more in various areas than younger adults (Ackerman & Rolfhus, 1999). Measures of crystallized intelligence predict scores on Advanced Placement tests and similar tests of knowledge better than the prediction from fluid intelligence tests (Ackerman et al., 2001).

The distinction between fluid and crystallized intelligence has contributed to research on the ways that heredity and experience combine to develop a variety of intelligences, not simply a single general factor, and how intelligence changes over the course of life (e.g., McArdle et al., 2002). One intriguing finding is that, although some cognitive abilities generally decline with age, this is not inevitable; the elderly who continue to use certain abilities intensively do not show a decline (Baltes, Sowarka, & Kliegl, 2001; Masunaga & Horn, 2001), supporting the popular "use it or lose it" motto. In addition, theorists who focus on development in adulthood have suggested that the development of crystallized intelligence and development of coping abilities (generally considered separate from intelligence) may be interconnected (Labouvie-Vief & Diehl, 2000), which is consistent with the emphasis on cognition in adult personality.

fluid intelligence the part of intelligence that is the innate ability to learn, without including the effects of specific learning

crystallized intelligence intelligence influenced by education, so it measures what has been learned

Culture Fair Intelligence Test a test designed to measure fluid intelligence only

In keeping with his aim to devise new and purer tests, Cattell devised the **Culture Fair Intelligence Test** to measure only fluid intelligence. It aims to provide a better assessment of the intelligence of people who may be educationally deprived—for example, the poor. Unfortunately, experience does influence scores. For example, an educational intervention that taught cognitive skills to seventh-grade children in low socioeconomic schools in Venezuela not only increased performance on tests of school-related abilities but also produced improved scores on the Cattell Culture Fair Intelligence Test, suggesting the test is not completely free of educational effects (Herrnstein et al., 1986). Furthermore, a review of IQ test scores in 14 countries shows that the average IQ can increase 25 points in one generation and these changes are larger on tests of fluid intelligence. Because genetic factors cannot explain such changes, the reviewer concludes that the tests do not measure fluid intelligence as intended but are also subject to environmental influences (Flynn, 1987). Perhaps fluid and crystallized intelligence do not correspond to the effects of heredity and environment, as Cattell intended, but are simply different abilities (Horn, 1984).

Cattell concluded that about 80% of the variation in intelligence is determined by heredity (in other words, is fluid) and only 20% by experience (in other words, is crystallized). Based on his belief that intelligence is largely hereditary, he supported the eugenics movement, fearing a general decline in the intelligence of the British population because of the greater birthrate of less intelligent people (Cattell, 1937; Horn, 1984). Subsequent research has not confirmed Cattell's fears (Loehlin, 1984); intelligence among British children was found to be rising, rather than falling (Cattell, 1957; Lynn, Hampson, & Mullineux, 1987). Historical and cultural factors, in addition to genetics, influence measured intelligence.

Educators are concerned not only with intelligence but also with learning disabilities. These can be investigated by looking for patterns of abilities. In one study, schoolchildren who were low achieving at mathematics took intelligence tests diagnostic of skills in the Cattell-Horn-Carroll theory of cognitive abilities, and they were found, surprisingly, to have no consistent area in which they scored low that would explain their poor school performance in math. This result suggested to the investigators that, at least in this one sample, the so-called math disability might not be caused by an underlying cognitive impairment at all but could perhaps be as simple as lack of adequate education and practice (Proctor, Floyd, & Shaver, 2005). In that case, remediation seems hopeful.

Although the distinction between fluid and crystallized intelligence has stimulated considerable research, other models of intelligence have been proposed (e.g., Johnson & Bouchard, 2005).

TEMPERAMENT TRAITS

Temperament traits are largely constitutional (inherited) source traits that determine the "general style and tempo with which [a person] carries out whatever he [or she] does" (Cattell, 1965, p. 165). Cattell (1950, p. 35) gave as examples "high-strungness, speed, energy, and emotional reactivity." Many researchers are seeking to understand the concept of temperament further because it is a key concept for understanding how biological influences, which are inherited, play a role in shaping personality (e.g., Bates & Wachs, 1994; Kagan, 1994).

DYNAMIC TRAITS

Dynamic traits are motivational; they provide the energy and direction to action. Like many other theorists, Cattell recognized that some motivations are innate and others are learned. He called these types of dynamic traits: ergs (innate) and metaergs (learned).

Ergs

Cattell accepted the concept from many previous psychologists that people have some innate motivational traits or, in his language, constitutional dynamic source traits. He called them **ergs**. (The term comes from a Greek word meaning "energy.") They are comparable to animal instincts and involve "an innate reactivity toward a goal, though stimuli and means are learned" (Cattell, 1957, p. 893). Cattell listed several human ergs: anger, curiosity, fear, greed, hunger, loneliness, pity, pride, sensuousness, and sex.

erg a constitutional dynamic source trait

Individual differences occur in various ways. For one thing, the level of an ergic trait may vary in different individuals because of genetics. In addition, the ways in which ergs are channeled into complex behaviors vary widely from person to person. For example, one person seeks security through brute force, another through financial planning.

Metaergs

Ergs, with their energy, are channeled into learned patterns, called **metaergs**. Metaergs are environmental-mold dynamic source traits. These learned motivations can range from the very general, like love of country and esteem of education, to the very specific, like opposition to a particular political candidate. Cattell called the more general metaergs *sentiments*. He used the term *attitudes* to refer to more specific responses to particular stimulus situations.

metaerg environmental-mold dynamic source traits; includes sentiments and attitudes

Sentiments.   Sentiments are deep underlying dynamic structures in personality that are formed early and are generally enduring. They include sentiments toward home, family, hobbies, and religion, among others. The most important sentiment is the *self-sentiment* that Cattell referred to as a *master motive*. Research showing greater attention to self-relevant information (e.g., Warren, Hughes, & Tobias, 1985) seems to confirm the centrality of the self-sentiment.

Attitudes.   Attitudes are the more specific expressions of sentiments. Cattell (1965, p. 175) defined an attitude as "an interest in a course of action, in a given situation." An example would be "like to spend Thanksgiving with the family." Because attitudes are so specific, no broad list is feasible. As discussed later, the concept is important in considering how broader dimensions of personality—the sentiments and ergs—are actually expressed.

Ergs and metaergs are dynamic, motivational traits that are activated by situations (Boyle & Cattell, 1984). They help people select goals and provide the energy to pursue goals. They stimulate emotional responses to certain objects: hope, fear, expectation, and so forth. These motivational traits also cause people to perceive selective opportunities for satisfying goals. When the hunger erg is aroused, we notice restaurants on a street where we may never have noticed them before, and even a rock seems like a pillow if we are tired enough.

Subsidiation

Through a process of learning, basic drives (ergs) are satisfied by multistep sequences of purposive activities. The environment demands this kind of learning. Instrumental acts must be completed before basic goals can be met. Cattell (1950, p. 156) noted, for example, that we must work to eat. Working serves (or, to use Cattell's jargon, is "subsidiary to") the motivation to eat. In general, metaergs are subsidiary to ergs. Attitudes are subsidiary to sentiments because attitudes are more particular, more remote from the basic ergs. The instrumental goals along the way may be called "subsidiary goals" or "means-end activities" (p. 156).

This idea that the fundamental motivations are constitutional and that learning channels them into specific forms of expression is found in many personality theories. Freud, of course, assumed this (Herrnstein et al., 1986) in his assertion that all energy flows from the id and the ego channels this energy. Murray named the concept **subsidiation**, and it was from Murray that Cattell borrowed the idea. Even learning theory makes such assumptions with the concept of primary reinforcement. Hence the concept of subsidiation, although not always so named, is an idea that crosses theoretical boundaries. It has not always received the attention it deserves, however.

subsidiation the pattern of interrelationships among ergs, metaergs, and sentiments (as diagrammed in the dynamic lattice)

The Dynamic Lattice

Cattell diagrammed these subsidiation relationships in the **dynamic lattice** (see Figure 8.2). Attitudes (on the left) are subsidiary to sentiments (in the middle), which are subsidiary to ergs (on the right). The channels show the connections among these dynamic (motivational) levels. Cattell (1950) explained how to interpret this diagram:

dynamic lattice Cattell's diagram to show motivational dynamics

> The man's attitude . . . to his bank account has the direction that he wants to increase it. The lines of subsidiation . . . indicate that he wants to do so in order to protect his wife . . . to satisfy self-assertion . . . to assuage his fear of insecurity . . . and to satisfy hunger. . . . This attitude or sentiment to his bank account is served by an attitude of annoyance toward higher taxation . . . by an intention to keep company with his business friend . . . and by an attitude of avoidance to New York, where he spends too much money. (p. 188)

Metaergs (attitudes and sentiments) are learned. Their connections with one another and with the ergs are affected by learning. Sentiments may be connected to many ergs; through development, these connections change. Ergs are generally satisfied indirectly through metaergs. This indirect satisfaction of ergs is called long-circuiting. (In contrast, artificial stimulation of the pleasure centers of the brain through electrical stimulation in the laboratory, or drug use on the street, could be thought of as short-circuiting.)

Certain types of learning involve reorganizing or coordinating various traits. We may learn certain behaviors that can satisfy many motivations (many metaergs and ergs) at the same time. This is called **confluence learning**. For example, learning to ski might satisfy various social and physical motivations.

confluence learning learning behaviors that satisfy more than one motivation

Predicting Behavior

Recall that Cattell defined personality as that which permits the prediction of behavior. Let us examine his model for making predictions about how individuals will behave in particular situations.

Figure 8.2 The Dynamic Lattice

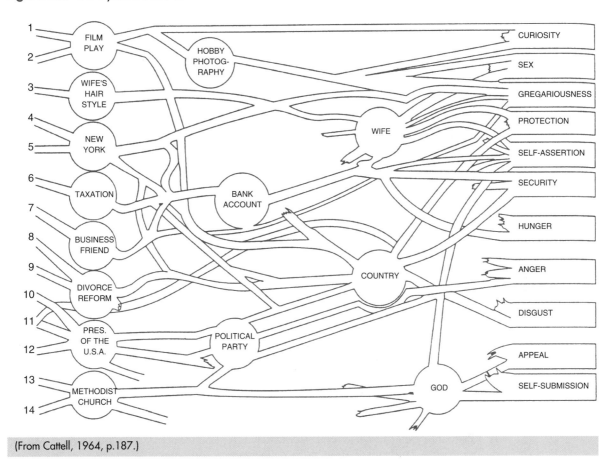

(From Cattell, 1964, p.187.)

THE SPECIFICATION EQUATION

Various traits are combined in a predictive mathematical equation, called the **specification equation**. In principle, all behavior can be predicted from such equations. The specific terms, of course, would vary depending on the application. To predict which university football players would play the most games, an equation can be formed from four personality traits assessed by the 16PF (group-dependence, tough-mindedness, extraversion, and emotional stability) and five coaching variables (autocratic behavior, training and instruction, rewarding behavior, democratic behavior, and social support) (Garland & Barry, 1990). To predict the performance of airline cabin crew members, an equation would give positive weights to the 16PF factors of emotional stability, conscientiousness, and tough-mindedness (Furnham, 1991). These equations are determined by research in specific settings.

Source traits are entered into the predictive equation if they are relevant for predicting the particular behavior. These may include ability traits, temperament traits, ergic tensions, and metaergs (sentiments and attitudes). Situational and temporary factors may also be added to the equation if they help predict the particular behavior. Situational factors include such factors as the roles called for in the situation. Temporary factors include states like fatigue and anxiety. Here is the full specification equation:

$$P_{ij} = S_{1j}T_{1i} + S_{2j}T_{2i} + \cdots + S_{Nj}T_{Ni} + S_j T_{ji}$$

specification equation mathematical expression that shows how personality and situational variables combine to predict a specific behavior

The behavior being predicted, the performance of the individual *i* in situation *j,* is referred to as *Pij.* For example, if a person is running a race, *P* might represent the time to run the course.

Each predictive trait is referred to as a *T* in the specification equation. Subscripts identify the particular trait and the particular individual. Thus T_{2i} refers to the second trait and the *i*th individual. Individual differences in the strength of each trait are reflected in different *T*'s for each person. The letter *S* refers to a situational index, that is, the extent to which the trait *T* is relevant in predicting the performance *P* in this situation. These situational indexes are the same in the equation for each person whose behavior is being predicted.

Consider a simple example: trying to predict how fast a person runs a race, based on knowledge of the person's athletic ability and motivation. Because there are only two predictive traits, we could use a short specification equation:

$$P_{ij} = S_{1j}T_{1i} + S_{2j}T_{2i}$$

In this case, *Pij* is the running speed of the *i*th individual in this situation (*j*). T_{1i} is the first trait, athletic ability. It is weighted by its situational index, S_{1j}, which would be the same constant for each subject. To indicate that it is quite important as a predictor, let's say that S_{1j} equals 0.8 (on a scale that has 1 as a maximum). The second predictive trait, T_{2i}, is the motivation of each subject, *i*. It is weighted by its situational index, S_{2j}. It is less important than athletic ability as a predictor, so let's say it is 0.2. To predict running speed, then, we would multiply a person's athletic ability by 0.8 and add that to the person's motivation multiplied by 0.2. Ability and motivation are not equal contributors to running speed; the more important predictor (ability) gets a higher situational index (0.8) than the less important predictor (motivation, 0.2). A near-Olympian athlete running with moderate effort is going to beat the klutz, however motivated. An average runner would have to be very, very motivated to surpass a veteran runner, and the veteran runner would have to be very unmotivated.

Research determines which predictors are necessary and the appropriate weight of each. This is the sort of prediction that colleges sometimes use to predict the potential success of each applicant from high school grades, Scholastic Aptitude Test (SAT) scores, letters of recommendation, and so forth. Cattell simply extended the concept of prediction to many more nonacademic behaviors. In some applications, however, clinicians and occupational psychologists have particular specification equations for diagnosis and selection (Cattell, 1990b).

Notice that situations also play an important role in prediction. Cattell called for more descriptions of situations to be developed (a taxonomy of the environment) because situations combine with personality to predict behavior (Cattell, 1979, p. 273). Although measurement of situations is far behind measurement of personality as a priority for researchers, there has been some attention to this important issue. What must be measured is not the objective physical environment but instead the "psychological environment" or "life space" as the person sees it (Lewin, 1951). Applying this idea to college students, researchers have tried to measure the life space by counting environmental variables such as photographs of friends and of parents, health and diet books, and so on (Mayer, Carlsmith, & Chabot, 1998), but so far the measure of life space looks rather cluttered. That is, we do not know yet how to measure situations. It must be done, however, if we are to truly learn from Cattell's theory.

The specification equation described assumes that each person's traits are stable, which has been the usual assumption of trait theories in personality. In a theoretical article published after his death, however, Cattell and colleagues proposed a modification of the equation that would allow for some variation in a person's traits over time, reflecting the impact of learning on personality (Cattell, Boyle, & Chant, 2002). Considering all the determinants of behavior we can imagine, let alone measure accurately, it is a theoretician's delight, but a practical impossibility, to predict all behavior.

NOMOTHETIC AND IDIOGRAPHIC APPROACHES: R-TECHNIQUE AND P-TECHNIQUE

Most of Cattell's research involved the nomothetic method, or to use Cattell's terminology, the *R-technique*. In this technique, many subjects are analyzed together, comparing their scores. Cattell also adapted his analysis to the intensive investigation of a single subject. This *P-technique* analyzes scores taken from a single person, comparing scores across time. Thus, in theory, it can discover unique individual traits. (Gordon Allport was, incidentally, skeptical that Cattell's approach corresponded to his own concept of unique traits.)

P-technique research requires so many measurements on the same individual across time that, at the outset, researchers could get only their spouses to serve as subjects. The in-house joke was that only married students could study the single subject. Cattell's wife served as his subject in the first P-technique experiment, published in 1947 (Cattell, 1984, p. 141). Cattell (1979) reported the P-technique in graphical form (see Figure 8.3). Each line reflects a particular trait as it rises and falls each day, illustrating the general principle that "ergic tension levels do alter considerably with time and circumstances" (p. 159).

Cattell (1957, p. 643) suggested one promising application of the P-technique: the investigation of psychosomatic conditions in individuals. Dean Keith Simonton (1998), although not citing Cattell, found that King George III of Great Britain typically experienced ill health about 9 months after times of extreme stress, giving insights into the cause of his breakdowns.

Researchers are searching for improved methods for examining variability within individuals, expanding on the methods suggested by Cattell's P-technique. Nesselroade (2001) reviews some intriguing findings of previous research: People's variation in internality predicts mortality, and variations in self-esteem predict depression. The detailed analysis envisioned by Cattell's P-technique has even greater potential for the study of detailed interactions over time between the individual and the environment.

SYNTALITY

Paralleling individual differences described by the term *personality,* Cattell offered a term to describe group differences: **syntality** (Cattell & Brennan, 1984). Cattell reported that compared to the British, U.S. undergraduates are more extraverted, more radical, and have a higher superego, whereas the British have higher ego strength and are more conservative (Cattell & Warburton, 1961). Nations also vary in emotionality. Cattell (1965) reported that Americans were less emotional than many other nationalities and that people in countries on the border between capitalism and communism had higher emotionality scores, presumably because of environmental pressures.

syntality group (e.g., national) differences in personality

Other researchers, too, report differences in personality characteristics among nations (Skinner & Peters, 1984) and ethnic groups (Whitworth & Perry, 1990). Such differences suggest that we be cautious when interpreting the personalities of individuals from other cultures. Unless we know what the "typical" personality of that culture is like, we are apt to make individual interpretations of traits that seem unusual to us but in fact may be

Figure 8.3 Illustration of P-Technique

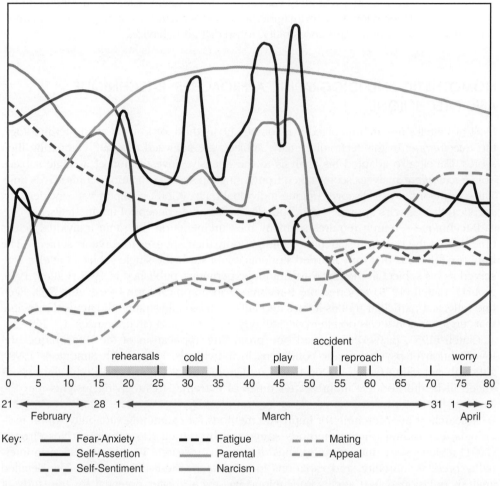

Ergic tension (and sentiment) response to stimulus (*S*), internal state (*P*), and goal satisfaction (*G*).

(From Cattell, 1965, p. 229.)

quite typical for the other culture. Research also raises intriguing questions about the extent to which personality is influenced by larger cultural forces that change from one generation to another. Jean Twenge and colleagues report that birth cohort explains up to 20% of the variance in several personality traits, including neuroticism and extraversion (Twenge, 2000, 2001a; Twenge & Campbell, 2001).

constitutional trait
a trait influenced by heredity

environmental-mold trait a trait influenced by learning

Determinants of Personality: Heredity and Environment

Where do traits, so useful for prediction, originate? Cattell distinguishes between **constitutional traits**, which originate in biological causes (especially genetics), and **environmental-mold traits**, which are the result of learning and social experience.

Cattell (1960) developed a statistical technique, the **Multiple Abstract Variance Analysis (MAVA)**, to analyze the effects of heredity and environment. It examines the similarity of relatives (identical twins, fraternal twins, siblings, and unrelated children) raised together, compared with the variation occurring when relatives are raised apart, and also with variation in the general population. To the extent that genetics determines a trait, relatives will be more similar than nonrelatives. The MAVA is an extension of the more restricted twin method of studying heredity, which examines twins reared together and apart but not other relatives. On the basis of these studies, Cattell (1973) estimated the **heritability** *(H)* of various traits, which he defined as "the fraction of the total measured variance of the trait X in the population that is due to hereditary differences in individual makeup" (p. 145). He found that many traits have high heritability.

Multiple Abstract Variance Analysis (MAVA) statistical technique for assessing how much of a trait is determined by heredity and how much by environment

heritability the extent to which a trait is influenced by genetics

The Role of Theory in Cattell's Empirical Approach

Cattell has been accused of being atheoretical, that is, of doing empirical work blindly and predicting without a guiding theory. He disputed this characterization. Cattell (1979) aimed to be not simply a methodologist but also a psychologist who used statistical methodology to address substantive questions. He acknowledged the groundwork laid down by earlier personality theories, used their ideas to interpret his factors, and urged students to have a background in Freudian and Jungian theory. He noted convergence of his results with the psychoanalytic concepts of the conscious and unconscious, ego strength, and impulse control. Others, too, have also noted the apparent convergence of factors derived from Cattell's measures with such psychoanalytic concepts as superego, ego strength, and anxiety (J. F. Campbell, 1988). Cattell's metatheoretical assumptions, which emphasize holism, motivation, and functionalism, are close to the mainstream theories, including Allport and Murray (Wiggins, 1984).

Although Cattell (1984, p. 158) denied being atheoretical, he remarked, "I have always felt justifiably suspicious of theory built much ahead of data." Cattell (1957, p. 50) claimed that his multivariate approach, which aspires to examine the entire sphere of personality systematically, resulted in many more discoveries in a briefer time than alternative approaches guided by theory. Not all researchers are satisfied with his factors, however. One of the biggest obstacles to consensus is disagreement about how many traits are necessary to describe personality. Currently, there is much enthusiasm for a five-factor model sometimes referred to as the Big Five, to which we now turn.

The Five-Factor Theory: McCrae and Costa

The method of factor analysis, which was the basis for Cattell's research, has been the tool of many other personality researchers. Often it is used in a limited way to develop personality tests that measure a particular trait of personality. (Factor analysis helps test developers be sure that their tests do not include extraneous dimensions or factors that are not intended.) The grand scope of Cattell's vision—that of proposing an empirically supported model of traits that could encompass the full spectrum of personality—has been again captured in a more recent model: the **Big Five**. Although many researchers

Big Five the five-factor model of personality, consisting of Extraversion, Agreeableness, Neuroticism, Conscientiousness, and Openness

have studied these five factors, the two leading proponents today are Paul Costa, Jr. and Robert McCrae. Their primary focus is on the description of personality, not on its causes.

As its name indicates, the Big Five model of personality asserts there are five basic factors of personality. The five factors originally were developed from factor analysis of the words people use in everyday language to describe personality, the *lexical approach* to personality (Goldberg, 1981, 1982; Norman, 1963). There is a good reason for starting with everyday language. If we assume people are tuned in to personality differences, because these differences are meaningful for everyday life, then the language of everyday speech should, over centuries, have come to reflect important dimensions of personality. (Recall that Allport and his colleague Odbert had also analyzed everyday language for personality traits, as described in Chapter 7.) Researchers report that even professionals who are attempting simply to describe behavior without coming to conclusions, as part of an employment screening, cannot help using trait language in their descriptions (Lievens, De Fruyt, & Van Dam, 2001).

The factors have been called by various names and have been replicated by factor analyzing many different personality tests and ratings of personality by outside observers (see Table 8.3). Many researchers are convinced that these five factors constitute the major dimensions of personality and thus a sensible descriptive foundation on which further personality research can be based (John, 1990). Other researchers, however, disagree: Cattell, because he prefers more narrow traits, as described earlier, and Jack Block (1995), because of methodological doubts.

PAUL COSTA, JR.

ROBERT MCCRAE

The Big Five consist of five broad personality traits: Extraversion, Agreeableness, Neuroticism, Conscientiousness, and Openness. (Students may find that the word "ocean" is a convenient mnemonic for helping to remember the Big Five, if the letters are scrambled, because each factor begins with one of the letters in "ocean.") A self-report questionnaire has been developed to measure people's standing on each factor by computing how much they agree that various statements describe them. This questionnaire, the NEO-PI (Costa & McCrae, 1985, 1992b), was named for the three factors measured in its first edition (neuroticism, extraversion, and openness); soon conscientiousness and agreeableness were added.

Let's consider the five factors so central to the description of personality. Each factor has been studied extensively, and each is correlated with many behaviors. In fact, if you know a person's standing on all five factors, you will have quite a clear awareness of that person's personality, although you will not be able to predict behavior perfectly in every situation that the person may confront.

TABLE 8.3	The Big Five Factors of Personality	
Factor	*Description of High Scorer*	*Description of Low Scorer*
Extraversion (E)	Talkative	Quiet
	Passionate	Unfeeling
	Active	Passive
	Dominant	
	Sociable	
Agreeableness (A)	Good-natured	Irritable
	Soft-hearted	Ruthless
	Trusting	Suspicious
Neuroticism (N)	Worrying	Calm
	Emotional	Unemotional
	Vulnerable	Hardy
	Anxious	Self-controlled
		Sense of well-being
Openness (O)	Creative	Uncreative
	Imaginative	Down-to-earth
	Prefers variety	Prefers routine
Conscientiousness (C)	Conscientious	Negligent
	Hardworking	Lazy
	Ambitious	Aimless
	Responsible	Irresponsible

(Adapted from McCrae, 1990, p. 402 and McCrae, Costa, & Piedmont, 1993.)

Extraversion

The first factor, **Extraversion**, has also been called both dominance-submissiveness and "surgency" (John, 1990). It is not surprising that extraversion is one of the Big Five. In fact, it is routinely found whenever factor analyses of personality questionnaires are conducted (Watson & Clark, 1997). Obviously an important dimension of personality, extraversion predicts many social behaviors.

Ask an extravert what he or she values in life, and the answer will often be cheerfulness and an exciting life (Dollinger, Leong, & Ulicni, 1996). Extraverted subjects, in a study in which they kept records of their social interactions, interacted with more people than did those low in extraversion; they also reported having more control and intimacy in those interactions (Barrett & Pietromonaco, 1997). Their peers consider extraverted people to be friendly, fun-loving, affectionate, and talkative (McCrae & Costa, 1987). Fellow group members perceive extraverted members as making valuable contributions to group projects (Barry & Stewart, 1997). Among both white and Asian American college

Extraversion factor of personality, typified by sociability, cheerfulness, and activity

students, extraverts are more willing to have sexual contact without commitment, and they report more sexual experience, compared to introverts (Wright & Reise, 1997).

Extraversion predicts the development of social relationships during college. Not surprisingly, those who are high on the trait of Extraversion make friends more quickly than those who are low. One facet of Extraversion, low *shyness,* also predicts falling in love. After a year in college, about one in three shy students, compared to three out of four nonshy students, reported being in love. Longitudinal research demonstrates that shy children in Sweden and the United States do not marry as early in adulthood as their less shy peers (Kerr, Lambert, & Bem, 1996).

Extraverts often seem happy, and it has been proposed that positive emotional experience is a core feature of Extraversion; perhaps the extravert is even biologically more responsive to pleasure than others are (Watson & Clark, 1997). It is not a serene happiness, but an active, energetic happiness that characterizes the typical extravert.

Agreeableness

Agreeableness
factor of personality,
typified by a friendly,
compliant personality

Agreeableness, which is sometimes instead called Social Adaptability or Likability (John, 1990), indicates a friendly, compliant personality, one who avoids hostility and tends to go along with others. Their friends find them sympathetic and softhearted, in contrast to those low in Agreeableness, who are described as suspicious, ruthless, and uncooperative (McCrae & Costa, 1987). On a survey of values, people scoring high in Agreeableness report that they value being helpful, forgiving, and loving (Dollinger et al., 1996). They report little conflict in their interpersonal relationships; when conflict occurs, it reduces their self-esteem (Barrett & Pietromonaco, 1997). People high in Agreeableness avoid direct attempts to assert power as a means of resolving conflict with other people, but large sex differences have also been found. Men, even those high in Agreeableness (who use less power to resolve conflict than men low in Agreeableness), are more likely to assert power than women (Graziano, Jensen-Campbell, & Hair, 1996).

In one study, students high on the trait of Agreeableness reported more interactions with their family and very few open conflicts with opposite-sex peers. We can only speculate how this avoidance of conflict might affect the development of relationships over a longer period than the 18 months of this study (Asendorpf & Wilpers, 1998).

Neuroticism

Neuroticism factor of
personality, typified by
negative emotionality

Neuroticism describes people who frequently are troubled by negative emotions such as worry and insecurity (McCrae & Costa, 1987). Emotionally, they are labile (readily aroused) instead of stable, like their low-scoring peers; thus the factor, turning attention to its opposite pole—low Neuroticism—has also been called Emotional Stability, Emotional Control, and Ego Strength (John, 1990). People who score low on Neuroticism are happier and more satisfied with life than those who score high (DeNeve & Cooper, 1998; Hills & Argyle, 2001; Schmutte & Ryff, 1997), and they are more satisfied with their marriage (Bouchard, Lussier, & Sabourin, 1999). Global well-being is higher among those with lower levels of Neuroticism in Germany and the United States (Staudinger, Fleeson, & Baltes, 1999). In marriage, high Neurotics are unhappy and dissatisfied with life (McCrae & Costa, 1991). Besides difficulties in relationships and commitment (Karney & Bradbury, 1995; Kurdek, 1997), they often suffer low self-esteem (Costa, McCrae, & Dye, 1991).

Another study reports that adults in the community who scored high on neuroticism also reported—in a diary in which they checked life events that had occurred each day— that more unpleasant events with family and friends, leisure, and finance had happened to them, which may explain why their mood was generally negative (David et al., 1997). Neuroticism is higher in people with diverse types of disturbances, whose specifics can be understood by considering their other personality factors (Claridge & Davis, 2001).

Conscientiousness

Conscientiousness, also called Dependability, Impulse Control, and Will to Achieve (John, 1990), describes differences in people's orderliness and self-discipline. Conscientious people value cleanliness and ambitiousness (Dollinger et al., 1996). Described by their peers as well organized, punctual, and ambitious (McCrae & Costa, 1987), the student who has a neat notebook and list of assignments and who keeps up with reading and completes work on time would score high on Conscientiousness. Conscientious students are generally motivated to achieve; they achieve high grade-point averages (Digman, 1989) and perform better in medical school (Ferguson et al., 2000). School and many other settings reward conscientious individuals, contributing to their generally high self-esteem (Costa et al., 1991).

> **Conscientiousness** factor of personality, typified by hard work, orderliness, and self-discipline

Conscientiousness predicts higher job satisfaction, income, and occupational status (Judge et al., 1999). Conscientious workers achieve more and set higher goals (Barrick & Mount, 1991; Barrick, Mount, & Strauss, 1993), receive better evaluations from their bosses (Barrick & Mount, 1996), and are also satisfied with their lives (DeNeve & Cooper, 1998). Conscientious employees have better attendance records (Judge, Martocchio, & Thoresen, 1997). Among police officers, low conscientiousness is associated with more job disciplinary actions for various kinds of misconduct, including sexual misconduct, insubordination, theft, and other unprofessional behavior (Sarchione et al., 1998).

We may note that, in addition to the strong evidence for Conscientiousness as a favorable personality contributor to job-related measures, other factors are also helpful for many jobs: low Neuroticism and Extraversion for jobs requiring social interaction and sometimes Agreeableness and Openness; when people are out of work, those high in Extraversion and Conscientiousness are more effective in searching for a new job (Kanfer, Wanberg, & Kantrowitz, 2001).

Beyond work and school, Conscientiousness also relates to family relationships and health behavior. Young married people who score high on Conscientiousness are less susceptible to sexual infidelity than those who score low (Buss & Shackelford, 1997c). Conscientious women are more likely to have a mammogram, despite their fear of breast cancer (Schwartz et al., 1999).

Openness

The factor **Openness** to experience is perhaps the most difficult to describe because it does not correspond to everyday language as well as the other factors (McCrae, 1990). Experts have given this factor various names: Culture, Intellect, Intellectual Interests, Intelligence, and Imagination (John, 1990; Sneed et al., 1998). Laypeople recognize it by the terms *artistic, curious, imaginative, insightful, original,* and *wide interests* (Sneed et al., 1998). Liberal values often go along with this factor (Costa & McCrae, 1992a). On the Rokeach Values Survey, people scoring high on Openness report that they value

> **Openness** factor of personality, typified by artistic, imaginative, and intellectual interests

imaginativeness, broadmindedness, and a world of beauty. People low in Openness, in contrast, value cleanliness, obedience, and national security (Dollinger et al., 1996).

Openness is conducive to personal growth, according to questionnaires (Schmutte & Ryff, 1997). Creative achievements are greater among people scoring high on Openness and low in Agreeableness (King, Walker, & Broyles, 1996). People who are creative, curious, or open to experience are more likely to find intelligent solutions to problems. In the workplace, this creativity is most likely to be manifested when the high Openness employee has flexibility, or even ambiguity, in the goals to be achieved and the way to achieve them, instead of having a highly structured set of expectations (George & Zhou, 2001).

More about These Five Factors

The five factors each consist of components called *facets,* which can be measured separately. Each facet is a somewhat more precise and focused trait of personality than the larger factor to which it belongs, yet all the facets that belong to one factor are positively correlated with one another (see Table 8.4).

Why should these particular factors have been chosen? As described earlier, the factors originated from analysis of language. The rationale for this approach is that people will have developed words to describe the aspects of personality that are most important to them as they interact with one another (Goldberg, 1981). According to David Buss (1997), who describes an evolutionary approach to personality, it is important for people to know how others with whom they interact will behave in the quest for social dominance. The factor Extraversion taps behavior related to social dominance, so it has become an important factor in all comprehensive trait models. Another issue is important in social interaction: our expectations that others will cooperate, perhaps to form alliances. The factor Agreeableness reflects cooperative tendencies, so it, too, has become an important factor when people talk about one another. It is not difficult to understand that people would also find it useful to label others as dependable or not (Conscientiousness) and as emotional or not (Neuroticism). Openness is less well represented in everyday language than the other factors, but even here, knowing who is intellectual and aesthetic would be essential in any social grouping that values the mind and the arts.

Alternative measures of these five factors have been developed. An interview measure has been devised especially for studying clinic populations. This procedure permits the interviewer to follow up on personality trends to see whether they are maladaptive for the individual. For example, a person who seems high in the Agreeableness factor by affirmatively answering the question, "Do you often go out of your way to help others who are in need?" will then be asked, "Do you do this at the sacrifice of your own best interests?" (Trull et al., 1998).

Self-ratings, ratings by friends, and even ratings by interviewers who are just getting to know a person tend to agree. When people are trying to present themselves in a particular way—being conscientious for a mock job interviewer, for example—this strategic self-presentation may reduce the accuracy of an interviewer's impression (Barrick, Patton, & Haugland, 2000).

The five-factor theory claims legitimacy in part because the same factors emerge in factor analysis despite variations in how data are obtained. Vary the specific statistical techniques used in factor analysis: not much effect. Analyze data based on self-report questionnaires: Five factors emerge. Analyze data based on ratings by peers: Again, the same five factors emerge. Vary the age of subjects studied, and the same five factors emerge, whether adults or children are measured. Study people in different countries

TABLE 8.4   Specific Facets of the Big Five Factors of Personality

Factor	Facets
Extraversion (E)	Warmth
	Gregariousness
	Assertiveness
	Activity
	Excitement-seeking
	Positive emotions
Agreeableness (A)	Trust
	Straightforwardness
	Altruism
	Compliance
	Modesty
	Tender-mindedness
Neuroticism (N)	Anxiety
	Hostility
	Depression
	Self-consciousness
	Impulsiveness
	Vulnerability
Openness (O)	Fantasy
	Aesthetics
	Feelings
	Actions
	Ideas
	Values
Conscientiousness (C)	Competence
	Order
	Dutifulness
	Achievement striving
	Self-discipline
	Deliberation

Note: Each of the five factors in the left column is composed of the six facets of that factor in the right column. The facets are positively correlated with one another, and scores on the facets are summed to obtain a score on the corresponding factor. (Adapted from Costa, McCrae, & Dye, 1991.)

(Germany, Italy, the Netherlands, Spain, the Philippines, Turkey, the United States, and others), speaking different languages, and again, the same five factors emerge, with perhaps more variation on the fifth factor, Openness (Caprara et al., 2000; Church & Katigbak, 2000; De Raad, 1998; McCrae et al., 1998; Somer & Goldberg, 1999; Wiggins & Trapnell, 1997). According to Robert McCrae (2000), "factor analyses show very similar five-factor solutions in German, Spanish, Portuguese, French, Italian, Dutch, Croatian, Russian, Hebrew, Japanese, Chinese, Korean, and Filipino . . .—every culture in which the structure has been examined" (p. 16). Clearly the Big Five are robust.

The five-factor theory has prompted researchers to reexamine many earlier personality tests to see whether they can be reinterpreted from this new perspective. In many cases, they can. The five factors described by the Big Five model are found in analyses of the California Personality Inventory (McCrae, Costa, & Piedmont, 1993), the Eysenck Personality Inventory (McCrae & Costa, 1982), the Myers-Briggs Type Inventory (McCrae, 1991) the Personality Research Form (Costa & McCrae, 1988), the Adjective Check List (Craig et al., 1998), and other tests. This approach has made it possible for researchers to infer a person's scores on these five factors, based on data collected using other tests. For example, such recoding has permitted researchers to consider the five-factor model in longitudinal research spanning 45 years, reaching back in time to data collected before the model was fully developed. They concluded that these personality factors were relatively stable from the first test at the end of college to retest in the men's 60s and that they predicted adult adjustment and behavior (Soldz & Vaillant, 1999).

In addition to analyzing the more focused facets of the five factors, researchers have asked whether they can be described as fewer, more general higher-order factors. Digman (1997) suggests that two such higher-order factors exist, one that reflects high Agreeableness, Conscientiousness, and Emotional Stability, and the other the factors of Extraversion and Openness.

Often the five-factor model is referred to as a theory, but it is probably more accurate simply to describe it as a model for organizing our observations about people's traits—that is, a descriptive taxonomy and not an explanatory theory (John & Srivastava, 1999; Ozer & Reise, 1994). For some factors, compelling theories have been offered, such as the biological theories for extraversion and neuroticism, described in Chapter 9. For the factor of Agreeableness, a systematic theoretical explanation is still emerging; perhaps a key to the explanation is individual differences in controlling and expressing anger (Ahadi & Rothbart, 1994; Graziano, Jensen-Campbell, & Hair, 1996). A learning theory or social cognitive explanation, using theories in the next two perspectives in this book, may help us understand this important personality factor. Despite these theoretical limitations, a clear description of personality is essential to understanding personality, and the Big Five claim respect as such a descriptive framework.

Summary

- Cattell defined *personality* simply as "that which permits a prediction of what a person will do in a given situation."
- Cattell developed a great number of *personality tests*.
- His research obtained data from three sources: self-report questionnaires (*Q-data*); objective tests, including projective tests and behavioral measures (*T-data*); and life history information (*L-data*). He sought convergence across these sources of data.
- Cattell used *multivariate* research methods, particularly *factor analysis*.

- He described the *surface traits* of people and, through more intensive statistical analysis, sought the underlying *source traits* that determine personality.
- His *16PF* personality test builds on this research and measures the 16 major source traits of personality. These scores can be presented in a *profile* for each individual.
- A *second-order factor analysis* of these scores results in five more general factors, including extraversion and anxiety.
- Cattell distinguished various types of traits: *dynamic, temperament,* and *ability.*
- He differentiated *fluid intelligence* (innate potential) from *crystallized intelligence* (influenced by experience) and developed ways to measure fluid intelligence.
- Cattell's *dynamic lattice* presents the relationship among *ergs* (constitutional dynamic source traits) and *metaergs* (environmental-mold dynamic source traits), which include *sentiments* and *attitudes.*
- These are related according to the principle of *subsidiation.*
- In principle, behavior can be predicted by the *specification equation,* which includes traits, situational factors, and temporary factors.
- Although most of his research was nomothetic *(R-technique),* Cattell also explored a *P-technique* for idiographic research.
- He offered the concept of *syntality* to describe group differences, such as national character.
- He developed the *MAVA technique* to investigate the impact of heredity on personality.
- Although his approach has been criticized for being atheoretical, Cattell drew on other theorists' concepts in interpreting his results, and he argued that extensive empirical work such as his had much to contribute to theoretical advances in personality.
- Another factor theory, the *five-factor model,* includes Extraversion, Agreeableness, Neuroticism, Conscientiousness, and Openness as factors derived from analysis of language.
- The Big Five factors correspond to Cattell's second-order factors of personality.
- These factors, assessed by self-report or peer report, are correlated with behavior as would be expected, and researchers report that they are heritable.

Thinking about Factor Analytic Trait Theories

1. Gordon Allport had an office near Raymond Cattell's office, and he reported that students were often confused by the differences between their approaches to personality. Why might this be so? Do you view factor analysis as an esteemed scientific tool or (like Allport) as "methodolatry"?

2. What is your opinion about the causes of intelligence, especially the extent to which heredity and experience influence intelligence?

3. Discuss why people may have a difficult time being objective and unemotional when discussing the role of heredity as a determinant of intelligence and personality.

4. If you have traveled to another country, have you observed any cross-cultural differences that could be labeled syntality? Describe them.

5. Cattell urges using mathematics in part because without it, we have difficulty keeping several causes of behavior in mind simultaneously. How multivariate can you be without math? Try to explain a particular behavior (e.g., working through the lunch hour), using as many variables as you can keep in mind at once.

6. Compare the five-factor model with Cattell's model. Based on this comparison, does it seem broad enough to encompass all the major dimensions of personality?

7. Propose a research study to investigate the impact of the social environment on any one specific hereditary dimension of personality. For example, how might an inherited predisposition for high levels of anxiety lead to maladaptive personality in one environment but not in another?

Study Questions

1. How did Cattell define personality?
2. Describe Cattell's contributions to personality testing.
3. List and explain the three sources of data that Cattell included in his research. Give an example of each.
4. Explain what is meant by multivariate research.
5. Distinguish between surface traits and source traits.
6. Describe Cattell's 16PF. Why is it said to measure source traits rather than surface traits?
7. What is factor analysis? What is second-order factor analysis?
8. Summarize Cattell's contributions to the measurement of intelligence. Include a description of his concepts of fluid intelligence and crystallized intelligence.
9. What did Cattell report about the inheritance of intelligence?
10. Distinguish between ergs and metaergs. Give examples of each.
11. Explain the principle of subsidiation in Cattell's dynamic lattice. Give an example.
12. What is the purpose of the specification equation? What terms are included? (Explain in words.)
13. Explain the P-technique. How is it different from the more common R-technique? Which method would you use if you wanted to study one individual in depth to determine what circumstances triggered that person's asthma?
14. Explain syntality. Give an example.
15. What is the purpose of the MAVA technique of data analysis? What findings have resulted from this technique?
16. Discuss the accusation that Cattell's work is atheoretical.
17. List the Big Five factors and describe each briefly.
18. How are the Big Five factors measured?
19. How does the Big Five factor model of personality compare with Cattell's model? How are they different?

Evolution and Temperament
Biological Theories

Chapter Overview

Preview: Overview of Biological Theories
Evolutionary Approaches
Emotions
Altruism
Sexual Behavior
Parental Behavior
Aggression and Dominance
Culture
Language and Thought
Genetics and Personality
Temperament

Biological Contributors to Personality
The Brain
Emotional Arousal
Cortical Arousal
Biological Factor Theories: Eysenck, Gray, and Others
Eysenck's "PEN" Biological Model
Gray's Reinforcement Sensitivity Theory
Cloninger's Tridimensional Model
Biological Mechanisms in Context
Summary

ILLUSTRATIVE BIOGRAPHY

Hillary Rodham Clinton

Although personality theorists have long acknowledged that biological factors influence personality, and biological abnormalities have long been identified for extreme pathologies, only recently have detailed mechanisms described the variations that we find in normal personality. Why is one person shy and another bold, one anxious and another confident? Why does one person recoil from criticism, whereas another laughs it off? Now we understand the role that biology plays (in combination with environment and upbringing) to create this diversity of human personalities.

Hillary Rodham Clinton, the former First Lady who became an elected official in her own right, a senator from New York, has been an active and controversial figure. Much in her life story speaks powerfully of the importance of upbringing and environment in determining personality. Yet these for her, as for all of us, did not act on a *tabula rasa* but rather on a person with a temperament, a biological potential that would interact with her experience to create a unique style of being human. Although the evidence is indirect—we have no bioassays or brain scans to offer—and the interpretations admittedly speculative, her life story illustrates the emerging biological models of personality presented in this chapter.

Hillary Rodham was born in 1947, the first child to hard-working parents in Illinois. She and her four brothers were disciplined with love and high standards for achievement. Impressive academic and extracurricular activities won her entrance to prestigious Wellesley College, where she encountered liberal attitudes that contrasted with her conservative Republican upbringing. Graduating as valedictorian, she publicly criticized the conservative Republican speaker who had preceded her, receiving a 7-minute standing ovation (Brock, 1996) and nationwide attention as a voice of the liberal segment of the baby boom generation, those critical of the Nixon administration. She then attended Yale Law School, where she met her future husband William Jefferson Clinton, whose career as Arkansas governor and then U.S. president detracted (some say) from Hillary's own promising career as a young lawyer. Public controversy and defeat followed her ambitious and unprecedented proposal for national health care reform. This active role in government as an unelected First Lady was either a bonus or an intrusion, depending on the perspective of her supporters or opponents. Her husband, whose extramarital sexual activities had plagued their relationship for years, was publicly humiliated when a White House intern, Monica Lewinsky, exposed their liaison. After two terms in the White House, the couple reversed public roles; Hillary became the elected politician, winning the election to represent New York in the U.S. Senate. The young Republican in Illinois had now clearly transformed into a Democratic leader, with speculation that her ambitions included a presidential run for herself.

Biology

Biological theorists describe brain areas and neurotransmitters that influence personality. So far, much attention has focused on emotions, both positive and negative. These activate different brain areas (more left hemisphere activation for positive emotions and also for anger; more right hemisphere for negative ones), and they are implicated in the formation of memory, so they have particular promise for understanding development and, ideally, therapy. Another biological approach, the evolutionary approach, is based on the adaptive implications of personality variations, at least for our ancestors. This approach suggests different predispositions for women and men on sexual

issues: a greater tendency toward sexual promiscuity among men than women because women who are more sexually selective have a greater chance of conceiving and raising more genetically fit children. Evolutionary theory also suggests an appetite for greater sexual promiscuity in men than women and more female concern with nurturing children.

Public images more often capture Hillary Rodham Clinton in smiling or assertive/angry poses than in sad ones, suggesting a prevalence of the positive and right hemisphere emotions. The implications of this require considering personality development, as we do in a moment. The evolutionary argument about gender differences in sexual promiscuity is consistent with the evidence. In this marriage, it is the husband who was the philanderer.

Description

Hillary Rodham Clinton, in the words of one biographer, "seems to have been born ambitious" (Olson, 1999, p. 23). Temperament refers to the innate biological predispositions of personality; some people are bold and assertive, whereas others are timid and shy (and many others, somewhere in between). An assertive personality is more influenced by rewards than punishment. For other people, the pain of punishment seems greater because negative emotions, such as fear, are accentuated by their brain functioning, and so they act more cautiously.

From childhood onward, Hillary Rodham was more assertive and bold than timid, although not to an extreme. She recalls a childhood incident in which, with her mother's encouragement, at age 4 she stood up to a neighborhood bully who teased her (Clinton, 2003). In elementary school, Hillary reports that she was considered a tomboy and had a reputation for being able to stand up to unruly male classmates (Clinton, 2003, p. 15). For a less assertive person, fear would have precluded many of the choices that Hillary made in her life: leaving her Illinois home for a distant, not yet seen college on the East Coast; approaching a male classmate (her future husband, as it turns out) in the Yale library to introduce herself; presenting an ambitious health care reform proposal to a skeptical audience; embarking on her own elective political career. But fear is muted in Hillary Rodham Clinton's personality, an innate temperamental quality. This quality is also helpful in dealing with events outside her own choices. Her husband's infidelity and the ensuing media frenzy could have produced retreat into the safety of a private life, but it did not.

Development

Understanding the development of personality from a biological perspective highlights the impact of experience on diverse temperamental beginnings. Biological theories specify genetically based variants in the brain's functioning that predispose variations in the emotional responses that shape personality. All of us seek what feels pleasant to us and recoil from what is punishing, but the inner experience of these emotions is enhanced or muted, depending on our biological makeup. These subtle variations tweak personality in one direction or another. As experiences in life are rewarded and punished, the impact of these experiences are muted for some and magnified for others.

Kagan's model of temperament, described in this chapter, says that the outcome of a hereditary predisposition can be one of good or poor adjustment, depending on the experience of an appropriate child-rearing experience for that temperament type. For temperamentally bold children, clear guidance and discipline are important, so the lure of rewards does not lead to ill-chosen behavior. That is the sort of environment that Hillary Rodham's loving and hardworking parents provided, according to her autobiography.

Still, it is the rewards rather than the punishments that seem to have made the greatest impression. Here is a childhood recollection that illustrates her attention to rewards. In sixth grade, Hillary was co-captain of the school safety patrol. A friend's mother commented that she would have fixed lunch for them instead of leaving them to make their own sandwiches, if she had known of Hillary's status, which Hillary described as "my first lesson in the strange ways some people respond to electoral politics" (Clinton, 2003, p. 15). There are rewards to be gained from politics.

Adjustment

Emotional reactions cause adjustment problems if they are extreme. Those people whose anxiety or depressive reactions are predisposed by heredity to be greater risk developing adjustment problems, although the occurrence of such problems is also affected by life experience. The same life experience may push one person over a threshold to dysfunction, whereas another remains stable, depending on their different biological predispositions. In contrast, positive emotions provide the incentive for assertive behavior, although if they are extreme and untempered by negative experiences, they can lock a person into maladapted addictive patterns.

Hillary Rodham Clinton's life attests to an ability to withstand the trials that provoke anxiety and tears and to be more strongly influenced by potential rewards and achievements. In part, the greater influence of positive than negative emotions is the product of heredity (as Gray's Behavioral Activation System and Behavioral Inhibition System, described in this chapter, explain). Society's judgments are influenced by the role expectations, including gender roles, and there certainly was a time when the assertive style of behavior was judged maladjusted in a woman. Such judgments still occur in some circles.

Cognition

Heredity influences cognitive as well as emotional aspects of personality. Intelligence is under genetic control (although of course it requires educational opportunity to fulfill its potential). Cognition, though, is more than simply intelligence. Researchers have even found that attitudes toward social issues, inclinations toward liberalism or conservatism, are influenced by heredity, although undoubtedly by indirect mechanisms, and in interaction with experience.

Hillary Rodham Clinton's academic credentials attest to high intelligence. She was near the top of her high school class, missing the top spot, according to one biographer, because some of her energies were expended on extracurricular involvements. She was the valedictorian of her college class at rigorous Wellesley College. Attitudes of liberalism and conservatism are influenced by both heredity and experience. In studying a single case, it is not possible to know which of these influences was more important. Did Hillary become more liberal in college because of the experiences in that environment? Or could some of the suppressed heredity from her mother, a secret liberal Democrat in a conservative Republican family and town, have been freed for expression in that more permissive environment? We can only speculate, with one case.

Society

Biology is expressed in a social context, and for humans, our shared biological predispositions have prepared us to play a role in a social environment. The ability to communicate with other people, to cooperate and to compete with them, is fundamental to our nature. We also learn from one another, and these lessons are passed down from one generation to the next, changing with each generation's experience, producing what can be called "cultural evolution." Thus the life experience of a person must be understood within a particular society and time.

The society and time that Hillary Rodham Clinton experienced is the postwar baby boom generation of America: a time of increased opportunities for women to participate in public life, and a time of disenchantment with the nation's political leadership that was particularly salient during Hillary's high school and college years, over the Vietnam War. As she points out in her autobiography (Clinton, 2003), women's colleges, such as her alma mater Wellesley College, have a track record of cultivating leadership in women. And so she emerged into young adulthood, prepared by the current culture's influence to be more flexible than previous generations of women in the style of her femininity. Traditional maternal concerns for children are an example. She could try (although unsuccessfully) to care for the nation's children through expanded government health programs. Societal considerations can also help her understand the intensity of anti-Hillary feeling that her critics voice. Dominance is characteristically a male trait, whether by evolutionary selection or cultural teaching or some combination of these. A woman with low levels of fear, who seizes the opportunities of this place and time to assert dominance, is thus unusual, and much psychological research indicates that people generally prefer the familiar to the new.

Final Thoughts

Although this chapter focuses on biological influences, it is clear from this brief analysis of Hillary Rodham Clinton that culture, too, must be considered. Theorists no longer present debates of nature versus nurture. They seek models to integrate the two. How does the environment enhance or suppress the possibilities that each person's biology predisposes? Thinking in these terms, the assertive, ambitious, and resilient Hillary Rodham Clinton is a product of both her biology and her familial and cultural environment. Using a phrase that is part of the curriculum in the women's college where I teach, we may call her a "woman of influence," as one who is not only product but also producer of our evolving culture.

Preview: Overview of Biological Theories

Biological theories have implications for major theoretical questions, as presented in Table 9.1. They have generated many empirical studies, ranging from correlational investigations to determine the reliability of categorizing people into particular temperament or other biological categories to empirical investigations that examine the relationship of these categories to biological measures such as brain activity. Evolutionary theorists have observed animals and surveyed college students. The concreteness of biological concepts (in contrast to statistically derived factors discussed in Chapter 8) further adds to the scientific status of this approach by suggesting clear operational definitions of theoretical constructs. The biological approach adds to the comprehensiveness of other trait approaches by connecting personality theory to natural science understandings of evolution and neurobiology. The potential for applied value in a biological approach is considerable, although the approach is still too new to have produced notable applications. If reliable and valid assessments of personality predispositions in early life are developed, this approach may help identify the particular optimal "nurture" environment for people with different genetic "nature," thus permitting intervention to improve personality. There are risks to application as well, labeling individuals and groups with prejudicial terms. We begin our consideration of biological approaches to personality with evolutionary theory, which offers an explanation of universal human tendencies. Then we consider theories that focus on individual differences described as inherited temperament and biological personality factors.

Evolutionary Approaches

Imagine a small group of our ancient human ancestors. They are almost all related in some way, with a few women who have been coaxed or kidnapped from other clans. They seldom see other humans, and when they do, they are apprehensive and aggressive.

TABLE 9.1	Preview of Biological Theories
Individual Differences	Individuals differ in their hereditary predispositions and in the traits that develop from the interaction of these predispositions with experience. Several factor theories describe individual differences.
Adaptation and Adjustment	Some biological factors, such as Neuroticism, are differences in emotional instability that predispose some people to anxiety and other adjustment problems. Differences in responses to rewards and punishments, based on biological differences, can predispose people to addiction, depression, and other problems.
Cognitive Processes	Evolutionary theory points to human language and cognitive abilities as adaptations characteristic of our species because of natural selection. Cognitive processes can be influenced by biological processes and hereditary differences.
Society	Society channels inherited traits and provides the cultural context for their expression through learning.
Biological Influences	Biological factors are the central focus of this approach, including evolutionary selection, heredity, hormonal, brain, and neurotransmitter effects.
Development	Temperament is observable in infancy and later, as an early indicator of the individual's inherited biologically based personality. Some early experiences can sensitize particular neural pathways (e.g., for stress reactions). Biologically based personality factors are generally stable in adulthood.

One man is clearly the privileged one when it comes to food and mating. There is relative peace, except for occasional sexual jealousy or rivalry for status. The women gather food, with their superior memory for locations of fruits and berries found in the past, and care for their children. Some of the men have gone to hunt, using their superior spatial abilities so useful for throwing spears. The children watch and imitate the skills their parents know. The adults speak with one another, telling tales of past hunting successes or talking about one another's social behavior.

Are these ancient ancestors so different from us? Probably not, according to evolutionary theorists. The groups are much smaller—a few dozen people—and the advances that would come with the evolution of culture had not yet accumulated modern technology, but the fundamental emotions and behavioral impulses were, nonetheless, remarkably like our own. This is the lesson of **evolutionary psychology**, which theorizes that natural selection—well known in biology because of the work of Charles Darwin and others—has produced a human species with certain identifiable genetically based characteristics that affect personality and social behavior. The fundamental assumption of the evolutionary approach is that genetic variations in body and behavior that enhance the reproductive success of the organism will become more frequent over generations as a result of natural selection.

Evolutionary theory, according to its advocates, offers a genuinely new paradigm for the study of personality (Buss, 1995a; Buss et al., 1998; Cervone, 1999). In fact, advocates

evolutionary psychology the perspective that applies the evolutionary principles of natural selection to understanding human psychology, including personality

claim that the evolutionary approach has the potential to provide theoretical coherence to replace the current disunity in psychology. It embeds the study of personality in a theoretical framework that does not have the exaggerated dualisms of "body and mind, human and animal, and nature and culture" that burden much of psychology (de Waal, 2002, p. 187).

Evolutionary personality psychology focuses on universal, or near-universal, aspects of "human nature," such as our language capacity, aggression, and sexual behaviors. It seeks insights from the proposed effects of selective pressure over long spans of time, in which traits that confer adaptive fitness become increasingly widespread in a population: the survival of the fittest (Darwin, 1859/1909).

Although the core idea of survival and reproductive advantage is easy enough to understand, the theory strikes many as highly speculative when applied to personality, often politically incorrect (cf. Buss, 1995b) and—from a primatologist's point of view (de Waal, 2002)—overly simplified. Contrary to what many seem to think, evolutionary theory does not propose that every trait that now exists has adaptive value. Circumstances may have changed from what they were at the time of evolutionary selection (Buss et al., 1998). For example, our current environment in much of the developed world provides more calories than we need, yet people still crave fat and sweets—cravings that long ago ensured they would seek out high-caloric food to sustain life. In the personality domain, the aggressive behavior that may have favored our remote ancestors' survival does not have the same effect today.

Emotions

Evolution is not limited to physical characteristics and basic drives. For the field of personality, emotional reactions and social behaviors are especially important. Because of evolutionary selection, many emotional reactions are innate, and therefore more efficient and reliable for survival, such as fear of snakes and of strangers. By coming prewired with reactions such as this, or at least with the predisposition to learn them quickly ("prepared learning"), our ancestors had better survival prospects. Emotions tap deep evolutionary roots. Laughter, for example, has precursors in the chirping vocalizations of happy rats (Panksepp, 2000).

Modern evolutionary psychology is especially concerned with social behavior, including altruism, aggression, and sex differences in courtship (Archer, 1996; Cronin, 1991). In social behavior, emotions are communicated to others, with universally understood innate expressions of fear, happiness, anger, and other emotions (Ekman, 1993). Embarrassment, an emotion that presumes awareness of self, has its own distinct and recognizable facial display, including downward and then shifting eye gaze and partially controlled smiling (Keltner & Anderson, 2000).

Communication of emotions between people, and by animals too (through such expressions as bared fangs to show anger), was regarded as quite important by Darwin, who wrote *The Expression of Emotions in Man and Animals* (1872/1979) as well as *The Origin of Species* (1859/1909). Communication of emotions by unlearned, stereotyped universal facial expressions is one aspect of our evolutionary legacy that makes society and culture possible. But what triggers emotions? According to David Buss (2000), "Human anguish in modern minds is tethered to the events that would have caused fitness failure in ancestral times" (p. 18), that is, loss of social status, rejection by sexual partners, death of a child, and so on. Emotions and their communications make human social living possible: We know when others are angry, friendly, and so on, and can adjust our own behavior appropriately. This protects us and helps us achieve our own best interests, as well as solidifying the social ties that contribute to survival in a variety of ways: by sharing the fruits of one another's labor, cooperating to protect from threat, and even enhancing immune functioning through the calming effect of social support.

Altruism

The concept of **inclusive fitness** assumes that evolution will select for genes that increase the survival of the individual and his or her genetic relatives (Caporeal, 2001; Dawkins, 1976; Kenrick, 2001; Trivers, 1971). Examples include genes that enhance parental investment in their children and those that produce altruistic behavior, especially toward relatives. Evolutionary approaches explain altruistic behavior according to two principles: kin altruism and reciprocal altruism. The principle of **kin altruism** asserts that natural selection favors those who act altruistically toward their genetic relatives because the genes they save are (in part) identical to their own. Helping nonrelatives is explained by the concept of **reciprocal altruism**, whereby members of a group have evolved tendencies to help one another, even if they are unrelated. An individual's risk of harm while helping someone else is compensated by the increased benefit when others help him or her, so the net result is, on average, greater probability of survival. The maximum survival probability would belong to those who are surrounded by reciprocally altruistic others but who themselves would not help in an emergency.

These "cheaters" threaten others, whose risk by helping is not compensated by the benefits of being helped, and so mechanisms to control them are brought into play: scorn for free riders and honor to heroes. Human emotions are positive toward those who cooperate on group endeavors and negative (punitive) toward those who act as free riders, benefiting from group effort without contributing to it (Price, Cosmides, & Tooby, 2002). We are prepared by evolution to be on the alert for signs that people are not trustworthy by being skeptical about their motivations when there are reasons to think they may be deceiving us (Andrews, 2001). From a behavioral point of view, people could gradually learn which people are trustworthy and which are likely to exploit others through experience with the other people. This rather slow process, though, does not seem to be necessary. Instead, our brains come prewired to readily understand social nuances of cooperation and competition.

Altruism is not a rationally calculated act. It flows from a basic and unlearned psychological process, empathy. When we identify psychological mechanisms that have an evolutionary survival function, we are more certain to have identified basic universal processes influenced by heredity, so there is more probability of building a universally applicable personality theory—although we may still be on the lookout for cultural variations. But because they emerged to solve particular adaptive problems, evolutionary mechanisms are many and diverse and do not go together in a unified way. Thus when an individual has an odd quirk of personality, if it stems from an evolutionary trait, it may be quite unrelated to the rest of personality. For example, the common human fear of snakes had adaptive value for our ancestors, who risked illness or death from snake bites, so there is no need to try to understand such fears from a symbolic, Freudian point of view. These mechanisms are basic and unconscious but not personal.

inclusive fitness the evolutionary principle that traits that increase the survival of the individual and his or her genetic relatives will become more frequent by natural selection

kin altruism the principle that natural selection favors those who risk their own lives or welfare to improve the survival and reproductive prospects of their genetic relatives

reciprocal altruism the evolutionary principle whereby members of a group take risks to help the survival and reproductive prospects of others, even nonrelatives, with the (not necessarily conscious) expectation of being helped in return

TABLE 9.2	Examples of Evolved Psychological Mechanisms
Sexual jealousy	Functions to help ensure men that they are the genetic fathers of their mate's child
Sexual attraction based on physical appearance	Functions to ensure a healthy mate and one with effects of hormones (estrogen or testosterone) that indicate fertility
Sexual attraction based on man's ability to provide resources	Functions to ensure women that their mates will be able to provide resources needed for the survival of their children
Sexual attraction based on youth	Functions to optimize the number of remaining years of fertility
Imitation	Functions to enable children to learn culture and to profit from the experience of adults

evolved psychological mechanisms specific psychological processes that have evolved because they solved particular adaptive problems (e.g., sexual jealousy, dealing with the problem of paternal uncertainty)

David Buss (1999) describes **evolved psychological mechanisms**, which are specific psychological processes that have evolved because they solve particular adaptive problems of survival or reproduction (see Table 9.2). Sexual jealousy evolved as a psychological mechanism to deal with the problem of uncertain paternity. Other psychological mechanisms include female preference for mates who can supply economic resources, serving the function of providing for children, and male preferences for youth and variety in sexual partners, serving the functions of increasing the fertility and number of sexual partners (Buss, 1995a).

Sexual Behavior

Reproduction is of primary concern to evolutionary theory, and psychologists have used evolutionary arguments to explain attraction to potential sexual partners, maintaining relationships, and caring for children. What is exciting about these analyses is that they are beginning to be integrated with ideas, such as attachment, that theorists from other personality perspectives have already explored.

Freud described libido as driving sexual behavior, but where does this libido come from, and why (other than childhood experience) is it focused more on some objects than others? Evolutionary theory asserts that the goal is to pass on one's genes; thus sexual attraction that can culminate in reproduction would have a natural advantage. Yet it is not the mind's knowledge but evolved psychological mechanisms, which operate unconsciously, that nature uses for this purpose.

Consider sexual attraction. The gene race is won by those who mate with fertile partners. Both sexes prefer physically attractive partners, whose good looks are signals of health. Men prefer youthful females, who have more reproductive years ahead. Many studies of attraction in a variety of societies, both in laboratory environments and by analyzing such real-world evidence as advertisements for dating introductions, confirm these predictions (Buss, 1989; Campos, Otta, & Siqueira, 2002). Details of physical attractiveness have been investigated. Bodies and faces that are more symmetrical on the left and right sides are found more attractive (by both men and women); symmetry, because of biological mechanisms, is produced by good genetic quality (Fink & Penton-Voak, 2002; Hume & Montgomerie, 2001).

Attractive features also serve as "hormone markers," indicating higher levels of estrogen in females and testosterone in males. Research generally supports the evolutionary hypothesis that men prefer women with a low waist-to-hip ratio, an observable cue to high estrogen levels associated with greater fertility. In most studies, the ideal ratio of waist to hips is near the 0.7 that experts consider optimal for reproduction, but in Uganda, even larger hips attract men, probably as part of a general preference in that culture for large-bodied women (Bereczkei, 2000; Furnham, Moutafi, & Baguma, 2002). For their part, women are attracted to men whose faces show masculine bone structure features, such as a strong chin, that are produced by higher testosterone levels—especially when the women respond to researchers' questions during their most fertile phase (Fink & Penton-Voak, 2002).

Evolution selects for different traits in males and females because of different **parental investment** for the two sexes (Buss, 1988; Trivers, 1972). A woman can produce only a limited number of children in her lifetime because of the 9 months of gestation and, in ancestral times, diminished fertility after birth when the baby is being breastfed. Because of the greater costs in time and lost alternative opportunities with each conception, it is adaptive for the woman to be particularly selective about her choice of mate. To conceive a genetically inferior child who might die or fail to carry on the genetic line would waste her reproductive opportunity, and evolution would selectively remove such unselective women from the population. The woman, then, must be sure that she mates with the man who provides the highest quality genes for her investment in maternity. In addition, because of the dangers to a vulnerable child and mother, she also looks for a man who will stay to help protect them and to provide resources.

In contrast, a man's reproductive potential is much greater because sperm cells are so much more abundant than ova and the reduced reproductive potential after each conception is measured in hours, not years. This view probably exaggerates men's reproductive potential, relative to women (Einon, 1998), but even so, it suggests that by their nature, men are more opportunistic and women more selective in their sexual behavior. Research confirms this observation. Buss and Schmitt (1993), for example, asked undergraduates on a questionnaire how long they would wait before being willing to have sexual intercourse with a hypothetical person of the opposite sex they had just met. Women would wait for 3 months before becoming as willing as the man was after only 1 day; by 3 months, the man was as ready as the woman would be after 2 years.

The promiscuous strategy is not the only one men have, and it brings risks. His children may not survive, given the harsh environment for unprotected mothers and the danger of child killing by competing men. Many men would leave no offspring if all adopted this promiscuous strategy. An alternative is available: to become bonded with the mother and stay to ensure that his children will survive. The increased survival of these children compensates for lost reproductive opportunities elsewhere. Some research surveying college students finds that 99% of both men and women report wanting to settle down in a monogamous sexual relationship (Pedersen et al., 2002).

Because all his reproductive potential is invested in this one relationship (with perhaps a few surreptitious exceptions, if opportunity permits—to increase his reproductive potential), a new issue arises: Are the children really his, or has another man conceived them? This **paternal uncertainty** that the children actually are his genetic offspring has no parallel in a woman's experience (because she has carried the child during pregnancy), so sexual jealousy is greater in men. Confirming this idea, several studies find that male college students in a variety of countries report greater distress than women at the hypothetical scenario of their dating partner having sex with another man; in contrast,

parental investment the expenditure of time and resources to reproduce each child, especially emphasizing the amount of one's reproductive potential that is expended for each child

paternal uncertainty evolutionary proposal that men cannot be sure they are the biological fathers of the children born to their mates

women were more disturbed at the prospect of their partner having an emotional relationship with another woman, theoretically because it might entice the male protector away from her (Buss et al., 1992; Wiederman & Kendall, 1999). Based on reports of their actual personal experiences, though, another researcher reports no sex differences in the pain of emotional and sexual partner infidelity, either in heterosexual or homosexual respondents (C. R. Harris, 2002).

The image of the selective and committed female and the unselective, promiscuous male sexual styles is of course an oversimplification, even within evolutionary theory. Men are more willing to report infidelities on self-report measures, but actual behavioral measures show less difference between the sexes. Women, too, engage in sexual relationships outside of their primary relationship, especially when the alternative partner is superior and when they are fertile (Drigotas & Barta, 2001). Theoretical arguments explain that it sometimes is in the best reproductive interest of the woman to reproduce with a more genetically fit man, even if he is not willing to stay to protect the child (Buss, 1999; Gangestad & Simpson, 1990).

The specific strategies that humans use to attract a mate are less stereotyped than in lower animals, and they reflect the alternatives of seeking a long-term mate or a short-term partner (Buss & Schmitt, 1993). Based on questionnaires answered by undergraduates, Schmitt and Buss (1996) report that people use different sexual strategies to attract a partner to a short-term relationship (e.g., emphasizing sexual availability) or a long-term one (e.g., emphasizing future resource potential). Male status and dominance are more important for short-term relationships, including efforts to "poach" women who are already in a relationship with someone else; but dominance is less important for longer-term commitments, where loyalty matters (Schmitt & Buss, 2001). Among married couples, various strategies are used to retain the mate, ranging from appearance enhancement (more common in women) to threatening competitors (more common in men). Wives' youth and attractiveness and husbands' status striving and income predict mate retention (Buss & Shackelford, 1997a). Culture matters, too; when cultures have more equal status between the sexes, gender differences in sexual attraction—women's preference for high-status men and men's preference for youthful women, for example—are reduced (Eagly & Wood, 1999).

Most of the data supporting male promiscuity and female commitment come from questionnaires to undergraduates, whereas the actual behavior of adults later shows more long-term relationships in both sexes. An alternative model suggests that both sexes are primarily drawn to long-term mating as an extension of the attachment process of earlier life. Under conditions of adversity, children are less likely to be raised in the sort of stable family that is conducive to secure attachment. This teaches them a less desirable strategy, but one that is adaptive under conditions of scarce resources, that is, to mate opportunistically, instead of counting on stable pair-bonds and high investment in parenting (Bereczkei, 2000). When the situation is more stable, the attachment model portrays both parents caring for children, offering an evolutionary advantage in the survival of the offspring during a long period of immaturity. Mates also provide emotional security to one another, as in the mother–child bond, and there are even parallels at the biological level: the hormone **oxytocin** is released both in nursing and in sexual intercourse, and it stimulates cuddling or contact comfort in both cases (Hazan & Diamond, 2000). Animal studies, using mice and voles, also point to the role of oxytocin (and vasopressin) in social attachment (LeDoux, 2002; Young, 2002). Human females, according to Shelley Taylor and colleagues (2000), respond to stress with a "friend-and-befriend" attachment and caregiving mode, mediated by oxytocin, in addition to the "fight-or-flight" mode that occurs in both sexes. This caregiving response to stress would have had evolutionary value in protecting children.

oxytocin hormone released by nursing females and in sexual intercourse; thought to promote caretaking and cuddling

In portraying this evolutionary picture, we should not oversimplify. After all, many behaviors have no simple, obvious evolutionary advantage, and many genes combine to produce a great variety of outcomes in various individuals. Consider homosexuality, a sexual orientation influenced by a number of genes. The component genes, it has been argued, produce such traits as empathy and sensitivity, which are attractive to women and enhance fathering. When a great many of these genes are present, they produce homosexuality, which confers no reproductive advantage on the individual but which, argues E. M. Miller (2000), is consistent with evolutionary selection because of the positive contribution of the component genes on cooperation and other social traits. Celibacy is another sexual pattern that seems inconsistent with the evolutionary impetus to reproduce, but it, too, can fit evolutionary models. Our genes, after all, are not exclusively our own. If we enhance the survival of our siblings' children, these shared genes are well served. A celibate aunt or uncle (or other relative) whose relatives gain sufficient survival advantage from his or her altruistic behavior may more than compensate for the genes lost by celibacy. Consistent with this reasoning, religious communities that mandate celibacy, from diverse traditions that include Christianity, Buddhism, and Islam, often refer to one another using kin terms, such as "sisters" or "brothers," and they dress and groom themselves to appear similar, as relatives would. These behaviors invoke evolutionary kin recognition mechanisms to encourage altruistic behavior (Qirko, 2004).

Parental Behavior

Parents who nurture their children enhance the survival of their genes. Other family members, aunts and uncles, grandparents and others, who share some of these genes, also have an investment in the child's survival to reproductive maturity. Stepchildren, who are not the genetic offspring of the parent, are more often abused or neglected (Belsky, 1993) and they receive less financial support for education (Zvoch, 1999). Families can provide a supportive environment for the mother and child, with long-term consequences for the child's psychological health. In contrast, children who are exposed to stressed or depressed mothers during their preschool years have elevated cortisol levels later, indicating that they have developed a physiological sensitization to stress (Essex et al., 2002). Animal studies show that young rats who are deprived of maternal contact for as few as 3 hours per day develop permanent deficits in the hippocampus that could affect later learning and memory and make them (and humans too, if the result generalizes across species) more vulnerable to depression (Karten, Olariu, & Cameron, 2005). Because of the impact of early maternal care, the same genotype can be programmed into different adult phenotypes (Meaney & Szyf, 2005). This plasticity, which is clearly documented in studies of rats (where experimental control is possible), should make us less pessimistic about apparent "bad genes." Given different early parenting, the outcome can be changed.

Although passing on one's genes to the next generation and beyond is clearly an important evolutionary outcome, sometimes the parents and children have divergent interests. It is not genetically advantageous to fully invest in parenthood at all times. Evolutionary models describe selection for deferring parenthood when conditions are not favorable to their survival (Boone & Kessler, 1999). It may at times be beneficial, from the perspective of passing on one's genes, for parents not to safeguard the survival of one particular child, to invest their limited resources in other children who have been born or may be born in the future. The one child may have genetic shortcomings or the environmental context may not be favorable for survival (such as in times of famine). Even when times are not so austere, the interests of parent and child may diverge. Jay Belsky (1993) gives the example of a toddler's best interest through continuing breastfeeding, but a mother's interest in weaning in order to provide for other children or to conceive another child.

An extended period of dependency in childhood has been described as a consequence of our evolving large brain. Left to mature longer in the uterus, the brain would soon become too large to fit through the birth canal. Children's extended period of immaturity makes them vulnerable, but it also permits a long period for learning, thus encouraging transmission of language and culture (Bjorklund, 1997).

Aggression and Dominance

Aggressive behavior, from an evolutionary point of view, serves several functions: "co-opting the resources of others, defending against attack, inflicting costs on same-sex rivals, negotiating status and power hierarchies, deterring rivals from future aggression, deterring mates from sexual infidelity, and reducing resources expended on genetically unrelated children" (Buss & Shackelford, 1997b, p. 605). Studies of the elderly find that power remains more significant to the life satisfaction of men than of women, who are more affected by affiliation (Halisch & Geppert, 2001).

Competition among men for reproductive opportunities makes social dominance a male issue and leads to much higher rates of aggression among men than among women, particularly among young men who are at an age when competition with other men serves the evolutionary purpose of selecting the fittest and enforcing on women their exclusive sexual access to them (D. Jones, 1999; Mesquida & Wiener, 1996). In some studies, testosterone levels are higher, on average, in boys and men who are more aggressive (Chance et al., 2000) and who are diagnosed with antisocial personality disorder and alcoholism (Stålenheim et al., 1998). The evolutionary selection for aggression in men does not mean, however, that male aggression today is necessarily tied to competition over women. A review suggests that, more often, men are concerned with status and respect from other men (Fischer & Mosquera, 2001). Whether this means that the theorized sexual motivation is incorrect or whether culture has simply replaced brute force with more culturally evolved mechanisms of establishing dominance is a matter of debate.

Culture

Oddly, one of the most important evolutionary legacies is the ability of humans to form cultures. This irony illustrates how modern evolutionary theory challenges the biology–culture distinction that many take for granted. Cultural transmission of ideas from one generation to another is described in modern evolutionary theory and includes elaborate symbolic representations, such as religion (Boyer, 2000). An evolutionary genetic change permitted humans to accumulate culture that continued to develop and change over many generations through learning, without the requirement of further genetic change (Tomasello, 1999). Children's propensity to imitate what they see facilitates the learning of culture.

In contrast to Freud's description of conflict between animal nature and civilization, evolutionary theorists describe human nature as inherently prepared for culture through such human abilities as language and other symbols, tools and technologies, and social organizations. Each personality develops in an environment shaped by cumulative **cultural evolution**. In fact, because biological evolution has continued among our human ancestors who had culture, including mystical and religious aspects, we may refer to both culture and biology in a conjoint way, as a *biocultural* paradigm or model (de Nicolas, 1998).

> **cultural evolution**
> evolution through trans-mitted learning from one generation to another

Evolutionary selective pressures can explain cultural practices. Consider the taboo against eating beef and oxen in cultures that needed those animals to plow fields. Over time, those who ate their animals were more likely to lose their farms and ultimately starve; those who kept the animals despite famine, if they survived, could plant the next crop (Alessi, 1992). Cultural practices coevolve with genetic evolution. Individual behaviors influence societal-level cultural practices; these in turn influence individual behavior, so the relationship between culture and the individual is one of mutual influence (Bereczkei, 2000).

Language and Thought

Language gives humans our capacity for a unique kind of consciousness (LeDoux, 2002). Culture builds on human language capacity, which makes it possible to weave narratives of past experiences—for example, by telling others about successful hunting (Premack & Premack, 2003).

Our human nature has given us the capacity to develop a "theory of mind," that is, an understanding of the thoughts and intentions of others. Chimpanzees also have a rudimentary theory of mind (Premack & Premack, 2003): For example, they respond differently to a person who fails to give them an expected treat because of accidentally spilling it as compared to a person who intentionally poured it on the ground. But the human child's capacity to infer what others know and want is greater than our simian relatives. Evidence that it is a discrete brain mechanism, unrelated to intelligence, comes from observing autistic children, who lack this understanding—not from low intelligence or lack of experience, but from (we think) a genetic defect (Pinker, 2002).

The human mind has evolved to be capable of symbolic thought, which has made a tremendous difference in our capacity. By manipulating symbols in the mind, we are freed from the limitations of concrete objects. Consider our close relative, the chimpanzee. With careful training, chimps can learn rudimentary symbols, for example, numbers. In one study, researchers found that chimpanzees could be taught that if they picked the smaller of two numbers, they would receive a large food reward. If they picked the larger number, they would receive the smaller food reward, and another chimp would get the bigger one. The chimps learned this quickly when the choice was between two numbers, and they picked the smaller number to receive more food. However, if the choice was between a smaller and a larger amount of candy, instead of between numbers corresponding to the amount of candy, despite repeated trials the animals never learned. They kept choosing the bigger amount of candy and continued to see their choice given to another animal while they were left with the smaller amount (Boysen et al., 1996). That choice was, of course, the one that evolution would have favored in the natural environment of the chimpanzee, although it was not the optimal choice in the contrived experimental laboratory (Berntson & Cacioppo, 2000). The problem that they could not solve with these actual arrays of candy could be solved when symbols were used instead, freeing them from the automatic choices triggered by the actual food. How much more freedom from immediate situations must be available to humans with our sophisticated symbolic abilities!

The way that people think of abstract problems, however, is still embedded in an evolutionary context. Consider a classic framing problem studied by cognitive psychologists: the Asian disease problem. Tversky and Kahneman (1981) posed the question of choosing between two possible medical treatments to attempt to save 600 anonymous people infected by a fatal disease. Plan A guaranteed saving a third of the people; the other 400 would die. Plan B offered a one in three probability that all patients would be saved, and two in three that all would die. Mathematically, both plans are identical in offering a one-third probability of success for each patient. A classic finding is the *framing effect:* People offered a version of plan A phrased to indicate that one third will be saved, go for that plan; but if plan A is phrased to indicate that two thirds will die, they choose the other plan. This framing effect is often cited to illustrate the irrationality of human cognition.

Consider, now, a variation of this problem based on evolutionary thought. Our ancestors evolved in much smaller groups than 600, so any prewired social understandings assume smaller groups and are probably influenced by sensitivity to kinship. Subjects who are presented with the framing problem, but with groups of 6 or of 60 instead of 600, responded in the same way whether the question was framed as one third saved or two thirds die—that is, they did not show the framing effect. In either phrasing, they chose the risky plan (plan B), in which all would either live or die—especially if they were told that the hypothetical people were close relatives. In fact, they would take greater risks to possibly save everyone. Evolution seems to have prepared us for thinking in terms of small groups—and in that context, if two thirds of the group perished, the others would be more vulnerable by the absence of their support. Experience living in larger groups with extended kin relationships can probably increase the number of people we can consider while still maintaining this evolutionary "all-or-none" solution, based on the finding from cross-cultural research that Chinese respondents do not switch to the framing effect at 600 but rather at large numbers compared to U.S. respondents (Rode & Wang, 2000).

Automatic processing uses evolved modules, making many tasks routine and efficient. In the unusual situations that experimenters pose, automatic processing can lead to strange and erroneous behavior. Consider the familiar Stroop test, which requires subjects to ignore the words printed before them but simply call out the color of the ink with which they are printed. Our automatic habit of reading causes us to stumble over our words and make errors. A similar phenomenon happens if the stimuli are positive or negative emotional words and the interference is a picture of an emotionally expressive face behind the word. When they try to focus on evaluating the words, subjects are impaired when the irrelevant facial expression is happy for a sad word or a sad face for a happy word (Stenberg, Wiking, & Dahl, 1998).

The mind's workings are also in other ways out of kilter with the evolved adaptation to small living communities. We compare ourselves with many others beyond our immediate circle, including media personalities. These comparisons make us dissatisfied with ourselves and our companions, contributing to depression. In addition, we are likely more distant from supportive families than our remote ancestors are. More temptations that threaten intimate bonds surround us (Buss, 2000).

Genetics and Personality

Imagine being able to look at a person's genes and know what kind of personality he or she would possess. That molecular genetic approach, even as a vision, is oversimplified because personality develops from a combination of biological and environmental influences. But there are intriguing hints about the role of particular genes for personality. One recent study obtained DNA samples from preschool children and correlated those analyses with data obtained from their mothers' reports and from observations of peer play at age 4. They found that children with long repeat alleles of the DRD4 gene, which regulates a form of dopamine, were described by their mothers as having problems with aggression (Schmidt et al., 2002).

Studies of twins and other relatives have established that scores on many personality tests show substantial genetic influences, usually with **heritability** estimates of about 0.50 (Bouchard & Loehlin, 2001; L. A. Clark & Watson, 1999; Loehlin, McCrae, & Costa, 1998). The heritability estimate is a description of how much of the variability of a trait, studied in a particular population, can be attributed to the genetic variation in that population, based on studies of twins and other relatives who are raised together or apart. One review concludes that "virtually every trait that has ever been examined. . . has a substantial genetic component" (L. A. Clark & Watson, 1999, p. 411). Studies that consider whether twins and other relatives have been raised together or adopted out into different homes make it clear that it is the genetic influence, and not the fact of having been raised by the same parents, that produces similarity among siblings.

It is surprising how many characteristics, besides the usual personality factor tests, show significant heritability: coping styles (Busjahn et al., 1999); ego development (Newman, Tellegen, & Bouchard, 1998); happiness, or subjective well-being (Lykken & Tellegen, 1996); the likelihood of divorce (McGue & Lykken, 1992); authoritarian attitudes (McCourt et al., 1999); and other social attitudes (Tesser, 1993).

Sometimes individuals seem quite different from the rest of the family, and we may wonder how this can be. One genetic interpretation is that traits we observe (phenotypic traits) are composed of combinations of many different genes, and these combinations are not simply additive in their effect in the case of **emergenic traits** (Lykken et al., 1992). Among emergenic traits are extraordinary mathematical genius that can emerge in some individuals, such as Karl Gauss and the Hindu mathematician Srivinvasa Ramanujan, without evidence of particular talent in that area among other family members. Thus the impact of genetics on personality cannot be studied only by documenting similarity in observable personality among those who are genetic relatives. In addition, biological studies make it clear that the genes we possess are not always active. Like computer programs that do nothing until they are executed (much to the relief of those who find computer viruses on their machines that have not yet been activated), genes can be turned on and off in their expression by a variety of environmental factors that are just beginning to be understood. Ultimately, we will need to understand the mechanisms by which genes, in their environmental context, influence personality.

heritability the statistic that shows what proportion of the variability of a trait in a particular population is associated with genetic variability

emergenic traits phenotypic traits caused by a constellation of many genes and so may not appear to run in families

Temperament

Biological influences on personality have always been acknowledged but only recently have they become a mature approach that promises to be integrated with the rest of the discipline. Ever since ancient Greece in the second century, when Galen suggested that the four bodily humors described 600 years earlier by Hippocrates influenced personality, the body has been thought to have consequences for personality. Galen suggested that four humors were determinants: an excess of blood produced an energetic, optimistic "sanguine" personality; an excess of yellow bile made one irritable, or "choleric"; an excess of black bile made one depressed, or "melancholic"; and an excess of phlegm made one apathetic, or "phlegmatic." This ancient model has been superseded by modern biological analyses, but even modern theorists (Eysenck, described later) agree with its description of individual differences, although they replace outmoded humors with modern neuroscience and are open to the impact of experience.

temperament the biologically based foundation of personality, including such characteristic patterns of behavior as emotionality, activity, and sociability

Temperament is the biologically foundation of personality, based on a child's inherited predisposition for characteristic patterns of emotionality, activity, and sociability. It also includes inherited tendencies toward self-regulation (Rothbart, Ahadi, & Evans, 2000), such as neural processes that prevent emotions from becoming excessive. A person's temperament is observable early in life, and it is at least moderately stable throughout life and across situations (Kagan, 1994). Genetic studies, using subjects of various ages and measurement techniques, show that temperament is highly heritable (Bates & Wachs, 1994; Goldsmith, Buss, & Lemery, 1997; Rowe, 1997). The specific dimensions of temperament vary somewhat, depending on the researcher.

An often-cited model, based on observations of 151 infants in the New York Longitudinal Study (NYLS), described about 40% of the infants as *easy* babies—they were happy and interactive with new objects. Others withdrew from unfamiliar objects and seemed mildly distressed; these 15% were called *slow to warm up*. Another 10% were called *difficult children;* they withdrew from the unfamiliar, were irritable, and were at high risk for psychiatric symptoms in childhood. Some babies did not fit any of these categories (Thomas & Chess, 1977). Another typology, the EASI model, proposes four dimensions: emotionality, activity, sociability, and impulsivity (A. Buss & Plomin, 1975). Even the Big Five personality factors (see Chapter 8) have been described as genetically based temperament dimensions (McCrae et al., 2000).

Let's focus our attention on a temperament model presented by Jerome Kagan (1994) because he proposes connections with specific biological variables. In studies of young children, Kagan and his colleagues have found a variety of behavior patterns when the children are tested in standard novel situations (Garcia-Coll, Kagan, & Reznick, 1984; Kagan, 1994). In one study, 21-month-old children played with toys while their mother was with them. After a few minutes, an experimenter entered and played with the toys and then left. What would the child do? Some imitated the experimenter's play behavior (e.g., by having a doll talk on a telephone). Others did not; some even cried. Next, another woman entered and sat on a chair briefly, and then she spoke to the child and invited interaction on some developmental tasks. Most children at first stared at the strange woman; some approached and participated in the tasks, whereas others withdrew to their mother and would have nothing to do with the stranger. Then the experimenter returned and showed the child a robot; some children played with it, whereas others would not and stayed with their mothers. As a final test, the experimenter and the child's mother both left the room to see what the child would do when left alone.

inhibited type temperament type (described by Kagan) that is shy and nonassertive around strangers, proposed to have high levels of norepinephrine and an activation of the amygdala

The children's reactions confirmed the expectation that two temperament types could be distinguished (although some children did not fit into either group). One pattern, the **inhibited type**, interacted less with the experimenter and with the strange woman, and they often cried and clung to their mothers during these novel experiences. (Kagan compared this group with Thomas and Chess's slow-to-warm-up group.) Another group of children, the

uninhibited type, interacted more with the experimenter, were more likely to approach the strange woman, and were more likely to approach and touch the toy robot that the experimenter showed them. (They were like the *easy* temperament group.) Other research using somewhat older toddlers (31 months) and different novel situations (interacting with a child they did not know) also found these two types. These early behaviors predicted the child's behavior at age 7 when inhibited children shyly watched while other children played, and uninhibited children initiated interaction and seemed happier to play with other kids (Kagan, 1994, p. 132). Other studies also show relative stability of a child's behavior over time and indicate that children's talkativeness with people they do not know is one key behavior indicating whether they are shy, inhibited types or outgoing, uninhibited types.

These temperament types have a genetic basis, with heritabilities of 0.5 or higher (Kagan, 1994). Inhibited children are especially afraid of unfamiliar stimuli, according to Kagan, because their genetic makeup produces high levels of norepinephrine and/or corticotropin-releasing hormone. These in turn lead to stimulation of the **amygdala** and other brain areas involved in fear, which then produces greater sympathetic nervous system activity: acceleration in heart rate, rise in blood pressure, dilation of pupils, and evidence through urinalysis of more norepinephrine (see Figure 9.1). Neuroendocrinologists are now identifying the specific mechanisms of fear, which is influenced by glucocorticoids, and what sustains it for a longer time in some individuals than in others (Schulkin, Morgan, & Rosen, 2005).

uninhibited type temperament type (described by Kagan) that is outgoing and low in fear, proposed to have lower sympathetic nervous system activity

amygdala brain area involved in fear, theorized (by Kagan) to contribute to inhibited temperament

Figure 9.1   Inhibited and Uninhibited Temperament in Kagan's Model

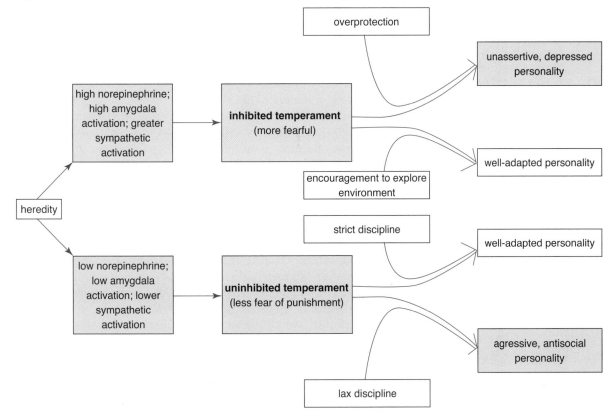

Conversely, the uninhibited children have less activity in the amygdala and low levels of the neurotransmitter norepinephrine. Consequently, they are low in sympathetic nervous system reactivity, which makes them less fearful. Researchers have noted low heart rates in such adolescents and adults (Kagan, 1994, p. 53). As they develop through childhood and beyond, the uninhibited children are less affected by fear of punishment than their inhibited peers. Therefore, they are more disposed to become aggressive and antisocial, and in some cases criminals. Kagan warns that the uninhibited children, unless carefully disciplined, "may acquire a permissive superego" (Kagan, 1994, p. 240). Inhibited 3-year-olds, in contrast, are likely to become unassertive, depressed adults with little social support (Caspi, 2000). Although genetic inheritance influences personality, it does not alone determine personality. A child with an inherited tendency toward an inhibited temperament may not develop in that direction, depending on the environment. Perhaps surprisingly, if the environment is very calming and predictable, with mothers who hold their infants a lot and do not call out warnings to them, the infants develop their predisposition toward inhibition. However, if the mothers give their infants more latitude to explore the world, by not holding them so much and by calling out explicit warnings when they do something forbidden, these clear limits produce a child who is less inhibited (Kagan, 1994, p. 205). Here's a comparison that may help make this clear: Imagine you are walking through a woods and some of the plants have painful but invisible thorns. You would be inhibited, keeping a distance from all plants. But if you had a guide who reliably called out a warning when you got near the dangerous plants, you would explore more freely. Kagan's genetically inhibited group, then, seems to be the one for whom Alfred Adler's warning about the dangers of "pampering" is good advice.

Even children who are not physiologically predisposed to fear and anxiety can develop conditioned fears, if experience is especially traumatic. Kagan (1994, p. 123) gives the example of a child who developed in this way when her father committed suicide. Emotional experience is a key to the influence that temperament has on adult personality (L. A. Clark & Watson, 1999). Children with temperaments characterized by low levels of negative emotionality often develop into sympathetic children, sensitive to others' emotions (Eisenberg et al., 1998). So may those with higher levels of negative emotionality, if they learn to optimally regulate their emotions (Eisenberg et al., 2000).

So far there has been little description of the specific way this development occurs during childhood (Shiner, 1998). Presumably, social interaction is a key process. Individual temperamental dispositions cause infants and young children to behave in various ways that are then subject to the influences of family and larger social environments. Children with different temperaments behave differently, and in turn they are treated differently by others, including adults. In most cases the way a parent or other caretaker treats a child is probably reflective of the expectations they have made from observing the child's temperament (Graziano, Jensen-Campbell, & Sullivan-Logan, 1998). A child with an easygoing disposition is likely to have positive interactions with adults and with other children and become confident and sociable as a result. Of course, there is no guarantee that a child's temperament will always produce a predictable reaction. For example, an impulsive child may be disciplined or, in another family, indulged, and each will have a different adult personality as a result.

genotype the inherited genetic profile of an individual

phenotype the developed characteristics that can be observed in an individual, based on both genetic and environmental influences

The inherited genetic profile, called the **genotype**, does not always produce the same observed characteristics, or **phenotype**, because of environmental influences. Furthermore, the effect of this experience is not limited to behavior; it can change biology. Animal experiments show that experience influences the development of the brain. The density of glucocorticoid receptors in the hippocampus of newborn rats' brains is changed if they are handled by humans daily for 15 minutes for 3 weeks

(Kagan, 1994, p. 35). Thus both genetic inheritance and early experience influence the physiology of the brain, and this combination of influences produces an individual's temperament.

Biological Contributors to Personality

Evidence of heredity and relatively stable temperament differences constitute strong evidence that biology affects personality, but how? The brain's functioning is a prime candidate. The profound personality change that occurred when a railroad construction accident caused severe brain injury in Phineas Gage, turning a well-liked, well-behaved man into an impulsive misfit, is part of the standard curriculum for introductory psychology students (Harlow & Miller, 1939/1993).

The Brain

Personality depends on the brain. Somehow we are not surprised to learn that people diagnosed with antisocial personality disorder have less gray matter in their prefrontal cerebral cortex than other people (Raine et al., 2000). Sometimes rather dramatic claims are made, based on correlations with brain functioning. For example, during religious meditation and contemplation, brain changes are observed on SPECT brain-imaging devices, leading to the rash claim that humans are "hardwired for God" ("Hardwired for God?" 2001). Although such claims go far beyond what careful science would assert, there are brain areas that are of particular relevance for personality.

The brain is now generally described as functioning by modules that each serves a specialized function. Such social phenomena as recognizing people's faces, understanding their facial expressions of emotion, and wanting to communicate with others have neural mechanisms that neuroscientists can now locate (Brothers, 1996; Kesler/West et al., 2001). Humans with damage to the amygdala, a structure involved in fear, lose the ability to judge, in an experiment, which faces appear to be unapproachable and untrustworthy, even though they have no trouble telling one face from another, and even though they judge accurately when information is presented in words instead of visually. In real life, these brain-damaged individuals act indiscriminately trusting (Adolphs, Tranel, & Damasio, 1998). Areas of the medial prefrontal cortex and of the temporoparietal junction are active when we attribute mental states (such as emotion, pain, or the feeling of being tickled) to others or think about our own mental states (Frith & Frith, 2001). When we look at images of ourselves, the left fusiform gyrus of the cerebral cortex is particularly active (Kircher et al., 2000).

The frontal lobe of the right hemisphere is more active when people are experiencing negative emotions—depression, anxiety, and fear—and the left frontal lobe is more active when positive emotions are experienced. People with greater self-reported psychological well-being show greater left hemisphere functioning on electroencephalograph (EEG) recordings (Urry et al., 2004). Different social judgments are influenced by presentation of stimuli to right or left cerebral hemispheres; the left hemisphere is more involved in "in-group favoritism," whereas the right hemisphere facilitates "the mere exposure effect" (Zarate, Sanders, & Garza, 2000).

The subcortical levels of the brain, especially, function in a modular way, whereas the newer cortical levels are less devoted to specific innate functions and more built up by experience (Quartz & Sejnowski, 1997, 2000). The modular efficiency of the brain gives an adaptive advantage by allowing it to function more quickly, with less need for individual learning, but it also brings the potential for dissociations among functions and conflict with our conscious experience. The amygdala, for example, is involved in the experience of fear, and it produces this emotion even without conscious awareness. This helps us quickly detect emotional expressions on others' faces (Öhman, 2002), an important process in social interaction. It has obvious survival advantage when it is associated with seeing a dangerous predator but risks the development of the irrational fears that we call phobias (Öhman & Mineka, 2001). The efficiencies that come with inherited modules also bring a loss of flexibility. These brain modules improve our functioning when used for the tasks they were designed to accomplish but thwart our attempts to adapt to new problems in environments our ancestors never faced.

Brain activity occurs when chemical neurotransmitters activate specialized neural pathways in the central nervous system. A few neurotransmitters are familiar to many students of psychology: dopamine, epinephrine, serotonin, for example. This is a very abbreviated list, however. According to Jerome Kagan (1994, p. 32), "The brain contains over 150 different chemicals—monoamines, amino acids, hormones, and peptides. . . . The number of combinations of these molecules exceeds ten million." Obviously, there is considerable potential for diversity in both major and subtle influences on behavior. Neurotransmitters influence changes in brain structure, too, by sensitizing neural pathways to function more efficiently in the future, depending on a person's individual experience.

One of the most studied neurotransmitters for personality, as we see later in this chapter, is **dopamine**. There are actually several kinds of dopamine, each with specific neural pathways. Excess levels in many of these dopamine pathways are found in the serious mental disturbance, schizophrenia, whereas low levels are characteristic of Parkinson's disease. Dopamine produces rewarding experiences. Variations in the dopamine system predispose some people to become more vulnerable to tobacco addiction, and others—who have less craving for novelty based on questionnaire scores—less likely to smoke or more able to stop once they have started (Sabol et al., 1999).

dopamine
neurotransmitter involved in many brain functions, including rewarding experiences, novelty seeking, schizophrenia (high levels), and Parkinson's disease (low levels)

Emotional Arousal

Emotions are a core to human personality and motivation (Damasio, 1994). Many theories make this assumption; for example, Freud's hedonic hypothesis asserts that people seek pleasure, and various learning theories explicitly or implicitly consider positive and negative emotions as the basis for reinforcement and punishment. The process of personality development must include learning emotional intelligence (Salovey & Mayer, 1990) as we learn to deal with our emotions and to interpret the emotions of others. Furthermore, individuals differ in how much they are drawn to emotional experience or prefer to avoid strong emotions (Maio & Esses, 2001).

The diagnosis of antisocial personality disorder is often applied to criminals, and many studies indicate brain functioning that is abnormal in this group (Abbott, 2001; "Antisocial Personality," 2001). People with a diagnosis of antisocial personality show less response to experimental situations designed to elicit stress, such as the threat of an electric shock, and a weaker than normal startle reflex to loud noise or to pictures of dead bodies or guns pointed at them. When they hear emotionally loaded words (such as "death"), their EEGs do not show the usual difference from neutral words (such as "paper"). Psychopaths show less empathy than normal controls; this enables them to make judgments more quickly in some laboratory tests where emotion slows down ordinary people. At the neurotransmitter level, lower than normal levels of serotonin are typical of those with an antisocial personality.

Neuroscientists have been studying the brain mechanisms of emotion. Consider people's tendency to approach emotionally pleasant stimuli and to avoid emotionally unpleasant stimuli. Approach and avoidance, pleasure and pain, are not simply two extremes on the same scale; they are neurologically distinct. Studies of brain waves, using EEG recordings, find that the left cerebral hemisphere is more active during pleasant emotional experiences and the right cerebral hemisphere during unpleasant emotional experiences (Davidson et al., 1990; Ekman, Davidson, & Friesen, 1990; Gross, 1999; Tomarken, Davidson, & Henriques, 1990). Not surprisingly, the left hemisphere is also more active when individuals are motivated to approach, and the right when they are motivated to avoid (Harmon-Jones & Allen, 1997; Sutton & Davidson, 1997). People with a history of depression, and those with family history of depression, have less activity in the left hemisphere (Harmon-Jones & Allen, 1997).

What is being registered, though: the pleasantness or the tendency to approach it, in the left hemisphere? Or the unpleasantness or the tendency to move away from it, in the right hemisphere? Anger provides an important clue. Anger activates the left hemisphere, suggesting that motivation, not emotion, is the key to left–right asymmetry. Anger, among the emotions, may have a unique role in helping people confront fear, depression, and other inhibiting negative emotions, without being immobilized (Harmon-Jones & Allen, 1998; Izard, 1991). Anger has been of interest to personality theorists such as Dollard and Miller (see Chapter 11) and to those who study the relationship between emotions and physical illness, such as cardiovascular problems (Hodapp, Heiligtag, & Störmer, 1990; Houston, Smith, & Cates, 1989). Important for personality, the asymmetries are not only activated during transient emotional experiences in a laboratory, but they are also stable over time and correlated with people's typical emotions (Tomarken et al., 1992). Research suggests that specific cerebral differences, observable from infancy onward (Dawson et al., 1992), make important contributions to personality.

Cortical Arousal

In addition to emotional arousal is another kind of arousal: from thinking. We respond to interesting or exciting stimuli by becoming aroused from our relaxed state. People vary in how rapidly this arousal of the brain's cortex (*cortical arousal*) occurs and to what extent. The idea of cortical stimulation is based on the work of the Russian physiologist Ivan Pavlov. Pavlov noticed that the dogs in his classical conditioning studies increased their conditioned responses with increasing conditioned stimuli up to a certain point; after that, even stronger stimuli led to a decline in the strength of conditioning. Pavlov reasoned that when the stimulus was too intense, the nervous system protected itself by some sort of inhibitory process to counterbalance the intense excitatory process set in action by the stimulus. Pavlov made one more intriguing observation: Dogs varied in the point at which inhibition kicked in. Some—who Pavlov said had a **strong nervous system**—increased the strength of their conditioning to much more intense levels of the stimulus than others, whose inhibitory processes were already decreasing the strength of conditioning. Because these others could tolerate only weaker stimuli, they were said to have a **weak nervous system**. These types of nervous systems, however, were described by Pavlov in strictly functional terms (what processes occurred—activation and inhibition), and not in terms of the underlying brain structures (see Figure 9.2).

strong nervous system in Pavlov's theory, a nervous system that forms stronger conditioned responses and tolerates higher intensities of stimulation; said by other theorists to produce extraversion

weak nervous system in Pavlov's theory, a nervous system that forms weaker conditioned responses and does not tolerate high intensities of stimulation; said by other theorists to produce introversion

Figure 9.2 Pavlov's Model of the Nervous System and Implications for Personality

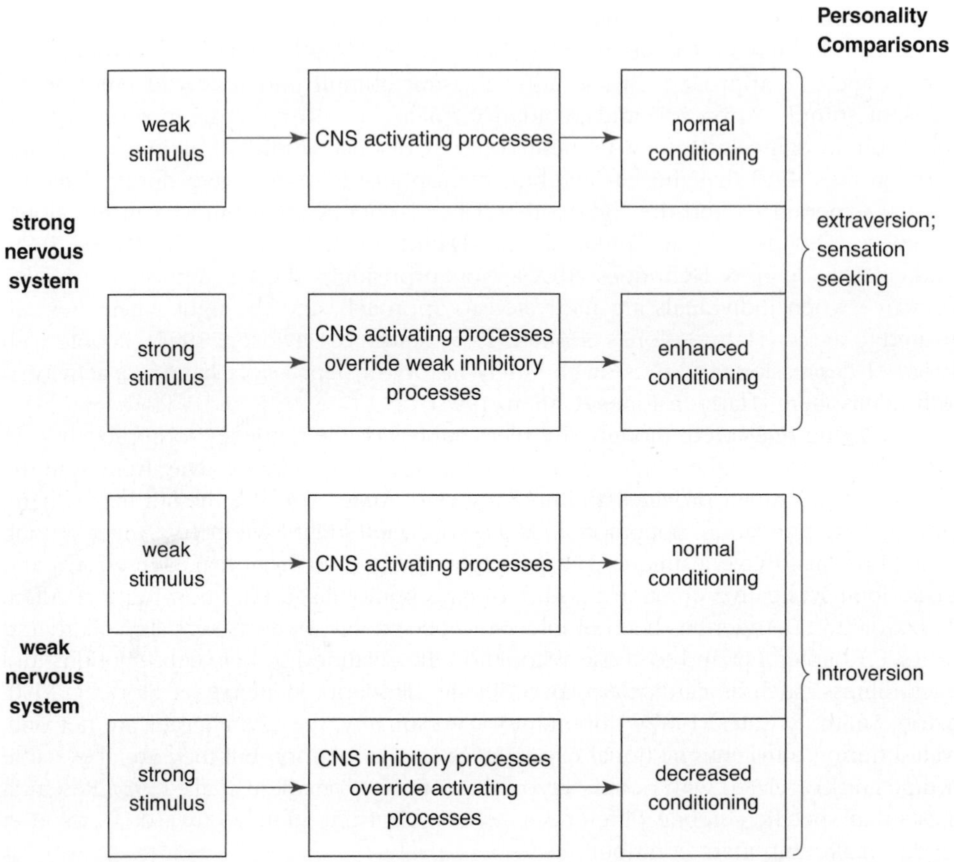

People, too, vary from one to another in whether they tend to overreact or underreact to stimuli, and this physiological difference has implications for personality. We seek to compensate for our nervous system variations by behavior. Several theories have proposed arousal-related personality concepts, including a trait called **sensation seeking** (Zuckerman, 1994). Sensation seeking is "the seeking of varied, novel, complex, and intense sensations and experiences, and the willingness to take physical, social, legal, and financial risks for the sake of such experience" (Zuckerman, 1994, p. 27). Highly influenced by genetics, this trait is thought to involve the enzyme monamine oxidase (MAO), which is low in sensation seekers, and two monoamine neurotransmitters that it regulates: dopamine (high) and serotonin (low) (Zuckerman & Kuhlman, 2000). College students who score high on the Sensation Seeking Scale typically prefer more arousing music (McNamara & Ballard, 1999). They are more likely to drink, smoke, use illegal drugs, gamble, and drive recklessly; and they are more likely to engage in risky sexual behaviors, such as unprotected sex and many sexual partners, that put them at risk for HIV infection (Hoyle, Fejfar, & Miller, 2000; Zuckerman & Kuhlman, 2000). Zuckerman's Impulsive Sensation Seeking scale is highly correlated ($r = +0.68$) with the Novelty Seeking scale of the Tridimensional Personality Questionnaire, part of Cloninger's theory considered later in this chapter (Zuckerman & Cloninger, 1996). Other theoretical approaches, including those presented by Hans Eysenck and J. A. Gray, also include arousal as a key concept, as we will see.

sensation seeking
trait, proposed by Zuckerman, of seeking varied, novel, complex and intense sensations and experiences, even if that requires risk

Biological Factor Theories: Eysenck, Gray, and Others

Several theorists have proposed comprehensive factor models of personality that specify biological underpinnings of the major dimensions along which personality varies. In one sense, they correspond to the factor models we considered in Chapter 8, but instead of building only on a description of personality through verbal reports, they correlated it from the outset with biological variation.

Eysenck's "PEN" Biological Model

HANS EYSENCK

Hans Eysenck (1967; Eysenck & Eysenck, 1985) and others who expanded his approach (Gray, 1999) built their biological models of personality on Pavlov's analysis (described earlier) of strong and weak nervous systems (Strelau, 1997). Like Pavlov's laboratory dogs, each person has both excitatory and inhibitory processes in the nervous system that (respectively) respond to, or defend against, incoming stimuli. Physiological measures, such as brain scan recordings to varying flashes of light or auditory stimuli, have been used to measure these differences (Buckingham, 2002). Variations in excitatory and inhibitory processes produce interesting implications for personality. Specifically, people whose excitatory processes are stronger (who have a "strong nervous system") are extraverts, whereas those with relatively greater inhibitory processes (who have a "weak nervous system") are introverts.

Extraversion is the first of Eysenck's three proposed factors of personality. The others, also based on biological differences between people, are Neuroticism and Psychoticism. (Rearranging the first letters of these factors gives the acronym "PEN.") The first two factors, when combined, bear a striking similarity to the ancient Greek temperaments described earlier in this chapter (Robinson, 2001). The melancholic type is an introvert who is high on neuroticism (E−N+); the phlegmatic type is an introvert who is low on neuroticism (E−N−); the choleric type is an extravert who is high on neuroticism (E+N+); and the sanguine type is an extravert who is low on neuroticism (E+N−) (see Table 9.3).

The first factor, **Extraversion**, with its opposite pole Introversion, illustrates how subtle differences in the balance of biological processes (excitation and inhibition, in this case) can have great implications for personality. A person with a "strong" nervous system, quick to inhibit stimuli, can tolerate relatively intense stimuli without being overwhelmed by them, including the stimuli that come from social interactions. Because they readily tune out the arousing inputs from social situations, they can tolerate having a lot of activity and many people around them. In fact, they crave such stimulation, and in seeking it, they act like extraverts. Introverts, in contrast, have a "weak" nervous system that is quickly overwhelmed by intense stimuli. In the presence of other people, they readily are stimulated above the level at which they can function well, so they take behavioral measures to control overstimulation; they withdraw from overly stimulating environments. (By analogy, compare this to a person with sensitive ears, who protects by wearing earplugs or by moving to a quieter room—although hearing in particular is not an issue, but cortical

extraversion
tolerance for high levels of stimulation because of a strong nervous system that inhibits incoming stimulation, leading to sociability in Eysenck's theory

TABLE 9.3 Eysenck's Extraversion and Neuroticism Factors and the Ancient Greek Temperaments

Greek humors	Greek temperament	Description	Eysenck factors
Excess of yellow bile	Choleric	Irritable	Unstable (high Neuroticism) extravert (high Extraversion)
Excess of black bile	Melancholic	Depressed	Unstable (high Neuroticism) introvert (low Extraversion)
Excess of blood	Sanguine	Energetic, optimistic	Stable (low Neuroticism) extravert (high Extraversion)
Excess of phlegm	Phlegmatic	Apathetic	Stable (low Neuroticism) introvert (low Extraversion)

Note: Correspondences are based on Eysenck & Eysenck, 1975, and L. A. Clark & Watson, 1999.

reaction to all incoming stimuli.) This includes withdrawing from situations where there is too much stimulation from other people; hence these individuals become introverts.

Eysenck identifies the ascending reticular activating system of the brain (ARAS), which senses arousal messages from the brainstem to higher brain levels, as a pathway for this arousal. We generally define introverts and extraverts in terms of their behavior, but Eysenck's assertion that they differ biologically as well is supported by laboratory observations (Eysenck, 1967; Stelmack, 1997). In one study, researchers monitored subjects' responses to auditory stimuli. Hearing a click automatically causes an evoked neural response in the brain, which the experimenters recorded through electrodes placed on the subject's head. Computers analyzed the recordings to focus on the brain's particular responses that are known to indicate activation by the brainstem (which Eysenck's theory identifies as important). Subjects who were extraverts, according to their personality tests, were slower to generate activity in response to the auditory stimuli (longer latency) and the waves were farther apart in time (greater interpeak interval)—in other words, extraverts were less reactive to the stimuli (Swickert & Gilliland, 1998). This finding offers support for Eysenck's theory that extraverts need more stimulation to become aroused, to overcome their innate neural dampening of incoming stimulation. Also supporting the theory, when given an opportunity to choose the level of background noise during an experimental task, extraverts chose more noise than introverts, and they performed better at higher levels of noise (Geen, 1997). When tasks require a great deal of attentiveness—for example, keeping watch for a relatively infrequent stimulus to respond to it—extraverts perform poorly compared to introverts, who are better able to maintain attention with lower levels of stimulation (Brebner, 2000). Brain monitoring studies show higher blood flow to the temporal lobes among introverts (especially among anxious introverts) (Stenberg et al., 1990; Stenberg, Wendt, & Risberg, 1993). Extraverts responded to a visual task with larger amplitude P300 waves in the right hemisphere (Stenberg, 1994). Other patterns of brain wave activity are associated with impulsivity (Stenberg, 1992). Rammsayer (1998) reports that under the influence of a drug that blocks certain dopamine receptors (mesolimbocortical DA D2 receptors), introverts were more impaired on a reaction-time task than were extraverts, supporting the case that introverts and extraverts have differences in their dopamine system that affect behavior.

The second factor in Eysenck's model is **Neuroticism**. Greater activity in the limbic system causes some people to become more emotionally aroused when they are threatened or placed in stressful situations. These people are high in the factor of Neuroticism. Others, low on that factor, do not become so emotional in the same situation. Greater emotional arousal can, in turn, cause neurotics to make use of defense mechanisms; hence the term *neuroticism.* (Notice that the factor of extraversion-introversion corresponds to cortical arousal, in contrast to the emotional arousal that is at issue in neuroticism.) On written personality tests, people with high neuroticism scores report that they are less self-accepting than those with lower scores (McCroskey, Heisel, & Richmond, 2001).

Eysenck's third factor refers to a tendency toward nonconformity or social deviance (Zuckerman, Kuhlman, & Camac, 1988). Eysenck (1992) labeled this factor **Psychoticism**, an unfortunate label because it exaggerates the image of pathology. In fact, people who are creative tend to have high Psychoticism scores (Eysenck, 1993, 1994). Although psychotic patients score high on this factor, so do creative people who are not suffering from disorders. In fact, one study that measured the Psychoticism scores of college students found that, 10 years later, those scoring high had no increased risk of psychosis (Chapman, Chapman, & Kwapil, 1994). On average, those who score high on the Psychoticism scale do have characteristics that put them at risk for deviance: They are more impulsive, hostile, sadistic, and unempathic than those who score low (Eysenck & Eysenck, 1991). People trying to climb Mount Everest score high on Psychoticism, and also on Extraversion, but low on Neuroticism (Egan & Stelmack, 2003). Research suggests that those who score high on Psychoticism prefer to watch violent videos and that they view it as more enjoyable and comical than those who score lower. Their physiological responses show quicker desensitization to the violence (Bruggemann & Barry, 2002). Physically, Psychoticism scores are correlated with the gastrointestinal system. Those scoring high show more saliva flow in response to taste stimuli, and they are relatively unlikely to become seasick (Gordon et al., 1994).

Eysenck's theory has stimulated thousands of research studies (Geen, 1997). Many of them are noteworthy in that they find significant relationships between biological variables and personality. Caffeine, for example, makes people act more like introverts, with conditioning like those with a weak nervous system, and extraverts are quicker to become fatigued and make errors on a vigilance task (Pickering, 1997). High Neuroticism scores are correlated with greater limbic system activity, whereas lower Extraversion scores (introversion) are correlated with higher levels of cortical arousal. Other findings are summarized in Table 9.4. In itself, isolated findings are not momentous, but the accumulation of experimental evidence relating personality measures with biological measures and performance on laboratory tasks is nothing short of astonishing.

Among the most intriguing aspects of Eysenck's theory is the prediction that people who, because of their nervous system, do not readily form conditioned responses to punishment and are at increased risk for becoming criminals. The argument is simple: Fear and pain, such as that administered when a parent spanks a child, become the basis for learned emotional reactions that stop us from misbehaving. That twinge of conscience at the thought of doing something forbidden is a conditioned anxiety response. If some people are less likely to form such conditioned responses, they will be less inhibited

neuroticism tendency toward high levels of emotional arousal; the second factor in Eysenck's factor model

Psychoticism in Eysenck's model, factor related to nonconformity or social deviance

TABLE 9.4   Experimental Findings Relating Eysenck's Extraversion and Neuroticism Factors to Biological and Performance Measures

	high N (N+): neurotic	*low N (N−): emotionally stable*
Autonomic nervous system (ANS) reactivity	Greater (labile)	Less (stable)
Limbic system activity (hippocampus, amygdala, cingulum, septum, and hypothalamus)	High activation	Low activation
Emotions (response to emotion-arousing events)	More intense (moody, anxious, worried)	Less intense (calm, controlled, well adjusted)
Temporal lobe activity	Greater	Less
Preparation for novel stimuli	Reduce focus of attention	Do not reduce focus of attention
	low E (E−): introverted	*high E (E+): extraverted*
Brain's cortical emphasis	Excitation (rapid, strong response to stimuli)	Inhibition (slow, weak, brief response to stimuli)
Brainstem area responsible	Ascending reticular activating system (ARAS) leads to excitation	Descending reticular activating system (ARAS) leads to inhibition
Basal level of cortical arousal	Higher (leading to greater risk of overstimulation)	Lower (tolerates stronger stimuli)
Sensory response to low levels of stimulation	Greater	Less
Perceptual sensitivity, assessed by brain's event-related potentials (ERPs) to auditory and visual stimuli on vigilance tasks	Greater perceptual sensitivity; stronger ERPs; more attention; slower habituation to repeated stimuli; better performance at vigilance tasks	Less perceptual sensitivity; weaker ERPs; less attention (more lapses of attention); greater habituation to repeated stimuli; worse performance on vigilance tasks
Typical coping with incoming stimuli	Avoid overstimulation; focus on narrower range of stimuli	Augment stimuli; attend to a broader range of stimuli
Involuntary rest pauses (IRPs) during massed practice	Less frequent	More frequent

Source: Prepared from information in Taub (1998).

about misbehavior. Evidence supports this prediction. Criminals, psychopaths, and conduct-disordered children have weaker conditioned emotional responses than other people (Raine, 1993). Among adolescents who have early criminal records, those who have stronger conditioned emotional responses are more likely to turn away from crime, whereas those with weaker conditioned emotional responses become adult criminals (Raine, Venables, & Williams, 1996).

Slightly different from Eysenck's model is another three-factor model proposed by L. A. Clark and Watson (1999). They propose factors similar to Eysenck's Neuroticism and Extraversion but emphasize the specific emotions involved in each. One factor, which they call Neuroticism/Negative Emotionality (N/NE), emphasizes negative emotions such as distress and threat, as well as instability of emotions. A second factor, called Extraversion/Positive Emotionality (E/PE), describes extraverts' cheerfulness and confidence in approaching life, one aspect of which is interpersonal involvement. As expected, college students with high scores on the N/NE factor report more negative moods currently in their lives, whereas those scoring high on the E/PE factor report more positive moods and more active social lives. The third factor, Disinhibition versus Constraint (DvC), focuses on impulsive behavior based on immediate feelings, as contrasted with carefully planned action that considers long-term consequences. Students scoring high on this scale are more likely than others to sleep late, stay up late, engage in casual sex with more partners, drive recklessly, and use alcohol, tobacco, and illegal drugs (L. A. Clark & Watson, 1999).

Gray's Reinforcement Sensitivity Theory

J. A. Gray (1987) proposes a biological theory of personality that builds on Eysenck's theory. Gray proposes that individuals vary in motivational systems related to positive and negative reinforcement (approach and avoidance). Some people emphasize approach and positive emotions, whereas others emphasize avoidance and negative emotions (Heubeck, Wilkinson, & Cologon, 1998). In the laboratory, mood induction procedures ask subjects to imagine positive events (winning a lot of money and taking a vacation) or negative events (being expelled from school). It is easier to induce positive moods in extraverts and negative moods in neurotics (Larsen & Ketelaar, 1991). Functional magnetic resonance imaging (fMRI) of the brain shows that extraverts (measured from the NEO-PI) have more brain reactivity to emotionally positive pictures and neurotics have more to emotionally negative pictures (Canlin et al., 1998), but Gray's theory proposes more specific reward and punishment mechanisms, which occur especially in the phylogenetically older processes related to emotion and motivation, instead of in the higher cognitive processes that are described by many personality theorists (Corr, Pickering, & Gray, 1997).

Gray describes a **Behavioral Activation System (BAS)** that comes into play when rewarding experiences happen, causing us to approach them. It is involved in extraversion, sexual behavior, and aggressive behavior and thought to be associated with the neurotransmitter dopamine, which stimulates the brain's reward and pleasure center in the nucleus accumbens. This system produces greater happiness when research subjects anticipate a reward (Carver & White, 1994). The BAS can be expressed by impulsive behavior, especially in neurotic extraverts. It is improperly regulated in people who suffer from bipolar disorder, whose symptoms increase after they achieve goals that they have been striving toward (Johnson et al., 2000). High BAS scores are associated with greater craving for alcohol (Franken, 2002), which at least initially increases dopamine release and so enhances pleasurable emotion (L. A. Clark & Watson, 1999, p. 415). Low BAS sensitivity, in contrast, predisposes people to depression (Harmon-Jones & Allen, 1997). BAS scores are measured by responses to questions, such as "I crave excitement and new sensations" and "When I get something I want, I feel excited and energized."

Another system is measured by answers to questions like "Criticism or scolding hurts me quite a bit." Gray's **Behavioral Inhibition System (BIS)** comes into play when feared

Behavioral Activation System (BAS) in Gray's model, tendency of personality related to the approaching of rewarding experiences

Behavioral Inhibition System (BIS) in Gray's model, tendency of personality related to reactions to aversive stimuli

or aversive or surprising stimuli occur: when a snake slithers across the path in front of you or when you touch a hot object and feel pain. When the BIS is activated, the person becomes aroused, attentive, afraid, and inhibits behavior. Some people are particularly sensitive to punishment and activation of the BIS and are therefore anxiety prone, more impaired on an emotional Stroop test, and less able to disengage from tasks that involve aversive cues. They also are quicker to learn aversive associations (Avila, 2001). They become more nervous when anticipating punishment, and they are more vulnerable to anxiety disorders (Carver & White, 1994; Caseras, Torrubia, & Farre, 2001). Women who have been treated for breast cancer and who expect it to reoccur are particularly distressed if they also have high BIS levels (Carver, Meyer, & Antoni, 2000). The BIS is postulated to involve the neurotransmitter norepinephrine and the brain's hippocampus and septum.

The ability to inhibit behavior is essential for healthy psychological functioning. Underactivation of the BIS presumably contributes to impulsive behavior, excessive risk taking, and difficulty delaying gratification, and it has been suggested as a contributor to attention-deficit/hyperactivity disorder, ADHD (Avila & Parcet, 2001; Quay, 1997). Violent criminal behavior is more common in youth who have low norepinephrine levels; physiologically, they seem calm (low heart rates), which may mean they have been less impacted by efforts to discipline them because their physiology makes them less afraid (Kagan, 1994). Excessive activation of this system, though, contributes to such problems as anxiety.

BAS and BIS scores are not limited to emotional feelings; they also predict people's cognitive processing of emotional stimuli. In one study, subjects were presented with words that had some missing letters and told to fill in the blanks to make a word. On positive emotional words, such as *e_a_ed,* the approach-oriented (high BAS) scorers were more likely than the low BAS scorers to see *elated* instead of *erased*. Other emotional word tasks produced similar results (Gomez & Gomez, 2002). This finding is consistent with other research showing that emotional thoughts are more readily activated when the person is in the emotional state that corresponds to the thought or memory, so it makes theoretical sense. It also has practical implications, showing how people with strong approach orientation may, over time, build up cognitions that enhance this predisposition, and that conversely, avoidance-oriented people may become stronger in that direction through cognitions that emphasize the negative.

Fight-Flight System (FFS) biological personality factor proposed by Gray that produces rage and panic

Gray also describes a separate **Fight-Flight System (FFS)** (J. A. Gray, 1987) that produces rage and panic (see Table 9.5).

According to Gray's theory, extraverts are more influenced by reward, introverts by punishment. As predicted by this theory, in an experimental task in which auditory signals

TABLE 9.5	Gray's Model of the Biological Basis of Personality		
	BAS: Behavioral Activation System	**BIS: Behavioral Inhibition System**	**FFS: Fight-Flight System**
Neurotransmitter	Dopamine	Norepinephrine	
Implications for learning	Sensitivity to reward	Sensitivity to punishment (or nonreward)	
Psychological implications	Impulsivity; positive affect (in response to reward)	Anxiety; attention and arousal	Panic; rage

Note: The fight-flight system is less clearly described in Gray's model than the BAS and the BIS.

sometimes signaled reward and sometimes punishment, introverts showed more brain wave reaction to signals of punishment for an incorrect response, and extraverts showed more brain wave reaction to signals of reward for a correct response (Bartussek et al., 1993). Activation of the BAS and BIS does not simply produce pleasant and unpleasant emotion, but it also guides learning. Rewards and punishments are cues that teach us what to approach and what to avoid. In a study of male prisoners, physiological indicators were influenced by reward and punishment manipulations while subjects tried to earn money (reward) or avoid losing money (punishment) by determining which two-digit numbers were the "good" ones. When punishment was involved in the learning task, activation of the BIS produced an increase in skin conductance; when the BAS system was activated by the possibility of reward, heart rate sped up (Arnett & Newman, 2000). Because of their greater sensitivity to punishment, anxious subjects learn more quickly in a laboratory computer learning task involving punishment (verbal feedback and loss of money), whereas low anxious people learn more slowly (Corr, Pickering, & Gray, 1997).

The search for distinct neurobiological mechanisms of personality, such as particular neurotransmitters, is more likely to succeed if personality factors can be identified that are quite homogeneous (in contrast to very general factors). For example, in the case of extraversion, combining the components of assertiveness and impulsivity, which are not closely related (as many models of extraversion do), makes it harder to find a simple neurobiological mechanism (Depue & Collins, 1999). Depue and Collins prefer to focus on the first of these, which they refer to as the agency factor and that includes several closely related traits, including social dominance, achievement, and activity. Based on animal research, they then suggest (in keeping with Gray's model) that dopamine regulates this factor—specifically the ventral tegumental area dopamine projection system—resulting in behavioral facilitation of goal-directed behavior. It becomes active when an animal is hungry, for example, or when other drives (e.g., social or sexual) are activated. The animal (or person) moves toward positive incentives. Animal research using drugs that are agonists (activating) and antagonists (reducing) of dopamine, and monitoring dopamine neural responses shows that the neurotransmitter dopamine carries these positive incentive messages in the brain. Biological changes occur with experience. Dopamine signals become conditioned to incentive stimuli that are associated in the environment with reward. With repeated experience, these neural pathways work more efficiently, so goal-directed behavior, with its associated extraversion and pleasure, is facilitated (Depue & Collins, 1999). Combining biological mechanisms with the impact of learning, as Gray's theory does, offers considerable promise for understanding personality as it is inherited and as it changes with experience.

Cloninger's Tridimensional Model

C. R. Cloninger's (1986, 1987a, 1987b) tridimensional model proposes three biologically based personality traits, each resulting from the relative level of a particular neurotransmitter in a person's central nervous system. These three dimensions can be considered temperament types, the biological foundation on which personality, through experience, is developed.

The first temperament trait, **novelty seeking**, is proposed to be related to levels of the neurotransmitter dopamine (with low levels of dopamine producing greater novelty seeking). It serves as a behavioral activation system. People high in novelty seeking become more excited in response to novel stimuli, and they explore their environments more. They report that they often try new things for the thrill of it and they seek excitement. In a double-blind placebo-control study, people with higher Novelty Seeking scores reported greater mood elevation to amphetamine than those scoring low (Sax & Strakowski, 1998).

novelty seeking
biological trait proposed by Cloninger that activates people to explore new things; related to dopamine levels

In mice, exploratory behavior (which is analogous to human novelty seeking) increases when dopamine is increased (Sabol et al., 1999). Novelty seeking, which can lead to impulsive behavior, tends to run in families (Sher & Wood, 1995). Novelty seeking is higher among those with drug abuse, although sometimes substance abuse is produced by the second genetic trait, harm avoidance (Berman et al., 2002).

harm avoidance
biological dimension proposed by Cloninger that inhibits behavior; related to serotonin levels

The second temperament trait, **harm avoidance**, is related to high levels of the neurotransmitter serotonin. It serves as a behavioral inhibition system. People high in this trait are highly influenced by aversive stimuli or by signals indicating they will be punished, and so they act to avoid pain. They report that they worry and feel tense. Conversely, low serotonin activity is associated with impulsive acts of aggression, including murder, suicide, and arson (Coccaro et al., 1989). Incidentally, in monkeys, serotonin is higher in dominant monkeys, and dominance can be experimentally increased or decreased by drugs that change the level of serotonin in the monkey (Buck, 1999). High serotonin functioning is associated with grooming and other sociable behaviors; low serotonin is associated with aggression (Rogeness & McClure, 1996).

reward dependence
biological dimension proposed by Cloninger that maintains behavior through seeking rewards; related to nor-epinephrine levels

The third temperament trait, **reward dependence**, results from low levels of the neurotransmitter norepinephrine. It serves as a behavioral maintenance system, making people continue to behave in ways that produce reward, especially reward through warm social attachments (Stallings et al., 1996). People who are high in reward dependence report that they are hardworking and keep working even if others have given up.

One aspect of reward dependence, a subscale named persistence, may be a separate temperament dimension. Some evidence indicates that it is separately inherited. This temperament trait can lead to perfectionism and overachievement (Cloninger & Svrakic, 1997; Stallings et al., 1996).

These temperament dimensions are scored from a self-report measure, the Tridimensional Personality Questionnaire (TPQ). Here are some examples of items (listed by Stallings et al., 1996):

> *I do things spontaneously.* (Novelty Seeking)
> *I get tense and worried in unfamiliar situations.* (Harm Avoidance)
> *Others think I am too independent.* (disagree; Reward Dependence)
> *I often push myself to exhaustion.* (Persistence component of Reward Dependence)

These temperamental dimensions can occur in any combination, leading to a diversity of biological predispositions. They influence a person's risk for particular psychiatric diagnoses. A temperament, though, is only a starting point for personality. Social learning builds on this foundation, producing adult personality that is more intentional and reflective than the automatic habits of temperament (Cloninger & Svrakic, 1997).

Cloninger's theory helps explain different types of alcohol abuse. Type I alcoholics are high in harm avoidance and reward dependence and low in novelty seeking, and they become alcoholic in response to environmental stress. Type II alcoholics are high in novelty seeking and low in the other two traits, and they are likely to begin drinking earlier (Cloninger, Sigvardsson, & Bohman, 1988; Wills, Windle, & Cleary, 1998). However, traits in the tridimensional model do not have a direct, automatic influence on people's lives. Experience matters. One of the most important experiences for predicting adolescent substance use is having friends who use drugs. The trait of novelty seeking, in Cloninger's model, predicts having such friends, but without them, novelty seeking alone does not lead to substance use (Wills et al., 1998).

Biological Mechanisms in Context

Personality is influenced by heredity and biology, without doubt. The sense that we make of this, however, is challenging. Many traditional ways of thinking are not helpful. Much of Western philosophy presumed a separation between the physical and the mental, and that tradition does not help us integrate the two, as we must if we are to make sense of new findings in behavioral genetics and neuroscience. Nor is it helpful to turn to biology as a more developed science, replacing primitive psychology. Why not?

One consideration is that all psychological behavior is biological, requiring a body to occur. This does not mean we should try to understand it at the biological level, any more than a computer scientist would analyze a program at the level of electronic circuits. Turkheimer (1998) refers to this indiscriminant biological involvement as "weak biologism," in contrast to "strong biologism," which occurs when biological variables explain psychological phenomena. (A computer analogy of strong biologism is to understand a computer failure in terms of a defective hard drive, in contrast to a programming bug. In this case, of course, the hard drive is not biological, but it is physical.)

Although we often presume that biology is basic and experience is added to it but does not change it (much as a computer program is added to a computer but does not change its hardware), this is not true. Experience changes biology. The brains of animals and humans develop greater differentiation when they are stimulated by enriched experience, and groups that begin with different biological characteristics (such as the two sexes) can exaggerate this difference by having different experiences—for example, the greater spatial abilities of males may become exaggerated when they spend more time on video games that involve spatial skills (Halpern, 1997). Harmful effects can come from experience. The brain's normal fear mechanisms can become sensitized so pathological anxiety results (Rosen & Schulkin, 1998). Animal studies show that maternally deprived monkeys develop abnormal norepinephrine systems that may have long-lasting developmental effects. Evidence suggests this also occurs in humans. Neglect also causes abnormalities in human dopamine systems. These findings mean that neglect of children in early life causes biological damage, which may help us understand the biological mechanism of its psychological effects (Galvin et al., 1991; Kraemer, 1992; Rogeness & McClure, 1996). Early mother–infant interaction, some theorize, is necessary for the normal development of the brain (Steklis & Walter, 1991) and for the personality that depends on the brain. Neuroscientist Joseph LeDoux (2002) argues that experiences (nurture) and heredity (nature) both have their effect by changing the synaptic organization of the brain; in this way, both nature and nurture "actually speak the same language" (p. 3).

The effects of individual experience, LeDoux acknowledges, build on innate species characteristics but shape them to the specifics of an individual's life. Monogamous pair bonding or attachment, for example, occurs in animals (although only a few species, including only 3% of mammals). Experiments with two species of voles suggest that bonding to the mate occurs because of the release of specific hormones during mating: specifically, oxytocin in the female and vasopressin in the male (LeDoux, 2002, pp. 230–233). Perhaps human pair bonding is influenced by the same hormones as in these small rodents. If it is, does that mean that oxytocin or vasopressin pills could cement a relationship? Clearly, that is an oversimplified idea. The hormone alone does not make for pair bonding; what it does is to prepare the nervous system to respond to experience with the mate by forming an exclusive and protective attachment, mediated by synaptic changes in the brain. In a similar way, as LeDoux describes it, when medication is effective in therapy for depression or schizophrenia, it works by preparing the brain to make permanent changes in response to specific learning, which must be provided by the experiences of life or of therapy. This is a reason why some medications take time to become effective: The learning that they facilitate occurs over time. Furthermore, LeDoux suggests that traumatic experience, such as childhood abuse, impedes brain development by limiting the emotional system, causing it to focus on fear systems at the expense of positive emotional systems; this limits the repertoire of neural circuits that are developed to prepare for future behavior.

Biological predispositions are shaped by experience to form adult personality. The same predispositions can be molded into a variety of outcomes, just as clay can be made into a pot or a vase or a plate. Consider the example of behavioral inhibition (Rubin, 1998). This temperament style has biological implications: faster heartbeat, higher salivary cortisol levels, and brain wave differences. Such children do not assert themselves by taking initiative in social situations, but what happens to them then? It depends on the environment. Cross-cultural developmental researchers have found that two children with the same biological predisposition—a wary, fearful reaction to unfamiliar people and situations—will develop quite differently in U.S. or Chinese cultures. In the United States, such a child has a difficult time because the cultural value for more assertive and competitive social interactions leaves the child on the sidelines or even a target of ridicule. They have difficulty with friendships and are at risk for loneliness and depression. In the People's Republic of China, however, such a reticent child encounters a more accepting reaction. This culture values collective outcomes, in contrast to the individualism of U.S. culture, and the shy child is not at a disadvantage here; in fact, this child's submissiveness and restraint may be an asset. In China, such a child is likely to have positive relationships with peers and high self-esteem.

No doubt biological understandings will continue to transform personality theory, but they must be considered in relation to culture and experience. Biological explanations will not make personality theory obsolete by explaining all the phenomena of interest in terms of neuroscience. That would be *reductionism*. Carried to the extreme, reductionism would also make neuroscience obsolete by reducing all explanations to the level of physics (Gold & Stoljar, 1999). To understand personality, we will always need a multilevel theory that considers biological explanation in relation to cognition and experience.

Summary

- Biological understandings of personality have been offered from the evolutionary shared traits of our species to individual differences in genetic inheritance and brain functioning.
- At the level of *evolution,* natural selection based on reproductive success offers explanations for sexual selectivity and jealousy, aggression, altruism, and nurturance; many of these traits vary between males and females.
- The immaturity of human young, combined with human capacity for language and imitation, prepare for considerable influence of experience.
- *Cultural evolution* supplements biological changes.
- *Heredity* has widespread influences on individual differences in personality.
- *Temperament* differences are observable early in life, and they are the basis for adult personality differences.
- Studies of the brain and nervous system find specific areas for many human traits. Emotion and arousal are particularly important.

- Several biological factor theories have been proposed (including those by Eysenck, Gray, and Cloninger).
- Eysenck's *PEN model* describes Extraversion, Neuroticism, and Psychoticism.
- Gray's *reinforcement sensitivity theory* proposes a *Behavioral Activation System (BAS)* that emphasizes rewards and a *Behavioral Inhibition System (BIS)* that emphasizes punishments.
- Cloninger's *tridimensional model* describes three factors: Novelty Seeking, Harm Avoidance, and Reward Dependence.
- All of these biological aspects of personality are subject to influences from experience and culture.

Thinking about Biological Personality Theories

1. If an ancient human newborn were brought to our current time (by some science fiction time travel device) and raised with a contemporary family, would he or she fit in? How would this help us evaluate the evolutionary theory of personality?
2. Discuss how the concept of cumulative cultural evolution brings learning and experience into evolutionary theory.
3. Propose a research study to investigate the impact of the social environment on any one specific hereditary dimension of personality, such as a particular temperament type.
4. Considering the importance of biochemical influences (such as neurotransmitters) on personality from childhood on, do you think drugs should be used to modify or correct imbalances of these influences in children?
5. Many different biological factor theories have been described. What are the overall biological differences, considering all of them, that you would include in one model of personality?
6. Several biological models offer three components. Compare these models. In what ways are they similar? In what ways are they different?
7. Given the importance of biology for personality, do you expect there will be less attention to childhood experience and to culture in future theories?

Study Questions

1. In explaining personality (and other) characteristics in humans today, what does evolutionary psychology assume?
2. Describe the evolutionary explanation of social behaviors such as altruism and aggression.
3. What is an "evolved psychological mechanism"? Give examples.
4. How does evolutionary psychology explain the differences between men and women in sexual and parental behavior?
5. Why are people aggressive, according to evolutionary psychology?
6. What is cultural evolution? How is it related to language and symbolism?
7. How strong is the impact of heredity on personality, according to genetic research?
8. What is temperament? Describe Kagan's categories of temperament.
9. Describe how the brain and neurotransmitters influence personality.
10. How does emotional arousal influence personality? Describe the distinction between positive and negative emotions and the emotion of anger.
11. Describe cortical arousal and its relationship to Pavlov's strong and weak nervous systems.
12. What is sensation seeking?
13. List and describe the three factors in Eysenck's PEN theory.
14. How does Eysenck's model relate to criminal behavior?
15. Summarize Gray's reinforcement sensitivity theory and the different functions of the Behavioral Activation System and the Behavioral Inhibition System. How does this theory interpret introversion and extraversion?

The Learning Perspective

Behaviorism has been one of the major perspectives in modern psychology. Radical behaviorism insists that only observable behaviors should be included in a scientific theory. Historically, this represented a departure from the introspective methods of Titchener and the psychoanalytic method of Freud (Rilling, 2000), and it still serves as a reminder to attend to what people actually do and to the circumstances in which they do it. Early in the twentieth century, John B. Watson (1924/1970) proposed that personality is determined by the environment. He made an often-quoted claim:

> Give me a dozen healthy infants, well-formed, and my own specified world to bring them up in and I'll guarantee to take any one at random and train him to become any type of specialist I might select—doctor, lawyer, artist, merchant-chief and, yes, even beggar-man and thief—regardless of his talents, penchants, tendencies, abilities, vocations, and race of his ancestors. (p. 104)

Read in context, it is clear that Watson was exaggerating to make a point of the importance of experience, which can overcome the effects of genetic endowments. The "talents, penchants, tendencies, [and] abilities" that Watson said could be overcome by environment are what most people mean by personality. Watson, though, defined personality in terms of behavior. Habitual behaviors constitute personality. They are modified and expanded throughout life. Personality change comes about through learning, which is more rapid early in life when habit patterns are forming. Watson believed the study of personality required extensive observation of individuals. What should be observed? Watson listed several factors: education, achievements, psychological tests, recreational activities, and emotions in daily life (p. 279).

The behavioral perspective makes distinctive assumptions about personality:

1. Personality is defined in terms of behavior. What a person does constitutes his or her personality (Richards, 1986; Watson, 1924/1970).
2. Behavior (and therefore personality) is determined by external factors in the environment, specifically reinforcements and discriminative stimuli.
3. Behaviorism claims that it is possible to influence people for the better by changing environmental conditions, including social changes.
4. Behaviorism asserts that change can occur throughout a person's life.
5. Behaviorism studies the individual person (idiographic approach). It does not presume that the factors influencing one person will necessarily have similar influences on someone else.

The behavioral approach has little difficulty explaining individual differences, although that is not its usual emphasis. Each person experiences a somewhat different environment, with different conditions of learning. Inevitably, different behaviors are learned. Personality consists of behaviors that are built into extensive repertoires of behavior through a lifetime (Staats, 1996). Some researchers have incorporated this behavioral emphasis into personality assessment, measuring personality traits by counting the frequency of behaviors in a trait-relevant category. This is called the act frequency approach (Buss & Craik, 1980, 1983).

A behavioral perspective considers subjective experience only to the extent that the experience is manifested in observable behavior. The early behaviorist John Watson (1913/1994) suggested it is possible to know, without asking for a report of the introspective experience, whether a person or an animal can tell the difference between two colors: Punish a response to one color but not to the other. If the person or animal learns to avoid the punished color but not the other, it evidence of color vision. Behaviorists frequently conduct research with animals rather than with humans in their search for a general theory of behavior, and they are not generally concerned with the particular responses studied (Thompson, 1994).

Behaviorism assumes that people's actions are determined by external factors, not by forces within the individual. This assumption of determinism has led to a long-standing debate between behaviorists, particularly B. F. Skinner, and humanists (presented later), who claim that people are free to choose their actions. Skinner declared that behaviorism represents a scientific revolution against earlier conceptions, which sought the causes of behavior within the individual. Yet behaviorism itself is not free of the influences on thought that derive from outside of science. Behaviorism contains themes that are part of modern thought more generally: Problems can be solved through technology, reason prevails over emotion, morality is relative rather than absolute, and the world can be improved (Woolfolk & Richardson, 1984).

To a large extent, behavioral approaches today have built on the earlier, more external versions emphasized by Watson and Skinner, incorporating internal factors such as thinking. Staats and, earlier, Dollard and Miller, whose theories are covered in the next two chapters, include cognition, as do theories presented in Part V. Scientific theories are expected to change with the influence of new data, so these changes are not criticisms of the learning perspective but rather evidence of its impact on our thinking about personality.

Study Questions

1. What are the distinguishing assumptions of the learning perspective?
2. What position does behaviorism take on the idiographic-nomothetic controversy?

Skinner and Staats
The Challenge of Behaviorism

Chapter Overview

Preview: Overview of Skinner's and Staats's Theories

Radical Behaviorism: Skinner

Behavior as the Data for Scientific Study

Learning Principles

Schedules of Reinforcement

Applications of Behavioral Techniques

Radical Behaviorism and Personality Theory: Some Concerns

Psychological Behaviorism: Staats

Reinforcement

Basic Behavioral Repertoires

Situations

Psychological Adjustment

The Nature-Nurture Question from the Perspective of Psychological Behaviorism

Personality Assessment from a Behavioral Perspective

The Act Frequency Approach to Personality Measurement

Contributions of Behaviorism to Personality Theory and Measurement

Summary

ILLUSTRATIVE BIOGRAPHY

Tiger Woods

Both Skinner and Staats propose that personality consists of learned behaviors. The earlier theory by B. F. Skinner describes the principles of learning, whereas the later theory by Arthur Staats goes into detail about how this applies specifically to the behaviors that help us understand personality.

Tiger Woods, by his extraordinary youthful achievements, has transformed the image of professional golf. Consider these achievements in his first quarter century of life: He is the youngest player (by 2 years) to have won all four of modern golf's so-called major tournaments—the Masters, the United States Open, the British Open, and the PGA Championship. He is the only player in history to have won all four in succession, holding those championships simultaneously. And, as if all that were not enough, he holds the all-time scoring record in three of them and shares it in the other. His golf earnings have made him a multimillionaire.

His golf achievements have made him a celebrity, and that began very early. Already he appeared swinging a golf club on television at age 2, and he was featured in a golf magazine at age 5. At age 8, Tiger won the Junior World Championship, and he repeated this feat four more times by age 14 (Owen, 2001; "Tiger Woods Profile," 2006).

Tiger Woods was born on December 30, 1975. His ancestors are diverse: black, white, Native American, and Asian on his father's side and Asian on his mother's side (Owen, 2001, pp. 187–188). This diversity adds to his media appeal as the world struggles to find models of diversity. Along the way, though, he was sometimes not permitted to play on golf courses that were restricted to whites.

From the start of his life, his father Earl fostered interest in golf, and the family continued to support Tiger both emotionally and materially. His parents sacrificed considerably for their son, taking out tens of thousands of dollars in loans to provide him with the opportunity to play golf competitively in his childhood and adolescence.

Tiger attended high school in Southern California and college at California's prestigious Stanford University (until he stopped to become a full-time golf professional). Woods was married to his wife Elin in 2004. His father, who was so closely involved as a career mentor and—according to Tiger's description—best friend, died in 2006.

Development

Personality develops by learning. The basic principle of learning is reinforcement. Skinner's radical behavioral theory emphasizes that the behavior must occur and be followed by reward (reinforcement). The more frequently and immediately this occurs, the stronger the behavioral tendency becomes. Staats accepted these principles and also added additional considerations.

Tiger Woods's father Earl directed his son's learning. He set up a high chair for Tiger while he practiced golf swings, and soon Tiger was climbing down from the chair to imitate him with a plastic golf club (Owen, 2001, pp. 59–60). In the beginning, we would expect the reward would be his father's approval, but with time, as he learned to judge his own performance, reinforcement came from knowing he had hit well (i.e., the ball went where it was intended). In Staats's theory, motor activities such as golf provide reinforcement by directly seeing the effect of the swing on the movement of the ball and also by feedback from observers.

Frequency of behavior and of reinforcement also influence the strength of learning. The intensive practice that has been a routine part of Tiger's life provides reinforcement in the form of feedback with every swing of the club. Even after winning many championships, Tiger continues to practice intensively and to seek expert trainers to improve his near-perfect swing.

As he puts it, "My dad always told me that there are no shortcuts, . . . and that if you want to become the best you're going to have to be willing to pay your dues" (Owen, 2001, p. 131). In addition, the approval of a greater audience and, after several years, the financial rewards of golf achievement have contributed to the persistence of Woods's behavior in golf by increasing the reinforcement. In the adult championship phase of his life, additional reinforcements come into play: fame, admiration of fans, multimillion dollar contracts from *Golf Digest* magazine, Nike sports equipment, and championship purses.

Staats's theory of psychological behaviorism describes the basic behavior repertoires (BBRs), which people learn early in life, that provide the basis for later personality. What we learn early is the foundation on which later learning builds. Golf is not the only thing a child needs to learn, as Staats's theory makes clear. While supporting his golf, Tiger's parents also were concerned that he might be missing other important experiences. Nonetheless, they let their son follow his own motivation and supported him. Tiger's mother Kultida used the time-honored method of reinforcement to get Tiger to do his school homework. She would not permit him to practice golf until the homework was done. Such a reinforcement procedure only works because practicing golf had itself become a reward, as a result of learning. Without the systematic observation of behavior required by learning theorists, we can only speculate what learning history caused this to occur. A likely possibility, given the close relationship between Tiger and his father, is that his father's attention was paired with Tiger's early golf swings, leading the golf itself to become reinforcing.

Description

Of the two theorists in this chapter, Staats gives the more extensive descriptive categories for understanding personality. He proposes that personality consists of learned behaviors. He categorizes them into behaviors that have to do with language and cognition, those that have to do with emotion and motivation, and those that have to do with sensory and motor behavior. Each of these groups is called a "repertoire," or "Basic Behavioral Repertoire (BBR)," for the components learned early in life, to indicate it is the foundation for later personality.

Consider the Sensory-Motor repertoire. As a child, Tiger's ability to watch the ball (sensory) and to hit it (motor) established the foundation of this repertoire. Over time, it has expanded to include all of his diverse golf shots, designed to propel the ball toward the hole in a variety of winds and other environmental conditions. Tiger continues to develop new shots, which can best be appreciated by those who know the sport well, like keeping the ball low in windy conditions. His golf swing is now so fast, 120 miles per hour, that even a Hulcher camera designed to take stop-action photographs of missiles for the U.S. government has difficulty capturing an image of his club hitting the ball (Owen, 2001, pp. 124–125). Besides the golf strokes, Tiger works out with weights to develop his muscles further. The basic components of the Sensory-Motor repertoire were learned early. Additional behaviors continue to be added.

Adjustment

The behaviors that belong to Staats's Emotional-Motivational repertoire are relevant to adjustment. These include such skills as emotional control, including management of anxiety and anger. In a competitive sport such as golf, emotional self-management is essential for success. Golfers confront emotional situations when they miss a shot or when something disrupts their concentration, and learning how to manage these situations is an important behavioral skill.

To control his emotions, by adulthood Woods had developed an elaborate warm-up behavioral sequence before tournaments that he had learned made his swings more reliable. He arrives early at golf tournaments to go through a series of practice shots in a standard sequence, thus calming himself. He says this reduces his nervousness (Owen, 2001, p. 23). Skinner's theory (at least in its original formulation) would avoid such internal subjective states as "nervousness" that cannot be verified by external observers. Staats, however, permits emotional language in his expanded learning theory. A ritual sequence of behaviors like Tiger developed would produce a reliable stimulus environment for the golf shot, making the well-practiced behavior more reliably performed.

What about distractions? For a golfer, distractions such as comments from the audience can interfere with performance. Fortunately, we can train for this by including distractions during learning. During the intensive training for golf that his father provided, his father verbally hazed him, subjecting him to the sort of distractions that might occur in a real game to give Tiger an opportunity to learn to play through such conditions without losing his concentration. "Earl would tee up his own ball on the wrong side of the markers, improve his lie, jingle coins in his pockets as Tiger was preparing to putt, clap his hands, make rude noises, and do everything he

could think of to break his son's concentration" (Owen, 2001, pp. 66–67). So when similar situations happened in a real tournament, Tiger's well-learned automatic self-control kept him focused.

Certainly there are some exceptions, however. A demanding sport such as golf produces considerable frustration, even for a world-class player like Tiger Woods, when the ball rolls short of the target or beyond it. He has been seen throwing his club to the ground and heard swearing when the game goes badly (Owen, 2001, p. 151). Yet for the most part Tiger displays self-control and good manners on the golf course, and his emotional expressions, which are common among golfers, pass quickly.

In addition to controlling nervousness, the emotional repertoire includes ways of obtaining pleasure. When his parents worried that Tiger was too competitive to enjoy the game of golf, he replied, "That's how I enjoy myself, by shooting low scores" (Owen, 2001, p. 81). Probably his focus on the possibility of winning, rather than on the risk of losing, kept his emotions positive.

Cognition

Cognitive elements of personality are included in what Staats calls the Language-Cognitive repertoire. These include intelligence, planning, and so on.

Tiger Woods is academically intelligent. He attended highly selective Stanford University but left before graduating to turn professional.

As part of the Language-Cognitive behavioral repertoire he learned under his father's tutelage, Tiger was gradually taught to take responsibility for travel arrangements to his golf tournaments. In this, he not only learned the practical arrangements required to book transportation and hotels, he also learned the confidence that comes from being self-sufficient. Incidentally, such independence training is thought by researchers to be the basis for learning achievement motivation.

Society

Learning is done by individuals, but the social context influences it, and a person's learned behaviors can also have an impact on society. Cultural factors in his parents' background undoubtedly made them better teachers of emotional self-control. Both his parents deserve credit for teaching him alternatives to aggressive outbursts. As described earlier, his father purposely made remarks and noises during practice sessions to give his son practice in putting up with such events. His mother, raised a Buddhist, taught him the nonviolent self-control that is better developed in that tradition than in the U.S. culture in which Tiger was raised. In an interview, Tiger praised Buddhism: "It's based on discipline and respect and personal responsibility. I like Asian culture better than ours because of that. Asians are much more disciplined than we are. Look how well behaved their children are. It's how my mother raised me. You can question, but talk back? *Never.*" (Owen, 2001, p. 88).

Besides the usual emotional issues in golf, his race brought additional issues. As a minority in a predominantly white neighborhood in Southern California, he was targeted for attacks, like being tied to a tree on the first day of kindergarten (Owen, 2001, p. 87). Later, some golf clubs refused him permission to play because of race. Because of the emotional self-control he had learned, these societal obstacles were manageable.

The image of golf has been changed in the public eye, less what Tiger described as "a wussy sport" (Owen, 2001, p. 175), as it was when he was a kid and now attractive to young people who in the past might have been drawn to other sports, such as basketball. Golf was also historically a whites-only sport, although that was already changing because of the success of black American golfers such as Lee Elder and Calvin Peete. Tiger's success has further contributed to the inclusiveness of the sport. For nonwhite kids, biographer David Owen describes Tiger Woods as "the fearless conqueror of a world that has never wanted anything to do with them" (2001, p. 195).

From a learning perspective, Tiger is a teacher as well as a learner. Since 1996, he has run the Tiger Woods Foundation, which teaches children about golf, career opportunities, and personal attributes such as courtesy and hard work that make people better off the golf course as well as on it. His father was an active participant in the establishment of this foundation, and now commercial enterprises have donated millions of dollars to establish learning centers to help youth identify and achieve their goals.

Biology

Learned behavior can be limited by biological factors, especially when it requires an overt behavior, such as athletic performance. A combination of genetic gifts and lifestyle choices, including extensive practice, has been essential to developing this world-class athlete. Staats describes biological factors that can potentially affect a person before, during, and after learning (as we see later in this chapter).

Final Thoughts

The particular behaviors that are learned vary from one person to another, creating a diversity of personalities. It is not always so clear, as it is in the case of this extensively tutored champion, what contributed to learning. Additionally, learning can produce some unfortunate behaviors that produce disturbed personalities. In Tiger Woods's case, the positive behaviors are not limited to the game of golf. In the words of Tiger's father, "Golf is a game in which you learn about life" (Owen, 2001, p. 44). This thought is what makes the story of Tiger Woods's golf career also the story of the development of his personality.

Preview: Overview of Skinner's and Staats's Theories

Skinner's theory and Staats's theory, both offering behavioral interpretations of personality, have implications for major theoretical questions, as presented in Table 10.1. One of the greatest strengths of these and other behavioral perspectives is its clear statement of scientifically verifiable hypotheses. Because the causes of behavior can be manipulated, this approach more closely approximates the models of science derived from laboratories in other scientific disciplines. Adding reinforcers, eliminating them, adding punishments—such manipulations are predicted to change the rate of responses, and these can be readily counted to test whether the predictions are confirmed. Staats's theory goes further than Skinner's in defining in advance what would be reinforcing (stimuli that produce emotional responses). In extending the basic behavioral concepts beyond animal models, Staats describes responses that have particular importance to humans, including language

TABLE 10.1	Preview of Skinner's and Staats's Theories
Individual Differences	Individuals differ in their behaviors owing to differences in reinforcement histories. In Staats's theory, biological predispositions are also acknowledged.
Adaptation and Adjustment	Rather than considering "health" or "illness," it is more profitable to specify which behaviors should be eliminated and which increased, and to change them through learning therapies (behavior modification).
Cognitive Processes	Mental processes are difficult to study because the scientist does not have access to them. In principle, mental processes can be explained in behavioral terms. In practice, according to radical behaviorists such as Skinner, it probably is not worth the trouble; instead, the focus should be on observable behavior. According to Staats, cognitive processes can be studied by self-report measures, and thought processes are important behaviors.
Society	Society provides the conditions of learning, and therefore shapes personality. Behavioral principles suggest that some aspects of society should be improved (e.g., education). A society can be envisioned in which more effective use of reinforcement makes people happier and more productive, using rewards rather than punishments or coercion to control behavior.
Biological Influences	Species differences influence response capabilities and the effectiveness of various reinforcements. According to Staats, individuals, too, have biological differences that influence but are also influenced by learning.
Development	Children learn which behaviors will lead to positive reinforcement and which to punishment, and they respond accordingly. Stimulus control and schedules of reinforcement influence this learning. Childhood development provides the basis for later learning, according to Staats. Adult development is explained according to the same principles as child development. It builds on earlier learning.

and cognition, emotion and motivation, and sensory-motor behaviors. He explains in detail how development builds from these basics to adaptive or maladaptive adult behaviors. Implications for treatment follow from both approaches, but with more flexibility in Staats's model because of the greater comprehensiveness of behaviors that it encompasses. Both theorists offer idiographic approaches, respecting that each individual is unique.

Radical Behaviorism: Skinner

B. F. Skinner proposed a theory of behavior based on principles of reinforcement. This theory describes how behavior is influenced by its effects, popularly referred to as reward and punishment. Although most of his work was with animals, particularly rats, Skinner wrote extensively about the implications of behaviorism for humans. His animal model of learning is widely respected, but the implications he has drawn for humans are controversial and (compared to later behavioral theories) limited.

BIOGRAPHY OF B. F. SKINNER

Burrhus Frederic Skinner was born March 20, 1904, in the railroad town of Susquehanna, Pennsylvania. He was named Burrhus after his mother's maiden name. She and her husband William, an attorney, raised Burrhus and a younger son, Ebbe. Skinner's brother died suddenly of an acute illness (probably a massive cerebral hemorrhage) while Fred Skinner, as he was generally called, was visiting his hometown (at that time, Scranton) during his freshman year at college.

B. F. SKINNER

Childhood had been happy for Skinner. He explored the countryside around Susquehanna, showing an inventive interest through various devices. These included a flotation contraption to separate ripe elderberries from green ones, a perpetual motion machine, and a device to remind himself to hang up his pajamas (B. F. Skinner, 1967, 1976).

Besides inventing things, Skinner was interested in writing. He wrote poetry and prose at Hamilton College in upstate New York, where he majored in English. He sent three short stories to Robert Frost, who had invited submissions when he visited the campus. Frost's response was encouraging, and Skinner was serious enough (and, thanks to his father's hard work, affluent enough) to take a year off after graduation to try to write a novel. The project failed as his parents had anticipated. Later he concluded, "I had failed as a writer because I had had nothing important to say" (B. F. Skinner, 1967, p. 395). At the time, though, he felt the fault was not his but rather the limitations of the "literary method" for understanding human behavior.

A better method, he decided, was psychology, although he had not taken a single course in psychology as an undergraduate. Much to the relief of his parents, Skinner decided to return to school, studying psychology as a graduate student at Harvard in 1928. He read extensively, making up for the lack of previous courses, devouring many primary sources in psychology, physiology, and philosophy in their original languages (French and German). At Harvard, Skinner encountered important personality theorists. He enrolled in Henry Murray's course in the psychology of the individual and reported that they became great friends. Gordon Allport joined the faculty in time to hear Skinner defend his dissertation but too late for Skinner to take any courses with him.

Skinner's first experimental animal was, strangely enough, a squirrel. He soon turned to laboratory rats. He investigated learning in the new apparatus he invented (which Hull later named the Skinner box). The device was intended to isolate particular aspects of learning, which were confounded in the mazes that dominated learning studies at the time. Already Skinner was working on a new theory of conditioning, in contrast to that of Pavlov.

Skinner received his doctorate from Harvard University in 1931. His studies at Harvard were extended by postdoctoral fellowships from the National Research Council (1931–1933) and the Harvard Society of Fellows (1933–1936) in the midst of the Great Depression. He married Yvonne Blue just before beginning his first teaching job at the University of Minnesota (1936–1945). They had two daughters and raised the younger in her early years in a modified crib he called an Air Crib, designed to provide an environmentally controlled environment (B. F. Skinner, 1945) (see Figure 10.1). Several hundred

Figure 10.1 An Air Crib

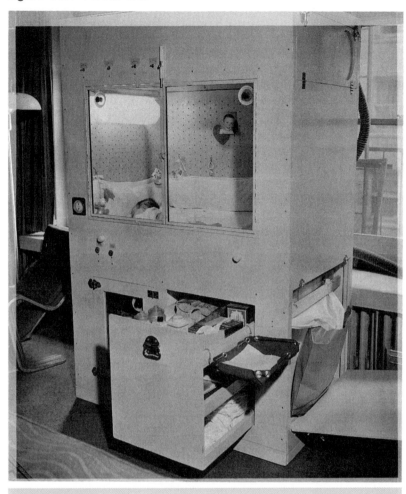

(Culver Pictures, Inc.)

such Air Cribs were marketed, although critics felt it was inhumane to place a human in a modified Skinner box.

One of the most unusual of Skinner's efforts was Project Pigeon. During World War II, he trained pigeons to guide missiles toward their targets, which were enemy warships on the ocean. Although an unusual technology, preliminary work showed it was effective. The government abandoned the project, however, before it was implemented, and efforts were instead channeled into the development of the atom bomb (D. Cohen, 1977).

Although Skinner's primary interest remained conditioning, evidence of his earlier interests is found in his course "The Psychology of Literature." Besides his scientific writing, he wrote a novel, *Walden Two* (B. F. Skinner, 1948), and made extensive notes in a journal that he kept for many years (1958a). In 1945 Skinner accepted a position as chair of the Department of Psychology at Indiana University. He was enticed back to Harvard in 1948 with the offer of a full professorship and laboratory support and remained there, continuing his research, theory building, and teaching until his death from leukemia on August 18, 1990, at age 86.

Skinner was one of the most influential psychologists of the 20th century, according to surveys of psychologists (e.g., Heyduk & Fenigstein, 1984). He received many professional awards, including the American Psychological Association's Distinguished Scientific Contribution Award (American Psychological Association, 1958) and an unprecedented honor, the Citation for Outstanding Lifetime Contribution to Psychology, awarded by the American Psychological Association just before Skinner's death (American Psychological Association, 1990).

Behavior as the Data for Scientific Study

Unlike the theorists considered so far in this book, Skinner did not propose causes of behavior within the personality of the individual. In fact, he dismissed personality as a discipline that had not become fully scientific but was still contaminated with prescientific philosophical assumptions. The idea that behavior is caused by forces within an individual (traits, thoughts, needs, and so on) should be abandoned, according to Skinner, in favor of more scientific explanations outside the person. Thus his theory does not present a concept of personality in the usual sense but rather a challenge to the idea that a theory of personality can be part of science.

Skinner's behavioral approach focuses on predicting and controlling overt, observable behavior. Such behavior can be reliably observed by independent observers, who can count or otherwise measure it. In addition, it argues that the causes of behavior are external to the individual, in contrast to personality theory, which has traditionally looked for causes within people: traits, needs, and the like. Skinner argued that it is illogical to consider personality traits (such as extraversion) or inner motives (such as self-actualization and anxiety) to be the causes of behavior because inner causes involve circular reasoning. Traits are inferred from behavior, whether from anecdotal observation or more formal analysis. Traits are therefore simply summary descriptions of behaviors. To say that (1) "John is aggressive because he hits people" (an inference) and (2) "John hits people because he is aggressive" (an explanation) is circular reasoning and logically indefensible.

Skinner argued that moving from internal explanations, such as traits, to external explanations, such as reinforcements and stimuli, was a scientific step forward. External variables are convenient for science. The researcher can manipulate them so their status as causes of behavior is not in doubt. Skinner's behaviorism is more thoroughly external than other behavioral approaches. It is called *radical behaviorism* to distinguish it from learning theories that include some internal causes of behavior, such as drives (per theorists Dollard and Miller) and cognitive variables (per Mischel and Bandura). To most modern behaviorists, this radical refusal to consider intervening variables (variables not directly observable) is unnecessary and impedes the development of psychological theory (e.g., Kimble, 1994).

Common sense tells us that thoughts can cause behavior. "I thought about my friend, so I phoned." Intention is also often offered as an explanation: A person intends to do something, and the intention is regarded as the "cause" of the action. Why would Skinner rule out thoughts, intentions, and other inner states as causes in his theory? First, mental states are not available for observation by others. They are private experiences and can only be inferred from behavior, such as self-reports. An empirical science should be based on direct observations. Second, the individual does not know his or her inner states very accurately. Self-reports are often flawed.

Skinner (e.g., 1963, 1975, 1990) argued that scientific progress in psychology requires abandoning *mentalism,* which explains behavior in terms of internal mental states. The inner life of feelings and thoughts should not be regarded as causing observable behavior. Rather, inner thoughts and feelings are simply "collateral products" (e.g., B. F. Skinner, 1975, p. 44) of the environmental factors causing overt behavior.

Besides focusing on observable behavior and external causes, Skinner emphasized the importance of control over behavior. If science can provide ways of controlling behavior, we can be sure it has identified the causes of behavior. Traits and other inner determinants allow prediction and explanation of behavior, but not control, and so are inconsistent with Skinner's behaviorist orientation (Zuriff, 1985).

THE EVOLUTIONARY CONTEXT OF OPERANT BEHAVIOR

Humans are adaptable. More than lower animals, who respond to environments largely with fixed instincts, humans can learn to respond in different ways, depending on what is effective in a given situation. Evolution is a process by which adaptive characteristics are selected in response to the environment, through natural selection, but it is a slow process that takes generations. Skinner argued that adaptive behavior can also be selected within the experience of one individual. In fact, the human capacity to adapt to the environment may be its most salient species characteristic. The basic idea is that behavior is determined by the environmental outcomes contingent on the behavior—that is, those that follow regularly from the behavior. Skinner described **operant conditioning** as the selection of behavior through its consequences.

operant conditioning learning in which the frequency of responding is influenced by the consequences that are contingent on a response

THE RATE OF RESPONDING

To analyze the learning process into small steps, Skinner realized it was necessary to select a dependent measure carefully. Earlier work, such as Thorndike's puzzle boxes, confounded several processes so it was difficult to know just what changes were occurring as learning progressed. In addition, Skinner was interested in the actions of the whole organism, so he did not want to choose a mere physiological component, such as a muscle twitch, or the neurological reflexes to which theorists in the Pavlovian tradition referred.

rate of responding the number of responses emitted in a period of time; a change in this rate is taken as evidence of learning

Skinner (1950, 1953b) argued that the best operant behaviors for research purposes are those that occur distinctly and repeatedly, so they can be clearly observed and counted. Learning is then measured by changes (increases or decreases) in the **rate of responding**. To achieve control of extraneous influences, Skinner studied primarily lower animals, especially rats and pigeons, whose lives could be highly controlled. He invented a new apparatus, which has come to be known as a **Skinner box**, to provide an environment in which **operant responses**, responses freely emitted by the organism (as contrasted with elicited classical responses such as salivation), could be readily observed and automatically recorded. He devised the apparatus as a graduate student through a series of rather drastic modifications of the mazes popular in learning studies of the period. Over time, the apparatus became more sophisticated, incorporating automatic recording and reinforcing devices. Each time the experimental animal makes a **response** (a rat presses a lever or a pigeon pecks a disk), the response is automatically recorded, enabling researchers to determine whether the rate of responding is changing to indicate learning.

Skinner box a device that provides a controlled environment for measuring learning

operant responses behaviors freely emitted by an organism

response a discrete behavior by an organism

Learning Principles

In contrast to the one-way influence of the environment on reflexive behavior, operant behavior involves mutual responsiveness of the person (or other organism) and the environment. The person's behavior leads to a contingent change in the environment; in turn, the person's behavior changes. Thousands of hours of observation resulted in Skinner's description of the fundamental principles of this adaptive behavior. The rate of responding can be increased by reinforcement and decreased by punishment or extinction.

REINFORCEMENT: INCREASING THE RATE OF RESPONDING

Behavior that is adaptive in a given environment is strengthened. Skinner's research indicates it is the immediate short-term consequences of behavior that are influential rather than any long-term vision of the consequences of behavior. In the real world, often the immediate consequences of our behavior are different from the long-term consequences; for example, indulging in drugs brings short-term pleasure but long-term failure to achieve important life goals. Impulsive behavior can result, unless people learn to delay immediate gratification (Critchfield & Kollins, 2001). Sometimes people, of course, do consider long-term consequences, and later revision of behavioral theory suggests models for both immediate and long-term consequences as determinants of behavior (Dragoi & Staddon, 1999).

positive reinforcer an outcome stimulus that is presented contingent on a response and that has the effect of increasing the rate of responding

Reinforcement corresponds to what we would commonly label reward. (Skinner did not use the term *reward* because it had connotations, such as pleasure, that were not directly observable.) A **positive reinforcer** is "any stimulus the presentation of which strengthens the behavior upon which it is made contingent" (B. F. Skinner, 1953a, p. 185). That is, there is an increase in the rate of responding compared to the **base rate** (the rate of responding before any reinforcement). Pigeons pecked at a disk more often when the pecking was followed by food. If a reinforcer follows a behavior, the organism will repeat that behavior again and again.

base rate the rate of responding before conditioning

Some reinforcers, such as food, are innate; these are called **primary reinforcers**. Other reinforcers, such as money and praise, only become effective reinforcers after their value is learned; these learned rewards are called **secondary reinforcers**. There is no guarantee that either kind of reinforcer will be beneficial in the long run in an individual case. Some people eat lots of junk food, reinforced by its taste, but they suffer ill health in the long run. Other people, reinforced by money or praise, work themselves to an early death.

primary reinforcer a reinforcer that is not learned (i.e., innate)

secondary reinforcer a reinforcer that is learned

People do not all respond in the same way to a specific environmental consequence of their action. If a teacher praises a student for asking a question, and if the frequency of asking questions increases, praise has reinforced the response of asking questions. The same praise, however, would not be called a reinforcer if it did not increase the frequency (rate) of the behavior. (Some students may prefer that the teacher not focus attention on them.) There is nothing inherent about any consequence that makes it always a reinforcer. Only by observing the effects of a contingent stimulus outcome on the rate of behavior can we determine whether that contingent outcome is a reinforcer in a particular situation for a particular individual. Skinner's focus on studying the individual organism corresponds to the idiographic approach to personality.

For clarity, reinforcers such as these, which are added to (+) the situation as a result of the behavior, are termed *positive reinforcers,* to distinguish them from another kind of reinforcer, which increases the rate of responding by being removed from (−) the situation. To put it in terms suggested by Skinner's evolutionary metaphor, the caveman had to find food (positive reinforcer) and come in out of the cold (negative reinforcer). A **negative reinforcer** is "any stimulus the withdrawal of which strengthens behavior" (B. F. Skinner, 1953a, p. 185). For example, taking drugs to reduce unpleasant symptoms constitutes negative reinforcement, and it strengthens the drug-taking habit (e.g., Blume, 2001).

Negative reinforcement is different from punishment. Both are aversive, but they have different effects on behavior. All forms of reinforcement, positive and negative, increase the rate of responding. If your skin is burning and you touch a cool object that relieves the burning, you will continue to touch that object because of negative reinforcement (removal of the aversive burning).

negative reinforcer an outcome stimulus that ends when a response occurs; it has the effect of increasing the rate of responding

PUNISHMENT AND EXTINCTION: DECREASING THE RATE OF RESPONDING

In contrast, **punishment** reduces the rate of responding. It is an aversive stimulus that is presented following a response. In contrast to the negative reinforcement example just cited, if touching an object *produced* a burning sensation in your skin, you would stop touching it because the burning is a punishment. Examples of punishment abound because it is "the commonest technique of control in modern life" (B. F. Skinner, 1953a, p. 182). For example, parents reduce the frequency of misbehavior by their children by scolding when they observe misbehavior. Punishment is used by parents, educators, governments, and even religion, which threatens aversive consequences in the afterlife.

punishment a stimulus contingent on a response and that has the effect of decreasing the rate of responding

The immediate effect of punishment is to reduce the frequency of an operant behavior. Animals in Skinner boxes learn quickly to stop doing whatever brings a punishing electric shock. Unfortunately, punishment also has unintended adverse effects that make it a generally undesirable technique for controlling behavior. Punishment produces emotional reactions, including fear and anxiety, which remain even after the undesirable behavior has ceased. These emotions often generalize to other situations. For example, children punished for sexual exploration may experience anxiety later, even under circumstances when sexual behavior would be appropriate. Children punished for talking back to their parents may become nervous when they want to state an opinion later, even when speaking up would be desirable. Punishment is often effective in the short run in reducing behavior, but unless the controlling agent is able to stay to administer continuing punishments as a "reminder," in the long run the behavior often returns.

Skinner was critical of punishment and urged society to find more effective and humane ways of controlling behavior. One alternative is to substitute desired behaviors. By reinforcing alternative behaviors, which are incompatible with the undesired behavior, behavior can be eliminated without punishment. For example, children may be rewarded for playing cooperative games rather than punished for fighting.

Another way to reduce the frequency of a behavior is to simply stop reinforcing it. For example, a child may tease a playmate, reinforced by the playmate's signs of embarrassment. If the playmate stops reacting, eventually the child will stop teasing. This reduction of responding when reinforcement ceases is called **extinction**. Skinner's first investigation of experimental extinction began when the food-dispensing apparatus on his Skinner box accidentally jammed (B. F. Skinner, 1979, p. 95). (Serendipity can be a fortuitous teacher!) Sometimes a behavior that has undergone extinction may later return spontaneously (Rachman, 1989). Perhaps this is the organism's way of testing whether the environment has changed back to its earlier, reinforcing mode.

extinction reduction in the rate of responding when reinforcement ends

ADDITIONAL BEHAVIORAL TECHNIQUES

Behaviorists have many additional techniques available to further describe how experience can change behavior, including shaping, chaining, discrimination, and generalization training.

The techniques just considered can increase or decrease the rate of existing behavior, but what about learning new behavior? To increase the frequency of a response that has a base rate of zero in the laboratory, special procedures are necessary. After all, it is impossible to reinforce a response that does not occur. Skinner developed a method called **shaping**, which involves reinforcing successive approximations of the desired response. At first, a response that is only roughly similar to the ultimate desired response occurs. It might be a slight raising of a paw by a rat who will be taught to press a bar or a marginally courteous statement by a child who is to be taught to speak respectfully to adults. This response is reinforced, and therefore it increases in frequency, but naturally there are minor variations from one repetition to another. Gradually, the experimenter or parent reinforces only those responses that are increasingly similar to the desired behavior—the paw that is a little higher or the more civil of the child's utterances. Thus, by a method of successive approximations, a response with a base rate of zero can be made to occur more frequently.

Complex sequences of behavior can be established using operant conditioning—like teaching a rat to run up a ladder, across a board, down a slide, and then press a bar for food. If the rat has already learned to press the bar, then teaching it to go down the slide will bring it near the bar and the final bar-pressing will occur; next add the prior step, and so gradually teach the sequence from back to front. Skinner (1953a) describes **chaining** as occurring when one response of the organism produces or alters the variables that control another response. For example, effective studying may begin with entering the library. This response changes the surrounding stimuli, providing a quiet and book-filled environment that makes the next response, opening a book, more likely. Seeing the book open, in turn, stimulates reading and note taking. This chain of behavior is actually a complex series of responses, each making the next more likely. By chaining together patterns of behavior like this, people learn a variety of adaptive behaviors, including self-control (Skinner, 1953a).

The behaving organism, whether a pigeon or a person, learns to behave in ways appropriate to a changing situation through discrimination learning. If pecking, or pleading, sometimes leads to desirable outcomes and sometimes not, the organism learns to take advantage of stimuli in the environment that signal whether the behavior will pay off this time. These environmental signals are called *discriminative stimuli*. Skinner demonstrated **discrimination learning** in pigeons by reinforcing them with food when a signal light was on but not when the light was off. The pigeons learned to peck only when the discriminative stimulus (the light) was present. Such behavior is said to be under stimulus control.

Discrimination occurs frequently in human behavior. Motorists drive more slowly when they see a police car nearby than when they do not. Shoppers buy more when "sale" signs are present. Socially mature adults know when to speak and when to keep silent. Responding to discriminative stimuli is an essential aspect of adaptive behavior. Much of what other theorists describe as ego skills or coping with the environment would, from a learning theory point of view, be described as discrimination learning.

Unless careful discrimination training is undertaken, responding is not restricted to the discriminative stimuli present during training. Stimuli similar to the discriminative stimulus also produce responses. A dog trained to bark when his master says, "Speak" will probably

shaping reinforcement of successive approximations of a response to increase the frequency of a response that originally has a zero base rate

chaining operant technique for developing sequences of responses by teaching the last one, then adding the next to last, and so on, with each response producing the stimuli that control the next response

discrimination learning learning to respond differentially, depending on environmental stimuli

also bark when his master says, "Spit." This process is called *stimulus generalization* or, more simply, **generalization**. The more closely the stimulus resembles the discriminative stimulus that was present during conditioning, the more likely the behavior is to occur. It is sensible that generalization would occur. Even a stimulus that is objectively the same varies from one presentation to the next, depending on such conditions as the surrounding light, the angle from which it is seen, and so forth. Without generalization, it would be impossible for an organism to identify stimuli as the same from one presentation to another.

The concepts of stimulus discrimination and generalization help explain personality consistency and change. On the one hand, environmental stability leads to behavioral stability because similarity of situations produces generalization. On the other hand, when situations change, stimulus discrimination allows the person to recognize new contingencies of behavior. People can behave quite differently as they move back and forth among various situations (home, work, social situations, etc.). Experience in particular environments can produce either generalization of responding (as simple trait approaches imply) or context-specific behavior (as discrimination learning produces), as some more recent trait approaches (like Mischel's) describe.

generalization responding to stimuli that were not present during learning as though they were the discriminative stimuli present during learning

Schedules of Reinforcement

In adapting to the environment, the organism is exquisitely modifying its behavior in response to the frequency and timing of reinforcements. The term **schedule of reinforcement** refers to the specific contingency between a response and a reinforcement. Is every response reinforced? Are only some reinforced? If only some, which? Skinner (e.g., 1953a) explored this question in detail. In fact, his classic book (Ferster & Skinner, 1957) on schedules of reinforcement reports "on 70,000 hours of continuously recorded behavior composed of about one quarter of a billion responses" (B. F. Skinner, 1972, p. 167).

Responses that always produce reinforcement are said to be on a **continuous reinforcement (CR) schedule**. This occurs if a rat receives food every time the bar is pressed or if a customer receives a can of soda every time money is deposited in the machine. Continuous reinforcement schedules produce quick learning, provided that reinforcement follows the response immediately. However, extinction is also rapid. Strategies that have always worked in the past are quickly abandoned when they fail. How many college freshmen who had an easy time succeeding in high school have given up quickly when studying no longer brought the reward of good grades? Skinner's work suggests that a few earlier failures would produce greater persistence.

Partial reinforcement schedules occur when only some of the responses are followed by reinforcement. Although they produce slower learning, partial reinforcement schedules bring about greater resistance to extinction than CR schedules. To combine the advantages of both schedules, those who apply behavioral techniques may produce quick learning by using a continuous schedule of reinforcement and then thinning out the schedule, reinforcing fewer and fewer responses to make the behavior resistant to extinction.

Skinner described a variety of partial reinforcement schedules. **Fixed ratio (FR) schedules** reinforce according to the number of responses that have been emitted. In the FR-15 schedule, for example, the organism is reinforced after every 15th response (i.e., after response 15, after response 30, after response 45, etc.). By responding quickly, it is possible to earn more reinforcements, which is what a hungry pigeon does, pecking for

schedule of reinforcement the specific contingency between a response and a reinforcement

continuous reinforcement (CR) schedule a reinforcement schedule in which every response is reinforced

partial reinforcement schedule a reinforcement schedule in which only some responses are reinforced

fixed ratio (FR) schedule a reinforcement schedule in which a reinforcement follows every Nth response (e.g., in FR-15, every 15th response is reinforced)

food pellets. Skinner (1972, p. 134) reported that one bird responded nonstop for 2 months! Employees who are paid on a piecework basis also work at a very high rate, which makes for difficult working conditions. Rather than explaining such behavior as the result of an inner trait of persistence or an inner drive, Skinner's theory explains it in terms of the external history of reinforcements.

Under a **variable ratio (VR) schedule**, reinforcements are given according to the number of responses the organism has made, but the exact number of responses that must be made for each reinforcement varies randomly around a predetermined average. Under a VR-15 schedule, the organism will, in the long run, receive 1 reinforcement for each 15 responses. Sometimes, however, a reinforcement will follow the previous one by only 5 responses or 6 or 7; and sometimes 20 or 30 or more responses must be made between reinforcements. Like the FR schedule, a VR schedule produces a high rate of responding, although it is more resistant to extinction than is the FR schedule. We might explain this as a result of the organism's decreased awareness of the change from reinforcement to extinction, although Skinner would not have used such "mentalistic" terms.

Fixed interval (FI) schedules reinforce responses based on the passage of time. An FI-10 schedule, for example, will reinforce the organism at the end of each 10-second interval, as long as at least one response has occurred during that interval. No extra reinforcements can be obtained by responding more than once during the interval. Hence lower rates of responding occur, compared with ratio schedules. Fixed interval schedules produce a distinctive record. Few responses are made at the beginning of each interval, and response rates increase dramatically toward the end. A pigeon reinforced every 10 seconds will find other things to do during the first several seconds but pecks rapidly at the end of each interval. A college student in a class with weekly quizzes on Friday will typically study very little early in the week but will energetically cram on Thursday. This pattern, however, is not found consistently in studies of humans; some students, after all, study throughout the week, probably because of language and planning (Michael, 1984; Poppen, 1982).

A **variable interval (VI) schedule** reinforces according to time intervals that change from reinforcement to reinforcement. Sometimes reinforcements follow one another rapidly (as long as at least one response has been made in the interval). At other times, long intervals pass between reinforcements. Without a constant interval, the scalloping (slow-then-fast pattern) of the FI schedule is smoothed.

Although Skinner claimed that the behavioral principles he was investigating apply to real life, the phenomena are extraordinarily complex, even in principle. Many behaviors occur, and they are reinforced by many different schedules, which are themselves subject to change. Critics are skeptical that reinforcement principles can be applied to humans except in special highly controlled situations. To them, the assertion that everyday life can be explained in behavioral terms alone, without some higher-order theoretical concepts, seems reductionistic.

Applications of Behavioral Techniques

Skinner's theory of operant behavior has been applied widely, particularly in therapy and in education, to design strategies for increasing desired behavior and decreasing problematic behavior. For example, research on preschool children ages 4 and 5 shows that cooperative behavior is increased during play periods after the children have participated in cooperative games. After competitive games, children are more aggressive during free-play periods (Bay-Hinitz, Peterson, & Quilitch, 1994). Teachers who wish to encourage

---

variable ratio (VR) schedule a reinforcement schedule in which a reinforcement follows, on the average, every *N*th response, (e.g., in VI-15, one reinforcement is given for every 15 responses, but sometimes fewer than 15 responses occur between reinforcements and sometimes more)

fixed interval (FI) schedule a reinforcement schedule in which a reinforcement follows every *N* units of time (e.g., in FI-15, one reinforcement is given every 15 seconds if a response has occurred at least once)

variable interval (VI) schedule a reinforcement schedule in which a reinforcement follows, on the average, every *N* units of time, (e.g., in VI-15, one reinforcement is given every 15 seconds on the average if a response has occurred at least once, but sometimes the time span is under 15 seconds between reinforcements and sometimes more)

cooperation have a useful strategy. On a broader scale, behavioral techniques have been applied in several settings in an inner-city children's project in Kansas for over a quarter of a century (Greenwood et al., 1992). Many interventions were included in this project, ranging from increasing compliance with medical instructions to improving children's language usage at home to improving spelling. In keeping with Skinner's advice, current behavior analysts prefer to use positive reinforcements whenever possible. For example, Strand (2001) contrasts the fears of many parents of disruptive children that if they are too rewarding, they will spoil their children, with the evidence of scientific studies that show rewarded behavior generally persists even when reinforcements are withdrawn, and that "such [positively reinforced] behavior is likely to become more effective at generating its own rewards due to practice. This makes it self-sustaining" (p. 174).

THERAPY

Behavior therapy offers effective treatment for a variety of problems. For researchers, behavior therapy has the advantage of providing straightforward measures of therapeutic effectiveness: the increased rate of desired behavior and the decreased rate of undesired behavior.

Behavior modification is the therapeutic approach that systematically applies learning principles to change behavior. The first step is to make a **functional analysis** of the behavior to be changed by carefully identifying the stimuli and reinforcements influencing the behavior. Does the behavior occur more often in certain settings? What consequences (such as attention or a change of activity) follow the behavior? A careful observation of behavior can overcome the errors of human clinical judgment (Moran & Tai, 2001) and provide insights to problem behavior without using excessively powerful or artificial reinforcements or punishments (Mace, 1994). The specific contingencies can be rather subtle. For example, one researcher (Fisher, 2001) reports that parents of autistic and mentally retarded children who were being evaluated for self-injurious behavior were reinforcing the behavior by becoming more responsive to another of the children's behavior, namely, asking the parents for something, such as ice cream. (Such verbal requests are called "mands.") That is, the undesired self-injurious behavior was reinforced by changing the schedule of reinforcement for the child's verbal behavior. Only a careful behavioral analysis would identify such a subtle effect.

Second, intervention is planned. If the behavior occurs in some situations but not in others, it may be possible to change the behavior by controlling the situation. Desirable behavior often is strengthened by adding reinforcements, and undesirable behavior is decreased by withholding reinforcements (extinction) or, if necessary, by punishment. For example, a child who cries at bedtime might be placed on an extinction schedule. Parents are instructed not to provide attention that has been reinforcing the undesired bedtime tears. Behaviors to be increased are reinforced, either with primary reinforcements like food or secondary reinforcements like tokens (e.g., points or gold stars), which can later be exchanged for desired rewards. **Token economies**, which systematically reward behavior with tokens in a group setting, have been used to treat many populations, from children in school to psychiatric inpatients (Kazdin, 1982; O'Leary & Drabman, 1971). Despite the effectiveness of this technique, there is a danger. People may learn to work only for the tokens, losing intrinsic interest in the behavior itself and thus not behaving as desired when the tokens are removed (Levine & Fasnacht, 1974). Furthermore, maintaining a token economy requires considerable careful control, and that is not always feasible—for example when mental patients are released from a psychiatric hospital into the community (Liberman, 2000).

behavior modification the application of learning principles to therapy

functional analysis preparatory to behavior modification, careful observation to identify the stimuli and reinforcements influencing behavior

token economy setting in which reinforcement of behavior is systematically applied in a group setting through the use of tokens, which can later be exchanged for rewards or privileges

Behavior modification techniques have been applied to an astonishing range of behaviors, including oral hygiene, social skills training, weight control, classroom management and teaching, organizational management, pain control, and even creativity. Behavior modification interventions are often suitable for special populations who cannot participate in traditional psychotherapy because of their inability or refusal to talk with sufficient focus: delinquents, hyperactive children, autistic children, the retarded or developmentally disabled, patients with neurological injuries, and psychiatric patients. Behavioral therapy is an effective mode of treatment for many patients and many problems. It is particularly appropriate for clients whose verbal functioning is inadequate for traditional psychotherapy. Behavioral therapy requires less time and money than many alternative therapies, including psychoanalysis, and it provides an objective behavioral record of success, which facilitates the evaluation of treatment effectiveness (Lundin, 1969).

EDUCATION

Skinner (1954, 1984, 1989) advocated his behavioral technology to improve education. He developed and popularized a teaching machine, which presents material in small increments and provides frequent reinforcement (B. F. Skinner, 1958b, 1968). Early teaching machines were based on a crude mechanical apparatus that scrolled paper through a window that presented information and asked questions. The principle of programmed instruction, as his method was called, is much more easily implemented with computers, which can individualize the pacing of a student's work. Skinner did not intend instructional technology to replace teachers but instead to free them from having to present routine information, so they could spend more time interacting with higher level discussions with students, although the public image of his science emphasized the mechanistic aspects instead of the humane aspects of his technology (Rutherford, 2000).

Skinner recommended programmed instruction to facilitate learning and behavior modification to prevent classes from being disrupted by unruly, bored students. Many educators discipline students by using explicitly behavioral methods (Render, Padilla, & Krank, 1989). Skinner debated his ideas about education with the humanist Carl Rogers (Rogers & Skinner, 1956) and claimed that behaviorism had been the more effective approach for improving education (Evans, 1981a, pp. 24–25).

Radical Behaviorism and Personality Theory: Some Concerns

Skinner's work focused on animals. He argued that the fundamental principles of behavior are the same in rats and humans, but does his model adequately address the issues that personality theory should consider? Critics claim that Skinner's theory neglects the unique capacities of the human organism, such as language and intelligent thought. Skinner (1938, 1971) always intended his theory to apply to humans, and behaviorists have undertaken to explain even creative behavior by the operant conditioning model (Eisenberger, Armeli, & Pretz, 1998; R. Epstein, 1991; Winston & Baker, 1985). To most personality psychologists, however, such applications seem stretched. Critics also say Skinner overestimated the potential of any behavior to be learned and underestimated genetic contributions to personality, such as inherited temperament and intellect (Todd & Morris, 1992).

What about relationships among people? In theory, behavioral principles can extend to complex settings. Social relationships, from a behaviorist viewpoint, can be understood by considering the mutual reinforcements each person provides for the other (Schmitt, 1984). It seems extremely reductionistic, however, to have no more elaborate concepts than this for interpersonal relationships, which are so important to human personality.

Probably the most popular objection to Skinner's theory is that, with its emphasis on situational control, it describes people as not free (Garrett, 1985; Hillstrom, 1984). This objection is ironic because Skinner did not advocate highly controlling societies; in fact, he strongly objected to coercion and provided alternative ways of influencing behavior that are much closer to libertarian than to totalitarian politics (Dinsmoor, 1992). Societies should be designed, argued Skinner, in such a way that reinforcements cause people to behave in desirable ways, so that little coercion would be necessary. Skinner (1948) explored the question of how a culture should be designed in his utopian novel **Walden Two**, in which planned reinforcers coaxed people voluntarily to behave as good citizens. Although the community he described was fictional, it inspired actual communities designed more or less on his principles, including Los Horcones in Mexico (Holland, 1992).

> **Walden Two** the novel about Skinner's imagined utopian community based on learning principles

Language was of great interest to Skinner, who called it "verbal behavior." For 23 years, as he tells it, Skinner (1967) labored over his book *Verbal Behavior* (1957). There, and in other writings, he argued that human language and thought could be analyzed into component operant behaviors that could be understood through the principles emerging from his animal studies. Most psychologists, however, are not convinced that language and thought can be understood as operant behaviors (Chomsky, 1959; Paniagua, 1987).

Because of these serious objections, many are convinced that Skinner's theory is not a theory of personality. It focuses too much on the environment and too little on the person (Schnaitter, 1987; Zuriff, 1985). If we require that a personality theory describe the internal characteristics of the individual, clearly Skinner's theory is not a personality theory. Skinner's influence is not restricted to and not even primarily concerned with personality, yet his work poses a challenge to its fundamental assumptions. If the behavior of individuals can be fully explained as a consequence of the environment, is personality theory necessary? Richard I. Evans (1981a, p. 123) says of Skinner that "he can [not] in any sense be called a 'personality psychologist,' but . . . he represents historically the most important alternative to a personality psychology." Of particular value for personality psychology, though, Skinner always emphasized the importance of observing individuals, rather than groups, offering a truly idiographic approach.

Psychological Behaviorism: Staats

Although Skinner's theory challenged personality psychologists to pay attention to overt behavior and to its environmental determinants, the gap between his laboratory studies of animals and the concerns of personality psychologists is immense. Another behaviorist, Arthur Staats, has provided a much more detailed theory of human personality. Unlike Skinner, Staats has not simply thrown out personality concepts but has translated personality concepts into behavioral language. As with any translation, the concepts are changed or refined by the translation, which often makes them more precise.

Arthur Staats (1986, 1993, 1996) has developed a theory of **psychological behaviorism** (earlier called *paradigmatic behaviorism;* cf. Tryon, 1990) that contributes behavioral insights to an understanding of personality. He criticizes the Skinnerian radical behaviorism

> **psychological behaviorism** behavioral theory, proposed by Staats, that includes traditional personality concerns (e.g., emotion, testing) as well as behavior

tradition for neglecting issues of personality: individual differences and psychological tests. His model addresses these ideas, and, in addition, it incorporates biological influences. In fact, the framework that Staats builds is one he argues can provide a unified vision for many disparate fields within psychology (e.g., Staats, 1991). Therapy, social psychology, biological approaches, personality, developmental psychology: All fit within the psychological behaviorism he sketches, though, as Staats admits, many aspects of the framework have yet to be filled in. In his analysis, the study of personality rests on more fundamental levels that include biology, learning, social interaction, and child development. In turn, psychological measurement, abnormal psychology, and therapy draw on personality as a more fundamental level of psychological study (Staats, 1996, p. 19). The basic idea is that human personality is built up through learning. Even with the attention drawn in recent years to neuroscience, Staats maintains that the central unifying principle is not biology (cf. Wilson, 1998), but learning (Staats, 1999). This learning occurs through the principles described by Skinner and other behaviorists: reinforcement, extinction, generalization, discrimination, and so on, and including classical conditioning as well as operant conditioning. Beyond that, Staats describes human learning principles—especially the extended and incremental nature of the process—in far more detail than Skinner or other behaviorists.

BIOGRAPHY OF ARTHUR STAATS

Arthur Staats was born in New York in 1924, the youngest among four children. His Jewish mother, whose maiden name was Jennie Yollis, came from Tetiev, Russia. Her grandfather was a Talmudic scholar, devoted only to study. Her father, after his own study, became an atheist and radical thinker. When Staats was 3 months old, his father Frank died suddenly, several days after the family arrived in Los Angeles after a voyage through the Panama Canal; his mother never remarried.

ARTHUR STAATS

Through primary and secondary schools he scored very high on standardized tests but remained, by his account, a bored underachiever and a disappointment to his teachers. An otherwise happy childhood was devoted mostly to omnivorous reading and athletic play. With a family tradition of radical thought, he was exposed, especially by his sister and an uncle, to leftist progressive literature and discussions, and he began to form at a very early age a worldview and an interest in political-social-economic affairs that has continued throughout his life. Raised in a family that was very poor, atheist in a Jewish ethnic tradition, vegetarian, and politically radical, Staats always felt different. He thought differently than his peers, he read different things, he questioned ideas that others accepted, and progressively he became a radical and original thinker, in ways that permeated every aspect of his life, including his various fields of study.

After serving in the navy in World War II, Staats became a serious college student. In graduate school at the University of California at Los Angeles (UCLA), his wide interests, combined with his drive for analysis in terms of basic principles, led him to complete the requirements for a PhD in clinical psychology while taking his degree in general-experimental psychology. With his objective view of human behavior, he found valuable elements in behaviorism's science philosophy and conditioning principles. However, he saw deep and widespread weaknesses also, including behaviorism's focus on animal research, its rejection of traditional psychology, and its divisive internecine rivalry. While still in graduate school, he began a research program to extend learning principles broadly in the systematic study of human behavior, a new development. The approach he constructed was a behaviorism, but not an ordinary behaviorism. It became "psychologized" because it incorporated essential elements of psychology, but it "behaviorized" those elements, so it remained a consistent, unified approach, later called psychological behaviorism.

In 1955 he became an instructor at Arizona State University (ASU), advancing to the rank of professor in 5 years. Beginning his own human behavioral program, within a few years he also succeeded in bringing in Jack Michael, Israel Goldiamond, and Arthur Bachrach to help begin the predominant center of the time for psychological behaviorism and radical behaviorism. While conducting intensive research in selected areas, he habitually placed it conceptually in a broad framework that lay the foundations for general development; then he would move on to the next needed development. For example, at ASU he began a human-oriented behaviorism that provided a critical foundation for the fields of behavior modification, behavior therapy, behavior analysis, and behavioral assessment. By the early 1960s, when others were just beginning to use reinforcement to change human behavior, he had been using it for 10 years. He was already laying the foundations for developments into areas such as cognitive behavior therapy, behavioral assessment, personality, and personality measurement.

He had met his wife Carolyn at UCLA. When he went to ASU, she became his assistant, completed her dissertation on a study in his research program, and contributed to two chapters in his first book. When they had a daughter in 1960, he soon devised training procedures to study and produce her language-cognitive and sensory-motor development, using his psychological behaviorism principles. He states that his children—Jennifer Kelley, a child psychiatrist, and Peter, an associate professor in pain medicine at Johns Hopkins—were the first children raised systematically within behaviorism. In this and other "experimental-longitudinal" child research, Staats claims invention of the "time-out" procedure that today is a household word, as well as the token reinforcer (token economy) system that he used in training dyslexic children.

His psychological behaviorism is set in a conceptual framework that involves unification with the biological sciences, from below, and the social sciences and humanities, from above. That perspective yields a philosophy of science, called unified positivism. Within the theoretical and philosophical paradigm, Staats projects significant developments for many areas of psychology, including personality. In 1998 the Arthur W. Staats Unifying Psychology Lecture was established in the American Psychological Association as an annual event to foster such developments.

Reinforcement

Accepting behaviorism's assertion that behavior is maintained by reinforcement, Staats considered the implications of this concept for human behavior. Two of the interventions he used early on have become widespread. One of these was described earlier in this chapter: a token-reinforcer or token-economy system, in which desired behavior is reinforced with tokens that can be exchanged later for other reinforcers (O'Leary & Drabman, 1971). The other is a **time-out procedure**. Staats reasoned that a child who is misbehaving is being reinforced for that behavior. Taking the child out of the environment where the problematic behavior occurs will often remove the reinforcer, and with a "time out

time-out procedure
a procedure or environment in which no reinforcements are given in an effort to extinguish unwanted behavior

from reinforcement," the troublesome behavior is diminished or eliminated. Staats reports introducing the concept of time-out with his own daughter in 1961–1962 and describing it to colleagues, who began using time-out procedures in their research (Staats, 1971). The procedure has become commonplace in elementary schools, where undesirable behavior can be controlled without using aversive punishment. Disruptive students are placed in time-out rooms, where they will not be reinforced for misbehavior.

In contrast to Skinner's (1975) radical behaviorism, which did not specify in advance what would be reinforcing but left that to empirical analysis, Staats asserts that stimuli that elicit emotional responses have the additional function of serving as reinforcers in new learning (Staats et al., 1973; Staats, 1988). It is because a stimulus elicits an emotional response that it will serve as a reinforcer. If a positive emotional response occurs, behavior is strengthened; if a negative emotional response, behavior is weakened. The stimuli to which we respond in everyday life are more emotional than the lights and geometric shapes that often serve as discriminative stimuli in a Skinner box. In addition to reinforcing behavior, emotional responses can provide incentives that cause us to approach or, in the case of negative emotions, to avoid them. Anything we feel emotional about can either reward or punish us, as well as attract or repel us. These basic principles make our emotional responding a very central determinant of our behavior. In addition, the theoretical recognition of emotions permits behaviorism to include classical as well as operant conditioning, and thus to be a more comprehensive theory (Staats, 1988).

Basic Behavioral Repertoires

The behaviors of interest to personality psychologists are built up through extensive learning experiences, beginning early in life and continuing onward for decades. Skinner (as described earlier) suggested that many human behaviors are developed by chaining, but this theoretical statement needs to be supplemented by a detailed description of the particular behaviors that humans develop. Staats answers this need, proposing that personality consists of *behavioral repertoires,* which, like traits, vary from one person to another and lead to different behaviors (see Figure 10.2). Most important are those repertoires that are the stepping-stones for subsequent learning: **basic behavioral repertoires (BBRs)**, built up through learning from birth onward.

basic behavioral repertoires (BBRs) learned behaviors fundamental to later learning of more complex behavior, in three categories: language-cognitive, emotional-motivational, and sensory-motor

Figure 10.2 Personality as a Basic Behavioral Repertoire

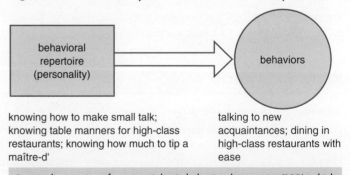

knowing how to make small talk; knowing table manners for high-class restaurants; knowing how much to tip a maître-d'

talking to new acquaintances; dining in high-class restaurants with ease

Personality consists of a person's basic behavioral repertoire (BBR), which is produced by past environmental experiences. Together with the current environment, personality influences current behavior. (Adapted from Staats, 1996, p. 177)

Staats agrees with traditional personality approaches that personality (in the form of BBRs) is a cause of behavior. By identifying some behavioral repertoires as "basic," he provides a behaviorist's version of a concept expressed by psychoanalytic and other theories: Early human learning has special importance for personality. Learning does not end with these basic behavioral repertoires; learning is "long term, cumulative, and very complex" (1996, p. 35). Typically, behavior is built up of combinations of component behaviors, including aspects from each of the three types of BBRs described here later (Riedel, Heiby, & Kopetskie, 2001). If the basics are not learned, later learning is necessarily

TABLE 10.2   Staats's Three Basic Behavioral Repertoires (BBRs)

Basic Behavioral Repertoires	*Examples of Behaviors*	*Examples of Related Personality Tests*
Language-Cognitive	Speech Reading Thinking Planning Social interaction	Intelligence tests (many items) Reading readiness tests
Emotional-Motivational	Responses to punishment and reward Emotional responses to social interactions with friends and family Sexual arousal Enjoying work and recreation Religious values Depression Anxiety Reinforcing or punishing self-talk Emotional responses to music and art Type-A behavior[a]	Interest tests (Strong Vocational Interest Blank) Values tests (Allport-Vernon-Lindzey Study of Values) Edwards Personal Preference Schedule Motivation tests Attitude tests Anxiety tests Depression tests
Sensory-Motor	Feeding Toilet training Writing Aggressive behavior Active-passive behavior Behavior judged "masculine" or "feminine" Athletic activities Social skills	Intelligence tests (some items, such as Geometric Design and Mazes) Behavioral assessments[a] Sensation-Seeking Scale[a] Expressive behavior measures[a]

(Adapted in part from Staats, 1986, 1993; Staats & Burns, 1981; and Staats & Heiby, 1985. Some items, indicated by superscript a, are the suggestions of this author.)

compromised. Fortunately, through carefully planned interventions, it is sometimes possible to teach the basics in remedial programs. For example, adolescents suffering from Down syndrome have been taught basic social skills, such as saying hello and introducing themselves, through a behavioral intervention that includes modeling and role playing (Soresi & Nota, 2000).

Staats identifies three types of BBRs: the *language-cognitive,* the *emotional-motivational,* and the *sensory-motor* (see Table 10.2). As basic behavioral repertoires, behaviors in these categories, once learned, provide the basis for later, more complicated learning. Unless a child knows the fundamentals of holding a pencil, for example, learning to write will be impossible, and performance on intelligence tests will suffer. Intervention to teach such fundamentals leads to improved scores on relevant intelligence scales (Staats & Burns, 1981). Similarly, certain emotional responses must be learned before more elaborate motivations can be formed. Whether because of a neglecting early environment or a neurological deficit, a child who does not learn basic experiences of pleasure in interpersonal situations will not develop normal social behaviors. Once we have analyzed the crucial basic behaviors, we are in a better position to deal with life tasks, such as raising children, as well as to develop appropriate interventions to change behavior, based on learning principles (cf. Staats & Eifert, 1990).

THE EMOTIONAL-MOTIVATIONAL REPERTOIRE

Each human, with a unique set of environmental conditions, learns emotional responses to a huge number of stimuli. That constitutes the individual's unique emotional-motivational BBR. Some of the emotional responses to stimuli are built into us by biology: positive emotional responses to food, negative emotional responses to painful stimuli. Other stimuli come to elicit emotional responses in us through classical conditioning (Staats, 1996, p. 40). This emphasis on classical conditioning illustrates the greater breadth of Staats's theory, compared to Skinner's. It explains, for example, how people can develop learned fears (see Figure 10.3).

The infant learns to love the parent because the parent is paired with food, warmth, caresses, play, and relief from negative stimuli. If a parent frowns when the infant feels pain, the parental frown becomes, by conditioning, a stimulus that elicits a negative emotion. Subsequently, because the child has a negative emotional response to seeing her

Figure 10.3 Classical Conditioning of One Emotional Response (Fear)

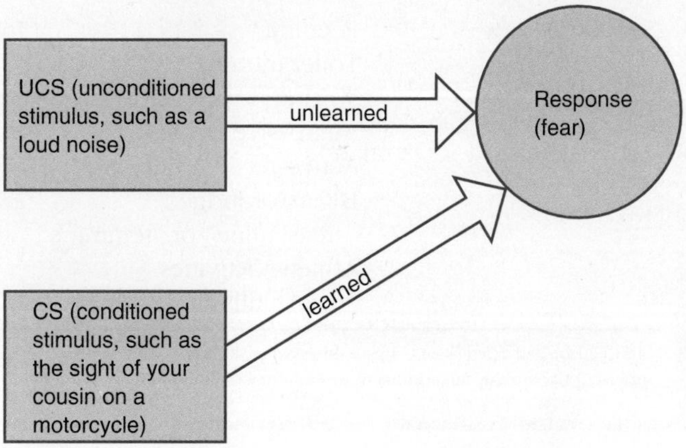

parent frown at her, that will act as a punishment for whatever she is doing. Some people go to symphony concerts because the music elicits a positive emotional response in them that reinforces their behavior of buying a ticket and driving to the concert hall. Other people go to church because the stimuli there elicit a positive emotional response in them or reduce their experience of a negative emotional response, both of which reinforce the behavior of attendance. So the individual's emotional learning, via simple or higher-order classical conditioning, produces the emotional-motivational repertoire, and that repertoire plays a very powerful role in determining the individual's behavior in almost every life situation that will be encountered.

As a result of learning, people approach pleasant stimuli and avoid unpleasant ones. The stronger the emotion, the stronger the tendency to approach or to avoid. It is the fear learned from its mother's behavior, according to Staats (1996, p. 51), that motivates a young deer to flee from the scent of a mountain lion. This is an example of higher-order conditioning; the conditioned fear, itself a product of learning, becomes a motivator that can reinforce new learning (running away). Imagine how much more important human emotions, learned from adults, must be in directing human behavior. A father's frown, because learning has made it elicit a negative emotion in the child, can now become the stimulus that teaches the child to avoid doing what makes Dad frown. Notice that fear and anxiety are not simply unpleasant remnants of past learning, but they function as stimuli to direct current behavior. Whether they will be adaptive depends on the specific learning. A wise parental guide can direct adaptive behavior through smiles and frowns. An unwise abusive parent is the source of maladaptive learned behavior, instead.

Because of different learning experiences, people develop a variety of emotions and motivations about hobbies, work, and even more biological activities, such as food and sex. Eating and sexual behaviors vary widely, supporting the importance of learning. People can even learn that "industriousness," that is, working with high effort, is a desirable behavior, so they become more generally industrious across different kinds of behavior (Eisenberger, 1992). Social circumstances and individual experience shape these potentials into diverse patterns. Emotional learning is also involved in less biological areas. Interests and values, such as those measured in some personality tests, predispose a person toward certain careers. Religion incorporates emotional learning. Positive emotions foster friendship. In contrast, social prejudice against minorities includes the learning of negative emotions against them. Cultural differences in social interaction occur; for example, Chinese people generally learn more positive emotional responses to older people than Americans do (Staats, 1996, p. 127).

The theory of paradigmatic behaviorism proposes that basic emotional-motivational responses build the foundation for more mature behavior. Early in life we learn to approach things that we enjoy or pull them toward us, as a baby grabs for a toy. We also learn to push away what is repulsive, spitting out undesired food or shoving a disliked object (or sibling!) away from us. These basic approach and avoidance behaviors form the foundation for more mature motivational-emotional processes. An experiment illustrates this (Staats & Burns, 1982). Subjects were presented with stimuli, words associated with religion and words associated with transportation. Several weeks earlier, they had taken a personality test (the Allport-Vernon-Lindzey Study of Values, described in Chapter 7), allowing the researchers to classify each subject as high-religious or low-religious in values. They were then administered a learning task that required the subjects to learn to respond differentially to words related to religion and to a nonreligious topic (transportation). Unknown to the subjects, their speed of responding was measured (and constituted the dependent variable). Some subjects were required to pull a handle toward them

Figure 10.4 Interaction of Religious Orientation and Task Demands on Performance on an Experimental Task

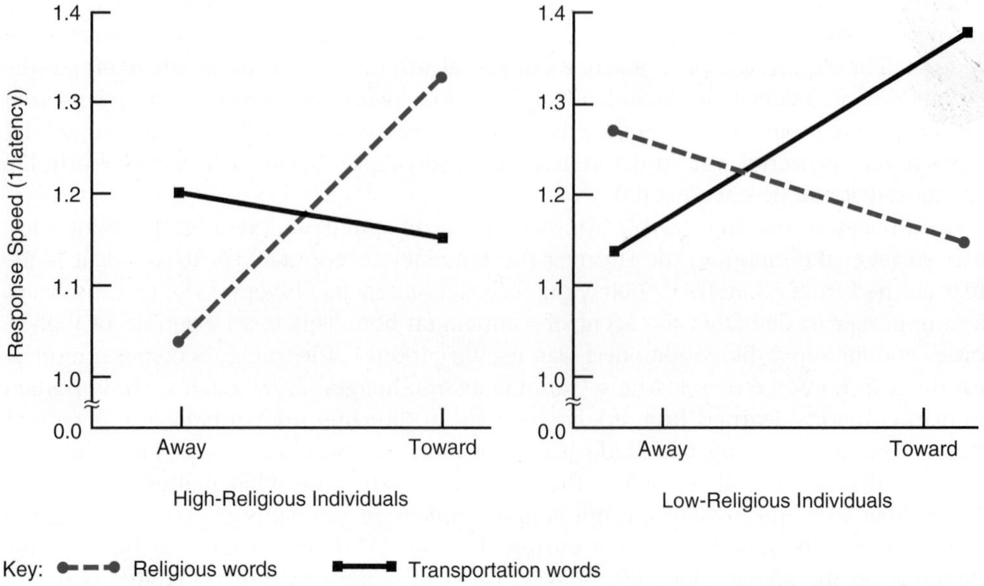

High-Religious Individuals

Low-Religious Individuals

Key: ●– –● Religious words   ■——■ Transportation words

Speed with which the religious and transportation words were approached or avoided by the high- and low-religious individuals, higher scores indicating a more rapid response.

(From A. W. Staats & G. L. Burns (1982). Emotional personality repertoire as cause of behavior: Specification of personality and interaction principles. *Journal of Personality and Social Psychology*, 43, 873–881. Copyright 1982 by the American Psychological Association. Reprinted by permission.)

when they were shown a religious word and push the handle away for a transportation word. The researchers found that highly religious subjects responded quickly on this task. For other subjects, the task was reversed: to push away when shown religious words and to pull toward when shown transportation words. Highly religious subjects were slower on this task. For subjects low on religious values, the results were reversed (see Figure 10.4). This study shows that reactions to religious values, which are part of the emotional-motivational repertoire, build on earlier, more basic behaviors in this repertoire: approach ("pull toward") and avoidance ("push away") behaviors. When the experimenters required a highly religious subject to approach what they value or a nonreligious subject to reject what they did not value, the task was easier than when the reverse was required. That is, we learn more quickly when our earlier learning, our basic behavioral repertoire, has prepared us for the new demands.

THE LANGUAGE-COGNITIVE REPERTOIRE

Language is essential to human personality, enabling us to communicate with others and to think. Normal social interaction requires us to understand and respond to what others say. A person's own thoughts and self-directed speech can also direct behavior, permitting foresight and judgments. Consider the phrases "sex is dirty and sinful," and "abortion is murder" (Staats, 1996, p. 83). These statements elicit emotions and influence behavior. Language has important emotional functions.

Language is primarily cognitive. Words conjure up images. Analysis of education and the development of intelligence suggest that children who learn to visualize objects and ideas when they hear or read words can build on these basic responses with additional learning. Those who are less able to visualize verbal concepts will have a more difficult time understanding what they read, and so they will be handicapped in various educational tasks, including reading and mathematics (e.g., word problems). Parents, by speaking to their children, and by more self-conscious educational interactions such as flashcards for letters of the alphabet, teach these language skills. Children learn to imitate the words spoken by adults, and this basic response of imitation helps children learn more complex language. Building on language for concrete objects such as cookies and cars, children can ultimately develop concepts for more abstract ideas such as God and flying saucers (Staats, 1996, p. 95).

Artists, musicians, dancers, and others in specialized areas have particular strengths in concepts related to their fields. These competencies are learned. Staats challenges the necessity of proposing innate talents to explain why one person is an accomplished musician, another a reader, and so on.

THE SENSORY-MOTOR REPERTOIRE

Using tools, performing work, combing hair, and cleaning the house are among the behaviors in our sensory-motor repertoire. These skills vary from one person to another, as a comparison of Tiger Woods on the golf course and Michael Tyson in the boxing ring makes clear. Tiger Woods learned his golf skills through extensive practice from early childhood, guided by his father: clear support for the importance of learning. Even our body movements, whether masculine or feminine, self-assured or timid, are learned motor patterns. Educators who teach the accents of foreign languages are training sensory-motor responses. In these various kinds of learning, the ability to imitate a model is an important basic response that facilitates later learning. Extensive practice is the basis for competent behavior—more important than genetic talent in producing champions, according to Staats.

Staats argues that children's early motor development is more influenced by learning, and less by innate predispositions, than most people believe. He illustrates this argument with pictures of his own children walking without support at 9 months of age, considerably earlier than most children, as a consequence of the learning opportunities provided by their behaviorist father (1996, p. 137). He also expresses the opinion that whether a child becomes right- or left-handed is largely a matter of early learning, not brain predisposition. Children also learn to be toilet trained, to avoid bed wetting, to pay attention, to swim, and a variety of other behaviors that contribute to their social adjustment.

Situations

Situations can have three different kinds of implications on behavior, according to what Staats has variously termed "three-function learning theory" or "A-R-D theory" (Riedel, Heiby, & Kopetskie, 2001; Staats, 1975). Situations can arouse affects and attitudes ("A"), as when an exam room elicits anxiety. They can provide reinforcements ("R"), as when the attention of an audience reinforces a performer who is on stage. They can direct ("D") behavior, as when a well-organized study directs a student to the next academic task.

Psychological Adjustment

Staats describes his theory as one that "specifically aims to construct theory bridges that go from the scientific to practice in a bidirectional development, . . . that . . . has been formulated with respect to the goals of unification, including that of science and practice" (1993, p. 59). To function as a well-adjusted person, much learning is needed. People who fail to learn the basics, the important components of higher learning that constitute the basic behavioral repertoire, behave in ways that are maladjusted. Conversely, full-blown maladaptive patterns build on earlier components—for example, cruelty to animals in childhood is a stepping-stone to violence toward people (C. Miller, 2001).

Deficits in the emotional-motivational repertoire lead to many psychological disorders. For example, maladaptive emotions take the form of phobias (irrational fears), depression, and anxiety. Autistic children are deficient emotionally, lacking affection for their parents. Language-cognitive repertoire behavior is deficient in mental retardation, defense mechanisms, and paranoid delusions. The sensory-motor repertoire is inadequate in people who lack social skills and work skills, people who are violent, and in some excessive self-stimulation behavior of autistic children.

Behaviors in the language-cognitive repertoire include self-statements that lead to depression and other pathologies or that affirm health. A positive self-concept, core to health in many theories, occurs when favorable self-statements become habitual. Such mood-elevating positive statements must, however, be balanced with more cautionary statements, lest a person spiral into a maladaptive manic condition (Riedel et al., 2001). A healthy person also learns reinforcing behaviors, corresponding to an effective emotional-motivational repertoire. Socially competent behavior requires appropriate learning. Our behavior functions as a stimulus to other people, so a child must learn to behave in a way that will produce desired responses in others: taking turns, sharing toys, and so on. If this happens, continued social learning with playmates occurs; if not, such learning is stifled, and a cascade of problems may result. Later, learning the behaviors of adult friendship and love, of work relationships and leadership, builds on these childhood skills.

The defense mechanisms, as described by psychoanalysts (see Chapter 2), are products of learning. The language-cognitive repertoire reflects defensive learning in those who rationalize the failures, making excuses for what they have not done. Such labels can undermine efforts to improve and are thus maladaptive (Staats, 1996, p. 170). Repression, from a behavioral viewpoint, may be understood as the avoidance of making statements (including thinking) that elicit negative emotions. Staats suggests that even some serious psychological symptoms can be understood as products of learning. A hallucination occurs when someone sees or hears something that is not present. This bizarre symptom, indicative of serious mental disturbance, can be a conditioned response to stimuli, according to a behavioral interpretation (Burns, Heiby, & Tharp, 1983; Staats, 1996).

Perfectionism has also been interpreted from a behavioral viewpoint (Slade & Owens, 1998). An unhealthy form of perfectionism may occur when a person adopts rigid rules, enforced through language directed toward oneself, that state unrealistically high standards for behavior. Sometimes parents teach such unrealistic standards. However, adaptive high standards are also possible, as when a person responds realistically to the standards of a reasonable work environment.

Whatever the specific type of psychological disorder, behavioral interventions can be targeted to modify the identified deficient behavior. Over the years, behaviorists have developed interventions for many disorders: learning deficits, self-care among retarded and psychotic children and adults, social skills in various populations, depression, anxiety, and the whole gamut of psychological disturbances. Interventions often are planned in close conjunction with behavioral assessment of the problem, which facilitates planning of the intervention and evaluating its effectiveness. This perspective provides a different understanding of some issues described in other therapies: transference, for example, which occurs because of stimulus generalization, if the therapist resembles a parent or other important person from the patient's past (Staats, 1996, p. 329). Cognitive therapy, and talk therapy generally, can have powerful effects on language-related basic behavioral repertoires. The behavioral emphasis on conditions of learning suggests the importance of prevention, through changing social conditions, which is also a focus in community psychology (Staats, 1996, p. 332).

The Nature-Nurture Question from the Perspective of Psychological Behaviorism

Sometimes we think of learning and biology as competing explanations of personality: The more important one is, the less important the other. That competition between the two explanations is often called the *nature-nurture question*. Arthur Staats (1996) criticizes this position. He reasons that biological evolution has contributed to human survival by making our species highly adaptable. That way, we can survive in a variety of different environments, by learning to behave in ways that are adaptive in each particular environment. We adapt through learning. Biology has made learning important. In addition, learning can often influence biology, changing our hormonal and even neurological processes and structures.

Staats has also considered the impact of biological factors on learning as it affects individuals. His analysis is consistent with common sense, and it provides a framework within which physiological approaches to personality may be integrated with behavioral approaches. Learning is stored in biological representations, and so biological factors can influence learning either by having an impact on the process of new learning or by influencing the biological storage of past learning. A stroke or other physical trauma can eradicate influences of past learning. Such interference can be permanent, as from a stroke, or temporary, as from the transient effects of many drugs (see Figure 10.5).

During the process of learning, biological factors may facilitate or impede certain types of learning. Staats suggests that many biologically based disorders, such as Down syndrome, affect learning. People with these biological variations may be able to learn more slowly or with different sequences of tasks and reinforcements than others. They can learn, however, if their environment provides the opportunity. By recognizing that biological differences do not directly cause the typical symptoms of these disorders but only change the circumstances of learning, the theory provides direction for effective intervention.

What about variations in intelligence among people who are not affected by Down syndrome or other known sources of low intelligence? Are such variations simply a matter of heredity (cf. Cattell, Chapter 8)? Without denying that heredity has an effect, Staats describes many ways of interacting with children that enhance their intelligence. He taught his daughter numbers by holding up one or two raisins and saying the numbers, rewarding imitation of these numbers with (naturally) the raisins (1996, p. 148). He taught letters of the alphabet using cards (p. 147). Children with preschool experiences such as these are likely to surpass their classmates in the earliest years of school, and this makes

Figure 10.5 Various Points at Which Biological Factors Influence Personality and Behavior from a Psychological Behaviorist Position

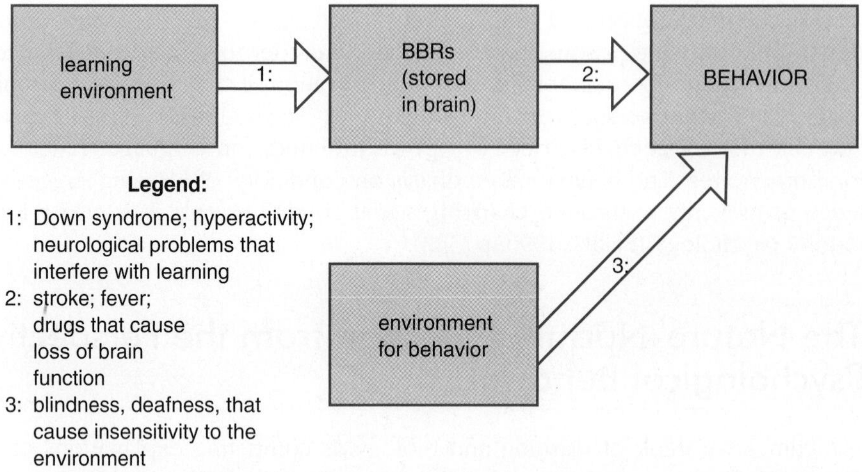
learning environment
1:
BBRs (stored in brain)
2:
BEHAVIOR
3:
environment for behavior
Legend:
1: Down syndrome; hyperactivity; neurological problems that interfere with learning
2: stroke; fever; drugs that cause loss of brain function
3: blindness, deafness, that cause insensitivity to the environment

(Adapted from Staats, 1996, p. 182.)

later lessons easier as well, compounding the advantage. Staats even argues that intelligence tests do not tap an innate ability to learn but rather the basic behavioral repertoire required for educational success—such as the effect of these preschool preparatory lessons. Systematic training of 4-year-old children from culturally deprived backgrounds resulted in improved reading, writing, and number skills and an average IQ score gain of 12 points (Staats, 1968). On a larger scale, private tutorial programs are available commercially.

As we saw in Chapter 9, whether a person is shy is thought related to a biologically based temperament. Staats challenges this view, however. He points out that parents vary in their interactions with children, and until we study more thoroughly the differences in such parenting—for example, in playful and reassuring interactions—he regards it as premature to assume that early differences in temperament must be biological and not learned. Even if partly biological, the impact of small differences in a child's sociability can be magnified by the different reactions of adults to a warm smiling infant or a hesitant shy one—and by different reactions of peers in childhood, adolescence, and beyond. Looks also matter. Observations of mothers with their newborns document the importance of a child's appearance. Cute newborns received more positive interactions from their mothers: holding them close, cooing and talking to them, checking their diapers, and so on (Langlois et al., 1995). The advantage of good looks does not end after infancy, either.

Personality Assessment from a Behavioral Perspective

In contrast to radical behaviorism, which finds personality tests to be useless, psychological behaviorism considers many personality tests to offer useful information about behavioral repertoires. Although self-report measures obviously do not provide the sort of objective behavioral assessment that an observer could produce, they do often summarize basic behavioral repertoires closely enough to have value, according to Staats

(1996). Intelligence tests assess behaviors that have been shown to predict academic success, thus necessarily measuring basic behaviors that provide a foundation for school learning (Staats, 1996, p. 211).

Behaviorism (in the more general sense—not only Staats's psychological behaviorism) has stimulated some personality theorists to develop new theoretical concepts and measurement methods. Donald Fiske (1988, p. 815) refers to behavior as "personality in action." Most personality research in the past has relied on questionnaires, which ask many questions about thoughts and feelings but very few about behavior. On Cattell's 16PF, for example, only 22% of the items ask about behavior (Buss & Craik, 1989; Werner & Pervin, 1986).

The Act Frequency Approach to Personality Measurement

Personality theorists assume that personality traits predict or cause behavior. Why not put a different angle on this relationship and use behavior to measure personality? If a person behaves in a distinctive way frequently, surely this is evidence of personality. Someone who frequently gives gifts and spends time helping others can be said to be generous. Managers may informally assess which of their workers are motivated by achievement needs and which by affiliation needs by watching to see who strives to do better than before and who chooses to work with friends rather than alone (Chusmir, 1989).

The **act frequency approach (AFA)** to personality measurement uses systematic procedures for assessing the frequency of prototypical behaviors to infer an individual's personality traits (Buss & Craik, 1980, 1983). Several steps are needed to be sure that the behaviors are relevant to the trait. First, research participants (undergraduates, typically) are asked to nominate acts that are good examples of the category under consideration. For example, they might be asked to describe an act by a friend that is typical of dominance or gregariousness. Next, a separate group of judges evaluates the nominated acts for their relevance, and their judgments are pooled. From the many acts nominated, a small number of prototypical acts are selected that have been judged characteristic of the particular trait (e.g., dominance) and not of any other. These acts then are used as the act frequency measure. Subjects are asked how often they have behaved in this way, or they rate the frequency with which someone else, such as their spouse, has behaved in this way. This produces the act frequency measure of the trait (Buss & Craik, 1985).

Researchers have used the act frequency method to assess a variety of traits, including agreeableness, aloofness, dominance, gregariousness, helplessness, quarrelsomeness, and submissiveness (Angleitner, Buss, & Demtröder, 1990; Buss & Craik, 1980; Peterson, 1993). What behaviors would you nominate as typical of each of these traits? Some differences in judgments of acts as prototypical of particular traits have been observed cross-culturally, comparing West German subjects with those in the United States. West Germans are more likely to judge acts as prototypical of agreeableness if a person helps someone else more than duty requires, for example, "She tried to help a stranger with his problems." In contrast, Americans judged behavior as agreeable if a person yielded to someone else, for example, "He left the party when his date wanted to, even though he wanted to stay" (Angleitner et al., 1990, p. 192).

Asking about behavior is more objective than asking about feelings or beliefs, but how do we know that self-reports of behavior are accurate? People, after all, sometimes overestimate the frequency with which they do desirable behaviors and underestimate their

act frequency approach measuring personality traits by assessing the frequency of prototypical behaviors

faults—especially people who are narcissistic (Gosling et al., 1998). Strict behaviorists have researchers observe behavior, which would be difficult in measuring personality (although some studies do observe behavior for brief periods of time in controlled laboratory settings). Act frequency approaches often improve on the self-report method by having friends of subjects report the subjects' behavior (e.g., Moskowitz, 1990).

The act frequency approach has contributed observability to personality assessment, but it has not gone unchallenged. Jack Block (1989) points out that it is based on retrospective self-reports and ignores the context and meaning of behavioral acts. Others object to the implicit assumption that all traits are behavioral dispositions (Vollmer, 1993). What about mental dispositions such as beliefs, desires, and abilities?

Contributions of Behaviorism to Personality Theory and Measurement

The behavioral approach has emerged from its early position of conflict with personality theory. As the act frequency approach illustrates, behaviorists have stimulated more precise operational definitions of personality concepts. Some behaviorists have even suggested that personality trait measures be included in planning behavioral treatment (Collins & Thompson, 1993). Behaviorists remind us emphatically that situations matter. They challenge the development of measurement of a person's "life space," the environment in which a particular individual functions, to better understand that person's behavior (Mayer, Carlsmith, & Chabot, 1998). If traits were redefined to be more specific to situations, they could be particularly useful (Haynes & Uchigakiuchi, 1993). People learn how to behave in particular situations, and the impact of particular stimuli and reinforcers (such as a mother's praise) may vary depending on the setting in which they are given to the individual (Wahler & Castlebury, 2002).

Psychological theory has, since early behaviorism, become decidedly more cognitive, and versions of behaviorism such as that proposed by Skinner, which exclude considering people's thoughts, are thereby less integrated with theoretical advances in the field, despite their many applications (DeGrandpre, 2000). By contrast, Staats's theory explicitly includes meanings and is thereby more comprehensive and better able to be unified with other theoretical insights in psychology. One way to understand these idiosyncratic meanings would be to study people's narratives, their telling of their life story (Wahler & Castlebury, 2002), although strict behaviorists would also want to assess behavior and environments by objective observation. Whatever the particular aspects of personality and situations that ultimately proves most helpful, theoretical analysis of personality development and change is more specific in behaviorism than in many theories. The picture is still far from complete, though. Arthur Staats acknowledges that "many of the BBRs involved in personality have not been identified yet" (1996, p. 368). For example, a child's love for the parent, important in many theories of personality, is still not measured (p. 381). The research agenda, though, has been prepared.

Summary

- B. F. Skinner proposed a *radical behavioral theory* of individual behavior in terms of environmental determinants, without referring to unobservable internal characteristics such as traits.

- He described *operant behavior* as behavior selected by the environment. This provides a mechanism for adaptation in the life of an individual, parallel to evolutionary selection that occurs over generations.

- Skinner's theory of *operant conditioning* describes the acquisition of behaviors through *reinforcement* and their elimination through *extinction* and *punishment*.

- Various *schedules of reinforcement* produce characteristic effects. Variable ratio schedules produce a high rate of responding. Fixed interval schedules produce a scalloped effect (alternating high and low rates of responding).

- New behaviors can be produced through *shaping*.

- *Discrimination learning* brings behavior under the control of environmental stimuli, and *generalization* produces similar responding in various environments.

- Skinner's model suggested interventions in the treatment of the mentally disturbed and developmentally disabled, as well as educational interventions for normal children. He argued that society could be improved by planned application of behavioral principles.

- Critics have argued that many uniquely human phenomena cannot be understood in terms of Skinner's model, which is overly reductionistic and deterministic. It is criticized for ignoring important differences between humans and other species, particularly human language capacities and the complexity of the social world.

- Arthur Staats has presented a theory of *psychological behaviorism* that fills in many of the pieces missing in Skinner's theory to make it more precise as a behavioral approach to personality.

- Staats proposes that personality consists of *basic behavioral repertoires,* learned behaviors that have broad effects on personality and are the basis of later learning.

- Three categories of such basic behaviors are the *emotional-motivational repertoire,* the *language-cognitive repertoire,* and the *sensory-motor repertoire.*

- Effective learning produces psychological adjustment, whereas inadequate learning leaves a person maladjusted.

- Instead of regarding personality as innate, psychological behaviorism describes it as learned, leaving open the possibility that innate differences may contribute to personality but only through their effect on learned behavior.

- Instead of dispensing with personality tests, psychological behaviorism accepts them as useful because they often tap basic behavioral repertoires.

Thinking about Skinner's Theory

1. If you were to apply operant conditioning principles to improve some aspect of life, what would you do? Describe the behavior(s) you would wish to change and describe the reinforcers that might achieve this goal.

2. Suppose an observer watched infants and their mothers in the strange-situation experiment. What might a behaviorist observe by paying attention to the mother as well as to the infant? How might this help understand the development of infant personality?

3. Would you recommend using an Air Crib (Figure 10.1) to care for an infant? Why or why not?

4. Have you observed any use of operant conditioning techniques in education? Describe them. If not, what uses would you propose?

Thinking about Staats's Theory

1. Of the three kinds of basic behavioral repertoires proposed by Staats, which do you think is most important for personality? Why?

2. Do you find Staats's arguments about early learning plausible, or do you think he underestimates the impact of biology (heredity, temperament)?

3. Give examples of basic behaviors that you think are not sufficiently developed in the repertoire of people whose personalities are not well adjusted. Can you suggest therapeutic interventions or changes in child-rearing practices to deal with these problems?

4. How different would you say Staats's theory is from Skinner's?

Study Questions

1. Explain what is meant by the term *radical behaviorism*. Why does this theory not consider a personality trait to be an acceptable theoretical construct? How does radical behaviorism explain individual differences?

2. What observations are appropriate data for a scientific theory of psychology, according to Skinner? How are these data different from personality test scores or transcripts of psychotherapy?

3. Summarize the basic principles of operant conditioning—that is, how do reinforcement, punishment, and extinction influence the rate of responding?

4. Explain the differences among a positive reinforcer, a negative reinforcer, and punishment.

5. Describe how shaping builds new behaviors.

6. Explain discrimination learning. Devise an example to demonstrate how this type of learning could help one cope in a particular environment.

7. Explain generalization. How might this concept explain the defense mechanism of displacement?

8. List and explain continuous reinforcement and the four partial schedules of reinforcement. What are the typical effects of each on behavior?

9. How might one schedule of reinforcement produce steady, frequent behavior and another produce inconsistent behavior?

10. Describe the implications of operant conditioning for understanding pathology and providing therapy.

11. Discuss applications of Skinner's ideas to education.

12. Explain why the differences between humans and other species make some psychologists criticize Skinner's theory as an appropriate model for personality.

13. Summarize the objections to Skinner's ideas as a theory of human personality. What are its strengths as a theory of human personality?

14. What is meant by the term *basic behavioral repertoire?*

15. Give examples of behaviors in the emotional-motivational repertoire, the language-cognitive repertoire, and the sensory-motor repertoire.

16. Using the "A-R-D" model, describe the three functions by which situations influence behavior. Give examples.

17. Describe Staats's psychological behaviorism as an approach for understanding personality adjustment in behavioral terms.

18. What are the implications of Staats's theory for the nature-nurture question?

19. Describe the act frequency approach to measuring personality.

Dollard and Miller
Psychoanalytic Learning Theory

Chapter Overview

Preview: Overview of Dollard and Miller's Theory
Four Fundamental Concepts about Learning
The Learning Process
Learning by Imitation
The Four Critical Training Periods of Childhood
Conflict
Frustration and Aggression

Language
Neurosis
Psychotherapy
Suppression
Psychoanalytic Learning Theory Reconsidered
Summary

ILLUSTRATIVE BIOGRAPHY

Eleanor Roosevelt

Eleanor Roosevelt, wife of the President Franklin Delano Roosevelt, was not only First Lady but also a politically and socially active personality in her own right. She also faced considerable frustration and conflict, and it is for this reason that her life story provides an opportunity to introduce the theory that John Dollard and Neal Miller devised, a theory that explicitly deals with conflict and frustration from a learning viewpoint.

Eleanor Roosevelt was born on October 11, 1884, the oldest child of a New York City society family. Her mother teased Eleanor repeatedly, unfortunately, about her appearance and serious expression, calling her "Grandma" and

making her feel inferior. Her childhood was disrupted by the deaths of all her family except one brother. Her mother died at age 29, when Eleanor was 8, and her father (who had been away from the family for several years, in treatment for alcoholism) when she was 9. One of her two younger brothers died of diphtheria shortly before her father's death. After her mother's death, Eleanor was raised by her grandmother.

In her teens, Eleanor spent 3 years at a boarding school in England. The formal curriculum was traditional and further developed Eleanor's already promising ability with several languages. The informal lessons were liberal and encouraged independent thinking. Eleanor was a favorite of the headmistress, Mlle. Souvestre, who inspired her not only to learn the social skills expected for her role in society but also to think intelligently about the larger world.

At 19, Eleanor Roosevelt married Franklin D. Roosevelt, a distant cousin who shared her last name. Her uncle, President Theodore Roosevelt, attended the ceremony. The couple later had four sons and a daughter. A sixth child died in the first few weeks of life. A close relationship with her mother-in-law aroused conflicting feelings of affection and resentment. Early in the marriage, her sense of self was defined primarily by her role as mother and wife. She presided over the large household, staffed by servants (for they were affluent), and supported her husband as he rose politically from assistant secretary of the navy to governor of New York, ultimately to become the thirty-second president of the United States (1933–1945).

The marriage between these two strong personalities was threatened by her husband's affair with Lucy Mercer, Eleanor's own friend and social secretary. Eleanor Roosevelt offered him a divorce. Out of concern for his political career, she thought, he refused. In her autobiography, she described this crisis as a turning point in her life. Thereafter, she involved herself in interests outside the home, writing for magazines and speaking on the radio and in lectures and, according to one biographer, finding love as well, although the details have been kept from public scrutiny (Cook, 1993). She continued these activities as First Lady and thereafter. Yet her activities were closely intertwined with those of her husband. She became a sounding board and an informal access route to the presidency during the White House years. Although she had not attended college, she spoke many languages and was acquainted with European cultures, so she could facilitate personal relationships between the president and the heads of state of several European nations. As the president's wife, she was an important partner, not simply a source of emotional support, although she did encourage him through the crippling effects of polio, which were largely kept from the public eye. In fact, her political influence seems to have diminished her capacity for purely emotional support. She would not permit her husband to rest, any more than she herself would place personal enjoyment ahead of duty. Franklin Roosevelt is said to have prayed, "O Lord, make Eleanor tired" (Lash, 1972, p. 162).

When her husband died in office, only months before the end of World War II, many expected that Eleanor Roosevelt's public life would subside. It did not. She continued her newspaper column and served as a delegate to the United Nations. There she continued her efforts to combat racism. She chaired the committee that prepared a statement on human rights, negotiating vigorously with the Russians, who objected to the emphasis on individual rights over economic issues. She won the respect of those who had questioned her appointment and

ultimately saw the adoption of a statement on human rights by the UN General Assembly, which recognized her contribution with a standing ovation. She died in 1962.

Development

Dollard and Miller's theory uses learning principles, such as reinforcement, to explain how personality develops, but they turned to Freud's psychoanalytic theory to describe the issues that are important in child development.

We may suggest some of the reinforcers that influenced Eleanor. As a child, she was raised in financial comfort but family emotional disruption. Thus the reinforcers she strived to attain were love and approval, secondary reinforcers. Because she was belittled in her family—her mother mocking her and calling her "Grandma"—she found that behaviors at school were more successful in earning these reinforcers, which led to her academic persistence and success.

A father is particularly important in a young girl's development, as Freud proposed, and Dollard and Miller accepted this idea. As a young girl, Eleanor was protected from the fact of her father's disease, and she would have developed a romanticized image of him (having been, as a child, protected from the truth of his alcoholism, and too young to understand the evidence that she witnessed firsthand). Later, Eleanor was drawn to men who, like her father, needed nurturing. This common pattern is explained by the learning principle of generalization. If little girls are, as Freud proposed, rivals with their mother for their father's love, it must have been momentous and guilt producing that Eleanor's mother died so young and with her father gone (for alcohol rehabilitation).

Undoubtedly the habits that must have been developed in childhood, of hiding her disappointment and embarrassment, gave her the ability to generalize those behaviors to a different situation later in life when her husband's publicized affair with Lucy Mercer challenged her public image. She also needed to be interpersonally skilled not to arouse criticism in her childhood family, which contributed to the development of her political finesse in adulthood. She maintained her dignity in public and earned the honor and support of the public.

Description

This theory does not present a standard catalog of traits, but some issues frequently arise from childhood experience. Some issues that are results of early training, described later in this chapter, are apathy or sociability (resulting from the feeding or oral period), conformity and guilt (resulting from cleanliness training), anxiety over sex and authority (from early sex training), and conflict between anger and anxiety (from the fourth training period).

Based on her social class, Eleanor would have been raised by governesses, without excessive warmth. In such a cold and controlling atmosphere, childhood apathy and guilt and anxiety are common. Fortunately, what is learned early can be relearned, and so the quite different atmosphere that Eleanor experienced during her boarding school years in England were transformative, making her confident, sociable, and assertive. In a learning approach such as this, we must remember that personality is not fixed, and so descriptions are subject to change, with new experience.

Adjustment

Dollard and Miller describe neurosis as a learned behavior, one in which people are miserable because they cannot get their needs met, often because they do not accurately label their experience. Dollard and Miller theorize that the symptoms described by psychoanalysts as neurosis occur when a person does not know the behavioral responses that will be effective: a condition they label the "stupidity-misery syndrome," but which we would more often refer to as learned helplessness.

Throughout her life, Eleanor Roosevelt experienced the punishing embarrassment of family scandal. Biographer Blanche Wiesen Cook tells us, "The 'Victorian' world of her father, and subsequently her young uncles and aunts, involved alcoholism, adultery, child molestation, rape, abandonment. [Eleanor] grew up with scandal, understood its nuances, and hated it" (1993, p. 15). This understanding was not complete, though. Her family did not tell her about her father's alcoholism, so she knew only what she overheard from adult conversation (Cook, 1993). So she knew there were difficult emotional issues but was taught to keep quiet and suppress her feelings. Nonetheless, she was subject to moodiness, melancholy, and childhood tantrums. Suppression does not eliminate negative emotions but only drives them from consciousness.

Eleanor Roosevelt learned early not to express her emotions openly. She was ridiculed by her mother for her serious demeanor but not encouraged to express the pleasures and pains openly that children feel. Building on these early learned patterns, "she scolded her children and grandchildren when they seemed to her emotionally self-indulgent. She once became very annoyed at a child who seemed to be crying all over the White House halls, and insisted he find a bathtub to sit in until he was through" (Cook, 1993, p. 16).

Conflict occurs when we must make behavioral choices that will have at least some negative consequences. When she learned her husband was involved in a serious extramarital affair with a close friend, Eleanor had to choose whether to remain in the marriage or leave. According to Dollard and Miller's analysis of conflict, people seek to leave situations that threaten punishment, but whether she stayed or left, there would be pain. She had many positive incentives for remaining in the marriage, including her respect for her husband and devotion to their children and their political causes, but to stay meant remaining with the betrayal. Leaving would be painful for them both, and a divorce would have compromised Franklin's political career. What to do? Dollard and Miller's analysis of avoidance gradients (explained later in this chapter) suggests that the painful aspects of a situation can be reduced by distancing from it, and that is what Mrs. Roosevelt did. Although she remained married, she literally distanced herself from the marital home by setting up her own separate house at Val-Kill cottage, which remains a tourist attraction today.

Cognition

Dollard and Miller emphasized the importance of language to label our experience. Words serve as cues for our behavior. If we label someone's criticism as an insult, for example, we may express anger; if we label it as a misunderstanding, we will likely behave more calmly. So correct labeling makes behavior more adapted.

In her childhood, Eleanor Roosevelt was unable to label much experience correctly because of family secrets. They did not tell her that her father was away for treatment of alcoholism, so to a young girl, it may have felt like an abandonment. The words that her mother offered were not helpful. Ample evidence indicates that Eleanor Roosevelt felt inferior because of her mother's negative messages about her physical appearance. Her mother was sorry that her daughter was not beautiful, as she herself had been. Her mother encouraged her to develop her intelligence and personality as a compensation for her lack of beauty. Later in life, her mother-in-law also expressed considerable criticism, returning Eleanor to the childhood feelings of self-doubt after a respite of success at boarding school.

There is considerable evidence of self-doubt in Eleanor Roosevelt's early life, subjected as she was to explicit messages from her mother about her lack of worth and from abandonment by her alcoholic father. Fortunately, her intelligence prepared her to become a favorite pupil and recipient of clear positive messages during her adolescent years as a student under Mlle. Souvestre at school in England, giving Eleanor a sense of her own worth that prepared her for monumental achievements and self-acceptance. In schoolwork and in likableness, Eleanor achieved excellence and social recognition in an atmosphere that valued her talents and intelligence.

As difficult as it must have been to know that her husband had betrayed her with sexual infidelity, and with her friend and social secretary at that, at least this experience could be correctly labeled. The public knew of the affair, and Eleanor received sympathy and support, and so she could go on with her own efforts without having the burden of denying what had happened.

Society

John Dollard, one of the two theorists who collaborated in formulating this theory, was a sociologist, and so he was tuned into the importance of social influences on personality, such as social class.

Although she came from an affluent and respected background, Eleanor was not protected from many of the serious social issues that cross class lines, including alcoholism, abuse, and sexual impropriety. Perhaps it was exposure to this pain that gave Eleanor a passion for eradicating social injustice. Although unable openly to express emotion herself or support it in individuals, Eleanor had a highly developed passion for social welfare. She worked for human rights on behalf of workers, veterans, women, children, and racial minorities. Perhaps it is because she came to grips with emotional experiences later in life, when her capacity for more systematic social thought was developed, that her emotionality took the form of social conscience and human rights activities instead of one-on-one emotional empathy.

Learning theorists like Dollard and Miller interpret the defense mechanism of displacement differently from psychoanalysts, who emphasize the expression of unconscious energy. Instead, from a learning point of view, a behavior is expressed toward a substitute stimulus. From this perspective, Eleanor Roosevelt's efforts on behalf of human rights may be interpreted as displacement from her own frustrated need to assert her own rights. At home, she had not been permitted to assert rebellious independence, instead playing the role of an obedient child. Later, as a wife, she fell under the restrictive influence of her mother-in-law, who was in charge of the household. In her maturity, though, she was a dedicated activist for social change, supporting controversial causes such as workers' rights and affiliating with communist causes, thus becoming the target of extensive investigations by the FBI. Could it be that her original drive, the desire for her own independent rights, became transformed to fuel her efforts on behalf of the oppressed among humanity?

Biology

Biology is a factor in the early experience of a child when the conditions of drive satisfaction (feeding, toileting, and early sexual explorations) set the stage for learned behaviors. Biology provides the drive, comparable to Freud's concept of libido. The theory focuses on the conditions of learning, with drive satisfaction providing the reinforcement.

As already described, the conditions of learning in Eleanor's early life set her on a more passive and restricted course, until new experience in adolescence provided an opportunity for new learning. Biology had also given her certain physical characteristics, but it was in her family that these were labeled (as not beautiful, by her mother). Words matter.

Final Thoughts

Many women, including other American first ladies, have lauded her as a role model for the grace and dignity with which she coped with her conflicts and frustrations. Moving from a restrictive childhood environment where open discussion was discouraged, to a boarding school where she was labeled in more positive terms and encouraged to take initiative, freed her to develop into a person of great stature in the world. Theorist Abraham Maslow, whose theory is described in a later chapter, gave her high praise in saying that she was self-actualized (Maslow, 1976; cf. Piechowski & Tyska, 1982).

Preview: Overview of Dollard and Miller's Theory

Dollard and Miller's theory has implications for major theoretical questions, as presented in Table 11.1. It offered a major scientific advance over psychoanalysis by translating the clinical insights of that theory into verifiable theoretical language, offering

TABLE 11.1   Preview of Dollard and Miller's Theory

Individual Differences	Individuals differ in behaviors and in conscious and unconscious processes due to learning.
Adaptation and Adjustment	Neurosis is reconceptualized as learned conflict. Learning principles suggest therapy techniques, such as discrimination learning.
Cognitive Processes	Much motivation is unconscious because of inadequate labeling. Suppression of thought can sometimes be a valuable skill.
Society	Personality development occurs in a social context. Social applications are explored, especially aggressive behavior.
Biological Influences	Biological drive satisfaction is the basis of early personality development. (Miller also did later work on biological mechanisms of motivation.)
Development	Freud's stages of early child development are reconceptualized in terms of learning theory and involve conflict. A fourth stage is added. Learning occurs throughout life, although adult development is less important than childhood development. Therapy can produce change in adulthood.

hypotheses to be tested in laboratory studies using animals. Dollard and Miller described aggression as a behavior produced by clearly defined stimulus situations (frustration or blockage in goal seeking), an idea that stimulated considerable research. Their description of neurosis as a failure to make adaptive behavioral responses made this clinical concept easier to study scientifically. The theory is comprehensive enough to include language in more detail than other behavioral theories of their time, and behavioral approaches to therapy since then have also continued this insight. Cultural conditions were also recognized by the theory. The approach has useful application to therapeutic interventions and to understanding the problem of aggression in society.

Dollard and Miller took on an ambitious challenge: to translate Freud's theory into the concepts of learning theory, which they regarded as more scientific, and then to test this new theory in the laboratory. Such an approach is based on the belief that Freud had worthwhile clinical insights but his theory was phrased in largely untestable terms. By more clearly defining his theory, and then actually manipulating the causes of behavior in an animal laboratory, Dollard and Miller hoped to refine and validate the fundamental ideas of psychoanalytic theory.

BIOGRAPHIES OF JOHN DOLLARD AND NEAL MILLER

John Dollard was born in Menasha, Wisconsin, in 1900. He did his undergraduate work at the University of Wisconsin and graduate work in sociology at the University of Chicago, where he was awarded a doctorate in 1931. He also studied psychoanalysis at the Berlin Institute.

Dollard taught anthropology at Yale University for a year, then joined the new Institute of Human Relations, which was interdisciplinary in focus. Besides anthropology, he also taught psychology and sociology and for many years was a research associate. He retired from Yale in 1969, becoming professor emeritus, until his death in 1980.

JOHN DOLLARD

Besides their joint work, Dollard and Miller had individual research interests. Dollard researched the sociological issues of race relations and social class. He also explored biographical analyses, suggesting what should be included in biographical materials to permit sound psychological studies, and he researched various topics related to sociology and culture, as well as psychoanalysis. According to Dollard (1949, p. 17) much can be predicted without knowing anything about the individual, simply from a knowledge of the culture into which the person is born. Sociological variables, such as social class, influence a person's particular learning experiences. Sarason (1989) credits John Dollard (1949, 1937/1957) for this vision. Dollard recognized the necessity of considering actual human social conditions—also frequently ignored by psychoanalysts—and not simply abstract psychological principles that could be studied in a context-impoverished laboratory setting.

NEAL MILLER

Neal E. Miller was born in Milwaukee, Wisconsin, on August 3, 1909. The family moved to Bellingham, Washington, so his father, an educational psychologist, could teach at Western Washington State College. Neal Miller received a BS degree in psychology from the University of Washington in 1931. He did graduate work at Stanford University (from which he received a master's degree in 1932) and Yale University (where he earned his PhD in 1935). At Yale, he studied learning theory from Clark Hull, whose concepts of drive reduction influenced Miller's later theorizing. Miller married Marion Edwards in 1948, and they had two children, York and Sara.

Like Dollard, Miller also studied psychoanalysis. He went to Vienna in 1936, funded by the Social Science Research Council. There, he was analyzed for 8 months by Heinz Hartmann, an eminent Freudian. He could not afford the higher fees ($20 an hour) required to be analyzed by Freud himself (Moritz, 1974). Returning to the United States, Miller joined the faculty at the Institute of Human Relations at Yale University (1936–1941), where he collaborated with Dollard and others on the books *Frustration and Aggression* (1939) and *Social Learning and Imitation* (1941). These works explored a learning theory reconceptualization of psychoanalytic insights. In 1950, they jointly published a more mature and comprehensive version of their theoretical work: *Personality and Psychotherapy: An Analysis in Terms of Learning, Thinking and Culture*. In addition, they explored anxiety among soldiers in World War II.

In 1966 Miller founded the Laboratory of Physiological Psychology at Rockefeller University in New York, where he conducted basic research on animals. He encouraged psychologists to communicate with neuroscientists because physical processes in the brain influence human problems (Miller, 1995). Miller performed extensive basic research on physiological mechanisms of motivation, using rats and other animals. In 1969 he began applying the work to humans (Moritz, 1974). This work contributed to the development of biofeedback (Miller, 1985, 1989; Miller & Dworkin, 1977) by showing that autonomic nervous system functions such as heart rate, gastric vascular responses, and blood pressure could be influenced by operant learning (e.g., Carmona, Miller, & Demierre, 1974; DiCara & Miller, 1968; Miller, 1963, 1969; Miller & Banuazizi, 1968). This concept contradicted the prevailing assumption that the autonomic nervous system involves only classical (not operant) conditioning. Although later research by Miller and others was not able to reproduce these effects reliably (Dworkin & Miller, 1986; Evans, 1976), biofeedback remains an accepted and effective treatment technique, and Miller continued his research on the learning of autonomic nervous system responses (Grasing & Miller, 1989). In 1991 the American Psychological Association (1992) presented Neal Miller with one of its most prestigious awards, the Citation for Outstanding Lifetime Contribution to Psychology. The award cited his cumulative record of research, using basic scientific methods and animal models to understand social learning, psychopathology, health, and other important topics. In his acceptance of the award, Miller (1992a) emphasized the importance of the scientific method to solve theoretical disagreements and to ameliorate social problems such as the care of the mentally ill. He died on March 23, 2002.

This chapter does not attempt to discuss all of Miller's and Dollard's work but rather focuses on the collaborative effort of the two theorists, which is the learning theory reinterpretation of psychoanalytic theory.

Four Fundamental Concepts about Learning

Dollard and Miller drew on various theories of learning, including those of Pavlov, Thorndike, Hull, and Skinner. From these theorists, they borrowed the basic principles of conditioning: stimulus, response, reward, generalization, discrimination, and extinction. Miller and Dollard (1941) summed up the primary concepts of learning theory by suggesting that "in order to learn one must want something, notice something, do something, and get something" (p. 2). These conditions correspond to the learning theory concepts of drive (want something), cue (notice something), response (do something), and reward (get something).

DRIVE: WANTING SOMETHING

Freudian theory regarded libido as the driving force behind all action, but Dollard and Miller preferred the concept of **drive**, from Hullian learning theory, to refer to the motivating force. In common language, a drive is a need, such as hunger, thirst, sleep, money, or recognition, and so on. More formally, Miller and Dollard (1941, p. 18) defined a drive as "a strong stimulus which impels action." (This behavioral language avoids the logical problems of whether we truly need something or simply believe that we do.) Drive stimuli may be of various kinds: not only external environmental stimuli but also internal physical stimuli or even thought processes. Physical needs serve as primary drives, for example, hunger, thirst, fatigue, loud noises, cold, and pain. Drives can also be learned. For example, rats who originally show no preference for a black or white experimental chamber will acquire a drive of anxiety if they are shocked in the white chamber, and they will learn to press a bar or turn a wheel to escape to the now-preferred black chamber (Miller, 1941a, 1948/1992c). Many human drives are learned, or acquired: anxiety, the need for money, the need for approval, ambition, anger, gregariousness, and so on. Different acquired needs are developed in different learning circumstances. For example, Dollard and Miller theorized that ambition is fostered more in the middle class than in the lower class.

drive what a person wants, which motivates learning

CUE: NOTICING SOMETHING

cue what a person notices, which provides a discriminative stimulus for learning

Cues are discriminative stimuli that a person notices at the time of behavior. Distinctive sights, sounds, smells, and so forth, may serve as cues. Hidden intrapsychic stimuli, such as thoughts, are also important cues. Once drives activate a person, cues "determine when he will respond, where he will respond, and which response he will make" (Miller & Dollard, 1941, p. 21). Learning consists of strengthening the cue–response connection, so that a person's tendency to respond in a particular way in the presence of certain cues or stimuli is increased. People can learn to respond to patterns of stimuli, as well as to isolated stimuli. For example, children respond differently when their mother is calling (cue$_1$) and they remember leaving their bike on the driveway (cue$_2$) than when their mother is calling (cue$_1$) and they are hungry (cue$_3$).

RESPONSE: DOING SOMETHING

response what a person does, which can be learned

Responses are aspects of a person's behavior. Any behavior that can be changed by learning can be considered a **response**. These include not only overt, readily observable behaviors, such as shouting or fainting, but also covert, or hidden, behaviors, like thinking. In any situation, some responses occur more frequently than others. For example, 2-year-old Jason, hearing it is bedtime, is more likely to cry than to go quietly to bed. A list of all the responses that may occur in a given situation, arranged in order from the highest probability to the lowest probability, is termed a **response hierarchy**. In this example, the response hierarchy might include the following responses:

response hierarchy list of all the responses a person could make in a given situation, arranged from most likely to least likely

$$R_1 \text{ (most likely)} = \text{cry}$$
$$R_2 = \text{grab teddy bear}$$
$$R_3 = \text{hide}$$
$$R_4 = \text{demand Daddy}$$
$$R_5 = \text{go quietly to bed}$$

dominant response a person's most likely response in a given situation

The most likely response in the hierarchy is called the **dominant response**. In this example, crying is the dominant response. The dominant response will occur unless circumstances prevent it. For example, the parent might threaten the child or bribe the child to prevent crying on a particular occasion. In this case, the second response in the hierarchy will occur. If it is blocked, the third response will occur, and so forth.

resultant hierarchy a response hierarchy after it has been modified by learning

With learning, responses change their positions in the hierarchy. By the time a child is 8 or 10, given successful discipline, R_5 should be the most likely response. The new hierarchy, revised by learning, is termed the **resultant hierarchy**. Not surprisingly, rewards make responses move higher in the response hierarchy, whereas punishment and extinction make responses move lower.

REWARD: GETTING SOMETHING

reward what a person gets as a result of a response in the learning sequence, which strengthens responses because of its drive-reducing effect

Dollard and Miller's concept of **reward** makes sense, given their interest in psychoanalytic theory. Unlike Skinner's theory, which did not make any a priori assumptions about what would be reinforcing, Miller and Dollard (1941) preferred the alternative assumption of Hull's learning theory: Drive reduction is reinforcing. They asserted that "reward is impossible in the absence of drive" (p. 29). This assumption provided a ready link with libido in psychoanalysis. As did other learning theorists, Dollard and Miller recognized that rewards may be either innate (primary) or learned (secondary).

The Learning Process

If drives are satisfied by the dominant response, no learning will occur. If, however, the dominant response does not bring about drive reduction, there is a **learning dilemma**: a situation in which the existing responses are not rewarded. This produces change. A new response can be learned if there is a drive and if the new response occurs and is rewarded (i.e., leads to reduction of the drive). Thus it is important to arrange the situation so the desired new response will occur. This may involve simplifying the situation (to reduce cues for competing responses), coaxing the desired response, providing models to be imitated, or any of a variety of strategies used by parents, teachers, and therapists.

Many of the learning principles that Dollard and Miller described are already familiar: punishment, extinction, generalization and discrimination, for example. Others may not be: spontaneous recovery and the gradients of reward and punishment.

Undesirable responses can be eliminated by immediate *punishment*. Then another response from the response hierarchy will occur, and if it is reinforced it will move up in the hierarchy. However, punishment may not work as intended because the person may resume the punished response when the situation changes. A child, for example, can learn to avoid teasing a sibling when the parents, who punish, are present. The absence of the parents provides a cue that indicates that no punishment will be given, so the child may learn to tease only when the parents are absent.

If the sibling did not react, there would be no joy in the teasing, and it would soon be abandoned. When a response is not rewarded, it becomes less frequent and gradually stops occurring. This is **extinction**. For well-learned responses (that have been rewarded in the past), extinction may be a very slow process. Whereas overt behaviors seem to extinguish completely, fear does not. Fear and anxiety may diminish with extinction but never be completely eliminated. This is consistent with clinical evidence of the enduring problems created by traumatic experiences.

Even after a response has extinguished, it will occasionally reoccur (**spontaneous recovery**). A child who has not cried at bedtime for many weeks may, once in a while, do so again. Learning principles do not require an explanation for the return of the extinguished response on that particular occasion. As seen in research with animals, it is simply a characteristic of extinguished responses that they do, occasionally, return. If not rewarded, these responses disappear again quickly.

Although responses have been learned in one stimulus situation, they also occur in other situations that provide cues similar to those present when learning occurred. This phenomenon is called **stimulus generalization**. For example, a child who has learned to be afraid of one dog, who bit the child, will also be afraid of other dogs—the fear generalizes to other dogs. The response (fear, in this example) will be more likely or stronger for cues that are quite similar to the cues present at learning and less likely or weaker to less similar cues. If bitten by a large dog, the child will be more afraid of other large dogs than of small dogs. Generalization contributes to other behaviors as well. The tendency to follow leaders is based on stimulus generalization; childhood tendencies to obey parents generalize so that leaders provide cues for obedience.

Discrimination means responding only to particular cues. The more a response generalizes, the less discrimination there is. If repeated learning experiences occur in which responses are rewarded only to highly specific cues, and not to other, similar ones, the learner will discriminate among these stimulus cues. For example, if only one cat in the household purrs when petted, the child will learn to pet only that one cat.

When should a reward be given? Obviously, if the cat begins purring immediately, the response of petting will be strengthened more than if the cat waits several minutes to

learning dilemma a situation in which existing responses are not rewarded, which leads to change

extinction reduction in the frequency of a nonrewarded response

spontaneous recovery return of a response that was previously extinguished

stimulus generalization occurrence of a response to a stimulus other than the one that was a cue during learning

discrimination responding only to particular cues

gradient of reward the greater strengthening of responses that are immediately followed by reward; that is, delayed reward is less effective than immediate reward

gradient of punishment the greater weakening of responses that are most closely followed by punishment; that is, delayed punishment is less effective than immediate punishment

anticipatory response tendency of responses that precede reward to occur earlier and earlier in the behavioral sequence

imitation learning by observing the actions of others

same behavior a person's behavior being the same as that of a model, considering the cues and reinforcements as well as the response

copying learning to behave in the same way as a model, but not in response to the same cues as the model, in order to be rewarded by perceived similarity to the model

purr. The concept of the **gradient of reward** states that the more closely the response is followed by reward, the more it is strengthened. Similarly, the more immediately that punishment follows misbehavior, the more effective it is in reducing the strength of the tendency to misbehave: the **gradient of punishment**.

For human beings, the capacity to think and to use language makes it possible to create greater closeness between the response and the reward or punishment, even if time has passed. By talking about a child's misbehavior before a punishment, the parent causes the child to think about the misbehavior, and this response of thinking about the behavior is thus brought to greater immediacy with the punishment. The next time the child is in a situation like the one that led to the misbehavior, he or she is less likely, because of the punishment, to think about the misdeed. This makes the punishment more effective.

Similarly, talking about a praised behavior can effectively bring it into a higher position on the gradient, strengthening laudable behaviors that a parent may not have praised at the moment of their occurrence. To make this effective, it is important to evoke as many thoughts about the act as possible. Thus a parent who simply praises a child for getting an A on a paper will be less effective than one who, before praising, talks about the studying, the place where studying occurred, the books read, the rewriting, and so forth.

Responses that precede reward are strengthened, and as they are strengthened they tend to occur earlier and earlier as the behavioral sequence is repeated. That is, they become **anticipatory responses**. This tendency of responses to become anticipatory is often adaptive; we learn to pull the hand away from a hot stove faster and faster so that eventually we do not even touch it. Behavior becomes more efficient.

Learning by Imitation

Dollard and Miller advanced learning theory by suggesting that learning can occur by **imitation**, an attempt to phrase the psychoanalytic concept of identification in terms of learning theory. Their analysis distinguished three specific processes, or varieties of identification.

SAME BEHAVIOR

For a child to emit the **same behavior** as the person being imitated, it is necessary not only for the behavior to be the same but also for the controlling cues to be the same. Miller and Dollard (1941, p. 92) cited the example of two people who take the same bus (response), each having independently read the schedule (cue). Or imagine a little boy playing basketball like his father. Is this really the "same behavior"? What appears on the surface to be the same behavior may, if analyzed, actually be controlled by different cues—it may be a case of copying or perhaps of matched dependent behavior. In both cases, the cues for the learner come from the person being imitated.

COPYING

Often what is learned by imitation is not precisely the same as what the model has learned. In **copying**, the learner is aware of the discrepancy between his or her behavior and that of the model and is trying to reduce it. Often there has been a past reward for similarity.

A young child who is trying to be like his father, talking like he talks, shooting baskets like Dad, and so on, is copying. Despite the similarity, the child's behavior is not controlled by the same cues, so it is not the "same behavior." In the case of copying, the cues come from the model's behavior, and the reinforcement is recognition of response similarity to the model. Social conformity is produced by such copying (Miller & Dollard, 1941, p. 163).

MATCHED DEPENDENT BEHAVIOR

In **matched dependent behavior**, as in copying, the learner produces a response that matches the model's response and depends on the model to provide a cue for the behavior. However, there is a different reinforcement. Miller and Dollard (1941) provided the example of an older brother (model) who runs (response) to greet his father upon hearing his father's footsteps (cue). His younger brother runs just like the model (matched response) but has not yet learned to recognize his father's footsteps as an appropriate cue for the behavior. Instead, his response is cued by seeing his brother running (dependent cue). If the younger brother is rewarded by candy from his father, this is a case of matched dependent behavior. If the reward was seeing that he is like his older brother, it would be a case of copying.

These distinctions indicate the conceptual clarity with which Dollard and Miller approached their task. Obviously, not all behaviors that we might loosely call imitation or identification stem from the same processes.

matched dependent behavior learning to make the same response as a model, in response to a cue from the model

The Four Critical Training Periods of Childhood

The development of personality in childhood can be understood in terms of these learning principles. Dollard and Miller credited Freud with pointing out the importance of childhood and its conflicts. They described the three psychosexual conflicts that Freud enunciated, translated into the language of learning theory. They also added a fourth important childhood conflict, focusing on anger. In considering these four stages, keep in mind that the learning analysis has not been tested systematically.

FEEDING

Because eating reduces the hunger drive, it is rewarding. The responses an infant has made just before being fed are therefore strengthened. The presence of the mother, who is repeatedly on hand at these times, becomes a secondary reward. The circumstances of an infant's feeding determine what responses are reinforced. A hungry child who is consistently left to cry without being fed learns not to cry for food; crying as a response is extinguished. General character traits of apathy and apprehensiveness develop. A child fed appropriately (when hungry and in a warm interpersonal context) develops love for the mother and, by generalization, a sociable personality.

CLEANLINESS TRAINING

This period, corresponding to Freud's anal stage, is a time of learning that may produce conflict between the individual and society's demands. The young child has learned to connect the internal physical cues of a full bladder and bowel with the responses of urinating and defecating. However, cleanliness training demands that these cue–response connections be weakened so that more complex behavior (going to the bathroom, undressing, and sitting on the potty) may take place. These new complex behaviors, then, provide new cues (seeing the bathroom and feeling the toilet seat on one's thighs) that must be connected with the voiding responses (Dollard & Miller, 1950, p. 137).

If this stage is rushed, excessive conformity and guilt may be learned. Additionally, the child may learn to avoid the parents in order to avoid punishment. Dollard and Miller (1950, p. 141) suggest that the anxiety and guilt of this stage correspond to the early development of what Freud called the superego. The complex learning of this stage is easier and less likely to produce anxiety and anger if toilet training is delayed until language develops sufficiently to provide mediating cues.

EARLY SEX TRAINING

Early sex training often consists of punishment for masturbation, which results in conflict; sexual impulses remain tempting but also arouse anxiety. By generalization, a child may develop a bed phobia because masturbation frequently occurs and is punished in bed. Dollard and Miller describe a child whose masturbation was discovered and punished and who subsequently tried to avoid his bed by protesting bedtime, sleeping in the hallway, and finally even putting on two pairs of pajamas to limit access to the forbidden pleasure. Dollard and Miller (1950) favor a more permissive attitude because punishment simply "sets up in the child the same sex-anxiety conflict which the adults have" (p. 142). Dollard and Miller regard their learning analysis as consistent with Freud's ideas about Oedipal rivalry and castration fear. Besides developing conflict over sexual impulses, a child at this stage may learn a fear of authority figures, generalized from experience with the punishing parents (especially the father).

ANGER-ANXIETY CONFLICTS

Dollard and Miller thought that anger-anxiety conflict was sufficiently important to add it, as a fourth critical training period, to those that correspond to Freud's first three psychosexual stages. Because childhood produces many frustrations—including those that come from childhood dependency, mental limitations, and sibling rivalry—children must learn to deal with anger. When children express their anger overtly, perhaps by hitting or throwing things, they are punished. In this way, they learn to be anxious about anger. To some extent this is a necessary and desirable result because it helps the child learn self-control. It can be overdone, however, eliminating even appropriately assertive behavior.

Anger becomes a learned drive that motivates behavior. If it is unacknowledged and unlabeled, it is likely to lead to undifferentiated responses like repression. Angry feelings can be mislabeled; a child who has been punished for angry outbursts may come to label anger as "bad feelings" rather than "angry feelings." Guilt, rather than assertion, will follow. If properly labeled, anger can provide discriminative cues for behaviors appropriate in the real world.

Conflict

Intrapsychic conflict was a key idea in psychoanalytic theory, and Dollard and Miller offered extensive learning analyses of conflict. A situation may provide cues for more than one response. If both responses can occur, there is no particular difficulty. For example, busy professionals find that eating lunch and conducting business negotiations are compatible responses. However, if a situation provides cues for two incompatible responses (i.e., responses that cannot both occur at the same time), there is conflict.

Conflicts assume many forms. We sometimes must choose between two desirable responses: Which favorite meal should we order at a restaurant? At other times the choices are unpleasant: Would you rather die by firing squad or lethal injection? Or the same situation may cue both approach and avoidance responses: Charlie Brown wants to flirt with the little redheaded girl, but his fear of rejection makes him want to run away. In all of these cases, a choice between incompatible responses must be made. Thus these are situations of **conflict**.

conflict a situation in which cues for two incompatible responses are provided

GRADIENTS OF APPROACH AND AVOIDANCE RESPONSES

The concept of gradients, reflecting the strength of the tendency to make a response depending on the distance from the goal, provided Dollard and Miller with a powerful conceptual tool for understanding conflicts, including the intrapsychic conflicts central to psychoanalytic theory. By considering the gradients for two or more possible responses to the same cue, it was possible to illustrate how people could face difficult conflicts.

Dollard and Miller (1950) postulated four basic assumptions about the **gradient of approach** and the **gradient of avoidance**:

gradient of approach the greater tendency to approach a goal, the closer one is to it

1. The tendency to approach a goal is stronger the nearer the subject is to it. This . . . [is] called the gradient of approach.
2. The tendency to avoid a feared stimulus is stronger the nearer the subject is to it. This . . . [is] called the gradient of avoidance.
3. . . . The gradient of avoidance is steeper than that of approach.
4. . . . An increase in drive raises the height of the entire gradient. (pp. 352–353)

gradient of avoidance the greater tendency to avoid a goal, the closer one is to it

These principles have been verified in animal studies in which the strength of the motivational tendency was measured by the speed with which rats ran and even the pressure with which they pulled harnesses.

FOUR TYPES OF CONFLICT

A variety of conflict situations can be analyzed by applying these principles. As a person moves nearer to or further from the goal, the strengths of the approach and avoidance tendencies change. Distance can refer literally to distance, as when a person walks to school or toward the dinner table. Distance can also be time, as when the calendar brings an event closer. Choices that seem easy at some distance from the goal can trigger conflict when they are closer. For example, Bill considers signing up for a vacation trip to an exotic location that promises great enjoyment (approach) but also a big bill (avoidance). What decision will prevail? It depends. If the approach tendency is higher, Bill will sign up. If the avoidance tendency is higher, he will not. In some cases, the choice is easy because one tendency is higher than the other throughout the gradients. In one case, positive tendencies outweigh negative ones at all points. In the other, avoidance tendencies are so great that they are always stronger than approach tendencies. In either of these two cases, no conflict is experienced. Other situations, though, produce conflict.

Approach-Avoidance Conflict

approach-avoidance conflict
conflict in which an organism simultaneously wishes to approach and to avoid the same goal

In an **approach-avoidance conflict**, a person has competing tendencies to both approach and to avoid the same goal because the same course of action will lead to both reward and punishment. Because an avoidance gradient is steeper than an approach gradient, the two may cross. In this case, the approach tendency will be higher further from the goal; when the trip is several weeks away, Bill signs up. But the avoidance tendency is higher near the goal; as the departure date nears, Bill backs out. People can behave quite inconsistently in approach-avoidance conflicts. When the gradients cross like this, anxiety is acutely felt at the crossover point, where approach and avoidance tendencies are equally strong.

Avoidance-Avoidance Conflict

avoidance-avoidance conflict
conflict in which an organism must choose between two goals, both of which it finds undesirable, but is constrained from leaving the field (abandoning the situation)

In an **avoidance-avoidance conflict**, the person must choose between two goals, both of which are undesirable. If possible, the person will avoid both. If constrained to stay in the situation, the person will become immobilized partway between the two goals, where the two avoidance gradients cross, because movement in either direction would increase anxiety. Such decisions invite postponement and procrastination.

A punitive approach to controlling the behavior of children (or employees or students or anyone) often produces such immobilizing conflict. The only way to produce a response may be to increase one of the avoidance tendencies by escalating the threat of punishment. Because this makes escape even more appealing, constraints must also be increased.

Approach-Approach Conflict

approach-approach conflict
conflict in which an organism simultaneously wishes to approach two incompatible goals

If two goals are both associated with approach tendencies, there is very little conflict (**approach-approach conflict**). At the midway point, a brief equilibrium exists, and we could describe the situation as one of minimal conflict because the opposing tendencies are in equilibrium. It is momentarily uncertain which goal will be chosen, although any movement, however minimal, toward either goal tips the balance by making that tendency stronger, drawing the person toward that goal. Because even brief thoughts serve as such a movement, choice is easy. As Dollard and Miller (1950, p. 366) put it, "Donkeys do not starve midway between two equally desirable stacks of hay."

Double Approach-Avoidance Conflict

double approach-avoidance conflict
conflict in which an organism must choose between two options, both of which have positive and negative aspects

Indecisiveness is a sign that there is an avoidance aspect to a choice. Sometimes this avoidance may be understood simply as "the need to renounce the other goal" (Dollard & Miller, 1950, p. 366). When a person must choose between two options, each of which has both desirable and undesirable aspects, the situation is called a **double approach-avoidance conflict**. The strength of each avoidance tendency increases more steeply than the approach tendency as the person comes nearer the goal. Thus, when the person is far from either goal, little conflict is experienced and the positive hopes of approach prevail. After the choice is made and the person moves toward a goal, avoidance tendencies increase. If they become strong enough, the approach and avoidance gradients cross, and the person stops, hesitantly and anxiously, no longer moving toward the goal. Because real life offers many more choices, and many more sources of approach and avoidance, it would be complicated, indeed, to graph.

Reducing Conflict

A person who stays far from situations that cue avoidance will not feel conflict. This is often impractical, however, because the same situations that cue avoidance are often essential to fulfilling our approach tendencies (i.e., satisfying our drives). An actor may be nervous about a stage performance, but avoiding the situation would preclude any applause.

If the avoidance tendency can be reduced enough so it no longer crosses the approach tendency, the person will be able to continue approaching the goal. Therapy may do this. Tranquilizing drugs may allow approach by reducing the avoidance tendency. For that matter, alcohol also has this effect; in animal studies, hungry rats who normally avoid a feeding area where they have been shocked will dare to approach it if they have been injected with alcohol, and frightened cats prefer a little alcohol in their milk (Dollard & Miller, 1950, pp. 185–186). Humans, too, turn to alcohol after failure, or if they are thinking about their disappointments (Baumeister, 1997b; Hull & Young, 1983; Hull, Young, & Jouriles, 1986). Unfortunately, some of the avoidance tendencies that alcohol numbs in drunken humans are the inhibitions that are a necessary part of adaptive social behavior (Steele & Josephs, 1990). Drugs are nonspecific, reducing avoidance tendencies generally. Thus they may have undesirable effects in other aspects of life. Psychotherapy, in contrast to drugs, can teach fear reduction that is specific to the problematic choice, although it is slower.

Frustration and Aggression

Dollard and Miller's hypothesis relating frustration and aggression is probably their most often cited idea. They acknowledged Freud's influence on this hypothesis, with his concepts of Thanatos and of the conflict between libidinal impulses and the restraining forces of civilization. Dollard and Miller, however, explained aggression as the result of frustration, that is, of failure to reach goals, rather than a death instinct.

THE FRUSTRATION-AGGRESSION HYPOTHESIS

Dollard and Miller began with the assumption that "aggression is always a consequence of frustration" and, in addition, "the existence of frustration always leads to some form of aggression" (Dollard et al., 1939, p. 1). They defined *frustration* as occurring when obstacles interfere with drive reduction. For example, it would be frustrating to be hungry and sit down to a meal, only to have the phone ring and call you away from the table. Might you be ruder toward the caller than usual? *Aggression* is defined as behavior intended to injure the person toward whom it is directed. Aggression is more likely when the blocked drive is strong, when the interference is more complete, and when the frustration is repeated.

The **frustration-aggression hypothesis**, that frustration causes aggression, has many implications for individual and social behavior. It implies, for example, that adolescent aggression is caused by the increased frustrations of that stage of life (caused, at least in part, by the increase in sexual drive). Poverty brings many frustrations, and therefore crime rates are higher in poor neighborhoods. Economic deprivations contribute to authoritarian attitudes and prejudice and aggression against minority groups in society (Doty, Peterson, & Winter, 1991; Grossarth-Maticek, Eysenck, & Vetter, 1989).

frustration-aggression hypothesis the hypothesis that frustration always leads to aggression, and aggression is always caused by frustration

The precise statement of hypotheses about aggression makes experimental verification possible. Several studies have exposed subjects to frustration and then provided an opportunity for them to express aggression. Frustration often takes the form of failure or blockage in meeting a desired goal, such as earning money in an experiment. Aggression is often operationally defined in research studies by having subjects administer electric shocks to another subject under the pretext that it is punishment being delivered in a learning experiment. By manipulating other variables, it is possible to investigate under what circumstances frustration leads to aggression and when it does not.

Modifications to the Frustration-Aggression Hypothesis

Although the simple cause-and-effect relationship was a fruitful working hypothesis to begin their research, Dollard and Miller soon revised it, and other theorists have also suggested modifications.

Learning Responses to Frustration Dollard and Miller's revised theory acknowledged that aggression is only one possible response to frustration and that its position in the response hierarchy depends on past experience (Miller, 1941b). Aggression is frequently rewarded; thus it often becomes a dominant response to frustration. However, this is a learned rather than an innate or inevitable connection. Nonaggressive responses may be learned instead, such as by taking adaptive steps to change the situation that produced the anger, for example (Tangney, Hill-Barlow, et al., 1996).

Displacement and Catharsis Under some circumstances, aggression can be displaced, that is, directed toward another target besides the source of the frustration (Miller, 1948). Experimental research has evaluated the displacement concept through a variety of manipulations—for example, insulting the research subject to see whether he acts more aggressively toward someone he later encounters. A review of this research confirms that displaced aggression occurs, especially when the target of the aggression is similar to the original person who aroused the aggressive feelings and when the aggressor and the target interacted in a negative setting (Marcus-Newhall et al., 2000). Berkowitz (1989), however, theorizes that displaced aggression does not fully reduce aggressive drives; only direct aggression against the source of the aggression does so.

Psychoanalytic theory proposes reduction of drives through catharsis. Can aggressive tendencies be reduced through competitive games? Leonard Berkowitz (1962, 1989) concluded that competition is more likely to increase aggression than to reduce it, contrary to the concept of catharsis, which is now rejected by many clinicians in favor of other ways of treating anger (cf. Lewis & Bucher, 1992).

Hostile Aggression and Instrumental Aggression Some theorists (Feshbach, 1964) have distinguished another type of aggression in addition to the *hostile aggression* described by Dollard and Miller, in which the primary goal is to injure someone. In contrast, instrumental aggression is a means toward some other goal. A mugger, for example, may injure someone in order to steal that person's money. Dollard and Miller's theory explains hostile but not *instrumental aggression* (Berkowitz, 1989). Although the distinction between these two types of aggression is widely cited, the accumulation of research on aggression has made these categories, too, inadequate for the more sophisticated questions theorists can now address, such as the way multiple motives combine to produce aggression and the way cognitive processes influence aggression (Bushman & Anderson, 2001).

Aggressive Cues   Many situational factors can influence whether aggressive behavior occurs (Berkowitz, 1983). Subjects who are exposed to aggressive cues, such as seeing guns or violent movies, behave more aggressively (Anderson, Benjamin, & Bartholow, 1998; Berkowitz & LePage, 1967; Gustafson, 1986). Other situations can have a more benign influence, decreasing aggression (Berkowitz, 1986). Mitigating circumstances can reduce aggression. Aggressive tendencies can be inhibited by social rules, fear of punishment, ego strength, and one's understanding of the situation, among other factors (Berkowitz, 1989). For example, knowing that someone who angers us has just received a bad grade on an important exam reduces aggression toward that person (Johnson & Rule, 1986).

The Role of Emotion   According to Leonard Berkowitz, frustration does not directly lead to aggression. Rather, frustration produces anger and other types of negative emotions, such as sadness, disappointment, threats to identity, depression, and physical pain. These negative emotions, in turn, produce anger (Berkowitz, 1962, 1983, 1989; Melburg & Tedeschi, 1989). Some people are more prone to anger than others; people who feel ashamed of themselves as globally not a worthwhile person are more prone to anger and to maladaptive responses. In contrast, those who feel guilty about particular behavior are more likely to cope constructively (Tangney, Wagner, et al., 1996).

Another emotion that can lead to aggression is anxiety about death. After they were made conscious of their own mortality by writing thoughts about dying when told to do so by an experimenter, subjects in one experiment behaved more aggressively toward a supposed fellow subject. Under the pretext of a study of taste preferences, they gave more of a painfully hot pepper sauce to someone who had expressed political views contrary to their own and who had also expressed a dislike for spicy foods—a behavior interpreted as aggressive by the researchers. If they were given an opportunity to express their negative opinion of the potential target of aggression beforehand, by indicating on a questionnaire that the person was unintelligent, unknowledgeable, and so on, then they were less aggressive (McGregor et al., 1998). The researchers theorize that there is a specific cause-and-effect relationship between "mortality salience" (thinking about one's own death) and defending one's worldview, which may be political liberalism-conservatism (as in the study just cited) or patriotism toward country (in Arndt et al., 1997). The more experiential our frame of mind when considering death, the more such defenses are activated. Conversely, the more rational we are, the less defensive we become (Simon et al., 1997). (It is no wonder that, in advocating military action, leaders speak emotionally.) If other ways of defending that view are unavailable, we may do so with aggression, as researchers have demonstrated in the laboratory and as history attests in the real world.

INDIVIDUAL DIFFERENCES IN AGGRESSIVE RESPONSES

Research on aggression indicates that frustration often produces aggression but some people are more likely to become aggressive than others. Many of the childhood predictors of later aggressive behavior are consistent with psychoanalytic ideas that aggression results from some failure of ego development that lets aggressive instincts get out of control. Problems with early attachment predict aggressive behavior (Lyons-Ruth, 1996). Childhood physical abuse predicts later violence (Malinosky-Rummell & Hansen, 1993). People whose self-esteem is challenged, often because it is inflated and vulnerable, are more likely to become angry and violent in response to ego threats— that is, aggression is a reaction to a narcissistic wound (Baumeister, Smart, & Boden, 1996;

Bushman & Baumeister, 1998). One kind of ego threat is a threat to masculinity, which can produce violence in relationships (Jakupcak, Lisak, & Roemer, 2002).

Dollard and Miller's experimental evidence for the frustration-aggression relationship came from animal studies, in which mice who were shocked while confined in a cage became aggressive against various targets (including other mice and dolls). Although in an abstract way these studies show that frustration (the shock) leads to aggression (attacking the target), in the human, many more options exist. Aggression is influenced by situations and by individual differences in personality. Clearly people learn how to respond to life's frustrations.

Biological influences also occur. Animal research on frustration did not end with Dollard and Miller, either. Abram Amsel (1992) suggests that the early development of the limbic system of the brain influences the way rats, and presumably also humans, respond to frustration. Biological influences, including prenatal exposure to alcohol, along with other adverse influences on brain development, can thus influence tolerance of frustration in later life.

Language

Language provides important discriminative cues for learning how to deal with various situations. Behavior that Freud understood as ego controlled is, for the most part, under the control of verbal cues. In contrast, the Freudian id and primary process describe experiences not under verbal control—for example, the visual imagery of dreams (Dollard & Miller, 1950, pp. 122–123).

The unconscious consists not only of repressed experiences but also of those that have never been verbally labeled. Many of these unlabeled experiences occurred early in development, before language skills were developed. Others simply were not given appropriate verbal labels. Often such unlabeled, and therefore unconscious, experiences are emotional, and they may be evidenced by physiological reactions that can be monitored to improve therapy (Miller, 1992b; Rendon, 1988).

People can learn through trial and error, but this is a slow process. Language permits much faster learning, which occurs through insight. Also, language-mediated learning facilitates generalization to new situations. For example, learning to apply the label "tests of character" to situations that arouse the impulses to cheat, yell, and exploit others facilitates the generalization of responses of self-control across all such situations. Self-control, once learned in one situation, does not have to be tediously relearned in each new situation. Humans can learn behaviors in socializing environments that are very different from the later situations in which these behaviors will be needed. Responses learned on the sports field, in a scout troop, and in school can be applied later in quite different situations if language connects the two.

Language also facilitates problem-solving skills through reasoning and planning. People can mentally imagine a trial-and-error process of solving a problem, thus avoiding the necessity of going through a tedious trial-and-error process in actual behavior. (A student may do this, for example, when considering where to find a quiet place to study for an exam. Would studying in the dorm work? No, too noisy. How about the library? No, too likely to see Jan and have to talk about our personal difficulties. A vacant classroom, perhaps?) Symbolic trial-and-error techniques allow for faster problem solving.

In addition, symbolic problem solving can, in effect, reverse time. Problem solvers can focus on the goal and work backward, allowing the discovery of new ways of approaching the goal. Dollard and Miller (1950, pp. 111–113) proffered the example of a driver, stuck in traffic, who is in a long line of vehicles waiting to turn left. By imagining the intersection where the turn must be made, it occurs to the driver that a right-hand turn there, from the other direction, would be easy. Aha! The problem is solved: Change lanes, go past the intersection, make a U-turn, and then come back and turn right. This creative and effective solution to the problem was made possible by symbolic processes.

Conscious, verbally cued behavior is quite different from prelanguage responses. The latter, like Freud's unconscious, are less discriminating, less future oriented, timeless, and illogical (cf. Dollard & Miller, 1950, p. 220). Learning implements Freud's recommendation "Where there was id, there shall be ego" by providing words that correctly label experience. Inaccurate and misleading language compromises effective action, whether it comes from the sort of political thought control portrayed in George Orwell's novel *1984* (Lucca & Jennings, 1993) or the marketing campaigns of advertisers.

Neurosis

Many types of maladaptive learning can produce neurotic symptoms. Fear, conflict, and repression play major roles in this process. Because repression interferes with higher mental processes, problems are not adequately solved and high drive remains undischarged. Thus neurosis can be called a *stupidity-misery syndrome*.

Many neuroses can be understood as learned ways of avoiding anxiety. Phobias develop when a fear-producing experience generalizes to produce fear in similar situations. For example, a fighter pilot, after combat, became afraid of everything connected with airplanes (Dollard & Miller, 1950, p. 158). He shunned all contact with aircraft to avoid anxiety. Compulsive behaviors are also interpreted as anxiety motivated. Compulsive handwashing may be a way of avoiding anxiety about contamination. Alcoholism can result from the anxiety-reducing physiological effect of drinking.

The concept of response hierarchies, described earlier, also helps explain neuroses. Whenever the dominant response in a situation is blocked or punished, the next response in the hierarchy is tried. This next response is often behavior from an earlier period in development, in which case the result may be called *regression*. For example, a child who has learned to behave properly may, if the parents are distracted by the demands of a new baby, fail to be reinforced for good behavior; hence the next response down in the hierarchy, having a temper outburst or wetting the bed, may occur.

Displacement is also understandable in learning terms. Behavior is directed toward a substitute target because of generalization based on similarity. For example, children seek and receive the love of their parents. When they are older, a romantic partner "just like" Mom or Dad is often chosen. Although this displacement may be the basis of a normal and happy outcome, it may also lead to maladaptive choices—for example, if the parent was alcoholic or abusive.

Psychotherapy

The problems that cause people to seek therapy are learned. "Neurotic conflicts are taught by parents and learned by children" (Dollard & Miller, 1950, p. 126). Therapeutic relearning experiences can correct them. Like all learning, psychotherapy requires drive reduction. For that reason, it helps to have a patient who is miserable at the beginning of therapy; a contented client would have little incentive to change. One of the things therapists do is to encourage patients to stay in conflictful situations rather than to avoid them. This permits extinction of fear to occur (Wachtel, 1978).

Dollard and Miller (1950) describe the therapist as using approval strategically to reward specific aspects of the patient's behavior. "The therapist . . . makes the patient work for approval" (p. 395). The therapist is also, at times, permissive, allowing the patient to express feared material without reprimand. This allows fears to undergo extinction. Both approval and permissiveness are dispensed according to learning principles to increase or decrease tendencies the patient has just been exhibiting. The timing of approval and permissive acceptance is quite important, and Dollard and Miller comment that most therapists are not disciplined enough to be maximally effective.

For the patient, the extinction of fear that occurs during therapy can open up new creativity (cf. Dollard & Miller, 1950, p. 252). By eliminating maladaptive dominant responses, the person becomes free to try a greater variety of behaviors, including new ways of thinking. Psychotherapy uses the powerful discriminations possible with language, teaching the patient more adaptive ways to label situations and inner emotional states. The statement "You seem angry" provides cues for a new set of behaviors. Repressed experiences are made available to conscious control through free association and new labeling.

Ultimately, the success of therapy must also be measured in the real world. The goal of therapy is to enable "real-world action which alone can reduce misery" (Dollard & Miller, 1950, p. 459). Dollard and Miller criticized psychologists for underestimating the impact of social conditions, including those associated with social class. Behaviors appropriate among the middle class may not be adaptive among lower-class individuals. Therapists' effectiveness is limited if they are unaware of the sociological facts of life.

Suppression

suppression willfully putting thoughts out of consciousness

The patient must learn to control thinking to act in the real world. **Suppression** is willful control of thinking, purposely putting thoughts out of consciousness. Dollard and Miller recommended that therapists pay more attention to teaching this skill. Contrary to their recommendation, however, recent research consistently shows that "suppression is not simply an ineffective tactic of mental control; it is counterproductive, helping assure the very state of mind one had hoped to avoid" (Wenzlaff & Wegner, 2000, p. 83). Although research continues, Wenzlaff and Wegner suggest that suppression may contribute to various problems, including depression, posttraumatic stress disorder, physical pain, and a compromised immune system. They suggest that other forms of controlling thought would be more effective.

Suppression is one of several patterns of coping that people use to deal with stress (Lazarus & Folkman, 1984). You might avoid thinking about an upcoming dental appointment so you can concentrate on studying, for example. People also suppress their attitudes to strive for approval of new social groups; for example, suppression of prejudice (by not laughing at jokes that demean racial or other groups) is a tactic people adopt to fit in with new groups that disapprove of that prejudice (Crandall, Eshleman, & O'Brien, 2002).

In laboratory research (Wegner et al., 1987), subjects were told to avoid thinking about a white bear. Unfortunately, that was difficult to do; thoughts of white bears intruded into their later thinking. That classic study provided the name for a self-report measure used to measure suppression, the White Bear Suppression Inventory, which is correlated with obsessive thoughts, depression, and anxiety (Wegner & Zanakos, 1994). Laboratory research indicates that people can learn to suppress unwanted thoughts. However, a rebound effect often occurs later, and the unwanted thoughts return with greater frequency (Kelly & Nauta, 1997; Wegner, Erber, & Zanakos, 1993). Rebound effects have been demonstrated for many different phenomena, including emotional stimuli, memories, stereotypes, and cravings for tobacco and alcohol (Wenzlaff & Wegner, 2000). Furthermore, people who are suffering from posttraumatic stress disorder following rape and people suffering high levels of anxiety after an automobile accident have particularly high levels of rebound after they have tried to suppress their memories for the events (Wenzlaff & Wegner, 2000). A meta-analysis of research reports that this rebound effect is generally small to moderate (Abramowitz, Tolin, & Street, 2001).

Not surprisingly, suppression of personal emotional issues is more difficult than suppression of mundane events (Wenzlaff & Wegner, 2000). It seems plausible that thoughts that simply won't go away may symbolize something that we should pay attention to. Undoubtedly, this is sometimes the case, but even trivial, arbitrarily assigned ideas in laboratory studies show this failure of suppression. Thus it is the process of suppression, not the content of the ideas, that makes them intrusive (Wenzlaff & Wegner, 2000). The rebound effect can be reduced by changing the context or the person's mood, which has potential implications for therapy (Wegner et al., 1991; Wenzlaff, Wegner, & Klein, 1991). Experimentation also shows that allowing previously suppressed thoughts to be expressed prevents the rebound effect on subsequent testing, as though a motivation to express the suppressed material had been satisfied (Liberman & Förster, 2000).

In one study, introductory psychology students were instructed to suppress their overt displays of emotional responses to a disgusting film (portraying an arm amputation or treatment of a burn victim) so an observer would not know their feelings. Subjects reacted physiologically, with increased sympathetic nervous system arousal (Gross & Levenson, 1993). Research with other films indicates that suppressing amusement, as well as sadness, also increases sympathetic nervous system activity (Gross & Levenson, 1997). Thought is also impaired. When subjects watched films of people who had been accidentally injured, under instructions to suppress their emotion, they do not remember the details of the film as well. However, if they are instructed to think about the emotional material differently (e.g., taking on the detached perspective of a medical professional), using a coping technique called "cognitive reappraisal," their memory is not impaired (Richards & Gross, 2000).

Suppressed emotion contributes to the risk of various diseases including hypertension, cancer, and impaired immune system functioning, whereas expressing emotions through writing has positive health benefits (Contrada, Cather, & O'Leary, 1999; Giese-Davis & Spiegel, 2001; Pennebaker, 1993; Petrie, Booth, & Pennebaker, 1998; Smyth, 1998). Researchers have demonstrated the beneficial effects of writing about personal topics. Such writing helps some people, especially those who have difficulty expressing emotions, to avoid depression when dealing with the death of a loved one (Stroebe, Schut, & Stroebe, 2006). Writing about their anxiety and other feelings about upcoming exams required for admission to graduate school, even though for less than half an hour, reduced students' level of depression during the days before the exam (Lepore, 1997). James Pennebaker and his colleagues found that first-year college students who wrote about personal thoughts and feelings had better health during subsequent months than those who wrote about less personally relevant topics (Pennebaker, Colder, & Sharp, 1990). In a psychiatric prison population, those suffering pain who participated in an intervention of writing about their traumatic experiences had fewer medical visits afterward, suggesting a therapeutic effect of confronting emotion (Richards et al., 2000). Writing about emotional experiences improves immune functioning, whereas suppressing thoughts leads to unhealthy changes in the immune system (Petrie et al., 1998). However, beneficial effects do not always occur. If the writing explores events that are too traumatic, opening them up without therapeutic support can backfire, leading to more visits to the health service instead of fewer (Honos-Webb et al., 2000). Researchers, naturally, are investigating the mechanisms by which the cognitive processes of suppression and of emotional expression are related to the physical condition of the body. Besides the sympathetic nervous system with its implications for immune system functioning, the opiate system, which has effects on pain or its control, may be involved (Jamner & Leigh, 1999). Suppression can influence our social perception, too. If we suppress thinking about people in stereotyped ways, the stereotyped images are nonetheless activated below the level of consciousness, and they are ready to spring into action to influence our subsequent perception (Wyer & Radvansky, 1999).

Psychoanalytic Learning Theory Reconsidered

Dollard and Miller argued that personality conflicts are learned, and they provided an analysis in terms of drives and conflicts, but drive theories within psychology fell out of favor, which blunted later researchers' interest in their model. Perhaps the marriage of psychoanalysis and learning theory that they attempted was premature. Modern research on emotion and the body and cognition have been influenced, probably without sufficient recognition, by psychoanalytic theory and the sorts of scientific analysis of that theory that Dollard and Miller, and others, proposed (cf. Bucci, 2000). Now, however, the biological understandings of learning have progressed considerably, and an exciting new approach is emerging: a neuroscience learning approach. The exciting possibilities for personality are moving in the direction that Neal Miller, who continued his research on physiological effects of experience, and John Dollard, who insisted on also considering culture, set forth decades ago.

Summary

- Dollard and Miller proposed a learning theory that could explain the clinical phenomena observed by psychoanalysts.
- Four learning concepts are fundamental: *drive, cue, response,* and *reward.*
- At any given time, various responses are possible in a given stimulus situation. These can be arranged in order of probability, with the *dominant response* at the top of this *response hierarchy.* Learning occurs when the response hierarchy is changed.
- Both primary (innate) and secondary (learned) rewards can produce learning.
- Learning only occurs if the dominant response does not produce drive reduction, a situation termed a *learning dilemma.*
- Behaviors are increased in frequency by reward and reduced in frequency by extinction and punishment.
- Behaviors that have been eliminated can return without being again rewarded, a phenomenon called *spontaneous recovery.*
- Reward and punishment have their greatest effects on behavior near the goal, producing *approach and avoidance tendencies.* The avoidance gradient is steeper than the approach gradient.

- Dollard and Miller reinterpreted several psychoanalytic concepts in terms of their learning theory. *Identification* was reinterpreted in terms of imitation. Freud's first three psychosexual stages were reinterpreted as learning concerned with *feeding, cleanliness training*, and *early sex training*. A fourth stage, concerned with *anger-anxiety conflicts*, was added.

- Intrapsychic conflict was reinterpreted as conflict among *incompatible responses*. Various types of *conflict* were identified: *approach-approach, approach-avoidance, avoidance-avoidance*, and *double approach-avoidance*.

- Their *frustration-aggression hypothesis*, which has been revised to include learning, emotion, and other variables, described the cause of aggressive behavior.

- Language is an important species-specific human behavior that offers cues for behavior and permits a learning theory interpretation of levels of consciousness.

- Various defense mechanisms can be understood from a learning perspective (e.g., displacement as a consequence of generalization).

- Psychotherapy should take into account principles of learning theory by understanding and modifying the cues that produce various responses and by teaching new behaviors.

- Dollard and Miller's discussion of *suppression* has been followed by research that demonstrates its adverse effects.

Thinking about Dollard and Miller's Theory

1. Using the concept of response hierarchy and resultant hierarchy, analyze the learning that occurs when a student decides, after doing poorly on the first exam, to study alone in the library instead of with friends.

2. Two friends dress very similarly. How would you be able to tell whether this is a case of same behavior, copying, or matched dependent behavior?

3. Do you agree with the advice Dollard and Miller give for raising children in each of the four critical training periods of childhood? Why or why not?

4. Using the concepts of gradient of approach and gradient of avoidance, analyze the conflict experienced by an adult who is ambivalent about visiting his or her childhood home.

5. Based on the concept of frustration, discuss why people might become more annoyed to receive telephone solicitations at dinnertime than at other times. What might be the effect on their behavior?

6. Give an example of a person attempting to use suppression to control thought or emotion. Do you think this would be effective?

Study Questions

1. Describe the relationship between Dollard and Miller's theory and psychoanalysis.

2. List and explain the four fundamental concepts about learning.

3. Explain what is meant by response hierarchy. Give an example.

4. Explain the difference between a primary reward and a secondary reward.

5. What is a learning dilemma? Give an example.

6. Discuss how behaviors may be eliminated by using the techniques of punishment and extinction.

7. Explain what is meant by spontaneous recovery. Give an example.

8. Explain what is meant by the gradient of reward and the gradient of punishment.

9. Discuss Dollard and Miller's analysis of imitation as a learning model for identification. Explain the differences among same behavior, copying, and matched dependent learning.

10. List the four critical training periods of childhood. Explain what is learned in each stage.

11. What differences would be expected between children raised with scheduled feeding and those raised with feeding on demand?

12. What additional stage of childhood did Dollard and Miller add to the three psychosexual stages proposed by Freud?

13. Describe various types of conflict: approach-avoidance, approach-approach, avoidance-avoidance, and double approach-avoidance. Compare the ease or difficulty with which each is resolved.

14. Explain the effects of anxiety-reducing drugs on conflict. Compare and contrast this effect with those of psychotherapy.

15. What is predicted in Dollard and Miller's frustration-aggression hypothesis? Give an example of aggression that is predicted by this model.

16. Explain the role of emotion in predicting the relationship between frustration and aggression, according to Berkowitz's hypothesis.

17. What role does language play in Dollard and Miller's model of personality development and neurosis?

18. Explain why neurosis is called the "stupidity-misery syndrome."

19. What suggestions do Dollard and Miller offer for psychotherapy?

20. What is Dollard and Miller's attitude about suppression? What does research show about the effects of suppression?

The Cognitive Social Learning Perspective

The cognitive social learning perspective expands on themes in Dollard and Miller's theory: the importance of language and the social environment. According to this learning perspective, to describe people's overt behaviors without paying attention to what they are thinking cannot provide an adequate model of personality. To study only the physiological aspects of emotion, for example, without considering what people are thinking when they are frightened, angry, or otherwise emotionally aroused cannot lead to a full understanding of human personality (Staats & Eifert, 1990).

Cognitive psychology studies mental processes and their effects on behavior. Sometimes those who describe the history of our discipline describe the "cognitive challenge" posed to traditional behaviorism. Zettle (1990) summarizes the cognitive challenge as "the proposition that cognitive psychology, with its appeal to mental processes, offers a more complete and adequate account of human behavior than that provided by behavior analysis" (p. 41). Many behaviorists have responded to this challenge by including cognitive aspects within learning theory.

Theorists in the cognitive behavioral perspective share some important assumptions with the behaviorists considered in Part IV. They maintain that personality is formed through interaction with the environment, and they agree that behavior, to a large extent, is environmentally determined and situation specific. In addition, the cognitive behavioral perspective has distinctive emphases:

1. These theorists include much more elaborate descriptions of mental processes than the theorists discussed in Part IV.
2. These theorists assume that people differ from one another in the ways they think about themselves and the people around them and that these cognitions are key variables in understanding personality differences. These theorists attempt to measure cognitions in a systematic way.
3. These theorists assert that cognitive change is the key to personality change.

Besides their purely theoretical interest, cognitive approaches have led to new strategies of therapy (e.g., Försterling, 1985) and different research methods used to study therapy (O'Donohue & Houts, 1985). Behavioral approaches employ primarily single-subject research designs and thus are idiographic. Cognitive approaches use primarily group designs and thus are nomothetic. Yet this latter approach avoids global traitlike constructs. Instead, recognizing that situations have important influences, questions are specific to situations or domains of behavior and thought (Bandura, 1989a). In addition, theorists in this perspective emphasize modeling as a planned method of influencing behavior (Decker & Nathan, 1985).

This perspective offers enhanced potential for understanding uniquely human experiences because higher cognitive processes cannot be studied in the animal models so central to earlier behaviorism. The cognitive social learning perspective is one of the most active areas of theory and research in current personality theory.

Study Questions

1. What are the fundamental assumptions of the cognitive social learning perspective?
2. Contrast cognitive social learning with traditional behaviorists (in the tradition of B. F. Skinner).

Mischel and Bandura
Cognitive Social Learning Theory

Chapter Overview

Preview: Overview of Mischel's and Bandura's Theories

Traits in Cognitive Social Learning Theory: Mischel

The Trait Controversy: Mischel's Challenge

Cognitive Person Variables

Delay of Gratification

Performance in Cognitive Social Learning Theory: Bandura

Reciprocal Determinism

Self-Regulation of Behavior: The Self-System

Self-Efficacy

Processes Influencing Learning

Observational Learning and Modeling

Therapy

The Person in the Social Environment

Summary

ILLUSTRATIVE BIOGRAPHY

Frida Kahlo

The cognitive social learning perspective, exemplified in this chapter by Albert Bandura and Walter Mischel, focuses on the cognitions that people have learned in their life experience. These cognitions, which may be quite nuanced in taking aspects of the environment into account, determine life choices and striving (or, for others, giving up). One woman whose life could have taken many directions but whose cognitions propelled her to an original and creative artistic life, is Mexican painter Frida Kahlo.

Frida Kahlo was born on July 6, 1907, in an old residential area on the outskirts of Mexico City. Her childhood was a time of war. The Mexican Revolution broke out in 1910 when Frida was only 3 years old, and guerrilla armies led by Pascual Orozco, Pancho Villa, and Emiliano Zapata began an uprising that continued for a decade, finally leading to the inauguration of revolutionary president Alvaro Obregón.

When Frida was 6, she contracted the crippling disease polio, and her right leg remained very weak for the rest of her life. Self-conscious of the deformity, she wore layers of socks and later long skirts to hide it. On the advice of doctors, she remained physically active. When Frida was 18 years old, an accident further damaged her body and changed her life. Riding in a bus home from school in Mexico City, a collision with a streetcar impaled her on a metal bar, fracturing her spine, crushing her pelvis, and breaking one foot. During her forced bed rest, she began to paint to relieve the boredom. For the rest of her life, she endured at least 32 surgeries, pain, and fear of infection. The accident left her unable to carry children to term successfully.

Frida left her small village in 1922 to attend the National Preparatory School in Mexico City, where she was offered an excellent education and the companionship of Mexico's intellectual elite. She was not intimidated, but actively participated, was somewhat of a prankster, and fell passionately in love with an artist commissioned to paint murals in the auditorium. She and Diego Rivera, more than 20 years older than Frida, later married (1929) and became internationally

Frida Kahlo (1907–1954), "Self Portrait with Monkey", 1938. Oil on Masonite, overall: 16" × 12" (40.64 × 30.48 cm). ©Banco de Mexico Diego Rivera & Frida Kahlo Museums Trust. Av. Cinco de Mayo No. 2, Col. Centro, Del. Cuauhtemoc 06059, Mexico, D.F. Reproduction authorized by the Instituto Nacional de Bellas Artes and Literature. Courtesy of Albright-Knox Art Gallery, Buffalo, New York, Bequest of A. Conger Goodyear, 1966.

bed at age 47, writing in her diary, "I hope the leaving is joyful and I hope never to return."

Development

Personality develops by learning. We learn behaviors, and we learn what to expect when we behave in particular ways. One important source of learning, in Bandura's theory, is by observing models of behavior. We also learn because of other people's reactions to our behavior.

Obviously Frida Kahlo learned the technical craft of her painting, but she also learned what themes to paint. For Frida Kahlo, her father was an important model. She was his favorite child, and they were bonded not only by temperament but by physical problems (he was epileptic). Her father was a photographer, and from his pictures she saw images of Mexican indigenous culture, undoubtedly inspiring her own great interest, which influenced her painting and also her choice of clothing. The long skirts also hid her legs, helping avoid embarrassment from her physical deformity. Her interest in self-portraiture likely stems from the many months of bedrest, when she could see little except her own reflection in a mirror that was hung over her bed. Whatever the origins of her nonconformist and extraverted social behavior, perhaps in part from the civil unrest that prevails during a revolution, her lively pranks earned attention, reinforcing her for nonconformity.

Description

Instead of listing traits, Bandura and Mischel describe the cognitive constructs of a person, using detailed categories that are further explained in this chapter. These include beliefs about what he or she is capable of doing and expectations about what would be reinforcing.

Despite her physical suffering, Frida did not take on the role of a victim. Quite the contrary; behaviorally, she was assertive to the point of being abrasive. This strength derived in part from a feeling of connection with strong Mexican peasants and a rejection of the European-based influence. The personal construct she had of nurturance is beautifully portrayed in her 1949 pointing, *The Love Embrace of the Universe, the Earth (Mexico), Diego, Me and Señor Xolotl*. While she is being embraced by the Mexican earth mother, she in turn is embracing her husband, who seems more like an adult child. If a person does not think of herself as a victim, she is not, whatever misfortune has come to her.

Mischel's theory describes behaviors as situationally variable because of the different constructs that people apply in

known as an artist couple. Frida painted colorful and symbolic images of herself and her family. Many self-portraits portrayed her physical deformities (crippled leg, injured spine) and contained symbols, including images of herself as a fetus in her mother's body and as a cactus flower being pollinated by the wind. She also painted cultural themes of native and colonial people in Mexico.

Frida's artistic fame was second to that of her husband, whose career took him to the United States, where he was commissioned to paint murals for Henry Ford and others. And their physical appearance, petite Frida and immense Diego, conveys this discrepancy—except that Frida's behavior was outgoing and often outrageous, enlarging her in a metaphorical sense. She also wore unusual clothes for her circle: traditional Mexican long colorful dresses.

Her one art exhibition in Mexico came in 1953. In ill health, she was brought by ambulance on a stretcher to the gallery. Her typical good humor kept her joking and drinking with the crowd, who loved Frida and her art. Soon her health declined even further. Her right leg was amputated because of infection, and she became depressed. She died at home in

various situations. Frida's affectionate behavior toward close friends and audiences, contrasted with her abrasive incivility toward those she construed as overly ambitious and shallow, illustrates this situational specificity.

Cognition

As mentioned earlier, cognition is the central focus in these theories. A person's *competencies* describe what he or she is able to do. Mischel and Bandura use the term *self-efficacy* to refer to a person's confidence in being able to do something, asserting that without self-efficacy in a particular domain of behavior, performance will be limited. Knowing that one can do a behavior does not, in itself, ensure the behavior will occur. It also must be expected to lead to some desired outcome.

Frida Kahlo's competencies include her artistic ability, learned undoubtedly from observing her father's photographs and practiced in her long period of forced bedrest as she recovered from the streetcar accident that nearly took her life. The persistence of Frida's artistic effort attests to her sense of self-efficacy for painting. Experience taught Frida that she would earn approval from those in her artistic circle and from those who admired it without themselves being artists, and it was especially the opinion of the artistic elite whose opinion she valued. Without the approval of these, including her husband Diego Rivera, her art might have languished.

Because there is such a gap between the tastes of the vanguard of artists and that of most of the population, it is no surprise that artists like Frida and Diego were particularly drawn to a bohemian circle of friends. Was it, perhaps, uncertainty about the less predictable reactions of those who did not really understand art but simply consumed it, as part of their lifestyle, that led Frida to be verbally aggressive toward them? That, at least, would lead to predictable outcomes of attention and awe.

Adjustment

Through elaborate learning, people develop self-systems that permit them to pursue goals effectively. Bandura calls these self-regulatory systems and plans.

The self-regulatory system that organized Frida Kahlo's striving was uniquely hers (as a cognitive social learning perspective would predict). Her sexual promiscuity reflected her own values and those of her bohemian friends. Her artistic goals and self-judgments were obviously unique, as even casual examination of her paintings reveals. For despite similarities to surrealistic painters, she was obviously not trying to imitate someone else's style but rather exploring vividly colorful and symbolically haunting images of ancestors and political celebrities, deformed bodies and fetuses, and herself in many poses and costumes. (Cognitive social learning theorists do not engage in symbolic interpretation of artistic images, unlike psychoanalysts, but some of these are obvious, such as the portrayal of her damaged spine with the architectural image described in the title of her 1944 painting, *The Broken Column*.)

Society

Personality is learned in a cultural context, so naturally the expectations and values of the society influence the individual. It is probably a reflection of American cultural values that so much research inspired by these theories focuses on what a person can accomplish—for example, self-efficacy expectations. When people join together to pursue goals that they can achieve as a group but not alone, they exhibit what Bandura calls *collective efficacy*.

Frida Kahlo bore close allegiance to the indigenous culture of Mexico, and when she was in the United States, she rejected the ambitious values that she observed, even in the art community. What of her political convictions? A child during the time of the Mexican revolution, she witnessed models of revolutionary rejection of established authority that neglected the interests of the people. Powerful established authority did not have legitimacy in these childhood lessons, and her communist and socialist sympathies later echoed this message of rebellion and the moral authority of the people at large, not the elite at the top. Participation in this circle must have provided predictable social rewards and a sense of fellowship, not to mention lovers. It also reflected a sense of collective efficacy, that they could together overcome those who would exploit the common people.

Culture brings odd combinations of people: Frida and her husband Diego were politically active, supporting communism and liberal causes. As successful artists, they were invited to social functions by well-to-do society people, where she acted outrageously, used obscene language, spoke disrespectfully of religion in the home of Catholics, and praised communism in the home of capitalist Henry Ford's sister (Herrera, 1983, p. 135). Frida did not share the cultural values she saw in the United States, especially the rampant ambitiousness. She did not think of her painting from the perspective of a business, even when she became financially successful. She seemed content to have her husband Diego be the publicly more esteemed artist, although it is not clear how much of this was a gender role restriction and how much a simple expression of her personal values.

She tolerated his many sexual infidelities (and responded with her own, with both men—including Trotsky—and women). Their relationship was stormy, and they even divorced for a year but reunited.

Bandura's concept of reciprocal determinism reminds psychologists that not only are people shaped by their environment, but they also have an impact on it, as this artist did on the art world.

Biology

No theory can deny the impact of biology on personality, and cognitive social behaviorists have found some positive associations between high efficacy expectations and health.

Perhaps Frida's efficacy expectations helped her endure her physical pain and infections better than she could have done if she had adopted a victim mentality instead. With a single case, one can never be sure.

Final Thoughts

This theory makes a general point that is easy to grasp: Our beliefs are powerful determinants of our behavior. The elaborate details that follow are more at home in research journals than in life narratives. However, without knowing what a person, in this case Frida Kahlo, believes about herself and expects as a result of her behavior, we cannot truly grasp her personality.

Preview: Overview of Mischel's and Bandura's Theories

Walter Mischel and Albert Bandura analyze personality in the tradition of learning theory, but focus particularly on cognitive variables because the human capacity to think is central to personality. Although Mischel and Bandura have many similar theoretical orientations, have cited one another's work, and have collaborated (Bandura & Mischel, 1965), most of their formal theoretical developments and research have been published independently. Mischel's social cognitive alternative to trait explanations takes the particular context into account. Bandura emphasizes how behavior is impacted by cognition, especially thoughts about one's goals and abilities.

Mischel's and Bandura's theories have implications for major theoretical questions, as presented in Table 12.1. Their theories are evolving statements within an ongoing, active research perspective shared by many researchers. Its basic tenets—the processes of learning and the relevance of cognition for behavior—are well established. Unlike some of the more historical theories, these ideas are not so much being validated as they are being used to generate refined hypotheses and to organize research in studies of many populations, ranging from young children to old people. The theory is comprehensive in covering various life stages and both normal and problematic behavior, although only a few relationships with biological variables have been reported. The applied value of the perspective includes its suggestions for therapy and for businesses and for understanding more effective strategies for education and child development.

Traits in Cognitive Social Learning Theory: Mischel

Behaviorism emphasizes the importance of situations as determinants of behavior. This poses a challenge to traditional psychoanalytic and trait approaches, and Walter Mischel took on the challenge. It was not easily resolved. A heated theoretical controversy about the relative importance of personality traits and situations in predicting behavior stimulated personality researchers to ask how personality and situations both contribute to behavior.

TABLE 12.1	Preview of Mischel's and Bandura's Theories
Individual Differences	Individuals differ in behaviors and in cognitive processes because of learning.
Adaptation and Adjustment	New therapies using modeling and other techniques to treat phobias and other disorders have been found effective. Techniques to increase self-efficacy are effective.
Cognitive Processes	Cognitive processes (including expectancies and self-efficacy) are central to personality.
Society	Modeling has major implications for society, including TV violence, which promotes aggression.
Biological Influences	Although the theory does not focus on biological phenomena, Bandura found that self-efficacy improves immune functioning among phobic subjects.
Development	Children learn much through modeling, as demonstrated in research using children as subjects. Learning can occur throughout life. Expectancies and other cognitive learning variables can change as a result of experience.

BIOGRAPHY OF WALTER MISCHEL

Walter Mischel was born in 1930 in Vienna, Austria. His family fled Europe to avoid the Nazi persecutions at the beginning of World War II, when he was a young boy. Like many Europeans, they immigrated to New York City, where Mischel later studied at the City College of New York. He became a social worker, focusing on juvenile delinquents.

Mischel's graduate work at Ohio State University in the 1950s had an effect on his developing cognitive emphasis. In particular, he was influenced by the work of his mentors, George Kelly and Julian Rotter (Mischel, 1984b). He used in his own theory the concept of personal construct, an idea developed by George Kelly (presented in Chapter 13). After several

WALTER MISCHEL

brief faculty positions, Mischel moved to Stanford University, where he taught and did research from 1962 to 1983. Since 1983, he has been on the faculty of Columbia University.

The Trait Controversy: Mischel's Challenge

Traditional personality theories, including trait and psychodynamic approaches, assumed that individual differences consist of global characteristics affecting a wide variety of behaviors (Mischel, 1973). Walter Mischel (1968) startled the field by questioning this fundamental assumption, contributing to a paradigm crisis in personality theory (Epstein & O'Brien,

1985; Mischel, 1973, p. 254). He stated, after examining the research literature, "With the possible exception of intelligence, highly generalized behavioral consistencies have not been demonstrated, and the concept of personality traits as broad predispositions is thus untenable" (p. 140). The average relationship between self-report personality measures and behavior was only $r = 0.30$, which Mischel termed the **personality coefficient**. It is low, accounting for less than 10% of the variability in behavior.

personality coefficient the average relationship between self-report personality measures and behavior, estimated by Mischel at $r = 0.30$

Personality psychologists commonly believe that "people are characterized by broad dispositions resulting in extensive cross-situational consistency, [but] the research in the area has persistently failed to support that intuition" (Mischel, 1984a, p. 357). In a much-cited study, Walter Mischel and Philip Peake (1982) examined the consistency of college students on two characteristics, conscientiousness and friendliness. Although common sense would seem to predict that each student would behave consistently across situations, depending on their traits of friendliness and conscientiousness, the results indicated there was virtually no tendency for intersituational consistency ($r = 0.13$). Critics objected that this result could be related to methodological faults, but Mischel believed that the lack of consistent behavior across situations required revision of the theory of traits.

THE CONSISTENCY PARADOX

consistency paradox the mismatch between intuition, which says that people are consistent, and research findings, which say they are not

This discrepancy between the intuition that people are consistent and empirical findings that they are not poses a **consistency paradox**. People who are honest in the classroom may cheat on taxes; children who wait patiently in the presence of a parent may act impulsively when the situation changes. That is, behavior is not determined by general personality traits, but is situation specific. Even the religious beliefs and worldviews of elderly people, studied in longitudinal research, vary considerably from one testing to another (Kim, Nesselroade, & Featherman, 1996).

A social learning approach does not predict that behavior will be consistent across situations. Behavior depends on the consequences (rewards and punishments) it produces. If the same behavior in different situations produces different consequences (e.g., talking in a restaurant or talking in a library), adaptive responses will vary from situation to situation. Consistency is expected only when the same behavior is reinforced in a variety of situations or if a person is unable to discriminate among situations. For example, a child who is rewarded at play by friends, at school by teachers, and at home by parents for speaking will learn to speak in a great variety of situations. A child who cannot tell when speaking will result in punishment and when it will not may learn to be quiet all the time. When such consistency is found, social learning theory explains it as a consequence of a particular learning history, without resorting to a concept of traits, like extraversion or introversion.

That does not mean, though, that we must discard the concept of traits, provided we are aware of its limitations. Mischel pointed out that laypeople have always made trait attributions. Traits constitute summaries of multiple behavioral observations and may have some descriptive usefulness for salient characteristics, although they exaggerate consistency and make inferences about unobserved behavior (Carlson & Mulaik, 1993; Hayden & Mischel, 1976; Mischel, 1973). For Mischel, traits are not causes but merely summary labels. They describe, but do not explain, personality.

Mischel's challenge to an overgeneralized conceptualization of traits was not intended to displace traits entirely from personality theory. Rather, he advocated replacing overgeneralized trait concepts with more refined analyses and to understand when people behave consistently and when they discriminate among situations (Mischel, 1983a, 1984b;

Mischel & Peake, 1983; Peake & Mischel, 1984). Perhaps it will not surprise those who view the field from a distance that the consistency question has bothered personality theorists more than the average person. When people are given personality information in laboratory tasks, they can often reconcile inconsistent information readily. Told that a particular individual is both "generous" and "thrifty," observers do not find these traits inconsistent but reason that the individual is generous in situations that call for that, and thrifty when other circumstances make thrift sensible (Hampson, 1998).

THE SITUATIONAL CONTEXT OF BEHAVIOR

Consider the following research that Mischel and colleagues conducted with college students. You are asked to vividly imagine yourself having gotten a poor grade on an important paper. Next, you fill in the blanks on a questionnaire, with items like: "I am _____ when._____" This procedure, the researchers assume, will put you in the frame of mind of imagining that your characteristics vary from one situation to another. Compared to other subjects, who go through the same imaginary exercise but have fill-in-the-blank questions that do not refer to situations ("I am_____ ."), you will be less extreme in thinking that one failure means you are overall a failure; the imaginary exercise will have a less devastating effect on your self-concept. That is what Mischel and his colleagues predicted, and found (Mendoza-Denton et al., 2001). Keeping the situational context in mind helps prevent people from making overgeneralized conclusions about their failure—or, for that matter, success, or stereotypes about people.

Knowing that traits are oversimplified explanations unless they take situations into account, Mischel and his colleagues have developed sophisticated models of how traits affect behavior in situations (e.g., Mischel & Shoda, 1995; Wright & Mischel, 1987). For example, even aggressive people do not hit and yell all the time, and helpful people may act no different from others unless they see someone in need. The relationship between traits and behavior takes situations into account (see Figure 12.1). A given trait, such as aggressiveness, influences behavior only under certain conditions. For example, the trait of aggressiveness will influence behavior (hitting, yelling, etc.) only under certain conditions: when a person feels angry or frustrated and when people threaten or criticize.

This situational context for behavior makes a great deal of sense, if we think of traits as learned ways of adapting to situations. Situations activate thoughts and emotions that were developed as a result of prior experience with that situation (Mischel, 1973; Mischel & Shoda, 1995). Moods, fantasies, plans, goals, and other internal reactions are triggered by specific situations. The psychological situation that a person is in is therefore not simply the objective situation but the subjective amalgam of that plus internal reactions to it. In fact, by ruminating about situations, people activate these dynamics themselves. In so doing, one individual may be particularly sensitive to rejection, responding to the slightest hint of abandonment with an exaggerated, even aggressive, response. Another may exaggerate the romantic possibilities of encounters (Mischel & Shoda, 1995).

The situational approach is consistent with people's everyday descriptions of behavior. When individuals describe other people's behavior, they hedge their statements with pronouncements about the conditions under which traits will be manifested (Wright & Mischel, 1988). For example, they may say, "Johnny will hit back [aggressive behavior] when he is teased [conditional modifier, or hedge]." Conditional statements about the expression of dispositionally relevant behaviors take the form "Person does x when y." When people describe behavior, they do not use trait terms (e.g., aggressive) in a global, overly simplified manner that ignores the situation.

Figure 12.1 Illustration of a Dispositional Construct (Aggressive) as an If-Then Linkage between a Category of Conditions and a Category of Behaviors

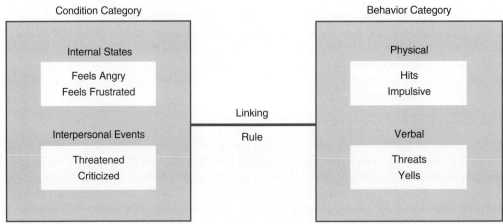

Behavior results from a set of conditions, rather than from a trait alone. Only under certain conditions does a trait of "aggressiveness" influence behavior.

(From J. C. Wright & W. Mischel (1987). A conditional approach to dispositional constructs: The local predictability of social behavior. *Journal of Personality and Social Psychology, 53,* 1159–1177. Copyright 1987 by the American Psychological Association. Reprinted by permission.)

What happens when people are presented with information about behavior that occurs in situations in which it is unlikely to occur naturally? Data from such a study strengthen Mischel's argument that situations are always relevant to trait judgments. Accurate situational descriptions of children's behavior (e.g., "child hits when provoked") were perceived meaningfully. However, descriptions that distorted the situational context of behavior in unnatural ways (e.g., "child hits when praised") yielded descriptions of children as odd, withdrawn, or psychotic (Shoda, Mischel, & Wright, 1989). Judges labeled the children as aggressive or as odd depending on the situations that provoked the hitting. People have distinctive patterns of situation–behavior relationships. In a study of perceptions of children at a summer camp, extensive records were kept of each child's behavior and of situations as they changed hour by hour over the 6-week camp session. These were analyzed idiographically, in the behavioral tradition, to show the behavior of each individual child separately for various kinds of situations. Individual differences emerged. One child, for example, was verbally aggressive when punished by an adult. Another child was verbally aggressive when warned by an adult but less so when actually punished. A third child was verbally aggressive when approached by another child. Thus there are consistent individual differences in situation–behavior relationships. Furthermore, these consistent patterns were independent of the average level of the behavior (verbal aggression) across all situations, strengthening Mischel's contention that it is situation–behavior relationships, rather than overall behavior, that defines traits (Shoda, Mischel, & Wright, 1994).

Situational variation should not be considered a problem for personality theory. In fact, the ability to discriminate among situations is characteristic of people who are well adapted (Mischel, 1968, 1973, 1984a). The assumption of global personality traits was an oversimplified theory that did not even include the wisdom of everyday people, who implicitly know that situations matter. One intriguing finding comes from an unlikely source: a genetic study of temperament in twin toddlers. The children were observed in standard laboratory situations to see how they responded to toys, to adults, and so on. Emotional reactions, activity, and other behaviors were observed—not simply for overall traits of temperament but to find situation-specific reactions. For example, sometimes during the cognitive tests one twin became more sociable toward the experimenter, and the other became less sociable but more fussy. These individual differences were consistent with parents' reports of how the twins responded at home. Statistical analyses suggest that reactions to specific situations are influenced by both genetics and experience (Phillips & Matheny, 1997).

Another theoretical development suggests that people are best described by a distribution of trait-related behavior not by simply their typical behavior. Consider conscientiousness behavior, for example: An individual may be very conscientious sometimes (carefully proofreading a term paper), moderately conscientious at other times, and not at all careful at others. The situational context influences this variability. An overly simplified concept of a trait score does not convey this variability; thinking, instead, of traits as distributions of behaviors, with a central or typical score for an individual plus a distribution around that middle, is a newer suggestion (Fleeson, 2001).

Cognitive Person Variables

Instead of global traits, Mischel (1973) proposes that personality psychologists consider several psychological processes within a person that determine how a particular situation will influence a person's behavior. These aspects of personality enable adaptation to the environment, in the unique style of an individual. He calls these concepts *cognitive social learning person variables* because they are derived from cognition and from social learning. More briefly, we may call them **cognitive person variables**.

cognitive person variables cognitive factors within a person, less global than traits, which influence how an individual adapts to the environment

ENCODING STRATEGIES AND PERSONAL CONSTRUCTS

Trait terms, which people use to describe themselves and other people, are called **personal constructs**. They are personal both in the sense that they describe individuals and in the sense that they vary from one person to another. Personal constructs that people use to describe themselves may be termed a *self-system*. They are unique to each person.

Besides personal constructs, people also have other kinds of **encoding strategies**, including concepts for describing situations and events. Because of their different learning histories, the meaning of situations varies from person to person. Behavior is influenced by environmental stimuli, but it is a person's unique interpretation of these stimuli, rather than objective aspects, that matters. Mischel (1968) suggests, "Assessing the acquired meaning of stimuli is the core of social behavior assessment" (p. 190). For this purpose, it is necessary to rely on subjects' reports because only they have access to their cognitions (Mischel, 1973).

Personal constructs are different from the traits of personality theories. Rather than judging personality consistency based on similar behavior across many situations (as a researcher might), the average person looks for consistency across time in a small number of behaviors that are seen as particularly characteristic (prototypical) of a given trait (Mischel, 1984b). In formal logic and in the simplified environment of a Skinner box, events either do or do not belong to a particular category. Logical reasoning demands that we are able to say that something either is A or not A, and it seems the two choices

personal constructs trait terms that people use to describe themselves and other people

encoding strategies person variables concerned with how a person construes reality

cover all options. In a Skinner box, a discriminative stimulus may consist of a signal light, which is either on or off. But what if the light is flickering? What if the thing we are judging as A or not A is an ostrich, and A is the category bird? Suddenly, things are not so easy, and we turn from logical categories to prototypes, which permit us to convey that some birds (robins and canaries) are more birdlike than others (ostriches and turkeys). A **prototype** is a typical example of a category.

We also have "personality prototypes—abstract representations of particular personality types" (Cantor & Mischel, 1979b, p. 188)—such as introverts and extraverts. We judge whether a particular individual is an introvert or an extravert based on similarity to the prototype. Some people are difficult to classify, just as the ostrich is difficult to categorize as a bird or not a bird (Cantor & Mischel, 1979a). Prototypes include social stereotypes, such as redneck, and do-gooder, although researchers generally use more value-neutral labels, such as comedian type or pet-owner type (Andersen & Klatzky, 1987). We also have prototypes of various kinds of love: romantic love, maternal love, self-love, and so on (Aron & Westbay, 1996; Fehr & Russell, 1991).

Prototypes range from very broad categories (e.g., extravert) to narrow ones (e.g., door-to-door salesperson). Broader categories are distinctive, with little overlap among categories, and they correspond to broad personality types (cf. Chapter 1). Narrower categories are more vivid and concrete, conjuring up clearer visual images and trait descriptions (Cantor & Mischel, 1979a). It is more difficult to recall information about people who do not consistently fit a prototype (Cantor & Mischel, 1979b).

prototype a typical example of an object or type of person; a "fuzzy concept" typical of the categories people use in perceiving others

COMPETENCIES

What can a person do? What can a person think? These are the person's cognitive and behavioral construction **competencies**. These competencies "to construct (generate) diverse behaviors under appropriate conditions" (Mischel, 1973, p. 265) vary widely from person to person, "as becomes obvious from even casual comparison of the different competencies, for example, of a professional weight lifter, a distinguished chemist, a retardate, an opera star, or a convicted forger" (Mischel, 1977, p. 342). Leaders of neighborhood block organizations have higher construction competencies for skills relevant to leadership, including talking in front of a group and being able to get others to follow one's ideas (Florin, Mednick, & Wandersman, 1986).

Construction competencies include many learned behaviors and concepts (see Table 12.2). They refer to what a person knows or is able to do (not what the person actually does). Therefore, assessing competencies requires providing incentives for the performance of the behavior. Competencies have better stability across time and situations than do many of the personality traits that Mischel (1973, p. 267) criticizes because they are free of the variable factors that determine whether a person will do what he or she can do. Such factors include various expectancies about the situation.

competencies person variables concerned with what a person is able to do

EXPECTANCIES

Whether people will behave in a particular way depends not only on whether they know how (their competencies) but also on their **expectancies**. Mischel said that internal subjective expectancies determine performance. Several kinds of expectancies can be distinguished: behavior-outcome expectancies, stimulus-outcome expectancies, and self-efficacy expectancies.

Will racing to the corner in 11 seconds result in catching the bus, or will the driver ignore me and not stop? Will opening a door for a woman result in a "thank you" or a

expectancies subjective beliefs about what will happen in a particular situation (including behavior outcomes, stimulus outcomes, and self-efficacies)

TABLE 12.2	Examples of Cognitive and Behavioral Construction Competencies

Sexual gender identity

Knowing the structure of the physical world

Social rules and conventions

Personal constructs about self and others

Rehearsal strategies for learning

(Adapted from Mischel, 1973, p. 266.)

reprimand for sexist assumptions? A **behavior-outcome expectancy** is an expectation about what will happen if a person behaves in a particular way. Such expectancies are already evident in preschool children (Hegland & Galejs, 1983; Mischel, Zeiss, & Zeiss, 1974), although of course they can change with experience.

People also develop expectancies about how events will develop in the world, aside from their own actions. These are termed **stimulus-outcome expectancies**. "If the number 10 bus has just left, the number 23 must be coming soon." "If Jerry is shouting, he may soon hit someone." Although not always directly connected with immediate behavior, these expectancies are important in maintaining a person's ongoing awareness of the environment. Sometimes they may motivate an individual to change environments.

"Can I even make it to the bus stop in 11 seconds, or will I fall flat on my face trying?" Expectancies about whether one actually can do the behavior are termed **self-efficacy expectancies**. They are different from behavior-outcome expectancies, as any student knows who believes that 12 hours of straight study would result in an A on an exam (high behavior-outcome expectancy) but who also believes that such a feat would not be possible (low self-efficacy expectancy). Self-efficacy expectancies are central to the cognitive social learning approach and have been discussed by both Walter Mischel (e.g., 1981b, p. 349) and Albert Bandura (as we see later in this chapter). An idea this important has, not surprisingly, been expressed in other theories as well, although not always by the same name and not always identical in meaning: Julian Rotter (1966, 1990) describes internal-external locus of control; Martin Seligman (1992) describes helplessness (which corresponds closely to low self-efficacy); Carol Dweck describes mastery orientation (Dweck & Leggett, 1988). All of these theoretical concepts share the idea that people's beliefs about what they can accomplish influence behavior in important ways.

These various types of expectancies that Mischel described, behavior-outcome, stimulus-outcome, and self-efficacy, develop from experience in various situations. When a person is in a new situation, his or her expectancies are derived from past experience in similar situations (Mischel & Staub, 1965). Such generalized expectancies are replaced by specific situational expectancies when experience permits. A child will expect that a new baby-sitter will ignore obscene language if past baby-sitters have done so, but with experience the child may learn that she punishes such utterances.

SUBJECTIVE STIMULUS VALUES

Not all people value the same outcomes. The term **subjective stimulus value** refers to the extent to which a person regards an outcome as desirable or undesirable—that is, a person's goals or values. In learning terms, it is the value of the reward. Mischel (1981a)

behavior-outcome expectancy expectancy about what will happen if a person behaves in a particular way

stimulus-outcome expectancies expectancies about how events will develop in the world, i.e., what events will follow other environmental stimuli

self-efficacy expectancies (or self-efficacy) subjective beliefs about what a person will be able to do

subjective stimulus value how much an outcome is valued by an individual

offers the example of a teacher's praise. This outcome may have high subjective stimulus value for a student trying to get good grades but would have quite a different value for a rebellious adolescent who rejects school.

SELF-REGULATORY SYSTEMS AND PLANS

self-regulatory systems and plans
ways that a person works on complicated behavior (e.g., by setting goals and by self-criticism)

Among the most important cognitive person variables are **self-regulatory systems and plans**. These are internal mechanisms that have powerful implications for behavior. People set performance goals for themselves (whether it is running a 4-minute mile, skiing an advanced slope, or graduating with honors); they reward themselves; they criticize themselves; they pass by immediate pleasure for long-term goals (delay of gratification). All these are self-regulatory systems "through which we can influence our environment substantially, overcoming 'stimulus control' (the power of the situation)" (Mischel, 1981b, p. 350). One important self-regulatory system is the ability to delay gratification.

Delay of Gratification

delay of gratification the ability to give up immediate gratifications for larger, more distant rewards

Modern culture offers instant gratification of many needs and tempts consumers with a barrage of advertisements for immediate happiness (Goldman, 1996). Our own impulses, too, beg for immediate gratification. In the face of these temptations, **delay of gratification**, the ability to defer present gratification for larger future goals, is an important adaptational skill that develops in childhood. Mischel and his colleagues explored this self-regulatory system in several studies (e.g., Mischel, 1966, 1974). They gave young children the choice of receiving a small reward (e.g., one marshmallow) immediately or a larger reward (two marshmallows) later. Some children were tested with pretzels instead of marshmallows. By manipulating aspects of the situation and by teaching the children strategies for waiting, Mischel and his colleagues learned what facilitates delay of gratification and what prevents it.

Delay is more difficult if the rewards are visible (Mischel & Ebbesen, 1970) and if the child is thinking about how wonderful the marshmallow will taste (Mischel & Baker, 1975). If the marshmallows are out of sight (Mischel & Ebbesen, 1970) and if the child is thinking about something else (Mischel, Ebbesen, & Zeiss, 1972), delay of gratification is easier. Paying attention to pictures of the rewards (that is, symbolically presented rewards) instead of the actual rewards increases delay of gratification (Mischel & Moore, 1973). By age 5, children develop effective strategies that enable them to wait for rewards: covering the rewards (marshmallows) and thinking about something else (H. N. Mischel & Mischel, 1983). Children can be taught to think about other things, which improves their ability to delay gratification (Mischel et al., 1972). Adolescents who have difficulty controlling aggression can be taught to use imagery as a technique for increasing self-control (Lennings, 1996). The ability to delay gratification can also be improved by exposure to models who delay their own gratification (Bandura & Mischel, 1965; Mischel & Liebert, 1966).

Research on delay of gratification adds wisdom beyond that known intuitively by parents. When mothers of preschool children were asked to predict which techniques would be most effective, they underestimated the value of distraction in producing delay of gratification. They predicted that tasting a desired marshmallow would help children wait longer for it—when in fact that technique had the opposite effect (Hom & Knight, 1996).

Fortunately, children can be taught to delay gratification. When mothers are more author-itative, providing direction, their children develop more ability to delay gratification, com-pared to those whose mothers are more permissive (Mauro & Harris, 2000). Children diagnosed with attention-deficit/hyperactivity disorder are prime candidates because of their impulsive behavior. An intervention with three children, ages 3 to 5, was successful in teaching them to forgo immediate rewards (such as a chocolate chip cookie) in favor of delayed but larger rewards (Binder, Dixon, & Ghezzi, 2000).

The delay of gratification research seems to be tapping a core ego strength (as it would be called in psychoanalytic language). When children learn to delay gratification, they are mastering a skill with important consequences for their future. Preschool children who waited longer for marshmallows or pretzels were rated higher by parents on cognitive and social competence years later when they were juniors and seniors in high school (Mischel, 1983b, 1984a; Mischel, Shoda, & Peake, 1988; Mischel, Shoda, & Rodriguez, 1989) (see Table 12.3). Preschoolers who delayed gratification longer had higher SAT ver-bal and math scores in high school. They were described by their parents as better able to concentrate and to cope with frustration and stress (Shoda et al., 1990). In contrast, children who are impulsive, who have temper tantrums more often than other children in late childhood (age 8 to 10), have poorer life outcomes later, with more frequent divorce and less successful occupational lives than their better controlled peers (Caspi, Elder, & Bem, 1987). Even among adults, some continue to choose small immediate reinforcers (such as briefly playing a video game) in favor of larger, delayed reinforcers (having a longer play time) (Navarick, 1998).

Longitudinal studies find that young children's ability to control their impulses, called *ego control*, is stable over time (J. Block, 1993). A related construct, *ego resiliency*, is the ability to modify one's behavior according to the demands of the situation (J. H. Block & J. Block, 1980). This ability helps people learn from experience, further developing their personality in healthy directions. For example, ego resiliency measured at age 7 predicts which children will have more advanced understanding of friendship and higher moral judgment 8 years later (Hart et al., 1998).

Personality is adaptational, and the personality characteristics proposed by Mischel prepare an individual to cope with situations. Mischel's research inspires intervention programs for children who do not develop normal abilities to delay gratification, such as those who are aggressive or hyperactive (Mischel, Shoda, & Rodriguez, 1989; Rodriguez, Mischel, & Shoda, 1989). Inhibition of behaviors, although a valuable ego skill, sometimes comes at a price, resulting in emotional distress and even ill health (Polivy, 1998). Such

TABLE 12.3	Examples of High School Behavior Ratings Predicted from Preschool Delay of Gratification

Is attentive and able to concentrate.

Is verbally fluent, can express ideas well.

Uses and responds to reason.

Tends to go to pieces under stress, becomes rattled. (disagree)

Reverts to more immature behavior under stress. (disagree)

(From W. Mischel (1984a). Convergences and challenges in the search for consistency. *American Psychologist, 39,* 351–364. Copyright 1984 by the American Psychological Association. Adapted by permission.)

costs underscore the importance of learning more about both healthy and inadequate development of people's capacity to seek gratifications in the long term as well as the short term.

The mature resolution of the conflict over delay of gratification within the individual is still being explored. It has been theorized as essentially a battle for cognition over emotion, with a hot "go" emotional system that urges the person to go for the immediate pleasure and a cool "know" cognitive system that inspires restraint (Metcalfe & Mischel, 1999). A tempting stimulus activates the "go" emotional system, so delay of gratification constitutes overcoming stimulus control. Young children, because of their immaturity, have not yet developed the "cool" system sufficiently to be able to delay gratification. Metcalfe and Mischel speculate that this may be because the hippocampus and frontal lobes of the brain are not yet developed enough to take over this function, leaving the "hot" amygdala less controlled; but they do not commit to particular neural structures in their model. They also suggest that at very high levels of stress, the "cool" function becomes less effective, leaving more impulsive behavior. This model is exciting, not only because of the possibility of integrating with neuroscience, but also because it treats delay of gratification as a process and not simply a developmental level. That is, in addition to the many studies of individual differences in delay of gratification that have been reported, the model helps us understand why the same person will sometimes be able to delay gratification and other times (e.g., under high stress), will not.

Mischel's model of personality offers a way of integrating two competing approaches in personality: the approach that seeks to identify personality traits or dispositions as stable determinants of behavior and the approach that minimizes individual differences and focuses instead on personality dynamics, the processes by which all of us are influenced in similar ways by situations (Mischel & Shoda, 1998). Mischel's focus on competencies and other cognitive person variables emphasizes the adaptational function of personality. His research on the delay of gratification shows how individual children learn to overcome the power of situations to gain self-control (e.g., Mischel, 1984a, p. 353). Mischel has offered an exciting and practical theory, rich with implications for research and intervention.

Performance in Cognitive Social Learning Theory: Bandura

Albert Bandura, like Walter Mischel, recognizes the importance of the social context for personality and presents a detailed description of cognitive variables that can be used instead of traits to describe personality and to predict behavior in various situations. Bandura's theoretical contributions permit personality theory to resolve a difficult dilemma: whether to treat people as pawns, whose behavior and experience are determined from the outside, or whether to treat them as the causes of their own behavior. Much is at stake. As Bandura puts it (2001b, p. 1), "The capacity to exercise control over the nature and quality of one's life is the essence of humanness."

BIOGRAPHY OF ALBERT BANDURA

Albert Bandura was born on December 4, 1925, in northern Alberta, Canada. Elementary and high school were combined in one school in the small town of Mundare. Bandura worked on the Alaska highway before entering the University of

British Columbia, graduating in 3 years. He did his graduate work at the University of Iowa, finishing his doctorate in clinical psychology in 1952. There he met his future wife, Virginia Varns, who taught in the School of Nursing. After a postdoctoral internship at the Wichita Guidance Center, he went to Stanford University in California, where he has been on the faculty his entire career, becoming a full professor in 1964 and holder of an endowed chair from 1974. He headed the Department of Psychology from 1976 to 1977.

ALBERT BANDURA

His interests have been broad, including not only the therapeutic concerns that might have been anticipated from his clinical training but also broad issues in child development and social problems. He was president of the American Psychological Association in 1974 and has received many professional honors for his scholarly work, including the American Psychological Association's Award for Distinguished Scientific Contributions in 1980 (American Psychological Association, 1981).

Bandura has two daughters. In addition to research, he enjoys hiking in the mountains and attending the opera.

Reciprocal Determinism

Many psychological approaches deal with only some aspects of the complex network of interacting causes, describing how situations influence behavior (as behaviorism does) or how personality traits influence behavior (as trait approaches do). Bandura (1978, 1984b) expanded these more limited cause-and-effect models with his concept of **reciprocal determinism**. This concept recognizes that the person, the environment, and behavior all influence one another, as illustrated in Figure 12.2.

> **reciprocal determinism** the interacting mutual influences of the person, the environment, and the behavior

The concept of reciprocal determinism recognizes that the environment influences behavior, as behaviorism has always suggested. (Libraries are conducive to studying; the student lounge is not.) It also recognizes that characteristics within a person influence behavior, as trait approaches have traditionally emphasized. (Conscientious students study more.) Reciprocal determinism goes beyond these approaches, pointing out that behavior also causes changes in the environment (studying instead of spending time with friends reduces social pressures or invitations to go out) and in the individual (studying increases academic self-confidence). The environment is not only a cause of behavior but also an effect of behavior. One way in which personality influences situations is that people choose situations differently, depending on their personalities (Emmons, Diener, & Larsen, 1985).

A complete understanding of personality requires the recognition of all of these mutual influences among personality, situation, and behavior. In addition, fortuitous chance also plays a role in determining the paths that we take through life—as in the example of a professional who by chance took an empty chair at a conference presentation, whereupon he met, in the adjacent chair, the woman who was to become his wife (Bandura, 1998). Determinist science must be salted with a few grains of unpredictability.

Figure 12.2 Reciprocal Determinism

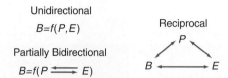

Schematic representation of three alternative conceptions of interaction. *B* signifies behavior, *P* the cognitive and other internal events than can affect perceptions and actions, and *E* the external environment.

(From A. Bandura (1978). The self system in reciprocal determinism. *American Psychologist, 33,* 344–358. Copyright 1978 by the American Psychological Association. Reprinted by permission.)

Self-Regulation of Behavior: The Self-System

People have considerable control over their own behavior. They vary, of course, in how effectively they exert this control. Sometimes they procrastinate, putting off projects rather than working on them; sometimes people engage in self-handicapping, doing work in ways that make it difficult to succeed, such as trying to study in a place that has too many distractions (Lay, Knish, & Zanatta, 1992). In contrast, other people make the most of their potential. A study of gifted students reports that they are more likely than other students to take responsibility for their own learning. Thomas Edison, for example, read almost all the books in the local library, if his own report is accurate (Risemberg & Zimmerman, 1992). By teaching us about the processes by which people regulate their own behavior, Bandura's theory promises to give people more control over their own lives.

To contrast with the old behavioral model of a person who simply responds to the environment, or even a complicated information-processing system, Bandura speaks of *human agency*. In this mode, people act with intention, forethought, self-reactiveness, and self-reflectiveness (Bandura, 2001b). Humans are conscious beings, and we act intentionally, with a desire to achieve some end (although sometimes our intentional acts do not work out as we plan). By anticipating the future and adopting goals, people become, in essence, self-directed. As they progress toward these goals, they monitor their progress, evaluate how they are doing, and correct their course. Personal values and identity come into play here.

> **self-system** personal constructs that people use to describe themselves; cognitive structures and subfunctions for perceiving, evaluating, and regulating behavior (not a psychic agent that controls action)

The processes are cognitive, and they are collectively called the **self-system**. "A self-system within the framework of social learning theory comprises cognitive structures and subfunctions for perceiving, evaluating, and regulating behavior, not a psychic agent that controls action" (Bandura, 1978, p. 344). These cognitive processes are outlined in Figure 12.3. Notice that self-regulation is more than simply giving oneself reinforcements, which alone does not work very well (Sohn & Lamal, 1982).

Choosing goals is an important step in self-regulation. Higher goals generally produce higher performance. In the applied psychology research literature, one of the most replicated findings is that people who are given higher goals perform at a higher level than those given lower goals (Phillips & Gully, 1997). In many instances, people set their own goals. Setting subgoals generally enhances performance, especially if there is some flexibility about immediate tasks as we work toward longer-term goals (Kirschenbaum, 1985).

People can self-regulate their emotions as well as their behavior. Life's events surely contribute to our happiness or sadness, and other emotions, but we also can feel differently by internal processes of self-regulation. People in laboratory situations were shown unpleasant videotapes about mass destruction caused by an atomic bomb. Naturally, they

Figure 12.3 Self-Regulation Processes

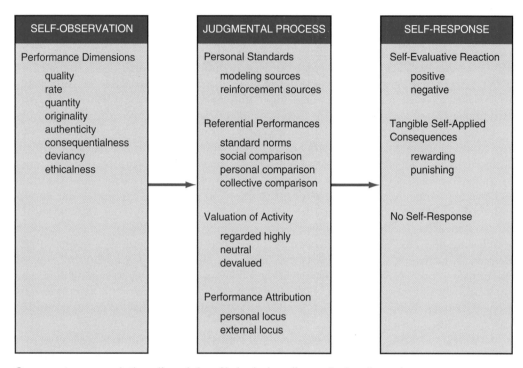

Component processes in the self-regulation of behavior by self-prescribed contingencies.

(From A. Bandura (1978). The self system in reciprocal determinism. *American Psychologist, 33*, 344–358. Copyright 1978 by the American Psychological Association. Reprinted by permission.)

experienced unpleasant emotions, but some of them defended against this unpleasantness by conjuring up pleasant memories (Boden & Baumeister, 1997). The ability to avoid thinking about unpleasant things can be adaptive; for example, it helps bereaved adults cope with the death of their spouse (Bonanno et al., 1995). At other times, putting a positive spin on events may prevent us from dealing with unpleasantries that need attention.

Self-Efficacy

Self-efficacy means believing "that one can organize and execute given courses of action required to deal with prospective situations" (Bandura, 1980). A person who has a high self-efficacy expectation in a particular situation is confident of mastery. For example, a tennis player who believes his or her serve is reliably excellent has a high self-efficacy expectation. A person who doubts that he or she can do the required behavior has a low self-efficacy expectation. A stage-frightened performer, who believes the first lines will be spoken with a squeaky voice, suffers from low self-efficacy. High self-efficacy leads to effort and persistence at a task and setting higher goals, whereas low self-efficacy produces discouragement and giving up (Bandura, 1989b; Phillips & Gully, 1997). Homeless people higher in self-efficacy are more persistent in seeking housing and employment; those with lower scores give up sooner (Epel, Bandura, & Zimbardo, 1999). Parents with high self-efficacy for parenting do a better job of it (Jones & Prinz, 2005).

Health depends considerably on lifestyle, and the lifestyle choices that people make are matters of self-regulation, largely determined by efficacy (Bandura, 2001b). Health interventions, such as programs for weight loss, exercise, and stopping smoking, are more likely to succeed if self-efficacy is high (Desharnais, Bouillon, & Godin, 1986; Dzewaltowski, 1989; Garcia, Schmitz, & Doerfler, 1990; O'Leary, 1985, 1992; Weinberg et al., 1984; Wojcik, 1988). Self-efficacy helps people to control pain (Dolce, 1987; Kores et al., 1990). Self-defense programs for women increase their self-efficacy, which leads participants to feel safer so their mobility is no longer unreasonably restricted by fear (Ozer & Bandura, 1990).

Efficacy is key to successful health-related prevention programs, including adolescents' resistance to using alcohol and other drugs (Bandura, 1999b; Hays & Ellickson, 1990). Sexual behavior, including the use of condoms to prevent the spread of HIV and other sexually transmitted diseases, is influenced by self-efficacy (O'Leary, 1992). Bandura (1990a) recommends developing AIDS-prevention programs that recognize the importance of self-efficacy, which is particularly low among runaway teens (Kaliski et al., 1990). Rehearsal of relevant behaviors—for example, through role playing of condom purchasing and HIV testing—can increase preventive behavior (Fisher & Fisher, 1992), perhaps by increasing self-efficacy for these behaviors. Among college students, self-efficacy about using condoms has been increased by a relay race that involved putting condoms on models of penises (J. Hayden, 1993), surely an illustration of two important concepts from Bandura's theory: Self-efficacy is specific to a particular behavior and self-efficacy can be changed through learning.

Although some researchers measure general self-efficacy, a broad trait applicable to a variety of behaviors (Shelton, 1990), Bandura recommends using measures self-efficacy specifically for a particular domain of behavior (e.g., Wells-Parker, Miller, & Topping, 1990). A public health survey confirms that health self-efficacy comprises several specific dimensions (nutrition, medical care, and exercise), as Bandura predicted, rather than one global dimension (Hofstetter, Sallis, & Hovell, 1990). Measures of efficacy that refer to a particular situation predict better than global measures (Wollman & Stouder, 1991). If intervention programs, such as programs to reduce tobacco use in youth, are to succeed, they should target their teaching toward the specific problem—for example, teaching adolescents the cognitive and behavioral skills needed to resist pressure to smoke (J. A. Epstein, Botvin, & Diaz, 1999).

outcome expectations the belief about what desirable or undesirable things will occur if a behavior is successfully performed

Bandura (like Mischel) distinguishes between self-efficacy (the belief that one has the ability to perform the behavior) and **outcome expectations** (see Figure 12.4). The latter refers to the belief that if the behavior is successfully done, it will lead to desirable outcomes. If I am confident that I can put my coins in a soda machine but doubt the machine will deliver my chosen soda, I have low outcome expectations despite high efficacy expectations. Obviously, both types of expectations must be high for a person to attempt a specific behavior.

The concept of efficacy has been applied to many areas of life. Mothers who are higher in self-efficacy for specific problems in caring for their infants were rated higher in maternal competence by observers who watched them interact with their children (Teti & Gelfand, 1991). Low self-efficacy is associated with negative emotions, including depression (Bandura, 1989a; Davis-Berman, 1990). Politically active citizens scored higher on a measure of political efficacy (Zimmerman, 1989). People with high-efficacy expectations about computers are less anxious and use them more (Compeau, Higgins, & Huff, 1999). In organizations, where theories are evaluated by their practical contribution to corporate profitability, self-efficacy and other social cognitive concepts help predict career aspirations and job performance (Lent & Hackett, 1987; Stajkovic & Luthans, 1998).

Figure 12.4 Diagrammatic Representation of the Difference between Efficacy Expectations and Outcome Expectations

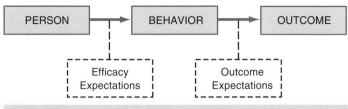

(From A. Bandura (1977). Self-efficacy: Toward a unifying theory of behavioral change. *Psychological Review, 84,* 191–215. Copyright 1977 by the American Psychological Association. Reprinted by permission.)

EFFICACY AND STRIVING TOWARD GOALS

People vary in the goals that they value, whether health, wealth, a college degree, and so on; but striving toward goals is characteristically human and a major concern in personality, with implications for our emotional well-being (Austin & Vancouver, 1996; Brunstein, Schultheiss, & Grässmann, 1998; Emmons, 1997). Self-efficacy promotes striving toward goals. Students who have higher self-efficacy beliefs are more persistent in their academic work and achieve higher levels of academic performance (Multon, Brown, & Lent, 1991). Occupational choice is influenced by efficacy. In a study of high school equivalency students, those who had a broader generality of self-efficacy considered a wider possible range of occupations; they also had a greater range of interests (Bores-Rangel et al., 1990).

Athletes who are more confident perform better, and elite coaches use a variety of techniques to build such a sense of efficacy, including enhancing performance through drilling, modeling of confidence, and encouraging positive talk (Gould et al., 1989). Self-efficacy promotes good performance among graduate students in business in simulated managerial decision making (Bandura & Wood, 1989; Wood, Bandura, & Bailey, 1990). A sense of self-efficacy leads to persistence in the face of setbacks. Persistence, in turn, ultimately leads to greater success (Wood & Bandura, 1989b). Leading subjects in a managerial task to believe that performance is a skill that can be learned, rather than a stable ability trait, makes them more persistent, so early failures do not lead to giving up (Wood & Bandura, 1989a).

Efficacy is increased if subjects gradually improve their performance on a task. This efficacy, in turn, improves later decision making (Bandura & Jourden, 1991). At least under some circumstances, breaking a large task into smaller subgoals beneficially affects performance because it increases a sense of efficacy. Stock and Cervone (1990) found that subjects who worked toward proximal subgoals on complex problems had increased self-efficacy and persisted longer than those who worked only toward more remote goals. Students with low self-efficacy are especially likely to perform better if they are instructed to set goals for each day's work (Tuckman, 1990). Sexton and Tuckman (1991) studied female college students on a series of mathematics tasks. Based on changes over time, they proposed that self-efficacy beliefs are especially important at the beginning of a task. Thereafter, the behaviors themselves become more important than cognitive variables.

Considerable evidence exists that efficacy expectations and similar positive expectations (such as optimism) contribute to effective functioning in a variety of ways. Before signing up for a motivational "think positive" seminar, though, we should keep some cautions in mind. First, Bandura warns that efficacy expectations should be grounded in experience, or they may not last. Second, it is possible to have unrealistically high efficacy expectations that are harmful, for example, when we expect to be able to stop a bad habit cold and are therefore unprepared to deal with a relapse (Litt, 1988). Or unrealistically high efficacy expectations may cause us to commit to actions that are beyond our ability and therefore harmful or dangerous, such as skiing down a mountain beyond our competence. Third, high efficacy expectations for undesirable behavior (such as aggression) will facilitate those actions, unfortunately (Crick & Dodge, 1994). High efficacy expectancies are helpful, provided they are realistic and the behavior is desirable.

PHYSIOLOGICAL CORRELATES OF EFFICACY

When a person has low self-efficacy, the body, as well as the mind, responds. The autonomic nervous system is aroused (Bandura, Reese, & Adams, 1982). In one study, women phobically afraid of spiders confronted spiders in the laboratory. Sometimes the task was one that the subjects felt they had high efficacy to accomplish (e.g., seeing a spider at a distance); other tasks were more difficult. The women's level of efficacy predicted changes in plasma catecholamine secretion (epinephrine, norepinephrine, and DOPAC). When therapy increased their efficacy expectations, the physiological indicators also changed (Bandura et al., 1985).

Stressors can enhance or suppress immune system functioning. When subjects in a laboratory had low self-efficacy about performing the tasks they were given, their endogenous opioid systems were activated (Bandura et al., 1988; Bandura et al., 1987), which can interfere with the immune system. When subjects who had snake phobias developed self-efficacy to control phobic stressors (because of an experimental manipulation), immune functioning was enhanced (Wiedenfeld et al., 1990).

Although the relationship of efficacy and goal striving more generally to biological variables is only scant, this seems a direction for potential further developments. Self-directed motivated behavior, according to brain development research, plays a role in shaping the brain itself (Bandura, 2001b). Bandura clearly states, though, that psychological analysis cannot be reduced to biological explanation. Changes in such major characteristics as gender roles and a country's peaceful or warlike nature can occur rapidly, as a result of cultural change, not biological or evolutionary mechanisms (Bandura, 2001a; Bussey & Bandura, 1999). As part of an increasingly multilevel approach to theory in personality, the control beliefs described by Bandura (and others) serve an important bridge because they connect to both biological level variables and societal level outcomes (Haidt & Rodin, 1999).

Processes Influencing Learning

Bandura considered in some detail how cognitive person variables such as efficacy are developed. Much more occurs in learning than an automatic "stamping in" of preceding responses, based on reinforcement. His early studies, described here, showed that children could learn aggressive behaviors simply by observing models perform them, without reinforcement. Learning without reinforcement required a new theoretical explanation, which Bandura (1986b) offers: a set of theoretical concepts for understanding the complex events within people that must occur for observed models to produce changes in performance. Briefly, the learner must observe the behavior, remember it, be able to do it, and be motivated to do it. Let's examine these processes in more detail (see Table 12.4).

TABLE 12.4	Processes in Observational Learning

1. ATTENTIONAL PROCESSES: Noticing the Model's Behavior.

The Model: Distinctive

Affective Valence

Complexity

Prevalence

Functional Value

The Observer: Sensory Capacities

Arousal Level

Motivation

Perceptual Set

Past Reinforcement

2. RETENTION PROCESSES: Putting the Behavior into Memory.

Symbolic Coding

Cognitive Organization

Symbolic Rehearsal

Motor Rehearsal

3. MOTOR REPRODUCTION PROCESSES: Being Able to Do It.

Physical Capabilities

Availability of Component Responses

Self-Observation of Reproductions

Accuracy Feedback

4. MOTIVATIONAL PROCESSES: Deciding It Is Worth Doing.

External Reinforcement

Vicarious Reinforcement

Self-Reinforcement

(Albert Bandura, *Social Foundations of Thought & Action: A Social Cognitive Theory.* © 1986, p. 2. Reprinted by permission of Prentice Hall, Englewood Cliffs, New Jersey.)

ATTENTIONAL PROCESSES: OBSERVING THE BEHAVIOR

Nothing will be learned that is not observed. People who have difficulty remembering names, for example, often simply do not pay attention to them in the first place. Several characteristics of the model and of the observer influence modeling. Models catch our attention more when they look distinctive because of their clothes or other aspects of their physical appearance, when they are liked or disliked, and when they are seen repeatedly, as advertisers well know. All these are examples of **attentional processes**. Characteristics of the observer, too, influence attention, including sensory capacities, arousal level, motivation, perceptual set, and past reinforcement.

attentional processes noticing the model's behavior (a prerequisite for learning by modeling)

RETENTION PROCESSES: REMEMBERING IT

retention process
remembering what a
model has done

As any student knows who has paid attention to a classroom lecture or film, not all that is observed is retained. The **retention process** occurs through imaginational representations (such as images of places or people that are familiar) and through verbal coding, which can be much more efficient. Symbolic coding facilitates retention, as cognitive psychology suggests it should. In academic settings, pedagogues teach students to work actively with material to remember it. The same advice applies in other settings as well (e.g., Bandura, Grusec, & Menlove, 1966). Additional factors influencing retention include cognitive organization, symbolic rehearsal, and motor rehearsal.

MOTOR REPRODUCTION PROCESSES: DOING IT

**motor reproduction
process** being able to
do what one has seen a
model do

The behavior being modeled must then be reproduced from its remembered encoding **(motor reproduction process)**. No response can be emitted that is beyond the physical capacity of the individual. Complex behaviors can be reproduced by combining their component response elements, if they are known. Feedback about our performance, such as an athletic trainer's comments or videotaped images of our own play, improve this motor reproduction phase of learning.

MOTIVATIONAL PROCESSES: WANTING IT

**motivational
process** deciding
whether it is worthwhile
to behave as a model
has behaved

Coaches also give pep talks, recognizing the importance of **motivational processes** to learning. Bandura clearly distinguishes between learning and performance. Unless motivated, a person will not produce learned behavior. This motivation can come from external reinforcement, such as the experimenter's promise of reward in some of Bandura's studies, or the bribe of a parent. Or it can come from vicarious reinforcement, based on the observation that models are rewarded. High-status models can affect performance through motivation. For example, girls age 11 to 14 performed better on a motor performance task when they thought it was demonstrated by a high-status cheerleader than by a low-status model (McCullagh, 1986).

Observational Learning and Modeling

We are so aware today of the importance of good models that it is easy to overlook the theoretical advance that occurred when modeling was introduced to the learning-theory paradigm within personality. Radical learning theory, in the Skinnerian tradition, required that responses must occur and be reinforced to be strengthened. Even Neal Miller and John Dollard (1941), for all their theoretical innovation, assumed that responses must be reinforced to be learned. Laboratory rats and pigeons in Skinner boxes were subjected to exhausting shaping interventions to bring about those necessary conditions for learning. If elaborate procedures were necessary to trigger relatively simple motor responses, how could learning theory possibly explain the much more extensive developments that occur in human personality formation?

Humans learn by observing. This is the simple answer that Bandura proposed. Intuitively, it is obvious. However, observational learning violates a traditional assumption of learning theory—that learning can occur only if there is reinforcement. Bandura asserted that learning and performance could be distinguished. Reinforcement provides incentives necessary for performance, but it is not necessary for learning.

Behavioral changes that result from exposure to models are variously called **modeling**, imitative learning, observational learning, or vicarious learning. These terms are interchangeable in Bandura's usage. He defines **vicarious learning** as learning in which

> new responses are acquired or the characteristics of existing response repertoires are modified as a function of observing the behavior of others and its reinforcing consequences, without the modeled responses being overtly performed by the viewer during the exposure period. (Bandura, 1965c, p. 3)

modeling learning by observing others; also called vicarious learning

vicarious learning learning by observing others, without being directly rewarded oneself

In everyday experience, a child may see a friend grab a ball away from a classmate and learn to grab as a result. Or a TV viewer may see a mass murder on television and later imitate the crime. More positively, exposure to competent and socialized adults teaches children desirable behaviors. Bandura's laboratory investigations show that exposure to adult models can lead to diverse effects, including the elevation of the level of moral reasoning (Bandura, 1969; Bandura & McDonald, 1963) or, conversely, an increase in aggressive behavior.

Bandura's interest in modeling had roots in other theoretical traditions. Psychoanalytic approaches emphasize identification with parents as the basis for much personality development. Previous researchers reasoned that children may identify with parents because of their power (as controllers of rewards) or because of their status (as recipients of rewards). Bandura designed a laboratory experiment to test these proposed causes of identification. Preschool children observed various kinds of models, some powerful, called *controller models* (because they controlled access to highly desirable toys) and some high status, called *consumer models* (because they received rewards). The children observed the models engaging in playful behavior with several distinctive components, such as putting on a hat backward or walking and saying, "Left, right, left, right."

Then the children played with the same toys, and observers counted the number of responses patterned after each model. Children modeled their behavior more after the controller models, not the consumer models. In a traditional family, with a working father and a homemaker mother, this would produce greater identification with the father, as much psychoanalytically derived research has suggested. Other family power structures exist, of course, and were explored in this study. Whether the controller model was male or female and whether the subjects were boys or girls, the controller model was imitated more than the consumer model. Overall, the research indicates that power leads to identification (Bandura, Ross, & Ross, 1963a). Other research has confirmed that models that dispense rewards to children have more effect on children's learning than nonrewarding models do (Grusec & Mischel, 1966).

Models also can influence children's development of standards for behavior (cf. Mischel, 1966). How good does a performance have to be before self-congratulations are deserved? Bandura and Whalen (1966) exposed 8- to 11-year-olds to models who rewarded themselves for their scores on a bowling task, giving themselves praise and candy according to a performance criterion that varied for different groups of subjects. Some models rewarded themselves only for superior performance; others demanded of themselves moderately good performance; and lenient models rewarded themselves for all but the very worst scores. When the children later played the game themselves, they demanded very high performance before rewarding themselves only if their models had set high standards. Even the most permissive models, however, produced self-reward standards higher than a control group of children who had not observed any model. Later research (Bandura, Grusec, & Menlove, 1967a) found that children were influenced by peer models who set high standards, as well as adult models.

Aggression, too, is learned by modeling (Bandura, 1965a, 1965b, 1973). Boys and girls, age 3 to 5, watched a film in which adults played with a variety of toys, including a large inflated Bobo doll. The adult models engaged in distinctive aggressive behaviors that the children would not have seen before to provide an opportunity to learn new responses.

> First, the model laid the Bobo doll on its side, sat on it, and punched it in the nose while remarking, "Pow, right in the nose, boom, boom." The model then raised the doll and pommeled it on the head with a mallet. Each response was accompanied by the verbalization, "Sockeroo . . . stay down." Following the mallet aggression, the model kicked the doll about the room, and these responses were interspersed with the comment, "Fly away." Finally, the model threw rubber balls at the Bobo doll, each strike punctuated with a "Bang." This sequence of physically and verbally aggressive behavior was repeated twice. (Bandura, 1965b, pp. 590–591)

For some children, this was the end of the film (no consequences condition). Other children saw the film continue, ending with the model being punished by another adult for his aggression (model punished condition) or with another adult praising the aggressive model for being a "strong champion" and rewarding him with food (model rewarded condition).

To test for modeling, the children were brought to a playroom similar to the one they had seen on the film. Observers counted the number of aggressive responses the children imitated from the film. As predicted, there was less imitation in the model-punished condition than in the other two conditions. There was no difference between the model-rewarded condition and the no-consequences condition. These modeling effects were similar for boys and for girls, although the girls behaved less aggressively overall (see Figure 12.5), consistent with other studies finding greater aggression in boys. Whether these sex differences were caused by different learning experiences for boys and girls or from the influence of biological differences such as hormones (Collaer & Hines, 1995) could not be answered from this study.

It is tempting to conclude that aggressive television is no danger as long as the villain is punished in the end. Although observing a model who is punished can sometimes inhibit aggression (Bandura, Ross, & Ross, 1963b), such a conclusion is not always warranted. Bandura included another feature in this study, which discredits this erroneous conclusion. For some children in each condition Bandura offered incentives (stickers and juice) if they could behave like the model they had seen. These children showed high levels of learning of the aggressive behaviors in all conditions. Thus punishing the villain may temporarily suppress the performance of imitative aggression, but the behaviors have been learned and may emerge later when incentive conditions change.

Ever since Bandura's early research, hundreds of studies using a variety of research methods have examined the relationship between TV violence and behavior. The overwhelming finding is that in the real world, as well as in the laboratory, models do teach aggression. Fortunately, as other studies show, models can also teach high standards and other positive social behaviors.

Modeling is not limited to childhood. Industrial psychologists use principles of learning through modeling to train workers (Decker & Nathan, 1985). In a field experiment, female college students who were in a car were more likely to use a seat belt if the driver did so (Howell, Owen, & Nocks, 1990). Even the Philadelphia Zoo has increased the attention of visitors to its exhibits, causing them to linger instead of moving quickly on to the next by placing strategic models who expressed interest in various exhibits (Koran & Camp, 1998). Modeling is a powerful determinant of the sorts of behaviors that have traditionally interested personality theorists. Bandura's clear theoretical specification of the processes involved in modeling and other forms of learning makes a precise, verifiable theory.

Figure 12.5 Modeling of Aggression

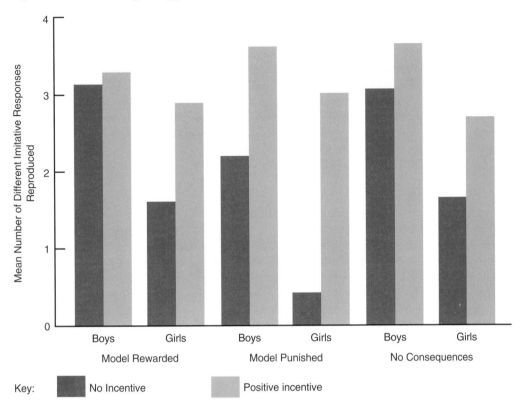

Mean number of different matching responses reproduced by children as a function of positive incentives and the model's reinforcement contingencies.

(From A. Bandura (1965). Influences of models' reinforcement contingencies on the acquisition of imitative responses. *Journal of Personality and Social Psychology, 1,* 589–595. Copyright 1965 by the American Psychological Association. Reprinted by permission.)

Therapy

Bandura (1961) criticizes therapy based only on talking, when known learning principles could improve outcomes. This evaluation is widely shared; cognitive behavioral approaches in therapy have been the most rapidly growing citations in recent years (Killgore, 2000), and cognitive behavioral therapy has demonstrated success in treating a variety of problems, including depression, eating disorders, and several kinds of anxiety disorders, and it even has value in treating sexual offenders and those who suffer from schizophrenia (Butler et al., 2004). Programs to increase clients' ability to avoid relapse after giving up alcohol have been devised, using social learning principles to individualize treatment for each alcoholic's high-risk situations (Annis, 1990). Efficacy expectations help people stop using marijuana (Stephens, Wertz, & Roffman, 1995).

Therapy that uses social learning principles such as modeling can successfully treat adults and children who suffer from phobias, including excessive fear of snakes, without any need for symbolic interpretation of the snake phobia (Bandura, Adams, & Beyer, 1977; Bandura & Barab, 1973; Bandura, Blanchard, & Ritter, 1969; Bandura, Grusec, & Menlove,

1967b; Bandura, Jeffery, & Wright, 1974; Bandura & Menlove, 1968). Other studies confirm that therapies based on learning principles are effective for various phobias, including agoraphobia, a fear of public places (Bandura et al., 1980). These findings contradict the prediction of psychoanalytic theory that only resolution of deep-seated unconscious conflicts could bring about a cure. They are consistent, though, with a study of the thoughts of agoraphobic people as they faced enclosed places, which they feared. These patients thought much more about their ability or inability to manage their anxiety than they did about any danger in the situation (Williams et al., 1997). Bandura (1961) argues that psychotherapy should be regarded as a learning process. More systematic application of learning principles (including reward, extinction, and discrimination learning, among others) can improve therapeutic outcomes.

In Bandura's view, changing self-efficacy expectations are key to successful therapy for fears and avoidant behavior (Bandura, 1977, 1984a; Bandura et al., 1980). Bandura suggests that phobias result from low efficacy expectations, not low outcome expectations. A person with a fear of flying may be convinced that, if only it were possible to get on the plane, life would be improved by desirable recreational and business outcomes (high outcome expectation). But as long as it seems impossible to board the plane and sit calmly in a seat during a flight (low efficacy expectation), that person will not be able to fly. Bandura stated, "treatments that are most effective are built on an empowerment model. If you really want to help people, you provide them with the competencies, build a strong self-belief, and create opportunities for them to exercise those competencies"

Figure 12.6 Changing Efficacy Expectations Through Therapy

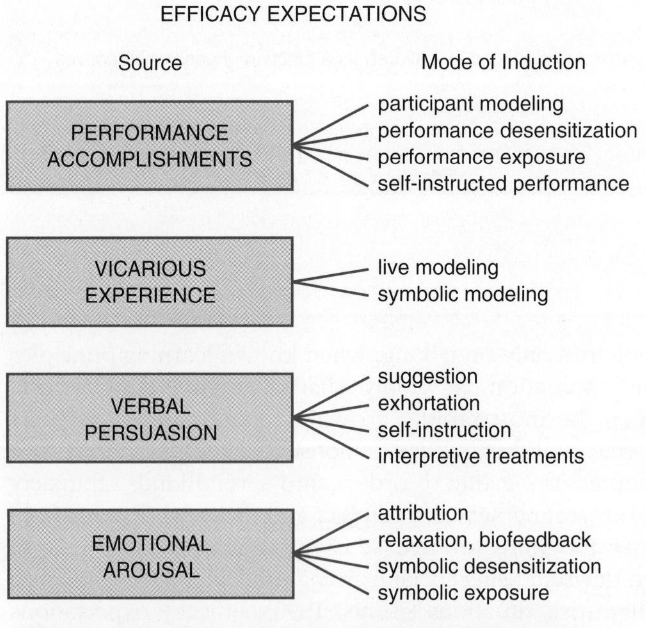

EFFICACY EXPECTATIONS

Major sources of efficacy information and the principal sources through which different modes of treatment operate.

(From A. Bandura (1977). Self-efficacy: Toward a unifying theory of behavioral change. *Psychological Review, 84,* 191–215. Copyright 1977 by the American Psychological Association. Reprinted by permission.)

(R. I. Evans, 1989, p. 16). Therapy will succeed if it increases self-efficacy. Bandura suggests that various therapy techniques, including talk therapy, are effective for a common reason: They change dysfunctional expectancies. People avoid actions that they do not expect they are able to do (Bandura, 1986a, 1989a, 1991a). Behavioral therapies, according to Bandura, are the most efficient and effective ways to raise efficacy expectations and therefore are the treatment of choice for phobias. Other techniques may be effective but only to the extent that efficacy expectations are raised. Even depth psychoanalysis can change dysfunctional expectancies but slowly. After many months or years, a patient may come to expect that adult life will be improved because problems are seen as stemming from childhood conflicts that are considered resolved. Figure 12.6 lists some of the therapeutic alternatives for increasing efficacy expectations.

Sometimes increasing efficacy is simple but nonetheless effective. Naval cadets who were simply told that they would probably not become seasick, and that if they did, it would probably not interfere with their work, in fact experienced less seasickness as a result (Eden & Zuk, 1995). Usually, though, more extensive therapeutic intervention is required to modify efficacy expectations. Knowing its importance, researchers who evaluate the effectiveness of therapies, such as interventions to help people with disabilities, now include measures of empowerment as one desirable outcome of their interventions (Zimmerman & Warschausky, 1998). We can think of increased empowerment or efficacy as a *nonspecific* outcome of therapy, in contrast to *specific* outcomes, such as a reduction in fear (Frank, 1982; Keijsers, Schaap, & Hoogduin, 2000).

The Person in the Social Environment

Many of the terms we have been using—*self* and *goals*, for example—conjure up images of the individual pursuing selfish goals with no thought of others, but that misperception probably comes from the overwhelming individualism of the culture in which most of us were raised. In fact, the environment in Bandura's three-part reciprocal determinism does more than simply provide an arena for individual accomplishments. It is a place of community, with goals and values that we share with others; of social responsibility, where our efficacy and ability can be put to work on behalf of others.

In addition to individual efficacy, Bandura suggests that a sense of **collective efficacy** occurs when groups believe that they, as a group, can do what needs to be done (R. I. Evans, 1989). Working together, they exert collective agency, in contrast to individual agency (Bandura, 2001b). As expected, the higher the sense of collective efficacy, the more groups mobilize toward their goals and resist obstacles, and the more they accomplish (Bandura, 2000).

collective efficacy the sense that a group can do what is to be done

Bandura (1990b, 1991b) warns that individuals often fail to regulate their own behavior in ways that live up to high moral standards. They exploit others, commit aggressive acts, pollute the atmosphere, and engage in many other behaviors that violate moral standards. This is a problem of **moral disengagement** (Bandura, 1978, 2001b; R. I. Evans, 1989). People can turn off, or disengage, their moral standards by a variety of techniques: convincing themselves that the ends justify the means, using euphemistic language that does not convey the immorality of the action, comparing with far worse behavior, displacing responsibility onto others, dehumanizing the victims, and so on (Bandura, 2001b). Like defense mechanisms described by psychoanalysts, these maneuvers protect from guilt. What is more, though, the social sensitivity of this theory makes a point that intrapsychic psychoanalytic theory does not: The moral disengagement mechanisms

moral disengagement failure to regulate one's behavior to live up to high moral standards

facilitate immoral behavior against others. Measures of moral disengagement (e.g., agreeing with the statement "If people are careless where they leave things, it is their own fault if they get stolen") predict that people will commit more transgressions (Bandura et al., 2001). Bandura (1999a) argues that societies must exert social control to supplement individuals' undependable moral self-control.

Fortunately, there is not a conflict between individual efficacy and moral responsibility. In fact, Bandura (2001b) reports that children who are high in efficacy are more cooperative and helpful to others, not less.

Summary

- Mischel challenged the assumption of *global personality traits* that led to consistent behavior across many situations, finding inconsistency instead. Behavior is much more situationally variable than trait theory had assumed.
- Instead of traits, Mischel proposed *cognitive person variables*, including *competencies, encoding strategies*, and *personal constructs*.
- Mischel has investigated children's development of a capacity to *delay gratification*. Cognitive variables are important in this development. Children learn such strategies as thinking about something else to avoid impulsive behavior.
- Bandura's concept of *reciprocal determinism* describes the mutual influences among the person, the environment, and behavior.
- Bandura has divided learning into four processes, allowing more precise prediction of when learning will occur. These are *attentional, retention, motor reproduction*, and *motivational processes*.
- Bandura demonstrated that children are influenced by *models* of desirable and undesirable behavior. They can learn to delay gratification or to be aggressive by watching adults in real life and on television.
- *Self-efficacy* refers to the belief that one can perform a particular behavior.
- Extensive research shows that *efficacy beliefs* affect the choice and persistence of behavior.
- Efficacy beliefs can be increased in *therapy*, and this is the mechanism by which therapy is effective, according to Bandura.

Thinking about Mischel's and Bandura's Theories

1. Do you think that cognitive social learning theory is capable of describing the most important human personality characteristics, or is it too focused on cognition?

2. Do you believe that people are consistent or not consistent? Explain.

3. How would you determine whether competencies and expectancies are the causes of behavior or the effects?

4. Compare delay of gratification to what psychoanalysts meant by the ego; compare modeling with identification.

5. Do you believe that media violence contributes to aggression in society? If so, what should be done about it?

6. How do schools and/or parents influence children's sense of self-efficacy? What advice would you give?

Study Questions

1. Summarize the trait controversy and Mischel's role in it.
2. Explain the term *personality coefficient*. Why does it present a problem for traditional personality theory that this number is low?
3. Explain Mischel's concept of situational hedges. How is this concept relevant to the trait versus situation controversy?
4. Explain what Mischel meant by cognitive person variables as alternatives to traits. Give examples.
5. Explain what is meant by competencies. How are they different from expectancies?
6. Define self-efficacy. Why are self-efficacy expectancies important?
7. Explain how expectancies can be influenced by experience.
8. What is the function of self-regulatory systems and plans in personality? Give an example.
9. Summarize research on delay of gratification. What evidence shows the importance of developing this capacity in early life?
10. Diagram and explain Bandura's concept of reciprocal determinism. Discuss how this concept is different from Skinner's concept of environmental determinism.
11. What is a self-system, in Bandura's theory?
12. What is self-efficacy? How is it related to behavior?
13. What evidence has Bandura presented to indicate that self-efficacy affects the body?
14. List and explain Bandura's four processes that influence learning. Give an example of each process as it might influence a person who is learning to act like a famous athlete.
15. Summarize Bandura's research on modeling. Explain the relevance of this research for personality development.
16. Describe the evidence Bandura presented that indicates a relationship between seeing aggressive models and behaving aggressively. Why can aggression still result, even if the aggressive model is punished?
17. What has cognitive social learning theory contributed to psychotherapy?
18. How does self-efficacy change during therapy?
19. What is collective efficacy? Give an example from your own observation.
20. Explain what Bandura meant by moral disengagement. How does this process raise problems that must be solved by society, and not simply by changing individuals?

13

Kelly
Personal Construct Theory

Chapter Overview

Preview: Overview of Kelly's Theory

Constructive Alternativism

The Process of Construing

The Structure of Construct Systems

The Social Embeddedness of Construing Efforts

The Role Construct Repertory (REP) Test

Cognitive Complexity

Personality Change

Therapy

Research Findings

Constructivism, Social Constructionism, and Postmodernism

Summary

ILLUSTRATIVE BIOGRAPHY

Richard Nixon

Richard Nixon, remembered as the U.S. president who resigned from office in 1974 in the face of almost certain impeachment, provides an interesting case study for personal construct theory. The ideas that drove his personality are central to understanding how he succeeded politically and why he faced a disgraceful end to a long political career. George Kelly's personal construct theory provides a framework for understanding concepts such as these. It is distinct from many of the other analyses of this man because it focuses squarely on his thinking.

Richard Milhous Nixon, born in 1913, was elected the 37th president of the United States (1969–1974). His administration was widely praised for increasing contact with communist China, which earlier had been closed to Western visitors and business, but most Americans remember him for the disgrace that ended his presidency. He resigned under the threat of impeachment initiated by the Watergate scandal, a bungled act of political espionage, in which his Republican party tried to steal documents from the Democratic offices at the Watergate Hotel complex and then lied in an attempt to cover up the burglary.

Richard Nixon was the second child of five boys. His older brother, Arthur, died of meningitis in 1925, and a younger brother, Harold, died of tuberculosis in 1933. Nixon was raised (after age 9) in Whittier, California, where he worked in the family store. His mother's family was Quaker, and this background influenced his upbringing by emphasizing emotional control, modesty, and hard work. His father (not a Quaker) was more emotional and punitive, and Nixon became interested in politics because of his influence

(Ambrose, 1987). At times, Nixon avoided his father when the atmosphere became too tense, often going off somewhere alone to read.

Nixon enjoyed debate. His first formal debate was in seventh grade (Ambrose, 1987, p. 39). He continued with this interest at Whittier College. (Although he had been admitted to Harvard University and awarded a scholarship there, he could not afford to attend. His brother's bout with tuberculosis had been costly.) After college, Nixon attended Duke University Law School on a scholarship; he was an excellent student. He later became an attorney in California. During World War II, he volunteered for the navy, although as a Quaker he would have qualified for conscientious

objector status. (At that time in history, there was a military draft in the United States, not a volunteer military.) Nixon was popular in this structured environment. He was also very good at poker, winning enough to start a political campaign for Congress when the war ended.

Elected to public office, Nixon became nationally known for his role in the House Committee on Un-American Activities, where he forcefully investigated Alger Hiss, who had served in the State Department, for secret communist associations and espionage. Nixon served in the House and then in the Senate before becoming vice president under Dwight Eisenhower (1953–1961). He had a reputation for dirty campaign tactics and was disliked by many because of his personality, seeming to be insincere and calculating (Ambrose, 1987). In 1960 he lost a close election for the presidency to John F. Kennedy, and 2 years later he lost a bid to become governor of California. He seemed to have retired from politics. However, he garnered the Republican presidential nomination in 1968 and won the general election that November. In the 1972 election, Nixon was reelected by one of the widest margins on record, defeating Democratic presidential candidate George McGovern.

As president, Richard Nixon grappled with the Vietnam War, but like his predecessor, Lyndon Johnson, he could not easily end it. He opened diplomatic relations with communist China and signed an historic Strategic Arms Limitation Treaty with the Soviet Union. Despite these bold initiatives in foreign policy, most Americans remember Nixon primarily for the Watergate scandal. It began as a fumbled political espionage caper, with burglars hired by the Committee to Reelect the President breaking into the Washington, D.C., headquarters of the Democratic National Committee at the Watergate apartment-office complex. As the case developed, the break-in became less salient than Nixon's involvement in a coverup of the operation, a coverup documented in his own tape recordings of conversations in the president's Oval Office. Ultimately, threatened with impeachment, Nixon resigned from office on August 9, 1974 (Woodward & Bernstein, 1976). It is ironic that a third-rate act of domestic political espionage could bring down such a leader. During the years before his death in 1994, Nixon continued as an elder statesman and wrote about his public life and foreign policy.

Description

Personality, in Kelly's theory, consists of the ideas, the concepts, that a person uses to understand and predict his or her experience. He provided an elaborate description of the nature of such constructs, as we see later in this chapter. In Kelly's approach, there is no one objective, accurate way to construe situations. It is the unique concepts that each person applies, that constitute personality.

Nixon's actions stunned many, who wondered what he could have been thinking, in the elaborate political espionage and coverup of Watergate. In foreign affairs, he thought differently about our then enemies, the communist countries of the Soviet Union and mainland China. (It was a different era then. Current students are not likely to appreciate how much distrust and fear those countries aroused.) People wondered how he could make overtures of peace and trade with these enemies. Obviously Nixon thought differently.

Cognition

Kelly's theory offers an elaborate framework for describing a person's cognition. The concepts, called constructs, that we use to understand and predict the world are dichotomous, consisting of two opposite poles. We may not always know both sides of these concepts, consciously.

Richard Nixon's speeches give ample evidence of the dichotomous poles of his constructs. He described people by the construct of "we" (patriotic Americans; the working class; his supporters) versus "they" (the spoiled rich).

Hard work was a theme that resonated with the working class, especially when portrayed against the spoiled rich. Richard Nixon aimed for success, working long hours on his election campaigns and before that in law school, surviving on little sleep. Winter and Carlson (1988) concluded, from a content analysis of Nixon's first inaugural address, that he was high in achievement motivation. How did he define success? It was not in financial terms; he regularly gave speaking fees to charity (Ambrose, 1987). He considered success to be achievable by hard work. Some of his important personal constructs, then, concerned hard work. Perhaps his expression of this work ethic was a factor in his political success among middle-class and working-class voters.

Ambrose (1987, p. 614) describes the divisiveness of Nixon's campaign speeches. "He wanted to divide the community into 'us' and 'them,' and he succeeded." Nixon's construct of us versus them applied to domestic politics (Republicans versus the opposition) and to international relations (the United States versus the communists). Patriotism was an important theme, with the Vietnam war still on the nation's mind. Nixon's dogged investigations of communists early in his political career when he was a member of the House Committee on Un-American Activities reflects the *us* (patriotic Americans) versus *them* (communist sympathizers) construct. In his successful 1968 campaign for the presidency, Nixon defined *us* as "the Silent Majority, Middle America, the white, comfortable, patriotic, hawkish 'forgotten Americans'" (Ambrose, 1989, p. 222). *Them* included long-haired antiwar protesters and the elite who attended Ivy League schools. At other times, the press was the enemy (p. 250). Nixon's reputed vindictiveness also stems from an

us-versus-them construct system. Ambrose described Nixon as "a vindictive man, with a long memory and a deep capacity to hate" (p. 172; cf. also p. 267). He maintained an "enemies list" of political opponents. Secretary of Defense Elliot Richardson suggested that Nixon was unable to stop thinking of others as enemies, which impeded his effectiveness as chief executive (T. H. White, 1975, p. 180). *We-they* may work as a construct in political campaigns (and Nixon was a dedicated campaigner), but it is a divisive construct for a sitting president.

How did he conceptualize the role of politician? Nixon's interpersonal manner was cold toward others, including his wife, at least in public. For Nixon, loneliness was inevitable for a politician. As he said, "Politics is not a team sport" (Nixon, 1990, p. 32). Yet Ambrose (1987, p. 618) argues that other politicians, including Dwight Eisenhower, were in fact gregarious, so there is nothing universal about Nixon's ideas. For Nixon, the construct of politician included, on the positive pole, loneliness; close interpersonal relationships belonged to the contrast pole, which for Nixon would also include the dimension of insecurity, given the death of two of his brothers and the absence of his mother during significant periods of his youth (Levey, 1986). The constructs of politician by others did not include this loneliness component. It is noteworthy that in other conditions, in which he was not vulnerable, Nixon showed a friendly, considerate side of himself (Winter & Carlson, 1988). For example, he was especially considerate to hired help at the White House. Such fragmentation is consistent with Kelly's Fragmentation Corollary, which says constructs are applied in only some settings, not all.

Another aspect of Nixon's construct of a successful politician was pragmatism (Ambrose, 1989, p. 171; Nixon, 1990, chap. 32). Political realism or pragmatism could produce changes of opinion and illegal actions that others, with other construct systems, would regard as unprincipled (cf. Winter & Carlson, 1988). Nixon's construct system facilitated his bold initiatives in foreign affairs, most notably his visit to the People's Republic of China in 1972 and arms reduction negotiations with the Soviet Union.

The construct of privacy or secrecy was important for Richard Nixon. He seemed to regard secret activities as more effective and public ones less effective, the latter for show but not for effective action. Public behavior called for a politician to behave as an actor (Nixon, 1990). He often made executive decisions with little consultation. For example, his secretary of state learned of his plan to visit China by reading it in the newspaper (Ambrose, 1989, p. 454). Nixon preferred to negotiate in "back-channel" communications, where fewer people were involved. He often acted through National Security Adviser Henry Kissinger rather than through the State Department. He is remembered for favoring covert operations, including wiretaps and the infamous break-in of the headquarters of the Democratic National Committee in the Watergate office complex in Washington, D.C.

Kelly's Sociality Corollary asserts that understanding another person's construct system makes possible a relationship with that person. Nixon and Kissinger understood one another. According to Ambrose (1989), "They shared a love of eavesdropping on others (the taps and the tapes), of secrecy, of surprises, of conspiracy, of backbiting, of power plays. They were alike in their utter cynicism, and in their contempt for everyone else, including each other" (pp. 490–491).

Adjustment

Constructs vary from one person to another, but some produce better adjustment than others. If we think of our constructs as ways of making predictions—what will happen, if I do thus and so—then some construct systems will produce more accurate predictions than others. A well-adjusted person has construct systems that make accurate predictions, and having a variety of construct systems ("cognitive complexity") suggests that the person is more likely to have one to fit any particular situation.

Nixon's greatest presidential achievements were, it is generally acknowledged, in foreign affairs. His knowledge was immense in this area. He eschewed simple tactics and criticized simplistic slogans about war and peace (Nixon, 1990, p. 346) and simplistic approaches to combating communism (Nixon, 1962, pp. 287–291). In Kelly's language, we may conclude that Nixon's construct system in foreign affairs was cognitively complex and served to predict accurately. In this area, he functioned commendably. In domestic affairs, his constructs did not lead to accurate predictions, or there would never have been the tragedy of Watergate. His "we–they" polarizations did not give him the flexibility needed to work with the people he needed to influence.

Society

In Kelly's theory, you must understand the constructs of other people if you are to work effectively with them. It is not necessary that you have the same ideas, but you must understand the other.

The polarizing constructs of Nixon's construct system, just described, tended to dismiss the other's point of view, preventing effective dialogue, at least in the domestic arena. Nixon's success in opening new relationships with communist countries implies that he could understand their concepts. His own preference for secrecy and intolerance for dissent may be key to this understanding. Besides this theoretical point, when we are dealing with the actions of the president of the United States, it is obvious that his behavior has an impact on society both at home and abroad (e.g., the changed relationship with China).

Development

Kelly's theory says relatively little about development. He does assert that constructs change with experience. If you use a construct and it makes a usable prediction (confirmation), you keep it. If the construct leads to a false prediction (disconfirmation), you abandon or modify it, although people do have ways of blinding themselves to disconfirmation.

Cognitive expectations influence our behavior, and if they are incomplete or inaccurate, adverse consequences may happen in the real world. This was the case in the infamous end of Nixon's presidency. Behavior that he thought of little consequence—approving domestic political espionage into the secrets of the opposing Democratic party and then ordering coverup of the crime of the Watergate break-in—led to public scandal and his forced resignation from office. Clearly, his constructs had been disconfirmed, but it was too late to take back those actions.

Biology

Kelly's theory says little about biology. One idea he offers is the idea of a "preverbal construct," which is not represented in language but rather in emotion or a physical symptom. Nixon's reported psychosomatic symptoms in times of crisis can be explained as preverbal constructs (Volkan, Itzkowitz, & Dod, 1997). They may have begun in his conflicted childhood.

Final Thoughts

In many ways, the life of Richard Nixon illustrates both the positive and the negative effects of our cognitively based personality. On the positive side, high beliefs in his potential for success inspired Nixon to climb from unremarkable origins to world fame. On the negative side, the fact that some of these cognitions were based on a shaky foundation led to his downfall. The great tragedy of Nixon's fall from the office of president came from a cognitive error, a miscalculation. He approved a scheme to steal political secrets, and when it was discovered, he misjudged that he could lie and make the accusations go away. These errors and their resultant behavior resulted in severe damage to his reputation, and they placed the federal government in disarray. The constructs by which he judged behavior such as domestic spying as simply expedient were judged by others to be unethical. If we want to know what another person will do, we must know what they think.

Preview: Overview of Kelly's Theory

George Kelly's theory has implications for major theoretical questions, as presented in Table 13.1. Like the cognitive theories of Mischel and Bandura, who were influenced by his earlier work, Kelly analyzed personality in a way that suggested measurement techniques, especially his much-used Role Construct Repertory test. Predictions based on his theory, though, are not always precise because of the difficulty of making allowance for idiosyncrasies, a problem inherent in all approaches that use an idiographic, as opposed

TABLE 13.1	Preview of Kelly's Theory
Individual Differences	Individuals differ in the personal constructs (cognitions) they apply to experience. Other differences (emotions, behavior) follow from this.
Adaptation and Adjustment	Constructs that can predict a broad variety of experience accurately are more adaptive than constructs that predict only limited experience. Many therapeutic techniques are presented, including fixed-role therapy.
Cognitive Processes	Cognition is central to personality. Cognitive processes are elaborately described in Kelly's theory. Behaviors and emotions follow from cognitions.
Society	Social relationships require that one person can understand the other's personal constructs. Kelly does not consider broader social institutions.
Biological Influences	Kelly does not consider biological factors explicitly. However, his concept of "preverbal constructs" and ideas about the relationship between construct change and emotions have potential implications for health and disease.
Development	Although Kelly does not focus on childhood, children develop constructs for making sense of their experience, especially their experience with people. Adults continue to use the personal constructs developed earlier, changing them when they do not predict accurately.

to a nomothetic, approach. The theory is rather narrowly cognitive; although Kelly suggested preverbal constructs with bodily implications, explicit connections with particular biological functions have not been made. As an applied theory, Kelly's work on role constructs has been widely applied in business and organizations.

George Kelly proposed a theory of personality that emphasizes the individual's thoughts. When it was proposed, it was outside the mainstream of psychology. Despite the fact that a cognitive revolution has taken place within psychology and that the need for cognition has been studied as a personality variable (Cacioppo et al., 1996), Kelly's theory is still relatively isolated from other theories, perhaps because of its idiographic emphasis and its teleological orientation (G. S. Howard, 1988; B. Warren, 1991). It focuses on the individual personality, rather than on the situation, inspiring Kelly to refer to his theory as a **jackass theory** of personality. By this, he meant that the theory concerns the "nature of the animal" rather than environmental forces that push ("pitchfork theories") or pull ("carrot theories") the individual (Kelly, 1958). Like his unpretentious phrase, Kelly's theory is not caught up in abstract and unobservable theoretical constructs; rather, it focuses on the phenomenological experience of the individual (cf. B. M. Walker, 1990), as do the humanistic theories in the next two chapters (cf. Epting & Leitner, 1992). Despite the theory's emphasis on a person's thoughts, some argue that it is not a cognitive theory (W. G. Warren, 1990a, 1990b), and Kelly (1955) agreed. He argued for a holistic, even humanistic (Kelly, 1969) integration of cognition with other processes, usually separately considered as emotional and motivational. Broadly speaking, Kelly's view is similar to that of Alfred Adler. In fact, he published some of his work in the Adlerian journal, *Individual Psychology* (Kelly, 1963b, 1964), and, like Adler, cited the philosopher Hans Vaihinger (Kelly, 1964). People are not pawns in the face of reality. They make their own destiny by how they interpret events.

jackass theory
Kelly's phrase to indicate that his theory concerns the "nature of the animal" rather than of the environment

BIOGRAPHY OF GEORGE KELLY

George A. Kelly was born in 1905 on a farm in Perth, Kansas, the only child in a family headed by a Presbyterian minister. In college, Kelly first studied engineering but then changed to education, completing his degree at the University of Edinburgh, Scotland, in 1930. In graduate school, he turned his attention to "learn[ing] something about sociology and labor relations" (Kelly, 1963a, p. 47). While a graduate student, he taught in many nonpsychological fields, including oratory, public speaking, dramatics, and government. Kelly's first reading of Freud led to "the mounting feeling of incredulity that anyone could write such nonsense, much less publish it. It was not the pansexualism that makes Freud objectionable to some new readers, but the elastic meanings and arbitrary syntax that disturbed me" (p. 47). Kelly reported spending only 9 months studying psychology before completing his doctorate at the University of Iowa. This left him free to develop a theory that was quite original, not closely tied to that of any earlier theorist.

GEORGE KELLY

For 12 years, Kelly taught at a small college in western Kansas. Although his training was in education rather than clinical psychology, he saw many students in a free counseling clinic that he set up. This clinic became the laboratory for his emerging theory.

He served as a traveling psychologist for many rural Kansas schools during this time and so should be recognized as a school psychologist, although this is usually overlooked (Guydish et al., 1985). Also often forgotten is his early use of bipolar adjective ratings, which did not become popular until many years later (Jackson et al., 1988). He reports that he never, even later, charged for his consultations. Kelly (1963a) was aware of the impact of the Great Depression on his students, but he felt that psychology had an important role, "to generate the imagination needed to envision. . . possibilities" of overcoming the limitations of circumstances (p. 50). Thus, despite his scientific background as an engineer, the dramatist's imagination played an important role in his sense of what psychology should be, and he integrated this approach with science. As he alternated between seeing clients and supervising graduate students, Kelly came to view both as doing similar cognitive work. "Man-the-scientist" became his metaphor for therapeutic work.

After a year at the University of Maryland, Kelly moved to Ohio State University, where he took Carl Rogers's former position heading the clinical training program. It was there that Kelly (1955) wrote his two-volume work, *The Psychology of Personal Constructs*, explaining his theory and its clinical implications.

Kelly influenced the training of clinicians not only in Ohio and Kansas but also nationwide. He was president of the American Board of Examiners for Professional Psychologists from 1951 to 1953, a member of the Special Advisory Group for the Veterans Administration from 1955 to 1960, and a member of the Training Committee of the National Institute for Mental Health and the National Institutes of Health from 1958 to 1967. In the final year of his life, he accepted the invitation of Abraham Maslow to a position at Brandeis University. Kelly died on March 6, 1967.

Constructive Alternativism

personal construct a person's concept for predicting events

Drawing on his experiences as both a clinician and a faculty member in a research discipline, Kelly developed a metaphor of personality that described a human being as a scientist. Just as a scientist uses theories to plan observations, a person uses **personal constructs** to predict what will happen in life. Like a scientist seeking a theory with maximum predictive ability, the person tries to develop concepts that will make personal life, especially in the realm of interpersonal relationships, most predictable. Accurate predictions permit control. The person, like the scientist, finds that predictions are not always confirmed by experience, so he or she must sometimes revise these personal concepts. This, then, is Kelly's (1955, p. 4) metaphor of **man-the-scientist**.

man-the-scientist Kelly's metaphor for human personality

Kelly did not postulate some motivation or force to get a person moving. That is, no motivational theory was necessary, no concept akin to Freud's libido or learning theorists' reward. The person is already active, and the direction of this activity is determined by "the ways in which he anticipates events." Thus the person is actively adapting in a future-oriented way. To continue with his "man-the-scientist" metaphor, the person is hypothesizing future events as best he or she can.

constructive alternativism the assumption that people can interpret the world in a variety of ways

Kelly (1955, p. 15) makes the philosophical position behind his theory explicit: "We assume that all of our present interpretations of the universe are subject to revision or replacement." He calls this assumption **constructive alternativism**. Because we could construe the world differently, our beliefs do not have the status of objective truth. Instead, we should emphasize the act of construing, realizing that our concepts are never identical with ultimate reality but always tentative and subject to revision (McWilliams, 1993).

This uncertainty can bring freedom rather than anxiety. Rather than being determined, as stimulus-response theories and psychoanalytic theory assume, people are free to the extent that they are able to construct alternate "interpretations of the universe."

The theory is stated clearly and explicitly in 12 succinct statements. These dozen statements consist of one Fundamental Postulate and 11 corollaries.

THE FUNDAMENTAL POSTULATE

Kelly's **Fundamental Postulate** states:

> A person's processes are psychologically channelized by the ways in which he anticipates events. (Kelly, 1955, p. 46)

Fundamental Postulate Kelly's main assumption, which stresses the importance of psychological constructs

We prepare for the events that we anticipate. Our actions, thoughts, and emotions are determined by this anticipation, whether accurate or inaccurate. Imagine that you expect to win the lottery tomorrow; now, imagine that you expect the world to end tomorrow. Such anticipations have different effects, do they not? If events occur as they are anticipated, **validation** has occurred. If not, there has been invalidation (Landfield, 1988). This cycle of construing events and having the construction confirmed or not is repeated, sometimes with revision of the construct system (see Figure 13.1). Learning from experience through confirmation or disconfirmation of hypotheses is, of course, the scientist's way.

validation confirmation of an anticipation by events

Are people really like scientists in their personal lives? Although the metaphor of the scientist has become popular even beyond Kelly's theory (e.g., D. Kuhn, 1989), people are not very good scientists in their everyday lives. For one thing, they seek confirmation of their beliefs, whereas the scientist seeks evidence that could be disconfirming (Klayman & Ha, 1987). In fact, people sometimes turn to nonscientific astrology to become more certain about their beliefs (Lillqvist & Lindeman, 1998). We generally live so that our prophecies become self-fulfilling. Life frequently offers enough evidence on both sides to permit the confirmation of mutually contradictory expectations, depending on where we look. This selective viewing is suggested by the popular image of the "half-empty, half-full" glass, which confirms either optimistic or pessimistic expectations. Optimism is maintained by optimistic expectations and a tendency to overlook negatives. Depressed people, in contrast, maintain their depression by self-confirmation (Andrews, 1989). For example, a depressed person may expect that others will not want to have a close friendship and therefore will avoid looking for disconfirmation (e.g., by suggesting to spend time together) but rather will look for confirmation (e.g., evidence that the person has other friends).

The validation and invalidation of personal constructs is certainly less precise than the careful experiments of scientists. In fact, experience that an outsider sees as clear evidence against a person's constructs may not sway our imperfect scientist. Milton Rokeach (1964) describes his efforts to dissuade three psychiatric patients from their claim to be Christ by bringing them all together to be housed in the same ward of a hospital. Wouldn't you expect that confronting other Christs would be convincing evidence that one's own delusion was wrong? Although that seems logical, each of the three patients retained his belief.

Beverly Walker (1992) suggests that the scientist metaphor is a goal, rather than a description, of human nature. By daring to test our beliefs, we can eradicate the errors and move toward more accurate understanding of ourselves and our world.

Figure 13.1 The Experience Cycle

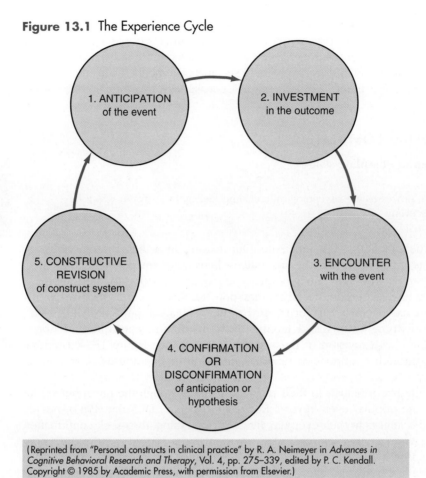

(Reprinted from "Personal constructs in clinical practice" by R. A. Neimeyer in *Advances in Cognitive Behavioral Research and Therapy*, Vol. 4, pp. 275–339, edited by P. C. Kendall. Copyright © 1985 by Academic Press, with permission from Elsevier.)

The Process of Construing

Because anticipating (or construing) events is so important, Kelly described this process in detail. Four of Kelly's corollaries explain the process of construing (R. A. Neimeyer, 1987).

THE CONSTRUCTION COROLLARY

Construction Corollary Kelly's statement that people anticipate replications of events

According to the **Construction Corollary**:

> A person anticipates events by construing their replications. (Kelly, 1955, p. 50)

Like a scientist who anticipates that observations will confirm a stated research hypothesis, we anticipate confirmation of our constructs (cf. Mancuso, 1998). We base our expectations of the next football game on our experiences of previous ones, of the next concert by previous ones, and so on. Events, more or less similar, occur repeatedly, and our plans for the future are based on the lessons of the past. Of course, there is always some difference. Events do not repeat themselves exactly. Nonetheless, adaptation would be impossible if we did not identify sufficient similarity among events to allow prediction of the future. We accomplish this by applying constructs to various events.

Events is a broad, inclusive term. It can be applied to events in the usual sense of the word; for example, "New Year's Eve is a time for celebration" applies the construct "a time for celebration" to the event "New Year's Eve." Most often, though, Kelly's concept of events is used to refer to people. Thus, if we say that "Hitler was disturbed," we are applying the construct "disturbed" to the event (in this case a person) "Hitler."

The language of constructs and prediction sounds quite cognitive and has been criticized as being overly intellectualized, ignoring the emotional side of human experience (Bruner, 1956; Rogers, 1956). Kelly intended these processes to be understood more broadly (cf. J. Adams-Webber, 1990). Unverbalized and unconscious anticipations are also included. Kelly (1955, p. 459) refers to a **preverbal construct** as "one which continues to be used even though it has no consistent word symbol." Constructs may be experienced as emotions (Landfield & Epting, 1987, p. 15). If a person becomes tense every time his or her father is present, that is evidence for a construct relating to the father, even if the individual is unaware of any ideas about it and cannot verbalize it. One therapist quotes a patient who has developed a preverbal construct as a consequence of sexual victimization in childhood: "When my husband touches me, I feel a chill go through me. I don't know why, as he is a really caring man and I know he would not hurt me" (Cummins, 1992, p. 360). The "chill" is evidence of her construct, which she cannot express in more precise language. Although such preverbal constructs are difficult and painful to uncover, they are important keys to personality. Many psychosomatic disorders (headaches, stomach or bowel problems, etc.) result from unverbalized constructs; the body expresses constructs in its own language. In therapy, the client may learn to verbalize such constructs. For example, one patient with frequent chest pains learned to verbalize her anger, and the pains rapidly improved (Leitner & Guthrie, 1993). We might compare such preverbal constructs with the unconscious emotional experiences described by psychoanalysts—experiences in which emotions occur without accompanying conscious content (Shean, 2001).

> **preverbal construct**
> a construct that is not conscious

THE EXPERIENCE COROLLARY

Constructs can change. The **Experience Corollary** is Kelly's (1955, p. 72) statement of a developmental principle. It says:

> A person's construction system varies as he successively construes the replications of events.

> **Experience Corollary** Kelly's statement about personality development

Briefly, people change with experience. The directions of this change vary individually and can be understood from the other corollaries, to be explained later (including elaboration of constructs, constriction, and slot movement). Perhaps Kelly's theory is as interesting for what he does not say about change. Some theorists have proposed universal stages of development (e.g., Freud and Erikson); Kelly does not. Unlike stage theorists, Kelly does not propose that development must occur in a fixed sequence or toward a particular direction (Vaughn & Pfenninger, 1994). Nor does he emphasize the role of the environment in producing change. Nonetheless, personal construct theory as proposed by Kelly and expanded by others does describe development, particularly in adulthood as people use and revise their personal constructs (Berzonsky, 1992; Viney, 1992).

THE CHOICE COROLLARY

Choice Corollary
statement that people
choose the pole of a
construct that promises
greater possibility of
extending and defining
the system of constructs

How do we decide which of our constructs to apply to an event? Kelly's (1955) **Choice Corollary** states:

> A person chooses for himself that alternative in a dichotomized construct through which he anticipates the greater possibility for extension and definition of his system. (p. 64)

elaborative choice
a choice that allows a
construct system to be
extended; the Choice
Corollary says this
choice will be selected

(The term *dichotomized* is explained later, when we consider the Dichotomy Corollary.) Like a scientist whose theory has worked so far, the individual seeks to extend his or her predictions. A person, in Kelly's terminology, always makes the **elaborative choice** (p. 65). Sometimes the elaborative choice involves extending the construct system. The emphasis, however, is on the action or choice, not on cognitive elaboration: on daring to do something different (Butt, 1998). Even drug use and addiction are, in a personal construct approach, ways of constructing meaning, of exploring a new, substance-centered self (Burrell & Jaffe, 1999). In the absence of threat we may explore and experiment, developing new constructs in the process. If threat is too great, however, a person will instead act in the same way as before, a choice called *sedimentation*. Although less healthy, sedimentation protects against the overly threatening choice of change, which feels as though it could destroy the system (Butt, 1998). It is not easy to predict what choice an individual will make. The elaborative choice may take various forms, as Kelly (1955) notes:

> One may anticipate events by trying to become more and more certain about fewer and fewer things or by trying to become vaguely aware of more and more things on the misty horizon. (p. 67)

THE MODULATION COROLLARY

Modulation Corollary statement
that the permeability of
constructs sets limits to
construction possibilities

How extensively can a person's constructs be applied to new experiences? That is the question addressed by Kelly's (1955) **Modulation Corollary**:

> The variation in a person's construction system is limited by the permeability of the constructs within whose ranges of convenience the variants lie. (p. 77)

permeable construct a construct
that can be extended to
include new elements

A construct that can be applied to new elements is called a **permeable construct**:

> A construct is permeable if it will admit to its range of convenience new elements which are not yet construed within its framework. (Kelly, 1955, p. 79)

For example, imagine that a person thinks of many people as "able to read my mind" and of others as "not able to read my mind." Among his friends and acquaintances, each is categorized as a mind reader or not. Now the person meets someone new. Will he or she apply the construct of "mind reader or not" to the new person? If so, the construct is permeable. Permeable constructs can be used to construe new experiences.

concrete construct
a construct that cannot
be extended to include
new elements

The opposite of a permeable construct is a **concrete construct**. It is part of a person's construct system, but it is not open to new elements. A person would have the mind reader construct as a concrete construct if he or she believed there used to be mind readers in the past, but there are not anymore. In contrast, a person who does not think of people as mind readers or not, even a closed set of people without the possibility of adding new ones, would not have this as a construct, not a concrete construct or any other kind. Another example of a concrete construct was suggested by George Kelly (1955, p. 1076): Most people regard the age of miracles as the past, even those who accept that miracles once occurred.

Kellian therapists sometimes deal with problematic constructs (or poles) by working with a client to make constructs more concrete, or impermeable, so that they, with their devastating effects, will not be applied to new experiences. Other types of construct system change—changes in the structure of construct systems—are also made during constructivist therapy.

The Structure of Construct Systems

Four of Kelly's corollaries explain the structure of construct systems (R. A. Neimeyer, 1987).

THE DICHOTOMY COROLLARY

Constructs are always bipolar. Kelly's (1955) **Dichotomy Corollary** states:

> A person's construction system is composed of a finite number of dichotomous constructs. (p. 59)

Dichotomy Corollary statement that constructs are bipolar

Good–bad, popular–unpopular, intelligent–stupid, and so on, are examples of dichotomous constructs. Either one pole or the other may be applied to an event (person). It is also possible for the construct itself to be deemed irrelevant (see the Range Corollary later) and neither pole be applicable to a particular event. One side of the bipolar construct is typically used more often than the other. The poles are referred to as the *likeness end* and the *contrast end* because of the way they are measured in the REP test (discussed later in the chapter). The likeness end is generally most used and describes how several people are seen to be alike. The contrast end tells how other people are seen as different. The nature of an individual's dichotomies may come as a surprise to the individual. It is generally the contrast end that is less available, or submerged.

When people change, especially in response to stress, the dichotomous nature of constructs has important predictive implications for Kellian therapists. Under stress, people often change from one pole to the opposite pole of a dichotomous construct. Such changes can be manifested as religious conversions, turning sober after being alcoholic, or in literature, the transformation of miserly Scrooge to a more generous soul in Dickens's *Christmas Carol* (Vaillant, 2002). Kelly (1955, p. 938) offers the example of a client who changes from kindly to hostile. Another example is the police officer who becomes a lawbreaker (D. A. Winter, 1993). Such changes from one pole to another are called **slot movement**. Kellian therapists are especially attentive to the client's often unstated opposites because these are directions in which change may occur, especially when stress (either in therapy or in the world) makes current patterns inadequate. With a detailed understanding of the particular individual's constructs, a therapist can make an educated guess of the direction that person will move when currently operating choices cease being validated. This may offer an advance warning of dangerous change. On the positive side, a therapist armed with such information can use planned invalidation of

slot movement abrupt change from one pole of a construct to its opposite, often precipitated by stress

currently operative constructs to trigger change in a client, when it is judged that such change would be in a safe and desirable direction.

Both poles of the construct must be understood from the individual's point of view. Often dichotomies are not strictly logical. The opposite of *ambitious*, for example, may be *happy*. Dichotomies vary from one person to another. Alvin Landfield (1982) cites the example of two people with quite different contrasts to *liveliness*. For one, the contrast was *exhaustion;* for the other, *suicide*. The implications of these different dichotomous constructs are obvious.

THE ORGANIZATION COROLLARY

Having many constructs, a person must have some way of selecting the relevant one or ones to anticipate various events. As an effective mechanic keeps his or her tools well organized, so a person keeps his or her constructs well organized. The comparison is apt because constructs, after all, are tools for psychological adaptation to the world.

Organization Corollary describes the hierarchical relationships among constructs

According to the **Organization Corollary**,

> Each person characteristically evolves, for his convenience in anticipating events, a construction system embracing ordinal relationships between constructs. (Kelly, 1955, p. 56)

superordinate construct a construct that applies broadly and subsumes lower-order constructs

Superordinate constructs, which apply broadly to several lower-order constructs, are more abstract. The superordinate concept *vegetables* encompasses several lower-order concepts: carrots, beans, corn, and so on. If some things are true of all vegetables (e.g., they provide vitamins and little fat), it is more convenient to have a superordinate concept than to have only more limited constructs. Conversely, adding subordinate categories to break down a larger concept can lead to more correct anticipations. Consider mushrooms: Developing subcategories of edible mushrooms and poisonous mushrooms is adaptive and potentially lifesaving. Similarly, constructs about people may need to be elaborated on in such a hierarchical arrangement to improve adaptation. For example, we distinguish between trustworthy people and con artists. This sort of cognitive elaboration can be an important goal of therapy.

core constructs constructs central to a person's identity and existence

The term **core constructs** refers to constructs central to a person's identity and existence (Kelly, 1955, p. 482). They are superordinate constructs, encompassing others lower in the hierarchy. They constitute stabilizing elements within the personality, and they are slower to change than less comprehensive **peripheral constructs**. Developing more superordinate, abstract concepts helps an individual to transcend contradictions. These higher-order constructs vary from person to person. "One man may resolve the conflicts between his anticipations by means of an ethical system. Another may resolve them in terms of self-preservation" (p. 56). If these core constructs are not adaptive, it may be possible for therapy to change them.

peripheral constructs constructs not central to one's identity

THE FRAGMENTATION COROLLARY

Fragmentation Corollary statement describing the inconsistency of people

People are not always consistent. Kelly's (1955) **Fragmentation Corollary** helps us understand inconsistency:

> A person may successively employ a variety of construction subsystems which are inferentially incompatible with each other. (p. 83)

Not all of a person's constructs are operative at the same moment. One moment we may be a ruthless competitor and the next, a loving friend. This potential for fragmentation suggests that observers may err if they infer personality from a limited sample of behavior.

THE RANGE COROLLARY

Any construct has only limited usefulness. Kelly's (1955) **Range Corollary** states:

> A construct is convenient for the anticipation of a finite range of events only. (p. 68)

Range Corollary statement that a construct applies only to some events, not to all

The **range of convenience** of a construct refers to the events to which it applies. If either pole of a dichotomous construct describes the event (or person), that event is within the range of convenience of the construct. Apples, bananas, yogurt, and Cholesterol Clusters are all within the range of convenience of the dichotomous construct nutritious food versus junk food, but cement is outside of it. Examples with personal constructs are more problematic because each of us has somewhat different constructs. Most people, probably, would agree that Saddam Hussein, Adolf Hitler, and Mother Teresa are within the range of convenience of the construct villain versus saint. They might disagree about whether other individuals fall within its scope.

range of convenience the events to which a construct applies

The Social Embeddedness of Construing Efforts

Personal constructs are particularly important for understanding interpersonal behavior. Kelly's remaining three corollaries place the construing process in its social context (R. A. Neimeyer, 1987).

THE INDIVIDUALITY COROLLARY

Kelly's (1955) **Individuality Corollary** states:

> Persons differ from each other in their constructions of events. (p. 55)

Individuality Corollary Kelly's assertion that different people use different constructs

It is in these constructions that individual differences, so important for any personality theory, are to be found. They are not to be found in different environments or different histories, although such factors may contribute to their formation. Only through the construction processes of individuals do such external events have an effect.

THE COMMONALITY COROLLARY

Although each person is unique, there are some similarities from person to person. Kelly's **Commonality Corollary** (1955) suggests where we should look for them:

> To the extent that one person employs a construction of experience which is similar to that employed by another, his psychological processes are similar to those of the other person. (p. 90)

Commonality Corollary statement describing similarity between people

In contrast to what we might infer from other theories, similarity between persons is not a necessary consequence of similar experiences. It is the sense made of that experience that is critical. In this, Kelly sounds Adlerian.

THE SOCIALITY COROLLARY

Kelly's (1955) theory emphasizes interpersonal relationships. This last corollary addresses such relationships and allows Kellian therapists to establish a therapeutic relationship with their clients. The **Sociality Corollary** states:

Sociality Corollary statement that describes understanding another person or being understood as a prerequisite for a social process with that person

> To the extent that one person construes the construction processes of another, he may play a role in a social process involving the other person. (p. 95)

Note that psychological similarity, addressed in the Commonality Corollary, is not necessary for a social interaction to occur. Understanding, rather than similarity, is necessary. This understanding may be mutual, as between two friends, or it may be unilateral, as between a parent and a child or a therapist and a client. For example, a therapist for clients who have problems with alcohol or other drugs will be more effective in the therapeutic role if he or she understands how the client thinks about alcohol and/or drugs. This understanding is often greater if the therapist has personally recovered from problems with addiction. If neither person in an interaction can "construe the construction processes" of the other, a social process is not possible. This mutual construction failure may occur, for example, between a psychotic and a so-called normal person or between two people from vastly differing backgrounds.

Kelly (1955) defines *role* "as a psychological process based on the role player's construction of aspects of the construction systems of those with whom he attempts to join in a social enterprise" (p. 97). Psychotherapy involves role relationships, as the therapist comes to understand the client's construct system (Leitner & Guthrie, 1993). We also form role relationships with friends, lovers, and others, and in many cases the role constructions are mutual; each understands the other.

The Role Construct Repertory (REP) Test

Kelly devised a measuring instrument to assess a person's constructs. This **Role Construct Repertory (REP) Test** is easily adapted to particular clients. It has been widely used in research as well as in clinical and applied settings.

Role Construct Repertory (REP) Test instrument for measuring a person's constructs

The REP test identifies the constructs a person uses to understand others. The first step in the test is to list several particular people with whom the client or subject is acquainted. (See Table 13.2 for an example.) The subject is sometimes, but not always, included on this list. Next, three of the persons identified are selected by the researcher or therapist. The subject is instructed to identify one way in which two of these individuals are the same and different from the third. The word or phrase used by the subject to identify how two individuals are the same is termed the *construct*. The word or phrase used to describe how the third person is different is termed the *contrast*. In keeping with Kelly's theory, these do not need to be logical opposites, and often they are not. Additional constructs are elicited by repeating the preceding step for several different triads of persons.

TABLE 13.2	Role Specifications for One Version of the REP Test

1. mother
2. father
3. brother
4. sister
5. spouse (or girlfriend/boyfriend)
6. same-sex friend
7. work partner who disliked you
8. person you feel uncomfortable with
9. someone you would like to know better
10. teacher whose viewpoint you accepted
11. teacher whose viewpoint was objectionable
12. unsuccessful person
13. successful person
14. happy person
15. unhappy person

(Adapted from Landfield & Epting, 1987, p. 33, who give more detailed descriptions of these roles.)

Repertory tests provide counselors with qualitative impressions of clients as they progress through therapy. In addition, they can be scored in a variety of ways. For example, the discrepancy between the ideal self and the real, current self can be computed to look for change (Leach et al., 2001).

Figure 13.2 shows examples of constructs elicited by one subject, a therapy client.

Under standard instructions, the circles in each row would nominate two individuals to the construct pole in column 1, indicated by "1" in the cell, and one individual to the contrast pole in column 2, indicated by "2." (The subject in Figure 13.2, however, refused to name anyone by the contrast pole, "Someone I hate.") A zero, as in the lower right of the figure, indicates that neither pole applies. After several constructs have been elicited, the subject is instructed to consider each person for every construct–contrast dimension and to indicate which pole applies. This creates a grid, rating each person on every construct.

Even without further analysis, the grid and list of constructs may offer insights. The subject or client may be surprised to learn what constructs come to mind through this technique. A clinician may use these results to identify material for further exploration in psychotherapy sessions. For example, Robert Neimeyer (1992) notes that many of the client's constructs in Figure 13.2 refer to emotional reactions from other people (e.g., "sensitive," "impatient," and "emotional") and that a suggestion of conflict between being "committed to family" or "independence" could be relevant for the individual's current life decisions.

The grid, however, virtually begs for mathematical analysis. A variety of scoring methods have been devised. Because of the diversity of scoring techniques, it is advisable to seek empirical validation for the measures, for example, by comparing grid analyses with clinical judgments (e.g., Chambers et al., 1986). Constructs are judged to be similar or different not simply from the verbal labels but also from the way they are applied to

Figure 13.2 Example of One Client's Personal Constructs

RESPONSE SHEET

Column 1	Mother	Father	Happy Person	Successful Person	Andy (self)	Brian (son)	Mike (son)	Sharon (wife)	Beth (lover)	Therapist	Column 2	
1 Someone I love	1	1	1	1	2	1	1	1	1	1	Someone I hate	1
2 Lack sensitivity	1	2	1	2	2	2	2	2	2	2	Sensitive	2
3 Committed to family	1	1	1	1	1	1	2	2	2	2	Independent	3
4 Understanding	2	1	1	1	1	2	1	2	1	1	Impatient	4
5 Bright	1	1	1	1	2	1	1	1	1	1	Just average	5
6 Very inward	1	1	2	1	1	1	1	2	2	1	Very outspoken	6
7 Childlike inside	2	1	2	1	1	1	1	2	1	2	Get what you see	7
8 Have real communication	2	2	2	2	2	2	1	1	1	1	Aloof	8
9 Easy going	2	1	1	1	1	1	1	2	1	1	Emotional	9
10 Unaffectionate	2	2	1	1	2	2	2	1	2	0	Likes to touch	10

(By Robert A. Neimeyer in *Handbook of Constructivist Assessment* edited by G. J. Neimeyer. Copyright © 1992 by Sage Publications, Inc. Reprinted by permission of Greg Neimeyer.)

the persons being rated. For example, a person may propose two constructs, rich–poor and happy–unhappy. The words alone do not reliably disclose whether these are entirely different constructs. If all or nearly all of the individuals rated as rich are also rated as happy, whereas all or nearly all of those rated as poor are rated as unhappy, these are essentially the same construct, although with more than one way of referring to them in words. One pole of the construct is "rich and happy," while the contrast pole is "poor and unhappy."

Cognitive Complexity

cognitive complexity elaborateness of a person's construct system, reflected in a large number of different constructs

The **cognitive complexity** of a person is reflected by the number of different constructs he or she uses in describing people (Bieri, 1955). Cognitively complex people are able to view social behavior from several different dimensions and thus have greater flexibility. This helps them adapt to new challenges. First-year university students who have greater cognitive complexity, for example, typically adjust to college more easily (Pancer et al., 2000). General Robert E. Lee won many military battles for the Confederate army during the U.S. Civil War, despite having fewer forces, because of his higher complexity, as inferred from his military documents (Suedfeld, Corteen, & McCormick, 1986). Peace overtures, as well as military victory, can come from cognitive complexity. During the 1970s, when Egyptian leaders spoke in more complex ways about their traditional enemy, Israel, their behavior became more cooperative (Maoz & Astorino, 1992).

Cognitive complexity is desirable, but it is not the sole criterion of an adaptive construct system. In addition, healthy development requires that people learn to integrate their various constructs. Complexity without integration is an unhealthy sign (e.g., Landfield & Epting, 1987). *Integrative complexity* can be developed as people think and write about the challenges of negative life events and explore ways to resolve contradictions (Suedfeld & Bluck, 1993), although there is no guarantee of such a healthy outcome. Complicating research on this topic, many measures of cognitive complexity based on the REP test and other instruments have been proposed, which unfortunately do not necessarily correlate with one another.

Personality Change

Personal constructs can change. Sometimes change is necessitated by life events. When a loved one dies, for example, we grieve, not only mourning our loss, but also struggling to reconstruct a new set of meanings—that is, to revise our personal constructs to accommodate to a world without the one who has died (R. A. Neimeyer, 1999). Change does not come automatically, however, and sometimes when events discredit our old constructs, a person is not able to find new constructs for the new situation. This happened in the tragic case of a U.S. naval officer who had risen to become chief of naval operations and won acclaim for his success, rising from a humble background. However, when news reports accused him of wearing an unearned combat ribbon on his uniform, he was cast in the role of a liar and fraud. Unable to continue with his old successful constructs, he was also unable to find new constructs for his new situation. What to do? Unfortunately, he took the only course he saw available and committed suicide (Mancuso, 1998). Less dramatically but still tragically, people who have witnessed a mass murder or soldiers who have served in combat risk suffering posttraumatic stress responses if they cannot integrate these horrific experiences into their personal construct systems in an integrated, elaborate way (Sewell, 1996; Sewell et al., 1996).

Kelly considered in some detail the possible types of change. These concepts were particularly interesting to him because they suggested both possibilities and dangers in psychotherapy. The same principles of change operate outside of therapy, in life itself.

EMOTIONS RELATED TO CHANGE

Personality change leads to strong emotions. **Threat** is "the awareness of imminent comprehensive change in one's core structures" (Kelly, 1955. p. 489). Once we have become dislodged from our core role structures, we experience *guilt* (Kelly, 1955, 1962). Guilt, as used by Kelly, is not identical to its usual meaning concerning the violation of a culturally accepted standard of morality. Consider the case studies of two women who, having been sexually victimized themselves, were arrested or imprisoned for committing violent acts against the men in their lives. During therapy, as they came to think of themselves as victims as well as abusers, counterintuitively they experienced an increased sense of guilt (Pollock & Kear-Colwell, 1994).

Threat may be caused by major life changes, including the anticipation of death (Moore & Neimeyer, 1991; R. A. Neimeyer, Moore, & Bagley, 1988). Both music students performing for an evaluation in front of faculty (Tobacyk & Downs, 1986) and counselors in training conducting sessions for evaluation by faculty (Froehle, 1989) face threat,

threat awareness of imminent comprehensive change in one's core structures which in turn, produces anxiety. Therapy that leads to changes in core constructs also arouses threat. Because people have different core structures, they find different situations threatening. For example, the possibility of becoming a homosexual is more threatening to some people than to others (Leitner & Cado, 1982). Threat is not always triggered by negative events. Kelly (1955) supplies an example: "A prisoner of twenty years, while eager, is nevertheless threatened on the last day by the imminence of his release" (p. 490). Personality developments in psychotherapy are (presumably) desired, yet still threatening.

When core constructs are changed by new incidental (rather than comprehensive) constructs, *fear* is experienced (rather than threat). The less we think about a matter, the more likely we are to experience fear; the more we think about it, the more likely we are to experience threat. *Anxiety* occurs when we recognize that we are confronted by events outside the range of convenience of our construct system. Our constructs are not adequate to deal with events, and we know this. Anxiety is a sign of construct failure and the need for change.

People do not change their constructs easily and sometimes continue to try to make them work. Kelly (1955, p. 510) defined **hostility** as "the continued effort to extort validational evidence in favor of a type of social prediction which has already proved itself a failure." One example is a man who became violent toward his wife when she wanted to divorce him, an idea he could not accept (Leitner & Pfenninger, 1994). Can this explanation of hostility also contribute to our understanding of wars and other violent acts? This seems reasonable. According to one analysis, individual hostility is especially likely to occur under alienating societal conditions, such as among groups that are minorities or marginalized (Kalekin-Fishman, 1993).

hostility continuing to try to validate constructs that have already been invalidated

EFFECTIVE ACTION: THE C-P-C CYCLE

Kelly's theory is based on pragmatic philosophy, paying particular attention to how people behave and offering the potential for improving effective behavior in the social world (Butt, 2001). A person who is making a decision about how to act typically engages in a three-step process called the **C-P-C Cycle**. In the first stage, **circumspection**, the person "employs a series of propositional constructs in dealing with the elements at hand" (Kelly, 1955, p. 515). That is, he or she tries out several available constructs tentatively to see how they might fit in that situation. (For example, is a new teacher a slave driver, a mentor, or what?)

C-P-C Cycle the three-step process leading to effective action

circumspection the first stage in the C-P-C Cycle, in which various constructs are tentatively explored

The second phase, **preemption**, involves selecting which of the constructs to actually use. The person selects which construct to apply to that situation. (After the first exam, some students decide "slave driver" applies.) The third phase, **control**, involves action. (The student may study harder or drop the course.) Kelly (1966) emphasized, though, that action or behavior is not simply an outcome, a "dependent variable" in the scientific metaphor. Instead, he argued, "Behavior is man's independent variable in the experiment of creating his own existence" (p. 36). Behavior, after all, produces consequences that permit hypothesis testing and, therefore, confirmation or revision of a person's constructs (as Bandura recognized in his concept of reciprocal determinism, presented in Chapter 12).

preemption the second stage in the C-P-C Cycle, in which a construct is selected

control the third stage in the C-P-C Cycle; the way in which the person acts

Each step contributes to effective action. Some people are less effective because they do not devote enough attention to the circumspection phase, deciding impulsively to act. Others continue considering alternatives long after the time for decision has arrived. A therapist can help a client act more effectively by noticing which stages are inadequate and working on those.

LOOSENING AND TIGHTENING CONSTRUCTS: THE CREATIVITY CYCLE

Although the C-P-C Cycle enables us to select constructs for action, it does not change those constructs. The **Creativity Cycle**, in contrast, involves the development of constructs. It occurs in therapy, which Kelly (1955, p. 529) calls "a creative process." Tight construing means that a large number of situations are construed in the same way, so the individual is insensitive to differences among them. Psychotherapy patients who use defense mechanisms (denial, rationalization, and turning against the object) also show tight construing (Catina, Gitzinger, & Hoeckh, 1992). Loosening these constructs should facilitate change. The first stage of the Creativity Cycle involves loosened construction, or **loosening**. Constructs are applied in ways that may seem to make little sense, as illustrated in brainstorming sessions. Kelly (1955, p. 529) remarked that "creativity always arises out of preposterous thinking." In therapy, techniques to loosen constructs include free association, fantasy, dream reporting, and silence (p. 484). The constructs involved are often preverbal.

In the next phase, one variation of the construct is selected, tightened, and applied in action. Without validation in action, the cycle is not complete, and the person is left with loose constructs that are no doubt too unclear to be adaptive. The creativity cycle occurs outside of therapy, too. It can be used in brainstorming sessions to aid problem solving. For example, the creativity cycle was invoked by a structured problem-solving exercise among graduate students to develop a strategic plan for the development of their educational program (Morçöl & Asche, 1993).

> **Creativity Cycle** the process of changing constructs by loosening and tightening them

> **loosening** applying constructs in ways that seem not to make sense, such as in brainstorming and free association

Therapy

Constructivist therapy is not a single method or school but has a variety of methods influenced by Kelly's work and emphasizing that the meanings are constructed (R. A. Neimeyer, 1993). Several therapists practice personal construct therapy based on Kelly's foundation (Bannister, 1975; Epting, 1984; Neimeyer & Neimeyer, 1987). The aim is to help clients improve their construct system. Personal construct therapy has been used with diverse populations: schizophrenics (Bannister et al., 1975), elderly people suffering from anxiety and depression (Viney, Benjamin, & Preston, 1989), patients with HIV and AIDS coping with their psychological adjustment (Viney et al., 1992), and of course clients at a university, where Kelly's theory originated (Raz-Duvshani, 1986). Although the therapeutic use of the REP test is individualized, some research illustrates its potential. One study, for example, finds that a few males with a history of having been sexually abused had REP grids that showed they identified themselves with their victimizer, rather than with the victimized child. Therapy changed this and helped relieve depression (Clarke & Pearson, 2000).

Kelly's therapy typically was brief, ranging from six sessions completed within 2 weeks to as long as 3 months. Of course, he was in college counseling, so his clients were already functioning reasonably well, compared with some other clinical populations. He claimed, however, that the method itself is more efficient: "[Fixed-role therapy is] a method of substituting whole new prefabricated constructions. . . rather than "analyzing away" old rickety structures [as in psychoanalysis]—thus it takes less time" (Kelly, 1955, p. 682). Kelly (1960, p. 347) takes another gibe at psychoanalysis by noting that "Insight is what you are left with after you have been stripped of your imagination."

One constructivist therapist undoubtedly speaks for many, in reminding us that therapy is not a process with a clear and unambiguous set of directions. He invites trust in the therapeutic process, even in the absence of definitive empirical results and the pervasive uncertainty of our postmodern era in which certainty is not to be found (R. A. Neimeyer, 2001).

UNDERSTANDING THE CLIENT'S CONSTRUCTS

Personal construct theory traces disturbances to faulty constructs. Talk therapy is an obvious treatment for developing better constructs (Raskin & Epting, 1993). Kelly's therapy requires the therapist "to understand the client in the client's own terms" (Landfield & Epting, 1987, p. 275). If the therapist cannot understand the client, he or she will not be able to enter into a role, even a therapeutic role, with the client (cf. the Sociality Corollary). This does not mean that the therapist will agree with the client. Instead, the therapist should have a construct system (largely developed from Kelly's theory) that will allow him or her to subsume the client's construct system under the therapist's own construct system.

Kelly recommended a spirit of cooperative problem-solving techniques between client and therapist. Both therapist and client work to understand, test, and improve the client's constructs. This task-centered focus prevents the client from developing an overly dependent relationship with the therapist. In fact, Kelly discouraged his own clients from disclosing too much personal material early in the therapy, until they came to understand what his mode of therapy was all about.

EXPLORING AND CHANGING CONSTRUCTS

A variety of therapeutic techniques can be used to explore and then to change constructs. The REP test is used early in therapy to explore the client's construct system. Robert Neimeyer (1992) describes techniques for laddering constructs to explore their hierarchical organization into superordinate and subordinate constructs (see the Organization Corollary).

Later, when constructs are being revised, several techniques can be used. Therapeutic techniques to tighten constructs include *time binding* and *word binding* (Kelly, 1955, pp. 484, 1074–1076). Elicited constructs can be made less harmful in the present by learning to say, for example, "That happened long ago and does not happen anymore" (an example of time binding) or "That is really exploitation, not love" (an example of word binding). Constructs are developed to be more complex and to have greater hierarchical organization.

Besides conversations with the therapist, interacting with others stimulates the creation of our inner selves, our personal constructs (Shotter, 1997). For that reason, interactions in therapeutic role playing are important techniques for change in personal construct therapy (Buirs & Martin, 1997).

FIXED-ROLE THERAPY

fixed-role therapy
Kelly's method of therapy, based on role playing

One therapeutic technique suggested by Kelly is **fixed-role therapy**. In this technique, the client experiments with new constructs by role-playing a fictitious personality specifically devised by the therapist. For example, Linda Viney (1981) described a case study in which a bright and attractive female client, Susan, age 24, sought counseling for anxiety that focused on her limited social life. Her therapist worked with the client to devise the following fixed role for her, using constructs elicited from her REP test. As Kelly recommended, this fictitious personality was given a different name (Mary Jones), so that Susan could experiment with this role without losing her own identity or committing herself to change before she was ready.

> Mary Jones is a friendly young woman who is open and frank with the people she meets. She enjoys giving to these people and the feelings of companionship she has with them. She sees herself as united with her fellows, as part of the world with them.
>
> Mary is a down-to-earth kind of person, and most of the time she is calm and relaxed. She is able to be patient with the people she knows and is not very critical of them.
>
> Mary is also searching and inquisitive about her world. She can be forceful when the occasion demands it and lively too.
>
> Mary is the kind of person people like to know. (pp. 274–275)

As therapy progressed, the client changed in the direction of this role, as was evident on the REP test and, although more subjectively, in life.

Development of the fixed role is a significant collaborative effort between client and therapist. It generally involves the discovery of new constructs and not merely the realignment of the individual in relation to existing constructs. The client practices the role in therapy. Sometimes the roles are reversed, so the client plays the other person while the therapist plays the role of the client. Besides teaching the client to view the situation from the other's viewpoint, this allows the therapist to model the new role. The new role is enacted in an exploratory way. Kelly (1955, p. 373) thought that the protection of "make-believe. . . is probably man's oldest protective screen for reaching out into the unknown." The attitude of experimentation facilitates self-directed change after the end of formal therapy.

CONSTRUCTS IN CONTEXT: PERSONAL STORIES

Roles are only one aspect of the drama of life. Robert Neimeyer (1994) emphasizes the importance of *narratives*, or stories that the client develops in therapy, often with the assistance of the therapist. They take many forms, ranging from personal stories and even poetry presented to the therapist to the self-discoveries that occur in a personal journal. Such narratives describe the context for one's personal constructs. They may function as a personal myth, giving meaning and predictability to life (cf. G. S. Howard, 1991; Mair, 1988). Because each person is unique, the meaning of a specific life event, like the death of a loved one, varies from person to person. The impact of bereavement cannot be understood from some standard formula but must be viewed with the meanings provided by an individual's personal life story (Romanoff, 1999). Life narratives have become a popular area of attention among psychologists outside therapy, too, as a way of understanding adult development (Pasupathi, 2001).

Research Findings

Kelly's theory has generated a great deal of research in a variety of settings.

CLINICAL POPULATIONS

Researchers have found that various clinical populations have disturbed personal constructs. Different kinds of faulty constructs are characteristic of schizophrenia and paranoia (Lorenzini, Sassaroli, & Rocchi, 1989). Schizophrenics show impaired perceptions of themselves, as well as of others (Gara, Rosenberg, & Mueller, 1989). Their constructs about people and psychological phenomena are particularly disturbed, compared to constructs about objects and the physical world (Bannister & Salmon, 1966; McPherson, Barden, & Buckley, 1970; McPherson & Buckley, 1970).

Among nonpsychotics, constructs have been studied in relationship to anxiety (McPherson & Gray, 1976), phobias (Huber & Altmaier, 1983), and eating disorders (G. J. Neimeyer & Khouzam, 1985). Physical disorders, too, are related to personal constructs. Hypertensive men have constructs about dependency that prevent them from turning to others for help that might reduce their stress (Talbot, Cooper, & Ellis, 1991).

BUSINESS APPLICATIONS AND VOCATIONAL CHOICE

Kelly's theory is popular in many business fields—for example, with industrial-organizational psychologists, management development specialists, and occupational counselors (Jankowicz, 1987; V. Stewart & Stewart, 1982). Market researchers use REP grids to understand consumers' preferences (Marsden & Littler, 2000). Many studies have used repertory grids to describe what experienced workers have learned, so that these lessons can be more readily taught to others (Jankowicz, 1987; Jankowicz & Hisrich, 1987; Salmon & Lehrer, 1989). In a complementary way, grid analysis shows how a new school psychologist learns the role of consultant under a mentor's guidance (Salmon & Fenning, 1993). An analysis of repertory grids completed by those who train counselors illustrates how such training information can be useful for more clearly defining job requirements: They described good versus bad counseling trainees using the constructs "open–closed," "personable–aloof," "secure–insecure," and "professional skilled–unskilled" (Wheeler, 2000).

Research on vocational development is an extension of the more general theory that Kelly offered (G. J. Neimeyer, 1988; Neimeyer & Metzler, 1987). Several studies suggest that cognitive complexity is associated with a more appropriate vocational choice (Bodden, 1970; Harren et al., 1979; G. J. Neimeyer, 1988). People can evaluate careers on a repertory grid, instead of evaluating people on the REP test, to reveal the constructs they are using in making career decisions (G. J. Neimeyer, 1992). In addition, structured exercises based on personal construct theory have been developed to improve the vocational choice process (Forster, 1992). Job performance can also be enhanced by cognitive complexity; salespeople, for example, can be more effective because of a wider repertoire of sales strategies (Porter & Inks, 2000).

OTHER RESEARCH

Personal construct theory has been extended to other topics as well, including biofeedback therapy (Zolten, 1989) and hypnosis (Burr & Butt, 1989). Researchers have explored the relationship between personal constructs and measures of identity (Berzonsky, 1989; Berzonsky & Neimeyer, 1988; Berzonsky, Rice, & Neimeyer, 1990);

sex roles (Baldwin et al., 1986); and values and beliefs (Horley, 1991). In education, repertory grids document the changing concepts of elementary school students as they learn about science (B. L. Shapiro, 1991), as well as the concepts that university students learn, both personally relevant understanding and course facts (Fromm, 1993). In summary, Kelly's theory has implications for a variety of applied and theoretical issues.

Constructivism, Social Constructionism, and Postmodernism

In contrast to George Kelly's theory, which is little known outside of its limited psychological audience, the term *postmodern* is popular in educated circles much more widely. It is well represented in magazines and newspapers, as well as providing a topic of academic discourse. Kelly's theory has been described as a forerunner of postmodern thought (Botella, 1995; Butt, 1998), but one that remains psychological (Raskin, 2001). Postmodern thought draws on philosophy, rather than psychology, but like Kelly's constructivism, postmodernism rejects the idea that there is an objective reality that applies to everyone. People's reality depends on the meaning they construct, in the context of their lives. This approach is popular in an era that is sensitive to cultural pluralism or multiculturalism.

Another term in this dialogue over the larger perspectives is *social constructionism*. A theory within the social sciences, social constructivism holds that people create social reality, influenced by their interactions and conversations with others (e.g., Berger & Luckmann, 1966). In this, Kelly (a constructivist) would agree, but social constructionism emphasizes the shared meanings with others in society and the creation of meanings through social interaction—for example, the male gender role, with its potentially restrictive implications (Courtenay, 2000). This social basis of constructionism contrasts with the more individual constructions that Kelly described (Gergen, 1985; Martin & Sugarman, 1997; Stam, 1998).

Summary

- Kelly proposed a theory of personal constructs based on the fundamental postulate of *constructive alternativism*, which says that people can interpret any event in a variety of ways.

- His metaphor for personality was *man-the-scientist*.

- He elaborated on this model in a formal theory, which consists of a *Fundamental Postulate* and 11 corollaries. The *Fundamental Postulate* states that "a person's processes are psychologically channelized by the ways in which he anticipates events."

- The process of construing is described in four corollaries *(Construction Corollary, Experience Corollary, Choice Corollary,* and *Modulation Corollary)*. These statements describe how constructs are formed and chosen to apply to a particular situation. People choose a particular way of construing events that offers the best possibility for extending the construct system.

- Four corollaries describe the structure of construct systems: *Dichotomy Corollary, Organization Corollary, Fragmentation Corollary,* and *Range Corollary*.

- *Dichotomous constructs* vary in their centrality and organization within the construct system.

- With development, constructs become expanded into hierarchical arrangements.

- Incompatible constructs may be applied in succession.
- *Each construct has only a limited* range of convenience.
- Finally, the social context of construing is described by the *Individuality Corollary*, *Commonality Corollary*, and *Sociality Corollary*.
- People have different construct systems, and personalities are judged to be similar if they use similar construct systems.
- Interpersonal relationships depend on at least one of the parties understanding the constructs used by the other.
- Personality change produces a variety of emotions, including anxiety and threat.
- The *C-P-C Cycle* describes the process by which a person selects a construct to apply in a particular instance.
- The *Creativity Cycle* describes the progressive loosening and tightening of constructs that occurs during change, including during therapy.
- Kelly developed a *Role Construct Repertory (REP) Test* to measure personal constructs.
- *Cognitive complexity*, which is considered adaptive, can be measured from the REP Test. It has been used to measure change as a result of therapy and has been modified for applications in industry.
- Kelly used *fixed-role therapy* to produce change through the development and practice of new constructs, and additional therapeutic techniques have also been developed.
- Besides therapy, Kelly's theory has stimulated research in business, group processes, social perception, and other areas.

Thinking about Kelly's Theory

1. The dichotomous nature of constructs emphasizes the importance of the opposite of usual experience. Have you noticed this theme in any other theorists (e.g., Freud's reaction formation or Jung's shadow)?
2. Kelly refers to identity as a core construct. What other theorists have had similar ideas about the importance of identity or a sense of self?
3. What are the implications of Kelly's Commonality Corollary for psychological testing? (In a nomothetic research study, one that compares individuals, what sorts of questions are consistent with the Commonality Corollary?)
4. Do you think that cognitive complexity is a general personality trait or a characteristic that can vary considerably, depending on the specific subject matter that a person is thinking about?
5. Based on Kelly's theory and the technique of fixed-role therapy, what do you think would be the effects of acting (as in movies or the theater)? How is such acting different from fixed-role therapy?
6. Have you observed or heard of anyone changing dramatically in ways that could be described by Kelly's concept of slot movement?
7. Propose a researchable hypothesis about cognitive complexity or some other concept from personal construct theory.

Study Questions

1. Explain Kelly's concept of constructive alternativism.
2. What is meant by Kelly's metaphor of man-the-scientist? In what ways are people like scientists? In what ways are they not?
3. Explain the difference between a verbal construct and a preverbal construct. Give examples to illustrate each.
4. What concepts from Kelly are relevant in understanding personality development? Contrast this approach with theories that propose stages of development.
5. Why do we make the choices we do, according to Kelly's Choice Corollary? Give an example to illustrate the idea of the elaborative choice.

6. Explain the difference between a permeable construct and a concrete construct. Give examples of each.

7. What concept from Kelly's theory would be relevant for understanding why a person makes a radical change in personality—for example, a criminal who repents and becomes a born-again Christian? Explain how this concept is relevant to the dichotomous nature of constructs.

8. Describe the hierarchical organization of constructs, from core superordinate constructs to peripheral subordinate constructs. How does this organization relate to identity?

9. What does Kelly's Fragmentation Corollary suggest about the situational stability of behavior?

10. What is the range of convenience of a construct?

11. According to Kelly's Individuality Corollary and Commonality Corollary, what is the main way in which individuals differ from one another? In what way can they be evaluated as similar?

12. How can personal constructs facilitate or prevent a social relationship from occurring?

13. Describe the REP Test. What information does it offer to a therapist to help understand a client?

14. Summarize research on cognitive complexity. Why is this an adaptive characteristic?

15. How does personal construct theory explain the emotions of threat, fear, anxiety, and hostility?

16. Explain the C-P-C Cycle of effective action. In what ways can it be distorted to interfere with effective action?

17. How does personal construct theory explain creativity?

18. How does a therapist learn about a client's constructs?

19. Describe techniques for changing constructs.

20. What is fixed-role therapy?

21. How do clients' stories (narratives) relate to personal constructs?

22. Summarize some research using personal construct theory or its measures outside of the clinical setting.

PART

VI

The Humanistic Perspective

The humanistic perspective in personality theory represents a "third force" (Maslow, 1968b), established to combat the deterministic and fragmenting tendencies of psychoanalysis and of behaviorism. It began as an informal network of psychologists who, organized by Abraham Maslow, exchanged mimeographed papers representing ideas not welcome in the established psychology journals (DeCarvalho, 1990b). Several of these humanists held their first meeting in 1957 and formally organized in 1961, founding the organization now known as the Association of Humanistic Psychology (Moustakas, 1986). Among the first members were Gordon Allport, Erich Fromm, George Kelly, Abraham Maslow, Rollo May, Henry Murray, and Carl Rogers (DeCarvalho, 1990b; Wertheimer, 1978). Today, most psychologists remember Gordon Allport as a trait psychologist, forgetting his association with humanistic psychology. This is ironic because Allport is probably the first one to have used the term *humanistic psychology*, and he was closely involved with the movement until his death (DeCarvalho, 1990c, 1990d).

The early self-proclaimed humanistic psychologists had a close affinity with Adlerians. Before their separate organization was founded, humanists had been invited to express their ideas in the Adlerian journal, the *American Journal of Individual Psychology*, under the editorship of Heinz Ansbacher (DeCarvalho, 1990b). The two humanists we consider in the following chapters, Abraham Maslow and Carl Rogers, both studied with Adler. Rogers was taught by Adler during the former's internship at the Institute for Child Guidance in New York City in 1927–1928. Maslow regularly attended Adler's informal seminars in his home in New York in 1935 (Ansbacher, 1990b). Both humanists acknowledged Adler's influence on their ideas. It was Adler's emphasis on holism, choice, and the intentions and subjective experience of the individual that most influenced the humanists. Other significant influences included Karen Horney and Kurt Goldstein, who found that brain-injured patients can best be understood as striving whole organisms rather than as collections of part-brain processes. Furthermore, the early developments of humanistic psychology were closely connected with the academic developments in personality by Gordon Allport, George Kelly, Henry Murray, and others, although over time this connection weakened (Taylor, 2000).

The major distinguishing characteristics of the humanistic perspective derive from its commitment to the value of personal growth:

1. The humanistic perspective focuses on "higher," more developed, and healthier aspects of human experience and their development. Among these are spirituality, creativity, and tolerance.

2. The humanistic perspective values the subjective experience of the individual, including emotional experience. This is sometimes called a phenomenological approach.

395

3. Humanistic psychologists emphasize the present rather than the past or the future.

4. Humanists stress that each individual is responsible for his or her own life outcomes. No past conditions predetermine the present. A person's capacity for self-reflection enhances healthy choice.

5. The humanistic perspective seeks to apply its findings to the betterment of the human condition by changing the environment in which people develop. It assumes that, given appropriate conditions, individuals will develop in a desirable direction.

Humanists describe a "true self" that contains the potential for optimal growth. Alienation from this true self results from unhealthy socialization when other people define what one should do. The view of humanism that one should be guided by one's true self, or "daimon," is an old idea, with roots in eudaemonistic philosophy as old as Aristotle (A. S. Waterman, 1990). Humanistic psychology has served as an ideology, rather than science, for many (Geller, 1982; M. B. Smith, 1990). It has been compared with religious traditions (H. Smith, 1985), including Hinduism and Buddhism, although these Eastern approaches describe self-actualization as requiring considerably more effort than humanism (Das, 1989). Closer to home, humanism is compatible with the individualism and optimism of U.S. culture (Fuller, 1982). It served as an ideology for many people in the counterculture of the 1960s who were attracted to its emphasis on experience and self-disclosure (M. B. Smith, 1990). In contrast to psychoanalysis, which regards instincts as dangerous and needing suppression for civilization to function, humanists assume our human nature is inherently good and that suppression itself causes difficulties (Wallach, 2004).

Humanists have been criticized for underestimating the evil in humankind. They say that people are intrinsically good and cite environmental causes to explain evil (Das, 1989). Some critics suggest the idea of self-actualization fosters selfishness or narcissism rather than promoting what Adler called "social interest" (Geller, 1982; Wallach & Wallach, 1983). Rogers (1982b) expressed dismay at this indictment, which he regarded as undeserved.

Humanistic psychologists are more interested in process and change than in measuring individual differences. In clinical settings, therapists of the humanistic orientation prefer not to make a diagnosis if possible (e.g., Munter, 1975). By emphasizing the goals of behavior rather than the mechanisms by which behavior occurs, humanists are teleological (future oriented) as opposed to deterministic. Teleology searches for the overall design or purpose toward which things are developing. In contrast, the predominant philosophy of science, logical positivism, insists on determinism—that is, explanation in terms of past or present, not future, causes. The challenge to humanism is to be able to be rigorously, scientifically teleological (Rychlak, 1977).

As Seligman and Csikszentmihalyi (2000) point out, humanistic psychologists failed to produce a cumulative, empirical body of research. Humanists are generally uncomfortable with the constraints of the traditional scientific method. To many, cognitive behaviorism pushes the scientific method as far toward the directions of interest to humanists as one can go, without abandoning science. M. Brewster Smith (1990), writing from a humanistic perspective, suggests that theoretical developments within the cognitive social learning perspective (Part V, Chapters 12 and 13) can be reconciled with the concerns of humanistic psychology:

> Albert Bandura has stretched his social learning theory to accommodate central humanistic concerns in developing a theory of reciprocal determinism in which

he manages to take into account self-control and personal initiative in constituting one's environment (p. 15).

Others disagree, saying that cognitive behaviorism is still too deterministic to meet the needs of personality theory (Rychlak, 1984a, 1988) or that it fails to describe the self adequately (Malm, 1993). The tension between the constraints of the scientific method, on the one hand, and interest in the whole healthy human, on the other, will be felt throughout our consideration of the humanistic perspective. Ongoing efforts to add science to the humanistic emphasis on well-being are consolidating under a movement called *positive psychology* (Seligman & Csikszentmihalyi, 2000).

Study Questions

1. What are the fundamental assumptions of the humanistic perspective?
2. Should the humanistic perspective be considered a scientific approach, an ideology, or both? What considerations will be relevant as you consider this question while reading the following chapters? (Chapter 1 presents criteria for a theory that may apply.)

CHAPTER

14

Rogers
Person-Centered Theory

Chapter Overview

Preview: Overview of Rogers's Theory
The Actualizing Tendency
The Self
Development
Therapy
Other Applications
Criticisms of Rogers's Theory
Summary

ILLUSTRATIVE BIOGRAPHY

Maya Angelou

Maya Angelou, writer, actress, civil rights activist, and more, struggled with some of the issues that are central to Rogers's theory: issues of self-acceptance and esteem and fulfilling her potential despite life's challenges. Her writings and teachings inspire affirmation of life and love for all beings.

Maya Angelou is a U.S. writer of prose and poetry who has published several autobiographical works (1969, 1974, 1976, 1981, 1986, 1993, 1998, 2002). Her vivid descriptions of her own experience make it rather easy for the reader to understand life from her point of view, as Rogers urges for those who would truly understand another person. She was born in 1928 to parents who soon divorced and sent her at age 3 with her 4-year-old brother, Bailey, from Southern California to live with their grandmother in Stamps,

Arkansas. They grew up in the black section of this poor community, helping their grandmother in her grocery store. From her they learned pride and discipline. Although poor, they were relatively better off than the other blacks, who picked cotton. For a time, they lived with their other grandmother and then with their mother and her boyfriend, Mr. Freeman, in St. Louis. Angelou (1969) describes being raped by him when she was 8 years old. For this, he was convicted and sentenced to jail, but he was lynched before serving time. Afterward, Maya developed psychogenic mutism, and after a time she and Bailey were sent back to Stamps.

During her adolescence and young adulthood, Angelou lived in various places: in Stamps with her grandmother, in Los Angeles with her father, and in San Francisco with her mother (a prostitute). For a while she lived in an abandoned car in a junkyard. At 16 she had a son. She held a variety of jobs: waitress, cook, dancer, singer, prostitute, music store clerk, and San Francisco cable car operator. She worked for Martin Luther King, Jr.'s Southern Christian Leadership

Conference (SCLC). She has been an actress. Above all, she is a writer. She lived for a time in Ghana, where her son attended college. She married and divorced a Greek, Tosh Angelos, and later an African freedom fighter, a relationship that also ended but taught her about her African heritage. After the end of another marriage, she moved from the San Francisco Bay Area to North Carolina, where she is a professor at Wake Forest University. Throughout these varied experiences, her primary career is writing.

Intelligent, talented as a dancer and actress as well as a writer, Maya Angelou frankly reveals her multifaceted self in autobiographical books that are also noteworthy for their artistic merit. The tension between the true self and the self that others can accept has been part of her life journey, with the real self prevailing, as Rogers would advocate. Being nonwhite in America places people at risk for alienation from the true self because of prejudice. Maya Angelou describes some of the cruelties of white children that she experienced in childhood, the sort of discrimination that assaults self-esteem. Her grandmother insisted that Angelou act courteously toward whites, even when she felt angry. Such incongruence between felt emotion and overt behavior is inconsistent with Rogers's advice, but it was adaptive under the social conditions of racial prejudice in which Maya grew up because blacks who expressed their feelings openly risked attack, even lynching. As a child, when Maya met some whites who treated her as an equal, she found that "the old habits of withdrawing into righteous indignation or lashing out furiously against insults were not applicable in this circumstance" (Angelou, 1976, p. 75). Positive regard, as Rogers would say, can be transformative.

Development

In Carl Rogers's theory, the most important childhood experience is to be loved, wholly and unconditionally. As a young child, only 3 years old, when she and her brother were sent from their mother's home to live with their grandmother, Maya could not have understood that this abandonment was not her fault. Experientially, it was rejection. Once in Arkansas, she experienced a loving and stable environment from a protective grandmother who loved her granddaughter with few "conditions of regard." That is, as Rogers advocates, she was loved for who she was, providing a solid foundation for self-esteem. She returned to her grandmother's home for a time later, during a difficult time when she needed that love again. Throughout her varied careers and love relationships, Maya Angelou has tasted richly of life's opportunities, exploring many facets of her own evolving self and resisting the limitations that would be imposed if she abandoned her own voice.

Description

A person's sense of self is key to Rogers's theory. He describes most people as split, aware of a part of themselves that is acceptable to others but unaware of a deeper "real self" that has the potential for health and vitality. Self-esteem suffers when the real self is not affirmed by others.

Adjustment

Rogers's concept of process proposes that at higher levels of development, people become more spontaneous in discovering and accepting aspects of themselves and their feelings. They censor less, both from others' view and from themselves. Self-acceptance is more likely if a person has been accepted unconditionally by others (the parents, ideally; if not, then remedially in therapy). This acceptance helps a person maintain touch with the inner voice from the self, called the *organismic valuing process.*

Maya Angelou's self-disclosures, rich in emotional feeling, fit the higher levels of process (described later in this chapter). They do so in a way that is not self-indulgent, as some autobiographical works can be, but that reflects on the wisdom gained from her family and African and American culture. Her self-acceptance is clear from the way she rejoices in even the aspects of her life that seem like mistakes—the passions that led to failed marriages, for example.

She describes seeking therapy, in young adulthood, and finding that the white male therapist had little help to offer (Angelou, 1976). She quickly concluded that the wealth and social class of this man would make it impossible for him to understand her, and she turned instead to a friend. Rogers insisted that a therapist, to be effective, must empathically understand as well as accept the client. This is more difficult when ethnicity or other differences separate the life experience of the client and therapist.

Cognition

Accurate awareness of the true self is impeded by other people's messages about what is acceptable, what sort of self we must be to be loved by them.

Along the way, though, Angelou did not always follow her organismic valuing process; it conflicted with her need to be loved. For example, she decided to marry Thomas Allen, a bail bondsman, despite misgivings about his presumption that he could make all the important decisions. "I ignored the twinge which tried to warn me that I should stop and do some serious thinking" (Angelou, 1981, p. 103). Soon, though, another man won her heart and prevented the practical but subjectively troublesome marriage from taking place. Another relationship, too, conflicted with her inner sense, when her African lover, Sheikhali, demanded that she become less impatient, more submissive, more traditionally female (Angelou, 1986).

Often, though, Angelou was guided by her organismic valuing process, which made her a nonconformist but also saved her from mishap. When the singers in the cast of *Porgy and Bess* had their hair straightened in Italy, Angelou insisted that the chemicals, which burned intensely, be washed out of her hair; she was the only one who did not have her hair fall out as a consequence of this overly harsh chemical treatment. The lessons of the healthy nature of that inner voice, the organismic valuing process, are usually not quite so concrete as this!

Society

In Rogers's approach, society's problems can be addressed by helping people accept their true selves. This would reduce racial prejudice and international conflict and transform educational institutions by giving students more responsibility for their intellectual explorations.

In exploring her own identity as a black American, both in the United States and in travel to Africa, Maya Angelou describes the importance of society's messages about race. In Africa, Angelou (1986) met proud black tribal leaders and learned from these models to accept being black with pride. The power of her feelings attests to the importance of the acceptance of other people as nourishment for self-actualization. In contrast, in America she encountered blatant racism. As an active participant in the civil rights movement, she has helped change that blight. She reminds us of our history, of slavery, of continuing poverty, and also of the tremendous strength that black Americans have shown and continue to show. The brutal honesty of her own self-examination is a model for a societal honesty that can also help us discover truth and healing. She asserts, "If it is true that a chain is only as strong as its weakest link, isn't it also true a society is only as healthy as its sickest citizen and only as wealthy as its most deprived? I think so" (1998, p. 108)

Biology

Rogers uses a biological metaphor when he describes self-actualization as an innate tendency to grow, to fulfill one's potential. His theory, though, does not describe the actual biological details of this process.

Like Rogers's therapy clients, Angelou wrestles with biological urges, particularly sexuality, in her journey toward self-actualization. She celebrates that aspect of selfhood and urges that it continue into old age (Angelou, 1998). Psychologists sometimes emphasize our intellectualization of the self, forgetting its biological reality. The self is biological in more than a metaphorical sense.

Final Thoughts

Rogers's theory teaches us that health requires self-understanding and self-acceptance. Maya Angelou's autobiographical self-explorations and her explicit lessons about poverty and race not only exemplify Rogers's theory; they also extend its promise.

Preview: Overview of Rogers's Theory

Rogers's theory has implications for major theoretical questions, as presented in Table 14.1. In the history of personality theories that have major relevance for psychotherapy, Rogers's theory holds a special place. It is the one theory of effective therapy that was first extensively tested by empirical research. Rogers, rightly, took pride that he had specified the conditions needed to be created in the therapy process for them to be measured by observers, to say whether they were present in a particular therapy session. Further, he defines the outcomes of therapy so they could be measured. This contribution alone, opening up psychotherapy to empirical verification, would make Rogers's theory stand out, but in addition, many of his theoretical assertions have withstood the test. The theory is not limited to therapy but is comprehensive enough to have also been extended to other settings, including business organizations, and it offers advice to parents and others who rear children about how to be effective in that important job. The applied value of the theory thus extends to business and child development, and also (Rogers argued) to the political arena, where it offers suggestions for reducing political conflict

TABLE 14.1	Preview of Rogers's Theory
Individual Differences	Rogers did not focus on stable individual differences, although individuals can be said to differ in their level of development and in the conditions they perceive must be met to be approved by others. Other researchers have recently developed scales to measure aspects of his theory that may be comparable to personality traits.
Adaptation and Adjustment	Rogers describes in detail his client-centered therapeutic technique. Individual therapy and group therapy, including encounter groups, lead to progress through stages of functioning, leading to greater openness to feelings, the present, and choice.
Cognitive Processes	Thought and feeling may be impeded by accepting others' messages about what we should be.
Society	The person-centered approach has implications for the improvement of society, including education, marriage, work roles, and group conflict (including conflict among nations).
Biological Influences	Rogers did not consider biological factors, though his actualizing process is based on a biological metaphor.
Development	Children become alienated from the growth forces within them if they are raised with conditions of worth. Parents should raise their children with unconditional positive regard. People can change in adulthood, becoming freer.

(although some question whether a psychological theory, without the insights from political science levels of understanding, can accomplish all that much).

Carl Rogers, probably the best known spokesperson for humanistic psychology, was one of the first members of the Association of Humanistic Psychology. Like other humanists, his ideas built on Alfred Adler's belief that people have a fundamental tendency to develop in healthy directions. This is particularly understandable in that Rogers, as an intern, studied with Adler, a visiting professor, in 1927–1928 in New York (Watts, 1996). Rogers believed that all human beings are motivated fundamentally by a growth-directed process, which he called the actualizing tendency (Rogers, 1963). Rogers tackled the problem of providing empirical evidence for humanistic psychology through research, although perhaps not as objectively and scientifically as one might wish (Feltham, 1999).

BIOGRAPHY OF CARL ROGERS

CARL ROGERS

Carl R. Rogers was born in Oak Park, Illinois (near Chicago), on January 8, 1902. He was the fourth of six children. His father was part owner of a successful contracting and civil engineering business and a cold disciplinarian (Cohen, 1997). The family atmosphere valued hard work and fundamentalist Christianity, adhering to strict rules of behavior. "We did not dance, play cards, attend movies, smoke, drink, or show any sexual interest" (Rogers, 1967, p. 344). The family moved to a farm so the children would not encounter the temptations of close contact with others in the city or suburbs. This "gently suppressive family atmosphere" (p. 352), however, took its toll. Rogers and two siblings developed ulcers.

Rogers always enjoyed reading. He read at a fourth-grade level when he first entered school, and he loved to be alone and to read when he was growing up and even later. As one might expect, his grades were always high. Chores on the family farm led to his interest in scientific farming. He enrolled in the agriculture program at the University of Wisconsin. He was active in a church-related student volunteer movement and spent more than 6 months in China on a YMCA (Young Men's Christian Association) program for young people. This was a very important transition experience for Rogers because for the first time he was distant from family members and their influence. Letters at that time moved by ship, so communication took months. He grew increasingly tolerant of different customs that his parents could not challenge.

Rogers graduated from college in 1924 with a bachelor's degree in history (having lost interest in agriculture). Ironically, he had taken only one psychology course as an undergraduate. That summer he married his fiancée of nearly 2 years, Helen, a commercial artist, although his family objected that it would be better to wait until his postgraduate studies were over. Helen gave up her work as a commercial artist, and they went to New York City, where they both entered graduate school. Rogers studied at Union Theological Seminary, continuing the religious interest that had been a major theme in his life. He also took courses at Teachers College at Columbia University and decided to do graduate work there in psychology. For his doctoral dissertation, Rogers developed a test to measure children's personality adjustment. Researchers used this test for many years thereafter (Cain, 1987).

For several years after completing his graduate studies in 1928, Rogers worked with children. His first position was at the Rochester (New York) Society for the Prevention of Cruelty to Children, where he worked with delinquent and underprivileged youths. He headed the Rochester Guidance Center when it first opened in 1938, although traditionally a psychiatrist would fill such a position. He struggled for many years over the status of psychologists within the mental health care establishment (Rogers, 1974c). He reported feeling alienated from the mainstream of psychology, which emphasized animal laboratory studies. Not constrained by disciplinary loyalty, Rogers felt more akin to social workers and participated actively in their professional organizations.

In 1940, after 12 years at Rochester, Rogers and his wife and two children moved to Ohio, where he took his first academic appointment: full professor at Ohio State University. It is highly unusual for a faculty member to begin at the top academic rank, but Rogers had just published an influential book, *Clinical Treatment of the Problem Child*. In his lectures, he came to realize that his ideas about therapy were new, and he developed these ideas in another book, *Counseling and Psychotherapy* (Rogers, 1942a). It contained the first published verbatim transcript of a therapy case, opening this private process for study (see also Rogers, 1942b). The text has become a classic. Opening therapy sessions to the scrutiny of research required persistence because the therapeutic community objected, but the practice eventually was accepted (Gendlin, 1988). His students learned not only in the classroom but also through practicum experience. This was revolutionary: "the first instance in which supervised therapy was carried on in a university setting. . . . Neither Freud nor any other therapist had ever managed to make supervised experience in the therapeutic relationship a part of academic experience" (Rogers, 1967, p. 362).

In 1945 Rogers went to the University of Chicago to establish a new counseling center. An active and collegial atmosphere developed there, and during this time Rogers (1951) wrote another of his classic books, *Client-Centered Therapy*. In 1957 Rogers accepted a joint appointment in psychology and psychiatry at the University of Wisconsin, where he found a competitive and nonsupportive atmosphere. Only one out of seven students who began the doctoral program in psychology remained to complete the degree requirements. This conflicted with his own humanistic convictions. He protested in 1963 by resigning his appointment in the Department of Psychology. (He retained his position in psychiatry.) He published his criticisms of the competitive environment, suggesting a more humanistic approach (Rogers, 1969).

His next move was away from university life. For the third time in his career, Rogers gave up a tenured appointment to begin a new phase of his professional development. In 1964 he went to the Western Behavioral Sciences Institute in La Jolla, California. With others, he formed, in 1968, the Center for the Studies of the Person. In these years, he explored encounter groups and sensitivity training. According to one biographer, these group experiences were times of personal exploration for Rogers; he had begun drinking heavily. In his 70s he had a relationship with one of the women in a group (although he was married), and he was unkind in dealing with his wife and family (Cohen, 1997). Some of his projects aimed to achieve international peace in such areas of conflict as Central America, South Africa, and Northern Ireland. He offered a workshop in the Soviet Union in 1986, influencing therapists there (Bondarenko, 1999).

Rogers was a leader in professional organizations throughout his career. He served as president of the American Association for Applied Psychology (1944–1945) and of the American Psychological Association (1946–1947). He received two prestigious awards from the American Psychological Association: the Distinguished Scientific Contribution

Award in 1956 (American Psychological Association, 1957) and the first Distinguished Professional Contribution Award in 1972 (American Psychological Association, 1973). He was the first (and as of 1987, only) psychologist to receive both honors (Cain, 1987). Rogers was also nominated for the Nobel Peace Prize in 1987. Rogers died in 1987, at age 85, of a heart attack.

The Actualizing Tendency

Rogers (1961a) theorized that all motivation is subsumed under a fundamental process, the **actualizing tendency**, that is:

> the directional trend which is evident in all organic and human life—the urge to expand, extend, develop, mature—the tendency to express and activate all the capacities of the organism, or the self. (p. 351)

The broad, general tendency toward development in nature he called the *formative tendency*. He contrasted it with a tendency toward randomness (entropy) and suggested that the tendency to move from simpler to more complex forms is just as powerful in nature (Rogers, 1979). The specific human aspect of the formative tendency is the actualizing tendency, which describes humans and all other organisms, animals, and even plants. Biological motivations, such as hunger and thirst, are part of this actualizing tendency, as are the "higher" human motivations.

We do not behave irrationally, as psychoanalysis assumed. Rather, "our behavior is exquisitely rational, moving with subtle and ordered complexity toward the goals the organism is endeavoring to achieve" (Rogers, 1983, p. 292). The actualizing tendency leads to differentiation (complexity), independence, and social responsibility. For Rogers (1986a), the motivation intrinsic to each person is basically good and healthy. More negative views of human motivation prevail in psychoanalysis, Christianity, and educational institutions. In contrast, Rogers's optimism "is profoundly radical" (p. 127).

THE ORGANISMIC VALUING PROCESS

A self-actualizing person is in touch with the inner experience that is inherently growth producing, the **organismic valuing process**. It is a subconscious guide that evaluates experience for its growth potential. It draws the person toward experiences that produce growth and away from those that inhibit growth. Even activities that might seem fun or profitable to conscious experience will be avoided if they feel wrong to this inner guide. Thus internal experience, rather than external rules, directs choices. This inner valuing process is natural in the infant, who values food and security. Although this is not usually emphasized, some have interpreted Rogers's organismic valuing process in terms of the body, interpreting physical symptoms and healthy functioning as evidence of contact with the organismic valuing process (Fernald, 2000). With development, people unfortunately substitute external rules for inner experience as they learn values from society that interfere with psychological development (Rogers, 1964).

What about people who are emotionally disturbed or criminals? Many people do not seem to be healthy and mature. How can this occur if the actualizing tendency motivates everyone? Rogers blamed social forces that cause a person to lose touch with inner growth processes. People distrust their inner feelings because they repeatedly hear that these feelings are bad. Such messages come from parents, schools, and even psychoanalysts. It is people's fear and defensiveness, rather than innate evil forces, that cause them to become destructive.

THE FULLY FUNCTIONING PERSON

A person who pays attention to the organismic valuing process is self-actualizing or **fully functioning**. Such a person does not lose the use of some human functions through adverse socialization messages. A potentially creative person may lose touch with that capacity by being taught that idle drawing is a waste of time. Similarly, a potentially empathic person may lose touch with that capacity by being taught that showing feelings is a sign of weakness.

fully functioning Rogers's term for a mentally healthy person

The person who is fully functioning, who is most healthy, has several characteristics, which Rogers lists. These characteristics can be interpreted as signs of mental health.

Openness to Experience

The fully functioning person is *open to experience*, receptive to the subjective and objective happenings of life. Others may censor experience through defenses (e.g., not recognizing an insult or the anger it provokes). In contrast, the fully functioning person accurately perceives such events. In this sense, one might describe such a person as having an expanded consciousness. This openness includes the ability to tolerate ambiguity in experience. A situation that seems to be one way at one moment may seem to be different another time.

Existential Living

A person open to experience shows "an increasing tendency to live fully in each moment" (Rogers, 1961a, p. 188). Experience changes, and each moment allows the real self to emerge, possibly changed by the new experience. Part of the person is participating in each moment of existential living, but part is an observer of the process. This "means. . . a maximum of adaptability. . . a flowing, changing organization of self and personality" (Rogers, 1983, p. 288). The self is experienced as a fluid process rather than a fixed entity. Experience is not rigid and structured.

Organismic Trusting

A person with *organismic trust* (also called the "organismic valuing process," described more fully later in this chapter) relies on inner experience at each moment to guide behavior. This experience is accurate. The person perceives inner needs and emotions and various aspects of the social situation without distortion. Dysfunction comes when a person loses touch with inner feelings and values (J. B. Watson & Greenberg, 1998). The individual integrates all these facets of experience and comes to an inner sense of what is right for him or her. This sense is trustworthy; it is not necessary to depend on outside authorities to say what is right.

Experiential Freedom

The fully functioning person experiences freedom, in each moment, to choose. Such *experiential freedom* is subjective and does not deny there is determinism in the world.

Viktor Frankl described concentration camp prisoners, each free to choose at least an attitude toward the experiences of life (Rogers, 1969). In most circumstances, there is considerable behavioral freedom as well.

Creativity

The fully functioning person lives *creatively*. He or she finds new ways of living at each moment, instead of being locked into past, rigid patterns no longer adaptive. Rogers (1961a, p. 194) described fully functioning humans as the best able to adapt to new conditions, the "vanguard of human evolution."

SUBJECTIVE EXPERIENCE, VALUES, AND SCIENCE

Rogers experienced a conflict between the model of science, in which the therapy client would be viewed objectively, and his experience as a therapist, in which a subjective stance worked better (Barresi, 1999; Rogers, 1955). In his later writing, Rogers went further in his emphasis on subjectivity. Participants in his workshops sometimes described the experience in terms of spirituality. This suggests a transpersonal dimension to human experience. Experiences of altered states of consciousness and mysticism are something like self-actualization. Many therapists have found Rogers's approach, and other humanistic-existential approaches, compatible with spirituality (e.g., Benjamin & Looby, 1998), although not with traditional organized religion (Van Kalmthout, 1995). Rogers (1979) suggested that he might have underestimated the "mystical, spiritual dimension" of experience. Fritz Capra's (1975) comparison of modern physics with Eastern mysticism validated Rogers's belief that subjective experience could be compatible with science (cf. Bozarth, 1985). He wrote sympathetically about mysticism and suggested that paranormal phenomena should be explored in empirical research (Rogers, 1973, 1979, 1980). A scale measuring belief in Transcendental Mental Powers has been developed from Rogers's theory (Cartwright, 1989). His approach challenges us to consider the role of subjectivity within a scientific framework, even in areas that seem to contradict science.

Values are explicitly important in Rogers's theory (DeCarvalho, 1989), as in humanistic theory generally. Rogers (1964) argued that values emerge for each individual, and for humankind as a whole, from the process of experiencing. This position offends those who hold that science should be value free and others who regard it as an invitation to selfishness, in which no one is held to an external standard of right and wrong. How ironic that Rogers, who disagreed with psychoanalysis, should be criticized along with Freud, who challenged religious values (cf. Fuller, 1982).

The Self

Much of personality growth, including that occurring in therapy, involves changes in the self. Rogers hesitated to introduce this term into his theory, but clients would say, for example, "I'm not sure I'm being my real self." At first reluctantly, Rogers accepted the necessity of including the concept self in his theory but was amazed that it became so popular in psychology. Walter Mischel (1992), reviewing the history of the study of personality, credited Carl Rogers with his influential recognition of the importance of the self as an organizing unit of personality.

The self that is healthy, though, is not the self that is carefully built up by success and approved by others. That self can, in fact, be an impediment to health. That self, it can be said, must (metaphorically) "die" for the true, healthy self to emerge (Van Kalmthout, 1995). We are familiar with the terms *ideal self* and *real self* from psychoanalytic theory (especially Karen Horney's theory). Rogers used these terms too. He observed that many people experience a discrepancy between the two. They wish to be like the **ideal self**; perhaps they even pretend to be like it. The real self is different; it contains a person's true or real qualities, including the actualizing tendency. The organismic valuing process leads to health; the ideal self leads to disturbance. Rogers used the term *incongruence* to describe the experience of conflict between the **real self** and the ideal self. When a person is incongruent, he or she experiences the real self as threatening. To prevent this, defense mechanisms distort and deny experience. "Me? Angry? Never!" "Lie? Never, not me!" "Tired? No—I always have energy to help a friend!" and so on. The real self may be suppressed.

Most people use the term *self-actualization* loosely to refer to the healthy actualizing process. Rogers (1951) himself did not distinguish between *self-actualization* and *actualization* in his early work. Later, however, he described self-actualization as a "subaspect" of the actualization process. If the person has forsaken the real self, actualization and self-actualization are in conflict. A phony self-actualization impedes the healthy actualization process. *Self-actualization*, in the more precise sense of the term, is an unhealthy tendency when a person is in a state of incongruence because the self that is being actualized is defined by society, not by the individual. Actualization, the more general tendency, is always healthy (Ford & Maas, 1989; Rogers, 1959). This complicated distinction, according to Roy DeCarvalho (1990b), means that everyone is "becoming," but only for some does growth become a truly individual, self-chosen process.

One of the legacies of Rogers's work has been increased recognition that self-esteem is important. Rogers did make a person's basic self-acceptance central to his theory, and he would likely take exception to the implicit assumption in some measures that self-esteem is "earned" by behavior or accomplishments. His emphasis on "the self" as a core of psychological health has made a lasting impression.

> **ideal self** what a person feels he or she ought to be like

> **real self** the self that contains the actualizing tendency

Development

To understand why incongruence occurs, consider how the self-concept develops. Adults tell children to "be good." Rogers described such pressures in his own childhood: Be hardworking, be respectful to adults, and so forth. "Bad" behavior leads to punishment or is simply ignored. Rogers called this kind of socialization *conditional positive regard*. That is, parents will love (regard positively) children only to the extent that the children live up to their **conditions of worth**. As a result of this socialization, children come to think of themselves as having only the "good" qualities; they disown the "bad" qualities. Despite the good intentions of parents, this socialization does not work out for the best. Unfortunately, some of the "bad" qualities parents discourage are really healthy potentials.

Parents have different styles of raising their children. Some, called *authoritarian parents*, place a high priority on respect and obedience (Baumrind, 1971). Although well intentioned, such a style of parenting works against the child's inherent tendency toward self-actualization. College students who report that their parents used authoritarian parenting techniques were less self-actualized than those whose parents gave them direction

> **conditions of worth** the expectations a person must live up to before receiving respect and love

without harsh restrictions, an *authoritative parenting style* (Dominguez & Carton, 1997). Consider a child who has learned not to challenge the parents' authority. The ideal self is obedient and respectful. The real self would question and rebel, but it has been suppressed. As the person grows up, feelings of rebellion or questioning of authority, when they begin to surface, feel dangerous, so the person turns away from them. What the young child learned to be "good" becomes a rigid, maladaptive trait in the adult, who relies on authority figures for direction and does not think independently.

The problem with overly restrictive parenting, as Rogers envisioned it, is that only those aspects of potential selfhood that are compatible with these conditions of worth develop. A better alternative would be to impose no conditions of worth. That is, give the child **unconditional positive regard**, which means loving the child regardless of his or her behavior. This allows the child to explore all his or her potentials. Because Rogers viewed human beings as essentially good, the outcome is the development of a fully functioning person. Critics argue that such advice is impractical and neglectful. Indeed, parents who have humanistic values are more likely to have children who report experimenting with drugs, although they are unlikely to engage in delinquent behaviors (Garnier & Stein, 1998). Surely, Rogers did not advocate abdicating parental responsibilities to direct and teach their children, yet he contended that feeling loved, fully and unconditionally, is essential to healthy development.

Early research suggested to Rogers that inner resources of the child are more important than external influences in determining healthy outcomes. He reported research on delinquent children in which inner influences were far more predictive of later behavior than were outer influences, including the family environment, health, economic background, intelligence, and heredity. More important than any of these was a measure that tapped various inner influences, "the degree of the child's self-understanding, self-insight; the realistic acceptance of self and the realistic appraisal of the situation in which he found himself; and the acceptance of responsibility for oneself" (Rogers, 1989, p. 204).

Outside the family, the larger society also can reject children, through racism and other prejudices. These messages, too, interfere with healthy development, although a loving family can largely protect children. Conversely, when children are not completely accepted by their family, others may support their development by providing love.

unconditional positive regard accepting and valuing a person without requiring particular behaviors as a prerequisite

DEVELOPMENT OF CREATIVITY

Creativity is one of the qualities that emerges from healthy development. Rogers (1954) considered what sort of environment encourages creativity. Creativity requires three psychological qualities: "openness to experience, an internal locus of evaluation, and the ability to toy with elements and concepts" (Harrington, Block, & Block, 1987). Harrington and colleagues studied 106 children and their parents from preschool through adolescence. Results confirmed predictions based on Rogers's ideas. Preschool parent–child interactions correlated, about a decade later, with creative potential in early adolescence. Parents of preschool children who later became creative agreed with statements such as these:

"I respect my child's opinions and encourage him to express them."
"I encourage my child to be curious, to explore and question things."

They disagreed with statements such as these:

> "I do not allow my child to get angry with me."
> "I feel my child is a bit of a disappointment to me."

The parents taught tasks to their preschoolers in the research laboratory. Creativity-facilitating parents encouraged and praised their children. Parents who criticized and who controlled or structured the tasks instead of allowing the child to work independently raised less creative children. Because the study was correlational, we cannot be certain whether the parents caused their children to become creative or not. For example, the children may have already been different, causing the parents to behave differently, rather than vice versa. Nonetheless, the results support Rogers's conceptualization of creativity.

What about creativity later in life? Later, too, exposure to Rogerian-type leadership enhances creativity. Students at a technological university were assigned to groups with either a Rogerian leader, a structured leader, or a considerate leader, and they worked on an engineering problem, designing a way to provide fresh water to their dog, who was left at home while the family went on a vacation. The group with Rogerian leadership solved the problem more creatively (Fodor & Roffe-Steinrotter, 1998).

Therapy

Not everyone is fortunate enough to have been raised by ideal accepting parents and to have developed according to the innate actualizing potential. Can remedial therapy help overcome unhealthy tendencies? Carl Rogers is best known as a therapist, and he had much to say about effective therapy. He developed a new therapeutic approach that he called client-centered therapy, and he pioneered the scientific investigation of the effectiveness of therapy.

CLIENT-CENTERED THERAPY

Rogers considered therapy to be an experience that could help people reconnect with their organismic valuing process, which guides healthy development. In fact, disconnection from the organismic valuing process is the universal source of maladjustment, in his view (Van Kalmthout, 1995). Because this approach takes its direction from the client rather than from the therapist's insights, it was called nondirective therapy, later client-centered therapy or sometimes person-centered therapy. It turns the focus to the client's experience, particularly toward feelings (Mahrer & Fairweather, 1993), to mobilize the growth-producing force of the actualizing tendency (Bozarth & Brodley, 1991). In contrast to therapies based on the medical model, which objectifies those who are to be treated and presumes that wisdom comes from the authority of the therapist (Kahn, 1999), client-centered therapy is a noncoercive approach that honors the client's experience. Thus it is true to a vision of psychotherapy as the cure of souls (Szasz, 1998).

Rogers developed his therapeutic technique over many years in a practical setting, away from academia. He was thus guided by "what works" rather than by considerations of theory. He described, for example, an early therapeutic encounter when he was still following his early training in psychoanalytic theory. He helped a pyromaniac boy discover that his motivation for setting fires stemmed from sexual desire, only to be crushed when this insight did not prevent recurrence of the behavior. Psychoanalysis taught that *insight* brought a cure; clinical experience taught otherwise.

Rogers became convinced that theoretical preconceptions interfere with therapeutic progress. He dropped theoretical formulas, such as the sexual-drive-leads-to-pyromania formulation, which had failed him, and instead listened to what his clients were telling him. Their experience provided worthwhile directions for growth. Because of this emphasis on the client's experience and direction, Rogers called his technique **client-centered therapy**.

Drawing on his therapeutic experience, Rogers (1957a) listed six conditions that lead to therapeutic progress (see Table 14.2). Foremost among these conditions were *unconditional positive regard, congruence,* and *empathic understanding,* conditions he regarded as necessary and sufficient for therapeutic progress.

client-centered therapy therapy based on the belief that the person seeking help is the best judge of the direction that will lead to growth

Unconditional Positive Regard

Rogers found that clients are most likely to make progress when they feel accepted by the therapist. Obviously, a therapist cannot approve of maladaptive behaviors. Yet it is possible to convey a feeling of warmth and acceptance, of *unconditional positive regard,* offering the client acceptance that is not contingent on particular behaviors. (This is the same quality that Rogers advocated for effective parenting, described earlier.) Unconditional positive regard means the therapist accepts the client but not necessarily that the therapist approves. Somehow, even if the client behaves in abhorrent ways that may be criminal or racist or whatever, the therapist must find a nonjudgmental, accepting connection with the inner experience of that client.

prizing characteristic of a good therapist, which involves positively valuing the client; also called unconditional positive regard

Rogers expressed his **prizing** (another term for unconditional positive regard) of a patient, Gloria, in a training film when he said to her, "You look to me like a pretty nice daughter" (Shostrom, 1965). Feeling positively valued by the therapist, the client becomes more accepting of herself or himself. Aspects of the real self that were previously repressed because of childhood conditions of worth become available. The client begins to trust personal experience, the inner organismic valuing process. Therapeutic progress results from this prizing of the client.

Unconditional positive regard has sometimes been compared to *agape,* divine love. Although Rogers identified three conditions for effective therapy, one therapist argues that unconditional positive regard is the most important one; the other two conditions simply make it credible (Wilkins, 2000). If the therapist does not seem to be genuine

---

TABLE 14.2   Necessary and Sufficient Conditions for Therapeutic Process

1. Two persons are in psychological contact.
2. The first, whom we shall term the client, is in a state of incongruence, being vulnerable or anxious.
3. The second person, whom we shall term the therapist, is congruent or integrated in the relationship.
4. The therapist experiences unconditional positive regard for the client.
5. The therapist experiences an empathic understanding of the client's internal frame of reference and endeavors to communicate this experience to the client.
6. The communication to the client of the therapist's empathic understanding and unconditional positive regard is to a minimal degree achieved.

(From Rogers, 1957a.)

(congruence) or does not seem to understand the client emotionally, then positive regard may not be credible. In fact, in the unusual case where a therapist simply does not like the client, Rogers recommended that the therapist acknowledge anger or even dislike of the client rather than pretend acceptance. That sort of dishonesty would violate the second condition of effective psychotherapy.

Congruence

A second condition for successful psychotherapy is that the therapist behave with **congruence** in the interaction. That is, the therapist's behavior should match his or her inner experience. The therapist should be genuine and to a large extent transparent, so the client can, as it were, see inside the therapist's experience rather than see only a facade or mask that hides the real person of the therapist. As one expert explained it, "Through the therapist's willingness to risk [being genuine in the relationship], and his or her confidence in the client, the therapist makes it easier for the client to take the plunge into the stream of experiencing" (Friedman, 1994, p. 50). How can one expect the client to become a person open to experience if the therapist is not? This congruency or genuineness or authenticity does not mean, though, that the therapist passively lets every thought be known; it is an active disclosure, taking the client's well-being into consideration (Tudor & Worrall, 1994).

congruence a feeling of consistency between the real self and the ideal self

Empathic Understanding

A third condition for successful psychotherapy is **empathic understanding**. That is, the therapist should be able to understand the experience of the client. Whereas other approaches seek to reduce a client's pain, the client-centered approach also seeks to share that experience empathically (Gruen, 1998). Largely because of Rogers, empathy has become a major topic of discussion among therapists (Bohart & Greenberg, 1997). Empathic understanding is easier to teach than the other two therapeutic requirements, according to Rogers. It often involves restating the client's communications in a way that has been criticized as "parroting" plus a change of pronoun. (Client: "I am sad." Therapist: "You feel sad.") The criticism is too hasty. Empathic understanding involves more than mechanical restatement. Consider Rogers's reflection of one client's statement, "[I]t would be much better for me to. . . ": he reflected back "'I need and must have. . . ,' thus placing more emphasis on the client's underlying need" and taking her deeper into experience that she brought as unfinished business from her past (Gundrum, Lietaer, & Van Hees-Matthijssen, 1999, p. 472). Such therapeutic skill requires what Peter Salovey and John Mayer (1990) call "emotional intelligence." When empathy is present, the therapist may be able to verbalize feelings that the client has been not able to express or even fully experience, which gives the client permission to view himself from a new vantage point, almost introducing the client to himself. One client said of her therapist, "Jack understood me more than I understood me" (Myers, 2000, p. 162). The therapist's ability to understand such unstated feelings empathically has been called "inferential empathy," and Rogers was a master of that ability (Cain, 1996). Thus hidden, unacknowledged feelings such as anger and rejection can be named or, as Rogers would say, "symbolized." Hence these parts of the real self are no longer unknown. Research suggests that it is not so much what the therapist does but rather the client's perception of being understood empathically that matters (Hill & Corbett, 1993). Because of the empathic response of the therapist, the client is treated as "a self that is an authentic source of experience" (Bohart & Greenberg, 1997, p. 6), and thus comes to accept as valid his or her own experience.

empathic understanding the ability of the therapist to understand the subjective experience of the client

Other psychoanalysts, including Freud and Kohut, include empathy as an important psychotherapeutic technique (Emery, 1987; Kahn, 1985, 1987; Tobin, 1991). In fact, the psychoanalyst Heinz Kohut, who developed a theory of self psychology, may have been influenced by Rogers when they were both at the University of Chicago (Kahn & Rachman, 2000). However, for psychoanalysts, empathy is an intellectual tool aimed to increase insight about the patient's psychodynamics. For Kohut (and also for Freud), empathy is cold and impersonal (Rogers, 1986a), a tool for identifying aspects of pathology. In contrast, for Rogers, empathy occurs in a context of unconditional positive regard; in fact, the unconditional positive regard may be a natural outgrowth of deep empathy (Hart, 1999). Although the therapist does not necessarily agree with the client's experience, no judgment is pronounced and the client is valued (Bohart, 1988). When Rogers analyzed a woman, Ellen West, based on her diaries and letters, as well as the psychiatric analyses of this case by others, he criticized those who had been her therapists for analyzing her as an object, rather than genuinely relating to her as a person (Friedman, 1994; Rogers, 1961b), which in Rogers's view is essential for therapy to be effective.

Empathy as a counseling technique may need to be augmented when the counselor and client come from different cultural backgrounds. In many cases, minority clients, treated by therapists from the majority white culture, experience "empathic failure" and so do not form effective working alliances with the therapist (Jenkins, 1997). Rogers conducted a videotaped therapy demonstration with a black man in the 1970s that has been used as a training film, demonstrating that effective therapy can be conducted across racial lines (Moodley, 2000). However, counselors may not understand people accurately whose cultural background is quite different from their own because they have different assumptions about reality. How can this problem be addressed? One approach is to select counselors whose background matches that of their clientele, but this approach is not always feasible. Counselors can be trained to be sensitive to cultural issues (Laungani, 1997). Emotional empathy can be supplemented by cognitive empathy techniques, such as explicitly asking clients about their culture, so the counselor can accurately understand the experience of the client (Scott & Borodovsky, 1990). Ethnic and cultural diversity has many implications for the process of psychotherapy (e.g., B. A. Greene, 1985, 1993; Homma-True et al., 1993).

RESEARCH ON THERAPY

The concepts in Rogers's theory are challenging to study scientifically. Self-actualization is an elusive potentiality. Empathy and genuineness refer to phenomena within an individual; how is an observer to record them? Among his critics was B. F. Skinner, who claimed that many of the concepts used by Rogers could not be defined operationally in scientific terms. Despite these formidable challenges, Rogers (1959) was committed to empirical research, recognizing that no theory is without error when first formulated. He took pride in his scientific research and criticized therapists who did not test their theories (Rogers, 1968, 1986a). Research leads to theoretical revision toward greater validity and accuracy.

Rogers described his theoretical constructs with as much precision as possible to make it possible for them to be operationally defined, and he (1986a) explained behavior in terms of factors present at that time. In contrast, many clinical approaches (especially psychoanalysis) focus on the distant past, leading to theories "that are of necessity speculative and untestable" (p. 137). Rogers especially objected to interpretations of the therapeutic relationship in terms of transference (Bohart, 1991; Rogers, 1986c; Weinrach, 1991). The concept of transference denies the real and present relationship between the client and the therapist, instead making the current situation simply a blank projective screen for past experience.

By turning attention away from the present time and the current relationship (between therapist and client), such notions as transference discourage research on the process of psychotherapy. In stark contrast to the hidden mysterious process of psychoanalysis, Rogers tape-recorded therapy sessions to open the process for examination by researchers.

The Process of Psychotherapy

Guided by his vision, many of Rogers's students and colleagues developed measuring instruments to study the events that occur during therapy (Hill & Corbett, 1993). Using these instruments, judges code the behaviors of the therapist and of the client. For example, are feelings expressed? What tone of voice is used? Other instruments ask the client and the therapist to describe their experiences of therapy sessions. As Rogers came to describe effective counseling techniques more fully, scales to assess therapist effectiveness made it possible to evaluate and improve counselor training programs (Carkhuff, 1969; Ivey, 1971).

Early research supported Rogers's "necessary and sufficient conditions" for therapeutic progress. Rogers asserted that if these conditions (unconditional positive regard, congruence, and empathic understanding) were present, regardless of the theoretical orientation of the therapist, progress would occur. He was correct on both counts. In fact, therapists from other orientations produce these same conditions in their therapy sessions, to a large extent, and the three conditions do lead to improvement in therapy (Keijsers, Schaap, & Hoogduin, 2000). Other factors may be necessary, in addition to these three "necessary and sufficient conditions," for therapeutic effectiveness (Hill & Corbett, 1993; W. H. Lockhart, 1984). For example, it may be helpful to more actively encourage clients to reflect consciously on their goals and evaluate means of reaching them, a reflexivity that requires going beyond the organismic valuing process (Watson & Rennie, 1994).

Rogers and other therapists modeled their therapeutic techniques in instructional films. Rogers was, as we would expect, distinctively different from other therapists in what he said to clients in these films (Essig & Russell, 1990; Mahrer et al., 1988). He frequently reflected or restated what the client said, and he often offered encouragement, approval, and reassurance (Lee & Uhlemann, 1984). He offered more interpretation than we might expect (Weinrach, 1990; but see the rebuttal by Bohart, 1991), and he was not always so nondirective as client-centered therapy typically is portrayed (Bowen, 1996). In one case, for example, he was uncharacteristically directive in his counseling of a black man, thereby helping the client to express his anger about society's mistreatment of him, aided by Rogers's empathic connection with that unexpressed anger (Brodley, 1996).

Detailed microanalyses of client and therapist behavior help us understand how therapists can get clients to focus on the internal subjective experiences that are critical to growth (Wiseman & Rice, 1989). Therapy sessions that therapists rate as indicating improvement tend to be preceded by sessions in which there is a particularly positive emotional bond between therapist and client and are followed by sessions in which the client reports insight (Sexton, 1993). The most important question, though, is whether the effects of therapy carry over to life after therapy.

Outcomes of Psychotherapy

Rogers proposed that when a therapeutic climate is created that has the three crucial characteristics just described (unconditional positive regard, congruence, and empathic understanding), a positive therapeutic outcome will result. In such a case, the client will develop more of the healthy characteristics of self-actualizing people, including openness to experience, self-acceptance, and trust of organismic experience (Rogers, 1961a).

Rogers reported empirical studies demonstrating the effectiveness of psychotherapy. In one study, self-concept was measured by a Q-technique. Subjects sorted 100 self-perception statements—for example, "I often feel resentful," "I feel relaxed and nothing really bothers me"—into nine piles, indicating how well the statements described themselves. These sortings were done for the actual self (as perceived by the subject) and for the ideal self (how the subject would like to be). Before therapy, the real self and the ideal self were quite different. They correlated $r = -0.47$, indicating that clients before therapy saw themselves as unlike their ideal selves. After therapy, the real self and the ideal self were much more similar ($r = 0.59$). Thus therapy produced greater self-acceptance (Butler & Haigh, 1954). This heightened self-acceptance sprang from changes in both the actual self, which came to have more desirable qualities, and the ideal self, which came to include previously unappreciated qualities that the person already possessed.

In recent years, therapists have been increasingly required to demonstrate that their interventions are effective within the shortest feasible time. This demand, reasonable from the perspective of those who pay the bills, has brought increased attention to therapy outcome studies. In principle, such research is straightforward. Because the goal of the research is to show that treatment produces a positive outcome, a simple experimental study (as described in Chapter 1) seems advisable, in which an experimental group receives therapy and a control group does not. (To compare different types of therapy, the control group may receive a different form of treatment, instead of no treatment at all.) However, actually conducting sound research in this area requires carefully considering a fundamental requirement of experimental research: namely, that except for the treatment, everything else is kept equal for the two groups. Client expectations must be controlled: Simply being aware that you are, or are not, receiving treatment (or a particular kind of treatment) can influence you positively or negatively. Aspects of your personality, or of your life circumstance, also can influence the outcome of therapy. Thus the only way to ensure that these are made equal is to assign clients randomly to either the treatment or control group. Therapy studies that use correlational methods, instead of true experiments, leave uncertainty about cause-and-effect relationships (D. Cramer, 1990c).

Even when therapy outcome studies control for expectations and for other client characteristics, another issue remains: Can we agree on the goals of therapy, that is, what constitutes a "good outcome"? Some outcomes are relatively easy to agree on: that people should be able to function more satisfactorily in their work and families after therapy than before and that their troubling symptoms should be eliminated or at least reduced. However, humanistic therapists have a vision of therapy that emphasizes healthy growth from the subjective point of view of the client and less from the perspective of outside observers. A client should come to feel more free, more self-accepting, more willing to experience life as it presents itself. Such goals are not shared by all therapies, and they are not well represented as outcome criteria in studies that compare the effectiveness of various types of therapy, so the contributions of humanistic therapy may be underestimated by such studies (Bohart, O'Hara, & Leitner, 1998; Rychlak, 1998).

STAGES OF PROCESS

Process Scale
measuring instrument to assess how far along an individual is to the goal of becoming a fully functioning person

Personality change in psychotherapy occurs gradually. Rogers devised a way of measuring the types of changes that occur in psychotherapy. The **Process Scale** constitutes a seven-stage description of the process of change (see Table 14.3). Rogers said that therapy is generally involved in stages 3 to 6 on this continuum. Before stage 3, individuals are generally unwilling to participate in therapy, not perceiving problems in themselves.

TABLE 14.3 Seven Stages of Process

Stage	Characteristic Behaviors
1.	Communicates about externals, rather than self; feelings not recognized or owned; rigid perceptions ("constructs"); fear of close relationships; no desire to change
2.	Problems seen as external to self; no sense of responsibility about problems; some feelings described in past or belonging to others; unaware of contradictions
3.	Much talk about self and past feelings; present feelings not accepted; recognition of contradictions; constructs less rigid; choices seen as ineffective
4.	Present feelings acknowledged and expressed, but feared and only partly accepted; more open constructs about experience; recognition of incongruence between experience and self; self acknowledged as responsible for problems
5.	Feelings expressed freely in the present; feelings are surprising and frightening; discovery of new personal constructs; desire to be the "real me," even if imperfect
6.	Immediate experience of previously "stuck" feeling; rich immediacy of experience, and acceptance of it; self experienced as existentially living in the moment, not as an object; physiological "loosening" (tears, sighs, muscle relaxation); subjective experience replaces defined "problems"
7.	New feelings experienced richly and immediately; experience is new and present, not related to past structures; self is the awareness of experiencing, not an object; constructs are tentative and loosely held, to be tested; feelings match ideation; rich experience of choice

(Adapted from Rogers, 1961b, pp. 132–155.)

The transition from stage 6 to stage 7 (when it occurs) involves continuing growth, often after the termination of successful therapy.

At the outset of therapy, the client generally experiences problems in the past and external to the self. As therapy progresses, the client experiences a greater immediacy and ownership of experience. These changes are carried over to life outside the consulting room, so the client increasingly lives according to the organismic valuing process rather than according to rigid ideas that may not correspond well to subjective experience.

ENCOUNTER GROUPS

Therapeutic change may be brought about in groups, as well as in individual psychotherapy. Rogers reported that the first such groups were developed by Kurt Lewin in the 1940s. The group movement continued; for example, the National Training Laboratories (NTL) offered training to business organizations to enhance the performance of managers and executives (Rogers, 1970). Groups often serve as growth-enhancing experiences for healthy people rather than as a means of treatment for those with emotional problems.

encounter group
growth-enhancing technique in which a group of people openly and honestly express their feelings and opinions

facilitator the leader of an encounter group

Rogers labeled his groups **encounter groups**. They provide experiences intended to produce personal growth and to improve interpersonal functioning. The groups have a **facilitator**, who directs participants. Rogers (1970) preferred a relatively unstructured format. He opened his groups with very little structure, often something as simple as the statement, "Here we are. We can make of this group experience exactly what we wish" (pp. 46–47). Too much structure through highly programmed group exercises, according to Rogers, is essentially a power play by the group leader. It keeps the locus of responsibility for the group with the leader instead of sharing it with the members. Groups should be member centered, just as therapy is client centered.

Betty Meador (in Rogers, 1970) reported the study of an encounter group that met for 16 hours over an intensive weekend, led by group facilitators. Each of the eight participants was filmed in ten 2-minute segments, two during each of the five group sessions. These segments were rated by judges on Rogers's Process Scale. On the average, participants moved up one and a half stages on the Process Scale during this weekend. Of course, these data do not address the question of whether this change affected behavior when participants returned to their everyday lives.

Treatment groups have become accepted modes of intervention for a variety of personal problems, including drug and alcohol abuse. Just as acceptance by a therapist facilitates change in individual psychotherapy, acceptance by group members promotes healing. Acceptance by other group members can help alcoholics acknowledge their drinking problem, an important first step toward change (Rugel & Barry, 1990).

Other Applications

Principles that guide client-centered therapy have also been applied outside of the therapy setting, to a greater extent than some other therapy traditions (Kahn, 1996). Rogers (1986a, p. 138) commented, "I find a deep satisfaction in discovering that some of my basic learnings in psychotherapy apply to other areas of life." Let us examine some of these other areas.

HUMANISTIC EDUCATION

person-centered
Rogers's orientation to therapy and education, which focuses on the experience of the client or student rather than the therapist or teacher

Rogers wrote at length about the implications of his **person-centered** approach for education (DeCarvalho, 1991b; Rogers, 1957b, 1969, 1974a, 1974b). (Outside of therapy the term *person centered* is more appropriate than *client centered*.) Humanistic education has implications for both the relationship between teacher and student and the content of education. It nurtures the personal as well as professional development of unique individuals (Shapiro, 1997, 1998).

Traditionally, the teacher decides what should be learned, and students are treated as though they would do nothing productive if not motivated by external demands and threats of poor grades. Hence students are afraid—of failure, of embarrassment, of punishment. Such an atmosphere can undermine the motivation of even competent, creative scholars such as Albert Einstein (Rogers, 1969). By focusing on the authority of the teacher, rather than on the needs and experience of the learner, traditional education violates the fundamental value advocated by Rogers: namely, *making each person the evaluator and guide to his or her own experience.* Rogers (1969) believed that an ideal educational system would trust students to develop their own programs of learning, either in cooperation with other students or alone. The aim is to foster students' creativity, in which intrinsic interest in learning provides motivation, grades, and requirements.

In the ideal classroom, the authority of the teacher would be reduced. A better term for that new role would be *facilitator of education.* Such a facilitator of education would provide resources to students based on students' interests. These resources could include books, community experiences (because the classroom would not be so isolated from life as it is now), and personal experience. In a humanistic educational environment, the teacher would be perceived as an integrated and authentic person; would freely express and accept feelings; would treat students with unconditional positive regard; would understand students' experiences empathically; and would communicate his or her congruence, acceptance, and empathy, thus having the characteristics of an effective therapist (DeCarvalho, 1991b; Roscoe & Peterson, 1982).

Traditional education addresses only the intellect, ignoring feelings and distrusting experiential learning (Rogers, 1973, 1987). Rogers argued that feelings are part of the whole person and to educate only the mind is unnecessarily limiting. In contrast, B. F. Skinner, who excluded feelings and other internal states from his behavioral theory, emphasized educational technology (Rogers & Skinner, 1956). Humanistically oriented educators have attempted to transform classrooms to be more consistent with Rogers's principles—for example, through values clarification exercises (Richards & Combs, 1992). Another strategy is the use of narratives—for example, teaching students about gerontology through the stories of older people, an approach that engages students emotionally as well as intellectually (Gattuso & Saw, 1998). Some classes that are specifically designated as personal development classes can now be found in many schools (e.g., Ware & Perry, 1987). Some even claim that "the *real* purpose of higher education [is to develop] self-actualizing personalities" (Cangemi, 1984, p. 51).

MARRIAGE AND RELATIONSHIPS

Rogers's humanistic approach also has implications for marriage. He noted that modern marriage occurs in a new context, compared to past generations, in which people live longer and have more choice to limit family size. Other factors affecting modern marriage are the social acceptability of divorce, family mobility, wives who have jobs and careers, and sexual freedom (Rogers, 1977). Rogers advocated a person-centered relationship with mutual trust, tolerance of separate as well as shared interests, and focus on the uniqueness of each partner rather than on impersonal expectations about roles. Greater mutuality and equality result, and communication between partners is more honest.

Humanistic openness may produce more mature interaction, but there are risks (as in any change). Partners may form **satellite relationships**, significant secondary relationships that sometimes involve extramarital sex. Although these seem, to the individuals who choose them, to meet significant growth needs, they obviously challenge trust and risk jealousy. A theory placing the locus of evaluation of experience within the individual makes choices such as these more frequent and may seem to endorse them.

Among dating couples, being loved and supported helps partners to grow toward self-actualization, becoming closer to their ideals (Ruvolo & Brennan, 1997). In several studies, Duncan Cramer (1985, 1986, 1990a, 1990b) has examined both romantic relationships

satellite relationships side relationships, which supplement a person's primary committed relationship

and friendship. These studies support the growth-producing qualities of relationships identified by Rogers. Cramer (1990a) reported that high school and college students had higher self-esteem if their romantic partners possessed the characteristics that Rogers identified as facilitating growth (unconditional acceptance, empathy, and congruence). Growth-facilitating qualities of friends were also associated with higher self-esteem but not so strongly as those of romantic partners. Unconditional acceptance seems to be a particularly important quality (Cramer, 1990b). Friends appear able to be relatively directive—that is, giving advice—while still having growth-facilitating qualities, in contrast to the nondirective mode advocated by person-centered therapists (Cramer, 1986). Having a friendship characterized by understanding, congruence, and unconditional acceptance is (at least among women) correlated with higher scores on measures of psychological adjustment and self-esteem (Cramer, 1985). Of course, in correlational studies, the direction of causality is debatable. Perhaps psychological adjustment produces better friendships rather than the other way around.

SOCIAL WELFARE PROGRAMS

Programs that support individuals and families who are poor or homeless can also change their usual bureaucratic approach, in which experts with power and authority dispense help to those in need. A client-centered approach would take a different course, in which the system instead provides resources and in which the clients are empowered (Novotny, 2000).

BUSINESS

Rogers and other humanistic psychologists have also influenced industrial-organizational psychology, providing business managers with a model to guide their dealings with employees (Massarik, 1992). Rogers reasoned that relationships between administration and staff, like those between therapist and client, parent and child, and teacher and student, will be growth promoting if the three characteristics of genuineness (congruence), acceptance (prizing), and empathic understanding are present (Rogers, 1979). Organizations, including industrial enterprises, are traditionally based on patterns of authority that would change under Rogers's humanistic vision of human relationships. In addition to encounter groups (described earlier), Rogers described an industrial experiment in sharing power and decision making with workers that was so successful it boosted the profit margin substantially, so much so that it was regarded as a trade secret (Rogers, 1977, pp. 101–102).

POLITICAL CONFLICT, WAR, AND PEACE

With his focus on the individual person and abhorrence of authority, Rogers presented a perspective that was essentially democratic (Kahn, 1999). In the political realm, Rogers (1982a) suggested ways of dealing with conflict through encounter groups: to facilitate discussions between the National Health Council, made up of representatives of medical professions, and poor people concerned with their access to health care; in Northern Ireland, between Protestants and Catholics in their long-standing conflict; and in 1985, when government officials, academicians, and others from 17 countries met in Austria, aiming to reduce political tensions (Rogers, 1986b). Rogers suggested that psychological principles, including those discovered in his encounter groups, could even help avert the threat of nuclear annihilation (Rogers & Ryback, 1984).

Criticisms of Rogers's Theory

Although it has enthusiastic supporters, Rogers's theory has been dismissed by others as naive about human nature. Carl Rogers the therapist reminds some of Fred Rogers, the sensitive, accepting neighbor on children's television (Palmer & Carr, 1991). It is tempting to base our evaluation of his theory simply on whether we like or dislike his message about the potential goodness and creativity in everyone. This approach, of course, is not adequate to evaluate a therapy or a theory. As a therapy, the approach should show treatment effectiveness. As a theory, the approach should provide hypotheses that can be tested and that are confirmed by research. These evaluations bring mixed results. Client-centered therapy is effective but not more effective than alternative treatments. If its assertions about human nature were more accurate than those of other therapies (psychoanalytic and behavioral, for example), we might expect client-centered therapy to produce better treatment results.

Rogers's theory is more optimistic about the essential goodness of people than most of us probably believe (Downey, 1998). Critics accuse Rogers of being too optimistic about human nature, not recognizing the extent of the human capacity for evil (Friedman, 1982; May, 1982; Rogers, 1982b). This criticism was made from a theological perspective, by the theologian-philosopher Martin Buber (Friedman, 1994) and by social scientists, who point out that Rogers pays little attention to the social forces that influence a person (Kensit, 2000; Ryan, 1995).

Rollo May (1982) points out that the issue of excessive optimism about human nature is not simply a philosophical disagreement but has implications for therapy. According to May, their neglect of the evil side of human nature has left client-centered therapists unprepared to deal adequately with negative emotions, including anger and hostility, in their clients. He says that culture, through its values and myths, must provide positive direction for people's growth because human growth is not always toward the good, contrary to the hypothesized actualizing tendency. Growth can also be, like cancer, destructive (DeCarvalho, 1992). David Bakan (1982) suggests a resolution of the philosophical side of the issue. He distinguishes between the level of the individual and the collective level. Behavior that is "good" at an individual level (e.g., responsibly doing one's job) may be "evil" when considered collectively (e.g., the Nazis exterminating masses of Jews in concentration camps). It is unclear, though, how this insight could guide a therapist, who is treating an individual rather than a society. Should the therapist become a social critic or political activist within therapy sessions? Some have taken that position, but that is not the position of client-centered therapy. Perhaps there is a role for humanistic psychologists as social activists on causes like overpopulation (Howard, 1992) but outside of the therapy setting.

Aside from its therapy, how does Rogers's approach fare when evaluated as a theory that guides research? Here, too, results are mixed. Desmond Cartwright and Chise Mori (1988) have developed the Feelings, Reactions, and Beliefs Survey (FRBS) to measure several aspects of personality described by Rogers. These aspects make up nine scales, named here according to the revised titles reported in Cartwright, DeBruin, and Berg (1991): Focusing Conscious Attention, Open to Feelings in Relationships, Fully Functioning Person, Feeling Uncomfortable with People, Feeling Ambivalent in Relationships, Struggling with Feelings of Inferiority, Trust in Self as an Organism, Openness to Transcendent Experiences, and Religio-spiritual Beliefs.

Cartwright and Mori (1988) found that the scales of this survey are correlated with other personality measures and with self-reported autobiographical information among college freshmen. For example, the Fully Functioning Person scale correlated positively

($r = +0.55$) with the Time-Competence scale of the Personal Orientation Inventory, a measure of self-actualization based on Abraham Maslow's theory (Shostrom, 1974). Scales correlate also with self-reported biographical information. For example, students who scored high on the Focusing Conscious Attention scale reported doing better in school, and a group of religious devotees scored higher on the Religio-spiritual Beliefs scale (Cartwright et al., 1991). These studies support the validity of the scales. This multifaceted measurement now enables researchers to explore the details of the theory and to extend it. Such an empirical approach is certainly in keeping with Rogers's openness to scientific investigation of his theory and of his treatment techniques. Perhaps it is fitting to conclude that, like the humans it describes, Rogers's personality theory is still in process.

Summary

- Carl Rogers offered a theory in which the person actively seeks higher development, motivated by the *actualizing tendency* rather than being passively determined by external forces.
- He described the characteristics of a healthy person, whom he called a *fully functioning person*.
- His client-centered therapy emphasized three factors that contribute to therapeutic success: *unconditional positive regard, congruence*, and *empathic understanding*.
- Rogers specified his theoretical constructs in ways that could be measured, so the theory could be *empirically verified*. Furthermore, he conducted groundbreaking research on the therapeutic process.
- Rogers (1986a) acknowledged that he focused far more on personality *change* than on the development or structure of personality. He elaborated on the change process in therapy, groups, education, and political conflict.
- However, he did not offer a general scheme for understanding personality differences.
- Despite these limitations, as one of the founders of the Division of Humanistic Psychology of the American Psychological Association, Rogers, together with Abraham Maslow and others, provided a forum for psychologists who believe that concepts such as *free will* and the meaning of life should not be ruled out of the discipline that aims to study human nature.

Thinking about Rogers's Theory

1. Discuss the experience of freedom, contrasting Carl Rogers's concept of experiential freedom with B. F. Skinner's criticism of the concept of free will.

2. Imagine you are talking to a person who is about to become a parent, who asks your advice about how to raise a well-adjusted child. Based on Rogers's theory, what would you recommend? Give examples of particular issues that are likely to become potential problems in your cultural setting. How would you recommend resolving them?

3. Do you believe it is important for a therapist to come from the same ethnic and cultural background as the client? If someone from another background was to be your therapist, what would it be important for that therapist to understand to be able to act with empathy toward you?

4. Recall Adler's concept of social interest. Do you agree that Rogers's concept of unconditional positive regard is similar to saying that a therapist should have an attitude of social interest toward the client (cf. Watts, 1996)?

5. Compare Rogers's therapeutic empathic understanding with Kelly's Sociality Corollary (Chapter 13).

6. What values from Rogers's theory are relevant to marriage and other intimate relationships? How do your own ethical beliefs compare with the implications of these values?

7. Do you believe that political conflict can be reduced by using encounter groups or other humanistic techniques? Or does this suggestion reflect political naïveté?

Study Questions

1. Explain what Rogers meant by the actualizing tendency.

2. Discuss Rogers's idea that people are basically good, and the criticism this optimism has elicited.

3. Describe the organismic valuing process. Give an example.

4. List and explain the characteristics of a fully functioning person.

5. Discuss Rogers's attitude toward subjective experience.

6. Explain how Rogers used the concept of self to understand personal growth.

7. Explain Rogers's concept of congruence and incongruence. Include the terms *real self* and *ideal self* in your discussion. What are the implications for psychological well-being?

8. Describe the confusion between self-actualization and actualization.

9. What does it mean to be raised with unconditional positive regard? What are the effects of such child rearing?

10. What sort of environment encourages the development of creativity?

11. Why is Rogers's theory called client centered?

12. List and explain the three major conditions necessary for therapeutic progress.

13. Discuss the difficulties of therapists in using empathy as a counseling technique when treating clients with different backgrounds from their own.

14. Describe research into the effectiveness of client-centered therapy.

15. Describe some of the important changes measured by the Process Scale.

16. Describe an encounter-group experience. List some of the uses of these groups.

17. Describe Rogers's approach to education. Why is it called a person-centered approach?

18. How did Rogers's humanistic approach influence his beliefs about marriage and relationships? What are satellite relationships?

19. Describe the implications of Rogers's approach for business.

20. Describe the application of Rogers's theory to problems of international tensions.

21. Summarize the major criticisms of Rogers's theory of personality.

22. Describe research outside of the clinical setting that investigates Rogers's theory.

15

Maslow
Need Hierarchy Theory

Chapter
Overview

Preview: Overview of Maslow's Theory
Need Hierarchy Theory: Maslow
Maslow's Vision of Psychology
Hierarchy of Needs
Self-Actualization
Applications and Implications of Maslow's Theory
Maslow's Challenge to Traditional Science
Other Growth Themes in Psychological Theory
Self-Determination Theory and Intrinsic Motivation
Positive Psychology
Summary

ILLUSTRATIVE BIOGRAPHY

David Pelzer

Abraham Maslow's theory describes an ordered sequence of human needs. When each one is met, the person may move to a higher level of motivation, ultimately reaching the highest level (self-actualization). Deprivation of a need holds one back. The case of David Pelzer is an inspirational life in which the force to move upward to higher potential is shown to be extraordinary because he has endured unspeakable childhood abuses and still found the courage to move on.

David Pelzer grew up in an abusive home in Daly City, just south of San Francisco, California. His alcoholic and mentally disturbed mother singled him out, among his brothers, for abuse that was one of the most extreme in California history. Ultimately, in 1973, at the age of 12, school officials intervened and, with court action, he was removed from the home and placed in foster care. His life story after that epitomizes a heroic struggle for healthy development against immense obstacles. Dave Pelzer describes his life in four autobiographical works, describing his childhood abuse (1995), his rescue to foster care (1997), his adolescence (2004), and his young adulthood (1999).

His mother's abuse was extreme. She forced David to sleep in the cold basement, on a cot, where he struggled for warmth. He was commanded to get up before her in order to sweep and do other household chores. She deprived him of food, so he stole from other children's lunch boxes at school, from a grocery store, and even ate from garbage cans and from the family dog's dish. His clothes were ragged and dirty, causing other children to make fun of him. His mother assaulted him physically, once in a drunken rage stabbed him with a knife, forced him to drink spoonfuls of ammonia and breathe toxic fumes from an ammonia and Clorox mixture, and pushed him down the stairs, leading to a neck injury that made it difficult for him to breathe. He was regularly at the school nurse's office to be examined for cuts and bruises and relate fabricated explanations of accidents that his mother devised to explain his injuries, trying to keep the abuse secret.

detracted from his academic efforts. After many difficulties, including a brief stay at a reform school, he dropped out of high school to work. He joined the Air Force at age 18 and served for 13 years, beginning as a cook and finally working on a flight crew to refuel the F-117 Stealth Fighter and other aircraft, serving in Desert Storm and other combat operations. He also worked assiduously on behalf of abused children in several capacities, as a counselor, lecturer, adviser, and board member. He has received several national and international awards for his activities, including one of The Outstanding Young Persons of the World.

Along with the physical abuse, his mother belittled him and told him he was bad and less than human. She called him "It" instead of using his name. David was the designated scapegoat; his four brothers were treated more humanely, allowed food, new clothes, and toys while David was excluded from family activities; they were permitted to sleep upstairs and were not subjected to the physical or mental abuse, while being told that David was bad. (Once he was removed by social services from the home, however, his other brothers became targets of abuse.)

His father was a firefighter, and David admired him as a hero and cherished memories of his attention. In truth, though, such moments were rare. His father retreated to alcohol and was powerless to protect his son or to maintain semblance of a loving family. Memories of better times in his early life seem to have given Pelzer hope through the difficult times that came later, as he struggled to escape the abusive side of his mother that he refers to as "The Mother," in contrast to the better, "Mommy" side of her (Pelzer, 1999, p. 107). Like many abused children, he fantasized both escape and rescue.

David was fortunate to spend some of his time in foster care in the home of a loving and supportive family, beginning at age 13. This was no easy time, though. He got into trouble with stealing, which he did to impress other kids, and was suspected of starting a fire at school (although he claims to have been trying to put it out). He was placed in a juvenile detention facility for a while. During high school, he worked long hours, trying to save enough money to make something of his life (because he knew that when he reached age 18, he would be done with the foster system and on his own), which

Development

The fundamental idea behind Maslow's need hierarchy theory is that satisfaction of lower-order needs leads, inevitably, to movement toward higher-order needs. It would seem that if lower-order needs are not met, the human spirit would be kept from developing, but that prediction is difficult to reconcile with the story of Dave Pelzer's life.

His most basic needs for safety and food were chronically dissatisfied by his mentally ill, alcoholic mother. In fact, she actively impeded the satisfaction of those needs. Instead of providing adequate food, she deprived him and made him vomit what food he may have eaten at school. Instead of keeping him safe, she burned him on the gas stove, pushed him down the basement stairs, and stabbed him in a drunken accident. Instead of providing satisfaction of his need for love, she hated him. Instead of fostering his esteem needs, she mocked him and told him he was worthless. His father had little power to protect him.

Description

Maslow's theory does not list descriptive traits at the lower levels of the need hierarchy (although it does give descriptors of self-actualized people, which we consider later.) He does mention that, as they develop, people often must choose between safety and growth.

From the outside, the boy Dave Pelzer must have seemed wretched: disheveled, smelly, skinny, isolated, furtively seeking to steal food. He had obvious unmet needs at many levels. But another aspect of his personality must also be described: the courage, the will to live, that enabled him to use his wits to keep alive in childhood and then, with help, to become a proud and loving adult. As he describes his childhood experience, this courage is apparent: "Mother can beat me all she wants, but I haven't let her take away my will to somehow survive" (Pelzer, 1995, p. 4).

Adjustment

Adjustment is built on need satisfaction and motivates movement up the hierarchy to concentrate on the next sequential need. Maslow's theory describes many characteristics of self-actualized (very healthy) individuals, including accurate perception of reality, spontaneity, creativity, and many others described in the chapter.

Obviously children require parents or others to supply their lower-order needs, and so it was not until he was removed from his parents' home that David Pelzer could move beyond a survival mentality. Ultimately, the school nurse, teachers, and administrators contacted the police and judicial system and had Dave removed from his abusive home, finally protecting his most basic needs for food and safety. As Maslow's theory predicts, this provision for basic need satisfaction finally opened the possibility of healthy growth. He was fortunate to be placed with loving foster parents who, through words and deeds, showed him that they loved him and would support him. In adolescence, he made friends. Later, as a member of the U.S. Air Force, he describes achieving a "sense of pride and belonging that until then, I had never known" (1995, p. 158), reflecting movement toward satisfaction of Maslow's third and fourth stages.

A social worker offered him safety and love, and loving foster parents provided the child and adolescent Dave with what he needed to break free from fear and self-loathing. They not only provided food and shelter but love and compassion. Not uncommon for abused children, Dave's behavior tested this love through misbehavior, including minor theft. His foster father, even when facing the accusation that Dave had been involved in setting a fire at school (which he denied), for which he was to be sent to reform school, said, "No matter what happens, I want you to know that we care

for you" (Pelzer, 1995, p. 187). It takes many instances of such support, though, to heal deep wounds, and when David was old enough for marriage, his low self-esteem left him vulnerable to an unwise marriage, which depleted his savings and challenged his self-discipline. However, this experience also taught him something of love and fatherhood, which he took quite seriously as he strove to be a better father for his son Stephan than his own father had been for him.

Cognition

The lower four stages of the need hierarchy can be described as cognitions: I know I have food (or not); I know I am safe (or not); I know I am loved (or not); I know I am worthwhile (or not). At the highest stage, self-actualization, Maslow describes some cognitive elements more explicitly: accurate perception, creativity, and peak experiences.

It is clear that the lower-order cognitions were all challenged in Dave Pelzer's upbringing, although he could have temporary positive cognitions when he found (or stole) food, escaped from physical assault, and so on. His foster parents gave him the positive love message, repeatedly. The feeling of being worthwhile, positive self-esteem, is one of the most important legacies of childhood and adolescence that underlies future success. It builds on knowing you are loved, adding the esteem that comes from personal achievement. Pelzer (1997) describes his subjective experience: "I have no home. I am a member of no one's family. I know deep inside that I do not now, nor will I ever, deserve any love, attention, or even recognition as a human being. I am a child called 'It'" (p. 5). He describes "standing in front of the bedroom mirror yelling at myself, 'I'm a bad boy! I'm a bad boy!' over and over again" (Pelzer, 1999, p. 121). Even at age 23, with an Air Force career, he describes himself as having "the self-esteem of an ant" when dealing with women (1999, p. 143).

Society

Abraham Maslow envisioned a utopian society in which people's needs would be adequately met so they would naturally move toward healthier personalities. One place that this could occur is at work. But he recognized that society as we know it has the effect of diminishing the human potential.

The foster care system, although it is often overburdened, provided the societal support that Dave Pelzer needed. It was not, of course, the "system" that turned the tide but the particular loving foster parents to whom he expresses gratitude. In turn, Pelzer has contributed to many abused children through speeches and programs. He became an autobiographer and a motivational speaker, inspiring others to improve their lives. Instead of narcissistically focusing on his own needs, he serves the needs of others—of his son, with a parental protection that he had not experienced (until foster care), and of others through his service and speeches.

His books do not detail all of the abuses he suffered, according to his second wife (although he tells enough to bring tears), and they only hint at the help he received from therapy. The message is consistent with Maslow's perspective: Turn away from the forces that diminish the human spirit and toward growth and health. Pelzer (2000) explicitly warns people not to place too much emphasis on seeking other people's approval and to love yourself and create your own future. He also emphasizes the importance of choice and of positive emotions, consistent with current themes in positive psychology and Maslow's theory.

Biology

Maslow's theory considers biology only from the need-fulfillment viewpoint. He is more interested in the sorts of growth that occur once our biological needs have been satisfied.

Consistent with that emphasis, Dave Pelzer's life story begins with severe deprivation of biological needs, and then moves on to the "higher-order" needs that are more psychological.

Final Thoughts

Maslow was more a visionary and a prophet than a scientist. He frequently expressed dissatisfaction with the scientific model of prediction and research. He called attention to people's intrinsic potential for growth, as though with this force we can step beyond the constraints of predictable neurosis and into the freedom of self-actualization. Although this vision does not fit traditional science, it does provide a framework for understanding the life of Dave Pelzer—and hope for the growth potential in all of us.

Preview: Overview of Maslow's Theory

Maslow's theory has implications for major theoretical questions, as presented in Table 15.1.

In contrast to recognition of the importance of scientific verification that Rogers expressed and that is reemerging in current *positive psychology* (see later in this chapter), Maslow thought the methods of science were far too restrictive to be useful for his vision of a growth-oriented psychology. This has seriously detracted from his role in mainstream psychology, although the appeal of humanistic theoretical ideas remains as a reoccurring issue. Because of his focus on the most healthy (self-actualized) individuals, Maslow's theory is less comprehensive than one would want for a general theory of personality, neglecting detailed description of the vast majority of people who do not fit his goal of self-actualization. The theory is comprehensive enough to apply to business and to ideas about adult healthy functioning, although not with the precision we might wish. Even more than Rogers's theory, Maslow's ideas of self-actualization have been applied to business, undoubtedly because of his own background in his family business and the insights that gave him. He did not, however, apply his theory explicitly to therapy in the detailed way that Rogers undertook.

Need Hierarchy Theory: Maslow

Abraham Maslow believed that people develop through various levels toward their full potential. A few reach the highest level of development and are called self-actualized. Most, however, stop at a lower level along the way, stuck in needs that cannot be adequately met. Maslow's greatest interest was in the few who become most highly developed,

TABLE 15.1	Preview of Maslow's Theory
Individual Differences	Individuals can be said to differ in their position in the need hierarchy, that is, their level of development toward self-actualization. Self-actualized people develop their unique potentials.
Adaptation and Adjustment	Only a few people reach the highest developmental stage, self-actualization. Maslow describes these individuals in detail.
Cognitive Processes	Self-actualized people perceive the world accurately and are creative.
Society	A better society can be imagined (Eupsychia). Changes in schools, work settings, and religious institutions should be made. Growth centers can be established to foster development.
Biological Influences	Biological motivations are the foundation of personality, but once satisfied, they become unimportant. Sex differences are influenced by biology.
Development	Children's physiological, safety, love, and esteem needs should be met. Changes in schools could facilitate growth. Few adults develop to their full potential. Transformations in the workplace and elsewhere could change this.

rather than the majority of folks. He saw these few as beacons, directing humankind toward its full potential.

BIOGRAPHY OF ABRAHAM MASLOW

Abraham Maslow was born on April 1, 1908, in Brooklyn, New York. His parents were Russian immigrants, poor and uneducated, but hoping for something better for their son. His father was a cooper (a barrel maker). Abraham grew up, the oldest of seven children, in the only Jewish family in the neighborhood, and he "was not always sure where his next meal was coming from" (Maddi & Costa, 1972, p. 159). He described the experience as lonely: "I grew up in libraries and among books, without friends" (Maslow, 1968a, p. 37). In his family, too, he was regarded as physically ugly and so developed a sense of inferiority (Nicholson, 2001).

Maslow was intellectually gifted. His IQ was measured at an astonishing 195 (Maslow, 1954/1987, p. xxxvi). In college, he at first studied law, as his father wished. However, this did not appeal to him

ABRAHAM MASLOW

and he abandoned it after 2 weeks. He turned to a broader course of studies at Cornell and then transferred to the University of Wisconsin in 1928 to study psychology. While still in college, he married his high school sweetheart (and cousin), Bertha, when she was 19 and he 20. His wife was an artist and undoubtedly fostered Maslow's ongoing respect for more global and integrative approaches to knowledge.

Ironically, given the later direction of his theorizing, Maslow was at first very excited about the behaviorism he was studying at the University of Wisconsin. His doctoral work was supervised by Harry Harlow in the primate laboratory at Wisconsin. (Harlow is famous for the "cloth mother" studies that established the importance of contact comfort for monkeys.) Maslow's dissertation was an observational study of sexual behavior in monkeys, which, he reported, was influenced by dominance. Furthermore, in establishing dominance hierarchies, monkeys communicate primarily by visual cues rather than by fighting. Harlow evaluated Maslow's work very highly (Lowry, 1973, p. 1). Maslow later tried to investigate sexuality in a parallel way with female undergraduates, which proved more difficult (Nicholson, 2001).

Behaviorism and animal psychology did not continue to hold Maslow's interest. He read psychoanalysis and Gestalt psychology and philosophy, and these paved the way for an experiential conversion.

> Then when my baby was born that was the thunderclap that settled things. I looked at this tiny, mysterious thing and felt so stupid. I was stunned by the mystery and by the sense of not really being in control. I felt small and weak and feeble before all this. I'd say that anyone who had a baby couldn't be a behaviorist. (Maslow, 1968a, p. 56)

Maslow and his wife had two daughters. (He reported that his wife warned him not to experiment on them!)

Following successful completion of his dissertation, Maslow remained at the University of Wisconsin as assistant instructor and teaching fellow (1930–1935) before going to Columbia University as a Carnegie fellow (1935–1937). While at Columbia, he interviewed female college students about their sex lives (Maslow, 1942), extending to humans his earlier observations of monkeys. This research caused some controversy and may have inspired the Kinsey studies of sexuality that began several years later. Maslow was associate professor at Brooklyn College (1937–1951), where he was especially popular among the many students who came from immigrant families. He met many eminent psychologists who came to the United States to escape Nazism, including Alfred Adler, Karen Horney, and Kurt Goldstein. Besides his academic career, Maslow also was plant manager in a family company from 1947 to 1949 (Maddi & Costa, 1972). He became professor and chair of the Psychology Department at the new Brandeis University (1951–1969).

Despite his success, Maslow experienced anxiety. He describes an incident during the first year of graduate school:

> I was a very timid boy—very shy, very easily frightened, very isolated, an outsider. . . . I think I was a first-year graduate student, and I offered a paper that would still be worthy of doing. It was called "Psychoanalysis and Mental Hygiene as Status Quo Social Philosophy." And I was to give that, but when the day came I was so frightened, so timid, that I just fled. I just didn't show up for the meeting and didn't give my paper, but that was the first paper I . . . you know, if I had given it, that would have been the first paper I would have published. (Frick, 2000, p. 131)

Maslow reported that he suffered anxious dreams when he presented new ideas in public:

> I remember one dream. . . . It was sort of a recurrent dream whenever I'd say something publicly that had been worked out privately. It was a typical dream and it sums up this whole courage and fear thing—of being in the street and then somebody yells, "Hey, lions and tigers are loose," and then I would get frightened and run to the door behind which is my family—not the blood family but somehow the whole clan—and bang on the door, crying "let me in, let me in!" And the door is locked, and they don't let me in, and it was definitely the American Psychological Association. I was always figuring, "My God, they're going to throw me out!" or "I'll be cast out," and this, I think, may be a universal fear. If you say something that contradicts the people you've admired and learned from, something that contradicts your teachers, this is kind of a cosmic, eternal thing. (Frick, 2000, pp. 133–134)

He again experienced a difficult period in about 1965, which he described as "a long spell of insomnia and . . . a writing block" (Maslow, 1966, p. xix) that responded to a brief period of psychotherapy. While on a leave of absence, working on the implications of humanistic psychology for broader social values, Maslow died of a heart attack (not his first, according to Frick, 2000) in 1970, at age 62.

Abraham Maslow was a member and officer in several professional organizations, including the Society for the Psychological Study of Social Issues, the New York Academy of Sciences, the American Psychological Association, and of course the Association for Humanistic Psychology (of which he was one of the founding members, with Rollo May, Carl Rogers, and others, in 1962).

Maslow's vision of psychology was influenced by Asian traditions, as evidenced in the "Taoist" vision of psychology described in this chapter. In turn, Maslow's work helped bring attention in the West to these Asian traditions (Cleary & Shapiro, 1996). Maslow (1987) supported the human potential movement, in particular the Esalen Institute in Big Sur, California, "the world's first growth center" (p. xi). He gave workshops at Esalen but was not comfortable with the much more emotional expression of Fritz Perls, who disrupted Maslow's first talk at Esalen by crawling toward an attractive woman, saying, "You are my mother; I want my mother" (p. xi). Maslow's work was directed toward society at large, which he hoped to improve, more than to academic audiences, whose methodological rigidity and lack of vision he criticized. He described himself as having a "missionary" concern for improving the world and pointed to the utopian concerns of his own Jewish background (Frick, 2000). His later books have been described as "both humanistic and Messianic" (Maddi & Costa, 1972, p. 150).

Maslow's Vision of Psychology

Abraham Maslow (1966) distrusted the methods of mainstream psychology. Rather than enlightening us, he said, traditional scientific methods prevent full knowledge of human nature. Psychological theory and research are not focused on the most important areas of human nature, the higher functions that raise us above the animals. To be sure, like animals, we eat, we reproduce, we learn. However, people are capable of developing beyond these primitive processes. A theory limited to these levels cannot explain a healthy person, any more than a theory of color vision can explain what we see in a

Picasso painting. In addition, Maslow criticized theories based on clinical experience with neurotic individuals who have not achieved full human potential. Health is more than simply the absence of disease or disorder.

Psychology strives for scientific rigor, and Maslow argued that this effort had undermined the purpose of psychological work. Rigorous science could study only certain phenomena, leaving out much of interest. Traditional scientific methodology is **method centered**. Human experiences that cannot be investigated in the traditional fashion are ruled "nonscientific." Maslow recommended, instead, a **problem-centered** approach in which the issues to be investigated would be given higher priority than would the methods. Other humanists, such as Carl Rogers, shared this view. Gordon Allport, although generally classified as a trait theorist, also argued for a problem-centered emphasis. Maslow expressed his rejection of a method-centered approach by suggesting that "what isn't worth doing, isn't worth doing well" (Maslow, 1966, p. 14).

> **method centered** an approach to science that emphasizes procedure over content

> **problem centered** an approach to science that emphasizes subject matter over procedure

Both scientific determinism and logical positivism as a philosophy of science failed to direct psychology toward the uniquely human experiences that personality theorists and clinicians face. Maslow (1968b) suggested existentialism as an alternative philosophy because of its emphasis on **experiential knowledge** (based on personal experience) and the search for identity. For psychology to understand the profound meaningfulness of life, the "ultimate aloneness of the individual" (p. 14) and the real uncertainty of the future, it must go beyond the more limited deterministic theories available in behaviorism and in psychoanalysis. A **third force** psychology, much influenced by existentialism, was being developed. Maslow is widely acclaimed as the spiritual father of American humanism, of this new third force.

> **experiential knowledge** what we know because we have experienced it for ourselves

> **third force** Maslow's term for his theory, emphasizing its opposition to psychoanalysis and behaviorism

Maslow did not want to throw out traditional scientific methods entirely. Rather, he wanted to supplement them with a more honest acknowledgment of the experiential basis of the problems being investigated. Rather than focusing on externally observed symptoms and behaviors, Maslow asked what people were experiencing subjectively. Then, on this experiential knowledge, the empirical methods of hypothesis testing should be built. Either emphasis alone is inadequate: methodology without "soul" or experiential knowledge without the cross validation of the scientific method. The two approaches are less antagonistic, in Maslow's (1966) vision, than is commonly supposed. "Emotion is not always an enemy of truth and objectivity," he observed (p. 140).

To understand normal personality, innovative methods must be devised because traditional methodology is inadequate. Maslow (1966, p. 95) struggled to define such a new approach. He described his vision as **Taoist Science**, which he contrasted with "Controlling Science." Taoist Science would be subjective and experiential, not objective and abstract. It would honor and even love the subject matter rather than being coolly indifferent. It would be interpersonal (in the spirit of Martin Buber's I-Thou approach), truly engaged in a meaningful interaction with the object of study. It would not insist on a false separation of the observer and the subject. Rather, it could be described as "fusion-knowledge." Furthermore, it would be explicitly concerned with values. All of these notions violate traditional assumptions of scientific methods that, Maslow argued, cannot study healthy personalities adequately.

> **Taoist Science** Maslow's alternative to the traditional scientific method, emphasizing values and subjectivity (instead of objectivity)

One obstacle to the development of such a science is the limited development of scientists as human beings. Traditional science sometimes functions as a defense mechanism, offering safety and predictability. When studying the highest human potentials, scientists are likely to experience resistance against the truth because this subject matter challenges them personally, whereas nonhuman or clinical topics do not (Maslow, 1966).

Hierarchy of Needs

Maslow postulated that people begin development with basic needs (motives) that are not noticeably different from animal motivation. As they mature and as their lower-order needs are satisfied, people develop more uniquely human motivations. Thus motivation changes as we progress upward through a **hierarchy of needs**, or motives. This hierarchy consists of five levels: four levels of deficiency motivation and a final, highly developed level called being motivation, or self-actualization.

DEFICIENCY MOTIVATION

The first four levels of the need hierarchy can be understood as motivation to overcome the feeling of a deficiency and are collectively called **deficiency motivation**. A **basic need** at any of these four levels, if unmet, leads to a craving, and it directs action to get the need fulfilled. This fulfillment brings pleasure. Subjective experiences of "craving" and "pleasure" would, of course, not be possible to measure operationally in the animal studies that were the basic research approach of behaviorists under whom Maslow studied. Humans, though, can be asked to report their experiences—and they should be asked to do so, according to Maslow.

What are these basic needs? Maslow listed four of them and asserted that they emerge in a particular order (see Figure 15.1). Each need must be met, more or less adequately, before the individual is free to move on to a "higher" need. "More or less adequately" is not so precise a statement as one might prefer. The same events might satisfy one person's need but not another. Maslow offers some guidance by suggesting that deprivation that threatens personality is more serious—for example, sexual frustration when it is interpreted as rejection or inferiority (Maslow, 1941). Without those added threats to self-worth, deprivation is more easily tolerated and presumably would not interfere with progress up the hierarchy of needs.

Generally, the need hierarchy is understood as an "up-only" path, but some have argued that people may move down as well as up the hierarchy (Rowan, 1999). Moving upward may give more sense of the direction of our growth, and moving downward may

Figure 15.1 Maslow's Hierarchy of Needs

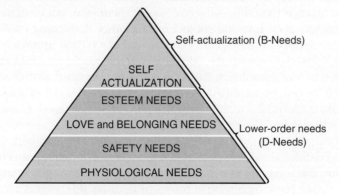

As each level of need is satisfied, the person moves up
the hierarchy. If needs are not satisfied, growth stops.

Margin glossary terms:

hierarchy of needs ordered progression of motives, from basic physical needs upward to motives of the most developed human beings

deficiency motivation motivation at lower levels of development

basic need a fundamental deficiency need

ground us more in the realities of our living. Or perhaps conditions of extreme deprivation of a previously satisfied need may move us backward, as regression. Unfortunately, empirical evidence does not address this issue adequately.

Physiological Needs

At the lowest level of the need hierarchy are physiological needs—the needs for food, water, sleep, and sex. These needs are essential to human and animal survival. If unmet, they dominate motivation, regardless whether other, higher-order needs are also unmet. "For the man who is extremely and dangerously hungry, no other interests exist but food," Maslow (1943) asserted (in Lowry, 1973, p. 156).

Lower animals may always live at this level, but humans, under normal conditions, have their physiological needs predictably met. If these needs are met adequately (although not necessarily leading to complete satisfaction), the next need level becomes salient. If, after moving on, the person encounters a situation in which the physiological needs are no longer met, these needs will once again become the predominant motivation. In Maslow's terminology, needs that are dominant at a particular time are called **prepotent**. Before dinner, hunger is a prepotent need; after eating, it is not. Something else dominates attention and thus is prepotent.

Maslow (1943) suggested that a person's history—as well as the current level—of need satisfaction is important. He hypothesized that "it is precisely those individuals in whom a certain need has always been satisfied who are best equipped to tolerate deprivation of that need in the future, and those who have been deprived in the past will react differently to current satisfactions than the one who has never been deprived" (in Lowry, 1973, p. 157). Research on the effects of dieting on food metabolism offers support for his claim at the physiological level; those who have dieted in the past convert food to fat more quickly than those who have not dieted. Could those who have been deprived of love or of security also hoard these satisfactions when they are available?

> **prepotent** currently most powerful; said of a need that because it is unmet is most powerful at the moment

Safety Needs

At the next level, the person's predominant motivation is to ensure a safe situation. Familiarity is perceived as safe, so the young child feels threatened when new situations occur (loud noises, strange animals, parental quarrels or divorce, etc.). Physical violence, of course, also threatens safety for both children and adults. For the most part, the safety needs of adults are met in an ordered society, but safety is threatened by emergencies, such as "war, disease, natural catastrophes. crime waves, societal disorganization, neurosis, brain injury, [and a] chronically bad situation" (Maslow, 1943; in Lowry, 1973, p. 160).

Maslow interpreted some neuroses as attempts to ensure a feeling of safety. Compulsive and obsessive neurotics, especially, try to keep life quite predictable, although it impedes their higher-level functioning. For others, money seems to promise safety. For example, someone whose business enterprises bring great wealth but little love may continue to strive for a feeling of safety through compulsive financial dealings.

Belongingness and Love Needs

If safety and physiological needs are met adequately, the next level to become prepotent is the need for love and belongingness. At this level, the person seeks love and friendship. Maslow included the need to give love, as well as to receive it. He described these needs as a frequent source of maladjustment in our society.

Sex is an issue at this level to the extent that it is an expression of affection; but sex can also function at a purely physiological level (i.e., the first level of the hierarchy). Maslow was interested in human sexuality, extending his doctoral studies in which he observed sexuality in animals. He interviewed 120 women about their sexuality, in the context of a broader study of their individual personalities. He also planned to study prostitutes but did not complete that research. Late in his life, he said, "If I were beginning all over again, I'd study homosexuality. . . as a means to a profound understanding of humanity" (Maslow, 1968a, p. 54). His work predated the rise of sexology, and it was less statistical than the later work of Alfred Kinsey and others. He described sexual dissatisfaction as an important "deficiency need," and dreamed, "If I could discover a way to improve the sexual life of even one percent, then I could improve the whole species" (p. 54).

Esteem Needs

The next need to emerge in the hierarchy is the need for self-respect and the esteem of others. Esteem should be "stable [and] firmly based," by which Maslow meant that it should result from our actual abilities and achievements. Reputation based on false premises would not meet this need.

We can interpret achievement strivings as manifestations of the esteem needs because society honors those who achieve. Many successful entrepreneurs, for example, whose physiological, safety, and love needs are met sufficiently, turn their motivation to career success. Maslow's hierarchical conception also suggests that people who feel unloved, perhaps sensing parental rejection, continue to function at the third level of the hierarchy and are not motivated by esteem needs.

When these needs are not met, we feel inferior. Maslow (1943) noted that Adler, who wrote so much about feelings of inferiority, paid more attention to the esteem needs than Freud. If the needs are met, we feel "self-confidence, worth, strength, capability and adequacy of being useful and necessary in the world" (in Lowry, 1973, p. 162). Research supports this idea; undergraduates who scored high on a measure of self-actualization (the Personal Orientation Inventory, described later) also scored higher on a measure of Physical Self-Presentation Confidence than those less self-actualized (Ryckman et al., 1985).

Although esteem needs are the highest of Maslow's deficiency motivations, they are still only the fourth of five developmental steps. The highest level, self-actualization, is so different from the others that it stands alone as a nondeficiency motive.

BEING MOTIVATION

being motivation
higher-level motivation in which the need for self-actualization predominates

Once the deficiency needs are more or less adequately met, the person functions at a higher level, which Maslow called **being motivation**, as opposed to deficiency motivation. This level is the pinnacle of development and the primary focus of Maslow's theory. It is described briefly here and more fully later in the chapter.

The Need for Self-Actualization

At this highest stage, the person is no longer motivated by deficiencies but rather by the need to "actualize" or fulfill his or her potential. "A musician must make music, an artist must paint, a poet must write, if he is to be ultimately happy. What a man can be, he must be. This need we may call self-actualization" (Maslow, 1943; in Lowry, 1973, p. 162). It is the desire "to become everything that one is capable of becoming" (p. 163). Subjectively, the person feels bored if lower-order needs are met, and this boredom motivates and is relieved by self-actualization striving. Some support for this proposal comes from the research finding that spirituality is correlated with high boredom proneness, as assessed on self-report scales (MacDonald & Holland, 2002).

Because humans have different potentials (compared to their similar physiological needs), the particular behaviors motivated by self-actualization needs vary from person to person. For Maslow (1968b, p. 33), "self-actualization is idiosyncratic since every person is different." This step seems to have been influenced by Carl Jung's description of the individuation process in adulthood (Schott, 1992).

DIFFERENCES BETWEEN D-MOTIVATION AND B-MOTIVATION

Lower-order needs occur earlier in the development of the individual and lower in the phylogenetic chart (which compares species). Because they are necessary for survival, lower-order needs cannot be postponed as easily as higher-order needs, and they feel more urgent when unmet. Maslow (1954/1987, p. 57) cited an example: "Respect is a dispensable luxury when compared with food or safety." Luxury or not, living at the level of higher-order needs brings better physical health and greater subjective happiness and serenity.

To stress the difference from deficiency motivation, Maslow described people at the level of self-actualization as **metamotivated**. At this level they are motivated by "meta-needs" or "B-values" ("B" for "becoming") such as beauty, truth, and justice. They are not motivated in the traditional sense of the term—that is, seeking to reduce a need to restore homeostasis. At this highest level, there is less determinism (based on environmental availability of need satisfaction) and more psychological freedom (Maslow, 1955). Perception is no longer focused, looking for objects to satisfy needs; it can be more passive and receptive. This is B-motivation, in contrast to D-motivation (deficiency motivation). Interpersonal relationships take on a very different quality at the level of B-motivation. Maslow described **B-love** as nonpossessive and enjoyable. In contrast, **D-love** is often contaminated by jealousy and anxiety. B-love allows the partners more independence and autonomy and it facilitates the growth of each person (Maslow, 1955).

It would be tempting to interpret Maslow's hierarchy in a simple way: that each need prevails until it is met and then disappears. However, this interpretation, which would mean that self-actualization does not appear as a need until the top of the hierarchy, is oversimplified (Maslow, 1968b, p. 26). The difficulty is that elements of self-actualization appear even at the earlier levels of the hierarchy—for example, curiosity and creative tendencies and talents. Thus self-actualization tendencies can be found throughout life. We do not, however, become dominated by them unless and until we reach the highest level of the need hierarchy. Because we do not get to that high level unless lower-order needs are sufficiently met, the hierarchy of needs provides a list of prerequisites for becoming a fully developed human being. Based on this hierarchy of needs, we can claim that people have certain rights or entitlements, such as the right to safety and to respect, if they are to develop to their full potential, even if they are handicapped by various disabilities (Schultz, 1996). Such a list of needs can guide those who provide care for people adjusting to disabling conditions, by pointing out the psychological needs that become salient to their patients (Calabro, 1997). Beyond that, a need hierarchy offers a model for society to set priorities in striving to provide for its members, to facilitate their development as humans: food, safety, respectable work, and so on.

metamotivated motivated by needs at the top of the hierarchy

B-love nonpossessive love, characteristic of a self-actualized person

D-love selfish love, characteristic of a person who is not self-actualized

RESEARCH TESTING THE NEED HIERARCHY

A fundamental postulate of Maslow's theory is that the five needs emerge in the sequence he described. We would expect hunger and poverty to prevent higher functioning, but many contrary examples have been reported. Psychiatrist Robert Coles (e.g., 1971a, 1971b) has observed people in dire economic conditions who, in apparent contradiction to the concept of a need hierarchy, seem to function at higher levels of human potential. Nazi concentration camps, for all their atrocities, did not cause all prisoners to regress to the lowest levels of human functioning, as Maslow's hierarchical theory would predict. People commit suicide, clearly compromising their safety needs; starving people refuse to cannibalize humans or to eat sacred cows when their religious beliefs do not permit these actions. Soldiers die for political causes. These examples, as well as empirical research (reviewed by Wahba & Bridwell, 1976), suggest to some that the need hierarchy should be abandoned (Fox, 1982).

Nonetheless, other research has been presented in support of the postulate of a need hierarchy. William Graham and Joe Balloun (1973) surveyed a cross-section of people in a community. The higher needs in the hierarchy were judged less satisfied than were the lower needs, and needs perceived as less satisfied were judged more desirable to satisfy. The researchers interpreted these findings as evidence for the hierarchical model. Ratings by college students indicate that they would feel worse if they failed to attain goals low in the hierarchy than those high. Conversely, they would feel more positive about attaining goals higher in the hierarchy than lower ones (Wicker et al., 1993). Evidence from cross-cultural anthropological records is also consistent with the model: People attend to their physiological needs before their safety needs (Davis-Sharts, 1986). An examination of Chinese history and literature is consistent with Maslow's concept of a need hierarchy—periods of peace, which provide more safety, a good life, and freedom to writers, have been associated with greater literary genius for over 2,000 years (Kuo, 1987).

Other researchers have measured the satisfaction of some or all of the five need levels in Maslow's hierarchy. This strategy has resulted in some evidence that the needs are sequentially important in different age groups, as Maslow's hierarchical theory suggests. Physiological needs are more important in childhood, whereas belongingness is more important in adolescence and adulthood (Haymes & Green, 1982). Self-actualization has been reported to increase with age (Hyman, 1988). Older people are more likely than younger ones to express humanistic values (Prager, 1998). Some inconsistencies in age sequencing are reported, however. Among the very old (ages 68–84), self-actualization scores on some subscales are reported to be lower than among those less old (ages 56–67) in one study (Plouffe & Gravelle, 1989). Such a finding can be explained in terms of Maslow's theory, however, by age-related changes that reduce the satisfaction of basic needs among the very old.

Other studies show that mental health is higher when basic needs are satisfied. Undergraduates who report that their needs are satisfied score lower on neuroticism (Lester, 1990) and higher on belief in internal locus of control than do those who report less need satisfaction (Lester et al., 1983). Need gratification assessed by the Maslowian Assessment Survey (MAS) was positively related to self-esteem and negatively related to neuroticism and depression (D. E. Williams & Page, 1989).

Although not proposed on the basis of Maslow's theory, another research study also supports the idea that higher-order needs can be pleasurable. Subjects engaged in cognitive activity, playing a game of video golf on a computer and trying to understand poems, reported greater pleasure when they were performing better. The researchers interpret that mental pleasure is—like physiological need satisfaction—an adaptive mechanism selected by evolution (Cabanac, Pouliot, & Everett, 1997).

Self-Actualization

Maslow preferred the term **self-actualization** to such terms as *psychological health* (or illness). His term refers to the full development of human potential, based on biological nature. It connotes the full potential of being human. Unlike the term *adjustment*, it does not mean adjusting to a particular cultural situation. Maslow (1968b, p. vii) suggested that instead of referring to "illness," we should speak of "human diminution or stunting," at least in psychology generally. He did acknowledge that psychotherapy may need more specific terminology. From his perspective, illness strikes if the person denies his or her inner potential, going against one's own nature. Karen Horney made a similar point in describing the alienation from the real self in neurosis, and Maslow credited her as a theorist whose ideas were in the direction he advocated for psychology.

> **self-actualization** development of a person's full potential

When a person's basic needs (the first four levels of the need hierarchy) have been met, motivation is directed toward self-actualization, which Maslow (1968b) defined as

> ongoing actualization of potentials, capacities and talents, as fulfillment of mission (or call, fate, destiny, or vocation), as a fuller knowledge of, and acceptance of, the person's own intrinsic nature, as an unceasing trend toward unity, integration or synergy within the person. (p. 25)

Maslow (1954/1987) was convinced that it was necessary for psychology to study its healthiest, most developed people if it was to learn about human potential. He remarked that

> healthy people are so different from average ones, not only in degree but in kind as well, that they generate two very different kinds of psychology. It becomes more and more clear that the study of crippled, stunted, immature, and unhealthy specimens can yield only a cripple psychology and a cripple philosophy. The study of self-actualizing people must be the basis for a more universal science of psychology. (p. 149)

Maslow reported a study of self-actualized people, selected from his personal acquaintances and friends and from public figures, both current and historical. In a survey of some 3,000 college students, he found only one subject who met his criterion for being self-actualized. This is not surprising, for few people become self-actualized, and a young college sample would not be likely to include many who have achieved that level of personal growth. Maslow (1968b) estimated that fewer than 1% of all people are self-actualized.

His decision about whether a person was self-actualized was subjective, of course. He included Rorschach tests when practical (obviously not for historical figures). Early in his observations, he found that "Possible subjects, when informed of the purpose of the research, became self-conscious, froze up, laughed off the whole effort, or broke off the relationship. As a result, since this early experience, all older subjects have been studied indirectly, indeed almost surreptitiously" (Maslow, 1954/1987, p. 127).

Among the public figures, Maslow included Abraham Lincoln and Thomas Jefferson, both "fairly sure" to have been self-actualized, and seven others whom he said were "probably" self-actualized: Albert Einstein, Eleanor Roosevelt, Jane Addams, William James, Albert Schweitzer, Aldous Huxley, and Benedict de Spinoza. Nominating individuals as exemplars of mental health is instructive for readers of the theory because prototypes are easier to consider than abstract concepts. Studies of individuals, such as one study of Eleanor Roosevelt, also reveal characteristics that are not reflected in self-report measures of self-actualization, such as problem centering and compassion, and traits overlooked in Maslow's description, such as humility and equitableness (Piechowski & Tyska, 1982). Describing individuals as self-actualized is, however, a risky strategy. Everett Shostrom (1972), writing for a popular audience, named Richard Nixon, then at the height of his prestige as president, as an example of a self-actualized person. The later scandal of Watergate, leading to Nixon's resignation to avoid impeachment, discredited this assessment and highlighted the danger of equating public success with self-actualization (Anderson, 1975; Shostrom, 1975). The concept of self-actualization is difficult to define precisely. Psychologists may erroneously label successful people as self-actualized. In fact, many successful people do not meet Maslow's criteria.

CHARACTERISTICS OF SELF-ACTUALIZED PEOPLE

Based on his observations, Maslow identified a number of characteristics of self-actualized people.

Efficient Perception of Reality

Self-actualized people have "an unusual ability to detect the spurious, the fake, and the dishonest in personality, and in general to judge people correctly and efficiently" (Maslow, 1954/1987, p. 128). They are less likely than others to be misled by their own defense mechanisms, wishes, expectations, or stereotypes. Rather, like the boy in the fairy tale, they are likely to see that the emperor has no clothes if, in fact, he has none. This accuracy perhaps develops because they are not threatened by the unknown and because their focus is not narrowed by unfilled needs (Maslow, 1955).

Acceptance

Maslow's self-actualized subjects were more accepting of themselves, of others, and of nature than the average person, including acceptance of their "animal level"; they eat well, sleep well, and enjoy sex. They accept both the bad and the good and are thus tolerant. Research suggests that self-actualized people (measured by low discrepancies between the self and the ideal self) have less fear of death (R. A. Neimeyer, 1985).

Spontaneity

Self-actualized people behave spontaneously, simply, and naturally, although generally they are not outwardly unconventional. This spontaneity derives from being in close touch with their inner impulses and subjective experience. They do not hide behind a social mask. Research finds that in older women, self-actualization (measured by the Personal Orientation Inventory) and impulsiveness are positively correlated, but this is not so among men (Plouffe & Gravelle, 1989).

Problem Centered

Self-actualized people focus on problems outside themselves. They are problem centered, not self-centered. The tasks may come from a sense of social obligation.

Need for Privacy (Solitude)

More than most people, self-actualized individuals like privacy. Maslow hypothesized that they would endure sensory deprivation (conducted by experimental psychologists) more easily than others. They are capable of high levels of concentration, and they make up their own minds rather than letting others make decisions for them.

Independence of Culture and Environment (Autonomy)

Self-actualized people do not depend on other people or the world for need satisfaction. They are "self-contained" and resilient in the face of difficulties. Because the self-actualized person is motivated by internal needs, rather than responding to the external world, such a person feels more "psychological freedom" (Maslow, 1968b, p. 35).

Freshness of Appreciation

The sense of awe and wonder at life remains always fresh with self-actualized individuals. This may come from aesthetic experiences, social encounters, or other sources. For many of Maslow's subjects, sexual pleasure provided a "kind of basic strengthening and revivifying that some people derive from music or nature" (Maslow, 1954/1987, p. 137).

Peak Experiences

Probably the best known characteristic that Maslow described is the capacity for mystical experiences, which he called **peak experiences**. Maslow (1954/1987) described these as

> feelings of limitless horizons opening up to the vision, the feeling of being simultaneously more powerful and also more helpless than one ever was before, the feeling of great ecstasy and wonder and awe, the loss of placing in time and space with, finally, the conviction that something extremely important and valuable has happened, so that the subject is to some extent transformed and strengthened even in daily life by such experiences. (p. 137)

peak experiences mystical states of consciousness, characteristic of many but not all self-actualized people

A variety of events may trigger such experiences. Sometimes they occur in response to nature; sometimes they are religious experiences; sometimes they occur during meditation; sometimes they are even sexual encounters. Not all self-actualized people are "peakers," however, who are more poetic, musical, philosophical, and religious. Nonpeakers are more practical, working in the social world through reform, politics, and other real-world arenas. Maslow seemed to have more admiration for peakers, whom he called "transcending," than for nonpeakers. whom he called "merely healthy" (p. 138).

People often do not report their peak experiences to others because they are very personal (Davis, Lockwood, & Wright, 1991). Gayle Privette (1983, 1985, 1986) writes that people's reports of peak experience convey distinctive characteristics: "joy, fulfillment, and lasting significance . . . and for some, spiritual . . . clarity of process marked by absorption, intention, sense of self, freedom, and spontaneity" (1986, p. 241). Although the peak experience itself is transitory, it often has a long-lasting, even life-transforming, effect (Lanier et al., 1996).

Self-reported peak experiences are correlated with hypnotic susceptibility and romantic love (Mathes, 1982). Additional research on altered states of consciousness in relationship to mental health might answer unresolved issues. College students, artists, and realtors, despite differences in age and in triggering events, report peak experiences in similar terms (Lanier et al., 1996; Yeagle, Privette, & Dunham, 1989). Are these peak experiences simply doing something very well? They are not. Subjects' descriptions of peak experiences are different from their descriptions of peak performances, in which they perform excellently (Privette & Bundrick, 1987). These attempts to quantify subjective experience are commendable, but it is not clear that Maslow's peak experiences exactly coincide with these or with descriptions based on interpersonal communication (Gordon, 1985) or on the experience of residents of a yoga ashram (Wilson & Spencer, 1990).

Maslow did not claim that peak experiences occur only among the self-actualized, but he did assert that these experiences are more frequent among such individuals (Daniels, 1982; Maslow, 1968b, 1969) and that they open the door to a transcendence of the ego, which is life transforming (Frick, 2000). In his later theorizing, Maslow acknowledged that some people have peak experiences in childhood, when they could not yet be self-actualized, and retrospective reports by adults confirm this assertion (E. Hoffman, 1998). Stamatelos (1984) reports that peak experiences can occur even among the developmentally delayed. Perhaps such episodes would be among the exceptions that Maslow noted when he remarked that not all peak experiences are truly "Being-cognition," that is, evidence of self-actualization (Maslow, 1968b, p. 100). Although it seems reasonable that some people stuck at lower levels of development would be too rigid to allow themselves to experience the altered states Maslow described as peak experiences, it is by no means demonstrated that such experiences occur exclusively among the self-actualized.

States of consciousness also are influenced by psychoactive drugs, of course. The idea that such drug-induced altered states of consciousness could provide insights into the functioning of the human mind, perhaps even offering therapeutic value, has been suggested (e.g., Boorstein, 1980; Masters & Houston, 2000), although it is not generally accepted within therapeutic practice.

Human Kinship

Self-actualizing people identify with human beings in general, feeling a sense of kinship with the human race. Because they identify with all humans rather than only one particular group, they are not prejudiced.

Humility and Respect

Self-actualizing people are humble, feeling they can learn from many different people, even those of a different class or race. They are democratic, rather than authoritarian, and do not insist on maintaining their status over others.

Interpersonal Relationships

Self-actualized people are capable of "more fusion, greater love, more perfect identification, more obliteration of the ego boundaries than other people would consider possible" (Maslow, 1954/1987, p. 140). They are discriminating, however, seeking out other self-actualized people, so they have deep relationships with a few people rather than many more superficial relationships. They also tend to attract admirers, who may be quite devoted, even becoming disciples, although self-actualized people do not encourage this reverence.

Ethics and Values

Self-actualized people have strong ethical standards, although their standards are often not conventional standards of right and wrong. They are not concerned with what Maslow (1954/1987) regarded as trivial ethical issues, such as "card playing, dancing, wearing short dresses, exposing the head (in some churches) or not exposing the head (in others), drinking wine, or eating some meats and not others, or eating them on some days but not on others" (p. 147). Their values emerge from acceptance of human nature and of their own nature, including their unique potentials.

Discrimination between Means and Ends

Maslow's subjects were clearly focused on the ends or goals of their efforts and subordinated the means to the end. Nonetheless, they could appreciate the pleasure of the means.

Sense of Humor

Self-actualizers have a nonhostile sense of humor, not laughing at other people's expense. Their sense of humor is more philosophical than that of most people, laughing at the human condition. Overall, though, Maslow's subjects were more serious than humorous.

Creativity

Creativity is the one characteristic Maslow claimed was present in all of his self-actualized subjects, without exception. He did not mean creativity in the sense we often use it. It does not necessarily involve any creative product such as a work of art or music, which Maslow (1954/1987, p. 160) calls "special talent creativeness," as contrasted with "self-actualizing creativeness." "There can be creative shoemakers or carpenters or clerks. . . . One can even see creatively as the child does" (p. 143).

Although Maslow's creativity does not require expression in the traditional arts, the arts can foster such creativity and self-actualization for many people. One study, for example, reports that artistic activities foster self-acceptance and openness, two important aspects of self-actualization (Manheim, 1998). Researchers report correlations between measures of self-actualization and creativity, including judged creativity of written and art projects (Buckmaster & Davis, 1985), and creativity measured by a written test (Runco, Ebersole, & Mraz, 1991). The creativity of a self-actualized person emerges naturally out of the other characteristics: spontaneity, resistance to enculturation, efficiency of perception, and so forth. It is a capacity in all children but is lost by many, as both neurosis and what psychoanalysts call secondary process displace earlier creativity (Maslow, 1958).

Resistance to Enculturation

Self-actualized people do not "adjust" to society at the expense of their own character, but rather "maintain a certain inner detachment from the culture in which they are immersed" (Maslow, 1954/1987, p. 143). They are conventional when it is easier or less disruptive to be so, but this is a superficial adaptation that readily gives way to their autonomous nature. At other times, they are not easily influenced. Undergraduates who scored high on a measure of self-actualization were less influenced, in their performance on a reasoning test, by statements leading them to believe they would do well or poorly than were those who were less self-actualized (Bordages, 1989).

Resolution of Dichotomies

Self-actualized people do not see in either-or terms, as less healthy people often do. Maslow (1954/1987, p. 149) offered several examples of dichotomies that to self-actualized people no longer seem so—for example, reason versus emotion, selfish versus unselfish, serious versus humorous, active versus passive, and masculine versus feminine. Rather than seeing conflict between what is good for the individual and what serves others, the two operate together, with "synergy" (Maslow, 1964). This fusion of self-interest and social interest can occur at a cultural level, too, leading to a better society, a utopia, or to use the term Maslow preferred, **Eupsychia**. Consciously thinking and acting in terms of synergy, highly developed people can help solve some of the social problems that have been produced by less developed, dichotomous thinking (Carlsen, 1996).

Eupsychia a utopian society in which individual and societal needs are both met and where society supports individual development

Despite having so many admirable characteristics, Maslow (1954/1987) noted that his subjects were not perfect.

> They too are equipped with silly, wasteful, or thoughtless habits. They can be boring, stubborn, irritating. They are by no means free from a rather superficial vanity, pride, partiality to their own productions, family, friends, and children. Temper outbursts are not rare. (p. 146)

And because of their autonomy, they "are occasionally capable of an extraordinary and unexpected ruthlessness," for example, when terminating a friendship or a marriage or when recovering quickly (too quickly, most people would say) from the death of a loved one (p. 146).

Maslow's list of characteristics of self-actualized people serves as a description of mental health, of what people become if they develop their full potential. Willard Mittelman (1991) interpreted these characteristics as consequences of an "open" personality, in the sense of taking in information and experience nondefensively.

MEASUREMENT AND RESEARCH ON SELF-ACTUALIZATION

Maslow did not devote much effort to the development of measuring instruments, preferring for the most part to observe people more holistically, in keeping with his concept of a receptive or Taoist scientific method. He did, however, collaborate with his wife to devise the Maslow Art Test "to test for holistic perception and intuition by testing the ability to detect the style of an artist" (Maslow, 1966, p. 62). This ability, which may perhaps be described as an intuitive cognitive style, does not necessarily improve with art training and may even sometimes be impaired by it. Maslow valued the receptive ability measured by the test and felt that, combined with an ability to think in the abstract, nomothetic terms of traditional science, it could enable psychologists to develop the new approach he envisioned.

Maslow (1968b) realized that his ideas were in the early stages of scientific validation. He acknowledged that his work "is full of affirmations which are based on pilot researches, bits of evidence, on personal observation, on theoretical deduction and on sheer hunch. . . . They are hypotheses, i.e., presented for testing rather than for final belief" (p. ix). Others have carried these ideas the logical next step. The key concept in Maslow's theory is self-actualization. Whereas Maslow explored this construct through observation, rather than formal measurement, others have attempted to assess self-actualization by a questionnaire.

Personal Orientation Inventory

The **Personal Orientation Inventory (POI)** (Shostrom, 1964) is a 150-item multiple-choice inventory that provides two primary scores derived from Maslow's theory. The **Inner Directed Supports** scale measures the degree to which the subject provides his or her own support (as opposed to turning to others). The **Time Competence** scale measures the degree to which the subject lives in the present. In addition, there are subscales to measure self-actualizing values, existentiality, feeling reactivity, spontaneity, self-regard, self-acceptance, the nature of people, synergy, acceptance of aggression, and capacity for intimate contact.

Everett Shostrom (1964) reported that his inventory distinguished between groups nominated by clinicians to be self-actualized or not self-actualized and that meaningful changes in scores occurred during the course of psychotherapy. Several studies have validated the POI through criterion group studies; that is, groups thought to be more self-actualized score higher than those assumed to be less self-actualized (Hattie & Cooksey, 1984). For example, medical patients score higher than alcoholics, who score higher than schizophrenics (Murphy, DeWolfe, & Mozdzierz, 1984). Researchers have often used the Personal Orientation Inventory as a criterion measure of mental health. Scores increase as a result of various therapeutic interventions (Duncan, Konefal, & Spechler, 1990; Elizabeth, 1983; Peterson-Cooney, 1987) and less formal interventions to improve psychological health, such as meditation, reading self-help books, and even exercise (Delmonte, 1984; Forest, 1987; Gondola & Tuckman, 1985). However, hypothesized increases are not always found (Giltinan, 1990).

The Personal Orientation Inventory correlates positively with many other measures of mental health (J. M. Campbell et al., 1989; Hageseth & Schmidt, 1982; Ramanaiah, Heerboth, & Jinkerson, 1985; Yonge, 1975). Some evidence indicates that self-actualization on the POI is correlated with greater spirituality, as measured by a written test (Tloczynski, Knoll, & Fitch, 1997). High scorers among married couples also report greater sexual enjoyment (McCann & Biaggio, 1989). A short form of the Personal Orientation Inventory, consisting of only 15 items, has been developed (Jones & Crandall, 1986), as have other measures of self-actualization (e.g., Buckmaster & Davis, 1985; Sumerlin & Bundrick, 1996, 1998), but none are so widely used as the POI.

Personal Orientation Inventory the most popular measure of self-actualization

Inner Directed Supports scale of the Personal Orientation Inventory measuring a person's tendency to obtain support from himself or herself rather than from other people

Time Competence a scale of the Personal Orientation Inventory that measures a person's concern with the present rather than the past or future

OBSTACLES TO SELF-ACTUALIZATION

If self-actualization is an innate potential, why is it not universally developed? Human beings repeatedly confront situations in which they must choose between growth and safety. Safety choices are appealing, but only growth choices move us toward self-actualization. If we think of the positive attractions rather than the dangers of growth, and of the potential boredom rather than the social approval of what appears to be the safe choice, our choices will move us more often toward self-actualization. To encourage such choices in

Figure 15.2 Choice between Safety and Growth

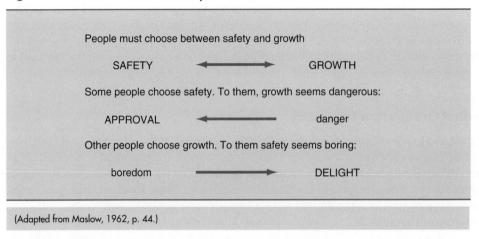

People must choose between safety and growth

SAFETY   ⟵⟶   GROWTH

Some people choose safety. To them, growth seems dangerous:

APPROVAL   ⟵   danger

Other people choose growth. To them safety seems boring:

boredom   ⟶   DELIGHT

(Adapted from Maslow, 1962, p. 44.)

children, parents are wise to avoid both overprotection (which orients the child toward safety) and excessive approval (which focuses the child on others' opinions rather than on his or her own experience). When all goes well, the child finds that the growth choice offers delight, and the safety choice leads to boredom. Under less ideal circumstances, the growth choice seems dangerous and the safety choice offers approval (see Figure 15.2). This postulate is confirmed by a study that reports lower levels of boredom proneness on a self-report scale among undergraduates scoring high on the Short Index of Self-Actualization (McLeod & Vodanovich, 1991).

Besides this intrapsychic pull against self-actualization, there are other reasons why self-actualization is not more frequent. Higher-order needs emerge only if favorable external conditions (such as adequate food and housing) allow satisfaction of the earlier needs. Also, higher-order needs are weaker than lower-order needs; hence they must compete with them.

External forces can more readily obscure our inner motivations than is the case for animals.

> Humans no longer have instincts in the animal sense, powerful, unmistakable inner voices which tell them unequivocally what to do, when, where, how and with whom. All that we have left are instinct-remnants. And furthermore, these are weak, subtle and delicate, very easily drowned out by learning, by cultural expectations, by fear, by disapproval. (Maslow, 1968b, p. 191)

instinctoid weakly instinctive motives characteristic of humans

To indicate the weakness of human instincts, Maslow (1955, 1965) added the diminutive ending -*oid*, calling them **instinctoid**. The weakness of higher instinctoid impulses means that they are sometimes inadequate to lead us fully to self-actualization.

Jonah complex not developing one's full potential because of a belief that it is impossible to do anything very important

In addition, people sometimes have a **Jonah complex**—that is, they are convinced it is impossible to do anything very important and so avoid developing to their full potential. Maslow (1976) chided his students for not aspiring to important contributions in their field. He asked them, "If not you, then who else?" (p. 35). He warned them that failure to aspire to their highest potential, to self-actualization, would leave them profoundly unhappy.

Applications and Implications of Maslow's Theory

Because Maslow's aim was to improve the human condition through his theorizing, it is appropriate that his ideas have been applied to diverse areas. Taken together, these applications are part of the **human potential movement**, which strives to improve the human condition by fostering the development of individuals to their highest potential through special training centers and through the transformation of social institutions like places of employment and schools.

> **human potential movement** social trend to foster the full development of individuals, reflected in the development of growth centers and in transformation of social institutions

THERAPY

Within psychology, Maslow's theory has implications for psychotherapy. Many people, according to Maslow, turn to psychotherapy because their love and belongingness needs are unfulfilled. Therapeutic progress requires that these needs be met. Maslow believed the therapeutic approach should be tailored to the particular patient. For seriously disturbed neurotics, a traditional Freudian approach might be appropriate. For more healthy individuals, group therapy and encounter groups would be more suitable.

Building on the ideas of Maslow and others, *transpersonal therapists* work with a worldview that encompasses a larger domain than the individual who is suffering. There are many varieties of transpersonal therapy (Boorstein, 2000). They draw not only from traditional therapies but also from religious and spiritual traditions and techniques of healing, valuing states of consciousness that are outside of everyday experience. Sometimes meditation techniques are included in therapy. Claims of paranormal insights are sometimes offered to support the validity of the transpersonal approach. In keeping with Maslow's emphasis on the higher human functions, transpersonal therapists are concerned with positive emotions as well as painful ones: "Transpersonal psychotherapy attempts to open awareness to . . . psychic realms where joy, love, serenity, and even ecstasy are present" (Boorstein, 2000, p. 413).

GROWTH CENTERS

Growth centers, devoted to the development of human potential, are using Maslow's ideas. The best known is the Esalen Institute in Big Sur, California. At these centers, group experiences as well as lifestyle changes, often involving communal living, enhance human potential.

> **growth centers** places where people come together to develop their full potential (e.g., Esalen)

WORKPLACE

Maslow's need hierarchy has become a major concept for industrial-organizational psychologists (Massarik, 1992). Those who help people choose their careers can counsel more effectively, even helping people become more self-actualized in the process, by taking into account clients' levels on the need hierarchy (Sackett, 1998). The workplace is a major area for the development of self-actualization, and workers are more effective when they function at the level of the higher needs while avoiding dissatisfaction based on unmet lower-order needs.

In 1962 Maslow was a visiting fellow at a high-tech corporation in California, NonLinear Systems. Among self-actualized managers, he found positive, supportive interpersonal relationships with subordinates and more productive and creative work. These were the managers who were more likely to believe that people are trustworthy, responsible, curious, open to change, and intrinsically interested in work (cf. Payne, 2000). Unfortunately, many managers are not self-actualized but rather are motivated by neurotic power needs. The challenge for business is to fill management positions with the most highly developed individuals, despite the fact that self-actualized people may not be particularly attracted to those positions (Schott, 1992).

Customer satisfaction is important in the business realm, and Maslow's theory offers suggestions to satisfy not only employees but also customers and to maintain loyalty: Businesses should aim to meet lower-order needs while also appealing to higher-order needs (Maslow, 1998; Tuten & August, 1998).

CONSUMERISM

To sell products and services, advertisers slant their communications in ways that appeal to potential customers. Maslow's need hierarchy provides a framework for reaching potential customers (Kahle & Chiagouris, 1997). Many products can be considered from various need levels. Food, for example, fulfills physiological needs but also is relevant to esteem needs, as a friend of mine recognized when choosing a gourmet brand of bottled mushrooms instead of a less expensive, but equally nutritious, store brand of mushroom stems and pieces.

In addition, however, Maslow's need hierarchy suggests another implication: that people whose needs are satisfied are able to turn away from consumer values to seek satisfaction of other needs. Research indicates that money does not raise people's level of happiness, except, of course, for the poor, for whom additional money does increase happiness by permitting need satisfaction (L. A. King & Napa, 1998; Myers & Diener, 1995). In social circumstances that are economically secure, a movement toward "voluntary simplicity" often emerges, in which people voluntarily turn away from consumption toward other values, including the arts and education—choices that have beneficial consequences for the environment and for the economic well-being of those less well off (Etzioni, 1998).

RELIGION AND SPIRITUALITY

Maslow thought at length about religion, considering how the values emerging from his theory compared with religious traditions and urging a more spiritual approach within psychology. Indeed, his voice was one of a chorus of advocates of a spiritualized psychotherapy, often one that added insights from Eastern religious tradition to the Judeo-Christian backgrounds of Western psychotherapists. Although there are similarities in their concern for growth and healing, self-actualization and spirituality are not interchangeable concepts (Benjamin & Looby, 1998; DeHoff, 1998). Clinical and counseling psychologists who agree with Christian beliefs generally prefer other (cognitive-behavioral) therapy orientations, instead of humanistic or existential approaches to therapy, which are preferred by those whose religious beliefs are more mystical and Eastern (Bilgrave & Deluty, 1998). The religious traditions that most influenced humanism and existentialism were, in fact, the mystical traditions (Martinez, 1998). As history has repeatedly demonstrated, religion has often been the rallying cry of those who persecute others outside their own group, although it need not take on such a prejudiced form (Burris & Tarpley, 1998). Maslow strongly opposed dogmatic views in religion, as in other fields.

He interpreted the experiences of religious prophets as peak experiences. Such moments bring important insights, useful to humankind in general and not simply to the individual. The task of religion is to communicate these insights to their members. Unfortunately, it often happens that institutionalized religions are filled with "nonpeakers" who cannot communicate prophetic experiences and who substitute dogmatic rigidity for vision (Maslow, 1970). Some of this failure is inevitable because it is difficult to translate right-brain mediated transcendental experience into language, which is a left-brain function (Frank, 1977).

Although he did not support traditional institutionalized religion, Maslow lamented the **desacralization** of human experience by professionals (including psychologists and physicians) as well as others. Removing a sense of the sacred—of the awesome, highest human values—and treating humans as animal-like or robotlike, was a profound loss. He hoped that psychology would contribute to the "resacralization" of human experience, even if it meant experimenting with new forms, such as publishing poetry and personal testimonials in scientific journals.

desacralization loss of a sense of the sacred or spiritual

EDUCATION

Maslow (1976) described the goal of education to be "the 'self-actualization' of a person, the becoming fully human, the development of the fullest height the human species can stand up to or that the particular individual can come to" (p. 162). This is surely a different aim from the mere acquisition of technical skills. Maslow realized that his theory implied drastic changes in educational practice, similar to the changes proposed by Carl Rogers. Humanistic education should foster, rather than sedate, the natural curiosity of children. In most classrooms, children learn to behave in ways that please the teacher rather than being encouraged to think creatively.

The ideal college would have much more self-directed learning. Students would follow their own inner directions in meaningful and honest dialogue with faculty. "There would be no credits, no degrees, and no required courses" (Maslow, 1976, p. 175). For such a system to succeed, of course, students and faculty would need to be self-actualizing so their choices would indeed be directed toward growth.

GENDER

Maslow (1954/1987) encouraged women, as well as men, to live up to their full potential. Self-actualized people are not constrained by rigid sex roles. Both men and women can be both active and passive, in lovemaking and in life (p. 153), a challenge to traditional gender assumptions that was embraced by feminist Betty Friedan (Nicholson, 2001). Nonetheless, Maslow believed there are inherent, biologically based sex differences. (It seems unlikely that a psychologist whose doctoral work was based on the observation of sexual behavior in monkeys would give up this concept.) Evidence indicates that the Personal Orientation Inventory, a measure of self-actualization, may be biased in favor of the masculine role; at any rate, scores are correlated positively with masculinity and negatively with femininity on the Bem Sex-Role Inventory (Faulkender, 1991). Maslow envisioned men and women achieving self-actualization along different routes or paths, a concept accepted by some feminist psychologists (e.g., Gilligan, 1982), but not all. If there are different, gender-related paths to self-actualization, it may be helpful to develop better measures to reflect them.

Maslow's Challenge to Traditional Science

Traditional scientific objectivity and methods are always more difficult to apply when humans are the object of inquiry. Humanistic psychology, in particular, because of its emphasis on subjective experience and its valuing of experience and growth, regularly faces the dilemma of a scientific method that seems inadequate to study the phenomena that really matter. Maslow articulated this problem, and he went further than many humanistic psychologists—certainly further than Carl Rogers—in questioning the relevance of traditional science for the study of human psychology.

Consider prayer, for example. Does praying for patients in a hospital lead to their improved recovery—even if they do not know they are receiving this "treatment"? Researchers have attempted the test, in some cases claiming scientific validation of the value of prayer (W. S. Harris et al., 1999), but critics have expressed scientific doubts about the adequacy of their research methods and the failure of attempted replications (Christopher, 2002; Hoover, 2000). Perhaps replication of the experiments, addressing critics' methodological concerns, would settle the issue one way or the other. Or perhaps it would be wiser to refrain from testing religious issues such as this with the methods of science (Chibnall, 2001).

Maslow has been accused of allowing his own values, rather than scientific observations, to dictate his description of the concept of self-actualization. That is, his list of characteristics of self-actualized persons may simply be a list of qualities that Maslow admires (cf. McClelland, 1955). For example, his emphasis on mystical, nonrational experience, rather than reason, may reflect personal bias (Daniels, 1988; M. B. Smith, 1973). It has been suggested that the values represented in the need hierarchy are Western cultural values only. An alternate hierarchy has been proposed to reflect Chinese values, in which the highest level is "self-actualization in the service of society" rather than individual self-actualization (Nevis, 1983).

Maslow's concept of self-actualization clearly has meaning that extends beyond its status as an academic personality theory. It has been described as a myth to foster individual development and social change (Daniels, 1988), although with limited ability to support some political agendas (Prilleltensky, 1992; Sipe, 1987). Michael Daniels describes the concept of self-actualization as "one of the most optimistic and life-affirming [concepts] ever proposed within psychology" (p. 19). Such a mythic function, however, goes beyond the standards by which scientific personality theory is ordinarily evaluated (cf. Chapter 1).

Maslow responded to accusations of not following traditional methodology, not providing statistics to support his assertions, and allowing values to influence his work so blatantly. He claimed it did not bother him:

> I have a secret. I talk over the heads of the people in front of me to my own private audience. I talk to people I love and respect. To Socrates and Aristotle and Spinoza and Thomas Jefferson and Abraham Lincoln. And when I write, I write for them. This cuts out a lot of crap. (Maslow, 1968a, p. 56)

Contrary to the stated aim of a valid scientific theory to make predictions, Maslow expected, paradoxically, that his approach would make people less predictable. Humanistic science would increase people's ability to make choices and to express their spontaneity.

Surely Maslow was aware of the powers of science to persuade. In his preface to his book *Toward a Psychology of Being*, he remarked, "Science is the only way we have of shoving truth down the reluctant throat" (Maslow, 1968b, p. viii). Or as his former student assistant, Kendler, puts it more diplomatically, "Maslow considered psychology to be a *prescriptive* science, capable of providing moral values that should guide human conduct . . . [as opposed to] a *descriptive* science . . . , which describe[s] the world as it is, not as it ought to be" (Kendler, 2002, p. 56). He thought that his beliefs about human nature, if true, "promise a scientific ethics, a natural value system, a court of ultimate appeal for the determination of good and bad, of right and wrong" (p. 4). A new ethics would emerge from his view of human nature (Maslow, 1955; McClelland, 1955).

Maslow's (1968b) vision went beyond his third force psychology with its emphasis on human values.

> I . . . consider Humanistic, Third Force Psychology to be transitional, a preparation for a still "higher" Fourth Psychology, transpersonal, transhuman, centered in the cosmos rather than in human needs and interest. (pp. iii–iv)

To adopt a genuinely cosmic point of view leaves an uncertain role for simply human concerns; perhaps Maslow simply meant to call attention to the potential for highly developed people to transcend their own individual needs in favor of universal values like justice and truth (Koltko-Rivera, 1998). In the present day, with its awareness of global planetary issues, Maslow's vision of a "Fourth Psychology" seems prophetic. Yet he has not persuaded mainstream psychology that it should abandon the traditional scientific method for his more Taoist-receptive, intuitive model of experiential knowledge. The traditional scientific method has proved too valuable to convince even many dedicated humanists to abandon it now in the name of humanism or feminism or postmodern thought or any other currently popular new way of thinking (M. B. Smith, 1994). As a sketch of the direction in which psychological science should move, Maslow's vision of humanistic research needs to be supplemented by clear operational definitions (McClelland, 1955; Rychlak, 1988) if it is to transform the science of psychology. Many humanistic psychologists are actively developing research methodology so that personality research can remain scientific without having to abandon the person as a whole, healthy, thriving being (Giorgi, 1992; Polkinghorne, 1992).

Will it ever be possible to resolve this tension between objective science and subjectivity in humanistic, transpersonal approaches? Probably not. But if Maslow was correct in his assertion that "Without the transpersonal, we get sick, violent, and nihilistic, or else hopeless and apathetic" (1968b, pp. iii–iv), then we must permit psychology to tolerate, if not to fully understand, such points of view.

Other Growth Themes in Psychological Theory

The themes that Maslow described are represented in other psychological theory and research, too, including research on intrinsic motivation and a newer theme, positive psychology.

Self-Determination Theory and Intrinsic Motivation

Edward Deci offers a different theoretical analysis that corresponds to the thrust of Maslow's argument that there is a fundamental motivation within individuals that is healthy. Building on his concept of intrinsic motivation (Deci, 1975) is a more refined theoretical model, *self-determination theory* (SDT) (Ryan & Deci, 2000). The advantage of this analysis is that it has inspired a fertile line of empirical research, which Maslow's less precise approach did not. Deci's best known theoretical concept, **intrinsic motivation**, refers to "doing an activity for the inherent satisfaction of the activity itself" (Ryan & Deci, 2000, p. 71).

intrinsic motivation motivation to perform an activity for its inherent satisfaction (rather than as a means to some other goal)

Self-determination theory proposes that people innately have three important psychological needs: competence, autonomy, and relatedness (Ryan & Deci, 2000). All of these needs must be satisfied if an individual is to thrive. When these basic needs are satisfied, self-motivation is enhanced: People work more persistently, perform better, and are more creative. They have a higher self-esteem and sense of well-being. Mental health improves. However, when these needs are not satisfied, well-being suffers and motivation decreases.

Whether people are self-motivated or apathetic depends, according to Ryan and Deci (2000), on the situation. Rewards can be designed to encourage intrinsic motivation by providing feedback about performance, or they can override a person's inner motives. Most of the research on this theory relates to achievement-type concepts, but the more recent developments extend the theory into interpersonal concerns, reminiscent of Maslow's love and belongingness needs and explicitly related (Ryan & Deci, 2000) to the childhood attachment literature. They suggest that attachments to others, such as parents, and interpersonal supports help people develop from less mature external motivations to more internalized motivations. As the individual's motivation becomes more autonomous, it does not necessarily become independent of other people, contrary to what most of us probably think, immersed as we are in the individualism of Western culture. Instead, "within SDT, autonomy refers not to being independent, detached, or selfish but rather to the feeling of volition that can accompany any act, whether dependent or independent, collectivist or individualist" (Ryan & Deci, 2000, p. 74). Individuality and the sort of intrinsic motivation that is comparable to Maslow's concept of self-actualization is nurtured by the support of others.

Positive Psychology

A number of psychologists who currently express the emphasis on health and self-actualization that Maslow and other humanists advocated have recently rallied behind the term **positive psychology**. A key similarity between Maslow's theory and current positive psychology is the emphasis on immediate experience as an aspect of healthy functioning (Rathunde, 2001).

positive psychology current movement in psychology that emphasizes healthy functioning, with concern for immediate experience and positive emotions such as happiness

Martin Seligman and Mihaly Csikszentmihalyi (2000) describe positive psychology this way:

> The field of positive psychology at the subjective level is about valued subjective experiences: well-being, contentment, and satisfaction (in the past); hope and optimism (for the future); and flow and happiness (in the present). At the individual

level, it is about positive individual traits: the capacity for love and vocation, courage, interpersonal skill, aesthetic sensibility, perseverance, forgiveness, originality, future mindedness, spirituality, high talent, and wisdom. At the group level, it is about the civic virtues and the institutions that move individuals toward better citizenship: responsibility, nurturance, altruism, civility, moderation, tolerance, and work ethic. (p. 5)

Positive psychology includes the humanistic themes of a proactive personality, seeking growth—themes that also appeared in the theories of Adler and Allport. We know that health does not come automatically by simply avoiding known causes of ill health but must rather be fostered and nourished. Positive psychology aims to help us do that.

Happiness is not simply the absence of unhappiness. Even at a neurological level, as we saw in Chapter 9, positive and negative emotions are served by different brain pathways. At the level of a life narrative, happiness is fostered by finding meaning in one's life (Ryan & Deci, 2001). Warm and supportive interpersonal relationships also contribute substantially to subjective well-being. George Vaillant (2000) integrates his research on defense mechanisms with positive psychology by noting that in contrast to immature defenses, the mature defenses—such as altruism, suppression, humor, anticipation, and sublimation—are quite relevant to positive psychology. Other researchers (Bonanno et al., 2005) report that some individuals are unusually resilient in coping with even very stressful life events, such as the loss of a spouse or life partner. Even in the face of major loss, they are not overcome with grief but express positive emotions, according to their friends.

Positive psychology aims to expand on the humanistic legacy by making it more scientific. Building a foundation of solid research can provide more certain guidance for actualizing the positive visions of humanism in the real world where personality lives.

Summary

- Maslow proposed a *third force* humanistic psychology that is less deterministic and more focused on values than psychoanalysis or behaviorism.
- Maslow proposed that people develop through five levels of a *need hierarchy:* physiological, safety, love and belongingness, esteem, and self-actualization.
- At the four lower stages, a person is motivated by deficiencies. At the highest stage, *self-actualization*, the person is motivated by *being motivation* and has distinctive characteristics, foremost of which is creativity.
- *Peak experiences* are mystical states of consciousness that are particularly common among self-actualized people.
- Maslow's theory has implications for many fields and is closely associated with the *human potential movement.*
- Maslow urged religion to be less dogmatic and more concerned with growth. In addition to psychotherapy, his work prompted the development of growth centers, such as Esalen, where people could live in a community that promoted self-actualization.
- Maslow urged employers to be more concerned with the growth needs of their employees and educators to encourage personal growth and creativity among students. He urged psychology to be more concerned with human values.

- Maslow criticized mainstream psychology for being method centered rather than problem centered, and he argued that scientific investigation of the highest human potentials requires the development of new models of science.

Thinking about Maslow's Theory

1. Maslow found only 1 out of 3,000 undergraduates to be self-actualized. Do you think there would be fewer, more, or the same number today, considering changes in the student population (such as more students returning to school at later ages and a greater ethnic and racial diversity)?

2. Discuss the implications of Maslow's hierarchy of needs for current society. Are there factors (e.g., poverty or crime) that can be interpreted in terms of deficiency motivation?

3. Maslow suggested that sexuality is partly a physiological need and partly a belongingness need. Are any other levels of the need hierarchy relevant to understanding sexuality in the context of current society? Explain.

4. Compare Maslow's deficiency motivation with Adler's inferiority striving, and Maslow's Jonah complex with Adler's inferiority complex.

5. Are any of the listed characteristics of self-actualized people not indicators, in your opinion, of a high level of development?

6. Contrast Maslow's description of Taoist Science with the description of science in Chapter 1.

7. Thinking about all the psychology you have studied (in this and other courses), is the emphasis on positive psychology and healthy functioning unusual?

Study Questions

1. What is third force psychology?

2. Contrast Maslow's view of psychology with that of mainstream psychology. In particular, how important is scientific methodology? What else is important?

3. Discuss the role of values and experiential knowledge in Maslow's theory.

4. List and explain the levels of Maslow's hierarchy of needs. What is implied by having them arranged in a hierarchy?

5. Contrast deficiency motivation with being motivation. Include the differences between D-love and B-love.

6. Explain the term *metamotivation*.

7. Summarize research testing the concept of a hierarchy of needs.

8. What is self-actualization? How is it different from mental health? From public success?

9. List and explain characteristics of a person who is self-actualized.

10. What are peak experiences? Discuss the types of people who experience them.

11. From his description of self-actualized people, discuss Maslow's attitude toward both religion and ethics.

12. Explain what Maslow meant by creativity as a characteristic of a self-actualized person. How is this different from musical or artistic talent?

13. How is self-actualization measured?

14. Discuss research testing Maslow's concept of self-actualization.

15. How common is self-actualization? Why is it not more common?

16. What did Maslow mean to convey by describing human instincts as instinctoid?

17. What is a Jonah complex?

18. Discuss implications of Maslow's theory for therapy.

19. Describe a growth center.

20. Discuss implications of Maslow's theory for the workplace.

21. Explain what Maslow meant by desacralization and what he suggested be done about it.

22. Discuss implications of Maslow's theory for education.

23. Discuss implications of Maslow's theory for gender roles and sex differences.

24. What is intrinsic motivation?

25. What is positive psychology?

16

Buddhist Psychology
Lessons from Eastern Culture

Chapter Overview

Preview: Overview of Buddhist Psychology

The Relevance of Buddhism for Personality Psychology

A Brief History of Buddhism

The Buddhist Worldview: The Four Noble Truths

Buddhism and Personality Concepts

Spiritual Practices

Buddhism and Psychotherapy

The Importance of the Dialogue, and Some Cautions

Summary

ILLUSTRATIVE BIOGRAPHY

The Dalai Lama

Buddhist approaches to personality are derived from a religious tradition dating back two and a half millennia. This rich tradition has many practices and writings that are closer to personality theory than to religious practice as we in modern Western cultures think of religion. Buddhism emphasizes exploration and control of the mind, so it is a cognitive approach. It also has much to say about ethical behavior. The current leader of Tibetan Buddhism, the 14th Dalai Lama, travels widely and collaborates with psychologists and others. His autobiographical writings give insights into this personality approach.

In the remote and mountainous Asian country of Tibet, a succession of Tibetan Buddhist leaders, whose title "Dalai Lama" means "Ocean of Wisdom" (Bstan-dzin-rgya-mtsho, 1989),

lived in isolation from the rest of the world and provided spiritual and political guidance for their people. This changed with the invasion of the country by China in the middle of the 20th century. After many failed attempts to keep Tibet free from Chinese rule, on May 31, 1959, the 23-year-old 14th Dalai Lama (whose personal name is Tenzin Gyatso but spelled Bstan-dzin-rgya-mtsho in conventional library usage and so in the references at the end of this book) fled his palace in Lhasa, Tibet. He was disguised and, with a group of supporters, established a community of Tibetan refugees in neighboring India, where the city of Dharamsala has become the seat of the Tibetan government-in-exile (Bstan-dzin-rgya-mtsho, 1990). Thrust into the larger world, unlike all the earlier Dalai Lamas, he has met with political and religious leaders throughout the world and has engaged in dialogues on political freedom, modern science, and religion, bringing the tradition of Buddhism with its insights to the problems of the modern world. Tibet, too, has lost its isolation, with the completion of a railroad connection between Lhasa, Tibet, and Qinghai, China, in the summer of 2006 (Kahn, 2006).

Description

Because the emphasis is not on stable personality—the very idea of which is considered an illusion (Kamilar, 2002)—but rather on spiritual progress, personality description is closely connected with ideas of development and adaptation (or spiritual progress). People who have risen to higher levels of development are calm and compassionate. Those who remain less developed have more troubled traits.

The Dalai Lama would certainly be described as highly developed, which translates into the trait term of *compassionate*. Those who have observed him and his effect on people give many examples of this compassion: listening to people with a variety of troubles; taking time to greet hotel staff individually instead of looking past them as invisible persons of no consequence, the way so many guests do; turning from a crowd of people to offer individual attention to a man showing the telltale physical tremors of long-term mental illness treatment. Despite his status, as a person the Dalai Lama is described as approachable and practical, answering questions in thoughtful and often commonsense ways, and unafraid to say, "I don't know" when that is the case. His sense of *peace* is contagious. He frequently smiles and makes jokes. Despite his high status, he is unpretentious and lives the humble, celibate, reflective life of a Buddhist monk. In his autobiographical writings, the Dalai Lama also reports aspects of his personality that would be of interest to other personality theories: an interest in mechanics that from childhood had him tinkering with mechanical things, including watches and cars, and led him to comment that if he had another career than Dalai Lama, he might be an engineer (Knight, 2004). His interest in science made him receptive to some cultural modernization trends, and he muses that this scientific interest led to Chairman Mao of China's underestimation of spiritual dedication when the two met, before the Chinese invasion and occupation forced his exile from Tibet (Bstan-dzin-rgya-mtsho, 1990).

Adjustment

Buddhism describes adaptation and adjustment in spiritual terms. Poor adjustment is reflected in ways familiar to Western psychologists: impulsive and addictive behavior, selfishness, anxiety, and other adverse emotional states. (Of course, these descriptions come from Buddhist dialogue with Westerners, especially therapists. Within Tibetan Buddhist cultures, different descriptions may well be used.) In Buddhist teaching, healthy growth requires clear and undistorted perception of reality as it is, which requires giving up the illusory notion of a separate self and recognizing the interrelationships of all people and all that exists in the natural world. Other theories have described narcissism as unhealthy self-absorption, but the Buddhist approach goes much further, teaching that the individualism generally regarded as normal and healthy in our culture is inherently unhealthy and a cause of suffering. Behaviorally, acts of unkindness and selfishness show evidence of shortcomings. Happiness is the reward for spiritual growth and ethical living.

In both Buddhist teaching and Western psychotherapy, healthy functioning requires undistorted perception. Much that the Dalai Lama says reflects his *openness to reality*. He is open to new information. Instead of adhering to a dogmatic viewpoint, he has welcomed dialogue with modern brain researchers to explore the relationships between meditation and brain functioning (as described later in this chapter). Emotional well-being reflects adjustment, and he claims to be happy, despite a variety of adversities, including exile from his homeland and the death of many family members and friends. The Dalai Lama does recount childhood immaturities: impatience and conflict with his brother, confessing that he was the aggressor, and he notes that in childhood he played with toy soldiers. As an adult, however, his patience and calmness are well known.

Cognition

Cognitive processes receive considerable emphasis in this ancient discipline. Through meditation, with disciplined examination of the contents of consciousness, centuries of insights have detailed the ways in which people think and perceive the world in distorted ways, leading them to act foolishly or unethically. The fundamental error that leads to suffering is "our passionate desire for and attachment to things that we misapprehend as enduring entities" (Bstan-dzin-rgya-mtsho, 1989). Things are constantly changing, but we do not realize how transient everything is. One particular cognition is a milestone for spiritual growth: becoming aware of suffering (the first of the Four Noble Truths), including the reality of death. Buddhist tradition urges people to meditate, to be aware of their perceptions, and to question the validity of what they think they know, to come closer to true reality.

In keeping with Buddhist practices, the Dalai Lama spends considerable time in meditation. He reports that he prays 4 hours a day (Bstan-dzin-rgya-mtsho & Cutler, 1998). He connects with suffering humanity, bringing the pain of others into his own consciousness. The Dalai Lama describes his education as rich in many ways but without exposure to modern science. His writings reflect an unusual degree of intellectual curiosity and open-mindedness to new ideas. For example, earlier in his life, he saw visible shadows on the moon's surface, and so acknowledged that the moon did not emit light as classic Buddhist texts said but rather reflected it. Now he engages in enthusiastic dialogues with modern neuroscientists about the nature of consciousness. One place that such interchange between Buddhism and science occurs is at the Mind and Life Institute in Colorado, established to promote such a dialogue (http://www.mindandlife.org). Ironically, sometimes neuroscientists have opposed having a religious figure speak at scientific gatherings (Reed, 2006; Schmidt, 2005).

Despite his openness to scientific analysis of Buddhist practices, the Dalai Lama rejects the Western tendency to see biology as the fundamental cause of mental processes. Instead, he argues for the Buddhist emphasis on thought as a cause and challenges the tendency of reducing it to biological or neural processes as a Western prejudice. Science and Buddhism, he argues, can each learn from the other. Scientists can learn more about consciousness by including, among their research participants, those who have developed their consciousness to high levels through Buddhist meditation. Conversely, he expresses openness to integrating the findings of modern science into his Buddhist beliefs, and he says he would change those beliefs if science can prove them wrong (Goleman, 2004). This is not a man who sees science and religion as antithetical. Nor does he place science over religion. He maintains that science must be

supplemented by a spiritual understanding if human-created problems and suffering are to be alleviated (Bstan-dzin-rgya-mtsho, 1989).

Biology

Buddhist sages and Western neuroscientists are now actively collaborating to understand consciousness. In contrast to the tendency in modern psychology to think of the body and brain as determinants or limiters of psychological functioning, Buddhism suggests a more interactive model. As the Dalai Lama describes it, Buddhist medicine teaches that "the root causes of disease are Ignorance, Desire or Hatred" (Bstan-dzin-rgya-mtsho, 1990, p. 218). Mental processes can be truly causal, changing biology, in this model. This does not deny the role of biology, though. Diet and behavior are the first line of treatment for disease, but Tibetan medicine also uses organic medicines, acupuncture and heat treatments, and surgery (Bstan-dzin-rgya-mtsho, 1990, p. 219). The Buddhist worldview regards a person's status and characteristics in this lifetime as bearing the results of past lives, so that whatever Western approaches describe as the hereditary aspects of personality would, from a Buddhist viewpoint, be the morally legacy of past lives.

According to this doctrine, the selection of Tenzin Gyatso as the next Dalai Lama recognized his entitlement to this high position. Buddhist rebirth teaching says that the previous Dalai Lama chose to be reborn in this child. In the context of a tradition that regards the idea of a separate individual self or soul as illusory, this is a difficult idea to conceptualize. The attitude created by the doctrine, however, is clear: The Dalai Lama's high position is an entitlement and so should not provoke envy, in the way that random genetic gifts can seem unfair. In terms of his own biology, the Dalai Lama has led a healthy life, following the Buddhist practices of healthy eating, avoiding alcohol, and practicing meditation. He attributes his energy to his lifestyle. He confesses that his diet is not strictly vegetarian, his health having suffered when he tried (after observing a chicken being slaughtered) to give up meat (Bstan-dzin-rgya-mtsho, 1990). Tibetan people have traditionally incorporated meat in their diet, reportedly because of the harsh mountain climate that makes a purely vegetarian diet inadequate. As a child, he savored the meat dishes that his family was accustomed to eating, over the disapproval of the monks who were training him to be the next Dalai Lama.

Society

Although individuals are responsible for their behavior and development, society is also important in Buddhist teaching. The individual influences others and has a responsibility to help reduce others' suffering. Buddhists are concerned with ethics; in modern times Buddhists are involved in such humanitarian concerns as peace and environmentalism. The individual's relationship to society goes in the reverse direction also. The society in which the individual is developing can help or hinder individual development, so it is important to put oneself in a healthy community environment (*sangha*). Even apparently adverse environments and people, though, can be reinterpreted by the individual in such a way as to foster spiritual development. An apparent enemy, for example, can be a source of growth lessons, making us aware of our unhealthy attachments and misconceptions.

Beginning with the invasion of his homeland by the Chinese, the Dalai Lama was impelled to deal with larger social issues. His exile has facilitated connections with people around the world, including cultures that he did not know while isolated in Tibet. Like many other modern Buddhists, he has voiced insights about some of the world's most difficult problems, including war, starvation, the environment, sexuality, and abortion. He affirms a common humanity across cultures and socioeconomic divisions. His identity and loyalty for his homeland, Tibet, have prompted him to advocate that it be restored to independence. He tries to maintain Tibetan culture through education and cultural practices in the exile communities in India and elsewhere. He proposed a peace plan between Tibet and China in 1987 that would have (among other provisions) removed armaments from Tibet, stopping its use as a place to produce nuclear weapons and store nuclear waste. His proposal would have preserved Tibet's cultural identity by stopping the influx of Chinese people, who now outnumber native Tibetans. Although not implemented, this proposal was influential in his nomination for the Nobel Peace Prize, awarded in 1989. His discussions of peace do not satisfy some critics because he stops short of demanding full political independence of Tibet from China, and once the United States invaded Iraq, he did not demand cessation of hostilities there either, despite having objected to the war ahead of time (Goodstein, 2003; Zupp, 2004). These positions, however, can be understood from the Buddhist principle of accepting reality as it is. Once China invaded Tibet and the United States invaded Iraq, he accepted those realities and discussed, as a realist, what should happen next.

The Dalai Lama has met with diverse religious leaders all over the planet, working toward spiritual goals that are shared by the world's religions. Although embracing Buddhism for himself, the Dalai Lama recognizes the value of many religious traditions, and he does not wish for everyone to become a Buddhist. Other religions may be better suited for other people (Bstan-dzin-rgya-mtsho & Cutler, 1998). His tolerance extends to the nonreligious as well, recognizing the secularization of society, and he argues that individuals can be spiritual even if they do not identify with a formal religious tradition.

Development

Development is a major theme in Buddhist psychology, which emphasizes continued growth. The emphasis is not on external determinants, such as the influence of family or society, but rather on the choices of the individual. An individual's own actions can foster continued development. In the model of development that Buddhism proposes (and Buddhism is not alone; Hinduism has related ideas), development spans not only one lifetime but also time before birth in past lives and after death in the next rebirth. Intentional acts that are virtuous boost the individual toward higher states, according to the principle of moral causality (karma), and also have beneficial consequences for others because all the world is interrelated.

Other approaches to personality development would find, in the 14th Dalai Lama, evidence of an active, assertive childhood. The Dalai Lama reports that he fought with his brother, resisted school lessons, ate what was not permitted, and only in adolescence fully appreciated the Buddhist legacy and its scholarship. (This nicely fits the stage of identity formation, in Erik Erikson's theory.) Despite his status and world respect, he confesses to foibles, such as memory errors and occasional misjudgments.

Beyond this normal developmental pattern, the Buddhist approach outlines a larger developmental perspective, spanning multiple lifetimes. Born into a farming family, the almost 3-year-old Lhamo Thondup (his birth name) was identified by a delegation of Buddhist monks to be the reincarnation of the previous Dalai Lama. Their evidence consisted of visions and signs, including the child's identification of objects that had belonged to the now dead Dalai Lama as "mine" (Bstan-dzin-rgya-mtsho, 1990; 1997). On the issue of rebirth, the Dalai Lama describes his life from the perspective of the

Buddhist tradition, telling anecdotes from childhood that seem premonitions of his high destiny. For example, as a child he insisted on sitting at the head of the table, and he fantasized a trip to the city of Lhasa, location of the palace of the Dalai Lama (Bstan-dzin-rgya-mtsho, 1990). Despite being chosen for his leadership role, he still faced many years of demanding education and examinations before officially becoming a Buddhist monk. As an adult, his continued study and service to humanity are evidence of continued development. In the Buddhist worldview, if that development reaches a sufficient level, after death he would be free of the cycle of rebirth.

Final Thoughts

This is a unique illustrative biography, not only because of the cross-cultural focus of the subject matter, but because the Dalai Lama is a spokesperson for the theory and so mixes teaching with his life story. An issue to consider, which will not be resolved here but only suggested, is this: Are the concepts about personality universal in their application? That is, do Buddhist insights apply to a Western audience? Conversely, could we apply our Western theories to the Dalai Lama (as in the identity suggestion earlier), or are the cultures so different that they require different theories?

Preview: Overview of Buddhist Psychology

Buddhism has implications for major theoretical questions in personality psychology, as presented in Table 16.1. It presents an elaborate model of psychological development with traditional practices, especially meditation, to foster healthy growth. It emphasizes universal potentialities in the human condition, rather than individual differences in stable characteristics. Buddhism teaches nonjudgmental acceptance of experience, including the experience of human suffering, and emphasizes change and the transitory nature of experience, including the experience of the self. Its influence on Western psychology, especially therapy, is increasing.

The Relevance of Buddhism for Personality Psychology

William James, one of the primary founders of American psychology who is remembered for his writing about the self, admired the psychological ideas contained in Buddhism and predicted that psychology would soon be influenced by Buddhism (Michalon, 2001). His prediction was perhaps premature but not wrong. Several of the theorists described in earlier chapters in this book included mention of Buddhist concepts in their own writing. Karen Horney studied Zen Buddhism at the end of her life (Morvay, 1999; Westkott, 1998). Carl Jung was visited in 1958 at his home by Buddhist Zen master Hisamatsu Shin'ichi, and the two discussed their areas of common interest, although the difference between the two views was immense (Haule, 2000; Heisig, 2002).

As a religion, Buddhism has been neglected by researchers who have developed measures of religious orientation, such as those mentioned in Chapter 7 (Tsang & McCullough, 2003). Here we study it as a psychology, not a religion. That is not as strange as it might appear. Buddhism is in many ways more comparable to Western psychotherapy than to Western religion; it may be misconstrued if we make Western assumptions about religion (Muramoto, 2002). Buddhism provides ways of knowing about reality based on personal experience, and it does not ask people to accept the idea of a god or the teachings of a dogma or of any particular teacher. The practices that Buddhism

TABLE 16.1	Preview of Buddhist Personality Theory
Individual Differences	Buddhist approaches emphasize the commonalities among people. Differences occur in the specific content of consciousness, but these are transient, and the emphasis is on a common developmental progression.
Adaptation and Adjustment	Buddhism explains suffering and its causes, and offers an Eightfold Path to alleviate suffering and bring happiness. It offers detailed practices for improving mental functioning, through various kinds of yoga and meditation.
Cognitive Processes	Wrong thinking is a fundamental cause of suffering. Meditation improves cognitive functioning. The idea of a stable, enduring self is seen as an illusion with adverse consequences.
Society	The individual is not separate from others or the world as a whole, and individual development has positive consequences for the world. Conversely, a supportive community improves individual functioning.
Biological Influences	The Buddhist worldview does not see the body and mind as separate but rather as closely related, so improved consciousness has beneficial health effects.
Development	Development results from systematic and intensive spiritual practices, and is an individual responsibility. In contrast to other approaches, Buddhism does not look to external causes, such as the family or the environment, as the cause of development or developmental failures.

espouses, such as meditation, are methods for achieving experience that will reveal what is true. The separation between the sacred and the secular, which has been part of Western culture for hundreds of years, is not characteristic of Eastern cultures. Additionally, Buddhism takes as a major goal the task of alleviating suffering, which makes it comparable to psychotherapy.

Many of the concepts in Buddhism, including the self, are also important ideas in theories of psychotherapy in particular and personality theory more generally. Buddhism urges self-control and disciplined understanding of the self through meditation. In contrast to humanistic approaches that are sometimes criticized as simplistic, urging people simply to become aware of their true self and follow its guidance, the Buddhist approach emphasizes mental discipline and restraint.

Although the subject matter of Buddhism and psychology have considerable overlap, it is obviously not complete. Like any long tradition, Buddhism includes many teachings about cosmology, including spirits and rebirth, that are foreign to psychological science and to the West. Furthermore, although there are strong empirical practices in Buddhism, these rely on self-observation of individual phenomenological experience, not on recruiting experimental subjects who can be treated as objects by a researcher. In addition, the Buddhist tradition assumes that mind is central and causal, and it does not try to reduce it to physical structures and processes, as psychology today often (although not always) does.

Buddhism and Western psychology stem from separate cultures. It is all too tempting to try to reduce Buddhist ideas to those forms of explanation that are assumed in Western culture, and thus to miss aspects of its message that our Western ears cannot hear. We must be cautious about this *etic* approach, one that looks at a culture (in this case, Buddhist) from the outside, from another culture's perspective (in this case, from the Western scientific perspective). In the past, for example, cultural biases caused Western mental health experts to compare Buddhist practices with schizophrenia (Walsh & Shapiro, 2006)! Fortunately, several current Western scientists have also studied Buddhism and practiced meditation, and so they are better able to understand Buddhism from an *emic* perspective, that is, from the culture's own point of view.

Although the psychological community is now more open to Buddhist practices, even incorporating meditation into a variety of treatment strategies, misunderstanding is still an issue. This occurs, for example, when the evidence of specific brain functioning in meditative states is taken to mean that the brain *causes* those experiences. The Dalai Lama, surely an authority on Buddhism, criticizes such interpretations as Western prejudice and argues that the mental phenomena are the causes. These different perspectives are the topic of exciting current research on the mind and the brain, the mental and the physical, and both psychology and Buddhism are being challenged by this dialogue.

A Brief History of Buddhism

Buddhism is one of the major Eastern world religions, with roots in the much older Hinduism. Buddhism began in India about 2,500 years ago, when a man on a spiritual quest, named **Siddhartha Gautama**, reportedly reached enlightenment after years of searching. Siddhartha rejected many aspects of Hinduism, including the Hindu gods and the inequalities of the caste system, and he emphasized compassion and an individual quest for enlightenment. The name of the religion is based on the name, the **Buddha**, meaning "the Awakened One," which was given to Siddhartha Gautama after he had attained enlightenment (Richards & Bergin, 1997). Other people who have become awakened are also called "buddhas." Buddhism is not a deistic religion; it does not depend on a divine presence for wisdom or salvation. Rather it describes the way in which people can become enlightened. It is quite psychological, describing human nature and emphasizing ethics (Finn & Rubin, 2000).

One fundamental idea that Buddhism and Hinduism share is the concept of **rebirth**. Existence is continuous, extending beyond death and before birth. The condition in which a person is born depends on intentional actions in past lives. One aspect of this idea is that cause and effect continue beyond the death of the individual. This aspect of the rebirth concept is not so strange to those who have pondered Western religions' descriptions of heaven and hell. There is an important difference, however. In Western religious ideas, the individual self or soul continues after death. In contrast, Buddhism teaches (as we see later in this chapter) that the individual self is unreal, an illusion, a false perception; so what continues beyond death is a broader reality, of which the individual is only one brief and fleeting component. This idea is often conveyed by the metaphor of a wave on an ocean: The individual self is like a wave that rises and falls, but that is in reality not separate from the ocean but only a transitory form.

Siddhartha Gautama the historical Buddha, whose spiritual journey provided the foundation for Buddhism; also called Sakyamuni

Buddha Awakened one; the term often refers to Siddhartha Gautama (Sakyamuni Buddha), who lived in India about 2,500 years ago; in some forms of Buddhism, it is held that everyone can attain buddha status (become a buddha) by following the path, although it may take more than one lifetime to achieve this

rebirth continuation of the effects of karma in previous lifetimes into the present

Since its origins, Buddhism has spread to many parts of the world, and in so doing, it has been transformed into local variations, which should not be confused with one another (Kearney, n.d.). The differences have emerged in part because of the sort of sectarian arguments that happen also in other religions (Finn & Rubin, 2000), and in part because of the influences that occur when the tradition spreads to new places, with variations developing as Buddhist practices are adapted to new parts of the world. In the United States, for example, the relationships between American Buddhism and psychotherapy are making for a more democratic (less hierarchical) structure, one more open to equality of the sexes (Finn & Rubin, 2000).

Many histories describe two major schools of Buddhism. *Theravada* Buddhism ("Way of the Elders," also called *Hinayana*, "common or lesser vehicle" to emphasize the individual) was the older form; it emphasizes simple living. **Mahayana Buddhism** ("The Greater Vehicle" or "Great Raft" to emphasize its universality and the goal of liberating everyone from suffering) developed about 500 years later and emphasizes compassion. Tibetan Buddhism (Vajrayana Buddhism), the form that the Dalai Lama represents, added to these two traditions a more elaborate description of enlightenment and emphasis on a guru or teacher (Kamilar, 2002). (Sometimes it is classified as a separate category, and sometimes as a type of Mahayana Buddhism.) **Zen Buddhism**, a form of Mahayana Buddhism, is popular in Japan and emphasizes meditation and characteristic koans (described later). Immigration has brought these types of Buddhism to the United States, where Buddhists now number about 2 million (Keller, 2000).

Mahayana Buddhism the major East Asian Buddhist tradition, which pays particular attention to the Buddha and to devotional practices that assist others to follow his path to Enlightenment

Zen Buddhism type of Buddhism found particularly in Japan, which uses koans to overcome limitations of thought

BIOGRAPHY OF SIDDHARTHA GAUTAMA

Buddhism traces its origins to a man whose spiritual path inspired others to follow. About 2,500 years ago, in or around 563 BC, a wealthy and privileged young prince in northern India ventured out from his overprotective paternal home, leaving his wife of 13 years and his child. He saw, for the first time, people suffering and dying. Instead of retreating back into his shelter, as his father wished, he began a lengthy quest for understanding suffering and happiness that ultimately led to his enlightenment and to the founding of a new religious tradition that has become widespread. This man was Siddhartha Gautama (Knierim, n.d.).

According to legend, Siddhartha's father had a particular incentive to protect his son because prophecy predicted one of two destinies: He would become either a political leader or a religious ascetic. The father, Suddhodana, thought that preventing Gautama from seeing life's misery would preclude the religious ascetic path, but he did not succeed. Siddhartha left the palace to see the world, and to his shock, he realized that the sheltered life of the palace was not all there was to existence. Outside, people were ill. People became old, and they died. These aspects of the human condition had been hidden from him before, but now he had witnessed human suffering, and it troubled him. He also saw a religious man, who seemed at peace—suggesting a path that could provide an alternative to disillusionment. So he left his home, abandoning his family, and immediately began a spiritual journey.

For 6 years Siddhartha wandered, studying under Hindu teachers and subjecting himself to strict discipline as a monk. He was brutal at self-mortification. But this did not satisfy his spiritual quest, and he tried other approaches. At one point, he indulged in the opposite extreme, enjoying many pleasures in a life of luxury. Neither extreme satisfied. He turned to a life of meditation and self-examination. Tradition has it that while meditating in the lotus position under a Bodhi-tree, he finally and suddenly achieved

enlightenment, understanding how to get rid of suffering by giving up illusions and desire. During his remaining long life, Siddhartha taught his insights to many disciples in northern India, dying at the age of 80.

Siddhartha followed the tradition of yoga in his quest to deal with the pain of seeing suffering around him. Thus Buddhism incorporates many Hindu practices and shares some beliefs (including rebirth). Many schools of Buddhism have developed. They agree on fundamental teachings that describe the nature of the mind in the *Abhidhamma* ("higher teaching") doctrine. The core ideas are the Four Noble Truths and the Eightfold Path.

Enlightenment
higher stage of consciousness that results from following the Eightfold Path; sometimes also used synonymously with Awakening

The Buddhist Worldview: The Four Noble Truths

Siddhartha Gautama conveyed the wisdom of his enlightenment through teaching the **Four Noble Truths**, which convey the view of reality that, if accepted, produces positive psychological and spiritual change. Unlike most religions, Buddhism does not expect these truths to be accepted on the basis of authority. Instead, the approach is one of natural law, and people are encouraged to test the truths for themselves.

We are ignorant of the true nature of things, the **dharma**, mistaking appearances for reality (Mahathera, 1982). This ignorance is often called **delusion**. The true nature of things can be discovered through Buddhist teachings and practices, especially meditation. To an enlightened person, the dharma appears everywhere: in beautiful natural objects, in a baby crying, and even in unexpected places such as horseshit because nothing is rejected (Nhat Hanh, 1996, p. 24). Even things that we might rather deny, even suffering, is part of the dharma. Instead of embracing the good and rejecting evil, this approach accepts reality in its entirety.

Four Noble Truths
that there is suffering, that it has a cause, that suffering can cease, and that there is a path to end suffering

dharma the true, intrinsic nature of things

delusion ignorance or false beliefs about the nature of reality

THE FIRST NOBLE TRUTH: THERE IS SUFFERING

The first fundamental lesson is that "there is suffering." The original Pali language word that has been translated as "suffering" is **duhkha**, which has other possible translations, including "unsatisfactoriness," "disharmony," and "painfulness" (de Silva, 1990). Or we could refer to "frustration" (Hayes, 2003), of wanting what we do not have and being blocked in attaining it—a translation that seems particularly apt for psychology because so many of our theories describe human "needs" or "drives" and the efforts to satisfy them. Although unhappiness exists, ordinary people are not aware of the extent of suffering. They are not yet aware, in a traditional Buddhist image, that "the pretty, colored rope that one has found and treasures is actually a very poisonous snake" (Chen, 1999, p. 15). We are under the illusion that things are better than they are. The realization and acceptance of the fact of suffering motivates following the Buddha path.

duhkha suffering, which is accepted in the First Noble Truth

Surely psychologists will not disagree there is suffering. It is all around, and those who are therapists see additional suffering walk in the door with each patient. Helping clients to accept the reality of their lives that causes pain is an important therapeutic step. Therapist and theorist Karen Horney (see Chapter 5) compared *duhkha* with the "basic anxiety" that she proposed in her own theory (Westkott, 1998). What is distinct, though, is the Buddhist attitude of permitting suffering into consciousness. We tend to put it out of our minds, suppressing or repressing painful experiences. In the physical realm, we avoid doing things that produce suffering or pain and flee, if possible; that is the principle of punishment that is fundamental to learning theory. The first noble truth insists that the suffering be permitted to enter consciousness, not pushed aside (Sumedho, 1992). The attitude of acceptance of the suffering is challenging because our natural impulse would be to end the suffering, to satisfy the desire; our natural impulse would be to be motivated to action, not to focus on the *duhkha*. If escape is impossible, we might at least feel sorry for ourselves, but that is not the Buddhist way. The focus is on the experience, not on the self, for as we see later, the self is an illusion.

Although acceptance of suffering is in some ways consistent with psychological insights, as when clinicians help clients, there are other themes within psychology that seem at odds with this idea. Psychologists have reported studies that show an optimistic bias is associated with positive outcomes, including avoidance of depression. If we accept this first Buddhist truth, we will have to look beyond the apparent adaptation that such cognitive bias produces and see what it may cost.

THE SECOND NOBLE TRUTH: THE ORIGIN OF SUFFERING

attachment craving for a variety of things, including physical objects and even the self; the source of suffering (according to the Second Noble Truth)

The Second Noble Truth identifies the origin of suffering: craving, or **attachment** to desire. At root, the problem is ignorance because we are deluded about what would make us happy, and so we crave the wrong things (Bstan-dzin-rgya-mtsho, 2000). We are fixated on, or attached to, these mistaken desires. There is a cause-and-effect relationship between this attachment to desire and the consequent suffering. Consider addiction: If a craving for tobacco (or another drug) can be eliminated, the suffering of not having it will disappear. Similarly, if a desire for fame and fortune can be eliminated, the suffering of being ordinary and poor will disappear. Ordinary people, not yet enlightened, are caught up in **samsara**, the "wheel of suffering" in which the consequences of ignorant craving and bad behavior cause continued suffering and prevent attaining nirvana and liberation from the cycle of rebirth.

samsara the wheel of suffering, in which the consequences of unenlightened action lock a person into a cycle of rebirth instead of permitting liberation to nirvana

Buddhism lists three kinds of desire: for sensory pleasure *(kama tanha)*; to become or continue to exist *(bhava tanha)*, including ambitions; and for annihilation *(vibhava tanha)*, or to get rid of something, such as annoying people or a troubling emotion (de Silva, 1990; Sumedho, 1992). These three desires may seem more familiar if we note that they are similar, respectively, to libido, ego, and thanatos in Freud's theory (de Silva, 1990). Letting go of these desires is the challenge; we must give up our attachments if we wish to end suffering—because eliminating the cause will eliminate the effect.

This teaching finds the cause of suffering within the person and not in external circumstances. It is not the absence of a satisfying object in the external world but rather the person's craving and, furthermore, attachment to craving (unwillingness to give it up), that produces suffering.

THE THIRD NOBLE TRUTH: THE END OF SUFFERING

Because craving or desire is the cause of suffering, ending the craving will end the suffering. *Detachment* from craving is the key. This includes detachment from the craving for material goods. It also includes detachment from possessiveness of other people, but it does not imply giving up on loving them, although sometimes the idea of detachment is misinterpreted that way (Ghose, 2004). Psychological studies of unhealthy or "desperate" love are easily reconcilable with this teaching; it is not healthy to cling possessively to another person, even in the name of love. We must also give up attachments to fixated ideas and attitudes to be more open to present experience and new information. The individual ego or self is relinquished because it is not real but only an illusion. This difficult concept is more fully discussed later.

Attachments do not disappear easily. Meditation allows them to appear, be examined, and be released. Some of the persistent intrusions in meditation come from previously unacknowledged attachments, fears, ideas, and so on. They must be allowed to become conscious before they can be let go.

A person who has attained the end of the cycle of suffering is an *arahant* and has value to society through acts of compassion and in the role of teacher or adviser (de Silva, 1990). Ancient Buddhist teachings describe the *arahant* as not indulging in certain behaviors: "taking life, stealing, sexual contact, uttering falsehoods, enjoying the comforts of wealth, and going astray through desire, through hate, through delusion, and through fear" (de Silva, 1990). It is not that they have suppressed or denied part of themselves to be "good," but rather the ethical implications that are part of Buddhism flow naturally from truly understanding the nature of reality. Goodness is not imposed by some supernatural entity opposed to natural law. Ethical behavior is intrinsic to the process of psychological development (Walsh, 1988). The problems that humans suffer come from ignorance, not from sin. In fact, Buddhism holds that people are basically good (Trungpa, 2005).

TABLE 16.2   The Eightfold Path

Step	Description
Right view	Accurate perception, not distorted by prejudice or prior conceptualization, such as a negative self-concept or inaccurate assumptions about other people
Right intention	Intention based on acceptance of what really is, rather than wishing for something better (intending to achieve unrealistic goals) or believing that things are worse than they really are (intending to avoid exaggerated or inaccurate dangers)
Right speech	True and direct, assertive, respectful statements
Right action	Living simply and behaving respectfully toward others (not in a spirit of self-denial but out of our basic goodness)
Right livelihood	Work that is meaningful and consistent with ethical and spiritual principles
Right effort	Being disciplined but not overly severe toward oneself, so that there is room for playfulness and rejuvenation
Right mindfulness	Maintaining awareness of the larger picture, instead of only the immediate perception or project
Right concentration	Full involvement in the moment, in a nondualistic way that does not see the self and the other or the environment as separate entities

THE FOURTH NOBLE TRUTH: THE EIGHTFOLD PATH

Eightfold Path the method for achieving an end of suffering, described in the Fourth Noble Truth

Middle Way description of the path to Enlightenment by avoiding extremes, such as extreme asceticism or extreme self-indulgence

Suffering exists; it will end if craving ends; craving can end. How? The Fourth Noble Truth outlines an **Eightfold Path** for achieving this: right view, right intention, right speech, right action, right livelihood, right effort, right mindfulness, and right concentration (see Table 16.2). This path is sometimes called "the **Middle Way**" because it avoids the extremes of either self-indulgence or self-mortification (de Silva, 1990), as Siddhartha learned when he realized that neither extreme asceticism nor extreme indulgence brought lasting satisfaction. He nearly died from an excess of asceticism by not eating enough to sustain life; he then accepted food, even asking for more—although other monks criticized his weakness (Nhat Hanh, 1996).

Sumedho (1992) notes that the body can be used as a memory aid for these eight components. The head reminds us of the importance of right view and right intention. The body reminds us of the importance of right speech, action, and livelihood. The heart reminds us of the importance of right effort, mindfulness, and concentration.

The responsibility for following the path and attaining the goal of nirvana rests with each person. Teachers show the way, but neither they nor any higher power grants salvation. This is one instance in which Buddhism is much closer to Western psychology than religion.

Buddhism and Personality Concepts

Buddhism's understanding of human personality is rich indeed. It offers insights into many of the topics that personality psychologists have included in their theories, including the self, behavior, emotions, social relationships, and more.

SELF OR EGO

Thinking positively of our selves seems so very important, yet many people lack self-esteem. The Dalai Lama was astonished when he asked a gathering, including many psychology professionals, how many of them had experienced a lack of self-esteem, and many raised their hands (Kamilar, 2002). Self-esteem requires self-acceptance, yet our culture teaches self-doubt. (Carl Rogers's concept of conditional positive regard makes this point.)

"Who am I?" is a familiar question in the Western psychological tradition; it is the basis for measuring the self concept and an indicator of our identity. Western psychology generally accepts the idea of a stable self, one that is gradually discovered in many Western personality theories; and some Western religions describe a soul that endures even beyond physical death. In contrast, Buddhism teaches that the self, like everything else in the universe, is impermanent (Paranjpe, 1998). There is no enduring separate self. The Lotus Sutra, a major teaching in Mahayana Buddhism, teaches "that the universe and the individual self are one and the same; that is, that our life is itself the macrocosm" (Dudley-Grant, 2003, p. 109). The self can be compared to a wave on an ocean; it appears, then disappears, and is part of the whole, not a separate entity.

Buddhism teaches that we do not know ourselves. We may not be quite as wrong as a deluded mental patient who claims to be God, but we are nonetheless deluded. Each time we think we know ourselves, we are wrong. We are not our thoughts, not our wishes, not our reputation. All these are fleeting. Before enlightenment, people grasp, mistakenly, at various aspects that they take for a self. Traditional Buddhist teaching lists five such nonself aspects described in the Buddha's teachings: the physical body, feelings, perceptions, intention or will, and consciousness (Williams, 2000). The Buddhist idea of **anatta**, or "no-self," says that in reality, there is only a sequence of changes and not a stable, permanent self. Buddhist monk and teacher Chögyam Trungpa (2005) describes the Buddhist view as "egolessness." Attachment to illusory ideas of self impedes progress toward the goal of liberation from the cycle of rebirth (e.g., Williams, 2000).

> *anatta* no-self; the doctrine that there is, in reality, no fixed, stable, enduring self (although the illusion of one may be constructed from fleeting impressions)

According to early (Hinayana) Buddhist teachings, the self is an obstacle because the self is attached to illusion, constructed on a false or wishful foundation. What is this illusion? Young-Eisendrath (2002) describes it as "the illusion that the individual self is enduring and needs to be protected" (p. 71). There is no role for defense mechanisms from this viewpoint. Geshe Thupten Jinpa, who has translated works of the Dalai Lama, puts it this way: "The existence of self as an independent, eternal, and atemporal unifying principle is an illusion; [and] . . . the grasping at such a notion of self lies at the root of our suffering and bondage, i.e. our unenlightened existence" (2000, pp. 10–11). Zen Buddhism, which often uses language to show the folly of our conceptions, describes a concept of self as unnecessary, as like "adding legs to a snake" (Gaskins, 1999, p. 209).

The goal of development is **nirvana** "which represented the final annihilation of all 'selfhood' and attachments, the causes of suffering" (Dudley-Grant, 2003, p. 108). The term *nirvana* is derived from a Sanskrit word referring to extinguishing a flame; it is the fire of desire that is extinguished. This goal includes eliminating craving for interpersonal attachments such as those described by attachment theorists (cf. Chapter 6).

> *nirvana* the goal of spiritual development, in which there is no attachment, and therefore suffering has ended

Western tradition, including psychology, emphasizes the development of an independent, autonomous self. This sense of separateness from others, although it has been central to our Western traditional views of psychological health in our individualistic society, is coming under attack. Harris (2004) asserts that "Almost every problem we have can be ascribed to the fact that human beings are utterly beguiled by their feelings of separateness" (p. 214). Depression is one common form of suffering that can be understood as stemming from a cultural overemphasis on individualism. Even so, because the self has been so central to a person's development in our culture, renouncing the self by precipitously adopting a Buddhist perspective can be threatening because there is so little to replace it (Michalon, 2001).

TRANSIENCE AND MORTALITY

In contrast to the illusion of, and the longing for, a stable self, Buddhism teaches that things are constantly changing. Our perception, for example, is a sequence of transient moments in sequence. Thought, too, is one transient image after another. We may assemble these transient thoughts into what appears to be a stable world of matter, but reality is more accurately described as *momentariness*. Meditation allows a person "to deconstruct the apparent stability of things, and to see directly the world as a *process*, a *flow*" (Williams, 2000, p. 85). This is true not only on the scale of everyday life, and of the seasons, and of the life span. It is also true on a cosmic scale. Instead of one origin of the universe—a point about which even literal creationists and "big bang" cosmologists agree—Buddhism teaches that the universe has been created and destroyed many times, and this continues to occur.

Buddhist scholars have given considerable attention to causality, both in the realm of human personality and in a more general sense. The arguments are deeply philosophical and difficult, but it is clear that they do accept the basic premise of cause and effect and have considered in detail the transitory nature of experience and how change occurs over time (e.g., Brown, 1999). Observations of mental states during meditation contribute to this knowledge, especially as they focus on awareness of the present moment.

Without recognizing the transitory nature of existence, many people cling to various states of existence, fearing loss, fearing death. In contrast, in the Buddhist worldview, patterns repeat: There is rebirth. Yet it is not an endless cycle. There can be spiritual progression from one lifetime to the next (although regression is also possible). The current condition is higher or lower, depending on the level of spiritual development attained in one's previous lives; this is one aspect of karma.

The awareness of mortality is one of the primary reasons why people turn to religion. But whereas most religions deal with this by describing an immortal soul that does not die, Buddhism does not, and in this way it is more comparable to modern psychology, which is silent on the issue of a soul (cf. Loy, 2002). Psychoanalyst Erich Fromm, one of many Western psychoanalysts who studied Buddhism, described a Zen-inspired meditation in which he practiced his own death, merging with the great cosmic oneness that psychoanalysts call an "oceanic feeling" of infantile unity with the mother, and which Buddhists conceptualize as relinquishing the illusion of an individual self (Maccoby, 1995).

BEHAVIOR: ITS CAUSES AND CONSEQUENCES

Behavior is produced by thought and intention, whether wise or unwise; the mind is causal in this theory. Behavior, including antisocial or maladaptive behavior, can be changed by stopping the underlying thoughts. The emphasis on thought as a cause of behavior is also an important theme in psychology's cognitive behaviorism. Buddhist practices include various techniques that are similar to some modern behavioral methods of control, including rewards, modeling, aversion, and thought stopping, among other techniques (de Silva, 1990; Dudley-Grant, 2003). But for Buddhism, it is not simply a matter of substituting other thoughts, as some Western psychological techniques suggest. Rather change requires ceasing the chronic egoistic self-observation that is the habit of an undisciplined mind.

Action is not always necessary. When one Western academician met the Tibetan Buddhist teacher Chogyam Trungpa and remarked that, because of upheavals in his life he did not know what to do, the monk's reply was "Why do you want to do something? How about doing nothing?" (Goleman, 2004, p. 308).

Consequences of Behavior: Karma

Buddhism assumes that people have free will and make choices about their lives and these choices have consequences. Mental training to purify intention is central to Buddhism (Williams, 2000).The term **karma** refers to intention and to volitional activity. Such willful action has consequences, called *Vipaka*. (Many people use the term *karma* to refer to both the action and its consequences—as when a child climbs on a stool to take a forbidden cookie—karma—but falls down and gets hurt in the process.)

Intentions, good and bad, have results, not only in this lifetime but beyond. Buddhism (like Hinduism) assumes rebirth. Unlike the Christian notion of heaven, rebirth occurs in the ordinary physical world. The circumstances of rebirth depend on the karma of the prior life. Prior good acts elevate the circumstances of rebirth in the next life; bad behavior will

karma intentional or willed activity, which produces consequences (positive or negative, depending on the action)

have the opposite effect. Depending on one's karma, rebirth can be to various states: in hell or purgatory, as an animal, a ghost (these three being lower than human, a result of bad karma), a human, a god, or a jealous anti-god (Williams, 2000). The gods in this worldview are not perfect or enlightened, although some are higher than others; many have some of the same faults that humans possess: anger, pride, and so on. From the human state, if enlightenment is attained, then the cycle of rebirth ends.

Westerners have difficulty understanding rebirth because we assume an individual self. Buddhism, in contrast, views the idea of a fixed individual self as an illusion. Rebirth is not the repackaging of an individual in another body; there is no fixed self or soul to be repackaged. What is reborn is not what we know as the individual person, not a "fixed soul," according to Paranjpe (1998, p. 124), but rather the karmic consequences of the past life. Put differently, "at death the psychophysical bundle reconfigures" (Williams, 2000, p. 69). The physical death of an individual does not stop the karmic consequences of that person's intentional behavior.

The idea of karma provides an incentive for good behavior, but it can also be used to tolerate the plight of those who are unfortunate in social status, reasoning that they deserve their suffering. Survey data of Indian college students indicate that those from higher castes are more likely to accept statements like this: "It is proper to bear without complaining our current miseries as rightful dues for our deeds in a previous life" (Paranjpe, 1998, p. 340). Lower caste college students reject such statements, which after all would undermine their dissatisfaction with their unfairly low status.

Dependent Origination

Although karma states an important causal principle, the result of intentional action, it is not the only cause-and-effect relationship. Another principle is that of *dependent origination*. This idea comes from Hinduism, where the "Net of Indra" describes a jeweled net, full of reflections of every jewel in every other jewel. Everything is interconnected; nothing is separate (e.g., Thomson, 2000). In Buddhism, the doctrine of dependent origination emphasizes that many interconnected factors determine any condition. Isolated causes do not exist. The individual's attitude is one factor in this field of interconnected causes, and it is one that the individual can and should control by free will (cf. karma). But the idea of dependent origination also acknowledges other causes, which may include biological predispositions, social factors, and so on.

MIND AND BODY

Buddhism asserts that the physical world and consciousness are not distinct, in contrast to the general assumption in the West of the separation of body and mind. Neuroscientists and philosophers, sometimes in discussions with Buddhists, have been deliberating how physical processes in the brain are related to conscious experience. Is the physical process primary, with consciousness an effect? Is consciousness primary? When I think that my choice is causing me to act in a particular way (as common sense tells me), is that true or perhaps only an illusion (Nahmias, 2005; Wegner & Wheatley, 1999)?

Psychology and medicine recognize that psychological factors influence the body. Stress predisposes to illness, for example, and psychological factors influence recovery from illness (e.g., Nelson et al., 1989). The Buddhist worldview goes further. Because mind and body are not two separate entities, there does not need to be a physical intermediary as part of every explanation. For example, the Buddhist monk Thich Nhat Hanh

(2001) asserts that anger can be caused (in part) by eating angry chickens, those who have been caged inhumanely and who suffer from confinement. Our Western mentality would either take this statement as a metaphor or would look for some physical mechanism for the connection—a molecule in the chicken that can be ingested and absorbed by people, for example. In the Buddhist view, in contrast, the body and the mind are not separate but linked as a "body/mind formation *namarupa . . .* the psychesoma, the body-mind as one entity. The same reality sometimes appears as mind, and sometimes appears as body" (Nhat Hanh, 2001, p. 14). Furthermore, the separateness of the chicken and the chicken eater is questioned.

Consciousness

Ordinary consciousness is chaotic, with ideas rapidly jumping from one thought to another. The undisciplined mind can be considered to be like a wild horse (Trungpa, 2005) or a drunken monkey that has been stung by a scorpion (cf. Saraswati, 2002). This undesirable condition can be improved by meditation (discussed later). Buddhism does not confine itself to ordinary waking consciousness, unlike most Western approaches, which are suspicious of "mystical" thought (Paranjpe, 1998). Buddhism encourages altered consciousness through meditation, and according to Walsh (1988), Tibetan Buddhists have practiced lucid dreaming, in which the dreamer is conscious of dreaming and able to exert some control over the dream, for over 1,200 years.

Buddhism advocates a transformation of consciousness, conveyed by the metaphor of awakening. The term *budhi*, the root of Buddhism, means "to wake up" (Dhammika, 2005). A classic story of the Buddha conveys this awakening image. After attaining his insight, he seemed to radiate some special quality, causing people to ask what he was—some kind of special spirit, a god, a wizard, or what? His response: "I am awake."

At other times, the change is called "enlightenment." One critic characterizes this as a poor translation, one reflecting the Western enlightenment era but that distorts the meaning (Kearney, n.d.). Others describe enlightenment as a higher stage than awakening. **Awakening** involves recognizing the true nature of things and the path to achieving Buddhahood (one's true nature), whereas enlightenment comes later, when one has overcome imperfections and delusions by following the path (Chen, 1999).

> **Awakening** a transformation from ordinary consciousness in which a person recognizes the true nature of things and the path to spiritual progress

A model proposed within the Transcendental Meditation program describes seven distinct states of consciousness. The state attained in Transcendental Meditation is midway up the hierarchy. Below it are three states that are familiar to us: deep sleep, dreaming sleep, and waking state. After the transitional fourth state of transcendental consciousness come three that are even higher: cosmic consciousness, God consciousness, and unity consciousness. At these higher states, the self is no longer separate from the rest of the universe (Alexander, 2005).

The puzzle of what is real is not easily resolved. Like many traditions, Buddhism offers explanations through stories. Consider the following traditional story, recounted by Shore (2003, p. 30):

> Once Chuang Chou dreamt he was a butterfly, a butterfly flitting and fluttering around, happy with himself and doing as he pleased. He didn't know he was Chuang Chou. Suddenly he woke up and there he was, solid and unmistakable Chuang Chou. But he didn't know if he was Chuang Chou who had dreamt he was a butterfly, or a butterfly dreaming he was Chuang Chou. Between Chuang Chou and a butterfly there must be *some* distinction! This is called the Transformation of Things. (*Chuang Tzu*, chap. 2; quoted in Watson, 1968: 49)

Am I a butterfly? A man dreaming of a butterfly? Escape from the presumptions of the familiar self, upon awakening, can be quite confusing—an identity crisis beyond the usual sense of the term.

EMOTIONS

All personality theories deal with emotion in one way or another. Buddhism offers insights as well. Emotions can interfere with growth, but happiness is the natural consequence of following the right spiritual path. Emotions can be made more healthy through learning, and a collaborative project between Buddhists and Western scientists and educators has developed a curriculum, called Cultivating Emotional Balance, to teach emotional health in eight sessions that include both meditation and Western psychological techniques (Mind and Life Institute, 2006).

Happiness

The goal that individuals should seek, according to the Dalai Lama, is happiness. By this he means not momentary pleasure but the lasting happiness that Tibetan Buddhism calls *sukha*. This happiness comes from an internal source, not from external things or experiences. It requires long years of discipline to achieve (Ekman et al., 2005). Although it sounds simple—after all, who doesn't want to be happy—Buddhist tradition teaches that genuine happiness is not easily obtained. Things that seem to bring happiness in the short run often have opposite consequences farther along: junk food, drugs, and passionate encounters, to name a few. If only we knew the true nature of reality, we would make wiser choices and so would be happier. Buddhism provides a path for learning the true nature of things, so the delusions and illusions that obscure our understanding and cause suffering can be overcome.

Current psychological research supports Buddhist teaching that happiness does not come, in any lasting way, from material possessions. However, there are differences, too, such as psychology's current emphasis on biological mechanisms of happiness, including genetics and brain biochemistry (e.g., Davidson, 2003; Klein, 2006).

Anger

Buddhism is labeled as one of the world's "unangry religions," according to a classic analysis (Stratton, 1923/2005). Buddhism strives for tranquility and peace. In contrast, religions categorized as angry religions, including Christianity and Islam, accept and even encourage some aggressive acts. Holy wars have been fought in both religious traditions, whereas Buddhism has a history of pacifism.

Buddhism describes people who are possessed by anger as being in a "hell realm" marked by aggression against enemies and their retaliation. Looking at the world today, it does feel very much like such a hell realm. How can this end? As Buddhist teaching is summarized by Scott Kamilar, "the only way out of this realm is to observe one's feelings of anger and hatred clearly. This is symbolically represented by the Boddhisattva of Compassion holding a mirror" (p. 93). Anger diminishes when a person's sense of self expands to include compassionate identification with others. Without clinging to desires and without protecting an individual self, the individual is not provoked to anger.

Buddhism offers techniques for dealing with anger: "the method of mindful breathing, the method of mindful walking, the method of embracing our anger, the method of looking deeply into the nature of our perceptions, and the method of looking deeply into the other person to realize that she also suffers a lot and needs help" (Nhat Hanh, 2001, pp. 24–25). Notice that none of these techniques rejects the anger. Anger must not be set apart from the self, isolated as a rejected bad self, to be overpowered by the accepted good self. Instead, it must be brought to awareness and treated with compassion, as one would a loved but immature brother or sister (Nhat Hanh, 1996). Acceptance and understanding of one's anger transforms it, removing the delusion or ignorance that is its cause.

Brain scans show that people are able to regulate their emotions, at least to some extent, when they choose to do so. People who have been instructed to continue thinking about the negative emotion elicited by a picture they have just seen, compared to those who turn their thoughts elsewhere, show different brain activity. Neuroscience expert Richard Davidson suggests that people who have difficulty controlling their anger have been influenced not only by physical causes such as genetics, but also by early social experience; he proposes that training experiences could be developed, based on understanding the brain circuitry involved, to teach such people to control their emotions better (Davidson, Putnam, & Larson, 2000). In one case, an institutionalized, mildly mentally retarded adult learned to control his aggressive impulses so successfully that he was released to the community. He was taught to focus attention on the soles of his feet instead of on whatever had triggered his anger (Singh et al., 2003).

Love and Other Emotions

It's not only negative emotions like anger and hatred that are eschewed in Buddhism, however. Even pleasant emotions can be problematic, under some conditions, because they interfere with an accurate perception of reality. In linking our positive emotions to some person or object in the outside world, we lose touch with the truth that happiness truly comes from within (Ekman et al., 2005). Buddhism warns against sexual passion (although accepting sexual relationships in the context of love and commitment), and even attachment to family and friends, because all of these disturb the calm and unattached mind. Early Buddhism rejected even joy and love, but modern Buddhism is more accepting of these emotions (Stratton, 1923/2005). Emotion, like so many other aspects of human experience, needs to be guided by the Middle Way, avoiding excesses.

It is interesting that both aggression or anger and passion are two of "three poisons" named by Buddhist teaching at one stage of development of the self. Passion tries to possess what we desire, whether a person or object. Aggression rejects the object or person. The third poison is ignorance, in which we avoid or are indifferent to something (Kamilar, 2002). Don't these three bear a similarity to Karen Horney's three interpersonal orientations: moving toward, moving against, and moving away?

INTERPERSONAL RELATIONSHIPS AND SOCIETY

People who have come to grips with emotions and have grown beyond the illusion of a separate self are also transformed in their interpersonal relationships.

Compassion

Compassion *(karuna)* is a central concept in Buddhism. Compassion is similar to the term *love* in Western approaches (McDargh, 2000). We might also compare compassion to empathy, the term more often used by psychologists, or to Adler's concept of social interest.

Compassion for others comes as a natural consequence of realizing that the separate self is an illusion (Loy, 2002), and so the selfish desires of the individual have no merit. When there is no separate self, the suffering of others is not separate from and outside the self. The Dalai Lama portrays a mother breastfeeding her infant as a powerful symbol of this love, conveying the innateness of compassion to human nature (Bstan-dzin-rgya-mtsho, 2001). Intriguingly, the relationship of early life social experience to happiness has additional support from neuroscience. Researchers measured the prefrontal brain activity of 10-month-old infants. Those whose right hemispheres were relatively more active were more likely to cry when they were briefly separated from their mothers, whereas left hemisphere activity predicted not crying (Davidson & Fox, 1989). In rats, those exposed to early maternal licking and grooming—care that is more frequent when the mothers are themselves less stressed—developed physiological changes (including increased receptors for benzodiazepine in the amygdala and locus ceruleus) that made them more able to cope with stress in later life (Davidson, 2000; Francis & Meaney, 1999). Early social experience shapes the brain.

In the tradition of Mahayana Buddhism, as described in the Lotus Sutra, the individual self and the universe are the same. So one should not seek so much to deny the self as to expand or enlarge one's concept of self so it is connected with the universe and all others (Dudley-Grant, 2003). This begins with smaller networks of friends and gradually expands to include more and more people, all humans, and all creatures (Hayes, 2003). The environmental concerns of Buddhists today flow from this compassion because harm to the earth produces harm to living creatures.

Spiritual progression is accompanied by increased compassion, not only for fellow humans but also for other creatures. Buddhist monks filter their drinking water to remove bugs, not for fear of their own welfare but out of compassion for the insects that could be swallowed. Perhaps the ultimate compassion is shown by a **bodhisattva**, one whose spiritual progress would enable him or her to be released from the cycle of rebirth, out of the world of suffering, but who remains back out of compassion to help those who have not attained that degree of development. A bodhisattva is described by McDargh (2000) as "the one 'whose essence is perfected wisdom.' " This definition makes clear that the compassion is a consequence of knowledge; conversely, lack of compassion is caused by wrong views of reality.

> **bodhisattva** a spiritually enlightened person who remains in the world to help others on their spiritual path

Intergroup prejudice and violence, understood from a Buddhist perspective, stems from attachment to difference—in the language of social psychology, to social identity and in-group bias (Dockett & North-Schulte, 2003). Buddha argued against the Hindu practice of categorizing people by their caste of birth, regarding their own level of development as more important; and more recently, activists in India found greater support in Buddhism than in Hinduism for efforts to eliminate caste-based prejudice (Chappell, 2003). Group identity is a slightly expanded version of attachment to the individual self but still falls short of the compassion for all living creatures to which Buddhists aspire.

Peace

Although the focus of Buddhist practice is on individuals, its impact permeates throughout the world. In the Buddhist worldview, all individuals are reflected in all others (cf. the Net of Indra, explained earlier). An individual who personally moves toward inner peace creates a more peaceful world. To scientific ears, this is a metaphorical statement that requires specifying the mechanisms. Does a peaceful world come about through certain kinds of interpersonal interactions, for example, such as the greater ability of the more peaceful individual to listen empathically to others, producing in turn their reduced animosity?

Some claims for the peace-producing potential of meditation cannot be reconciled with science as we know it. For example, some researchers report that by assembling a critical number of meditators in a violent area of the world, they can change the collective consciousness or stress level enough to produce a measurable reduction in acts of violence. Such a strategy was reported in the Middle East, where meditators in locations as distant as the United States were credited with reducing war-related acts of violence and death in Lebanon and Israel (Davies & Alexander, 2005).

Peace interventions also take a more comprehensible form. Buddhist monk Thich Nhat Hanh left his native Vietnam, one of several monks who became engaged in humanitarian and peace efforts as a result of the war in Vietnam, and he has applied Buddhist ideas to the search for peace and offered many workshops to Westerners. He has met with world leaders, including Pope Paul VI, Dr. Martin Luther King, Jr., and American secretary of defense McNamara (Nhat Hanh, 1996), and he was nominated for the Nobel Peace Prize. He has offered retreats and workshops to help peace activists learn how Buddhist practices, including the anger management practices described earlier, can help reduce the suffering of war.

Community

sangha a community living in harmony and awareness

Although Buddhism stresses the development of the individual's consciousness, this is not done in isolation, and its benefits are not limited to the individual. The term **sangha** refers to "the community that lives in harmony and awareness" (Nhat Hahn, 1996). The individual is not isolated and is affected not only by his or her own actions but also by others (Nhat Hahn, 1996).

Another lesson about community may be drawn from the story of Siddhartha, described earlier. Recall that he practiced extreme asceticism before finding the Middle Way. He learned to be needy in relationship to other people and to accept their support. Nearly starving, he accepted milk from a milkmaid. A young boy tending buffaloes thought he had nothing to give, but at Siddhartha's suggestion, he gave him grass from which to make a cushion to sit on (Nhat Hahn, 1996). Only after accepting these gifts did Siddhartha's meditation result in his final enlightenment. This may be a noteworthy lesson for those who seem to be more psychologically advanced than others, to whom others turn for help (including psychotherapists). We must receive as well as give. Sometimes this insight is easier to understand in the language of self or identity; if one's self-perception is focused on being strong and helping others, then clinging to this self-image is one sort of attachment that must be let go.

Other Social Issues

Americans, consistent with the individualism of our culture, have focused more on Buddhism's implications for personal development than on its implications for social transformation, although environmentalism and the peace movement have strong Buddhist support. Yet some Buddhists work actively for social change in political and economic spheres, and in that aspect of their work they may be closer to community psychologists than to psychotherapists (Dockett, 2003). The later Mahayana school of Buddhism is more involved in such social action than is the older, more introspective Theravada Buddhism (Jason & Moritsugu, 2003).

Environmental problems stem from human selfishness, from attachment to individual desires that lead to exploitation of the environment. This attitude reflects ignorance of the interdependence of all things, which is a fundamental Buddhist teaching, a teaching that in Chinese and Japanese Buddhism describes aspects of nature, including plants and mountains, as having a Buddha-nature (Yamamoto, 2003). A higher consciousness would not spew toxins out of smokestacks or degrade the landscape with strip mining or clear cutting of forests. Most Buddhists do not eat animals, either, although some Tibetan Buddhists are not vegetarian (owing to the harsh mountain climate that makes nutrition more problematic).

Spiritual Practices

Eastern religions offer various paths to spiritual development. Meditation is a basic practice that has been the focus of considerable research, so it receives particular attention here.

In a broad sense, the term **yoga** refers to any of several spiritual self-development paths. The most familiar to Westerners are the paths that involve physical postures, but there are other yoga types. Even the physical posture types of yoga are not solely, or even mainly, about physical fitness but are paths to spiritual development (see Table 16.3).

yoga spiritual practice; various forms exist

Buddhism, like Hinduism, provides guidance through various exercises and the direction of a **guru**, a spiritual teacher. Various teachers offer different kinds of practices to stimulate awareness. Zen Buddhism calls our logic into question by posing riddles, or **koans** (literally meaning "test," according to Kamilar, 2002) that cannot be resolved through the usual methods of logics. One famous example: What is the sound of one hand clapping? (The traditional answer is for the student to slap the teacher's face.) The goal is not to engage in scholarly Olympics, though, but to cut through obstacles that arise because of thinking. Simple actions, unimpeded by thought, are encouraged. Often stories make the point:

guru teacher; spiritual adviser

koan in Zen Buddhism, a riddle that is posed for the purpose of overcoming preconceptions and so furthering spiritual enlightenment

> A monk said to Chao-Chou, "I have just entered this monastery. Please teach me."
> Chao-Chou said, "Have you eaten your rice gruel?"
> The monk said, "Yes I have."
> Chao-Chou said, "Wash your bowl." (Aitken, 1990, p. 54; quoted in Gaskins, 1999, p. 209)

TABLE 16.3	Some Types of Yoga Practices
Yoga Type	**Description**
Bhakti yoga	Cultivates love by contemplating a saint, teacher, or God
Hatha yoga	Disciplines the body through exercises and postures
Karma yoga	Serves others, thus relinquishing egocentric motivation and addiction
Jnana yoga	Through contemplation, relinquishes false self-concepts and explores reality

In another story, Chü-Chih, a Zen master, had an attendant who imitated his master's habit of holding up one finger (as the master did when he was asked a question). Imitation is not what a teacher wants; enlightenment must be individually experienced. Chü-Chih dealt with this imitation by cutting off the boy's finger, causing great pain. The boy ran off but returned when his master called and, seeing the master raising his finger, is said to have become enlightened (Heine, 2002). The goal of enlightenment cannot be achieved by imitating an authority; teachers only facilitate the learner on the path.

MEDITATION

meditation a practice in which attention is consciously regulated to enhance serenity and well-being

Meditation is a fundamental practice in Buddhism in which attention is consciously regulated to achieve insight and enhance well-being. Depending on the form of meditation, consciousness may be focused on a particular object (such as breathing) or it may be more passive, attending to whatever thoughts and sensations arise spontaneously. With practice, the "drunken monkey" of consciousness is tamed, and power of the mind over consciousness and the body increases. With meditation, the grosser layers of consciousness driven by passions and by outside stimuli are calmed, and the more "subtle" layers of consciousness can be experienced. These can harness powerful forces (Bstan-dzin-rgya-mtsho, 1989).

Many varieties of meditation exist, each with particular practices and, to some extent, distinct outcomes. In general (with some exceptions), they have a calming and joyful effect. Meditation focuses on regulating attention, producing calmness and enhanced awareness, without harmful distractions. Because much everyday thought is nonproductive and even counterproductive, with worry and distraction, the result is expected to be improved cognitive functioning. The Dalai Lama quotes an ancient Buddhist saying: "If the problem is such that there is a solution, there is no need to worry about it; if there is no solution, then there is no point in being overwhelmed and paralyzed" (Bstan-dzin-rgya-mtsho, 2003). This focus on only productive thought may be the basis for his response, when asked how he could not be angry at all that the Chinese had taken from him and from his country: "Why should I give them my mind as well?" (Lefebure, 2005, p. 84).

concentrative meditation a form of meditation in which attention is focused on a particular object, such as the breath or a word or phrase (mantra), one of the best known being the mantra "om"

Two major types of meditation—concentrative and mindfulness meditation—are often distinguished (although there are variations that cross these categories). **Concentrative meditation** focuses attention on an object, often the breath, but sometimes a sound or an image. This helps reduce distractions that come from external stimuli and also reduces one's own distracting thoughts. *Transcendental Meditation* (TM) is a concentrative form of meditation that was developed a half century ago and is copyrighted and marketed; it aims to convey ancient practices to the modern world in schools, businesses, architecture, and other settings (The Transcendental Meditation program, 2005). **Mindfulness meditation** allows thoughts to appear as they will and observes them without judgment. Zen meditation, called **zazen**, and Vipassana meditations are types of mindfulness meditation.

mindfulness meditation a form of meditation in which thoughts are observed but not judged

The Process of Meditation

zazen meditation; sitting meditation; practiced in Zen Buddhism

Meditation frequently focuses attention on breathing or sometimes an external object. An advantage of breathing as a focus is that it is always present, and it comes to be a conditioned stimulus for the meditative mindset, carrying some of the benefits into everyday life. The body is held in a position that aids concentration, typically a seated, cross-legged lotus position. During meditation, awareness is maintained and monitored, but the usual duality of self and other is removed. A frequent metaphor for the effect of meditation on the mind is water. Without meditation, the surface of the water is full of waves and turmoil that prevent us from seeing what is below. With meditation, the surface of the water becomes calm and still. The depths can now be seen. Thus meditation permits knowing the deeper contents of the mind, the "subtle" consciousness, that is obscured by the frenzy of unregulated attention.

Meditation turns focus away from external objects, inward. Instead of pleasure produced by the external world, meditators report experiences of inner joy. The blissful state reported by experienced meditators has been compared to that produced by opiates; perhaps it results from a release of these endogenous brain chemicals, the endorphins (Austin, 1998). One Transcendental Meditator described states of "deep, unbounded silence, during which I am completely aware and awake, but no thoughts are present. There is no awareness of where I am, or the passage of time. I feel completely whole and at peace" (Travis & Pearson, 2000, p. 81). This description illustrates the "pure consciousness" that is the goal of the meditation. The person is alert and aware but not disturbed by specific content of consciousness. According to Travis and Pearson (2000), such states can be attained without meditation and are a natural potential of human nature that has been described in diverse cultures. They describe physiological correlates of such states, including decreased autonomic activity and increased peak power of the EEG (a sign of alertness).

During meditation, a person notices thoughts that arise, without clinging to them or rejecting them, without judgment. Sensations from the body are observed. Teachers warn meditation students not to judge whether a meditation has been successful or not but simply to observe and to continue the practice on a regular basis. A variety of subjective experiences, some pleasant and some troubling, occur naturally. First beginning to meditate, people may experience intrusions of many thoughts that have been previously suppressed, some of them from the distant past. Sometimes the presence of another being, a spiritual visitor of some sort defined by the person's tradition, is reported. Rarely, psychiatric difficulties precipitated by meditation have been reported, and the opportunity for exploitation of their followers by unscrupulous meditation gurus has sometimes marred both traditional Eastern and newer Western practices (Andresen, 2000).

Although the experiential reporting of meditators is rich, it is hard to quantify. Researchers have devised a scale consisting of Likert-type items to measure mindfulness, the Freiburg Mindfulness Inventory. It consists of items such as this: "I watch my feelings without getting lost in them" (Walach et al., 2006, p. 1553). Scores increased, as expected, with meditation practice.

Meditation and the Control of Attention and Perception

During meditation, attention is focused. What about afterward? Some research supports the idea that focused attention improves after meditation. In one study, a group who had practiced meditation twice daily was compared with a wait-list control of aspiring meditators who had not yet begun (but who sat quietly each day). After 3 months, the meditating group had become more accurate on two perceptual tasks; the control group remained unchanged. The experimental group became more accurate in judging whether a vertical rod was exactly vertical, despite the distraction of a misaligned surrounding frame (the Rod and Frame Test). They also could locate more hidden pictures in the Embedded Figures Test (Austin, 1998). Other research also provides evidence that meditation improves performance on tests of creativity, practical intelligence, field independence, and other cognitive tasks (So & Orme-Johnson, 2001) and that it helps the elderly maintain their intellectual abilities (Nidich, Schneider, et al., 2005).

Subjective experience is not determined by external input alone but by a person's response to it. The practice of meditation teaches a person to observe and change that response, thereby gaining control over subjective experience. Ordinarily, when sensory input—what we see or hear, for example—comes in, we immediately respond to it. In the language of psychology, *sensation* (the incoming light or sound waves that trigger neural response) is immediately followed by *perception*, the meaning we impute to those sensations (perceiving a snake or a rope, for example). It is so immediate that the sound of a class-ending bell and the perception "class is over" have no pause in between for reflection!

Perceptions, however, are not the stimulus (sensation) but rather our creation of it, and they can be wrong or incomplete. That point is clear in the familiar story, told in Buddhism and other cultures, of the several blind men who touch various parts of an elephant. The specific details vary from one telling to another, but the point is clear: Each perceives a different reality, based on partial information. The man who touches the elephant's leg describes the beast as like a pillar or a tree trunk; the one touching the elephant's side says it is like a wall. The one who touches the ear likens the elephant to a large basket or a huge leaf. The one at the tail end describes a snakelike animal. The tusk led another other to say it was like a plowshare. Each has only a partial view of the elephant; perception is limited. Obviously perception (the sense we make of our sensations) can be wrong. In this example, the blind men each came to a different conclusion, and the story is often used to encourage the listener to honor other people's perspectives, which may be based on information that they themselves lack.

Consider another interpretation of this story of the blind men and the elephant: that if each of the blind men had not been so hasty to identify the incoming sensations, he might have remained open himself to more information, perhaps exploring more of the elephant's body. By pausing longer between sensation and perception, we may make fewer errors. We should not remain fixated or attached to our perceptions of reality. In a translation of the original Buddhist story of the blind men and the elephant, the Buddha is said to have characterized the quarreling blind men, and the quarreling religious scholars about whom the parable was told, as "attached" (Bhikkhu, 1994). Attachment to perception is one of the kinds of attachment that must be forfeited in following the Buddhist path to enlightenment.

Attachment to the self, as discussed earlier, must also be given up. Measurement of brain changes during meditation help us conceptualize the experience of being conscious and aware but not focused on the self or on any specific content of experience—that is, "pure conscious experience," or awareness of only consciousness itself. Brain studies show that when meditators report being in this state, they show increased alpha waves, increased frontal blood flow, and decreased blood flow in the visual regions of the brain; they are more autonomically aroused by sudden, unexpected stimuli (Taylor, 2002).

An interpretation by Austin (2000) suggests that the sense of self (or, rather, various aspects of the sense of self: I, me, and mine) are constructed by processes in the brain that involve sensory input. We know that neural firing is subject to inhibition as well as activation, and Austin suggests that meditation practices can produce such inhibition, thus preventing the inputs that are necessary to experience a self. Some of the brain areas that he suggests play a role are structures in the temporal lobe that give us a sense of self in space, including the emotionally important hippocampus and the amygdala; and parts of the parietal and frontal lobes involved in attention, intentional acts, and awareness of time. He proposes that a small area of the thalamus can close the "gate" of incoming sensory information that normally provides input to the sense of self. Similar to the lack of such information that people experience under sensory deprivation conditions or in the transition into sleep, experienced meditators can "close the gate" to these sensory inputs and so experience a nonself state, the *anatta* described earlier. Austin suggests that endogenous opioids and acetylcholine could achieve this inhibition, noting that the opioids are especially interesting because morphine has some similar effects to the proposed meditation outcome: fearlessness, pain reduction, and euphoria. Even the ecstatic mystical phenomena sometimes reported in meditation could be caused by endogenous opioids (Austin, 1998). Without the experience of self, the meditator experiences peace, joy, timelessness, and connection to a world that is experienced more purely, without the distortions of attachment to self. How profound a change this is from normal consciousness; our sense of self, developed over a lifetime of interaction with the world and carrying with it the legacy of traumas and fears and misperceptions, is temporarily set aside!

Self and nonself, brain chemistry and the like, are interesting but a bit abstract. Consider the following very concrete and somewhat amusing study of perception. This study, not surprisingly, caused some of the Tibetan Buddhist monks who were research subjects to express "mild bewilderment towards the study's aims and motivations" (Carter et al., 2005b, p. R1). Researchers presented monks, during meditation, with a binocular rivalry task. Horizontal lines were presented to one eye and vertical lines to another, through a device strapped to their heads. Typically people perceive each of these images sequentially, and the perception fluctuates back and forth as the brain tries to coordinate the input from the left and right eyes. Could the monks, experienced through meditation in controlling incoming stimuli, experience something different? Indeed they did. The meditating monks reported that the images stabilized in one or the other (horizontal or vertical) form for much longer periods of time than was typical for this task. One reported that he could hold one of the stabilized images indefinitely. These effects occurred for only one type of meditation, one that focuses attention on an object. Compassion meditation did not produce the effect, even in the same monks (Carter et al., 2005a). It seems clear that meditation practice, lasting for several decades in some of these monks, does indeed alter perception.

The 17 Moments of Perception.   The distinction between unprocessed incoming sensation and meaningful consequent perception is analyzed far more extensively in Buddhist teaching than in psychology. The introspection that early psychologists, a century or so ago, used as a tool is about as similar to Buddhist teachings about perception as a child's reader is to Shakespeare.

According to Buddhist teachings, mental processes create the illusion of something that is solid and permanent, from transient sensations. The classic Buddhist texts, the Pali canon, describe 17 successive moments of perception, which can be made known through carefully trained introspection (Lancaster, 1997). Beginning with unawareness or unconsciousness of the object of sensation, it is not until the 6th moment in this sequence that the person "receives" the object, described by Lancaster as "a simple feeling tone . . . which at this stage is merely 'agreeable,' 'disagreeable' or 'neutral'" (p. 126). At this point, the person has not yet identified the object. At stage 8, the mind responds to the object but has still not identified it (Lancaster, 1997).

Consistent with this ancient teaching, current psychological studies have found that research subjects can respond to the emotional tone of a stimulus without knowing consciously what the object is. If, indeed, emotional reaction to an object comes before identification of the object, then psychoanalytic defense mechanisms become more understandable, particularly because the process of perception can be stopped at this stage, without progressing to full awareness (Lancaster, 1997).

The Dalai Lama challenges us to become aware of some of these stages that usually pass so quickly that we are unaware of them. If we can hold them in awareness, we may be able to experience a state called *pure awareness*, before perception. At this point, our notion of "self" has not yet entered into the process. In a catchy title, Mark Epstein (1995) describes this as *Thoughts without a Thinker*. Stopping at this point, though, is not easy. Not only is this difficult to achieve, but with the emphasis in modern Western psychology on "the self," it even seems that our discipline is moving in the opposite direction, inserting the self into many psychological processes instead of considering that it might be an impediment.

Observations by neurologists document kinds of mental functioning that do not fit our ordinary concept of consciousness, that may correspond to the Buddhist description of the earlier stages of perception, including blindsight and implicit memory (Lancaster, 1997). In Western science, though, these phenomena are observed through cases of people with brain damage (blindsight) or through contrived experimental tasks (implicit memory), not through trained introspection. Thus Western science had not considered that such states could be produced willfully.

Mindfulness meditation "shift[s] the focus of attention progressively earlier in the perceptual or thought process" (Lancaster, 1997, p. 139). This makes it possible to experience incoming sensory input before they are processed in terms of the self system, the awareness of "I," which in the Buddhist worldview distorts them. Lancaster (1997) proposes that Buddhist descriptions of incomplete processes, where sensory input does not proceed all the way to conscious perception, correspond to various phenomena that have been observed in modern psychological studies. The sort of implicit processing that happens in amnesia, he suggests, corresponds to the *abhidhamma* tradition of a "great object," in which perception proceeds only to the 15th stage. The last two stages, when conscious awareness of the object would occur, do not happen. Lacking the last two stages, which involve the concept of self (or "I"), memory is impaired. Nonetheless, enough perception has occurred to affect behavior.

Another correspondence is to the phenomenon of subliminal perception, which corresponds to the *abhidhamma* tradition of a "slight object," in which processing is incomplete at an even earlier stage, before the sensory stimulus has been interpreted and before its self-relevance has been interpreted.

Emotions do not require full progression through all 17 stages of perception. Positive and negative emotions are activated at earlier stages. As research continues, we may discover that mood disturbances, such as depression, could be treated by teaching specific kinds of control over these stages of perception. We may learn that the dissociation of consciousness that occurs in hypnosis and in some diagnostic categories reflects a condition in which part of the perceptual process stops earlier while a related process continues further. In hypnosis experiments, a subject denies feeling pain but a "hidden observer" is able to report the pain that a nonhypnotized person feels when subjected to the pain test, immersion of a hand in ice water. Meditation may provide a way to understand and make therapeutic use of the discrepancies between what people know consciously and how they feel and behave, allowing clearer understanding of defense mechanisms.

Brain Measurement during Meditation

The meeting of Eastern spiritual traditions with Western scientific technology has resulted in many observations of brain activity while people—both relative novices and decades-long practitioners—meditate. Benson and his colleagues (1990) reported that Tibetan monks living in India were able to reduce their resting metabolism to 64%, or increase it by 61%, through meditation. Meditation has been compared to the lowered metabolic state of hibernation in other species (Young & Taylor, 1998). In 1992 the Dalai Lama (Tenzin Gyatso, the 14th Dalai Lama of Tibet) and the American neuroscientist Richard Davidson, himself a meditator, began studying longtime meditating monks with neuroscientific measurements (Hall, 2003). The brain's functioning may well be different in a person who has only been meditating a few weeks or months and a person who has been meditating for decades, so access to these world-class meditators provides an unprecedented and irreplaceable opportunity to assess the potential of meditation.

Meditation generally produces slower EEG activity, increased alpha wave activity (and increased feelings of calmness associated with this pattern), both during meditation and thereafter, and also increased theta waves during meditation. Over time, meditation changes the way that the brain responds to stimuli (Cahn & Polich, 2006).

Although alpha and theta waves are the usual finding, EEG gamma waves, too, have been reported elevated among long-term meditators (Lutz et al., 2004). In this study the type of meditation was one of compassion and loving kindness, without a specific object. Different forms of meditation produce a variety of neural activity patterns, and results are also affected by the experience of the meditators and the particular tasks presented (Cahn & Polich, 2006). Even within a single form of meditation, it is not a steady state but can change as it progresses. One meditator was being recorded when he experienced a state of ecstasy, and the recordings showed a sudden increase in autonomic activation (Andresen, 2000).

Researchers have explored the metabolism of various brain areas using positron emission tomography (PET) techniques, functional magnetic resonance imaging (*f*MRI), and blood flow using single-photon emission computed tomography (SPECT) imaging. These measurements offer more detailed evidence of brain activity than EEG measures. Many brain areas change during various meditation studies, including the thalamus, the basal ganglia, the frontal, temporal, and parietal lobes, and others. The specific findings vary depending on the type of meditation and the experience of the practitioners (Andresen, 2000; Ritskes et al., 2003). There is so much excitement about measuring the brain during meditation, but it is far too soon to say that this type of brain wave, in that particular location, is the locus of enlightenment. Suffice it to say that clearly meditation has effects on the brain.

Habituation. *Habituation* means that, with repetition, the same stimulus no longer triggers the response that it earlier did. Typically, when a relaxed person with high alpha activity is confronted with a stimulus, such as a noise, there is a decrease in alpha activity (*alpha blocking*) as the brain's cortex processes the stimulus. (Relaxation interrupted; what was that stimulus?) A classic study of Zen meditators found that with repeated auditory click stimuli, the meditators continued to show this alpha blocking, evidence that they remained open to the moment and continued to respond to each new stimulus. In contrast, control subjects became habituated to the stimulus quickly and it no longer triggered the alpha blocking (Kasamatsu & Hirai, 1973).

Later studies sometimes replicated this finding of nonhabituation in meditators and sometimes did not. Variation in these results can be attributed (at least in part) to the kinds of meditation. Those that focus on fully experiencing each moment (mindfulness meditation, including Zen meditation) do not show alpha blocking habituation; the stimulus continues to interrupt alpha activity. However, forms of meditation that emphasize concentration do show alpha blocking habituation as the meditator tunes out the interruption and focuses on the object of meditation (Cahn & Polich, 2006). Thus the choice of meditation technique tells the brain how to respond: a case of mind over matter.

Processing Emotional Stimuli.   What about emotional stimuli? That would be of particular importance for personality. According to Richard Davidson (2005), who has frequently discussed Buddhist meditative practices and their relationship to science with the Dalai Lama, happiness can be increased by meditation. People can, at least to some extent, regulate their emotion, and doing so increases their resiliency to adversity (Davidson, 2005). He has confirmed this using brain-imaging studies. Research subjects who were shown upsetting pictures, such as a infant with a tumor on its eye, showed more activation of the amygdala when they focused on the negative emotions and less activation when they were instructed to think positively, that the tumor was successfully removed (Davidson, 2005). Another study shows that subjects who were instructed to continue the negative emotion induced by a stimulus (such as a picture of a gun pointed toward them), after the picture was removed, maintained their elevated amygdala activity longer, confirming the impact of voluntary focus of conscious attention (such as occurs during meditation) on brain activity (Schaefer et al., 2002).

A Russian laboratory found that experienced Sahaja Yoga meditators (a form of mindfulness meditation) were less affected by an emotionally distressing video clip (a scene from the film *Funny Games* in which two young people are abusing a family), compared to a control group of nonmeditators (Aftanas & Golosheykin, 2005). Both subjects' subjective ratings and their brain activity showed the meditators to be less distressed. Brain EEG recordings showed that the meditators had larger alpha and theta waves (indicative of relaxation, bliss, and inward concentration or the meditative goal of thoughtless awareness). These differences occurred even though the meditators were not instructed to meditate during these film viewings, which is consistent with other evidence that the effects of meditation endure into ongoing life.

Emotions are also involved during the stages of perception described earlier. When perception is delayed—for example, when we are unable immediately to recognize a sound as a bell or a siren—we are vigilant and especially attentive. The heightened vigilance can be pleasant, as a stimulant drug or an exciting sports activity is pleasant. That seems to be what meditation practitioners have managed to learn to do, and it could explain the positive emotion and heightened awareness produced by meditation. Brain mechanisms that could contribute to this attentiveness have been suggested: inhibition of incoming sensory stimuli from the posterior thalamus (similar to what happens normally in sleep) and vigilance because of stimulation from the sciatic nerve as a result of the usual cross-legged sitting posture of meditation (Austin, 1998). Specific neurotransmitters could also play a role, including dopamine, acetylcholine, and serotonin (Austin, 1998; Kjaer et al., 2002; Newberg & Iversen, 2003).

Clearly meditation produces change in the functioning of the brain. Could it also change its structure, as (by analogy) exercise changes not only the functioning of muscles but also their bulk? Comparing a group of Western meditators who regularly practiced Buddhist insight meditation with a control group of 15 nonmeditators, MRI showed that the meditators had greater cortical thickness in certain brain areas, those associated with attention, interoception, and sensory processing (Lazar et al., 2005). Although the study was cross-sectional, and so rests on the assumption that the matched control group did not differ except in meditation experience in ways that could produce these effects, the researchers suggest that meditation influences the physical structure of the brain. This is consistent with other studies showing that the brain responds structurally to use.

Ongoing collaboration between experienced meditators and neuroscientists promises to identify more rigorously specific brain mechanisms that have been brought under voluntary control through the discipline of meditation. What an exciting expansion of biological approaches that promises: biology not as simply the cause of subjective experience (as in the attribution of depression or anxiety to an imbalance of neurotransmitters) but as the mechanism by which human will and practice can achieve control of subjective life.

Psychological and Health Effects of Meditation

Meditation has been used as a method for treating an astonishing variety of medical and psychological problems (see Table 16.4), and a meta-analysis confirms its overall value in improving health (Grossman et al., 2004). Some claim that meditation can reduce the cost of health care (Herron & Cavanaugh, 2005).

Meditation offers an alternative, nonpharmacological approach for the treatment of attention deficit disorder (Arnold, 2001). Perhaps it is not surprising that improved ability to concentrate attention, achieved through meditation, has also been found to improve memory, intelligence, and academic performance (Walsh & Shapiro, 2006).

TABLE 16.4	Examples of Conditions for which Meditation has been Used as Treatment
Anxiety	
Asthma	
Atherosclerosis	
Cancer	
Chronic pain	
Criminal behavior	
Diabetes	
Drug abuse	
Fibromyalgia	
High cholesterol	
Hypertension (blood pressure)	
Infertility	
Insomnia	
Irritable bowel syndrome	
Learning disabilities	
Muscle and joint pain	
Premenstrual dysphoric disorder	
Psoriasis	
Psychiatric conditions (inpatients)	
Stress disorders	
Stuttering	

Source: Information from several sources, including Carlson et al., 2004; Grossman et al., 2004; Kamilar, 2002; Keefer & Blanchard, 2002; Monk-Turner, 2003; Seeman, Dubin, & Seeman, 2003; Walsh & Shapiro, 2006.

Meditation has become a popular alternative treatment for a variety of stress-related disorders, including hypertension, headaches, and insomnia, and it is reported to also reduce pain (Andresen, 2000). Self-report measures indicate increased relaxation (Gillani & Smith, 2001). Indeed, the "relaxation response" popularly described by Benson (1975) describes the stress-reducing effect of meditation. Later critics suggest that it is an over-simplification to describe meditation as a relaxation response (Austin, 1998), although it often has that effect. However, sometimes meditators become more responsive to exper-imental stimuli, consistent with a heightened state of awareness, and this can increase stress reactions instead of decreasing stress.

During meditation, physiological indicators typically (but not always) show reduced stress and increased relaxation: lower heart rate and respiration rate, lower levels of cor-tisol, plasma lactate, and catecholamines (e.g., MacLean et al., 1997; Travis, 2001). Immune response improves (Aftanas & Golosheykin, 2005). An experimental study of healthy biotechnology employees documented reduced stress and improved immune activity as a result of meditation. Some were trained to meditate and then compared with a randomly assigned wait-list control group (Davidson et al., 2003). After only 8 weeks of mindfulness meditation training, these new meditators not only reported that they were less anxious; they also showed a significantly greater rise in antibody titers when they were given an influenza vaccine, evidence of improved immune system functioning. The immune system improvement is particularly impressive because self-reported anxiety reduction could theoretically be an artifact of demand characteristics, a potential source of error in research that occurs when subjects respond (consciously or not) in ways that they think the researcher expects or wants (Austin, 1998).

Meditation produces physiological changes that indicate reduced stress and lower arousal of the sympathetic nervous system: lowered blood pressure and heart rate, reduced oxygen consumption, slower breathing, and reduced levels of lactic acid (Barnes, Treiber, & Davis, 2001; Barnes, Treiber, & Johnson, 2004; de Silva, 1990; Wenneberg et al., 1997). Most impressively, the death rate of hypertensive older people who were randomly assigned to Transcendental Meditation interventions was significantly decreased, by 30% for cardiovascular causes and also significantly for cancer (Schneider, Alexander, Staggers, et al., 2005). Findings such as these, which have been replicated in other studies, suggest that meditation could be an effective additional strategy for pre-venting and treating cardiovascular disease, which is of particular value for populations at high risk for such health problems, such as African Americans (Schneider, Alexander, Salerno, et al., 2005).

The dramatic results of meditation surprised researchers who were monitoring, for research purposes, the impact of a drug that increases sympathetic nervous system func-tioning. One subject showed an unprecedented dramatic drop in heart rate of 17 beats per minute at a time in the procedure when it should have been increasing by about 21 beats. What was going on? She reported that she had been meditating. When the proce-dure was repeated without meditation, her heart rate increased instead, as it had for the other subjects (Dimsdale & Mills, 2002).

Besides physical health benefits, meditation has psychological effects, too. The goal of a meditative retreat described by Davidson (2001) is to enhance one's own personal happiness and to cultivate compassion toward other people, especially those with whom one has had conflict and those who are suffering. Meditation produces a change in the sense of self, moving the experience away from the experience of a self separate from others, and toward a state that encompasses all that is around, a state described by some as "transcendental" in which an individual is more an aware witness than a sepa-rate being (Cahn & Polich, 2006). This state of consciousness, it is argued, moves people to higher levels of moral development, for example to a seventh stage that Lawrence Kohlberg added to his influential stage model of moral development (Nidich, Nidich, & Alexander, 2005).

Another study compared meditators at a school where Transcendental Meditation is a major part of the curriculum with matched undergraduates at other schools, and reported that over 10 years, those from the meditating college showed significantly greater gains in ego development and moral reasoning (Chandler, Alexander, & Heaton, 2005). Measures of defense mechanisms improved after an intensive, but only 7-day, meditation retreat in Thailand using Buddhist Vipassana techniques that encourage recognizing the self is only transient. Participants developed increased maturity of ego defense mechanisms and greater tolerance for common stressors (Emavardhana & Tori, 1997).

Some of the experiences reported during meditation, however, are strange. People sometimes experience dramatic emotional reactions that may be accompanied by physical experiences such as trembling and painful sensations. These are traditionally taken as evidence of progress in meditation. More speculatively, they have been interpreted as reenactments of memories of birth (Bache, 1981). By stopping the later developed ways of thinking, it is plausible that earlier modes of consciousness can surface, and those that predate language would be especially likely to be expressed in physiological and emotional terms. Indeed, one model of meditation and other altered states of consciousness (including dreaming, hypnosis, long-distance running, and some drug-induced states) suggested that deregulation of various functions of the prefrontal cortex, a higher-order integrative structure of the brain, occurs in these states, accounting for such experiences as time distortion and loss of the sense of self in meditation (Dietrich, 2002).

Effects of meditation can permeate everyday life. We generally think of meditation as a very separate activity: sitting in a special position, stopping our regular activity. However, a meditative state of mind can be present during everyday activities, increasing mindfulness. An experimental study (Kohlmetz, Kopiez, & Altenmüller, 2003) found that an experienced musician and meditator could play complex music (Erik Satie's *Vexations*) on the piano while meditating, and brain recordings indicated a trance. People who practice Transcendental Meditation regularly have reported that the states of consciousness first experienced in such meditative states then begin to coexist with their waking and sleeping states of consciousness, and EEG recordings are consistent with these reports of experience (Mason et al., 1997; Travis et al., 2002). So meditation does not necessarily mean stopping everything else. In fact, some spiritual advisers recommend maintaining a meditative state during everyday activities.

Buddhism and Psychotherapy

Among psychologists, psychotherapists are often enthusiastic supporters of the Buddhist viewpoint and of meditation. This seems reasonable; both approaches expect dramatic improvements in a person's well-being to come from changes in consciousness. Let us consider first the contributions that Buddhism offers to understanding psychotherapy more generally. Then we turn to one common issue: addiction.

APPLICATIONS TO PSYCHOTHERAPY

Jungian psychoanalyst Polly Young-Eisendrath (2002) succinctly describes the similar goals of therapy and Buddhism as a decrease in personal suffering and an increase in compassion for others. Mindfulness meditation allows thoughts to appear and be recognized but not judged, a practice that is in many ways similar to the free association practiced by Freudian psychoanalysts (Kamilar, 2002). Other types of therapy, too, value a nonjudgmental stance (Miller, 2002).

There are, of course, differences. Therapy focuses attention more on symptoms than on health, and so it is more helpful when people have particular psychopathologies (Khong, 2003). Buddhist practices are suitable for people who function at too high a level to be thought candidates for psychotherapy (Ekman et al., 2005).

Cognitive behaviorists have incorporated aspects of meditation into their treatments for a variety of disorders, including eating disorders, phobias, addiction, and obsessive-compulsive disorders ("Integrating," 2002; "Meditation in Psychotherapy," 2005). *Dialectical behavior therapy* treats borderline personality disorder by integrating Zen Buddhist principles, including acceptance and mindfulness meditation, to a cognitive behavioral approach (Robins, 2002). Different clients have different needs. Clients who are relatively disturbed may require ego-strengthening work; the detachment from an inflated ego, using a Buddhist approach, may be more helpful to those whose difficulties come from a later developmental point, including midlife crises (Michalon, 2001).

Although meditation offers an alternative to medication, it also can work in conjunction with it. Because meditation heightens awareness of a person's own physiological condition, it can be a useful tool for measuring the effect of antidepressant medication, so that changes in type or dosage of medication can be made more precisely (Bitner et al., 2003). Effects of antidepressants may include beneficial changes, including reduction in anxiety and depression, but also undesirable ones, including reduction in positive emotions such as happiness and love, and a reduced frequency of peak experiences, those ecstatic and transpersonal states described by Maslow and experienced more frequently by meditators (Walsh, Victor, & Bitner, 2006). The experience of meditators has the potential for use as an instrument for learning about these various effects of medicines.

Meditation is useful for therapists to cope with their own stress and avoid burnout (Shapiro et al., 2005). It can improve their ability to listen to their clients, without distortions based on their own preconceptions (Finn & Rubin, 2000; Michalon, 2001). It improves their ability to tolerate problematic emotions and helps them deal with countertransference issues (Thomson, 2000). Thus meditation helps therapists to set aside their own needs and their theoretical preconceptions in order to be truly present with the client.

In one sense, the meeting of psychoanalysis with Buddhism is surprising because psychoanalysts seek to strengthen the self, whereas Buddhists challenge it (Morgan, 1996); but there is self and then there is self: one, a deluded, sick self that Buddhists challenge and psychoanalysts attempt to "shrink," and another a real self, however dimly known, however different from what we usually think of as "self," that is revealed when delusions and fixations are dispensed with.

MOTIVATION AND DESIRE: UNDERSTANDING AND TREATING ADDICTION

Buddhism asserts that desire or craving produces suffering. Surely addiction can be thought of as a problem of unhealthy craving. A healthy growth pattern is to experience the patterns of desire and seeking fulfillment but then to move on to something higher. (Here, the psychology of Abraham Maslow's need hierarchy is similar. In his approach, once lower-order needs are met, a person is no longer preoccupied by them but moves toward higher-order needs.) But at a less developed level, once the temporary pleasure has passed, we seek the next source of pleasure—another consumer product or sexual partner or drug hit, for example—instead of moving up to a higher level of consciousness. Addiction occurs when a person becomes fixated on fulfilling one type of need and does not move higher. The satiation does not recede in value but remains salient (Dudley-Grant, 2003).

Why does this occur? Biological approaches, such as those described in Chapter 9, suggest that the genetically determined physiology of some people makes them particularly susceptible to reward, including the pleasure produced by drugs. Such an interpretation, although quite comfortable to most modern psychologists, does not represent the worldview of Buddhist psychology. It does not deny physical processes by any means, but it does not seek explanation of human experience and development at that level either.

Sometimes the term *addiction* is applied to behaviors, such as "sex addiction" or "workaholism," that do not have an obvious physiological component. Critics of this terminology suggest that such maladaptive behaviors should be described in behavioral terms, as habits. Buddhist teachings are relevant to both physiological addictions and behavioral patterns. Both kinds of craving are included in a level described as the **hungry ghosts**. The term *preta* is used in Buddhism to refer to the hungry ghost realm, which is one of six realms or styles of experience (see Table 16.5). The hungry ghosts have gigantic and empty bellies, but they cannot eat enough to be satisfied because their mouths are tiny. This imagery describes a variety of cravings: physiological cravings that cannot be satisfied, and also, at a somewhat higher level, the sorts of behavioral "addictions" just listed. Interpersonal attachments, the desire for fame and fortune, or any compulsive hoarding can be encompassed in this model of unhealthy craving.

The Buddhist model offers an alternative sort of spirituality to the one implied by the idea of a Higher Power, which is the model assumed by 12-step approaches to treating addiction (such as Alcoholics Anonymous). Buddhism does not include a god in its worldview, and so it may be more acceptable to those who reject deism (Dudley-Grant, 2003).

Buddhism offers advice about dealing with cravings, and so it has practical value for alcoholism and other addictions. One intervention to treat addiction and consequent HIV-risky behavior was developed by integrating Buddhist principles, such as mindfulness

hungry ghosts
(pretas) one of several realms of existence in Buddhist teaching, characterized by persistent, unsatisfied cravings

---

TABLE 16.5   The Six Realms of Experience

Realm	*Characteristic emotions and experience*
Realm of the gods	Pride; ego striving; self-consciousness
Realm of the jealous gods	Paranoia; distrust; defensive pride
Realm of humans	Passion; striving for high ideals; intellectual concerns
Realm of animals	Lack of self-consciousness; egocentrism; stubbornness
Realm of the hungry ghosts	Neediness; vulnerability to addictive substances and behaviors
Realm of hell	Anger; aggression; hatred

Prepared from information in Trungpa (2005).

and compassion, with cognitive behavioral techniques (Avants & Margolin, 2004). Meditation provides a time of respite from the pressure of everyday life, and it is a ritual that often strengthens a person's commitment to self-improvement and spiritual growth. Meditation may displace unhealthy ways of dealing with stress and anxiety, including the use of drugs and alcohol. Especially if accompanied by cognitive therapy, meditation is more effective than attempts at suppressing thoughts about desiring drugs; the thought is observed and then let go (Kavanagh, Andrade, & May, 2004).

In describing his clinical work with addiction, Marlatt (2002) notes that several Buddhist teachings facilitate a therapeutic result. The idea of impermanence emphasizes that no drug "high" can last permanently. The eightfold path offers a curriculum for the gradual and multifaceted changes that need to be made. The Buddhist concept of the "Middle Way" offers an important insight for those who have relapsed from sobriety. By recognizing a difference between one episode and a full-blown return to being controlled by the drug, the addict has more hope of combating the disorder.

Although Buddhist principles in general and meditation in particular are promising for treating addicted people, the idea needs further research to determine whether it is effective, and if so, how it should be implemented. One study of a small sample of randomly assigned residents in recovery found no improvement for substance abuse patients with 8 weeks of mindfulness meditation training, when it was added to standard treatment (Alterman et al., 2004). Perhaps that was not long enough.

The Importance of the Dialogue, and Some Cautions

Science and religion have not always been happy partners. In the name of religion, scientific theories of the solar system (Copernicus), of evolution (Darwin), and of the so-called big bang that started the universe have all been criticized, and sometimes their supporters were persecuted. Scientists have also sometimes demeaned religious proponents.

Buddhism, however, is different. It is, among the world's religions, distinctly receptive to science (Young-Eisendrath, 2003). Buddhism provides insights into higher-order spiritual and moral issues, as do other great religions, but it is not dogmatic. As one consequence of its renunciation of attachments (detachment in this case from ideas), it does not cling to a particular set of scientific beliefs. Thus it remains receptive to new scientific knowledge, reinterpreting its own teachings to be consistent with advances in science over the centuries (Ratanakul, 2002). This openness to science may be why the eminent physicist Albert Einstein found Buddhism appealing:

> The religion of the future will be a cosmic religion. It should transcend a personal God and avoid dogmas and theology. Covering both natural and spiritual, it should be based on a religious sense arising from the experience of all things, natural and spiritual and a meaningful unity. Buddhism answers this description. If there is any religion that would cope with modern scientific needs, it would be Buddhism. (quoted in Dhammika, 2005, p. 9)

The dialogue between Buddhism (and other religions, too) and the science and practice of psychology is important; each gains from the interaction. What does Buddhism, and what does a religious or spiritual community more generally, have to gain from discussions with psychology? The Dalai Lama argues that mature ethics depend on a correct understanding of human nature (Bstan-dzin-rgya-mtsho, 1999, 2001) and psychology contributes to this understanding. How much free will or choice does a person have over behavior at any given moment? How does this choice increase or decrease, depending on the consequences of past behaviors? Arguably, too, the popularity of psychology offers Buddhists an inroad to achieve their aim of fostering the spiritual development of others.

Psychology, for its part, gains from the wisdom of the centuries, a wisdom that reflects considerable empirical observation (although without modern statistical evaluation and research design, through most of that history). The long Buddhist tradition of systematic observation of consciousness through meditation is a rich resource, offering a far more developed technique than the introspectionist methods of early psychology. Meditation practices have been fine-tuned and repeated by many people, and the effects are in large part predictable. Furthermore, the impact of meditation does not depend on acceptance of Buddhist beliefs. Somewhat similar processes occur in other religious traditions, including various mystical traditions and Christian prayer (d'Aquili & Newberg, 2000; Newberg et al., 2003). From these observations based on meditation, psychologists could devise better ways of observing subjective experience, an area that has been relatively neglected in recent years (Lancaster, 1997; Young-Eisendrath, 2003).

In considering Buddhist psychology, we must be aware of the many levels of understanding that are possible in trying to understand personality, from very objective traditional scientific studies of physical processes, to higher-order investigation of functioning persons, which encompasses a range of levels of understanding—the highest levels being spiritual and transpersonal. These multiple levels have intrigued and sometimes troubled personality psychologists throughout our history. Some tradeoff between science and a wholistic understanding of the person seems inevitable. Given this ongoing dilemma, the current conversations between wholistic Buddhism and neuroscience, the quintessential "science" for psychology, is truly exciting. Studies of brain functioning during meditation and prayer are sometimes interpreted zealously as providing evidence for the existence of God (Newberg, d'Aquili, & Rause, 2001), a claim that is dismissed by critics who instead understand such phenomena as unusual or even abnormal brain functioning, not the action of a deity (Pigliucci, 2004). We must not, however, leap prematurely to conclusions across the levels of understanding.

The science of physics, too, has been brought into the dialogue. Modern physicists describe large amounts of empty space within atoms, once considered solid and indivisible, which is sometimes interpreted as evidence supporting Buddhist claims of emptiness. Buddhists in dialogue with physicists have challenged the unidirectionality of time (Ricard & Thuan, 2001). Time, in the worldview in which Buddhism developed, is not always moving forward but is cyclical, in contrast to the assumption of progression forward that underlies psychology—for example, the forward movement toward self-actualization in humanistic psychology (Paranjpe, 1998). Subatomic physics has even been proposed as a mechanism for understanding the soul, angels, and precognition (the ability to foretell the future), by those ready to leap from physics to phenomenology (Benford, 2001). Although it is too great a leap to take subatomic physics as proof of spiritual claims, the imagery can facilitate changes in awareness of more psychological and spiritual domains. In a dialogue between Buddhists and physicists, Matthieu Ricard puts it this way:

> Buddhists don't want to determine the mass and the charge of particles, but instead to break down the notion that things are permanent and solid, so as to

> liberate us from the vicious circle of illusions that cause our suffering. . . . The impermanence of the macroscopic world is obvious to everyone, but reflection about subtle impermanence has deeper consequences. Phenomena contain the seeds of their own transformation, and the universe can contain no immutable entities. It's this very malleability of phenomena and of consciousness that allows us to undertake the process of transformation that finally leads to enlightenment. (Ricard & Thuan, 2001, p. 112)

Undoubtedly there are still many lessons to be learned as Buddhism and psychology, with other sciences, continue their dialogue. We need to be cautious about leaping from one level of explanation to another prematurely. Physics and neuroscience are of great value, but psychological assessments help fill the gap between these physical measures and the spiritual language of Buddhism. For example, self-reported mindfulness (on the Mindful Attention Awareness Scale, the MAAS) is correlated with psychological well-being and self-regulation (Brown & Ryan, 2003). Buddhist approaches offer new ways to think about the cognitions described by other personality approaches. How exciting is this dialogue!

Summary

- Buddhism, although a religion, makes many statements that are closer to psychology than to religion as Westerners understand religion.
- It describes the universal human condition of *suffering* and its causes, and it offers methods for ending suffering, in teachings called the *Four Noble Truths* and the *Eightfold Path*.
- Clinging to the idea of stability, including a stable self, is said to be ignorant and a cause of suffering.
- Buddhism is a religious tradition that has developed religious practices, especially *meditation*, based on understandings of phenomena that are of interest to personality theory: thought, the self, emotion, behavior and its consequences, to name a few.
- Meditation is now used by some Western psychotherapists and medical practitioners in conjunction with other therapeutic interventions to deal with stress, anxiety, and many other disorders.
- Neuroscientists studying meditating monks and other meditating subjects have found that the practice does change brain functioning in various ways, depending on the type of meditation and experience of the meditator.
- These effects support the Buddhist claim of increased positive emotions from meditation.
- Benefits to physical health and to society are claimed to result from individual spiritual practice and development.
- Psychotherapists have incorporated meditation into their practice, including treatments for addiction, and neuroscientists are exploring the relationship of meditation to brain functioning.
- Changes in consciousness are central to the Buddhist approach.

Thinking about Buddhist Psychology

1. Which theories from earlier in the book are most similar to Buddhist psychology? How are they similar? How are they different?

2. Why do you suppose that Buddhist ideas have become popular among some therapists?

3. Compare and contrast the idea of the self in Buddhism with ideas that have been presented earlier in this text (e.g., Horney, Allport, Bandura, Rogers). Do you think that Western psychology's ideas of the self are based on illusion?

4. Can you propose a method for testing whether the concept of "past lives" is factually accurate? If so, how? If not, does it have value as a metaphor for experience, or should it be discarded?

5. Do you agree that Buddhism has a role to play within psychology, or should it be kept strictly as a religion?

6. Do you think a person who has trouble focusing attention and who is easily distracted (e.g., by sounds when taking an exam) would be helped more by concentrative meditation or by mindfulness meditation? Why?

7. Discuss the challenges and benefits of applying a theory to a different culture than that in which it was formulated. Do you think it makes sense to apply Buddhist ideas to Western culture? What about applying Western psychological ideas to Eastern cultures?

Study Questions

1. If Buddhism is a religion, why is it of interest to psychologists? Which psychologists, historically, have been interested in it?

2. Describe the life of Siddhartha Gautama and his role in the history of Buddhism.

3. What are the Four Noble Truths?

4. What are some of the translations of "suffering"? What are the implications of these translations for psychological statements?

5. What is the Eightfold Path?

6. What does Buddhism teach about the self?

7. Discuss stability versus change from a Buddhist viewpoint.

8. What is the relationship between the mind (especially intention) and behavior, in the Buddhist approach?

9. What is karma?

10. Explain the concept of dependent origination. How does this relate to the idea that there are multiple causes for events?

11. Does Buddhism describe the body and mind as separate, or not?

12. How does meditation aim to change consciousness?

13. What is Enlightenment? How is it different from Awakening?

14. How does Buddhism view emotions? In particular, what is the Buddhist attitude toward anger?

15. How does Buddhism view compassion? What produces compassion? What are its implications for interpersonal relationships?

16. Compare neuroscience research on emotion with Buddhist ideas.

17. Describe claims of the power of meditation to produce peace. Do you believe these claims? Why or why not?

18. What does Buddhism say about the individual in a community?

19. What is a *koan*?

20. Describe meditation. How is mindfulness meditation different from concentrative meditation?

21. Describe research, especially neuroscience research, on meditation. Does it support the Buddhist model?

22. What health claims are made for mediation?

23. How have psychotherapists used meditation? What are its effects on psychological problems, such as addiction?

24. How has modern physics been compared with Buddhist ideas? Do the similarities prove Buddhist ideas? Why or why not?

17

Conclusion

Chapter Overview

Contributions of the Theories to Various Topics
Choosing or Combining Theories
Theories as Metaphors
What Lies Ahead?
Summary

Many theories have been devised to explain personality. Why so many? Do they offer competing explanations of the same phenomena? Sometimes they do. More often, though, they address different issues, trying to explain divergent facets of personality. Theorists often portray personality differently because of their different observations— some in clinical consulting rooms, others in experimental laboratories, and many through self-report, written questionnaires. It is no wonder that emotional conflict and troublesome personal histories figure centrally in clinically derived theories, whereas others emphasize behavior, or conscious self-concept and beliefs about the world.

STATUS OF PERSONALITY THEORY

If there were widespread agreement in the field of personality on which theoretical concepts were most useful, we could say that a dominant paradigm prevailed (T. S. Kuhn, 1970). Agreement on a common paradigm would guide personality researchers in their choice of research questions and methods. However, no such agreement exists, as the diversity of theories in this text attests. Various perspectives compete: the psychoanalytic perspective and its sociocultural variant, the trait perspective, the learning perspective, cognitive behaviorism, and the humanistic perspective. No one perspective has been able to replace the others by demonstrating its clear superiority in explaining and predicting relevant observations. Indeed, lack of agreement about which observations are relevant makes it difficult to imagine the kind of direct scientific competition that would allow a critical test among theories.

Lacking a shared theoretical understanding, the field of personality is fragmented, although there are increasing movements toward integration. Multiplicity of theory is not necessarily undesirable (Koch, 1981). Having a number of limited-range theories, each developing concepts to understand a relatively narrow range of phenomena, may at some stages of scientific development lead to faster advances than a more comprehensive, but less precise, theory. Now, though, personality seems to be moving toward more communication among its component parts. Developmental processes of learning are building on biological foundations that include descriptions of individual differences (e.g., J. A. Gray's theory). Trait descriptions are being considered in an integrated way with dynamics of social interactions (e.g., Walter Mischel's theory).

The field is moving in the direction of a multilevel theory, not only combining insights from traditional personality theories but also drawing on findings from other fields (Caprara, 1996). At the level of biology, brain structure and function and the impact of heredity are beginning to suggest mechanisms by which development and dynamic processes occur, including documenting changes in brain function during meditation. Contributions come from systematic large-scale scientific projects, such as the investigation of heredity and personality (e.g., Loehlin, 1992). From earlier studies—for example, Cattell's findings about a genetic contribution to neuroticism—the way pointed to the relevance of genetics to the clinical behaviors that psychoanalysts and other therapists treat, but the earlier theories did not provide theoretical constructs for discussing such evidence. To be sure, Freud believed that inherited temperament influenced the development of psychological problems (Freud, 1908/1953; cited in Westen, 1998a), but that insight was not elaborated with a theory of *how* such hereditary influence occurs. After decades of development along separate lines, psychodynamic approaches and genetic approaches are now mature enough for meaningful dialogue.

Learning approaches and cultural approaches also contribute to the discussion. We can begin to understand that therapy problems represent emotional conflict, often about interpersonal relationships, that build on negative and positive emotionality stemming not only from biology but also from the cumulative impact of learning in the environment presented by particular families and cultures. Genetics contributes to the readiness with which a person becomes emotionally aroused; learning approaches describe the kinds of experiences that produce learned emotional responses that may be troublesome (and, not incidentally, the kinds of remedial experiences that alleviate such distress); and culture provides situations and social messages that make both kinds of learning experiences more or less likely.

Humanistic and cognitive social theories remind us that a self-aware person is at the heart of personality. The self-regulation of behavior builds on more basic levels (e.g., genetics and learning) in the process of building personality, but without conscious awareness, human personality is incomprehensible. That is not to say, of course, that all processes, or even most processes, are conscious but the way that individuals adapt to the world is, given its unique imprint by a sense of self. The heavy reliance of personality research on self-report measures is more understandable and less problematic when we are exploring this level of personality, the self-reflection made possible by human language.

Contributions of the Theories to Various Topics

Throughout this text the contributions of each theory to certain substantive questions have been summarized. (See the preview tables in Chapter 2 to 16.) Let us now review these contributions, looking for major themes.

INDIVIDUAL DIFFERENCES

How important are differences among people? Some theories emphasize the ways in which individuals are unique; others focus more on similarities. Trait approaches usually emphasize the identification of differences among people (with the exception of Allport's individual traits, Cattell's P-technique, and a few others). Learning theories traditionally analyze the behavior of individual organisms rather than making comparisons across individuals, but psychological behaviorism describes universal categories of learning that are the basis of personality, and cognitive learning theories compare individuals on such characteristics as self-efficacy and cognitive complexity. In the clinically derived theories of psychoanalysis and its revisions, differences are defined according to coping mechanisms (or diagnostic categories), but these are developed from shared universal conflicts. Many other theories, including the humanistic theories and Buddhist psychology, focus on dynamics common to all people.

What constitutes evidence of individual differences? Most personality research relies on self-report psychological tests for this measurement. Other evidence comes from observer ratings, measures of behavior in real life or in laboratory settings, clinical observation, and physiological measurement. As personality develops toward an explicit multilevel theory, we are beginning to appreciate the contributions of each data source for particular levels of study.

ADAPTATION AND ADJUSTMENT

Personality can be evaluated along a dimension of health or adjustment. In fact, some personality approaches consider the adaptive function of personality to be central to its definition (e.g., Allport). Many of these theories were developed in a clinical context, including those of Freud, Jung, Adler, Horney, Erikson, Rogers, and Kelly. Others, developed outside the clinical setting, have suggested new forms of therapy. These include the theories proposed by Skinner and Bandura, which suggest improving adaptation by teaching people more effective behaviors and (in cognitive approaches) more effective ways of thinking about oneself and life's tasks. Even Cattell's empirical theory has examined neurosis and psychosis and produced clinical diagnostic questionnaires. A few theorists criticize excessive theoretical concentration on maladjustment. Humanists and Buddhists are particularly concerned with the development of full human potential, and they call attention to the more integrated and developed self.

Healthy functioning is generally portrayed as integrated or unified—that is, with little conflict—and adaptive in the social world. Psychoanalytic theorists described intrapsychic conflict as evidence of maladjustment, and Dollard and Miller explained such conflict in learning terms. Allport also emphasized integration or unity. Many theorists, notably Freud, warn that unconscious processes, set in action by earlier maladaptive learning, can undermine healthy personality functioning. The unconscious has its advocates, though; Jung argued for a balance between the conscious ego and the unconscious aspects of the psyche, and Buddhists have long probed the deeper or "subtle" levels of consciousness.

Although most personality theories focus on the individual rather than considering society, a few theorists (e.g., Adler, Allport) have suggested that healthy personalities contribute more to society or bring fewer prejudices to social interaction than less healthy personalities. The evaluation of healthy functioning is affected by cultural values, as well as scientific considerations, because cultural values are implicit in personality theories.

Various therapy techniques have been developed that reflect the different theoretical interpretations of adjustment. Psychoanalysis, which emphasizes the unconscious, seeks increases in consciousness through insight. Rogers developed client-centered therapy and encounter groups to help restore the true self through unconditional acceptance by others. Learning theorists emphasize behavioral interventions through systematic reinforcement and through such techniques as discrimination learning. Cognitive learning theories identify expectancies as critical focal points for therapeutic intervention.

COGNITIVE PROCESSES

Theoretical developments in psychology generally and in personality in particular have often emphasized cognitive processes. Mischel and Bandura exemplify this tendency: They argue that cognitive concepts (e.g., person variables) are the most useful concepts for understanding personality. Realistic cognition is described as a criterion of mental health by many theorists (e.g., Freud, Allport, Rogers, Maslow, and Bandura). Many warn of unconscious forces that make such realism difficult (e.g., Freud, Horney), although others assert that conscious experience is generally trustworthy (e.g., Adler, Allport). Psychoanalysts also consider dreams and symbolic thought, which express the unconscious. Jung's work on the collective unconscious represents an extensive consideration of symbolic thought. Maslow, too, was interested in these less rational modes of cognition, including mystical experiences. Buddhist meditation practices explore depths of experience unmatched in Western approaches, with the expectation that this exploration will facilitate healthy development.

Individual differences in what are sometimes considered to be cognitive styles have also been explored. Jung described different cognitive functions (sensation and intuition, thinking and feeling), asserting that people vary in their use of these functions but that all should be fully developed for optimal functioning. Cattell's interest in intelligence resulted in improved scales for measuring mental abilities. Further, some of the scales of his 16PF reflect differences in cognitive styles.

Language is a significant concern of many theorists. It has been described as the key to making experience conscious and in making discriminations possible, thus facilitating healthy adaptation (e.g., Dollard and Miller, Staats, and other learning theorists). Cognition is central to Kelly's theory, which asserts that behaviors and emotions follow from a person's personal constructs. Mischel and Bandura further developed this idea, describing the cognitive processes of personality, including expectancies and self-efficacy.

SOCIETY

Personality is expressed through behavior in the social world. Healthy personality can have a positive impact on society, as Buddhists in particular emphasize. Failure in social behavior can motivate people to seek therapy to improve their personality, and personality tests are used to select people for social roles such as particular jobs. Allport's contributions to social psychology (prejudice, rumor, and religion) testify to his recognition of the importance of society in personality. Other trait theorists have compared trait scores cross-culturally (e.g., Cattell and Five Factor theorists). Learning theorists consistently attend to the social environment in their explanations of personality because it provides reinforcements and discriminative stimuli that direct behavior.

Society affects personality development. It provides tasks and models, and it influences the way parents raise children. Dollard and Miller described the importance of the social context for personality learning, and they explored social applications, including aggression. Erikson featured society throughout his life-span developmental theory; people develop by mastering psychosocial tasks, and cultural institutions continue to support ego strengths throughout life. Horney noted that changes that had taken place in society since the time of Freud affected the types of problems patients brought to therapy.

Increasingly, psychologists are focusing attention on the impact of historical, cultural, and socioeconomic conditions on personality (e.g., Baumeister, 1987; Markus & Kitayama, 1991; Marsella et al., 2000; McCrae, 2000; Zarate, Uleman, & Voils, 2001). Exploration of personality theories from other cultures and traditions—such as Buddhism (Nitis, 1989) and other Eastern approaches (Atwood & Maltin, 1991)—challenges us to recognize that the personality theories we have studied are biased by the individualistic assumptions of Western culture (cf. Bock, 2000; Cooper & Denner, 1998; Heine et al., 1999; Triandis, 1989).

BIOLOGICAL INFLUENCES

Personality theories have traditionally focused on the effects of experience and not of biology (cf. Steklis & Walter, 1991). Many theorists in the past recognize that biological motives provide a foundation for personality (e.g., Freud's libido, Maslow's lowest needs, some of Cattell's ergs). Only in recent years, with developments in neuroscience, are these vague statements moving toward precise theoretical assertions about specific neurotransmitter influences on such personality dimensions as impulsiveness and emotionality (cf. Chapter 9) and brain function correlates of altered states of consciousness (cf. Chapter 16).

Research on behavior genetics underscores the role of heredity on personality, including Cattell's personality factors and the Five Factor model. Studies of heredity can easily be misinterpreted, however. Depending on the environment, the effects of heredity can be magnified, for example, when the environment responds very differently to people with different genetics, as it may by providing different educational experiences to bright and less intelligent children or by putting children into environments where the energetic impulsive ones are likely to have difficulty adjusting while the quiet ones are praised. Or the effects of heredity may be minimized, if the environment does not provide opportunities for an inherited quality to be expressed.

Temperament differences, long studied by developmental psychologists, are being integrated into an understanding of adult personality, and descriptions of temperament are no longer simply behavioral but describe underlying biological bases (Kagan, 1994). Although biologically determined temperament undoubtedly affects personality, Chess (1986) cautions that temperament must be considered in its social context. The "goodness of fit" between an individual (including temperament and other aspects of personality) and "environmental opportunities, demands, and stresses" (p. 134) is a more useful model than simply temperament alone.

DEVELOPMENT

Most theorists agree that important personality development occurs in childhood. Psychoanalysis, in particular, considers the experience of the early years to be critical to personality throughout life, based on family experience (e.g., Freud, Adler, Horney). Rogers, from a humanistic perspective, also emphasizes the importance of parental behavior toward the child (unconditional positive regard). From a learning perspective, Staats challenges us to focus attention on the basic behaviors, learned early, which are the necessary precursors of later adjustment. Cognitive learning theorists have described the learning of adaptive behaviors such as the capacity to delay gratification (Mischel) and the ability to set high standards for performance (Bandura), calling attention to modeling and other learning influences. Many theorists describe a sequence of stages in which distinct developmental tasks are accomplished (e.g., Freud, Dollard and Miller, Erikson, Allport). The specific role that parents play in the child's personality development has been questioned (Harris, 1995, 2000).

Adult personality development builds on the foundation of personality developed in childhood. For many theorists, personality is largely stable in adulthood, the major developments having occurred earlier in life (e.g., psychoanalytic theories). To varying degrees, though, theorists would agree that significant personality change can occur in adulthood. Buddhism provides practices, such as yoga and meditation, to bring about this change. Jung described the individuation process of midlife. Erikson continued his life-span approach to development, proposing four stages of development from adolescence to old age. Cattell investigated personality change across time, finding that some traits change in adulthood (including anxiety and some types of intelligence), whereas others do not. Learning approaches suggest that relearning can occur at any time, although this relearning may not be able to build an entirely different personality. Like an architectural renovation of a building, which may add access ramps and new facades, but not change the basic structure of an edifice, relearning can improve personality but probably not undo the effects of decades of earlier learning.

The impetus for adult personality development can occur from external, societal sources or from within the individual. Some theorists emphasize external sources. Erikson said that adults, like children, develop by facing psychosocial crises and adjusting to the age-specific expectations of society. Learning theorists emphasize external determinants. Changes in reinforcements produce changes in behavior. Cognitive social learning theorists believe that subjective variables, such as self-efficacy, determine behavior. Because behavior in turn leads to reinforcements, these internal variables are indirect causes of development. Other theorists, like the Buddhists, Jung, and humanistic theorists, describe change as motivated directly by internal forces. It is not always easy to determine whether change or consistency should be attributed to causes in the environment or in the person. For example, people tend to marry those who are similar to them in personality. This similarity contributes to consistency of personality in adulthood (Caspi & Herbener, 1990), but which is the cause, the original personality or the spousal influence? As Bandura's model of reciprocal determinism suggests, mutual influences from the person and the environment occur. Change and stability in adulthood, then, occur for reasons that include both personal and environmental causes in complex interaction.

Choosing or Combining Theories

How many theories of personality are needed? Should we try to select the one best theory or devise a new single theory to guide the field? Or is it better to have the coexistence of several theories? Various opinions have been offered.

ECLECTICISM

One way of dealing with the diversity of theories is to advocate **eclecticism**. To be eclectic is to value selected contributions from diverse theories, without accepting any theory completely. For example, we could value psychoanalytic understanding of symbolism in art while at the same time accepting the usefulness of behavioral methods of treating

eclecticism combining ideas from a variety of theories

phobias. It certainly seems reasonable to use the best available theoretical tool when trying to understand a particular issue or when choosing the best form of therapy for a particular client (cf. Lazarus, 1989), so it is not surprising that many mental health professionals consider themselves to be eclectic (Jensen, Bergin, & Greaves, 1990). Eclecticism has limitations as a theory, however; it does not provide a systematic framework for understanding personality, so it cannot be verified as an overall theory. It does not offer a rationale for deciding when to select from among the diverse models. Nonetheless, because the available theories have such different areas of strength and weakness, many personality psychologists consider themselves to be eclectic.

PLURALISM

pluralism the coexistence of various theories without attempting to combine them

Various paradigms can coexist, each maintaining its theoretical distinctiveness. This is theoretical **pluralism.** At present, psychology is a pluralistic discipline (Walsh & Peterson, 1985), as should be apparent from this text. Many psychologists consider this to be the desirable condition, at least for the present. Terry Smith (1983) argues that it would be undesirable to focus entirely on one theoretical approach because we cannot be certain which one would be most productive:

> Given our current lack of knowledge, we should not be staking everything on what, through the dark glass of our ignorance, looks to be the best available alternative; but rather we should take a more experimental approach . . . and ask what alternatives are worth trying. Presumably there will be more than one. (p. 148)

Premature integration makes it difficult to define theoretical concepts clearly, and that impedes research and theoretical progress (London, 1988; Russell, 1986).

UNIFIED THEORY

unified theory a theory that combines diverse aspects from various approaches, indicating how they are organized and related

As sciences mature, they develop integrated theories. There have been many calls for the development of a multilevel unified theory that incorporates the various levels of explanation that personality psychologists have explored (e.g., biological, cognitive, and social). Arthur Staats (1981, 1991, 1996) argues that the time has come for psychology to develop a **unified theory**. In his view, all sciences progress from disunity to unity, as seen, for example, in physics. He says that it is time for psychology to search for links among phenomena that are now explained by diverse theories, and he urges greater respect for alternative points of view to encourage the discovery of conceptual bridges.

Several attempts to integrate theories have been made. Dollard and Miller, for example, combined psychoanalysis with learning theory, and many behaviorists since have advocated behaviorism as the unifying paradigm for all of personality theory (cf. Ardila, 1992). Convergence has also been explored between psychoanalysis and personal construct theory (B. Warren, 1990), between Adlerian individual psychology and behaviorism (Pratt, 1985), and between the theories of Erikson and Kelly (G. J. Neimeyer & Rareshide, 1991). Modern psychodynamic theory, which describes unconscious aspects of interpersonal relationships, has untapped implications for currently popular social cognitive theories (Westen, 1991) and many findings in laboratory studies of memory and emotion converge with clinical insights expressed by Freud and other psychoanalytic theorists (Westen, 1998b).

These convergences are still far from the vision of an integrated psychological theory, but such explorations are moving the field in that direction, and increasing numbers of personality researchers are venturing beyond narrower paradigms and asking larger questions: about emotion, about early experience, about people's self-concept, and so on.

One way to make sense of the diversity of theories is to recognize that they explain different phenomena, often at different levels. A unified theory will then be a **multilevel theory** (e.g., Hyland, 1985; Staats & Eifert, 1990). It is not unusual for important phenomena to be explained from diverse levels of explanation. In trying to understand why parents sometimes neglect and abuse their children, theorists have offered explanations at the historical level (e.g., attitudes toward privacy in families), at the current sociological level (e.g., poverty), and at the psychological level (e.g., the characteristics of the abusers), among others. Focusing on traits, such as neuroticism, and states, such as emotional reactions to the stresses of parenting, are two different levels of analysis for understanding parental abuse (Belsky, 1993). People simultaneously exist at several levels: as biological beings, as conscious and thinking humans, as behaving organisms, and so on. A theory may be more precise if it restricts consideration to only one level of explanation, but this restriction limits the comprehensiveness of the theory. Perhaps, though, a restricted one-level theory can be merged into a more comprehensive framework (much as Newtonian physics was incorporated into Einstein's more comprehensive theory).

Ultimately, personality theorists may be able to develop theories that include various levels of explanation. In the abstract, such an aspiration is not too difficult to imagine. Consider, for example, the humanistic idea of self-actualization. This high-level concept seems remote from a biological explanation, but at least one hypothetical model of brain functioning has been proposed: that the brain has two modules of neurons, one evaluating the present state and another evaluating an imagined alternative. If the imagined alternative is better, this discrepancy activates motivation to strive for that improved condition, and this motivation is parallel to self-actualization motivation (Levine, 1997). It is, however, a long way from this suggestion to a fully developed model that would offer detailed descriptions of all the processes involved.

> **multilevel theory**
> a unified theory that integrates various levels of explanation (e.g., biological, cognitive, social)

CRITERIA OF A GOOD THEORY: REVISITED

Recall from Chapter 1 the criteria of a good theory: verifiability, comprehensiveness, and applied value. Often, there are trade-offs among these requirements. Psychoanalytic, social psychoanalytic, and humanistic approaches attempt to explain a broad range of behaviors (comprehensiveness) but have concepts (e.g., libido and self-actualization) that are imprecise and not readily verified. Rogers's description of conditions of effective therapy, however, is phrased precisely and has stimulated research. Behavioral and cognitive behavioral theories have also engendered considerable research.

Besides the criteria generally accepted for evaluating theories, other standards are sometimes applied. For example, cognitive social learning approaches stand up well when evaluated for verifiability and applied value. Yet they have been criticized by humanistic psychologists for continuing a scientific model that objectifies people rather than enabling them to achieve their full potential. This criticism is directed at the ideological or philosophical implications of a theory and does not correspond to any of the criteria defining a sound scientific theory. This does not necessarily invalidate the criticism but makes it a matter of professional values.

Perhaps personality theory is not well served by the traditional model of science. Science is supposed to be objective and value free. Maslow questioned this assumption with his proposal of a Taoist Science. Others also question whether such a value-free stance is desirable, or even possible, for personality theory (Kukla, 1982; Sampson, 1977, 1978). Could it be that our traditional understanding of scientific objectivity is inadequate?

Theories as Metaphors

If a scientific theory modeled after the physical sciences could be devised for personality, would people be dehumanized? Perhaps the physical sciences provide the wrong metaphor for the scientific study of personality. We often express our thoughts by using metaphors (figures of speech that imply comparisons). For example, we may refer to the elderly as experiencing the "sunset of their years" or to bad news as a "bitter pill." Scientific theories can also be understood as metaphors. A **root metaphor**, according to Stephen Pepper (1942), provides a model for understanding phenomena, and it is often unconscious. He suggests six worldviews, each based on a different root metaphor (see Table 17.1). The concept of root metaphor provides another basis for comparing theories, besides the scientific criteria discussed earlier. It also helps to explain why some of the theories seem so incompatible with one another. If two theories are based on different

root metaphor the underlying assumptions of a theoretical position, expressed in terms of an image

TABLE 17.1 Pepper's Root Metaphors with Examples from Personality Theory

Worldview (based on Root Metaphor)	Explanation	Examples
Animism (*spiritualism*) of a human or a spirit.	The world has the characteristics of a human or a spirit.	(None)
Mysticism (*revelation*)	Knowledge is acquired through revelation of experience, such as through symbols or love.	Synchronicity (Jung)
Formism (*artisan making products from the same plan*)	Forms exist in nature that are manifested in entities, making them similar (if the same form) or different (if different forms).	Personality traits and types (Allport, Cattell); archetypes (Jung)
Mechanism (*the machine*)	Forces are transmitted to produce effects.	Learning (Skinner, Dollard and Miller); energy transformation (Freud)
Organicism (*the organism*)	Stages of development result in the emergence of the previously concealed organic structure.	Self-actualization (Maslow); personal growth (Rogers); the epigenetic principle (Erikson); becoming (Allport)
Contextualism (*the historical event or present event*)	Situations change as events unfold through episodes that influence other events.	Narrative metaphor (Sarbin); biographial approaches; identity (Erikson); case histories (Freud and others)

This elaboration of Pepper's (1942) concepts of a world view (world hypothesis) and root metaphor is based in part on information in Sarbin (1986) and Polkinghorne (1988) as well as Pepper (1942). Some personality theories have aspects of more than one world view or root metaphor. Others do not correspond well to any of these models. Personality theories are not based on the world view of animism and (with the exception of some aspects of Jung's theory) are not based on mysticism.

root metaphors, their unstated assumptions will be incompatible. Personality theories are based on some of the metaphors suggested by Pepper, as well as others.

THE MECHANISTIC METAPHOR

The **mechanistic metaphor** presumes that personality is determined with the same external, decisive determinism that propels physical objects through space. It has been called "the dominant world view in Western civilization" (Sarbin, 1986). This metaphor, adopted from the physical sciences (Rychlak, 1984b; Wolman, 1971), historically has appealed to psychologists because it makes psychology seem more rigorous. The mechanistic metaphor underlies theories as diverse as Freudian theory and behaviorism (although Theodore Sarbin suggests that Freud's warring id, ego, and superego departed from the mechanistic model).

However, critics point out that psychologists are using an outdated metaphor borrowed from the physical sciences. Many psychologists continue to model their philosophy of science after 18th-century Newtonian physics, despite the fact that physicists themselves have dismissed this model as outdated (Atwood & Maltin, 1991; Oppenheimer, 1956; Slife, 1981). In Newton's 18th-century physics, the world could be understood mechanically. Objects did not move unless they were acted on by outside forces, and then the change was continuous, in proportion to the outside force. With Einstein's formulation of the interrelationship between energy and matter (his famous $E = mc^2$ equation) and with the development of quantum theory, all that has changed. In modern physics, energies within matter can produce change without outside intervention, and change can occur in discontinuous quantum leaps within the atom (Einstein & Infeld, 1938/1961). In contrast to the false dichotomy between the person and the environment (and other false dichotomies, such as between free will and determinism or mind and matter), the new physics proposes an integrated field approach (Midgley & Morris, 1988). Even the assumption that time moves in one direction has been questioned (Slife, 1981). If a mechanistic metaphor is inadequate for understanding physical matter, should it be the model for personality?

mechanistic metaphor an image that calls attention to the immediate, direct forces that determine personality and behavior

THE ORGANIC METAPHOR

What about a biological metaphor? The **organic metaphor** compares personality with the growth of plants and animals. Rogers used this metaphor when he described the actualizing tendency, and it is also the underlying metaphor of Erikson's epigenetic principle. Potentials for development are located by this metaphor within the person rather than externally. The environment is seen not as a determining force, as in the mechanistic metaphor, but rather as an environment either conducive to the inherent growth of the personality or an impediment, just as a seed may fall on good or poor soil. This metaphor emphasizes the potential inherent in every person, as part of his or her nature. The role of the environment is to nurture growth, not to cause it.

organic metaphor an image that calls attention to the potential for growth and form that is inherent within every person, nurtured by growth-producing circumstances

THE INFORMATION-PROCESSING METAPHOR

The **information-processing metaphor** calls attention to people's capacity to function differently, depending on what they think. It is represented in cognitive theories, such as those of Kelly, Bandura, and Mischel. Unlike the organic metaphor, which implies only one healthy potential, this metaphor recognizes multiple potentials without focusing only on external determinants (as the mechanistic metaphor does). It recognizes developmental

information-processing metaphor an image that calls attention to the cognitive aspects of personality, which can take many forms and therefore can produce many personality outcomes

change because personal constructs (like computer programs) can develop and change over time. Many current psychological theories emphasize cognition (Pervin, 1985). Older approaches question the necessity of a separate cognitive approach, arguing that cognitive processes can be fully explained by environmental events (e.g., Skinner) or in terms of neuronal events. The "consciousness revolution" (R. W. Sperry, 1988, 1990), in contrast, regards higher mental functioning, including subjective experience, as causal in its own right.

THE NARRATIVE METAPHOR

narrative metaphor an image that calls attention to the stories people create that give meaning and direction to their lives

Theodore Sarbin (1986) suggests that the **narrative metaphor** underlies much of psychology. Personality can be thought of as the story of a person's life. When personality changes, we in effect rewrite our life stories, perhaps changing the future or telling the past from a different viewpoint. A narrative has a plot, characters, time progression, and important episodes. So does the story of a person's life. The dramatic role playing of George Kelly's theory obviously fits this metaphor.

Narratives distinguish human experience from descriptions of inanimate matter and so provide an alternative to the mechanistic metaphor of physical science. Are they too much like nonscientific fields, like literature and religion, for example? If we do not test them, surely narrative metaphors can be nonscientific, but the same is true of other metaphors. If we test these metaphors, using the scientific methods of operational definitions and hypothesis testing, making sure that our observations are based on appropriate subjects and are replicated adequately, there is no reason why narrative metaphors cannot be the basis of a scientific theory. They may, in fact, suggest hypotheses overlooked by other metaphors.

THE METAPHOR OF THE EMERGENT SELF

emergent self metaphor an image that calls attention to the higher-order characteristics of purpose and will that are produced by the culmination of lower-order deterministic forces

The **emergent self metaphor** suggests that a self-directed, willful personality emerges from the more deterministic and predictable forces described by the earlier metaphors. In science fiction, computers and robots are sometimes portrayed as evolving to a willful state, reflecting this image that self-will can emerge from parts that are, in less complex form, determined. This metaphor describes Adler's emphasis on choice and striving, as well as humanistic psychology's discussions of free will. It highlights people's purposeful behavior (cf. Sappington, 1990; Ziller, 1990). It can be considered **teleological** to convey that it focuses attention on the direction toward which a person is moving rather than on the past forces that are determining the present.

teleological viewing phenomena in terms of their overall purpose, design, or intent (rather than in terms of the mechanisms by which they occur)

This metaphor, suggesting the study of striving and willful activity, underlies many recent theoretical developments. Seymour Epstein (1980, 1985) has proposed a cognitive-experiential self-theory that derives concepts from Kelly's theory of constructive alternativism, learning theory, psychoanalysis, and other approaches. Roger Sperry (1988) has argued that micro control from neurological processes now is accompanied with macro control from higher levels, from emergent mental processes. This higher control can be called **emergent determinism**. Joseph Rychlak's (1977, 1986, 1988) logical learning theory proposes the concept of a telosponse, "behavior done for the sake of a premised reason (purpose, intention, etc.)" (Rychlak, 1984b, p. 92). He compares his approach to aspects of several of the theories included in this text: "the Freudian wish, the Adlerian prototype, the Jungian archetype, [and] the Kellyian construct" (Rychlak, 1986, p. 757), as well as the humanists Rogers and Maslow (Rychlak, 1977). Gian Vittorio Caprara (1996) proposes that personality is an emergent self-regulatory system.

emergent determinism causation or determinism from higher mental processes, such as thought, in contrast to lower-order determinism, such as from neurological process

Most psychologists maintain that teleology is incompatible with science, which requires the assumption of determinism. In response, Joseph Rychlak (1977, 1984b) charges that psychologists have not adequately differentiated between theory and method. Although experimentation requires a causal rather than a teleological model, theory does not. Rychlak argues that teleological ideas have been an important part of human thought throughout history, from before Aristotle up to 20th-century physics. Psychology is unduly narrow to rule them out of its theorizing. Many factors must be considered to understand personality, and some of these factors are teleological (e.g., purpose and free will). To permit them adequate representation within a personality theory requires a shift of paradigm, not borrowed from physics or another science but developed explicitly to understand human personality.

THE METAPHOR OF THE TRANSCENDENT SELF

Finally, the **transcendent self metaphor** is suggested by Jung's mysticism, by the suggestions of experience beyond individual ego that Maslow and Rogers mentioned, and by the Buddhist approach. It implies that individuals are not so separate and self-contained as we usually assume them to be, but rather they are connected in some plane of shared experience. This metaphor, however, has few advocates within Western personality theory, which is still struggling to understand the experience of individuals.

transcendent self metaphor an image that calls attention to the shared experience of people that is not limited by their individual separateness

What Lies Ahead?

Many personality theorists and researchers are satisfied with the particular theories that organize their own work, but as a whole the field lacks coherence. Personality theorists have not yet achieved a coherent, shared **paradigm** to organize research in the field. Perhaps that will never happen, but the effort seems likely to continue. As we move toward new theoretical developments, it is well that some researchers continue to pay attention to people's real-life experiences (e.g., Baumeister, Stillwell, & Wotman, 1990), life stories (e.g., G. S. Howard, 1991; Vitz, 1990), and biographical analyses. Theory, after all, should not be imposed on the data but should emerge from it. Data from the laboratory, too, is stimulating personality theory in new directions. As we learn more about the brain, neuroscientists are helping clarify the discrete yet interrelated processes that must be integrated to forge a personality. As we learn more about the field from many sources, ranging from the subjective to the neurological, it seems safe to predict that some theoretical pronouncements will appear prophetic and others dubious.

paradigm a general framework that provides direction to a field of science, within which theoretical concepts are extended and empirical work is conducted

Summary

- The field of personality, although it has many perspectives and theories, lacks a shared *paradigm* to direct research.
- Several theoretical perspectives toward personality have been discussed in this text.
- They are here reviewed for their contributions and assumptions on several topics of interest to the field of personality: individual differences, adaptation and adjustment, cognitive processes, society, biological influences, and development.

- Alternative solutions to the dilemma of many theories include *eclecticism,* which selects aspects from various theories; *unified theory,* which aims for an integrated and systematic theory combining diverse elements; and *pluralism,* which allows diverse theories to exist while maintaining their separate integrity.
- The criteria of a good theory presented in Chapter 1 are considered briefly and found not to be applied as systematically in practice as in principle.
- The concept of *root metaphor* suggests that some theories may disagree because of unstated fundamental assumptions.
- Several metaphors have been applied to personality theories, including the mechanistic metaphor, the organic metaphor, the information-processing metaphor, the narrative metaphor, the metaphor of the emergent self, and the metaphor of the transcendent self.

Thinking about Personality Theory

1. Evaluate the theories in the text according to the criteria for a good scientific theory presented in Chapter 1.
2. Which metaphor do you consider most appropriate for personality theory? Why?
3. Can you suggest any additional metaphors for personality theory?
4. In your opinion, what issues are most important for personality theorists and researchers to examine next?

Study Questions

1. What is a theoretical paradigm? Does personality theory have a dominant paradigm?
2. Summarize the current status of personality theory.
3. Summarize theoretical contributions to the issue of individual differences.
4. Summarize theoretical contributions to the issue of adaptation and adjustment.
5. Summarize theoretical contributions to the issue of cognitive processes.
6. Summarize theoretical contributions to the issue of society.
7. Summarize theoretical contributions to the issue of biological influences.
8. Summarize theoretical contributions to the issue of development.
9. Discuss the ways in which one can deal with theoretical diversity, including eclecticism, pluralism, and the search for a unified theory.
10. How can the concept of multiple levels of explanation justify theoretical diversity?
11. Explain Pepper's concept of a root metaphor. List and explain two (or more) of his root metaphors and associate each of them to a personality concept from a particular theory.
12. Describe the mechanistic metaphor of personality.
13. Describe the organic metaphor of personality.
14. Describe the information-processing metaphor of personality.
15. Describe the narrative metaphor of personality.
16. Describe the emergent self metaphor of personality.
17. Describe the transcendent self metaphor of personality.

Glossary

16PF Cattell's questionnaire designed to measure the major source traits of normal personality

act frequency approach measuring personality traits by assessing the frequency of prototypical behaviors

active imagination technique for exploring the unconscious by encouraging waking fantasies

actual self what a person really is at a given time, seen objectively

actualizing tendency the force for growth and development that is innate in all organisms

adaptation coping with the external world

aggressive drive one of Adler's terms for positive striving, emphasizing anger and competitiveness

Agreeableness factor of personality, typified by a friendly, compliant personality

amplification elaboration of dream images as a step toward dream interpretation

amygdala brain area involved in fear, theorized (by Kagan) to contribute to inhibited temperament

anal character personality type resulting from fixation at age 1 to 3, characterized by orderliness, parsimony, and obstinacy

anal stage the second psychosexual stage of development, from age 1 to 3

anatta no-self; the doctrine that there is, in reality, no fixed, stable, enduring self (although the illusion of one may be constructed from fleeting impressions)

anima the femininity that is part of the unconscious of every man

animus the masculinity that is part of the unconscious of every woman

anticipatory response tendency of responses that precede reward to occur earlier and earlier in the behavioral sequence

applied research research intended for practical use

applied value the ability of a theory to guide practical uses

approach-approach conflict conflict in which an organism simultaneously wishes to approach two incompatible goals

approach-avoidance conflict conflict in which an organism simultaneously wishes to approach and to avoid the same goal

arbitrary rightness secondary adjustment technique in which a person rigidly declares that his or her own view is correct

archetype a primordial image in the collective unconscious; an innate pattern that influences experience of the real world

attachment (psychoanalysis) bonds of affection in which an infant turns to the mother or other caretaker for comfort and security; by extension, close interpersonal styles in adulthood

attachment (Buddhism) craving for a variety of things, including physical objects and even the self; the source of suffering (according to the Second Noble Truth)

attentional processes noticing the model's behavior (a prerequisite for learning by modeling)

autonomy the positive pole of the second psychosocial stage

auxiliary function the second most developed function of an individual's personality

avoidance-avoidance conflict conflict in which an organism must choose between two goals, both of which it finds undesirable, but is constrained from leaving the field (abandoning the situation)

Awakening a transformation from ordinary consciousness in which a person recognizes the true nature of things and the path to spiritual progress

base rate the rate of responding before conditioning

basic anxiety feeling of isolation and helplessness resulting from inadequate parenting in infancy

basic behavioral repertoires (BBRs) learned behaviors fundamental to later learning of more complex behavior, in three categories: language-cognitive, emotional-motivational, and sensory-motor

basic hostility feeling of anger by the young child toward the parents, which must be repressed

basic need a fundamental deficiency need

basic research research intended to develop theory

behavior modification the application of learning principles to therapy

Behavioral Activation System (BAS) in Gray's model, tendency of personality related to the approaching of rewarding experiences

Behavioral Inhibition System (BIS) in Gray's model, tendency of personality related to reactions to aversive stimuli

behavior-outcome expectancy expectancy about what will happen if a person behaves in a particular way

being motivation higher-level motivation in which the need for self-actualization predominates

Big Five the five-factor model of personality, consisting of Extraversion, Agreeableness, Neuroticism, Conscientiousness, and Openness

blind spots secondary adjustment technique in which a person is unaware of behavior inconsistent with the idealized self-image

B-love nonpossessive love, characteristic of a self-actualized person

bodhisattva a spiritually enlightened person who remains in the world to help others on their spiritual path

Buddha Awakened one; the term often refers to Siddhartha Gautama (Sakyamuni Buddha), who lived in India about 2,500 years ago; in some forms of Buddhism, it is held that everyone can attain buddha status (become a buddha) by following the path, although it may take more than one lifetime to achieve this

cardinal trait a pervasive personality trait that dominates nearly everything a person does

care ability to nurture the development of the next generation; the basic virtue developed during the seventh psychosocial stage

case study an intensive investigation of a single individual

castration anxiety fear that motivates male development at age 3 to 5

catharsis therapeutic effect of a release of emotion when previously repressed material is made conscious

cathexis investment of psychic energy in an object

central trait one of the half dozen or so traits that best describe a particular person

chaining operant technique for developing sequences of responses by teaching the last one, then adding the next to last, and so on, with each response producing the stimuli that control the next response

Choice Corollary statement that people choose the pole of a construct that promises greater possibility of extending and defining the system of constructs

circumspection the first stage in the C-P-C Cycle, in which various constructs are tentatively explored

client-centered therapy therapy based on the belief that the person seeking help is the best judge of the direction that will lead to growth

cognitive complexity elaborateness of a person's construct system, reflected in a large number of different constructs

cognitive person variables cognitive factors within a person, less global than traits, which influence how an individual adapts to the environment

collective efficacy the sense that a group can do what is to be done

collective unconscious the inherited unconscious

collectivism values, predominant in some cultures, of social cooperation and group goals

common trait a trait characterizing many people (i.e., a trait considered from the nomothetic point of view)

Commonality Corollary statement describing similarity between people

compartmentalization secondary adjustment technique in which incompatible behaviors are not simultaneously recognized

compensation principle of the relationship between the unconscious and consciousness, by which the unconscious provides what is missing from consciousness to make a complete whole

competence sense of workmanship, of perfecting skills; the basic virtue developed during the fourth psychosocial stage

competencies person variables concerned with what a person is able to do

complexes emotionally charged networks of ideas (such as those resulting from unresolved conflicts)

comprehensiveness the ability of a theory to explain a broad variety of observations

concentrative meditation a form of meditation in which attention is focused on a particular object, such as the breath or a word or phrase (mantra), one of the best known being the mantra "*om*"

concrete construct a construct that cannot be extended to include new elements

condensation combining of two or more images; characteristic of primary processes (e.g., in dreams)

conditions of worth the expectations a person must live up to before receiving respect and love

conflict a situation in which cues for two incompatible responses are provided

confluence learning learning behaviors that satisfy more than one motivation

congruence a feeling of consistency between the real self and the ideal self

Conscientiousness factor of personality, typified by hard work, orderliness, and self-discipline

conscious aware; cognizant; mental processes of which a person is aware

consistency paradox the mismatch between intuition, which says that people are consistent, and research findings, which say they are not

constitutional trait a trait influenced by heredity

construct a concept used in a theory

construct validity the usefulness of a theoretical term, evidenced by an accumulation of research findings

Construction Corollary Kelly's statement that people anticipate replications of events

constructive alternativism the assumption that people can interpret the world in a variety of ways

continuous reinforcement (CR) schedule a reinforcement schedule in which every response is reinforced

control group in an experiment, the group not exposed to the experimental treatment

control the third stage in the C-P-C Cycle; the way in which the person acts

conversion hysteria form of neurosis in which psychological conflicts are expressed in physical symptoms (without actual physical damage)

copying learning to behave in the same way as a model, but not in response to the same cues as the model, in order to be rewarded by perceived similarity to the model

core constructs constructs central to a person's identity and existence

correlation coefficient a measure of the association between two variables, in which 0 indicates no association, and +1 or −1 a strong association (positive or negative)

correlation matrix a chart of the correlations between all pairs of a set of variables

correlational research research method that examines the relationships among measurements

countertransference the analyst's reaction to the patient, as distorted by unresolved conflicts

C-P-C Cycle the three-step process leading to effective action

creative self the person who acts to determine his or her own life

Creativity Cycle the process of changing constructs by loosening and tightening them

crystallized intelligence intelligence influenced by education, so it measures what has been learned

cue what a person notices, which provides a discriminative stimulus for learning

cultural evolution evolution through transmitted learning from one generation to another

Culture Fair Intelligence Test a test designed to measure fluid intelligence only

cynicism secondary adjustment technique in which the moral values of society are rejected

defense mechanisms ego strategies for coping with unconscious conflict

deficiency motivation motivation at lower levels of development

delay of gratification the ability to give up immediate gratifications for larger, more distant rewards

delusion ignorance or false beliefs about the nature of reality

denial primitive defense mechanism in which material that produces conflict is simply repressed

dependent variable the effect in an experimental study

deprecation complex unhealthy way of seeking superiority by belittling others

desacralization loss of a sense of the sacred or spiritual

description theoretical task of identifying the units of personality, with particular emphasis on the differences between people

despair the negative pole of the eighth psychosocial stage

determinism the assumption that phenomena have causes that can be discovered by empirical research

development formation or change (of personality) over time

dharma the true, intrinsic nature of things

Dichotomy Corollary statement that constructs are bipolar

disconfirmation evidence against a theory; observations that contradict the predictions of a hypothesis

discrimination responding only to particular cues

discrimination learning learning to respond differentially, depending on environmental stimuli

displacement defense mechanism in which energy is transferred from one object or activity to another

D-love selfish love, characteristic of a person who is not self-actualized

dominant function a person's predominant psychological function

dominant response a person's most likely response in a given situation

dopamine neurotransmitter involved in many brain functions, including rewarding experiences, novelty seeking, schizophrenia (high levels), and Parkinson's disease (low levels)

double approach-avoidance conflict conflict in which an organism must choose between two options, both of which have positive and negative aspects

drive what a person wants, which motivates learning

dubkha suffering, which is accepted in the First Noble Truth

dynamic lattice Cattell's diagram to show motivational dynamics

dynamics the motivational aspect of personality

eclectic combining ideas from a variety of theories

eclecticism combining ideas from a variety of theories

ego inflation overvaluation of ego consciousness, without recognizing its limited role in the psyche

ego the most mature structure of personality; mediates intrapsychic conflict and copes with the external world

ego-extensions objects or people that help define a person's identity or sense of self

Eightfold Path the method for achieving an end of suffering, described in the Fourth Noble Truth

elaborative choice a choice that allows a construct system to be extended; the Choice Corollary says this choice will be selected

elusiveness secondary adjustment technique in which a person avoids commitment to any opinion or action

emergenic traits phenotypic traits caused by a constellation of many genes and so may not appear to run in families

emergent determinism causation or determinism from higher mental processes, such as thought, in contrast to lower-order determinism, such as from neurological process

emergent self metaphor an image that calls attention to the higher-order characteristics of purpose and will that are produced by the culmination of lower-order deterministic forces

empathic understanding the ability of the therapist to understand the subjective experience of the client

empirical based on scientific observations

encoding strategies person variables concerned with how a person construes reality

encounter group growth-enhancing technique in which a group of people openly and honestly express their feelings and opinions

Enlightenment higher stage of consciousness that results from following the Eightfold Path; sometimes also used synonymously with Awakening

environmental-mold trait a trait influenced by learning

epigenetic principle the principle for psychosocial development, based on a biological model, in which parts emerge in order of increasing differentiation

erg a constitutional dynamic source trait

Eros the life instinct

Eupsychia a utopian society in which individual and societal needs are both met and where society supports individual development

evolutionary psychology the perspective that applies the evolutionary principles of natural selection to understanding human psychology, including personality

evolved psychological mechanisms specific psychological processes that have evolved because they solved particular adaptive problems (e.g., sexual jealousy, dealing with the problem of paternal uncertainty)

excessive self-control secondary adjustment technique in which emotions are avoided

expansive solution attempting to solve neurotic conflict by seeking mastery; moving against people

expectancies subjective beliefs about what will happen in a particular situation (including behavior outcomes, stimulus outcomes, and self-efficacies)

Experience Corollary Kelly's statement about personality development

experiential knowledge what we know because we have experienced it for ourselves

experimental group in an experiment, the group exposed to the experimental treatment

expressive traits traits concerned with the style or tempo of a person's behavior

externalization defense mechanism in which conflicts are projected outside

extinction reduction in the frequency of a nonrewarded response

extinction reduction in the rate of responding when reinforcement ends

Extraversion factor (in several factor theories) of personality, typified by sociability, cheerfulness, and activity

extraversion tolerance for high levels of stimulation because of a strong nervous system that inhibits incoming stimulation, leading to sociability in Eysenck's theory

extrinsic religious orientation attitude in which religion is seen as a means to a person's other goals (such as status or security)

facilitator the leader of an encounter group

factor a statistically derived, quantitative dimension of personality that is broader than most traits

factor analysis statistical procedure for determining a smaller number of dimensions in a data set from a large number of variables

family constellation the configuration of family members, including the number and birth order of siblings

feeling psychological function in which decisions are based on the emotions they arouse

fictional finalism a person's image of the goal of his or her striving

fidelity ability to sustain loyalties freely pledged; the basic virtue developed during the fifth psychosocial stage

Fight-Flight System (FFS) biological personality factor proposed by Gray that produces rage and panic

fixation failure to develop normally through a particular developmental stage

fixed interval (FI) schedule a reinforcement schedule in which a reinforcement follows every *N* units of time (e.g., in FI-15, one reinforcement is given every 15 seconds if a response has occurred at least once)

fixed ratio (FR) schedule a reinforcement schedule in which a reinforcement follows every Nth response (e.g., in FR-15, every 15th response is reinforced)

fixed-role therapy Kelly's method of therapy, based on role playing

fluid intelligence the part of intelligence that is the innate ability to learn, without including the effects of specific learning

Four Noble Truths that there is suffering, that it has a cause, that suffering can cease, and that there is a path to end suffering

Fragmentation Corollary statement describing the inconsistency of people

free association psychoanalytic technique in which the patient says whatever comes to mind, permitting unconscious connections to be discovered

Freudian slip a psychologically motivated error in speech, hearing, behavior, and so forth (e.g., forgetting the birthday of a disliked relative)

frustration-aggression hypothesis the hypothesis that frustration always leads to aggression, and aggression is always caused by frustration

fully functioning Rogers's term for a mentally healthy person

functional analysis preparatory to behavior modification, careful observation to identify the stimuli and reinforcements influencing behavior

functional autonomy a trait's independence of its developmental origins

Fundamental Postulate Kelly's main assumption, which stresses the importance of psychological constructs

generalization responding to stimuli that were not present during learning as though they were the discriminative stimuli present during learning

generativity the positive pole of the seventh psychosocial stage

genital character healthy personality type

genital stage the adult psychosexual stage

genotype the inherited genetic profile of an individual

gerotranscendence the ninth stage of psychosocial development, referring to the very elderly

gradient of approach the greater tendency to approach a goal, the closer one is to it

gradient of avoidance the greater tendency to avoid a goal, the closer one is to it

gradient of punishment the greater weakening of responses that are most closely followed by punishment; that is, delayed punishment is less effective than immediate punishment

gradient of reward the greater strengthening of responses that are immediately followed by reward; that is, delayed reward is less effective than immediate reward

growth centers places where people come together to develop their full potential (e.g., Esalen)

guilt the negative pole of the third psychosocial stage

guru teacher; spiritual adviser

harm avoidance biological dimension proposed by Cloninger that inhibits behavior; related to serotonin levels

heritability the extent to which a trait is influenced by genetics; the statistic that shows what proportion of the variability of a trait in a particular population is associated with genetic variability

hierarchy of needs ordered progression of motives, from basic physical needs upward to motives of the most developed human beings

hope fundamental conviction in the trustworthiness of the world; the basic virtue developed during the first psychosocial stage

hostility continuing to try to validate constructs that have already been invalidated

human potential movement social trend to foster the full development of individuals, reflected in the development of growth centers and in transformation of social institutions

hungry ghosts (*pretas*) one of several realms of existence in Buddhist teaching, characterized by persistent, unsatisfied cravings

hypothesis a prediction to be tested by research

I Ching ancient Chinese method of fortune-telling

id the most primitive structure of personality; the source of psychic energy

ideal self what a person feels he or she ought to be like

idealized self an image of what a person wishes to be

identification defense mechanism in which a person fuses or models after another person

identity achievement status representing optimal development during the fifth (adolescent) psychosocial stage

identity confusion the negative pole of the fifth psychosocial stage

identity diffusion the negative pole of the fifth psychosocial stage (earlier terminology)

identity foreclosure inadequate resolution of the fifth psychosocial stage, in which an identity is accepted without adequate exploration

identity sense of sameness between one's meaning for oneself and one's meaning for others in the social world; the positive pole of the fifth psychosocial stage

idiographic focusing on one individual

imitation learning by observing the actions of others

implicit theories of personality ideas about personality that are held by ordinary people (not based on formal theory)

inclusive fitness the evolutionary principle that traits that increase the survival of the individual and his or her genetic relatives will become more frequent by natural selection

independent variable in an experiment, the cause that is manipulated by the researcher

individual differences qualities that make one person different from another

individual trait a trait that characterizes only the one person who has it (i.e., a trait considered from the idiographic point of view)

individualism values, predominant in many Western cultures, of individual goals and achievement (in contrast to shared group goals and cooperation)

Individuality Corollary Kelly's assertion that different people use different constructs

individuation the process of becoming a fully developed person, with all psychic functions developed

industry the positive pole of the fourth psychosocial stage

inferiority complex stagnation of growth in which difficulties seem too immense to be overcome

inferiority the negative pole of the fourth psychosocial stage

information processing metaphor an image that calls attention to the cognitive aspects of personality, which can take many forms and therefore can produce many personality outcomes

inhibited type temperament type (described by Kagan) that is shy and nonassertive around strangers, proposed to have high levels of norepinephrine and an activation of the amygdala

initiative the positive pole of the third psychosocial stage

Inner Directed Supports scale of the Personal Orientation Inventory measuring a person's tendency to obtain support from himself or herself rather than from other people

insight conscious recognition of one's motivation and unconscious conflicts

instinctoid weakly instinctive motives characteristic of humans

integrity the positive pole of the eighth psychosocial stage

intellectualization defense mechanism in which a person focuses on thinking and avoids feeling

intimacy the positive pole of the sixth psychosocial stage

intrapsychic conflict conflict within the personality, as between id desires and superego restrictions

intrinsic motivation motivation to perform an activity for its inherent satisfaction (rather than as a means to some other goal)

intrinsic religious orientation attitude in which religion is accepted for its own sake rather than as a means to an end

intuition psychological function in which material is perceived with a broad perspective, emphasizing future possibilities rather than current details

isolation (psychoanalysis) defense mechanism in which conflictful material is kept disconnected from other thoughts

isolation (Erikson) the negative pole of the sixth psychosocial stage

jackass theory Kelly's phrase to indicate that his theory concerns the "nature of the animal" rather than of the environment

jackdaw eclecticism considering concepts from diverse theories, without making careful selection from and evaluation of these concepts

Jonah complex not developing one's full potential because of a belief that it is impossible to do anything very important

karma intentional or willed activity, which produces consequences (positive or negative, depending on the action)

kin altruism the principle that natural selection favors those who risk their own lives or welfare to improve the survival and reproductive prospects of their genetic relatives

koan in Zen Buddhism, a riddle that is posed for the purpose of overcoming preconceptions and so furthering spiritual enlightenment

latent content the hidden, unconscious meaning of a dream

L-data objective information about the life history of the individual

learning dilemma a situation in which existing responses are not rewarded, which leads to change

libido psychic energy, derived from sexuality

loosening applying constructs in ways that seem not to make sense, such as in brainstorming and free association

love ability to form an intimate mutual relationship with another person; the basic virtue developed during the sixth psychosocial stage

Mahayana Buddhism the major East Asian Buddhist tradition, which pays particular attention to the Buddha and to devotional practices that assist others to follow his path to Enlightenment

mandala symbolic representation of the whole psyche, emphasizing circles and/or squares

manifest content the surface meaning of a dream

man-the-scientist Kelly's metaphor for human personality

masculine protest one of Adler's terms for positive striving, emphasizing manliness

matched dependent behavior learning to make the same response as a model, in response to a cue from the model

mechanistic metaphor an image that calls attention to the immediate, direct forces that determine personality and behavior

meditation a practice in which attention is consciously regulated to enhance serenity and well-being

metaerg environmental-mold dynamic source traits; includes sentiments and attitudes

metamotivated motivated by needs at the top of the hierarchy

method centered an approach to science that emphasizes procedure over content

Middle Way description of the path to Enlightenment by avoiding extremes, such as extreme asceticism or extreme self-indulgence

mindfulness meditation a form of meditation in which thoughts are observed but not judged

mistrust the negative pole of the first psychosocial stage

modeling learning by observing others; also called vicarious learning

Modulation Corollary statement that the permeability of constructs sets limits to construction possibilities

moral disengagement failure to regulate one's behavior to live up to high moral standards

moratorium period provided by society when an adolescent is sufficiently free of commitments to be able to explore identity; also, a stage of identity development when such exploration is occurring, before identity achievement

motivational process deciding whether it is worthwhile to behave as a model has behaved

motor reproduction process being able to do what one has seen a model do

moving against interpersonal orientation emphasizing hostility

moving away interpersonal orientation emphasizing separateness from others

moving toward interpersonal orientation emphasizing dependency

multilevel theory a unified theory that integrates various levels of explanation (e.g., biological, cognitive, social)

Multiple Abstract Variance Analysis (MAVA) statistical technique for assessing how much of a trait is determined by heredity and how much by environment

multivariate a research strategy that includes many variables

Myers-Briggs Type Indicator (MBTI) psychological test for measuring the psychic functions in an individual

narcissism unhealthy self-focus that impairs the ability to have healthy, empathic relationships with other people

narrative metaphor an image that calls attention to the stories people create that give meaning and direction to their lives

negative identity identity based on socially devalued roles

negative reinforcer an outcome stimulus that ends when a response occurs; it has the effect of increasing the rate of responding

neglect parental behavior in which a child's needs are not adequately met

Neuroticism factor of personality, typified by negative emotionality

neuroticism tendency toward high levels of emotional arousal; the second factor in Eysenck's factor model

nirvana the goal of spiritual development, in which there is no attachment, and therefore suffering has ended

nomothetic involving comparisons with other individuals; research based on groups of people

novelty seeking biological trait proposed by Cloninger that activates people to explore new things; related to dopamine levels

numinous experience of spiritual or transpersonal energies

object relations term used in psychoanalysis for relationships with people, based originally on the idea that people serve as objects to satisfy libidinal drives

Oedipus conflict conflict that males experience from age 3 to 5 involving sexual love for the mother and aggressive rivalry with the father

Openness factor of personality, typified by artistic, imaginative, and intellectual interests

operant conditioning learning in which the frequency of responding is influenced by the consequences that are contingent on a response

operant responses behaviors freely emitted by an organism

operational definition procedure for measuring a theoretical construct

oral character personality type resulting from fixation in the first psychosexual stage; characterized by optimism, passivity, and dependency

oral stage the first psychosexual stage of development, from birth to age 1

organic metaphor an image that calls attention to the potential for growth and form that is inherent within every person, nurtured by growth-producing circumstances

organismic valuing process inner sense within a person, which guides him or her in the directions of growth and health

Organization Corollary describes the hierarchical relationships among constructs

outcome expectations the belief about what desirable or undesirable things will occur if a behavior is successfully performed

oxytocin hormone released by nursing females and in sexual intercourse; thought to promote caretaking and cuddling

pampering parental behavior in which a child is overindulged or spoiled

paradigm a basic theoretical model, shared by various theorists and researchers

paradigm a general framework that provides direction to a field of science, within which theoretical concepts are extended and empirical work is conducted

parapraxis (plural: **-es**) a psychologically motivated error, more commonly called a *Freudian slip*

parental investment the expenditure of time and resources to reproduce each child, especially emphasizing the amount of one's reproductive potential that is expended for each child

partial reinforcement schedule a reinforcement schedule in which only some responses are reinforced

paternal uncertainty evolutionary proposal that men cannot be sure they are the biological fathers of the children born to their mates

peak experiences mystical states of consciousness, characteristic of many but not all self-actualized people

peripheral constructs constructs not central to one's identity

permeable construct a construct that can be extended to include new elements

persona a person's social identity

personal construct (Kelly) a person's concept for predicting events

personal constructs (Mischel) trait terms that people use to describe themselves and other people

Personal Orientation Inventory the most popular measure of self-actualization

personal unconscious that part of the unconscious derived from an individual's experience

personality coefficient the average relationship between self-report personality measures and behavior, estimated by Mischel at $r = 0.30$

personality for Gordon Allport, "the dynamic organization within the individual of those psychophysical systems that determine his unique adjustment to the environment"

personality the underlying causes within the person of individual behavior and experience

person-centered Rogers's orientation to therapy and education, which focuses on the experience of the client or student rather than the therapist or teacher

phallic stage the third psychosexual stage of development, from age 3 to 5

phenotype the developed characteristics that can be observed in an individual, based on both genetic and environmental influences

pleasure principle the id's motivation to seek pleasure and to avoid pain

pluralism the coexistence of various theories without attempting to combine them

positive psychology current movement in psychology that emphasizes healthy functioning, with concern for immediate experience and positive emotions such as happiness

positive reinforcer an outcome stimulus that is presented contingent on a response and that has the effect of increasing the rate of responding

preconscious mental content of which a person is currently unaware but that can readily be made conscious

preemption the second stage in the C-P-C Cycle, in which a construct is selected

prepotent currently most powerful; said of a need that because it is unmet is most powerful at the moment

preverbal construct a construct that is not conscious

primary process unconscious mental functioning in which the id predominates; characterized by illogical, symbolic thought

primary reinforcer a reinforcer that is not learned (i.e., innate)

prizing characteristic of a good therapist, which involves positively valuing the client; also called unconditional positive regard

problem centered an approach to science that emphasizes subject matter over procedure

Process Scale measuring instrument to assess how far along an individual is to the goal of becoming a fully functioning person

profile the pattern of a person's scores on several parts of a personality test

projection defense mechanism in which a person's own unacceptable impulse is incorrectly thought to belong to someone else

projective test a test that presents ambiguous stimuli such as inkblots or pictures, so responses will be determined by the test taker's unconscious

propriate striving effort based on a sense of selfhood or identity

proprium all aspects of a person that make for unity; a person's sense of self or ego

prototype a typical example of an object or type of person; a "fuzzy concept" typical of the categories people use in perceiving others

pseudospeciation the exaggerated sense of many groups, especially national and ethnic groups, that they are different from others, leading to conflict among groups

psychoanalysis Freud's theory and its application in therapy

psychobiography the application of a personality theory to the study of an individual's life; different from a case study because of its theoretical emphasis

psychological behaviorism behavioral theory, proposed by Staats, that includes traditional personality concerns (e.g., emotion, testing) as well as behavior

psychological type a person's characteristic pattern of major personality dimensions (introversion-extraversion, thinking-feeling, and sensation-intuition)

psychosocial Erikson's approach to development, offered as an alternative to Freud's psychosexual approach

Psychoticism in Eysenck's model, factor related to nonconformity or social deviance

punishment a stimulus contingent on a response and that has the effect of decreasing the rate of responding

purpose orientation to attain goals through striving; the basic virtue developed during the third psychosocial stage

Q-data data from self-report tests or questionnaires

quantitative measures measures that permit expression of various amounts of something, such as a trait

Range (Corollary) statement that a construct applies only to some events, not to all

range of convenience the events to which a construct applies

rate of responding the number of responses emitted in a period of time; a change in this rate is taken as evidence of learning

rational coper a stage in middle childhood in which problem-solving ability is important to one's sense of self

rationalization (Freud) defense mechanism in which reasonable, conscious explanations are offered rather than true unconscious motivations

rationalization (Horney) secondary adjustment technique in which a person explains behaviors in socially acceptable ways

reaction formation defense mechanism in which a person thinks or behaves in a manner opposite to the unacceptable unconscious impulse

real self the self that contains the actualizing tendency; the vital, unique center of the self, which has growth potential

reality principle the ego's mode of functioning in which there is appropriate contact with the external world

rebirth continuation of the effects of karma in previous lifetimes into the present

reciprocal altruism the evolutionary principle whereby members of a group take risks to help the survival and reproductive prospects of others, even nonrelatives, with the (not necessarily conscious) expectation of being helped in return

reciprocal determinism the interacting mutual influences of the person, the environment, and the behavior

relational approach approach in modern psychoanalysis that emphasizes interpersonal relationships

reliability consistency, as when a measurement is repeated at another time or by another observer, with similar results

repression defense mechanism in which unacceptable impulses are made unconscious

resignation solution attempting to solve neurotic conflict by seeking freedom; moving away from people

response (Skinner) a discrete behavior by an organism

response (Dollard & Miller) what a person does, which can be learned

response hierarchy list of all the responses a person could make in a given situation, arranged from most likely to least likely

resultant hierarchy a response hierarchy after it has been modified by learning

retention process remembering what a model has done

reward what a person gets as a result of a response in the learning sequence, which strengthens responses because of its drive-reducing effect

reward dependence biological dimension proposed by Cloninger that maintains behavior through seeking rewards; related to norepinephrine levels

ritual cultural practice or tradition that supports ego strengths

ritualism an individual's maladaptive repetitive actions intended to make up for weak aspects of ego development

Role Construct Repertory (REP) Test instrument for measuring a person's constructs

root metaphor the underlying assumptions of a theoretical position, expressed in terms of an image

same behavior a person's behavior being the same as that of a model, considering the cues and reinforcements as well as the response

samsara the wheel of suffering, in which the consequences of unenlightened action lock a person into a cycle of rebirth instead of permitting liberation to nirvana

sangha a community living in harmony and awareness

satellite relationships side relationships, which supplement a person's primary committed relationship

schedule of reinforcement the specific contingency between a response and a reinforcement

scientific method the method of knowing based on systematic observation

secondary process conscious mental functioning in which the ego predominates; characterized by logical thought

secondary reinforcer a reinforcer that is learned

secondary trait a trait that influences a limited range of behaviors

second-order factor analysis factor analysis in which the data are factor scores (rather than raw data); produces more general personality factors

Self the total integrated personality

self as knower a stage in adulthood in which a person integrates the self into a unified whole

self-actualization development of a person's full potential

self-effacing solution attempting to solve neurotic conflict by seeking love; moving toward people

self-efficacy expectancies (or self-efficacy) subjective beliefs about what a person will be able to do

self-regulatory systems and plans ways that a person works on complicated behavior (e.g., by setting goals and by self-criticism)

self-system personal constructs that people use to describe themselves; cognitive structures and subfunctions for perceiving, evaluating, and regulating behavior (not a psychic agent that controls action)

sensation psychological function in which material is perceived concretely, in detail

sensation seeking trait, proposed by Zuckerman, of seeking varied, novel, complex and intense sensations and experiences, even if that requires risk

shadow the unconscious complement to a person's conscious identity, often experienced as dangerous and evil

shame the negative pole of the second psychosocial stage

shaping reinforcement of successive approximations of a response to increase the frequency of a response that originally has a zero base rate

Siddhartha Gautama the historical Buddha, whose spiritual journey provided the foundation for Buddhism; also called Sakyamuni

Skinner box a device that provides a controlled environment for measuring learning

slot movement abrupt change from one pole of a construct to its opposite, often precipitated by stress

social interest innate potential to live cooperatively with other people

Sociality Corollary statement that describes understanding another person or being understood as a prerequisite for a social process with that person

socially useful type a personality that is well adjusted

source traits basic, underlying personality traits

specification equation mathematical expression that shows how personality and situational variables combine to predict a specific behavior

spontaneous recovery return of a response that was previously extinguished

stagnation the negative pole of the seventh psychosocial stage

stimulus generalization occurrence of a response to a stimulus other than the one that was a cue during learning

stimulus-outcome expectancies expectancies about how events will develop in the world, i.e., what events will follow other environmental stimuli

strong nervous system in Pavlov's theory, a nervous system that forms stronger conditioned responses and tolerates higher intensities of stimulation; said by other theorists to produce extraversion

style of life a person's consistent way of striving

subjective stimulus value how much an outcome is valued by an individual

sublimation defense mechanism in which impulses are expressed in socially acceptable ways

subsidiation the pattern of interrelationships among ergs, metaergs, and sentiments (as diagrammed in the dynamic lattice)

superego structure of personality that is the internal voice of parental and societal restrictions

superiority complex a neurotic belief that one is better than others

superiority striving effort to achieve improvement in oneself

superordinate construct a construct that applies broadly and subsumes lower-order constructs

suppression willfully putting thoughts out of consciousness

surface traits traits as defined simply at the level of observable behavior

synchronicity the acausal principle, in which events are determined by transpersonal forces instead of by causes generally understood by science

syntality group (e.g., national) differences in personality

Taoist Science Maslow's alternative to the traditional scientific method, emphasizing values and subjectivity (instead of objectivity)

T-data data collected from objective tests, such as reaction times

teleological viewing phenomena in terms of their overall purpose, design, or intent (rather than in terms of the mechanisms by which they occur)

temperament consistent styles of behavior and emotional reactions present from early life onward, presumably caused by biological factors; innate emotional aspects of personality; the biologically based foundation of personality, including such characteristic patterns of behavior as emotionality, activity, and sociability

Thanatos the death instinct

theoretical proposition theoretical statement about relationships among theoretical constructs

theory a conceptual tool, consisting of systematically organized constructs and propositions, for understanding certain specified phenomena

thinking psychological function in which decisions are based on logic

third force Maslow's term for his theory, emphasizing its opposition to psychoanalysis and behaviorism

threat awareness of imminent comprehensive change in one's core structures

Time Competence a scale of the Personal Orientation Inventory that measures a person's concern with the present rather than the past or future

time-out procedure a procedure or environment in which no reinforcements are given in an effort to extinguish unwanted behavior

token economy setting in which reinforcement of behavior is systematically applied in a group setting through the use of tokens, which can later be exchanged for rewards or privileges

trait a characteristic of a person that makes a person unique, with a unique style of adapting to stimuli in the world; personality characteristic that makes one person different from another and/or that describes an individual's personality

trait (Cattell) that which defines what a person will do in a particular situation

transcendent function the process of integrating all opposing aspects of personality into a unified whole

transcendent self metaphor an image that calls attention to the shared experience of people that is not limited by their individual separateness

transference in therapy, the patient's displacement onto the therapist of feelings based on earlier experiences (e.g., with the patient's own parents)

transformation modification of psychic energy to higher purposes (e.g., through ritual)

true experimental research research strategy that manipulates a cause to determine its effect

trust the positive pole of the first psychosocial stage

type a category of people with similar characteristics

tyranny of the shoulds inner demands to live up to the idealized self

unconditional positive regard accepting and valuing a person without requiring particular behaviors as a prerequisite

unconscious mental processes of which a person is unaware

unified theory a theory that combines diverse aspects from various approaches, indicating how they are organized and related

unifying philosophy of life an attitude or set of values, often religious, that gives coherence and meaning to life

uninhibited type temperament type (described by Kagan) that is outgoing and low in fear, proposed to have lower sympathetic nervous system activity

unique trait a trait that only one person has (also called individual trait)

unitas multiplex the Latin phrase indicating that a person makes a unified whole out of many diverse aspects of personality

validation confirmation of an anticipation by events

validity desirable characteristic of a test, indicating it actually does measure what it is intended to measure

variable in research, a measurement of something across various people (or times or situations), which takes on different values

variable interval (VI) schedule a reinforcement schedule in which a reinforcement follows, on the average, every N units of time, (e.g., in VI-15, one reinforcement is given every 15 seconds on the average if a response has occurred at least once, but sometimes the time span is under 15 seconds between reinforcements and sometimes more)

variable ratio (VR) schedule a reinforcement schedule in which a reinforcement follows, on the average, every Nth response, (e.g., in VI-15, one reinforcement is given for every 15 responses, but sometimes fewer than 15 responses occur between reinforcements and sometimes more)

verifiable the ability of a theory to be tested by empirical procedures, resulting in confirmation or disconfirmation

vicarious learning learning by observing others, without being directly rewarded oneself

Walden Two the novel about Skinner's imagined utopian community based on learning principles

weak nervous system in Pavlov's theory, a nervous system that forms weaker conditioned responses and does not tolerate high intensities of stimulation; said by other theorists to produce introversion

will conviction that what one wants to happen can happen; the basic virtue developed during the second psychosocial stage

wisdom mature sense of the meaningfulness and wholeness of experience; the basic virtue developed during the eighth psychosocial stage

womb envy men's envy of women's reproductive capacity (the complement of Freud's penis envy)

Word Association Test method devised by Jung to reveal complexes by asking people to say whatever comes to mind when they hear a word

yoga spiritual practice; various forms exist

zazen meditation; sitting meditation; practiced in Zen Buddhism

Zen Buddhism type of Buddhism found particularly in Japan, which uses koans to overcome limitations of thought

References

Abbott, A. (2001, March 15). Into the mind of a killer. *Nature, 410,* 296–298.

Abraham, K. (1986). Ego identity differences among Anglo-American and Mexican-American adolescents. *Journal of Adolescence, 9,* 151–167.

Abramowitz, J. S., Tolin, D. F., & Street, G. P. (2001). Paradoxical effects of thought suppression: A meta-analysis of controlled studies. *Clinical Psychology Review, 21,* 683–703.

Abrams, S. (1995). False memory syndrome vs. total repression. *Journal of Psychiatry and Law, 23,* 283–293.

Ackerman, P. L., Bowen, K. R., Beier, M. E., & Kanfer, R. (2001). Determinants of individual differences and gender differences in knowledge. *Journal of Educational Psychology, 93,* 797–825.

Ackerman, P. L., & Rolfhus, E. L. (1999). The locus of adult intelligence: Knowledge, abilities, and nonability traits. *Psychology and Aging, 14,* 314–330.

Acklin, M. W., Bibb, J. L., Boyer, P., & Jain, V. (1991). Early memories as expressions of relationship paradigms: A preliminary investigation. *Journal of Personality Assessment, 57,* 177–192.

Acklin, M. W., Sauer, A., Alexander, G., & Dugoni, B. (1989). Predicting depression using earliest childhood memories. *Journal of Personality Assessment, 53,* 51–59.

Adams, G. R., & Fitch, S. A. (1982). Ego stage and identity status development: A cross-sequential analysis. *Journal of Personality and Social Psychology, 43,* 574–583.

Adams, H. E., Wright, L. W., Jr., & Lohr, B. A. (1996). Is homophobia associated with homosexual arousal? *Journal of Abnormal Psychology, 105,* 440–445.

Adams-Webber, J. (1990). Personal construct theory and cognitive science. *International Journal of Personal Construct Psychology, 3,* 415–421.

Adkins, K. K., & Parker, W. (1996). Perfectionism and suicidal preoccupation. *Journal of Personality, 64,* 529–543.

Adler, A. (1927). *Understanding human nature* (W. B. Wolfe, Trans.). New York: Fawcett. (Original work published 1921)

Adler, A. (1929). *The practice and theory of individual psychology* (P. Radin, Trans.) (2nd ed.). London: Routledge & Kegan Paul. (Original work published 1923)

Adler, A. (1958). Suicide. *Journal of Individual Psychology, 14,* 57–61. (Original work published 1937)

Adler, A. (1964). *Social interest: A challenge to mankind.* New York: Capricorn. (Original work published 1936)

Adler, A. (1978). *Co-operation between the sexes: Writings on women and men, love and marriage, and sexuality* (H. L. Ansbacher & R. R. Ansbacher, Eds. and Trans.). New York: Norton.

Adler, A. (1982a). The fundamental views of Individual Psychology. *Individual Psychology, 38,* 3–6. (Original work published 1935)

Adler, A. (1982b). The progress of mankind. *Individual Psychology, 38,* 13–17. (Original work published 1937)

Adler, A. (1988a). The child's inner life and a sense of community. *Individual Psychology, 44,* 417–423. (Original work published 1917)

Adler, A. (1988b). Personality as a self-consistent unity. *Individual Psychology, 44,* 431–440. (Original work published 1932)

Adler, A. (1988c). Problem children. *Individual Psychology, 44,* 406–416. (Original work published 1926)

Adler, A. (1998). Understanding children with emotional problems [based on 1932–1933 lectures]. *Journal of Humanistic Psychology, 38,* 121–127.

Adolphs, R., Tranel, D., & Damasio, A. R. (1998). The human amygdala in social judgment. *Nature, 393,* 470–474.

Aftanas, L., & Golosheykin, S. (2005). Impact of regular meditation practice on EEG activity at rest and during evoked negative emotions. *International Journal of Neuroscience, 115,* 893–909.

Agger, E. M. (1988). Psychoanalytic perspectives on sibling relationships. *Psychoanalytic Inquiry, 8,* 3–30.

Agor, W. H. (1991). How intuition can be used to enhance creativity in organizations. *Journal of Creative Behavior, 25,* 11–19.

Agronick, G. S., & Duncan, L. E. (1998). Personality and social change: Individual differences, life path, and importance attributed to the women's movement. *Journal of Personality and Social Psychology, 74,* 1545–1555.

Ahadi, S. A., & Rothbart, M. K. (1994). Temperament, development, and the Big Five. In C. F. Halverson, G. A. Kohnstamm, & R. P. Martin (Eds.), *The developing structure of temperament and personality from infancy to adulthood* (pp. 189–208). Hillsdale, NJ: Erlbaum.

Ainsworth, M. D. S. (1972). Attachment and dependency. In J. L. Gewirtz (Ed.), *Attachment and dependency* (pp. 97–137). Washington, DC: Winston.

Ainsworth, M. D. S., Blehar, M. C., Waters, E., & Wall, S. (1978). *Patterns of attachment: A psychological study of the Strange Situation.* Hillsdale, NJ: Erlbaum.

Alessi, G. (1992). Models of proximate and ultimate causation in psychology. *American Psychologist, 47,* 1359–1370.

Alexander, I. E. (1988). Personality, psychological assessment, and psychobiography. *Journal of Personality, 56,* 265–294.

Alexander, I. E. (1990). *Personology: Method and content in personality assessment and psychobiography.* Durham, NC: Duke University Press.

Alexander, V. K. (2005). Applications of Maharishi Vedic science to developmental psychology. *Journal of Social Behavior and Personality, 17,* 9–20.

Allan, J., & Brown, K. (1993). Jungian play therapy in elementary schools. *Elementary School Guidance and Counseling, 28,* 30–41.

Allers, C. T., White, J., & Hornbuckle, D. (1990). Early recollections: Detecting depression in the elderly. *Individual Psychology, 46,* 61–66.

Allison, K. W., Crawford, I., Echemendia, R., Robinson, L. V., & Knepp, D. (1994). Human diversity and professional competence: Training in clinical and counseling psychology revisited. *American Psychologist, 49,* 792–796.

Allport, G. W. (1931). What is a trait of personality? *Journal of Abnormal and Social Psychology, 25,* 368–371.

Allport, G. W. (1937a). The functional autonomy of motives. *American Journal of Psychology, 50,* 141–156.

Allport, G. W. (1937b). *Personality: A psychological interpretation.* New York: Henry Holt.

Allport, G. W. (1940). The psychologist's frame of reference. *Psychological Bulletin, 37,* 1–28.

Allport, G. W. (1950a). *The individual and his religion.* New York: Macmillan.

Allport, G. W. (1950b). *The nature of personality: Selected papers.* Cambridge, MA: Addison-Wesley.

Allport, G. W. (1954). *The nature of prejudice.* Cambridge, MA: Addison-Wesley.

Allport, G. W. (1955). *Becoming: Basic considerations for a psychology of personality.* New Haven, CT: Yale University Press.

Allport, G. W. (1959). Religion and prejudice. *Crane Review, 2,* 1–10.

Allport, G. W. (1961). *Pattern and growth in personality.* New York: Holt, Rinehart & Winston.

Allport, G. W. (1962). Prejudice: Is it societal or personal? *Journal of Social Issues, 18*(2), 120–134.

Allport, G. W. (1963). Behavioral science, religion, and mental health. *Journal of Religion and Health, 2,* 187–197.

Allport, G. W. (1964). Mental health: A generic attitude. *Journal of Religion and Health, 4,* 7–21.

Allport, G. W. (Ed.). (1965). *Letters from Jenny.* New York: Harcourt Brace Jovanovich.

Allport, G. W. (1966a). The religious context of prejudice. *Journal for the Scientific Study of Religion, 5,* 447–457.

Allport, G. W. (1966b). Traits revisited. *American Psychologist, 21,* 1–10.

Allport, G. W. (1967). Gordon W. Allport. In E. G. Boring & G. Lindzey (Eds.), *A history of psychology in autobiography* (Vol. 5, pp. 3–25). Englewood Cliffs, NJ: Prentice-Hall.

Allport, G. W., & Allport, F. H. (1921). Personality traits: Their classification and measurement. *Journal of Abnormal and Social Psychology, 16,* 6–40.

Allport, G. W., & Odbert, H. S. (1936). Trait-names: A psycholexical study. *Psychological Monographs, 47*(211).

Allport, G. W., & Postman, L. (1947). *The psychology of rumor.* New York: Henry Holt.

Allport, G. W., & Ross, J. M. (1967). Personal religious orientation and prejudice. *Journal of Personality and Social Psychology, 5,* 432–443.

Allport, G. W., & Vernon, P. E. (1931). *A study of values.* Boston: Houghton Mifflin.

Allport, G. W., & Vernon, P. E. (1933). *Studies in expressive movement.* New York: Macmillan.

Allport, G. W., Vernon, P. E., & Lindzey, G. (1951). *Study of values: A scale for measuring the dominant interests in personality* (Rev. ed.). New York: Houghton Mifflin.

Alter-Reid, K., Gibbs, M. S., Lachenmeyer, J. R., Sigal, J., & Massoth, N. A. (1986). Sexual abuse of children: A review of the empirical findings. *Clinical Psychology Review, 6,* 249–266.

Alterman, A. I., Koppenhaver, J. M., Mulholland, E., Ladden, L. J., & Baime, M. J. (2004). Pilot trial of effectiveness of mindfulness meditation for substance abuse patients. *Journal of Substance Use, 9,* 259–268.

Alvarez, A. N., & Helms, J. E. (2001). Racial identity and reflected appraisals as influences on Asian Americans' racial adjustment. *Cultural Diversity and Ethnic Minority Psychology, 7,* 217–231.

Amaral, D. G. (2002). The primate amygdala and the neurobiology of social behavior: Implications for understanding social anxiety. *Biological Psychiatry, 51,* 11–17.

Ambrose, S. E. (1987). *Nixon: Vol. 1. The education of a politician, 1913–1962.* New York: Simon & Schuster.

Ambrose, S. E. (1989). *Nixon: Vol. 2. The triumph of a politician, 1962–1972.* New York: Simon & Schuster.

American Psychiatric Association. (1994). *Diagnostic and statistical manual of mental disorders* (4th ed.). Washington, DC: Author.

American Psychological Association. (1957). The American Psychological Association Distinguished Scientific Contribution Awards for 1956. *American Psychologist, 12,* 125–133.

American Psychological Association. (1958). Distinguished Scientific Contribution Awards. *American Psychologist, 13,* 729–738.

American Psychological Association. (1973). Distinguished Professional Contribution Award for 1972. *American Psychologist, 28,* 71–74.

American Psychological Association. (1981). Awards for distinguished scientific contributions: 1980. Albert Bandura. *American Psychologist, 36,* 27–34.

American Psychological Association. (1990). Citation for outstanding lifetime contribution to psychology: Presented to B. F. Skinner, August 10, 1990. *American Psychologist, 45,* 1204–1205.

American Psychological Association. (1992). American Psychological Association citation for outstanding lifetime contribution to psychology: Presented to Neal E. Miller, August 16, 1991. *American Psychologist, 47,* 847.

American Psychological Association. (1997). Gold medal award for life achievement in psychological science. *American Psychologist, 52,* 797–799.

Amerikaner, M., Elliot, D., & Swank, P. (1988). Social interest as a predictor of vocational satisfaction. *Individual Psychology, 44,* 316–323.

Amirkhan, J. H. (1990). A factor analytically derived measure of coping: The Coping Strategy Indicator. *Journal of Personality and Social Psychology, 59,* 1066–1074.

Amirkhan, J. H. (1994). Criterion validity of a coping measure. *Journal of Personality Assessment, 62,* 242–261.

Amsel, A. (1992). Frustration theory: Many years later. *Psychological Bulletin, 112,* 396–399.

Andersen, S. M., & Klatzky, R. L. (1987). Traits and social stereotypes: Levels of categorization in person perception. *Journal of Personality and Social Psychology, 53,* 235–246.

Anderson, C. A., Benjamin, A. J., Jr., & Bartholow, B. D. (1998). Does the gun pull the trigger? Automatic priming effects of weapon pictures and weapon names. *Psychological Science, 9,* 308–314.

Anderson, W. (1975). The self-actualization of Richard M. Nixon. *Journal of Humanistic Psychology, 15*(1), 27–34.

Andresen, J. (2000). Meditation meets behavioral medicine: The story of experimental research on meditation. In J. Andresen & R. K. C. Forman (Eds.), *Cognitive models and spiritual maps: Interdisciplinary explorations of religious experience* (pp. 17–73). Bowling Green, OH: Imprint Academic.

Andrews, J. D. (1989). Psychotherapy of depression: A self-confirmation model. *Psychological Review, 96,* 576–607.

Andrews, P. W. (2001). The psychology of social chess and the evolution of attribution mechanisms: Explaining the fundamental attribution error. *Evolution and Human Behavior, 22,* 11–29.

Angelou, M. (1969). *I know why the caged bird sings.* New York: Bantam.

Angelou, M. (1974). *Gather together in my name.* New York: Bantam.

Angelou, M. (1976). *Singin' and swingin' and gettin' merry like Christmas.* New York: Bantam.

Angelou, M. (1981). *The heart of a woman.* New York: Bantam.

Angelou, M. (1986). *All God's children need traveling shoes.* New York: Vintage.

Angelou, M. (1993). *Wouldn't take nothing for my journey now.* New York: Random House.

Angelou, M. (1998). *Even the stars look lonesome.* New York: Bantam.

Angelou, M. (2002). *A song flung up to heaven.* New York: Random House.

Angleitner, A., Buss, D. M., & Demtröder, A. I. (1990). A cross-cultural comparison using the act frequency approach (AFA) in West Germany and the United States. *European Journal of Personality, 4,* 187–207.

Angleitner, A., Ostendorf, F., & John, O. P. (1990). Towards a taxonomy of personality descriptors in German: A psycho-lexical study. *European Journal of Personality, 4,* 89–118.

Annis, H. M. (1990). Relapse to substance abuse: Empirical findings within a cognitive-social learning approach. *Journal of Psychoactive Drugs, 22,* 117–124.

Ansbacher, H. L. (1982). Alfred Adler's views on the unconscious. *Individual Psychology, 38,* 32–41.

Ansbacher, H. L. (1988). Dreikurs's four goals of children's disturbing behavior and Adler's social interest-activity typology. *Individual Psychology, 44,* 282–289.

Ansbacher, H. L. (1989). Adlerian psychology: The tradition of brief psychotherapy. *Individual Psychology, 45,* 26–33.

Ansbacher, H. L. (1990a). Alfred Adler, pioneer in prevention of mental disorders. *Journal of Primary Prevention, 11,* 37–68.

Ansbacher, H. L. (1990b). Alfred Adler's influence on the three leading cofounders of humanistic psychology. *Journal of Humanistic Psychology, 30,* 45–53.

Ansbacher, H. L. (1992). Alfred Adler, pioneer in prevention of mental disorders. *Individual Psychology, 48,* 3–34.

Ansbacher, H. L., & Ansbacher, R. R. (Eds.). (1956). *The individual psychology of Alfred Adler: A systematic presentation in selections from his writings.* New York: Harper Torchbooks.

Antisocial personality—Part II. (2001, January). *Harvard Mental Health Letter, 17*(7), 1, 4.

Antrobus, J. (1991). Dreaming: Cognitive processes during cortical activation and high afferent thresholds. *Psychological Review, 98,* 96–121.

Apostal, R., & Marks, C. (1990). Correlations between the Strong-Campbell and Myers-Briggs scales of introversion-extraversion and career interests. *Psychological Reports, 66,* 811–816.

Archer, J. (1996). Sex differences in social behavior: Are the social role and evolutionary explanations compatible? *American Psychologist, 51,* 909–917.

Archer, S. L. (1982). The lower age boundaries of identity development. *Child Development, 53,* 1551–1556.

Archer, S. L. (1989). Gender differences in identity development: Issues of process, domain and timing. *Journal of Adolescence, 12,* 117–138.

Archer, S. L., & Waterman, A. S. (1988). Psychological individualism: Gender differences or gender neutrality? *Human Development, 31,* 65–81.

Ardila, R. (1992). Toward unity in psychology: The experimental synthesis of behaviour. *International Journal of Psychology, 27,* 299–310.

Arlow, J. A. (1977). Psychoanalysis as scientific method. In M. M. Rahman (Ed.), *The Freudian paradigm: Psychoanalysis and scientific thought* (pp. 345–353). Chicago: Nelson-Hall.

Arnau, R. C., Green, B. A., Rosen, D. H., Gleaves, D. H., & Melancon, J. G. (2003). Are Jungian preferences really categorical? An empirical investigation using taxometric analysis. *Personality and Individual Differences, 34,* 233–251.

Arndt, J., Greenberg, J., Solomon, S., Pyszczynski, T., & Simon, L. (1997). Suppression, accessibility of death-related thoughts, and cultural worldview defense: Exploring the psychodynamics of terror management. *Journal of Personality and Social Psychology, 73,* 5–18.

Arnett, J. J. (2002). The psychology of globalization. *American Psychologist, 57,* 774–783.

Arnett, P. A., & Newman, J. P. (2000). Gray's three-arousal model: An empirical investigation. *Personality and Individual Differences, 28,* 1171–1189.

Arnold, L. E. (2001). Alternative treatments for adults with attention-deficit hyperactivity disorder (ADHD). In J. Wasserstein, L. E. Wolf, & F. F. LeFever (Eds.), *Adult attention deficit disorder: Brain mechanisms and life outcomes* (pp. 310–341, Annals of the New York Academy of Sciences, Vol. 931). New York: New York Academy of Sciences.

Aron, A., & Westbay, L. (1996). Dimensions of the prototype of love. *Journal of Personality and Social Psychology, 70,* 535–551.

Asendorpf, J. B., & Wilpers, S. (1998). Personality effects on social relationships. *Journal of Personality and Social Psychology, 74,* 1531–1544.

Atkinson, R. (1991). A new myth of humanity. *Humanistic Psychologist, 19,* 354–358.

Atwood, J. D., & Maltin, L. (1991). Putting Eastern philosophies into Western psychotherapies. *American Journal of Psychotherapy, 45,* 368–382.

Auerhahn, N. C., & Laub, D. (1998). The primal scene of atrocity: The dynamic interplay between knowledge and fantasy of the holocaust in children of survivors. *Psychoanalytic Psychology, 15,* 360–377.

Austin, J. H. (1998). *Zen and the brain: Toward an understanding of meditation and consciousness.* Cambridge, MA: MIT Press.

Austin, J. H. (2000). Consciousness evolves when the self dissolves. In J. Andresen & R. K. C. Forman (Eds.), *Cognitive models and spiritual maps: Interdisciplinary explorations of religious experience* (pp. 209–230). Bowling Green, OH: Imprint Academic.

Austin, J. T., & Vancouver, J. B. (1996). Goal constructs in psychology: Structure, process, and content. *Psychological Bulletin, 120,* 338–375.

Avants, S. K., & Margolin, A. (2004). Development of spiritual self-schema (3-S) therapy for the treatment of addictive and HIV risk behavior: A convergence of cognitive and Buddhist psychology. *Journal of Psychotherapy Integration, 14,* 253–289.

Avila, C. (2001). Distinguishing BIS-mediated and BAS-mediated disinhibition mechanisms: A comparison of disinhibition models of Gray (1981, 1987) and of Patterson and Newman (1993). *Journal of Personality and Social Psychology, 80,* 311–324.

Avila, C., & Parcet, M. A. (2001). Personality and inhibitory deficits in the stop-signal task: The mediating role of Gray's anxiety and impulsivity. *Personality and Individual Differences, 31,* 975–986.

Aylesworth, A. B., Goodstein, R. C., & Kalra, A. (1999). Effect of archetypal embeds on feelings: An indirect route to affecting attitudes? *Journal of Advertising, 28,* 73–81.

Bache, C. H. (1981). On the emergence of perinatal symptoms in Buddhist meditation. *Journal for the Scientific Study of Religion, 20,* 339–350.

Baird, L. L. (1990). A 24-year longitudinal study of the development of religious ideas. *Psychological Reports, 66,* 479–482.

Bakan, D. (1982). On evil as a collective phenomenon. *Journal of Humanistic Psychology, 22*(4), 91–92.

Baker, J. E. (2001). Mourning and the transformation of object relationships: Evidence for the persistence of internal attachment. *Psychoanalytic Psychology, 18,* 55–73.

Baker, R. (1993). Some reflections on humour in psychoanalysis. *International Journal of Psychoanalysis, 74,* 951–960.

Balay, J., & Shevrin, H. (1988). The subliminal psychodynamic activation method: A critical review. *American Psychologist, 43,* 161–174.

Baldwin, A. C., Critelli, J. W., Stevens, L. C., & Russell, S. (1986). Androgyny and sex role measurement: A personal construct approach. *Journal of Personality and Social Psychology, 51,* 1081–1088.

Baltes, P. B., Sowarka, D., & Kliegl, R. (2001). Cognitive training research on fluid intelligence in old age: What can older adults achieve by themselves? *Psychology and Aging, 4,* 217–221.

Bandura, A. (1961). Psychotherapy as a learning process. *Psychological Bulletin, 58,* 143–159.

Bandura, A. (1965a). Behavioral modifications through modeling procedures. In L. Krasner & L. Ullmann (Eds.), *Research in behavior modification* (pp. 310–340). New York: Holt, Rinehart & Winston.

Bandura, A. (1965b). Influences of models' reinforcement contingencies on the acquisition of imitative responses. *Journal of Personality and Social Psychology, 1,* 589–595.

Bandura, A. (1965c). Vicarious processes: A case of no-trial learning. In L. Berkowitz (Ed.), *Advances in experimental social psychology* (Vol. 2, pp. 1–55). New York: Academic Press.

Bandura, A. (1969). Social learning of moral judgments. *Journal of Personality and Social Psychology, 11,* 275–279.

Bandura, A. (1973). *Aggression: A social learning analysis.* Englewood Cliffs, NJ: Prentice-Hall.

Bandura, A. (1977). Self-efficacy: Toward a unifying theory of behavioral change. *Psychological Review, 84,* 191–215.

Bandura, A. (1978). The self system in reciprocal determinism. *American Psychologist, 33,* 344–358.

Bandura, A. (1980). Gauging the relationship between self-efficacy judgment and action. *Cognitive Therapy and Research, 4,* 263–268.

Bandura, A. (1984a). Recycling misconceptions of perceived self-efficacy. *Cognitive Therapy and Research, 8,* 231–255.

Bandura, A. (1984b). Representing personal determinants in causal structures. *Psychological Review, 91,* 508–511.

Bandura, A. (1986a). Fearful expectations and avoidant actions as coeffects of perceived self-inefficacy. *American Psychologist, 41,* 1389–1391.

Bandura, A. (1986b). *Social foundations of thought and action: A social cognitive theory.* Englewood Cliffs, NJ: Prentice-Hall.

Bandura, A. (1989a). Human agency in social cognitive theory. *American Psychologist, 44,* 1175–1184.

Bandura, A. (1989b). Regulation of cognitive processes through perceived self-efficacy. *Developmental Psychology, 25,* 729–735.

Bandura, A. (1990a). Perceived self-efficacy in the exercise of control over AIDS infection. *Evaluation and Program Planning, 13,* 9–17.

Bandura, A. (1990b). Selective activation and disengagement of moral control. *Journal of Social Issues, 46*(1), 27–46.

Bandura, A. (1991a). Human agency: The rhetoric and the reality. *American Psychologist, 46,* 157–162.

Bandura, A. (1991b). Social cognitive theory of self-regulation. *Organizational Behavior and Human Decision Processes, 50,* 248–287.

Bandura, A. (1998). Exploration of fortuitous determinants of life paths. *Psychological Inquiry, 9,* 95–115.

Bandura, A. (1999a). Moral disengagement in the perpetration of inhumanities. *Personality and Social Psychology Review, 3,* 193–209.

Bandura, A. (1999b). A sociocognitive analysis of substance abuse: An agentic perspective. *Psychological Science, 10,* 214–217.

Bandura, A. (2000). Exercise of human agency through collective efficacy. *Current Directions in Psychological Science, 9,* 75–78.

Bandura, A. (2001a). The changing face of psychology at the dawning of a globalization era. *Canadian Psychology, 42,* 12–24.

Bandura, A. (2001b). Social cognitive theory: An agentic perspective. *Annual Review of Psychology, 52,* 1–26.

Bandura, A., Adams, N. E., & Beyer, J. (1977). Cognitive processes mediating behavioral change. *Journal of Personality and Social Psychology, 35,* 125–139.

Bandura, A., Adams, N. E., Hardy, A. B., & Howells, G. N. (1980). Tests of the generality of self-efficacy theory. *Cognitive Therapy and Research, 4,* 39–66.

Bandura, A., & Barab, P. G. (1973). Processes governing disinhibitory effects through symbolic modeling. *Journal of Abnormal Psychology, 82,* 1–9.

Bandura, A., Blanchard, E. B., & Ritter, B. (1969). The relative efficacy of desensitization and modeling approaches for inducing behavioral, affective, and attitudinal changes. *Journal of Personality and Social Psychology, 13,* 173–199.

Bandura, A., Caprara, G. V., Barbaranelli, C., Pastorelli, C., & Regalia, C. (2001). Sociocognitive self-regulatory mechanisms governing transgressive behavior. *Journal of Personality and Social Psychology, 80,* 125–135.

Bandura, A., Cioffi, D., Taylor, C. B., & Brouillard, M. E. (1988). Perceived self-efficacy in coping with cognitive stressors and opioid activation. *Journal of Personality and Social Psychology, 55,* 479–488.

Bandura, A., Grusec, J. E., & Menlove, F. L. (1966). Observational learning as a function of symbolization and incentive set. *Child Development, 37,* 499–506.

Bandura, A., Grusec, J. E., & Menlove, F. L. (1967a). Some social determinants of self-monitoring reinforcement systems. *Journal of Personality and Social Psychology, 5,* 449–455.

Bandura, A., Grusec, J. E., & Menlove, F. L. (1967b). Vicarious extinction of avoidance behavior. *Journal of Personality and Social Psychology, 5,* 16–23.

Bandura, A., Jeffery, R. W., & Wright, C. L. (1974). Efficacy of participant modeling as a function of response induction aids. *Journal of Abnormal Psychology, 83,* 56–64.

Bandura, A., & Jourden, F. J. (1991). Self-regulatory mechanisms governing the impact of social comparison on complex decision making. *Journal of Personality and Social Psychology, 60,* 941–951.

Bandura, A., & McDonald, F. J. (1963). The influence of social reinforcement and the behavior of models in shaping children's moral judgments. *Journal of Abnormal Psychology, 67,* 274–281.

Bandura, A., & Menlove, F. L. (1968). Factors determining vicarious extinction of avoidance behavior through symbolic modeling. *Journal of Personality and Social Psychology, 8,* 99–108.

Bandura, A., & Mischel, W. (1965). Modification of self-imposed delay of reward through exposure to live and symbolic models. *Journal of Personality and Social Psychology, 2,* 698–705.

Bandura, A., O'Leary, A., Taylor, C. B., Gauthier, J., & Gossard, D. (1987). Perceived self-efficacy and pain control: Opioid and nonopioid mechanisms. *Journal of Personality and Social Psychology, 53,* 563–571.

Bandura, A., Reese, L., & Adams, N. E. (1982). Microanalysis of action and fear arousal as a function of differential levels of perceived self-efficacy. *Journal of Personality and Social Psychology, 43,* 5–21.

Bandura, A., Ross, D., & Ross, S. A. (1963a). A comparative test of the status envy, social power, and secondary reinforcement theories of identificatory learning. *Journal of Abnormal and Social Psychology, 67,* 527–534.

Bandura, A., Ross, D., & Ross, S. A. (1963b). Vicarious reinforcement and imitative learning. *Journal of Abnormal and Social Psychology, 67,* 601–607.

Bandura, A., Taylor, C. B., Williams, S. L., Mefford, I. N., & Barchas, J. D. (1985). Catecholamine secretion as a function of perceived coping self-efficacy. *Journal of Consulting and Clinical Psychology, 53,* 406–414.

Bandura, A., & Whalen, C. K. (1966). The influence of antecedent reinforcement and divergent modeling cues on patterns of self-reward. *Journal of Personality and Social Psychology, 3,* 373–382.

Bandura, A., & Wood, R. (1989). Effect of perceived controllability and performance standards on self-regulation of complex decision making. *Journal of Personality and Social Psychology, 56,* 805–814.

Bannister, D. (1975). Personal construct theory psychotherapy. In D. Bannister (Ed.), *Issues and approaches in the psychological therapies* (pp. 31–47). Chichester, UK: Wiley.

Bannister, D., Adams-Webber, J. R., Penn, W. I., & Radley, A. R. (1975). Reversing the process of thought-disorder: A serial validation experiment. *British Journal of Social and Clinical Psychology, 14,* 169–180.

Bannister, D., & Salmon, P. (1966). Schizophrenic thought disorder: Specific or diffuse? *British Journal of Medical Psychology, 39,* 215–219.

Barenbaum, N. B. (2000). How social was personality? The Allports' "connection" of social and personality psychology. *Journal of the History of the Behavioral Sciences, 36,* 471–487.

Barends, A., Westen, D., Leigh, J., Silbert, D., & Byers, S. (1990). Assessing affect-tone of relationship paradigms from TAT and interview data. *Psychological Assessment, 2,* 329–332.

Barnard, C. P., & Hirsch, C. (1985). Borderline personality and victims of incest. *Psychological Reports, 57,* 715–718.

Barnes, V. A., Treiber, F. A., & Davis, H. (2001). Impact of Transcendental Meditation® on cardiovascular function at rest and during acute stress in adolescents with high normal blood pressure. *Journal of Psychosomatic Research, 51,* 597–605.

Barnes, V. A., Treiber, F. A., & Johnson, M. H. (2004). Impact of transcendental meditation on ambulatory blood pressure in African-American adolescents. *American Journal of Hypertension, 17,* 366–369.

Baron, S. H., & Pletsch, C. (Eds.). (1985). *Introspection in biography.* Hillsdale, NJ: Erlbaum.

Barresi, J. (1999). On becoming a person. *Philosophical Psychology, 12,* 79–98.

Barrett, D., & Fine, H. J. (1990). The Gnostic syndrome: Anorexia nervosa. *Psychoanalytic Psychotherapy, 4,* 263–270.

Barrett, L. F., & Pietromonaco, P. R. (1997). Accuracy of the five-factor model in predicting perceptions of daily social interactions. *Personality and Social Psychology Bulletin, 23,* 1173–1187.

Barrick, M. R., & Mount, M. K. (1991). The Big Five personality dimensions and job performance: A meta-analysis. *Personnel Psychology, 44,* 1–26.

Barrick, M. R., & Mount, M. K. (1996). Effects of impression management and self-deception on the predictive validity of personality constructs. *Journal of Applied Psychology, 81,* 261–272.

Barrick, M. R., Mount, M. K., & Strauss, J. P. (1993). Conscientiousness and performance of sales representatives: Test of the mediating effects of goal setting. *Journal of Applied Psychology, 78,* 715–722.

Barrick, M. R., Patton, G. K., & Haugland, S. N. (2000). Accuracy of interviewer judgements of job applicant personality traits. *Personnel Psychology, 53,* 925–951.

Barry, B., & Stewart, G. L. (1997). Composition, process, and performance in self-managed groups: The role of personality. *Journal of Applied Psychology, 82,* 62–78.

Barry, G. M. (1991). Consulting with contrary types. *Organization Development Journal, 9*(1), 61–66.

Bartholomew, K. (1990). Avoidance of intimacy: An attachment perspective. *Journal of Social and Personal Relationships, 7,* 147–178.

Bartholomew, K., & Horowitz, L. M. (1991). Attachment styles among young adults: A test of a four-category model. *Journal of Personality and Social Psychology, 61,* 226–244.

Bartussek, D., Diedrich, O., Naumann, E., & Collet, W. (1993). Introversion-extraversion and event-related potential (ERP): A test of J. A. Gray's theory. *Personality and Individual Differences, 14,* 565–574.

Bass, M. L., Curlette, W. L., Kern, R. M., & McWilliams, A. E., Jr. (2002). Social interest: A meta-analysis of a multidimensional construct. *Journal of Individual Psychology, 58,* 4–34.

Bassoff, E. S., & Glass, G. V. (1982). The relationship between sex roles and mental health: A meta-analysis of twenty-six studies. *Counseling Psychologist, 10,* 105–112.

Bates, J. E., & Wachs, T. D. (Eds.). (1994). *Temperament: Individual differences at the interface of biology and behavior.* Washington, DC: American Psychological Association.

Batson, C. D. (1976). Religion as prosocial: Agent or double agent? *Journal for the Scientific Study of Religion, 15*, 29–45.

Batson, C. D. (1990). Good Samaritans—or priests and Levites? Using William James as a guide in the study of religious prosocial motivation. *Personality and Social Psychology Bulletin, 16*, 758–768.

Batson, C. D., Eidelman, S. H., & Higley, S. L. (2001). "And who is my neighbor?": II: Quest religion as a source of universal compassion. *Journal for the Scientific Study of Religion, 40*, 39–50.

Batson, C. D., Floyd, R. B., Meyer, J. M., & Winner, A. L. (1999). "And who is my neighbor?": Intrinsic religion as a source of universal compassion. *Journal for the Scientific Study of Religion, 38*, 445–457.

Batson, C. D., & Schoenrade, P. A. (1991a). Measuring religion as quest: I. Validity concerns. *Journal for the Scientific Study of Religion, 30*, 416–429.

Batson, C. D., & Schoenrade, P. A. (1991b). Measuring religion as quest: II. Reliability concerns. *Journal for the Scientific Study of Religion, 30*, 430–447.

Batson, C. D., Schoenrade, P., & Ventis, W. L. (1993). *Religion and the individual*. New York: Oxford University Press.

Bauer, P. J. (1996). What do infants recall of their lives? *American Psychologist, 51*, 29–41.

Baumeister, R. F. (1987). How the self became a problem: A psychological review of historical research. *Journal of Personality and Social Psychology, 52*, 163–176.

Baumeister, R. F. (1990). Suicide as escape from self. *Psychological Review, 97*, 90–113.

Baumeister, R. F. (1991). On the stability of variability: Retest reliability of metatraits. *Personality and Social Psychology Bulletin, 17*, 633–639.

Baumeister, R. F. (1997a). Esteem threat, self-regulatory breakdown, and emotional distress as factors in self-defeating behavior. *Review of General Psychology, 1*, 145–174.

Baumeister, R. F. (1997b). Identity, self-concept, and self-esteem: The self lost and found. In R. Hogan, J. Johnson, & S. Briggs (Eds.), *Handbook of personality psychology* (pp. 681–710). San Diego: Academic Press.

Baumeister, R. F., Bratslavsky, E., Muraven, M., & Tice, D. M. (1998). Ego depletion: Is the active self a limited resource? *Journal of Personality and Social Psychology, 74*, 1252–1265.

Baumeister, R. F., Dale, K., & Sommer, K. L. (1998). Empirical findings in modern social psychology: Reaction formation, projection, displacement, undoing, isolation, sublimation, and denial. *Journal of Personality, 68*, 1081–1124.

Baumeister, R. F., Heatherton, T. F., & Tice, D. M. (1993). When ego threats lead to self-regulation failure: Negative consequences of high self-esteem. *Journal of Personality and Social Psychology, 64*, 141–156.

Baumeister, R. F., Smart, L., & Boden, J. M. (1996). Relation of threatened egotism to violence and aggression: The dark side of high self-esteem. *Psychological Review, 103*, 5–33.

Baumeister, R. F., Stillwell, A., & Wotman, S. R. (1990). Victim and perpetrator accounts of interpersonal conflict: Autobiographical narratives about anger. *Journal of Personality and Social Psychology, 59*, 994–1005.

Baumeister, R. F., & Tice, D. M. (1988). Metatraits. *Journal of Personality, 56*, 571–598.

Baumrind, D. (1967). Child care practices anteceding three patterns of preschool behavior. *Genetic Psychology Monographs, 75*, 43–88.

Baumrind, D. (1971). Current patterns of parental authority. *Developmental Psychology Monograph, 4*(1), part 2.

Bay-Hinitz, A. K., Peterson, R. F., & Quilitch, H. R. (1994). Cooperative games: A way to modify aggressive and cooperative behaviors in young children. *Journal of Applied Behavior Analysis, 27*, 435–446.

Becker, E. (1973). *The denial of death*. New York: Free Press.

Beebe, J. (1996). Jungian illumination of film. *Psychoanalytic Review, 83*, 579–587.

Beebe, J., Cambray, J., & Kirsch, T. B. (2001). What Freudians can learn from Jung. *Psychoanalytic Psychology, 18*, 213–242.

Behrends, R. S. (1986). The integrated personality: Maximal utilization of information. *Journal of Humanistic Psychology, 26*(1), 27–59.

Bell, A. J., & Cook, H. (1998). Empirical evidence for a compensatory relationship between dream content and repression. *Psychoanalytic Psychology, 15*, 154–163.

Bellak, L. (1993). *Psychoanalysis as a science*. Boston: Allyn & Bacon.

Belsky, J. (1993). Etiology of child maltreatment: A developmental-ecological analysis. *Psychological Bulletin, 114*, 413–434.

Bem, D. J., & Allen, A. (1974). On predicting some of the people some of the time: The search for cross-situational consistencies in behavior. *Psychological Review, 81*, 506–520.

Benford, M. S. (2001). Can a theory derived from recent experimental data explain precognition and other mysterious spiritual phenomena? *Journal of Religion and Psychical Research, 24*, 132–141.

Benjamin, L. T., Jr., & Dixon, D. N. (1996). Dream analysis by mail: An American woman seeks Freud's advice. *American Psychologist, 51*, 461–468.

Benjamin, P., & Looby, J. (1998). Defining the nature of spirituality in the context of Maslow's and Rogers's theories. *Counseling and Values, 42*(2), 92–100.

Benson, H. (1975). *The relaxation response*. New York: Morrow.

Benson, H., Malhotra, M. S., Goldman, R. F., Jacobs, G. D., & Hopkins, P. J. (1990). Three case reports of the metabolic and electroencephalographic changes during advanced Buddhist meditation techniques. *Behavioral Medicine, 16*, 90–95.

Bereczkei, T. (2000). Evolutionary psychology: A new perspective in the behavioral sciences. *European Psychologist, 5*, 175–190.

Berger, P. L., & Luckmann, T. (1966). *The social construction of reality: A treatise in the sociology of knowledge*. New York: Doubleday.

Berkowitz, L. (1962). *Aggression: A social psychological analysis*. New York: McGraw-Hill.

Berkowitz, L. (1983). Aversively stimulated aggression: Some parallels and differences in research with animals and humans. *American Psychologist, 38*, 1135–1144.

Berkowitz, L. (1986). Situational influences on reactions to observed violence. *Journal of Social Issues, 42*(3), 93–106.

Berkowitz, L. (1989). Frustration-aggression hypothesis: Examination and reformulation. *Psychological Bulletin, 106*, 59–73.

Berkowitz, L., & LePage, A. (1967). Weapons as aggression-eliciting stimuli. *Journal of Personality and Social Psychology, 7*, 202–207.

Berman, S., Ozkaragoz, T., Young, R. M., & Noble, E. P. (2002). D2 dopamine receptor gene polymorphism discriminates two kinds of novelty seeking. *Personality and Individual Differences, 33*, 867–882.

Bernal, M. E., & Castro, F. G. (1994). Are clinical psychologists prepared for service and research with ethnic minorities? Report of a decade of progress. *American Psychologist, 49*, 797–805.

Berntson, G. G., & Cacioppo, J. T. (2000). Psychobiology and social psychology: Past, present, and future. *Personality and Social Psychology Review, 4*, 3–15.

Berr, S. A., Church, A. H., & Waclawski, J. (2000). The right relationship is everything: Linking personality preferences to managerial behaviors. *Human Resource Development Quarterly, 11*(2), 133–157.

Berzonsky, M. D. (1989). The self as a theorist: Individual differences in identity formation. *International Journal of Personal Construct Psychology, 2*, 363–376.

Berzonsky, M. D. (1992). "Can we see ourselves changing? Toward a personal construct model of adult development": Commentary. *Human Development, 35*, 76–80.

Berzonsky, M. D., & Neimeyer, G. J. (1988). Identity status and personal construct systems. *Journal of Adolescence, 11*, 195–204.

Berzonsky, M. D., Rice, K. G., & Neimeyer, G. J. (1990). Identity status and self-construct systems: Process X structure interactions. *Journal of Adolescence, 13*, 251–263.

Bettelheim, B. (1976). *The uses of enchantment: The meaning and importance of fairy tales*. New York: Knopf.

Bhikkhu, T. (Trans.). (1994). Tittha Sutta: Various sectarians (1) [Translation from the Pali canon of *Udana 6.4, Sutta Pitaka*]. Available online at http://www.accesstoinsight.org/tipitaka/kn/ud/ud.6.04.than.html

Bieling, P. J., Summerfeldt, L. J., Israeli, A. L., & Antony, M. M. (2004). Perfectionism as an explanatory construct in comorbidity of Axis I disorders. *Journal of Psychopathology and Behavioral Assessment, 26,* 193–201.

Bieri, J. (1955). Cognitive complexity-simplicity and predictive behavior. *Journal of Abnormal and Social Psychology, 51,* 263–268.

Bilgrave, D. P., & Deluty, R. H. (1998). Religious beliefs and therapeutic orientations of clinical and counseling psychologists. *Journal for the Scientific Study of Religion, 37,* 329–349.

Binder, L. M., Dixon, M. R., & Ghezzi, P. M. (2000). A procedure to teach self-control to children with attention deficit hyperactivity disorder. *Journal of Applied Behavior Analysis, 33,* 233–237.

Birch, M. (1998). Through a glass darkly: Questions about truth and memory. *Psychoanalytic Psychology, 15,* 34–48.

Bitner, R., Hillman, L., Victor, B., & Walsh, R. (2003). Subjective effects of antidepressants: A pilot study of the varieties of antidepressant-induced experiences in meditators. *Journal of Nervous and Mental Disease, 191,* 660–667.

Bjorklund, D. F. (1997). The role of immaturity in human development. *Psychological Bulletin, 122,* 153–169.

Blackmore, S. (1994). Psi in psychology. *Skeptical Inquirer, 18,* 351–355.

Blackwood, N. J., Howard, R. J., Bentall, R. P., & Murray, R. M. (2001). Cognitive neuropsychiatric models of persecutory delusions. *American Journal of Psychiatry, 158,* 527–539.

Blagrove, M. (1993). The structuralist analysis of dream series. *Journal of Mental Imagery, 17*(3 & 4), 77–90.

Blankfield, R. P. (1991). Suggestion, relaxation, and hypnosis as adjuncts in the care of surgery patients: A review of the literature. *American Journal of Clinical Hypnosis, 33,* 172–186.

Blashfield, R. K., & Livesley, W. J. (1991). Metaphorical analysis of psychiatric classification as a psychological test. *Journal of Abnormal Psychology, 100,* 262–270.

Blatt, S. J. (1995). The destructiveness of perfectionism: Implications for the treatment of depression. *American Psychologist, 50,* 1003–1020.

Block, J. (1989). Critique of the act frequency approach to personality. *Journal of Personality and Social Psychology, 56,* 234–245.

Block, J. (1993). Studying personality the long way. In D. C. Funder, R. D. Parke, C. Tomlinson-Keasey, & K. Widaman (Eds.), *Studying lives through time: Personality and development* (pp. 4–41). Washington, DC: American Psychological Association.

Block, J. (1995). A contrarian view of the five-factor approach to personality description. *Psychological Bulletin, 117,* 187–215.

Block, J. H., & Block, J. (1980). The role of ego-control and ego-resiliency in the organization of behavior. In W. A. Collins (Ed.), *The Minnesota Symposia on Child Psychology: Vol. 13. Development of cognition, affect, and social relations.* (pp. 39–101). Hillsdale, NJ: Erlbaum.

Bloland, S. E. (2005). *In the shadow of fame: A memoir by the daughter of Erik H. Erikson.* New York: Viking.

Blomberg, J., Lazar, A., & Sandell, R. (2001). Long-term outcome of long-term psychoanalytically oriented therapies: First findings of the Stockholm outcome of psychotherapy and psychoanalysis study. *Psychotherapy Research, 11,* 361–382.

Blouin, A. G., & Goldfield, G. S. (1995). Body image and steroid use in male bodybuilders. *International Journal of Eating Disorders, 18,* 159–165.

Blum, G. S. (1953). *Psychoanalytic theories of personality.* New York: McGraw-Hill.

Blum, H. P. (1994). Dora's conversion syndrome: A contribution to the prehistory of the Holocaust. *Psychoanalytic Quarterly, 63,* 518–535.

Blume, A. W. (2001). Negative reinforcement and substance abuse: Using a behavioral conceptualization to enhance treatment. *Behavior Analyst Today, 2,* 86–90.

Blume, E. S. (1995). The ownership of truth. *Journal of Psychohistory, 23*(2), 131–140.

Blustein, D. L., Devenis, L. E., & Kidney, B. A. (1989). Relationship between the identity formation process and career development. *Journal of Counseling Psychology, 36,* 196–202.

Bochner, S. (1994). Cross-cultural differences in the self concept: A test of Hofstede's individualism/collectivism distinction. *Journal of Cross-Cultural Psychology, 25,* 273–283.

Bock, P. K. (2000). Culture and personality revisited. *American Behavioral Scientist, 44,* 32–40.

Bodden, J. C. (1970). Cognitive complexity as a factor in appropriate vocational choice. *Journal of Counseling Psychology, 17,* 364–368.

Boden, J. M., & Baumeister, R. F. (1997). Repressive coping: Distraction using pleasant thoughts and memories. *Journal of Personality and Social Psychology, 73,* 45–62.

Bohart, A. C. (1988). Empathy: Client centered and psychoanalytic. *American Psychologist, 43,* 667–668.

Bohart, A. C. (1991). The missing 249 words: In search of objectivity. *Psychotherapy, 28,* 497–503.

Bohart, A. C., & Greenberg, L. S. (Eds.). (1997). *Empathy reconsidered: New directions in psychotherapy.* Washington, DC: American Psychological Association.

Bohart, A. C., O'Hara, M., & Leitner, L. M. (1998). Empirically violated treatments: Disenfranchisement of humanistic and other psychotherapies. *Psychotherapy Research, 8*(2), 141–157.

Bolen, J. S. (1984). *Goddesses in everywoman: A new psychology of women.* San Francisco: Harper & Row.

Bonanno, G. A., Keltner, D., Holen, A., & Horowitz, M. J. (1995). When avoiding unpleasant emotions might not be such a bad thing: Verbal-autonomic dissociation and midlife conjugal bereavement. *Journal of Personality and Social Psychology, 69,* 975–989.

Bonanno, G. A., Moskowitz, J. T., Papa, A., & Folkman, S. (2005). Resilience to loss in bereaved spouses, bereaved parents, and bereaved gay men. *Journal of Personality and Social Psychology, 88,* 827–843.

Bond, M. (1995). The development and properties of the Defense Style Questionnaire. In H. R. Conte & R. Plutchik (Eds.), *Ego defenses: Theory and measurement* (pp. 202–220). New York: Wiley.

Bondarenko, A. F. (1999). My encounter with Carl Rogers: A retrospective view from the Ukraine. *Journal of Humanistic Psychology, 39*(1), 8–14.

Boon, J. C., & Davis, G. M. (1987). Rumours greatly exaggerated: Allport and Postman's apocryphal study. *Canadian Journal of Behavioural Science, 19,* 430–440.

Boone, J. L., & Kessler, K. L. (1999). More status or more children? Social status, fertility reduction, and long-term fitness. *Evolution and Human Behavior, 20,* 257–277.

Boorstein, S. (Ed.). (1980). *Transpersonal psychotherapy.* Palo Alto, CA: Science and Behavior Books.

Boorstein, S. (2000). Transpersonal psychotherapy. *American Journal of Psychotherapy, 54,* 408–423.

Bordages, J. W. (1989). Self-actualization and personal autonomy. *Psychological Reports, 64,* 1263–1266.

Bores-Rangel, E., Church, A. T., Szendre, D., & Reeves, C. (1990). Self-efficacy in relation to occupational consideration and academic performance in high school equivalency students. *Journal of Counseling Psychology, 37,* 407–418.

Borkenau, P. (1990). Traits as ideal-based and goal-derived social categories. *Journal of Personality and Social Psychology, 58,* 381–396.

Bornstein, R. F. (1992). The dependent personality: Developmental, social, and clinical perspectives. *Psychological Bulletin, 112,* 3–23.

Bornstein, R. F. (1996). Beyond orality: Toward an object relations/interactionist reconceptualization of the etiology and dynamics of dependency. *Psychoanalytic Psychology, 13,* 177–203.

Bornstein, R. F. (1997). Dependent personality disorder in the DSM-IV and beyond. *Clinical Psychology: Science and Practice, 4,* 175–187.

Bornstein, R. F. (1998). Interpersonal dependency and physical illness: A meta-analytic review of retrospective and prospective studies. *Journal of Research in Personality, 32,* 480–497.

Bornstein, R. F. (2000). From oral fixation to object relations: Changing perspectives on the psychodynamics of interpersonal dependency and illness. In P. R. Duberstein & J. M. Masling (Eds.), *Psychodynamic perspectives on sickness and health* (pp. 3–37). Washington, DC: American Psychological Association.

Bornstein, R. F., & Masling, J. M. (Eds.). (2005). *Scoring the Rorschach: Seven validated systems.* Mahwah, NJ: Erlbaum.

Botella, L. (1995). Personal construct psychology, constructivism and postmodern thought. In R. A. Neimeyer & G. J. Neimeyer (Eds.), *Recent advances in personal construct psychology* (Vol. 3, pp. 3–36). New York: Springer.

Bottome, P. (1947). *Alfred Adler: Apostle of freedom* (J. Linton & R. Vaughan, Trans.). London: Faber & Faber.

Bouchard, G., Lussier, Y., & Sabourin, S. (1999). Personality and marital adjustment: Utility of the five-factor model of personality. *Journal of Marriage and the Family, 61,* 651–660.

Bouchard, T. J., Jr., & Hur, Y. (1998). Genetic and environmental influences on the continuous scales of the Myers-Briggs Type Indicator: An analysis based on twins reared apart. *Journal of Personality, 66,* 135–149.

Bouchard, T. J., Jr., & Loehlin, J. C. (2001). Genes, evolution, and personality. *Behavior Genetics, 31,* 243–273.

Bowen, M. V. B. (1996). On being nondirectiveness: The case of Jill. In B. A. Farber, D. C. Brink, & P. M. Raskin (Eds.), *The psychotherapy of Carl Rogers: Cases and commentary* (pp. 84–94). New York: Guilford.

Bowers, K. S. (1985). On being unconsciously influenced and informed. In K. S. Bowers & D. Meichenbaum (Eds.), *The unconscious reconsidered* (pp. 227–272). New York: Wiley.

Bowers, K. S. (1994). A review of Ernest R. Hilgard's books on hypnosis, in commemoration of his 90th birthday. *Psychological Science, 5,* 186–189.

Bowers, K. S., & Farvolden, P. (1996). Revisiting a century-old Freudian slip—from suggestion disavowed to the truth repressed. *Psychological Bulletin, 119,* 355–380.

Bowlby, J. (1988a). Developmental psychiatry comes of age. *American Journal of Psychiatry, 145,* 1–10.

Bowlby, J. (1988b). *A secure base: Parent-child attachment and healthy human development.* New York: Basic Books.

Boyer, P. (2000). Evolutionary psychology and cultural transmission. *American Behavioral Scientist, 43,* 987–1000.

Boyle, G. J., & Cattell, R. B. (1984). Proof of situational sensitivity of mood states and dynamic traits—ergs and sentiments—to disturbing stimuli. *Personality and Individual Differences, 5,* 541–548.

Boyle, G. J. (1989). Re-examination of the major personality-type factors in the Cattell, Comrey and Eysenck scales: Were the factor solutions by Noller et al. optimal? *Personality and Individual Differences, 10,* 1289–1299.

Boysen, S. T., Berntson, G. G., Hannan, M. B., & Cacioppo, J. T. (1996). Quantity-based interference and symbolic representations in chimpanzees (Pan troglodytes). *Journal of Experimental Psychology: Animal Behavior Processes, 22,* 76–86.

Bozarth, J. D. (1985). Quantum theory and the person-centered approach. *Journal of Counseling and Development, 64,* 179–182.

Bozarth, J. D., & Brodley, B. T. (1991). Actualization: A functional concept in client-centered therapy. *Journal of Social Behavior and Personality, 6*(5), 45–59.

Bradley, C. L., & Marcia, J. E. (1998). Generativity-stagnation: A five-category model. *Journal of Personality, 66,* 39–64.

Bradshaw, C. K. (1990). A Japanese view of dependency: What can amae psychology contribute to feminist theory and therapy? *Women and Therapy, 9,* 67–86.

Brainerd, C. J., Stein, L. M., & Reyna, V. F. (1998). On the development of conscious and unconscious memory. *Developmental Psychology, 34,* 342–357.

Brebner, J. (2000). Comment: "The personality theories of H. J. Eysenck and J. A. Gray: A comparative review." [G. Matthews and K. Gilliland (1999), *Personality and Individual Differences, 26,* 583–626.] *Personality and Individual Differences, 28,* 1191–1192.

Bremner, J. D., Krystal, J. H., Charney, D. S., & Southwick, S. M. (1996). Neural mechanisms in dissociative amnesia for childhood abuse: Relevance to the current controversy surrounding the "false memory syndrome." *American Journal of Psychiatry, 153,* 71–82.

Bremner, J. D., Krystal, J. H., Southwick, S. M., & Charney, D. S. (1995). Functional neuroanatomical correlates of the effects of stress on memory. *Journal of Traumatic Stress, 8,* 527–553.

Brems, C., & Johnson, M. E. (1990). Reexamination of the Bem Sex-Role Inventory: The Interpersonal BSRI. *Journal of Personality Assessment, 55,* 484–498.

Brennan, K. A., & Shaver, P. R. (1998). Attachment styles and personality disorders: Their connections to each other and to parental divorce, parental death, and perceptions of parental caregiving. *Journal of Personality, 66,* 835–878.

Brenneis, C. B. (1997). On the relationship of dream content, trauma, and mind: A view from the inside out or outside in? In E. R. Shapiro (Ed.), *The inner world and the outer world: Psychoanalytic perspectives* (pp. 59–76). New Haven: Yale University Press.

Brenneis, C. B. (2000). Evaluating the evidence: Can we find authenticated recovered memory? *Psychoanalytic Psychology, 17,* 61–77.

Brent, D. A. (1989). The psychological autopsy: Methodological considerations for the study of adolescent suicide. *Suicide and Life Threatening Behavior, 19,* 43–57.

Breuer, J., & Freud, S. (1955). Studies on hysteria. In J. Strachey (Ed. and Trans.), *The standard edition of the complete psychological works of Sigmund Freud* (Vol. 2, pp. xxxix–xxxi, 1–335). London: Hogarth Press. (Original work published 1895)

Breuer, J., & Freud, S. (1955). *Studies on hysteria. The standard edition of the complete psychological works of Sigmund Freud* (Vol. 2) (J. Strachey, Ed. & Trans.). London: Hogarth Press. (Original work published 1925)

Brewer, M. B. (1999). The psychology of prejudice: Ingroup love or outgroup hate? *Journal of Social Issues, 55,* 429–444.

Brian, D. (1996). *Einstein: A life.* New York: Wiley.

Bringhurst, N. C. (2001). How assessing personality type can benefit you and your practice. *Journal of Financial Planning, 14*(1), 104–113.

Brock, D. (1996). *The seduction of Hillary Rodham.* New York: Free Press.

Brodley, B. T. (1996). Uncharacteristic directiveness: Rogers and the "anger and hurt" client. In B. A. Farber, D. C. Brink, & P. M. Raskin (Eds.), *The psychotherapy of Carl Rogers: Cases and commentary* (pp. 310–321). New York: Guilford.

Brody, G. H. (1998). Sibling relationship quality: Its causes and consequences. *Annual Review of Psychology, 49,* 1–24.

Brody, N. (1987). Introduction: Some thoughts on the unconscious. *Personality and Social Psychology Bulletin, 13,* 293–298.

Broehl, W. G., Jr., & McGee, V. E. (1981). Content analysis in psychohistory: A study of three lieutenants in the Indian Mutiny, 1957–58. *Journal of Psychohistory, 8,* 281–306.

Brogden, H. E. (1972). Some observations on two methods in psychology. *Psychological Bulletin, 77,* 431–437.

Brothers, L. (1996). Brain mechanisms of social cognition. *Journal of Psychopharmacology, 10,* 2–8.

Brown, C., & Lowis, M. J. (2003). Psychosocial development in the elderly: An investigation into Erikson's ninth stage. *Journal of Aging Studies, 17,* 415–426.

Brown, J. W. (1999). Microgenesis and Buddhism: The concept of momentariness. *Philosophy East and West, 49,* 261–277.

Brown, K. W., & Ryan, R. M. (2003). The benefits of being present: Mindfulness and its role in psychological well-being. *Journal of Personality and Social Psychology, 84,* 822–848.

Browne, A., & Finkelhor, D. (1986). Impact of child sexual abuse: A review of the research. *Psychological Bulletin, 99,* 66–77.

Bruggemann, J. M., & Barry, R. J. (2002). Eysenck's P as a modulator of affective and electrodermal responses to violent and comic film. *Personality and Individual Differences, 32,* 1029–1048.

Bruhn, A. R. (1990). Cognitive-perceptual theory and the projective use of autobiographical memory. *Journal of Personality Assessment, 55,* 95–114.

Bruhn, A. R. (1992a). The Early Memories Procedure: A projective test of autobiographical memory, Part 1. *Journal of Personality Assessment, 58,* 1–15.

Bruhn, A. R. (1992b). The Early Memories Procedure: A projective test of autobiographical memory, Part 2. *Journal of Personality Assessment, 58,* 326–346.

Bruner, J. S. (1956). A cognitive theory of personality. *Contemporary Psychology, 1,* 355–359.

Brunstein, J. C., Schultheiss, O. C., & Grässmann, R. (1998). Personal goals and emotional well-being: The moderating role of motive dispositions. *Journal of Personality and Social Psychology, 75,* 494–508.

Bstan-dzin-rgya-mtsho, Dalai Lama XIV. (1989). *Ocean of wisdom: Guidelines for living.* San Francisco: Harper & Row.

Bstan-dzin-rgya-mtsho, Dalai Lama XIV. (1990). *Freedom in exile: The autobiography of the Dalai Lama.* New York: HarperCollins.

Bstan-dzin-rgya-mtsho, Dalai Lama XIV. (1997). *My land and my people: The original autobiography of His Holiness the Dalai Lama of Tibet.* New York: Warner Books.

Bstan-dzin-rgya-mtsho, Dalai Lama XIV. (1999). *Ethics for the new millennium.* New York: Riverhead Books.

Bstan-dzin-rgya-mtsho, Dalai Lama XIV. (2000). *A simple path: Basic Buddhist teachings by His Holiness the Dalai Lama* (G. T. Junpa, Trans.; D. Side, Ed.). London: Thorsons.

Bstan-dzin-rgya-mtsho, Dalai Lama XIV. (2001). Understanding our fundamental nature. In R. J. Davidson & A. Harrington (Eds.), *Visions of compassion: Western scientists and Tibetan Buddhists examine human nature.* (pp. 66–80). Cary, NC: Oxford University Press.

Bstan-dzin-rgya-mtsho, Dalai Lama XIV. (2003). Cultivating peace as an antidote to violence: Sincere practice is important for promotion of religious harmony. *Vital Speeches of the Day,* 742–743. [Speech delivered to the Washington National Cathedral, Washington, DC, September 11, 2003].

Bstan-dzin-rgya-mtsho, Dalai Lama XIV, & Cutler, H. C. (1998). *The art of happiness: A handbook for living.* New York: Riverhead Books.

Bubenzer, D. L., Zimpfer, D. G., & Mahrle, C. L. (1990). Standardized individual appraisal in agency and private practice: A survey. *Journal of Mental Health Counseling, 12,* 51–66.

Bucci, W. (2000). The need for a "psychoanalytic psychology" in the cognitive science field. *Psychoanalytic Psychology, 17,* 203–224.

Buck, R. (1999). The biological affects: A typology. *Psychological Review, 106,* 301–336.

Buckingham, R. M. (2002). Extraversion, neuroticism and the four temperaments of antiquity: An investigation of physiological reactivity. *Personality and Individual Differences, 32,* 225–246.

Buckmaster, L. R., & Davis, G. A. (1985). ROSE: A measure of self-actualization and its relationship to creativity. *Journal of Creative Behavior, 19,* 30–37.

Bucko, R. A. (2000). The sacred pipe: An archetypal theology. *American Indian Quarterly, 24,* 311–312.

Budd, B. E., Clance, P. C., & Simerly, D. E. (1985). Spatial configurations: Erikson reexamined. *Sex Roles, 12,* 571–577.

Buirs, R. S., & Martin, J. (1997). The therapeutic construction of possible selves: Imagination and its constraints. *Journal of Constructivist Psychology, 10,* 153–166.

Burn, S. M., & Busso, J. (2005). Ambivalent sexism, scriptural literalism, and religiosity. *Psychology of Women Quarterly, 29,* 412–418.

Burns, C. E., Heiby, E. M., & Tharp, R. G. (1983). A verbal behavior analysis of auditory hallucinations. *Behavior Analyst, 6,* 133–143.

Burr, V., & Butt, T. W. (1989). A personal construct view of hypnosis. *British Journal of Experimental and Clinical Hypnosis, 6,* 85–90.

Burrell, M. J., & Jaffe, A. J. (1999). Personal meaning, drug use, and addiction: An evolutionary constructivist perspective. *Journal of Constructivist Psychology, 12,* 41–63.

Burris, C. T., & Jackson, L. M. (1999). Hate the sin/love the sinner, or love the hater? Intrinsic religion and responses to partner abuse. *Journal for the Scientific Study of Religion, 38,* 160–174.

Burris, C. T., Jackson, L. M., Tarpley, W. R., & Smith, G. J. (1996). Religion as quest: The self-directed pursuit of meaning. *Personality and Social Psychology Bulletin, 22,* 1068–1076.

Burris, C. T., & Tarpley, W. R. (1998). Religion as being: Preliminary validation of the Immanence scale. *Journal of Research in Personality, 32,* 55–79.

Busch, F. N., Milrod, B. L., Rudden, M., Shapiro, T., Roiphe, J., Singer, M., & Aronson, A. (2001). How treating psychoanalysts respond to psychotherapy research constraints. *Journal of the American Psychoanalytic Association, 49,* 961–984.

Bushman, B. J., & Anderson, C. A. (2001). Is there time to pull the plug on the hostile versus instrumental aggression dichotomy? *Psychological Review, 108,* 273–279.

Bushman, B. J., & Baumeister, R. F. (1998). Threatened egotism, narcissism, self-esteem, and direct and displaced aggression: Does self-love or self-hate lead to violence? *Journal of Personality and Social Psychology, 75,* 219–229.

Busjahn, A., Faulhaber, H. D., Freier, K., & Luft, F. C. (1999). Genetic and environmental influences on coping styles: A twin study. *Psychosomatic Medicine, 61,* 469–475.

Buss, A., & Plomin, R. (1975). *A temperament theory of personality development.* New York: Wiley-Interscience.

Buss, D. M. (1988). The evolution of human intrasexual competition: Tactics of mate attraction. *Journal of Personality and Social Psychology, 54,* 616–628.

Buss, D. M. (1989). Sex differences in human mate preferences: Evolutionary hypotheses tested in 37 cultures. *Behavioral and Brain Sciences, 12,* 1–49.

Buss, D. M. (1995a). Evolutionary psychology: A new paradigm for psychological science. *Psychological Inquiry, 6,* 1–30.

Buss, D. M. (1995b). The future of evolutionary psychology. *Psychological Inquiry, 6,* 81–87.

Buss, D. M. (1997). Evolutionary foundations of personality. In R. Hogan, J. Johnson, & S. Briggs (Eds.), *Handbook of personality psychology* (pp. 317–344). San Diego: Academic Press.

Buss, D. M. (1999). Human nature and individual differences: The evolution of personality. In L. A. Pervin & O. P. John (Eds.), *Handbook of personality: Theory and research* (2nd ed., pp. 31–56). New York: Guilford.

Buss, D. M. (2000). The evolution of happiness. *American Psychologist, 55,* 15–23.

Buss, D. M., & Craik, K. H. (1980). The frequency concept of dispositions: Dominance and dominant acts. *Journal of Personality, 48,* 379–392.

Buss, D. M., & Craik, K. H. (1983). The act frequency approach to personality. *Psychological Review, 90,* 105–126.

Buss, D. M., & Craik, K. H. (1985). Why not measure that trait? Alternative criteria for identifying important dispositions. *Journal of Personality and Social Psychology, 48,* 934–946.

Buss, D. M., & Craik, K. H. (1989). On the cross-cultural examination of acts and dispositions. *European Journal of Personality, 3,* 19–30.

Buss, D. M., Haselton, M. G., Shackelford, T. K., Bleske, A. L., & Wakefield, J. C. (1998). Adaptations, exaptations, and spandrels. *American Psychologist, 53,* 533–548.

Buss, D. M., Larsen, R. J., Westen, D., & Semmelroth, J. (1992). Sex differences in jealousy: Evolution, physiology, and psychology. *Psychological Science, 3,* 251–255.

Buss, D. M., & Schmitt, D. P. (1993). Sexual strategies theory: An evolutionary perspective on human mating. *Psychological Review, 100,* 204–232.

Buss, D. M., & Shackelford, T. K. (1997a). From vigilance to violence: Mate retention tactics in married couples. *Journal of Personality and Social Psychology, 72,* 346–361.

Buss, D. M., & Shackelford, T. K. (1997b). Human aggression in evolutionary psychological perspective. *Clinical Psychology Review, 17,* 605–619.

Buss, D. M., & Shackelford, T. K. (1997c). Susceptibility to infidelity in the first year of marriage. *Journal of Research in Personality, 31,* 193–221.

Buss, H. M. (1990). The different voice of Canadian feminist autobiographers. *Biography, 13,* 154–167.

Bussey, K., & Bandura, A. (1999). Social cognitive theory of gender development and differentiation. *Psychological Review, 106,* 676–713.

Butcher, J. N., & Rouse, S. V. (1996). Personality: Individual differences and clinical assessment. *Annual Review of Psychology, 47,* 87–111.

Butler, A. C., Chapman, J. E., Forman, E. M., & Beck, A. T. (2004). The empirical status of cognitive-behavioral therapy: A review of meta-analyses. *Clinical Psychology Review, 26,* 17–31.

Butler, J. M., & Haigh, G. V. (1954). Changes in the relation between self-concepts and ideal concepts consequent upon client-centered counseling. In C. R. Rogers & R. F. Dymond (Eds.), *Psychotherapy and personality change* (pp. 55–75). Chicago: University of Chicago Press.

Butt, T. (1998). Sedimentation and elaborative choice. *Journal of Constructivist Psychology, 11,* 265–281.

Butt, T. (2001). Social action and personal constructs. *Theory and Psychology, 11,* 75–95.

Byrd, K. R. (1994). The narrative reconstructions of incest survivors. *American Psychologist, 49,* 439–440.

Cabanac, M., Pouliot, C., & Everett, J. (1997). Pleasure as a sign of efficacy of mental activity. *European Psychologist, 2,* 226–234.

Cacioppo, J. T., Petty, R. E., Feinstein, J. A., & Jarvis, W. B. G. (1996). Dispositional differences in cognitive motivation: The life and times of individuals varying in need for cognition. *Psychological Bulletin, 119,* 197–253.

Cahill, C., Llewelyn, S. P., & Pearson, C. (1991). Long-term effects of sexual abuse which occurred in childhood: A review. *British Journal of Clinical Psychology, 30,* 117–130.

Cahn, B. R., & Polich, J. (2006). Meditation states and traits: EEG, ERP, and neuroimaging studies. *Psychological Bulletin, 132,* 180–211.

Cain, D. J. (1987). Carl Rogers's life in review. *Person-Centered Review, 2,* 476–506.

Cain, D. J. (1996). Rogers and Sylvia: An intimate and affirming encounter. In B. A. Farber, D. C. Brink, & P. M. Raskin (Eds.), *The psychotherapy of Carl Rogers: Cases and commentary* (pp. 275–283). New York: Guilford.

Calabro, L. E. (1997). "First things first": Maslow's hierarchy as a framework for REBT in promoting disability adjustment during rehabilitation. *Journal of Rational Emotive and Cognitive Behavior Therapy, 15,* 193–213.

Campbell, J. (1949). *The hero with a thousand faces.* New York: Pantheon.

Campbell, J. (1972). *Myths to live by.* New York: Viking.

Campbell, J. B., & Heller, J. F. (1987). Correlations of extraversion, impulsivity and sociability with sensation seeking and MBTI-introversion. *Personality and Individual Differences, 8,* 133–136.

Campbell, J. F. (1988). The primary personality factors of younger adolescent Hawaiians. *Genetic, Social, and General Psychology Monographs, 114,* 141–171.

Campbell, J. M., Amerikaner, M., Swank, P., & Vincent, K. (1989). The relationship between the Hardiness Test and the Personal Orientation Inventory. *Journal of Research in Personality, 23,* 373–380.

Campos, L. S., Otta, E., & Siqueira, J. O. (2002). Sex differences in mate selection strategies: Content analyses and responses to personal advertisements in Brazil. *Evolution and Human Behavior, 23,* 395–406.

Cangemi, J. P. (1984). The real purpose of higher education: Developing self-actualizing personalities. *Education, 105,* 151–154.

Canlin, T., Zhao, Z., Desmond, J. E., Kang, E., Gross, J., & Gabrieli, J. D. E. (1998). An fMRI study of personality influences on brain reactivity to emotional stimuli. *Behavioral Neuroscience, 115,* 33–42.

Cann, D. R., & Donderi, D. C. (1986). Jungian personality typology and the recall of everyday and archetypal dreams. *Journal of Personality and Social Psychology, 50,* 1021–1030.

Cantor, N., & Mischel, W. (1979a). Prototypes in person perception. In L. Berkowitz (Ed.), *Advances in experimental social psychology* (Vol. 12, pp. 3–52). New York: Academic Press.

Cantor, N., & Mischel, W. (1979b). Prototypicality and personality: Effects on free recall and personality impressions. *Journal of Research in Personality, 13,* 187–205.

Cantril, H., & Allport, G. W. (1935). *The psychology of radio.* New York: Harper.

Caplan, P. J. (1979). Erikson's concept of inner space: A data-based reevaluation. *American Journal of Orthopsychiatry, 49,* 100–108.

Caplan, P. J. (1984). The myth of women's masochism. *American Psychologist, 39,* 130–139.

Caporeal, L. R. (2001). Evolutionary psychology: Toward a unifying theory and a hybrid science. *Annual Review of Psychology, 52,* 607–628.

Capps, D. (2004). The decades of life: Relocating Erikson's stages. *Pastoral Psychology, 53,* 3–32.

Capra, F. (1975). *The Tao of physics.* Boston: Shambhala.

Caprara, G. V. (1996). Structures and processes in personality psychology. *European Psychologist, 1,* 14–26.

Caprara, G. V., Barbaranelli, C., Bermudez, J., Maslach, C., & Ruch, W. (2000). Multivariate methods for the comparison of factor structures in cross-cultural research: An illustration with the Big Five Questionnaire. *Journal of Cross-Cultural Psychology, 31,* 437–464.

Carich, M. S., & Willingham, W. (1987). The roots of family systems theory in individual psychology. *Individual Psychology, 43,* 71–78.

Carkhuff, R. R. (1969). *Human and helping relations* (Vols. 1 and 2). New York: Holt, Rinehart & Winston.

Carlsen, M. B. (1996). Engaging synergy: Kindred spirits on the edge. *Journal of Humanistic Psychology, 36*(3), 85–102.

Carlson, J. G. (1985). Recent assessments of the Myers-Briggs Type Indicator. *Journal of Personality Assessment, 49,* 356–365.

Carlson, L. E., Speca, M., Patel, K. D., & Goodey, E. (2004). Mindfulness-based stress reduction in relation to quality of life, mood, symptoms of stress and levels of cortisol, dehydroepiandrosterone sulfate (DHEAS) and melatonin in breast and prostate cancer outpatients. *Psychoneuroendocrinology, 29,* 448–474.

Carlson, M., & Mulaik, S. A. (1993). Trait ratings from descriptions of behavior as mediated by components of meaning. *Multivariate Behavioral Research, 28,* 111–159.

Carlson, R. (1971). Where is the person in personality research? *Psychological Bulletin, 75,* 203–219.

Carlson, R. (1981). Studies in script theory: I. Adult analogs of a childhood nuclear scene. *Journal of Personality and Social Psychology, 40,* 501–510.

Carlson, R. (1988). Exemplary lives: The uses of psychobiography for theory development. *Journal of Personality, 56,* 105–138.

Carmona, A., Miller, N. E., & Demierre, T. (1974). Instrumental learning of gastric vascular tonicity responses. *Psychosomatic Medicine, 36,* 156–163.

Carp, C. E. (1998). Clown therapy: The creation of a clown character as a treatment intervention. *Arts in Psychotherapy, 25,* 245–255.

Carter, O. L., Presti, D. E., Callistemon, C., Ungerer, Y., Lin, G. B., & Pettigrew, J. D. (2005a). Meditation alters perceptual rivalry in Tibetan Buddhist monks. *Current Biology, 15,* R412–R413.

Carter, O. L., Presti, D. E., Callistemon, C., Ungerer, Y., Lin, G. B., & Pettigrew, J. D. (2005b). Supplemental data: Meditation alters perceptual rivalry in Tibetan Buddhist monks. *Current Biology, 15,* R1.

Cartwright, D. (1989). Concurrent validation of a measure of transcendental powers. *Journal of Parapsychology, 53,* 43–59.

Cartwright, D., DeBruin, J., & Berg, S. (1991). Some scales for assessing personality based on Carl Rogers' theory: Further evidence of validity. *Personality and Individual Differences, 12,* 151–156.

Cartwright, D., & Mori, C. (1988). Scales for assessing aspects of the person. *Person-Centered Review, 3,* 176–194.

Carver, C. S., Meyer, B., & Antoni, M. H. (2000). Responsiveness to threats and incentives, expectancy of recurrence, and distress and disengagement: Moderator effects in women with early stage breast cancer. *Journal of Consulting and Clinical Psychology, 68,* 965–975.

Carver, C. S., & White, T. L. (1994). Behavioral inhibition, behavioral activation, and affective responses to impending reward and punishment: The BIS/BAS Scales. *Journal of Personality and Social Psychology, 67,* 319–333.

Caseley-Rondi, G., Merikle, P. M., & Bowers, K. S. (1994). Unconscious cognition in the context of general anesthesia. *Consciousness and Cognition, 3,* 166–195.

Caseras, X., Torrubia, R., & Farre, J. M. (2001). Is the Behavioural Inhibition System the core vulnerability for Cluster C personality disorders? *Personality and Individual Differences, 31,* 349–359.

Caspi, A. (2000). The child is father of the man: Personality continuities from childhood to adulthood. *Journal of Personality and Social Psychology, 78,* 158–172.

Caspi, A., Elder, G. H., & Bem, D. J. (1987). Moving against the world: Life-course patterns of explosive children. *Developmental Psychology, 23,* 308–313.

Caspi, A., & Herbener, E. S. (1990). Continuity and change: Assortative marriage and the consistency of personality in adulthood. *Journal of Personality and Social Psychology, 58,* 250–258.

Catina, A., Gitzinger, I., & Hoeckh, H. (1992). Defense mechanisms: An approach from the perspective of personal construct psychology. *Personal Construct Psychology, 5,* 249–257.

Cattell, H. E. P., & Schuerger, J. M. (2003). *Essentials of 16PF assessment.* Hoboken, NJ: Wiley.

Cattell, R. B. (1937). *The fight for our national intelligence.* London: King.

Cattell, R. B. (1943a). The description of personality: Basic traits resolved into clusters. *Journal of Abnormal and Social Psychology, 38,* 476–506.

Cattell, R. B. (1943b). The description of personality: I. Foundations of trait measurement. *Psychological Review, 50,* 559–594.

Cattell, R. B. (1950). *Personality: A systematic theoretical and factual study.* New York: McGraw-Hill.

Cattell, R. B. (1957). *Personality and motivation structure and measurement.* Yonkers, NY: World.

Cattell, R. B. (1960). The multiple abstract variance analysis equations and solutions: For nature-nurture research on continuous variables. *Psychological Review, 67,* 353–372.

Cattell, R. B. (1964). *Personality and social psychology.* San Diego: Robert R. Knapp.

Cattell, R. B. (1965). *The scientific analysis of personality.* Baltimore: Penguin.

Cattell, R. B. (1971). *Abilities: Their structure, growth and action.* Boston: Houghton Mifflin.

Cattell, R. B. (1973). *Personality and mood by questionnaire.* San Francisco: Jossey-Bass.

Cattell, R. B. (1974). Raymond B. Cattell. In G. Lindzey (Ed.), *A history of psychology in autobiography* (Vol. 6, pp. 59–100). Englewood Cliffs, NJ: Prentice-Hall.

Cattell, R. B. (1978). *The scientific use of factor analysis.* New York: Plenum.

Cattell, R. B. (1979). *Personality and learning theory: Vol. 1. The structure of personality in its environment.* New York: Springer-Verlag.

Cattell, R. B. (1984). The voyage of a laboratory, 1928–1984. *Multivariate Behavioral Research, 19,* 121–174.

Cattell, R. B. (1990a). Advances in Cattellian personality theory. In L. A. Pervin (Ed.), *Handbook of personality: Theory and research* (pp. 101–110). New York: Guilford.

Cattell, R. B. (1990b). The birth of the Society of Multivariate Experimental Psychology. *Journal of the History of the Behavioral Sciences, 26,* 48–57.

Cattell, R. B., Boyle, G. J., & Chant, D. (2002). Enriched behavioral prediction equation and its impact on structured learning and the dynamic calculus. *Psychological Review, 109,* 202–205.

Cattell, R. B., & Brennan, J. (1984). The cultural types of modern nations, by two quantitative classification methods. *Sociology and Social Research, 68,* 208–235.

Cattell, R. B., Eber, H. W., & Tatsuoka, M. M. (1970). *Handbook for the 16 Personality Factor Questionnaire.* Champaign, IL: IPAT.

Cattell, R. B., & Warburton, F. W. (1961). A cross-cultural comparison of patterns of extraversion and anxiety. *British Journal of Psychology, 52,* 3–16.

Ceci, S. J., & Bruck, M. (1993). Suggestibility of the child witness: A historical review and synthesis. *Psychological Bulletin, 113,* 403–439.

Ceci, S. J., & Bruck, M. (1995). *Jeopardy in the courtroom: A scientific analysis of children's testimony.* Washington, DC: American Psychological Association.

Celani, D. P. (1999). Applying Fairbairn's object relations theory to the dynamics of the battered woman. *American Journal of Psychotherapy, 53,* 60–73.

Cella, D. F., DeWolfe, A. S., & Fitzgibbon, M. (1987). Ego identity status, identification, and decision-making style in late adolescents. *Adolescence, 22,* 849–861.

Cervone, D. (1999). Evolutionary psychology and explanation in personality psychology. *American Behavioral Scientist, 43,* 1001–1014.

Chambers, W. V., Olson, C., Carlock, J., & Olson, D. (1986). Clinical and grid predictions of inconsistencies in individuals' personal constructs. *Perceptual and Motor Skills, 62,* 649–650.

Chance, S. E., Brown, R. T., Dabbs, J. M., Jr., & Casey, R. (2000). Testosterone, intelligence and behavior disorders in young boys. *Personality and Individual Differences, 28,* 437–445.

Chandler, H. M., Alexander, C. N., & Heaton, D. P. (2005). The Transcendental Meditation program and postconventional self-development: A 10-year longitudinal study. *Journal of Social Behavior and Personality, 17,* 93–121.

Chang, E. C. (1998). Cultural differences, perfectionism, and suicidal risk in a college population: Does social problem solving still matter? *Cognitive Therapy and Research, 22,* 237–254.

Chang, E. C. (2003). On the perfectibility of the individual: Going beyond the dialectic of good versus evil. In E. C. Chang & L. J. Sanna (Eds.), *Virtue, vice, and personality: The complexity of behavior* (pp. 125–144). Washington, DC: American Psychological Association.

Chaplin, C. (1964). *My autobiography.* New York: Simon & Schuster.

Chaplin, W. F., John, O. P., & Goldberg, L. R. (1988). Conceptions of states and traits: Dimensional attributes with ideals as prototypes. *Journal of Personality and Social Psychology, 54,* 541–557.

Chapman, J. P., Chapman, L. J., & Kwapil, T. R. (1994). Does the Eysenck Psychoticism Scale predict psychosis? A ten year longitudinal study. *Personality and Individual Differences, 17,* 369–375.

Chappell, D. W. (2003). Buddhist social principles. In K. H. Dockett, G. R. Dudley-Grant, & C. P. Bankart (Eds.), *Psychology and Buddhism: From individual to global community* (pp. 259–274). Secaucus, NJ: Kluwer Academic.

Cheek, J. (1982). Aggregation, moderator variables, and the validity of personality tests: A peer-rating study. *Journal of Personality and Social Psychology, 43,* 1254–1269.

Chen, J., & Goldsmith, L. T. (1991). Social and behavioral characteristics of Chinese only children: A review of research. *Journal of Research in Childhood Education, 5,* 127–139.

Chen, T. (1999). *The fundamentals of meditation practice.* (L. To, Trans.; S. Landberg & F. G. French, Eds.). Available online at http://www.buddhanet.net/pdf_file/chanmed1.pdf

Cheng, S. H., & Kuo, W. H. (2000). Family socialization of ethnic identity among Chinese American pre-adolescents. *Journal of Comparative Family Studies, 31,* 463–484.

Chess, S. (1986). Early childhood development and its implications for analytic theory and practice. *American Journal of Psychoanalysis, 46,* 123–148.

Chetwynd, T. (1982). *A dictionary of symbols.* London: Paladin.

Chibnall, J. T. (2001). Experiments on distant intercessory prayer: God, science, and the lesson of Massah. *Archives of Internal Medicine, 161,* 2529–2536.

Chomsky, N. (1959). Review of Skinner's verbal behavior. *Language, 35,* 26–58.

Christopher, K. (2002). 'No effect' prayer study from Mayo Clinic ignored by media. *Skeptical Inquirer, 26*(2), 5–6.

Church, A. T., & Katigbak, M. S. (2000). Trait psychology in the Philippines. *American Behavioral Scientist, 44,* 73–94.

Chusmir, L. H. (1989). Behavior: A measure of motivation needs. *Psychology: A Journal of Human Behavior, 26*(2–3), 1–10.

Ciardiello, J. A. (1985). Beethoven: Modern analytic views of the man and his music. *Psychoanalytic Review, 72,* 129–147.

Cicogna, P., Cavallero, C., & Bosinelli, M. (1991). Cognitive aspects of mental activity during sleep. *American Journal of Psychology, 104,* 413–425.

Cirlot, J. E. (1971). *A dictionary of symbols* (2nd ed.) (J. Sage, Trans.). New York: Philosophical Library.

Claridge, G., & Davis, C. (2001). What's the use of neuroticism? *Personality and Individual Differences, 31,* 383–400.

Clark, C., & O'Donnell, J. (1999). *Becoming and unbecoming White: Owning and disowning a racial identity.* Westport, CT: Bergin & Garvey.

Clark, J. M., & Paivio, A. (1989). Observational and theoretical terms in psychology: A cognitive perspective on scientific language. *American Psychologist, 44,* 500–512.

Clark, L. A., & Watson, D. (1999). Temperament: A new paradigm for trait psychology. In L. A. Pervin & O. P. John (Eds.), *Handbook of personality: Theory and research* (2nd ed., pp. 399–423). New York: Guilford.

Clark, P. A. (1985). *Individual education: Application of Adler's personality theory.* (ERIC Document Reproduction Service No. EJ325150)

Clark, R. W. (1984). *Einstein: The life and times.* New York: Avon Books. (Original work published 1971)

Clarke, S., & Pearson, C. (2000). Personal constructs of male survivors of childhood sexual abuse receiving cognitive analytic therapy. *British Journal of Medical Psychology, 73,* 169–177.

Clarkson, P., & Nippoda, Y. (1997). The experienced influence or effect of cultural/racism issues on the practice of counselling psychology—a qualitative study of one multicultural training organization. *Counselling Psychology Quarterly, 10,* 415–437.

Cleary, T. S., & Shapiro, S. I. (1996). Abraham Maslow and Asian psychology. *Psychologia: An International Journal of Psychology in the Orient, 39,* 213–222.

Clinton, H. R. (2003). *Living history.* New York: Scribner.

Cloninger, C. R. (1986). A unified biosocial theory of personality and its role in the development of anxiety states. *Psychiatric Developments, 3,* 167–226.

Cloninger, C. R. (1987a). Neurogenetic adaptive mechanism in alcoholism. *Science, 236,* 410–416.

Cloninger, C. R. (1987b). A systematic method for clinical description and classification of personality variants: A proposal. *Archives of General Psychiatry, 44*(6), 573–588.

Cloninger, C. R., Sigvardsson, S., & Bohman, M. (1988). Childhood personality predicts alcohol abuse in young adults. *Alcoholism Clinical and Experimental Research, 12,* 494–505.

Cloninger, C. R., & Svrakic, D. M. (1997). Integrative psychobiological approach to psychiatric assessment and treatment. *Psychiatry, 60,* 120–141.

Coan, R. W. (1989). Dimensions of masculinity and femininity: A self-report inventory. *Journal of Personality Assessment, 53,* 816–826.

Coccaro, E. F., Siever, L. J., Klar, H. M., Maurer, G., Cochrane, K., Cooper, T. B., Mohs, R. C., & Davis, K. L. (1989). Serotonergic studies in patients with affective and personality disorders. *Archives of General Psychiatry, 46,* 587–599.

Cohen, A. B., Pierce, J. D., Jr., Chambers, J., Meade, R., Gorvine, B. J., & Koenig, H. G. (2005). Intrinsic and extrinsic religiosity, belief in the afterlife, death anxiety, and life satisfaction in young Catholics and Protestants. *Journal of Research in Personality, 39,* 307–324.

Cohen, C. R., Chartrand, J. M., & Jowdy, D. P. (1995). Relationships between career indecision subtypes and ego identity development. *Journal of Counseling Psychology, 42,* 440–447.

Cohen, D. (1977). *Psychologists on psychology.* New York: Taplinger.

Cohen, D. (1997). *Carl Rogers: A critical biography.* London: Constable.

Cohen, J. B. (1967). An interpersonal orientation to the study of consumer behavior. *Journal of Marketing Research, 4,* 270–278.

Coles, R. (1970). *Erik H. Erikson: The growth of his work.* Boston: Little, Brown.

Coles, R. (1971a). *Children of crisis. Vol. 2. Migrants, sharecroppers, mountaineers.* Boston: Atlantic-Little, Brown.

Coles, R. (1971b). *Children of crisis. Vol. 3. The South goes north.* Boston: Atlantic-Little, Brown.

Collaer, M. L., & Hines, M. (1995). Human behavioral sex differences: A role for gonadal hormones during early development? *Psychological Bulletin, 118,* 55–107.

Collins, F. L., & Thompson, J. K. (1993). The integration of empirically derived personality assessment data into a behavioral conceptualization and treatment plan: Rationale, guidelines, and caveats. *Behavior Modification, 17,* 58–71.

Compeau, D., Higgins, C. A., & Huff, S. (1999). Social cognitive theory and individual reactions to computing technology: A longitudinal study. *MIS Quarterly, 23,* 145–158.

Connors, M. E., & Morse, W. (1993). Sexual abuse and eating disorders: A review. *International Journal of Eating Disorders, 13,* 1–11.

Conrad, H. S. (1932). The validity of personality ratings of preschool children. *Journal of Educational Psychology, 23,* 671–680.

Contrada, R. J., Cather, C., & O'Leary, A. (1999). Personality and health: Dispositions and processes in disease susceptibility and adaptation to illness. In L. A. Pervin & O. P. John (Eds.), *Handbook of personality: Theory and research* (2nd ed., pp. 576–604). New York: Guilford.

Conway, M. A., & Pleydell-Pearce, C. W. (2000). The construction of autobiographical memories in the self-memory system. *Psychological Review, 107,* 261–288.

Cook, B. W. (1993). *Eleanor Roosevelt. Vol. 1, 1884–1933.* New York: Penguin.

Coolidge, F. L., Moor, C. J., Yamazaki, T. G., Stewart, S. E., & Segal, D. L. (2001). On the relationship between Karen Horney's tripartite neurotic type theory and personality disorder features. *Personality and Individual Differences, 30,* 1287–1400.

Coolidge, F. L., Segal, D. L., Benight, C. C., & Danielian, J. (2004). The predictive power of Horney's psychoanalytic approach: An empirical study. *American Journal of Psychoanalysis, 64,* 363–374.

Cooper, C. R., & Denner, J. (1998). Theories linking culture and psychology: Universal and community-specific processes. *Annual Review of Psychology, 49,* 559–584.

Cooper, S. H. (1998). Changing notions of defense within psychoanalytic theory. *Journal of Personality, 66,* 947–964.

Corcoran, K. O., & Mallinckrodt, B. (2000). Adult attachment, self-efficacy, perspective taking, and conflict resolution. *Journal of Counseling and Development, 78,* 473–483.

Cornett, C. (2000). Ideas and identities: The life and work of Erik Erikson [Book review]. *Clinical Social Work Journal, 28,* 123–128.

Corr, P. J., Pickering, A. D., & Gray, J. A. (1997). Personality, punishment, and procedural learning: A test of J. A. Gray's anxiety theory. *Journal of Personality and Social Psychology, 73,* 337–344.

Corsini, R. J. (1989). *Manual: Corsini 4-R System of Individual Education.* Chicago: North American Society of Adlerian Psychology.

Costa, P. T., Jr., & McCrae, R. R. (1985). *The NEO Personality Inventory manual.* Odessa, FL: Psychological Assessment Resources.

Costa, P. T., Jr., & McCrae, R. R. (1988). From catalog to classification: Murray's needs and the five-factor model. *Journal of Personality and Social Psychology, 55,* 258–265.

Costa, P. T., Jr., & McCrae, R. R. (1992a). Four ways five factors are basic. *Personality and Individual Differences, 13,* 653–665.

Costa, P. T., Jr., & McCrae, R. R. (1992b). *Revised NEO Personality Inventory (NEO-PI-R) and NEO Five-Factor Inventory (NEO-FFI) professional manual.* Odessa, FL: Psychological Assessment Resources.

Costa, P. T., Jr., McCrae, R. R., & Dye, D. A. (1991). Facet scales for agreeableness and conscientiousness: A revision of the NEO Personality Inventory. *Personality and Individual Differences, 12,* 887–898.

Côté, J. E. (1993). Foundations of a psychoanalytic social psychology: Neo-Eriksonian propositions regarding the relationship between psychic structure and cultural institutions. *Developmental Review, 13,* 31–53.

Côté, J. E., & Levine, C. (1988a). A critical examination of the ego identity status paradigm. *Developmental Review, 8,* 147–184.

Côté, J. E., & Levine, C. (1988b). On critiquing the identity status paradigm: A rejoinder to Waterman. *Developmental Review, 8,* 209–218.

Côté, J. E., & Levine, C. (1988c). The relationship between ego identity status and Erikson's notions of institutionalized moratoria, value orientation stage, and ego dominance. *Journal of Youth and Adolescence, 17,* 81–99.

Côté, J. E., & Levine, C. (1989). An empirical test of Erikson's theory of ego identity formation. *Youth and Society, 20,* 388–414.

Côté, J. E., & Levine, C. G. (1992). The genesis of the humanistic academic: A second test of Erikson's theory of identity formation. *Youth and Society, 23,* 387–410.

Courtenay, W. H. (2000). Engendering health: A social constructionist examination of men's health beliefs and behaviors. *Psychology of Men and Masculinity, 1,* 4–15.

Covington, C. (2001). The future of analysis. *Journal of Analytical Psychology, 46,* 325–334.

Cowan, D. A. (1989). An alternative to the dichotomous interpretation of Jung's psychological functions: Developing more sensitive measurement technology. *Journal of Personality Assessment, 53,* 459–471.

Coward, H. (1989). Jung's conception of the role of religion in psychological development. *Humanistic Psychologist, 17,* 265–273.

Craig, R. J., Loheidi, R. A., Rudolph, B., Leifer, M., & Rubin, N. (1998). Relationship between psychological needs and the five-factor model of personality classification. *Journal of Research in Personality, 32,* 519–527.

Craik, K. H. (1988). Assessing the personalities of historical figures. In W. M. Runyan (Ed.), *Psychology and historical interpretation.* New York: Oxford University Press.

Cramer, D. (1985). Psychological adjustment and the facilitative nature of close personal relationships. *British Journal of Medical Psychology, 58,* 165–168.

Cramer, D. (1986). An item factor analysis of the revised Barrett-Lennard Relationship Inventory. *British Journal of Guidance and Counselling, 14,* 314–325.

Cramer, D. (1990a). Disclosure of personal problems, self-esteem, and the facilitativeness of friends and lovers. *British Journal of Guidance and Counselling, 18,* 186–196.

Cramer, D. (1990b). Self-esteem and close relationships: A statistical refinement. *British Journal of Social Psychology, 29,* 189–191.

Cramer, D. (1990c). Towards assessing the therapeutic value of Rogers's core conditions. *Counselling Psychology Quarterly, 3,* 57–66.

Cramer, P. (1991). Anger and the use of defense mechanisms in college students. *Journal of Personality, 59,* 39–55.

Cramer, P. (1997). Evidence for change in children's use of defense mechanisms. *Journal of Personality, 65,* 233–247.

Cramer, P. (1998a). Coping and defense mechanisms: What's the difference? *Journal of Personality, 66,* 919–946.

Cramer, P. (1998b). Freshman to senior year: A follow-up study of identity, narcissism, and defense mechanisms. *Journal of Research in Personality, 32,* 156–172.

Cramer, P. (1998c). Threat to gender representation: Identity and identification. *Journal of Personality, 66,* 335–357.

Cramer, P. (2000). Defense mechanisms in psychology today: Further processes for adaptation. *American Psychologist, 55,* 637–646.

Cramer, P. (2001). Identification and its relation to identity development. *Journal of Personality, 69,* 667–688.

Cramer, P. (2002). Defense mechanisms, behavior, and affect in young adulthood. *Journal of Personality, 70,* 103–126.

Cramer, P., & Blatt, S. J. (1990). Use of the TAT to measure change in defense mechanisms following intensive psychotherapy. *Journal of Personality Assessment, 54,* 236–251.

Cramer, P., & Block, J. (1998). Preschool antecedents of defense mechanism use in young adults: A longitudinal study. *Journal of Personality and Social Psychology, 74,* 159–169.

Cramer, P., & Gaul, R. (1988). The effect of success and failure on children's use of defense mechanisms. *Journal of Personality, 56,* 729–742.

Crandall, C. S., Eshleman, A., & O'Brien, L. (2002). Social norms and the expression and suppression of prejudice: The struggle for internalization. *Journal of Personality and Social Psychology, 82,* 359–378.

Crandall, J. E. (1991). A scale for social interest. *Individual Psychology, 47,* 106–114. (Original work published 1975)

Crick, F., & Mitchison, G. (1986). REM sleep and neural nets. *Journal of Mind and Behavior, 7,* 229–250.

Crick, N. R., & Dodge, K. A. (1994). A review and reformulation of social information-processing mechanisms in children's social adjustment. *Psychological Bulletin, 115,* 74–101.

Critchfield, T. S., & Kollins, S. H. (2001). Temporal discounting: Basic research and the analysis of socially important behavior. *Journal of Applied Behavior Analysis, 34,* 101–122.

Crockett, J. B., & Crawford, R. L. (1989). The relationship between Myers-Briggs Type Indicator (MBTI) Scale scores and advising style preferences of college freshmen. *Journal of College Student Development, 30,* 154–161.

Cronbach, L. J. (1957). The two disciplines of scientific psychology. *American Psychologist, 12,* 671–684.

Cronbach, L. J. (1975). Beyond the two disciplines of scientific psychology. *American Psychologist, 30,* 116–127.

Cronbach, L. J., & Meehl, P. E. (1955). Construct validity in psychological tests. *Psychological Bulletin, 52,* 281–302.

Cronin, H. (1991). *The ant and the peacock: Altruism and sexual selection from Darwin to today.* Cambridge, UK: Cambridge University Press.

Cross, H. J., & Allen, J. G. (1970). Ego identity status, adjustment, and academic achievement. *Journal of Consulting and Clinical Psychology, 34,* 288.

Cross, W. E., Jr. (1991). *Shades of black: Diversity in African-American identity.* Philadelphia: Temple University Press.

Cummins, P. (1992). Construing the experience of sexual abuse. *Journal of Personal Construct Psychology, 5,* 355–365.

Cuny, H. (1965). *Albert Einstein: The man and his theories.* New York: Eriksson.

Curry, C., Trew, K., Turner, I., & Hunter, J. (1994). The effect of life domains on girls' possible selves. *Adolescence, 29,* 133–150.

Curtis, J. M., & Cowell, D. R. (1993). Relation of birth order and scores on measures of pathological narcissism. *Psychological Reports, 72,* 311–315.

d'Aquili, E. G., & Newberg, A. B. (2000). The neuropsychology of aesthetic, spiritual, and mystical states. *Zygon, 35,* 39–51.

Dalton, R, (2004, October 21). Quarrel over book leads to call for misconduct inquiry. *Nature, 431*(7011), 889.

Daly, M. (1978). *Gyn/Ecology: The metaethics of radical feminism.* Boston: Beacon Press.

Damasio, A. R. (1994). *Descartes' error: Emotion, reason, and the human brain.* New York: Putnam.

Daniels, M. (1982). The development of the concept of self-actualization in the writings of Abraham Maslow. *Current Psychological Reviews, 2,* 61–75.

Daniels, M. (1988). The myth of self-actualization. *Journal of Humanistic Psychology, 28*(1), 7–38.

Darwin, C. (1909). *The origin of species.* In *Harvard classics* (Vol. 11). New York: P. F. Collier. (Original work published 1859)

Darwin, C. (1979). *The expression of emotions in man and animals* (S. J. Rachman, Trans.). New York: St. Martin's Press. (Original work published 1872)

Das, A. K. (1989). Beyond self-actualization. *International Journal for the Advancement of Counselling, 12,* 13–27.

David, J. P., Green, P. J., Martin, R., & Suls, J. (1997). Differential roles of neuroticism, extraversion, and event desirability for mood in daily life: An integrative model of top-down and bottom-up influences. *Journal of Personality and Social Psychology, 73,* 149–159.

Davidow, S., & Bruhn, A. R. (1990). Earliest memories and the dynamics of delinquency: A replication study. *Journal of Personality Assessment, 54,* 601–616.

Davidson, K., & MacGregor, M. W. (1998). A critical appraisal of self-report defense mechanism measures. *Journal of Personality, 66,* 965–992.

Davidson, R. J. (2000). Affective style, psychopathology, and resilience: Brain mechanisms and plasticity. *American Psychologist, 55,* 1196–1214.

Davidson, R. J. (2001). Toward a biology of positive affect and compassion. In R. J. Davidson & A. Harrington (Eds.), *Visions of compassion: Western scientists and Tibetan Buddhists examine human nature.* (pp. 107–130). Cary, NC: Oxford University Press.

Davidson, R. J. (2003). Darwin and the neural basis of emotion and affective style. *Annals of the New York Academy of Sciences, 1000,* 316–336.

Davidson, R. J. (2005). Emotion regulation, happiness, and the neuro-plasticity of the brain. *Advances, 21*(3–4), 25–29.

Davidson, R. J., Ekman, P., Saron, C. D., Senulis, J. A., & Friesen, W. V. (1990). Approach-withdrawal and cerebral asymmetry: I. Emotional expression and brain physiology. *Journal of Personality and Social Psychology, 58,* 330–341.

Davidson, R. J., & Fox, N. A. (1989). Frontal brain asymmetry predicts infants' response to maternal separation. *Journal of Abnormal Psychology, 98,* 127–131.

Davidson, R. J., Kabat-Zinn, J., Schumacher, J., Rosenkranz, M., Muller, D., Santorelli, S. F., Urbanowskik, F., Harrington, A., Bonus, K., & Sheridan, J. F. (2003). Alterations in brain and immune function produced by mindfulness meditation. *Psychosomatic Medicine, 65,* 564–570.

Davidson, R. J., Putnam, K. M., & Larson, C. L. (2000). Dysfunction in the neural circuitry of emotion regulation—A possible prelude to violence. *Science, 289,* 591–594.

Davies, J. L., & Alexander, C. N. (2005). Alleviating political violence through reducing collective tension: Impact assessment analyses of the Lebanon war. *Journal of Social and Behavior and Personality, 17,* 285–338.

Davis, C., Kaptein, S., Kaplan, A. S., Olmsted, M. P., & Woodside, D. B. (1998). Obsessionality in anorexia nervosa: The moderating influence of exercise. *Psychosomatic Medicine, 60,* 192–197.

Davis, D. L., Grove, S. J., & Knowles, P. A. (1990). An experimental application of personality type as an analogue for decision-making style. *Psychological Reports, 66,* 167–175.

Davis, J., Lockwood, L., & Wright, C. (1991). Reasons for not reporting peak experiences. *Journal of Humanistic Psychology, 31*(1), 86–94.

Davis, T. (1986). Book reviews. *Individual Psychology, 42,* 133–142.

Davis-Berman, J. (1990). Physical self-efficacy, perceived physical status, and depressive symptomatology in older adults. *Journal of Psychology, 124,* 207–215.

Davis-Sharts, J. (1986). An empirical test of Maslow's theory of need hierarchy using hologeistic comparison by statistical sampling. *Advances in Nursing Science, 9,* 58–72.

Dawes, R. M. (1994). *House of cards: Psychology and psychotherapy built on myth.* New York: Free Press.

Dawis, R. V. (1996). Vocational psychology, vocational adjustment, and the workforce: Some familiar and unanticipated consequences. *Psychology, Public Policy, and Law, 2,* 229–248.

Dawkins, R. (1976). *The selfish gene.* New York: Oxford University Press.

Dawson, G., Panagiotides, H., Klinger, L. G., & Hill, D. (1992). The role of frontal lobe functioning in the development of infant self-regulatory behavior. *Brain and Cognition, 20,* 152–175.

de Nicolas, A. T. (1998). The biocultural paradigm: The neural connection between science and mysticism. *Experimental Gerontology, 33,* 169–182.

de Silva, P. (1990). Buddhist psychology: A review of theory and practice. *Current Psychology, 9,* 236–254.

de St. Aubin, E. (1998). Truth against the world: A psychobiographical exploration of generativity in the life of Frank Lloyd Wright. In D. P. McAdams & E. de St. Aubin (Eds.), *Generativity and adult development: How and why we care for the next generation* (pp. 391–427). Washington, DC: American Psychological Association.

Dean, P. J., & Range, L. M. (1996). The escape theory of suicide and perfectionism in college students. *Death Studies, 20,* 415–424.

Deaux, K. (1993). Reconstructing social identity. *Personality and Social Psychology Bulletin, 19,* 4–12.

Deberry, S. T. (1989). The effect of competitive tasks on liking of self and other. *Social Behavior and Personality, 17,* 67–80.

DeCarvalho, R. J. (1989). Contributions to the history of psychology: LXII. Carl Rogers' naturalistic system of ethics. *Psychological Reports, 65,* 1155–1162.

DeCarvalho, R. J. (1990a). Contributions to the history of psychology: LXIX. Gordon Allport on the problem of method in psychology. *Psychological Reports, 67,* 267–275.

DeCarvalho, R. J. (1990b). The growth hypothesis and self-actualization: An existential alternative. *Humanistic Psychologist, 18,* 252–258.

DeCarvalho, R. J. (1990c). A history of the "third force" in psychology. *Journal of Humanistic Psychology, 30*(4), 22–44.

DeCarvalho, R. J. (1990d). Who coined the term "humanistic psychology"? *Humanistic Psychologist, 18,* 350–351.

DeCarvalho, R. J. (1991a). Gordon Allport and humanistic psychology. *Journal of Humanistic Psychology, 31*(3), 8–13.

DeCarvalho, R. J. (1991b). The humanistic paradigm in education. *Humanistic Psychologist, 19,* 88–104.

DeCarvalho, R. J. (1992). The humanistic ethics of Rollo May. *Journal of Humanistic Psychology, 32*(1), 7–18.

deChesnay, M. (1985). Father-daughter incest: An overview. *Behavioral Sciences and the Law, 3,* 391–402.

Deci, E. L. (1975). *Intrinsic motivation.* New York: Plenum.

Decker, P. J., & Nathan, B. N. (1985). *Behavior modeling training: Principles and applications.* New York: Praeger.

DeGrandpre, R. J. (2000). A science of meaning: Can behaviorism bring meaning to psychological science? *American Psychologist, 55,* 721–739.

DeHoff, S. L. (1998). In search of a paradigm for psychological and spiritual growth: Implications for psychotherapy and spiritual direction. *Pastoral Psychology, 46,* 333–346.

Della Selva, P. C., & Dusek, J. B. (1984). Sex role orientation and resolution of Eriksonian crisis during the late adolescent years. *Journal of Personality and Social Psychology, 47,* 204–212.

Delmonte, M. M. (1984). Psychometric scores and meditation practice: A literature review. *Personality and Individual Differences, 5,* 559–563.

DeNeve, K. M., & Cooper, H. (1998). The happy personality: A meta-analysis of 137 personality traits and subjective well-being. *Psychological Bulletin, 124,* 197–229.

Depue, R. A., & Collins, P. F. (1999). Neurobiology of the structure of personality: Dopamine, facilitation of incentive motivation, and extraversion. *Behavioral and Brain Sciences, 22,* 491–517.

de Quervain, D. J. F., Roozendaal, B., & McGaugh, J. L. (1998). Stress and glucocorticoids impair retrieval of long-term spatial memory. *Nature, 394,* 787–790.

De Raad, B. (1998). Five big, Big Five issues: Rationale, content, structure, status, and crosscultural assessment. *European Psychologist, 3,* 113–124.

Derakshan, N., & Eysenck, M. W. (1997). Repression and repressors: Theoretical and experimental approaches. *European Psychologist, 2,* 235–246.

Desharnais, R., Bouillon, J., & Godin, G. (1986). Self-efficacy and outcome expectations as determinants of exercise adherence. *Psychological Reports, 59,* 1155–1159.

de Waal, F. B. M. (2002). Evolutionary psychology: The wheat and the chaff. *Current Directions in Psychological Science, 11,* 187–191.

Dhammika, S. (2005). *Good question, good answer* (4th ed.). Singapore: Buddha Dhamma Mandala Society. Available online at http://www.buddhanet.net/pdf_file/gqga-4ed.pdf

DiCara, L. V., & Miller, N. E. (1968). Changes in heart rate instrumentally learned by curarized rats as avoidance responses. *Journal of Comparative and Physiological Psychology, 65,* 8–12.

Dickson, L. (1973). *Wilderness man: The strange story of Grey Owl.* Scarborough, Ont.: Signet.

Diehl, M., Elnick, A. B., Bourbeau, L. S., & Labouvie-Vief, G. (1998). Adult attachment styles: Their relations to family context and personality. *Journal of Personality and Social Psychology, 74,* 1656–1669.

Dien, D. (1992). Gender and individuation: China and the West. *Psychoanalytic Review, 79,* 105–119.

Diener, E., Suh, E. M., Lucas, R. E., & Smith, H. L. (1999). Subjective well-being: Three decades of progress. *Psychological Bulletin, 125,* 276–302.

Dietrich, A. (2002). Functional neuroanatomy of altered states of consciousness: The transient hypofrontality hypothesis. *Consciousness and Cognition, 12,* 231–256.

Digman, J. M. (1989). Five robust trait dimensions: Development, stability, and utility. *Journal of Personality, 57,* 195–214.

Digman, J. M. (1990). Personality structure: Emergence of the five-factor model. *Annual Review of Psychology, 41,* 417–440.

Digman, J. M. (1997). Higher-order factors of the Big Five. *Journal of Personality and Social Psychology, 73,* 1246–1256.

Dimsdale, J. E., & Mills, P. J. (2002). An unanticipated effect of meditation on cardiovascular pharmacology and physiology. *American Journal of Cardiology, 90,* 908–909.

Dinkmeyer, D., & Dinkmeyer, D., Jr. (1989). Adlerian psychology. *Psychology, 26,* 26–34.

Dinkmeyer, D., & McKay, G. (1976). *Systematic training for effective parenting.* Circle Pines, MN: American Guidance Service.

Dinkmeyer, D., McKay, G., & Dinkmeyer, J. (1982). *The next step: Effective parenting through problem solving.* Circle Pines, MN: American Guidance Service.

Dinsmoor, J. A. (1992). Setting the record straight: The social views of B. F. Skinner. *American Psychologist, 47,* 1454–1463.

Dockett, K. H. (2003). Buddhist empowerment: Individual, organizational, and societal transformation. In K. H. Dockett, G. R. Dudley-Grant, & C. P. Bankart (Eds.), *Psychology and Buddhism: From individual to global community* (pp. 173–196). Secaucus, NJ: Kluwer Academic.

Dockett, K. H., & North-Schulte, D. (2003). Transcending self and other: Mahayana principles of integration. In S. Muramoto & P. Young-Eisendrath (Eds.), *Awakening and insight: Zen Buddhism and psychotherapy* (pp. 215–238). New York: Brunner-Routledge.

Dolce, J. J. (1987). Self-efficacy and disability beliefs in behavioral treatment of pain. *Behaviour Research and Therapy, 25,* 289–299.

Dollard, J. (1949). *Criteria for the life history: With analyses of six notable documents.* New York: Peter Smith.

Dollard, J. (1957). *Caste and class in a southern town* (3rd ed.). Garden City, NY: Doubleday Anchor. (Original work published 1937)

Dollard, J., & Miller, N. E. (1950). *Personality and psychotherapy: An analysis in terms of learning, thinking, and culture.* New York: McGraw-Hill.

Dollard, J., Miller, N. E., Doob, L. W., Mowrer, O. H., Sears, R. R., et al. (1939). *Frustration and aggression.* New Haven, CT: Yale University Press.

Dollinger, S. J., Leong, F. T. L., & Ulicni, S. K. (1996). On traits and values: With special reference to openness to experience. *Journal of Research in Personality, 30,* 23–41.

Dollinger, S. J., Levin, E. L., & Robinson, A. E. (1991). The Word Association Implications Test. *Journal of Personality Assessment, 57,* 368–380.

Dominguez, M. M., & Carton, J. S. (1997). The relationship between self-actualization and parenting style. *Journal of Social Behavior and Personality, 12,* 1093–1100.

Domino, G., & Affonso, D. D. (1990). A personality measure of Erikson's life stages: The Inventory of Psychosocial Balance. *Journal of Personality Assessment, 54,* 576–588.

Domino, G., & Hannah, M. T. (1989). Measuring effective functioning in the elderly: An application of Erikson's theory. *Journal of Personality Assessment, 53,* 319–328.

Donahue, E. M., Robins, R. W., Roberts, B. W., & John, O. P. (1993). The divided self: Concurrent and longitudinal effects of psychological adjustment and social roles on self-concept differentiation. *Journal of Personality and Social Psychology, 64,* 834–846.

Donahue, M. J. (1985). Intrinsic and extrinsic religiousness: Review and meta-analysis. *Journal of Personality and Social Psychology, 48,* 400–419.

Doty, R. M., Peterson, B. E., & Winter, D. G. (1991). Threat and authoritarianism in the United States, 1978–1987. *Journal of Personality and Social Psychology, 61,* 629–640.

Douvan, E., & Adelson, J. (1966). *The adolescent experience.* New York: Wiley.

Downey, J. L. (1998). Ratings of perceptions related to phenomenological theory. *Perceptual and Motor Skills, 86,* 277–278.

Dragoi, V., & Staddon, J. E. R. (1999). The dynamics of operant conditioning. *Psychological Review, 106,* 20–61.

Dreikurs, R. (1950). *Fundamentals of Adlerian psychology.* Chicago: Alfred Adler Institute.

Dreikurs, R. (1982). Adleriana. *Individual Psychology, 38,* 7. (Original work published 1940)

Dreikurs, R., & Soltz, V. (1964). *Children: The challenge.* New York: Hawthorn.

Drigotas, S. M., & Barta, W. (2001). The cheating heart: Scientific explorations of infidelity. *Current Directions in Psychological Science, 10,* 177–180.

Drob, S. L. (1999). Jung and the Kabbalah. *History of Psychology, 2,* 102–118.

Dubow, E. F., Huesmann, L. R., & Eron, L. D. (1987). Childhood correlates of adult ego development. *Child Development, 58,* 859–869.

Dubow, E. F., Pargament, K. I., Boxer, P., & Tarakeshwar, N. (2000). Initial investigation of Jewish early adolescents' ethnic identity, stress, and coping. *Journal of Early Adolescence, 20,* 418–441.

Dudley-Grant, G. R. (2003). Buddhism, psychology, and addiction theory in psychotherapy. In K. H. Dockett, G. R. Dudley-Grant, & C. P. Bankart (Eds.), *Psychology and Buddhism: From individual to global community* (pp. 105–124). Secaucus, NJ: Kluwer Academic.

Duncan, R. C., Konefal, J., & Spechler, M. M. (1990). Effect of neurolinguistic programming training on self-actualization as measured by the Personal Orientation Inventory. *Psychological Reports, 66,* 1323–1330.

Dweck, C. S., & Leggett, E. L. (1988). A social-cognitive approach to motivation and personality. *Psychological Review, 95,* 256–273.

Dworkin, B. R., & Miller, N. E. (1986). Failure to replicate visceral learning in the acute curarized rat preparation. *Behavioral Neuroscience, 100,* 299–314.

Dzewaltowski, D. A. (1989). Toward a model of exercise motivation. *Journal of Sport and Exercise Psychology, 11,* 251–269.

Eacott, M. J., & Crawley, R. A. (1998). The offset of childhood amnesia: Memory for events that occurred before age 3. *Journal of Experimental Psychology: General, 127,* 22–33.

Eagle, M. (1997). Contributions of Erik Erikson. In Erik Erikson's clinical contributions: A symposium in memorial tribute. *Psychoanalytic Review, 84,* 337–347.

Eagly, A. H. (1987). *Sex differences in social behavior: A social-role interpretation.* Hillsdale, NJ: Erlbaum.

Eagly, A. H., Diekman, A. B., Johannesen-Schmidt, M. C., & Doenig, A. M. (2004). Gender gaps in sociopolitical attitudes: A social psychological analysis. *Journal of Personality and Social Psychology, 87,* 796–816.

Eagly, A. H., & Wood, W. (1991). Explaining sex differences in social behavior: A meta-analytic perspective. *Personality and Social Psychology Bulletin, 17,* 306–315.

Eagly, A. H., & Wood, W. (1999). The origins of sex differences in human behavior: Evolved dispositions versus social roles. *American Psychologist, 54,* 408–423.

Eckardt, M. H. (1991). Feminine psychology revisited: A historical perspective. *American Journal of Psychoanalysis, 51,* 235–243.

Eden, D., & Zuk, Y. (1995). Seasickness as a self-fulfilling prophecy: Raising self-efficacy to boost performance at sea. *Journal of Applied Psychology, 80,* 628–635.

Edinger, E. F. (1968). An outline of analytical psychology. *Quadrant, 1,* 1–12.

Edinger, E. F. (1972). *Ego and archetype: Individuation and the religious function of the psyche.* New York: Putnam.

Edinger, E. F. (1999). *Archetype of the apocalypse: A Jungian study of the book of Revelation.* Chicago: Open Court.

Edwards, D. J. A. (1998). Types of case study work: A conceptual framework for case-based research. *Journal of Humanistic Psychology, 38*(3), 36–70.

Egan, S., & Stelmack, R. M. (2003). A personality profile of Mount Everest climbers. *Personality and Individual Differences, 34,* 1491–1494.

Eidelson, R. J. (1997). Complex adaptive systems in the behavioral and social sciences. *Review of General Psychology, 1,* 42–71.

Einon, D. (1998). How many children can one man have? *Evolution and Human Behavior, 19,* 413–426.

Einstein, A., & Infeld, L. (1961). *The evolution of physics: The growth of ideas from early concepts to relativity and quanta.* New York: Simon & Schuster. (Original work published 1938)

Eisenberg, N. (1996). Meta-emotion and socialization of emotion in the family—a topic whose time has come: Comment on Gottman et al. (1996). *Journal of Family Psychology, 10,* 269–276.

Eisenberg, N., Fabes, R. A., Guthrie, I. K., & Reiser, M. (2000). Dispositional emotionality and regulation: Their role in predicting quality of social functioning. *Journal of Personality and Social Psychology, 78,* 136–157.

Eisenberg, N., Fabes, R. A., Shepard, S. A., Murphy, B. C., Jones, S., & Guthrie, I. K. (1998). Contemporaneous and longitudinal prediction of children's sympathy from dispositional regulation and emotionality. *Developmental Psychology, 34,* 910–924.

Eisenberger, R. (1992). Learned industriousness. *Psychological Review, 99,* 248–267.

Eisenberger, R., Armeli, S., & Pretz, J. (1998). Can the promise of reward increase creativity? *Journal of Personality and Social Psychology, 74,* 704–714.

Ekman, P. (1993). Facial expression and emotion. *American Psychologist, 48,* 376–379.

Ekman, P., Davidson, R. J., & Friesen, W. V. (1990). The Duchenne smile: II. Emotional expression and brain physiology. *Journal of Personality and Social Psychology, 58,* 342–353.

Ekman, P., Davidson, R. J., Ricard, M., & Wallace, B. A. (2005). Buddhist and psychological perspectives on emotion and well-being. *Current Directions in Psychological Science, 14,* 59–63.

Elizabeth, P. (1983). Comparison of psychoanalytic and a client-centered group treatment model on measures of anxiety and self-actualization. *Journal of Counseling Psychology, 30,* 425–428.

Ellenberger, H. F. (1970). *The discovery of the unconscious: The history and evolution of dynamic psychiatry.* New York: Basic Books.

Ellenberger, H. F. (1972). The story of "Anna O": A critical review with new data. *Journal of the History of the Behavior Sciences, 8,* 267–279.

Ellenberger, H. F. (1991). The story of Helene Preiswerk: A critical study with new documents. *History of Psychiatry, 2*(5, Pt 1), 41–52.

Elliott, D., Amerikaner, M., & Swank, P. (1987). Early recollections and the Vocational Preference Inventory as predictors of vocational choice. *Individual Psychology, 43,* 353–359.

Elliott, J. E. (1992). Compensatory buffers, depression, and irrational beliefs. *Journal of Cognitive Psychotherapy, 6,* 175–184.

Ellis, A. (1989). Using rational-emotive therapy (RET) as crisis intervention: A single session with a suicidal client. *Individual Psychology, 45,* 75–81.

Elms, A. C. (1988). Freud as Leonardo: Why the first psychobiography went wrong. *Journal of Personality, 56,* 19–40.

Elson, M. (Ed.). (1987). *The Kohut seminars on self psychology and psychotherapy with adolescents and young adults.* New York: Norton.

Emavardhana, T., & Tori, C. D. (1997). Changes in self-concept, ego defense mechanisms, and religiosity following seven-day Vipassana meditation retreats. *Journal for the Scientific Study of Religion, 36,* 194–206.

Emery, E. J. (1987). Empathy: Psychoanalytic and client centered. *American Psychologist, 42,* 513–515.

Emmerich, W. (1968). Personality development and concepts of structure. *Child Development, 39,* 671–690.

Emmons, R. A. (1997). Motives and life goals. In R. Hogan, J. Johnson, & S. Briggs (Eds.), *Handbook of personality psychology* (pp. 485–512). San Diego, CA: Academic Press.

Emmons, R. A., Diener, E., & Larsen, R. J. (1985). Choice of situations and congruence models of interactionism. *Personality and Individual Differences, 6,* 693–705.

Endler, N. S., & Magnusson, D. (Eds.). (1976). *Interactional psychology and personality.* New York: Wiley.

Engle, R. W., Tuholski, S. W., Laughlin, J. E., & Conway, A. R. A. (1999). Working memory, short-term memory, and general fluid intelligence: A latent-variable approach. *Journal of Experimental Psychology: General, 128,* 309–331.

Epel, E. S., Bandura, A., & Zimbardo, P. G. (1999). Escaping homelessness: The influences of self-efficacy and time perspective on coping with homelessness. *Journal of Applied Social Psychology, 29,* 575–596.

Epstein, J. A., Botvin, G. J., & Diaz, T. (1999). Social influence and psychological determinants of smoking among inner-city adolescents. *Journal of Child and Adolescent Substance Abuse, 8,* 1–19.

Epstein, M. (1995). *Thoughts without a thinker: Psychotherapy from a Buddhist perspective.* New York: Basic Books.

Epstein, R. (1991). Skinner, creativity, and the problem of spontaneous behavior. *Psychological Science, 2,* 362–370.

Epstein, S. (1980). The self-concept: A review and the proposal of an integrated theory of personality. In E. Staub (Ed.), *Personality: Basic issues and current research* (pp. 82–131). Englewood Cliffs, NJ: Prentice-Hall.

Epstein, S. (1983). A research paradigm for the study of personality and emotions. In M. M. Page (Ed.), *Personality—Current theory and research: 1982 Nebraska Symposium on Motivation* (pp. 91–154). Lincoln: University of Nebraska Press.

Epstein, S. (1985). The implications of cognitive-experimental self-theory for research in social psychology and personality. *Journal for the Theory of Social Behavior, 15,* 283–310.

Epstein, S., & O'Brien, E. J. (1985). The person-situation debate in historical and current perspective. *Psychological Bulletin, 98,* 513–537.

Epting, F. R. (1984). *Personal construct counselling and psychotherapy.* New York: Wiley.

Epting, F. R., & Leitner, L. M. (1992). Humanistic psychology and personal construct theory. *Humanistic Psychologist, 20,* 243–259.

Erikson, E. H. (1950). *Childhood and society.* New York: Norton.

Erikson, E. H. (1951a). Sex differences in the play configurations of preadolescents. *American Journal of Orthopsychiatry, 21,* 667–692.

Erikson, E. H. (1951b). Statement to the committee on privilege and tenure of the University of California concerning the California loyalty oath. *Psychiatry, 14,* 243–245.

Erikson, E. H. (1958a). On the nature of clinical evidence. *Daedalus, 87,* 65–87.

Erikson, E. H. (1958b). *Young man Luther: A study in psychoanalysis and history.* New York: Norton.

Erikson, E. H. (1959). Identity and the life cycle. Selected papers. *Psychological Issues, 1* (Monograph 1). New York: International Universities Press.

Erikson, E. H. (1961). The roots of virtue. In J. Huxley (Ed.), *The humanist frame* (pp. 145–165). New York: Harper & Brothers.

Erikson, E. H. (1963). *Childhood and society* (2nd ed.). New York: Norton.

Erikson, E. H. (1964). *Insight and responsibility: Lectures on the ethical implications of psychoanalytic insight.* New York: Norton.

Erikson, E. H. (1965). Inner and outer space: Reflections on womanhood. In R. J. Lifton (Ed.), *The woman in America* (pp. 1–26). Boston: Houghton Mifflin.

Erikson, E. H. (1968). *Identity: Youth and crisis.* New York: Norton.

Erikson, E. H. (1969). *Gandhi's truth: On the origins of militant nonviolence.* New York: Norton.

Erikson, E. H. (1975). *Life history and the historical moment.* New York: Norton.

Erikson, E. H. (1977). *Toys and reasons: Stages in the ritualization of experience.* New York: Norton.

Erikson, E. H. (1982). *The life cycle completed: A review.* New York: Norton.

Erikson, E. H. (1985). Pseudospeciation in the nuclear age. *Political Psychology, 6,* 213–217.

Erikson, E. H. (1988). Youth: Fidelity and diversity. *Daedalus, 117*(3), 1–24. (Original work published 1962)

Erikson, E. H. (1997). *The life cycle completed: Extended version with new chapters on the ninth stage by Joan M. Erikson.* New York: Norton.

Erikson, E. H., Erikson, J. M., & Kivnick, H. Q. (1986). *Vital involvement in old age.* New York: Norton.

Eriksson, C. (1992). Social interest/social feeling and the evolution of consciousness. *Individual Psychology, 48,* 277–287.

Essex, M. J., Klein, M. H., Cho, E., & Kalin, N. H. (2002). Maternal stress beginning in infancy may sensitize children to later stress exposure: Effects on cortisol and behavior. *Biological Psychiatry, 52,* 776–784.

Essig, T. S., & Russell, R. L. (1990). Analyzing subjectivity in therapeutic discourse: Rogers, Perls, Ellis and Gloria revisited. *Psychotherapy, 27,* 271–281.

Etzioni, A. (1998). Voluntary simplicity: Characterization, select psychological implications and societal consequences. *Journal of Economic Psychology, 19,* 619–643.

Evans, R. I. (1976). Neal Miller. In *The making of psychology: Discussions with creative contributors* (pp. 169–183). New York: Knopf.

Evans, R. I. (1981a). *Dialogue with B. F. Skinner.* New York: Praeger.

Evans, R. I. (1981b). *Dialogue with Gordon Allport.* New York: Praeger.

Evans, R. I. (1989). *Albert Bandura: The man and his ideas—A dialogue.* New York: Praeger.

Exner, J. E., & Andronikof-Sanglade, A. (1992). Rorschach changes following brief and short-term therapy. *Journal of Personality Assessment, 59,* 59–71.

Eysenck, H. J. (1954). The science of personality: Nomothetic! *Psychological Review, 61,* 339–342.

Eysenck, H. J. (1967). *The biological basis of personality.* Springfield, IL: Thomas.

Eysenck, H. J. (1990). Biological dimensions of personality. In L. A. Pervin (Ed.), *Handbook of personality: Theory and research* (pp. 244–276). New York: Guilford.

Eysenck, H. J. (1991). Dimensions of personality: 16, 5, or 3?—Criteria for a taxonomic paradigm. *Personality and Individual Differences, 12,* 773–790.

Eysenck, H. J. (1992). Four ways five factors are not basic. *Personality and Individual Differences, 13,* 667–673.

Eysenck, H. J. (1993). Creativity and personality: Suggestions for a theory. *Psychological Inquiry, 4,* 147–178.

Eysenck, H. J. (1994). Creativity and personality: Word association, origence, and psychoticism. *Creativity Research Journal, 7,* 209–216.

Eysenck, H. J., & Eysenck, M. W. (1985). *Personality and individual differences: A natural science approach.* New York: Plenum.

Eysenck, H. J., & Eysenck, S. B. G. (1975). *Manual of the Eysenck Personality Questionnaire.* San Diego, CA: Educational and Industrial Testing Service.

Eysenck, H. J., & Eysenck, S. B. G. (1991). *Manual of the Eysenck personality scales.* London: Hodder & Stoughton.

Fabrega, H., Jr. (1990). The concept of somatization as a cultural and historical product of Western medicine. *Psychosomatic Medicine, 52,* 653–672.

Fairfield, B. (1990). Reorientation: The use of hypnosis for life-style change. *Individual Psychology, 46,* 451–458.

Fakouri, M. E., & Hafner, J. L. (1984). Early recollections of first-borns. *Journal of Clinical Psychology, 40,* 209–213.

Falbo, T. (1987). Only children in the United States and China. *Applied Social Psychology Annual, 7,* 159–183.

Fancher, R. E. (1998). Biography and psychodynamic theory: Some lessons from the life of Francis Galton. *History of Psychology, 1,* 99–115.

Fanon, F. (1967). *Black skin, white masks.* New York: Grove Press.

Farwell, L., & Wohlwend-Lloyd, R. (1998). Narcissistic processes: Optimistic expectations, favorable self-evaluations, and self-enhancing attributions. *Journal of Personality, 66,* 65–83.

Faulkender, P. J. (1991). Does gender schema mediate between sex-role identity and self-actualization? *Psychological Reports, 68,* 1019–1029.

Feeney, B. C., & Kirkpatrick, L. A. (1996). Effects of adult attachment and presence of romantic partners on physiological responses to stress. *Journal of Personality and Social Psychology, 70,* 255–270.

Fehr, B., & Russell, J. A. (1991). The concept of love viewed from a prototype perspective. *Journal of Personality and Social Psychology, 60,* 425–438.

Feiring, C. (1984). Behavioral styles in infancy and adulthood: The work of Karen Horney and attachment theorists collaterally considered. *American Journal of Psychoanalysis, 44,* 197–208.

Feltham, C. (1999). Carl Rogers: A critical biography. *British Journal of Guidance and Counselling, 27,* 151.

Ferguson, E., Sanders, A., O'Hehir, F., & James, D. (2000). Predictive validity of personal statements and the role of the five-factor model of personality in relation to medical training. *Journal of Occupational and Organizational Psychology, 73,* 321–344.

Fernald, P. S. (2000). Carl Rogers: Body-centered counselor. *Journal of Counseling and Development, 78,* 172–179.

Ferster, C. B., & Skinner, B. F. (1957). *Schedules of reinforcement.* New York: Appleton-Century-Crofts.

Feshbach, S. (1964). The function of aggression and the regulation of aggressive drive. *Psychological Review, 71,* 257–272.

Fink, B., & Penton-Voak, I. (2002). Evolutionary psychology of facial attractiveness. *Current Directions in Psychological Science, 11,* 154–158.

Finkelhor, D., Hotaling, G., Lewis, I. A., & Smith, C. (1990). Sexual abuse in a national survey of adult men and women: Prevalence, characteristics, and risk factors. *Child Abuse and Neglect, 14,* 19–28.

Finn, M., & Rubin, J. B. (2000). Psychotherapy with Buddhists. In P. S. Richards & A. E. Allen (Eds.), *Handbook of psychotherapy and religious diversity* (pp. 317–340). Washington, DC: American Psychological Association.

Fischer, A. H., & Mosquera, P. M. R. (2001). What concerns men? Women or other men? A critical appraisal of the evolutionary theory of sex differences in aggression. *Psychology, Evolution and Gender, 3,* 5–25.

Fisher, J. D., & Fisher, W. A. (1992). Changing AIDS-risk behavior. *Psychological Bulletin, 111,* 455–474.

Fisher, S., & Greenberg, R. P. (1977). *The scientific credibility of Freud's theories and therapy.* New York: Basic Books.

Fisher, W. W. (2001). Functional analysis of precurrent contingencies between mands and destructive behavior. *Behavior Analyst Today, 2,* 176–181.

Fiske, D. W. (1988). From inferred personalities toward personality in action. *Journal of Personality, 56,* 815–833.

Fitzpatrick, J. J. (1976). Erik H. Erikson and psychohistory. *Bulletin of the Menninger Clinic, 40,* 295–314.

Fleeson, W. (2001). Toward a structure- and process-integrated view of personality: Traits as density distributions of states. *Journal of Personality and Social Psychology, 80,* 1011–1027.

Flett, G. L., Hewitt, P. L., Blankstein, K. R., & Gray, L. (1998). Psychological distress and the frequency of perfectionistic thinking. *Journal of Personality and Social Psychology, 75,* 1363–1381.

Florin, P., Mednick, M., & Wandersman, A. (1986). Cognitive social learning variables and the characteristics of leaders. *Journal of Applied Social Psychology, 16,* 808–830.

Flynn, J. R. (1987). Massive IQ gains in 14 nations: What IQ tests really measure. *Psychological Bulletin, 101,* 171–191.

Fodor, E. M., & Roffe-Steinrotter, D. (1998). Rogerian leadership style and creativity. *Journal of Research in Personality, 32,* 236–242.

Ford, J. G., & Maas, S. (1989). On actualizing person-centered theory: A critique of textbook treatments of Rogers's motivational constructs. *Teaching of Psychology, 16,* 30–31.

Ford, T. E. (2000). Effects of sexist humor on tolerance of sexist events. *Personality and Social Psychology Bulletin, 26,* 1094–1107.

Fordham, F. (1966). *An introduction to Jung's psychology* (3rd ed.). Baltimore: Penguin Books.

Forest, J. J. (1987). Effects on self-actualization of paperbacks about psychological self-help. *Psychological Reports, 60,* 1243–1246.

Forey, W. F., Christensen, O. J., & England, J. T. (1994). Teacher burnout: A relationship with Holland and Adlerian typologies. *Individual Psychology, 50,* 3–17.

Forster, J. R. (1992). Eliciting personal constructs and articulating goals. *Journal of Career Development, 18,* 175–185.

Försterling, F. (1985). Attributional retraining: A review. *Psychological Bulletin, 98,* 495–512.

Fosse, R., Stickgold, R., & Hobson, J. A. (2001). Brain-mind states: Reciprocal variation in thoughts and hallucinations. *Psychological Science, 12,* 30–36.

Fox, W. M. (1982). Why we should abandon Maslow's need hierarchy theory. *Journal of Humanistic Education and Development, 21,* 29–32.

Francis, D., & Meaney, M. J. (1999). Maternal care and development of stress responses. *Current Opinion in Neurobiology, 9*, 128–134.

Francis, L. J. (1991). Personality and attitude towards religion among adult churchgoers in England. *Psychological Reports, 69*, 791–794.

Francis, L. J. (1992). Is psychoticism really a dimension of personality fundamental to religiosity? *Personality and Individual Differences, 13*, 645–652.

Francis, L. J., & Bourke, R. (2003). Personality and religion: Applying Cattell's model among secondary school pupils. *Current Psychology: Developmental, Learning, Personality, Social, 22*, 125–137.

Francis, L. J., & Pearson, P. R. (1993). The personality characteristics of student churchgoers. *Personality and Individual Differences, 15*, 373–380.

Frank, G. (1999). Freud's concept of the superego: Review and assessment. *Psychoanalytic Psychology, 16*, 448–463.

Frank, J. D. (1977). Nature and functions of belief systems: Humanism and transcendental religion. *American Psychologist, 32*, 555–559.

Frank, J. D. (1982). Therapeutic components shared by all psychotherapies. In J. H. Harvey & M. M. Parks (Eds.), *Psychotherapy research and behavior change* (Vol. 1, pp. 5–37). Washington, DC: American Psychological Association.

Frank, J. D., & Frank, J. B. (1991). *Persuasion and healing: A comparative study of psychotherapy* (3rd ed.). Baltimore: Johns Hopkins University Press.

Frankel, F. H. (1987). Significant developments in medical hypnosis during the past 25 years. *International Journal of Clinical and Experimental Hypnosis, 35*, 231–247.

Franken, I. H. A. (2002). Behavioral approach system (BAS) sensitivity predicts alcohol craving. *Personality and Individual Differences, 32*, 349–355.

Franklin, A. J. (1999). Invisibility syndrome and racial identity development in psychotherapy and counseling African American men. *Counseling Psychologist, 27*, 761–793.

Freese, J., Powell, B., & Steelman, L. C. (1999). Rebel without a cause effect: Birth order and social attitudes. *American Sociological Review, 64*, 207–231.

Freud, A. (1935). *Psychoanalysis for teachers and parents* (B. Low, Trans.). New York: Emerson Books.

Freud, A. (1966). *The ego and the mechanisms of defense* (Rev. ed.). New York: International Universities Press. (Original work published 1936)

Freud, S. (1953). Character and anal eroticism. In J. Strachey (Ed. and Trans.), *The standard edition of the complete psychological works of Sigmund Freud* (Vol. 9, pp. 169–175). London: Hogarth Press. (Original work published 1908)

Freud, S. (1953). The interpretation of dreams. In J. Strachey (Ed. and Trans.), *The standard edition of the complete psychological works of Sigmund Freud* (Vols. 4 and 5). London: Hogarth Press. (Original work published 1900)

Freud, S. (1957). Leonardo da Vinci and a memory of his childhood. In J. Strachey (Ed. and Trans.), *The standard edition of the complete psychological works of Sigmund Freud* (Vol. 11, pp. 59–137). London: Hogarth Press. (Original work published 1910)

Freud, S. (1958). *On creativity and the unconscious.* New York: Harper & Row. (Original work published 1925)

Freud, S. (1962a). The aetiology of hysteria. In J. Strachey (Ed. and Trans.), *The standard edition of the complete psychological works of Sigmund Freud* (Vol. 3, pp. 187–221). London: Hogarth Press. (Original work published 1896)

Freud, S. (1962b). *The ego and the id* (J. Riviere, Trans.; J. Strachey, Ed.). New York: Norton. (Original work published 1923)

Freud, S. (1962c). Three essays on the theory of sexuality. In J. Strachey (Ed. and Trans.), *Sigmund Freud: Three essays on the theory of sexuality* (pp. 1–130). New York: Basic Books. (Original work published 1905)

Freud, S. (1963a). *An autobiographical study* (J. Strachey, Trans.). New York: Norton. (Original work published 1935)

Freud, S. (1963b). *Jokes and their relation to the unconscious* (J. Strachey, Ed. and Trans.). New York: Norton. (Original work published 1916)

Freud, S. (1966a). *The complete introductory lectures on psychoanalysis* (J. Strachey, Ed. and Trans.). New York: Norton. (Original work published 1933)

Freud, S. (1966b). Project for a scientific psychology. In J. Strachey (Ed. and Trans.), *The standard edition of the complete psychological works of Sigmund Freud* (Vol. 1, pp. 283–397). London: Hogarth Press. (Original work published 1895)

Freud, S. (1978). The psychogenesis of a case of homosexuality in a woman. In P. Reif (Ed.) & B. Low & R. Gabler (Trans.), *Sexuality and the psychology of love.* New York: Macmillan. (Original work published 1920)

Freud, S., & Bullitt, W. C. (1966). *Thomas Woodrow Wilson: A psychological study.* Boston: Houghton Mifflin.

Freyd, J. J. (1994). Betrayal trauma: Traumatic amnesia as an adaptive response to childhood abuse. *Ethics and Behavior, 4*, 307–329.

Freyd, J. J. (1996). *Betrayal trauma: The logic of forgetting childhood abuse.* Cambridge, MA: Harvard University Press.

Frick, W. B. (1993). Subpersonalities: Who conducts the orchestra? *Journal of Humanistic Psychology, 33*(2), 122–128.

Frick, W. B. (2000). Remembering Maslow: Reflections on a 1968 interview. *Journal of Humanistic Psychology, 40*(2), 128–147.

Friedman, H. S., & Booth-Kewley, S. (1987). Personality, Type A behavior, and coronary heart disease: The role of emotional expression. *Journal of Personality and Social Psychology, 53*, 783–792.

Friedman, M. (1982). Comment on the Rogers-May discussion of evil. *Journal of Humanistic Psychology, 22*, 93–96.

Friedman, M. (1994). Reflections on the Buber-Rogers dialogue. *Journal of Humanistic Psychology, 34*(1), 46–65.

Frith, U., & Frith, C. (2001). The biological basis of social interaction. *Current Directions in Psychological Science, 10*, 151–155.

Froehle, T. C. (1989). Personal construct threat as a mediator of performance anxiety in a beginning course in counseling techniques. *Journal of College Student Development, 30*, 536–540.

Fromm, M. (1993). What students really learn: Students' personal constructions of learning items. *International Journal of Personal Construct Psychology, 6*, 195–208.

Fudin, R. (1986). Subliminal psychodynamic activation: Mommy and I are not yet one. *Perceptual and Motor Skills, 63*, 1159–1179.

Fudin, R. (2001). Problems in Silverman's work indicate the need for a new approach to research on subliminal psychodynamic activation. *Perceptual and Motor Skills, 92*(3, Pt 1), 611–622.

Fuller, R. C. (1982). Carl Rogers, religion, and the role of psychology in American culture. *Journal of Humanistic Psychology, 22*, 21–32.

Fullerton, C. S., Ursano, R. J., Wetzler, H. P., & Slusarcick, A. (1989). Birth order, psychological well-being, and social supports in young adults. *Journal of Nervous and Mental Disease, 177*, 556–559.

Fulton, A. S., Gorsuch, R. L., & Maynard, E. A. (1999). Religious orientation, antihomosexual sentiment, and fundamentalism among Christians. *Journal for the Scientific Study of Religion, 38*, 14–22.

Funder, D. C. (1991). Global traits: A neo-Allportian approach to personality. *Psychological Science, 2*, 31–39.

Furnham, A. (1990a). The development of single trait personality theories. *Personality and Individual Differences, 11*, 923–929.

Furnham, A. (1990b). The fakeability of the 16PF, Myers-Briggs and FIRO-B personality measures. *Personality and Individual Differences, 11*, 711–716.

Furnham, A. (1991). Personality and occupational success: 16PF correlates of cabin crew performance. *Personality and Individual Differences, 12*, 87–90.

Furnham, A., Moutafi, J., & Baguma, P. (2002). A cross-cultural study on the role of weight and waist-to-hip ratio on female attractiveness. *Personality and Individual Differences, 32*, 729–745.

Furnham, A., & Stringfield, P. (1993). Personality and work performance: Myers-Briggs Type Indicator correlates of managerial performance in two cultures. *Personality and Individual Differences, 14*, 145–153.

Gaines, S. O., & Reed, E. S. (1995). Prejudice: From Allport to DuBois. *American Psychologist, 50*, 96–103.

Gallo, E. (1994). Synchronicity and the archetypes. *Skeptical Inquirer, 18*, 396–403.

Galvin, M., Shekhar, A., Simon, J., Stilwell, B., Ten Eyck, R., Laite, G., Karwisch, G., & Blix, S. (1991). Low dopamine beta-hydroxylase: A biological sequela of abuse and neglect? *Psychiatry Research, 39,* 1–11.

Gandhi, M. K. (1957). *An autobiography: The story of my experiments with truth.* Boston: Beacon Press.

Gangestad, S. W., & Simpson, J. A. (1990). Toward an evolutionary theory of female sociosexual variation. *Journal of Personality, 58,* 69–96.

Gara, M. A., Rosenberg, S., & Mueller, D. R. (1989). Perception of self and other in schizophrenia. *International Journal of Personal Construct Psychology, 2,* 253–270.

Garcia, M. E., Schmitz, J. M., & Doerfler, L. A. (1990). A fine-grained analysis of the role of self-efficacy in self-initiated attempts to quit smoking. *Journal of Consulting and Clinical Psychology, 58,* 317–322.

Garcia-Coll, C., Kagan, J., & Reznick, J. S. (1984). Behavioral inhibition in young children. *Child Development, 55,* 1005–1009.

Garden, A. M. (1991). The purpose of burnout: A Jungian interpretation. *Journal of Social Behavior and Personality, 6,* 73–93.

Gardner, W. L., & Martinko, M. J. (1996). Using the Myers-Briggs Type Indicator to study managers: A literature review and research agenda. *Journal of Management, 22,* 45–83.

Garland, D. J., & Barry, J. R. (1990). Personality and leader behaviors in collegiate football: A multidimensional approach to performance. *Journal of Research in Personality, 24,* 355–370.

Garnier, H. E., & Stein, J. A. (1998). Values and the family: Risk and protective factors for adolescent problem behaviors. *Youth and Society, 30,* 89–120.

Garrett, K. R. (1985). Elbow room in a functional analysis: Freedom and dignity regained. *Behaviorism, 13,* 21–36.

Garrison, D. (1981). Karen Horney and feminism. *Signs, 6,* 672–691.

Garrow, D. J. (1986). *Bearing the cross: Martin Luther King, Jr., and the Southern Christian Leadership Conference.* New York: Vintage Books.

Gaskins, R. W. (1999). "Adding legs to a snake": A reanalysis of motivation and the pursuit of happiness from a Zen Buddhist perspective. *Journal of Educational Psychology, 91,* 204–215.

Gattuso, S., & Saw, C. (1998). Humanistic education in gerontology—a case study using narrative. *Educational Gerontology, 24,* 279–285.

Gedo, P. M. (1999). Single case studies in psychotherapy research. *Psychoanalytic Psychology, 16,* 274–280.

Geen, R. G. (1997). Psychophysiological approaches to personality. In R. Hogan, J. Johnson, & S. Briggs (Eds.), *Handbook of personality psychology* (pp. 387–414). San Diego: Academic Press.

Geher, G. (2000). Perceived and actual characteristics of parents and partners: A test of a Freudian model of mate selection. *Current Psychology, 19*(3), 194–214.

Geisler, C. (1985). Repression: A psychoanalytic perspective revisited. *Psychoanalysis and Contemporary Thought, 8,* 253–298.

Geller, L. (1982). The failure of self-actualization theory: A critique of Carl Rogers and Abraham Maslow. *Journal of Humanistic Psychology, 22*(2), 56–73.

Gendlin, E. T. (1988). Carl Rogers (1902–1987). *American Psychologist, 43,* 127–128.

Genia, V. (1993). A psychometric evaluation of the Allport-Ross I/E Scales in a religiously heterogeneous sample. *Journal for the Scientific Study of Religion, 32,* 284–290.

Genoni, T., Jr. (1994). American Psychological Association statement addresses the debate over assisted memory. *Skeptical Inquirer, 18,* 342–343.

Genoni, T., Jr. (1995). Exploring mind, memory, and the psychology of belief: Part II: Perception, memory and the courtroom. *Skeptical Inquirer, 19*(2), 7–12.

George, J. M., & Zhou, J. (2001). When openness to experience and conscientiousness are related to creative behavior: An interactional approach. *Journal of Applied Psychology, 86,* 513–524.

Geppert, U., & Halisch, F. (2001). Genetic vs. environmental determinants of traits, motives, self-referential cognitions, and volitional control in old age: First results from the Munich Twin Study (GOLD). In A. Efklides, J. Kuhl, & R. M. Sorrentino (Eds.), *Trends and prospects in motivation research* (pp. 359–387). New York: Kluwer Academic.

Gergen, K. J. (1985). The social constructionist movement in modern psychology. *American Psychologist, 40,* 266–275.

Gergen, M. M. (1990). Finished at 40: Women's development within the patriarchy. *Psychology of Women Quarterly, 14,* 471–493.

Ghose, L. (2004). A study in Buddhist psychology: Is Buddhism truly pro-detachment and anti-attachment? *Contemporary Buddhism, 5,* 105–120.

Gibson, H. B. (1991). Can hypnosis compel people to commit harmful, immoral and criminal acts? A review of the literature. *Contemporary Hypnosis, 8,* 129–140.

Giese-Davis, J., & Spiegel, D. (2001). Suppression, repressive-defensiveness, restraint, and distress in metastatic breast cancer: Separable or inseparable constructs? *Journal of Personality, 69,* 417–449.

Gigerenzer, G. (1991). From tools to theories: A heuristic of discovery in cognitive psychology. *Psychological Review, 98,* 254–267.

Gilbert, D. T., & Malone, P. S. (1995). The correspondence bias. *Psychological Bulletin, 117,* 21–38.

Gillani, N. B., & Smith, J. C. (2001). Zen meditation and ABC relaxation theory: An exploration of relaxation states, beliefs, dispositions, and motivations. *Journal of Clinical Psychology, 57,* 839–846.

Gilligan, C. (1982). *In a different voice.* Cambridge, MA: Harvard University Press.

Gilman, S. L. (2001). Karen Horney, M. D., 1885–1952. *American Journal of Psychiatry, 158,* 1205.

Giltinan, J. M. (1990). Using life review to facilitate self-actualization in elderly women. *Gerontology and Geriatrics Education, 10,* 75–83.

Giorgi, A. (1992). The idea of human science. *Humanistic Psychologist, 20,* 202–217.

Girelli, S. A., & Stake, J. E. (1993). Bipolarity in Jungian type theory and the Myers-Briggs Type Indicator. *Journal of Personality Assessment, 60,* 290–301.

Gleaves, D. H., & Hernandez, E. (1999). Recent reformulations of Freud's development and abandonment of his seduction theory: Historical/scientific clarification or a continued assault on truth? *History of Psychology, 2,* 324–354.

Gleser, G. C., & Ihilevich, D. (1969). An objective instrument for measuring defense mechanisms. *Journal of Consulting and Clinical Psychology, 33,* 51–60.

Glucksman, M. L. (2000). Affect dysregulation: Defense or deficit? *Journal of the American Academy of Psychoanalysis, 28,* 263–273.

Goebel, B. L., & Boeck, B. E. (1987). Ego integrity and fear of death: A comparison of institutionalized and independently living older adults. *Death Studies, 11,* 193–204.

Goertzel, M. G., Goertzel, V., & Goertzel, T. G. (1978). *Three hundred eminent personalities.* San Francisco: Jossey-Bass.

Gold, I., & Stoljar, D. (1999). A neuron doctrine in the philosophy of neuroscience. *Behavioral and Brain Sciences, 22,* 809–830.

Goldberg, L. R. (1981). Language and individual differences: The search for universals in personality lexicons. In L. Wheeler (Ed.), *Review of personality and social psychology* (Vol. 2, pp. 141–165). Beverly Hills, CA: Sage.

Goldberg, L. R. (1982). From Ace to Zombie: Some explorations in the language of personality. In C. D. Spielberger & J. N. Butcher (Eds.), *Advances in personality assessment* (Vol. 1, pp. 203–234). Hillsdale, NJ: Erlbaum.

Goldfried, M. R., Greenberg, L. S., & Marmar, C. (1990). Individual psychotherapy: Process and outcome. *Annual Review of Psychology, 41,* 659–688.

Goldman, L. (1996). Mind, character, and the deferral of gratification. *Educational Forum, 60,* 135–140.

Goldsmith, H. H., Buss, K. A., & Lemery, K. S. (1997). Toddler and childhood temperament: Expanded content, stronger genetic evidence, new evidence for the importance of environment. *Developmental Psychology, 33,* 891–905.

Goldwert, M. (1986). Childhood seduction and the spiritualization of psychology: The case of Jung and Rank. *Child Abuse and Neglect, 10,* 555–557.

Goldwert, M. (1991). Contributions to psychohistory: XVII. Bridging the great divide: Psychology and history. *Psychological Reports, 68,* 719–722.

Goleman, D. (2004). *Destructive emotions: A scientific dialogue with the Dalai Lama.* Westminster, MD: Bantam Books.

Gomez, A., & Gomez, R. (2002). Personality traits of the behavioural approach and inhibition systems: Associations with processing of emotional stimuli. *Personality and Individual Differences, 32,* 1299–1316.

Gondola, J. C., & Tuckman, B. W. (1985). Effects of a systematic program of exercise on selected measures of creativity. *Perceptual and Motor Skills, 60,* 53–54.

Gonzalez-Balado, J., & Playfoot, J. N. (Eds.). (1985). *My life for the poor: Mother Teresa of Calcutta.* New York: Ballantine Books.

Goodspeed, R. B., & DeLucia, A. G. (1990). Stress reduction at the worksite: An evaluation of two methods. *American Journal of Health Promotion, 4,* 333–337.

Goodstein, L. (2003, September 18). Dalai Lama says terror may need a violent reply. *New York Times,* p. A18.

Gordon, C. R., Ben-Aryeh, H., Spitzer, O., Doweck, I., Gonen, A., Melamed, Y., & Shupak, A. (1994). Seasickness susceptibility, personality factors, and salivation. *Aviation, Space, and Environmental Medicine, 65,* 610–614.

Gordon, R. D. (1985). Dimensions of peak communication experiences: An exploratory study. *Psychological Reports, 57,* 824–826.

Gorsuch, R. L., & McPherson, S. E. (1989). Intrinsic/extrinsic measurement: I/E-revised and single-item scales. *Journal for the Scientific Study of Religion, 28,* 348–354.

Gosling, S. D., John, O. P., Robins, R. W., & Craik, K. H. (1998). Do people know how they behave? Self-reported act frequencies compared with on-line codings by observers. *Journal of Personality and Social Psychology, 74,* 1337–1349.

Gottman, J. M., Katz, L. F., & Hooven, C. (1996). Parental meta-emotion philosophy and the emotional life of families: Theoretical models and preliminary data. *Journal of Family Psychology, 10,* 243–268.

Gould, D., Hodge, K., Peterson, K., & Giannini, J. (1989). An exploratory examination of strategies used by elite coaches to enhance self-efficacy in athletes. *Journal of Sport and Exercise Psychology, 11,* 128–140.

Gould, M. S., King, R., Greenwald, S., Fisher, P., Schwab-Stone, M., Kramer, R., Flisher, A. J., Goodman, S., Canino, G., & Shaffer, D. (1998). Psychopathology associated with suicidal ideation and attempts among children and adolescents. *Journal of the American Academy of Child and Adolescent Psychiatry, 37,* 915–923.

Graham, W. K., & Balloun, J. (1973). An empirical test of Maslow's need hierarchy theory. *Journal of Humanistic Psychology, 13,* 97–108.

Grand, S., & Alpert, J. L. (1993). The core trauma of incest: An object relations view. *Professional Psychology: Research and Practice, 24,* 330–334.

Grasing, K. W., & Miller, N. E. (1989). Self-administration of morphine contingent on heart rate in the rat. *Life Sciences, 45,* 1967–1976.

Gray, J. (1999). Ivan Petrovich Pavlov and the conditioned reflex. *Brain Research Bulletin, 50,* 433.

Gray, J. A. (1987). *The psychology of fear and stress.* Cambridge, UK: Cambridge University Press.

Graziano, W. G., Jensen-Campbell, L. A., & Hair, E. C. (1996). Perceiving interpersonal conflict and reacting to it: The case for agreeableness. *Journal of Personality and Social Psychology, 70,* 820–835.

Graziano, W. G., Jensen-Campbell, L. A., & Sullivan-Logan, G. M. (1998). Temperament, activity, and expectations for later personality development. *Journal of Personality and Social Psychology, 74,* 1266–1277.

Greasley, P. (2000). Handwriting analysis and personality assessment: The creative use of analogy, symbolism, and metaphor. *European Psychologist, 5,* 44–51.

Greenberg, J., & Mitchell, S. (1983). *Object relations in psychoanalytic theory.* Cambridge, MA: Harvard University Press.

Greenberg, J. R. (1986). Theoretical models and the analyst's neutrality. *Contemporary Psychoanalysis, 22,* 89–106. (Reprinted, with Editors'

Introduction and Afterword, in S. A. Mitchell & L. Aron (1999). *Relational psychoanalysis: The emergence of a tradition* (pp. 131–152). Hillsdale, NJ: Analytical Press.)

Greenberg, R. P., & Fisher, S. (1978, September). Testing Dr. Freud. *Human Behavior,* pp. 28–33.

Greene, B. A. (1985). Considerations in the treatment of black patients by white therapists. *Psychotherapy, 22,* 389–393.

Greene, B. A. (1993). Human diversity in clinical psychology: Lesbian and gay sexual orientations. *Clinical Psychologist, 46,* 74–82.

Greenwald, A. G. (1992). New look 3: Unconscious cognition reclaimed. *American Psychologist, 47,* 766–779.

Greenwood, C. R., Carta, J. J., Hart, B., Kamps, D., Terry, B., Arreaga-Mayer, C., Atwater, J., Walker, D., Risley, T., & Delquadri, J. C. (1992). Out of the laboratory and into the community: 26 years of applied behavior analysis at the Juniper Gardens Children's Project. *American Psychologist, 47,* 1464–1474.

Greever, K. B., Tseng, M. S., & Friedland, B. U. (1973). Development of the Social Interest Index. *Journal of Consulting and Clinical Psychology, 41,* 454–458.

Grey, W. (1994). Philosophy and the paranormal. Part 1: The problem of "psi." *Skeptical Inquirer, 18,* 142–149.

Gross, J. J. (1999). Emotion and emotion regulation. In L. A. Pervin & O. P. John (Eds.), *Handbook of personality: Theory and research* (2nd ed., pp. 525–552). New York: Guilford.

Gross, J. J., & Levenson, R. W. (1993). Emotional suppression: Physiology, self-report, and expressive behavior. *Journal of Personality and Social Psychology, 64,* 970–986.

Gross, J. J., & Levenson, R. W. (1997). Hiding feelings: The acute effects of inhibiting negative and positive emotion. *Journal of Abnormal Psychology, 106,* 95–103.

Grossarth-Maticek, R., Eysenck, H. J., & Vetter, H. (1989). The causes and cures of prejudice: An empirical study of the frustration-aggression hypothesis. *Personality and Individual Differences, 10,* 547–558.

Grossman, C. L. (2001, October 22). Experts seek clues in a bioterrorist's penmanship. *USA Today,* p. D3.

Grossman, P., Niemann, L., Schmidt, S., & Walach, H. (2004). Mindfulness-based stress reduction and health benefits: A meta-analysis. *Journal of Psychosomatic Research, 57,* 35–43.

Grotstein J. S. (1993). A reappraisal of W. R. D. Fairbairn. Bulletin of the Menninger Clinic; 57, 421–450.

Grove, W. M., & Meehl, P. E. (1996). Comparative efficiency of informal (subjective, impressionistic) and formal (mechanical, algorithmic) prediction procedures: The clinical-statistical controversy. *Psychology, Public Policy, and Law, 2,* 293–323.

Gruber, H. E. (1989). The evolving systems approach to creative work. In D. B. Wallace & H. E. Gruber (Eds.), *Creative people at work: Twelve cognitive case studies* (pp. 3–43). New York: Oxford University Press.

Gruen, A. (1998). Reductionistic biological thinking and the denial of experience and pain in developmental theories. *Journal of Humanistic Psychology, 38*(2), 84–102.

Grünbaum, A. (1984). *The foundations of psychoanalysis: A philosophical critique.* Berkeley: University of California Press.

Grünbaum, A. (1990). "Meaning" connections and causal connections in the human sciences: The poverty of hermeneutic philosophy. *Journal of the American Psychoanalytic Association, 38,* 559–577.

Grusec, J., & Mischel, W. (1966). Model's characteristics as determinants of social learning. *Journal of Personality and Social Psychology, 4,* 211–215.

Grych, J. H., & Fincham, F. D. (1992). Interventions for children of divorce: Toward greater integration of research and action. *Psychological Bulletin, 111,* 434–454.

Guastello, D. D., & Guastello, S. J. (2002, June). Birth category effects on the Gordon Personal Profile variables. *Journal of Articles in Support of the Null Hypothesis, 1*(1) [Electronic journal]. Retrieved June 28, 2002, from http://www.jasnh.com/a1.htm

Guisinger, S., & Blatt, S. J. (1994). Individuality and relatedness: Evolution of a fundamental dialectic. *American Psychologist, 49,* 104–111.

Gundrum, M., Lietaer, G., & Van Hees-Matthijssen, C. (1999). Carl Rogers' responses in the 17th session with Miss Mun: Comments from a process-experiential and psychoanalytic perspective. *British Journal of Guidance and Counselling, 27,* 461–482.

Gustafson, R. (1986). Alcohol, frustration, and aggression: An experiment using the balanced placebo design. *Psychological Reports, 59,* 207–218.

Guydish, J., Jackson, T. T., Markley, R. P., & Zelhart, P. F. (1985). George A. Kelly: Pioneer in rural school psychology. *Journal of School Psychology, 23,* 297–304.

Haaken, J. (1993). From Al-Anon to ACOA: Codependence and the reconstruction of caregiving. *Signs, 18,* 321–345.

Habermas, T., & Bluck, S. (2000). Getting a life: The emergence of the life story in adolescence. *Psychological Bulletin, 126,* 748–769.

Hageseth, J. A., & Schmidt, L. D. (1982). Self-actualization and conceptual structures. *Psychological Reports, 51,* 672.

Haidt, J., & Rodin, J. (1999). Control and efficacy as interdisciplinary bridges. *Review of General Psychology, 3,* 317–337.

Halisch, F., & Geppert, U. (2001). Motives, personal goals, and life satisfaction in old age: First results from the Munich Twin Study (GOLD). In A. Efklides, J. Kuhl, & R. M. Sorrentino (Eds.), *Trends and prospects in motivation research* (pp. 389–409). New York: Kluwer Academic.

Hall, C. S. (1966). *The meaning of dreams.* New York: McGraw-Hill.

Hall, C. S., & Nordby, V. J. (1973). *A primer of Jungian psychology.* New York: Mentor Books.

Hall, S. S. (2003, September 14). Is Buddhism good for your health? *New York Times Magazine,* p. 46.

Halpern, D. F. (1997). Sex differences in intelligence: Implications for education. *American Psychologist, 10,* 1091–1102.

Hampson, S. E. (1998). When is an inconsistency not an inconsistency? Trait reconciliation in personality description and impression formation. *Journal of Personality and Social Psychology, 74,* 102–117.

Han, J. J., Leichtman, M. D., & Wang, Q. (1998). Autobiographical memory in Korean, Chinese, and American children. *Developmental Psychology, 34,* 701–713.

Hankoff, L. D. (1987). The earliest memories of criminals. *International Journal of Offender Therapy and Comparative Criminology, 31,* 195–201.

Hanlon, R. P., Jr. (2000). The use of typology in financial planning. *Journal of Financial Planning, 13*(7), 96–112.

Hanna, F. J. (1996). Community feeling, empathy, and intersubjectivity: A phenomenological framework. *Individual Psychology, 52,* 22–30.

Hannah, M. T., Domino, G., Figueredo, A. J., & Hendrickson, R. (1996). The prediction of ego integrity in older persons. *Educational and Psychological Measurement, 56,* 930–950.

Hanson, G. (2001). Ideas and identities: The life and work of Erik Erikson [Book review]. *American Journal of Psychiatry, 158,* 1941–1943.

Hardaway, R. A. (1990). Subliminally activated symbiotic fantasies: Facts and artifacts. *Psychological Bulletin, 107,* 177–195.

Hardwired for God? (2001, April). *U.S. Catholic, 66*(4), p. 11.

Harlow, J. M., & Miller, E. (1993). Recovery from the passage of an iron bar through the head. *History of Psychiatry, 4,* 271–281. (Original work published 1939)

Harmon-Jones, E., & Allen, J. J. B. (1997). Behavioral activation sensitivity and resting frontal EEG asymmetry: Covariation of putative indicators related to risk for mood disorders. *Journal of Abnormal Psychology, 106,* 159–163.

Harmon-Jones, E., & Allen, J. J. B. (1998). Anger and frontal brain activity: EEG asymmetry consistent with approach motivation despite negative affective valence. *Journal of Personality and Social Psychology, 74,* 1310–1316.

Harren, V. A., Kass, R. A., Tinsley, H. E. A., & Moreland, J. R. (1979). Influence of gender, sex-role attitudes, and cognitive complexity on gender-dominant career choices. *Journal of Counseling Psychology, 26,* 227–234.

Harrington, D. M. (1993). Child-rearing antecedents of suboptimal personality development: Exploring aspects of Alice Miller's concept of the *poisonous pedagogy.* In D. C. Funder, R. D. Parke, C.

Tomlinson-Keasey, & K. Widaman (Eds.), *Studying lives through time: Personality and development* (pp. 289–313). Washington, D. C.: American Psychological Association.

Harrington, D. M., Block, J. H., & Block, J. (1987). Testing aspects of Carl Rogers's theory of creative environments: Child-rearing antecedents of creative potential in young adolescents. *Journal of Personality and Social Psychology, 52,* 851–856.

Harrington, R., & Loffredo, D. A. (2001). The relationship between life satisfaction, self-consciousness, and the Myers-Briggs Type Inventory dimensions. *Journal of Psychology, 135,* 439–450.

Harris, C. R. (2002). Sexual and romantic jealousy in heterosexual and homosexual adults. *Psychological Science, 13,* 7–12.

Harris, J. R. (1995). Where is the child's environment? A group socialization theory of development. *Psychological Review, 102,* 458–489.

Harris, J. R. (2000). Socialization, personality, and the child's environments: Comment on Vandell (2000). *Developmental Psychology, 36,* 711–723.

Harris, S. (2004). *The end of faith: Religion, terror, and the future of reason.* New York: Norton.

Harris, W. S., Gowda, M., Kolb, J. W., Strychacz, C. P., Vacek, J. L., Jones, P. G., Forker, A., O'Keefe, J. H., & McCallister, B. D. (1999). A randomized, controlled trial of the effects of remote, intercessory prayer on outcomes in patients admitted to the coronary care unit. *Archives of Internal Medicine, 159,* 2273–2278.

Hart, D., Keller, M., Edelstein, W., & Hofmann, V. (1998). Childhood personality influences on social-cognitive development: A longitudinal study. *Journal of Personality and Social Psychology, 74,* 1278–1289.

Hart, T. (1999). The refinement of empathy. *Journal of Humanistic Psychology, 39*(4), 111–125.

Hartmann, E. (1998). Nightmare after trauma as a paradigm for all dreams: A new approach to the nature and functions of dreaming. *Psychiatry: Interpersonal and Biological Processes, 61,* 223–238.

Hartmann, E., Zborowski, M., Rosen, R., & Grace, N. (2001). Contextualizing images in dreams: More intense after abuse and trauma. *Dreaming: Journal of the Association for the Study of Dreams, 11,* 115–126.

Hartmann, H. (1958). *Ego psychology and the problem of adaptation* (D. Rapaport, Trans.). New York: International Universities Press. (Original work published 1939)

Harvey, R. J., & Hammer, A. L. (1999). Item response theory. *Counseling Psychologist, 27,* 353–383.

Hattie, J., & Cooksey, R. W. (1984). Procedures for assessing the validities of tests using the "known-groups" method. *Applied Psychological Measurement, 8,* 295–305.

Haule, J. R. (2000). Jung's practice of analysis: A Euro-American parallel to Ch'an Buddhism. *Journal of Individual Psychology, 56,* 353–365.

Haupt, A. L., & Leary, M. R. (1997). The appeal of worthless groups: Moderating effects of trait self-esteem. *Group Dynamics: Theory, Research, and Practice, 1,* 124–132.

Hayden, J. (1993). The condom race. *Journal of American College Health, 42*(3), 133–136.

Hayden, T., & Mischel, W. (1976). Maintaining trait consistency in the resolution of behavioral inconsistency: The wolf in sheep's clothing? *Journal of Personality, 44,* 109–132.

Hayes, R. P. (2003). Classical Buddhist model of a healthy mind. In K. H. Dockett, G. R. Dudley-Grant, & C. P. Bankart (Eds.), *Psychology and Buddhism: From individual to global community* (pp. 161–170). Secaucus, NJ: Kluwer Academic.

Haymes, M., & Green, L. (1982). The assessment of motivation within Maslow's framework. *Journal of Research in Personality, 16,* 179–192.

Haynes, S. N., & Uchigakiuchi, P. (1993). Incorporating personality trait measures in behavioral assessment: Nuts in a fruitcake or raisins in a mai tai? *Behavior Modification, 17,* 72–92.

Hays, R. D., & Ellickson, P. L. (1990). How generalizable are adolescents' beliefs about pro-drug pressures and resistance self-efficacy? *Journal of Applied Social Psychology, 20,* 321–340.

Hazan, C., & Diamond, L. M. (2000). The place of attachment in human mating. *Review of General Psychology, 4,* 186–204.

Hazan, C., & Shaver, P. (1987). Romantic love conceptualized as an attachment process. *Journal of Personality and Social Psychology, 52,* 511–524.

Hazan, C., & Shaver, P. (1994). Attachment as an organizational framework for research on close relationships. *Psychological Inquiry, 5,* 1–22.

Heckhausen, H., & Beckmann, J. (1990). Intentional action and action slips. *Psychological Review, 97,* 36–48.

Hegland, S. M., & Galejs, I. (1983). Developmental aspects of locus of control in preschool children. *Journal of Genetic Psychology, 143,* 229–239.

Heine, S. (2002). *Opening a mountain: Koans of the Zen masters.* New York: Oxford University Press.

Heine, S. J., Lehman, D. R., Markus, H. R., & Kitayama, S. (1999). Is there a universal need for positive self-regard? *Psychological Review, 106,* 766–794.

Heiserman, A., & Cook, H. (1998). Narcissism, affect, and gender: An empirical examination of Kernberg's and Kohut's theories of narcissism. *Psychoanalytic Psychology, 15,* 74–92.

Heisig, J. W. (2002). Jung, Christianity, and Buddhism. In S. Muramoto & P. Young-Eisendrath (Eds.), *Awakening and insight: Zen Buddhism and psychotherapy* (pp. 45–66). New York: Brunner-Routledge.

Helms, J. E. (1990). *Black and White racial identity: Theory, research, and practice.* Westport, CT: Greenwood Press.

Helson, R., & Picano, J. (1990). Is the traditional role bad for women? *Journal of Personality and Social Psychology, 59,* 311–320.

Helson, R., & Wink, P. (1987). Two conceptions of maturity examined in the findings of a longitudinal study. *Journal of Personality and Social Psychology, 53,* 531–541.

Henning, K., Ey, S., & Shaw, D. (1998). Perfectionism, the imposter phenomenon and psychological adjustment in medical, dental, nursing and pharmacy students. *Medical Education, 32,* 456–464.

Henry, J. (1967). Discussion of Erikson's eight ages of man. In *Current Issues in Psychiatry* (Vol. 2). New York: Science House.

Herek, G. M. (1987). Religious orientation and prejudice: A comparison of racial and sexual attitudes. *Personality and Social Psychology Bulletin, 13,* 34–44.

Hermans, H. J. M. (1987). The dream in the process of valuation: A method of interpretation. *Journal of Personality and Social Psychology, 53,* 163–175.

Hermans, H. J. M. (1988). On the integration of nomothetic and idiographic research methods in the study of personal meaning. *Journal of Personality, 56,* 785–812.

Hermans, H. J. M., & Oles, P. K. (1996). Value crisis: Affective organization of personal meanings. *Journal of Research in Personality, 30,* 457–482.

Herrera, H. (1983). *Frida: A biography of Frida Kahlo.* New York: HarperCollins.

Herrnstein, R. J., Nickerson, R. S., de Sánchez, M., & Swets, J. A. (1986). Teaching thinking skills. *American Psychologist, 41,* 1279–1289.

Herron, R. E., & Cavanaugh, K. L. (2005). Can the Transcendental Meditation program reduce the medical expenditures of older people? A longitudinal cost-reduction study in Canada. *Journal of Social Behavior and Personality, 17,* 415–442.

Herron, W. G. (1995). Development of the ethnic unconscious. *Psychoanalytic Psychology, 12,* 521–532.

Hettman, D. W., & Jenkins, E. (1990). Volunteerism and social interest. *Individual Psychology, 46,* 298–303.

Heubeck, B. G., Wilkinson, R. B., & Cologon, J. (1998). A second look at Carver and White's (1994) BIS/BAS scales. *Personality and Individual Differences, 25,* 785–800.

Hewitt, P. L., Flett, G. L., & Ediger, E. (1996). Perfectionism and depression: Longitudinal assessment of a specific vulnerability hypothesis. *Journal of Abnormal Psychology, 105,* 276–280.

Hewitt, P. L., Newton, J., Flett, G. L., & Callander, L. (1997). Perfectionism and suicide ideation in adolescent psychiatric patients. *Journal of Abnormal Child Psychology, 25,* 95–101.

Heyduk, R. G., & Fenigstein, A. (1984). Influential works and authors in psychology: A survey of eminent psychologists. *American Psychologist, 39,* 556–559.

Hicks, L. E. (1985). Is there a disposition to avoid the fundamental attribution error? *Journal of Research in Personality, 19,* 436–456.

Higgins, E. T. (1997). Beyond pleasure and pain. *American Psychologist, 52,* 1280–1300.

Hilgard, E. R. (1976). Neodissociation theory of multiple cognitive control systems. In G. E. Schwartz & D. Shapiro (Eds.), *Consciousness and self-regulation: Advances in research* (Vol. 1, pp. 137–171). New York: Plenum.

Hilgard, E. R. (1994). Neodissociation theory. In S. J. Lynn & J. W. Rhue, *Dissociation: Clinical, theoretical and research perspectives* (pp. 32–51). New York: Guilford.

Hill, A. B. (1976). Methodological problems in the use of factor analysis: A critical review of the experimental evidence for the anal character. *British Journal of Medical Psychology, 49,* 145–159.

Hill, C. E., & Corbett, M. M. (1993). A perspective on the history of process and outcome research in counseling psychology. *Journal of Counseling Psychology, 40,* 3–24.

Hillman, J. (1980). Egalitarian typologies versus the perception of the unique. *Eranos Lectures* (Vol. 4). Dallas: Spring.

Hills, P., & Argyle, M. (2001). Emotional stability as a major dimension of happiness. *Personality and Individual Differences, 31,* 1357–1364.

Hillstrom, E. (1984). Human personality: Deterministic or merely predictable? *Journal of Psychology and Christianity, 3,* 42–48.

Hobson, J. A. (1988). *The dreaming brain.* New York: Basic Books.

Hobson, J. A., Pace-Schott, E. F., & Stickgold, R. (2000). Dreaming and the brain: Toward a cognitive neuroscience of conscious states. *Behavioral and Brain Sciences, 23,* 793–842, 904–1018, 1083–1121.

Hobson, J. A., & Leonard, J. (2001). *Out of its mind: Psychiatry in crisis.* Cambridge, MA: Perseus.

Hobson, J. A., & McCarley, R. W. (1977). The brain as a dream state generator: An activation-synthesis hypothesis of the dream process. *American Journal of Psychiatry, 134,* 1335–1348.

Hobson, J. A., & Stickgold, R. (1994). Dreaming: A neurocognitive approach. *Consciousness and Cognition, 3,* 1–15.

Hocoy, D. (1999). The validity of Cross's model of black racial identity development in the South African context. *Journal of Black Psychology, 25,* 131–151.

Hodapp, V., Heiligtag, U., & Störmer, S. W. (1990). Cardiovascular reactivity, anxiety and anger during perceived controllability. *Biological Psychology, 30,* 161–170.

Hodgson, J. W., & Fischer, J. L. (1979). Sex differences in identity and intimacy development in college youth. *Journal of Youth and Adolescence, 8,* 37–50.

Hoffman, M. L. (1975). Developmental synthesis of affect and cognition and its implications for altruistic motivation. *Developmental Psychology, 11,* 607–622.

Hoffman, C., & Tchir, M. A. (1990). Interpersonal verbs and dispositional adjectives: The psychology of causality embodied in language. *Journal of Personality and Social Psychology, 58,* 765–778.

Hoffman, E. (1997). *The drive for self: Alfred Adler and the founding of individual psychology.* Reading, MA: Addison-Wesley.

Hoffman, E. (1998). Peak experiences in childhood: An exploratory study. *Journal of Humanistic Psychology, 38*(1), 109–120.

Hoffman, L. W. (1991). The influence of the family environment on personality: Accounting for sibling differences. *Psychological Bulletin, 110,* 187–203.

Hofstetter, C. R., Sallis, J. F., & Hovell, M. F. (1990). Some health dimensions of self-efficacy: Analysis of theoretical specificity. *Social Science and Medicine, 31,* 1051–1056.

Hogan, R., Hogan, J., & Roberts, B. W. (1996). Personality measurement and employment decisions: Questions and answers. *American Psychologist, 51,* 469–477.

Holland, J. G. (1992). B. F. Skinner (1904–1990) [obituary]. *American Psychologist, 47,* 665–667.

Holland, J. L. (1996). Exploring careers with a typology: What we have learned and some new directions. *American Psychologist, 51,* 397–406.

Hollis, J. (2000). *The archetypal imagination.* College Station, TX: Texas A & M University Press.

Holt, R. R. (1962). Individuality and generalization in the psychology of personality. *Journal of Personality, 30,* 377–404.

Hom, H. L., & Knight, H. (1996). Delay of gratification: Mothers' predictions about four attentional techniques. *Journal of Genetic Psychology, 157,* 180–190.

Homma-True, R., Greene, B., Lòpez, S. R., & Trimble, J. E. (1993). Ethnocultural diversity in clinical psychology. *Clinical Psychologist, 46,* 50–63.

Honos-Webb, L., Harrick, E. A., Stiles, W. B., & Park, C. L. (2000). Assimilation of traumatic experiences and physical-health outcomes: Cautions for the Pennebaker paradigm. *Psychotherapy: Theory, Research, Practice, Training, 37,* 307–314.

Hoover, D. R. (2000). Questions on the design and findings of a randomized, controlled trial of the effects of remote, intercessory prayer on outcomes in patients admitted to the coronary care unit [letter]. *Archives of Internal Medicine, 160,* 1875–1876.

Hopkins, J. R. (1995). Erik Homburger Erikson (1902–1994) [obituary]. *American Psychologist, 50,* 796–797.

Horley, J. (1991). Values and beliefs as personal constructs. *International Journal of Personal Construct Psychology, 4,* 1–14.

Horn, J. (1984). Genetical underpinnings. *Multivariate Behavioral Research, 19,* 307–309.

Horn, J. (2001). Raymond Bernard Cattell (1905–1998) [obituary]. *American Psychologist, 56,* 71–72.

Horner, A. J. (1994). In search of ordinariness: The dissolution of false pride. *American Journal of Psychoanalysis, 54,* 87–93.

Horner, M. S. (1972). Toward an understanding of achievement-related conflicts in women. *Journal of Social Issues, 28*(2), 157–175.

Horney, K. (1937). *The neurotic personality of our time.* New York: Norton.

Horney, K. (1939). *New ways in psychoanalysis.* New York: Norton.

Horney, K. (1942). *Self-analysis.* New York: Norton.

Horney, K. (1945). *Our inner conflicts: A constructive theory of neurosis.* New York: Norton.

Horney, K. (1950). *Neurosis and human growth: The struggle toward self-realization.* New York: Norton.

Horney, K. (1967a). The flight from womanhood: The masculinity complex in women as viewed by men and by women. In H. Kelman (Ed.), *Feminine psychology* (pp. 54–70). New York: Norton. (Original work published 1926)

Horney, K. (1967b). On the genesis of the castration complex in women. In H. Kelman (Ed.), *Feminine psychology* (pp. 37–53). New York: Norton. (Original work published 1923)

Horney, K. (1967c). Inhibited femininity: Psychoanalytical contribution to the problem of frigidity. In H. Kelman (Ed.), *Feminine psychology* (pp. 71–83). New York: Norton. (Original work published 1926)

Horney, K. (1967d). The neurotic need for love. In H. Kelman (Ed.), *Feminine psychology* (pp. 245–258). New York: Norton. (Original work published 1937)

Horney, K. (1967e). The problem of feminine masochism. In H. Kelman (Ed.), *Feminine psychology* (pp. 214–233). New York: Norton. (Original work published 1935)

Horwitz, N. M. (2001). Why do people stay in hateful relationships? The concept of malignant vindictiveness. *American Journal of Psychoanalysis, 61,* 143–160.

Houston, B. K., Smith, M. A., & Cates, D. S. (1989). Hostility patterns and cardiovascular reactivity to stress. *Psychophysiology, 26,* 337–342.

Howard, G. S. (1985). The role of values in the science of psychology. *American Psychologist, 40,* 255–265.

Howard, G. S. (1988). Kelly's thought at age 33: Suggestions for conceptual and methodological refinements. *International Journal of Personal Construct Psychology, 1,* 263–272.

Howard, G. S. (1991). Culture tales: A narrative approach to thinking, cross-cultural psychology, and psychotherapy. *American Psychologist, 46,* 187–197.

Howard, G. S. (1992). Projecting humanistic values into the future: Freedom and social activism. *Humanistic Psychologist, 20,* 260–272.

Howard, J. A., Blumstein, P., & Schwartz, P. (1986). Sex, power, and influence tactics in intimate relationships. *Journal of Personality and Social Psychology, 51,* 102–109.

Howe, M. L., & Courage, M. L. (1993). On resolving the enigma of infantile amnesia. *Psychological Bulletin, 113,* 305–326.

Howell, R. H., Owen, P. D., & Nocks, E. C. (1990). Increasing safety belt use: Effects of modeling and trip length. *Journal of Applied Social Psychology, 20,* 254–263.

Hoyle, R. H., Fejfar, M. C., & Miller, J. D. (2000). Personality and sexual risk taking: A quantitative review. *Journal of Personality, 68,* 1203–1231.

Huber, J. W., & Altmaier, E. M. (1983). An investigation of the self-statement systems of phobic and nonphobic individuals. *Cognitive Therapy and Research, 7,* 355–362.

Hudson, V. M. (1990). Birth order of world leaders: An exploratory analysis of effects on personality and behavior. *Political Psychology, 11,* 583–601.

Huffman, J. R. (1989). Young man Johnson. *American Journal of Psychoanalysis, 49,* 251–265.

Hui, C. H., & Triandis, H. C. (1986). Individualism-collectivism: A study of cross-cultural researchers. *Journal of Cross-Cultural Psychology, 17,* 225–248.

Hull, J. G., & Young, R. D. (1983). Self-consciousness, self-esteem, and success-failure as determinants of alcohol consumption in male social drinkers. *Journal of Personality and Social Psychology, 44,* 1097–1109.

Hull, J. G., Young, R. D., & Jouriles, E. (1986). Applications of the self-awareness model of alcohol consumption: Predicting patterns of use and abuse. *Journal of Personality and Social Psychology, 51,* 790–796.

Hume, D. K., & Montgomerie, R. (2001). Facial attractiveness signals different aspects of "quality" in women and men. *Evolution and Human Behavior, 22,* 93–112.

Huntley, C. W., & Davis, F. (1983). Undergraduate study of value scores as predictors of occupation 25 years later. *Journal of Personality and Social Psychology, 45,* 1148–1155.

Huston, H. L., Rosen, D. H., & Smith, S. M. (1999). Evolutionary memory. In D. Rosen & M. Luebbert (Eds.), *The evolution of the psyche.* Westport, CT: Praeger.

Hutton, P. H. (1983). The psychohistory of Erik Erikson from the perspective of collective mentalities. *Psychohistorical Review, 12,* 18–25.

Hyland, M. E. (1985). Do person variables exist in different ways? *American Psychologist, 40,* 1003–1010.

Hyman, R. B. (1988). Four stages of adulthood: An exploratory study of growth patterns of inner-direction and time-competence in women. *Journal of Research in Personality, 22,* 117–127.

Immelman, A. (1993). The assessment of political personality: A psychodiagnostically relevant conceptualization and methodology. *Political Psychology, 14,* 725–741.

Ingram, D. H. (2001). The Hofgeismar lectures: A contemporary overview of Horneyan psychoanalysis. *American Journal of Psychoanalysis, 61,* 113–141.

Integrating Buddhist philosophy with cognitive and behavioral practice [Special series]. (2002). *Cognitive and Behavioral Practice, 9,* 38–78.

Ivancevich, J. M., Matteson, M. T., & Gamble, G. O. (1987). Birth order and the Type A coronary behavior pattern. *Individual Psychology, 43,* 42–49.

Ivey, A. E. (1971). *Microcounseling: Innovations in interviewing training.* Springfield, IL: Thomas.

Izard, C. E. (1991). *The psychology of emotions.* New York: Plenum Press.

Jackson, L. M., & Hunsberger, B. (1999). An intergroup perspective on religion and prejudice. *Journal for the Scientific Study of Religion, 38,* 509–523.

Jackson, T. T., Markley, R. P., Zelhart, P. F., & Guydish, J. (1988). Contributions to the history of psychology: XLV. Attitude research: George A. Kelly's use of polar adjectives. *Psychological Reports, 62,* 47–52.

Jacobo, M. C. (2001). Revolutions in psychoanalytic theory of lesbian development: Dora to dykes and back again. *Psychoanalytic Psychology, 18,* 667–683.

Jacobsen, T., Edelstein, W., & Hofmann, V. (1994). A longitudinal study of the relation between representations of attachment in childhood and cognitive functioning in childhood and adolescence. *Developmental Psychology, 30,* 112–124.

Jaffe, L. S. (1990). The empirical foundations of psychoanalytic approaches to psychological testing. *Journal of Personality Assessment, 55,* 746–755.

Jaffe, L. S. (1992). The impact of theory on psychological testing: How psychoanalytic theory makes diagnostic testing more enjoyable and rewarding. *Journal of Personality Assessment, 58,* 621–630.

Jakupcak, M., Lisak, D., & Roemer, L. (2002). The role of masculine ideology and masculine gender role stress in men's perpetration of relationship violence. *Psychology of Men and Masculinity, 3,* 97–106.

Jamner, L. D., & Leigh, H. (1999). Repressive/defensive coping, endogenous opioids and health: How a life so perfect can make you sick. *Psychiatry Research, 85,* 17–31.

Jankowicz, A. D. (1987). Whatever became of George Kelly? Applications and implications. *American Psychologist, 42,* 481–487.

Jankowicz, A. D., & Hisrich, R. (1987). Intuition in small-business lending decisions. *Journal of Small Business Management, 25,* 45–52.

Jason, L. A., & Moritsugu, J. (2003). The role of religion and spirituality in community building. In S. Muramoto & P. Young-Eisendrath (Eds.), *Awakening and insight: Zen Buddhism and psychotherapy* (pp. 197–214). New York: Brunner-Routledge.

Jefferson, T., Jr., Herbst, J. H., & McCrae, R. R. (1998). Associations between birth order and personality traits: Evidence from self-reports and observer ratings. *Journal of Research in Personality, 32,* 498–509.

Jenkins, A. H. (1997). The empathic context in psychotherapy with people of color. In A. C. Bohart & L. S. Greenberg (Eds.), *Empathy reconsidered: New directions in psychotherapy* (pp. 321–341). Washington, DC: American Psychological Association.

Jensen, J. P., Bergin, A. E., & Greaves, D. W. (1990). The meaning of eclecticism: New survey and analysis of components. *Professional Psychology: Research and Practice, 21,* 124–130.

Jinpa, G. T. (2000). The foundations of a Buddhist psychology of awakening. In G. Watson, S. Batchelor, & G. Claxton (Eds.), *The psychology of awakening: Buddhism, science, and our day-to-day lives* (pp. 10–22). York Beach, ME: Samuel Weiser.

Joe, V. C., McGee, S. J., & Dazey, D. (1977). Religiousness and devaluation of a rape victim. *Journal of Clinical Psychology, 33,* 64.

John, O. P. (1990). The "Big Five" factor taxonomy: Dimensions of personality in the natural language and in questionnaires. In L. A. Pervin (Ed.), *Handbook of personality: Theory and research* (pp. 66–100). New York: Guilford.

John, O. P., Angleitner, A., & Ostendorf, F. (1988). The lexical approach to personality: A historical review of trait taxonomic research. *European Journal of Personality, 2,* 171–203.

John, O. P., & Srivastava, S. (1999). The big five trait taxonomy: History, measurement, and theoretical perspectives. In L. A. Pervin & O. P. John (Eds.), *Handbook of personality: Theory and research* (2nd ed., pp. 102–138.). New York: Guilford.

Johnson, B. T., & Nichols, D. R. (1998). Social psychologists' expertise in the public interest: Civilian morale research during World War II. *Journal of Social Issues, 54,* 53–77.

Johnson, N. B. (1991). Primordial image and the archetypal design of art. *Journal of Analytical Psychology, 36,* 371–392.

Johnson, S. L., Sandrow, D., Meyer, B., Winters, R., Miller, I., Solomon, D., & Keitner, G. (2000). Increases in manic symptoms after life events involving goal attainment. *Journal of Abnormal Psychology, 109,* 721–727.

Johnson, T. E., & Rule, B. G. (1986). Mitigating circumstance information, censure, and aggression. *Journal of Personality and Social Psychology, 50,* 537–542.

Johnson, W., & Bouchard, T. J., Jr. (2005). The structure of human intelligence: It is verbal, perceptual, and image rotation (VPR), not fluid and crystallized. *Intelligence, 33,* 393–416.

Jones, M. M. (1980). Conversion reaction: Anachronism or evolutionary form? A review of the neurologic, behavioral, and psychoanalytic literature. *Psychological Bulletin, 87,* 427–441.

Jones, A., & Crandall, R. (1986). Validation of a short index of self-actualization. *Personality and Social Psychology Bulletin, 12,* 63–73.

Jones, D. (1999). Evolutionary psychology. *Annual Review of Anthropology, 28,* 553–575.

Jones, E. E., & Windholz, M. (1990). The psychoanalytic case study: Toward a method for systematic inquiry. *Journal of the American Psychoanalytic Association, 38,* 985–1015.

Jones, T. L., & Prinz, R. J. (2005). Potential roles of parental self-efficacy in parent and child adjustment: A review. *Clinical Psychology Review, 25,* 341–363.

Jones, W. H., Couch, L., & Scott, S. (1997). Trust and betrayal: The psychology of getting along and getting ahead. In R. Hogan, J. Johnson, & S. Briggs (Eds.), *Handbook of personality psychology* (pp. 465–482). San Diego: Academic Press.

Jones, R. A. (2000). On the empirical proof of archetypes: Commentary on Maloney. *Journal of Analytical Psychology, 45,* 599–605.

Josselson, R. (1973). Psychodynamic aspects of identity formation in college women. *Journal of Youth and Adolescence, 2,* 3–52.

Josselson, R. (1987). *Finding herself: Pathways to identity development in women.* San Francisco: Jossey-Bass.

Joubert, C. E. (1989a). Birth order and narcissism. *Psychological Reports, 64,* 721–722.

Joubert, C. E. (1989b). The Famous Sayings test: Sex differences and some correlations with other variables. *Psychological Reports, 64,* 763–766.

Judge, T. A., Higgins, C. A., Thoresen, C. J., & Barrick, M. R. (1999). The big five personality traits, general mental ability, and career success across the life span. *Personnel Psychology, 52,* 621–652.

Judge, T. A., Martocchio, J. J., & Thoresen, C. J. (1997). Five-factor model of personality and employee absence. *Journal of Applied Psychology, 82,* 745–755.

Jung, C. G. (1954). Marriage as a psychological relationship. In C. G. Jung, *The development of personality* (pp. 187–201) (W. McGuire, Ed.; R. F. C. Hull, Trans.). Princeton, NJ: Princeton University Press. (Original work published 1931)

Jung, C. G. (1959). *Aion: Researches into the phenomenology of the self* (2nd ed.) (R. F. C. Hull, Trans.). Princeton, NJ: Princeton University Press.

Jung, C. G. (1960a). *The psychogenesis of mental disease* (R. F. C. Hull, Trans.). Princeton, NJ: Princeton University Press.

Jung, C. G. (1960b). *Synchronicity: An acausal connecting principle* (R. F. C. Hull, Trans.). Princeton, NJ: Princeton University Press.

Jung, C. G. (1961). *Memories, dreams, reflections* (A. Jaffe, Ed.; R. Winston & C. Winston, Trans.). New York: Random House.

Jung, C. G. (1964). *Civilization in transition* (R. F. C. Hull, Trans.). Princeton, NJ: Princeton University Press.

Jung, C. G. (1968a). *Alchemical studies* (R. F. C. Hull, Trans.). Princeton, NJ: Princeton University Press.

Jung, C. G. (1968b). *Psychology and alchemy* (2nd ed.) (R. F. C. Hull, Trans.). Princeton, NJ: Princeton University Press. (Original work published 1944)

Jung, C. G. (1969). *Four archetypes: Mother, rebirth, spirit, trickster* (R. F. C. Hull, Trans.). Princeton, NJ: Princeton University Press.

Jung, C. G. (1970). *Mysterium coniunctionis: An inquiry into the separation and synthesis of psychic opposites in alchemy* (2nd ed.) (R. F. C. Hull, Trans.). Princeton, NJ: Princeton University Press.

Jung, C. G. (1971). *Psychological types* (R. F. C. Hull and H. G. Baynes, Trans.). Princeton, NJ: Princeton University Press.

Jung, C. G. (1973). *Experimental researches* (L. Stein & D. Riviere, Trans.). Princeton, NJ: Princeton University Press.

Jung, C. G. (1974). The practical use of dream-analysis. In C. G. Jung, *Dreams* (pp. 87–109), (W. McGuire, Ed.; R. F. C. Hull, Trans.). Princeton, NJ: Princeton University Press.

Jung, C. G. (1987). The association method: Lecture III. *American Journal of Psychology, 100,* 489–509. (Original work published 1910)

Jung, C. G. (1989). *Analytical psychology: Notes of the seminar given in 1925.* Princeton, NJ: Princeton University Press.

Kagan, J. (1989). Temperamental contributions to social behavior. *American Psychologist, 44,* 668–674.

Kagan, J. (1990). Validity is local. *American Psychologist, 45,* 294–295.

Kagan, J. (1994). *Galen's prophecy: Temperament in human nature.* New York: Westview Press.

Kagan, J., & Snidman, N. (1991a). Infant predictors of inhibited and uninhibited profiles. *Psychological Science, 2,* 40–44.

Kagan, J., & Snidman, N. (1991b). Temperamental factors in human development. *American Psychologist, 46,* 856–862.

Kahle, L. R., & Chiagouris, L. (Eds.). (1997). *Values, lifestyles, and psychographics.* Mahwah, NJ: Erlbaum.

Kahn, E. (1985). Heinz Kohut and Carl Rogers: A timely comparison. *American Psychologist, 40,* 893–904.

Kahn, E. (1987). A reply to Emery's comments. *American Psychologist, 42,* 515–516.

Kahn, E. (1996). The intersubjective perspective and the client-centered approach: Are they one at their core? *Psychotherapy, 33,* 30–42.

Kahn, E. (1999). A critique of nondirectivity in the person-centered approach. *Journal of Humanistic Psychology, 39*(4), 94–110.

Kahn, E., & Rachman, A. W. (2000). Carl Rogers and Heinz Kohut: A historical perspective. *Psychoanalytic Psychology, 17,* 294–312.

Kahn, J. (2006, July 2). Last stop, Lhasa: Rail link ties remote Tibet to China. *New York Times.* Pp. 1, 8.

Kalekin-Fishman, D. (1993). The two faces of hostility: The implications of personal construct theory for understanding alienation. *International Journal of Personal Construct Psychology, 6,* 27–40.

Kaliski, E. M., Rubinson, L., Lawrance, L., & Levy, S. R. (1990). AIDS, runaways, and self-efficacy. *Family and Community Health, 13*(1), 65–72.

Kamilar, S. (2002). A Buddhist psychology. In R. P. Olson (Ed.), *Religious theories of personality and psychotherapy: East meets West* (pp. 85–139). New York: Haworth Press.

Kandel, E. R. (1999). Biology and the future of psychoanalysis: A new intellectual framework for psychiatry revisited. *American Journal of Psychiatry, 156,* 505–524.

Kanfer, R., Wanberg, C. R., & Kantrowitz, T. M. (2001). Job search and employment: A personality-motivational analysis and meta-analytic review. *Journal of Applied Psychology, 86,* 837–855.

Kaplan, H. A. (1997). Moral outrage: Virtue as a defense. *Psychoanalytic Review, 84,* 55–71.

Kaplan, H. B. (1991). Sex differences in social interest. *Individual Psychology, 47,* 120–123.

Kaplan, S. J., & Schoeneberg, L. A. (1987). Personality theory: The rabbinic and Adlerian paradigm. *Individual Psychology, 43,* 315–318.

Karney, B. R., & Bradbury, T. N. (1995). The longitudinal course of marital quality and stability: A review of theory, method, and research. *Psychological Bulletin, 118,* 3–34.

Karon, B. P., & Widener, A. J. (1997). Repressed memories and World War II: Lest we forget! *Professional Psychology: Research and Practice, 28,* 338–340.

Karten, Y. J. G., Olariu, A., & Cameron, H. A. (2005). Stress in early life inhibits neurogenesis in adulthood. *Trends in Neurosciences, 28,* 171–172.

Kasamatsu, A., & Hirai, T. (1973). An electroencephalographic study on the Zen meditation (zazen). *Journal of the American Institute of Hypnosis, 14,* 107–114.

Kaser-Boyd, N. (1993). Rorschachs of women who commit homicide. *Journal of Personality Assessment, 60,* 458–470.

Kast, V. (1996). The clinical use of fairy tales by a "classical" Jungian analyst. *Psychoanalytic Review, 83,* 509–523.

Katz, I. (1991). Gordon Allport's *The Nature of Prejudice. Political Psychology, 12,* 125–157.

Kavanagh, D. J., Andrade, J., & May, J. (2004). Beating the urge: Implications of research into substance-related desires. *Addictive Behaviors, 29,* 1359–1372.

Kazdin, A. E. (1982). The token economy: A decade later. *Journal of Applied Behavior Analysis, 15,* 431–445.

Kearney, P. (n.d.). Still crazy after all these years: Why meditation isn't psychotherapy. http://www.buddhanet.net/crazy.htm

Keefer, L., & Blanchard, E. B. (2002). A one year follow-up of relaxation response meditation as a treatment for irritable bowel syndrome. *Behaviour Research and Therapy, 40,* 541–546.

Keijsers, G. P. J., Schaap, C. P. D. R., & Hoogduin, C. A. L. (2000). The impact of interpersonal patient and therapist behavior on outcome in cognitive-behavior therapy, *Behavior Modification, 24,* 264–297.

Keller, R. R. (2000). Religious diversity in North America. In P. S. Richards & A. E. Bergin (Eds.), *Handbook of psychotherapy and religious diversity* (pp. 27–55). Washington, DC: American Psychological Association.

Kelly, A. E., & Nauta, M. M. (1997). Reactance and thought suppression. *Personality and Social Psychology Bulletin, 23,* 1123–1132.

Kelly, G. A. (1955). *The psychology of personal constructs* (Vols. 1 and 2). New York: Norton.

Kelly, G. A. (1958). Man's construction of his alternatives. In G. Lindzey (Ed.), *The assessment of human motives* (pp. 33–64). New York: Holt, Rinehart & Winston.

Kelly, G. A. (1960). Epilogue: Don Juan. Reprinted in B. Maher (Ed.), *Clinical psychology and personality: The selected papers of George Kelly* (1969, pp. 333–351). New York: Wiley.

Kelly, G. A. (1962). Sin and psychotherapy. Temple University Symposium on Psychotherapy, Philadelphia, March 9, 1962. Reprinted in B. Maher (Ed.), *Clinical psychology and personality: The selected papers of George Kelly* (1969, pp. 165–188). New York: Wiley.

Kelly, G. A. (1963a). The autobiography of a theory. Reprinted in B. Maher (Ed.), *Clinical psychology and personality: The selected papers of George Kelly* (1969, pp. 46–65). New York: Wiley.

Kelly, G. A. (1963b). Nonparametric factor analysis of personality theories. *Journal of Individual Psychology, 19,* 115–147. Reprinted in B. Maher (Ed.), *Clinical psychology and personality: The selected papers of George Kelly* (1969, pp. 301–332). New York: Wiley.

Kelly, G. A. (1964). The language of hypotheses: Man's psychological instrument. *Journal of Individual Psychology, 20,* 137–152. Reprinted in B. Maher (Ed.), *Clinical psychology and personality: The selected papers of George Kelly* (1969, pp. 147–162). New York: Wiley.

Kelly, G. A. (1966). Ontological acceleration. Reprinted in B. Maher (Ed.), *Clinical psychology and personality: The selected papers of George Kelly* (1969, pp. 7–45). New York: Wiley.

Kelly, G. A. (1969). Humanistic methodology in psychological research. In B. Maher (Ed.), *Clinical psychology and personality: The selected papers of George Kelly* (pp. 133–146). New York: Wiley.

Kelman, H. C. (1999). The interdependence of Israeli and Palestinian national identities: The role of the other in existential conflicts. *Journal of Social Issues, 55,* 581–600.

Keltner, D., & Anderson, C. (2000). Saving face for Darwin: The functions and uses of embarrassment. *Current Directions in Psychological Science, 9,* 187–192.

Kendall-Tackett, K. A., Williams, L. M., & Finkelhor, D. (1993). Impact of sexual abuse on children: A review and synthesis of recent empirical studies. *Psychological Bulletin, 113,* 164–180.

Kendler, H. H. (2002). A personal encounter with psychology (1937–2002). *History of Psychology, 5,* 52–84.

Kenrick, D. T. (2001). Evolutionary psychology, cognitive science, and dynamical systems: Building an integrative paradigm. *Current Directions in Psychological Science, 10,* 13–17.

Kensit, D. A. (2000). Rogerian theory: A critique of the effectiveness of pure client-centred therapy. *Counselling Psychology Quarterly, 13,* 345–352.

Kern, C., & Roll, S. (2001). Object representations in dreams of Chicanos and Anglos. *Dreaming: Journal of the Association for the Study of Dreams, 11,* 149–166.

Kernberg, P. F. (1994). Mechanisms of defense: Development and research perspectives. *Bulletin of the Menninger Clinic, 58,* 55–87.

Kerr, M., Lambert, W. W., & Bem, D. J. (1996). Life course sequelae of childhood shyness in Sweden: Comparison with the United States. *Developmental Psychology, 32,* 1100–1105.

Kesler-West, M. L., Andersen, A. H., Smith, C. D., Avison, M. J., Davis, C. E., Kryscio, R. J., & Blonder, L. X. (2001). Neural substrates of facial emotion processing using fMRI. *Cognitive Brain Research, 11,* 213–226.

Keutzer, C. S. (1984). The power of meaning: From quantum mechanics to synchronicity. *Journal of Humanistic Psychology, 24*(1), 80–94.

Kewman, D. G., & Tate, D. G. (1998). Suicide in SCI: A psychological autopsy. *Rehabilitation Psychology, 43,* 143–151.

Khong, B. S. L. (2003). Role of responsibility in daseinsanalysis and Buddhism. In K. H. Dockett, G. R. Dudley-Grant, & C. P. Bankart (Eds.), *Psychology and Buddhism: From individual to global community* (pp. 139–159). Secaucus, NJ: Kluwer Academic.

Kiecolt-Glaser, J. K., McGuire, L., Robles, T. F., & Glaser, R. (2002). Psychoneuroimmunology: Psychological influences on immune function and health. *Journal of Consulting and Clinical Psychology, 70,* 537–547.

Kihlstrom, J. (1985). Conscious, subconscious, unconscious: A cognitive perspective. In K. S. Bowers & D. Meichenbaum (Eds.), *The unconscious reconsidered* (pp. 149–211). New York: Wiley.

Kihlstrom, J. F. (1987). The cognitive unconscious. *Science, 237,* 1445–1452.

Kihlstrom, J. F. (1990). The psychological unconscious. In L. A. Pervin (Ed.), *Handbook of personality: Theory and research* (pp. 445–464). New York: Guilford.

Kihlstrom, J. F. (1994). Hypnosis, delayed recall, and the principles of memory. *International Journal of Clinical and Experimental Hypnosis, 42,* 337–345.

Kihlstrom, J. F. (1995). The trauma-memory argument. *Consciousness and Cognition, 4,* 65–67.

Kihlstrom, J. F., Barnhardt, T. M., & Tataryn, D. J. (1992). The psychological unconscious: Found, lost, and regained. *American Psychologist, 47,* 788–791.

Killgore, W. D. S. (2000). Academic and research interest in several approaches to psychotherapy: A computerized search of literature in the past 16 years. *Psychological Reports, 87,* 717–720.

Kim, J. E., Nesselroade, J. R., & Featherman, D. L. (1996). The state component in self-reported worldviews and religious beliefs of older adults: The MacArthur successful aging studies. *Psychology and Aging, 11,* 396–407.

Kimball, M. M. (2000). From "Anna O." to Bertha Pappenheim: Transforming private pain into public action. *History of Psychology, 3,* 20–43.

Kimble, G. A. (1984). Psychology's two cultures. *American Psychologist, 39,* 833–839.

Kimble, G. A. (1994). A new formula for behaviorism. *Psychological Review, 101,* 254–258.

King, L. A., & Napa, C. K. (1998). What makes a good life? *Journal of Personality and Social Psychology, 75,* 156–165.

King, L. A., Walker, L. M., & Broyles, S. J. (1996). Creativity and the five-factor model. *Journal of Research in Personality, 30,* 189–203.

King, M. L., Jr. (1968). The role of the behavioral scientist in the civil rights movement. *American Psychologist, 23,* 180–186.

King, N. (1987). *Everybody loves Oprah! Her remarkable life story.* New York: William Morrow and Company.

Kiracofe, N. M., & Kiracofe, H. N. (1990). Child-perceived paternal favoritism and birth order. *Individual Psychology, 46,* 74–81.

Kircher, T. T. J., Senior, C., Phillips, M. L., Benson, P. J., Bullmore, E. T., Brammer, M., Simmons, A., Williams, S. C. R., Bartels, M., & David, A. S. (2000). Towards a functional neuroanatomy of self-processing: Effects of faces and words. *Cognitive Brain Research, 10,* 133–144.

Kirmayer, L. J. (1992). From the witches' hammer to the Oedipus complex: Castration anxiety in Western society. *Transcultural Psychiatric Research Review, 29,* 133–158.

Kirsch, I., & Lynn, S. J. (1995). The altered state of hypnosis: Changes in the theoretical landscape. *American Psychologist, 50,* 846–858.

Kirsch, I., & Lynn, S. J. (1998). Dissociation theories of hypnosis. *Psychological Bulletin, 123,* 100–115.

Kirsch, I., Montgomery, G., & Sapirstein, G. (1995). Hypnosis as an adjunct to cognitive behavioral psychotherapy: A meta-analysis. *Journal of Consulting and Clinical Psychology, 63,* 214–220.

Kirschenbaum, D. S. (1985). Proximity and specificity of planning: A position paper. *Cognitive Therapy and Research, 9,* 489–506.

Kiser, L. J., Heston, J., Millsap, P. A., & Pruitt, D. B. (1991). Physical and sexual abuse in childhood: Relationship with post-traumatic stress disorder. *Journal of the American Academy of Child and Adolescent Psychiatry, 30,* 776–783.

Kjaer, T. W., Bertelsen, C., Piccini, P., Brooks, D., Alving, J., & Lou, H. C. (2002). Increased dopamine tone during meditation-induced change of consciousness. *Cognitive Brain Research, 13,* 255–259.

Klayman, J., & Ha, Y. (1987). Confirmation, disconfirmation, and information in hypothesis testing. *Psychological Review, 94,* 211–228.

Klein, M. (1946). Notes on some schizoid mechanisms. In M. Klein, P. Heimann, S. Isaacs, & J. Riviere (Eds.), *Developments in psychoanalysis.* London: Hogarth Press.

Klein, S. (2006). (S. Lehmann, Trans.). *The science of happiness: How our brains make us happy—and what we can do to get happier.* New York: Marlowe & Company.

Klohnen, E. C., & Bera, S. (1998). Behavioral and experiential patterns of avoidantly and securely attached women across adulthood: A 31-year perspective. *Journal of Personality and Social Psychology, 74,* 211–223.

Kluckhohn, C., & Murray, H. A. (1953). Personality formation: The determinants. In C. Kluckhohn, H. Murray, & D. Schneider (Eds.), *Personality in nature, society and culture* (pp. 53–67). New York: Knopf.

Knierim, T. (n.d.). Introduction to Buddhism. Available online at http://thebigview.com/download/buddhism.pdf

Knight, J. (2004, December 9). Buddhism on the brain. *Nature, 432,* 670.

Knight, K., Elfenbein, M. H., Capozzi, L., Eason, H. A., & Bernardo, M. F. (2000). Relationship of connected and separate knowing to parental style and birth order. *Sex Roles, 43,* 229–240.

Knight, Z. G. (2005). The use of the "corrective emotional experience" and the search for the bad object in psychotherapy. *American Journal of Psychotherapy, 59,* 30–41.

Koch, S. (1981). The nature and limits of psychological knowledge: Lessons of a century qua "science." *American Psychologist, 36,* 257–269.

Kohlmetz, C., Kopiez, R., & Altenmüller, E. (2003). Stability of motor programs during a state of meditation: Electrocortical activity in a pianist playing "Vexations" by Erik Satie continuously for 28 hours. *Psychology of Music, 31,* 173–186.

Kohut, H. (1984). *How does analysis cure?* Chicago: University of Chicago Press.

Koltko-Rivera, M. E. (1998). Maslow's "transhumanism": Was transpersonal psychology conceived as "a psychology without people in it"? *Journal of Humanistic Psychology, 38*(1), 71–80.

Konik, J., & Stewart, A. (2004). Sexual identity development in the context of compulsory heterosexuality. *Journal of Personality, 72,* 815–844.

Koran, J. J., & Camp, B. D. (1998). On the effects of modeling. *Curator, 41*(4), 10–12.

Kores, R. C., Murphy, W. D., Rosenthal, T. L., Elias, D. B., & North, W. C. (1990). Predicting outcome of chronic pain treatment via a modified self-efficacy scale. *Behaviour Research and Therapy, 28,* 165–169.

Kraemer, G. W. (1992). A psychobiological theory of attachment. *Behavioral and Brain Sciences, 15,* 493–541.

Kraft, T. (1992). Counteracting pain in malignant disease by hypnotic techniques: Five case studies. *Contemporary Hypnosis, 9,* 123–129.

Kratochwill, T. R., & Martens, B. K. (1994). Applied behavior analysis and school psychology. *Journal of Applied Behavior Analysis, 27,* 3–5.

Kris, E. (1964). *Psychoanalytic explorations in art.* New York: Shocken. (Original work published 1952)

Kroger, J. (1986). The relative importance of identity status interview components: Replication and extension. *Journal of Adolescence, 9,* 337–354.

Krosnick, J. A., Betz, A. L., Jussim, L. J., & Lynn, A. R. (1992). Subliminal conditioning of attitudes. *Personality and Social Psychology Bulletin, 18,* 152–162.

Kuhn, D. (1989). Children and adults as intuitive scientists. *Psychological Review, 96,* 674–689.

Kuhn, T. S. (1970). *The structure of scientific revolutions* (2nd ed.). Chicago: University of Chicago Press.

Kukla, A. (1982). Logical incoherence of value-free science. *Journal of Personality and Social Psychology, 43,* 1014–1017.

Kull, S. (1983). Nuclear arms and the desire for world destruction. *Political Psychology, 4,* 563–591.

Kunzendorf, R. G., & Moran, C. (1993–1994). Repression: Active censorship of stressful memories vs. source amnesia for self-consciously dissociated memories. *Imagination, Cognition and Personality, 13,* 291–302.

Kuo, Y. (1987). Environmental factors associated with the growth of Chinese literary genius: A test of Rogerian assumption. *Creative Child and Adult Quarterly, 12,* 93–102, 132.

Kupfersmid, J. (1992). The "defense" of Sigmund Freud. *Psychotherapy, 29,* 297–309.

Kurdek, L. A. (1997). The link between facets of neuroticism and dimensions of relationship commitment: Evidence from gay, lesbian, and heterosexual couples. *Journal of Family Psychology, 11,* 503–514.

Kwan, V. S. Y., Bond, M. H., & Singelis, T. M. (1997). Pancultural explanations for life satisfaction: Adding relationship harmony to self-esteem. *Journal of Personality and Social Psychology, 73,* 1038–1051.

Kwan, K. K. (2000). The internal-external ethnic identity measure: Factor-analytic structures based on a sample of Chinese Americans. *Educational and Psychological Measurement, 60,* 142–152.

Labouvie-Vief, G., & Diehl, M. (2000). Cognitive complexity and cognitive-affective integration: Related or separate domains of adult development? *Psychology and Aging, 15,* 490–504.

Lacks, R. (1980). *Women and Judaism: Myth, history, and struggle.* Garden City, NY: Doubleday.

LaFromboise, T., Coleman, H. L. K., & Gerton, J. (1993). Psychological impact of biculturalism: Evidence and theory. *Psychological Bulletin, 114,* 395–412.

Lamborn, S. D., Mounts, N. S., Steinberg, L., & Dornbusch, S. (1991). Patterns of competence and adjustment among adolescents from authoritative, authoritarian, indulgent, and neglectful families. *Child Development, 62,* 1049–1065.

Lamiell, J. T. (1987). *The psychology of personality: An epistemological inquiry.* New York: Columbia University Press.

Lamiell, J. T. (1997). Individuals and the differences between them. In R. Hogan, J. Johnson, & S. Briggs (Eds.), *Handbook of personality psychology* (pp. 117–141). San Diego: Academic Press.

Lamke, L. K., & Peyton, K. G. (1988). Adolescent sex-role orientation and ego identity. *Journal of Adolescence, 11,* 205–215.

LaMothe, R., Arnold, J., & Crane, J. (1998). The penumbra of religious discourse. *Psychoanalytic Psychology, 15,* 63–73.

Lancaster, B. L. (1997). On the stages of perception: Towards a synthesis of cognitive neuroscience and the Buddhist abhidhamma tradition. *Journal of Consciousness Studies, 4,* 122–142.

Landfield, A. W. (1982). A construction of fragmentation and unity: The fragmentation corollary. In J. C. Mancuso & J. R. Adams-Webber (Eds.), *The construing person* (pp. 170–197). New York: Praeger.

Landfield, A. W. (1988). Personal science and the concept of validation. *International Journal of Personal Construct Psychology, 1,* 237–249.

Landfield, A. W., & Epting, F. R. (1987). *Personal construct psychology: Clinical and personality assessment.* New York: Human Sciences Press.

Landrine, H. (1992). Clinical implications of cultural differences: The referential versus the indexical self. *Clinical Psychology Review, 12,* 401–415.

Lang, P. J. (1994). The varieties of emotional experience: A meditation on James-Lange theory. *Psychological Review, 101,* 211–221.

Langer, W. (1972). *The mind of Adolph Hitler: The secret wartime report.* New York: Basic Books.

Langlois, J. H., Ritter, J. M., Casey, R. J., & Sawin, D. B. (1995). Infant attractiveness predicts maternal behaviors and attitudes. *Developmental Psychology, 31,* 464–472.

Langs, R. (1993). Psychoanalysis: Narrative myth or narrative science. *Contemporary Psychoanalysis, 29,* 555–594.

Lang-Takac, E., & Osterweil, Z. (1992). Separateness and connectedness: Differences between the genders. *Sex Roles, 27,* 277–289.

Lanier, L. S., Privette, G., Vodanovich, S., & Bundrick, M. (1996). Peak experiences: Lasting consequences and breadth of occurrences among realtors, artists, and a comparison group. *Journal of Social Behavior and Personality, 11,* 781–791.

Larsen, R. J., & Ketelaar, T. (1991). Personality and susceptibility to positive and negative emotional states. *Journal of Personality and Social Psychology, 61,* 132–140.

Lash, J. P. (1972). *Eleanor: The years alone.* New York: Signet.

Las Heras, A. (1992). Psychosociology of Jung's parapsychological ability. *Journal of the Society for Psychical Research, 58,* 189–193.

Lasko, J. K. (1954). Parent behavior toward first and second children. *Genetic Psychology Monographs, 49,* 97–137.

Laungani, P. (1997). Replacing client-centred counselling with culture-centred counselling. *Counselling Psychology Quarterly, 10,* 343–351.

Lauter, E., & Rupprecht, C. S. (Eds.). (1985). *Feminist archetypal theory: Interdisciplinary re-visions of Jungian thought.* Knoxville: University of Tennessee Press.

Lawrence, L. (1988). The covert seduction theory: Filling the gap between the seduction theory and the Oedipus complex. *American Journal of Psychoanalysis, 48,* 247–250.

Lay, C. H., Knish, S., & Zanatta, R. (1992). Self-handicappers and procrastinators: A comparison of their practice behavior prior to an evaluation. *Journal of Research in Personality, 26,* 242–257.

Lazar, S. W., Kerr, C. E., Wasserman, R. H., Gray, J. R., Greve, D. N., Treatway, M. T., McGarvey, M., Quinn, B. T., Dusek, J. A., Benson, H., Rauch, S. L., Moore, C. I., & Fischl, B. (2005). Meditation experience is associated with increased cortical thickness. *NeuroReport, 16,* 1893–1897.

Lazarsfeld, S. (1991). The courage for imperfection. *Individual Psychology, 47,* 93–96.

Lazarus, A. A. (1989). Why I am an eclectic (not an integrationist). *British Journal of Guidance and Counselling, 17,* 248–258.

Lazarus, R. S. (2000). Toward better research on stress and coping. *American Psychologist, 55,* 665–673.

Lazarus, R. S., & Folkman, S. (1984). *Stress, appraisal, and coping.* New York: Springer.

Leach, C., Freshwater, K., Aldridge, J., & Sutherland, J. (2001). Analysis of repertory grids in clinical practice. *British Journal of Clinical Psychology, 40,* 225–248.

Leak, G. K., & Fish, S. (1989). Religious orientation, impression management, and self-deception: Toward a clarification of the link between religiosity and social desirability. *Journal for the Scientific Study of Religion, 28,* 355–359.

Leak, G. K., & Gardner, L. E. (1990). Sexual attitudes, love attitudes, and social interest. *Individual Psychology, 46,* 55–60.

Leak, G. K., Gardner, L. E., & Pounds, B. (1992). A comparison of Eastern religion, Christianity, and social interest. *Individual Psychology, 48,* 53–64.

Leak, G. K., Millard, R. J., Perry, N. W., & Williams, D. E. (1985). An investigation of the nomological network of social interest. *Journal of Research in Personality, 19,* 197–207.

Leak, G. K., & Williams, D. E. (1989). Relationship between social interest, alienation, and psychological hardiness. *Individual Psychology, 45,* 369–375.

LeDoux, J. (2002). *Synaptic self: How our brains become who we are.* New York: Viking.

Lee, D. Y., & Uhlemann, M. R. (1984). Comparison of verbal responses of Rogers, Shostrom, and Lazarus. *Journal of Counseling Psychology, 31,* 91–94.

Lefebure, L. D. (2005). The contribution of H. H. the XIVth Dalai Lama to interfaith education. *Cross Currents,* 83–89.

Leifer, M., Shapiro, J. P., Martone, M. W., & Kassem, L. (1991). Rorschach assessment of psychological functioning in sexually abused girls. *Journal of Personality Assessment, 56,* 14–28.

Leitner, L. M., & Cado, S. (1982). Personal constructs and homosexual stress. *Journal of Personality and Social Psychology, 43,* 869–872.

Leitner, L. M., & Guthrie, A. J. (1993). Validation of therapist interventions in psychotherapy: Clarity, ambiguity, and subjectivity. *International Journal of Personal Construct Psychology, 6,* 281–294.

Leitner, L. M., & Pfenninger, D. T. (1994). Sociality and optimal functioning. *Journal of Constructivist Psychology, 7,* 119–135.

Lemire, D. (1998). Individual psychology and innovation: The de-Freuding of creativity. *Journal of Individual Psychology, 54,* 108–118.

Lennings, C. J. (1996). Adolescent aggression and imagery: Contributions from object relations and social cognitive theory. *Adolescence, 31,* 831–840.

Lent, R. W., & Hackett, G. (1987). Career self-efficacy: Empirical status and future directions. *Journal of Vocational Behavior, 30,* 347–382.

Lepore, S. J. (1997). Expressive writing moderates the relation between intrusive thoughts and depressive symptoms. *Journal of Personality and Social Psychology, 73,* 1030–1037.

Lerman, H. (1986a). From Freud to feminist personality theory: Getting here from there. *Psychology of Women Quarterly, 10,* 1–18.

Lerman, H. (1986b). *A mote in Freud's eye: From psychoanalysis to the psychology of women.* New York: Springer-Verlag.

Lerner, J. A. (1986). Contrasting views of felt aliveness. *American Journal of Psychoanalysis, 46,* 318–326.

Lester, D. (1990). Maslow's hierarchy of needs and personality. *Personality and Individual Differences, 11,* 1187–1188.

Lester, D., Hvezda, J., Sullivan, S., & Plourde, R. (1983). Maslow's hierarchy of needs and psychological health. *Journal of General Psychology, 109,* 83–85.

Levant, R. F. (1996). The new psychology of men. *Professional Psychology: Research and Practice, 27,* 259–265.

LeVay, S. (1991). A difference in hypothalamic structure between heterosexual and homosexual men. *Science, 253,* 1034–1037.

Levey, J. (1986). Richard Nixon as elder statesman. *Journal of Psychohistory, 13,* 427–448.

Levine, D. S. (1997). Don't just stand there, optimize something! In D. S. Levine & W. R. Elsberry (Eds.), *Optimality in biological and artificial networks? The International Neural Networks Society series* (pp. 3–18). Mahwah, NJ: Erlbaum.

Levine, F. M., & Fasnacht, G. (1974). Token rewards may lead to token learning. *American Psychologist, 29,* 816–820.

Levitz-Jones, E. M., & Orlofsky, J. L. (1985). Separation-individuation and intimacy capacity in college women. *Journal of Personality and Social Psychology, 49,* 156–169.

Levy, K. N., Blatt, S. J., & Shaver, P. R. (1998). Attachment styles and parental representations. *Journal of Personality and Social Psychology, 74,* 407–419.

Lewes, L. (1998). A special Oedipal mechanism in the development of male homosexuality. *Psychoanalytic Psychology, 15,* 341–359.

Lewin, K. (1951). Selected theoretical papers, *Field theory in social science* (D. Cartwright, Ed.). New York: Harper Torchbooks.

Lewis, C. A. (1993). Oral pessimism and depressive symptoms. *Journal of Psychology, 127,* 335–343.

Lewis, W. A., & Bucher, A. M. (1992). Anger, catharsis, the reformulated frustration-aggression hypothesis, and health consequences. *Psychotherapy, 29,* 385–392.

Liberman, N., & Förster, J. (2000). Expression after suppression: A motivational explanation of postsuppressional rebound. *Journal of Personality and Social Psychology, 79,* 190–203.

Liberman, R. P. (2000). Images in psychiatry: The token economy. *American Journal of Psychiatry, 157,* 1398.

Lievens, F., De Fruyt, F., & Van Dam, K. (2001). Assessors' use of personality traits in descriptions of assessment centre candidates: A five-factor model perspective. *Journal of Occupational and Organizational Psychology, 74,* 623–636.

Lilenfeld, L. R. R., Wonderlich, S., Riso, L. P., Crosby, R., & Mitchell, J. (2006). Eating disorders and personality: A methodological and empirical review. *Clinical Psychology Review, 26,* 299–320.

Lillqvist, O., & Lindeman, M. (1998). Belief in astrology as a strategy for self-verification and coping with negative life-events. *European Psychologist, 3,* 202–208.

Lindsay, D. S., & Read, J. D. (1995). "Memory work" and recovered memories of childhood sexual abuse: Scientific evidence and public, professional, and personal issues. *Psychology, Public Policy, and Law, 1,* 846–908.

Lisle, L. (1980). *Portrait of an artist: A biography of Georgia O'Keeffe.* New York: Seaview.

Litt, M. D. (1988). Cognitive mediators of stressful experience: Self-efficacy and perceived control. *Cognitive Therapy and Research, 12,* 241–260.

Lobel, T. E., & Gilat, I. (1987). Type A behavior pattern, ego identity, and gender. *Journal of Research in Personality, 21,* 389–394.

Lobel, T. E., & Winch, G. L. (1986). Different defense mechanisms among men with different sex role orientations. *Sex Roles, 15,* 215–220.

Lobel, T. E., & Winch, G. L. (1988). Psychosocial development, self-concept, and gender. *Journal of Genetic Psychology, 149,* 405–411.

Lockhart, W. H. (1984). Rogers' "necessary and sufficient conditions" revisited. *British Journal of Guidance and Counselling, 12,* 113–123.

Loehlin, J. C. (1984). R. B. Cattell and behavior genetics. *Multivariate Behavioral Research, 19,* 310–321.

Loehlin, J. C. (1992). *Genes and environment in personality development.* Newbury Park, CA: Sage.

Loehlin, J. C., McCrae, R. R., & Costa, P. T., Jr. (1998). Heritabilities of common and measure-specific components of the big five personality factors. *Journal of Research in Personality, 32,* 431–453.

Loevinger, J. (1966). The meaning and measurement of ego development. *American Psychologist, 21,* 195–206.

Loevinger, J. (1976). *Ego development: Conceptions and theories.* San Francisco: Jossey-Bass.

Loevinger, J. (1979). Construct validity of the sentence completion test of ego development. *Applied Psychological Measurement, 3,* 281–311.

Loevinger, J. (1985). Revision of the Sentence Completion Test for Ego Development. *Journal of Personality and Social Psychology, 48,* 420–427.

Loewenberg, P. (1988). Psychoanalytic models of history: Freud and after. In W. M. Runyan (Ed.), *Psychology and historical interpretation* (pp. 126–156). New York: Oxford University Press.

Loftus, E. F. (1993). The reality of repressed memories. *American Psychologist, 48,* 518–537.

Loftus, E. F., & Pickrell, J. E. (1995). The formation of false memories. *Psychiatric Annals, 25,* 720–725.

Lombardi, D. N., & Elcock, L. E. (1997). Freud versus Adler on dreams. *American Psychologist, 52,* 572–573.

London, P. (1988). Metamorphosis in psychotherapy: Slouching toward integration. *Journal of Integrative and Eclectic Psychotherapy, 7*(1), 3–12.

Lorenzini, R., Sassaroli, S., & Rocchi, M. T. (1989). Schizophrenia and paranoia as solutions to predictive failure. *International Journal of Personal Construct Psychology, 2,* 417–432.

Lorimer, R. (1976). A reconsideration of the psychological roots of Gandhi's Truth. *Psychoanalytic Review, 63,* 191–207.

Lorr, H. (1991). An empirical evaluation of the MBTI typology. *Personality and Individual Differences, 12,* 1141–1146.

Lowry, R. J. (Ed.). (1973). *Dominance, self-esteem, self-actualization: Germinal papers of A. H. Maslow.* Monterey, CA: Brooks/Cole.

Loy, D. R. (2002). *A Buddhist history of the West: Studies in lack.* Albany, NY: State University of New York Press.

Lubinski, D. (1995). Applied individual differences research and its quantitative methods. *Psychology, Public Policy, and Law, 2,* 187–203.

Lubinski, D., Schmidt, D. B., & Benbow, C. P. (1996). A 20-year stability analysis of the study of values for intellectually gifted individuals from adolescence to adulthood. *Journal of Applied Psychology, 81,* 443–451.

Lucca, C. A., & Jennings, J. L. (1993). The impoverishment of human experience and eidetic imagination through the manipulation of language: The systematic destruction of language in Orwell's 1994. *Journal of Mental Imagery, 17*(3 & 4), 141–157.

Lukoff, D. (1997). The psychologist as a mythologist. *Journal of Humanistic Psychology, 37*(3), 34–58.

Lundin, R. W. (1969). *Personality: A behavioral analysis.* London: Macmillan.

Lupfer, M. B., Clark, L. F., & Hutcherson, H. W. (1990). Impact of context on spontaneous trait and situational attributions. *Journal of Personality and Social Psychology, 58,* 239–249.

Lutz, A., Greischar, L. L., Rawlings, N. B., Ricard, M., & Davidson, R. J. (2004). Long-term meditators self-induce high-amplitude gamma synchrony during mental practice. *Proceedings of the National Academy of Sciences, 101*(46), 16369–16373. Available online at http://www.pnas.org/cgi/doi/10.1073/pnas.0407401101

Lykken, D., & Tellegen, A. (1996). Happiness is a stochastic phenomenon. *Psychological Science, 7,* 186–189.

Lykken, D. T., McGue, M., Tellegen, A., & Bouchard, T. J., Jr. (1992). Emergenesis: Genetic traits that may not run in families. *American Psychologist, 47,* 1565–1577.

Lynn, R., Hampson, S. L., & Mullineux, J. C. (1987). A long-term increase in the fluid intelligence of English children. *Nature, 328,* 797.

Lynn, S. J., Lock, T. G., Myers, B., & Payne, D. G. (1997). Recalling the unrecallable: Should hypnosis be used to recover memories in psychotherapy? *Current Directions in Psychological Science, 6,* 79–83.

Lyons-Ruth, K. (1996). Attachment relationships among children with aggressive behavior problems: The role of disorganized early attachment patterns. *Journal of Consulting and Clinical Psychology, 64,* 64–73.

Mabry, C. H. (1993). Gender differences in ego level. *Psychological Reports, 72,* 752–754.

Maccoby, M. (1995). The two voices of Erich Fromm: Prophet and analyst. *Society, 32*(5), 72–82.

MacDonald, D. A., & Holland, D. (2002). Spirituality and boredom proneness. *Personality and Individual Differences, 32,* 1113–1119.

Mace, F. C. (1994). The significance and future of functional analysis methodologies. *Journal of Applied Behavior Analysis, 27,* 385–392.

Mack, J. E. (1971). Psychoanalysis and historical biography. *Journal of the American Psychoanalytic Association, 19,* 143–179.

Mack, J. E. (1980). Psychoanalysis and biography: Aspects of a developing affinity. *Journal of the American Psychoanalytic Association, 28,* 543–562.

Mack, J. E. (1986). Nuclear weapons and the dark side of mankind. *Political Psychology, 7,* 223–233.

Mackavey, W. R., Malley, J. E., & Stewart, A. J. (1991). Remembering autobiographically consequential experiences: Content analysis of psychologists' accounts of their lives. *Psychology and Aging, 6,* 50–59.

MacLean, C. R. K., Walton, K. G., Wenneberg, S. R., Levitsky, D. K., Mandarino, J. P., Wazin, R., Hillis, S. L., & Schneider, R. H. (1997). Effects of the Transcendental Meditation program on adaptive mechanisms: Changes in hormone levels and responses to stress after 4 months of practice. *Psychoneuroendocrinology, 22,* 277–295.

Maddi, S. R., & Costa, P. T., Jr. (1972). *Humanism in personology: Allport, Maslow, and Murray.* Chicago: Aldine Atherton.

Mahalik, J. R., Cournoyer, R. J., DeFrank, W., Cherry, M., & Napolitano, J. M. (1998). Men's gender role conflict and use of psychological defenses. *Journal of Counseling Psychology, 45,* 247–255.

Mahathera, N. (1982). *Buddhism in a nutshell.* Kandy, Sri Lanka: Buddhist Publication Society. Available online at http://www.buddhanet.net/pdf_file/nutshell.pdf

Mahoney, M. F. (1966). *The meaning in dreams and dreaming: The Jungian viewpoint.* Secaucus, NJ: Citadel Press.

Mahony, P. J. (1986). *Freud and the Rat Man.* New Haven, CT: Yale University Press.

Mahrer, A. R., & Fairweather, D. R. (1993). What is "experiencing"? A critical review of meanings and applications in psychotherapy. *Humanistic Psychologist, 21,* 2–25.

Mahrer, A. R., Nadler, W. P., Stalikas, A., Schachter, H. M., & Sterner, I. (1988). Common and distinctive therapeutic change processes in client-centered, rational-emotive, and experiential psychotherapies. *Psychological Reports, 62,* 972–974.

Maidenbaum, A., & Thomson, L. (1989). Star Trek: In search of the essential John Lennon. *Quadrant, 22*(2), 87–91.

Maio, G. R., & Esses, V. M. (2001). The need for affect: Individual differences in the motivation to approach or avoid emotions. *Journal of Personality, 69,* 583–615.

Mair, G. (1994). *Oprah Winfrey: The real story.* New York: Birch Lane Press.

Mair, M. (1988). Psychology as storytelling. *International Journal of Personal Construct Psychology, 1,* 125–137.

Malik, R., Krasney, M., Aldworth, B., & Ladd, H. W. (1996). Effects of subliminal symbiotic stimuli on anxiety reduction. *Perceptual and Motor Skills, 82,* 771–784.

Malinosky-Rummell, R., & Hansen, D. J. (1993). Long-term consequences of childhood physical abuse. *Psychological Bulletin, 114,* 68–79.

Mallory, M. E. (1989). Q-sort definition of ego identity status. *Journal of Youth and Adolescence, 18,* 399–412.

Malm, L. (1993). The eclipse of meaning in cognitive psychology: Implications for humanistic psychology. *Journal of Humanistic Psychology, 33*(1), 67–87.

Malone, M. (1977). *Psychetypes: A new way of exploring personality.* New York: Pocket Books.

Maloney, A. (1999). Preference ratings of images representing archetypal themes: An empirical study of the concept of archetypes. *Journal of Analytical Psychology, 44,* 101–116.

Mancuso, J. C. (1998). Can an avowed adherent of personal-construct psychology be counted as a social constructionist? *Journal of Constructivist Psychology, 11,* 205–219.

Manheim, A. R. (1998). The relationship between the artistic process and self-actualization. *Art Therapy, 15*(2), 99–106.

Mansfield, V. (1991). The opposites in quantum physics and Jungian psychology: II. Applications. *Journal of Analytical Psychology, 36,* 289–306.

Mansfield, V., & Spiegelman, J. M. (1991). The opposites in quantum physics and Jungian psychology: I. Theoretical foundations. *Journal of Analytical Psychology, 36,* 267–287.

Maoz, Z., & Astorino, A. (1992). The cognitive structure of peacemaking: Egypt and Israel, 1970–1978. *Political Psychology, 13,* 647–662.

Marceil, J. C. (1977). Implicit dimensions of idiography and nomothesis: A reformulation. *American Psychologist, 32,* 1046–1055.

Marcia, J. E. (1966). Development and validation of ego-identity status. *Journal of Personality and Social Psychology, 3,* 551–558.

Marcia, J. E. (1967). Ego identity status: Relationship to change in self-esteem, "general maladjustment" and authoritarianism. *Journal of Personality, 35,* 118–133.

Marcovitz, E. (1982). Jung's three secrets: Slochower on "Freud as Yahweh in Jung's Answer to Job." *American Imago, 39,* 59–72.

Marcus-Newhall, A., Pedersen, W. C., Miller, N., & Carlson, M. (2000). Displaced aggression is alive and well: A meta-analytic review. *Journal of Personality and Social Psychology, 78,* 670–689.

Marks, S. G., & Koepke, J. E. (1994). Pet attachment and generativity among young adults. *Journal of Psychology, 128,* 641–650.

Markstrom-Adams, C. (1989). Androgyny and its relation to adolescent psychosocial well-being: A review of the literature. *Sex Roles, 21,* 325–340.

Markus, H. (1977). Self-schemata and processing information about the self. *Journal of Personality and Social Psychology, 35,* 63–78.

Markus, H. R., & Kitayama, S. (1991). Culture and the self: Implications for cognition, emotion, and motivation. *Psychological Review, 98,* 224–253.

Marlatt, G. A. (2002). Buddhist philosophy and the treatment of addictive behavior. *Cognitive and Behavioral Practice, 9,* 44–50.

Marsden, D., & Littler, D. (2000). Exploring consumer product construct systems with the repertory grid technique. *Qualitative Market Research, 3,* 127–143.

Marsella, A. J., Dubanoski, J., Hamada, W. C., & Morse, H. (2000). The measurement of personality across cultures: Historical, conceptual, and methodological issues and considerations. *American Behavioral Scientist, 44,* 41–62.

Marsh, C. S., & Colangelo, N. (1983). The application of Dabrowski's concept of multilevelness to Allport's concept of unity. *Counseling and Values, 27,* 213–228.

Marshall, G. N. (1991). Levels of analysis and personality: Lessons from the person-situation debate? *Psychological Science, 2,* 427–428.

Martin, J., & Sugarman, J. (1997). The social-cognitive construction of therapeutic change: Bridging social constructionism and cognitive constructivism. *Review of General Psychology, 1,* 375–388.

Martin, R. A., Berry, G. E., Dobranski, T., & Horne, M. (1996). Emotion perception threshold: Individual differences in emotional sensitivity. *Journal of Research in Personality, 30,* 290–305.

Martinez, T. J., III (1998). Anthropos and existence: Gnostic parallels in the early writings of Rollo May. *Journal of Humanistic Psychology, 38*(4), 95–109.

Martinez, T. J., III, & Taylor, E. (1998). "Yes, in you the tempest rages": The archetypal significance of America for Jung, 1909–1913. *Spring: A Journal of Archetype and Culture, 64,* 33–56.

Marx, D. M., Brown, J. L., & Steele, C. M. (1999). Allport's legacy and the situational press of stereotypes. *Journal of Social Issues, 55,* 491–502.

Masling, J., Weiss, L., & Rothschild, B. (1968). Relationships of oral imagery to yielding behavior and birth order. *Journal of Consulting and Clinical Psychology, 32,* 89–91.

Maslow, A. H. (1941). Deprivation, threat and frustration. *Psychological Review, 48,* 364–366.

Maslow, A. H. (1942). Self-esteem (dominance-feeling) and sexuality in women. *Journal of Social Psychology, 16,* 259–294.

Maslow, A. H. (1943). A theory of human motivation. *Psychological Review, 50,* 370–396. Reprinted in R. J. Lowry (Ed.), *Dominance, self-esteem, self-actualization: Germinal papers of A. H. Maslow* (1973, pp. 153–173). Monterey, CA: Brooks/Cole.

Maslow, A. H. (1955). Deficiency motivation and growth motivation. In M. R. Jones (Ed.), *Nebraska symposium on motivation* (pp. 1–30). Lincoln: University of Nebraska Press.

Maslow, A. H. (1958). Emotional blocks to creativity. *Journal of Individual Psychology, 14,* 51–56.

Maslow, A. H. (1962). *Toward a psychology of being.* Princeton, NJ: Van Nostrand.

Maslow, A. H. (1964). Synergy in the society and in the individual. *Journal of Individual Psychology, 20,* 153–164.

Maslow, A. H. (1965). Criteria for judging needs to be instinctoid. In M. R. Jones (Ed.), *Human motivation: A symposium* (pp. 33–47). Lincoln: University of Nebraska Press.

Maslow, A. H. (1966). *The psychology of science: A reconnaissance.* New York: Harper & Row.

Maslow, A. H. (1968a, July). A conversation with Abraham H. Maslow. *Psychology Today,* pp. 34–37, 54–57.

Maslow, A. H. (1968b). *Toward a psychology of being* (2nd ed.). New York: Van Nostrand.

Maslow, A. H. (1969). Theory Z. *Journal of Transpersonal Psychology, 1,* 31–47.

Maslow, A. H. (1970). *Religions, values, and peak-experiences.* New York: Viking.

Maslow, A. H. (1976). *The farther reaches of human nature* (2nd ed.). New York: Viking.

Maslow, A. H. (1987). *Motivation and personality* (3rd ed.). New York: Harper & Row. (Original work published 1954)

Maslow, A. H. (with Stephens, D. C., & Heil, G.). (1998). *Maslow on management.* New York: Wiley.

Mason, L. I., Alexander, C. N., Travis, F. T., Marsh, G., Orme-Johnson, D. W., Gackenbach, J., Mason, D. C., Rainforth, M. & Walton, K. G. (1997). Electrophysiological correlates of higher states of consciousness during sleep in long-term practitioners of the Transcendental Meditation program. *Sleep, 20,* 102–110.

Massarik, F. (1992). The humanistic core of industrial/organizational psychology. *Humanistic Psychologist, 20,* 389–396.

Massaro, T. M. (1997). The meanings of shame: Implications for legal reform. *Psychology, Public Policy, and Law, 3,* 645–704.

Masson, J. M. (1984). *The assault on truth: Freud's suppression of the seduction theory.* New York: Farrar, Straus & Giroux.

Masters, R., & Houston, J. (2000). *The varieties of psychedelic experience: The classic guide to the effects of LSD on the human psyche.* Rochester, VT: Park Street Press.

Masunaga, H., & Horn, J. (2001). Expertise and age-related changes in components of intelligence. *Psychology and Aging, 16,* 293–311.

Mathes, E. W. (1982). Mystical experiences, romantic love, and hypnotic susceptibility. *Psychological Reports, 50,* 701–702.

Mattoon, M. A. (1978). *Applied dream analysis: A Jungian approach.* New York: Wiley.

Mauro, C. F., & Harris, Y. R. (2000). The influence of maternal child-rearing attitudes and teaching behaviors on preschoolers' delay of gratification. *Journal of Genetic Psychology, 161,* 292–306.

May, R. (1982). The problem of evil: An open letter to Carl Rogers. *Journal of Humanistic Psychology, 22,* 10–21.

May, R. (1991). *The cry for myth.* New York: Norton.

Mayer, J. D., Carlsmith, K. M., & Chabot, H. F. (1998). Describing the person's external environment: Conceptualizing and measuring the life space. *Journal of Research in Personality, 32,* 253–296.

Mayes, C. (1999). Reflecting on the archetypes of teaching. *Teaching Education, 10*(2), 3–16.

McAdams, D. P. (1988). Biography, narrative, and lives: An introduction. *Journal of Personality, 56,* 1–18.

McAdams, D. P. (1990). Unity and purpose in human lives: The emergence of identity as a life story. In A. I. Rabin, R. A. Zucker, R. A. Emmons, & S. Frank (Eds.), *Studying persons and lives* (pp. 148–200). New York: Springer-Verlag.

McAdams, D. P., & de St. Aubin, E. (1992). A theory of generativity and its assessment through self-report, behavioral acts, and narrative themes in autobiography. *Journal of Personality and Social Psychology, 62,* 1003–1015.

McAdams, D. P., de St. Aubin, E., & Logan, R. L. (1993). Generativity among young, midlife, and older adults. *Psychology and Aging, 8,* 221–230.

McAdams, D. P., Diamond, A., de St. Aubin, E., & Mansfield, E. (1997). Stories of commitment: The psychosocial construction of generative lives. *Journal of Personality and Social Psychology, 72,* 678–694.

McAdams, D. P., Ruetzel, K., & Foley, J. H. (1986). Complexity and generativity at mid-life: Relations among social motives, ego development, and adults' plans for the future. *Journal of Personality and Social Psychology, 50,* 800–807.

McArdle, J. J., & Cattell, R. B. (1994). Structural equation models of factorial invariance in parallel proportional profiles and oblique cofactor problems. *Multivariate Behavioral Research, 29,* 63–113.

McArdle, J. J., Ferrer-Caja, E., Hamagami, F., & Woodcock, R. W. (2002). Comparative longitudinal structural analyses of the growth and decline of multiple intellectual abilities over the life span. *Developmental Psychology, 38,* 115–142.

McCann, J. T., & Biaggio, M. K. (1989). Sexual satisfaction in marriage as a function of life meaning. *Archives of Sexual Behavior, 18,* 59–72.

McCaulley, M. H. (1990). The Myers-Briggs Type Indicator: A measure for individuals and groups. *Measurement and Evaluation in Counseling and Development, 22,* 181–195.

McClelland, D. C. (1955). Comments on Professor Maslow's paper. In M. R. Jones (Ed.), *Nebraska symposium on motivation* (pp. 31–37). Lincoln: University of Nebraska Press.

McClelland, D. C., Koestner, R., & Weinberger, J. (1989). How do self-attributed and implicit motives differ? *Psychological Review, 96,* 690–702.

McClelland, D. C., & Winter, D. G. (1969). *Motivating economic achievement.* New York: Free Press.

McCourt, K., Bouchard, T. J., Jr., Lykken, D. T., Tellegen, A., & Keyes, M. (1999). Authoritarianism revisited: Genetic and environmental influences examined in twins reared apart and together. *Personality and Individual Differences, 27,* 985–1014.

McCrae, R. R. (1990). Traits and trait names: How well is openness represented in natural languages? *European Journal of Personality, 4,* 119–129.

McCrae, R. R. (1991). The five-factor model and its assessment in clinical settings. *Journal of Personality Assessment, 57,* 399–414.

McCrae, R. R. (2000). Trait psychology and the revival of personality and culture studies. *American Behavioral Scientist, 44,* 10–31.

McCrae, R. R., & Costa, P. T., Jr. (1982). Comparison of EPI and psychoticism scales with measures of the five-factor model of personality. *Personality and Individual Differences, 6,* 587–597.

McCrae, R. R., & Costa, P. T., Jr. (1984). *Emerging lives, enduring dispositions: Personality in adulthood.* Boston: Little, Brown.

McCrae, R. R., & Costa, P. T., Jr. (1987). Validation of the five-factor model of personality across instruments and observers. *Journal of Personality and Social Psychology, 52,* 81–90.

McCrae, R. R., & Costa, P. T., Jr. (1988). Recalled parent-child relations and adult personality. *Journal of Personality, 56,* 417–434.

McCrae, R. R., & Costa, P. T., Jr. (1989). Reinterpreting the Myers-Briggs Type Indicator from the perspective of the five-factor model of personality. *Journal of Personality, 57,* 17–40.

McCrae, R. R., & Costa, P. T., Jr. (1991). Adding Liebe und Arbeit: The full five-factor model and well-being. *Personality and Social Psychology Bulletin, 17,* 227–232.

McCrae, R. R., Costa, P. T., Jr., Del Pilar, G. H., Rolland, J. P., & Parker, W. D. (1998). Cross-cultural assessment of the five-factor model: The Revised NEO Personality Inventory. *Journal of Cross-Cultural Psychology, 29,* 171–188.

McCrae, R. R., Costa, P. T., Jr., Ostendorf, F., Angleitner, A., Høebíeková, M., Avia, M. D., Sanz, J., Sánchez-Bernardos, M. L., Kusdil, M. E., Woodfield, R., Saunders, P. R., & Smith, P. B. (2000). Nature over nurture: Temperament, personality, and life span development. *Journal of Personality and Social Psychology, 78,* 173–186.

McCrae, R. R., Costa, P. T., Jr., & Piedmont, R. L. (1993). Folk concepts, natural language, and psychological constructs: The California Psychological Inventory and the five-factor model. *Journal of Personality, 61,* 1–26.

McCroskey, J. C., Heisel, A. D., & Richmond, V. P. (2001). Eysenck's big three and communication traits: Three correlational studies. *Communication Monographs, 68,* 360–366.

McCullagh, P. (1986). Model status as a determinant of observational learning and performance. *Journal of Sport Psychology, 8,* 319–331.

McDargh, J. (2000). Spiritual conceptions of love. In A. E. Kazdin (Ed.), *Encyclopedia of Psychology* (Vol. 5, pp. 85–87). New York: Oxford University Press.

McGowan, D. (1994). *What is wrong with Jung.* Buffalo, NY: Prometheus Books.

McGrath, J. (1986). *Freud's discovery of psychoanalysis: The politics of hysteria.* Ithaca, NY: Cornell University Press.

McGregor, H. A., Lieberman, J. D., Greenberg, J., Solomon, S., Arndt, J., Simon, L., & Pyszczynski, T. (1998). Terror management and aggression: Evidence that mortality salience motivates aggression against worldview-threatening others. *Journal of Personality and Social Psychology, 74,* 590–605.

McGue, M., & Lykken, D. T. (1992). Genetic influence on risk of divorce. *Psychological Science, 3,* 368–373.

McGuire, W. (Ed.). (1974). *The Freud/Jung letters: The correspondence between Sigmund Freud and C. G. Jung* (R. Manheim & R. F. C. Hull, Trans.). Princeton, NJ: Princeton University Press.

McKay, J. R. (1991). Assessing aspects of object relations associated with immune function: Development of the Affiliative Trust-Mistrust coding system. *Psychological Assessment, 3,* 641–647.

McKee, K. J., Wilson, F., Chung, M. C., Hinchliff, S., Goudie, F., Elford, H., & Mitchell, C. (2005). Reminiscence, regrets and activity in older people in residential care: Associations with psychological health. *British Journal of Clinical Psychology, 44,* 543–561.

McLeod, C. R., & Vodanovich, S. J. (1991). The relationship between self-actualization and boredom proneness. *Journal of Social Behavior and Personality, 6*(5), 137–146.

McMullin, E. (1990). Can theory appraisal be quantified? *Psychological Inquiry, 1,* 164–166.

McNamara, L., & Ballard, M. E. (1999). Resting arousal, sensation seeking, and music preference. *Genetic, Social and General Psychology Monographs, 125,* 229–251.

McPherson, F. M., Barden, V., & Buckley, F. (1970). The use of "psychological" constructs by affectively flattened schizophrenics. *British Journal of Medical Psychology, 43,* 291–293.

McPherson, F. M., & Buckley, F. (1970). Thought-process disorder and personal construct subsystems. *British Journal of Social and Clinical Psychology, 9,* 380–381.

McPherson, F. M., & Gray, A. (1976). Psychological construing and psychological symptoms. *British Journal of Medical Psychology, 49,* 73–79.

McWilliams, S. A. (1993). Construct no idols. *International Journal of Personal Construct Psychology, 6,* 269–280.

Meaney, M. J., & Szyf, M. (2005). Maternal care as a model for experience-dependent chromatin plasticity? *Trends in Neurosciences, 28,* 456–463.

Meditation in psychotherapy. (2005, April). *Harvard Mental Health Letter, 21*(10), 1–4.

Meehl, P. E. (1990). Appraising and amending theories: The strategy of Lakotosian defense and two principles that warrant it. *Psychological Inquiry, 1,* 108–141.

Meissner, W. W. (1990). Foundations of psychoanalysis reconsidered. *Journal of the American Psychoanalytic Association, 38,* 523–557.

Melburg, V., & Tedeschi, J. T. (1989). Displaced aggression: Frustration or impression management? *European Journal of Social Psychology, 19,* 139–145.

Menaker, E. (1990). Discussion: The feminine self. *American Journal of Psychoanalysis, 50,* 63–65.

Mendolia, M., Moore, J., & Tesser, A. (1996). Dispositional and situational determinants of repression. *Journal of Personality and Social Psychology, 70,* 856–867.

Mendoza-Denton, R., Ayduk, O., Mischel, W., Shoda, Y., & Testa, A. (2001). Person X situation interactionism in self-encoding (*I Am . . . When . . .*): Implications for affect regulation and social information processing. *Journal of Personality and Social Psychology, 80,* 533–544.

Merenda, P. F. (1987). Toward a four-factor theory of temperament and/or personality. *Journal of Personality Assessment, 51,* 367–374.

Merritt, J. M., Stickgold, R., Pace-Schott, E., Williams, J., & Hobson, J. A. (1994). Emotion profiles in the dreams of men and women. *Consciousness and Cognition, 3,* 46–60.

Mesquida, C. G., & Wiener, N. I. (1996). Human collective aggression: A behavioral ecology perspective. *Ethology and Sociobiology, 17,* 247–262.

Metcalfe, J., & Mischel, W. (1999). A hot/cool-system analysis of delay of gratification: Dynamics of willpower. *Psychological Review, 106,* 3–19.

Meyer-Bahlburg, H. F. L., Ehrhardt, A. A., Rosen, L. R., Gruen, R. S., Veridiano, N. P., Vann, F. H., & Neuwalder, H. F. (1995). Prenatal estrogens and the development of homosexual orientation. *Developmental Psychology, 31,* 12–21.

Michael, J. (1984). Verbal behavior. *Journal of the Experimental Analysis of Behavior, 42,* 363–376.

Michalon, M. (2001). "Selflessness" in the service of the ego: Contributions, limitations, and dangers of Buddhist psychology for Western psychotherapy. *American Journal of Psychotherapy, 55,* 202–218.

Mickelson, K. D., Kessler, R. C., & Shaver, P. R. (1997). Adult attachment in a nationally representative sample. *Journal of Personality and Social Psychology, 73,* 1092–1106.

Midence; K., & Hargreaves, I. (1997). Psychosocial adjustment in male-to-female transsexuals: An overview of the research evidence. *Journal of Psychology; 131,* 602–614.

Midgley, B. D., & Morris, E. K. (1988). The integrated field: An alternative to the behavior-analytic conceptualization of behavioral units. *Psychological Record, 38,* 483–500.

Mihesuah, D. A. (1998). American Indian identities: Issues of individual choices and development. *American Indian Culture and Research Journal, 22.* (No. BHUM98030155)

Miletic, M. P. (2002). The introduction of a feminine psychology to psychoanalysis: Karen Horney's legacy. *Contemporary Psychoanalysis, 38,* 287–299.

Mikulincer, M. (1998a). Adult attachment style and individual differences in functional versus dysfunctional experiences of anger. *Journal of Personality and Social Psychology, 74,* 513–524.

Mikulincer, M. (1998b). Attachment working models and the sense of trust: An exploration of interaction goals and affect regulation. *Journal of Personality and Social Psychology, 74,* 1209–1224.

Mill, J. (1984). High and low self-monitoring individuals: Their decoding skills and empathic expression. *Journal of Personality, 52,* 372–388.

Miller, C. (2001). Childhood animal cruelty and interpersonal violence. *Clinical Psychology Review, 21,* 735–749.

Miller, D. B. (1999). Racial socialization and racial identity: Can they promote resiliency for African American adolescents? *Adolescence, 34,* 493–501.

Miller, E. M. (2000). Homosexuality, birth order, and evolution: Toward an equilibrium reproductive economics of homosexuality. *Archives of Sexual Behavior, 29,* 1–34.

Miller, G. (1969). Psychology as a means of promoting human welfare. *American Psychologist, 24,* 1063–1075.

Miller, J. B. (1976). *Toward a new psychology of women.* Boston: Beacon Press.

Miller, M. E. (2002). Zen and psychotherapy: From neutrality, through relationship, to the emptying space. In S. Muramoto & P. Young-Eisendrath (Eds.), *Awakening and insight: Zen Buddhism and psychotherapy* (pp. 81–92). New York: Brunner-Routledge.

Miller, M. J., Smith, T. S., Wilkinson, L., & Tobacyk, J. (1987). Narcissism and social interest among counselors-in-training. *Psychological Reports, 60,* 765–766.

Miller, N. E. (1941a). An experimental investigation of acquired drives. Abstract of paper presented at the 49th Annual Meeting of the American Psychological Association, September 3–6, 1941. *Psychological Bulletin, 38,* 534–535.

Miller, N. E. (with Sears, R. R., Mowrer, O. H., Doob, L. W., & Dollard, J.). (1941b). The frustration-aggression hypothesis. *Psychological Review, 48,* 337–342.

Miller, N. E. (1948). Theory and experiment relating psychoanalytic displacement to stimulus-response generalization. *Journal of Abnormal and Social Psychology, 43,* 155–178.

Miller, N. E. (1963). Some reflections on the law of effect produce a new alternative to drive reduction. In M. R. Jones (Ed.), *Nebraska symposium on motivation* (pp. 65–112). Lincoln: University of Nebraska Press.

Miller, N. E. (1969). Learning of visceral and glandular responses. *Science, 163,* 434–445.

Miller, N. E. (1985). Some professional and scientific problems and opportunities for biofeedback. *Biofeedback and Self Regulation, 10,* 3024.

Miller, N. E. (1989). Biomedical foundations for biofeedback. *Advances, 6*(3), 30–36.

Miller, N. E. (1992a). Introducing and teaching much-needed understanding of the scientific process. *American Psychologist, 47,* 848–850.

Miller, N. E. (1992b). Some examples of psychophysiology and the unconscious. *Biofeedback and Self Regulation, 17,* 3–16.

Miller, N. E. (1992c). Studies of fear as an acquirable drive: I. Fear as motivation and fear-reduction as reinforcement in the learning of new responses. *Journal of Experimental Psychology: General, 121,* 6–11. (Original work published 1948)

Miller, N. E. (1995). Clinical-experimental interactions in the development of neuroscience: A primer for nonspecialists and lessons for young scientists. *American Psychologist, 50,* 901–911.

Miller, N. E., & Banuazizi, A. (1968). Instrumental learning by curarized rats of a specific visceral response, intestinal or cardiac. *Journal of Comparative and Physiological Psychology, 65,* 1–7.

Miller, N. E., & Dollard, J. (1941). *Social learning and imitation.* New Haven, CT: Yale University Press.

Miller, N. E., & Dworkin, B. R. (1977). Effects of learning on visceral functions: Biofeedback. *New England Journal of Medicine, 296,* 1274–1278.

Miller, T. Q., Smith, T. W., Turner, C. W., Guijarro, M. L., & Hallet, A. J. (1996). Meta-analytic review of research on hostility and physical health. *Psychological Bulletin, 119,* 322–348.

Minarik, M. L., & Ahrens, A. H. (1996). Relations of eating and symptoms of depression and anxiety to the dimensions of perfectionism among undergraduate women. *Cognitive Therapy and Research, 20,* 155–169.

Mind and Life Institute. (2006). The Cultivating Emotional Balance program. Available online at http://www.mindandlife.org/ceb.program.html

Minton, H. L. (1968). Contemporary concepts of power and Adler's views. *Journal of Individual Psychology, 24,* 46–55.

Mischel, H. N., & Mischel, W. (1983). The development of children's knowledge of self-control strategies. *Child Development, 54,* 603–619.

Mischel, W. (1966). Theory and research on the antecedents of self-imposed delay of reward. In B. Maher (Ed.), *Progress in experimental personality research* (Vol. 3, pp. 85–132). New York: Academic Press.

Mischel, W. (1968). *Personality and assessment.* New York: Wiley.

Mischel, W. (1973). Toward a cognitive social learning reconceptualization of personality. *Psychological Review, 80,* 252–283.

Mischel, W. (1974). Processes in delay of gratification. In L. Berkowitz (Ed.), *Advances in experimental social psychology* (Vol. 7, pp. 249–292). New York: Academic Press.

Mischel, W. (1977). The interaction of person and situation. In D. Magnusson & N. S. Endler (Eds.), *Personality at the crossroads: Current issues in interactional psychology* (pp. 333–352). Hillsdale, NJ: Erlbaum.

Mischel, W. (1981a). *Introduction to personality* (3rd ed.). New York: Holt, Rinehart & Winston.

Mischel, W. (1981b). Personality and cognition: Something borrowed, something new? In N. Cantor & J. F. Kihlstrom (Eds.), *Personality, cognition, and social interaction.* Hillsdale, NJ: Erlbaum.

Mischel, W. (1983a). Alternatives in the pursuit of the predictability and consistency of persons: Stable data that yield unstable interpretations. *Journal of Personality, 51,* 578–604.

Mischel, W. (1983b). Delay of gratification as process and as person variable in development. In D. Magnusson & V. P. Allen (Eds.), *Human development: An interactional perspective* (pp. 149–165). New York: Academic Press.

Mischel, W. (1984a). Convergences and challenges in the search for consistency. *American Psychologist, 39,* 351–364.

Mischel, W. (1984b). On the predictability of behavior and the structure of personality. In R. A. Zucker, J. Aronoff, & A. I. Rabin (Eds.), *Personality and the prediction of behavior* (pp. 269–305). New York: Academic Press.

Mischel, W. (1992). Looking for personality. In S. Koch & D. E. Leary (Eds.), *A century of psychology as science* (pp. 515–526). Washington, DC: American Psychological Association.

Mischel, W., & Baker, N. (1975). Cognitive appraisals and transformations in delay behavior. *Journal of Personality and Social Psychology, 31,* 254–261.

Mischel, W., & Ebbesen, E. B. (1970). Attention in delay of gratification. *Journal of Personality and Social Psychology, 16,* 329–337.

Mischel, W., Ebbesen, E. B., & Zeiss, A. R. (1972). Cognitive and attentional mechanisms in delay of gratification. *Journal of Personality and Social Psychology, 21,* 204–218.

Mischel, W., & Liebert, R. M. (1966). Effects of discrepancies between observed and imposed reward criteria on their acquisition and transmission. *Journal of Personality and Social Psychology, 3,* 45–53.

Mischel, W., & Moore, B. (1973). Effects of attention to symbolically presented rewards on self-control. *Journal of Personality and Social Psychology, 28,* 172–179.

Mischel, W., & Peake, P. K. (1982). Beyond déjà vu in the search for cross-situational consistency. *Psychological Review, 89,* 730–755.

Mischel, W., & Peake, P. K. (1983). Some facets of consistency: Replies to Epstein, Funder, and Bem. *Psychological Review, 90,* 394–402.

Mischel, W., & Shoda, Y. (1995). A cognitive-affective system theory of personality: Reconceptualizing situations, dispositions, dynamics, and invariance in personality structure. *Psychological Review, 102,* 246–268.

Mischel, W., & Shoda, Y. (1998). Reconciling processing dynamics and personality dispositions. *Annual Review of Psychology, 49,* 229–258.

Mischel, W., Shoda, Y., & Peake, P. K. (1988). The nature of adolescent competencies predicted by preschool delay of gratification. *Journal of Personality and Social Psychology, 54,* 687–696.

Mischel, W., Shoda, Y., & Rodriguez, M. L. (1989). Delay of gratification in children. *Science, 244,* 933–938.

Mischel, W., & Staub, E. (1965). Effects of expectancy on working and waiting for larger rewards. *Journal of Personality and Social Psychology, 2,* 625–633.

Mischel, W., Zeiss, R., & Zeiss, A. (1974). Internal-external control and persistence: Validation and implications of the Stanford Preschool Internal-External Scale. *Journal of Personality and Social Psychology, 29,* 265–278.

Mitchell, S. A. (1999). The wings of Icarus: Illusion and the problem of narcissism. In S. A. Mitchell & L. Aron (Eds.), *Relational psychoanalysis: The emergence of a tradition* (pp. 153–179). Hillsdale, NJ: Analytical Press. (Reprinted from *Contemporary Psychoanalysis, 22,* 107–132, 1970)

Mitchell, S. A., & Aron, L. (Eds.). (1999). *Relational psychoanalysis: The emergence of a tradition.* Hillsdale, NJ: Analytic Press.

Mittelman, W. (1991). Maslow's study of self-actualization: A reinterpretation. *Journal of Humanistic Psychology, 31*(1), 114–135.

Mongrain, M. (1998). Parental representations and support-seeking behaviors related to dependency and self-criticism. *Journal of Personality, 66,* 151–173.

Monk-Turner, E. (2003). The benefits of meditation: Experimental findings. *Social Science Journal, 40,* 465–470.

Monte, C. F. (1980). *Beneath the mask: An introduction to theories of personality* (2nd ed.). New York: Henry Holt.

Moodley, R. (2000). The right to be desperate and hurt and anger in the presence of Carl Rogers: A racial/psychological identity approach. *Counselling Psychology Quarterly, 13,* 353–364.

Moore, M. K., & Neimeyer, R. A. (1991). A confirmatory factor analysis of the Threat Index. *Journal of Personality and Social Psychology, 60,* 122–129.

Moran, D. J., & Tai, W. (2001). Reducing biases in clinical judgment with single subject treatment design. *Behavior Analyst Today, 2,* 196–203.

Moran, J. R., Fleming, C. M., Somervell, P., & Manson, S. M. (1999). Measuring bicultural ethnic identity among American Indian adolescents: A factor analytic study. *Journal of Adolescent Research, 14,* 405–426.

Morçöl, G., & Asche, M. (1993). Repertory grid in problem structuring: A case illustration. *International Journal of Personal Construct Psychology, 6,* 371–390.

Morgan, A. C. (1997). The application of infant research to psychoanalytic theory and therapy. *Psychoanalytic Psychology, 14,* 315–336.

Morgan, D. (1996). If the Buddha were a psychoanalyst, or vice versa [Review of *Contemporary psychoanalysis and Eastern thought*]. *Contemporary Psychology: APA Review of Books, 41,* 279.

Moritz, C. (Ed.). (1974). Miller, Neal Edgar. *Current biography yearbook* (pp. 276–279). New York: W. H. Wilson.

Morris, C. (1997). Mental health matters: Toward a non-medicalized approach to psychotherapy with women. *Women and Therapy, 20*(3), 63–77.

Morris, M. G. (1997). Psychoanalytic and literary perspectives on procreation conflicts in women. *Psychoanalytic Review, 84,* 109–128.

Morse, C., Bockoven, J., & Bettesworth, A. (1988). Effects of DUSO-2 and DUSO-2-revised on children's social skills and self-esteem. *Elementary School Guidance and Counseling, 22,* 199–205.

Morvay, Z. (1999). Horney, Zen, and the real self: Theoretical and historical connections. *American Journal of Psychoanalysis, 59,* 25–35.

Mosak, H. H., & Dreikurs, R. (2000). Spirituality: The fifth life task. *Individual Psychologist, 5,* 16–11. Reprinted in *Journal of Individual Psychology, 56,* 257–265. (Original work published 1967)

Moskowitz, D. S. (1990). Convergence of self-reports and independent observers: Dominance and friendliness. *Journal of Personality and Social Psychology, 58,* 1096–1106.

Motley, M. T., Baars, B. J., & Camden, C. T. (1983). Polysemantic lexical access: Evidence from laboratory-induced double entendres. *Communication Monographs, 50,* 79–101.

Moustakas, C. (1986). Origins of humanistic psychology. *Humanistic Psychologist, 14,* 122–123.

Mozdzierz, G. J., Greenblatt, R. L., & Murphy, T. J. (1988). Further validation of the Sulliman Scale of Social Interest and the Social Interest Scale. *Individual Psychology, 44,* 30–34.

Mullen, M. K. (1994). Earliest recollections of childhood: A demographic analysis. *Cognition, 52,* 55–79.

Multon, K. D., Brown, S. D., & Lent, R. W. (1991). Relation of self-efficacy beliefs to academic outcomes: A meta-analytic investigation. *Journal of Counseling Psychology, 38,* 30–38.

Munter, P. O. (1975). The medical model revisited: A humanistic reply. *Journal of Personality Assessment, 39,* 4.

Muramoto, S. (2002). Buddhism, religion and psychotherapy in the world today. In S. Muramoto & P. Young-Eisendrath (Eds.), *Awakening and insight: Zen Buddhism and psychotherapy* (pp. 15–29). New York: Brunner-Routledge.

Muraven, M., Tice, D. M., & Baumeister, R. F. (1998). Self-control as limited resource: Regulatory depletion patterns. *Journal of Personality and Social Psychology, 74,* 774–789.

Murphy, T. J., DeWolfe, A. S., & Mozdzierz, G. J. (1984). Levels of self-actualization among process and reactive schizophrenics, alcoholics, and normals: A construct validity study of the Personal Orientation Inventory. *Educational and Psychological Measurement, 44,* 473–482.

Murray, H. A. (1938). *Explorations in personality.* New York: Oxford University Press.

Murray, H. A. (1943, October). Analysis of the personality of Adolph Hitler: With predictions of his future behavior and suggestions for dealing with him now and after Germany's surrender. Confidential report to the Office of Strategic Services. Available online at http://www.lawschool.cornell.edu/library/donovan/hitler/

Murray, J. B. (1990). Review of research on the Myers-Briggs Type Indicator. *Perceptual and Motor Skills, 70,* 1187–1202.

Muslin, H., & Desai, P. (1984). Ghandi [*sic*] and his fathers. *Psychohistory Review, 12,* 7–18.

Myers, D. G., & Diener, E. (1995). Who is happy? *Psychological Science, 6,* 10–19.

Myers, I. B., & McCaulley, M. H. (1985). *Manual: A guide to the development and use of the Myers-Briggs Type Indicator.* Palo Alto, CA: Consulting Psychologists Press.

Myers, L. B., Brewin, C. R., & Power, M. J. (1998). Repressive coping and the directed forgetting of emotional material. *Journal of Abnormal Psychology, 107,* 141–148.

Myers, S. (2000). Empathic listening: Reports on the experience of being heard. *Journal of Humanistic Psychology, 40*(2), 148–173.

Nadel, L., & Zola-Morgan, S. (1984). Infantile amnesia: A neuro-biological perspective. In M. Moscovitch (Ed.), *Infant memory* (pp. 145–172). New York: Plenum Press.

Nahmias, E. (2005). Agency, authorship, and illusion. *Consciousness and Cognition, 14,* 771–785.

Naifeh, S. C. (2001). Carl Gustav Jung, M.D., 1875–1961. *American Journal of Psychiatry, 158,* 173.

Nash, M. R. (1987). What, if anything, is regressed about hypnotic age regression? A review of the empirical literature. *Psychological Bulletin, 102,* 42–52.

Natsoulas, T. (1993). Freud and consciousness: VIII. Conscious psychical processes perforce involve higher-order consciousness—intrinsically or concomitantly? A current issue. *Psychoanalysis and Contemporary Thought, 16,* 597–631.

Natsoulas, T. (1994). A rediscovery of consciousness. *Consciousness and Cognition, 3,* 223–245.

Navarick, D. J. (1998). Impulsive choice in adults: How consistent are individual differences? *Psychological Record, 48,* 665–674.

Neher, A. (1996). Jung's theory of archetypes: A critique. *Journal of Humanistic Psychology, 36,* 61–91.

Neimeyer, G. J. (1988). Cognitive integration and differentiation in vocational behavior. *Counseling Psychologist, 16,* 440–475.

Neimeyer, G. J. (1992). Personal constructs in career counseling and development. *Journal of Career Development, 18*(3), 163–173.

Neimeyer, G. J., & Khouzam, N. (1985). A repertory grid study of restrained eaters. *British Journal of Medical Psychology, 58,* 365–367.

Neimeyer, G. J., & Metzler, A. E. (1987). The development of vocational structures. *Journal of Vocational Behavior, 30,* 26–32.

Neimeyer, G. J., & Rareshide, M. B. (1991). Personal memories and personal identity: The impact of ego identity on autobiographical memory recall. *Journal of Personality and Social Psychology, 60,* 562–569.

Neimeyer, R. A. (1985a). Actualization, integration, and fear of death: A test of the additive model. *Death Studies, 9,* 235–244.

Neimeyer, R. A. (1985b). Personal constructs in clinical practice. In P. C. Kendall (Ed.), *Advances in cognitive behavioral research and therapy,* Vol. 4 (pp. 275–339). New York: Academic Press.

Neimeyer, R. A. (1987). An orientation to personal construct therapy. In R. A. Neimeyer & G. J. Neimeyer (Eds.), *Personal construct therapy casebook* (pp. 3–19). New York: Springer.

Neimeyer, R. A. (1992). Constructivist approaches to the measurement of meaning. In G. J. Neimeyer (Ed.), *Constructivist assessment: A casebook* (pp. 58–103). Newbury Park, CA: Sage.

Neimeyer, R. A. (1993). An appraisal of constructivist psychotherapies. *Journal of Consulting and Clinical Psychology, 61,* 221–234.

Neimeyer, R. A. (1994). The role of client-generated narratives in psychotherapy. *International Journal of Personal Construct Psychology, 7,* 229–242.

Neimeyer, R. A. (1999). Narrative strategies in grief therapy. *Journal of Constructivist Psychology, 12,* 65–85.

Neimeyer, R. A. (2001). Unfounded trust: A constructivist meditation. *American Journal of Psychotherapy, 55,* 364–371.

Neimeyer, R. A., Moore, M. K., & Bagley, K. J. (1988). A preliminary factor structure for the Threat Index. *Death Studies, 12,* 217–225.

Neimeyer, R. A., & Neimeyer, G. J. (Eds.). (1987). *Personal construct therapy casebook.* New York: Springer.

Nelson, D. V., Friedman, L. C., Baer, P. E., Lane, M., & Smith, F. E. (1989). Attitudes to cancer: Psychometric properties of fighting spirit and denial. *Journal of Behavioral Medicine, 12,* 341–355.

Nelson, L. S., & Roberge, L. P. (1993). The relationship between psychological type and preference for career services: Implications for career development strategies. *College Student Journal, 27,* 312–321.

Nesselroade, J. R. (2001). Intraindividual variability in development within and between individuals. *European Psychologist, 6,* 187–193.

Neumann, E. (1963). *The great mother: An analysis of the archetype* (2nd ed.). Princeton, NJ: Princeton University Press.

Nevis, E. C. (1983). Using an American perspective in understanding another culture: Toward a hierarchy of needs for the People's Republic of China. *Journal of Applied Behavioral Science, 19,* 249–264.

Newberg, A., d'Aquili, E., & Rause, V. (2001). *Why God won't go away: Brain science and the biology of belief.* New York: Ballantine Books.

Newberg, A., Pourdehnad, M., Alavi, A., & d'Aquili, E. G. (2003). Cerebral blood flow during meditative prayer: Preliminary findings and methodological issues. *Perceptual and Motor Skills, 97,* 625–630.

Newberg, A. B., & Iversen, J. (2003). The neural basis of the complex mental task of meditation: Neurotransmitter and neurochemical considerations. *Medical Hypotheses, 61,* 282–291.

Newman, D. L., Tellegen, A., & Bouchard, T. J., Jr. (1998). Individual differences in adult ego development: Sources of influence in twins reared apart. *Journal of Personality and Social Psychology, 74,* 985–995.

Newman, L. S., Duff, K. J., & Baumeister, R. F. (1997). A new look at defensive projection: Thought suppression, accessibility, and biased person perception. *Journal of Personality and Social Psychology, 72,* 980–1001.

Newman, L. S., Higgins, E. T., & Vookles, J. (1992). Self-guide strength and emotional vulnerability: Birth order as a moderator of self-affect relations. *Personality and Social Psychology Bulletin, 18,* 402–411.

Newman, P. R., & Newman, B. M. (1988). Differences between childhood and adulthood: The identity watershed. *Adolescence, 23,* 551–557.

Nez, D. (1991). Persephone's return: Archetypal art therapy and the treatment of a survivor of abuse. *Arts in Psychotherapy, 18*(2), 123–130.

Nghe, L. T., & Mahalik, J. R. (2001). Examining racial identity statuses as predictors of psychological defenses in African American college students. *Journal of Counseling Psychology, 48,* 10–16.

Nhat Hanh, T. (1996). *Being peace.* Berkeley, CA: Parallax Press.

Nhat Hanh, T. (2001). *Anger.* New York: Riverhead Books.

Nicholson, I. (1997). Humanistic psychology and the intellectual identity: The "open" system of Gordon Allport. *Journal of Humanistic Psychology, 37*(3), 61–79.

Nicholson, I. A. M. (1998). Gordon Allport, character, and the "culture of personality," 1897–1937. *History of Psychology, 1,* 52–68.

Nicholson, I. A. M. (2001). "Giving up maleness": Abraham Maslow, masculinity, and the boundaries of psychology. *History of Psychology, 4,* 79–91.

Nichtern, S. (1985). Gandhi: His adolescent conflict of mind and body. *Adolescent Psychiatry, 12,* 17–23.

Nidich, R. J., Nidich, S. I., & Alexander, C. N. (2005). Moral development and natural law. *Journal of Social Behavior and Personality, 17,* 137–149.

Nidich, S. I., Schneider, R. H., Nidich, R. J., Foster, G., Sharma, H., Salerno, J., Goodman, R., & Alexander, C. N. (2005). Effect of the Transcendental Meditation program on intellectual development in community-dwelling older adults. *Journal of Social Behavior and Personality, 17,* 217–226.

Niemann, Y. F., Romero, A. J., Arredondo, J., & Rodriquez, V. (1999). What does it mean to be "Mexican"? Social construction of an ethnic identity. *Hispanic Journal of the Behavioral Sciences, 21,* 47–60.

Nigg, J. T., Lohr, N. E., Westen, D., Gold, L. J., & Silk, K. R. (1992). Malevolent object representations in borderline personality disorder and major depression. *Journal of Abnormal Psychology, 101,* 61–67.

Nissen, M. J., Knopman, D. S., & Schacter, D. L. (1987). Neurochemical dissociation of memory systems. *Neurology, 37,* 789–794.

Nitis, T. (1989). Ego differentiation: Eastern and Western perspectives. *American Journal of Psychoanalysis, 49,* 339–346.

Nixon, R. M. (1962). *Six crises.* Garden City, NY: Doubleday.

Nixon, R. M. (1990). *In the arena: A memoir of victory, defeat, and renewal.* New York: Simon & Schuster.

Nolen-Hoeksema, S. (1987). Sex differences in unipolar depression: Evidence and theory. *Psychological Bulletin, 101,* 259–282.

Nolen-Hoeksema, S., & Girgus, J. S. (1994). The emergence of gender differences in depression during adolescence. *Psychological Bulletin, 115,* 424–443.

Noll, R. (1994). *The Jung cult: Origins of a charismatic movement.* Princeton, NJ: Princeton University Press.

Norman, W. T. (1963). Toward an adequate taxonomy of personality attributes: Replicated factor structure in peer nomination personality ratings. *Journal of Abnormal and Social Psychology, 66,* 574–583.

Novotny, K. M. (2000). Experts in their own lives: Emphasizing client-centeredness in a homeless program. *Policy Studies Journal, 28,* 382–401.

Oates, S. B. (1982). *Let the trumpet sound: The life of Martin Luther King, Jr.* New York: Mentor Books.

Ochberg, R. L. (1988). Life stories and the psychosocial construction of careers. *Journal of Personality, 56,* 173–204.

Ochse, R., & Plug, C. (1986). Cross-cultural investigation of the validity of Erikson's theory of personality development. *Journal of Personality and Social Psychology, 50,* 1240–1252.

O'Connell, A. N. (1980). Karen Horney: Theorist in psychoanalysis and feminine psychology. *Psychology of Women Quarterly, 5,* 81–93.

O'Connell, A. N., & Russo, N. F. (1980). Models for achievement: Eminent women in psychology. *Psychology of Women Quarterly, 5,* 6–10.

O'Connell, W. (1990). Natural high theory and practice (NHTP) as a model of Adlerian holism. *Individual Psychology, 46,* 263–269.

O'Donohue, W. T., & Houts, A. C. (1985). The two disciplines of behavior therapy: Research methods and mediating variables. *Psychological Record, 35,* 155–163.

Ofshe, R., & Watters, E. (1994). *Making monsters: False memories, psychotherapy, and sexual hysteria.* New York: Charles Scribner's Sons.

Öhman, A. (2002). Automaticity and the amygdala: Nonconscious responses to emotional faces. *Current Directions in Psychological Science, 11,* 62–66.

Öhman, A., & Mineka, S. (2001). Fears, phobias, and preparedness: Toward an evolved module of fear and fear learning. *Psychological Review, 108,* 483–522.

Oishi, S. (2004). Personality *in* culture: A neo-Allportian view. *Journal of Research in Personality, 38,* 68–74.

Okagaki, L., & Moore, D. K. (2000). Ethnic identity beliefs of young adults and their parents in families of Mexican descent. *Hispanic Journal of Behavioral Sciences, 22,* 139–162.

Olds, D. D. (1992). Consciousness: A brain-centered, informational approach. *Psychoanalytic Inquiry, 12,* 419–444.

O'Leary, A. (1985). Self-efficacy and health. *Behavior Research and Therapy, 23,* 437–452.

O'Leary, A. (1992). Self-efficacy and health: Behavioral and stress-physiological mediation. *Cognitive Therapy and Research, 16,* 229–245.

O'Leary, K. D., & Drabman, R. (1971). Token reinforcement programs in the classroom: A review. *Psychological Bulletin, 75,* 379–398.

Olson, B. (1999). *Hell to pay: The unfolding story of Hillary Rodham Clinton.* Washington, DC: Regnery.

Olson, E. E. (1990). The transcendent function in organizational change. *Journal of Applied Behavioral Science, 26,* 69–81.

O'Neill, R. M., & Bornstein, R. F. (1990). Oral-dependence and gender: Factors in help-seeking response set and self-reported psychopathology in psychiatric inpatients. *Journal of Personality Assessment, 55,* 28–40.

O'Neill, R. M., Greenberg, R. P., & Fisher, S. (1992). Humor and anality. *Humor: International Journal of Humor Research, 5,* 283–291.

Oppenheimer, R. (1956). Analogy in science. *American Psychologist, 11,* 127–135.

Orbach, I. (1997). A taxonomy of factors related to suicidal behavior. *Clinical Psychology: Science and Practice, 4,* 208–224.

Orlofsky, J. L. (1978a). Identity formation, achievement, and fear of success in college men and women. *Journal of Youth and Adolescence, 7,* 49–62.

Orlofsky, J. L. (1978b). The relationship between intimacy and antecedent personality components. *Adolescence, 13,* 419–441.

Orlofsky, J. L., & Frank, M. (1986). Personality structure as viewed through early memories and identity status in college men and women. *Journal of Personality and Social Psychology, 50,* 580–586.

Orne, M. T. (1959). The nature of hypnosis: Artifact and essence. *Journal of Abnormal and Social Psychology, 58,* 277–299.

Orne, M. T. (1971). Hypnosis, motivation, and the ecological validity of the psychological experiment. In W. J. Arnold & M. M. Page (Eds.), *Nebraska symposium on motivation, 1970* (pp. 187–265). Lincoln: University of Nebraska Press.

O'Roark, A. M. (1990). Comment on Cowan's interpretation of the Myers-Briggs Type Indicator and Jung's psychological functions. *Journal of Personality Assessment, 55,* 815–817.

Otto, R. K., Poythress, N., Starr, L., & Darkes, J. (1993). An empirical study of the reports of APA's peer review panel in the congressional review of the U.S.S. *Iowa* incident. *Journal of Personality Assessment, 61,* 425–442.

Overton, R. K. (1958). Experimental studies of organ inferiority. *Journal of Individual Psychology, 14,* 62–63.

Owen, D. (2001). *The chosen one: Tiger Woods and the dilemma of greatness.* New York: Simon and Schuster.

Ozer, D. J., & Reise, S. P. (1994). Personality assessment. *Annual Review of Psychology, 45,* 357–388.

Ozer, E. M., & Bandura, A. (1990). Mechanisms governing empowerment effects: A self-efficacy analysis. *Journal of Personality and Social Psychology, 58,* 472–486.

Paige, J. M. (1966). Letters from Jenny: An approach to the clinical analysis of personality structure by computer. In P. J. Stone, D. C. Dunphy, M. S. Smith, & D. M. Ogilvie (Eds.), *The General Inquirer: A computer approach to content analysis* (pp. 431–451). Cambridge, MA: MIT Press.

Palmer, E. C., & Carr, K. (1991). Dr. Rogers, meet Mr. Rogers: The theoretical and clinical similarities between Carl and Fred Rogers. *Social Behavior and Personality, 19,* 39–44.

Pam, A., & Rivera, J. A. (1995). Sexual pathology and dangerousness from a Thematic Apperception Test protocol. *Professional Psychology: Research and Practice, 26,* 72–77.

Pancer, S. M., Hunsberger, B., Pratt, M. W., & Alisat, S. (2000). Cognitive complexity of expectations and adjustment to university in the first year. *Journal of Adolescent Research, 15,* 38–57.

Pandora, K. (1998). "Mapping the new mental world created by radio": Media messages, cultural politics, and Cantril and Allport's *The Psychology of Radio. Journal of Social Issues, 54,* 7–27.

Paniagua, F. A. (1987). "Knowing" the world within the skin: A remark on Skinner's behavioral theory of knowledge. *Psychological Reports, 61,* 741–742.

Panksepp, J. (2000). The riddle of laughter: Neural and psychoevolutionary underpinnings of joy. *Current Directions in Psychological Science, 9,* 183–186.

Paranjpe, A. C. (1998). *Self and identity in modern psychology and Indian thought.* New York: Kluwer Academic.

Paris, B. J. (1989). Introduction: Interdisciplinary applications of Horney. *American Journal of Psychoanalysis, 49,* 181–188.

Paris, B. J. (1999). Karen Horney's vision of the self. *American Journal of Psychoanalysis, 59,* 157–166.

Park, C., Cohen, L. H., & Herb, L. (1990). Intrinsic religiousness and religious coping as life stress moderators for Catholics versus Protestants. *Journal of Personality and Social Psychology, 59,* 562–574.

Park, H. S., & Murgatroyd, W. (1998). Relationship between intrinsic-extrinsic religious orientation and depressive symptoms in Korean Americans. *Counselling Psychology Quarterly, 11,* 315–324.

Pasupathi, M. (2001). The social construction of the personal past and its implications for adult development. *Psychological Bulletin, 127,* 651–672.

Patai, R. (1967). *The Hebrew goddess.* New York: Avon Books.

Paterson, D. G. (1999). A provocative treatise. *Journal of Higher Education, 70,* 621–623.

Patterson, D. R., Everett, J. J., Burns, G. L., & Marvin, J. A. (1992). Hypnosis for the treatment of burn pain. *Journal of Consulting and Clinical Psychology, 60,* 713–717.

Patton, C. J. (1992). Fear of abandonment and binge eating: A subliminal psychodynamic activation investigation. *Journal of Nervous and Mental Disease, 180,* 484–490.

Paul, R. (1985). Freud and the seduction theory: A critical examination of Masson's *The assault on truth. Journal of Psychoanalytic Anthropology, 8,* 161–187.

Paulhus, D. L., Fridhandler, B., & Hayes, S. (1997). Psychological defense: Contemporary theory and research. In R. Hogan, J. Johnson, & S. Briggs (Eds.), *Handbook of personality psychology* (pp. 543–579). San Diego: Academic Press.

Payne, R. L. (2000). Eupsychian management and the millennium. *Journal of Managerial Psychology, 15,* 219–226.

Peake, P. K., & Mischel, W. (1984). Getting lost in the search for large coefficients: Reply to Conley. *Psychological Review, 91,* 497–501.

Pedersen, W. C., Miller, L. C., Putcha-Bhagavatula, A. D., & Yang, Y. (2002). Evolved sex differences in the number of partners desired? The long and the short of it. *Psychological Science, 13,* 157–161.

Pelzer, D. (1995). *A child called "it": One child's courage to survive.* Deerfield Beach, FL: Health Communications.

Pelzer, D. (1997). *The lost boy: A foster child's search for the love of a family.* Deerfield Beach, FL: Health Communications.

Pelzer, D. (1999). *A man named Dave: A story of triumph and forgiveness.* New York: Plume.

Pelzer, D. (2000). *Help yourself: Celebrating the rewards of resilience and gratitude.* New York: Dutton.

Pelzer, D. (2004). *The privilege of youth: A teenager's story of longing for acceptance and friendship.* New York: Dutton.

Pennebaker, J. (1993). Putting stress into words: Health, linguistic, and therapeutic implications. *Behavioral Research Therapy, 31,* 539–548.

Pennebaker, J. W., Colder, M., & Sharp, L. K. (1990). Accelerating the coping process. *Journal of Personality and Social Psychology, 58,* 528–537.

Pepper, S. C. (1942). *World hypotheses: A study in evidence.* Berkeley: University of California Press.

Perlini, A. H., Haley, A., & Buczel, A. (1998). Hypnosis and reporting biases: Telling the truth. *Journal of Research in Personality, 32,* 13–32.

Perlman, M. (1983). Phaethon and the thermonuclear chariot. *Spring: An Annual of Archetypal Psychology and Jungian Thought* (pp. 87–108). Zürich: Spring.

Perry J. C., & Ianni, F. F. (1998). Observer-rated measures of defense mechanisms. *Journal of Personality, 66,* 994–1024.

Pervin, L. A. (1985). Personality: Current controversies, issues and directions. *Annual Review of Psychology, 36,* 83–114.

Peterson, B. E. (2006). Generativity and successful parenting: An analysis of young adult outcomes. *Journal of Personality, 74,* 847–869.

Peterson, B. E., & Klohnen, E. C. (1995). Realization of generativity in two samples of women at midlife. *Psychology and Aging, 10,* 20–29.

Peterson, B. E., Smirles, K. A., & Wentworth, P. A. (1997). Generativity and authoritarianism: Implications for personality, political involvement, and parenting. *Journal of Personality and Social Psychology, 72,* 1202–1216.

Peterson, B. E., & Stewart, A. J. (1990). Using personal and fictional documents to assess psychosocial development: A case study of Vera Brittain's generativity. *Psychology and Aging, 5,* 400–411.

Peterson, B. E., & Stewart, A. J. (1993). Generativity and social motives in young adults. *Journal of Personality and Social Psychology, 65,* 186–198.

Peterson, B. E., & Stewart, A. J. (1996). Antecedents and contexts of generativity motivation at midlife. *Psychology and Aging, 11,* 21–33.

Peterson, C. (1993). Helpless behavior. *Behaviour Research and Therapy, 31,* 289–295.

Peterson, C., Seligman, M. E. P., & Vaillant, G. E. (1988). Pessimistic explanatory style is a risk factor for physical illness: A thirty-five-year longitudinal study. *Journal of Personality and Social Psychology, 55,* 23–27.

Peterson-Cooney, L. (1987). Time-concentrated instruction as an immediate risk to self-actualization. *Psychological Reports, 61,* 183–190.

Petrie, K. J., Booth, R. J., & Pennebaker, J. W. (1998). The immunological effects of thought suppression. *Journal of Personality and Social Psychology, 75,* 1264–1272.

Pettigrew, T. F. (1999). Gordon Willard Allport: A tribute. *Journal of Social Issues, 55,* 415–427.

Phillips, A. S., Long, R. G., & Bedeian, A. G. (1990). Type A status: Birth order and gender effects. *Individual Psychology, 46,* 365–373.

Phillips, J. M., & Gully, S. M. (1997). Role of goal orientation, ability, need for achievement, and locus of control in the self-efficacy and goal-setting process. *Journal of Applied Psychology, 82,* 792–802.

Phillips, K., & Matheny, A. P., Jr. (1997). Evidence for genetic influence on both cross-situation and situation-specific components of behavior. *Journal of Personality and Social Psychology, 73,* 129–138.

Phillips, K. L. (1980). The riddle of change. In G. Epstein (Ed.), *Studies in non-deterministic psychology* (pp. 229–253). New York: Human Sciences Press.

Philogene, G. (1994). "African American" as a new social representation. *Journal for the Theory of Social Behaviour, 24,* 89–109.

Phinney, J. S. (1990). Ethnic identity in adolescents and adults: Review of research. *Psychological Bulletin, 108,* 499–514.

Phinney, J. S. (1991). Ethnic identity and self-esteem: A review and integration. *Hispanic Journal of Behavioral Sciences, 13,* 193–208.

Pichot, P. (1984). Centenary of the birth of Hermann Rorschach. *Journal of Personality Assessment, 48,* 591–596.

Pickering, A. D. (1997). The conceptual nervous system and personality: From Pavlov to neural networks. *European Psychologist, 2,* 139–163.

Piechowski, M. M., & Tyska, C. (1982). Self-actualization profile of Eleanor Roosevelt, a presumed nontranscender. *Genetic Psychology Monographs, 105,* 95–153.

Piers, C. (1998). Contemporary trauma theory and its relation to character. *Psychoanalytic Psychology, 15,* 14–33.

Pietikainen, P. (1998). Archetypes as symbolic forms. *Journal of Analytical Psychology, 43,* 325–343.

Pietikainen, P. (1999). Jung's psychology in the light of his "personal myth." *Psychoanalysis and History, 1,* 237–251.

Pietromonaco, P. R., & Barrett, L. F. (1997). Working models of attachment and daily social interactions. *Journal of Personality and Social Psychology, 73,* 1409–1423.

Pigliucci, M. (2004). God in the brain [Review of *Why God won't go away: Brain science and the biology of belief*]. *Skeptic, 10,* 82–83.

Pillemer, D. B., Picariello, M. L., & Pruett, J. C. (1994). Very long-term memories of a salient preschool event. *Applied Cognitive Psychology, 8,* 95–106.

Pinker, S. (2002). *The blank slate: The modern denial of human nature.* New York: Viking.

Planalp, S., & Fitness, J. (1999). Thinking/feeling about social and personal relationships. *Journal of Social and Personal Relationships, 16,* 731–750.

Plouffe, L., & Gravelle, F. (1989). Age, sex, and personality correlates of self-actualization in elderly adults. *Psychological Reports, 65,* 643–647.

Podd, M. H. (1972). Ego identity status and morality: The relationship between two developmental constructs. *Developmental Psychology, 6,* 497–507.

Podd, M. H., Marcia, J. E., & Rubin, R. (1970). The effects of ego identity and partner perception on a prisoner's dilemma game. *Journal of Social Psychology, 82,* 117–126.

Pois, R. A. (1990). The case for clinical training and challenges to psychohistory. *Psychohistory Review, 18,* 169–187.

Polivy, J. (1998). The effects of behavioral inhibition: Integrating internal cues, cognition, behavior, and affect. *Psychological Inquiry, 9,* 181–204.

Polkinghorne, D. E. (1988). *Narrative knowing and the human sciences.* Albany: State University of New York Press.

Polkinghorne, D. E. (1992). Research methodology in humanistic psychology. *Humanistic Psychologist, 20,* 218–242.

Pollock, P. H., & Kear-Colwell, J. J. (1994). Women who stab: A personal construct analysis of sexual victimization and offending behaviour. *British Journal of Medical Psychology, 67,* 13–22.

Pope, H. G., & Hudson, J. I. (1996). "Recovered memory" therapy for eating disorders: Implications of the Ramona verdict. *International Journal of Eating Disorders, 19,* 139–145.

Pope, K. S. (1993–1994). Multivariate personality and clinical assessment in court: Use of the Cattell tests in forensic proceedings. *Imagination, Cognition and Personality, 13,* 175–186.

Poppen, R. (1982). The fixed-interval scallop in human affairs. *Behavior Analyst, 5,* 127–136.

Porter, S. S., & Inks, L. W. (2000). Cognitive complexity and salesperson adaptability: An exploratory investigation. *Journal of Personal Selling and Sales Management, 20,* 15–21.

Prager, E. (1998). Men and meaning in later life. *Journal of Clinical Geropsychology, 4,* 191–203.

Pratt, A. B. (1985). Adlerian psychology as an intuitive operant system. *Behavior Analyst, 8,* 39–51.

Pratt, M. W., Danso, H. A., Arnold, M. L., Norris, J. E., & Filyer, R. (1994). Adult generativity and the socialization of adolescents: Relations to mothers' and fathers' parenting beliefs, styles, and practices. *Journal of Personality, 69,* 89–120.

Premack, D., & Premack, A. (2003). *Original intelligence: Unlocking the mystery of who we are.* New York: McGraw-Hill.

Prerost, F. J. (1989). Humor as an intervention strategy during psychological treatment: Imagery and incongruity. *Psychology, 26,* 34–40.

Pressley, M., & Grossman, L. R. (Eds.). (1994). Recovery of memories of childhood sexual abuse [Special issue]. *Applied Cognitive Psychology, 8*(4).

Price, M. (1994). Incest and the idealized self: Adaptations to childhood sexual abuse. *American Journal of Psychoanalysis, 54,* 21–36.

Price, M. E., Cosmides, L., & Tooby, J. (2002). Punitive sentiment as an anti-free rider psychological device. *Evolution and Human Behavior, 23,* 203–231.

Prilleltensky, I. (1992). Humanistic psychology, human welfare and the social order. *Journal of Mind and Behavior, 13,* 315–327.

Primavera, J. P., III, & Kaiser, R. S. (1992). Non-pharmacological treatment of headache: Is less more? *Headache, 32,* 393–395.

Privette, G. (1983). Peak experience, peak performance, and flow: A comparative analysis of positive human experiences. *Journal of Personality and Social Psychology, 45,* 1361–1368.

Privette, G. (1985). Experience as a component of personality theory. *Psychological Reports, 56,* 263–266.

Privette, G. (1986). From peak performance and peak experience to failure and misery. *Journal of Social Behavior and Personality, 1,* 233–243.

Privette, G., & Bundrick, C. M. (1987). Measurement of experience: Construct and content validity of the experience questionnaire. *Perceptual and Motor Skills, 65,* 315–332.

Proctor, B. E., Floyd, R. G., & Shaver, R. B. (2005). Cattell-Horn-Carroll broad cognitive ability profiles of low math achievers. *Psychology in the Schools, 42,* 1–12.

Progoff, I. (1975). *At a journal workshop.* New York: Dialogue House Library.

Protinsky, H. (1988). Identity formation: A comparison of problem and nonproblem adolescents. *Adolescence, 23,* 67–72.

Pryor, D. B., & Tollerud, T. R. (1999). Applications of Adlerian principles in school settings. *Professional School Counseling, 2,* 299–304.

Pulkkinen, L. (1992). Life-styles in personality development. *European Journal of Personality, 6,* 139–155.

Pulkkinen, L., & Rönkä, A. (1994). Personal control over development, identity formation, and future orientation as components of life orientation: A developmental approach. *Developmental Psychology, 30,* 260–271.

Pyszczynski, T., Greenberg, J., & Solomon, S. (1999). A dual-process model of defense against conscious and unconscious death-related thoughts: An extension of terror management theory. *Psychological Review, 106,* 835–845.

Qirko, H. (2004). Altruistic celibacy, kin-cue manipulation, and the development of religious institutions. *Zygon, 39,* 681–706.

Quartz, S., & Sejnowski, T. J. (1997). The neural basis of cognitive development: A constructivist manifesto. *Behavioral and Brain Sciences, 20,* 537–596.

Quartz, S., & Sejnowski, T. (2000). Constraining constructivism: Cortical and sub-cortical constraints on learning in development. *Behavioral and Brain Sciences, 23,* 785–792.

Quay, H. C. (1997). Inhibition and attention deficit hyperactivity disorder. *Journal of Abnormal Child Psychology, 25,* 7–13.

Quinn, S. (1988). *A mind of her own: The life of Karen Horney.* Reading, MA: Addison-Wesley.

Rachman, S. J. (1989). The return of fear: Review and prospect. *Clinical Psychology Review, 9,* 147–168.

Raine, A. (1993). *The psychopathology of crime: Criminal behavior as a clinical disorder.* San Diego, CA: Academic Press.

Raine, A., Lencz, T., Bihrle, S., LaCasse, L., & Colletti, P. (2000). Reduced prefrontal gray matter volume and reduced autonomic activity in antisocial personality disorder. *Archives of General Psychiatry, 57,* 120–127.

Raine, A., Venables, P. H., & Williams, M. (1996). Better autonomic conditioning and faster electrodermal half-recovery time at age 15 years as possible protective factors against crime at age 29 years. *Developmental Psychology, 32,* 624–630.

Ramanaiah, N. V., Heerboth, J. R., & Jinkerson, D. L. (1985). Personality and self-actualizing profiles of assertive people. *Journal of Personality Assessment, 49,* 440–443.

Rammsayer, T. H. (1998). Extraversion and dopamine: Individual differences in response to changes in dopaminergic activity as a possible biological basis of extraversion. *European Psychologist, 3,* 37–50.

Ramona v. Isabella et al., Napa Superior Court Case No. 61898, Napa, CA. (1994).

Rapaport, D. (1959). Introduction: A historical survey of psychoanalytic ego psychology. In E. H. Erikson, *Identity and the life cycle: Selected papers. Psychological Issues, 1* (pp. 5–17). New York: International Universities Press.

Raskin, J. D. (2001). The modern, the postmodern, and George Kelly's personal construct psychology. *American Psychologist, 56,* 368–369.

Raskin, J. D., & Epting, F. R. (1993). Personal construct theory and the argument against mental illness. *International Journal of Personal Construct Psychology, 6,* 351–369.

Ratanakul, P. (2002). Buddhism and science: Allies or enemies? *Zygon, 37,* 115–120.

Rathunde, K. (2001). Toward a psychology of optimal human functioning: What positive psychology can learn from the "experimental turns" of James, Dewey, and Maslow. *Journal of Humanistic Psychology, 41,* 135–141.

Ratican, K. L. (1996). A symptom-focused hypnotic approach to accessing and processing previously repressed/dissociated memories. *Journal of Child Sexual Abuse, 5*(2), 17–35.

Raz-Duvshani, A. (1986). Cognitive structure changes with psychotherapy in neurosis. *British Journal of Medical Psychology, 59,* 341–350.

Reed, C. (2006, February). Talking up enlightenment. *Scientific American, 294*(2), 23–24.

Reinsdorf, W. (1993–1994). Schizophrenia, poetic imagery and metaphor. *Imagination, Cognition and Personality, 13,* 335–345.

Reis, H. T., Lin, Y., Bennett, M. E., & Nezlek, J. B. (1993). Change and consistency in social participation during early adulthood. *Developmental Psychology, 29,* 633–645.

Reiser, M. F. (2001). The dream in contemporary psychiatry. *American Journal of Psychiatry, 158,* 351–359.

Render, G. F., Padilla, J. N. M., & Krank, H. M. (1989). Assertive discipline: A critical review and analysis. *Teachers College Record, 90,* 607–630.

Rendon, M. (1988). A cognitive unconscious? *American Journal of Psychoanalysis, 48,* 291–293.

Repp, A. (1994). Comments on functional analysis procedures for school-based behavior problems. *Journal of Applied Behavior Analysis, 27,* 409–411.

ReVille, S. (1989). Young adulthood to old age: Looking at intergenerational possibilities from a human development perspective. *Journal of Children in Contemporary Society, 20,* 45–53.

Reyher, J. (1962). A paradigm for determining the clinical relevance of hypnotically induced psychopathology. *Psychological Bulletin, 59,* 344–352.

Rhodewalt, F., Madrian, J. C., & Cheney, S. (1998). Narcissism, self-knowledge, organization, and emotional reactivity: The effect of daily experience on self-esteem and affect. *Personality and Social Psychology Bulletin, 24,* 75–87.

Rhodewalt, F., & Morf, C. C. (1998). On self-aggrandizement and anger: A temporal analysis of narcissism and affective reactions to success and failure. *Journal of Personality and Social Psychology, 74,* 672–685.

Rholes, W. S., Simpson, J. A., Blakely, B. S., Lanigan, L., & Allen, E. A. (1997). Adult attachment styles, the desire to have children, and working models of parenthood. *Journal of Personality, 65,* 357–385.

Ricard, M., & Thuan, T. X. (2001). *The quantum and the lotus: A journey to the frontiers where science and Buddhism meet.* Westminster, MD: Crown.

Rice, K. G., Ashby, J. S., & Slaney, R. B. (1998). Self-esteem as a mediator between perfectionism and depression: A structural equations analysis. *Journal of Counseling Psychology, 45,* 304–314.

Richards, N. (1986). A conception of personality. *Behaviorism, 14,* 147–157.

Richards, A. C., & Combs, A. W. (1992). Education and the humanistic challenge. *Humanistic Psychologist, 20,* 372–388.

Richards, J. M., Beal, W. E., Seagal, J. D., & Pennebaker, J. W. (2000). Effects of disclosure of traumatic events on illness behavior among psychiatric prison inmates. *Journal of Abnormal Psychology, 109,* 156–160.

Richards, J. M., & Gross, J. J. (2000). Emotion regulation and memory: The cognitive costs of keeping one's cool. *Journal of Personality and Social Psychology, 79,* 410–424.

Richards, P. S., & Bergin, A. E. (1997). *A spiritual strategy for counseling and psychotherapy.* Washington, DC: American Psychological Association.

Richardson, F. C., & Guignon, C. B. (1988). Individualism and social interest. *Individual Psychology, 44,* 13–29.

Richardson, F. C., & Manaster, G. J. (1997). Back to the future: Alfred Adler on freedom and commitment. *Individual Psychology, 53,* 286–309.

Richman, J. (2001). Humor and creative life styles. *American Journal of Psychotherapy, 55,* 420–428.

Rideout, C. A., & Richardson, S. A. (1989). A teambuilding model: Appreciating differences using the Myers-Briggs Type Indicator with developmental theory. *Journal of Counseling and Development, 67,* 529–533.

Riedel, H. P. R., Heiby, E. M., & Kopetskie, S. (2001). Psychological behaviorism theory of bipolar disorder. *Psychological Record, 51,* 507–532.

Riggio, R. E., Lippa, R., & Salinas, C. (1990). The display of personality in expressive movement. *Journal of Research in Personality, 24,* 16–31.

Rilling, M. (2000). John Watson's paradoxical struggle to explain Freud. *American Psychologist, 55,* 301–312.

Risemberg, R., & Zimmerman, B. J. (1992). Self-regulated learning in gifted students. *Roeper Review, 15,* 98–101.

Ritskes, R., Ritskes-Hoitinga, M., Stodkilde-Jorgensen, H., Baerentsen, K., & Hartman, T. (2003). MRI scanning during Zen meditation: The picture of enlightenment? *Constructivism in the Human Sciences, 8,* 85–90.

Roberts, B. W., & DelVecchio, W. F. (2000). The rank-order consistency of personality traits from childhood to old age: A quantitative review of longitudinal studies. *Psychological Bulletin, 126,* 3–25.

Roberts, B. W., & Donahue, E. M. (1994). One personality, multiple selves: Integrating personality and social roles. *Journal of Personality, 62,* 199–218.

Roberts, R. E., Phinney, J. S., Masse, L. C., Chen, Y. R., Roberts, C. R., & Romero, A. (1999). The structure of ethnic identity of young adolescents from diverse ethnocultural groups. *Journal of Early Adolescence, 19,* 301–322.

Robins, C. J. (2002). Zen principles and mindfulness practice in dialectical behavior therapy. *Cognitive and Behavioral Practice, 9,* 50–57.

Robinson, D. L. (2001). How brain arousal systems determine different temperament types and the major dimensions of personality. *Personality and Individual Differences, 31,* 1233–1259.

Rode, C., & Wang, X. (2000). Risk-sensitive decision making examined within an evolutionary framework. *American Behavioral Scientist, 43,* 926–939.

Rodriguez, M. L., Mischel, W., & Shoda, Y. (1989). Cognitive person variables in the delay of gratification of older children at risk. *Journal of Personality and Social Psychology, 57,* 358–367.

Roemer, W. W. (1987). An application of the interpersonal models developed by Karen Horney and Timothy Leary to Type A-B behavior patterns. *American Journal of Psychoanalysis, 47,* 116–130.

Rogeness, G. A., & McClure, E. B. (1996). Development and neurotransmitter-environmental interactions. *Development and Psychopathology, 8,* 183–199.

Rogers, C. R. (1942a). *Counseling and psychotherapy: Newer concepts in practice.* Boston: Houghton Mifflin.

Rogers, C. R. (1942b). The use of electrically recorded interviews in improving psychotherapeutic techniques. *American Journal of Orthopsychiatry, 12,* 429–434.

Rogers, C. R. (1951). *Client-centered therapy.* Boston: Houghton Mifflin.

Rogers, C. R. (1954). Towards a theory of creativity. *ETC: A Review of General Semantics, 11,* 249–260.

Rogers, C. R. (1955). Persons or science: A philosophical question. *American Psychologist, 10,* 267–278.

Rogers, C. R. (1956). Intellectualized psychotherapy. *Contemporary Psychology, 1,* 355–358.

Rogers, C. R. (1957a). The necessary and sufficient conditions of therapeutic personality change. *Journal of Consulting Psychology, 21,* 95–103.

Rogers, C. R. (1957b). Personal thoughts on teaching and learning. *Merrill-Palmer Quarterly, 3,* 241–243.

Rogers, C. R. (1959). A theory of therapy, personality, and interpersonal relationships, as developed in the client-centered framework.

In S. Koch (Ed.), *Psychology: A study of a science: Vol. 3. Formulations of the person and the social context* (pp. 185–256). New York: McGraw-Hill.

Rogers, C. R. (1961a). *On becoming a person: A therapist's view of psychotherapy.* Boston: Houghton Mifflin.

Rogers, C. R. (1961b). Ellen West—and loneliness. *Review of Existential Psychology and Psychiatry, 1,* 94–101.

Rogers, C. R. (1963). The actualizing tendency in relation to "motives" and consciousness. In M. R. Jones (Ed.), *Nebraska symposium on motivation* (Vol. 11, pp. 1–24). Lincoln: University of Nebraska Press.

Rogers, C. R. (1964). Toward a modern approach to values: The valuing process in the mature person. *Journal of Abnormal and Social Psychology, 68,* 160–167.

Rogers, C. R. (1967). Carl R. Rogers. In E. G. Boring & G. Lindzey (Eds.), *A history of psychology in autobiography* (Vol. 5, pp. 341–384). New York: Appleton-Century-Crofts.

Rogers, C. R. (1968). Some thoughts regarding the current presuppositions of the behavioral sciences. In W. Coulson & C. R. Rogers (Eds.), *Man and the science of man* (pp. 55–72). Columbus, OH: Chas. E. Merrill.

Rogers, C. R. (1969). *Freedom to learn: A view of what education might become.* Columbus, OH: Merrill.

Rogers, C. R. (1970). *Carl Rogers on encounter groups.* New York: Harper & Row.

Rogers, C. R. (1973). Some new challenges. *American Psychologist, 28,* 379–387.

Rogers, C. R. (1974a). Can learning encompass both ideas and feelings? *Education, 95,* 103–114.

Rogers, C. R. (1974b). The project at Immaculate Heart: An experiment in self-directed change. *Education, 95,* 172–196.

Rogers, C. R. (1974c). In retrospect: Forty-six years. *American Psychologist, 29,* 115–123.

Rogers, C. R. (1977). *Carl Rogers on personal power.* New York: Delacorte Press.

Rogers, C. R. (1979). The foundations of the person-centered approach. *Education, 100,* 98–107.

Rogers, C. R. (1980). *A way of being.* Boston: Houghton Mifflin.

Rogers, C. R. (1982a). A psychologist looks at nuclear war: Its threat, its possible prevention. *Journal of Humanistic Psychology, 22*(4), 9–20.

Rogers, C. R. (1982b). Reply to Rollo May's letter to Carl Rogers. *Journal of Humanistic Psychology, 22*(4), 85–89.

Rogers, C. R. (1983). *Freedom to learn for the 80's.* Columbus, OH: Merrill.

Rogers, C. R. (1986a). Rogers, Kohut, and Erickson: A personal perspective on some similarities and differences. *Person-Centered Review, 1,* 125–140.

Rogers, C. R. (1986b). The Rust workshop. *Journal of Humanistic Psychology, 26*(3), 23–45.

Rogers, C. R. (1986c). Transference. *Person-Centered Review, 2,* 182–188.

Rogers, C. R. (1987). Comments on the issue of equality in psychotherapy. *Journal of Humanistic Psychology, 27*(1), 38–40.

Rogers, C. R. (1989). What I learned from two research studies. In H. Kirschenbaum & V. L. Henderson (Eds.), *The Carl Rogers reader* (pp. 203–211). Boston: Houghton Mifflin.

Rogers, C. R., & Ryback, D. (1984). One alternative to nuclear planetary suicide. *Counseling Psychologist, 12,* 3–12.

Rogers, C. R., & Skinner, B. F. (1956). Some issues concerning the control of human behavior. *Science, 124,* 1057–1066.

Rokeach, M. (1964). *The three Christs of Ypsilanti: A psychological study.* New York: Columbia University Press.

Romanoff, B. (1999). Meaning reconstruction in the wake of loss [Book review]. *Death Studies, 23,* 465–472.

Romm, S., & Slap, J. W. (1983). Sigmund Freud and Salvador Dali: Personal moments. *American Imago, 40,* 337–347.

Roscoe, B., & Peterson, K. L. (1982). Teacher and situational characteristics which enhance learning and development. *College Student Journal, 16,* 389–394.

Rose, G. J. (1983). Sigmund Freud and Salvador Dali: Cultural and historical processes. *American Imago, 40,* 349–353.

Rosen, D. H. (1993). *Transforming depression: Healing the soul through creativity*. New York: Penguin.

Rosen, D. H. (1996). *The Tao of Jung: The way of integrity*. New York: Penguin.

Rosen, D. H., Smith, S. M., Huston, H. L., & Gonzalez, G. (1991). Empirical study of associations between symbols and their meanings: Evidence of collective unconscious (archetypal) memory. *Journal of Analytical Psychology, 36,* 211–228.

Rosen, J. B., & Schulkin, J. (1998). From normal fear to pathological anxiety. *Psychological Review, 105,* 325–350.

Rosenberg, B. G. (2000). Birth order and personality: Is Sulloway's treatment a radical rebellion or is he preserving the status quo? *Politics and the Life Sciences, 19,* 170–172.

Rosenberg, S. D., Schnurr, P. P., & Oxman, T. E. (1990). Content analysis: A comparison of manual and computerized systems. *Journal of Personality Assessment, 54,* 298–310.

Rosenman, S. (1989). Guardians, ferrets and defilers of the treasure: The Masson-Freudians controversy. *Journal of Psychohistory, 16,* 297–321.

Rosenstein, D. S., & Horowitz, H. A. (1996). Adolescent attachment and psychopathology. *Journal of Consulting and Clinical Psychology, 64,* 244–253.

Ross, L. (1977). The intuitive psychologist and his shortcomings: Distortions in the attribution process. In L. Berkowitz (Ed.), *Advances in experimental social psychology* (Vol. 10, pp. 173–220). New York: Academic Press.

Rothbart, M. K., Ahadi, S. A., & Evans, D. E. (2000). Temperament and personality: Origins and outcomes. *Journal of Personality and Social Psychology, 78,* 122–135.

Rothbaum, F., & Weisz, J. R. (1994). Parental caregiving and child externalizing behavior in nonclinical samples: A meta-analysis. *Psychological Bulletin, 116,* 55–74.

Rotter, J. B. (1966). Generalized expectancies for internal versus external control of reinforcement. *Psychological Monographs, 80* (Whole No. 609).

Rotter, J. B. (1990). Internal versus external control of reinforcement: A case history of a variable. *American Psychologist, 45,* 489–493.

Rowan, J. (1999). Ascent and descent in Maslow's theory. *Journal of Humanistic Psychology, 39,* 125–133.

Rowe, D. C. (1997). Genetics, temperament, and personality. In R. Hogan, J. Johnson, & S. Briggs (Eds.), *Handbook of personality psychology* (pp. 367–386). San Diego: Academic Press.

Rubin, K. H. (1998). Social and emotional development from a cultural perspective. *Developmental Psychology, 34,* 611–615.

Rubinstein, B. B. (1980). The problem of confirmation in clinical psychoanalysis. *Journal of the American Psychoanalytic Association, 28,* 397–417.

Ruffman, T., Perner, J., Naito, M., Parkin, L., & Clements, W. A. (1998). Older (but not younger) siblings facilitate false belief understanding. *Developmental Psychology, 34,* 161–174.

Rugel, R. P., & Barry, D. (1990). Overcoming denial through the group: A test of acceptance theory. *Small Group Research, 21,* 45–58.

Runco, M. A., Ebersole, P., & Mraz, W. (1991). Creativity and self-actualization. *Journal of Social Behavior and Personality, 6*(5), 161–167.

Runyan, W. M. (1981). Why did Van Gogh cut off his ear? The problem of alternative explanations in psychobiography. *Journal of Personality and Social Psychology, 40,* 1070–1077.

Runyan, W. M. (1982). The psychobiography debate: An analytical review. In L. Wheeler (Ed.), *Review of personality and social psychology* (Vol. 3, pp. 225–253). Beverly Hills, CA: Sage.

Runyan, W. M. (1983). Idiographic goals and methods in the study of lives. *Journal of Personality, 51,* 413–437.

Runyan, W. M. (1988). *Psychology and historical interpretation*. New York: Oxford University Press.

Runyon, R. S. (1984). Freud and Adler: A conceptual analysis of their differences. *Psychoanalytic Review, 71,* 413–421.

Russell, R. L. (1986). The inadvisability of admixing psychoanalysis with other forms of psychotherapy. *Journal of Contemporary Psychotherapy, 16,* 76–86.

Rutherford, A. (2000). Radical behaviorism and psychology's public: B. F. Skinner in the popular press, 1934–1990. *History of Psychology, 3,* 371–395.

Ruvolo, A. P., & Brennan, C. J. (1997). What's love got to do with it? Close relationships and perceived growth. *Personality and Social Psychology Bulletin, 23,* 814–823.

Ryan, R. M. (1995). Psychological needs and the facilitation of integrative processes. *Journal of Personality, 63,* 397–427.

Ryan, R. M., & Deci, E. L. (2000). Self-determination theory and the facilitation of intrinsic motivation, social development, and well-being. *American Psychologist, 55,* 68–78.

Ryan, R. M., & Deci, E. L. (2001). On happiness and human potentials: A review of research on hedonic and eudaimonic well-being. *Annual Review of Psychology, 52,* 141–166.

Ryan, R. M., Rigby, S., & King, K. (1993). Two types of religious internalization and their relations to religious orientations and mental health. *Journal of Personality and Social Psychology, 65,* 586–596.

Ryback, D. (1983). Jedi and Jungian forces. *Psychological Perspectives, 14,* 238–244.

Rychlak, J. F. (1977). *The psychology of rigorous humanism*. New York: Wiley-Interscience.

Rychlak, J. F. (1984a). Logical learning theory: Kuhnian anomaly or medievalism revisited? *Journal of Mind and Behavior, 5,* 389–416.

Rychlak, J. F. (1984b). Newtonianism and the professional responsibility of psychologists: Who speaks for humanity? *Professional Psychology: Research and Practice, 15,* 82–95.

Rychlak, J. F. (1986). Logical learning theory: A teleological alternative in the field of personality. *Journal of Personality, 54,* 734–762.

Rychlak, J. F. (1988). *The psychology of rigorous humanism* (2nd ed.). New York: New York University Press.

Rychlak, J. F. (1998). How Boulder biases have limited possible theoretical contributions to psychotherapy. *Clinical Psychology: Science and Practice, 5,* 233–241.

Ryckman, R. M., Robbins, M. A., Thornton, B., Gold, J. A., & Kuehnel, R. H. (1985). Physical self-efficacy and actualization. *Journal of Research in Personality, 19,* 288–298.

Sabol, S. Z., Nelson, M. L., Fisher, C., Gunzerath, L., Brody, C. L., Hu, S., Sirota, L. A., Marcus, S. E., Greenberg, B. D., Lucas, F. R., IV, Benjamin, J., Murphy, D. L., & Hamer, D. H. (1999). A genetic association for cigarette smoking behavior. *Health Psychology, 18,* 7–13.

Sackett, S. J. (1998). Career counseling as an aid to self-actualization. *Journal of Career Development, 24,* 235–244.

Salmon, C. A., & Daly, M. (1998). Birth order and familial sentiment: Middleborns are different. *Evolution and Human Behavior, 19,* 299–312.

Salmon, D., & Fenning, P. (1993). A process of mentorship in school consultation. *Journal of Educational and Psychological Consultation, 4*(1), 69–87.

Salmon, D., & Lehrer, R. (1989). School consultant's implicit theories of action. *Professional School Psychology, 4,* 173–187.

Salovey, P., & Mayer, J. D. (1990). Emotional intelligence. *Imagination, Cognition and Personality, 9,* 185–211.

Saltman, V., & Solomon, R. (1982). Incest and the multiple personality. *Psychological Reports, 50,* 1127–1141.

Sampson, E. E. (1977). Psychology and the American ideal. *Journal of Personality and Social Psychology, 35,* 767–782.

Sampson, E. E. (1978). Scientific paradigms and social values: Wanted—A scientific revolution. *Journal of Personality and Social Psychology, 36,* 1332–1343.

Sampson, E. E. (1993). Identity politics: Challenges to psychology's understanding. *American Psychologist, 48,* 1219–1230.

Sanger, M. (1971). *Margaret Sanger: An autobiography*. New York: Dover. (Original work published 1938)

Sappington, A. A. (1990). Recent psychological approaches to the free will versus determinism issue. *Psychological Bulletin, 108,* 19–29.

Sarason, S. B. (1989). The lack of an overarching conception in psychology. *Journal of Mind and Behavior, 10,* 263–279.

Saraswati, N. (2002, May). Balancing the emotions. *Yoga Magazine*. Available online at http://www.yogamag.net/archives/2002/3may02/balemo.shtml

Sarbin, T. R. (1986). The narrative as a root metaphor for psychology. In T. R. Sarbin (Ed.), *Narrative psychology: The storied nature of human conduct* (pp. 3–21). New York: Praeger.

Sarchione, C. D., Cuttler, M. J., Muchinsky, P. M., & Nelson-Gray, R. O. (1998). Prediction of dysfunctional job behaviors among law enforcement officers. *Journal of Applied Psychology, 83,* 904–912.

Saunders, P., & Skar, P. (2001). Archetypes, complexes and self-organization. *Journal of Analytical Psychology, 46,* 305–323.

Sax, K. W., & Strakowski, S. M. (1998). Enhanced behavioral response to repeated d-amphetamine and personality traits in humans. *Biological Psychiatry, 44,* 1192–1195.

Schaefer, S. M., Jackson, D. C., Davidson, R. J., Aguirre, G. K., Kimberg, D. Y., & Thompson-Schill, S. L. (2002). Modulation of amygdalar activity by the conscious regulation of negative emotion. *Journal of Cognitive Neuroscience, 14,* 913–921.

Schaum, M. (2000). "Erasing angel": The Lucifer-trickster figure in Flannery O'Connor's short fiction. *Southern Literary Journal, 33*(1), 1–26.

Schachter, S. (1963). Birth order, eminence, and higher education. *American Sociological Review, 3,* 757–767.

Scheflin, A. W., & Brown, D. (1996). Repressed memory or dissociative amnesia: What the science says. *Journal of Psychiatry and Law, 24,* 143–188.

Schepeler, E. (1990). The biographer's transference: A chapter in psychobiographical epistemology. *Biography, 13,* 111–129.

Scherr, A. (2001). Leonardo Da Vinci, Sigmund Freud, and fear of flying. *Midwest Quarterly, 42,* 115–132.

Schiedel, D. G., & Marcia, J. E. (1985). Ego identity, intimacy, sex role orientation and gender. *Developmental Psychology, 24,* 149–160.

Schmidt, F. L., & Hunter, J. E. (1998). The validity and utility of selection methods in personnel psychology: Practical and theoretical implications of 85 years of research findings. *Psychological Bulletin, 124,* 262–274.

Schmidt, L. A., Fox, N. A., Rubin, K. H., Hu, S., & Hamer, D. H. (2002). Molecular genetics of shyness and aggression in preschoolers. *Personality and Individual Differences, 33,* 227–238.

Schmidt, L. E. (2005, Dec. 16). In the lab with the Dalai Lama. *Chronicle of Higher Education, 52*(7), B10–B11.

Schmitt, D. P., & Buss, D. M. (1996). Strategic self-promotion and competitor derogation: Sex and context effects on the perceived effectiveness of mate attraction tactics. *Journal of Personality and Social Psychology, 70,* 1185–1204.

Schmitt, D. P., & Buss, D. M. (2001). Human mate poaching: Tactics and temptations for infiltrating existing mateships. *Journal of Personality and Social Psychology, 80,* 894–917.

Schmitt, D. R. (1984). Interpersonal relations: Cooperation and competition. *Journal of the Experimental Analysis of Behavior, 42,* 377–383.

Schmutte, P. S., & Ryff, C. D. (1997). Personality and well-being: Reexamining methods and meanings. *Journal of Personality and Social Psychology, 73,* 549–559.

Schnaitter, R. (1987). Behaviorism is not cognitive and cognitivism is not behavioral. *Behaviorism, 15,* 1–11.

Schneider, R. H., Alexander, C. N., Salerno, J., Rainforth, M., & Nidich, S. (2005). Stress reduction in the prevention and treatment of cardiovascular disease in African Americans: A review of controlled research on the Transcendental Meditation program. *Journal of Social Behavior and Personality, 17,* 159–180.

Schneider, R. H., Alexander, C. N., Staggers, F., Rainforth, M., Salerno, J. W., Hartz, A., Arndt, S., Barnes, V. A., & Nidich, S. I. (2005). Long-term effects of stress reduction on mortality in persons ≥55 years of age with systemic hypertension. *American Journal of Cardiology, 95,* 1060–1064.

Schnell, R. L. (1980). Contributions to psychohistory: IV. Individual experience in historiography and psychoanalysis: Significance of Erik Erikson and Robert Coles. *Psychological Reports, 46,* 591–612.

Schore, A. N. (2001). The right brain as the neurobiological substratum of Freud's dynamic unconscious. In D. E. Scharff (Ed.) *The psychoanalytic century: Freud's legacy for the future* (pp. 61–88). New York: Other Press.

Schott, R. L. (1992). Abraham Maslow, humanistic psychology, and organization leadership: A Jungian perspective. *Journal of Humanistic Psychology, 32*(1), 106–120.

Schramski, T. G., & Giovando, K. (1993). Sexual orientation, social interest, and exemplary practice. *Individual Psychology, 49,* 199–204.

Schulkin, J., Morgan, M. A., & Rosen, J. B. (2005). A neuroendocrine mechanism for sustaining fear. *Trends in the Neurosciences, 28,* 629–635.

Schulman, E. (1998). Vulnerability factors in Sylvia Plath's suicide. *Death Studies, 22,* 597–613.

Schultz, G. S. (1996). Taxonomy of rights: A proposed classification system of rights for individuals with mental retardation or developmental disabilities. *Journal of Developmental and Physical Disabilities, 8,* 275–285.

Schurr, K. T., Ruble, V., Palomba, C., Pickerill, B., & Moore, D. (1997). Relationships between the MBTI and selected aspect of Tinto's model for college attrition. *Journal of Psychological Type, 40,* 31–34.

Schwartz, D. (1999). Is a gay Oedipus a Trojan horse? Commentary on Lewes's "A special Oedipal mechanism in the development of male homosexuality." *Psychoanalytic Psychology, 16,* 88–93.

Schwartz, L. K., & Simmons, J. P. (2001). Contact quality and attitudes toward the elderly. *Educational Gerontology, 27,* 127–137.

Schwartz, M. D., Taylor, K. L., Willard, K. S., Siegel, J. E., Lamdan, R. M., & Moran, K. (1999). Distress, personality, and mammography utilization among women with a family history of breast cancer. *Health Psychology, 18,* 327–332.

Scott, N. E., & Borodovsky, L. G. (1990). Effective use of cultural role taking. *Professional Psychology: Research and Practice, 21,* 167–170.

Sears, D. O. (1986). College sophomores in the laboratory: Influences of a narrow data base on social psychology's view of human nature. *Journal of Personality and Social Psychology, 51,* 515–530.

Seeman, T. E., Dubin, L. F., & Seeman, M. (2003). Religiosity/spirituality and health: A critical review of the evidence for biological pathways. *American Psychologist, 58,* 53–63.

Segura, D. A., & Pierce, J. L. (1993). Chicana/o family structure and gender personality: Chodorow, familism, and psychoanalytic sociology revisited. *Signs, 19,* 62–91.

Seligman, M. E. (1992). *Helplessness: On depression, development, and death* (Rev. ed.). New York: W. H. Freeman.

Seligman, M. E. P., & Csikszentmihalyi, M. (2000). Positive psychology: An introduction. *American Psychologist, 55,* 5–14.

Sewell, K. W. (1996). Constructional risk factors for a post-traumatic stress response after a mass murder. *Journal of Constructivist Psychology, 9,* 97–107.

Sewell, K. W., Cromwell, R. L., Farrell-Higgins, J., Palmer, R., Ohlde, C., & Patterson, T. W. (1996). Hierarchical elaboration in the conceptual structures of Vietnam combat veterans. *Journal of Constructivist Psychology, 9,* 79–96.

Sexton, H. (1993). Exploring a psychotherapeutic change sequence: Relating process to intersessional and posttreatment outcome. *Journal of Consulting and Clinical Psychology, 61,* 128–136.

Sexton, T. L., & Tuckman, B. W. (1991). Self-beliefs and behavior: The role of self-efficacy and outcome expectation over time. *Personality and Individual Differences, 12,* 725–736.

Shafran, R., & Mansell, W. (2001). Perfectionism and psychopathology: A review of research and treatment. *Clinical Psychology Review, 21,* 879–906.

Shamdasani, S. (1998). *Cult fictions: C. G. Jung and the founding of analytical psychology.* London: Routledge.

Shapiro, B. L. (1991). The use of personal construct theory and the repertory grid in the development of case reports of children's science learning. *International Journal of Personal Construct Psychology, 4,* 251–271.

Shapiro, J. P., Leifer, M., Martone, M. W., & Kassem, L. (1990). Multimethod assessment of depression in sexually abused girls. *Journal of Personality Assessment, 55,* 234–248.

Shapiro, K. (2002). Freudian slipage [Book review]. *Commentary, 113,* 60–63.

Shapiro, S. B. (1997). The UCSB Confluent Education Program: Its essence and demise. *Journal of Humanistic Psychology, 37*(3), 80–105.

Shapiro, S. B. (1998). *The place of confluent education in the human potential movement: A historical perspective.* Lanham, MD: University Press of America.

Shapiro, S. L., Astin, J. A., Bishop, S. R., & Cordova, M. (2005). Mindfulness-based stress reduction for health care professionals: Results from a randomized. trial. *International Journal of Stress Management, 12,* 164–176.

Sharpe, T. M., Killen, J. D., Bryson, S. W., Shisslak, C. M., Estes, L. S., Gray, N., Crago, M., & Taylor, C. B. (1998). Attachment style and weight concerns in preadolescent and adolescent girls. *International Journal of Eating Disorders, 23,* 39–44.

Sharpsteen, D. J., & Kirkpatrick, L. A. (1997). Romantic jealousy and adult romantic attachment. *Journal of Personality and Social Psychology, 72,* 627–640.

Shatz, S. M. (2004). The relationship between Horney's three neurotic types and Eysenck's PEN model of personality. *Personality and Individual Differences, 37,* 1255–1261.

Shaver, P. R., & Brennan, K. A. (1992). Attachment styles and the "big five" personality traits: Their connections with each other and with romantic outcomes. *Personality and Social Psychology Bulletin, 18,* 536–545.

Shean, G. (2001). A critical look at the assumptions of cognitive therapy. *Psychiatry, 64,* 158–164.

Shelton, S. H. (1990). Developing the construct of general self-efficacy. *Psychological Reports, 66,* 987–994.

Sher, K. J., & Wood, M. D. (1995). The Tridimensional Personality Questionnaire: Reliability and validity studies and derivation of a short form. *Psychological Assessment, 7,* 195–208.

Sherman, R., & Dinkmeyer, D. (1987). *Systems of family therapy: An Adlerian integration.* New York: Brunner/Mazel.

Shiflett, S. C. (1989). Validity evidence for the Myers-Briggs Type Indicator as a measure of hemisphere dominance. *Educational and Psychological Measurement, 49,* 741–745.

Shiner, R. L. (1998). How shall we speak of children's personalities in middle childhood? A preliminary taxonomy. *Psychological Bulletin, 124,* 308–332.

Shoda, Y., Mischel, W., & Peake, P. K. (1990). Predicting adolescent cognitive and self-regulatory competencies from preschool delay of gratification: Identifying diagnostic conditions. *Developmental Psychology, 26,* 978–986.

Shoda, Y., Mischel, W., & Wright, J. C. (1989). Intuitive interactionism in person perception: Effects of situation-behavior relations on dispositional judgments. *Journal of Personality and Social Psychology, 56,* 41–53.

Shoda, Y., Mischel, W., & Wright, J. C. (1994). Intraindividual stability in the organization and patterning of behavior: Incorporating psychological situations into the idiographic analysis of personality. *Journal of Personality and Social Psychology, 67,* 674–687.

Shore, J. (2003). A Buddhist model of the human self: Working through the Jung-Hisamatsu discussion. In P. Young-Eisendrath (Ed.), *Awakening and insight: Zen Buddhism and psychotherapy* (pp. 29–42). Florence, KY: Routledge.

Shostrom, E. L. (1964). An inventory for the measurement of self-actualization. *Educational and Psychological Measurement, 24,* 207–217.

Shostrom, E. L. (Producer). (1965). *Three approaches to psychotherapy* (part 1) [Motion picture]. Orange, CA: Psychological Films.

Shostrom, E. L. (1972). *Freedom to be: Experiencing and expressing your total being.* Englewood Cliffs, NJ: Prentice-Hall.

Shostrom, E. L. (1974). *Manual for the Personal Orientation Inventory.* San Diego, CA: Educational and Industrial Testing Service.

Shostrom, E. L. (1975). Rejoinder to Anderson's article. *Journal of Humanistic Psychology, 15*(1), 35.

Shotter, J. (1997). The social construction of our inner selves. *Journal of Constructivist Psychology, 10,* 7–24.

Shulman, D. G. (1990). The investigation of psychoanalytic theory by means of the experimental method. *International Journal of Psycho-Analysis, 71,* 487–498.

Shulman, D. G., & Ferguson, G. R. (1988). An experimental investigation of Kernberg's and Kohut's theories of narcissism. *Journal of Clinical Psychology, 44,* 445–451.

Siegel, B. (1982). Penis envy: From anatomical deficiency to narcissistic disturbance. *Bulletin of the Menninger Clinic, 46,* 363–376.

Silon, B. (1992). Dissociation: A symptom of incest. *Individual Psychology: Journal of Adlerian Theory, Research and Practice, 48,* 155–164.

Silverman, D. K. (1998). The tie that binds: Affect regulation, attachment, and psychoanalysis. *Psychoanalytic Psychology, 15,* 187–212.

Silverman, L. H. (1976). Psychoanalytic theory: "The reports of my death are greatly exaggerated." *American Psychologist, 31,* 621–635.

Silverman, L. H. (1983). The subliminal psychodynamic activation method: Overview and comprehensive listing of studies. In J. Masling (Ed.), *Empirical studies of psychoanalytic theories* (Vol. 1, pp. 69–100). Hillsdale, NJ: Analytic Press.

Silverman, L. H., Bronstein, A., & Mendelsohn, E. (1976). The further use of the subliminal psychodynamic activation method for the experimental study of the clinical theory of psychoanalysis: On the specificity of relationships between manifest psychopathology and unconscious conflict. *Psychotherapy: Theory, Research and Practice, 13,* 2–16.

Silverman, L. H., Frank, S. G., & Dachinger, P. (1974). A psychoanalytic reinterpretation of the effectiveness of systematic desensitization: Experimental data bearing on the role of merging fantasies. *Journal of Abnormal Psychology, 83,* 313–318.

Silverman, L. H., Kwawer, J. S., Wolitzky, C., & Coron, M. (1973). An experimental study of aspects of the psychoanalytic theory of male homosexuality. *Journal of Abnormal Psychology, 82,* 178–188.

Silverman, L. H., Martin, A., Ungaro, R., & Mendelsohn, E. (1978). Effect of subliminal stimulation of symbiotic fantasies on behavior modification treatment of obesity. *Journal of Consulting and Clinical Psychology, 46,* 432–441.

Silverman, L. H., Ross, D. L., Adler, J. M., & Lustig, D. A. (1978). Simple research paradigm for demonstrating subliminal psychodynamic activation: Effects of Oedipal stimuli on dart-throwing accuracy in college males. *Journal of Abnormal Psychology, 87,* 341–357.

Silverstein, S. M. (1993). Methodological and empirical considerations in assessing the validity of psychoanalytic theories of hypnosis. *Genetic, Social, and General Psychology Monographs, 119,* 5–54.

Simon, L., Greenberg, J., Harmon-Jones, E., Solomon, S., Pyszczynski, T., Arndt, J., & Abend, T. (1997). Terror management and cognitive-experiential self-theory: Evidence that terror management occurs in the experiential system. *Journal of Personality and Social Psychology, 72,* 1132–1146.

Simonton, D. K. (1998). Mad King George: The impact of personal and political stress on mental and physical health. *Journal of Personality, 66,* 443–466.

Singer, J. (1994). *Boundaries of the soul: The practice of Jung's psychology* (Rev. ed.). New York: Anchor.

Singh, N. N., Wahler, R. G., Adkins, A. D., & Myers, R. E. (2003). Soles of the feet: A mindfulness-based self-control intervention for aggression by an individual with mild mental retardation and mental illness. *Research in Developmental Disabilities, 24,* 158–169.

Sipe, R. B. (1987). False premises, false promises: A re-examination of the human potential movement. *Issues in Radical Therapy, 12*(4), 26–29, 49–53.

Sipps, G. J., & Alexander, R. A. (1987). The multifactorial nature of extraversion-introversion in the Myers-Briggs Type Indicator and Eysenck Personality Inventory. *Educational and Psychological Measurement, 47,* 543–552.

Sipps, G. J., & DiCaudo, J. (1988). Convergent and discriminant validity of the Myers-Briggs Type Indicator as a measure of sociability and impulsivity. *Educational and Psychological Measurement, 48,* 445–451.

Sizemore, C. C., & Huber, R. J. (1988). The twenty-two faces of Eve. *Individual Psychology, 44,* 53–62.

Skinner, B. F. (1938). *The behavior of organisms.* New York: Appleton-Century.

Skinner, B. F. (1945, October). Baby in a box. *Ladies' Home Journal*, p. 30.

Skinner, B. F. (1948). *Walden two*. New York: Macmillan.

Skinner, B. F. (1950). Are theories of learning necessary? *Psychological Review, 57,* 193–216.

Skinner, B. F. (1953a). *Science and human behavior*. New York: Free Press.

Skinner, B. F. (1953b). Some contributions to an experimental analysis of behavior and to psychology as a whole. *American Psychologist, 8,* 69–78.

Skinner, B. F. (1954). The science of learning and the art of teaching. *Harvard Educational Review, 24,* 86–97.

Skinner, B. F. (1957). *Verbal behavior*. New York: Appleton-Century-Crofts.

Skinner, B. F. (1958a). *Notebooks* (R. Epstein, Ed.). Englewood Cliffs, NJ: Prentice-Hall.

Skinner, B. F. (1958b). Teaching machines. *Science, 128,* 969–977.

Skinner, B. F. (1963). Behaviorism at fifty. *Science, 140,* 951–958.

Skinner, B. F. (1967). Autobiography. In E. G. Boring & G. Lindzey (Eds.), *A history of psychology in autobiography* (Vol. 5, pp. 385–413). New York: Appleton-Century-Crofts.

Skinner, B. F. (1968). *The technology of teaching*. New York: Appleton-Century-Crofts.

Skinner, B. F. (1971). *Beyond freedom and dignity*. New York: Knopf.

Skinner, B. F. (1972). *Cumulative record: A selection of papers* (3rd ed.). New York: Appleton-Century Crofts.

Skinner, B. F. (1975). The steep and thorny way to a science of behavior. *American Psychologist, 30,* 42–49.

Skinner, B. F. (1976). *Particulars of my life*. New York: Knopf.

Skinner, B. F. (1979). *The shaping of a behaviorist*. New York: Knopf.

Skinner, B. F. (1984). The shame of American education. *American Psychologist, 39,* 947–954.

Skinner, B. F. (1989). Teaching machines. *Science, 243,* 1535.

Skinner, B. F. (1990). Can psychology be a science of mind? *American Psychologist, 45,* 1206–1210.

Skinner, N. F., & Peters, P. L. (1984). National personality characteristics: Comparison of Canadian, American and British samples. *Psychological Reports, 54,* 121–122.

Slade, P. D., & Owens, R. G. (1998). A dual process model of perfectionism based on reinforcement theory. *Behavior Modification, 22,* 372–390.

Slife, B. D. (1981). Psychology's reliance on linear time: A reformulation. *Journal of Mind and Behavior, 2,* 27–46.

Slote, W. H. (1992). Oedipal ties and the issue of separation-individuation in traditional Confucian societies. *Journal of the American Academy of Psychoanalysis, 20,* 435–453.

Smith, C. P. (Ed.). (1992). *Handbook of thematic content analysis*. New York: Cambridge University Press.

Smith, H. (1985). The sacred unconscious, with footnotes on self-actualization and evil. *Journal of Humanistic Psychology, 25*(3), 65–80.

Smith, M. B. (1973). On self-actualization: A transambivalent examination of a focal theme in Maslow's psychology. *Journal of Humanistic Psychology, 13*(2), 17–33.

Smith, M. B. (1990). Humanistic psychology. *Journal of Humanistic Psychology, 30*(4), 6–21.

Smith, M. B. (1994). "Human science"—Really! A theme for the future of psychology. *Journal of Humanistic Psychology, 34*(3), 111–116.

Smith, T. L. (1983). Skinner's environmentalism: The analogy with natural selection. *Behaviorism, 11,* 133–153.

Smith, T. W. (1992). Changing racial labels: From "Colored" to "Negro" to "Black" to "African American." *Public Opinion Quarterly, 56,* 496–514.

Smyth, J. M. (1998). Written emotional expression: Effect sizes, outcome types, and moderating variables. *Journal of Consulting and Clinical Psychology, 66,* 174–184.

Sneed, C. D., McCrae, R. R., & Funder, D. C. (1998). Lay conceptions of the five-factor model and its indicators. *Personality and Social Psychology Bulletin, 24,* 115–126.

So, K., & Orme-Johnson, D. W. (2001). Three randomized experiments on the longitudinal effects of the Transcendental Meditation technique on cognition. *Intelligence, 29,* 419–440.

Sohier, R. (1985–1986). Homosexual mutuality: Variation on a theme by Erik Erikson. *Journal of Homosexuality, 12*(2), 25–38.

Sohlberg, S., Billinghurst, A., & Nylén, S. (1998). Moderation of mood change after subliminal symbiotic stimulation: Four experiments contributing to the further demystification of Silverman's "Mommy and I are one" findings. *Journal of Research in Personality, 32,* 33–54.

Sohlberg, S., Samuelberg, P., Sidén, Y., & Thörn, C. (1998). Caveat medicus—Let the subliminal healer beware: Two experiments suggesting conditions when the effects of Silverman's *Mommy and I are one* phrase are negative. *Psychoanalytic Psychology, 15,* 93–114.

Sohn, D., & Lamal, P. A. (1982). Self-reinforcement: Its reinforcing capability and its clinical utility. *Psychological Record, 32,* 179–203.

Soldz, S., & Vaillant, G. E. (1999). The Big Five personality traits and the life course: A 45-year longitudinal study. *Journal of Research in Personality, 33,* 208–232.

Somer, O., & Goldberg, L. R. (1999). The structure of Turkish trait-descriptive adjectives. *Journal of Personality and Social Psychology, 76,* 431–450.

Soresi, S., & Nota, L. (2000). A social skill training for persons with Down's syndrome. *European Psychologist, 5,* 33–43.

Spaccarelli, S. (1994). Stress, appraisal, and coping in child sexual abuse: A theoretical and empirical review. *Psychological Bulletin, 116,* 340–362.

Spanos, N. P. (1994). Multiple identity enactments and multiple personality disorder: A sociocognitive perspective. *Psychological Bulletin, 116,* 143–165.

Spanos, N. P., Burgess, C. A., Cocco, L., & Pinch, N. (1993). Reporting bias and response to difficult suggestions in highly hypnotizable hypnotic subjects. *Journal of Research in Personality, 27,* 270–284.

Spanos, N. P., Sims, A., de Faye, B., Mondoux, T. J., & Gabora, N. J. (1992–1993). A comparison of hypnotic and nonhypnotic treatments for smoking. *Imagination, Cognition and Personality, 12,* 12–43.

Spencer, M. B., & Markstrom-Adams, C. (1990). Identity processes among racial and ethnic minority children in America. *Child Development, 61,* 290–310.

Sperling, M. B., & Berman, W. H. (1991). An attachment classification of desperate love. *Journal of Personality Assessment, 56,* 45–55.

Sperling, M. B., Berman, W. H., & Fagen, G. (1992). Classification of adult attachment: An integrative taxonomy from attachment and psychoanalytic theories. *Journal of Personality Assessment, 59,* 239–247.

Sperry, L. (1992). Recent developments in neuroscience, behavioral medicine, and psychoneuroimmunology: Implications for physical and psychological well-being. *Individual Psychology, 48,* 480–487.

Sperry, R. W. (1988). Psychology's mentalist paradigm and the religion/science tension. *American Psychologist, 43,* 607–613.

Sperry, R. W. (1990). Structure and significance of the consciousness revolution. *Person-Centered Review, 5,* 120–129.

Spielberg, S. (Director), & Lustig, B. (Producer). (1993). *Schindler's list* [Motion picture]. Hollywood: Universal Pictures.

Spink, K. (1997). *Mother Teresa: A complete authorized biography*. New York: HarperCollins.

Spitz, R. A. (1945). Hospitalism. *Psychoanalytic Study of the Child, 2,* 53–74.

Staats, A. W. (1968). *Learning, language, and cognition*. New York: Holt, Rinehart & Winston.

Staats, A. W. (1971). *Child learning, intelligence and personality*. New York: Harper and Row.

Staats, A. W. (1975). *Social behaviorism*. Homewood, IL: Dorsey.

Staats, A. W. (1981). Social behaviorism, unified theory, unified theory construction methods, and the Zeitgeist of separatism. *American Psychologist, 36,* 239–256.

Staats, A. W. (1986). Behaviorism with a personality: The paradigmatic behavioral assessment approach. In R. O. Nelson & S. C. Hayes (Eds.), *Conceptual foundations of behavioral assessment* (pp. 242–296). New York: Guilford.

Staats, A. W. (1988). Skinner's theory and the emotion-behavior relationship: Incipient change with major implications. *American Psychologist, 43,* 747–748.

Staats, A. W. (1991). Unified positivism and unification psychology: Fad or new field? *American Psychologist, 46,* 899–912.

Staats, A. W. (1993). Personality theory, abnormal psychology, and psychological measurement: A psychological behaviorism. *Behavior Modification, 17,* 8–42.

Staats, A. W. (1996). *Behavior and personality: Psychological behaviorism.* New York: Springer.

Staats, A. W. (1999). Unifying psychology requires new infrastructure, theory, method, and a research agenda. *Review of General Psychology, 3,* 3–13.

Staats, A. W., & Burns, G. L. (1981). Intelligence and child development: What intelligence is and how it is learned and functions. *Genetic Psychology Monographs, 104,* 237–301.

Staats, A. W., & Burns, G. L. (1982). Emotional personality repertoire as cause of behavior: Specification of personality and interaction principles. *Journal of Personality and Social Psychology, 43,* 873–881.

Staats, A. W., & Eifert, G. H. (1990). The paradigmatic behaviorism theory of emotions. *Clinical Psychology Review, 10,* 539–566.

Staats, A. W., Gross, M. C., Guay, P. F., & Carlson, C. C. (1973). Personality and social systems and attitude-reinforcer-discriminative theory: Interest (attitude) formation, function, and measurement. *Journal of Personality and Social Psychology, 26,* 251–261.

Staats, A. W., & Heiby, E. M. (1985). Paradigmatic behaviorism's theory of depression: Unified, explanatory, and heuristic. In S. Reiss & R. R. Bootzin (Eds.), *Theoretical issues in behavior therapy* (pp. 279–330). New York: Academic Press.

Stajkovic, A. D., & Luthans, F. (1998). Self-efficacy and work-related performance: A meta-analysis. *Psychological Bulletin, 124,* 240–261.

Stålenheim, E. G., Eriksson, E., von Knorring, L., & Wide, L. (1998). Testosterone as a biological marker in psychopathy and alcoholism. *Psychiatry Research, 77,* 79–88.

Stallings, M. C., Hewitt, J. K., Cloninger, C. R., Heath, A. C., & Eaves, L. J. (1996). Genetic and environmental structure of the Tridimensional Personality Questionnaire: Three or four temperament dimensions? *Journal of Personality and Social Psychology, 70,* 127–140.

Stam, H. J. (1998). Personal-construct theory and social constructivism: Difference and dialogue. *Journal of Constructivist Psychology, 11,* 187–203.

Stamatelos, T. (1984). Peak and plateau experiences among persons labeled mentally retarded. *Arts in Psychotherapy, 11,* 109–115.

State v. Michaels, 264 N. J. Super. 579, 625 A.2d 489 (N.J. Super. Ad., 1993)

Staudinger, U. M., Fleeson, W., & Baltes, P. B. (1999). Predictors of subjective physical health and global well-being: Similarities and differences between the United States and Germany. *Journal of Personality and Social Psychology, 76,* 305–319.

Stava, L. J., & Jaffa, M. (1988). Some operationalizations of the neodissociation concept and their relationship to hypnotic susceptibility. *Journal of Personality and Social Psychology, 54,* 989–996.

Steblay, N. M., & Bothwell, R. K. (1994). Evidence for hypnotically refreshed testimony: The view from the laboratory. *Law and Human Behavior, 18,* 635–651.

Steele, C. M., & Josephs, R. A. (1990). Alcohol myopia: Its prized and dangerous effects. *American Psychologist, 45,* 921–933.

Stein, H. (1988). Twelve stages of creative Adlerian psychotherapy. *Individual Psychology, 44,* 138–143.

Stein, H. T., & Edwards, M. E. (1998). Classical Adlerian theory and practice. In *Psychoanalytic versions of the human condition and clinical practice: Philosophies of life and their impact on practice.* (P. Marcus & A. Rosenberg, Eds.). New York: New York University Press.

Steinem, G. (1986). *Marilyn: Norma Jeane.* New York: Signet.

Steklis, H. D., & Walter, A. (1991). Culture, biology, and human nature: A mechanistic approach. *Human Nature, 2,* 137–169.

Stelmack, R. M. (1997). The psychophysics and psychophysiology of extraversion and arousal. In H. Nyborg (Ed.), *The scientific study of human nature: Tribute to Hans J. Eysenck at eighty* (pp. 388–403). New York: Pergamon.

Stenberg, G. (1992). Personality and the EEG: Arousal and emotional arousability. *Personality and Individual Differences, 13,* 1097–1113.

Stenberg, G. (1994). Extraversion and the P300 in a visual classification task. *Personality and Individual Differences, 16,* 543–560.

Stenberg, G., Johansson, M., Olsson, A., Lindgren, M., & Rosen, I. (2000). Semantic processing without conscious identification: Evidence from event-related potentials. *Journal of Experimental Psychology: Learning, Memory, and Cognition, 26,* 973–1004.

Stenberg, G., Risberg, J., Warkentin, S., & Rosen, I. (1990). Regional patterns of cortical blood flow distinguish extraverts from introverts. *Personality and Individual Differences, 11,* 663–673.

Stenberg, G., Wendt, P. E., & Risberg, J. (1993). Regional cerebral blood flow and extraversion. *Personality and Individual Differences, 15,* 547–554.

Stenberg, G., Wiking, S., & Dahl, M. (1998). Judging words at face value: Interference in a word processing task reveals automatic processing of affective facial expressions. *Cognition and Emotion, 12,* 755–782.

Stephens, R. S., Wertz, J. S., & Roffman, R. A. (1995). Self-efficacy and marijuana cessation: A construct validity analysis. *Journal of Consulting and Clinical Psychology, 63,* 1022–1031.

Stern, P. J. (1976). *The haunted prophet.* New York: Delta Books.

Stevens, A. (1995). Jungian psychology, the body, and the future. *Journal of Analytical Psychology, 40,* 353–364.

Stewart, A. J., Franz, C., & Layton, L. (1988). The changing self: Using personal documents to study lives. *Journal of Personality, 56,* 41–74.

Stewart, R. B., Verbrugge, K. M., & Beilfuss, M. C. (1998). Sibling relationships in early adulthood: A typology. *Personal Relationships, 5,* 59–74.

Stewart, V., & Stewart, A. (1982). *Business applications of repertory grid.* London: McGraw-Hill.

Stifler, K., Greer, J., Sneck, W., & Dovenmuehle, R. (1993). An empirical investigation of the discriminability of reported mystical experiences among religious contemplatives, psychotic inpatients, and normal adults. *Journal for the Scientific Study of Religion, 32,* 366–372.

Stock, J., & Cervone, D. (1990). Proximal goal-setting and self-regulatory processes. *Cognitive Therapy and Research, 14,* 483–498.

Stone, A. A., Kessler, R. C., & Haythornthwaite, J. A. (1991). Measuring daily events and experiences: Decisions for the researcher. *Journal of Personality, 59,* 575–607.

Stone, A. A., Schwartz, J. E., Neale, J. M., Shiffman, S., Marco, C. A., Hickcox, M., Paty, J., Porter, L. S., & Cruise, L. J. (1998). A comparison of coping assessed by ecological momentary assessment and retrospective recall. *Journal of Personality and Social Psychology, 74,* 1670–1680.

Stone, L. (1981). *The past and the present.* Boston: Routledge & Kegan Paul.

Storm, L., & Thalbourne, M. A. (2001). Studies of the I Ching: I. A replication. *Journal of Parapsychology, 65,* 105–124.

Strand, P. S. (2001). Momentum, matching, and meaning: Toward a fuller exploitation of operant principles. *Behavior Analyst Today, 2,* 170–175.

Stratton, G. M. (2005). *Anger: Its religious and moral significance.* New York: Macmillan. (Reprinted electronic version from PsycBOOKS, Accession No. 2005–00637–000) (Original work published 1923)

Streitmatter, J. (1993). Gender differences in identity development: An examination of longitudinal data. *Adolescence, 28,* 55–66.

Strelau, J. (1997). The contribution of Pavlov's typology of CNS properties to personality research. *European Psychologist, 2,* 125–138.

Stroebe, M,, Schut, H., & Stroebe, W, (2006). Who benefits from disclosure? Exploration of attachment style differences in the effects of expressing emotions. *Clinical Psychology Review, 26,* 66–85.

Strube, M. J., & Ota, S. (1982). Type A coronary-prone behavior pattern: Relationship to birth order and family size. *Personality and Social Psychology Bulletin, 8,* 317–323.

Strupp, H. H. (2001). Implications of the empirically supported treatment movement for psychoanalysis. *Psychoanalytic Dialogues, 11,* 605–619.

Sudak, H. S. (2000). Current theories of psychoanalysis [Book review]. *American Journal of Psychiatry, 157,* 300–301.

Suedfeld, P., & Bluck, S. (1993). Changes in integrative complexity accompanying significant life events: Historical evidence. *Journal of Personality and Social Psychology, 64,* 124–130.

Suedfeld, P., Corteen, R. S., & McCormick, C. (1986). The role of integrative complexity in military leadership: Robert E. Lee and his opponents. *Journal of Applied Social Psychology, 16,* 498–507.

Sugarman, A. (1991). Where's the beef? Putting personality back into personality assessment. *Journal of Personality Assessment, 56,* 130–144.

Sugiyama, M. S. (2001). New science, old myth: An evolutionary critique of the Oedipal paradigm. *Mosaic: A Journal for the Interdisciplinary Study of Literature, 34,* 121–136.

Sullivan, G. (1990). Discrimination and self-concept of homosexuals before the gay liberation movement: A biographical analysis examining social context and identity. *Biography, 13,* 203–221.

Sullivan, H. S. (1953). *The interpersonal theory of psychiatry.* New York: Norton.

Sulloway, F. J. (1979). *Freud, biologist of the mind: Beyond the psychoanalytic legend.* New York: Basic Books.

Sulloway, F. J. (1996). *Born to rebel: Birth order, family dynamics, and creative lives.* New York: Vintage Books.

Sumedho, B. (1992). *The four noble truths.* Hertfordshire, UK: Amaravati. Available online at http://www.buddhanet.net/pdf_file/4nobltru.pdf

Sumerlin, J. R., & Bundrick, C. M. (1996). Brief Index of Self-Actualization: A measure of Maslow's model. *Journal of Social Behavior and Personality, 11,* 253–271.

Sumerlin, J. R., & Bundrick, C. M. (1998). Revision of the Brief Index of Self-Actualization. *Perceptual and Motor Skills, 87,* 115–125.

Summers, A. (1985). *Goddess: The secret lives of Marilyn Monroe.* New York: New American Library.

Sundberg, N. D. (1965). *The sixth mental measurements yearbook* (pp. 322–325). Highland Park, NJ: Gryphon Press.

Sutton, S. K., & Davidson, R. J. (1997). Prefrontal brain asymmetry: A biological substrate of the behavioral approach and inhibition systems. *Psychological Science, 8,* 204–210.

Swansbrough, R. H. (1994). A Kohutian analysis of President Bush's personality and style in the Persian Gulf crisis. *Political Psychology, 15,* 227–276.

Sweeny, T. J., & Myers, J. E. (1986). Early recollections: An Adlerian technique with older people. *Clinical Gerontologist, 4,* 3–12.

Swickert, R. J., & Gilliland, K. (1998). Relationship between the brain-stem auditory evoked response and extraversion, impulsivity, and sociability. *Journal of Research in Personality, 32,* 314–330.

Symonds, A. (1991). Gender issues and Horney theory. *American Journal of Psychoanalysis, 51,* 301–312.

Szasz, T. (2001). Mental illness: Psychiatry's phlogiston. *Journal of Medical Ethics, 27,* 297–301.

Szasz, T. S. (1998). The healing word: Its past, present, and future. *Journal of Humanistic Psychology, 38,* 8–20.

Talbot, R., Cooper, C. L., & Ellis, B. (1991). Uses of the dependency grid for investigating social support in stressful situations. *Stress Medicine, 7*(3), 171–180.

Tangney, J. P. (1990). Assessing individual differences in proneness to shame and guilt: Development of the Self-Conscious Affect and Attribution Inventory. *Journal of Personality and Social Psychology, 59,* 102–111.

Tangney, J. P. (1994). The mixed legacy of the superego: Adaptive and maladaptive aspects of shame and guilt. In M. J. Masling & R. F. Bornstein (Eds.), *Empirical perspectives on object relations theory.* Washington, DC: American Psychological Association.

Tangney, J. P., Hill-Barlow, D., Wagner, P. E., Marschall, D. E., Borenstein, J. K., Sanftner, J., Mohr, T., & Gramzow, R. (1996). Assessing individual differences in constructive versus destructive responses to anger across the lifespan. *Journal of Personality and Social Psychology, 70,* 780–796.

Tangney, J. P., Wagner, P. E., Hill-Barlow, D., Marschall, D. E., & Gramzow, R. (1996). Relation of shame and guilt to constructive versus destructive responses to anger across the lifespan. *Journal of Personality and Social Psychology, 70,* 797–809.

Tart, C. T. (1992). Perspectives on scientism, religion, and philosophy provided by parapsychology. *Journal of Humanistic Psychology, 32*(2), 70–100.

Taub, J. M. (1998). Eysenck's descriptive and biological theory of personality: A review of construct validity. *International Journal of Neuroscience, 94*(3–4), 145–198.

Taylor, E. (1998). Jung before Freud, not Freud before Jung: The reception of Jung's work in American psychoanalytic circles between 1904 and 1909. *Journal of Analytical Psychology, 43,* 97–114.

Taylor, E. (2000). "What is man, psychologist, that thou art so unmindful of him?": Henry A. Murray on the historical relation between classical personality theory and humanistic psychology. *Journal of Humanistic Psychology, 40,* 29–42.

Taylor, J. C., & Romanczyk, R. G. (1994). Generating hypotheses about the function of student problem behavior by observing teacher behavior. *Journal of Applied Behavior Analysis, 27,* 251–265.

Taylor, J. G. (2002). Paying attention to consciousness. *Trends in the Cognitive Sciences, 6,* 206–210.

Taylor, M. C., & Hall, J. A. (1982). Psychological androgyny: Theories, methods, and conclusions. *Psychological Bulletin, 92,* 347–366.

Taylor, S. E., Klein, L. C., Lewis, B. P., Gruenewald, T. L., Gurung, R. A. R., & Updegraff, J. A. (2000). Biobehavioral responses to stress in females: Tend-and-befriend, not fight-or-flight. *Psychological Review, 107,* 411–429.

Tegano, D. W. (1990). Relationship of tolerance of ambiguity and playfulness to creativity. *Psychological Reports, 66,* 1047–1056.

Teixeira, B. (1987). Comments on ahimsa (nonviolence). *Journal of Transpersonal Psychology, 19,* 1–17.

Tenopyr, M. L. (1995). The complex interaction between measurement and national employment. *Psychology, Public Policy, and Law, 2,* 348–362.

Tesser, A. (1993). The importance of heritability in psychological research: The case of attitudes. *Psychological Review, 100,* 129–142.

Teti, D. M., & Gelfand, D. M. (1991). Behavioral competence among mothers of infants in the first year: The mediational role of maternal self-efficacy. *Child Development, 62,* 918–929.

The Transcendental Meditation Program. (2005). Available at http://www.tm.org/

Thom, D. P., & Coetzee, C. H. (2004). Identity development of South African adolescents in a democratic society. *Society in Transition, 35,* 183–193.

Thomas, A., & Chess, S. (1977). *Temperament and development.* New York: Brunner-Mazel.

Thomas, C. B. (1988). Cancer and the youthful mind: A forty-year perspective. *Advances, 5*(2), 42–58.

Thompson, B., & Borrello, G. M. (1986). Construct validity of the Myers-Briggs Type Indicator. *Educational and Psychological Measurement, 46,* 745–752.

Thompson, R. F. (1994). Behaviorism and neuroscience. *Psychological Review, 101,* 259–265.

Thomson, N. F., & Martinko, M. J. (1995). The relationship between MBTI types and attributional style. *Journal of Psychological Type, 35,* 22–30.

Thomson, R. F. (2000). Zazen and psychotherapeutic presence. *American Journal of Psychotherapy, 54,* 531–548.

Thorne, B. M., Fyfe, J. H., & Carskadon, T. G. (1987). The Myers-Briggs Type Indicator and coronary heart disease. *Journal of Personality Assessment, 51,* 545–554.

Ticho, E. A. (1982). The alternate schools and the self. *Journal of the American Psychoanalytic Association, 30,* 849–862.

Tiger Woods profile. (2006). Available at http://www.tigerwoods.com/content/default.sps?iType=6266

Tillman, J. G., Nash, M. R., & Lerner, P. M. (1994). Does trauma cause dissociative pathology? In S. S. Lynn & J. W. Rhue (Eds.), *Dissociation: Clinical and theoretical perspectives* (pp. 395–414). New York: Guilford.

Tinling, L. (1990). Perpetuation of incest by significant others: Mothers who do not want to see. *Individual Psychology, 46,* 280–297.

Tloczynski, J. (1993). Is the self essential? Handling reductionism. *Perceptual and Motor Skills, 76,* 723–732.

Tloczynski, J., Knoll, C., & Fitch, A. (1997). The relationship among spirituality, religious ideology, and personality. *Journal of Psychology and Theology, 25,* 208–213.

Tobacyk, J. J., & Downs, A. (1986). Personal construct threat and irrational beliefs as cognitive predictors of increases in musical performance anxiety. *Journal of Personality and Social Psychology, 51,* 779–782.

Tobey, L. H., & Bruhn, A. R. (1992). Early memories and the criminally dangerous. *Journal of Personality Assessment, 59,* 137–152.

Tobin, S. A. (1991). A comparison of psychoanalytic self psychology and Carl Rogers's person-centered therapy. *Journal of Humanistic Psychology, 31*(1), 9–33.

Todd, J. T., & Morris, E. K. (1992). Case histories in the great power of steady misrepresentation. *American Psychologist, 47,* 1441–1453.

Tomarken, A. J., Davidson, R. J., & Henriques, J. B. (1990). Resting frontal brain asymmetry predicts affective responses to films. *Journal of Personality and Social Psychology, 59,* 791–801.

Tomarken, A. J., Davidson, R. J., Wheeler, R. E., & Doss, R. (1992). Psychometric properties of resting anterior EEG asymmetry: Temporal stability and internal consistency. *Psychophysiology, 29,* 576–592.

Tomasello, M. (1999). The human adaptation for culture. *Annual Review of Anthropology, 28,* 509–529.

Tori, C. D., & Bilmes, M. (2002). Multiculturalism and psychoanalytic psychology: The validation of a defense mechanisms measure in an Asian population. *Psychoanalytic Psychology, 19,* 701–721.

Torrey, J. W. (1987). Phases of feminist re-vision in the psychology of personality. *Teaching of Psychology, 14,* 155–160.

Townsend, F. (2000). Taking *Born to Rebel* seriously: The need for independent review. *Politics and the Life Sciences, 19,* 205–210.

Trappey, C. (1996). A meta-analysis of consumer choice and subliminal advertising. *Psychology and Marketing, 13,* 517–530.

Travis, F. (2001). Autonomic and EEG patterns distinguish transcending from other experiences during Transcendental Meditation practice. *International Journal of Psychophysiology, 42,* 1–9.

Travis, F., & Pearson, C. (2000). Pure consciousness: Distinct phenomenological and physiological correlates of "consciousness itself." *International Journal of Neuroscience, 100,* 77–89.

Travis, F., Tecce, J., Arenander, A., & Wallace, R. K. (2002). Patterns of EEG coherence, power and contingent negative variation characterize the integration of transcendental and waking states. *Biological Psychology, 61,* 293–319.

Treadway, M., & McCloskey, M. (1987). Cite unseen: Distortions of the Allport and Postman rumor study in the eyewitness testimony literature. *Law and Behavior, 11,* 19–25.

Triandis, H. C. (1988). Collectivism v. individualism: A reconceptualization of a basic concept in cross-cultural social psychology. In G. K. Verma & C. Bagley (Eds.), *Cross-cultural studies of personality, values, and cognition* (pp. 60–95). London: Macmillan.

Triandis, H. C. (1989). The self and social behavior in differing cultural contexts. *Psychological Review, 96,* 506–520.

Triandis, H. C. (1996). The psychological measurement of cultural syndromes. *American Psychologist, 51,* 407–415.

Triandis, H. C. (1997). Cross-cultural perspectives on personality. In R. Hogan, J. Johnson, & S. Briggs (Eds.), *Handbook of personality psychology* (pp. 439–464). San Diego: Academic Press.

Triandis, H. C. (2001). Individualism-collectivism and personality. *Journal of Personality, 69,* 907–924.

Triandis, H. C., McCusker, C., & Hui, C. H. (1990). Multimethod probes of individualism and collectivism. *Journal of Personality and Social Psychology, 59,* 1006–1020.

Tribich, D., & Messer, S. (1974). Psychoanalytic character type and status of authority as determiners of suggestibility. *Journal of Consulting and Clinical Psychology, 42,* 842–848.

Trickett, P. K., & Putnam, F. W. (1993). Impact of child sexual abuse on females: Toward a developmental, psychobiological integration. *Psychological Science, 4,* 81–87.

Trivers, R. (1972). Parental investment and sexual selection. In B. Campbell (Ed.), *Sexual selection and the descent of man: 1871–1971* (pp. 136–179). Chicago: Aldine.

Trivers, R. L. (1971). The evolution of reciprocal altruism. *Quarterly Review of Biology, 46,* 35–57.

Trull, T. J., Useda, J. D., Holcomb, J., Doan, B. T., Axelrod, S. R., Stern, B. L., & Gershuny, B. S. (1998). A structured interview for the assessment of the five-factor model of personality. *Psychological Assessment, 10,* 229–240.

Trungpa, C. (2005). *The sanity we are born with: A Buddhist approach to psychology.* Boston: Shambhala.

Tryon, W. W. (1990). Why paradigmatic behaviorism should be retitled psychological behaviorism. *Behavior Therapist, 13,* 127–128.

Tsang, J., & McCullough, M. E. (2003). Measuring religious constructs: A hierarchical approach to construct organization and scale selection. In S. J. Lopez & C. R. Snyder (Eds.), *Positive psychological assessment: A handbook of models and measures* (pp. 345–360). Washington, DC: American Psychological Association.

Tucker, I. F. (1991). Predicting scores on the Rathus Assertiveness Schedule from Myers-Briggs Type Indicator categories. *Psychological Reports, 69,* 571–576.

Tucker, J. S., Friedman, H. S., Schwartz, J. E., Cirqui, M. H., Tomlinson-Keasey, C., Wingard, D. L., & Martin, L. R. (1997). Parental divorce: Effects on individual behavior and longevity. *Journal of Personality and Social Psychology, 73,* 381–391.

Tuckman, B. W. (1990). Group versus goal-setting effects on the self-regulated performance of students differing in self-efficacy. *Journal of Experimental Education, 58,* 291–298.

Tudor, K., & Worrall, M. (1994). Congruence reconsidered. *British Journal of Guidance and Counselling, 22,* 197–206.

Turk, B. (1990). Kids with courage. *Individual Psychology, 46,* 178–183.

Turkheimer, E. (1998). Heritability and biological explanation. *Psychological Review, 105,* 782–791.

Turvey, C., & Salovey, P. (1993–1994). Measures of repression: Converging on the same construct? *Imagination, Cognition and Personality, 13,* 279–289.

Tuten, T. L., & August, R. A. (1998). Understanding consumer satisfaction in services settings: A bidimensional model of service strategies. *Journal of Social Behavior and Personality, 13,* 553–564.

Tversky, A., & Kahneman, D. (1981). The framing of decisions and the psychology of choice. *Science, 211,* 453–458.

Twenge, J. M. (2000). The age of anxiety? Birth cohort change in anxiety and neuroticism, 1952–1993. *Journal of Personality and Social Psychology, 79,* 1007–1021.

Twenge, J. M. (2001a). Birth cohort changes in extraversion: A cross-temporal meta-analysis, 1966–1993. *Personality and Individual Differences, 30,* 735–748.

Twenge, J. M. (2001b). Changes in women's assertiveness in response to status and roles: A cross-temporal meta-analysis, 1931–1993. *Journal of Personality and Social Psychology, 81,* 133–145.

Twenge, J. M. (2002). Birth cohort, social change, and personality: The interplay of dysphoria and individualism in the 20th century. In D. Cervone & W. Mischel (Eds.), *Advances in personality science* (pp. 196–218). New York: Guilford.

Twenge, J. M., & Campbell, W. K. (2001). Age and birth cohort differences in self-esteem: A cross-temporal meta-analysis. *Personality and Social Psychology Review, 5,* 321–344.

Twomey, H. B., Kaslow, N. J., & Croft, S. (2000). Childhood maltreatment, object relations, and suicidal behavior in women. *Psychoanalytic Psychology, 17,* 313–335.

Ungerer, J. A., Waters, B., & Barnett, B. (1997). Defense style and adjustment in interpersonal relationships. *Journal of Research in Personality, 31,* 375–384.

Urry, H. L., Nitschke, J. B., Dolski, I., Jackson, D. C., Dalton, K. M., Mueller, C. J., Rosenkranz, M. A., Ryff, C. D., Singer, B. H., & Davidson, R. J. (2004). Making a life worth living: Neural correlates of well-being. *Psychological Science, 15,* 367–372.

Utay, J. M., & Utay, C. M. (1996). Applications of Adler's theory in counseling and education. *Journal of Instructional Psychology, 23,* 251–256.

Vaillant, G. E. (1971). Theoretical hierarchy of adaptive ego mechanisms. *Archives of General Psychiatry, 24,* 107–118.

Vaillant, G. E. (1992). The historical origins and future potential of Sigmund Freud's concept of the mechanisms of defence. *International Review of Psychoanalysis, 19,* 35–50.

Vaillant, G. E. (1993). *The wisdom of the ego.* Cambridge, MA: Harvard University Press.

Vaillant, G. E. (1994). Ego mechanisms of defense and personality psychopathology. *Journal of Abnormal Psychology, 103,* 44–50.

Vaillant, G. E. (2000). Adaptive mental mechanisms and their role in a positive psychology. *American Psychologist, 55,* 89–98.

Vaillant, G. E., & Davis, J. T. (2000). Social/emotional intelligence and midlife resilience in schoolboys with low tested intelligence. *American Journal of Orthopsychiatry, 70,* 215–222.

Vaillant, G. E. (2002). Quantum change: When epiphanies and sudden insights transform ordinary lives [Book review]. *American Journal of Psychiatry, 159,* 1620–1621.

van der Kolk, B. A., & Fisler, R. (1995). Dissociation and the fragmentary nature of traumatic memories: Overview and exploratory study. *Journal of Traumatic Stress, 8,* 505–525.

Vandewater, E. A., Ostrove, J. M., & Stewart, A. J. (1997). Predicting women's well-being in midlife: The importance of personality development and social role involvements. *Journal of Personality and Social Psychology, 72,* 1147–1160.

Van Eenwyk, J. R. (1997). *Archetypes and strange attractors: The chaotic world of symbols.* Toronto, Canada: Inner City Books.

van Ijzendoorn, M. H., & Bakermans-Kranenburg, M. J. (1996). Attachment representations in mothers, fathers, adolescents, and clinical groups: A meta-analytic search for normative data. *Journal of Consulting and Clinical Psychology, 64,* 8–21.

Van Kalmthout, M. A. (1995). The religious dimension of Rogers's work. *Journal of Humanistic Psychology, 35*(4), 23–39.

Van Pelt, T. (1997). Symptomatic perfectionism: Ideal ego and ego ideal in the *Journals of Sylvia Plath. Literature and Psychology, 43,* 47–64.

Vaughn, C. M., & Pfenninger, D. T. (1994). Kelly and the concept of developmental stages. *Journal of Constructivist Psychology, 7,* 177–190.

Velmans, M. (1991). Is human information processing conscious? *Behavioral and Brain Sciences, 14,* 651–726.

Viney, L. L. (1981). Experimenting with experience: A psychotherapeutic case study. *Psychotherapy, 18,* 271–278.

Viney, L. L. (1992). Can we see ourselves changing? Toward a personal construct model of adult development. *Human Development, 35,* 65–75.

Viney, L. L., Allwood, K., Stillson, L., & Walmsley, R. (1992). Personal construct therapy for HIV seropositive patients. *Psychotherapy, 29,* 430–437.

Viney, L. L., Benjamin, Y. N., & Preston, C. A. (1989). An evaluation of personal construct therapy for the elderly. *British Journal of Medical Psychology, 62,* 35–41.

Vitz, P. C. (1990). The use of stories in moral development: New psychological reasons for an old education method. *American Psychologist, 45,* 709–720.

Vleioras, G., & Bosma, H. A. (2005). Are identity styles important for psychological well-being? *Journal of Adolescence, 28,* 397–409.

Vollmer, F. (1993). A theory of traits. *Philosophical Psychology, 6,* 67–79.

Volkan, V. D., Itzkowitz, N., & Dod, A. W. (1997). *Richard Nixon: A psychobiography.* New York: Columbia University Press.

von Franz, M. L. (1964). Conclusion: Science and the unconscious. In C. G. Jung (Ed.), *Man and his symbols* (pp. 304–310). Garden City, NY: Doubleday.

Vonk, R., & Heiser, W. J. (1991). Implicit personality theory and social judgment: Effects of familiarity with a target person. *Multivariate Behavioral Research, 26,* 69–81.

Vyse, S. A. (1990). Adopting a viewpoint: Psychology majors and psychological theory. *Teaching of Psychology, 17,* 227–230.

Wachtel, P. L. (1978). On some complexities in the application of conflict theory to psychotherapy. *Journal of Nervous and Mental Disease, 166,* 457–471.

Wahba, M. A., & Bridwell, L. G. (1976). Maslow reconsidered: A review of research on the need hierarchy theory. *Organizational Behavior and Human Performance, 15,* 212–240.

Wahler, R. G., & Castlebury, F. D. (2002). Personal narratives as maps of the social ecosystem. *Clinical Psychology Review, 22,* 297–314.

Waite, R. G. L. (1977). *The psychopathic God: Adolf Hitler.* New York: Basic Books.

Walach, H., Buchheld, N., Buttenmüller, V., Kleinknecht, N., & Schmidt, S. (2006). Measuring mindfulness—the Freiburg Mindfulness Inventory (FMI). *Personality and Individual Differences, 40,* 1543–1555.

Waldron, R. (1987). *Oprah!* New York: St. Martin's Press.

Walker, B. M. (1990). Construing George Kelly's construing of the person-in-relation. *International Journal of Personal Construct Psychology, 3,* 41–50.

Walker, B. M. (1992). Values and Kelly's theory: Becoming a good scientist. *International Journal of Personal Construct Psychology, 5,* 259–269.

Wallace, E. R., IV (1989). Pitfalls of a one-sided image of science: Adolf Grünbaum's *Foundations of Psychoanalysis. Journal of the American Psychoanalytic Association, 37,* 493–529.

Wallach, M. A. (2004). Humanism's heritage [Review of *Escape from Freedom* (2nd ed.)]. *PsycCRITIQUES.* Originally published in *Contemporary Psychology: APA Review of Books,* 1996, *41*(1), 7–11.

Wallach, M. A., & Wallach, L. (1983). *Psychology: Sanction for selfishness.* San Francisco: Freeman.

Wallerstein, R. S. (1989). The Psychotherapy Research Project of the Menninger Foundation: An overview. *Journal of Consulting and Clinical Psychology, 57,* 195–205.

Wallerstein, R. S., & Sampson, H. (1971). Issues in research in the psychoanalytic process. *International Journal of Psycho-Analysis, 42,* 11–50.

Walsh, B. W., & Peterson, L. E. (1985). Philosophical foundations of psychological theories: The issue of synthesis. *Psychotherapy, 2,* 145–153.

Walsh, R. (1988). Two Asian psychologies and their implications for Western psychotherapists. *American Journal of Psychotherapy, 42,* 543–560.

Walsh, R. (1994). The making of a shaman: Calling, training, and culmination. *Journal of Humanistic Psychology, 34*(3), 7–30.

Walsh, R., & Shapiro, S. L. (2006). The meeting of meditative disciplines and Western psychology. *American Psychologist, 61,* 227–239.

Walsh, R., Victor, B., & Bitner, R. (2006). Emotional effects of sertraline: Novel findings revealed by meditation. *American Journal of Orthopsychiatry, 36,* 134–137.

Ward, E. A. (1993). Generalizability of psychological research from undergraduates to employed adults. *Journal of Social Psychology, 133,* 513–519.

Ward, R. A., & Loftus, E. F. (1985). Eyewitness performance in different psychological types. *Journal of General Psychology, 112,* 191–200.

Ware, M. E., & Perry, N. W. (1987). Facilitating growth in a personal development course. *Psychological Reports, 60,* 491–500.

Warr, P., Miles, A., & Platts, C. (2001). Age and personality in the British population between 16 and 64 years. *Journal of Occupational and Organizational Psychology, 74,* 165–200.

Warren, B. (1990). Psychoanalysis and personal construct theory: An exploration. *Journal of Psychology, 124,* 449–463.

Warren, B. (1991). Concepts, constructs, cognitive psychology, and personal construct theory. *Journal of Psychology, 125,* 525–536.

Warren, M. W., Hughes, A. T., & Tobias, S. B. (1985). Autobiographical elaboration and memory for adjectives. *Perceptual and Motor Skills, 60,* 55–58.

Warren, W. G. (1990a). Is personal construct psychology a cognitive psychology? *International Journal of Personal Construct Psychology, 3,* 393–414.

Warren, W. G. (1990b). Personal construct theory and the Aristotelian and Galileian modes of thought. *International Journal of Personal Construct Psychology, 3,* 263–280.

Washburn, M. (1990). Two patterns of transcendence. *Journal of Humanistic Psychology, 30,* 84–112.

Waterman, A. S. (1982). Identity development from adolescence to adulthood: An extension of theory and a review of research. *Developmental Psychology, 18,* 341–358.

Waterman, A. S. (1988). Identity status theory and Erikson's theory: Commonalities and differences. *Developmental Review, 8,* 185–208.

Waterman, A. S. (1990). Personal expressiveness: Philosophical and psychological foundations. *Journal of Mind and Behavior, 11,* 47–73.

Waterman, A. S., & Waterman, C. K. (1970). The relationship between ego identity status and satisfaction in college. *Journal of Educational Research, 64,* 165–168.

Waterman, A. S., Geary, P. S., & Waterman, C. K. (1974). Longitudinal study of changes in ego identity status from the freshman to the senior year at college. *Developmental Psychology, 10,* 387–392.

Waterman, C. K., & Nevid, J. S. (1977). Sex differences in the resolution of the identity crisis. *Journal of Youth and Adolescence, 6,* 337–342.

Watkins, C. E., Jr., & Hector, M. (1990). A simple test of the concurrent validity of the Social Interest Index. *Journal of Personality Assessment, 55,* 812–814.

Watson, B. (Trans.) (1968). *The complete works of Chuang Tzu.* New York: Columbia University Press.

Watson, D., & Clark, L. A. (1997). Extraversion and its positive emotional core. In R. Hogan, J. Johnson, & S. Briggs (Eds.), *Handbook of personality psychology* (pp. 767–793). San Diego: Academic Press.

Watson, J. B. (1970). *Behaviorism.* New York: Norton. (Original work published 1924)

Watson, J. B. (1994). Psychology as the behaviorist views it. *Psychological Review, 101,* 248–253. (Original work published 1913)

Watson, J. B., & Greenberg, L. S. (1998). Humanistic and experiential theories of personality. In D. F. Barone, M. Hersen, & V. B. Van Hasselt (Eds.), *Advanced personality* (pp. 81–102). New York: Plenum Press.

Watson, J. C., & Rennie, D. L. (1994). Qualitative analysis of clients' subjective experience of significant moments during the exploration of problematic reactions. *Journal of Counseling Psychology, 41,* 500–509.

Watson, P. J., Hood, R. W., Morris, R. J., & Hall, J. R. (1984). Empathy, religious orientation, and social desirability. *Journal of Psychology, 117,* 211–216.

Watts, R. E. (1992). Biblical agape as a model of social interest. *Individual Psychology, 48,* 35–40.

Watts, R. E. (1996). Social interest and the core conditions: Could it be that Adler influenced Rogers? *Journal of Humanistic Counseling, Education, and Development, 34*(4), 165–170.

Wax, M. L. (2000). Oedipus as normative? Freud's complex, Hook's query, Malinowski's Trobrianders, Stoller's anomalies. *Journal of the American Academy of Psychoanalysis, 28,* 117–132.

Webster-Stratton, C. (1998). Preventing conduct problems in Head Start children: Strengthening parenting competencies. *Journal of Consulting and Clinical Psychology, 66,* 715–730.

Wegner, D. M., & Zanakos, S. (1994). Chronic thought suppression. *Journal of Personality, 62,* 615–640.

Wegner, D. M., Erber, R., & Zanakos, S. (1993). Ironic processes in the mental control of mood and mood-related thought. *Journal of Personality and Social Psychology, 65,* 1093–1104.

Wegner, D. M., Schneider, D. J., Carter, S. R., & White, T. L. (1987). Paradoxical effects of thought suppression. *Journal of Personality and Social Psychology, 53,* 5–13.

Wegner, D. M., Schneider, D. J., Knutson, B., & McMahon, S. R. (1991). Polluting the stream of consciousness: The effect of thought suppression on the mind's environment. *Cognitive Therapy and Research, 15,* 141–152.

Wegner, D. M., & Wheatley, T. (1999). Apparent mental causation: Sources of the experience of will. *American Psychologist, 54,* 480–492.

Wehr, G. (1987). *Jung: A biography* (D. M. Weeks, Trans.). Boston: Shambhala.

Wehr, G. S. (1987). *Jung and feminism.* Boston: Beacon Press.

Weinberg, R. S., Hughes, H. H., Critelli, J. W., England, R., & Jackson, A. (1984). Effects of preexisting and manipulated self-efficacy on weight loss in a self-control program. *Journal of Research in Personality, 18,* 352–358.

Weiner, I. B., & Exner, J. E., Jr. (1991). Rorschach changes in long-term and short-term psychotherapy. *Journal of Personality Assessment, 56,* 453–465.

Weinrach, S. G. (1990). Rogers and Gloria: The controversial film and the enduring relationship. *Psychotherapy, 27,* 282–290.

Weinrach, S. G. (1991). Rogers' encounter with Gloria: What did Rogers know and when? *Psychotherapy, 28,* 504–506.

Weiss, J. (1988). Testing hypotheses about unconscious mental functioning. *International Journal of Psycho-Analysis, 69,* 87–95.

Weiss-Rosmarin, T. (1990). Adler's psychology and the Jewish tradition. *Individual Psychology, 46,* 108–118. (Original work published 1958)

Wellingham-Jones, P. (1989). Evaluation of the handwriting of successful women through the Roman-Staempfli Psychogram. *Perceptual and Motor Skills, 69,* 999–1010.

Wells-Parker, E., Miller, D. I., & Topping, J. S. (1990). Development of control-of-outcome scales and self-efficacy scales for women in four life roles. *Journal of Personality Assessment, 54,* 564–575.

Wenneberg, S. R., Schneider, R. H., Walton, K. G., Maclean, C. R. K., Levitsky, D. K., Salerno, J. W., Wallace, R. K., Mandarino, J. V., Rainforth, M. V., & Waziri, R. (1997). A controlled study of the effects of the Transcendental Meditation® program on cardiovascular reactivity and ambulatory blood pressure. *International Journal of Neuroscience, 89,* 15–28.

Wenzlaff, R. M., & Wegner, D. M. (2000). Thought suppression. *Annual Review of Psychology, 51,* 59–91.

Wenzlaff, R. M., Wegner, D. M., & Klein, S. B. (1991). The role of thought suppression in the bonding of thought and mood. *Journal of Personality and Social Psychology, 60,* 500–508.

Werner, P. D., & Pervin, L. A. (1986). The content of personality inventory items. *Journal of Personality and Social Psychology, 51,* 622–628.

Wertheimer, M. (1978). Humanistic psychology and the humane but tough-minded psychologist. *American Psychologist, 33,* 739–745.

West, S. G. (1986). Methodological developments in personality research: An introduction. *Journal of Personality, 54,* 1–17.

Westen, D. (1991). Social cognition and object relations. *Psychological Bulletin, 109,* 429–455.

Westen, D. (1998a). The scientific legacy of Sigmund Freud: Toward a psychodynamically informed psychological science. *Psychological Bulletin, 124,* 333–371.

Westen, D. (1998b). Unconscious thought, feeling, and motivation: The end of a century-long debate. In R. F. Bornstein & J. M. Masling (Eds.), *Empirical perspectives on the psychoanalytic unconscious* (pp. 1–43). Washington, DC: American Psychological Association.

Westen, D., Klepser, J., Ruffins, S. A., Silverman, M., Lifton, N., & Boekamp, J. (1991). Object relations in childhood and adolescence: The development of working representations. *Journal of Consulting and Clinical Psychology, 59,* 400–409.

Westen, D., & Morrison, K. (2001). A multidimensional meta-analysis of treatments for depression, panic, and generalized anxiety disorder: An empirical examination of the status of empirically supported therapies. *Journal of Consulting and Clinical Psychology, 69,* 875–899.

Westen, D., Muderrisoglu, S., Fowler, C., Shedler, J., & Koren, D. (1997). Affect regulation and affective experience: Individual differences, group differences, and measurement using a Q-sort procedure. *Journal of Consulting and Clinical Psychology, 65,* 429–439.

Westkott, M. (1986a). *The feminist legacy of Karen Horney.* New Haven, CT: Yale University Press.

Westkott, M. (1986b). Historical and developmental roots of female dependency. *Psychotherapy, 23,* 213–220.

Westkott, M. (1989). Female relationship and the idealized self. *American Journal of Psychoanalysis, 49,* 239–250.

Westkott, M. (1998). Horney, Zen, and the real self. *American Journal of Psychoanalysis, 58,* 287–301.

Wheeler, M. A., Stuss, D. T., & Tulving, E. (1997). Toward a theory of episodic memory: The frontal lobe and autonoetic consciousness. *Psychological Bulletin, 121,* 331–354.

Wheeler, P. (2001). The Myers-Briggs Type Indicator and applications to accounting education research. *Issues in Accounting Education, 16,* 125–150.

Wheeler, S. (2000). What makes a good counsellor? An analysis of ways in which counsellor trainers construe good and bad counselling trainees. *Counselling Psychology Quarterly, 13,* 65–83.

Whitbourne, S. K., Zuschlag, M. K., Elliot, L. B., & Waterman, A. S. (1992). Psychosocial development in adulthood: A 22-year sequential study. *Journal of Personality and Social Psychology, 63,* 260–271.

White, T. H. (1975). *Breach of faith: The fall of Richard Nixon.* New York: Atheneum.

Whitfield, C. L. (1995). How common is traumatic forgetting? *Journal of Psychohistory, 23*(2), 119–130.

Whitley, B. E., Jr. (1984). Sex-role orientation and psychological well-being: Two meta-analyses. *Sex Roles, 12,* 207–225.

Whitmont, E. C. (1982). *Return of the goddess.* New York: Crossroad.

Whitworth, R. H., & Perry, S. M. (1990). Comparison of Anglo- and Mexican-Americans on the 16PF administered in Spanish or English. *Journal of Clinical Psychology, 46,* 857–863.

Wicker, F. W., Brown, G., Wiehe, J. A., Hagen, A. S., & Reed, J. L. (1993). On reconsidering Maslow: An examination of the deprivation/domination proposition. *Journal of Research in Personality, 27,* 118–133.

Wickett, J. C., Vernon, P. A., & Lee, D. H. (2000). Relationships between factors of intelligence and brain volume. *Personality and Individual Differences, 29,* 1095–1122.

Wiedenfeld, S. A., O'Leary, A., Bandura, A., Brown, S., Levine, S., & Raska, K. (1990). Impact of perceived self-efficacy in coping with stressors on components of the immune system. *Journal of Personality and Social Psychology, 59,* 1082–1094.

Wiederman, M. W., & Kendall, E. (1999). Evolution, sex, and jealousy: Investigation with a sample from Sweden. *Evolution and Human Behavior, 20,* 121–128.

Wiese, M. R. R., & Kramer, J. J. (1988). Parent training research: An analysis of the empirical literature 1975–1985. *Psychology in the Schools, 25,* 325–330.

Wiggins, J. S. (1984). Cattell's system from the perspective of mainstream personality theory. *Multivariate Behavioral Research, 19,* 176–190.

Wiggins, J. S., & Trapnell, P. D. (1997). Personality structure: The return of the big five. In R. Hogan, J. Johnson, & S. Briggs (Eds.), *Handbook of personality psychology* (pp. 737–765). San Diego: Academic Press.

Wilber, K. (1990). "Two patterns of transcendence": A reply to Washburn. *Journal of Humanistic Psychology, 30,* 113–136.

Wild, C. (1965). Creativity and adaptive regression. *Journal of Personality and Social Psychology, 2,* 161–169.

Wilhelm, H. (1960). *Change: Eight lectures on the I Ching.* Princeton, NJ: Princeton University Press.

Wilkins, P. (2000). Unconditional positive regard considered. *British Journal of Guidance and Counselling, 28,* 23–36.

Wilkinson, W. W. (2004). Religiosity, authoritarianism, and homophobia: A multidimensional approach. *International Journal for the Psychology of Religion, 14,* 55–67.

Williams, D. E., & Page, M. M. (1989). A multi-dimensional measure of Maslow's hierarchy of needs. *Journal of Research in Personality, 23,* 192–213.

Williams, D. I., & Irving, J. A. (1999). Why are therapists indifferent to research? *British Journal of Guidance and Counselling, 27,* 367–376.

Williams, E. N., & Hill, C. E. (2001). Evolving connections: Research that is relevant to clinical practice. *American Journal of Psychotherapy, 55,* 336–343.

Williams, L. M. (1994). Recall of childhood trauma: A prospective study of women's memories of child sexual abuse. *Journal of Consulting and Clinical Psychology, 62,* 1167–1176.

Williams, P., with Tribe, A. (2000). *Buddhist thought: A complete introduction to the Indian tradition.* London: Routledge.

Williams, S. L., Kinney, P. J., Harap, S. T., & Liebmann, M. (1997). Thoughts of agoraphobic people during scary tasks. *Journal of Abnormal Psychology, 106,* 511–520.

Williams, S. S., Kimble, D. L., Covell, N. H., Weiss, L. H., Newton, K. J., Fisher, J. D., & Fisher, W. A. (1992). College students use implicit personality theory instead of safer sex. *Journal of Applied Social Psychology, 22,* 921–933.

Wills, T. A., Windle, M., & Cleary, S. D. (1998). Temperament and novelty seeking in adolescent substance use: Convergence of dimensions of temperament with constructs from Cloninger's theory. *Journal of Personality and Social Psychology, 74,* 387–406.

Wilson, E. O. (1998). *Concilience: The unity of knowledge.* New York: Knopf.

Wilson, S. R., & Spencer, R. C. (1990). Intense personal experiences: Subjective effects, interpretations, and after-effects. *Journal of Clinical Psychology, 46,* 565–573.

Winston, A. S., & Baker, J. E. (1985). Behavior analytic studies of creativity: A critical review. *Behavior Analyst, 8,* 191–205.

Winter, D. A. (1993). Slot rattling from law enforcement to lawbreaking: A personal construct theory exploration of police stress. *International Journal of Personal Construct Psychology, 6,* 253–267.

Winter, D. G. (1993). Power, affiliation, and war: Three tests of a motivational model. *Journal of Personality and Social Psychology, 65,* 532–545.

Winter, D. G. (1997). Allport's life and Allport's psychology. *Journal of Personality, 65,* 723–731.

Winter, D. G., & Carlson, L. A. (1988). Using motive scores in the psychobiographical study of an individual: The case of Richard Nixon. *Journal of Personality, 56,* 75–103.

Winter, D. G., Hermann, M. G., Weintraub, W., & Walker, S. G. (1991a). The personalities of Bush and Gorbachev at a distance: Follow-up on predictions. *Political Psychology, 12,* 457–464.

Winter, D. G., Hermann, M. G., Weintraub, W., & Walker, S. G. (1991b). The personalities of Bush and Gorbachev measured at a distance: Procedures, portraits, and policy. *Political Psychology, 12*(2), 215–245.

Winter, D. G., John, O. P., Stewart, A. J., Klohnen, E. C., & Duncan, L. E. (1998). Traits and motives: Toward an integration of two traditions in personality research. *Psychological Review, 105,* 230–250.

Winter, S. (1999). *Freud and the institution of psychoanalytic knowledge.* Stanford, CA: Stanford University Press.

Wippich, W. (1994). Intuition in the context of implicit memory. *Psychological Research, 56,* 104–109.

Wiseman, H., & Rice, L. N. (1989). Sequential analyses of therapist-client interaction during change events: A task-focused approach. *Journal of Consulting and Clinical Psychology, 57,* 281–286.

Wittels, F. (1939). The neo-Adlerians. *American Journal of Sociology, 45,* 433–445.

Woike, B. A., Osier, T. J., & Candela, K. (1996). Attachment styles and violent imagery in thematic stories about relationships. *Personality and Social Psychology Bulletin, 22,* 1030–1034.

Wojcik, J. V. (1988). Social learning predictors of the avoidance of smoking relapse. *Addictive Behaviors, 13,* 177–180.

Wolfenstein, E. V. (1993). Mr. Moneybags meets the Rat Man: Marx and Freud on the meaning of money. *Political Psychology, 14,* 279–308.

Wollman, N., & Stouder, R. (1991). Believed efficacy and political activity: A test of the specificity hypothesis. *Journal of Social Psychology, 13,* 557–566.

Wolman, B. B. (1971). Does psychology need its own philosophy of science? *American Psychologist, 26,* 877–886.

Wolpe, J., & Rachman, S. (1960). Psychoanalytic "evidence": A critique based on Freud's case of Little Hans. *Journal of Nervous and Mental Disease, 131,* 135–148.

Wood, J. V., Saltzberg, J. A., Neale, J. M., Stone, A. A., & Rachmiel, T. B. (1990). Self-focused attention, coping responses, and distressed mood in everyday life. *Journal of Personality and Social Psychology, 58,* 1027–1036.

Wood, R., & Bandura, A. (1989a). Impact of conceptions of ability on self-regulatory mechanisms and complex decision making. *Journal of Personality and Social Psychology, 56,* 407–415.

Wood, R., & Bandura, A. (1989b). Social cognitive theory of organizational management. *Academy of Management Review, 14,* 361–384.

Wood, R., Bandura, A., & Bailey, T. (1990). Mechanisms governing organizational performance in complex decision-making environments. *Organizational Behavior and Human Decision Processes, 46,* 181–201.

Woodward, B., & Bernstein, C. (1976). *The final days.* New York: Avon Books.

Woolfolk, R. L., & Richardson, F. C. (1984). Behavior therapy and the ideology of modernity. *American Psychologist, 39,* 777–786.

Wright, J. C., & Mischel, W. (1987). A conditional approach to dispositional constructs: The local predictability of social behavior. *Journal of Personality and Social Psychology, 53,* 1159–1177.

Wright, J. C., & Mischel, W. (1988). Conditional hedges and the intuitive psychology of traits. *Journal of Personality and Social Psychology, 55,* 454–469.

Wright, T. M., & Reise, S. P. (1997). Personality and unrestricted sexual behavior: Correlations of sociosexuality in Caucasian and Asian college students. *Journal of Research in Personality, 31,* 166–192.

Wright, W. J. (1985). Personality profiles of four leaders of the German Lutheran Reformation. *Psychohistory Review, 14,* 12–22.

Wurgaft, L. D. (1976). Erik Erikson: From Luther to Gandhi. *Psychoanalytic Review, 63,* 209–233.

Wyer, R. S., & Collins, J. E. (1992). A theory of humor elicitation. *Psychological Review, 99,* 663–688.

Wyer, R. S., & Radvansky, G. A. (1999). The comprehension and validation of social information. *Psychological Review, 106,* 89–118.

Yamamoto, S. (2003). Environmental problems and Buddhist ethics: From the perspective of the consciousness-only doctrine. In S. Muramoto & P. Young-Eisendrath (Eds.), *Awakening and insight: Zen Buddhism and psychotherapy* (pp. 239–257). New York: Brunner-Routledge.

Yapko, M. D. (1994). Suggestibility and repressed memories of abuse: A survey of psychotherapists' beliefs. *American Journal of Clinical Hypnosis, 36*(3), 163–171.

Yeagle, E. H., Privette, G., & Dunham, F. Y. (1989). Highest happiness: An analysis of artists' peak experience. *Psychological Reports, 65,* 523–530.

Yeh, C. J., & Hwang, M. Y. (2000). Interdependence in ethnic identity and self: Implications for theory and practice. *Journal of Counseling and Development, 78,* 420–429.

Yehuda, R., & McFarlane, A. C. (1995). Conflict between current knowledge about posttraumatic stress disorder and its original conceptual basis. *American Journal of Psychiatry, 152,* 1702–1713.

Ying, Y. (2001). Migration and cultural orientation: An empirical test of the psychoanalytic theory in Chinese Americans. *Journal of Applied Psychoanalytic Studies, 3,* 409–430.

Yogev, S. (1983). Judging the professional woman: Changing research, changing values. *Psychology of Women Quarterly, 7,* 219–234.

Yonge, G. D. (1975). Time experiences, self-actualizing values, and creativity. *Journal of Personality Assessment, 39,* 601–606.

Young, J. D., & Taylor, E. (1998). Meditation as a voluntary hypometabolic state of biological estivation. *News in the Physiological Sciences, 13,* 149–153.

Young, L. J. (2002). The neurobiology of social recognition, approach, and avoidance. *Biological Psychiatry, 51,* 18–26.

Young-Bruehl, E. (Ed.). (1990). *Freud on women: A reader.* New York: Norton.

Young-Eisendrath, P. (2002). The transformation of human suffering: A perspective from psychotherapy and Buddhism. In S. Muramoto & P. Young-Eisendrath (Eds.), *Awakening and insight: Zen Buddhism and psychotherapy* (pp. 67–80). New York: Brunner-Routledge.

Young-Eisendrath, P. (2003). Suffering from biobabble: Searching for a science of subjectivity. In K. H. Dockett, G. R. Dudley-Grant, & C. P. Bankart (Eds.), *Psychology and Buddhism: From individual to global community* (pp. 125–138). Secaucus, NJ: Kluwer Academic.

Zahn-Waxler, C., & Radke-Yarrow, M. (1990). The origins of empathic concern. *Motivation and Emotion, 14*(2), 107–130.

Zahn-Waxler, C., Radke-Yarrow, M., Wagner, E., & Chapman, M. (1992). Development of concern for others. *Developmental Psychology, 28,* 126–136.

Zarate, M. A., Sanders, J. D., & Garza, A. A. (2000). Neurological dissociations of social perception processes. *Social Cognition, 18,* 223–251.

Zarate, M. A., Uleman, J. S., & Voils, C. I. (2001). Effects of culture and processing goals on the activation and binding of trait concepts. *Social Cognition, 19,* 295–323.

Zarski, J. J., Bubenzer, D. L., & West, J. D. (1986). Social interest, stress, and the prediction of health status. *Journal of Counseling and Development, 64,* 386–389.

Zborowski, M. J., & McNamara, P. (1998). Attachment hypothesis of REM sleep: Toward an integration of psychoanalysis, neuroscience, and evolutionary psychology and the implications for psychopathology research. *Psychoanalytic Psychology, 15,* 115–140.

Zettle, R. D. (1990). Rule-governed behavior: A radical behavioral answer to the cognitive challenge. *Psychological Record, 40,* 41–49.

Ziller, R. C. (1990). Environment-self behavior: A general theory of personal control. *Journal of Social Behavior and Personality, 5,* 227–242.

Zimmerman, M. A. (1989). The relationship between political efficacy and citizen participation: Construct validation studies. *Journal of Personality Assessment, 53,* 554–566.

Zimmerman, M. A., & Warschausky, S. (1998). Empowerment theory for rehabilitation research: Conceptual and methodological issues. *Rehabilitation Psychology, 43,* 3–16.

Zivkovic, M. (1982). Dream test. *Perceptual and Motor Skills, 55,* 935–938.

Zolten, A. J. (1989). Constructive integration of learning theory and phenomenological approaches to biofeedback training. *Biofeedback and Self-Regulation, 14,* 89–99.

Zosky, D. L. (1999). The application of object relations theory to domestic violence. *Clinical Social Work Journal, 27,* 55–69.

Zuckerman, M. (1994). *Behavioral expressions and biosocial bases of sensation seeking.* New York: Cambridge University Press.

Zuckerman, M., & Cloninger, C. R. (1996). Relationships between Cloninger's, Zuckerman's, and Eysenck's dimensions of personality. *Personality and Individual Differences, 21,* 283–285.

Zuckerman, M., & Kuhlman, D. M. (2000). Personality and risk-taking: Common biosocial factors. *Journal of Personality, 68,* 999–1029.

Zuckerman, M., Kuhlman, D. M., & Camac, C. (1988). What lies beyond E and N? Factor analyses of scales believed to measure basic dimensions of personality. *Journal of Personality and Social Psychology, 54,* 96–107.

Zupp, A. (2004, January/February). Why won't the Dalai Lama pick a fight? *Humanist,* pp. 5–6.

Zuriff, G. E. (1985). *Behaviorism: A conceptual reconstruction.* New York: Columbia University Press.

Zuroff, D. C. (1986). Was Gordon Allport a trait theorist? *Journal of Personality and Social Psychology, 51,* 993–1000.

Zvoch, K. (1999). Family type and investment in education: A comparison of genetic and stepparent families. *Evolution and Human Behavior, 20,* 453–464.

Zweig, C., & Wolf, S. (1997). *Romancing the shadow: A guide to soul work for a vital, authentic life.* New York: Ballantine.

Zweigenhaft, R. L., & von Ammon, J. (2000). Birth order and civil disobedience: A test of Sulloway's "born to rebel" hypothesis. *Journal of Social Psychology, 140,* 624–627.

Photo Credits

Page 25: Pearson Education/PH College
29: World Health Organization
64: Corbis/Bettmann
67: Corbis/Bettmann
95: AP Wide World Photos
99: Corbis/Bettmann
122: Corbis/Bettmann
127: Corbis/Bettmann
150: AP Wide World Photos
153: Culver Pictures, Inc.
185: Getty Images Inc. - Hulton Archive Photos
189: Stock Montage, Inc./Historical Pictures Collection
216: AP Wide World Photos
221: Raymond B. Cattell
236: National Institute on Aging
236: National Institute on Aging
245: AP Wide World Photos
267: Hans J. Eysenck, Ph.D, D.Sc.
281: AP Wide World Photos
286: B.F. Skinner Foundation
287: Culver Pictures, Inc.
298: Arthur Staats
313: Franklin D. Roosevelt Library
318: Yale University Library
318: AP Wide World Photos
340: Albright-Knox Art Gallery
343: Walter Mischel
353: Albert Bandura
369: The White House Photo Office
373: Brandeis University Photography Department
399: Corbis/Bettmann
402: Carl Rogers Memorial Library
423: D-Esprit
426: Corbis/Bettmann
452: Corbis/Reuters America LLC

Author Index

Abbott, A., 264
Abraham, K., 138, 395
Abramowitz, J. S., 333
Abrams, S., 55
Ackerman, P. L., 227
Acklin, M. W., 106
Adams, G. R., 144
Adams, H. E., 43
Adams, N. E., 358, 363
Adams-Webber, J., 377
Adelson, J., 142
Adkins, K. K., 161
Adler, A., 101–102, 104, 106, 109–110, 113–116, 118–119
Adolphs, R., 263
Affonso, D. D., 144–146
Aftanas, L., 478, 480
Agger, E. M., 109
Agor, W. H., 89
Agronick, G. S., 142
Ahadi, S. A., 242, 260
Ahrens, A. H., 161
Ainsworth, M. D. S., 174–175
Alessi, G., 257
Alexander, C. N., 470, 480–481
Alexander, I. E., 18
Alexander, R. A., 88
Alexander, V. K., 466
Allan, J., 82
Allen, A., 192
Allen, J. G., 144
Allen, J. J. B., 265, 271
Allers, C. T., 106
Allison, K. W., 166
Allport, F. H., 188
Allport, G. W., 3, 185–207, 210–211
Alpert, J. L., 173
Altenm?ller, E,, 481
Alterman, A. I., 484
Alter-Reid, K., 56
Altmaier, E. M., 390
Alvarez, A. N., 138
Amaral, D. G., 74
Ambrose, S. E., 369–371
American Psychiatric Association, 50, 173
American Psychological Association, 222, 225, 288, 319, 353, 403–404
Amerikaner, M., 106, 114
Amirkhan, J. H., 46
Amsel, A., 330
Andersen, S. M., 348
Anderson, C., 250
Anderson, C. A., 328–329
Anderson, W., 436
Andrade, J., 484
Andresen, J., 473, 477, 480
Andrews, J. D., 251, 375
Andronikof-Sanglade, A., 57
Angelou, M., 398–400
Angleitner, A., 195, 309
Annis, H. M., 363
Ansbacher, H. L., 98–107, 109–110, 113–118, 395

Ansbacher, R. R., 98–99, 101–103, 105–107, 109–110, 113–118
Antoni, M. H., 272
Antrobus, J., 35
Apostal, R., 88
Archer, J., 250
Archer, S. L., 142, 144
Ardila, R., 494
Argyle, M., 238
Arlow, J. A., 56
Armeli, S., 296
Arnau, R. C., 88
Arndt, J., 38, 329
Arnett, J. J., 140
Arnett, P. A., 273
Arnold, J., 119
Arnold, L. E., 479
Aron, A., 348
Aron, L., 169
Arredondo, J., 139
Asche, M., 387
Asendorpf, J. B., 238
Ashby, J. S., 161
Astorino, A., 384
Atkinson, R., 80
Atwood, J. D., 492, 497
Auerhahn, N. C., 48
August, R. A., 444
Austin, J. H., 473–475, 478, 480
Austin, J. T., 357
Avants, S. K., 484
Avila, C., 272
Aylesworth, A. B., 59

Baars, B. J., 58
Bache, C. H., 481
Bagley, K. J., 385
Baguma, P., 253
Bailey, T., 357
Baird, L. L., 197
Bakan, D., 419
Baker, J. E., 173, 296
Baker, N., 350
Baker, R., 118
Bakermans-Kranenburg, M. J., 178
Balay, J., 58
Baldwin, A. C., 390
Ballard, M. E., 266
Balloun, J., 434
Baltes, P. B., 227, 238
Bandura, A., 16, 337, 342, 350, 352–366
Bannister, D., 387, 390
Banuazizi, A., 319
Barab, P. G., 363
Barden, V., 390
Barenbaum, N. B., 206
Barends, A., 171
Barnard, C. P., 56
Barnes, V. A., 480
Barnett, B., 42
Barnhardt, T. M., 59
Baron, S. H., 18
Barresi, J., 132, 186, 202, 406
Barrett, D., 82

Barrett, L. F., 178, 237–238
Barrick, M. R., 239–240
Barry, B., 237
Barry, D., 416
Barry, G. M., 87
Barry, J. R., 231
Barry, R. J., 269
Barta, W., 254
Bartholomew, K., 177–178
Bartholow, B. D., 329
Bartussek, D., 273
Bass, M. L., 114
Bassoff, E. S., 166
Bates, J. E., 228, 260
Batson, C. D., 208–209
Bauer, P. J., 105
Baumeister, R. F., 41, 43, 46–47, 113, 173–174, 194, 327, 329–330, 355, 492, 499
Baumrind, D., 169, 407
Bay-Hinitz, A. K., 294
Becker, E., 38
Beckmann, J., 36
Bedeian, A. G., 110
Beebe, J., 69, 80, 82
Behrends, R. S., 202
Beilfuss, M. C., 111
Bell, A. J., 35, 69
Bellak, L., 57
Belsky, J., 168, 255–256, 495
Bem, D. J., 44, 192, 238, 351
Benbow, C. P., 197
Benford, M. S., 485
Benight, C. C., 158
Benjamin, A. J., Jr., 329
Benjamin, L. T., Jr., 35
Benjamin, P., 406, 444
Benjamin, Y. N., 387
Bennett, M. E., 133
Benson, H., 476, 480
Bera, S., 176, 178
Bereczkei, T., 253–254, 257
Berg, S., 419
Berger, P. L., 391
Berkowitz, L., 328–329
Berman, S., 274
Berman, W. H., 176
Bernal, M. E., 166
Bernstein, J., 369
Berntson, G. G., 258
Berr, S. A., 88
Berzonsky, M. D., 377, 390
Bettelheim, B., 79
Bettesworth, A., 117
Beyer, J., 363
Bhikkhu, T., 474
Biaggio, M. K., 441
Bieling, P. J., 161
Bieri, J., 384
Bilgrave, D. P., 444
Bilmes, M., 47
Binder, L. M., 351
Birch, M., 51, 55

Bitner, R., 482
Bjorklund, D. F., 256
Blackmore, S., 84
Blackwood, N. J., 61
Blagrove, M., 35
Blanchard, E. B., 363, 479
Blankfield, R. P., 33
Blashfield, R. K., 3
Blatt, S. J., 45, 113, 161, 176
Block, J., 43, 236, 310, 351, 408
Block, J. H., 351, 408
Bloland, S. E., 128
Blomberg, J., 54
Blouin, A. G., 161
Bluck, S., 132, 385
Blum, G. S., 50
Blum, H. P., 29
Blume, A. W., 291
Blume, E. S., 54
Blumstein, P., 165
Blustein, D. L., 144
Bochner, S., 166
Bock, P. K., 492
Bockoven, J., 117
Bodden, J. C., 390
Boden, J. M., 174, 329, 355
Boeck, B. E., 145
Boekamp, J., 171
Bohart, A. C., 411–414
Bohman, M., 274
Bolen, J. S., 80
Bonanno, G. A., 355, 449
Bond, M., 46
Bond, M. H., 159, 166
Bondarenko, A. F., 403
Boon, J. C., 210
Boone, J. L., 255
Boorstein, S., 438, 443
Booth, R. J., 196, 333
Booth-Kewley, S., 196
Bordages, J. W., 440
Bores-Rangel, E., 357
Borkenau, P., 183
Bornstein, R. F., 36, 49, 57, 159–160
Borodovsky, L. G., 412
Borrello, G. M., 88
Bosinelli, M., 35
Bosma, H. A., 143
Botella, L., 391
Bothwell, R. K., 34
Bottome, P., 99, 116, 118–119
Botvin, G. J., 356
Bouchard, G., 238
Bouchard, T. J., Jr., 90, 228, 259
Bouillon, J., 356
Bourke, R., 225
Bowen, M. V. B., 413
Bowers, K. S., 33, 55, 59
Bowlby, J., 174
Boxer, P., 139
Boyer, P., 256
Boyle, G. J., 183, 229, 233
Boysen, S. T., 257
Bozarth, J. D., 406, 409
Bradbury, T. N., 238

Bradley, C. L., 133
Bradshaw, C. K., 166
Brainerd, C. J., 59
Brebner, J., 268
Bremner, J. D., 60
Brems, C., 164
Brennan, C. J., 417
Brennan, J., 233
Brennan, K. A., 172, 177
Brenneis, C. B., 34, 55
Brent, D. A., 17
Breuer, J., 30, 32
Brewer, M. B., 206
Brewin, C. R., 46
Brian, D., 216–218
Bridwell, L. G., 434
Bringhurst, N. C., 89
Brock, D., 246
Brodley, B. T., 409, 413
Brody, G. H., 112
Brody, N., 58
Broehl, W. G., Jr., 196
Brogden, H. E., 16
Bronstein, A., 58
Brothers, L., 263
Brown, C., 133–134
Brown, D., 54
Brown, J. L., 206
Brown, J. W., 464
Brown, K., 82
Brown, K. W., 486
Brown, S. D., 357
Browne, A., 56
Broyles, S. J., 240
Bruck, M., 55
Bruggemann, J. M., 269
Bruhn, A. R., 105–106
Bruner, J. S., 377
Brunstein, J. C., 357
Bstan-dzin-rgya-mtsho, Dalai Lama
    XIV, 451–454, 460, 469, 472, 485
Bubenzer, D. L., 89, 115
Bucci, W., 334
Bucher, A. M., 328
Buck, R., 274
Buckingham, R. M., 267
Buckley, F., 390
Buckmaster, L. R., 439, 441
Bucko, R. A., 79
Buczel, A., 34
Budd, B. E., 141
Buirs, R. S., 388
Bullitt, W. C., 18
Bundrick, C. M., 438, 441
Burn, S. M., 209
Burns, C. E., 306
Burns, G. L., 301–304
Burr, V., 390
Burrell, M. J., 378
Burris, C. T., 209–210, 444
Busch, F. N., 54
Bushman, B. J., 174, 328, 330
Busjahn, A., 259
Buss, A., 260
Buss, D. M., 239–240, 249, 250,
    252–254, 256, 258, 280, 309
Buss, H. M., 17, 164
Buss, K. A., 260
Bussey, K., 358
Busso, J., 209

Butcher, J. N., 37
Butler, A. C., 363
Butler, J. M., 414
Butt, T., 378, 386, 391
Butt, T. W., 390
Byrd, K. R., 60

Cabanac, M., 435
Cacioppo, J. T., 258, 373
Cado, S., 386
Cahill, C., 56
Cahn, B. R., 477, 480
Cain, D. J., 402, 404, 411
Calabro, L. E., 433
Camac, C., 269
Cambray, J., 69
Camden, C. T., 58
Cameron, H. A., 255
Camp, B. D., 362
Campbell, J., 76, 80
Campbell, J. B., 88
Campbell, J. F., 235
Campbell, J. M., 441
Campbell, W. K., 6, 234
Campos, L. S., 252
Candela, K., 177
Cangemi, J. P., 417
Canlin, T., 271
Cann, D. R., 82, 88
Cantor, N., 348
Cantril, H., 189
Caplan, P. J., 51, 140
Caporeal, L. R., 251
Capps, D., 145
Capra, F., 406
Caprara, G. V., 242, 489, 498
Carich, M. S., 120
Carkhuff, R. R., 413
Carlsen, M. B., 440
Carlsmith, K. M., 232, 310
Carlson, J. G., 88
Carlson, L. A., 18, 196, 370
Carlson, L. E., 479
Carlson, M., 344
Carlson, R., 4, 18
Carmona, A., 319
Carp, C. E., 77
Carr, K., 419
Carskadon, T. G., 88
Carter, O. L., 475
Carton, J. S., 408
Cartwright, D., 406, 419–420
Carver, C. S., 271–272
Caseley-Rondi, G., 59
Caseras, X., 272
Caspi, A., 262, 351, 493
Castlebury, F. D., 310
Castro, F. G., 166
Cates, D. S., 265
Cather, C., 333
Catina, A., 387
Cattell, H. E. P., 226
Cattell, R. B., 183, 218, 220–235
Cavallero, C., 35
Cavanaugh, K. L., 479
Ceci, S. J., 55
Celani, D. P., 172
Cella, D. F., 142, 144
Cervone, D., 249, 357
Chabot, H. F., 232, 310

Chambers, W. V., 383
Chance, S. E., 256
Chandler, H. M., 481
Chang, E. C., 161
Chant, D., 233
Chaplin, C., 36, 39
Chaplin, W. F., 193
Chapman, J. P., 269
Chapman, L. J., 269
Chappell, D. W., 469
Chartrand, J. M., 144
Cheek, J., 194
Chen, J., 111
Chen, T., 459, 466
Cheney, S., 174
Cheng, S. H., 110
Chess, S., 142, 175, 179, 260, 492
Chetwynd, T., 78
Chiagouris, L., 444
Chibnall, J. T., 446
Chomsky, N., 297
Christensen, O. J., 110
Christopher, K., 446
Church, A. H., 88
Church, A. T., 242
Chusmir, L. H., 309
Ciardiello, J. A., 18
Cicogna, P., 35
Cirlot, J. E., 78
Clance, P. C., 141
Claridge, G., 239
Clark, C., 139
Clark, J. M., 10
Clark, L. A., 86, 237–238, 259, 262,
    268, 271
Clark, L. F., 12
Clark, P. A., 116
Clark, R. W., 215–218
Clarke, S., 387
Clarkson, P., 166
Cleary, S. D., 274
Cleary, T. S., 428
Clinton, H. R., 246–248
Cloninger, C. R., 266, 273–274
Coan, R. W., 72
Coccaro, E. F., 274
Coetzee, C. H., 138
Cohen, A. B., 209
Cohen, C. R., 144
Cohen, D., 287, 402–403
Cohen, L. H., 207
Colangelo, N., 202
Colder, M., 333
Coleman, H. L. K., 137
Coles, R., 125, 434
Collaer, M. L., 362
Collins, F. L., 310
Collins, J. E., 36
Collins, P. F., 273
Cologon, J., 271
Combs, A. W., 417
Compeau, D., 356
Connors, M. E., 56
Conrad, H. S., 194
Contrada, R. J., 333
Conway, M. A., 60
Cook, B. W., 314–315
Cook, H., 35, 69, 173
Cooksey, R. W., 14, 441
Coolidge, F. L., 157–158

Cooper, C. L., 390
Cooper, C. R., 492
Cooper, H., 238–239
Cooper, S. H., 170
Corbett, M. M., 411, 413
Corcoran, K. O., 176
Cornett, C., 146
Corr, P. J., 271, 273
Corsini, R. J., 116
Corteen, R. S., 384
Cosmides, L., 251
Costa, P. T., Jr., 8, 88, 168, 183, 186,
    236–239, 241–242, 259, 426–428
Côté, J. E., 136, 143, 146
Couch, L., 130
Courage, M. L., 104
Courtenay, W. H., 391
Covington, C., 53
Cowan, D. A., 88
Coward, H., 77
Cowell, D. R., 111
Craig, R. J., 242
Craik, K. H., 196, 203, 280, 309
Cramer, D., 414, 417–418
Cramer, P., 42–46, 132, 143–144
Crandall, C. S., 332
Crandall, J. E., 114, 332
Crandall, R., 332, 441
Crane, J., 119
Crawford, R. L., 89
Crawley, R. A., 104
Crick, F., 35
Crick, N. R., 358
Critchfield, T. S., 290
Crockett, J. B., 89
Croft, S., 172
Cronbach, L. J., 14, 18
Cronin, H., 250
Cross, H. J., 144
Cross, W. E., Jr., 139
Csikszentmihalyi, M., 396–397, 448
Cummins, P., 377
Cuny, H., 218
Curry, C., 142
Curtis, J. M., 111
Cutler, H. C., 453–454

d'Aquili, E. G., 485
Dachinger, P., 58
Dahl, M., 258
Dale, K., 47
Dalton, R., 112
Daly, M., 76, 110–111
Damasio, A. R., 263–264
Danielian, J., 158
Daniels, M., 438, 446
Darwin, C., 250
Das, A. K., 396
David, J. P., 56, 239
Davidow, S., 106
Davidson, K., 46
Davidson, R. J., 265, 467–469,
    478, 480
Davies, J. L., 470
Davis, C., 161, 239
Davis, D. L., 89
Davis, F., 197
Davis, G. A., 439, 441
Davis, G. M., 210
Davis, H., 480

Davis, J., 437
Davis, J. T., 42
Davis, T., 93
Davis-Berman, J., 356
Davis-Sharts, J., 434
Dawes, R. M., 223, 225
Dawis, R. V., 184
Dawkins, R., 251
Dawson, G., 265
Dazey, D., 209
De Fruyt, F., 236
de Nicolas, A. T., 257
de Quervain, D. J. F., 60
De Raad, B., 242
de Silva, P., 459–462, 464, 480
de St. Aubin, E., 136, 145
de Waal, F. B. M., 250
Dean, P. J., 161
Deaux, K., 138–139
Deberry, S. T., 164
DeBruin, J., 419
DeCarvalho, R. J., 80, 186, 198, 395, 406–407, 416–417, 419
deChesnay, M., 56
Deci, E. L., 448–449
Decker, P. J., 337, 362
DeGrandpre, R. J., 310
DeHoff, S. L., 444
Della Selva, P. C., 142
Delmonte, M. M., 441
DeLucia, A. G., 89
Deluty, R. H., 444
DelVecchio, W. F., 205
Demierre, T., 319
Demtröder, A. I., 309
DeNeve, K. M., 238–239
Denner, J., 492
Depue, R. A., 273
Derakshan, N., 46
Desai, P., 125
Desharnais, R., 356
Devenis, L. E., 144
DeWolfe, A. S., 142, 144, 441
Dhammika, S., 466, 484
Diamond, L. M., 254
Diaz, T., 356
DiCara, L. V., 319
DiCaudo, J., 88
Dickson, L., 44
Diehl, M., 178, 227
Dien, D., 164
Diener, E., 202, 353, 444
Dietrich, A., 481
Digman, J. M., 183, 239, 242
Dimsdale, J. E., 480
Dinkmeyer, D., 100, 108, 116–117
Dinkmeyer, D., Jr., 100, 108, 117
Dinkmeyer, J., 116
Dinsmoor, J. A., 297
Dixon, D. N., 35
Dixon, M. R., 351
Dockett, K. H., 469–470
Dod, A. W., 371
Dodge, K. A., 358
Doerfler, L. A., 356
Dolce, J. J., 356
Dollard, J., 318–320, 322–328, 330–332
Dollinger, S. J., 81, 237–240
Dominguez, M. M., 408
Domino, G., 144–146

Donahue, E. M., 202
Donahue, M. J., 207–208
Donderi, D. C., 82, 88
Doty, R. M., 327
Douvan, E., 142
Downey, J. L., 419
Downs, A., 385
Drabman, R., 295, 299
Dragoi, V., 290
Dreikurs, R., 107–108, 116, 119
Drigotas, S. M., 254
Drob, S. L., 69, 80
Dubin, L. F., 479
Dubow, E. F., 139, 169
Dudley-Grant, G. R., 462–464, 469, 483
Duff, K. J., 43
Duncan, L. E., 142
Duncan, R. C., 441
Dunham, F. Y., 438
Dusek, J. B., 142
Dweck, C. S., 349
Dworkin, B. R., 319
Dye, D. A., 238, 241
Dzewaltowski, D. A., 356

Eacott, M. J., 104
Eagle, M., 146
Eagly, A. H., 141, 164, 254
Ebbesen, E. B., 350
Eber, H. W., 225
Ebersole, P., 439
Eckardt, M. H., 155
Edelstein, W., 175
Eden, D., 365
Ediger, E., 161
Edinger, E. F., 69, 77, 80–81
Edwards, D. J. A., 17
Edwards, M. E., 102–103, 113, 117
Egan, S., 269
Eidelman, S. H., 208–209
Eidelson, R. J., 203
Eifert, G. H., 302, 337, 495
Einon, D., 253
Einstein, A., 497
Eisenberg, N., 179, 262
Eisenberger, R., 296, 303
Ekman, P., 250, 265, 467–468, 482
Elcock, L. E., 118
Elder, G. H., 351
Elizabeth, P., 441
Ellenberger, H. F., 30, 54, 68
Ellickson, P. L., 356
Elliot, D., 114
Elliot, L. B., 144
Elliott, D., 106
Elliott, J. E., 120
Ellis, A., 120
Ellis, B., 390
Elms, A. C., 18
Elson, M., 146
Emavardhana, T., 481
Emery, E. J., 412
Emmerich, W., 194
Emmons, R. A., 353, 357
Endler, N. S., 189
England, J. T., 110
Engle, R. W., 227
Epel, E. S., 355
Epstein, J. A., 356

Epstein, M., 476
Epstein, R., 296
Epstein, S., 5, 343, 498
Epting, F. R., 373, 377, 383, 385, 387–388
Erber, R., 333
Erikson, E. H., 18, 93, 122–137, 140–142
Erikson, J. M., 128–129, 136
Eriksson, C., 113
Eron, L. D., 169
Eshleman, A., 332
Esses, V. M., 264
Essex, M. J., 255
Essig, T. S., 413
Etzioni, A., 444
Evans, D. E., 260
Evans, R. I., 191, 198, 296–297, 319, 365
Everett, J., 435
Exner, J. E., 57
Exner, J. E., Jr., 57
Ey, S., 161
Eysenck, H. J., 183–184, 194, 267–269, 327
Eysenck, M. W., 46, 267
Eysenck, S. B. G., 268–269

Fabrega, H., Jr., 32
Fagen, G., 176
Fairfield, B., 119
Fairweather, D. R., 409
Fakouri, M. E., 111
Falbo, T., 110, 111
Fancher, R. E., 112
Fanon, F., 71, 72
Farre, J. M., 272
Farvolden, P., 55
Farwell, L., 173
Fasnacht, G., 295
Faulkender, P. J., 445
Featherman, D. L., 344
Feeney, B. C., 176
Fehr, B., 348
Feiring, C., 175
Fejfar, M. C., 266
Feltham, C., 402
Fenigstein, A., 288
Fenning, P., 390
Ferguson, E., 239
Ferguson, G. R., 16
Fernald, P. S., 404
Fernandez, M. E., 356
Ferster, C. B., 293
Feshbach, S., 328
Fincham, F. D., 117
Fine, H. J., 82
Fink, B., 253
Finkelhor, D., 56
Finn, M., 457–458, 482
Fischer, A. H., 256
Fischer, J. L., 142
Fish, S., 209
Fisher, J. D., 356
Fisher, S., 49–50, 54
Fisher, W. A., 356
Fisher, W. W., 295
Fiske, D. W., 309
Fisler, R., 60
Fitch, A., 441
Fitch, S. A., 144

Fitness, J., 87
Fitzgibbon, M., 142, 144
Fitzpatrick, J. J., 125, 128, 142
Fleeson, W., 238, 347
Fleming, C. M., 138
Flett, G. L., 161
Florin, P., 348
Floyd, R. G., 228
Flynn, J. R., 228
Fodor, E. M., 409
Foley, J. H., 145
Folkman, S., 332
Ford, J. G., 407
Ford, T. E., 36
Fordham, F., 85–86
Forest, J. J., 441
Forey, W. F., 110
Förster, J., 333
Forster, J. R., 390
Försterling, F., 337
Fosse, R., 35
Fox, N. A., 469
Fox, W. M., 434
Francis, D., 469
Francis, L. J., 208, 225
Frank, G., 40
Frank, J. B., 81
Frank, J. D., 81, 365, 445
Frank, M., 144
Frank, S. G., 58
Frankel, F. H., 33
Franken, I. H. A., 271
Franklin, A. J., 138
Franz, C., 18
Freese, J., 112
Freud, A., 41, 93
Freud, S., 18, 28, 30–32, 34–36, 38, 45, 50–53, 489
Freyd, J. J., 54
Frick, W. B., 204, 427–428, 438
Fridhandler, B., 42
Friedland, B. U., 114
Friedman, H. S., 196
Friedman, M., 411–412, 419
Friesen, W. V., 265
Frith, C., 263
Frith, U., 263
Froehle, T. C., 385
Fromm, M., 391
Fudin, R., 58
Fuller, R. C., 396, 406
Fullerton, C. S., 111
Fulton, A. S., 209
Funder, D. C., 13, 187
Furnham, A., 14, 89, 183, 231, 253
Fyfe, J. H., 88

Gaines, S. O., 202, 206
Galejs, I., 349
Gallo, E., 84
Galvin, M., 275
Gamble, G. O., 110
Gandhi, M. K., 123
Gangestad, S. W., 254
Gara, M. A., 390
Garcia, M. E., 356
Garcia-Coll, C., 260
Garden, A. M., 70
Gardner, L. E., 114
Gardner, W. L., 89

Garland, D. J., 231
Garnier, H. E., 408
Garrett, K. R., 297
Garrison, D., 163
Garrow, D. J., 63
Garza, A. A., 263
Gaskins, R. W., 463, 471
Gattuso, S., 417
Gaul, R., 46
Geary, P. S., 144
Gedo, P. M., 17
Geen, R. G., 268–269
Geher, G., 170
Geisler, C., 58
Gelfand, D. M., 356
Geller, L., 396
Gendlin, E. T., 403
Genia, V., 207
Genoni, T., Jr., 54–55
George, J. M., 240
Geppert, U., 133, 256
Gergen, K. J., 391
Gergen, M. M., 140
Gerton, J., 137
Ghezzi, P. M., 351
Ghose, L., 460
Gibson, H. B., 33
Giese-Davis, J., 333
Gigerenzer, G., 12
Gilat, I., 142
Gilbert, D. T., 192
Gillani, N. B., 480
Gilligan, C., 141, 165, 445
Gilliland, K., 268
Gilman, S. L., 155, 165
Giltinan, J. M., 441
Giorgi, A., 447
Giovando, K., 115
Girelli, S. A., 88
Girgus, J. S., 166
Gitzinger, I., 387
Glass, G. V., 166
Gleaves, D. H., 51
Gleser, G. C., 46
Glucksman, M. L., 168
Godin, G., 356
Goebel, B. L., 145
Goertzel, M. G., 111
Goertzel, T. G., 111
Goertzel, V., 111
Gold, I., 276
Goldberg, L. R., 193, 236, 240, 242
Goldfield, G. S., 161
Goldfried, M. R., 54
Goldman, L., 350
Goldsmith, H. H., 260
Goldsmith, L. T., 111
Goldwert, M., 17, 68
Goleman, D., 453, 464
Golosheykin, S., 478, 480
Gomez, A., 272
Gomez, R., 272
Gondola, J. C., 441
Gonzalez-Balado, J., 44
Goodspeed, R. B., 89
Goodstein, L., 454
Goodstein, R. C., 59
Gordon, C. R., 269
Gordon, R. D., 438
Gorsuch, R. L., 208–209
Gosling, S. D., 310

Gottman, J. M., 179
Gould, D., 357
Gould, M. S., 161
Graham, W. K., 434
Grand, S., 173
Grasing, K. W., 319
Grässmann, R., 357
Gravelle, F., 434, 436
Gray, A., 390
Gray, J., 267
Gray, J. A., 271, 273
Graziano, W. G., 238, 242, 262
Greasley, P., 195
Greaves, D. W., 494
Green, L., 434
Greenberg, J., 46, 54, 169
Greenberg, J. R., 179
Greenberg, L. S., 405, 411
Greenberg, R. P., 49–50, 54
Greenblatt, R. L., 114
Greene, B., 412
Greene, B. A., 412
Greenwald, A. G., 59
Greenwood, C. R., 295
Greever, K. B., 114
Grey, W., 84
Gross, J. J., 265, 333
Grossarth-Maticek, R., 327
Grossman, C. L., 196
Grossman, L. R., 55
Grossman, P., 479
Grotstein J. S., 169
Grove, S. J., 89
Grove, W. M., 225
Gruber, H. E., 18
Gruen, A., 411
Grünbaum, A., 57
Grusec, J., 361
Grusec, J. E., 360–361, 363
Grych, J. H., 117
Guastello, D. D., 110, 112
Guastello, S. J., 110, 112
Guignon, C. B., 113
Guisinger, S., 113
Gully, S. M., 354–355
Gundrum, M., 411
Gustafson, R., 329
Guthrie, A. J., 377, 382
Guydish, J., 374

Ha, Y., 375
Haaken, J., 165
Habermas, T., 132
Hackett, G., 356
Hafner, J. L., 111
Hageseth, J. A., 441
Haidt, J., 358
Haigh, G. V., 414
Hair, E. C., 238, 242
Haley, A., 34
Halisch, F., 133, 256
Hall, C. S., 34, 69, 83
Hall, J. A., 166
Hall, S. S., 477
Halpern, D. F., 275
Hammer, A. L., 88, 90
Hampson, S. E., 345
Hampson, S. L., 228
Han, J. J., 105
Hankoff, L. D., 106
Hanlon, R. P., Jr., 89

Hanna, F. J., 113
Hannah, M. T., 145–146
Hansen, D. J., 329
Hanson, G., 140
Hardaway, R. A., 58
Hardwired for God?, 263
Hargreaves, I., 45
Harlow, J. M., 263
Harmon-Jones, E., 265, 271
Harren, V. A., 390
Harrington, D. M., 88, 169, 408
Harris, C. R., 254
Harris, J. R., 493
Harris, S., 463
Harris, W. S., 446
Harris, Y. R., 351
Hart, D., 351
Hart, T., 412
Hartmann, E., 35, 128
Hartmann, H., 93
Harvey, R. J., 88, 90
Hattie, J., 14, 441
Haugland, S. N., 240
Haule, J. R., 76, 83, 455
Haupt, A. L., 173
Hayden, J., 356
Hayden, T., 344
Hayes, R. P., 459, 469
Hayes, S., 42
Haymes, M., 434
Haynes, S. N., 310
Hays, R. D., 356
Haythornthwaite, J. A., 224
Hazan, C., 176–178, 254
Heatherton, T. F., 173
Heaton, D. P., 481
Heckhausen, H., 36
Hector, M., 114
Heerboth, J. R., 441
Hegland, S. M., 349
Heiby, E. M., 301, 305–306
Heiligtag, U., 265
Heine, S., 472
Heine, S. J., 492
Heisel, A. D., 269
Heiser, W. J., 12
Heiserman, A., 173
Heisig, J. W., 455
Heller, J. F., 88
Helms, J. E., 138
Helson, R., 166, 202
Henning, K., 161
Henriques, J. B., 265
Henry, J., 137
Herb, L., 207
Herbener, E. S., 493
Herbst, J. H., 110–111
Herek, G. M., 207–208
Hermans, H. J. M., 5, 35, 193, 202
Hernandez, E., 51
Herrera, H., 341
Herrnstein, R. J., 228, 230
Herron, R. E., 479
Herron, W. G., 75
Hettman, D. W., 114
Heubeck, B. G., 271
Hewitt, P. L., 161
Heyduk, R. G., 288
Hicks, L. E., 88, 90
Higgins, C. A., 356
Higgins, E. T., 37, 110

Higley, S. L., 208–209
Hilgard, E. R., 33
Hill, A. B., 49
Hill, C. E., 57, 411, 413
Hill-Barlow, D., 328
Hillman, J., 90
Hills, P., 238
Hillstrom, E., 297
Hines, M., 362
Hirai, T., 477
Hirsch, C., 56
Hisrich, R., 390
Hobson, J. A., 35, 60
Hocoy, D., 139
Hodapp, V., 265
Hodgson, J. W., 142
Hoeckh, H., 387
Hoffman, C., 183
Hoffman, E., 100, 438
Hoffman, L. W., 110
Hoffman, M. L., 113
Hofmann, V., 175
Hofstetter, C. R., 356
Hogan, J., 184
Hogan, R., 184
Holland, D., 433
Holland, J. G., 297
Holland, J. L., 184, 433
Hollis, J., 83
Holt, R. R., 194
Hom, H. L., 350
Homma-True, R., 412
Honos-Webb, L., 334
Hoogduin, C. A. L., 365, 413
Hooven, C., 179
Hoover, D. R., 446
Hopkins, J. R., 127
Horley, J., 390
Horn, J., 222, 227–228
Hornbuckle, D., 106
Horner, A. J., 161
Horner, M. S., 164
Horney, K., 151–152, 155, 157–165,
    167–168
Horowitz, H. A., 176
Horowitz, L. M., 178
Horwitz, N. M., 162
Houston, B. K., 265
Houston, J., 438
Houts, A. C., 337
Hovell, M. F., 356
Howard, G. S., 12, 373, 389, 419, 499
Howard, J. A., 165
Howe, M. L., 104
Howell, R. H., 362
Hoyle, R. H., 266
Huber, J. W., 390
Huber, R. J., 118
Hudson, J. I., 55
Hudson, V. M., 111
Huesmann, L. R., 169
Huff, S., 356
Huffman, J. R., 161
Hughes, A. T., 229
Hui, C. H., 166
Hull, J. G., 327
Hume, D. K., 253
Hunsberger, B., 209
Hunter, J. E., 14
Huntley, C. W., 197
Hur, Y., 90

Huston, H. L., 79
Hutcherson, H. W., 12
Hutton, P. H., 125
Hwang, M. Y., 137
Hyland, M. E., 495
Hyman, R. B., 434

Ianni, F. F., 46
Ihilevich, D., 46
Immelman, A., 12
Infeld, L., 497
Ingram, D. H., 156, 161
Inks, L. W., 390
Irving, J. A., 57
Itzkowitz, N., 371
Ivancevich, J. M., 110
Iversen, J., 478
Ivey, A. E., 413
Izard, C. E., 265

Jackson, L. M., 209
Jackson, T. T., 374
Jacobo, M. C., 52
Jacobsen, T., 175
Jaffa, M., 33
Jaffe, A. J., 378
Jaffe, L. S., 53, 56
Jakupcak, M., 330
Jamner, L. D., 334
Jankowicz, A. D., 390
Jason, L. A., 470
Jefferson, T., Jr., 110–111
Jeffery, R. W., 364
Jenkins, A. H., 412
Jenkins, E., 114
Jennings, J. L., 331
Jensen, J. P., 494
Jensen-Campbell, L. A., 238, 242, 262
Jinkerson, D. L., 441
Jinpa, G. T., 463
Joe, V. C., 209
John, O. P., 183, 193, 195, 236–239, 242
Johnson, B. T., 210
Johnson, M. E., 164
Johnson, M. H., 480
Johnson, N. B., 82
Johnson, S. L., 271
Johnson, T. E., 329
Johnson, W., 228
Jones, A., 441
Jones, D., 75, 256
Jones, E. E., 54, 90
Jones, M. M., 32
Jones, T. L., 355
Jones, W. H., 130
Josephs, R. A., 327
Josselson, R., 142
Joubert, C. E., 111, 113
Jourden, F. J., 357
Jouriles, E., 327
Jowdy, D. P., 144
Judge, T. A., 239
Jung, C. G., 64, 67, 70, 72–74, 77–78, 80–83

Kagan, J., 6, 14, 190, 228, 260–264, 272, 492
Kahle, L. R., 444
Kahn, E., 409, 412, 416, 418
Kahn, J., 452
Kahneman, D., 258

Kaiser, R. S., 33
Kalekin-Fishman, D., 386
Kaliski, E. M., 356
Kalra, A., 59
Kamilar, S., 452, 458, 462, 467–468, 471, 479, 482
Kandel, E. R., 60
Kanfer, R., 239
Kantrowitz, T. M., 239
Kaplan, H. A., 43
Kaplan, H. B., 113
Kaplan, S. J., 114
Karney, B. R., 238
Karon, B. P., 55
Karten, Y. J. G., 255
Kasamatsu, A., 477
Kaser-Boyd, N., 57
Kaslow, N. J., 172
Kast, V., 79
Katigbak, M. S., 242
Katz, I., 206
Katz, L. F., 179
Kavanagh, D. J., 484
Kazdin, A. E., 295
Kear-Colwell, J. J., 385
Kearney, P., 458, 466
Keefer, L., 479
Keijsers, G. P. J., 365, 413
Keller, R. R., 458
Kelly, A. E., 333
Kelly, G. A., 373–382, 385–389
Kelman, H. C., 206
Keltner, D., 250
Kendall, E., 254
Kendall-Tackett, K. A., 56
Kendler, H. H., 447
Kenrick, D. T., 251
Kensit, D. A., 419
Kern, C., 171
Kern, G. M., 89
Kernberg, P. F., 42
Kerr, M., 238
Kesler/West, M. L., 263
Kessler, K. L., 255
Kessler, R. C., 178, 224
Ketelaar, T., 271
Keutzer, C. S., 84
Kewman, D. G., 17
Khong, B. S. L., 482
Khouzam, N., 390
Kidney, B. A., 144
Kiecolt-Glaser, J. K., 119
Kihlstrom, J., 34, 59
Kihlstrom, J. F., 34, 59
Killgore, W. D. S., 363
Kim, J. E., 344
Kimball, M. M., 30
Kimble, G. A., 18–19, 288
King, K., 202
King, L. A., 240
King, M. L., Jr., 65
King, N., 96
Kiracofe, H. N., 110
Kiracofe, N. M., 110
Kircher, T. T. J., 263
Kirkpatrick, L. A., 176–177
Kirmayer, L. J., 50
Kirsch, I., 33
Kirsch, T. B., 69
Kirschenbaum, D. S., 354
Kiser, L. J., 56

Kitayama, S., 492
Kivnick, H. Q., 128–129, 136
Kjaer, T. W., 478
Klatzky, R. L., 348
Klayman, J., 375
Klein, M., 23
Klein, S., 467
Klein, S. B., 333
Klepser, J., 171
Kliegl, R., 227
Klohnen, E. C., 145, 176, 178
Kluckhohn, C., 4
Knierim, T., 458
Knight, H., 350
Knight, J., 452
Knight, K., 111
Knight, Z. G., 179
Knish, S., 354
Knoll, C., 441
Knopman, D. S., 48
Knowles, P. A., 89
Koch, S., 488
Koepke, J. E., 145
Koestner, R., 37
Kohlmetz, C., 481
Kohut, H., 172
Kollins, S. H., 290
Koltko-Rivera, M. E., 447
Konefal, J., 441
Konik, J., 143
Kopetskie, S., 301, 305
Kopiez, R., 481
Koran, J. J., 362
Kores, R. C., 356
Kraemer, G. W., 275
Kraft, T., 33
Kramer, J. J., 108, 119
Krank, H. M., 296
Kratochwill, T. R., 119
Kris, E., 45
Kroger, J., 142
Krosnick, J. A., 59
Kuhlman, D. M., 266, 269
Kuhn, D., 375
Kuhn, T. S., 18, 488
Kukla, A., 496
Kull, S., 80
Kunzendorf, R. G., 56
Kuo, W. H., 110
Kuo, Y., 434
Kupfersmid, J., 51
Kurdek, L. A., 238
Kwan, K. K., 139
Kwan, V. S. Y., 159, 166
Kwapil, T. R., 269

Labouvie-Vief, G., 227
Lacks, R., 76
LaFromboise, T., 137–138
Lamal, P. A., 354
Lambert, W. W., 238
Lamborn, S. D., 169
Lamiell, J. T., 193–194
Lamke, L. K., 142
LaMothe, R., 119
Lancaster, B. L., 475–476, 485
Landfield, A. W., 375, 377, 380, 383, 385, 388
Landrine, H., 166
Lang, P. J., 59
Langer, W., 17

Langlois, J. H., 308
Langs, R., 57
Lang-Takac, E., 165
Lanier, L. S., 438
Larsen, R. J., 271, 353
Larson, C. L., 468
Las Heras, A., 68
Lash, J. P., 314
Lasko, J. K., 110
Laub, D., 48
Laungani, P., 412
Lauter, E., 80
Lawrence, L., 51
Lay, C. H., 354
Layton, L., 18
Lazar, A., 54
Lazar, S. W., 478
Lazarsfeld, S., 102
Lazarus, A. A., 494
Lazarus, R. S., 57, 332
Leach, C., 383
Leak, G. K., 114, 209
Leary, M. R., 173
LeDoux, J., 254, 257, 275
Lee, D. H., 227
Lee, D. Y., 413
Lefebure, L. D., 472
Leggett, E. L., 349
Lehrer, R., 390
Leichtman, M. D., 105
Leifer, M., 56
Leigh, H., 334
Leitner, L. M., 373, 377, 382, 386, 414
Lemery, K. S., 260
Lemire, D., 103
Lennings, C. J., 350
Lent, R. W., 356–357
Leonard, J., 60
Leong, F. T. L., 238
LePage, A., 329
Lepore, S. J., 333
Lerman, H., 141, 163
Lerner, J. A., 167
Lerner, P. M., 48
Lester, D., 434
Levant, R. F., 166
LeVay, S., 52
Levenson, R. W., 333
Levey, J., 370
Levin, E. L., 81
Levine, C., 136, 143, 146
Levine, C. G., 146
Levine, D. S., 495
Levine, F. M., 295
Levitz-Jones, E. M., 142
Levy, K. N., 176
Lewes, L., 52
Lewin, K., 232, 415
Lewis, C. A., 49
Lewis, W. A., 328
Liberman, N., 333
Liberman, R. P., 295
Liebert, R. M., 350
Lietaer, G., 411
Lievens, F., 236
Lifton, N., 171
Lilenfeld, L. R. R., 49
Lillqvist, O., 375
Lin, Y., 133
Lindeman, M., 375
Lindsay, D. S., 34, 54

Lindzey, G., 197
Lippa, R., 196
Lisak, D., 330
Lisle, L., 36
Litt, M. D., 358
Littler, D., 390
Livesley, W. J., 3
Llewelyn, S. P., 56
Lobel, T. E., 142, 144, 166
Lockhart, W. H., 413
Lockwood, L., 437
Loehlin, J. C., 228, 259, 489
Loevinger, J., 94, 128
Loewenberg, P., 27
Loffredo, D. A., 88
Loftus, E. F., 55, 89
Logan, R. L., 145
Lohr, B. A., 43
Lombardi, D. N., 118
London, P., 494
Long, R. G., 110
Looby, J., 406, 444
Lorenzini, R., 390
Lorimer, R., 125
Lorr, H., 88
Lowis, M. J., 133–134
Lowry, R. J., 427, 431–432
Loy, D. R., 464, 469
Lubinski, D., 184, 197
Lucca, C. A., 331
Luckmann, T., 391
Lukoff, D., 80–81
Lundin, R. W., 296
Lupfer, M. B., 12
Lussier, Y., 238
Luthans, F., 356
Lutz, A., 477
Lykken, D., 259
Lykken, D. T., 259
Lynn, R., 228
Lynn, S. J., 33–34
Lyons-Ruth, K., 329

Maas, S., 407
Mabry, C. H., 51
Maccoby, M., 464
MacDonald, D. A., 433
Mace, F. C., 295
MacGregor, M. W., 46
Mack, J. E., 17–18, 51, 80
Mackavey, W. R., 133
MacLean, C. R. K., 480
Maddi, S. R., 186, 426–428
Madrian, J. C., 174
Magnusson, D., 189
Mahalik, J. R., 139, 166
Mahathera, N., 459
Mahoney, M. F., 82
Mahony, P. J., 54
Mahrer, A. R., 409, 413
Mahrle, C. L., 89
Maidenbaum, A., 64
Maio, G. R., 264
Mair, G., 96
Mair, M., 389
Malik, R., 58
Malinosky-Rummell, R., 329
Malley, J. E., 133
Mallinckrodt, B., 176
Mallory, M. E., 143

Malm, L., 397
Malone, M., 87
Malone, P. S., 192
Maloney, A., 75
Maltin, L., 492, 497
Manaster, G. J., 113
Mancuso, J. C., 376, 385
Manheim, A. R., 439
Mansell, W., 161
Mansfield, V., 84
Manson, S. M., 138
Maoz, Z., 384
Marceil, J. C., 194
Marcia, J. E., 133, 142–145
Marcovitz, E., 68
Marcus-Newhall, A., 328
Margolin, A., 484
Marks, C., 88
Marks, S. G., 145
Markstrom-Adams, C., 138, 142
Markus, H., 194
Markus, H. R., 492
Marlatt, G. A., 484
Marmar, C., 54
Marsden, D., 390
Marsella, A. J., 492
Marsh, C. S., 202
Marshall, G. N., 184
Martens, B. K., 119
Martin, A., 58
Martin, J., 388, 391
Martin, R. A., 88
Martinez, T. J., III, 67, 444
Martinko, M. J., 89–90
Martocchio, J. J., 239
Marx, D. M., 206
Masling, J., 49
Masling, J. M., 37, 57
Maslow, A. H., 316, 395, 426–433, 435–440, 442, 444–447
Mason, L. I., 481
Massarik, F., 418, 443
Massaro, T. M., 135
Masson, J. M., 51
Masters, R., 438
Masunaga, H., 227
Matheny, A. P., Jr., 347
Mathes, E. W., 438
Matta, K. F., 89
Matteson, M. T., 110
Mattoon, M. A., 82
Mauro, C. F., 351
May, J., 80, 484
May, R., 80, 419
Mayer, J. D., 87, 232, 264, 310, 411
Mayes, C., 76
Maynard, E. A., 209
McAdams, D. P., 18, 81, 145
McArdle, J. J., 222, 227
McCann, J. T., 441
McCarley, R. W., 35
McCaulley, M. H., 85, 88–90
McClelland, D. C., 16, 37, 446–447
McCloskey, M., 210
McClure, E. B., 274–275
McCormick, C., 384
McCourt, K., 259
McCrae, R. R., 8, 13, 88, 110–111, 168, 183, 236–239, 241–242, 249, 259–260, 492

McCroskey, J. C., 269
McCullagh, P., 360
McCullough, M. E., 209, 455
McCusker, C., 166
McDargh, J., 468–469
McDonald, F. J., 361
McFarlane, A. C., 48
McGaugh, J. L., 60
McGee, S. J., 209
McGee, V. E., 196
McGowan, D., 67
McGrath, J., 51
McGregor, H. A., 329
McGue, M., 259
McGuire, W., 67
McKay, G., 108, 116
McKay, J. R., 172
McKee, K. J., 136
McLeod, C. R., 442
McMullin, E., 11
McNamara, L., 266
McNamara, P., 35
McPherson, F. M., 390
McPherson, S. E., 208
McWilliams, S. A., 374
Meaney, M. J., 255, 469
Mednick, M., 348
Meehl, P. E., 11, 14, 225
Meissner, W. W., 56
Melburg, V., 329
Menaker, E., 164
Mendelsohn, E., 58
Mendolia, M., 60
Mendoza-Denton, R., 345
Menlove, F. L., 360–361, 363–364
Merenda, P. F., 3
Merikle, P. M., 59
Merritt, J. M., 35
Mesquida, C. G., 256
Messer, S., 49
Metcalfe, J., 352
Metzler, A. E., 390
Meyer, B., 272
Meyer-Bahlburg, H. F. L., 52
Michael, J., 294
Michalon, M., 455, 463, 482
Mickelson, K. D., 178
Midence, K., 45
Midgley, B. D., 497
Mihesuah, D. A., 138–139
Mikulincer, M., 176–177
Miles, A., 205
Miletic, M. P., 167
Mill, J., 88
Miller, C., 306
Miller, D. B., 138
Miller, D. I., 356
Miller, E., 263
Miller, E. M., 255
Miller, G., 100
Miller, J. B., 165
Miller, J. D., 266
Miller, M. E., 482
Miller, M. J., 114
Miller, N. E., 318–320, 322–328, 330–332
Miller, T. Q., 159
Mills, P. J., 480
Minarik, M. L., 161
Mind and Life Institute, 453, 467

Mineka, S., 264
Minton, H. L., 107
Mischel, H. N., 350
Mischel, W., 16, 192, 342–352, 361, 406
Mitchell, S., 169
Mitchell, S. A., 169, 172
Mitchison, G., 35
Mittelman, W., 440
Mongrain, M., 169
Monk-Turner, E., 479
Monte, C. F., 105
Montgomerie, R., 253
Montgomery, G., 33
Moodley, R., 412
Moor, C. J., 158
Moore, B., 350
Moore, D. K., 139
Moore, J., 60
Moore, M. K., 385
Moran, C., 56
Moran, D. J., 295
Moran, J. R., 138
Morçöl, G., 387
Morf, C. C., 174
Morgan, A. C., 167
Morgan, D., 482
Morgan, M. A., 261
Mori, C., 419
Moritsugu, J., 470
Moritz, C., 318–319
Morris, C., 117
Morris, E. K., 296, 497
Morris, M. G., 51
Morrison, K., 54
Morse, C., 116
Morse, W., 56
Morvay, Z., 155, 455
Mosak, H. H., 116
Moskowitz, D. S., 310
Mosquera, P. M. R., 256
Motley, M. T., 58
Mount, M. K., 239
Moustakas, C., 395
Moutafi, J., 253
Mozdzierz, G. J., 114, 441
Mraz, W., 439
Mueller, D. R., 390
Mulaik, S. A., 344
Mullen, M. K., 104–105
Mullineux, J. C., 228
Multon, K. D., 357
Munter, P. O., 396
Muramoto, S., 455
Muraven, M., 41
Murgatroyd, W., 207
Murphy, T. J., 114, 441
Murray, H. A., 4–5, 25–27, 103
Murray, J. B., 88
Muslin, H., 125
Myers, D. G., 444
Myers, I. B., 88–90
Myers, J. E., 105
Myers, L. B., 46
Myers, S., 411

Nadel, L., 104
Nahmias E., 465
Naifeh, S. C., 67
Napa, C. K., 444

Nash, M. R., 34, 48
Nathan, B. N., 337, 362
Natsoulas, T., 59
Nauta, M. M., 333
Navarick, D. J., 351
Neher, A., 75, 78
Neimeyer, G. J., 144, 387, 390, 494
Neimeyer, R. A., 376, 379, 381, 383–385, 387–389, 436
Nelson, D. V., 89, 465
Nesselroade, J. R., 233, 344
Neumann, E., 76
Nevid, J. S., 142
Nevis, E. C., 446
Newberg, A., 485
Newberg, A. B., 478, 485
Newman, B. M., 132
Newman, D. L., 259
Newman, J. P., 273
Newman, L. S., 43, 110
Newman, P. R., 132
Nez, D., 82
Nezlek, J. B., 133
Nghe, L. T., 139
Nhat Hanh, T., 459, 462, 465–466, 468, 470
Nichols, D. R., 210
Nicholson, I., 186
Nicholson, I. A. M., 187, 426–427, 445
Nichtern, S., 125
Nidich, R. J., 481
Nidich, S. I., 473, 481
Niemann, Y. F., 139
Nigg, J. T., 172
Nippoda, Y., 166
Nisbett, R. E., 90
Nissen, M. J., 48
Nitis, T., 492
Nixon, R. M., 370–371
Nocks, E. C., 362
Nolen-Hoeksema, S., 166
Noll, R., 67–68, 74, 78, 81
Nordby, V. J., 69, 83
Norman, W. T., 236
North-Schulte, D., 469
Nota, L., 302
Novotny, K. M., 418
Nylén, S., 58

O'Brien, E. J., 343
O'Brien, L., 332
O'Connell, A. N., 154–155
O'Donnell, J., 139
O'Donohue, W. T., 337
O'Hara, M., 414
O'Leary, A., 295, 333, 356
O'Leary, K. D., 299
O'Neill, R. M., 49–50
O'Roark, A. M., 84, 88
Oates, S. B., 64
Ochberg, R. L., 18
Ochse, R., 138, 142, 144
Odbert, H. S., 3, 183, 195
Ofshe, R., 55
Öhman, A., 264
Oishi, S., 206
Okagaki, L., 139
Olariu, A., 255
Olds, D. D., 59
Oles, P. K., 202

Olson, B., 246
Olson, E. E., 89
Oppenheimer, R., 497
Orbach, I., 161
Orlofsky, J. L., 142, 144–145
Orme-Johnson, D. W., 473
Orne, M. T., 33
Osier, T. J., 177
Ostendorf, F., 195
Osterweil, Z., 165
Ostrove, J. M., 142
Ota, S., 110
Otta, E., 252
Otto, R. K., 17
Overton, R. K., 102
Owen, D., 282–284
Owen, P. D., 362
Owens, R. G., 306
Oxman, T. E., 196
Ozer, D. J., 242
Ozer, E. M., 356

Pace-Schott, E. F., 35
Padilla, J. N. M., 296
Page, M. M., 434
Paige, J. M., 196
Paivio, A., 10
Palmer, E. C., 419
Pam, A., 37
Pancer, S. M., 384
Pandora, K., 189
Paniagua, F. A., 297
Panksepp, J., 250
Paranjpe, A. C., 462, 465–466, 485
Parcet, M. A., 272
Pargament, K. I., 139
Paris, B. J., 156, 160–161
Park, C., 207
Park, H. S., 207
Parker, W., 161
Pasupathi, M., 389
Patai, R., 76
Paterson, D. G., 194
Patterson, D. R., 33
Patton, C. J., 58
Patton, G. K., 240
Paul, R., 51
Paulhus, D. L., 42
Payne, R. L., 444
Peake, P. K., 192, 344–345, 351
Pearson, C., 56, 387, 473
Pearson, P. R., 208
Pedersen, W. C., 253
Pelzer, D., 422–425
Pennebaker, J., 333
Pennebaker, J. W., 333
Penton-Voak, I., 253
Pepper, S. C., 496
Perlini, A. H., 34
Perlman, M., 80
Perry J. C., 46
Perry, N. W., 417
Perry, S. M., 233
Pervin, L. A., 309, 498
Peters, P. L., 233
Peterson, B. E., 144–145, 327
Peterson, C., 119, 309
Peterson, K. L., 417
Peterson, L. E., 494
Peterson, R. F., 294

Peterson-Cooney, L., 441
Petrie, K. J., 333–334
Pettigrew, T. F., 187, 206
Peyton, K. G., 142
Pfenninger, D. T., 377, 386
Phillips, A. S., 110
Phillips, J. M., 354–355
Phillips, K., 347
Phillips, K. L., 83
Philogene, G., 138
Phinney, J. S., 138
Picano, J., 166
Picariello, M. L., 104
Pichot, P., 57, 81
Pickering, A. D., 269, 271, 273
Pickrell, J. E., 55
Piechowski, M. M., 316, 436
Piedmont, R. L., 237, 242
Pierce, J. L., 164
Piers, C., 23, 48
Pietikainen, P., 68, 75
Pietromonaco, P. R., 178, 237–238
Pigliucci, M., 485
Pillemer, D. B., 104
Pinker, S., 257
Planalp, S., 87
Platts, C., 205
Playfoot, J. N., 44
Pletsch, C., 18
Pleydell-Pearce, C. W., 60
Plomin, R., 260
Plouffe, L., 434, 436
Plug, C., 138, 142, 144
Podd, M. H., 144
Polich, J., 477, 480
Polivy, J., 351
Polkinghorne, D. E., 447, 496
Pollock, P. H., 385
Pope, H. G., 55
Pope, K. S., 223
Poppen, R., 294
Porter, S. S., 390
Postman, L., 188–189, 210
Pouliot, C., 435
Pounds, B., 114
Powell, B., 112
Power, M. J., 46
Prager, E., 434
Pratt, A. B., 119, 145, 494
Pratt, M. W., 145
Premack, A., 257
Premack, D., 257
Prerost, F. J., 119
Pressley, M., 55
Preston, C. A., 387
Pretz, J., 296
Price, M., 161
Price, M. E., 251
Prilleltensky, I., 446
Primavera, J. P., III, 33
Prinz, R. J., 355
Privette, G., 437–438
Proctor, B. E., 228
Progoff, I., 82
Protinsky, H., 144
Pruett, J. C., 104
Pryor, D. B., 117
Pulkkinen, L., 107, 142
Putnam, F. W., 56

Putnam, K. M., 468
Pyszczynski, T., 46

Qirko, H., 255
Quartz, S., 264
Quay, H. C., 272
Quilitch, H. R., 294
Quinn, S., 154–155

Rachman, A. W., 412
Rachman, S., 54
Rachman, S. J., 291
Radke-Yarrow, M., 113
Radvansky, G. A., 334
Raine, A., 263, 270
Ramanaiah, N. V., 441
Rammsayer, T. H., 268
Range, L. M., 161
Rapaport, D., 93
Rareshide, M. B., 144, 494
Raskin, J. D., 388, 391
Ratanakul, P., 484
Rathunde, K., 448
Ratican, K. L., 60
Rause, V., 485
Raz-Duvshani, A., 387
Read, J. D., 34, 54
Reed, C., 453
Reed, E. S., 202, 206
Reese, L., 358
Reinsdorf, W., 45
Reis, H. T., 133
Reise, S. P., 238, 242
Reiser, M. F., 35
Render, G. F., 296
Rendon, M., 330
Rennie, D. L., 413
Repp, A., 119
ReVille, S., 129
Reyher, J., 58
Reyna, V. F., 59
Reznick, J. S., 260
Rhodewalt, F., 174
Rholes, W. S., 177
Ricard, M., 485–486
Rice, K. G., 161, 390
Rice, L. N., 413
Richards, A. C., 417
Richards, J. M., 333
Richards, N., 279
Richards, P. S., 457
Richardson, F. C., 113, 280
Richardson, S. A., 89
Richman, J., 118–119
Richmond, V. P., 269
Rideout, C. A., 89
Riedel, H. P. R., 301, 305–306
Rigby, S., 202
Riggio, R. E., 196
Rilling, M., 279
Risberg, J., 268
Risemberg, R., 354
Ritskes, R., 477
Ritter, B., 363
Rivera, J. A., 37
Roberge, L. P., 89
Roberts, B. W., 184, 202, 205
Roberts, R. E., 138
Robins, C. J., 482
Robinson, A. E., 81
Robinson, D. L., 267

Rocchi, M. T., 390
Rode, C., 258
Rodin, J., 358
Rodriguez, M. L., 351
Rodriquez, V., 139
Roemer, L., 330
Roemer, W. W., 159
Roffe-Steinrotter, D., 409
Roffman, R. A., 363
Rogeness, G. A., 274–275
Rogers, C. R., 296, 377, 396, 402–408, 410, 412–413, 415–419
Rokeach, M., 375
Rolfhus, E. L., 227
Roll, S., 171
Romanczyk, R. G., 119
Romanoff, B., 389
Romero, A., 139
Romero, A. J., 139
Romm, S., 45
Rönkä, A., 142
Roozendaal, B., 60
Roscoe, B., 417
Rose, G. J., 45
Rosen, D. H., 68, 71, 78–79
Rosen, J. B., 261, 275
Rosenberg, B. G., 112
Rosenberg, S., 390
Rosenberg, S. D., 196
Rosenman, S., 51
Rosenstein, D. S., 176
Ross, D., 361–362
Ross, D. L., 58
Ross, J. M., 207
Ross, L., 90
Ross, S. A., 361–362
Rothbart, M. K., 242, 260
Rothbaum, F., 107
Rothschild, B., 49
Rotter, J. B., 349
Rouse, S. V., 37
Rowan, J., 430
Rowe, D. C., 260
Rubin, J. B., 457–458, 482
Rubin, K. H., 276
Rubin, R., 144
Rubinstein, B. B., 56
Ruetzel, K., 145
Ruffins, S. A., 171
Ruffman, T., 111
Rule, B. G., 329
Runco, M. A., 439
Runyan, W. M., 4, 17–18, 194
Runyon, R. S., 99
Rupprecht, C. S., 80
Russell, J. A., 348
Russell, R. L., 413, 494
Russo, N. F., 155
Rutherford, A., 296
Ruvolo, A. P., 417
Ryan, R. M., 202, 419, 448–449, 486
Ryback, D., 80, 418
Rychlak, J. F., 11, 396–397, 414, 447, 497–499
Ryckman, R. M., 432
Ryff, C. D., 238, 240

Sabol, S. Z., 264, 274
Sabourin, S., 238
Sackett, S. J., 443
Salerno, J. W., 480

Salinas, C., 196
Sallis, J. F., 356
Salmon, C. A., 110–111
Salmon, D., 390
Salmon, P., 390
Salovey, P., 42, 46, 87, 264, 411
Saltman, V., 56
Sampson, E. E., 139, 496
Sampson, H., 54
Samuelberg, P., 58
Sandell, R., 54
Sanders, J. D., 263
Sanger, M., 44
Sapirstein, G., 33
Sappington, A. A., 498
Sarason, S. B., 318
Saraswati, N., 466
Sarbin, T. R., 496–498
Sarchione, C. D., 239
Sassaroli, S., 390
Sauer, A., 106
Saunders, P., 74
Saw, C., 417
Sax, K. W., 273
Schaap, C. P. D. R., 365, 413
Schachter, S., 111
Schacter, D. L., 48
Schaefer, S. M., 478
Schaum, M., 76
Scheflin, A. W., 54
Schepeler, E., 18
Scherr, A., 29
Schiedel, D. G., 142, 145
Schmidt, D. B., 197
Schmidt, F. L., 14
Schmidt, L. A., 259
Schmidt, L. D., 441
Schmidt, L. E., 453
Schmitt, D. P., 253–254
Schmitt, D. R., 297
Schmitz, J. M., 356
Schmutte, P. S., 238, 240
Schnaitter, R., 297
Schneider, R. H., 473, 480
Schnell, R. L., 125
Schnurr, P. P., 196
Schoeneberg, L. A., 114
Schoenrade, P., 209
Schoenrade, P. A., 209
Schore, A. N., 61
Schott, R. L., 433, 444
Schramski, T. G., 115
Schuerger, J. M., 226
Schulkin, J., 261, 275
Schulman, E., 161
Schultheiss, O. C., 357
Schultz, G. S., 433
Schurr, K. T., 89
Schut, H., 333
Schwartz, D., 52
Schwartz, L. K., 206
Schwartz, M. D., 239
Schwartz, P., 165
Scott, N. E., 412
Scott, S., 130
Sears, D. O., 4
Seeman, M., 479
Seeman, T. E., 479
Segal, D. L., 158
Segura, D. A., 164
Sejnowski, T., 264

Sejnowski, T. J., 264
Seligman, M. E., 349
Seligman, M. E. P., 119, 396, 397, 448
Sewell, K. W., 385
Sexton, H., 413
Sexton, T. L., 357
Shackelford, T. K., 239, 254, 256
Shafran, R., 161
Shamdasani, S., 68
Shapiro, B. L., 390
Shapiro, J. P., 56
Shapiro, K., 60
Shapiro, S. B., 416
Shapiro, S. I., 428
Shapiro, S. L., 457, 479, 482
Sharp, L. K., 333
Sharpe, T. M., 49
Sharpsteen, D. J., 177
Shatz, S. M., 158
Shaver, P., 176–178
Shaver, P. R., 172, 176–178
Shaver, R. B., 228
Shaw, D., 161
Shean, G., 377
Shelton, S. H., 356
Sher, K. J., 274
Sherman, R., 117
Shevrin, H., 58
Shiflett, S. C., 90
Shiner, R. L., 262
Shoda, Y., 345–346, 351–352
Shore, J., 466
Shostrom, E. L., 410, 420, 436, 441
Shotter, J., 388
Shulman, D. G., 16, 58
Sidén, Y., 58
Siegel, B., 165
Sigvardsson, S., 274
Silon, B., 56
Silverman, D. K., 176
Silverman, L. H., 16, 57–58
Silverman, M., 171
Silverstein, S. M., 33
Simerly, D. E., 141
Simmons, J. P., 206
Simon, L., 329
Simonton, D. K., 233
Simpson, J. A., 254
Singelis, T. M., 159, 166
Singer, J., 81
Singh, N. N., 468
Sipe, R. B., 446
Sipps, G. J., 88
Siqueira, J. O., 252
Sizemore, C. C., 118
Skar, P., 74
Skinner, B. F., 286–287, 289–294, 296–297, 300, 417
Skinner, N. F., 233
Slade, P. D., 306
Slaney, R. B., 161
Slap, J. W., 45
Slife, B. D., 497
Slote, W. H., 163
Smart, L., 174, 329
Smirles, K. A., 145
Smith, C. P., 15
Smith, H., 396
Smith, J. C., 480
Smith, M. A., 265
Smith, M. B., 396–397, 446–447

Smith, S. M., 79
Smith, T. L., 494
Smith, T. W., 138
Smyth, J. M., 333
Sneed, C. D., 13, 239
Snidman, N., 190
So, K., 473
Sohier, R., 136
Sohlberg, S., 58
Sohn, D., 354
Soldz, S., 242
Solomon, R., 56
Solomon, S., 46
Soltz, V., 107–108
Somer, O., 242
Somervell, P., 138
Sommer, K. L., 47
Soresi, S., 302
Sowarka, D., 227
Spaccarelli, S., 56
Spanos, N. P., 33
Spechler, M. M., 441
Spencer, M. B., 138
Spencer, R. C., 438
Sperling, M. B., 176
Sperry, L., 119
Sperry, R. W., 498
Spiegel, D., 333
Spiegelman, J. M., 84
Spielberg, S., 80
Spink, K., 185
Spitz, R. A., 174
Srivastava, S., 242
Staats, A. W., 8, 280, 297–298, 300–310, 337, 494–495
Staddon, J. E. R., 290
Staggers, F., 480
Stajkovic, A. D., 356
Stake, J. E., 88
Stålenheim, E. G., 256
Stallings, M. C., 274
Stam, H. J., 391
Stamatelos, T., 438
State v. Michaels, 55
Staub, E., 349
Staudinger, U. M., 238
Stava, L. J., 33
Steblay, N. M., 34
Steele, C. M., 206, 327
Steelman, L. C., 112
Stein, H., 117
Stein, H. T., 102–103, 113, 117
Stein, J. A., 408
Stein, L. M., 59
Steinem, G., 149–151
Steklis, H. D., 275, 492
Stelmack, R. M., 268–269
Stenberg, G., 59, 258, 268
Stephens, R. S., 363
Stern, P. J., 68
Stevens, A., 74
Stewart, A., 143, 390
Stewart, A. J., 18, 133, 142, 144–145
Stewart, G. L., 237
Stewart, R. B., 111
Stewart, S. E., 158
Stewart, V., 390
Stickgold, R., 35
Stifler, K., 45
Stillwell, A., 499
Stock, J., 357

Stoljar, D., 276
Stone, A. A., 46, 224
Stone, L., 18
Storm, L., 84
Störmer, S. W., 265
Stouder, R., 356
Strakowski, S. M., 273
Strand, P. S., 295
Stratton, G. M., 467–468
Strauss, J. P., 239
Street, G. P., 333
Streitmatter, J., 142
Strelau, J., 267
Stringfield, P., 89
Stroebe, M., 333
Stroebe, W., 333
Strube, M. J., 110
Strupp, H. H., 54
Stuss, D. T., 105
Sudak, H. S., 169
Suedfeld, P., 384–385
Sugarman, A., 23
Sugarman, J., 391
Sugiyama, M. S., 50
Sullivan, G., 17
Sullivan, H. S., 93
Sullivan-Logan, G. M., 262
Sulloway, F. J., 31, 52, 111–112
Sumedho, B., 460, 462
Sumerlin, J. R., 441
Sundberg, N. D., 87–88
Sutton, S. K., 265
Svrakic, D. M., 274
Swank, P., 106, 114
Swansbrough, R. H., 159
Sweeny, T. J., 105
Swickert, R. J., 268
Symonds, A., 154–155, 165
Szasz, T., 53
Szasz, T. S., 409
Szyf, M., 255

Tai, W., 295
Talbot, R., 390
Tangney, J. P., 51, 328–329
Tarakeshwar, N., 139
Tarpley, W. R., 210, 444
Tart, C. T., 84
Tataryn, D. J., 59
Tate, D. G., 17
Tatsuoka, M. M., 225
Taub, J. M., 270
Taylor, E., 67, 395, 477
Taylor, J. C., 119
Taylor, J. G., 474
Taylor, M. C., 166
Taylor, S. E., 254
Tchir, M. A., 183
Tedeschi, J. T., 329
Tegano, D. W., 88
Teixeira, B., 123
Tellegen, A., 259
Tenopyr, M. L., 184
Tesser, A., 60, 259
Teti, D. M., 356
Thalbourne, M. A., 84
Tharp, R. G., 306
The Transcendental Meditation
    program, 472
Thöm, C., 58
Thom, D. P., 138

Thomas, A., 260
Thomas, C. B., 57
Thompson, B., 88
Thompson, J. K., 310
Thompson, R. F., 280, 310
Thomson, L., 64
Thomson, N. F., 90, 482
Thomson, R. F., 465
Thoresen, C. J., 239
Thorne, B. M., 88
Thuan, T. X., 485–486
Tice, D. M., 41, 173, 194
Ticho, E. A., 68
Tiger Woods Profile, 282
Tillman, J. G., 48
Tinling, L., 118
Tloczynski, J., 204, 441
Tobacyk, J. J., 385
Tobey, L. H., 105
Tobias, S. B., 229
Tobin, S. A., 412
Todd, J. T., 296
Tolin, D. F., 333
Tollerud, T. R., 117
Tomarken, A. J., 265
Tomasello, M., 256
Tooby, J., 251
Topping, J. S., 356
Tori, C. D., 47, 481
Torrey, J. W., 73
Torrubia, R., 272
Townsend, F., 112
Tranel, D., 263
Trapnell, P. D., 242
Trappey, C., 59
Travis, F., 473, 480–481
Treadway, M., 210
Treiber, F. A., 480
Triandis, H. C., 6, 113, 166–167, 492
Tribich, D., 49
Trickett, P. K., 56
Trivers, R., 253
Trivers, R. L., 251
Trull, T. J., 240
Trungpa, C., 461, 463–464,
    466, 483
Tryon, W. W., 297
Tsang, J., 209, 455
Tseng, M. S., 114
Tucker, I. F., 88
Tucker, J. S., 178
Tuckman, B. W., 357, 441
Tudor, K., 411
Tulving, E., 105
Turk, B., 117
Turkheimer, E., 275
Turvey, C., 42, 46
Tuten, T. L., 444
Tversky, A., 258
Twenge, J. M., 6, 206, 234
Twomey, H. B., 172
Tyska, C., 316, 436

Uchigakiuchi, P., 310
Uhlemann, M. R., 413
Uleman, J. S., 492
Ulicni, S. K., 238
Ungerer, J. A., 42
Urry, H. L., 263
Utay, C. M., 108
Utay, J. M., 108

Vaillant, G. E., 42, 119, 242, 379, 449
Van Dam, K., 236
van der Kolk, B. A., 60
Van Eenwyk, J. R., 81
Van Hees-Matthijssen, C., 411
van Ijzendoorn, M. H., 178
Van Kalmthout, M. A., 406–407, 409
Van Pelt, T., 161
Vancouver, J. B., 357
Vandewater, E. A., 142
Vaughn, C. M., 377
Velmans, M., 59
Venables, P. H., 270
Ventis, W. L., 209
Vernon, P. A., 195, 197, 227
Vetter, H., 327
Victor, B., 482
Viney, L. L., 377, 387–389
Vitz, P. C., 499
Vleioras, G., 143
Vodanovich, S. J., 442
Voils, C. I., 492
Volkan, V. D., 371
Vollmer, F., 310
von Ammon, J., 112
von Franz, M. L., 84
Vonk, R., 12
Vookles, J., 110
Vyse, S. A., 11

Wachs, T. D., 228, 260
Wachtel, P. L., 332
Waclawski, J., 88
Wagner, P. E., 329
Wahba, M. A., 434
Wahler, R. G., 310
Waite, R. G. L., 26, 50
Walach, H., 473
Waldron, R., 97
Walker, B. M., 373, 375
Walker, L. M., 240
Wallace, E. R., IV, 57
Wallach, L., 396
Wallach, M. A., 396
Wallerstein, R. S., 54
Walsh, B. W., 494
Walsh, R., 57, 457, 461, 466, 479, 482
Walter, A., 275, 492
Wanberg, C. R., 239
Wandersman, A., 348
Wang, Q., 105
Wang, X., 258
Warburton, F. W., 233
Ward, E. A., 4
Ward, R. A., 89
Ware, M. E., 417
Warr, P., 205
Warren, B., 373, 494
Warren, M. W., 229
Warren, W. G., 373
Warschausky, S., 365
Washburn, M., 84
Waterman, A. S., 142–144, 396
Waterman, C. K., 142, 144
Waters, B., 42
Watkins, C. E., Jr., 114
Watson, B., 466
Watson, D., 86, 237–238, 259, 262,
    268, 271
Watson, J. B., 279–280

Watson, J. C., 405, 413
Watson, P. J., 208
Watters, E., 55
Watts, R. E., 114, 402
Wax, M. L., 50
Webster-Stratton, C., 108
Wegner, D. M., 332–333, 465
Wehr, D. S., 80
Wehr, G., 68
Weinberg, R. S., 356
Weinberger, J., 37
Weiner, I. B., 57
Weinrach, S. G., 412–413
Weiss, J., 54
Weiss, L., 49
Weiss-Rosmarin, T., 99
Weisz, J. R., 107
Wellingham-Jones, P., 196
Wells-Parker, E., 356
Wendt, P. E., 268
Wenneberg, S. R., 480
Wentworth, P. A., 145
Wenzlaff, R. M., 332–333
Werner, P. D., 309
Wertheimer, M., 395
Wertz, J. S., 363
West, J. D., 115
West, S. G., 16
Westbay, L., 348
Westen, D., 54, 170–173, 179, 489, 494
Westkott, M., 165, 455, 459
Whalen, C. K., 361
Wheatley, T., 465
Wheeler, M. A., 105
Wheeler, P., 89
Wheeler, S., 390
Whitbourne, S. K., 144
White, J., 106
White, T. H., 370
White, T. L., 271–272
Whitfield, C. L., 54
Whitmont, E. C., 80
Whitworth, R. H., 233
Wicker, F. W., 434
Wickett, J. C., 227
Widener, A. J., 55
Wiedenfeld, S. A., 358
Wiederman, M. W., 254
Wiener, N. I., 256
Wiese, M. R. R., 108, 119
Wiggins, J. S., 235, 242
Wiking, S., 258
Wilber, K., 84
Wild, C., 45
Wilhelm, H., 83
Wilkins, P., 410
Wilkinson, R. B., 271
Wilkinson, W. W., 209
Willard, K. S., 440
Williams, D. E., 114, 434
Williams, D. I., 57
Williams, E. N., 57
Williams, L. M., 55–56
Williams, M., 270
Williams, P., 463–465
Williams, S. L., 364
Williams, S. S., 13
Willingham, W., 120
Wills, T. A., 274
Wilpers, S., 238

Wilson, E. O., 298
Wilson, S. R., 438
Winch, G. L., 142, 144, 166
Windholz, M., 54
Windle, M., 274
Wink, P., 202
Winston, A. S., 296
Winter, D. A., 379
Winter, D. G., 16, 18, 37, 196, 198, 327, 370
Winter, S., 50
Wippich, W., 87
Wiseman, H., 413
Wittels, F., 98
Wohlwend-Lloyd, R., 173
Woike, B. A., 177
Wojcik, J. V., 356
Wolf, S., 71
Wolfenstein, E. V., 49
Wollman, N., 356
Wolman, B. B., 497

Wolpe, J., 54
Wood, J. V., 5
Wood, M. D., 274
Wood, R., 357
Wood, W., 141, 164, 254
Woodward, B., 369
Woolfolk, R. L., 280
Worrall, M., 411
Wotman, S. R., 499
Wright, C., 437
Wright, C. L., 364
Wright, J. C., 345–346
Wright, L. W., Jr., 43
Wright, T. M., 238
Wright, W. J., 18
Wurgaft, L. D., 127, 142, 146
Wyer, R. S., 36, 334

Yamamoto, S., 471
Yamazaki, T. G., 158
Yapko, M. D., 34

Yeagle, E. H., 438
Yeh, C. J., 137
Yehuda, R., 48
Ying, Y., 137
Yogev, S., 166
Yonge, G. D., 441
Young, J. D., 477
Young, L. J., 254
Young, R. D., 327
Young-Bruehl, E., 49
Young-Eisendrath, P., 463, 481, 484, 485

Zahn-Waxler, C., 113
Zanakos, S., 332–333
Zanatta, R., 354
Zarate, M. A., 263, 492
Zarski, J. J., 115
Zborowski, M. J., 35
Zeiss, A., 349
Zeiss, A. R., 350

Zeiss, R., 349
Zettle, R. D., 337
Zhou, J., 240
Ziller, R. C., 498
Zimbardo, P. G., 355
Zimmerman, B. J., 354
Zimmerman, M. A., 356, 365
Zimpfer, D. G., 89
Zivkovic, M., 81
Zola-Morgan, S., 104
Zolten, A. J., 390
Zosky, D. L., 173
Zuckerman, M., 266, 269
Zuk, Y., 365
Zupp, A., 454
Zuriff, G. E., 289, 297
Zuroff, D. C., 189
Zuschlag, M. K., 144
Zvoch, K., 255
Zweig, C., 71
Zweigenhaft, R. L., 112

Subject Index

1

16 Personality Factor Questionnaire (16PF), 223–225, 227, 231, 309

A

Ability traits, 227
Abuse of children, 54–55, 168, 172, 276, 329
  and attachment, 178
  and early memory, 105
  sexual, 47, 55–56
Abuse, substance (drug), 161, 176, 178, 274
Academic advisement, and psychological type, 89
Academic performance
  and meditation, 479
  and self-efficacy, 357
Acceptance. See also Unconditional positive regard.
  of suffering, 459–471
  parental acceptance, 169
  self-acceptance, 403, 436
Accomodating (second-order factor), 225
Acetylcholine, 475, 478
Achievement, 109, 273, 282, 448
  and esteem needs, 432
  and womb envy, 165
  gender roles, 164
  pride in, 204
Achievement motive, 16, 309
  motive to avoid success, 164
  projective test for, 37
Achievement, identity, 143
Acquired drives, 319
Act-frequency approach, 280, 309–310
Acting out (defense mechanism), 42, 79
Active imagination, 82
Activity (component of extraversion) 273
Activity (temperament), 203, 260, 269, 464
Actualization, 407
Actualizing tendency, 402, 404, 407, 409, 419
Adaptation and adjustment, 5, 113, 435
Addiction, 106
  Buddhist view, 482–483
Adjective Check List, 242
Adjustment. See also Fully Functioning; Mental Health.
  learning view, 306–307, 324
  Jung's view, 64
  to the environment, 192
Adler, Alfred
  biography, 99–100
  influence on humanistic theorists, 395
  theory of, 95–121
Adult development (Jung's theory of), 70–71
Aesop's fable, 159

Agency
  component of extraversion, 273
  component of generativity, 145
Agency (efficacy)
  human (Bandura), 354
  collective and individual, 365
Aggression, 250, 271, 327–328. See also Frustration-aggression hypothesis.
  and early memory, 105
  and self-esteem, 174
  and serotonin, 274
  and temperament, 262
  and testosterone, 256
  and Thanatos, 38
  animal studies, 330
  definition of, 327
  displacement of, 43
  hostile and instrumental, 328
  in dreams, 35
  individual differences, 329
  modeling of, 358, 361–362
  operational definition of, 328
Aggressive cues, 329
Aggressive drive, 102, 328
Aggressive impulses, 71
Aggressive type, 159, 163
Aggressive wishes (Freud's theory), 23
Agoraphobia, 364
Agreeableness, 236, 238, 309
AIDS, fear of, 50
Ainsworth, Mary, 174–175
Air Crib, 286
Alchemy, 84
Alcohol
  and attachment, 178
  and self-control, 163
  craving, 271, 333
  effect on conflict, 327
  prenatal exposure, 330
  treatment, 363
Alcohol and drug abuse, 56, 274
Alcohol and drug use, 271
Alcoholism, 106, 256
  family dynamics, 165
Allport, Gordon
  biography, 189–190
  compared with Cattell, 222
  compared with humanistic theory, 395, 429
  theory of, 185–214
Allport-Vernon-Lindzey Study of Values, 197, 303
Alpha blocking, 477
Altruism, 209, 250, 449
  defense mechanism, 42
  kin, 251
  reciprocal, 251
Amae, 166
Amnesia. See also Memory
  and hypnosis, 33
  and stages of perception, 476
  for traumatic events, 32, 48, 55, 60
Amphetamine, reactions to (individual differences), 273

Amplification (dream interpretation), 82
Amygdala, 74–75, 261–264, 352, 469, 474, 478
  and memory, 60
Anal character, 49–50
Anal stage
  psychoanalytic learning theory, 323
  psychoanalytic theory, 47
Anatta, 463, 475
Angelou, Maya (Illustrative Biography), 398–400
Anger, 102, 162, 168, 265, 323–324
  and Agreeableness factor, 242
  and attachment, 177
  Buddhist view, 466–467, 468, 470
  communication of, 250
  erg, 229
  in female development (Freud's view), 51
  in frustration-aggression relationship, 168, 328–329
  in Rogers's therapy case, 413
  learned drive, 324
Anger-anxiety conflict, 324
Anima and animus, 71–73, 75
Anna O., 30
Anorexia nervosa, 82
Antisocial personality disorder, 256, 263. See also Criminal; Delinquency.
  brain functioning, 264
Anxiety. See also Behavioral Inhibition System (BIS); Death: fear of.
  acquired drive, 319
  and anger, 324
  and attachment, 178
  and criminal predisposition, 269
  and culture, 6
  and defense mechanisms, 42
  and dependency, 159
  and dreams, 34–35
  and ego, 40
  and hypnosis, 33
  and identity development, 144
  and interpersonal relationships, 172
  and learning, 303
  and repression, 30–32, 46
  avoidance of, 331
  basic (Horney's theory), 155, 159–160, 459
  castration, 50–51
  cohort differences, 206
  in A-R-D theory, 305
  infantile, 171
  learned, 321, 324
  Maslow's own, 427
  moral, 42
  neurotic, 42, 226, 331
  reaction to punishment, 291
  reaction to threat, 386
  reality, 42
  sensitization to, 275
  second-order factor, 225

Anxiety-prone personality, 272
Apartheid, 139
Applied research, 12
Applied value (of theory), 12, 248, 342, 401, 495
Arbitrary rightness, 163
Archetypal Symbol Inventory, 78–79
Archetypes, 74–75
  of Self, 77
A-R-D theory, 305
Arousal, cortical and emotional, 265–269
Art
  and sublimation, 38, 44
  archetypes in, 76, 78
  Freud's view of, 45
  task of life, 116
Asian disease problem, 258
Assertiveness, 159, 166
  and psychological type, 88
  cohort differences, 206
  component of Extraversion, 273
Attachment
  adult, 174, 176–178, 254, 362, 448
  and interpersonal trust, 176
  and parental behavior, 178
  Buddhist view, 460–461, 470, 474–475
  dream function, 35
  infant, 170, 174–176, 275
  longitudinal studies, 178
  types of, 176–177
Attention Deficit Hyperactivity Disorder (ADHD), 272, 351, 479
Attention
  as reinforcer, 295
  consciousness and, 59, 173, 419, 472
  focused, 468, 473
  in social learning, 359
Attitudes, 229–230
  and birth order, 112
Autism, 257
Autonomy, 130, 135, 437, 448
  and birth order, 111
  and masculinity, 142
  functional (of motives), 201
Avoiding type, 106
Awakening, 457, 466–467
Awareness, pure, 476

B

Bandura, Albert
  biography, 352–353
  theory of, 352–366
Base rate (of responding), 290
Basic behavioral repertoires (BBRs), 300–302, 306, 308
Basic hostility, 155
Basic research, 12, 318
Becoming (Allport), 201
Behavior modification and behavior therapy, 295–296, 299, 302, 482

Behavior
  of autonomic responses, 319
  matched dependent, 322–323
  operant, 119, 289–291
  prediction of, 230, 232, 236, 352
  same, 322–323
Behavioral Activation System (BAS),
  271–273
Behavioral Inhibition System (BIS),
  271–273
Behavioral assessment, 254, 308–310
Behaviorism, 279, 296, 395
Belongingness and love (need for),
  431
Bem Sex-Role Inventory (BSRI), 44,
  145, 164, 166, 445
Big Five factors, 215, 225, 235–242,
  260
Biofeedback, 319, 390
Biological causes
  contributors to personality, 263–266
  cultural criticism, 453
  factor theories, 267–274
  in context, 275–276
  in psychological behaviorism, 298
Biological metaphor, 497
Biologism, strong and weak, 275
Biology and experience, 275–276
Birth order, See Family constellation.
Blind spots, 162, 168
Blindsight, 476
Bliss, 473
B-love, 433
Bobo doll study, 362
Bodhisattva, 469
Borderline personality disorder, 56,
  170, 172, 482
Bowlby, John, 174
Brain
  and collective unconscious, 74
  and consciousness, 59
  and delay of gratification, 352
  and dreams, 35
  and early memory, 104
  and emotion, 468
  and Freud's theory, 59–61
  and meditation, 476–477
  and sense of self, 474
  and sexual orientation, 52
  and stimulus categorization, 59
  and transcendental experience, 445
  ascending reticular activating
    system, 268
  limbic system, 269, 330
  neural imaging study, 60
  nucleus accumbens, 271
  response to punishment and
    reward, 273
  shaped by behavior, 358
  subcortical, 263
Breuer, Joseph, 30, 32
Bstan-dzin-rgya-mtsho, Dalai Lama
  IV, 457–458, 462–463, 467, 469,
  472, 476–478, 484
  (Illustrative Biography), 451–455
Buddha, 457, 463, 466, 469, 474
Buddha path, 459
Buddhism, history, 458
Buddhism, Zen, 455, 458, 463–464,
  471–472, 477, 482

Buddhist psychology, 451–487
Burnout (therapist), and meditation,
  482
Business
  and psychological type, 88
  applications of MBTI, 89
  applications of personal construct
    theory, 390
  humanistic applications, 418
  need hierarchy theory, 431

C

Caffeine, 269
California Personality Inventory, 14,
  145, 242
Care (psychosocial strength), 136
Career choice, and psychosocial
  development, 144
Case studies, 4, 17
  externalization, 162
  personal construct theory, 388
Castration anxiety, 50, 51
Catharsis, 53, 328
  case of Anna O., 30
Cathexis, 39
Cattell Culture Fair Intelligence
  Test, 228
Cattell, R. B., 183
  biography, 221–222
  theory of, 215–235
Cattell-Horn-Carroll theory, 228
Causation, biological vs. mental, 457
Cause-effect relationships
  in correlational and experimental
    research, 16
Celibacy, 255
Chaining, 292, 300
Charcot, Jean Martin, 30, 32
Children, 15, 110
  Adler's view, 115
  autistic, 257, 295–296, 306
  cross-cultural study, 171
  delinquent, 408
  dyslexic, 299
  early motor learning, 305
  first-born, 109, 110, 112
  Freudian view, 15, 110
  later-born, 111
  mentally retarded, 295
  middle, 111
  neglect of, 108, 155, 178, 275
  only, 110
  pampering of, 107, 262
  play, 131, 135, 140–141, 271, 294
  second-born, 109, 110
  therapy, 82
  youngest, 109
Children (parenthood), Erikson's
  view, 136
Choice corollary, 378
Circumspection, 386
Classical conditioning, 300
Cloninger tridimensional model,
  273–274
Client-centered therapy. See
  Psychotherapy: client-centered.
Clinical Analysis Questionnaire, 223
Clinton, Hillary Rodham (Illustrative
  biography), 245–248
Clown therapy, 77

Cognition
  effects of meditation, 473
  unconscious, 58–59
Cognitive challenge, 337
Cognitive complexity, 384, 390
Cognitive person variables, 347, 350,
  358
Cognitive processes, 5, 354, 491
  influence on aggression, 328
Cognitive reappraisal, 333
Cognitive social learning perspective,
  337–338
  compared with humanistic
    perspective, 396
Cognitive unconscious, 59
Collective efficacy, 365
Collective unconscious, 74
Collectivism, 139, 166
Commonality corollary, 381
Communion (component of genera-
  tivity), 145. See also
  Individualism.
Community psychology, 307
Community, feeling of, 113
Compartmentalization, 162
Compassion, 452, 457–458, 461,
  467–469, 480, 482
Compensation
  in Adler's theory, 102
  principle of (Jung), 69, 82
Competence, 448
  psychosocial strength, 135
  predicted by early delay of gratifi-
    cation, 351
Competencies, 348
  construction, 348
  learned, 305
Complexes, 75, 81
  deprecation, 106
  inferiority, 101, 102
  Jonah, 442
  Jung's studies of, 67
  masculinity, 51
  mother, 81, 110
  Oedipus, 50, 98, 108
  redeemer, 103
  superiority, 103
Compliant type, 158
Comprehensiveness (of theory),
  11–12, 185, 248, 495
  Jung's theory, 66
Concept, theoretical, 200, 488
Concrete construct, 378–379
Condensation, 35–36
Conditional positive regard, 407
Conditioning, classical, 265, 298,
  300, 302–303
Conditioning, operant, 289, 298, 300
  compared to Adlerian
    psychotherapy, 119
Conditions of worth (conditional
  positive regard), 407–408, 410
Conflict, 52, 128
  Adler and Freud views, 104
  approach and avoidance, 271,
    325–326
  basic, 155, 160
  civilization vs. biology (Freud's
    view), 52
  cultural view, 164

delayed or immediate
  gratification, 352
experimental arousal, 57–58
Freud's view, 32
impact on dreams, 34, 77
in Horney's theory, 156
in psychosexual
  development, 47
in psychosocial stages, 128
individual vs. society, 202
interpersonal, 86, 138, 155, 173, 238
intrapsychic, 41–42, 325
moral, 71
Oedipal, 50
political (Rogers's interventions),
  418
psychoanalytic social learning
  theory, 324–325
reduction of, 327
unawareness of, 162
unconscious, 23
working through, 53
Confluence learning, 230
Conformity
  learning analysis, 323
  oral fixation and, 49
Congruence, 410, 411, 413, 417–418
Conscientiousness, 236, 239
  consistency of, 344
Conscious striving (Adler's theory),
  101
Consciousness, 31–32, 37, 329, 332,
  334, 465, 465–466, 473, 481. See
  also Unconscious.
  altered states, 406, 438
  brain model, 59
  dissociated (hypnosis), 33
  dissociation of, 476
  drug effects, 438
  focusing in meditation, 472
  levels (Freud's theory), 31
  pure (brain correlates), 474
  subtle, 473
Consciousness revolution, 498
Conservative values, and birth order,
  109
Consistency in personality, 103, 189,
  197, 205, 293, 344, 347. See also
  Unity of personality.
Consistency paradox, 344
Construction corollary, 376
Constructive alternativism, 374
Constructs
  concrete, 378–379
  core, 380
  dichotomous, 379
  narrative context, 389
  peripheral, 380
  permeable, 378
  personal, 347, 374
  preverbal, 377, 387
  scientific (contrasted with every-
    day language) 183
  superordinate, 380
  theoretical, 8–10, 15
Consumerism, and need hierarchy
  theory, 444
Content analysis, 196, 198
Continuous reinforcement (CR), 293
Control, 72, 169

experimental, 255
in relationships, 158
of behavior, 295
of emotion, 468
of impulses, 226
of own life, 352
social, 366
stimulus, 292
vs. prediction of behavior, 72, 169, 289, 297
Control group, 16, 473, 480
Conversion hysteria, 32
Copying, 322–323
Corollaries. *See* Personal construct theory.
Coronary heart disease, and psychological type, 88
Correlation coefficient, 219–220
Correlation matrix, 220
Correlational research, 15–16
Correspondence bias, 192
Cortical arousal, 265
Corticotropin-releasing hormone, 261
Cortisol, 255, 276, 480
Costa, Jr., Paul. *See* Five-factor theory.
Countertransference, 53, 482
C-P-C Cycle, 386, 387
Craving (for tobacco or drugs), 460
Creationism, 80
Creative self, 103
Creativity, 240, 387, 395, 408–409, 417, 473
and intuition, 87–88
and self-actualization, 406, 439
and Psychoticism factor, 269
in behaviorism, 296
role of shadow, 72
Creativity cycle, 387
Criminals, 113, 115, 269–270, 272. *See also* Antisocial personality disorder; Delinquency.
Crisis, psychosocial, 128
Cross-cultural research, 258. *See also* Culture.
Cues, 253, 319–322
aggressive, 329
Cultivating Emotional Balance curriculum, 467
Cultural change, 358
Cultural evolution, 257
Cultural pluralism (multiculturalism), 391
Cultural scapegoats, 43
Culture, 6. *See also* Social class.
and act-frequency assessment, 309
and Asian disease problem, 258
and birth order effects, 111
and biology, 276
and defense mechanisms, 47
and early memory, 105
and empathy in psychotherapy, 412
and gender, 141
and learning, 303
and Oedipus conflict, 50
and personal unconscious, 75
and personality, 137
and psychoanalysis, 24
and psychobiography, 124

and psychosocial development, 134–135, 146
and self-esteem, 462
and Big Five factors, 242
and temperament, 276 and Trickster archetype, 76
bias in theory, 492
cognitive social learning view, 365
demographic changes, 136
design of, 297
effect on conversion hysteria, 32
etic and emic approaches, 457
evolutionary view, 256–257
gender roles (sex roles), 51–52, 80, 102, 164
global, 140
in psychoanalytic-social perspective, 93
individualism, 463
Jung's view, 65
psychoanalytic neglect of, 18
rituals, 137
values in humanistic psychology, 396
Culture Fair Intelligence Test, 223, 228
Cynicism (secondary adjustment technique), 163

D

Dalai Lama, *See* Bstan-dzin-rgya-mtsho, Dalai Lama IV.
Dali, Salvador, 45
Darwin, Charles, 112
Death
and career choice, 103
and Thanatos, 38
fear of, 105, 119, 145, 209, 436
of significant other, 173
Death anxiety, 46, 119
Decision-making, and psychological type, 89
Defense Mechanism Inventory, 46
Defense mechanisms, 42–47, 407, 436, 449. *See also* Neuroticism.
Adler's influence, 98
and gender roles, 166
Buddhist alternative, 463, 475–476
contrasted with adaptive functions, 204
empirical studies, 24, 45, 139, 144, 440, 481
Horney's theory, 160–163, 166
relational theory, 170
learning perspective, 306, 365
measurement, 45–46
science as, 429
Defense Style Questionnaire, 46
Deficiency motivation. *See* Motivation.
Delay of gratification, 350–352
Delinquency, 116. *See also* Antisocial personality disorder; Criminal.
and early memory, 106
prevention programs, 100
Delusion, 459, 461, 468
Denial (defense mechanism), 42–43, 47, 387
Dependency, 156, 158–159, 165, 256, 324, 390

and birth order, 111
and culture, 166
oral trait, 49
Dependent origination, 465
Dependent variable, 16
Deprecation complex, 106
Depression
and attachment, 176, 178
and early memory, 106
and ethnic identity, 138
and gender, 166
and self-efficacy, 356
behavioral view, 301, 306–307
brain activity, 255, 263, 265, 271, 275
cohort differences, 208
cognitive behavioral view, 356, 363, 375, 387
cultural differences, 276, 463
effect of religion, 209, 211
oral trait, 49
prediction of, 233
relational approach, 169
suppression, 332–333, 476
Desacralization, 445
Description (of personality), 2, 219, 236, 242, 352
lexical approach, 183
trait approach, 3
Desensitization, to violence, 269
Despair, 133
Detached type, 159
Detachment, 460, 484
Determinism, 8, 74, 280, 405, 433, 497, 499
Jung's view, 83
biological, 141, 163
emergent, 498
psychic, 30, 36
reciprocal, 353
scientific, 429
vs. teleology, 396
Dethronement, 109–110
Development
infant (Freud's view), 49
Development (of personality), 2, 6, 8, 492
learning analysis, 323
Dharma, 459
Dichotomies, resolution of and self-actualization, 440
Dichotomous construct, 379
Dichotomous thinking, 440
Dichotomy corollary, 379
Dictionary Study, 3, 183, 195
Disconfirmation of theory, 11, 191
Disconfirmation (invalidation) of personal constructs, 375
Discrimination, 292, 298, 321, 364
Discrimination learning. *See* Learning: discrimination.
Discrimination, stimulus, 292–293
Disinhibition versus Constraint (DvC), 271
Displacement, 162, 328, 331
defense mechanism, 42–43, 47
in dreams, 35
of castration anxiety, 50
Disposition. *See* Traits.

Dissociation (defense mechanism), 42, 48, 56
of Jung, 68
Distantiation, 133
Divorce
and attachment, 178
Dollard, John
biography, 317–318
theory of (with Neal Miller), 313–336
Dominance, 237, 240, 254, 309
and serotonin, 274
gender roles (sex roles), 164–165
striving, 102
DOPAC, 358
Dopamine, 259, 264, 266, 268, 271, 273, 275, 478
Dowl, Mildred, 34
Down syndrome, 302
Dreams, 76
Adler's view, 118
and collective unconscious, 74
biological view, 35
constructivist therapy, 387
Freud's associations, 67
Freud's view, 34
interpretation of, 34–35
Jungian approach, 81–83
lucid, 466
of Martin Luther King, Jr., 64
of nakedness, 71
of repressors, 69
recall of, 88
shadow images, 72
Dream-work, 35
Drive, 319, 325
instinctual, 39
reduction (reinforcement), 320–321
satisfaction, in Freud's theory, 41
tension, 227
undischarged, 331
Drive model, 104
Drug use, 274
Duhkha, 459, 460
Dynamic lattice, 230
Dynamics (of personality), 2, 5, 352
Dystonic resurgence, 133–134

E

Early Memories Procedure, 105
Eating disorders, 49, 54, 82, 363, 390, 482
experimental study of, 58
Eclectic approach, 18
Eclecticism, 493
Eclecticism, jackdaw and systematic, 211
Eclipsing, 160
Ecstasy, in meditation, 477
Edison, Thomas, 354
Education, 296, 390
and intelligence, 227
behavioral applications, 300, 305
humanistic, 445
individual (Adler), 116
metaerg, 229, 296
parental support, 255
person-centered, 416
EEG, 263–265, 477, 481

Efficacy, collective, 365. *See also* Self-efficacy.
Ego, 37–38, 40, 42, 172, 460–461
  identification with, 69
  in psychoanalytic-social perspective, 93, 146
  Jung's view, 70
Ego defenses. *See* Defense mechanisms.
Ego development, 128, 130, 133, 329, 481
  and culture, 137
  and parenting, 169
  heritability of, 259
  sex differences, 51
Ego ideal, 40
Ego identity, 132
Ego inflation, 69–70
Ego level, 202
Ego sacrifice, 72
Ego strength, 128–129, 133, 135, 137, 224, 227, 329, 351
  cultural bias, 137
Egocide, 72
Ego-control, 351
Ego-extension, 204
Ego-ideal, 98
Ego-resiliency, 351
Eightfold Path, 459, 462
Einstein, Albert, 416, 484
  (Illustrative Biography), 215–218
  psychetype of, 87
  self-actualization of, 436
Elaborative choice, 378
Elderly
  need hierarchy, 434
  psychosocial development, 133, 136
Elephant and blind men story, 474
Elusiveness, 163
Embedded Figures Test, 473
Emergenic traits, 259
Emergent determinism, 498
Emergent self metaphor, 498
Emotion
  and attachment, 176
  and perception, 476
  and reinforcement, 300
  and meditation, 478
  brain, 263, 265
  communication of, 250
  family messages, 179
  in dreams, 35, 118
  in frustration-aggression relationship, 329
  infant, 168
  negative, 238, 258, 264, 271, 303, 468
  positive, 238, 258, 271–272, 443, 449, 468
  reactivity, 60
  repression, 46
  stability, 224
  suppression, 333
Emotional intelligence, 87, 264, 411
Emotionality (temperament), 49, 203, 260, 262
Emotional-motivational repertoire, 302–304, 306
Empathy, 113, 166, 173, 251, 255, 410–413, 417–418

and religious orientation, 208
  compared to compassion, 468
  feminine value, 165
  in psychopaths, 264, 265
  in psychotherapy, 412
  sex differences, 51
Empirical, 8, 57, 431
Empirical approach (Cattell), 222
Empirical observation, 10
Empirical test, 11
  and psychoanalysis, 23
Empirically validated scales, 227
Empowerment, 364, 365
Encoding strategies, 347
Encounter groups, 403, 416, 418, 443
Endorphins, 473
Energy hypothesis, 41
Energy, psychic, 38–39, 41, 59, 60
Enlightenment, 457–459, 463, 465–466, 470, 472, 474, 486
  brain activity, 477
Epigenetic principle, 128, 141, 145
Epinephrine, 264, 358
Ergs, 229–230
Erikson, Erik
  biography, 126–128
  theory of, 122–148
Erogenous zones, 47, 49, 50
Eros, 27
Esalen Institute, 443
Esteem needs, 432
Ethical behavior, 461
Ethnicity. *See* Identity, ethnic and racial.
Eupsychia, 440
Evil
  ignored by Rogers, 419
  in Jungian shadow, 72
  underestimated by humanists, 396
Evoked neural response, 268
Evolution/evolutionary psychology, 435
  and creationism, 80
  collective unconscious, 74
  cultural, 257
  theory, 248–258
  view of incest, 50
Evolved psychological mechanisms, 252
Excitatory processes (nervous system), 265, 267
Existentialism, 429
Expansive solution, 156, 159
Expectancies, 348–349
  behavior-outcome, 348–349
  dysfunctional, 365
  outcome, 364
  self-efficacy, 348–349
  stimulus-outcome, 348–349
Expectation, influence on therapy, 17
Experience, 210, 227, 412, 429
  determinant of personality development, 37, 73–75, 104, 190, 279, 352, 429
  narrative interpretation, 51
  openness to, 405
  subjective, 395, 474
Experience corollary, 377
Experiential knowledge, 429, 447
Experimental group, 16, 473
Experimental research, 16

and psychoanalysis, 58
  in psychotherapy outcome studies, 414
  on defense mechanisms, 44
Expressive behavior, 193
Externalization, 162
Extinction, 290–291, 293, 295, 298, 320–321, 332
  of fear, 332
  resistance to, 293
Extrasensory perception (ESP), 83
Extraversion, 6, 84, 86, 88, 196, 236–238, 242, 269, 271
  and attachment, 177
  cohort differences, 206
  components of, 273
  distinguished from social interest, 113
  Eysenck factor, 267
  second-order factor, 225–226
Extraversion/Positive Emotionality (E/PE), 271
Eyewitness testimony, and psychological type, 89
Eysenck's "PEN" model, 267–271
Eysenck Personality Inventory, 158, 242

F
Facets of the Five Factors, 240
Facilitator, 416–417
Factor analysis, 183, 198, 220–221, 225, 235–236, 240
  of sex role measure, 164
  second-order, 225
Factor analytic trait theories, 221
Factors, 3, 174, 271
  Big Five, 240
  biological, 245, 307
Fairbairn, W. R. D., 172
Fairy tales, 79
False memory syndrome, 55
Family constellation, 109–112
Fantasies
  psychoanalytic view of, 27, 50–51
  in phallic stage (Freud's view), 47
  in constructivist therapy, 387
Fear, 261, 263, 321–332, 386
  evolutionary, 250
  generalization of, 321
  learned, 303
  neuroendocrine mechanisms, 261
  of success, 164
  reaction to punishment, 291
Feedback, 282, 448
Feeding, 47, 323, 327
Feeling (psychological function), 84–89
Feeling, social or community, 113
Feelings, Reactions, and Beliefs Survey (FRBS), 419
Felt minus and felt plus, 101–103
Feminine role (gender role). *See* Sex roles (gender).
Femininity, normal (Freudian view), 51
Feminist theory, 141, 155, 163–165
Fictional finalism, 103, 104
Fidelity (psychosocial strength), 132, 135
Field independence, 473

Fight-Flight System, 272
Five Factor Inventory, 169–170
Five-factor theory, 235–242
Fixation, 48, 51–52, 200
  Allport's criticism, 201
  anal, 49
  oral, 26, 49
Fixed interval schedule, 294
Fixed ratio schedule, 293
Fixed-role therapy, 387–388
Flow, 448
Flying saucers, 83
Foreclosure, identity, 132
Formative tendency, 404
Four Noble Truths, 453, 459
Fragmentation corollary, 380
Frankl, Viktor, 406
Free association, 53, 163, 332, 387, 482
Free will, 297
Freedom, 433, 437
  experiential, 405
Freiburg Mindfulness Inventory, 473
Freud, Sigmund
  and Adler's theory, 98
  Allport's meeting with, 188
  biography, 29–30
  psychetype of, 87
  relationship to Adler, 100
  theory of, 25–62
Freudian slips, 35, 58
Friedan, Betty, 445
Friend-and-befriend caregiving, 254
Friendliness, consistency of, 344
Friendship, 306, 418
  and psychosocial development, 145
  and social interest, 114
Fromm, Erich, 98, 155, 464
Frontal lobes, 474
Frustration, 459
Frustration-aggression hypothesis, 327
Fully functioning, 405–406, 408, *See also* Adjustment; Mental Health.
Function, auxiliary, 85, 88
Function, dominant, 84–85, 88
Functional analysis, 295
Functional autonomy, 200–201
Functional magnetic resonance imaging (fMRI), 271, 477
Fundamental attitude, in Jung's theory, 84
Fundamental attribution error, and psychological type, 90
Fundamental postulate (Kelly's theory), 375

G
Gandhi, Mahatma (Illustrative Biography), 122–125, 136
Gastrointestinal system, 269
Gender. *See* Sex roles (gender).
Generalization, 292–293, 298, 307, 321, 324, 331
Generativity (vs. stagnation), 133, 136, 145
Genetics and personality, 259. *See also* Heredity.
Genital character, 52

Genital constructions in children's play, 140
Genital erogenous zone, 50
Genital stage (Freud), 52
Genotype, 262
Gerotranscendence, 133, 134
Getting Type, 106
Ghosts, hungry, 483
Glove anesthesia, 32
Goldstein, Kurt, 395
Gradients of approach and avoidance, 325
Gradients of punishment and reward, 322
Grandiose self-image, 172
Graphology, 195
Great Mother archetype, 76
Grey Owl, 44
Group therapy, 443
Growth centers, 443
Guilt, 131, 135, 324, 365, 385
  and moral anxiety, 42
  and superego, 40–41
  sex differences, 51
Guru, 473
Gyatso, Tenzin, 451. *See also* Bstan-dzin-rgya-mtsho, Dalai Lama IV.

H

Habituation (in meditation), 477
Hallucinations (defense mechanism), 34, 58, 78
Handicaps, physical, 101
Happiness, 433, 448–449, 469
  and meditation, 478, 480
  biological causes, 467
  brain mechanism, 271
  heritability of, 259
  of extraverts, 88
Harm avoidance (trait), 274
Head Start, 108
Health (mental), and ego, 40
Health (physical), 119, 159, 233, 239, 333, 351, 356, 390, 433, 448, 480
  and meditation, 479, 480
  and sexual attraction, 252
  and social interest, 115
  self-efficacy dimensions, 356
Healthy personality, characteristics of, 201
Hedonic hypothesis, 37, 264
Helplessness, 158, 160–161, 309, 349
  and inferiority feeling, 101
Heredity, 6, 190–191, 203–204, 235, 261, 279
  of collective unconscious, 75, 78
Heritability, 235, 259
Hero archetype, 65, 76, 81
Heuristic value (of theory), 12
Hierarchy of needs, 430–431, 433, 482
Hippocampus, 104, 255, 262, 272, 474
  and memory, 60
Hippocrates, 260
History of science, 112
Hitler, Adolf, 17, 50, 103
  Erikson's analysis, 125–127
  (Illustrative Biography), 25–27.
Homosexuality. *See* Sexual orientation.
Hope (psychosocial strength), 134
Hormone markers, 253

Horney, Karen, 98, 395, 455
  biography, 153–155
  theory of, 149–169
Horney-Coolidge Type Indicator (HCTI), 157
Hostility, 156, 160, 173, 238, 386
  basic, 155
  repressed, 159
Hullian learning theory, 319–320
Human potential movement, 428, 443
Humanistic perspective, 395–397
Humor, 36, 202, 449
  Adler's view, 118–119
  anal, 49–50
  and self-actualization, 439
  defense mechanism, 42
  Freud's view, 36
  in psychotherapy, 118–119
Humors, ancient temperament, 260
Hungry ghosts, 483
Hypnosis, 30, 32–34, 119, 390, 476, 481
  study of unconscious, 58
Hypnotic susceptibility, 438
Hypothesis, 10, 429
  energy (Freud), 41
  frustration-aggression, 327
  seduction (Freud), 51
  structural (Freud), 38
  testing, 386
Hysteria, 51–52

I

I Ching, 83, 84
Iceberg metaphor, 31
Id, 37–38, 40
  in psychoanalytic social psychology, 146
Ideal prototype, and psychosocial development, 135
Ideal self, 407
Identification, 50, 322–323, 361
  Allport's analysis, 200–201
  and identity status, 143
  defense mechanism, 44
  ethnic, 139
  sex role (Freud's view), 52
  with the aggressor, 44
Identity, 132, 135
  achievement, 143
  change (Erikson's own), 127
  confusion, 143
  crisis, 123, 132
  diffusion, 143
  ethnic and racial, 110, 123, 136, 137–139
  foreclosure, 132, 143
  gender, 44, 138
  masculine, 164
  negative, 132
  persona, 69
  resolution, 132
  sex differences, 141, 142
  sex role (Freud's view), 51
  sexual, 45
  social, and prejudice, 469
  status, 138, 143
Ideology, 135, 143, 204
Idiographic approach, 4, 5, 194, 279, 285, 290, 297, 337, 372–373
Ignorance, 461

Imitation, 322–323
  behavioral approach, 305
  Buddhist story, 472
  rewarding of, 307
Immune system, 159, 332–334, 358, 480
  and object relationships, 172
Implicit theories of personality, 12–13
Impulsive Sensation Seeking scale, 266
Impulsivity, 268, 272
  and psychological type, 88
  component of Extraversion, 273
  temperament, 260
Incest, 161
  evolutionary view, 50
  Freud's view, 51
  real or fantasized, 55–56
  incest taboo, 47, 50
Inclusive fitness, 251
Incongruence, 407
Independent variable, 16
Individual differences, 3, 183, 280, 298, 352, 489–490
  Cattell's contribution, 222
  global traits, 343
  trait approach, 183
Individual education, 116
Individualism, 6, 113, 139, 142, 166, 206, 276, 365, 396, 448, 463, 470
  and masculinity, 142
Individuality corollary, 381
Individuation, 64–65, 70, 82
Industry vs. inferiority, 132
Infancy
  ego psychology vs. Freudian views, 93
  Erikson's theory, 130
  psychoanalytic view, 23, 47
Inferiority, 102, 109, 118, 132, 432
  complex, 101–102
Information processing metaphor, 497
In-group bias, 469
Inhibited temperament, 260
Inhibitory processes (nervous system), 265, 267
Initiative (vs. guilt), 131, 135, 276
Inner Directed Supports, 441
Insight, 53–54, 202, 412–413, 472
  clinical, 24
Instinct, 39, 74
  death (Thanatos), 27, 38, 460
  Freud's view of, 39
  id functioning, 40
  life (Eros), 27, 38
  psychic, 38, 74
Instinctoid, 442
Integration of personality, 200
Integrity, ego, 145
  vs. despair, 133
Intellectualization (defense mechanism), 42, 44
Intelligence, 190, 227, 302, 344, 473
  and meditation, 479
  behavioral interpretation, 305, 307–308
  crystallized, 227–228
  culture-fair, 222
  fluid, 227–228
  tests, 309
Interactionism, 189

Internal control, 107
Interpersonal orientations (Horney) 156–157, 160–161
  compared to Buddhism, 468
Interpersonal Potency scale, 164
Interpersonal relationships, 49, 130–131, 159, 169, 173, 238
  and attachment, 175
Interpersonal Sensitivity scale, 164
Interviews
  measurement of emotions in relationships, 171
Intimacy
  and attachment, 177
  motive, projective test for, 37
  vs. isolation, 133
Intrapsychic conflict, 41–42, 325
Intrinsic orientation, 208
Introspection, 475–476
Introversion, 84, 86, 88, 227, 269
  Eysenck, 267
  of Martin Luther King, Jr., 64
Intuition
  in psychoanalysis, 24
  psychological function, 84–88, 344
Invalidation of personal constructs, 375
Inventory of Psychosocial Balance, 144, 145
Isolation, 133
  defense mechanism, 42, 44, 47

J

Jackass theory, 373
Jackdaw eclecticism, 210–211
James, William, 455
Jealousy, 252, 433
  sex differences, 253–254
Jenny case study, 196, 198–199
Job satisfaction, and social interest, 114
Johnson, Lyndon, 161
Jokes. *See* Humor.
Jonah complex, 442
Judgments, 85–86
Jung, Carl
  biography, 67–68
  psychetype of, 87
  theory of, 63–91

K

Kahlo, Frida (Illustrative Biography), 339–342
Karma, 454, 464, 465
Kelly, George, 395
  biography, 373–374
  theory of, 368–393
Kin recognition mechanisms, 255
King George III, 233
King, Jr., Dr. Martin Luther 122, 398, 444, 470
  (Illustrative Biography) 63–65
Knowing Styles Inventory, 111
Koans, 471
Kohut, Heinz, 125, 146, 172, 412
Koro, 50

L

Labeling, in psychotherapy, 332
Laddering, 388

Language, 176, 257, 324, 337
  and ego control, 330–331
  behavioral approach, 305
  impact on learning, 322, 330
  in behaviorism, 296–297
  in Zen Buddhism, 463
  trait descriptions, 183
Language-cognitive repertoire, 302,
  304, 305, 306
Latency stage (Freud), 52
Latent content, 34
Law, and psychosocial development,
  135
L-data, 224
Learning, 293, 296, 309, 318
  and subsidiation, 230
  behavior change, 320
  brain involvement, 273
  discrimination, 292, 364
  evolutionary view, 256
  imitative, 361
  in specification equation, 233
  observational, 360–361
  prepared, 250
  vicarious, 361
Learning dilemma, 321
Learning disabilities, 228
Learning perspective, 280
Learning perspective, 279–280
Learning perspective, cognitive
  social, 337–338
Legal cases, child sexual abuse, 55
Leveling and sharpening, 210
Levels of explanation, 486
Lexical approach, 183, 236
Libido, 38–39, 47, 460. *See also*
  Psychic energy.
  compared with drive reduction,
  320
  plasticity of, 40
Life story, 132
Life Styles Inventory, 114
Likability, 238
Limbic system (brain), 269, 330
Locus of control, 142, 349, 434
  and birth order, 111
Logical positivism, 429
Logos, 72
Longitudinal research, 238
Loosening of constructs, 387
Los Horcones, 297
Love, 306
  agape, 410
  and Eros, 38
  B-love and D-love, 433
  for parents, 310
  Freud's view, 52
  Jung's theory, 73
  need for, 158, 431
  parental, 331
  predicting from personality, 238
  psychosocial strength, 136
  romantic, 438
  search for, 158
  sexual (Buddhist view), 468
  task of life, 115
Love styles
  storge and ludus, 114
  desperate, 176, 460
Loyola Generativity Scale, 145
Luther, Martin, 125

M

Machiavellian type, 163
Machismo, 164
Magnetic resonance imaging (MRI),
  478
Management (business), encounter
  groups, 416
Managers, self-actualized, 443–444
Mandala archetype, 77
Manifest content, 34
Man-the-scientist metaphor, 374
Marriage, 133, 136, 169, 238, 400
  Adler's view, 115
  and attachment, 178
  failed, 70
  Rogers's approach, 417
Marriage Counseling Report, 223
Masculine protest, 98, 102
Masculinity complex, 51
Maslow, Abraham
  biography, 426–428
  theory of, 422–447
Maslow Art Test, 440
Masochism, 165
  female trait (Freud's view), 51
Master motive, 229
Mastery orientation, 349
Masturbation, punishment of, 324
Maternal contact, 255
McCrae, Robert. *See* Five-factor
  theory.
Meador, Betty, 416
Measurement of personality, 13–14,
  232
  Cattell's contributions, 223
  direct self-report, 14
  indirect, 15
Mechanistic metaphor, 497
Medical model, 53, 409
Medication, effects of
  and meditation, 482
Meditation
  acceptance, 482
  and emotion, 478
  and stress reduction, 480
  Buddhist tradition, 452–453,
  455–459, 461, 463–464,
  466–467, 470–482, 484–485
  brain activity, 263, 476–477
  compassion type, 477
  concentration (concentrative)
  type, 472, 477
  effect on heart rate (case study),
  480
  insight type, 478
  mindfulness type, 472, 476–478,
  482
  peak experiences, 437
  psychological effects, 480–481
  therapy applications, 441, 443,
  479–482
  transcendental, 472
Memory. *See also* False memory
  syndrome.
  Adler's childhood, 99, 105
  and meditation, 479
  brain functioning and stress, 60
  early or first, 104–106, 111, 118,
  144, 173
  explicit and implicit, 59
  episodic, 105

implicit, 476
  malevolent, 172
  of abuse, 51
  of sexual abuse (recovered), 54–55
  semantic, 105
  traumatic, 32, 60
  working, 227
  unconscious effects on, 35
Mental health, 405, 436. *See also*
  Adjustment; Fully functioning.
  Adler's view, 115
  and gender, 166
  and need satisfaction, 434
  and religious orientation, 202
  culture and identity, 143
  Freud's view, 52, 53
Mental retardation, 306
Mentalism, 289
Metaergs, 229, 230
Metamotivated, 433
Metaphor, 496
  archeology (Freud), 52
  biological, 141
  emergent self, 498
  iceberg (Freud), 31
  information processing, 497
  interpretation of recovered
  memory, 55
  man-the-scientist, 374
  narrative, 498
  of driving (Freud), 38
  of physics (Freud), 41
  organic, 497
  root, 496
  transcendent self, 499
  wave, 457, 462
Method-centered, 198, 429
Methodology
  Allport's attitude, 187, 198
Middle Way, 462, 468, 470, 484
Miller, Alice, 169
Miller, Neal
  biography, 318–319
  theory of (with John Dollard),
  313–336
Mind, control of, 451
Mind-body relationship, 465, 479
Mindful Attention Awareness Scale
  (MAAS), 486
Minnesota Multiphasic Personality
  Inventory (MMPI), 14, 106,
  114, 202
Mischel, Walter
  biography, 343
  theory of, 342–352
Mistrust, 130, 134, 176
Model, energy (Freud), 58
Modeling, 113, 337, 360–362, 389.
  See also Imitation.
  of aggression, 358
  in sensory-motor repertoire, 305
Models, role, 138
Modulation corollary, 378
Molecular genetic approach, 259
Momentariness, 463
Monamine oxidase (MAO), 266
Monroe, Marilyn, 70, 87
  (Illustrative Biography) 149–152
Mood induction procedure, 271
Moral anxiety, 42
Moral development, 481

Moral disengagement, 365
Moral judgment and reasoning, 142,
  144, 351, 361, 481
Moratorium, 132, 143
Morphine, 475
Mortality
  awareness of, 464
  consciousness of, 329
  prediction of, 233
  salience, 329
Mother Teresa, 185
Motivation
  B-motivation (being motivation),
  430, 432–433
  D-motivation (deficiency motiva-
  tion), 430, 432–433
  intrinsic, 447–448
  unconscious, 32
Motivational process, 360
Motor reproduction process, 360
Moving against, 156, 159–160
  and attachment, 176
Moving away, 156, 160
Moving toward, 156, 159–160, 175
  and attachment, 176
Multiple Abstract Variance Analysis
  (MAVA), 235
Multiple personality disorder, 33, 48,
  56, 202
Multivariate approach, 224, 235
Murray, Henry, 127, 230, 395
Music preference, 266
Myers-Briggs Type Indicator (MBTI),
  88, 89, 90, 242
Mysticism, 45, 74, 80, 84, 406, 444,
  466, 475
  of Jung, 67–68
Mythology and myths, 57, 65–67,
  76–80, 82–83, 419, 446

N

Narcissism, 52, 114, 116, 157,
  173–174, 310, 329, 396
  and birth order, 110
Narrative memory, 105
Narrative metaphor, 498
Narrative, life, 449
Narrative, personal, 132
Nature-nurture question, 307–308
Need hierarchy, 425, 430–431, 433,
  482
Needs, 431, 433
  basic, 430
  esteem, 432
  physiological, 431, 433–434
  safety, 434
  self-actualization, 433
Neglect, parental, 108, 168
Neodissociation theory (hypnosis), 33
NEO-PI, 271
Nervous system, strong, 265, 267
Nervous system, weak, 265, 267, 269
Neuroscience, 260, 469, 485
  and Jung's theory, 74
  and Freud's theory, 60
  and learning, 334
  cognitive
Neurosis, 155, 160, 226, 331, 435
  development of, 52
  cultural determinants, 163
  lack of social feeling, 113

Neurotic anxiety, 42
Neuroticism, 236, 238–239, 242, 267, 269, 434
  and attachment, 177
  and culture, 6
  Eysenck's theory, 269
  impact on dreams, 82
  in parents, 168
Neuroticism Scale Questionnaire, 223
Neuroticism/Negative Emotionality (N/NE), 271
Neurotransmitters, 48, 264, 273, 478–479
  and dreams, 35
New York Longitudinal Study (NYLS), 260
Nirvana, 460, 462–463
Nixon, Richard (Illustrative Biography), 368–372
  psychetype of, 87
  self-actualization of, 436
Nomothetic approach, 4–5, 194, 197–199, 233, 337, 373
Nonconformity, 269
Nonconscious, 32, 59
Norepinephrine, 261–262, 272, 274–275, 358
Novelty seeking (trait), 273, 274
Numinous, 79, 82

O

Object, 39, 171, 472
  adult sexual, 52
  Freud's theory, 39
  great, 476
  mother, 49, 51
  slight, 476
Object relations. See Relational approach.
Observational learning, 360
Obsessional neurosis, 52
Obstinacy (anal trait), 49–50
Oceanic feeling, 464
Oedipus conflict and complex, 50, 52, 98, 108
  of Adolph Hitler, 26
Omnipotence, infant experience, 49
One-child policy (China), 111
Openness, 236, 417, 484
Openness to experience, 239–240, 408, 413
Operant behavior, 289
Operational definition, 9–11, 219, 248, 310
  in psychoanalytic theory, 24
Opiates, 334, 358, 473, 475
Optimism, 357, 396, 448
  oral trait, 49
Oral character, 49, 137
Oral stage, 49
  psychoanalytic theory, 47
Orderliness, 239
  anal trait, 49–50
Organ inferiority, 101–102
Organic metaphor, 497
Organismic valuing process, 404–405, 407, 409–410, 413, 415
Organization corollary, 380
Outcome expectations, 356
Oxytocin, 254, 275

P

P300 waves, 268
Pampered child, 106, 108–111
Pappenheim, Bertha, 30
Paradigm, 18, 494, 499
  biocultural, 257
  crisis of, 343
  dominant (or common), 488
  evolutionary, 249
  identity status, 143
  trait approach, 184
  unified positivism, 299
Paradigmatic behaviorism. See Psychological behaviorism.
Paranoia, development (Freud's view), 52
Paranormal phenomena, 83–84, 406, 443
Parapraxis, 35
Parenting and parental behavior, 107, 130, 168–169, 172, 254–255, 308, 355, 407–408, 410
  and attachment, 175
  and psychosocial development, 145
  evolutionary interpretation, 255–256
  memory of, 172
  parental investment, 251, 253
Parenting styles, 169
  authoritarian, 407
  authoritative, 408
Parenting training programs, 108, 119
Parietal lobes, 474
Parsimony (anal trait), 49–50
Parsimony (of theory), 12
Partial reinforcement schedule, 293
Passivity, 106
  female trait (Freud's view), 51
  oral trait, 49
Paternal uncertainty, 253
Patriotism
  and death anxiety, 46
  and mortality salience, 329
Pavlov, Ivan, 265, 267
Peace
  and Buddhism, 469–470
  humanistic perspective on, 434
Peak experiences, 437–438, 482
Pelzer, David (Illustrative Biography), 422–425
PEN biological model, 267–271
Penis (psychoanalytic view), 26, 50
  and homophobia, 43
Penis envy, 51, 154, 165
  cultural interpretation, 165
Perception, 474
  17 moments of, 475
  realistic, 202
  study of Buddhist monks, 475
Perfection striving, 101–102
Perfectionism, 49, 102, 159, 161, 274, 306
Peripheral construct, 380
Permeable construct, 378
Persistence, 274, 293, 355, 357, 448
Persona, 69–71
Personal construct, 347, 374–375
Personal construct theory, 368–393
Personal construct therapy, 387
Personal Orientation Inventory (POI), 420, 432, 436, 441, 445

Personal stories, 389
Personal unconscious, 73, 75
Personality
  definition, 2
  definition (Allport), 189
  definition (behavioral), 279
Personality coefficient, 344
Personality disorders, 157–158
  narcissistic, 173
Personality Research Form, 114, 242
Personality tests
  behavioral interpretation, 308–309
Pessimism, 223
  oral trait, 49
Pets, attachment to, 145
Phallic stage, 47, 50–51, 131
Phenomenological approach, 198, 395
Phenomenological experience, 456
Phenotype, 262
Philosophy of science, 299, 429
Phobias, 264, 306, 324, 331, 358, 364, 390, 482
  Allport anecdote, 187
  experimental study of, 58
  treatment, 363
Physics
  metaphor (Freud), 41
  model for personality theory, 84
  science of, 485
Plasticity, 40, 255
Pleasure, role of shadow, 72
Pleasure principle, 38–39, 47
Pluralism, 494
Political and social activism, and generativity, 145
Political leaders, and birth order, 111
Pons, and dreams, 35
Positive psychology, 397, 425, 447–449
Positivism, unified, 299
Positron emission tomography (PET), 477
Posthypnotic suggestion, 33
Postmodernism, 391
Posttraumatic stress disorder, 48, 56–57, 332–333
Power motive
  and generativity, 145
  projective test for, 37
Power (social), in couples, 165
Preconscious, 31
Predictive validity, 14
Preemption, 386
Prefrontal cortex, 481
Prejudice, 72, 123, 138, 189, 206–208, 469
  and frustration-aggression hypothesis, 327
  and humor, 36
  and intrapsychic conflict, 43
  and reaction formation, 43
  and religious orientation, 209–210
  learned, 303
Prepotent needs, 431
Present (time orientation), 396
Preta, 483
Prevention programs, 307, 356
Preverbal construct, 377
Primal scene, 47
Primary drives, 319
Primary process, 40

Privacy, need for, 437
Prizing. See Unconditional positive regard.
Problem-centered, 198, 429, 437
Process Scale, 414, 416
Process, primary, 40
Process, secondary, 40
Processes, attentional, 359
Profile, 225
Project Pigeon, 287
Projection (defense mechanism), 42–43, 47, 73, 162
  by Adolph Hitler, 27
  of anima and animus, 73
Projective tests, 15, 24, 36, 37
  Cattell's contribution, 221
  fear of success, 164
  measurement of emotions in relationships, 171
  of object relationships, 172
Promiscuity, 54
Proposition, theoretical, 8–10, 12
Propriate striving, 204
Proprium, 203–204
Prototype, 199, 348
  of buffalo hunter, 135
Pseudoscience
  Jung's work, 67
  psychoanalysis, 57
Pseudospeciation, 140
Psyche, 69
  Jung's view, 67
Psychetype. See Psychological type (psychetype).
Psychic determinism, 36, 53
Psychic energy, 38–39, 41, 59–60. See also Libido.
  Jung's theory, 66, 69
Psychic trauma, 47
Psychic wholeness, 77
Psychoanalysis (Freud), 31, 52- 54, 318, 395. See also Freud, Sigmund: theory of.
  and psychobiography, 18
  training analysis, 68
Psychoanalytic concepts, compared with Cattell, 235
Psychoanalytic perspective, 23–24
Psychoanalytic treatment. See Psychotherapy.
Psychoanalytic-social perspective, 93–94
Psychobiography and psychohistory, 17–18
  Erikson's contributions, 122, 125
Psychological behaviorism, 297, 299, 303, 308–309
Psychological health. See Adaptation and adjustment.
Psychological type (psychetype), 84–85, 88–89
Psychosexual stages, 47, 49, 52
  compared to psychosocial stages, 128
  psychoanalytic learning theory interpretation, 323–324
Psychosis, 34, 226–227, 269
Psychosocial development (Erikson), 126, 131, 134
Psychosocial stages, 128
  research, 144

Psychotherapists, cultural training of, 166
Psychotherapy, 307, 337, 358, 406, 482
Adlerian, 117, 118, 119
and Buddhism, 481
behavioral. *See* Behavior modification and behavior therapy.
client-centered, 409–410
cognitive social learning, 363
constructivist, 379–380, 383, 385–389
effect on defense mechanisms, 45
effectiveness, 54, 57, 296, 365, 409, 412, 414, 419
feminist, 165
for memory of abuse, 51
Horney's view, 167
implications for theory, 17
Jungian, 79, 81
learning interpretation, 331–332
learning process, 364
narrative approach, 81
play, 82
psychoanalytic, 23, 54
recorded sessions, 412–413
recovered memory, 54
relational approach, 179
research on, 412
outcomes of, 413
transpersonal, 443
Psychoticism (Eysenck's theory), 269
P-technique, 233
Punishment, 264, 272, 285, 290–291, 300, 303, 320–321. *See also* Reinforcement Sensitivity Theory.
Adler's view, 116
and superego development, 41
fear of, 262, 329
gradient of, 321
Gray's theory, 271
nonauthoritarian, 169
sensitivity to, 273
Purpose (psychosocial strength), 135

Q
Q-data, 223, 224
Quantitative measures, 3
Quasi-experiment, 16

R
Racism. *See* Prejudice.
Radical behaviorism, 279, 288, 297, 299, 300, 308
Ramona v. Isabella, 55
Random assignment, 17
Range corollary, 381
Range of convenience, 378, 381, 386
Rate of responding, 289–290, 291
Rational coper (rational agent), 204
Rationalization (defense mechanism), 42, 44, 163, 387
Reaction formation (defense mechanism), 42–43, 47, 49
Real self, 155, 160–161, 167, 172, 405–408, 410–411, 414, 435, 482. *See also* Self: true.
defined, 407
Reality anxiety, 42
Reality principle, 40

Rebirth, 453–457, 459–460, 463–465, 469
Rebound, after suppression, 333
Receptivity (second-order factor), 225
Reciprocal determinism, 353, 365
Memory 55, 272. *See also* Amnesia; False memory syndrome.
recovered memory, 55
Reductionism, 276
Regression, 331, 431
in the service of the ego, 45
Rehearsal, motor, 360
Rehearsal, symbolic, 360
Reinforcement, 264, 271, 285, 290, 293, 296, 298. *See also* Reward in psychological behaviorism, 300
schedules, 293
Reinforcement Sensitivity Theory 271–273
Reinforcer, negative, 291
Reinforcer, positive, 290
Reinforcer, primary, 290
Reinforcer, secondary, 290
Relatedness, 448
Eros and anima, 72
Relational approach, 49, 93, 153
theory of, 169–179
Relaxation response, 480
Reliability, 13, 223
alternate forms, 13
of diagnosis, 227
of projective tests, 57
split-half, 13
Religion, 79, 256, 406, 451
Adler's and Freud's views contrasted, 119
and death anxiety, 46
and identity, 142
and myth, 80
and prejudice, 206–207
and psychosocial development, 134
and social interest, 114
and spirituality (in Maslow's theory), 444
behavioral experiment, 303
Freud's view of, 41
punishment in, 291
sentiment, 229
unity of personality, 202
Religions, angry and unangry, 467
Religious Orientation Survey, 209
Religious orientations, 202, 208–209
immanence, 210
intrinsic and extrinsic, 207–210
quest, 209–210
Repression, 37–38, 41, 58, 60
caused by anger, 324
defense mechanism, 37, 42, 46, 104, 160
experimental studies, 43, 58
Repressive coping style, 46
Repressors, 46, 60, 69
dreams of, 35
Research
applied, 12
basic, 12, 318
correlational, 15–16
experimental, 16

in psychotherapy outcome studies, 414
relationship to theory, 12
Resignation solution, 157
Response, 269, 289–290, 292–293, 319–320, 322, 326
anticipatory, 322
dominant, 320–321, 331
emotional, 300, 302
evoked neural, 268
operant, 289
Response hierarchy, 320, 331
Response sets, 15
Resultant hierarchy, 320
Retention process, 360
Reward. *See also* Reinforcement, 272, 274, 285, 290, 293, 319–321
dependence (trait), 274
emotion relationship, 302
gradient of, 321
Gray's theory, 271
self, 350
Rituals and ritualisms, 137
of fasting, 82
Rod and Frame Test, 473
Rogers, Carl
biography, 402–404
theory of, 398–421
Rogers, Fred, 419
Rokeach Values Survey, 239
Role, 145, 174, 245
codependent, 165
female (Freud's view), 51
in personal construct theory, 382
social, 71
Role Construct Repertory Test (REP), 379, 382, 387–390
Role model, in psychosexual development, 45
Role-playing, 388
in hypnosis, 33
Roosevelt, Eleanor (Illustrative Biography), 313–316
self-actualization of, 436
Root metaphor, 496
Rorschach inkblot test, 15, 24, 36, 45, 57, 81, 435
oral imagery, 49
R-technique, 233
Rumor transmission, 189, 210

S
Sadism, oral, 49
Samasara, 460
Sangha, 470
Satellite relationships, 417
Satyagroha, 125
Schedules of Reinforcement. *See* Reinforcement: schedules.
Schizophrenia, 113, 264, 363, 390, 457
development (Freud's view), 52
Silverman's studies, 57–58
Schools 443, 472. *See also* Education.
Adler's contribution, 116–117
Scientific attitudes, 81
Scientific method, 8, 429, 446, 447, 498
and psychoanalysis, 56, 57
and psychological type, 90

constraints of, 396, 397
Jung's attitude toward, 66
Maslow's criticism, 428, 429
testing Jung's theory, 78–79
Scientific revolution, birth order effects, 112
Scientific thinking (psychetype interpretation), 84
Secondary adjustment techniques, 162
Secondary process, 40
Sedimentation, 378
Seduction hypothesis (Freud), 51
Self, 438, 455–456, 461, 463, 465, 470, 476. *See also* Real self.
actual self, 160, 414
and memory, 476
as knower, 204
bodily, 203
brain and sense of self, 474
creative self, 103
ideal, 383, 407–408, 414, 436
idealized, 160–163, 165, 167
illusion of separate, 469
in Allport's theory, 191, 202–204
in psychoanalytic-social perspective, 94
in psychotherapy vs. Buddhism, 482
individual, 457
internal representations, 169
Jung's theory, 69
Rogers's theory, 406–407
true, 161, 396, 456
Self psychology (Kohut), 412
Self-absorption, 129–130, 133
Self-acceptance, 413–414
Self-actualization, 114, 142, 396
characteristics of, 436–440
compared to Adler's theory, 102
empirical studies, 435, 440–441
Maslow's theory, 430, 435–436
obstacles to, 441
of Eleanor Roosevelt, 316
Rogers's theory, 406–407
workplace applications, 443–444
Self-actualizing, 405
Self-analysis, 168
Self-concept, 71, 104, 306, 407, 414
and culture, 166
and psychosocial development, 144
Self-control, 292, 324, 350, 352, 366, 456
excessive, 163
second order factor, 225
Self-determination theory, 448
Self-discipline, 239
Self-effacing solution, 156–157
Self-efficacy, 349, 355–358
change in psychotherapy, 364
domain specific, 356
parenting, 356
Self-esteem, 8–10, 56, 118, 158, 160–161, 170, 173, 201, 204, 233, 238–239, 276, 407, 418, 434, 448, 462
and aggression, 174, 329
and culture, 6, 142

and ethnic identity, 138
and interpersonal conflict, 178
cohort differences, 206
Self-extension, 201
Self-handicapping, 354
Self-identity, 203
Self-image, 71, 162, 173, 204
Self-injurious behavior, 295
Self-monitoring, in extraverts, 88
Self-objectification, 202
Self-presentation, 240
Self-regulation, 354
   aspect of temperament, 260
Self-regulatory systems and plans, 350
Self-report measures, 14, 57, 183, 223, 236, 254, 308–310, 436, 489
Self-sentiment, 224, 226, 229, 234
Self-system, 347, 354
Sensation, 474–475
   psychological function, 47, 84–90
Sensation seeking, 266
Sensation Seeking Scale, 266
Sensory deprivation, 475
Sensory-motor repertoire, 302, 305–306
Sentiment, master (Allport), 202
Sentiments, 229–230
Serotonin, 264, 266, 274, 478
   in antisocial personality, 265
Sex differences, 238
   aggression, 362
   courtship, 250
   Erikson's view (challenged), 140–141
   Freud's view, 50–52
   identity, 141
   jealousy, 253–254
   Jung's theory, 72
   moral development, 51
Sex roles (gender), 75, 93, 102, 107, 141, 164–166, 206, 390–391, 445. See also Sex differences.
   and identification, 44
   and mental health, 166
   and myths, 80
Sexual abuse, 55, 173. See also Abuse of children
   reported in therapy, 23
Sexual behavior, 266, 271
   dysfunctions, 115
   evolutionary explanation, 252–254
   impulses, 71
   inhibition, 51
   offenders, treatment of, 363
   promiscuity, 173
   sex differences, 253
Sexual identity disorder, 45
Sexual orientation, 167, 255, 432
   Freud's view, 51–52
   prejudice study, 208–209
Sexual pair bonding, 275
   and dreams, 35
Sexual wishes (Freud's theory), 23
Sexuality, 427
   adult (Freud's view), 52
   childhood, 131
   disturbances (Freud's view), 51
   Jung's view, 68
   Maslow's view, 432

Shadow, 70–72, 75, 77
   negative, 72
Shame, 131, 135
   sex differences, 51
Shaping, 292
Shyness, 238
Siddhartha Gautama, 457–459
Silverman's experiments, 16, 57–58
Sioux, rituals of, 137
Situational context of behavior, 345–346
Situation-behavior relationship, 346
Situations, predicting behavior, 232
Skinner box, 287, 289, 291, 300
Skinner, B. F.
   biography, 285–288
   criticism of Carl Rogers, 412
   theory of, 284–297
Slot movement, 377, 379
Snake fear or phobia, 251
   social learning view, 363
Sociability (temperament), 260
Social Adaptability, 238
Social class, 318, 332.
Social constructionism, 391
Social deviance, 269
Social dominance, 240, 256, 273
Social evolution, 136
Social interaction, 240, 267
   task of life, 115
Social interest, 99, 107, 113, 115, 117–118, 396
   compared to compassion, 468
   group differences, 114
   measurement of, 114
Social Interest Index, 114
Social Interest Scale, 114
Social psychology, psychoanalytic, 146
Social role of marriage, 133
Sociality corollary, 382
Socially useful type, 107
Society, 327, 461, 491
   and psychosocial development, 135
   and superego, 37, 40
   in Freud's theory, 27, 47
   in Jung's theory, 73
   influence on the self, 407
Socioeconomic status (value), 135
Specification equation, 231, 232
SPECT imaging, 477
Spiritual Father archetype, 76
Spiritual level, 485
Spirituality, 113, 116, 134, 395, 406, 433, 441, 449
   association with masculinity, 76
   of the unconscious (Jung's view), 65
   task of life, 116
Splitting (defense mechanism), 172
Spontaneous recovery, 321
Staats, Arthur
   biography, 298–299
   theory of, 297–308
Stagnation, 133
State vs. trait, 16
Stepchildren, 255
Stimulus generalization. See Generalization.

Stress
   and alcoholism, 274
   and attachment, 178
   and psychosocial development, 144
   combat, 55, 60
   effects on brain, 60, 469
   experimental study, 56
   impact of attachment, 176
   posttraumatic, 385
   traumatic, 48
Stress reduction, 480
   and psychological type, 89
   meditation, 480
Strong nervous system, 265, 267
Stroop test, 258
   emotional, 272
Structures of personality, 37
Stupidity-misery syndrome, 331
Style of life, 104–107, 118
   and early memory, 105
   healthy, 107
Subjective experience, 280, 395, 406, 413, 415, 436, 438, 446, 448, 474, 485
   and psychological type, 85
   fictional finalism, 103
   in meditation, 473
Subjective stimulus value, 349
Sublimation, 39, 52, 449
   and creativity, 45
Sublimation (defense mechanism), 42, 44, 47
Subliminal advertising, 59
Subliminal psychodynamic activation, 57. See also Silverman's experiments.
Subliminal stimuli, 59
Submissiveness, 309
Subsidiation, 230
Success, fear of, 164
Suffering, 452–456, 458–461, 463, 465, 467, 469–470, 481–482
Suggestion
   experimental studies, 55
   in hypnosis, 34
   in recovered memory therapy, 54–55
   posthypnotic, 33
Suicide, 17, 56–57, 106, 113, 172, 274, 380, 385, 434
   and attachment, 178
   and perfectionism, 161
   and Thanatos, 38
   impact of parental, 262
Sullivan, Harry Stack, 23, 98
Superego, 37–38, 40–41, 43, 50–51, 98, 131, 146, 324
Superiority complex, 103
Superiority striving, 102
Superordinate constructs, 380, 388
Suppression, 41–42, 332, 334, 449
   of instincts, 396
   emotional, 333
Symbolic life, 82
Symbolism in dreams, 35
Symbols, 258
   of unconscious, 78
Symmetry, bodily, 252
Sympathetic nervous system, 261–262, 333–334, 480

Symptom Checklist 90-Revised, 106
Synchronicity, 83
Syntality, 233

T

Taoist Science, 429
Tasks of life, 108, 115
T-data, 224
Teacher, authority of, 417
Teaching machine, 296
Technology, psychosocial development and, 136, 296
Teleological, 373, 396, 498–499
Television violence, 362
Telosponse, 498
Temperament, 6, 190, 260, 262
   ancient Greek model, 3, 267
   and attachment, 175
   behavioral alternative, 308
   Cattell's theory, 228
   heredity and experience, 263
   Kagan's model, 260–262
   theory, 259–263
Temporal lobe, 268, 474
Tension reduction, 39
Teresa, Mother (Illustrative Biography), 185–187
Terror management theory, 46
Thalamus, 474
Thanatos, 27, 38, 327, 460
Thematic Apperception Test (TAT), 15, 36, 44–45, 145, 177, 198
Theoretical construct, 8, 9, 10, 15, 191, 248, 489
   example of introversion and extraversion, 86
   measurement, 13
   trait, 183
   validity of, 14
Theoretical proposition, 8–10, 12
Theory, 9–10, 38, 57
   applied value of, 12, 248, 342, 401, 495
   comprehensiveness of, 11–12, 185, 248, 495
   criteria, 11–12, 28, 495
   heuristic value of, 12
   multilevel, 276, 358, 489–490, 494–495
   parsimony of, 12
   relationship to research, 12
   social role, 164
   testing of, 10
   unified, 19, 494–495
   verifiability of, 11–12, 56–57, 219, 495
Theory of mind, 257
Theory, neodissociation (hypnosis), 33
Thinking (psychological function), 84–90, 258, 320, 334
Thinking, in adolescence, 132
Third force psychology, 395, 429, 447
Threat, 378, 385–386
   and aggression, 330
   punishment, 326
   homosexual, experimental study of, 58
Three function learning theory, 305

Time binding, 388
Time Competence scale, 441
Time, unidirectional or cyclical, 485
Time-out, 299–300
Toilet training, 47, 49, 130, 324
Token economy, 295, 299
Tolerance, 395
Touch and attachment, 174
Trait, 3, 9, 228. *See also* Cognitive
    person variables.
    ability, 227
    cardinal, 199
    central, 194, 199
    circular reasoning, 193–194, 288
    common, 193–194
    constitutional, 234
    constitutional dynamic source,
        229
    constitutional source, 228
    contrasted with personal con-
        structs, 347
    definition (Allport), 193–194
    definition (Cattell), 222
    dynamic, 227, 229
    emergenic, 259
    environmental-mold, 229, 234
    environmental-mold dynamic
        source, 229
    expressive, 195–196
    genotypical, 197
    global, 347
    inconsistency, 197
    individual, 193–194, 233
    inferring, 192–195
    measurement, 198
    measurement (behavioral), 309
    personal, 183, 192
    predictive, 232
    secondary, 199
    source, 225
    surface, 225
    temperament, 227
    unique, 193–194, 233
    vs. state, 16
    vs. type, Jungian functions, 88
Trait perspective, 183–184
Trait theories
    Allport, 191
    assumption of stability, 232
    Big five, 183, 195
    Cloninger, 273–274
    Eysenck, 183, 267, 269

factor analytic, 219, 221
    Gray, 267, 271–273
Transcendent function, 70
Transcendent self metaphor, 499
Transcendental Meditation, 466, 472,
    480, 481
Transcendental Mental Powers, 406
Transference, 53, 118, 169, 179, 307,
    412
    in psychobiography, 18
Transformation, 78
Transience, 463
Transpersonal, 406, 447, 485
Transpersonal therapy, 443
Traumatic experience, 32, 276, 321
    effects on brain, 60
    in psychoanalysis, 26
    psychic, 47–48
    writing about, 333
Trickster archetype, 76, 77
Tridimensional model, 273–274
Tridimensional Personality
    Questionnaire, 266, 274
True experimental research, 16
Trust, 130, 134
    indiscriminant (brain damage), 263
    organismic. *See* Organismic valu-
        ing process.
Type, 3, 279
    aggressive, 159, 162–163
    avoiding, 106
    compliant, 158, 162–164
    detached, 159
    getting, 106
    Machiavellian, 163
    psychological (Jung's theory), 84,
        88–90
    ruling, 106
    socially useful, 107
    Type A (attachment), 175
    Type-A (cardiovascular), and birth
        order, 110
Tyranny of the shoulds, 161

U

Unconditional positive regard, 408,
    410, 412–413, 417–418
Unconscious, 23, 31–32, 35, 104
    and metaphor, 27
    cognition (cognitive), 58–59
    collective, 63–64, 68, 74–76,
        78–80, 83

compensatory relationship to con-
    sciousness, 69
contrasted with nonconscious, 32
dynamic, 23, 32, 59
ethnic and racial, 75
experimental study of, 16
Freud's theory, 30
identification with, 69
in dreams, 34
in fictional finalism, 103
Jung's theory, 63, 66
memory, 59
overvaluing, 70
personal, 73, 75, 78
psychoanalytic social learning
    interpretation, 330
wishes, 36
Unconditional positive regard,
    407–408, 410–411, 413–418
Undoing (defense mechanism), 47
Unified positivism, 299
Unified theory, 19, 494–495
Unifying philosophy of life,
    202, 209
Uninhibited temperament, 261
Unity of personality, 40, 104,
    202–203

V

Validation of personal constructs, 375
Validation, of measures, 383
Validity
    construct, 14
    of archetypal symbols, 79
    of handwriting analysis, 195
    of tests, 184, 219, 223–224, 227
    predictive, 14
Value, subjective stimulus, 349
Values
    and self-actualization, 439
    clarification, 417
    cultural, 47, 146
    feminine, 165
    in Maslow's theory, 446
    measure: Study of Values, 197
Variable, 16
    third, 15
Variable interval (VI) schedule, 294
Variable ratio (VR) schedule, 294
Variable, dependent, 16, 303, 386
Variable, independent, 16, 386
Vasopressin, 254, 275

Verifiability (of theory), 11–12, 219,
    495
    psychoanalytic theory, 24, 56, 57
    Bandura's theory, 362
Vicarious, 361
Violence, 306, 469
    and attachment, 177
    causes of, 329
    desensitization to, 269
    domestic, 173
    on television, 362
Vipassana (meditation), 472
Vocational choice and development,
    106, 390

W

Walden Two, 287, 297
Weak nervous system, 265, 267, 269
Weight loss, experimental study
    of, 58
West, Ellen, 412
White Bear Suppression Inventory,
    332
Will (will power), 135
Winfrey, Oprah (Illustrative
    Biography), 95–97
Wisdom (psychosocial strength),
    136
Wise old man archetype, 76
Wish, repressed, 34
Womb envy, 165
Woods, Tiger (Illustrative
    Biography), 281–284, 305
Word Association Test, 81
Word associations (Jung's empirical
    studies), 67
Word binding, 388
Work, 293, 296. *See also* Business.
    and birth order, 110
    and conscientiousness, 239
    and generativity, 133
    Freud's view, 52
    job burnout, 70
    task of life, 115
Wright, Frank Lloyd, 136
Writing (expressive), health benefits,
    333

Y

Yoga, 471

Z

Zazen (meditation), 472